M000208086

EVERYMAN'S LIBRARY

EVERYMAN,
I WILL GO WITH THEE,
AND BE THY GUIDE,
IN THY MOST NEED
TO GO BY THY SIDE

EDMUND BURKE

REFLECTIONS ON THE REVOLUTION IN FRANCE

AND OTHER WRITINGS

EDITED AND INTRODUCED
BY JESSE NORMAN

EVERYMAN'S LIBRARY
Alfred A. Knopf New York London Toronto

365

THIS IS A BORZOI BOOK
PUBLISHED BY ALFRED A. KNOPF

Reflections on the Revolution in France first included in Everyman's Library, 1910; all *Other Writings* first included in Everyman's Library, 2015
Introduction and Bibliography Copyright © 2015 by Jesse Norman
Chronology and Notes Copyright © 2015 by Everyman's Library
Typography by Peter B. Willberg
The Private Letters are from *The Correspondence of Edmund Burke*, ed. Thomas W. Copeland, 10 vols (Chicago and Cambridge: University of Chicago Press and Cambridge University Press, 1958–78). Used with permission.
'On Parties' and 'Considerations on a Militia', first published in *The Historical Journal*, vol. 55 (2012), are reproduced with the permission of Richard Bourke.

All rights reserved. Published in the United States by Alfred A. Knopf, a division of Penguin Random House LLC, New York, and in Canada by Penguin Random House of Canada Limited, Toronto. Distributed by Penguin Random House LLC, New York. Published in the United Kingdom by Everyman's Library, 50 Albemarle Street, London W1S 4BD and distributed by Penguin Random House UK Ltd.

www.randomhouse.com/everymans
www.everymanslibrary.co.uk

ISBN: 978-0-375-71253-1 (US)
978-1-84159-365-4 (UK)

A CIP catalogue reference for this book is available from the British Library

Book design by Barbara de Wilde and Carol Devine Carson

Typography by Peter B. Willberg

Typeset in the UK by Acc Computing, Wincanton, Somerset
and by Input Data Services,
17 King Square, Bridgwater, Somerset TA6 3DJ

Printed and bound in Germany by GGP Media GmbH, Pössneck

EDMUND BURKE

CONTENTS

vii

EDMUND BURKE

INTRODUCTION

Lord Randolph Churchill, father of Winston, once summarized Benjamin Disraeli's life as 'Failure, failure, failure, partial success, renewed failure, ultimate and complete triumph'. The same might be said of the great eighteenth-century philosopher-statesman Edmund Burke.

Edmund Burke was born, probably in 1730, on the banks of the Liffey in Dublin, the third of four children. His father was a solicitor, a difficult man described in an age before class analysis as of 'the middling sort', who practised in the superior courts, and a Protestant. His mother was calmer and kinder, and a Catholic. She came from a distinguished family, the Nagles of County Cork, Jacobites who had supported the claims of James II and his successors after the so-called Glorious Revolution of 1688–9, in which James went into exile and William III came to the throne amid a new constitutional settlement – a cause which had cost them both lands and grandeur.

Ireland at that time was in name a Kingdom, but in reality an English and Protestant dominion, in which the rights of Catholics were severely curtailed by the so-called Popery Laws. It was a place of huge disparities of wealth and wellbeing, compounding and in turn compounded by intense religious hatreds and political instability. It offered rich material for Burke's vivid moral and literary imagination, and for what proved to be his lifelong detestation of injustice.

Burke was educated first at a non-denominational school outside Dublin (1741–4), and then at Trinity College Dublin (1744–8). At school he was inspired by the intellectual and moral example of his schoolmaster, Abraham Shackleton, a Quaker and the father of his first great friend and early correspondent, Richard Shackleton. He was less enthused by Trinity, it seems, finding the teaching laborious and pedantic; his outlets lay elsewhere, in two short-lived literary societies which he helped to found, in three hours a day in the public library, and in poetry and other writing.

We know relatively little of Burke over the following seven years. He seems to have worked in his father's office, before arriving at the Middle Temple in London in May 1750 to read for the Bar, aged twenty. He had a year or two of ill-health and low spirits, which he sought to cure through extended journeys with his friend (but not it seems, relative) Will Burke. In 1755, to his father's apparent displeasure, he took the momentous decision to leave the law and try to live by his pen.

There followed an extraordinary burst of writing, sustained by the financial support and literary access given to Burke by Robert Dodsley, a noted publisher and bookseller. His wide-ranging early works included an almost too sophisticated parody, the literary polemic *A Vindication of Natural Society*; a highly influential work of aesthetics, *A Philosophical Inquiry into the Origin of our Ideas of the Sublime and Beautiful*; a social and historical survey, *An Account of the European Settlements in America* in collaboration with Will Burke; and *An Essay towards an Abridgment of the English History*, which broke off with Magna Carta in 1215 and was never completed.

By 1759 Burke had become the editor of Dodsley's new periodical, the *Annual Register*, and was married to Jane Nugent, with two infant sons, Richard and Christopher (the latter died in early youth). He was making a name for himself in literary circles, and in 1764 became a founder member of Dr Johnson's Club, alongside Johnson himself, Joshua Reynolds, Oliver Goldsmith and others. He had also taken his first steps into politics, as secretary to William Gerard Hamilton, whom he followed from the Board of Trade to Ireland, where Hamilton became Chancellor of the Exchequer in 1763. But Burke found himself impossibly constricted by Hamilton's demands, and by early 1765 they had parted.

Burke now had an extraordinary turn of luck. He was introduced to the Marquis of Rockingham, possibly the richest man in England and the leader of an important group of Whigs in Parliament. Britain had been wrestling with the financial after-effects of the Seven Years' War (1756–63), and its attempts to raise new revenues were proving highly controversial in the colonies. Moreover, George III, who had succeeded to the throne in 1760, saw his Hanoverian predecessors as having handed over the conduct of politics to Parliament, and sought to reassert the informal and prerogative rights of the Crown. The result was a political merry-go-round, in which a succession of administrations attempted to reconcile financial prudence and colonial management with parliamentary politics and the demands of the new monarch. By 1765, after several failed administrations, the King was reluctantly persuaded to approach Rockingham. Burke thus became private secretary to the new Prime Minister, and shortly afterwards a Member of Parliament, for the 'pocket borough' of Wendover, in his own right.

Rockingham's administration was short-lived; but Burke was an immediate success in Parliament, quickly gaining a formidable reputation for his speeches and skill in debate. He also developed a role over time as a party manager, helping to shape the Rockinghamites into what we can now see as the first genuine forerunner to the political parties of today. In 1770 he published *Thoughts on the Cause of the Present Discontents*, notable today because it drew a crucial distinction between mere factions and parties which are 'united, for promoting by their joint endeavours the national interest, upon some political principle in which they are all agreed'. The test comes when such a group is evicted from office. Founded on self-interest, factions will tend to disperse. Parties, however, will sustain themselves and their membership – on principle and shared values, on mutual commitments and on personal loyalties and friendship – until the opportunity to take power returns.

For many years this distinction, and the *Thoughts* itself, was denounced in some quarters as an apologia for the political power exercised by Rockingham and other great Whig magnates. However, recent research has demonstrated that Burke had formulated the key ideas in a hitherto unattributed essay of 1757, reproduced in this collection for the first time outside the scholarly journals.

The Rockinghamites had to wait until 1782 before they could resume office. The intervening sixteen years were a torrid time for them, a period dominated by Lord North's mishandling of the American colonies, by the long run-up to war, by war itself, and by their continuing attempts to restrain Crown influence and political patronage. Burke was active throughout, on issues ranging from political reform to religious matters to relief for Ireland, and in particular delivered two extraordinary speeches in 1774–5 on *American Taxation* and on *Conciliation with America*. Both are gems of political analysis and statesmanship. But they were also notable as some of the earliest occasions on which speeches had been published from a deliberate desire to build not merely a shared public understanding, but a degree of national and indeed international renown.

By 1774 Burke's political reputation was such that, with Wendover no longer available, he was elected as the MP for Bristol, then the second city of Britain. His backers doubtless expected the usual trite formulas of thanks, and perhaps a pledge by Burke to follow his constituents' instructions. But in his *Speech at the Conclusion of the Poll at Bristol*, Burke simply destroyed that radical idea at source, and gave what has become the classic statement of the duties of the political representative:

It ought to be the happiness and glory of a representative to live in the strictest union, the closest correspondence, and the most unreserved communication with his constituents ... but his unbiased opinion, his mature judgment, his enlightened conscience, he ought not to sacrifice to you, to any man, or to any set of men living ... Your representative owes you, not his industry only, but his judgment; and he betrays, instead of serving you, if he sacrifices it to your opinion.

Alas, by 1780 Burke himself had failed to build a political base in Bristol, and indeed had alienated many former supporters by refusing to support the government on the American war, and by favouring trade with Ireland and measures of relief for Catholics – the latter a cause which he pursued steadily, though at some cost, throughout his political career. But Rockingham eventually came to his aid, and installed him in a parliamentary seat at Malton in December 1780. There he remained until he left Parliament in 1794.

In 1780 Burke was fifty years of age, and at the height of his powers. We can catch glimpses of him in private: of the bespectacled Irishman with his wig off, who kept his red hair for many years and always spoke with an accent 'as strong as if he had never quitted the banks of the Shannon'; of the Christian Latitudinarian and respecter of dissent; of the husband,

'Ned', as Jane called him at home, who addressed his wife with the utmost tenderness as 'My dearest Jane', 'My dearest love', and 'My ever dear Jane'; of the father, whom one son's death had left almost too fond of the other, and who adored the company of children; of the host, never free of house guests but always entertaining with an open hand; of the patron, who knew the value of help to a young man, and who supported talented outsiders such as the painter James Barry and the poet George Crabbe; of the clubbable fellow who enjoyed puns and low jokes and conversation, but never quite mastered the art of wit or repartee; of the countryman, who loved nature and rejoiced in his vegetable garden and in 'scientific agriculture'; of the solitary thinker, who did not make close friends easily, who chafed at idleness and was prone to fits of melancholy.

As the war ground on, Burke's attention was increasingly drawn to two further issues, both of which he made into great personal causes. The first was 'economical reform': the attempt to control the spending and financial patronage of the Crown, and so push the monarchy back towards the settlement of 1688, long venerated by Whigs. This culminated in a great speech of 1780 in which Burke spoke for over three hours, laying out seven fundamental rules of good government, and a package of measures which included reforms to the office of Paymaster General, long used as a source of personal enrichment, and the abolition of the Board of Trade. But pioneering as they were, his proposals had few immediate practical consequences.

The other great cause was India. Since its foundation in 1600, the East India Company had grown from a trading enterprise to an instrument of empire, exercising political control over the whole of the Indian subcontinent. This raised profound moral questions. Revenue from mutually beneficial trade was being replaced by revenue from tribute and tax. Robert Clive, 'Clive of India', had been a brilliant commander, but he had not hesitated to bribe, coerce and where necessary deceive Indian nobles and merchants in order to achieve his goals. And such was its wealth and influence that the Company also exercised formidable political power at home. Initially Burke had opposed the measures of reform introduced by Lord North's government, seeing them as covert attacks on the institution of private property and an attempt to increase the Court's powers of patronage. He now threw himself into Indian affairs, becoming their acknowledged master in the Commons.

In 1782, the exhausted and discredited Lord North finally left office. The King cast about for alternatives, and at last reluctantly settled again on Rockingham. Politically, this was a highly equivocal victory, especially since Rockingham lacked an unfettered power to select his own cabinet. But it marked an extraordinary moment in the political history not merely of Britain but of the world.

Rockingham's group had been out of office since 1766. But they had not fragmented, as factions had fragmented before them. On the contrary, for sixteen years they had maintained a political grouping, a core of shared policies, and a coherent political identity in opposition. They had, in other words, created the first outlines of the modern political party. Power had passed entirely peacefully to this party, large numbers of office holders had been forced to leave, and the new government had arrived with well-understood legislative intent. In so doing, it had pushed the country one more step towards limited government and a constitutional democracy, and away from a purely personal monarchy. This remains a remarkable and woefully under-recognized achievement; and Edmund Burke was, intellectually and practically, at its centre.

Burke now became a Privy Councillor and Paymaster General, a position which he quickly reformed. He then pushed through several of his 'economical reforms' of 1780. The new government moved to end the war in America, and passed a range of measures granting relief to Ireland. The subordination of Dublin to Westminster was ended, allowing the Irish parliament to pass its own legislation without British assent; the Irish judiciary was made formally independent; and rights of appeal from Irish to English courts were abolished. Burke supported these reforms, but with substantial reservations. They strengthened the Protestant ascendancy, but would do nothing for Catholics. The Popery Laws remained in place.

But the new government did not last long, for in a cruel twist of fate Rockingham died suddenly after only three months in office; his role as *de facto* Whig leader was taken by Burke's sometime protégé, the wealthy, talented but dissolute Charles James Fox. The King then invited Lord Shelburne to form an administration, and Burke resigned. But a few months later Shelburne himself was forced out by a coalition which united North and Fox. The irony was telling: the Rockingham Whigs had taken office in 1782 after sixteen years in opposition, twelve of them fighting North. Now under Fox they had cast principle aside and allied themselves with their former foe. Little wonder that the Fox–North coalition was reviled from the outset.

Nevertheless, Burke was back in office. He reimmersed himself in India, and specifically in drafting a highly controversial measure of reform that became known as Fox's India Bill, on which he gave a memorable speech in December 1783. However, George III had now at last found a successor to North; that is, a politician of ability whom he felt he could trust. This was the younger William Pitt, then just twenty-four, the son of William Pitt, first Earl of Chatham, former Prime Minister and victor in the Seven Years' War. Seizing his opportunity, and casting constitutional protocol aside, the King engineered the defeat of Fox's India Bill and installed Pitt as Prime Minister. After an initial period of uncertainty while he consolidated power, Pitt was to hold office for nineteen of the next twenty-two years.

Burke was enraged and frustrated by the turn of events, which seemed to justify all his historic concerns about the excessive influence of the Crown. Thwarted yet again in domestic politics, he turned back to India; and specifically to the person of Warren Hastings, former Governor General of the East India Company. Hastings was a cultivated and accomplished man, and in some ways not unlike Burke himself. But Burke came to see him as the incarnation of the Company's harshness, self-enrichment, corruption and abuse of power. In February 1786 he brought formal proceedings against Hastings in Parliament, using the ancient procedure of impeachment. With the unexpected support of Pitt, this moved to formal trial in a richly bedecked Westminster Hall two years later. Burke's monumental (four-day) speech at the opening brilliantly laid out the charges and broader themes of the prosecution, which was to last for 149 sitting days over seven years.

By the end of 1788, however, the focus of Westminster was not on Hastings and India, but on a constitutional crisis rapidly engulfing the monarchy: George III, it seemed, was going mad. A series of mental episodes over the summer had been attributed to high spirits, but by November he appeared to be deranged. The political implications were profound, since both the King's death or a regency would bring the notoriously intemperate and thoroughly pro-Fox Prince of Wales to the throne. Pitt therefore stalled for time, while Fox hurriedly returned from a visit to Italy with his mistress, Mrs Armistead. Matters came to a head in a tumultuous parliamentary debate in December 1788, when Pitt proposed the creation of a committee to establish the relevant constitutional precedents. Fox unavailingly and unpersuasively blustered that the constitutional settlement of 1688 required a regency, while Burke delivered a rambling and hostile speech which badly misjudged the mood of the chamber.

In a further speech the following February, Burke drew lurid comparisons with asylum inmates who had recovered from insanity only to commit suicide or butcher their families, to the great distaste of his audience. This compounded the impression of him as a man visibly older, more brittle, self-righteous and out of touch, just as the King started to recover his mind, and the government its equilibrium. As the Regency Crisis ended, and a new generation of Whig politicians came to the fore around Fox, Burke seemed ever more a creature of another age.

Yet events were to prove otherwise: for the revolution in France was to give Burke the greatest triumph of his own lifetime. The revolution itself is still a subject of vigorous scholarly contention and cannot be easily summarized. It had many and mixed causes, including France's economic weakness, worsened by the vast accumulated debts of the Seven Years' War and the American War of Independence; her narrow, unfair and ineffectual tax system; her rigid social and religious hierarchies, which impeded advancement on merit and fomented dissent; and a succession of bad harvests. Louis XVI attempted a series of political manoeuvres designed to bolster the Exchequer, which only inflamed matters further. Popular anger erupted on 14 July 1789 with the storming of the Bastille. Within a kaleidoscopic sequence of shifting phases and moods, punctuated by unexpected pauses and sudden events, there then followed what we now think of as a revolution.

In Britain, the initial reaction to events in France was sanguine. Fox was exultant: 'How much the greatest event it is that ever happened in the world! And how much the best', he wrote in July. The revolution was regarded as a brief upheaval, which would quickly yield to good order, indeed a constitutional monarchy. Even Pitt declared to the Commons in February 1790 that 'The present convulsions of France must, sooner or later, terminate in general harmony ... thus circumstanced, France ... would enjoy just that kind of liberty which I venerate.'

But one man did not share the general optimism. Edmund Burke took pains to give events in France the benefit of the doubt, while expressing deep reservations. Yet by early 1790 his fears that French radicalism would cross the Channel were stoked by what he regarded as a highly incendiary sermon given by the dissenting preacher Dr Richard Price, arguing that Englishmen should see themselves not as rooted in a specific community, but as citizens of the world, and that the French revolution was the proper successor to the Glorious Revolution, itself unfinished, which had given the British people the right to cashier their governors and remove their own monarch from the throne.

On 1 November 1790 Burke published his reply, *Reflections on the Revolution in France*. The *Reflections*, and the works that accompany it, mark one of the greatest late flourishings not simply of any politician, but of any writer or thinker throughout history. They are filled with anger, indeed outrage. But gone is the aged irrelevance, the embarrassment, the much-derided pantaloon of the Regency Crisis. Instead we have Burke the Celtic *vates*, the seer, inspired by cold passion and intellectual energy, prophesying the future when all around are imbued in fantasy, folly and self-congratulation. This is no great event, he says, no general harmony, no liberty to be venerated; it is a catastrophe. It will not lead to good order, or the ideal society anticipated by the *bien pensants*, the radical intellectuals and their fellow travellers. No, the French revolution is not ended. What lie in store are violence, bloodshed, anarchy, terror and civil war. Far from settling down, France will spread an international spirit of sedition that will infect Britain, and the result of her revolution will be war.

So it proved, in almost every respect. The extraordinary quality of the *Reflections* was swiftly recognized: it was a great popular success, and spawned a vigorous immediate reaction from Burke's erstwhile admirer Thomas Paine in his *Rights of Man*, as well as a host of further pamphlets. Yet the *Reflections* is not merely a polemic, but a treasure trove of political wisdom and an enduring statement of what have come to be thought of as conservative principles. *Contra* Price, the Glorious Revolution was not, Burke insists, the exercise of the people's supposed right to choose their own monarch. It was necessary, not discretionary: 'a small and temporary deviation from the strict order of regular hereditary succession', and recognized at the time as such. As with all effective reforms, it was limited in scope and duration, and insulated from the rest of the body politic. Why? Because, as Burke memorably put it, 'A state without the means of some change is without the means of its conservation.' The true point of comparison for Burke is not the Glorious Revolution, but the civil war of the 1640s, with all its disorder and bloodshed.

The error of Dr Price and his friends was to follow the French doctrine of natural rights. This in turn led them to take the constitutional exception for the rule, and to support not gradual change, but revolution. They preferred their own imaginings to the settled idea of the constitution handed down through time 'in our histories, in our records, in our Acts of Parliament . . . and not in . . . sermons, or the after-dinner toasts of the Revolution Society'.

Individual foolishness thus supplanted shared wisdom. But such a supplanting, such a rejection was, in effect, a rejection of society itself, and of social institutions. Strikingly, Burke makes this point in something very close to the modern language and idea of 'social capital': 'We are afraid to put men to live and trade each on his own private stock of reason; because we suspect that this stock in each man is small, and that the individuals would do better to avail themselves of the general bank and capital of nations, and of ages.' Society was not the product of reason, but of affection, built up from below: 'To be attached to the subdivision, to love the little platoon ... is the first link in the series by which we proceed towards a love to our country and to mankind.' And its domain, its sphere of moral concern was not a person, or a group or class, or even a generation, but the social order itself, persisting over time. Society was 'a partnership not only between those who are living, but between those who are living, those who are dead, and those who are to be born.' Burke thus offers his own distinctively anti-rationalist and conservative version of the social contract, from within a context of Enlightenment social contract theory itself.

In the years that remained before his death in 1797 – and notably in the *Letter to a Member of the National Assembly, An Appeal from the New to the Old Whigs* and *Two Letters on the Prospect of a Regicide Peace* – Burke defended, elaborated and sharpened these themes still further. But he was overtaken by a mood of increasing melancholy and even despair, as Europe moved from war to what he saw as an inglorious peace, as his fears that Jacobinism would cross the Channel seemed to be realized, and as Ireland succumbed to violence and rebellion. In June 1794 he left Parliament, having given his oratorical swansong in a speech of some twenty-seven hours over nine days in closing the prosecution case against Hastings. By that time it was clear that Hastings would be acquitted, as he was the following year, on all the sixteen charges he faced.

Burke's sadness was briefly dispelled by the immediate election of his son Richard to his pocket borough seat of Malton on 18 July, a date Burke declared to be the happiest of his life. Yet the cruellest blow of all was still to come. Just ten days later Richard fell gravely ill, and four days after that he was dead, apparently of tuberculosis. Having lost their son Christopher in infancy, and now Richard in adulthood at his moment of greatest triumph, Edmund and Jane were absolutely desolate. And Burke's fears were magnified by his continuing financial indebtedness. No longer in Parliament, he could now be sued and potentially imprisoned for his debts;

and no son remained to manage and take over the estate he had bought at great cost. Unlike many politicians of the time, he had not used public office to enrich himself. Instead, he had fought a constant battle to reconcile his aspirations with his ideals: to square his desire for social status and public recognition with his insistence on personal accountability and independence of mind and action.

As a result, for nearly thirty years Burke's life had been a hand-to-mouth existence, forever sustained by credit and reliant on grants, sporadic fees, forgiven debts and bequests. At last, in July 1795, Pitt was able to settle on him a pension from the King – though not a peerage, as had been mooted before Richard's death – in recognition of his public service. Even this, however, did not escape controversy. Paine had denounced him earlier as one 'accustomed to kiss the aristocratical hand that hath purloined him from himself'. And was not Burke renowned for a lifetime's opposition to the extension of Crown patronage, and for his wide-ranging proposals for economical reform in 1780–82?

The charge was unfair, since Burke had never opposed pensions for good service. But he was roundly mocked in the House of Lords by two young Foxite aristocrats, the Duke of Bedford and the Earl of Lauderdale. He responded with *A Letter to a Noble Lord*, which Somerset Maugham called 'the finest piece of invective in the English language'. Burke puts the two peers firmly in their place, before offering a proud recapitulation and defence of his own career: 'I have, through life, been willing to give everything to others; and to reserve nothing for myself . . . I do not say I saved my country; I am sure I did my country important service.'

The contrast with the young Duke was manifest: 'I was not, like his Grace of Bedford, swaddled, and rocked, and dandled into a legislator . . . I was not made for a minion or a tool . . . At every step of my progress in life . . . I was obliged to show my passport.' As he turns to Richard, Burke's tone is poignant and elegiac. 'Had it pleased God to continue to me the hopes of succession, I should have been . . . a sort of founder of a family: I should have left a son, who, in all the points in which personal merit can be viewed . . . would not have shown himself inferior to the Duke of Bedford, or to any of those whom he traces in his line ... I live in an inverted order. They who ought to have succeeded me are gone before me. They who should have been to me as posterity are in the place of ancestors.'

Burke died in the small hours of 9 July 1797, and is buried next to his son and brother in Beaconsfield church. His coffin was borne on the shoulders of his most distinguished friends and admirers, including the Dukes of Portland and Devonshire, the Earls Fitzwilliam and of Inchiquin, and the Speaker of the House of Commons. His will left his estate in full to 'my entirely beloved, faithful ... affectionate ... and incomparable wife'. Jane lived on at Gregories until 1812 on a life interest, having sold the property and paid off the family's debts at last.

But, though his body be dead, Edmund Burke remains alive and vigorous today in every other way that matters – in thought and words, and in the continuing relevance and importance of his ideas. From the outset of his political career, he was acknowledged as an orator and writer of enormous power and intellectual imagination. James Boswell once said of him, 'It was astonishing how all kinds of figures of speech crowded upon him. He was like a man in an orchard where boughs loaded with fruit hung around him, and he pulled apples as fast as he pleased and pelted the Ministry.' The great critic William Hazlitt remarked that 'Burke's was a union of untameable vigour and originality'.

As a prose stylist, Burke ranks with the very greatest writers in the English language. Ironically, his most famous supposed quote – 'All that is necessary for evil to triumph is that good men do nothing' – does not seem to be by him; the closest he comes is 'When bad men combine, the good must associate; else they will fall, one by one, an unpitied sacrifice in a contemptible struggle', from the *Thoughts*. But such is the range and abundance of his writing that this matters not at all. Often Burke's writing works at several levels: for example, as an emotional appeal to the reader, as political propaganda, and as a concealed philosophical or historical argument. He is no wit, as Johnson was; his endless quotability lies in the union of language and intellectual substance, and his work is studded with gems such as these:

An Englishman is the unfittest person on earth to argue another Englishman into slavery. [*Speech on Conciliation*]

People crushed by law, have no hopes but from power. If laws are their enemies, they will be enemies to laws; and those who have much to hope and nothing to lose, will always be dangerous. [*Letter to Fox*, 1777]

Because half a dozen grasshoppers under a fern make the field ring with their importunate chink, whilst thousands of great cattle, reposed beneath the shadow of the British oak, chew the cud and are silent, pray do not imagine that those who make the noise are the only inhabitants of the field; that, of course, they are many in number; or that, after all, they are other than the little, shrivelled, meagre, hopping, though loud and troublesome, insects of the hour. [*Reflections*]

It cannot at this time be too often repeated; line upon line; precept upon precept; until it comes into the currency of a proverb, *to innovate is not to reform*. [*Letter to a Noble Lord*]

And most famously of all:

It is now sixteen or seventeen years since I saw the queen of France ... at Versailles; and surely never lighted on this orb, which she hardly seemed to touch, a more delightful vision ... little did I dream that I should have lived to see such disasters fallen upon her in a nation of gallant men, in a nation of men of honour, and of cavaliers. I thought ten thousand swords must have leaped from their scabbards to avenge even a look that threatened her with insult. But the age of chivalry is gone. That of sophisters, economists, and calculators, has succeeded; and the glory of Europe is extinguished for ever. [*Reflections*]

As a politician, Burke's record of practical achievement was mixed. He often overreached himself, he rarely exercised real power, and he was variously denounced as vainglorious, a blowhard and an irrelevance. Yet as a political thinker and statesman Burke will be forever remembered.

The extraordinary fact is not that Burke was occasionally wrong, but that he was so often right. Not only that, he was right for the right reasons – not through luck but because his powers of analysis, imagination and empathy gave him an extraordinary gift of prophecy. Thus he foresaw the effects of British rule in Ireland; the loss of the American colonies; the overreach of the East India Company; and the disastrous consequences of revolution in France. He is the first great framer of the modern conception of representative government, and of the political party.

But Burke also foresaw some of the greatest discontents of the modern age. From a Burkean perspective, the extreme liberalism and individualism of the present day now appear to be in crisis. Various disasters have gravely undermined conventional beliefs in the moral primacy of the individual, in the power of human reason alone to resolve political and economic problems, and in the capacity of unfettered individual freedom to deliver personal or social wellbeing.

In his own time, Burke regarded as his greatest achievement his campaign to restrain the crony capitalism of the East India Company, and to insist on the accountability of private power to legitimate public authority. In effect, he offers a profound critique of the market fundamentalism now prevalent in Western society. But this comes not from the left of the political spectrum, but from the right. Markets are not idolized, but treated as cultural artefacts mediated by trust and tradition. Capitalism becomes, not a one-size-fits-all ideology of consumption, but a spectrum of different models to be evaluated on their own merits.

Burke may have described himself as a Whig in politics, two generations before the word 'conservative' came into political usage. His thought bears little relation to most of the modern-day political ideologies that call themselves conservative. Yet it is profoundly 'small-c' conservative. He reminds us that the individual is not simply a compendium of wants, human happiness is not simply a matter of satisfying individual wants, and the purpose of politics is not to satisfy the interests of individuals living now: it is to preserve a social order which is shaped by the needs of generations past, present and future.

The paradox of Burke's conservatism is thus that, properly understood, it is intrinsically modest, while extreme liberalism appears to promote arrogance and selfishness. Burke's conservatism constrains rampant individualism and the tyranny of the majority, while extreme liberalism threatens to worsen their effects. Burke tempts us to the heretical thought that the route to a better politics may not be through managerial claims – 'we can do it better' – but through a deep change of viewpoint.

In his own political life, he was devoted to an ideal of public service and duty, and deplored the tendency to individual or generational arrogance, and the 'ethics of vanity'. His thought is imbued with the importance of history and memory, and an Orwellian detestation of those that would erase them. He insists on the importance of human allegiance and identity, and on manners, sentiment and 'prejudice', often inherited and not invented, and embedded in social institutions and networks. He emphasizes the human self as an active social force, not the passive vehicle for happiness of the utilitarians, or the individual atoms of much modern economics. Government itself cannot simply be a matter of utility and effectiveness. It must have some continuing purchase on our affections and allegiance.

Finally, Burke also leads us to question the self-image of the present political and media class, in which there is no truth, but only different kinds of 'narrative' deployed in the service of power. Instead, he offers principles that do not change, the sanction of history and the moral authenticity of those willing to give up power to principle. He gives us again the lost language of politics: a language of honour, loyalty, duty and wisdom, which can never be adequately captured in any spreadsheet or economic model.

As the Western world seeks to reset its political and economic course for the twenty-first century, it is this vision of human possibility and renewed social value that may prove to be Burke's greatest legacy.

Jesse Norman

A NOTE ON THE TEXT

Burke's was a life lived through speaking and writing, and his published works are very substantial: they include ten volumes of *Correspondence* published by Chicago/Cambridge University Press (1958–78), and nine volumes of *Writings and Speeches* still in process of publication by Oxford University Press. There have been numerous other editions of his works ever since his death.

This is a text for the general reader, not a scholarly edition. Where possible I have sought to include whole works, or whole sections rather than mere excerpts, so that the reader can see the cast of Burke's thought in each case. Every selection must inevitably offer a partial view. Burke himself regarded the impeachment of Hastings as his greatest achievement, but his speeches and writings on India alone would fill this volume.

Instead, I have tried to do justice to Burke's intellectual multiplicity, his very wide range of interests, his mastery of different rhetorical styles and the depth of his political engagement as well as to his campaigning passions over Ireland, the American colonies, domestic reform, India and revolutionary France. To show the underlying stability and continuity of Burke's thought, I have included a wide selection from his early writings, alongside better-known later works. Gladstone wrote of Burke's writings that they were a 'magazine of wisdom', and he was right: almost every page here attests to it.

A notable feature of this volume is the inclusion of two essays, 'On Parties' and 'Considerations on a Militia', which are newly attributed to Burke and published here in book form for the first time. The essay on parties is significant, since it demonstrates that, far from inventing a convenient theory of parties to suit his aristocratic Whig patrons as was alleged by his detractors, Burke had a recognizably modern working theory of political parties as early as 1757, eight years before he entered politics, and thirteen years before the publication of his seminal *Thoughts on the Cause of the Present Discontents*. I am

grateful to Richard Bourke, who made the original attribu-
tions, for drawing both essays to my attention. I am also very
glad to be able to include the remarkable eulogy placed on
Rockingham's tomb, as well as a small but fascinating representative selection of Burke's letters.

I would like to thank the Chicago/Cambridge University
Press for permission to use selected letters. Unfortunately we
have not been able to use the new OUP texts of the other
writings. For these the texts used in this volume have been
drawn largely from the George Bell & Sons edition of 1901, in
eight volumes, which reprints the Bohn Standard Library text
(1854–89). This has been supplemented by the John C. Nimmo
edition, in twelve volumes, of 1887. Cobbett's *Parliamentary
History* (36 volumes, 1806–20) is the source for several of
Burke's shorter speeches made in the course of debate in the
House of Commons.

Burke's spelling was not consistent, and these prior editions
were not edited or typeset in a consistent way. A few obvious
items have been silently corrected. But otherwise these idiosyn-
crasies have been left to exercise their charm as in the original
editions.

This has been a substantial project, and I would like to thank
my family for their forbearance; my agent, Caroline Michel;
the excellent team at Everyman; Richard Bourke, David Bromwich, Paddy Bullard, Stephen Farrell, Patrick Geoghegan and
Ian Harris for their suggestions for items for inclusion; and
Jonathan Clark, Harvey Mansfield, Michael Sandel and David
Womersley for other kindnesses. Needless to say, none is
responsible for what remains.

SELECT BIBLIOGRAPHY

This bibliography lists works of general interest relating to Burke's life, times and thought, and their influence and interpretation. For more detail see the scholarly bibliographies in Clark's edition of the *Reflections* and the works by Bourke, Bromwich and Lock.

WORKS BY BURKE

Correspondence, ed. THOMAS COPELAND et al., 10 vols, Chicago/Cambridge University Press, 1958–78.

Reflections on the Revolution in France: A Critical Edition, ed. J. C. D. CLARK, Stanford University Press, 2001.

Works, 8 vols, Bohn's Standard Library, London, 1854–89.

Writings and Speeches, ed. PAUL LANGFORD et al., 9 vols to date, Oxford University Press, 1981–.

ANTHOLOGIES

DAVID BROMWICH, *On Empire, Liberty and Reform: Speeches and Letters of Edmund Burke*, Yale University Press, 2000.

ROSS HOFFMAN and PAUL LEVACK, *Burke's Politics: Selected Writings and Speeches of Edmund Burke on Reform, Revolution and War*, Knopf, 1949.

ISAAC KRAMNICK, *The Portable Edmund Burke*, Viking, 1999.

HAROLD LASKI, *Letters of Edmund Burke: A Selection*, Oxford University Press, 1922.

HARVEY MANSFIELD, *Selected Letters of Edmund Burke*, University of Chicago Press, 1984.

PETER STANLIS, *Edmund Burke: Selected Writings and Speeches*, Doubleday, 1963, updated edition Transaction Publishers, 1999.

BIOGRAPHIES OF BURKE

RICHARD BOURKE, *Empire and Revolution: The Political Life of Edmund Burke*, Princeton University Press, 2015.

DAVID BROMWICH, *The Intellectual Life of Edmund Burke: From the Sublime and Beautiful to American Independence*, Harvard University Press, 2014.

IAN HARRIS, 'Edmund Burke', entry in *Stanford Encyclopaedia of Philosophy*, 2010.

RUSSELL KIRK, *Edmund Burke: A Genius Reconsidered*, Arlington House, 1967.

F. P. LOCK, *Edmund Burke*, 2 vols, Oxford University Press, 1998 and 2006.

EDMUND BURKE

JESSE NORMAN, *Edmund Burke: Philosopher, Politician, Prophet*, William Collins, 2013.

CONOR CRUISE O'BRIEN, *The Great Melody*, University of Chicago Press, 1992.

NICHOLAS K. ROBINSON, *Edmund Burke: A Life in Caricature*, Yale University Press, 1996.

OTHER WORKS

PAUL BEW, *Ireland: The Politics of Enmity 1789–2006*, Oxford University Press, 2007.

ROBERT BLAKE, *A History of the Conservative Party from Peel to Major*, Heinemann, 1997.

RICHARD BOURKE, 'Party, Parliament, and Conquest in Newly Ascribed Burke Manuscripts', *Historical Journal*, vol. 55, Cambridge University Press, 2012.

PADDY BULLARD, *Edmund Burke and the Art of Rhetoric*, Cambridge University Press, 2011.

HERBERT BUTTERFIELD, *George III and the Historians*, William Collins, 1957.

ARTHUR CASH, *John Wilkes: The Scandalous Father of Civil Liberty*, Yale University Press, 2006.

ALFRED COBBAN, *Edmund Burke and the Revolt against the Eighteenth Century*, Allen and Unwin, 1929.

THOMAS COPELAND, *Edmund Burke: Six Essays*, Jonathan Cape, 1950.

WILLIAM DOYLE, *The Oxford History of the French Revolution*, Oxford University Press, 2002.

DAVID DWAN and CHRISTOPHER INSOLE (eds), *The Cambridge Companion to Burke*, Cambridge University Press, 2012.

LUKE GIBBONS, *Edmund Burke and Ireland*, Cambridge University Press, 2003.

WILLIAM HAGUE, *William Pitt the Younger*, HarperCollins, 2004.

CHRISTOPHER HIBBERT, *King Mob*, Longman, 1958.

ELIZABETH R. LAMBERT, *Edmund Burke of Beaconsfield*, University of Delaware Press, 2003.

PAUL LANGFORD, *A Polite and Commercial People*, Oxford University Press, 1994.

PAUL LANGFORD, *Walpole and the Robinocracy*, Chadwyck-Healey, 1986.

W. E. H. LECKY, *A History of England in the Eighteenth Century*, 8 vols, London, 1878–90.

YUVAL LEVIN, *The Great Debate: Edmund Burke, Thomas Paine, and the Birth of Right and Left*, Basic Books, 2014.

L. G. MITCHELL, *Charles James Fox*, Penguin, 1997.

LEWIS NAMIER, *The Structure of Politics at the Accession of George III*, Macmillan, 1929.

SELECT BIBLIOGRAPHY

JESSE NORMAN, *The Achievement of Michael Oakeshott*, Duckworth, 1992.

JESSE NORMAN, *The Big Society*, University of Buckingham Press, 2010.

FRANK O'GORMAN, *Edmund Burke: His Political Philosophy*, Allen & Unwin, 1973.

FRANK O'GORMAN, *The Emergence of the British Two-Party System 1760–1832*, Edward Arnold, 1982.

NOËL O'SULLIVAN, *Conservatism*, Everyman, 1976.

RICHARD PARES, *King George III and the Politicians*, Oxford University Press, 1953.

J. G. A. POCOCK, *Virtue, Commerce and History*, Cambridge University Press, 1985.

NICK ROBINS, *The Corporation that Changed the World*, Pluto Press, 2006.

ROGER SCRUTON, *The Meaning of Conservatism*, Penguin, 1980.

P. D. G. THOMAS, *The House of Commons in the Eighteenth Century*, Oxford University Press, 1971.

LIONEL JAMES TROTTER, *Warren Hastings: A Biography*, London, 1878.

CHRONOLOGY

DATE	AUTHOR'S LIFE	LITERARY CONTEXT
1727		
1728		Pope: *The Dunciad.* Swift: *A Short View of the State of Ireland.*
1729		Swift: *A Modest Proposal.*
1730	Edmund Burke born on New Year's Day in Dublin, son of Richard Burke, a prosperous middle-class Protestant lawyer, and his wife Mary Nagle, from a family of impoverished Catholic gentry. He is the third of four surviving children; the boys are brought up as Protestants, their sister as a Catholic. The family home is on Arran Quay, by the river Liffey.	Thomson: *The Seasons.*
1731		Pope: *Moral Essays* (to 1735).
1733		Voltaire: *Lettres philosophiques.*
1736	Edmund sent to live with Patrick Nagle, his maternal uncle, in Ballyduff, Co. Cork, where he remains for four or five years.	Butler: *The Analogy of Religion.*
1739		Swift: *Verses on the Death of Dr Swift.* Hume: *Treatise of Human Nature.*
1740		Richardson: *Pamela.*
1741	Attends a non-denominational Quaker school at Ballitore (to 1744), run by Abraham Shackleton, whose son Richard becomes a close friend.	Hume: *Essays Moral and Political.* Middleton: *Life of Cicero.*
1742		Fielding: *Joseph Andrews; Shamela.*
1744	Uninspired by his studies at Trinity College, Dublin. Supplements them by reading widely, particularly in modern history, politics and poetry.	Death of Pope. Berkeley: *Siris.*

Accession of George II. Famine in Ireland (to 1730).
Irish Catholic freeholders lose voting rights.

Pamphlet war against Irish bankers. North Dublin being developed by Luke Gardiner, Irish politician and property tycoon. Construction begins of new Irish parliament building on College Green, designed by Edward Lovett Pearce (to 1739), the world's first purpose-built bicameral parliament.

Dublin Society (later Royal Society) for the promotion of the arts, sciences, industry and agriculture.

William Pitt the Elder delivers his maiden speech in the British House of Commons. He quickly establishes himself as a leading spokesman of the 'Patriot' opposition to prime minister Robert Walpole.

War of Captain Jenkins' Ear between Britain and Spain.

Famine in Ireland (to 1741). War of Austrian Succession (to 1748).
David Garrick makes his London debut as Richard III.

First performance of Handel's *Messiah* takes place in Dublin. Fall of Walpole after twenty-one years in office.
Henry Pelham and his brother the Duke of Newcastle form the 'Broadbottom' administration and continue to exercise the same network of patronage as had flourished under Walpole.

DATE	AUTHOR'S LIFE	LITERARY CONTEXT
1745		Death of Swift.
1746	Burke family move to Lower Ormond Quay, Dublin. Made a scholar at Trinity.	
1747	Founds two undergraduate clubs, one for the writing of burlesques, the other, the 'Academy of Belles Lettres', to broaden literary knowledge and hone debating skills.	Diderot: *Pensées philosophiques.* Condillac: *Essai sur l'origine des connaissances humaines.* Voltaire: *Zadig.* Gray: *Ode on a Distant Prospect of Eton College.*
1748	Graduates from Trinity. Possibly employed in his father's office. Starts the short-lived *Reformer* magazine.	Montesquieu: *L'Esprit des Lois.* Hume: *Inquiry Concerning Human Understanding.* Richardson: *Clarissa.* Smollett: *Roderick Random.*
1749		Fielding: *Tom Jones.* Bolingbroke: *The Idea of a Patriot King.* Buffon: *Histoire naturelle de l'homme.* Condillac: *Traité des systèmes.*
1750	Goes to London to train as a barrister at the Middle Temple. Begins lifelong friendship with fellow student William Burke.	Rousseau: *Discours sur les sciences et les arts.* Johnson begins *The Rambler.*
1751	Suffering from ill health, visits Bath; meets Dr Christopher Nugent, an Irish Catholic physician and his teenage daughter Jane with whom he later falls in love.	Gray: *Elegy Written in a Country Churchyard.* Hume: *Inquiry Concerning the Principles of Morals.* Voltaire: *Le Siècle de Louis XIV.* *L'Encyclopédie*, ed. Diderot and d'Alembert, begins publication (to 1772).
1752		Hume: *Political Discourses.* Bolingbroke: *Letters on the Study and Use of History.*
1753		Hogarth: *The Analysis of Beauty.* O'Conor: *Dissertations on the Ancient History of Ireland.* Buffon: *Discours sur le style.*
1754		Bolingbroke: *Works* (ed. Mallett).

CHRONOLOGY

Construction of Leinster House in Dublin; south Dublin developed. Jacobite rebellion: Charles Edward Stuart, the 'Young Pretender', lands in Scotland and marches into England, advancing as far as Derby.

Jacobite army defeated by the Duke of Cumberland at Culloden; 'Bonnie Prince Charlie' escapes to the continent. Pitt joins the government, becoming Paymaster General.

Repressive measures taken to secure Scotland against Jacobitism. Kelly Riot at the Smock Alley Theatre, Dublin.

Peace of Aix-la-Chapelle ends the War of Austrian Succession, generally restoring the *status quo ante bellum*. Maria Theresa confirmed as Habsburg empress; Prussia established as a major European power. For Britain and France the peace treaty is little more than an armistice. Site of Pompeii discovered.

Bow Street Runners formed in London. Founding of Halifax, Nova Scotia. Handel's *Music for the Royal Fireworks* first performed.

Britain gives up Asiento right (granted by the Treaty of Utrecht, 1713) to supply unlimited numbers of slaves to Spanish colonies, instead receiving a lump sum and renewed trading privileges with Spain. Westminster Bridge opens.

Dupleix appointed Governor General of India where French and British interests increasingly conflict. Death of Frederick, Prince of Wales. Hogarth's *Beer Street* and *Gin Lane*. Franklin's *Experiments and Observations on Electricity*.

Lord Chesterfield's reform brings English calendar (Julian) in line with the continent (Gregorian). The eleven 'lost days' of September provoke riots.

Hardwicke's Marriage Act rules that all marriages should take place in an Anglican church. Designed to prevent abductions and 'Fleet' (debtors') marriages, it affects dissenters and Catholics as well (Jews and Quakers only are exempted).

Select Society founded in Edinburgh; members include David Hume, William Robertson and Adam Smith. Death of Henry Pelham; Newcastle takes over as First Lord of the Treasury.

DATE	AUTHOR'S LIFE	LITERARY CONTEXT
1754 *cont.*		Warburton: *View of Lord Bolingbroke's Philosophy.* Hume: *History of Great Britain* (to 1762). Condillac: *Traité des sensations.* Diderot: *Pensées sur l'interprétation de la nature.*
1755	Gives up his legal studies to devote himself to writing, which does not improve an already difficult relationship with his father.	Johnson: *Dictionary of the English Language.* Hutcheson: *A System of Moral Philosophy.* Rousseau: *Discours sur l'origine de l'inégalité.*
1756	*A Vindication of Natural Society* published by Robert Dodsley – the beginning of an important business relationship.	Voltaire: *Essai sure les moeurs et l'esprit des nations; Discours sur la religion naturelle; Poème sur le désastre de Lisbonne.*
1757	Establishes himself as a writer with his essay on aesthetics, *A Philosophical Inquiry into the Origins of our Ideas of the Sublime and Beautiful.* Marries Jane Nugent. Sets up home near London in Battersea, later moving to Wimpole Street. The household includes Jane's father and brother, Burke's younger brother Richard and his friend Will Burke. 'On Parties' and 'Considerations on a Militia' drafted.	Hume: *Four Dissertations.* Smollett: *History of England.* Home: *Douglas.* Gray: *Odes.*
1758	*An Account of the European Settlements in America* (with Will Burke). Signed up by the Dodsley brothers to edit and write for a new periodical, the *Annual Register* to which he contributes until 1788. Birth of two sons, Richard (Feb) and Christopher (Dec). Around this time meets the painter Sir Joshua Reynolds and the actor David Garrick, both of whom will become close friends.	Price: *A Review of the Principal Question in Morals.* Vattel: *The Law of Nations.* Blackstone: *A Discourse on the Study of the Law.* Johnson: *The Idler* begins. Rousseau: *Lettres à d'Alembert.* Helvétius: *De l'Esprit.*

CHRONOLOGY

Joseph Black discovers carbon dioxide.
James Lind's *Treatise on Scurvy*.

Lisbon earthquake. British force under General Braddock defeated by French and Indian forces in Virginia.

Diplomatic realignment in Europe: Britain allies with Prussia; Austria with France. Beginning of Seven Years' War. Siraj-ud-daula, Nawab of Bengal, seizes Calcutta; British prisoners held overnight in the 'black hole' at Fort William, many of them dying there. George II reluctantly brings in Pitt the Elder – 'the Great Commoner' – to conduct the war as Secretary of State; Pitt–Newcastle ministry.
Calcutta recaptured. Robert Clive of the East India Company defeats the Nawab of Bengal at the battle of Plassey. French army defeats the Duke of Cumberland and invades Hanover; Pitt pays Frederick the Great an annual subsidy to keep up the fight on the continent; Frederick wins major victories against the French at the battle of Rossbach (Nov) and the Austrians at Leuthen (Dec). Militia Bill passed: Britain now able to raise regiments for her own defence instead of relying on troops from Hanover and Hesse. Admiral Byng court martialled and shot for loss of Minorca (which is restored to Britain at the end of the war). Catholic Committee formed in Ireland by Charles O'Conor, John Curry, Thomas Wyse and others.

In North America the British fail to capture Fort Ticonderoga, but take Louisburg and Fort Duquesne. Ferdinand of Brunswick drives the French from Hanover. Some restrictions lifted on Irish exports to Britain.

DATE	AUTHOR'S LIFE	LITERARY CONTEXT
1759	Working on *Essay towards an Abridgment of the English History* (begun in 1757). Meets the historian David Hume. Becomes secretary to William Gerard Hamilton, a commissioner on the Board of Trade, achieving financial security and an introduction to the world of politics.	Smith: *The Theory of Moral Sentiments*. Robertson: *History of Scotland*. Sterne: *Tristram Shandy* (to 1767). Johnson: *Rasselas*. Voltaire: *Candide*.
1760		George Lyttelton & Elizabeth Montagu: *Dialogues of the Dead*.
1761	Burke and Hamilton accompany Lord Halifax (Hamilton's boss) to Dublin when he is made Lord Lieutenant. Burke is concerned at the Irish government's handling of the 'Whiteboys' disturbances; works on *Tracts relating to Popery Laws* (unfinished).	Rousseau: *La nouvelle Héloïse*.
1762	Abandons his *English History*.	Rousseau: *Du contrat social*; *Émile*. H. Walpole: *Anecdotes of Painting* (to 1780). Stuart & Revett: *Antiquities of Athens*. Hurd: *Letters on Chivalry and Romance*. Home: *Elements of Criticism*.
1763	Hamilton becomes Chancellor of the Exchequer for Ireland; Burke accepts a pension with some qualms as he is reluctant to benefit from patronage.	Publication of Lady Mary Wortley Montagu's 'Turkish Letters'. Churchill: *A Prophecy of Famine* (against Bute). Voltaire: *Traité sur la tolérance*.
1764	Death of his son, Christopher. Hamilton dismissed from his Irish post; falls out with Burke who requires more time for his writing. Burke resigns his pension. Founder member of 'the Club' with Reynolds,	Voltaire: *Dictionnaire philosophique*. Reid: *An Inquiry Into the Human Mind on the Principles of Common Sense*. Pownall: *The Administration of the Colonies*.

CHRONOLOGY

'Year of victories'. General Wolfe's victory at Quebec; successful British invasion of Guadeloupe; Admiral Hawke defeats French fleet at Quiberon Bay; Admiral Boscawen destroys French Toulon fleet at Lagos; Ferdinand of Brunswick victorious at the battle of Minden. Wedgwood begins manufacture of pottery in Staffordshire. Duke of Bridgewater's canal from his Worsley coalfield to Manchester heralds dawn of canal age. Opening of British Museum and Kew Botanical Gardens. John Harrison invents chronometer to calculate longitude.

Accession of George III, who issues proclamation 'For the encouragement of piety and virtue, and for the prevention of vice, profaneness, and immorality' and favours a policy of peace. General Amherst takes Montreal: Canada now in British hands. General Eyre Coote's victory at Wandewash drives the French from the Carnatic. Slave rebellion in Jamaica.
First major outbreak of 'Whiteboys' violence in Ireland (to 1763) severely suppressed by the authorities. In Great Britain the enclosure of arable land reaches a peak with 1,066 enclosure acts between 1761 and 1780.
Pondicherry taken from the French. George III's favourite, Lord Bute, brought into the Cabinet. Peace negotiations pursued. Family compact between France and Spain. Pitt resigns over question of war with Spain.

Resignation of Newcastle; Bute is made First Lord of the Treasury, with Henry Fox as manager of the House of Commons for the court party. Wildman's political club formed by the opposition. 'Massacre of the Pelhamite Innocents' begins (Dec): Bute removes Newcastle's supporters from their offices, major and minor. John Wilkes founds political periodical, *The North Briton*, which leads a press campaign against Bute. Celebrated equine artist George Stubbs paints life-size portrait of Rockingham's racehorse, *Whistlejacket*. Catherine the Great becomes Empress of Russia.

Peace of Paris redefines colonial interests to Britain's advantage, though concessions made to France (the return of Guadeloupe and Martinique, for example) are criticized. Britain gains the whole of Canada. Pitt denounces the government for abandoning Frederick II. Bute's cider tax provokes riots. He resigns and is replaced by George Grenville. Issue 45 of *The North Briton* denounced by the government as a seditious libel; Wilkes arrested under contentious general warrant.
Sugar Act passed – first attempt by Parliament to raise money from the colonies to finance their administration and defence. Currency Act: all colonies banned from issuing paper money. Wilkes, having fled to Paris, is tried *in absentia* and outlawed. Hargreaves invents the spinning jenny which in time leads to a substantial increase in textile production. 'Capability' Brown landscapes the grounds at Blenheim Palace.

DATE	AUTHOR'S LIFE	LITERARY CONTEXT
1764 *cont.*	Dr Johnson, playwright Oliver Goldsmith, and music critic Charles Burney amongst others.	H. Walpole: *The Castle of Otranto.*
1765	Burke and Hamilton part company. Burke engaged as private secretary by the Marquis of Rockingham, just before he becomes prime minister. Elected as MP for Wendover, a pocket borough in the gift of Lord Verney, a Buckinghamshire landowner and friend of Will Burke (Dec).	Blackstone: *Commentaries on the Laws of England.* Macpherson: *Works of Ossian.* Percy: *Reliques of Ancient English Poetry.* Wesley: *Journal.*
1766	Makes his maiden speech on the repeal of the Stamp Act (Jan), having previously organized a repeal campaign. Supports Declaratory Act. After Rockingham's fall (July), turns down employment under Grafton. His pamphlet *A Short Account of a Late Short Administration*, sums up the achievements of the Rockingham ministry. Extended visit to Ireland; successfully organizes defence of James Nagle, a distant relative accused of complicity with the Whiteboys.	Goldsmith: *The Vicar of Wakefield.* Smollett: *Travels through France and Italy.* Lessing: *Laokoon.*
1767	Together with his brother Richard, invests in the East India Company (a scheme of Will Burke's in which their patron Lord Verney is also involved). Keen to acquire social status, purchases Gregories, a Palladian house (complete with art collection) and country estate near Beaconsfield in Buckinghamshire, borrowing heavily in order to do so. Granted the Freedom of the City of Dublin.	Ferguson: *An Essay on the History of Civil Society.* Young: *The Farmer's Letters to the People of England.*

CHRONOLOGY

Grenville's Stamp Act introduced: the first internal tax to be imposed on the American colonies by the British Parliament, it raises a levy on financial papers, advertisements, newspapers, playing cards, etc., and is met with petitions and protests and a boycott of English goods. Fall of Grenville (July). The King calls on Rockingham to form a ministry with the Dukes of Newcastle and Cumberland. The young Mughal emperor Shah Alam grants the British legal title to Bengal and two neighbouring provinces; Clive becomes the new governor; the East India Company gains control of trade and vast tax revenues. Legal challenge to British slave trade begins when Granville Sharp takes up the case of Jonathan Strong. Lord Camden rules against general warrants.

Rockingham's government repeals the Stamp Act but passes a Declaratory Act affirming in principle Parliament's right to tax the colonies (though with no intention of enforcing the right). George III asks Pitt the Elder, now Earl of Chatham, to form a ministry. Chatham orders enquiry into East India Company with a view to claiming their territories for the Crown. Following sectarian disturbances in Co. Tipperary, execution of Father Nicholas Sheehy (a relative by marriage of Burke) for murder on highly suspect evidence.

Chatham absent from politics due to illness, his place taken by the Duke of Grafton. Rockingham declines to join the ministry. East India Company retains control of Indian revenues in return for an annual payment of £400,000 to the government. East India Company stock market bubble (to 1769). Charles Townshend, Chancellor of the Exchequer, imposes duties on tea, lead, glass, paper and other imports to America, opposed by Burke though not by the Rockingham party. George Townshend (brother of the above) becomes the first resident Lord Lieutenant in Ireland; attempts to reform the government, proroguing the Irish Parliament when his money bill is defeated (1769) and sacking the former parliamentary managers from their posts. He is strongly opposed by the Patriot party under Henry Flood. Priestley publishes *The History and Present State of Electricity*. John Wood begins the Royal Crescent, Bath.

EDMUND BURKE

DATE	AUTHOR'S LIFE	LITERARY CONTEXT
1768	Re-elected for Wendover. Active in the House of Commons, where he is now a renowned orator, speaking more than 400 times in the next six years. His particular interests are trade policy and opposing the growth of the King's prerogative powers. Supports the *Nullum Tempus* Bill. Disapproves of Wilkes's playing to the mob, but presses for an enquiry into the St George's Fields killings. Sets to work farming the 400 acres of land attached to his new property, joking that 'politics have almost slipped out of my mind'. The Burke household remains extended, and is seldom without guests.	First *Encyclopaedia Britannica* published. Priestley: *Essay on the First Principles of Government*. Sterne: *A Sentimental Journey*. Arthur Young's accounts of his tours through England and Wales (to 1771).
1769	East India shares crash with dire financial repercussions for all three Burkes, from which they never recover. *Observations on a Late Publication Entitled 'The Present State of the Nation'* defends the Rockingham group on trade and on America. Opposes expulsion of Wilkes from the House of Commons (Feb); involved in the Buckinghamshire petition (July); visits Rockingham in Yorkshire to discuss tactics there (Sept).	*Letters of Junius* (anonymous but possibly written by Burke's friend Philip Francis) criticizing the Grafton ministry (to 1772). Sharp: *The Injustice ... of Tolerating Slavery*. Robertson: *The History of the Reign of Emperor Charles V.* Elizabeth Montagu: *An Essay on the Writings and Genius of Shakespear*.
1770	*Thoughts on the Cause of the Present Discontents*, attacking the influence of the Crown and upholding the cause of the Rockingham Whigs, turns Burke into a national figure. The agriculturalist Arthur Young visits Burke's farm and praises his many innovations.	Goldsmith: *The Deserted Village*. Death of Chatterton. Birth of Wordsworth.
1771	Accepts a well-paid job as London agent of the New York	Smollett: *Humphrey Clinker*. Mackenzie: *The Man of Feeling*.

CHRONOLOGY

Massachusetts petitions against taxation without representation, urging other colonies to follow suit. In response to claims made against lands held by the Duke of Portland, the Rockingham party unite in support of a *Nullum Tempus* Bill, protecting property held for more than sixty years from being challenged by the Crown (defeated but passed in 1769). Wilkes returns to England and is elected MP for Middlesex in the general election (March); surrenders to imprisonment, provoking riots and a 'massacre' of his supporters at St George's Fields, London. Octennial Act passes in Ireland, allowing for more frequent parliaments (Burke opposes this). Royal Academy of Art founded with Sir Joshua Reynolds as president. Captain Cook's first round-the-world voyage with the botanist Joseph Banks (to 1771).

Famine in Bengal (to 1773). East India Company financial crash. Wilkes expelled from the Commons (Feb) and re-elected four times; the runner-up, Henry Luttrell, declared the victor (April). Wilkes founds the radical Society of supporters of the Bill of Rights (Feb) and encourages petitions to the King demanding the dissolution of Parliament. The Rockingham group become involved in the petitioning movement after the end of the session (May), endeavouring to steer the petitions towards moderation. By the end of the year approximately thirty petitions have been sent. Richard Arkwright patents the water frame which will lead to the setting up of factories and the revolutionizing of the cotton industry. By 1792 there are about one hundred cotton mills in England. James Watt patents the condenser (improved version of Newcomen's steam engine).

Resignation of Grafton (Jan). Lord North's ministry restores political stability and follows successful policy of financial retrenchment. Townshend duties except that on tea withdrawn. Dispute between England and Spain over the Falkland Islands. Boston 'Massacre': British soldiers fire on mob attacking customs house, killing five. Wilkes released from prison and admitted as an alderman of the City. Split in the Society of supporters of the Bill of Rights, John Horne (Tooke) founding the more radical Constitutional Society in 1771. Chatham clashes in the Lords with Lord Mansfield for his ruling in the trial of the publisher of *Junius* that the judge and not the jury should decide on the criminality of a libel.
Wilkes and his friends in the City take on the government in their demand for the right of printers to report debates; 'riots and tumults' outside the

DATE	AUTHOR'S LIFE	LITERARY CONTEXT
1771 *cont.*	Assembly. During controversy about the reporting of parliamentary debates, upholds the rights of the printers. Speaks against Sawbridge's first annual motion for triennial parliaments. Supports Dowdeswell's bill to reform the libel laws. Falsely and bitterly attacked as the writer of the *Junius* articles by an old friend, Bishop Markham.	C. Burney: *The Present State of Music in France and Italy.* Price: *Appeal to the Public on the Subject of the National Debt.*
1772	Moves to repeal old laws relating to dealers and middlemen in the corn market. Joins his party in support of a Dissenters' Relief Bill; parts company with them by opposing the petition of the Feathers Tavern Association. Offered by the East India Company a seat on a commission to visit India and advise on reform, but declines. Advises Rockingham against a policy of secession.	Verelst: *A View of the Rise, Progress and Present State of the English Government in Bengal.* Dow: 'A Dissertation on the Origin and Nature of Despotism in Hindostan'.
1773	Travels to France to place his son Richard with a French family at Auxerre in Burgundy. Stays at Paris en route, visiting Versailles, where he sees Marie Antoinette. Fearing a government attempt to secure more patronage to itself, opposes North's Regulating Act. Helps organize campaign against a proposed tax on absentee Irish landlords (Rockingham and other Whig aristocrats own estates there).	Goldsmith: *She Stoops to Conquer.* Flood, Grattan, Langrishe: *Baratariana: Fugitive Political Pieces, Published During the Administration of Lord Townshend in Ireland.*
1774	Makes celebrated speech on American taxation, calling for the repeal of the tax on tea and advising against a policy of coercion (April). Lord Verney, also suffering from the East India crash, is obliged to auction off Burke's seat before the	Chesterfield: *Letters to His Natural Son.* Wesley: *Thoughts on Slavery.* Jefferson: *A Summary View of the Rights of British America.* Young: *Political Arithmetic.* Home: *Sketches of the History of Man.*

HISTORICAL EVENTS

House of Commons. Prosecutions cease but Lord North continues to exclude reporters when he chooses. Dowdeswell's bill to reform the libel laws defeated when the opposition fail to co-operate. Public indignation at the scandalous divorce of the Duke of Grafton while prime minister in 1769 prompts a bill from the upper house to prevent divorced women from marrying their lovers (passes in the Lords but is defeated in the Commons, where Burke supports it). First measures for relief of Catholics pass in the Irish Parliament (Bogland Act).

Relief bill for dissenters passes in the Commons but is defeated in the Lords (a process repeated in 1773). The Feathers Tavern Association, a group of liberal Anglicans, seeks to present a petition to Parliament for clergymen to be relieved from subscribing to the Thirty-Nine Articles and for religious tests to be removed from the universities. It is turned down. Chief Justice Lord Mansfield's landmark ruling in the Somerset Case that no slave should be forcibly removed from Britain and sold into bondage in the colonies is popularly misinterpreted as ending slavery in England.

North's government passes Regulating Act to reform finance and administration of East India Company. Warren Hastings appointed Governor General and a Supreme Council of four set up in Bengal. The Nawab of Arcot, with the support of the British governor of Madras, annexes the small neighbouring state of Tanjore – an action disapproved by the Court of Directors in London. Tea Act allows the Company to export tea directly to America, to be available at a cheap price. Boston Tea Party: radicals dump 340 chests of tea in the harbour (Dec). Lord Harcourt, Lord Lieutenant of Ireland (1772–7) proposes a 10 per cent tax on absentee landlords (Jan); Rockingham campaigns effectively against it, North withdraws his support and the measure is narrowly defeated in the Irish House of Commons (Nov).

Parliament passes a series of coercive Acts to punish the colonists (March–June): Boston Port Act, Massachusetts Government Act, Administration of Justice Act, Quartering Act. The Quebec Act (June), already underway before the Tea Party, attempts to provide equitable government for French Canadians but is regarded as provocative by Americans. First Continental Congress at Philadelphia (Sept) resolves to work for the repeal of all British colonial legislation passed since 1763, embargoes trade with Britain and promotes formation of local militia units.

DATE	AUTHOR'S LIFE	LITERARY CONTEXT
1774 *cont.*	general election. Rockingham supplies a pocket borough – Malton, in Yorkshire – but Burke then stands and wins a more prestigious seat at Bristol (Nov). Delivers an unusual acceptance speech. Around this time becomes the friend and mentor of talented young politician Charles James Fox.	Goethe: *The Sorrows of Young Werther.*
1775	Objects to North's conciliatory propositions (Feb). Presents counter-proposals in his famous speech on Conciliation with America (March). Throughout the summer recess, continues to goad the party leadership into opposing war. A second speech on Conciliation (Nov) recommending even further concessions is once again defeated.	Sheridan: *The Rivals.* Curry: *A Historical and Critical Review of the Civil Wars in Ireland.* Johnson: *A Journey to the Western Islands of Scotland.* Tucker: *A Letter to Edmund Burke, Esq.* Beaumarchais: *Le Barbier de Séville.*
1776	His Shipwreck Bill – for preventing the plunder of shipwrecks (a matter of concern in Bristol) is defeated (April). Drafts an amendment to the proposed Address of Thanks for the King's Speech, protesting against the war in America (Oct); it is defeated in both Houses. Seconds Lord John Cavendish's motion (Nov) proposing repeal of all legislation offensive to the Americans (also defeated). Offers to go to Paris and negotiate with Benjamin Franklin; at the end of the year draws up an address to the King and an appeal to the colonists which party leaders approve but do not act upon.	Gibbon: *The Decline and Fall of the Roman Empire* (to 1788). Smith: *The Wealth of Nations.* Paine: *Common Sense.* Price: *Observations on the Nature of Civil Liberty.* Adams: *Thoughts on Government.* Bentham: *Fragment on Government.* Cartwright: *Take Your Choice* (advocating parliamentary reform). Campbell: *The Philosophy of Rhetoric.* Condillac: *Le Commerce et le gouvernement.* Klinger: *Sturm und Drang.*
1777	Supports the Rockinghamite secession (Feb–April). His *Letter*	Sheridan: *The School for Scandal.*

HISTORICAL EVENTS

Philip Francis arrives in India as one of the Supreme Council, where he soon falls out with Warren Hastings. Bishop Hervey's Act enabling Catholics in Ireland to acknowledge allegiance to the King. Death of Louis XV; accession of Louis XVI. Priestley discovers oxygen.

North's conciliatory propositions passed by Parliament, arriving in America too late to prevent General Gage following orders to enforce the Coercive Acts. First clashes at Lexington and Concord (April). Second Continental Congress (May) votes to appoint George Washington commander-in-chief of the new continental army (May). Battle of Bunker Hill (June). North's proposals rejected in America (July). George III refuses to receive the Olive-branch Petition from Congress; issues proclamation declaring the colonies to be in 'open rebellion' (Aug). Bill passed prohibiting trade with the colonies, effectively ending any possibility of reconciliation (Nov). Renewed Whiteboys activity in Ireland. Henry Flood accepts office as vice-treasurer; Henry Gratton succeeds him as leader of the Patriot party. Harcourt secures permission of the Irish Parliament to send 4000 Irish troops to serve in America but their replacement by 4000 troops from Hesse is declined (Nov).

Embargo on Ireland exporting to America (Feb), causing widespread distress. Request from the Irish Parliament (spearheaded by the Patriot opposition) to raise a militia following the withdrawal of troops is refused by the British government (March). Wilkes introduces the first ever motion for Parliamentary reform (March). American colonies declare independence (4 July). British troops occupy New York City (Aug). Franklin arrives in Paris to secure a treaty between France and the United States (Oct).

Lord Pigot, newly appointed governor of Madras, returns Tanjore to the Rajah. Financier Paul Benfield, an employee of the East India Company, demands a share in the revenues of Tanjore which he claims was promised him by the Nawab of Arcot; Lord Pigot is imprisoned by his council in Madras and subsequently dies. Four members of the council recalled and prosecuted the following year, but get away with minimal fines.

The Rockingham group carry out a partial boycott of Parliament to demonstrate their disaffection with the government (Feb); it arouses little

DATE	AUTHOR'S LIFE	LITERARY CONTEXT
1777 *cont.*	*to the Sheriffs of Bristol* (May) fails to conciliate Bristol merchants, who find him an unsatisfactory constituency MP. Will Burke leaves for India where he finds work as an agent for the Rajah of Tanjore. After a heated Commons debate on the defeat at Saratoga, friends intervene to prevent a duel between Burke and the Solicitor General, Alexander Wedderburn (Dec).	Chatterton: *Poems.* Robertson: *History of America.*
1778	Speech condemning the employment of American Indians against the colonists (Feb). First public declaration on the inevitability of American independence (10 April). Supports Nugent's motion; helps frame the committee's resolutions to remove restrictions on Irish trade, in this instance prepared to co-operate with the government; defends his position on economic grounds to outraged Bristol merchants in two open letters (April–May); takes part in negotiating the final compromise. Busy behind the scenes smoothing the passage of the Catholic Relief Bill in Ireland (summer). In his speech on Army Estimates (Dec) explains his acceptance of American independence. Will Burke returns from India; Burke becomes interested in the plight of Tanjore and begins to study Indian affairs in depth.	Price: *Two Tracts on Civil Liberty* (challenges Burke's views on America). Fanny Burney: *Evelina.* Death of Voltaire and Rousseau.
1779	Drafts much of Admiral Keppel's defence for his court martial (Jan). Presents petition from Scottish Catholics asking for compensation for losses during riots in Edinburgh and Glasgow (March). Speaks in	Hume: *Dialogues Concerning Natural Religion.* Johnson: *Lives of the Poets* (to 1781). Franklin: *Political, Miscellaneous and Philosophical Pieces.*

CHRONOLOGY

public interest and is soon abandoned. Burgoyne defeated at Saratoga, first major American victory of the war (Sept & Oct); hopes of the Rockinghamites raised for a change of ministry. Necker becomes Director General of Finance in France.

Treaties of Alliance and of Amity and Commerce signed in Paris (Feb); France allies with America and enters war with Britain. Lord North dispatches Carlisle Peace Commission to negotiate with Congress (April); their terms are rejected. Rockinghamites adopt independence as a policy (April) opposed by Chatham in his last speech in the Lords. Death of Chatham (May).

US commander John Paul Jones captures HMS *Drake* in the Irish Sea. Irish Militia Act passes but proves too costly to be put into effect. Henry Grattan and the Earl of Charlemont mobilize and arm the loyalist Volunteers to act as a home guard for Ireland. Earl Nugent, an Irish lord sitting in the British House of Commons, successfully proposes a committee to review Irish trade. The planned concessions are reduced to a bare minimum after petitions pour in from the English commercial interest. Catholic Relief Act passed by the Irish Parliament, allowing Catholics to hold leases on land and pass land on to a single heir. A Catholic Relief Act (introduced in the British House of Commons by Sir George Savile and Lord Richard Cavendish, two Rockinghamites) allows Catholics to join the army and to purchase land provided they swear an oath of allegiance to the Crown.

Court-martial of Admiral Augustus Keppel for neglect of duty at the battle of Ushant; the charges against him are dismissed as 'malicious and ill-founded' (Jan). Spain enters war on the French side (June); siege of Gibraltar begins (to 1783). Britain is without allies.

Rioting in Edinburgh and Glasgow (Feb) when it is proposed to extend the Catholic Relief Act to Scotland. Lord George Gordon founds the Protestant Association. Dissenters Act (April) frees dissenting ministers from

DATE	AUTHOR'S LIFE	LITERARY CONTEXT
1779 *cont.*	support of the Dissenters Bill (April). Wary of Lord North's motions for more sweeping reform of Irish trade (Dec); the opposition's lack of commitment is criticized in Ireland. Accuses the government of provoking war with Spain. Drafts articles for the impeachment of Lord North, though does not pursue the matter.	W. Burke: *An Enquiry into the Policy of Making Conquests for the Mahometans.* Auckland: *Four Letters to the Earl of Carlisle.* Sheridan: *The Critic.* Cowper: *Olney Hymns.* Death of Garrick.
1780	Defends his silence on Irish trade in *Letter to Thomas Burgh* (Jan). Briefs Rockingham on his handling of the Yorkshire Association movement. His speech on economical reform (Feb) attracts considerable public interest. *Sketch of the Negro Code* drafted. Again opposes Sawbridge's motion for shorter parliaments – on which his own party is divided. Rockinghamites targeted during Gordon riots; Burke moves his household to safety but goes out into the streets to argue with the mob and favours treating rioters with clemency. Defends the Catholic Relief Act in Parliament. During the general election (Sept), withdraws from contest in Bristol; Rockingham reinstals him at Malton (Dec).	Priestley: *Letters to a Philosophical Unbeliever.* Bentham: *Introduction to the Principles of Morals and Legislation.* Young: *Tour in Ireland.* Lessing: *The Education of Mankind.*
1781	Active on parliamentary select committee reviewing the new Supreme Court in Calcutta and making important minor reforms. Speaks out against British conquest of St Eustatius and treatment of the inhabitants.	Crabbe: *The Library.* Rousseau: *Confessions* (to 1788). Kant: *Critique of Pure Reason.*
1782	*Letter to Lord Kenmare* (Feb) against the Irish penal laws.	Fanny Burney: *Cecilia.* Cowper: *Table-Talk.*

subscribing to the Thirty-Nine Articles.
Growth of Volunteer movement in Ireland; Presbyterians and Catholics are admitted. Free trade for Ireland demanded in the Irish Parliament and on the streets of Dublin. North gives way (Dec): his Irish Trade Act (Feb 1780) grants Ireland the right to trade freely with the colonies.
In Britain government mismanagement of the war combines with high taxation to spark a wave of national protest. Petitioning (Association) movement launched by Christopher Wyvill in Yorkshire (Dec).

Petitioning movement in the counties reaches its height; forty-one petitions delivered to the Commons (Feb–April). Opposition leaders involve themselves, the more cautious Rockinghamites emphasizing reforms to limit patronage and eliminate waste and corruption; Burke's proposals long debated in the House though only one passes (abolition of Board of Trade). John Dunning's motion 'that the influence of the Crown has increased, is increasing, and ought to be diminished' carried by 233 votes to 215 (April) but a subsequent challenge to the royal prerogative to prorogue or dissolve Parliament alarms independent members and Lord North regains control of the House. The Duke of Richmond splits from the Rockinghamites by proposing a far-reaching plan for parliamentary reform (June). Gordon organizes nationwide anti-Catholic petitions, which are presented to Parliament on 2 June; 'Gordon riots', a week of violence in London, put down by the army. Parliament unexpectedly dissolved on 1 September.
Grattan's speech calling for the legislative independence of Ireland (April). Repeal of 1704 Test Act allows dissenters to hold office in Ireland (May). League of Armed Neutrality formed by Russia, Denmark and Sweden to protect the ships of non-belligerents against the Royal Navy's policy of searching all shipping for contraband (March); Anglo-Dutch war breaks out (Dec). Army of Hayder Ali, Sultan of Mysore, overruns the Carnatic and attacks Tanjore.

St Eustatius seized and plundered by Admiral Rodney (Feb). General Cornwallis surrenders at Yorktown (Oct). General Eyre Coote defeats Hayder Ali at the battle of Porto Novo. Parliamentary select committee appointed to investigate complaints made against the East India Company. Thomas Rumbold, governor of Madras, leaves India with a fortune of some £750,000, much of it procured as bribes; Burke and colleagues press for an enquiry into his affairs but the government allows proceedings against him to be dropped in 1782. Pitt the Younger enters Parliament (Jan) as a supporter of Fox. Opening of the first iron bridge at Coalbrookdale, Shropshire.
Resignation of North (March). Rockingham becomes prime minister without a Cabinet majority, obliged to work with the radical Chathamite

DATE	AUTHOR'S LIFE	LITERARY CONTEXT
1782 *cont.*	Though excluded from the Cabinet, Burke is given the well-paid post of Paymaster General in the new Rockingham government, enabling him to introduce many of his economical reforms. He is also made a Privy Councillor. Finds government positions for his son, his brother and for Will Burke. Has misgivings about Irish constitutional reform. His behaviour is noted as becoming rather extreme: according to Sheridan, Burke attacks Pitt in 'a scream of passion' when he introduces a motion on parliamentary reform. Rockingham cancels all Burke's debts before he dies (July). Burke resigns from office when Shelburne, whom he loathes, becomes prime minister. Burke's committee produces eleven reports (to 1783), criticizing the conduct of the East India Company. Burke regards Governor General Warren Hastings as largely responsible and pursues him obsessively for the next twelve years.	Gilpin: *Observations on the River Wye.* Crèvecour: *Letters from an American Farmer.* Rousseau: *Les Rêveries du promeneur solitaire.*
1783	Returns as Paymaster during the Fox-North ministry (April–Dec). His defence of two members of his staff accused of embezzlement but found to be guilty, plays into the hands of his enemies. In the summer the Burkes go on their first ever pleasure trip, to Weymouth and Devon, taking in Stonehenge. Drafts Fox's East-India Bill and supports it eloquently in the Commons.	Crabbe: *The Village.*
1784	With the support of Earl Fitzwilliam (Rockingham's	Beaumarchais: *Le Mariage de Figaro.*

CHRONOLOGY

Lord Shelburne. Programme of economical reform carried through: Crewe's Act disenfranchises all revenue officers of the Crown; Clerke's Act disqualifies government contractors from sitting in the Commons; Burke's Civil Establishment Act subjects royal household expenditure to Treasury control; post of Colonial Secretary abolished; Secretaries of State for the Northern and Southern Department replaced by Home and Foreign Secretaries (Shelburne and Fox respectively); Paymaster's department reformed.

Two Catholic Relief Acts in Ireland, one allowing Catholics to act as teachers and guardians, the second allowing Catholics to buy land except in parliamentary boroughs (Feb). Volunteers' convention at Dungannon (15 Feb) demands legislative independence for Ireland, a demand repeated in the Irish Parliament by Grattan on 16 April and unanimously agreed to. Rockingham's government repeals Declaratory Act of 1719 (which asserted the right of the British Parliament to make laws binding in Ireland) and amends Poynings' Law so the British government can neither amend nor veto bills arising in the Irish Parliament. A Habeas Corpus Act and annual Mutiny Act are passed by 'Grattan's Parliament'. Bank of Ireland founded.

British surrender of Minorca (Feb). Rodney defeats French navy at the battle of the Saintes (April). Peace negotiations open in Paris (April).

Warren Hastings concludes the Treaty of Salbai, ending the first Anglo-Maratha war (May).

Wilkes finally carries his motion that the resolutions on the Middlesex election should be expunged from the journals of the House. Pitt the Younger's motion for an enquiry into the system of representation is defeated but he becomes known as an advocate of parliamentary reform (May). Death of Rockingham (July). When George III calls on Shelburne to head the ministry, Fox, Burke and others resign. Pitt becomes Chancellor of the Exchequer.

Fox and North combine to bring down Shelburne over the peace treaty (Feb); the King waits six weeks before calling on the Duke of Portland (nominal head of the Fox-North coalition) to take office. After further negotiations, Shelburne's treaty is eventually agreed (Sept). Peace of Paris recognizes American independence and largely restores the conquests of the Great Powers. George III ensures the defeat of Fox's East-India Bill in the Commons. Pitt becomes prime minister (Dec), leading a minority government.

Renunciation Act: Irish Parliament given the right to legislate for Ireland; independence of the judiciary guaranteed (April). Second Dungannon convention draws up proposals for parliamentary reform (Sept) but a subsequent bill fails in the Irish House of Commons.

Pitt is returned with a large majority in the general election (March–May); about a hundred coalition supporters defeated, dubbed 'Fox's Martyrs'.

DATE	AUTHOR'S LIFE	LITERARY CONTEXT
1784 *cont.*	nephew and heir) Burke retains his seat at Malton in the general election. Travels to Scotland to be installed as Lord Rector of Glasgow University. Visits Edinburgh en route where he dines with Adam Smith and William Robertson amongst others. Opposes Pitt's India Act. Expresses compassion for India in his speech on abuses of power in Oudh (30 July).	Herder: *Ideas Towards a Philosophy of a History of Mankind.* Young founds periodical *Annals of Agriculture.* Death of Diderot and Johnson.
1785	Opposes Pitt's commercial treaty with Ireland. In a four-hour speech on the Nawab of Arcot's debts, Burke denounces the speculator Paul Benfield (now an MP and influential supporter of Pitt) and accuses Pitt and Dundas of benefiting from the corrupt practices of others (Feb). Re-elected to the rectorship of Glasgow, travels to Scotland in August with his political disciple William Windham, staying at the homes of various opposition politicians en route, calling in on his Edinburgh friends and making a tour of the southern Highlands.	Cowper: *The Task.* Boswell: *The Journal of a Tour of the Hebrides.* Paley: *The Principles of Moral and Political Philosophy.* Reid: *Essays on the Intellectual Powers of Man.* Jefferson: *Notes on the State of Virginia.*
1786	Burke initiates impeachment proceedings against Hastings in the House of Commons (Feb). Indian affairs absorb most of his attention this year.	Burns: *Poems Chiefly in the Scottish Dialect.* Paine: *Dissertations on Government; the Affairs of the Bank; and Paper Money.* Clarkson: *An Essay on the Slavery and Commerce of the Human Species.* Hester Lynch Piozzi: *Anecdotes of Samuel Johnson.*
1787	Makes a personal attack on Pitt in his speech against the Commercial Treaty with France (Feb), considered by all to have gone too far. In a final House of Commons vote (May), receives a	Taylor: *Concerning the Beautiful.* Mary Wollstonecraft: *Thoughts on the Education of Daughters.* Bentham: *A Defence of Usury.*

CHRONOLOGY

Commutation Act (June) reduces duties on tea and other commodities to discourage smuggling and increase customs revenue; the window tax increased and placed on a graduated scale, becoming an important element in national finance. India Act (July) increases government control of East India Company and remains in force until 1858. The Company's creditors persuade Pitt and Dundas to rule that the Nawab of Arcot's debts are repayable in full.

End of Anglo-Mysore war (March); Warren Hastings resigns (Dec) and returns to England. John Wesley finally breaks with the Anglican Church, ordaining his own bishops. First meeting of Irish Academy (later Irish Royal Academy).

Pitt's proposals for free trade with Ireland welcomed by the Irish Parliament but strongly opposed by supporters of Fox and North, backed by the English commercial interest. Amended proposals are rejected in Ireland. Pitt introduces a private member's bill for parliamentary reform, disenfranchising thirty-six rotten and pocket boroughs, which is defeated by 248 to 174 (both government and opposition split over the vote; Burke as usual opposes). This is the best result for reform achieved in the eighteenth century. Pitt embarks on long-term programme to reduce sinecures, which are allowed to lapse on the death of the holder, and to create a leaner and fitter civil service; experiments with excise, introducing a series of new taxes on (for example) racehorses, stage-coach proprietors, hats, hair powder, female servants, dogs and clocks.

The civil list becomes subject to annual review by Parliament. Pitt reforms the sinking fund with a view to reducing the national debt and is largely successful until the outbreak of war in 1793. Commercial treaty between Britain and France. Death of Frederick the Great.

Granville Sharp and Thomas Clarkson set up the Abolition Society, starting a nationwide campaign to end the slave trade. Founding of colony for liberated slaves in Sierra Leone. Britain approves Frederick William II's intervention in the United Provinces to restore the Stadtholder who had been deposed by a revolution of the 'Patriots'; the following year Britain concludes treaties with both Prussia and the United Provinces, ending

DATE	AUTHOR'S LIFE	LITERARY CONTEXT
1787 *cont.*	go-ahead for the Hastings impeachment, with the unexpected support of Pitt.	Adams: *A Defence of the Constitutions of Government of the United States of America.*
1788	Delivers the speech in opening at Hastings' trial in Westminster Hall (13 February). Supports the Prince of Wales's right to be made Regent during the King's evident madness (Dec).	Madison: *The Federalist; or, the New Constitution.* Kant: *Critique of Practical Reason.*
1789	Attacks Pitt's bill for a limited regency (Feb). The violence of his language and his indecorous comments on insanity (he had been visiting madhouses researching the subject) causes general offence. His own sanity is called into question. Supports Wilberforce's resolutions against the slave trade (May). Receives letter from Charles Depont (Nov), asking for his views on the French Revolution about which he already has deep reservations.	Price: *A Discourse on the Love of our Country* (delivered at the Meeting House in Old Jewry, London). Blake: *Songs of Innocence.* White: *The Natural History of Selbourne.* Equiano: *The Interesting Narrative of the Life of Olaudah Equiano.* Sieyès: *Qu'est-ce que le Tiers-Etat?*
1790	Clashes with Sheridan over the Revolution during a debate on army estimates (Feb). With new caution opposes a full repeal of the Test and Corporation Act for dissenters and is accused of apostasy by Fox. Publishes his masterwork, *Reflections on the Revolution in France* (Nov) which becomes a huge popular success in both England and France. It inflames radical opinion outside the House and divides the Whigs within.	Kant: *The Critique of Judgement.* Mary Wollstonecraft: *A Vindication of the Rights of Men.* Blake: *The Marriage of Heaven and Hell.* Stanhope: *A letter from the Earl of Stanhope to the Rt. Hon. Edmund Burke.*

twenty years of isolation in Europe. Federal government established in the
United States. In France, Assembly of Notables reject Calonne's financial
reforms; Calonne is replaced by Brienne, whose proposals for a new land tax
and an end to tax exemptions bring the *parlements* into open confrontation
with the King.

Petitions against the slave trade received by Parliament; Pitt orders a Privy
Council enquiry (Jan). Impeachment of Warren Hastings for oppression and
corruption in India. The trial drags on for seven years; public excitement
swiftly subsides. George III suffers first bout of supposed insanity, prompting
Regency Crisis (Nov). The Prince of Wales's association with opposition
politicians, notably Fox, means that they stand to benefit from a regency
with full royal power, which they energetically support; the government
prefers a regency with conditions attached. The King recovers in February
1789, ending the argument. Louis XVI suspends the *parlements* in France.
Riots in Paris and Grenoble. Estates General convoked (Aug) and doubling
of Third Estate approved (Dec).

French Revolution. Meeting of the Estates General (May); Third Estate
renames itself the National Assembly. Storming of the Bastille (July);
abolition of feudal privileges; secularization of Church lands. Initial reaction
amongst reformers in Britain is generally positive; Fox is an enthusiastic
supporter. March on Versailles (5–6 Oct): royal family forced to accompany
the marchers to Paris. *Assignats* (paper currency) issued (Dec).

Privy Council reports on the slave trade; Wilberforce introduces motion for
abolition which is fiercely opposed in debate and postponed in favour of a
further enquiry. George Washington elected first president of the United
States with John Adams as vice-president. Mutiny on the *Bounty*. Lavoisier,
considered the founder of modern chemistry, publishes his *Traité élémentaire
de chimie*.

Henry Flood's motion for parliamentary reform (March) is not backed by
Pitt – as Burke's friend Windham observes, 'who would repair their house in
the hurricane season?' – and is withdrawn. Fox's motion to repeal the Test
and Corporations Act, the third in as many years, is opposed by a wider
margin than before as opinion hardens against reform (March). General
election in the summer strengthens the government. Burke's *Reflections*
instigate a 'pamphlet war' in which over 700 publications argue the
conservative and radical response to the French Revolution. Civil
constitution of the clergy in France. Abolition of nobility and titles.

DATE	AUTHOR'S LIFE	LITERARY CONTEXT
1791	Follows up with *A Letter to a Member of the National Assembly* (April). Publicly ends his long friendship with Fox during an emotional debate on the Quebec Bill (May), alienating himself from his own party. Defends his conduct against the charge of inconsistency and calls upon moderate Whigs to join him in *An Appeal from the New to the Old Whigs* (Aug). Burke and Windham holding informal meetings with Pitt and Grenville. *Thoughts on French Affairs*, calling for military action, drafted for ministers who prove unresponsive.	Paine: *Rights of Man* (to 1792). Franklin: *Autobiography*. Boswell: *Life of Johnson*. Wolfe Tone: *Argument of Behalf of the Catholics of Ireland*. E. Darwin: *The Botanic Garden*.
1792	Death of two old friends, Sir Joshua Reynolds and Richard Shackleton. Views on Ireland elaborated in *Letter to Sir Hercules Langrishe* and *Letter to Richard Burke*. Unsympathetic to the Unitarian petition (May). Spends two months in Bath (Sept–Oct) for Jane's health. Supports and publicizes a subscription for exiled French clergymen in England. Meets Pitt and presents him with a copy of *Heads for Consideration on the Present State of Affairs*, arguing that British neutrality is not practical (Nov).	Mary Wollstonecraft: *A Vindication of the Rights of Woman*. Young: *Travels in France*. Ferguson: *Principles of Moral and Political Science*. Wyvill: *A Defence of Dr Price and the Reformers of England*. Wordsworth: *Descriptive Sketches*. Paine: *Letter Addressed to the Addressers on the Late Proclamation*. Gilpin: *Three Essays on the Picturesque*.
1793	Pitt consults him over the French declaration of war (Feb). Resigns from the Whig Club when it states its unequivocal support of Fox. Works on Portland and Fitzwilliam to join Pitt, writing *Observations on the Conduct of the Minority* to that effect. Takes a close interest in the military situation on the	Godwin: *Political Justice*. Fanny Burney: *Brief Reflections relative to the Emigrant French Clergy*. Hannah More: *Village Politics*. Anna Laetitia Barbauld: *Sins of Government, Sins of the Nation*.

CHRONOLOGY

Catholic Relief Act (March) passes unopposed, granting Catholics in Britain freedom of worship, allowing them to own schools, to hold junior public offices, and to live in London. Wilberforce's motion to abolish the slave trade is finally put to the vote and defeated (April). Anti-Jacobin 'Church and King' riots in Birmingham (July); Priestley's house and dissenting meeting-houses attacked. Demonstrations in Dublin and Belfast mark the anniversary of the fall of the Bastille (July). Society of United Irishmen (including Catholics and Protestants) founded in Belfast by Wolfe Tone and others to press for parliamentary reform. Constitutional Act ('Quebec Bill') amends the constitution of 1774 to accommodate loyalist emigrants, creating two bicameral assemblies for Upper and Lower Canada and increasing the powers of the governor. Slave revolt in Saint Domingue. French royal family escape from Paris but are turned back at Varennes. Constitution of 1791 voted. Legislative Asssembly convened. Declaration of Pilnitz (Aug): Austria and Prussia declare support for Louis XVI.

Wilberforce's second motion for the abolition of the slave trade passes in the Commons (April) but is indefinitely delayed in the Lords. Pitt opens negotiations with the Portland Whigs (May), Fox's bill for relief of Unitarians defeated (May). Royal proclamation against Seditious Writings (May). Fox's Libel Act enables juries to determine the guilt of the defendant in libel cases, overturning Lord Mansfield's ruling of 1770 (June). Jury find against Tom Paine, tried in his absence for seditious libel (Dec) in part II of *Rights of Man*; the administration encouraged to proceed against his publishers the following year. Thomas Hardy founds the London Corresponding Society which adopts Paine's *Rights of Man* as its manifesto. The Society of Friends of the People set up by Lord Lauderdale, Earl Grey and others. In Ireland Langrishe's Catholic Relief Act enables Catholics to practise law; ban on intermarriage lifted.
France at war with Austria, Prussia and Sardinia. Insurrection in Paris and flight of Lafayette (Aug). September massacre of royalists. Meeting of the Convention; abolition of the monarchy (Sept). Convention promises assistance to all peoples who wish to recover their liberty (Nov). Trial of Louis XVI (Dec).
Execution of Louis XVI (Jan). France declares war on Britain, the United Provinces and Spain. First Coalition against France formed (Feb). Revolutionary tribunal set up. Counter-revolution in the Vendée breaks out (March). British force dispatched to seize French colonies in the West Indies (Burke disapproves). Jacobins seize power: Constitution of 1793 (June). Paine welcomed in France, becoming a French citizen (Aug) and a member of the Convention (Sept). Two Scottish radicals, Thomas Muir and Thomas Fyshe Palmer, sentenced to transportation to Botany Bay (Sept). Robespierre's reign of terror begins (Sept). Marie Antoinette executed (Oct). Anglo-Spanish force under Admiral Hood captures Toulon (Oct), linking up with royalists

DATE	AUTHOR'S LIFE	LITERARY CONTEXT

1793 *cont.* continent. Differs with Pitt on war aims; for Burke it is a crusade against Jacobinism and his aim is the restoration of the old regime. Bombards Pitt with letters of advice. Advocates British assistance in the Vendée headed by French émigré officers. Drafts memorandum, *Remarks on the Policy of the Allies*. Will Burke returns from India to live at Beaconsfield in broken health and considerable debt.

1794 Death of his younger brother Richard (Feb). Winds up the prosecution of Warren Hastings with a speech lasting twenty-seven hours (June). Retires from the House of Commons. Devastated by the death of his son Richard (Aug) for whom Fitzwilliam had kindly made available Burke's old pocket borough of Malton. Lobbying for Fitzwilliam to become Lord Lieutenant of Ireland.

Paine: *The Age of Reason* (to 1807).
Godwin: *Caleb Williams*; *Cursory Strictures on the Charge Delivered by Lord Chief Justice Eyre*.
Coleridge & Southey: *The Fall of Robespierre*.
E. Darwin: *Zoonomia* (to 1796).
Ann Radcliffe: *The Mysteries of Udolpho*.
Bishop Wakefield: *The Spirit of Christianity compared with the Spirit of the Time in Great Britain*.

1795 Involves himself in planned expedition to land émigré troops at Quiberon. Becomes concerned by waning public support for the war and by the possible effect of Auckland's pamphlet calling for peace. His financial embarrassments eased by a pension arranged by Pitt, as recognition of his public service. Drafts *Thoughts and Details on Scarcity*.

Thelwall: *The Natural and Constitutional Right of Britons to Annual Parliaments, Universal Suffrage, and the Freedom of Association*.

CHRONOLOGY

there (Burke approves but the city falls to the revolutionaries in December). Reformers hold national convention in Edinburgh (Dec) resulting in further arrests and punishments.

Catholic Committee presents a petition to George III which is well received. Catholic Relief Act – passed in Ireland under pressure from Pitt and Dundas (April) – gives Catholics the vote on the same term as Protestants (40 shilling freeholders); they are able to hold army commissions up to the rank of colonel, to take lower-level government jobs, and to study at Trinity College, Dublin. St Patrick's College, first Catholic higher education institution, opens in Carlow. A Militia Act passes raising a militia open to both Catholics and Protestants. Convention Act (July) bans associations seeking constitutional reform.

Portland and Fitzwilliam publicly break with Fox and support Pitt (Dec). Leading radicals arrested; Pitt suspends Habeas Corpus (May, until July 1795). Hardy, Horne Tooke and Thelwall tried for treason and acquitted (Dec); proceedings against nine others dropped. Failure of harvest, high food prices and social unrest. Portland Whigs enter into a coalition with Pitt, securing five Cabinet places (July). United Irishmen developing more radical agenda of independence and republicanism; first prosecutions; Dublin branch suppressed. Fall of Robespierre (July). French troops invade the United Provinces and Spain. Austrians defeated at battle of Fleurus. British successes in the West Indies.

France makes peace with the United Provinces, Prussia and Spain (March–April). Disastrous landings at Quiberon, off the coast of Brittany (July) in which 6000 émigré troops are captured and more than 700 executed. Constitution of the year III (Aug); royalist revolt of 13 *vendémiaire* put down by army commanded by Napoleon; dissolution of the Convention (Oct); Belgium incorporated with France (Oct); rule of Directory begins (Nov). Tory politician William Eden, 1st Baron Auckland, publishes *Some Remarks on the Apparent Circumstances of the War in the Fourth Week of October 1795*, arguing that peace with France would guarantee British security; the idea gains currency in Parliament. Seditious Meetings Act and Treasonable Practices Act passed. Another failed harvest. Food riots (to 1796). Government importing corn. Speenhamland system inaugurated. A year after his trial ends, Warren Hastings is acquitted on all charges.

Fitzwilliam, the new Lord Lieutenant, incautiously dismisses several members of the Irish government and backs Grattan's bill for further relief of Catholics, including the right to sit in Parliament; George III and Pitt disapprove and he is recalled. The bill is later defeated. Sectarian violence in Ireland. In Co. Armagh the battle of the Diamond (Sept) is followed by the formation of the Protestant Orange Order.

DATE	AUTHOR'S LIFE	LITERARY CONTEXT
1796	Replies to Foxite criticism of his pension in *A Letter to a Noble Lord* (Feb). Establishes a school at Penn, near his Beaconsfield home, for sixty French émigré boys who had lost their fathers at Quiberon. Publishes *Two Letters on a Regicide Peace* (Oct); embarks on a third letter (indicting the Malmesbury negotiations and criticizing Pitt) in December. Begins to suffer from a gastric illness; consults doctors in London and Bath.	Coleridge: *Poems on Various Subjects.* Lewis: *The Monk.* Bage: *Hermsprong.* Paine: *Agrarian Justice*; *The Decline and Fall of the English System of Finance.* Bishop Watson: *An Apology for the Bible* (against Paine's *Age of Reason*). Thelwall: *Sober Reflections* (response to Burke). Diderot: *Jacques le Fataliste.*
1797	Bath again. Dictates letter on Irish affairs. Dies 9 July and is buried at Beaconsfield.	Reynolds: *Discourses (1769–90).* Schelling: *Ideas Towards a Philosophy of Nature.* Chateaubriand: *Essai sur les révolutions.*
1798		Wordsworth & Coleridge: *Lyrical Ballads.*
1799 1801		

CHRONOLOGY

Insurrection Act in Ireland (Feb); suspension of Habeas Corpus (Sept). Wolfe Tone sails with French fleet in an abortive invasion of Ireland at Bantry Bay (Dec). Spain enters war on the French side. Revolt in the Vendée suppressed. Batavian Republic set up in the Netherlands. Sardinia defeated and granted peace at the price of Nice and Savoy. Napoleon defeats Austrian armies and overruns Italy. Lord Malmesbury's mission to discuss peace terms in Paris (Dec).

Naval mutinies at the Nore and Spithead. British naval victories against the Spanish at St Vincent and the Dutch at Camperdown. Fox and Charles Grey move resolutions for parliamentary reform, defeated 256 to 91; Foxites secede from Parliament. Army supports coup d'état of 18 fructidor, strengthening the power of the Directory (Sept). Peace of Campo Formio between France and Austria (Oct). First banknotes issued by Bank of England.

Failed republican uprisings in Ireland in Ulster and Leinster. Tone sentenced to death for treason; commits suicide. Pitt organizes Second Coalition against France.

Napoleon becomes First Consul for ten years.

Act of Union between England and Ireland.

REFLECTIONS
ON THE
REVOLUTION
IN FRANCE
AND OTHER
WRITINGS

From A VINDICATION OF NATURAL SOCIETY

1756

ADVERTISEMENT TO THE FIRST EDITION[1]

THE FOLLOWING LETTER appears to have been written about the Year 1748, and the Person to whom it is addressed need not be pointed out. As it is probable the Noble Writer had no Design that it should ever appear in Publick, this will account for his having kept no Copy of it, and consequently, for its not appearing amongst the rest of his Works. By what Means it came into the Hands of the Editor, is not at all material to the Publick, any farther than as such an Account might tend to authenticate the Genuineness of it, and for this it was thought it might safely rely on its own internal Evidence.

PREFACE

BEFORE THE PHILOSOPHICAL works of Lord Bolingbroke[2] had appeared, great things were expected from the leisure of a man, who, from the splendid scene of action in which his talents had enabled him to make so conspicuous a figure, had retired to employ those talents in the investigation of truth. Philosophy began to congratulate herself upon such a proselyte from the world of business, and hoped to have extended her power under the auspices of such a leader. In the midst of these pleasing expectations, the works themselves at last appeared in *full body*, and with great pomp. Those who searched in them for new discoveries in the mysteries of nature; those who expected something which might explain or direct the operations of the mind; those who hoped to see morality illustrated and enforced; those who looked for new helps to society and government; those who desired to see the characters and passions of mankind delineated; in short, all who consider such things as philosophy, and require some of them at least in every philosophical work, all these were certainly disappointed; they found the landmarks of science precisely in their former places: and they thought they received but a poor recompense for this disappointment, in seeing every mode of religion attacked in a lively manner, and the foundation of every virtue, and of all government, sapped with great art and much ingenuity. What advantage do we derive from such writings? What delight can a man find in employing a capacity which might be usefully exerted for the noblest purposes, in a sort of sullen labour, in which, if the author could succeed, he is obliged to own, that nothing could be more fatal to mankind than his success?

I cannot conceive how this sort of writers propose to compass the designs they pretend to have in view, by the instruments which they employ. Do they pretend to exalt the mind of man, by proving him no better than a beast? Do they think to enforce the practice of virtue, by denying that vice and virtue are distinguished by good or ill fortune here, or by happiness or misery hereafter? Do they imagine they shall increase our piety, and our reliance on God, by exploding his providence, and insisting that he is neither just nor good? Such are the doctrines which, sometimes concealed, sometimes openly and fully avowed, are found to prevail throughout the writings of Lord Bolingbroke; and such are the reasonings which this noble writer and several others have been pleased to dignify with the name of philosophy. If these are delivered in a specious manner, and in a style above the common, they cannot want a number of admirers of as much docility as can be wished for in disciples. To these the editor of the following little piece has addressed it: there is no reason to conceal the design of it any longer.

The design was, to show that, without the exertion of any considerable forces, the same engines which were employed for the destruction of religion, might be employed with equal success for the subversion of government; and that specious arguments might be used against those things which they, who doubt of everything else, will never permit to be questioned. It is an observation which I think Isocrates[3] makes in one of his orations against the sophists, that it is far more easy to maintain a wrong cause, and to support paradoxical opinions to the satisfaction of a common auditory, than to establish a doubtful truth by solid and conclusive arguments. When men find that something can be said in favour of what, on the very proposal, they have thought utterly indefensible, they grow doubtful of their own reason; they are thrown into a sort of pleasing surprise; they run along with the speaker, charmed and captivated to find such a plentiful harvest of reasoning, where all seemed barren and unpromising. This is the fairy land of philosophy. And it very frequently happens, that those pleasing impressions on the imagination, subsist and produce their effect, even after the understanding has been satisfied of their unsubstantial nature. There is a sort of gloss upon ingenious falsehoods, that dazzles the imagination, but which neither belongs to, nor becomes the sober aspect of, truth. I have met with a quotation in Lord Coke's Reports[4] that pleased me very much, though I do not know from whence he has taken it: "*Interdum fucata falsitas*, (says he,) *in multis est probabilior, et sæpe rationibus vincit nudam veritatem.*" In such cases, the writer has a certain fire and alacrity inspired into him by a consciousness, that, let it fare how it will with the subject, his ingenuity will be sure of applause; and this alacrity becomes much greater if he acts upon the offensive, by the impetuosity that always accompanies an attack, and the unfortunate propensity which mankind have to the finding and exaggerating faults. The editor is satisfied that a mind, which has no restraint from a sense of its own weakness, of its subordinate rank in the creation, and of the extreme danger of letting the imagination loose upon some subjects, may very plausibly attack everything the most excellent and venerable; that it would not be difficult to criticise the creation itself; and that if we were to examine the divine fabrics by our ideas of reason and fitness, and to use the same method of attack by which some men have assaulted revealed religion, we might with as good colour, and with the same success, make the wisdom and power of God in his creation appear to many no better than foolishness. There is an air of plausibility which accompanies vulgar reasonings and notions, taken from the beaten circle of ordinary experience, that is admirably suited to the narrow capacities of some, and to the laziness of others. But this advantage is in a great measure lost, when a painful, comprehensive survey of a very complicated matter, and which requires a great variety of considerations, is to be made; when we must seek in a profound subject, not only for arguments, but for new materials of argument, their measures and their method of arrangement; when we must go out of the sphere of our ordinary ideas, and when we can never walk sure, but by being sensible of our blindness. And this we must do, or we do nothing, whenever we examine the result of a reason which is not our own. Even in matters which are, as it were, just within our reach, what would become of the world, if the practice of all moral duties, and the foundations of society, rested upon having their reasons made clear and demonstrative to every individual?

The editor knows that the subject of this letter is not so fully handled as obviously it might; it was not his design to say all that could possibly be said. It had been inexcusable to fill a large volume with the abuse of reason; nor would such an abuse have been tolerable, even for a few pages, if some under-plot, of more consequence than the apparent design, had not been carried on.

Some persons have thought that the advantages of the state of nature ought to have been more fully displayed. This had undoubtedly been a very ample subject for declamation; but they do not consider the character of the piece. The writers against religion, whilst they oppose every system, are wisely careful never to set up any of their own. If some inaccuracies in calculation, in reasoning, or in method, be found, perhaps these will not be looked upon as faults by the admirers of Lord Bolingbroke; who will, the editor is afraid, observe much more of his Lordship's character in such particulars of the following letter, than they are likely to find of that rapid torrent of an impetuous and overbearing eloquence, and the variety of rich imagery for which that writer is justly admired.

A LETTER TO LORD ＊＊＊＊[5]

SHALL I VENTURE to say, my Lord, that in our late conversation, you were inclined to the party which you adopted rather by the feelings of your good nature, than by the conviction of your judgment? We laid open the foundations of society; and you feared that the curiosity of this search might endanger the ruin of the whole fabric. You would readily have allowed my principle, but you dreaded the consequences; you thought, that having once entered upon these reasonings, we might be carried insensibly and irresistibly farther than at first we could either have imagined or wished. But for my part, my Lord, I then thought, and am still of the same opinion, that error, and not truth of any kind, is dangerous; that ill conclusions can only flow from false propositions; and that, to know whether any proposition be true or false, it is a preposterous method to examine it by its apparent consequences.

These were the reasons which induced me to go so far into that inquiry; and they are the reasons which direct me in all my inquiries. I had, indeed, often reflected on that subject before I could prevail on myself to communicate my reflections to anybody. They were generally melancholy enough; as those usually are which carry us beyond the mere surface of things; and which would undoubtedly make the lives of all thinking men extremely miserable, if the same philosophy which caused the grief, did not, at the same time, administer the comfort.

On considering political societies, their origin, their constitution, and their effects, I have sometimes been in a good deal more than doubt, whether the Creator did ever really intend man for a state of happiness. He has mixed in his cup a number of natural evils, (in spite of the boasts of stoicism, they are evils,) and every endeavour which the art and polity of mankind has used from the beginning of the world to this day, in order to alleviate or cure them, has only served to introduce new mischiefs, or to aggravate and inflame the old. Besides this, the mind of man itself is too active and restless a principle ever to settle on the true point of quiet. It discovers every day some craving want in a body, which really wants but little. It every day invents some new artificial rule to guide that nature which, if left to itself, were the best and surest guide. It finds out imaginary beings prescribing imaginary laws; and then, it raises imaginary terrors to support a belief in the beings, and an obedience to the laws. Many things have been said, and very well undoubtedly, on the subjection in which we should preserve our bodies to the government of our understanding; but enough has not been said upon the restraint which our bodily necessities ought to lay on the extravagant sublimities and eccentric rovings of our minds. The body, or, as some love to call it, our inferior nature, is wiser in its own plain way, and attends its own business more directly, than the mind with all its boasted subtilty.

In the state of nature, without question, mankind was subjected to many and great inconveniences. Want of union, want of mutual assistance, want of a common arbitrator to resort to in their differences. These were evils which they could not but have felt pretty severely on many occasions. The original children of the earth lived with their brethren of the other kinds in much equality. Their diet must have been confined almost wholly to the vegetable kind; and the same tree, which in its flourishing state produced them berries, in its decay gave them an habitation. The mutual desires of the sexes uniting their bodies and affections, and the children which are the results of these intercourses, introduced first the notion of society, and taught its conveniences. This society, founded in natural appetites and instincts, and not in any positive institution, I shall call *natural society*. Thus far nature went and succeeded; but man would go farther. The great error of our nature is, not to know where to stop, not to be satisfied with any reasonable acquirement; not to compound with our condition; but to lose all we have gained by an insatiable pursuit after more. Man found a considerable advantage by this union of many persons to form one family; he therefore judged that he would find his account proportionably in an union of many families into one body politic. And as nature has formed no bond of union to hold them together, he supplied this defect by *laws*.

This is *political society*. And hence the sources of what are usually called states, civil societies, or governments; into some form of which, more extended or restrained, all mankind have gradually fallen. And since it has so happened, and that we owe an implicit reverence to all the institutions of our ancestors, we shall consider these institutions with all that modesty with which we ought to conduct ourselves in examining a received opinion; but with all that freedom and candour which we owe to truth wherever we find it, or however it may contradict our own notions, or oppose our own interests. There is a most absurd and audacious method of reasoning avowed by some bigots and enthusiasts, and through fear assented to by some wiser and better men; it is this: They argue against a fair discussion of popular prejudices, because, say they, though they would be found without any reasonable support, yet the discovery might be productive of the most dangerous consequences. Absurd and blasphemous notion! As if all happiness was not connected with the practice of virtue, which necessarily depends upon the knowledge of truth; that is, upon the knowledge of those unalterable relations which Providence has ordained that everything should bear to every other. These relations, which are truth itself, the foundation of virtue, and, consequently, the only measures of happiness, should be likewise the only measures by which we should direct our reasoning. To these we should conform in good earnest; and not think to force nature, and the whole order of her system, by a compliance with our pride and folly, to conform to our artificial regulations. It is by a conformity to this method we owe the discovery of the few truths we know, and the little liberty and rational happiness we enjoy. We have something fairer play than a reasoner could have expected formerly; and we derive advantages from it which are very visible.

The fabric of superstition has in this our age and nation received much ruder shocks than it had ever felt before; and, through the chinks and breaches of our prison, we see such glimmerings of light, and feel such refreshing airs of liberty, as daily raise our ardour for more. The miseries derived to mankind from superstition under the name of religion, and of ecclesiastical tyranny under the name of church government, have been clearly and usefully exposed. We begin to think and to act from reason and from nature alone. This is true of several, but still is by far the majority in the same old state of blindness and slavery; and much is it to be feared that we shall perpetually relapse, whilst the real productive cause of all this superstitious folly, enthusiastical nonsense, and holy tyranny, holds a reverend place in the estimation even of those who are otherwise enlightened.

Civil government borrows a strength from ecclesiastical; and artificial laws receive a sanction from artificial revelations. The ideas of religion and government are closely connected; and whilst we receive government as a thing necessary, or even useful to our well-being, we shall in spite of us draw in, as a necessary, though undesirable consequence, an artificial religion of some kind or other. To this the vulgar will always be voluntary slaves; and even those of a rank of understanding superior, will now and then involuntarily feel its influence. It is therefore of the deepest concernment to us to be set right in this point; and to be well satisfied whether civil government be such a protector from natural evils, and such a nurse and increaser of blessings, as those of warm imaginations promise. In such a discussion, far am I from proposing in the least to reflect on our most wise form of government; no more than I would, in the freer parts of my philosophical writings, mean to object to the piety, truth, and perfection of our most excellent church. Both I am sensible have their foundations on a rock. No discovery of truth can prejudice them. On the contrary, the more closely the origin of religion and government are examined, the more clearly their excellences must appear. They come purified from the fire. My business is not with them. Having entered a protest against all objections from these quarters, I may the more freely inquire, from history and experience, how far policy has contributed in all times to alleviate those evils which Providence, that perhaps has designed us for a state of imperfection, has imposed; how far our physical skill has cured our constitutional disorders; and whether it may not have introduced new ones, curable perhaps by no skill.

In looking over any state to form a judgment on it, it presents itself in two lights; the external, and the internal. The first, that relation which it bears in point of friendship or enmity to other states. The second, that relation which its component parts, the governing and the governed, bear to each other. The first part of the external view of all states, their relation as friends, makes so trifling a figure in history, that, I am very sorry to say, it affords me but little matter on which to expatiate. The good offices done by one nation to its neighbour;* the support given in public distress; the relief afforded in general calamity; the protection granted in emergent danger; the mutual return of kindness and civility, would afford a very ample and very pleasing subject for history. But, alas! all the history of all times, concerning all nations, does not afford matter enough to fill ten pages, though it should be spun out by the wire-drawing amplification of a Guicciardini[6] himself. The glaring side is that of enmity. War is the matter which fills all history, and consequently the only, or almost the only, view in which we can see the external of political society is in a hostile shape; and the only actions to which we have always seen, and still see, all of them intent, are such as tend to the destruction of one another. "War," says Machiavel,[7] "ought to be the only study of a prince;" and by a prince, he means every sort of state, however constituted. "He ought," says this great political Doctor, "to consider peace only as a breathing-time, which gives him leisure to contrive, and furnishes ability to execute military plans." A meditation on the conduct of political societies made old Hobbes[8] imagine, that war was the state of nature; and truly if a man judged of the individuals of our race by their conduct, when united and packed into nations and kingdoms, he might imagine that every sort of virtue was unnatural and foreign to the mind of man.

---

* Had his Lordship lived to our days, to have seen the noble relief given by this nation to the distressed Portuguese,[9] he had perhaps owned this part of his argument a little weakened; but we do not think ourselves entitled to alter his Lordship's words, but that we are bound to follow him exactly.

The first accounts we have of mankind are but so many accounts of their butcheries. All empires have been cemented in blood; and, in those early periods when the race of mankind began first to form themselves into parties and combinations, the first effect of the combination, and indeed the end for which it seems purposely formed, and best calculated, is their mutual destruction. All ancient history is dark and uncertain. One thing however is clear. There were conquerors and conquests in those days; and, consequently, all that devastation by which they are formed, and all that oppression by which they are maintained. We know little of Sesostris,[10] but that he led out of Egypt an army of above 700,000 men; that he overran the Mediterranean coast as far as Colchis; that, in some places, he met but little resistance, and of course shed not a great deal of blood; but that he found, in others, a people who knew the value of their liberties, and sold them dear. Whoever considers the army this conqueror headed, the space he traversed, and the opposition he frequently met, with the natural accidents of sickness, and the dearth and badness of provision to which he must have been subject in the variety of climates and countries his march lay through, if he knows anything, he must know that even the conqueror's army must have suffered greatly; and that, of this immense number, but a very small part could have returned to enjoy the plunder accumulated by the loss of so many of their companions, and the devastation of so considerable a part of the world. Considering, I say, the vast army headed by this conqueror, whose unwieldy weight was almost alone sufficient to wear down its strength, it will be far from excess to suppose that one half was lost in the expedition. If this was the state of the victorious, and, from the circumstances, it must have been this at the least; the vanquished must have had a much heavier loss, as the greatest slaughter is always in the flight, and great carnage did in those times and countries ever attend the first rage of conquest. It will therefore be very reasonable to allow on their account as much as, added to the losses of the conqueror, may amount to a million of deaths, and then we shall see this conqueror, the oldest we have on the records of history, (though, as we have observed before, the chronology of these remote times is extremely uncertain,) opening the scene by a destruction of at least one million of his species, unprovoked but by his ambition, without any motives but pride, cruelty, and madness, and without any benefit to himself (for

Justin[11] expressly tells us he did not maintain his conquests); but solely to make so many people, in so distant countries, feel experimentally how severe a scourge Providence intends for the human race, when he gives one man the power over many, and arms his naturally impotent and feeble rage with the hands of millions, who know no common principle of action, but a blind obedience to the passions of their ruler.

The next personage who figures in the tragedies of this ancient theatre is Semiramis:[12] for we have no particulars of Ninus, but that he made immense and rapid conquests, which doubtless were not compassed without the usual carnage. We see an army of about three millions employed by this martial queen in a war against the Indians. We see the Indians arming a yet greater; and we behold a war continued with much fury, and with various success. This ends in the retreat of the queen, with scarce a third of the troops employed in the expedition; an expedition which, at this rate, must have cost two millions of souls on her part; and it is not unreasonable to judge that the country which was the seat of the war must have been an equal sufferer. But I am content to detract from this, and to suppose that the Indians lost only half so much, and then the account stands thus: In this war alone, (for Semiramis had other wars,) in this single reign, and in this one spot of the globe, did three millions of souls expire, with all the horrid and shocking circumstances which attend all wars, and in a quarrel in which none of the sufferers could have the least rational concern.

The Babylonian, Assyrian, Median, and Persian monarchies must have poured out seas of blood in their formation, and in their destruction. The armies and fleets of Xerxes,[13] their numbers, the glorious stand made against them, and the unfortunate event of all his mighty preparations, are known to everybody. In this expedition, draining half Asia of its inhabitants, he led an army of about two millions to be slaughtered, and wasted by a thousand fatal accidents, in the same place where his predecessors had before by a similar madness consumed the flower of so many kingdoms, and wasted the force of so extensive an empire. It is a cheap calculation to say, that the Persian empire, in its wars against the Greeks and Scythians, threw away at least four millions of its subjects; to say nothing of its other wars, and the losses sustained in them. These were their losses abroad; but the war was brought home to them, first by Agesilaus, and afterwards by

Alexander.[14] I have not, in this retreat, the books necessary to make very exact calculations; nor is it necessary to give more than hints to one of your Lordship's erudition. You will recollect his uninterrupted series of success. You will run over his battles. You will call to mind the carnage which was made. You will give a glance at the whole, and you will agree with me, that to form this hero no less than twelve hundred thousand lives must have been sacrificed: but no sooner had he fallen himself a sacrifice to his vices, than a thousand breaches were made for ruin to enter, and give the last hand to this scene of misery and destruction. His kingdom was rent and divided; which served to employ the more distinct parts to tear each other to pieces, and bury the whole in blood and slaughter. The kings of Syria and of Egypt, the kings of Pergamus and Macedon, without intermission worried each other for above two hundred years; until at last a strong power, arising in the west, rushed in upon them and silenced their tumults, by involving all the contending parties in the same destruction. It is little to say, that the contentions between the successors of Alexander depopulated that part of the world of at least two millions.

The struggle between the Macedonians and Greeks, and, before that, the disputes of the Greek commonwealths among themselves, for an unprofitable superiority, form one of the bloodiest scenes in history. One is astonished how such a small spot could furnish men sufficient to sacrifice to the pitiful ambition of possessing five or six thousand more acres, or two or three more villages: yet, to see the acrimony and bitterness with which this was disputed between the Athenians and Lacedæmonians;[15] what armies cut off; what fleets sunk, and burnt; what a number of cities sacked, and their inhabitants slaughtered, and captived; one would be induced to believe the decision of the fate of mankind, at least, depended upon it! But these disputes ended, as all such ever have done, and ever will do, in a real weakness of all parties; a momentary shadow and dream of power in some one; and the subjection of all to the yoke of a stranger, who knows how to profit of their divisions. This at least was the case of the Greeks; and surely, from the earliest accounts of them to their absorption into the Roman empire, we cannot judge that their intestine divisions, and their foreign wars, consumed less than three millions of their inhabitants.

What an Aceldama,[16] what a field of blood, Sicily[17] has been

in ancient times, whilst the mode of its government was controverted between the republican and tyrannical parties, and the
possession struggled for by the natives, the Greeks, the Carthaginians, and the Romans, your Lordship will easily recollect. You
will remember the total destruction of such bodies as an army of
300,000 men. You will find every page of its history dyed in
blood, and blotted and confounded by tumults, rebellions, massacres, assassinations, proscriptions, and a series of horror beyond
the histories perhaps of any other nation in the world; though
the histories of all nations are made up of similar matter. I once
more excuse myself in point of exactness for want of books. But
I shall estimate the slaughters in this island but at two millions;
which your Lordship will find much short of the reality.

Let us pass by the wars, and the consequences of them, which
wasted Grecia-Magna,[18] before the Roman power prevailed in
that part of Italy. They are perhaps exaggerated; therefore I shall
only rate them at one million. Let us hasten to open that great
scene which establishes the Roman empire, and forms the grand
catastrophe of the ancient drama. This empire, whilst in its
infancy, began by an effusion of human blood scarcely credible.
The neighbouring little states teemed for new destruction: the
Sabines, the Samnites, the Æqui, the Volsci, the Hetrurians,
were broken by a series of slaughters which had no interruption,
for some hundreds of years; slaughters which upon all sides
consumed more than two millions of the wretched people. The
Gauls, rushing into Italy about this time, added the total destruction of their own armies to those of the ancient inhabitants.
In short, it were hardly possible to conceive a more horrid and
bloody picture, if that the Punic wars[19] that ensued soon after
did not present one that far exceeds it. Here we find that climax
of devastation and ruin, which seemed to shake the whole earth.
The extent of this war which vexed so many nations, and both
elements, and the havoc of the human species caused in both,
really astonishes beyond expression, when it is nakedly considered, and those matters which are apt to divert our attention
from it, the characters, actions, and designs of the persons concerned, are not taken into the account. These wars, I mean those
called the Punic wars, could not have stood the human race in
less than three millions of the species. And yet this forms but a
part only, and a very small part, of the havoc caused by the
Roman ambition. The war with Mithridates[20] was very little less

bloody; that prince cut off at one stroke 150,000 Romans by a massacre. In that war Sylla destroyed 300,000 men at Cheronea. He defeated Mithridates' army under Dorilaus, and slew 300,000. This great and unfortunate prince lost another 300,000 before Cyzicum. In the course of the war he had innumerable other losses; and having many intervals of success, he revenged them severely. He was at last totally overthrown; and he crushed to pieces the king of Armenia his ally by the greatness of his ruin. All who had connexions with him shared the same fate. The merciless genius of Sylla[21] had its full scope; and the streets of Athens were not the only ones which ran with blood. At this period, the sword, glutted with foreign slaughter, turned its edge upon the bowels of the Roman republic itself; and presented a scene of cruelties and treasons enough almost to obliterate the memory of all the external devastations. I intended, my Lord, to have proceeded in a sort of method in estimating the numbers of mankind cut off in these wars which we have on record. But I am obliged to alter my design. Such a tragical uniformity of havoc and murder would disgust your Lordship as much as it would me; and I confess I already feel my eyes ache by keeping them so long intent on so bloody a prospect. I shall observe little on the Servile, the Social, the Gallic, and Spanish wars; nor upon those with Jugurtha, nor Antiochus, nor many others equally important, and carried on with equal fury. The butcheries of Julius Cæsar[22] alone are calculated by somebody else; the numbers he has been the means of destroying have been reckoned at 1,200,000. But to give your Lordship an idea that may serve as a standard, by which to measure, in some degree, the others; you will turn your eyes on Judea; a very inconsiderable spot of the earth in itself, though ennobled by the singular events which had their rise in that country.

This spot happened, it matters not here by what means, to become at several times extremely populous, and to supply men for slaughters scarcely credible, if other well-known and well-attested ones had not given them a colour. The first settling of the Jews here was attended by an almost entire extirpation of all the former inhabitants. Their own civil wars, and those with their petty neighbours, consumed vast multitudes almost every year for several centuries; and the irruptions of the kings of Babylon and Assyria made immense ravages. Yet we have their history but partially, in an indistinct, confused manner; so that I shall

only throw the strong point of light upon that part which coincides with Roman history, and of that part only on the point of
time when they received the great and final stroke which made
them no more a nation;[23] a stroke which is allowed to have cut
off little less than two millions of that people. I say nothing of
the loppings made from that stock whilst it stood; nor from the
suckers that grew out of the old root ever since. But if, in this
inconsiderable part of the globe, such a carnage has been made
in two or three short reigns, and that this great carnage, great as
it is, makes but a minute part of what the histories of that people
inform us they suffered; what shall we judge of countries more
extended, and which have waged wars by far more considerable?

Instances of this sort compose the uniform of history. But
there have been periods when no less than universal destruction
to the race of mankind seems to have been threatened. Such was
that, when the Goths, the Vandals, and the Huns poured into
Gaul, Italy, Spain, Greece, and Africa, carrying destruction
before them as they advanced, and leaving horrid deserts every
way behind them. *Vastum ubique silentium, secreti colles; fumantia
procul tecta; nemo exploratoribus obvius*,[24] is what Tacitus calls *facies
victoriæ*. It is always so; but was here emphatically so. From the
north proceeded the swarms of Goths, Vandals, Huns, Ostro-
goths, who ran towards the south, into Africa itself, which
suffered as all to the north had done. About this time another
torrent of barbarians, animated by the same fury, and encouraged
by the same success, poured out of the south,[25] and ravaged all to
the north-east and west, to the remotest parts of Persia on one
hand, and to the banks of the Loire, or farther, on the other;
destroying all the proud and curious monuments of human art,
that not even the memory might seem to survive of the former
inhabitants. What has been done since, and what will continue
to be done while the same inducements to war continue, I shall
not dwell upon. I shall only in one word mention the horrid
effects of bigotry and avarice, in the conquest of Spanish America; a conquest, on a low estimation, effected by the murder of
ten millions of the species. I shall draw to a conclusion of this
part, by making a general calculation of the whole. I think I have
actually mentioned above thirty-six millions. I have not particularised any more. I do not pretend to exactness; therefore, for the
sake of a general view, I shall lay together all those actually slain
in battles, or who have perished in a no less miserable manner by

the other destructive consequences of war from the beginning of the world to this day, in the four parts of it, at a thousand times as much; no exaggerated calculation, allowing for time and extent. We have not perhaps spoke of the five-hundredth part; I am sure I have not of what is actually ascertained in history; but how much of these butcheries are only expressed in generals, what part of time history has never reached, and what vast spaces of the habitable globe it has not embraced, I need not mention to your Lordship. I need not enlarge on those torrents of silent and inglorious blood which have glutted the thirsty sands of Africa, or discoloured the polar snow, or fed the savage forests of America for so many ages of continual war. Shall I, to justify my calculations from the charge of extravagance, add to the account those skirmishes which happen in all wars, without being singly of sufficient dignity in mischief, to merit a place in history, but which by their frequency compensate for this comparative inno-cence; shall I inflame the account by those general massacres which have devoured whole cities and nations; those wasting pestilences, those consuming famines, and all those furies that follow in the train of war? I have no need to exaggerate; and I have purposely avoided a parade of eloquence on this occasion. I should despise it upon any occasion; else in mentioning these slaughters, it is obvious how much the whole might be height-ened, by an affecting description of the horrors that attend the wasting of kingdoms and sacking of cities. But I do not write to the vulgar, nor to that which only governs the vulgar, their passions. I go upon a naked and moderate calculation, just enough, without a pedantical exactness, to give your Lordship some feeling of the effects of political society. I charge the whole of these effects on political society. I avow the charge, and I shall presently make it good to your Lordship's satisfaction. The num-bers I particularised are about thirty-six millions. Besides those killed in battles I have said something, not half what the matter would have justified, but something I have said concerning the consequences of war, even more dreadful than that monstrous carnage itself, which shocks our humanity, and almost staggers our belief. So that allowing me in my exuberance one way for my deficiencies in the other, you will find me not unreasonable. I think the numbers of men now upon earth are computed at five hundred millions at the most. Here the slaughter of mankind, on what you will call a small calculation, amounts to upwards of seventy times the number of souls this day on the globe: a point which may furnish matter of reflection to one less inclined to draw consequences than your Lordship.

I now come to show, that political society is justly chargeable with much the greatest part of this destruction of the species. To give the fairest play to every side of the question, I will own that there is a haughtiness and fierceness in human nature, which will cause innumerable broils, place men in what situation you please; but owning this, I still insist in charging it to political regulations, that these broils are so frequent, so cruel, and attended with consequences so deplorable. In a state of nature, it had been impossible to find a number of men, sufficient for such slaughters, agreed in the same bloody purpose; or allowing that they might have come to such an agreement, (an impossible supposition,) yet the means that simple nature has supplied them with, are by no means adequate to such an end; many scratches, many bruises, undoubtedly would be received upon all hands; but only a few, a very few deaths. Society and politics, which have given us these destructive views, have given us also the means of satisfying them. From the earliest dawnings of policy to this day, the inventions of men have been sharpening and improving the mystery of murder, from the first rude essays of clubs and stones, to the present perfection of gunnery, cannoneering, bombarding, mining, and all these species of artificial, learned, and refined cruelty, in which we are now so expert, and which make a principal part of what politicians have taught us to believe is our principal glory.

How far mere nature would have carried us, we may judge by the example of those animals, who still follow her laws, and even of those to whom she has given dispositions more fierce, and arms more terrible, than ever she intended we should use. It is an incontestable truth, that there is more havoc made in one year by men of men, than has been made by all the lions, tigers, panthers, ounces, leopards, hyenas, rhinoceroses, elephants, bears, and wolves, upon their several species, since the beginning of the world; though these agree ill enough with each other, and have a much greater proportion of rage and fury in their composition than we have. But with respect to you, ye legislators, ye civilisers of mankind! ye Orpheuses, Moseses, Minoses, Solons, Theseuses, Lycurguses, Numas![26] with respect to you be it spoken, your regulations have done more mischief in cold blood, than all the rage of the fiercest animals in their greatest terrors, or furies, has ever done, or ever could do!

These evils are not accidental. Whoever will take the pains to consider the nature of society will find they result directly from its constitution. For as *subordination*, or, in other words, the reciprocation of tyranny and slavery, is requisite to support these societies; the interest, the ambition, the malice, or the revenge, nay, even the whim and caprice, of one ruling man among them, is enough to arm all the rest, without any private views of their own, to the worst and blackest purposes; and, what is at once lamentable and ridiculous, these wretches engage under those banners with a fury greater than if they were animated by revenge for their own proper wrongs.

It is no less worth observing, that this artificial division of mankind into separate societies, is a perpetual source in itself of hatred and dissension among them. The names which distinguish them are enough to blow up hatred and rage. Examine history; consult present experience; and you will find that far the greater part of the quarrels between several nations, had scarce any other occasion, than, that these nations were different combinations of people, and called by different names; to an Englishman, the name of a Frenchman, a Spaniard, an Italian, much more a Turk, or a Tartar, raises of course ideas of hatred and contempt. If you would inspire this compatriot of ours with pity, or regard, for one of these, would you not hide that distinction? You would not pray him to compassionate the poor Frenchman, or the unhappy German. Far from it; you would speak of him as a *foreigner*; an accident to which all are liable. You would represent him as a *man*; one partaking with us of the same common nature, and subject to the same law. There is something so averse from our own nature in these artificial political distinctions, that we need no other trumpet to kindle us to war and destruction. But there is something so benign and healing in the general voice of humanity, that, maugre all our regulations to prevent it, the simple name of man, applied properly, never fails to work a salutary effect.

This natural unpremeditated effect of policy on the unpossessed passions of mankind appears on other occasions. The very name of a politician, a statesman, is sure to cause terror and hatred; it has always connected with it the ideas of treachery, cruelty, fraud, and tyranny; and those writers, who have faithfully unveiled the mysteries of state-freemasonry, have ever been held in general detestation, for even knowing so perfectly a theory, so detestable. The case of Machiavel seems at first sight something hard in that respect. He is obliged to bear the iniquities of those whose maxims and rules of government he published. His speculation is more abhorred than their practice.

But if there were no other arguments against artificial society than this I am going to mention, methinks it ought to fall by this one only. All writers on the science of policy are agreed, and they agree with experience, that all governments must frequently infringe the rules of justice to support themselves; that truth must give way to dissimulation; honesty to convenience; and humanity itself to the reigning interest. The whole of this mystery of iniquity is called the reason of state. It is a reason which I own I cannot penetrate. What sort of a protection is this of the general right, that is maintained by infringing the rights of particulars? What sort of justice is this, which is enforced by breaches of its own laws? These paradoxes I leave to be solved by the able heads of legislators and politicians. For my part, I say what a plain man would say on such an occasion. I can never believe, that any institution, agreeable to nature, and proper for mankind, could find it necessary, or even expedient, in any case whatsoever, to do, what the best and worthiest instincts of mankind warn us to avoid. But no wonder, that what is set up in opposition to the state of nature should preserve itself by trampling upon the law of nature.

To prove that these sorts of policed societies are a violation offered to nature, and a constraint upon the human mind, it needs only to look upon the sanguinary measures, and instruments of violence, which are everywhere used to support them. Let us take a review of the dungeons, whips, chains, racks, gibbets, with which every society is abundantly stored; by which hundreds of victims are annually offered up to support a dozen or two in pride and madness, and millions in an abject servitude and dependence. There was a time, when I looked with a reverential awe on these mysteries of policy; but age, experience, and philosophy, have rent the veil; and I view this *sanctum sanctorum*, at least, without an enthusiastic admiration. I acknowledge, indeed, the necessity of such a proceeding in such institutions; but I must have a very mean opinion of institutions where such proceedings are necessary.

It is a misfortune, that in no part of the globe natural liberty and natural religion are to be found pure, and free from the mixture of political adulterations. Yet we have implanted in us by Providence, ideas, axioms, rules, of what is pious, just, fair, honest, which no political craft, nor learned sophistry, can entirely expel from our breasts. By these we judge, and we cannot otherwise judge, of the several artificial modes of religion and society, and determine of them as they approach to, or recede from, this standard.

From A PHILOSOPHICAL INQUIRY INTO THE ORIGIN OF OUR IDEAS OF THE SUBLIME AND BEAUTIFUL

1757

INTRODUCTION
ON TASTE

ON A SUPERFICIAL view, we may seem to differ very widely from each other in our reasonings, and no less in our pleasures: but notwithstanding this difference, which I think to be rather apparent than real, it is probable that the standard both of reason and taste is the same in all human creatures. For if there were not some principles of judgment as well as of sentiment common to all mankind, no hold could possibly be taken either on their reason or their passions, sufficient to maintain the ordinary correspondence of life. It appears indeed to be generally acknowledged, that with regard to truth and falsehood there is something fixed. We find people in their disputes continually appealing to certain tests and standards, which are allowed on all sides, and are supposed to be established in our common nature. But there is not the same obvious concurrence in any uniform or settled principles which relate to taste. It is even commonly supposed that this delicate and aërial faculty, which seems too volatile to endure even the chains of a definition, cannot be properly tried by any test, nor regulated by any standard. There is so continual a call for the exercise of the reasoning faculty, and it is so much strengthened by perpetual contention, that certain maxims of right reason seem to be tacitly settled amongst the most ignorant. The learned have improved on this rude science, and reduced those maxims into a system. If taste has not been so happily cultivated, it was not that the subject was barren, but that the labourers were few or negligent; for, to say the truth, there are not the same interesting motives to impel us to fix the one, which urge us to ascertain the other. And, after all, if men differ in their opinion concerning such matters, their difference is not attended with the same important consequences; else I make no doubt but that the logic of taste, if I may be allowed the expression, might very possibly be as well digested, and we might come to discuss matters of this nature with as much certainty, as those which seem more immediately within the province of mere reason. And indeed, it is very necessary, at the entrance into such an inquiry as our present, to make this point as clear as possible; for if taste has no fixed principles, if the imagination is not affected according to some invariable and certain laws, our labour is likely to be employed to very little purpose; as it must be judged a useless, if not an absurd undertaking, to lay down rules for caprice, and to set up for a legislator of whims and fancies.

The term taste, like all other figurative terms, is not extremely accurate; the thing which we understand by it is far from a simple and determinate idea in the minds of most men, and it is therefore liable to uncertainty and confusion. I have no great opinion of a definition, the celebrated remedy for the cure of this disorder. For, when we define, we seem in danger of circumscribing nature within the bounds of our own notions, which we often take up by hazard, or embrace on trust, or form out of a limited and partial consideration of the object before us; instead of extending our ideas to take in all that nature comprehends, according to her manner of combining. We are limited in our inquiry by the strict laws to which we have submitted at our setting out.

> – *Circa vilem patulumque morabimur orbem,*
> *Unde pudor proferre pedem vetat aut operis lex.*[1]

A definition may be very exact, and yet go but a very little way towards informing us of the nature of the thing defined; but let the virtue of a definition be what it will, in the order of things, it seems rather to follow than to precede our inquiry, of which it ought to be considered as the result. It must be acknowledged, that the methods of disquisition and teaching may be sometimes different, and on very good reason undoubtedly; but, for my part, I am convinced that the method of teaching which approaches most nearly to the method of investigation is incomparably the best; since, not content with serving up a few barren and lifeless truths, it leads to the stock on which they grew; it tends to set the reader himself in the track of invention, and to direct him into those paths in which the author has made his own discoveries, if he should be so happy as to have made any that are valuable.

But to cut off all pretence for cavilling, I mean by the word Taste no more than that faculty or those faculties of the mind, which are affected with, or which form a judgment of, the works of imagination and the elegant arts. This is, I think, the most general idea of that word, and what is the least connected with any particular theory. And my point in this inquiry is, to find whether there are any principles, on which the imagination is affected, so common to all, so grounded and certain, as to supply the means of reasoning satisfactorily about them. And such principles of taste I fancy there are; however paradoxical it may seem to those, who on a superficial view imagine, that there is so great a diversity of tastes, both in kind and degree, that nothing can be more indeterminate.

All the natural powers in man, which I know, that are conversant about external objects, are the senses; the imagination; and the judgment. And first with regard to the senses. We do and we must suppose, that as the conformation of their organs are nearly or altogether the same in all men, so the manner of perceiving external objects is in all men the same, or with little difference. We are satisfied that what appears to be light to one eye, appears light to another; that what seems sweet to one palate, is sweet to another; that what is dark and bitter to this man, is likewise dark and bitter to that; and we conclude in the same manner of great and little, hard and soft, hot and cold, rough and smooth, and indeed of all the natural qualities and affections of bodies. If we suffer ourselves to imagine, that their senses present to different men different images of things, this sceptical proceeding will make every sort of reasoning on every subject vain and frivolous, even that sceptical reasoning itself which had persuaded us to entertain a doubt concerning the agreement of our perceptions. But as there will be little doubt that bodies present similar images to the whole species, it must necessarily be allowed, that the pleasures and the pains which every object excites in one man, it must raise in all mankind, whilst it operates naturally, simply, and by its proper powers only; for if we deny this, we must imagine that the same cause, operating in the same manner, and on subjects of the same kind, will produce different effects; which would be highly absurd. Let us first consider this point in the sense of taste, and the rather, as the faculty in question has taken its name from that sense. All men are agreed to call vinegar sour, honey sweet, and aloes bitter; and as they are all agreed in finding these qualities in those objects, they do not in the least differ concerning their effects with regard to pleasure and pain. They all concur in calling sweetness pleasant, and sourness and bitterness unpleasant. Here there is no diversity in their sentiments; and that there is not, appears fully from the consent of all men in the metaphors which are taken from the sense of taste. A sour temper, bitter expressions, bitter curses, a bitter fate, are terms well and strongly understood by all. And we are altogether as well understood when we say, a sweet disposition, a sweet person, a sweet condition, and the like. It is confessed, that custom and some other causes have made many deviations from the natural pleasures or pains which belong to these several tastes: but then the power of distinguishing between the natural and the acquired relish remains to the very last. A man frequently comes to prefer the taste of tobacco to that of sugar, and the flavour of vinegar to that of milk; but this makes no confusion in tastes, whilst he is sensible that the tobacco and vinegar are not sweet, and whilst he knows that habit alone has reconciled his palate to these alien pleasures. Even with such a person we may speak, and with sufficient precision, concerning tastes. But should any man be found who declares, that to him tobacco has a taste like sugar, and that he cannot distinguish between milk and vinegar; or that tobacco and vinegar are sweet, milk bitter, and sugar sour; we immediately conclude that the organs of this man are out of order, and that his palate is utterly vitiated. We are as far from conferring with such a person upon tastes, as from reasoning concerning the relations of quantity with one who should deny that all the parts together were equal to the whole. We do not call a man of this kind wrong in his notions, but absolutely mad. Exceptions of this sort, in either way, do not at all impeach our general rule, nor make us conclude that men have various principles concerning the relations of quantity or the taste of things. So that when it is said, taste cannot be disputed, it can only mean, that no one can strictly answer what pleasure or pain some particular man may find from the taste of some particular thing. This indeed cannot be disputed; but we may dispute, and with sufficient clearness too, concerning the things which are naturally pleasing or disagreeable to the sense. But when we talk of any peculiar or acquired relish, then we must know the habits, the prejudices, or the distempers of this particular man, and we must draw our conclusion from those.

This agreement of mankind is not confined to the taste solely. The principle of pleasure derived from sight is the same in all.

Light is more pleasing than darkness. Summer, when the earth is clad in green, when the heavens are serene and bright, is more agreeable than winter, when everything makes a different appearance. I never remember that anything beautiful, whether a man, a beast, a bird, or a plant, was ever shown, though it were to a hundred people, that they did not all immediately agree that it was beautiful, though some might have thought that it fell short of their expectation, or that other things were still finer. I believe no man thinks a goose to be more beautiful than a swan, or imagines that what they call a Friezland hen excels a peacock. It must be observed too, that the pleasures of the sight are not near so complicated, and confused, and altered by unnatural habits and associations, as the pleasures of the taste are; because the pleasures of the sight more commonly acquiesce in themselves; and are not so often altered by considerations which are independent of the sight itself. But things do not spontaneously present themselves to the palate as they do to the sight; they are generally applied to it, either as food or as medicine; and, from the qualities which they possess for nutritive or medicinal purposes, they often form the palate by degrees, and by force of these associations. Thus opium is pleasing to Turks, on account of the agreeable delirium it produces. Tobacco is the delight of Dutchmen, as it diffuses a torpor and pleasing stupefaction. Fermented spirits please our common people, because they banish care, and all consideration of future or present evils. All of these would lie absolutely neglected if their properties had originally gone no further than the taste; but all these, together with tea and coffee, and some other things, have passed from the apothecary's shop to our tables, and were taken for health long before they were thought of for pleasure. The effect of the drug has made us use it frequently; and frequent use, combined with the agreeable effect, has made the taste itself at last agreeable. But this does not in the least perplex our reasoning; because we distinguish to the last the acquired from the natural relish. In describing the taste of an unknown fruit, you would scarcely say that it had a sweet and pleasant flavour like tobacco, opium, or garlic, although you spoke to those who were in the constant use of these drugs, and had great pleasure in them. There is in all men a sufficient remembrance of the original natural causes of pleasure, to enable them to bring all things offered to their senses to that standard, and to regulate their feelings and opinions by it. Suppose one who had so vitiated his palate as to take more pleasure in the taste of opium than in that of butter or honey, to be presented with a bolus of squills;[2] there is hardly any doubt but that he would prefer the butter or honey to this nauseous morsel, or to any other bitter drug to which he had not been accustomed; which proves that his palate was naturally like that of other men in all things, that it is still like the palate of other men in many things, and only vitiated in some particular points. For in judging of any new thing, even of a taste similar to that which he has been formed by habit to like, he finds his palate affected in a natural manner, and on the common principles. Thus the pleasure of all the senses, of the sight, and even of the taste, that most ambiguous of the senses, is the same in all, high and low, learned and unlearned.

Besides the ideas, with their annexed pains and pleasures, which are presented by the sense; the mind of man possesses a sort of creative power of its own; either in representing at pleasure the images of things in the order and manner in which they were received by the senses, or in combining those images in a new manner, and according to a different order. This power is called imagination; and to this belongs whatever is called wit, fancy, invention, and the like. But it must be observed, that this power of the imagination is incapable of producing anything absolutely new; it can only vary the disposition of those ideas which it has received from the senses. Now the imagination is the most extensive province of pleasure and pain, as it is the region of our fears and our hopes, and of all our passions that are connected with them; and whatever is calculated to affect the imagination with these commanding ideas, by force of any original natural impression, must have the same power pretty equally over all men. For since the imagination is only the representation of the senses, it can only be pleased or displeased with the images, from the same principle on which the sense is pleased or displeased with the realities; and consequently there must be just as close an agreement in the imaginations as in the senses of men. A little attention will convince us that this must of necessity be the case.

But in the imagination, besides the pain or pleasure arising from the properties of the natural object, a pleasure is perceived from the resemblance which the imitation has to the original: the imagination, I conceive, can have no pleasure but what results from one or other of these causes. And these causes operate pretty uniformly upon all men, because they operate by principles in nature, and which are not derived from any particular habits or advantages. Mr. Locke[3] very justly and finely observes of wit, that it is chiefly conversant in tracing resemblances: he remarks, at the same time, that the business of judgment is rather in finding differences. It may perhaps appear, on this supposition, that there is no material distinction between the wit and the judgment, as they both seem to result from different operations of the same faculty of *comparing*. But in reality, whether they are or are not dependent on the same power of the mind, they differ so very materially in many respects, that a perfect union of wit and judgment is one of the rarest things in the world. When two distinct objects are unlike to each other, it is only what we expect; things are in their common way; and therefore they make no impression on the imagination: but when two distinct objects have a resemblance, we are struck, we attend to them, and we are pleased. The mind of man has naturally a far greater alacrity and satisfaction in tracing resemblances than in searching for differences: because by making resemblances we produce *new images*; we unite, we create, we enlarge our stock; but in making distinctions we offer no food at all to the imagination; the task itself is more severe and irksome, and what pleasure we derive from it is something of a negative and indirect nature. A piece of news is told me in the morning; this, merely as a piece of news, as a fact added to my stock, gives me some pleasure. In the evening I find there was nothing in it. What do I gain by this, but the dissatisfaction to find that I have been imposed upon? Hence it is that men are much more naturally inclined to belief than to incredulity. And it is upon this principle, that the most ignorant and barbarous nations have frequently excelled in similitudes, comparisons, metaphors, and allegories, who have been weak and backward in distinguishing and sorting their ideas. And it is for a reason of this kind, that Homer and the Oriental writers, though very fond of similitudes, and though they often strike out such as are truly admirable, seldom take care to have them exact; that is, they are taken with the general resemblance, they paint it strongly, and they take no notice of the difference which may be found between the things compared.

Now, as the pleasure of resemblance is that which principally flatters the imagination, all men are nearly equal in this point, as far as their knowledge of the things represented or compared

extends. The principle of this knowledge is very much accidental, as it depends upon experience and observation, and not on
the strength or weakness of any natural faculty; and it is from this
difference in knowledge, that what we commonly, though with
no great exactness, call a difference in taste proceeds. A man to
whom sculpture is new, sees a barber's block, or some ordinary
piece of statuary; he is immediately struck and pleased, because
he sees something like a human figure; and, entirely taken up
with this likeness, he does not at all attend to its defects. No
person, I believe, at the first time of seeing a piece of imitation
ever did. Some time after, we suppose that this novice lights upon
a more artificial work of the same nature; he now begins to look
with contempt on what he admired at first; not that he admired it
even then for its unlikeness to a man, but for that general, though
inaccurate, resemblance which it bore to the human figure. What
he admired at different times in these so different figures, is
strictly the same; and though his knowledge is improved, his taste
is not altered. Hitherto his mistake was from a want of knowledge in art, and this arose from his inexperience; but he may
be still deficient from a want of knowledge in nature. For it is
possible that the man in question may stop here, and that the
masterpiece of a great hand may please him no more than the
middling performance of a vulgar artist: and this not for want of
better or higher relish, but because all men do not observe with
sufficient accuracy on the human figure to enable them to judge
properly of an imitation of it. And that the critical taste does not
depend upon a superior principle in men, but upon superior
knowledge, may appear from several instances. The story of the
ancient painter and the shoemaker is very well known. The shoemaker set the painter right with regard to some mistakes he had
made in the shoe of one of his figures, and which the painter,
who had not made such accurate observations on shoes, and
was content with a general resemblance, had never observed.
But this was no impeachment to the taste of the painter; it only
showed some want of knowledge in the art of making shoes.
Let us imagine, that an anatomist had come into the painter's
working-room. His piece is in general well done, the figure in
question in a good attitude, and the parts well adjusted to their
various movements; yet the anatomist, critical in his art, may
observe the swell of some muscle not quite just in the peculiar

action of the figure. Here the anatomist observes what the painter had not observed; and he passes by what the shoemaker had remarked. But a want of the last critical knowledge in anatomy no more reflected on the natural good taste of the painter or of any common observer of his piece, than the want of an exact knowledge in the formation of a shoe. A fine piece of a decollated head of St. John the Baptist was shown to a Turkish emperor;[4] he praised many things, but he observed one defect; he observed that the skin did not shrink from the wounded part of the neck. The sultan on this occasion, though his observation was very just, discovered no more natural taste than the painter who executed this piece, or than a thousand European connoisseurs, who probably never would have made the same observation. His Turkish Majesty had indeed been well acquainted with that terrible spectacle, which the others could only have represented in their imagination. On the subject of their dislike there is a difference between all these people, arising from the different kinds and degrees of their knowledge; but there is something in common to the painter, the shoemaker, the anatomist, and the Turkish emperor, the pleasure arising from a natural object, so far as each perceives it justly imitated; the satisfaction in seeing an agreeable figure; the sympathy proceeding from a striking and affecting incident. So far as taste is natural, it is nearly common to all.

In poetry, and other pieces of imagination, the same parity may be observed. It is true, that one man is charmed with Don Bellianis,[5] and reads Virgil coldly: whilst another is transported with the Eneid, and leaves Don Bellianis to children. These two men seem to have a taste very different from each other; but in fact they differ very little. In both these pieces, which inspire such opposite sentiments, a tale exciting admiration is told; both are full of action, both are passionate; in both are voyages, battles, triumphs, and continual changes of fortune. The admirer of Don Bellianis perhaps does not understand the refined language of the Eneid, who, if it was degraded into the style of the Pilgrim's Progress, might feel it in all its energy, on the same principle which made him an admirer of Don Bellianis.

In his favourite author he is not shocked with the continual breaches of probability, the confusion of times, the offences against manners, the trampling upon geography; for he knows nothing of geography and chronology, and he has never examined the grounds of probability. He perhaps reads of a shipwreck on the coast of Bohemia:[6] wholly taken up with so interesting an event, and only solicitous for the fate of his hero, he is not in the least troubled at this extravagant blunder. For why should he be shocked at a shipwreck on the coast of Bohemia, who does not know but that Bohemia may be an island in the Atlantic ocean? and after all, what reflection is this on the natural good taste of the person here supposed?

So far then as taste belongs to the imagination, its principle is the same in all men; there is no difference in the manner of their being affected, nor in the causes of the affection; but in the *degree* there is a difference, which arises from two causes principally; either from a greater degree of natural sensibility, or from a closer and longer attention to the object. To illustrate this by the proce-dure of the senses, in which the same difference is found, let us suppose a very smooth marble table to be set before two men; they both perceive it to be smooth, and they are both pleased with it because of this quality. So far they agree. But suppose another, and after that another table, the latter still smoother than the for-mer, to be set before them. It is now very probable that these men, who are so agreed upon what is smooth, and in the pleasure from thence, will disagree when they come to settle which table has the advantage in point of polish. Here is indeed the great difference between tastes, when men come to compare the excess or diminution of things which are judged by degree and not by measure. Nor is it easy, when such a difference arises, to settle the point, if the excess or diminution be not glaring. If we differ in opinion about two quantities, we can have recourse to a common measure, which may decide the question with the utmost exact-ness; and this, I take it, is what gives mathematical knowledge a greater certainty than any other. But in things whose excess is not judged by greater or smaller, as smoothness and roughness, hardness and softness, darkness and light, the shades of colours, all these are very easily distinguished when the difference is any way considerable, but not when it is minute, for want of some common measures, which perhaps may never come to be dis-covered. In these nice cases, supposing the acuteness of the sense equal, the greater attention and habit in such things will have the advantage. In the question about the tables, the marble-polisher will unquestionably determine the most accurately. But not-withstanding this want of a common measure for settling many disputes relative to the senses, and their representative the imagination, we find that the principles are the same in all, and that there is no disagreement until we come to examine into the pre-eminence or difference of things, which brings us within the province of the judgment.

So long as we are conversant with the sensible qualities of things, hardly any more than the imagination seems concerned; little more also than the imagination seems concerned when the passions are represented, because by the force of natural sympathy they are felt in all men without any recourse to reasoning, and their justness recognised in every breast. Love, grief, fear, anger, joy, all these passions have, in their turns, affected every mind; and they do not affect it in an arbitrary or casual manner, but upon certain, natural, and uniform principles. But as many of the works of imagination are not confined to the representation of sensible objects, nor to efforts upon the passions, but extend themselves to the manners, the characters, the actions, and designs of men, their relations, their virtues and vices, they come within the province of the judgment, which is improved by attention, and by the habit of reasoning. All these make a very considerable part of what are considered as the objects of taste; and Horace[7] sends us to the schools of philosophy and the world for our instruction in them. Whatever certainty is to be acquired in morality and the science of life; just the same degree of certainty have we in what relates to them in the works of imitation. Indeed it is for the most part in our skill in manners, and in the observances of time and place, and of decency in general, which is only to be learned in those schools to which Horace recommends us, that what is called taste, by way of distinction, consists; and which is in reality no other than a more refined judgment. On the whole it appears to me, that what is called taste, in its most general acceptation, is not a simple idea, but is partly made up of a perception of the primary pleasures of sense, of the secondary pleasures of the imagination, and of the conclusions of the reasoning faculty, concerning the various relations of these, and concerning the human passions, manners, and actions. All this is requisite to form taste, and the ground-work of all these is the same in the human mind; for as the senses are the great originals of all our ideas, and consequently of all our pleasures, if they are not uncertain and arbitrary, the whole ground-work of taste is common to all, and therefore there is a sufficient foundation for a conclusive reasoning on these matters.

Whilst we consider taste merely according to its nature and species, we shall find its principles entirely uniform; but the degree in which these principles prevail, in the several individuals of mankind, is altogether as different as the principles themselves are similar. For sensibility and judgment, which are the qualities that compose what we commonly call a *taste*, vary exceedingly in various people. From a defect in the former of these qualities arises a want of taste; a weakness in the latter constitutes a wrong or a bad one. There are some men formed with feelings so blunt, with tempers so cold and phlegmatic, that they can hardly be said to be awake during the whole course of their lives. Upon such persons the most striking objects make but a faint and obscure impression. There are others so continually in the agitation of gross and merely sensual pleasures, or so occupied in the low drudgery of avarice, or so heated in the chase of honours and distinction, that their minds, which had been used continually to the storms of these violent and tempestuous passions, can hardly be put in motion by the delicate and refined play of the imagination. These men, though from a different cause, become as stupid and insensible as the former; but whenever either of these happen to be struck with any natural elegance or greatness, or with these qualities in any work of art, they are moved upon the same principle.

The cause of a wrong taste is a defect of judgment. And this may arise from a natural weakness of understanding, (in whatever the strength of that faculty may consist,) or, which is much more commonly the case, it may arise from a want of proper and well-directed exercise, which alone can make it strong and ready. Besides that ignorance, inattention, prejudice, rashness, levity, obstinacy, in short, all those passions, and all those vices, which pervert the judgment in other matters, prejudice it no less in this its more refined and elegant province. These causes produce different opinions upon everything which is an object of the understanding, without inducing us to suppose that there are no settled principles of reason. And indeed, on the whole, one may observe, that there is rather less difference upon matters of taste among mankind, than upon most of those which depend upon the naked reason; and that men are far better agreed on the excellency of a description in Virgil, than on the truth or falsehood of a theory of Aristotle.

A rectitude of judgment in the arts, which may be called a

good taste, does in a great measure depend upon sensibility; because, if the mind has no bent to the pleasures of the imagina-tion, it will never apply itself sufficiently to works of that species to acquire a competent knowledge in them. But, though a degree of sensibility is requisite to form a good judgment, yet a good judgment does not necessarily arise from a quick sensibility of pleasure; it frequently happens that a very poor judge, merely by force of a greater complexional sensibility, is more affected by a very poor piece, than the best judge by the most perfect; for as everything new, extraordinary, grand, or passionate, is well calculated to affect such a person, and that the faults do not affect him, his pleasure is more pure and unmixed; and as it is merely a pleasure of the imagination, it is much higher than any which is derived from a rectitude of the judgment; the judgment is for the greater part employed in throwing stumbling-blocks in the way of the imagination, in dissipating the scenes of its enchantment, and in tying us down to the disagreeable yoke of our reason: for almost the only pleasure that men have in judging better than others, consists in a sort of conscious pride and superiority, which arises from thinking rightly; but then, this is an indirect pleasure, a pleasure which does not immediately result from the object which is under contemplation. In the morning of our days, when the senses are unworn and tender, when the whole man is awake in every part, and the gloss of novelty fresh upon all the objects that surround us, how lively at that time are our sensations, but how false and inaccurate the judgments we form of things? I despair of ever receiving the same degree of pleasure from the most excellent performances of genius, which I felt at that age from pieces which my present judgment regards as trifling and contemptible. Every trivial cause of pleasure is apt to affect the man of too sanguine a complexion: his appetite is too keen to suffer his taste to be delicate; and he is in all respects what Ovid says of himself in love,

> *Molle meum levibus cor est violabile telis,*
> *Et semper causa est, cur ego semper amem.*[8]

One of this character can never be a refined judge; never what the comic poet calls *elegans formarum spectator.*[9] The excellence and force of a composition must always be imperfectly estimated from its effect on the minds of any, except we know the temper and character of those minds. The most powerful effects of poetry and music have been displayed, and perhaps are still displayed, where these arts are but in a very low and imperfect state. The rude hearer is affected by the principles which operate in these arts even in their rudest condition; and he is not skilful enough to perceive the defects. But as the arts advance towards their perfection, the science of criticism advances with equal pace, and the pleasure of judges is frequently interrupted by the faults which are discovered in the most finished compositions.

Before I leave this subject I cannot help taking notice of an opinion which many persons entertain, as if the taste were a separate faculty of the mind, and distinct from the judgment and imagination; a species of instinct, by which we are struck naturally, and at the first glance, without any previous reasoning, with the excellencies, or the defects, of a composition. So far as the imagination and the passions are concerned, I believe it true, that the reason is little consulted; but where disposition, where decorum, where congruity are concerned, in short, wherever the best taste differs from the worst, I am convinced that the understanding operates, and nothing else; and its operation is in reality far from being always sudden, or, when it is sudden, it is often far from being right. Men of the best taste, by consideration, come frequently to change these early and precipitate judgments, which the mind, from its aversion to neutrality and doubt, loves to form on the spot. It is known that the taste (whatever it is) is improved exactly as we improve our judgment, by extending our knowledge, by a steady attention to our object, and by frequent exercise. They who have not taken these methods, if their taste decides quickly, it is always uncertainly; and their quickness is owing to their presumption and rashness, and not to any sudden irradiation, that in a moment dispels all darkness from their minds. But they who have cultivated that species of knowledge which makes the object of taste, by degrees, and habitually, attain not only a soundness, but a readiness of judgment, as men do by the same methods on all other occasions. At first they are obliged to spell, but at last they read with ease and with celerity; but this celerity of its operation is no proof that the taste is a distinct faculty. Nobody, I believe, has attended the course of a discussion, which turned upon matters within the sphere of mere naked reason, but must have observed the extreme readiness with which the whole process of the argument is carried on, the grounds discovered, the objections raised and answered, and the conclusions drawn from premises, with a quickness altogether as great as the taste can be supposed to work with; and yet where nothing but plain reason either is or can be suspected to operate. To multiply principles for every different appearance, is useless, and unphilosophical too in a high degree.

This matter might be pursued much further; but it is not the extent of the subject which must prescribe our bounds, for what subject does not branch out to infinity? It is the nature of our particular scheme, and the single point of view in which we consider it, which ought to put a stop to our researches.

PART I
SECTION I — NOVELTY

THE FIRST AND the simplest emotion which we discover in the human mind, is Curiosity. By curiosity, I mean whatever desire we have for, or whatever pleasure we take in, novelty. We see children perpetually running from place to place, to hunt out something new: they catch with great eagerness, and with very little choice, at whatever comes before them; their attention is engaged by everything, because everything has, in that stage of life, the charm of novelty to recommend it. But as those things, which engage us merely by their novelty, cannot attach us for any length of time, curiosity is the most superficial of all the affections; it changes its object perpetually, it has an appetite which is very sharp, but very easily satisfied; and it has always an appearance of giddiness, restlessness, and anxiety. Curiosity, from its nature, is a very active principle; it quickly runs over the greatest part of its objects, and soon exhausts the variety which is commonly to be met with in nature; the same things make frequent returns, and they return with less and less of any agreeable effect. In short, the occurrences of life, by the time we come to know it a little, would be incapable of affecting the mind with any other sensations than those of loathing and weariness, if many things were not adapted to affect the mind by means of other powers besides novelty in them, and of other passions besides curiosity in ourselves. These powers and passions shall be considered in their place. But whatever these powers are, or upon what principle soever they affect the mind, it is absolutely necessary that they should not be exerted in those things which a daily and vulgar use have brought into a stale unaffecting familiarity. Some degree of novelty must be one of the materials in every instrument which works upon the mind; and curiosity blends itself more or less with all our passions.

IT SEEMS THEN necessary towards moving the passions of people advanced in life to any considerable degree, that the objects designed for that purpose, besides their being in some measure new, should be capable of exciting pain or pleasure from other causes. Pain and pleasure are simple ideas, incapable of definition. People are not liable to be mistaken in their feelings, but they are very frequently wrong in the names they give them, and in their reasonings about them. Many are of opinion, that pain arises necessarily from the removal of some pleasure; as they think pleasure does from the ceasing or diminution of some pain. For my part, I am rather inclined to imagine, that pain and pleasure, in their most simple and natural manner of affecting, are each of a positive nature, and by no means necessarily dependent on each other for their existence. The human mind is often, and I think it is for the most part, in a state neither of pain nor pleasure, which I call a state of indifference. When I am carried from this state into a state of actual pleasure, it does not appear necessary that I should pass through the medium of any sort of pain. If in such a state of indifference, or ease, or tranquillity, or call it what you please, you were to be suddenly entertained with a concert of music; or suppose some object of a fine shape, and bright, lively colours, to be presented before you; or imagine your smell is gratified with the fragrance of a rose; or if without any previous thirst you were to drink of some pleasant kind of wine, or to taste of some sweetmeat without being hungry; in all the several senses, of hearing, smelling, and tasting, you undoubtedly find a pleasure; yet if I inquire into the state of your mind previous to these gratifications, you will hardly tell me that they found you in any kind of pain; or, having satisfied these several senses with their several pleasures, will you say that any pain has succeeded, though the pleasure is absolutely over? Suppose, on the other hand, a man in the same state of indifference, to receive a violent blow, or to drink of some bitter potion, or to have his ears wounded with some harsh and grating sound; here is no removal of pleasure; and yet here is felt in every sense which is affected, a pain very distinguishable. It may be said, perhaps, that the pain in these cases had its rise from the removal of the pleasure which the man enjoyed before, though that pleasure was of so low a degree as to be perceived only by the removal. But this seems to me a subtilty, that is not discoverable in nature. For if, previous to the pain, I do not feel any actual pleasure, I have no reason to judge that any such thing exists; since pleasure is only pleasure as it is felt. The same may be said of pain, and with equal reason. I can never persuade myself that pleasure and pain are mere relations, which can only exist as they are contrasted; but I think I can discern clearly that there are positive pains and pleasures, which do not at all depend upon each other. Nothing is more certain to my own feelings than this. There is nothing which I can distinguish in my mind with more clearness than the three states, of indifference, of pleasure, and of pain. Every one of these I can perceive without any sort of idea of its relation to anything else. Caius is afflicted with a fit of the colic; this man is actually in pain; stretch Caius upon the rack, he will feel a much greater pain: but does this pain of the rack arise from the removal of any pleasure? or is the fit of the colic a pleasure or a pain, just as we are pleased to consider it?

SECTION III — THE DIFFERENCE BETWEEN THE REMOVAL OF PAIN, AND POSITIVE PLEASURE

WE SHALL CARRY this proposition yet a step farther. We shall venture to propose, that pain and pleasure are not only not necessarily dependent for their existence on their mutual diminution or removal, but that, in reality, the diminution or ceasing of pleasure does not operate like positive pain; and that the removal or diminution of pain, in its effect, has very little resemblance to positive pleasure.* The former of these propositions will, I believe, be much more readily allowed than the latter; because it is very evident that pleasure, when it has run its career, sets us down very nearly where it found us. Pleasure of every kind quickly satisfies; and when it is over, we relapse into indifference,

---

* Mr. Locke [Essay on the Human Understanding, l. ii. c. 20, sect. 16] thinks that the removal or lessening of a pain is considered and operates as a pleasure, and the loss or diminishing of pleasure as a pain. It is this opinion which we consider here.

or rather we fall into a soft tranquillity, which is tinged with the agreeable colour of the former sensation. I own it is not at first view so apparent, that the removal of a great pain does not resemble positive pleasure; but let us recollect in what state we have found our minds upon escaping some imminent danger, or on being released from the severity of some cruel pain. We have on such occasions found, if I am not much mistaken, the temper of our minds in a tenor very remote from that which attends the presence of positive pleasure; we have found them in a state of much sobriety, impressed with a sense of awe, in a sort of tranquillity shadowed with horror. The fashion of the countenance and the gesture of the body on such occasions is so correspondent to this state of mind, that any person, a stranger to the cause of the appearance, would rather judge us under some consternation, than in the enjoyment of anything like positive pleasure.

> ὡς δ' ὅτ' ἂν ἄνδρ' ἄτη πυκινὴ λάβῃ, ὅς τ' ἐνὶ πάτρῃ
> φῶτα κατακτείνας ἄλλων ἐξίκετο δῆμον
> ἀνδρὸς ἐς ἀφνειοῦ, θάμβος δ' ἔχει εἰσορόωντας,

Iliad. 24

> As when a wretch, who, conscious of his crime,
> Pursued for murder from his native clime,
> Just gains some frontier, breathless, pale, amazed;
> All gaze, all wonder![10]

This striking appearance of the man whom Homer supposes to have just escaped an imminent danger, the sort of mixed passion of terror and surprise, with which he affects the spectators, paints very strongly the manner in which we find ourselves affected upon occasions any way similar. For when we have suffered from any violent emotion, the mind naturally continues in something like the same condition, after the cause which first produced it has ceased to operate. The tossing of the sea remains after the storm; and when this remain of horror has entirely subsided, all the passion, which the accident raised, subsides along with it; and the mind returns to its usual state of indifference. In short, pleasure (I mean anything either in the inward sensation, or in the outward appearance, like pleasure from a positive cause) has never, I imagine, its origin from the removal of pain or danger.

SECTION IV — OF DELIGHT AND PLEASURE, AS OPPOSED TO EACH OTHER

BUT SHALL WE therefore say, that the removal of pain or its diminution is always simply painful? or affirm that the cessation or
the lessening of pleasure is always attended itself with a pleasure?
By no means. What I advance is no more than this; first, that
there are pleasures and pains of a positive and independent
nature; and, secondly, that the feeling which results from the
ceasing or diminution of pain does not bear a sufficient resemblance to positive pleasure, to have it considered as of the same
nature, or to entitle it to be known by the same name; and,
thirdly, that upon the same principle the removal or qualification
of pleasure has no resemblance to positive pain. It is certain that
the former feeling (the removal or moderation of pain) has something in it far from distressing or disagreeable in its nature. This
feeling, in many cases so agreeable, but in all so different from
positive pleasure, has no name which I know; but that hinders
not its being a very real one, and very different from all others.
It is most certain that every species of satisfaction or pleasure,
how different soever in its manner of affecting, is of a positive
nature in the mind of him who feels it. The affection is
undoubtedly positive; but the cause may be, as in this case it certainly is, a sort of *Privation*. And it is very reasonable that we
should distinguish by some term two things so distinct in nature,
as a pleasure that is such simply, and without any relation from
that pleasure which cannot exist without a relation, and that too
a relation to pain. Very extraordinary it would be, if these affections, so distinguishable in their causes, so different in their
effects, should be confounded with each other, because vulgar
use has ranged them under the same general title. Whenever
I have occasion to speak of this species of relative pleasure, I call
it *Delight*; and I shall take the best care I can to use that word in
no other sense. I am satisfied the word is not commonly used in
this appropriated signification; but I thought it better to take up
a word already known, and to limit its signification, than to introduce a new one, which would not perhaps incorporate so well
with the language. I should never have presumed the least alteration in our words, if the nature of the language, framed for the
purposes of business rather than those of philosophy, and the
nature of my subject, that leads me out of the common track of

discourse, did not in a manner necessitate me to it. I shall make use of this liberty with all possible caution. As I make use of the word *Delight* to express the sensation which accompanies the removal of pain or danger; so when I speak of positive pleasure, I shall for the most part call it simply *Pleasure*.

SECTION V — JOY AND GRIEF

IT MUST BE observed, that the cessation of pleasure affects the mind three ways. If it simply ceases, after having continued a proper time, the effect is *indifference*; if it be abruptly broken off, there ensues an uneasy sense called *disappointment*; if the object be so totally lost that there is no chance of enjoying it again, a passion arises in the mind, which is called *grief*. Now there is none of these, not even grief, which is the most violent, that I think has any resemblance to positive pain. The person who grieves, suffers his passion to grow upon him; he indulges it, he loves it: but this never happens in the case of actual pain, which no man ever willingly endured for any considerable time. That grief should be willingly endured, though far from a simply pleasing sensation, is not so difficult to be understood. It is the nature of grief to keep its object perpetually in its eye, to present it in its most pleasurable views, to repeat all the circumstances that attend it, even to the last minuteness; to go back to every particular enjoyment, to dwell upon each, and to find a thousand new perfections in all, that were not sufficiently understood before; in grief, the *pleasure* is still uppermost; and the affliction we suffer has no resemblance to absolute pain, which is always odious, and which we endeavour to shake off as soon as possible. The Odyssey of Homer, which abounds with so many natural and affecting images, has none more striking than those which Menelaus raises of the calamitous fate of his friends, and his own manner of feeling it. He owns, indeed, that he often gives himself some intermission from such melancholy reflections; but he observes, too, that, melancholy as they are, they give him pleasure.

> ἀλλ' ἔμπης πάντας μὲν ὀδυρόμενος καὶ ἀχεύων
> πολλάκις ἐν μεγάροισι καθήμενος ἡμετέροισιν
> ἄλλοτε μέν τε γόῳ φρένα τέρπομαι, ἄλλοτε δ' αὖτε
> παύομαι: αἰψηρὸς δὲ κόρος κρυεροῖο γόοιο.

> Still in short intervals of *pleasing woe*,
> Regardful of the friendly dues I owe,
> I to the glorious dead, for ever dear,
> *Indulge* the tribute of a *grateful* tear.[11]

On the other hand, when we recover our health, when we escape an imminent danger, is it with joy that we are affected? The sense on these occasions is far from that smooth and voluptuous satisfaction which the assured prospect of pleasure bestows. The delight which arises from the modifications of pain confesses the stock from whence it sprung, in its solid, strong, and severe nature.

SECTION VI — OF THE PASSIONS WHICH BELONG TO SELF-PRESERVATION

MOST OF THE ideas which are capable of making a powerful impression on the mind, whether simply of Pain or Pleasure, or of the modifications of those, may be reduced very nearly to these two heads, *self-preservation* and *society*; to the ends of one or the other of which all our passions are calculated to answer. The passions which concern self-preservation, turn mostly on *pain* or *danger*. The ideas of *pain*, *sickness*, and *death*, fill the mind with strong emotions of horror; but *life* and *health*, though they put us in a capacity of being affected with pleasure, make no such impression by the simple enjoyment. The passions therefore which are conversant about the preservation of the individual turn chiefly on *pain* and *danger*, and they are the most powerful of all the passions.

SECTION VII — OF THE SUBLIME

WHATEVER IS FITTED in any sort to excite the ideas of pain and danger, that is to say, whatever is in any sort terrible, or is conversant about terrible objects, or operates in a manner analogous to terror, is a source of the *sublime*; that is, it is productive of the strongest emotion which the mind is capable of feeling. I say the strongest emotion, because I am satisfied the ideas of pain are much more powerful than those which enter on the part of pleasure. Without all doubt, the torments which we may be made to suffer are much greater in their effect on the body and mind, than any pleasures which the most learned voluptuary could suggest, or than the liveliest imagination, and the most sound and exquisitely sensible body, could enjoy. Nay, I am in great doubt whether any man could be found, who would earn a life of the most perfect satisfaction, at the price of ending it in the torments, which justice inflicted in a few hours on the late unfortunate regicide in France.[12] But as pain is stronger in its operation than pleasure, so death is in general a much more affecting idea than pain; because there are very few pains, how-ever exquisite, which are not preferred to death: nay, what generally makes pain itself, if I may say so, more painful, is, that it is considered as an emissary of this king of terrors. When danger or pain press too nearly, they are incapable of giving any delight, and are simply terrible; but at certain distances, and with certain modifications, they may be, and they are, delightful, as we every day experience. The cause of this I shall endeavour to investigate hereafter.

SECTION VIII — OF THE PASSIONS WHICH BELONG TO SOCIETY

THE OTHER HEAD under which I class our passions, is that of *society*, which may be divided into two sorts. 1. The society of the *sexes*, which answers the purpose of propagation; and next, that more *general society*, which we have with men and with other animals, and which we may in some sort be said to have even with the inanimate world. The passions belonging to the preser-vation of the individual turn wholly on pain and danger: those which belong to *generation* have their origin in gratifications and *pleasures*; the pleasure most directly belonging to this purpose is of a lively character, rapturous and violent, and confessedly the highest pleasure of sense; yet the absence of this so great an enjoy-ment scarce amounts to an uneasiness; and, except at particular times, I do not think it affects at all. When men describe in what manner they are affected by pain and danger, they do not dwell on the pleasure of health and the comfort of security, and then lament the *loss* of these satisfactions: the whole turns upon the actual pains and horrors which they endure. But if you listen to the complaints of a forsaken lover, you observe that he insists largely on the pleasures which he enjoyed, or hoped to enjoy, and on the perfection of the object of his desires; it is the *loss* which is always uppermost in his mind. The violent effects produced by love, which has sometimes been even wrought up to madness, is no objection to the rule which we seek to establish. When men have suffered their imaginations to be long affected with any idea, it so wholly engrosses them as to shut out by degrees almost every other, and to break down every partition of the mind which would confine it. Any idea is sufficient for the purpose, as is evident from the infinite variety of causes, which give rise to madness: but this at most can only prove, that the passion of love is capable of producing very extraordinary effects, not that its extraordinary emotions have any connexion with positive pain.

SECTION IX — THE FINAL CAUSE OF THE DIFFERENCE BETWEEN THE PASSIONS BELONGING TO SELF-PRESERVATION, AND THOSE WHICH REGARD THE SOCIETY OF THE SEXES

THE FINAL CAUSE of the difference in character between the passions which regard self-preservation, and those which are directed to the multiplication of the species, will illustrate the foregoing remarks yet further; and it is, I imagine, worthy of observation even upon its own account. As the performance of our duties of every kind depends upon life, and the performing them with vigour and efficacy depends upon health, we are very strongly affected with whatever threatens the destruction of either: but as we were not made to acquiesce in life and health, the simple enjoyment of them is not attended with any real pleasure, lest, satisfied with that, we should give ourselves over to indolence and inaction. On the other hand, the generation of mankind is a great purpose, and it is requisite that men should be animated to the pursuit of it by some great incentive. It is therefore attended with a very high pleasure; but as it is by no means designed to be our constant business, it is not fit that the absence of this pleasure should be attended with any considerable pain. The difference between men and brutes, in this point, seems to be remarkable. Men are at all times pretty equally disposed to the pleasures of love, because they are to be guided by reason in the time and manner of indulging them. Had any great pain arisen from the want of this satisfaction, reason, I am afraid, would find great difficulties in the performance of its office. But brutes, who obey laws, in the execution of which their own reason has but little share, have their stated seasons; at such times it is not improbable that the sensation from the want is very troublesome, because the end must be then answered, or be missed in many, perhaps for ever; as the inclination returns only with its season.

SECTION X — OF BEAUTY

THE PASSION WHICH belongs to generation, merely as such, is lust only. This is evident in brutes, whose passions are more unmixed, and which pursue their purposes more directly than ours. The only distinction they observe with regard to their mates, is that of sex. It is true, that they stick severally to their own species in preference to all others. But this preference, I imagine, does not arise from any sense of beauty which they find in their species, as Mr. Addison supposes, but from a law of some other kind, to which they are subject; and this we may fairly conclude, from their apparent want of choice amongst those objects to which the barriers of their species have confined them. But man, who is a creature adapted to a greater variety and intricacy of relation, connects with the general passion the idea of some *social* qualities, which direct and heighten the appetite which he has in common with all other animals; and as he is not designed like them to live at large, it is fit that he should have something to create a preference, and fix his choice; and this in general should be some sensible quality; as no other can so quickly, so power-fully, or so surely produce its effect. The object therefore of this mixed passion, which we call love, is the *beauty* of the *sex*. Men are carried to the sex in general, as it is the sex, and by the common law of nature; but they are attached to particulars by personal *beauty*. I call beauty a social quality; for where women and men, and not only they, but when other animals give us a sense of joy and pleasure in beholding them, (and there are many that do so,) they inspire us with sentiments of tenderness and affection towards their persons; we like to have them near us, and we enter willingly into a kind of relation with them, unless we should have strong reasons to the contrary. But to what end, in many cases, this was designed, I am unable to discover; for I see no greater reason for a connexion between man and several animals who are attired in so engaging a manner, than between him and some others who entirely want this attraction, or possess it in a far weaker degree. But it is probable, that Providence did not make even this distinction, but with a view to some great end; though we cannot perceive distinctly what it is, as his wisdom is not our wisdom, nor our ways his ways.

SECTION XI – SOCIETY AND SOLITUDE

THE SECOND BRANCH of the social passions is that which administers to *society in general*. With regard to this, I observe, that society, merely as society, without any particular heightenings, gives us no positive pleasure in the enjoyment; but absolute and entire *solitude*, that is, the total and perpetual exclusion from all society, is as great a positive pain as can almost be conceived. Therefore in the balance between the pleasure of general *society*, and the pain of absolute solitude, *pain* is the predominant idea. But the pleasure of any particular social enjoyment outweighs very considerably the uneasiness caused by the want of that particular enjoyment; so that the strongest sensations relative to the habitudes of *particular society* are sensations of pleasure. Good company, lively conversations, and the endearments of friendship, fill the mind with great pleasure; a temporary solitude, on the other hand, is itself agreeable. This may perhaps prove that we are creatures designed for contemplation as well as action; since solitude as well as society has its pleasures; as from the former observation we may discern, that an entire life of solitude contradicts the purposes of our being, since death itself is scarcely an idea of more terror.

SECTION XII – SYMPATHY, IMITATION, AND AMBITION

UNDER THIS DENOMINATION of society, the passions are of a complicated kind, and branch out into a variety of forms, agreeably to that variety of ends they are to serve in the great chain of society. The three principal links in this chain are *sympathy*, *imitation*, and *ambition*.

SECTION XIII – SYMPATHY

IT IS BY the first of these passions that we enter into the concerns of others; that we are moved as they are moved, and are never suffered to be indifferent spectators of almost anything which men can do or suffer. For sympathy must be considered as a sort of substitution, by which we are put into the place of another man, and affected in many respects as he is affected; so that this passion may either partake of the nature of those which regard self-preservation, and turning upon pain may be a source of the sublime; or it may turn upon ideas of pleasure; and then whatever has been said of the social affections, whether they regard society in general, or only some particular modes of it, may be applicable here. It is by this principle chiefly that poetry, painting, and other affecting arts, transfuse their passions from one breast to another, and are often capable of grafting a delight on wretchedness, misery, and death itself. It is a common observation, that objects which in the reality would shock, are in tragical, and such like representations, the source of a very high species of pleasure. This, taken as a fact, has been the cause of much reasoning. The satisfaction has been commonly attributed, first, to the comfort we receive in considering that so melancholy a story is no more than a fiction; and, next, to the contemplation of our own freedom from the evils which we see represented. I am afraid it is a practice much too common in inquiries of this nature, to attribute the cause of feelings which merely arise from the mechanical structure of our bodies, or from the natural frame and constitution of our minds, to certain conclusions of the reasoning faculty on the objects presented to us; for I should imagine, that the influence of reason in producing our passions is nothing near so extensive as it is commonly believed.

SECTION XIV – THE EFFECTS OF SYMPATHY IN THE DISTRESSES OF OTHERS

TO EXAMINE THIS point concerning the effect of tragedy in a proper manner, we must previously consider how we are affected by the feelings of our fellow-creatures in circumstances of real distress. I am convinced we have a degree of delight, and that no small one, in the real misfortunes and pains of others; for let the affection be what it will in appearance, if it does not make us shun such objects, if on the contrary it induces us to approach them, if it makes us dwell upon them, in this case I conceive we must have a delight or pleasure of some species or other in contemplating objects of this kind. Do we not read the authentic histories of scenes of this nature with as much pleasure as romances or poems, where the incidents are fictitious? The prosperity of no empire, nor the grandeur of no king, can so agreeably affect in the reading, as the ruin of the state of Macedon, and the distress of its unhappy prince.[13] Such a catastrophe touches us in history as much as the destruction of Troy does in fable. Our delight, in cases of this kind, is very greatly heightened, if the sufferer be some excellent person who sinks under an unworthy fortune. Scipio and Cato[14] are both virtuous characters; but we are more deeply affected by the violent death of the one, and the ruin of the great cause he adhered to, than with the deserved triumphs and uninterrupted prosperity of the other; for terror is a passion which always produces delight when it does not press too closely; and pity is a passion accompanied with pleasure, because it arises from love and social affection. Whenever we are formed by nature to any active purpose, the passion which animates us to it is attended with delight, or a pleasure of some kind, let the subject-matter be what it will; and as our Creator has designed that we should be united by the bond of sympathy, he has strengthened that bond by a proportionable delight; and there most where our sympathy is most wanted, – in the distresses of others. If this passion was simply painful, we would shun with the greatest care all persons and places that could excite such a passion; as some, who are so far gone in indolence as not to endure any strong impression, actually do. But the case is widely different with the greater part of mankind; there is no spectacle we so eagerly pursue, as that of some uncommon and grievous calamity; so that whether the misfortune is before our eyes, or whether they are turned back to it in history, it always touches with delight. This is not an unmixed delight, but blended with no small uneasiness. The delight we have in such things, hinders us from shunning scenes of misery; and the pain we feel prompts us to relieve ourselves in relieving those who suffer; and all this antecedent to any reasoning, by an instinct that works us to its own purposes without our concurrence.

SECTION XV — OF THE EFFECTS OF TRAGEDY

IT IS THUS in real calamities. In imitated distresses the only difference is the pleasure resulting from the effects of imitation; for it is never so perfect, but we can perceive it is imitation, and on that principle are somewhat pleased with it. And indeed in some cases we derive as much or more pleasure from that source than from the thing itself. But then I imagine we shall be much mistaken, if we attribute any considerable part of our satisfaction in tragedy to the consideration that tragedy is a deceit, and its representations no realities. The nearer it approaches the reality, and the farther it removes us from all idea of fiction, the more perfect is its power. But be its power of what kind it will, it never approaches to what it represents. Choose a day on which to represent the most sublime and affecting tragedy we have; appoint the most favourite actors; spare no cost upon the scenes and decorations, unite the greatest efforts of poetry, painting, and music; and when you have collected your audience, just at the moment when their minds are erect with expectation, let it be reported that a state criminal of high rank is on the point of being executed in the adjoining square; in a moment the emptiness of the theatre would demonstrate the comparative weakness of the imitative arts, and proclaim the triumph of the real sympathy. I believe that this notion of our having a simple pain in the reality, yet a delight in the representation, arises from hence, that we do not sufficiently distinguish what we would by no means choose to do, from what we should be eager enough to see if it was once done. We delight in seeing things, which, so far from doing, our heartiest wishes would be to see redressed. This noble capital, the pride of England and of Europe, I believe no man is so strangely wicked as to desire to see destroyed by a conflagration or an earthquake, though he should be removed himself to the greatest distance from the danger. But suppose such a fatal accident to have happened, what numbers from all parts would crowd to behold the ruins, and amongst many who would have been content never to have seen London in its glory! Nor is it, either in real or fictitious distresses, our immunity from them which produces our delight; in my own mind I can discover nothing like it. I apprehend that this mistake is owing to a sort of sophism, by which we are frequently imposed upon; it arises from our not distinguishing between what is indeed a necessary condition to our doing or suffering anything in general, and what is the cause of some particular act. If a man kills me with a sword, it is a necessary condition to this that we should have been both of us alive before the fact; and yet it would be absurd to say, that our being both living creatures was the cause of his crime and of my death. So it is certain, that it is absolutely necessary my life should be out of any imminent hazard, before I can take a delight in the sufferings of others, real or imaginary, or indeed in anything else from any cause whatsoever. But then it is a sophism to argue from thence, that this immunity is the cause of my delight either on these or on any occasions. No one can distinguish such a cause of satisfaction in his own mind, I believe; nay, when we do not suffer any very acute pain, nor are exposed to any imminent danger of our lives, we can feel for others, whilst we suffer ourselves; and often then most when we are softened by affliction; we see with pity even distresses which we would accept in the place of our own.

SECTION XVI — IMITATION

THE SECOND PASSION belonging to society is imitation, or, if you will, a desire of imitating, and consequently a pleasure in it. This passion arises from much the same cause with sympathy. For as sympathy makes us take a concern in whatever men feel, so this affection prompts us to copy whatever they do; and consequently we have a pleasure in imitating, and in whatever belongs to imitation merely as it is such, without any intervention of the reasoning faculty, but solely from our natural constitution, which Providence has framed in such a manner as to find either pleasure or delight, according to the nature of the object, in whatever regards the purposes of our being. It is by imitation far more than by precept, that we learn everything; and what we learn thus, we acquire not only more effectually, but more pleasantly. This forms our manners, our opinions, our lives. It is one of the strongest links of society; it is a species of mutual compliance, which all men yield to each other, without constraint to themselves, and which is extremely flattering to all. Herein it is that painting and many other agreeable arts have laid one of the principal foundations of their power. And since, by its influence on our manners and our passions, it is of such great consequence, I shall here venture to lay down a rule, which may

inform us with a good degree of certainty when we are to attribute the power of the arts to imitation, or to our pleasure in the
skill of the imitator merely, and when to sympathy, or some other
cause in conjunction with it. When the object represented in
poetry or painting is such as we could have no desire of seeing in
the reality, then I may be sure that its power in poetry or painting
is owing to the power of imitation, and to no cause operating in
the thing itself. So it is with most of the pieces which the painters
call still-life. In these a cottage, a dunghill, the meanest and most
ordinary utensils of the kitchen, are capable of giving us pleasure.
But when the object of the painting or poem is such as we should
run to see if real, let it affect us with what odd sort of sense it
will, we may rely upon it, that the power of the poem or picture
is more owing to the nature of the thing itself than to the mere
effect of imitation, or to a consideration of the skill of the imitator, however excellent. Aristotle has spoken so much and so
solidly upon the force of imitation in his Poetics, that it makes
any further discourse upon this subject the less necessary.

SECTION XVII — AMBITION

ALTHOUGH IMITATION IS one of the great instruments used by
Providence in bringing our nature towards its perfection, yet if
men gave themselves up to imitation entirely, and each followed
the other, and so on in an eternal circle, it is easy to see that there
never could be any improvement amongst them. Men must
remain as brutes do, the same at the end that they are at this day,
and that they were in the beginning of the world. To prevent
this, God has planted in man a sense of ambition, and a satisfaction arising from the contemplation of his excelling his fellows
in something deemed valuable amongst them. It is this passion
that drives men to all the ways we see in use of signalising themselves, and that tends to make whatever excites in a man the idea
of this distinction so very pleasant. It has been so strong as to
make very miserable men take comfort, that they were supreme
in misery; and certain it is, that, where we cannot distinguish
ourselves by something excellent, we begin to take a complacency in some singular infirmities, follies, or defects of one kind
or other. It is on this principle that flattery is so prevalent; for
flattery is no more than what raises in a man's mind an idea of a
preference which he has not. Now, whatever, either on good or

upon bad grounds, tends to raise a man in his own opinion, produces a sort of swelling and triumph, that is extremely grateful
to the human mind; and this swelling is never more perceived,
nor operates with more force, than when without danger we are
conversant with terrible objects; the mind always claiming to
itself some part of the dignity and importance of the things which
it contemplates. Hence proceeds what Longinus has observed of
that glorying sense of inward greatness, that always fills the reader
of such passages in poets and orators as are sublime; it is what
every man must have felt in himself upon such occasions.

SECTION XVIII – THE RECAPITULATION

TO DRAW THE whole of what has been said into a few distinct
points: – The passions which belong to self-preservation turn on
pain and danger; they are simply painful when their causes immediately affect us; they are delightful when we have an idea of pain
and danger, without being actually in such circumstances; this
delight I have not called pleasure, because it turns on pain, and
because it is different enough from any idea of positive pleasure.
Whatever excites this delight, I call *sublime*. The passions belonging to self-preservation are the strongest of all the passions.

The second head to which the passions are referred with relation to their final cause, is society. There are two sorts of societies.
The first is, the society of sex. The passion belonging to this is
called love, and it contains a mixture of lust; its object is the
beauty of women. The other is the great society with man and
all other animals. The passion subservient to this is called likewise
love, but it has no mixture of lust, and its object is beauty; which
is a name I shall apply to all such qualities in things as induce in
us a sense of affection and tenderness, or some other passion the
most nearly resembling these. The passion of love has its rise in
positive pleasure; it is, like all things which grow out of pleasure,
capable of being mixed with a mode of uneasiness, that is, when
an idea of its object is excited in the mind with an idea at the
same time of having irretrievably lost it. This mixed sense of
pleasure I have not called *pain*, because it turns upon actual pleasure, and because it is, both in its cause and in most of its effects,
of a nature altogether different.

Next to the general passion we have for society, to a choice in
which we are directed by the pleasure we have in the object, the

particular passion under this head called sympathy has the greatest extent. The nature of this passion is, to put us in the place of
another in whatever circumstance he is in, and to affect us in a
like manner; so that this passion may, as the occasion requires,
turn either on pain or pleasure; but with the modifications mentioned in some cases in section 11. As to imitation and preference, nothing more need be said.

SECTION XIX — THE CONCLUSION

I BELIEVED THAT an attempt to range and methodise some of
our most leading passions would be a good preparative to such
an inquiry as we are going to make in the ensuing discourse. The
passions I have mentioned are almost the only ones which it can
be necessary to consider in our present design; though the variety
of the passions is great, and worthy, in every branch of that
variety, of an attentive investigation. The more accurately we
search into the human mind, the stronger traces we everywhere
find of His wisdom who made it. If a discourse on the use of the
parts of the body may be considered as an hymn to the Creator;
the use of the passions, which are the organs of the mind, cannot
be barren of praise to him, nor unproductive to ourselves of that
noble and uncommon union of science and admiration, which
a contemplation of the works of infinite wisdom alone can afford
to a rational mind: whilst, referring to him whatever we find of
right or good or fair in ourselves, discovering his strength and
wisdom even in our own weakness and imperfection, honouring
them where we discover them clearly, and adoring their profundity where we are lost in our search, we may be inquisitive without
impertinence, and elevated without pride; we may be admitted,
if I may dare to say so, into the counsels of the Almighty by a
consideration of his works. The elevation of the mind ought to
be the principal end of all our studies; which if they do not in
some measure effect, they are of very little service to us. But,
beside this great purpose, a consideration of the rationale of our
passions seems to me very necessary for all who would affect
them upon solid and sure principles. It is not enough to know
them in general: to affect them after a delicate manner, or to
judge properly of any work designed to affect them, we should
know the exact boundaries of their several jurisdictions; we
should pursue them through all their variety of operations, and

pierce into the inmost, and what might appear inaccessible, parts of our nature,

Quod latet arcanâ non enarrabile fibrâ.[15]

Without all this it is possible for a man, after a confused manner, sometimes to satisfy his own mind of the truth of his work; but he can never have a certain determinate rule to go by, nor can he ever make his propositions sufficiently clear to others. Poets, and orators, and painters, and those who cultivate other branches of the liberal arts, have, without this critical knowledge, succeeded well in their several provinces, and will succeed: as among artificers there are many machines made and even invented without any exact knowledge of the principles they are governed by. It is, I own, not uncommon to be wrong in theory, and right in practice; and we are happy that it is so. Men often act right from their feelings, who afterwards reason but ill on them from principle: but as it is impossible to avoid an attempt at such reasoning, and equally impossible to prevent its having some influence on our practice, surely it is worth taking some pains to have it just, and founded on the basis of sure experience. We might expect that the artists themselves would have been our surest guides; but the artists have been too much occupied in the practice: the philosophers have done little; and what they have done, was mostly with a view to their own schemes and systems: and as for those called critics, they have generally sought the rule of the arts in the wrong place; they sought it among poems, pictures, engravings, statues, and buildings. But art can never give the rules that make an art. This is, I believe, the reason why artists in general, and poets principally, have been confined in so narrow a circle: they have been rather imitators of one another than of nature; and this with so faithful an uniformity, and to so remote an antiquity, that it is hard to say who gave the first model. Critics follow them, and therefore can do little as guides. I can judge but poorly of anything, whilst I measure it by no other standard than itself. The true standard of the arts is in every man's power; and an easy observation of the most common, sometimes of the meanest, things in nature, will give the truest lights, where the greatest sagacity and industry, that slights such observation, must leave us in the dark, or, what is worse, amuse and mislead us by false lights. In an inquiry it is almost everything to be once in a right road. I am satisfied I have done but little by these observations considered in themselves; and I never should have taken the pains to digest them, much less should I have ever ventured to publish them, if I was not convinced that nothing tends more to the corruption of science than to suffer it to stagnate. These waters must be troubled, before they can exert their virtues. A man who works beyond the surface of things, though he may be wrong himself, yet he clears the way for others, and may chance to make even his errors subservient to the cause of truth. In the following parts I shall inquire what things they are that cause in us the affections of the sublime and beautiful, as in this I have considered the affections themselves. I only desire one favour, – that no part of this discourse may be judged of by itself, and independently of the rest; for I am sensible I have not disposed my materials to abide the test of a captious controversy, but of a sober and even forgiving examination, that they are not armed at all points for battle, but dressed to visit those who are willing to give a peaceful entrance to truth.

PART II

SECTION I – OF THE PASSION CAUSED BY THE SUBLIME

THE PASSION CAUSED by the great and sublime in *nature*, when those causes operate most powerfully, is astonishment; and astonishment is that state of the soul, in which all its motions are suspended, with some degree of horror. In this case the mind is so entirely filled with its object, that it cannot entertain any other, nor by consequence reason on that object which employs it. Hence arises the great power of the sublime, that, far from being produced by them, it anticipates our reasonings, and hurries us on by an irresistible force. Astonishment, as I have said, is the effect of the sublime in its highest degree; the inferior effects are admiration, reverence, and respect.

SECTION II – TERROR

NO PASSION SO effectually robs the mind of all its powers of acting and reasoning as *fear*. For fear being an apprehension of pain or death, it operates in a manner that resembles actual pain. Whatever therefore is terrible, with regard to sight, is sublime too, whether this cause of terror be endued with greatness of dimensions or not; for it is impossible to look on anything as trifling, or contemptible, that may be dangerous. There are many animals, who though far from being large, are yet capable of raising ideas of the sublime, because they are considered as objects of terror. As serpents and poisonous animals of almost all kinds. And to things of great dimensions, if we annex an adventitious idea of terror, they become without comparison greater. A level plain of a vast extent on land, is certainly no mean idea; the prospect of such a plain may be as extensive as a prospect of the ocean: but can it ever fill the mind with anything so great as the ocean itself? This is owing to several causes; but it is owing to none more than this, that the ocean is an object of no small terror. Indeed, terror is in all cases whatsoever, either more openly or latently, the ruling principle of the sublime. Several languages bear a strong testimony to the affinity of these ideas. They frequently use the same word, to signify indifferently the modes of astonishment or admiration, and those of terror. $\theta\acute{\alpha}\mu\beta o\varsigma$ is in Greek, either fear or wonder; $\delta\varepsilon\iota\nu\grave{o}\varsigma$ is terrible or respectable; $\alpha\grave{\iota}\delta\acute{\varepsilon}\omega$, to reverence or to fear. *Vereor* in Latin, is what $\alpha\grave{\iota}\delta\acute{\varepsilon}\omega$ is in Greek. The Romans used the verb *stupeo*, a term which strongly marks the state of an astonished mind, to express the effect either of simple fear or of astonishment; the word *attonitus* (thunder-struck) is equally expressive of the alliance of these ideas; and do not the French *etonnement*, and the English *astonishment* and *amazement*, point out as clearly the kindred emotions which attend fear and wonder? They who have a more general knowledge of languages, could produce, I make no doubt, many other and equally striking examples.

SECTION III — OBSCURITY

TO MAKE ANYTHING very terrible, obscurity seems in general to be necessary. When we know the full extent of any danger, when we can accustom our eyes to it, a great deal of the apprehension vanishes. Every one will be sensible of this, who considers how greatly night adds to our dread, in all cases of danger, and how much the notions of ghosts and goblins, of which none can form clear ideas, affect minds which give credit to the popular tales concerning such sorts of beings. Those despotic governments, which are founded on the passions of men, and principally upon the passion of fear, keep their chief as much as may be from the public eye. The policy has been the same in many cases of religion. Almost all the heathen temples were dark. Even in the barbarous temples of the Americans at this day, they keep their idol in a dark part of the hut, which is consecrated to his worship. For this purpose too the Druids performed all their ceremonies in the bosom of the darkest woods, and in the shade of the oldest and most spreading oaks. No person seems better to have understood the secret of heightening, or of setting terrible things, if I may use the expression, in their strongest light, by the force of a judicious obscurity, than Milton.[16] His description of Death in the second book is admirably studied; it is astonishing with what a gloomy pomp, with what a significant and expressive uncertainty of strokes and colouring, he has finished the portrait of the king of terrors:

>   —The other shape,
>   If shape it might be called that shape had none
>   Distinguishable, in member, joint, or limb;
>   Or substance might be called that shadow seemed;
>   For each seemed either; black he stood as night;
>   Fierce as ten furies; terrible as hell;
>   And shook a deadly dart. What seemed his head
>   The likeness of a kingly crown had on.

In this description all is dark, uncertain, confused, terrible, and sublime to the last degree.

SECTION IV — OF THE DIFFERENCE BETWEEN CLEARNESS AND OBSCURITY WITH REGARD TO THE PASSIONS

IT IS ONE thing to make an idea clear, and another to make it *affecting* to the imagination. If I make a drawing of a palace, or a temple, or a landscape, I present a very clear idea of those objects; but then (allowing for the effect of imitation, which is something) my picture can at most affect only as the palace, temple, or landscape would have affected in the reality. On the other hand, the most lively and spirited verbal description I can give raises a very obscure and imperfect *idea* of such objects; but then it is in my power to raise a stronger *emotion* by the description than I could do by the best painting. This experience constantly evinces. The proper manner of conveying the *affections* of the mind from one to another, is by words; there is a great insufficiency in all other methods of communication; and so far is a clearness of imagery from being absolutely necessary to an influence upon the passions, that they may be considerably oper-ated upon, without presenting any image at all, by certain sounds adapted to that purpose; of which we have a sufficient proof in the acknowledged and powerful effects of instrumental music. In reality, a great clearness helps but little towards affecting the passions, as it is in some sort an enemy to all enthusiasms whatsoever.

SECTION [IV] – THE SAME SUBJECT CONTINUED

THERE ARE TWO verses in Horace's Art of Poetry, that seem to contradict this opinion; for which reason I shall take a little more pains in clearing it up. The verses are,

> *Segnius irritant animos demissa per aures,*
> *Quam quæ sunt oculis subjecta fidelibus.*[17]

On this the Abbé du Bos[18] founds a criticism, wherein he gives painting the preference to poetry in the article of moving the passions; principally on account of the greater *clearness* of the ideas it represents. I believe this excellent judge was led into this mistake (if it be a mistake) by his system; to which he found it more conformable than I imagine it will be found by experience. I know several who admire and love painting, and yet who regard the objects of their admiration in that art with coolness enough in comparison of that warmth with which they are animated by affecting pieces of poetry or rhetoric. Among the common sort of people, I never could perceive that painting had much influence on their passions. It is true, that the best sorts of painting, as well as the best sorts of poetry, are not much understood in that sphere. But it is most certain, that their passions are very strongly roused by a fanatic preacher, or by the ballads of Chevy-chace, or the Children in the Wood,[19] and by other little popular poems and tales that are current in that rank of life. I do not know of any paintings, bad or good, that produce the same effect. So that poetry, with all its obscurity, has a more general, as well as a more powerful, dominion over the passions, than the other art. And I think there are reasons in nature, why the obscure idea, when properly conveyed, should be more affecting than the clear. It is our ignorance of things that causes all our admiration, and chiefly excites our passions. Knowledge and acquaintance make the most striking causes affect but little. It is thus with the vulgar; and all men are as the vulgar in what they do not understand. The ideas of eternity and infinity are among the most affecting we have; and yet perhaps there is nothing of which we really understand so little, as of infinity and eternity. We do not anywhere meet a more sublime description than this justly celebrated one of Milton, wherein he gives the portrait of Satan with a dignity so suitable to the subject:

> —He above the rest
> In shape and gesture proudly eminent
> Stood like a tower; his form had yet not lost
> All her original brightness, nor appeared
> Less than archangel ruined, and th' excess
> Of glory obscured: as when the sun new risen
> Looks through the horizontal misty air
> Shorn of his beams; or from behind the moon
> In dim eclipse disastrous twilight sheds
> On half the nations; and with fear of change
> Perplexes monarchs.—[20]

Here is a very noble picture; and in what does this poetical picture consist? In images of a tower, an archangel, the sun rising through mists, or in an eclipse, the ruin of monarchs, and the revolutions of kingdoms. The mind is hurried out of itself, by a crowd of great and confused images; which affect because they are crowded and confused. For, separate them, and you lose much of the greatness; and join them, and you infallibly lose the clearness. The images raised by poetry are always of this obscure kind; though in general the effects of poetry are by no means to be attributed to the images it raises; which point we shall examine more at large hereafter. But painting, when we have allowed for the pleasure of imitation, can only affect simply by the images it presents; and even in painting, a judicious obscurity in some things contributes to the effect of the picture; because the images in painting are exactly similar to those in nature; and in nature, dark, confused, uncertain images have a greater power on the fancy to form the grander passions, than those have which are more clear and determinate. But where and when this observation may be applied to practice, and how far it shall be extended, will be better deduced from the nature of the subject, and from the occasion, than from any rules that can be given.

I am sensible that this idea has met with opposition, and is likely still to be rejected by several. But let it be considered, that hardly anything can strike the mind with its greatness, which does not make some sort of approach towards infinity; which nothing can do whilst we are able to perceive its bounds; but to see an object distinctly, and to perceive its bounds, is one and the same thing. A clear idea is therefore another name for a little idea. There is a passage in the book of Job[21] amazingly sublime, and this sublimity is principally due to the terrible uncertainty of the thing described: *In thoughts from the visions of the night, when deep sleep falleth upon men, fear came upon me, and trembling, which made all my bones to shake. Then a spirit passed before my face; the hair of my flesh stood up. It stood still*, but I could not discern the form thereof: *an image was before mine eyes, there was silence, and I heard a voice,—Shall mortal man be more just than God?* We are first prepared with the utmost solemnity for the vision; we are first terrified, before we are let even into the obscure cause of our emotion: but when this grand cause of terror makes its appearance, what is it? Is it not wrapt up in the shades of its own incomprehensible darkness, more awful, more striking, more terrible, than the liveliest description, than the clearest painting, could possibly represent it? When painters have attempted to give us clear representations of these very fanciful and terrible ideas, they have, I think, almost always failed; insomuch that I have been at a loss, in all the pictures I have seen of hell, to determine whether the painter did not intend something ludicrous. Several painters have handled a subject of this kind, with a view of assembling as many horrid phantoms as their imagination could suggest; but all the designs I have chanced to meet of the temptation of St. Anthony were rather a sort of odd, wild grotesques, than anything capable of producing a serious passion.[22] In all these subjects poetry is very happy. Its apparitions, its chimeras, its harpies, its allegorical figures, are grand and affecting; and though Virgil's

Fame[23] and Homer's Discord[24] are obscure, they are magnificent figures. These figures in painting would be clear enough, but I fear they might become ridiculous.

[...]

PART III.
SECTION I — OF BEAUTY

IT IS MY design to consider beauty as distinguished from the sublime; and, in the course of the inquiry, to examine how far it is consistent with it. But previous to this, we must take a short review of the opinions already entertained of this quality; which I think are hardly to be reduced to any fixed principles; because men are used to talk of beauty in a figurative manner, that is to say, in a manner extremely uncertain, and indeterminate. By beauty I mean that quality or those qualities in bodies, by which they cause love, or some passion similar to it. I confine this definition to the merely sensible qualities of things, for the sake of preserving the utmost simplicity in a subject, which must always distract us whenever we take in those various causes of sympathy which attach us to any persons or things from secondary considerations, and not from the direct force which they have merely on being viewed. I likewise distinguish love (by which I mean that satisfaction which arises to the mind upon contemplating anything beautiful, of whatsoever nature it may be) from desire or lust; which is an energy of the mind, that hurries us on to the possession of certain objects, that do not affect us as they are beautiful, but by means altogether different. We shall have a strong desire for a woman of no remarkable beauty; whilst the greatest beauty in men, or in other animals, though it causes love, yet excites nothing at all of desire. Which shows that beauty, and the passion caused by beauty, which I call love, is different from desire, though desire may sometimes operate along with it; but it is to this latter that we must attribute those violent and tempestuous passions, and the consequent emotions of the body, which attend what is called love in some of its ordinary acceptations, and not to the effects of beauty merely as it is such.

[...]

PART V
SECTION I — OF WORDS

NATURAL OBJECTS AFFECT us, by the laws of that connexion
which Providence has established between certain motions and
configurations of bodies, and certain consequent feelings in our
mind. Painting affects in the same manner, but with the super-
added pleasure of imitation. Architecture affects by the laws of
nature, and the law of reason: from which latter result the rules
of proportion, which make a work to be praised or censured, in
the whole or in some part, when the end for which it was
designed is or is not properly answered. But as to words; they
seem to me to affect us in a manner very different from that in
which we are affected by natural objects, or by painting or architecture; yet words have as considerable a share in exciting ideas
of beauty and of the sublime as many of those, and sometimes a
much greater than any of them: therefore an inquiry into the
manner by which they excite such emotions is far from being
unnecessary in a discourse of this kind.

SECTION II — THE COMMON EFFECTS OF POETRY,
NOT BY RAISING IDEAS OF THINGS

THE COMMON NOTION of the power of poetry and eloquence,
as well as that of words in ordinary conversation, is, that they
affect the mind by raising in it ideas of those things for which
custom has appointed them to stand. To examine the truth of this
notion, it may be requisite to observe, that words may be divided
into three sorts. The first are such as represent many simple ideas
united by nature to form some one determinate composition, as
man, horse, tree, castle, &c. These I call *aggregate words*. The
second are they that stand for one simple idea of such compositions, and no more; as red, blue, round, square, and the like.
These I call *simple abstract* words. The third are those which are
formed by an union, an *arbitrary* union, of both the others, and
of the various relations between them in greater or less degrees
of complexity; as virtue, honour, persuasion, magistrate, and the
like. These I call *compound abstract* words. Words, I am sensible,
are capable of being classed into more curious distinctions; but
these seem to be natural, and enough for our purpose; and they
are disposed in that order in which they are commonly taught,

and in which the mind gets the ideas they are substituted for. I shall begin with the third sort of words; compound abstracts, such as virtue, honour, persuasion, docility. Of these I am convinced, that whatever power they may have on the passions, they do not derive it from any representation raised in the mind of the things for which they stand. As compositions, they are not real essences, and hardly cause, I think, any real ideas. Nobody, I believe, immediately on hearing the sounds, virtue, liberty, or honour, conceives any precise notions of the particular modes of action and thinking together with the mixt and simple ideas, and the several relations of them for which these words are substituted; neither has he any general idea, compounded of them; for if he had, then some of those particular ones, though indistinct perhaps, and confused, might come soon to be perceived. But this, I take it, is hardly ever the case. For, put yourself upon analysing one of these words, and you must reduce it from one set of general words to another, and then into the simple abstracts and aggregates, in a much longer series than may be at first imagined, before any real idea emerges to light, before you come to discover anything like the first principles of such compositions; and when you have made such a discovery of the original ideas, the effect of the composition is utterly lost. A train of thinking of this sort is much too long to be pursued in the ordinary ways of conversation; nor is it at all necessary that it should. Such words are in reality but mere sounds; but they are sounds which being used on particular occasions, wherein we receive some good, or suffer some evil, or see others affected with good or evil; or which we hear applied to other interesting things or events; and being applied in such a variety of cases, that we know readily by habit to what things they belong, they produce in the mind, whenever they are afterwards mentioned, effects similar to those of their occasions. The sounds being often used without reference to any particular occasion, and carrying still their first impressions, they at last utterly lose their connexion with the particular occasions that give rise to them; yet the sound, without any annexed notion, continues to operate as before.

SECTION III — GENERAL WORDS BEFORE IDEAS

MR. LOCKE HAS somewhere observed, with his usual sagacity, that most general words, those belonging to virtue and vice, good and evil, especially, are taught before the particular modes of action to which they belong are presented to the mind; and with them, the love of the one, and the abhorrence of the other; for the minds of children are so ductile, that a nurse, or any person about a child, by seeming pleased or displeased with anything, or even any word, may give the disposition of the child a similar turn. When, afterwards, the several occurrences in life come to be applied to these words, and that which is pleasant often appears under the name of evil; and what is disagreeable to nature is called good and virtuous; a strange confusion of ideas and affections arises in the minds of many; and an appearance of no small contradiction between their notions and their actions. There are many who love virtue and who detest vice, and this not from hypocrisy or affectation, who notwithstanding very frequently act ill and wickedly in particulars without the least remorse; because these particular occasions never came into view, when the passions on the side of virtue were so warmly affected by certain words heated originally by the breath of others; and for this reason, it is hard to repeat certain sets of words, though owned by themselves unoperative, without being in some degree affected; especially if a warm and affecting tone of voice accompanies them, as suppose,

Wise, valiant, generous, good, and great.

These words, by having no application, ought to be unoperative; but when words commonly sacred to great occasions are used, we are affected by them even without the occasions. When words which have been generally so applied are put together without any rational view, or in such a manner that they do not rightly agree with each other, the style is called bombast. And it requires in several cases much good sense and experience to be guarded against the force of such language; for when propriety is neglected, a greater number of these affecting words may be taken into the service and a greater variety may be indulged in combining them.

SECTION IV — THE EFFECT OF WORDS

IF WORDS HAVE all their possible extent of power, three effects arise in the mind of the hearer. The first is, the *sound*; the second, the *picture*, or representation of the thing signified by the sound;

the third is, the *affection* of the soul produced by one or by both of the foregoing. *Compounded abstract* words, of which we have been speaking, (honour, justice, liberty, and the like,) produce the first and the last of these effects, but not the second. *Simple abstracts* are used to signify some one simple idea, without much adverting to others which may chance to attend it, as blue, green, hot, cold, and the like; these are capable of affecting all three of the purposes of words; as the *aggregate* words, man, castle, horse, &c., are in a yet higher degree. But I am of opinion, that the most general effect, even of these words, does not arise from their forming pictures of the several things they would represent in the imagination; because, on a very diligent examination of my own mind, and getting others to consider theirs, I do not find that once in twenty times any such picture is formed, and when it is, there is most commonly a particular effort of the imagination for that purpose. But the aggregate words operate, as I said of the compound-abstracts, not by presenting any image to the mind, but by having from use the same effect on being mentioned, that their original has when it is seen. Suppose we were to read a passage to this effect: "The river Danube rises in a moist and mountainous soil in the heart of Germany, where winding to and fro, it waters several principalities, until, turning into Austria, and leaving the walls of Vienna, it passes into Hungary; there with a vast flood, augmented by the Saave and the Drave, it quits Christendom, and rolling through the barbarous countries which border on Tartary, it enters by many mouths in the Black Sea." In this description many things are mentioned, as mountains, rivers, cities, the sea, &c. But let anybody examine himself, and see whether he has had impressed on his imagination any pictures of a river, mountain, watery soil, Germany, &c. Indeed it is impossible, in the rapidity and quick succession of words in conversation, to have ideas both of the sound of the word, and of the thing represented: besides, some words, expressing real essences, are so mixed with others of a general and nominal import, that it is impracticable to jump from sense to thought, from particulars to generals, from things to words, in such a manner as to answer the purposes of life; nor is it necessary that we should.

SECTION V — EXAMPLES THAT WORDS MAY
AFFECT WITHOUT RAISING IMAGES

I FIND IT very hard to persuade several that their passions are affected by words from whence they have no ideas; and yet harder to convince them, that in the ordinary course of conversation we are sufficiently understood without raising any images of the things concerning which we speak. It seems to be an odd subject of dispute with any man, whether he has ideas in his mind or not. Of this, at first view, every man, in his own forum, ought to judge without appeal. But, strange as it may appear, we are often at a loss to know what ideas we have of things, or whether we have any ideas at all upon some subjects. It even requires a good deal of attention to be thoroughly satisfied on this head. Since I wrote these papers, I found two very striking instances of the possibility there is that a man may hear words without having any idea of the things which they represent, and yet afterwards be capable of returning them to others, combined in a new way, and with great propriety, energy, and instruction. The first instance is that of Mr. Blacklock,[25] a poet blind from his birth. Few men blessed with the most perfect sight can describe visual objects with more spirit and justness than this blind man; which cannot possibly be attributed to his having a clearer conception of the things he describes than is common to other persons. Mr. Spence, in an elegant preface which he has written to the works of this poet, reasons very ingeniously, and, I imagine, for the most part, very rightly, upon the cause of this extraordinary phenomenon; but I cannot altogether agree with him, that some improprieties in language and thought, which occur in these poems, have arisen from the blind poet's imperfect conception of visual objects, since such improprieties, and much greater, may be found in writers even of a higher class than Mr. Blacklock, and who notwithstanding possessed the faculty of seeing in its full perfection. Here is a poet doubtless as much affected by his own descriptions as any that reads them can be; and yet he is affected with this strong enthusiasm by things of which he neither has nor can possibly have any idea further than that of a bare sound: and why may not those who read his works be affected in the same manner that he was, with as little of any real ideas of the things described? The second instance is of Mr. Saunderson,[26] professor of mathematics in the university of Cambridge. This learned man had acquired great knowledge in natural philosophy, in astronomy, and whatever sciences depend upon mathematical skill. What was the most extraordinary and the most to my purpose, he gave excellent lectures upon light and colours; and this man taught others the theory of these ideas which they had, and which he himself undoubtedly had not. But it is probable that the words red, blue, green, answered to him as well as the ideas of the colours themselves; for the ideas of greater or lesser degrees of refrangibility being applied to these words, and the blind man being instructed in what other respects they were found to agree or to disagree, it was as easy for him to reason upon the words, as if he had been fully master of the ideas. Indeed it must be owned he could make no new discoveries in the way of experiment. He did nothing but what we do every day in common discourse. When I wrote this last sentence, and used the words *every day* and *common discourse*, I had no images in my mind of any succession of time; nor of men in conference with each other; nor do I imagine that the reader will have any such ideas on reading it. Neither when I spoke of red, or blue, and green, as well as refrangibility, had I these several colours or the rays of light passing into a different medium, and there diverted from their course, painted before me in the way of images. I know very well that the mind possesses a faculty of raising such images at pleasure; but then an act of the will is necessary to this; and in ordinary conversation or reading it is very rarely that any image at all is excited in the mind. If I say, "I shall go to Italy next summer," I am well understood. Yet I believe nobody has by this painted in his imagination the exact figure of the speaker passing by land or by water, or both; sometimes on horseback, sometimes in a carriage; with all the particulars of the journey. Still less has he any idea of Italy, the country to which I propose to go; or of the greenness of the fields, the ripening of the fruits, and the warmth of the air, with the change to this from a different season, which are the ideas for which the word *summer* is substituted: but least of all has he any image from the word *next*; for this word stands for the idea of many summers, with the exclusion of all but one: and surely the man who says *next summer*, has no images of such a succession and such an exclusion. In short, it is not only of these ideas which are commonly called abstract, and of which no image at all can be formed, but even of particular, real beings, that we converse without having any idea of them excited in the imagination; as will certainly appear on a diligent examination of our minds. Indeed, so little does poetry depend for its effect on the power of raising sensible images, that I am convinced it would lose a very considerable part of its energy, if this were the necessary result of all description. Because that union of affecting words, which is the most powerful of all poetical instruments, would frequently lose its force, along with its propriety and consistency, if the sensible images were always excited. There is not perhaps in the whole Eneid a more grand and laboured passage than the description of Vulcan's cavern in Etna, and the works that are there carried on. Virgil dwells particularly on the formation of the thunder, which he describes unfinished under the hammers of the Cyclops. But what are the principles of this extraordinary composition?

> *Tres imbris torti radios, tres nubis acquosae*
> *Addiderant; rutili tres ignis, et alitis austri:*
> *Fulgores nunc terrificos, sonitumque, metumque*
> *Miscebant operi, flammisque sequacibus iras.*

This seems to me admirably sublime; yet if we attend coolly to the kind of sensible images which a combination of ideas of this sort must form, the chimeras of madmen cannot appear more wild and absurd than such a picture. "*Three rays of twisted showers, three of watery clouds, three of fire, and three of the winged south wind; then mixed they in the work terrific lightnings, and sound, and fear, and anger, with pursuing flames.*" This strange composition is formed into a gross body; it is hammered by the Cyclops, it is in part polished, and partly continues rough. The truth is, if poetry gives us a noble assemblage of words corresponding to many noble ideas which are connected by circumstances of time or place or related to each other as cause and effect, or associated in any natural way, they may be moulded together in any form and perfectly answer their end. The picturesque connexion is not demanded; because no real picture is formed; nor is the effect of the description at all the less upon this account. What is said of Helen by Priam and the old men of his council, is generally thought to give us the highest possible idea of that fatal beauty.

> οὐ νέμεσις Τρῶας καὶ ἐϋκνήμιδας Ἀχαιοὺς
> τοιῇδ' ἀμφὶ γυναικὶ πολὺν χρόνον ἄλγεα πάσχειν.
> αἰνῶς ἀθανάτῃσι θεῇς εἰς ὦπα ἔοικεν.

They cried, No wonder such celestial charms
For nine long years have set the world in arms;
What winning graces! what majestic mien!
She moves a goddess, and she looks a queen.

POPE

Here is not one word said of the particulars of her beauty; nothing which can in the least help us to any precise idea of her person; but yet we are much more touched by this manner of
mentioning her, than by those long and laboured descriptions of
Helen, whether handed down by tradition, or formed by fancy,
which are to be met with in some authors. I am sure it affects me
much more than the minute description which Spenser has given
of Belphebe;[27] though I own that there are parts in that description, as there are in all the descriptions of that excellent writer,
extremely fine and poetical. The terrible picture which
Lucretius[28] has drawn of religion, in order to display the magnanimity of his philosophical hero in opposing her, is thought to be
designed with great boldness and spirit.

> *Humana ante oculos fœdè cum vita jaceret,*
> *In terris, oppressa gravi sub religione,*
> *Quæ caput e cœli regionibus ostendebat*
> *Horribili super aspectu mortalibus instans;*
> *Primus Graius homo mortales tollere contra*
> *Est oculos ausus. –*

What idea do you derive from so excellent a picture? none at all,
most certainly: neither has the poet said a single word which
might in the least serve to mark a single limb or feature of the
phantom, which he intended to represent in all the horrors
imagination can conceive. In reality, poetry and rhetoric do not
succeed in exact description so well as painting does; their business is, to affect rather by sympathy than imitation; to display
rather the effect of things on the mind of the speaker, or of others,
than to present a clear idea of the things themselves. This is their
most extensive province, and that in which they succeed the best.

SECTION VI – POETRY NOT STRICTLY AN IMITATIVE ART

HENCE WE MAY observe that poetry, taken in its most general
sense, cannot with strict propriety be called an art of imitation.

It is indeed an imitation so far as it describes the manners and passions of men which their words can express; where *animi motus effert interprete lingua.*[29] There it is strictly imitation; and all merely *dramatic* poetry is of the soul. But *descriptive* poetry operates chiefly by *substitution*; by the means of sounds, which by custom have the effect of realities. Nothing is an imitation further than as it resembles some other thing; and words undoubtedly have no sort of resemblance to the ideas for which they stand.

SECTION VII – HOW WORDS INFLUENCE THE PASSIONS

NOW, AS WORDS affect, not by any original power, but by representation, it might be supposed, that their influence over the passions should be but light; yet it is quite otherwise; for we find by experience, that eloquence and poetry are as capable, nay indeed much more capable, of making deep and lively impressions than any other arts, and even than nature itself in very many cases. And this arises chiefly from these three causes. First, that we take an extraordinary part in the passions of others, and that we are easily affected and brought into sympathy by any tokens which are shown of them; and there are no tokens which can express all the circumstances of most passions so fully as words; so that if a person speaks upon any subject, he can not only convey the subject to you, but likewise the manner in which he is himself affected by it. Certain it is, that the influence of most things on our passions is not so much from the things themselves, as from our opinions concerning them; and these again depend very much on the opinions of other men, conveyable for the most part by words only. Secondly, there are many things of a very affecting nature, which can seldom occur in the reality, but the words that represent them often do; and thus they have an opportunity of making a deep impression and taking root in the mind, whilst the idea of the reality was transient; and to some perhaps never really occurred in any shape, to whom it is notwithstanding very affecting, as war, death, famine, &c. Besides, many ideas have never been at all presented to the senses of any men but by words, as God, angels, devils, heaven, and hell, all of which have however a great influence over the passions. Thirdly, by words we have it in our power to make such *combinations* as we cannot possibly do otherwise. By this power of combining, we are able, by the addition of well-chosen circumstances, to give a new life and force to the simple object. In painting we may represent any fine figure we please; but we never can give it those enlivening touches which it may receive from words. To represent an angel in a picture, you can only draw a beautiful young man winged: but what painting can furnish out anything so grand as the addition of one word, "the angel of the *Lord*?" It is true, I have here no clear idea; but these words affect the mind more than the sensible image did; which is all I contend for. A picture of Priam dragged to the altar's foot, and there murdered, if it were well executed, would undoubtedly be very moving; but there are very aggravating circumstances, which it could never represent:

Sanguine fœdantem *quos ipse saeraverat* ignes.[30]

As a further instance, let us consider those lines of Milton, where he describes the travels of the fallen angels through their dismal habitation:

– O'er many a dark and dreary vale
They passed, and many a region dolorous;
O'er many a frozen, many a fiery Alp;
Rocks, caves, lakes, fens, bogs, dens, and shades of death,
A universe of death. –[31]

Here is displayed the force of union in

Rocks, caves, lakes, dens, bogs, fens, and shades;

which yet would lose the greatest part of their effect, if they were not the

Rocks, caves, lakes, dens, bogs, fens, and shades –
— *Death*.

This idea or this affection caused by a word, which nothing but a word could annex to the others, raises a very great degree of the sublime; and this sublime is raised yet higher by what follows, a "*universe of Death*." Here are again two ideas not presentable but by language; and an union of them great and amazing beyond conception; if they may properly be called ideas which present no distinct image to the mind: – but still it will be difficult to conceive how words can move the passions which belong to real objects, without representing these objects clearly. This is difficult to us, because we do not sufficiently distinguish, in our observations upon language, between a clear expression and a strong expression. These are frequentiy confounded with each other, though they are in reality extremely different. The former regards the understanding; the latter belongs to the passions. The one describes a thing as it is; the latter describes it as it is felt. Now, as there is a moving tone of voice, an impassioned countenance, an agitated gesture, which affect independently of the things about which they are exerted, so there are words, and certain dispositions of words, which being peculiarly devoted to passionate subjects, and always used by those who are under the influence of any passion, touch and move us more than those which far more clearly and distinctly express the subject matter. We yield to sympathy what we refuse to description. The truth is, all verbal description, merely as naked description, though never so exact, conveys so poor and insufficient an idea of the thing described, that it could scarcely have the smallest effect, if the speaker did not call in to his aid those modes of speech that mark a strong and lively feeling in himself. Then, by the contagion of our passions, we catch a fire already kindled in another, which probably might never have been struck out by the object described. Words, by strongly conveying the passions, by those means which we have already mentioned, fully compensate for their weakness in other respects. It may be observed, that very polished languages, and such as are praised for their superior clearness and perspicuity, are generally deficient in strength. The French language has that perfection and that defect, whereas the Oriental tongues, and in general the languages of most unpolished people, have a great force and energy of expression; and this is but natural. Uncultivated people are but ordinary observers of things, and not critical in distinguishing them; but, for that reason, they admire more, and are more affected with what they see, and therefore express themselves in a warmer and more passionate manner. If the affection be well conveyed, it will work its effect without any clear idea, often without any idea at all of the thing which has originally given rise to it.

It might be expected from the fertility of the subject, that I should consider poetry, as it regards the sublime and beautiful, more at large; but it must be observed that in this light it has been often and well handled already. It was not my design to enter into the criticism of the sublime and beautiful in any art, but to attempt to lay down such principles as may tend to ascertain, to distinguish, and to form a sort of standard for them; which purposes I thought might be best effected by an inquiry into the properties of such things in nature, as raise love and astonishment in us; and by showing in what manner they operated to produce these passions. Words were only so far to be considered, as to show upon what principle they were capable of being the representatives of these natural things, and by what powers they were able to affect us often as strongly as the things they represent, and sometimes much more strongly.

BOOK III, CHAPTER VIII
REIGN OF JOHN[1]

AD 1199   WE ARE NOW arrived at one of the most memorable periods in the English story; whether we consider the astonishing revolutions which were then wrought, the calamities in which both the prince and people were involved, or the happy consequences, which, arising from the midst of those calamities, have constituted the glory and prosperity of England for so many years. We shall see a throne, founded in arms, and augmented by the successive policy of five able princes, at once shaken to its foundations; first made tributary by the arts of a foreign power; then limited, and almost overturned, by the violence of its subjects. We shall see a king, to reduce his people to obedience, draw into his territories a tumultuary foreign army, and destroy his country instead of establishing his government. We shall behold the people, grown desperate, call in another foreign army, with a foreign prince at its head, and throw away that liberty which they had sacrificed everything to preserve. We shall see the arms of this prince successful against an established king in the vigour of his years, ebbing in the full tide of their prosperity, and yielding to an infant; after this, peace and order and liberty restored; the foreign force and foreign title purged off, and all things settled as happily as beyond all hope.

Richard dying without lawful issue, the succession to his dominions again became dubious. They consisted of various territories, governed by various rules of descent, and all of them uncertain.[2] There were two competitors; the first was Prince John, youngest son of Henry II; the other was Arthur,[3] son of Constance of Bretagne by Geoffrey, the third son of that monarch. If the right of consanguinity were only considered, the title of John to the whole succession had been indubitable. If the right of representation had then prevailed which now universally prevails, Arthur, as standing in the place of his father Geoffrey, had a solid claim. About Brittany there was no dispute. Anjou, Poitou,

Touraine, and Guienne declared in favour of Arthur, on the principle of representation. Normandy was entirely for John. In England the point of law had never been entirely settled, but it seemed rather inclined to the side of consanguinity. Therefore in England, where this point was dubious at best, the claim of Arthur, an infant and a stranger, had little force against the pretensions of John, declared heir by the will of the late king, supported by his armies, possessed of his treasures, and at the head of a powerful party. He secured in his interests Hubert, archbishop of Canterbury, and Glanville, the chief justiciary;[4] and by them the body of the ecciesiastics and the law. It is remarkable also that he paid court to the cities and boroughs, which is the first instance of that policy; but several of these communities now happily began to emerge from their slavery, and, taking advantage of the necessities and confusion of the late reign, increased in wealth and consequence, and had then first attained a free and regular form of administration. The towns, new to power, declared heartily in favour of a prince who was willing to allow that their declaration could confer a right. The nobility, who saw themselves beset by the church, the law, and the burghers, had taken no measures, nor even a resolution; and therefore had nothing left but to concur in acknowledging the title of John, whom they knew and hated. But though they were not able to exclude him from the succession, they had strength enough to oblige him to a solemn promise of restoring those liberties and franchises which they had always claimed, without having ever enjoyed, or even perfectly understood. The clergy also took advantage of the badness of his title to establish one altogether as ill founded. Hubert, archbishop of Canterbury, in the speech which he delivered at the king's coronation, publicly affirmed that the crown of England was of right elective. He drew his examples in support of this doctrine, not from the histories of the ancient Saxon kings, although a species of election within a certain family had then frequently prevailed, but from the history of the first kings of the Jews; without doubt in order to revive those pretensions which the clergy first set up in the election of Stephen, and which they had since been obliged to conceal, but had not entirely forgotten. John accepted a sovereignty weakened in the very act by which he acquired it; but he submitted to the times. He came to the throne at the age of thirty-two. He had entered early into business; and had been often involved in difficult and arduous enterprises, in which he experienced a variety of men and fortunes. His father, whilst he was very young, had sent him into Ireland, which kingdom was destined for his portion, in order to habituate that people to their future sovereign, and to give the young prince an opportunity of conciliating the favour of his new subjects.[5] But he gave on this occasion no good omens of capacity for government. Full of the insolent levity of a young man of high rank, without education, and surrounded with others equally unpractised, he insulted the Irish chiefs; and, ridiculing their uncouth garb and manners, he raised such a disaffection to the English government, and so much opposition to it, as all the wisdom of his father's best officers and counsellors was hardly able to overcome. In the decline of his father's life he joined in the rebellion of his brothers, with so much more guilt, as with more ingratitude and hypocrisy. During the reign of Richard he was the perpetual author of seditions and tumults; and yet was pardoned and even favoured by that prince to his death, when he very unaccountably appointed him heir to all his dominions.

It was of the utmost moment to John, who had no solid title, to conciliate the favour of all the world. Yet one of his first steps, whilst his power still remained dubious and unsettled, was, on pretence of consanguinity, to divorce his wife Avisa,[6] with whom he had lived many years, and to marry Isabella of Angoulême, a woman of extraordinary beauty, but who had been betrothed to Hugh, Count of Marche;[7] thus disgusting at once the powerful friends of his divorced wife, and those of the Earl of Marche, whom he had so sensibly wronged.

The king of France, Philip Augustus, saw with pleasure these proceedings of John; as he had before rejoiced at the dispute about the succession. He had been always employed, and sometimes with success, to reduce the English power, through the reigns of one very able, and one very warlike, prince. He had greater advantages in this conjuncture, and a prince of quite another character now to contend with. He was therefore not long without choosing his part; and whilst he secretly encouraged the Count of Marche, already stimulated by his private wrongs, he openly supported the claim of Arthur to the duchies of Anjou and Touraine. It was the character of this prince readily to lay aside, and as readily to reassume, his enterprises, as his affairs demanded. He saw that he had declared himself too rashly, and that he was in danger of being assaulted upon every side. He saw it was necessary to break an alliance, which the nice circumstances and timid character of John would enable him to do. In fact, John was at this time united in a close alliance with the emperor and the Earl of Flanders;[8] and these princes were engaged in a war with France. He had then a most favourable opportunity to establish all his claims, and at the same time to put the king of France out of a condition to question them ever after. But he suffered himself to be over-reached by the artifices of Philip; he consented to a treaty of peace, by which he received AD 1200 an empty acknowledgment of his right to the disputed territories; and in return for which acknowledgment he renounced his alliance with the emperor.[9] By this act he at once strengthened his enemy, gave up his ally, and lowered his character with his subjects and with all the world.

This treaty was hardly signed, when the ill consequences of AD 1201 his conduct became evident. The Earl of Marche and Arthur immediately renewed their claims and hostilities, under the protection of the king of France, who made a strong diversion by invading Normandy. At the commencement of these motions, John, by virtue of a prerogative hitherto undisputed, summoned his English barons to attend him into France; but instead of a compliance with his orders, he was surprised with a solemn demand of their ancient liberties. It is astonishing that the barons should at that time have ventured on a resolution of such dangerous importance, as they had provided no sort of means to support them. But the history of those times furnishes many instances of the like want of design in the most momentous affairs; and shows that it is in vain to look for political causes for the actions of men, who were most commonly directed by a brute caprice, and were for the greater part destitute of any fixed principles of obedience or resistance. The king, sensible of the weakness of his barons, fell upon some of their castles with such timely vigour, and treated those whom he had reduced with so much severity, that the rest immediately and abjectly submitted. He levied a severe tax upon their fiefs; and, thinking himself more strengthened by this treasure than the forced service of his barons, he excused the personal attendance of most of them, and passing into Normandy he raised an army there. He found that his enemies had united AD 1202 their forces, and invested the castle of Mirabel, a place of importance, in which his mother, from whom he derived his right to

Guienne, was besieged.[10] He flew to the relief of this place with the spirit of a greater character, and the success was answerable. The Breton and Poitevin army was defeated; his mother was freed; and the young Duke of Brittany and his sister were made prisoners. The latter he sent into England, to be confined in the castle of Bristol;[11] the former he carried with him to Rouen. The good fortune of John now seemed to be at its highest point; but it was exalted on a precipice; and this great victory proved the occasion of all the evils which afflicted his life.

John was not of a character to resist the temptation of having the life of his rival in his hands. All historians are as fully agreed that he murdered his nephew as they differ in the means by which he accomplished that crime. But the report was soon spread abroad, variously heightened in the circumstances by the obscurity of the fact, which left all men at liberty to imagine and invent, and excited all those sentiments of pity and indignation which a very young prince of great hopes, cruelly murdered by his uncle, naturally inspire. Philip had never missed an occasion of endeavouring to ruin the king of England; and having now acquired an opportunity of accomplishing that by justice which he had in vain sought by ambition, he filled every place with complaints of the cruelty of John, whom, as a vassal to the Crown of France, the king accused of the murder of another AD 1203 vassal, and summoned him to Paris to be tried by his peers. It was by no means consistent either with the dignity or safety of John to appear to this summons. He had the argument of kings to justify what he had done. But as in all great crimes there is something of a latent weakness, and in a vicious caution something material is ever neglected, John, satisfied with removing his rival, took no thought about his enemy; but whilst he saw himself sentenced for non-appearance in the court of peers, whilst he saw the king of France entering Normandy with a vast army in consequence of this sentence, and place after place, castle after castle, falling before him, he passed his time at Rouen in the profoundest tranquillity; indulging himself in indolent amusements, and satisfied with vain threatenings and boasts, which only added greater shame to his inactivity. The English barons who had attended him in this expedition, disaffected from the beginning, and now wearied with being so long witnesses to the ignominy of their sovereign, retired to their own country, and there spread the report of his unaccountable sloth and cowardice. John quickly followed them; and returning into his kingdom, polluted with the charge of so heavy a crime, and disgraced by so many follies, instead of aiming by popular acts to re-establish his character, he exacted a seventh of their moveables from the barons, on pretence that they had deserted his service. He laid the same imposition on the clergy, without giving himself the trouble of seeking for a pretext. He made no proper use of these great supplies; but saw the great city of Rouen, always faithful to its sovereigns, and now exerting the most strenuous efforts in his favour, obliged at length to surrender without the least attempt to relieve it. Thus the whole duchy of Normandy, originally acquired by the valour of his ancestors, and the source from which the greatness of his family had been derived, after being supported against all shocks for 300 years, was torn for ever from the stock of Rollo,[12] and reunited to the Crown of France. Immediately all the rest of the provinces which he held on the continent, except a part of Guienne,[13] despairing of his protection, and abhorring his government, threw themselves into the hands of Philip.

Meanwhile the king by his personal vices completed the odium which he had acquired by the impotent violence of his government. Uxorious and yet dissolute in his manners, he made no scruple frequently to violate the wives and daughters of his nobility, that rock on which tyranny has so often split. Other acts of irregular power, in their greatest excesses, still retain the characters of sovereign authority; but here the vices of the prince intrude into the families of the subject; and whilst they aggravate the oppression, lower the character of the oppressor.

In the disposition which all these causes had concurred universally to diffuse, the slightest motion in his kingdom threatened the most dangerous consequences. Those things which in quiet times would have only raised a slight controversy, now, when the minds of men were exasperated and inflamed, were capable of affording matter to the greatest revolutions. The affairs of the church, the winds which mostly governed the fluctuating people, were to be regarded with the utmost attention. Above all, the person who filled the see of Canterbury, which stood on a level with the throne itself, was a matter of the last importance. Just at this critical time died Hubert, archbishop of that see; a man who had a large share in procuring the crown for John, and in weakening its authority by his acts at the ceremony of the coronation,

as well as by his subsequent conduct.[14] Immediately on the death
of this prelate, a cabal of obscure monks, of the abbey of St.
Augustine, assemble by night; and, first binding themselves by
a solemn oath not to divulge their proceedings until they should
be confirmed by the pope, they elect one Reginald, their sub-
prior, archbishop of Canterbury. The person elected immediately crossed the seas; but his vanity soon discovered the secret
of his greatness. The king received the news of this transaction
with surprise and indignation. Provoked at such a contempt of
his authority, he fell severely on the monastery, no less surprised
than himself at the clandestine proceeding of some of its
members. But the sounder part pacified him, in some measure,
by their submission. They elected a person recommended by the
king;[15] and sent fourteen of the most respectable of their body to
Rome to pray that the former proceedings should be annulled,
and the later and more regular confirmed. To this matter of contention another was added. A dispute had long subsisted between
the suffragan bishops of the province of Canterbury and the
monks of the abbey of St. Austin; each claiming a right to elect
the metropolitan. This dispute was now revived, and pursued
with much vigour. The pretensions of the three contending
parties were laid before the pope,[16] to whom such disputes were
highly pleasing; as he knew that all claimants willingly conspire
to flatter and aggrandise that authority from which they expect
a confirmation of their own. The first election he nulled, because
its irregularity was glaring. The right of the bishops was entirely
rejected. The pope looked with an evil eye upon those whose
authority he was every day usurping. The second election was
set aside, as made at the king's instance. This was enough to make
it very irregular. The canon law had now grown up to its full
strength. The enlargement of the prerogative of the pope was the
great object of this jurisprudence; a prerogative which, founded
on fictitious monuments, that are forged in an ignorant age,
easily admitted by a credulous people, and afterwards confirmed
and enlarged by these admissions, not satisfied with the supremacy, encroached on every minute part of church-government,
and had almost annihilated the episcopal jurisdiction throughout
Europe. Some canons had given the metropolitan a power of
nominating a bishop, when the circumstances of the election
were palpably irregular; and as it does not appear that there was
any other judge of the irregularity than the metropolitan himself,

the election below in effect became nugatory. The pope, taking the irregularity in this case for granted, in virtue of this canon, and by his plenitude of power, ordered the deputies of Canterbury to proceed to a new election. At the same time he recommended to their choice Stephen Langton,[17] their countryman; a person already distinguished for his learning, of irreproachable morals, and free from every canonical impediment. This authoritative request the monks had not the courage to oppose in the pope's presence, and in his own city. They murmured and submitted. In England this proceeding was not so easily ratified: John drove the monks of Canterbury from their monastery; and having seized upon their revenues, threatened the effects of the same indignation against all those who seemed inclined to acquiesce in the proceedings of Rome. But Rome had not made so bold a step with intention to recede. On the king's positive refusal to admit Langton, and the expulsion of the monks of Canterbury, England was laid under an interdict. Then divine service at once ceased throughout the kingdom: the churches were shut. The sacraments were suspended. The dead were buried without honour, in highways and ditches; and the living deprived of all spiritual comfort. On the other hand, the king let loose his indignation against the ecclesiastics; seizing their goods, throwing many into prison, and permitting or encouraging all sorts of violence against them. The kingdom was thrown into the most terrible confusion; whilst the people, uncertain of the object or measure of their allegiance, and distracted with opposite principles of duty, saw themselves deprived of their religious rites by the ministers of religion; and their king, furious with wrongs not caused by them, falling indiscriminately on the innocent and the guilty; for John, instead of soothing his people in this their common calamity, sought to terrify them into obedience. In a progress which he made into the north, he threw down the enclosures of his forests, to let loose the wild beasts upon their lands; and as he saw the papal proceedings increase with his opposition, he thought it necessary to strengthen himself by new devices. He extorted hostages, and a new oath of fidelity, from his barons. He raised a great army, to divert the thoughts of his subjects from brooding too much on their distracted condition. This army he transported into Ireland; and as it happened to his father in a simple dispute with the pope, whilst he was dubious of his hereditary kingdom, he subdued Ireland. At this time he is said to have established the English laws in that kingdom, and to have appointed itinerant justices.

At length the sentence of excommunication was fulminated against the king. In the same year the same sentence was pronounced upon the Emperor Otho; and this daring pope was not afraid at once to drive to extremities the two greatest princes in Europe. And, truly, nothing is more remarkable than the uniform steadiness of the court of Rome in the pursuits of her ambitious projects. For knowing that pretensions which stand merely in opinion cannot bear to be questioned in any part, though she had hitherto seen the interdict produce but little effect, and perceived that the excommunication itself could draw scarce one poor bigot from the king's service, yet she receded not the least point from the utmost of her demand. She broke off an accommodation just on the point of being concluded, because the king refused to repair the losses which the clergy had suffered, though he agreed to everything else, and even submitted to receive the archbishop, who, being obtruded on him, had in reality been set over him. But the pope, bold as politic, determined to render him perfectly submissive; and to this purpose brought out the last arms of the ecclesiastic stores, which were reserved for the most extreme occasions. Having first released the English subjects from their oath of allegiance, by an unheard-of presumption he formally deposed John from his throne and dignity; he invited the king of France to take possession of the forfeited crown; he called forth all persons from all parts of Europe to assist in this expedition, by the pardons and privileges of those who fought for the Holy Land.

This proceeding did not astonish the world. The king of France, having driven John from all he held on the continent, gladly saw religion itself invite him to further conquests. He summoned all his vassals, under the penalty of felony, and the opprobrious name of *culvertage*,* (a name of all things dreaded by both nations,) to attend in this expedition; and such force had this threat, and the hope of plunder in England, that a very great army was in a short time assembled. A fleet also rendezvoused in the mouth of the Seine, by the writers of these times said to consist of 1700 sail. On this occasion John roused all his powers. He called upon all his people, who, by the duty of their tenure

* A word of uncertain derivation, but which signifies some scandalous species of cowardice.

or allegiance, were obliged to defend their lord and king; and in his writs stimulated them by the same threats of *culvertage*, which had been employed against him. They operated powerfully in his favour. His fleet in number exceeded the vast navy of France; his army was in everything but heartiness to the cause equal, and, extending along the coast of Kent, expected the descent of the French forces. Whilst these two mighty armies overspread the opposite coasts, and the sea was covered with their fleets, and the decision of so vast an event was hourly expected, various thoughts rose in the minds of those who moved the springs of these affairs. John, at the head of one of the finest armies in the world, trembled inwardly when he reflected how little he possessed or merited their confidence. Wounded by the consciousness of his crimes, excommunicated by the pope, hated by his subjects, in danger of being at once abandoned by heaven and earth, he was filled with the most fearful anxiety. The legates of the pope had hitherto seen everything succeed to their wish. But having made use of an instrument too great for them to wield, they apprehended that, when it had overthrown their adversary, it might recoil upon the court of Rome itself; that to add England to the rest of Philip's great possessions was not the way to make him humble, and that, in ruining John to aggrandise that monarch, they should set up a powerful enemy in the place of a submissive vassal.

They had done enough to give them a superiority in any negotiation, and they privately sent an embassy to the king of England. Finding him very tractable, they hasted to complete the treaty. The pope's legate, Pandulph, was intrusted with this affair. He knew the nature of men to be such, that they seldom engage willingly if the whole of a hardship be shown them at first, but that having advanced a certain length, their former concessions are an argument with them to advance further, and to give all, because they have already given a great deal. Therefore he began with exacting an oath from the king, by which, without showing the extent of his design, he engaged him to everything he could ask. John swore to submit to the legate in all things relating to his excommunication. And first he was obliged to accept Langton as archbishop; then to restore the monks of Canterbury, and other deprived ecclesiastics, and to make them a full indemnification for all their losses. And now, by these concessions, all things seemed to be perfectly settled. The cause of the quarrel was entirely removed. But when the king expected for so perfect a submission a full absolution, the legate began a laboured harangue on his rebellion, his tyranny, and the innumerable sins he had committed; and in conclusion declared, that there was no way left to appease God and the church but to resign his crown to the holy see, from whose hands he should receive it purified from all pollutions, and hold it for the future by homage, and an annual tribute.

John was struck motionless at a demand so extravagant and unexpected. He knew not on which side to turn. If he cast his eyes toward the coast of France, he there saw his enemy Philip, who considered him as a criminal as well as an enemy, and who aimed not only at his crown but his life, at the head of an innumerable multitude of fierce people, ready to rush in upon him. If he looked at his own army, he saw nothing there but coldness, disaffection, uncertainty, distrust, and a strength in which he knew not whether he ought most to confide or fear. On the other hand, the papal thunders, from the wounds of which he was still sore, were levelled full at his head. He could not look steadily at these complicated difficulties; and truly it is hard to say what choice he had, if any choice were left to the kings in what concerns the independence of their crown. Surrounded, therefore, with these difficulties, and that all his late humiliations might not be rendered as ineffectual as they were ignominious, he took the last step; and, in the presence of a numerous assembly of his peers and prelates, who turned their eyes from this mortifying sight, formally resigned his crown to the pope's legate; to whom at the same time he did homage, and paid the first-fruits of his tribute. Nothing could be added to the humiliation of the king upon this occasion but the insolence of the legate, who spurned the treasure with his foot, and let the crown remain a long time on the ground before he restored it to the degraded owner.

In this proceeding the motives of the king may be easily discovered; but how the barons of the kingdom, who were deeply concerned, suffered, without any protestation, the independency of the Crown to be thus forfeited, is mentioned by no historian of that time. In civil tumults it is astonishing how little regard is paid by all parties to the honour or safety of their country. The king's friends were probably induced to acquiesce by the same motives that had influenced the king. His enemies, who were the most numerous, perhaps saw his abasement with pleasure, as they knew this action might be one day employed against him with effect. To the bigots it was enough that it aggrandised the pope. It is perhaps worthy of observation, that the conduct of Pandulph towards King John bore a very great affinity to that of the Roman consuls to the people of Carthage in the last Punic war; drawing them from concession to concession, and carefully concealing their design, until they made it impossible for the Carthaginians to resist. Such a strong resemblance did the same ambition produce in such distant times; and it is far from the sole instance in which we may trace a similarity between the spirit and conduct of the former and latter Rome in their common design on the liberties of mankind.

The legates, having thus triumphed over the king, passed back AD 1213 into France, but without relaxing the interdict or excommunication, which they still left hanging over him, lest he should be tempted to throw off the chains of his new subjection. Arriving in France, they delivered their orders to Philip with as much haughtiness as they had done to John. They told him that the end of the war was answered in the humiliation of the king of England, who had been rendered a dutiful son of the church: and that if the king of France should, after this notice, proceed to further hostilities, he had to apprehend the same sentence which had humbled his adversary. Philip, who had not raised so great an army with a view of reforming the manners of King John, would have slighted these threats, had he not found that they were seconded by the ill dispositions of a part of his own army. The Earl of Flanders,[18] always disaffected to his cause, was glad of this opportunity to oppose him; and only following him through fear, withdrew his force, and now openly opposed him. Philip turned his arms against his revolted vassal. The cause of John was revived by this dissension; and his courage seemed rekindled. Making one effort of a vigorous mind, he brought his fleet to an action of the French navy, which he entirely destroyed on the coast of Flanders, and thus freed himself from the terror of an invasion. But when he intended to embark and improve his success, the barons refused to follow him. They alleged that he was still excommunicated, and that they would not follow a lord under the censures of the church. This demonstrated to the king the necessity of a speedy absolution; and he received it this year from the hands of Cardinal Langton.

That archbishop no sooner came into the kingdom than he discovered designs very different from those which the pope had raised him to promote. He formed schemes of a very deep and extensive nature; and became the first mover in all the affairs which distinguished the remainder of this reign. In the oath which he administered to John on his absolution he did not confine himself solely to the ecclesiastical grievances, but made him swear to amend his civil government; to raise no tax without the consent of the great council; and to punish no man but by the judgment of his court. In these terms we may see the Great Charter traced in miniature. A new scene of contention was opened; new pretensions were started; a new scheme was displayed. One dispute was hardly closed when he was involved in another; and this unfortunate king soon discovered, that to renounce his dignity was not the way to secure his repose. For, being cleared from the excommunication, he resolved to pursue the war in France, in which he was not without a prospect of success; but the barons refused upon new pretences, and not a man would serve. The king, incensed to find himself equally opposed in his lawful and unlawful commands, prepared to avenge himself in his accustomed manner; and to reduce the barons to obedience by carrying war into their estates. But he found by this experiment that his power was at an end. The archbishop followed him; confronted him with the liberties of his people; reminded him of his late oath; and threatened to excommunicate every person who should obey him in his illegal proceedings. The king, first provoked, afterwards terrified, at this resolution, forbore to prosecute the recusants.

The English barons had privileges, which they knew to have been violated; they had always kept up the memory of the ancient Saxon liberty; and if they were the conquerors of Britain, they did not think that their own servitude was the just fruit of their victory. They had, however, but an indistinct view of the object at which they aimed; they rather felt their wrongs than understood the cause of them; and having no head nor council, they were more in a condition of distressing their king, and disgracing their country by their disobedience, than of applying any effectual remedy to their grievances. Langton saw these dispositions and these wants. He had conceived a settled plan for reducing the king; and all his actions tended to carry it into execution. This prelate, under pretence of holding an ecclesiastical synod, drew

AD 1214

together privately some of the principal barons to the church of St. Paul in London. There, having expatiated on the miseries which the kingdom suffered, and having explained at the same time the liberties to which it was entitled, he produced the famous charter of Henry I, long concealed, and of which, with infinite difficulty, he had procured an authentic copy. This he held up to the barons as the standard about which they were to unite. These were the liberties which their ancestors had received by the free concession of a former king; and these the rights which their virtue was to force from the present, if (which God forbid) they should find it necessary to have recourse to such extremities. The barons, transported to find an authentic instrument to justify their discontent, and to explain and sanction their pretensions, covered the archbishop with praises; readily confederated to support their demands; and, binding themselves by every obligation of human and religious faith to vigour, unanimity, and secrecy, they departed to confederate others in their design.

This plot was in the hands of too many to be perfectly concealed; and John saw, without knowing how to ward it off, a more dangerous blow levelled at his authority than any of the former. He had no resources within his kingdom, where all ranks and orders were united against him by one common hatred. Foreign alliance he had none among temporal powers. He endeavoured, therefore, if possible, to draw some benefit from the misfortune of his new circumstances; he threw himself upon the protection of the papal power, which he had so long and with such reason opposed. The pope readily received him into his protection; but took this occasion to make him purchase it by another and more formal resignation of his crown. His present necessities, and his habits of humiliation, made this second degradation easy to the king. But Langton, who no longer acted in subservience to the pope, from whom he had now nothing further to expect, and who had put himself at the head of the patrons of civil liberty, loudly exclaimed at this indignity, protested against the resignation, and laid his protestation on the altar.

This was more disagreeable to the barons than the first resignation, as they were sensible that he now degraded himself only to humble his subjects. They were, however, once more patient witnesses to that ignominious act, and were so much overawed by the pope, or had brought their design to so little maturity, that the king, in spite of it, still found means and authority to raise an army, with which he made a final effort to recover some part of his dominions in France. The juncture was altogether favourable to his design. Philip had all his attention abundantly employed in another quarter against the terrible attacks of the Emperor Otho, in a confederacy with the Earl of Flanders. John, strengthened by this diversion, carried on the war in Poitou for some time with good appearances. The battle of Bovines, which was fought this year, put an end to all these hopes. In this battle the imperial army, consisting of 150,000 men, were defeated by a third of their number of French forces. The emperor himself, with difficulty escaping from the field, survived but a short time a battle which entirely broke his strength.[19] So signal a success established the grandeur of France upon immovable foundations. Philip rose continually in reputation and power, whilst John continually declined in both; and as the king of France was now ready to employ against him all his forces, so lately victorious, he sued by the mediation of the pope's legate for a truce, which was granted to him for five years. Such truces stood in the place of regular treaties of peace, which were not often made at that time.

The barons of England had made use of the king's absence to bring their confederacy to form; and now, seeing him return with so little credit, his allies discomfited, and no hope of a party among his subjects, they appeared in a body before him at London. All in complete armour, and in the guise of defiance, they presented a petition, very humble in the language, but excessive in the substance; in which they declared their liberties, and prayed that they might be formally allowed and established by the royal authority. The king resolved not to submit to their demands; but being at present in no condition to resist, he required time to consider of so important an affair. The time, which was granted to the king to deliberate, he employed in finding means to avoid a compliance. He took the cross, by which he hoped to render his person sacred.[20] He obliged the people to renew their oath of fealty; and, lastly, he had recourse to the pope. Fortified by all the devices which could be used to supply the place of a real strength, he ventured, when the barons renewed their demands, to give them a positive refusal; he swore by the feet of God (his usual oath) that he would never grant them such liberties as must make a slave of himself.

The barons, on this answer, immediately fly to arms: they rise in every part; they form an army, and appoint a leader; and as they knew that no design can involve all sorts of people, or inspire them with extraordinary resolution, unless it be animated with religion, they called their leader the marshal of the army of God and holy church. The king was wholly unprovided against so general a defection. The city of London, the possession of which has generally proved a decisive advantage in the English civil wars, was betrayed to the barons. He might rather be said to be imprisoned than defended in the Tower of London, to which close siege was laid; whilst the marshal of the barons' army, exercising the prerogatives of royalty, issued writs to summon all the lords to join the army of liberty; threatening equally all those who should adhere to the king, and those who betrayed an indifference to the cause by their neutrality. John, deserted by all, had no resource but in temporising and submission. Without questioning in any part the terms of a treaty, which he intended to observe in none, he agreed to everything the barons thought fit to ask; hoping that the exorbitancy of their demands would justify in the eyes of the world the breach of his promises. The instruments by which the barons secured their liberties were drawn up in form of charters, and in the manner by which grants had been usually made to monasteries; with a preamble signifying, that it was done for the benefit of the king's soul, and those of his ancestors. For the place of solemnising this remarkable act, they chose a large field, overlooked by Windsor, called Running-mede, which in our present tongue signifies the meadow of council; a place long consecrated by public opinion, as that wherein the quarrels and wars which arose in the English nation, when divided into kingdoms or factions, had been terminated from the remotest times. Here it was that King John, on the 15th day of June, in the year of our Lord 1215, signed those two memorable instruments, which first disarmed the Crown of its unlimited prerogatives, and laid the foundation of English liberty. One was called the Great Charter; the other, the Charter of the Forest. If we look back to the state of the nation at that time, we shall the better comprehend the spirit and necessity of these grants.

Besides the ecclesiastical jurisprudence at that time, two systems of laws, very different from each other in their object, their reason, and their authority, regulated the interior of the kingdom: the Forest law, and the Common law. After the Northern nations had settled here and in other parts of Europe, hunting, which had formerly been the chief means of their subsistence, still continued their favourite diversion. Great tracts of each country, wasted by the wars in which it was conquered, were set apart for this kind of sport, and guarded in a state of desolation by strict laws and severe penalties. When such waste lands were in the hands of subjects, they were called chases; when in the power of the sovereign, they were denominated forests. These forests lay properly within the jurisdiction of no hundred, county, or bishoprick; and therefore being out both of the common and the spiritual law, they were governed by a law of their own, which was such as the king by his private will thought proper to impose. There were reckoned in England no less than sixty-eight royal forests, some of them of vast extent. In these great tracts were many scattered inhabitants; and several persons had property of wood-land, and other soil, enclosed within their bounds. Here the king had separate courts and particular justiciaries: a complete jurisprudence, with all its ceremonies and terms of art, was formed; and it appears that these laws were better digested, and more carefully enforced, than those which belonged to civil government. They had, indeed, all the qualities of the worst of laws. Their professed object was to keep a great part of the nation desolate. They hindered communication, and destroyed industry. They had a trivial object, and most severe sanctions; for as they belonged immediately to the king's personal pleasures, by the lax interpretation of treason in those days, all considerable offences against the forest law, such as killing the beasts of game, were considered as high treason, and punished, as high treason then was, by truncation of limbs, and loss of eyes and testicles. Hence arose a thousand abuses, vexatious suits, and pretences for imposition upon all those who lived in or near these places. The deer were suffered to run loose upon their lands; and many oppressions were used with relation to the claim of commonage, which the people had in most of the forests. The Norman kings were not the first makers of the forest law; it subsisted under the Saxon and Danish kings. Canute the Great composed a body of those laws, which still remains. But under the Norman kings they were enforced with greater rigour, as the whole tenor of the Norman government was more rigorous. Besides, new forests were frequently made, by which private property was outraged in a grievous manner. Nothing, perhaps, shows more clearly how little men are able to depart from the common course of affairs, than that the Norman kings, princes of great capacity, and extremely desirous of absolute power, did not think of peopling these forests; places under their own uncontrolled dominion, and which might have served as so many garrisons dispersed throughout the country. The Charter of the Forests had for its object the disafforesting several of those tracts; the prevention of future afforestings; the mitigation and ascertainment of the punishments for breaches of the forest law.

The common law, as it then prevailed in England, was in a great measure composed of some remnants of the old Saxon customs, joined to the feudal institutions brought in at the Norman conquest. And it is here to be observed, that the constitutions of Magna Charta are by no means a renewal of the laws of St. Edward, or the ancient Saxon laws, as our historians and law-writers generally, though very groundlessly, assert.[21] They bear no resemblance, in any particular, to the laws of St. Edward, or to any other collection of these ancient institutions. Indeed, how should they? The object of Magna Charta is the correction of the feudal policy, which was first introduced, at least in any regular form, at the conquest, and did not subsist before it. It may be further observed, that in the preamble to the Great Charter it is stipulated that the barons shall *hold* the liberties, there granted *to them and their heirs*, from the *king and his heirs*: which shows that the doctrine of an unalienable tenure was always uppermost in their minds. Their idea even of liberty was not (if I may use the expression) perfectly free; and they did not claim to possess their privileges upon any natural principle or independent bottom, but, just as they held their lands, from the king. This is worthy of observation.

By the feudal law all landed property is, by a feigned conclusion, supposed to be derived, and therefore to be mediately or immediately held, from the Crown. If some estates were so derived, others were certainly procured by the same original title of conquest, by which the crown itself was acquired; and the derivation from the king could in reason only be considered as a fiction of law. But its consequent rights being once supposed, many real charges and burdens grew from a notion made only for the preservation of subordination; and in consequence of this, a great power was exercised over the persons and estates of the tenants. The fines on the succession to an estate, called in the feudal language *Reliefs*, were not fixed to any certainty; and were therefore frequently made so excessive, that they might rather be considered as redemptions, or new purchases, than acknowledgments of superiority and tenure. With respect to that most important article of marriage, there was, in the very nature of the feudal holding, a great restraint laid upon it. It was of importance to the lord, that the person who received the feud should be submissive to him; he had therefore a right to interfere in the marriage of the heiress who inherited the feud. This right was carried further than the necessity required; the male heir himself was obliged to marry according to the choice of his lord; and even widows, who had made one sacrifice to the feudal tyranny, were neither suffered to continue in the widowed state, nor to choose for themselves the partners of their second bed. In fact, marriage was publicly set up to sale. The ancient records of the exchequer afford many instances where some women purchased, by heavy fines, the privilege of a single life; some the free choice of a husband; others the liberty of rejecting some person particularly disagreeable. And, what may appear extraordinary, there are not wanting examples, where a woman has fined in a considerable sum, that she might not be compelled to marry a certain man; the suitor on the other hand has outbid her; and solely by offering more for the marriage than the heiress could to prevent it, he carried his point directly and avowedly against her inclinations. Now, as the king claimed no right over his immediate tenants that they did not exercise in the same, or in a more oppressive, manner over their vassals, it is hard to conceive a more general and cruel grievance than this shameful market, which so universally outraged the most sacred relations among mankind. But the tyranny over women was not over with the marriage. As the king seized into his hands the estate of every deceased tenant in order to secure his relief, the widow was driven often by a heavy composition to purchase the admission to her dower, into which it should seem she could not enter without the king's consent.

All these were marks of a real and grievous servitude. The Great Charter was made not to destroy the root, but to cut short the overgrown branches, of the feudal service; first, in moderating, and in reducing to a certainty, the reliefs which the king's tenants paid on succeeding to their estate according to their rank;

and, secondly, in taking off some of the burdens which had been laid on marriage whether compulsory or restrictive, and thereby preventing that shameful market, which had been made in the persons of heirs, and the most sacred things amongst mankind.

There were other provisions made in the Great Charter, that went deeper than the feudal tenure, and affected the whole body of the civil government. A great part of the king's revenue then consisted in the fines and amercements[22] which were imposed in his courts. A fine was paid there for liberty to commence, or to conclude, a suit. The punishment of offences by fine was discretionary; and this discretionary power had been very much abused. But by Magna Charta things were so ordered, that a delinquent might be punished, but not ruined, by a fine or amercement, because the degree of his offence, and the rank he held, were to be taken into consideration. His freehold, his merchandise, and those instruments by which he obtained his livelihood, were made sacred from such impositions.

A more grand reform was made with regard to the administration of justice. The kings in those days seldom resided long in one place, and their courts followed their persons. This erratic justice must have been productive of infinite inconvenience to the litigants. It was now provided, that civil suits, called *Common Pleas*, should be fixed to some certain place. Thus one branch of jurisdiction was separated from the king's court, and detached from his person. They had not yet come to that maturity of jurisprudence as to think this might be made to extend to criminal law also; and that the latter was an object of still greater importance. But even the former may be considered as a great revolution. A tribunal, a creature of mere law, independent of personal power, was established, and this separation of a king's authority from his person was a matter of vast consequence towards introducing ideas of freedom, and confirming the sacredness and majesty of laws.

But the grand article, and that which cemented all the parts of the fabric of liberty, was this, "that no freeman shall be taken or imprisoned, or disseized,[23] or outlawed, or banished, or in any wise destroyed, but by judgment of his peers."

There is another article of nearly as much consequence as the former, considering the state of the nation at that time, by which it is provided, that the barons shall grant to their tenants the same liberties which they had stipulated for themselves. This prevented the kingdom from degenerating into the worst imaginable government, – a feudal aristocracy. The English barons were not in the condition of those great princes who had made the French monarchy so low in the preceding century; or like those who reduced the imperial power to a name. They had been brought to moderate bounds by the policy of the first and second Henrys, and were not in a condition to set up for petty sovereigns by an usurpation equally detrimental to the Crown and the people. They were able to act only in confederacy; and this common cause made it necessary to consult the common good, and to study popularity by the equity of their proceedings. This was a very happy circumstance to the growing liberty.

These concessions were so just and reasonable, that, if we except the force, no prince could think himself wronged in making them. But to secure the observance of these articles regulations were made, which, whilst they were regarded, scarcely left a shadow of regal power. And the barons could think of no measures for securing their freedom but such as were inconsistent with monarchy. A council of twenty-five barons was to be chosen by their own body, without any concurrence of the king, in order to hear and determine upon all complaints concerning the breach of the charter; and as these charters extended to almost every part of government, a tribunal of his enemies was set up, who might pass judgment on all his actions. And that force might not be wanting to execute the judgments of this new tribunal, the king agreed to issue his own writs to all persons, to oblige them to take an oath of obedience to the twenty-five barons, who were empowered to distress him by seizure of his lands and castles, and by every possible method, until the grievance complained of was redressed according to their pleasure: his own person and his family were alone exempted from violence.

By these last concessions it must be confessed he was effectually dethroned, and with all the circumstances of indignity which could be imagined. He had refused to govern as a lawful prince, and he saw himself deprived of even his legal authority. He became of no sort of consequence in his kingdom; he was held in universal contempt and derision; he fell into a profound melancholy. It was in vain that he had recourse to the pope, whose power he had found sufficient to reduce but not to support him. The censures of the holy see,[24] which had been fulminated at his desire, were little regarded by the barons, or even by the clergy, supported in this resistance by the firmness of their archbishop, who acted with great vigour in the cause of the barons, and even delivered into their hands the fortress of Rochester, one of the most important places in the kingdom. After much meditation, the king at last resolved upon a measure of the most extreme kind, extorted by shame, revenge, and despair; but, considering the disposition of the time, much the most effectual that could be chosen. He despatched emissaries into France, into the Low Countries, and Germany, to raise men for his service. He had recourse to the same measures to bring his kingdom to obedience which his predecessor William had used to conquer it. He promised to the adventurers in his quarrel the lands of the rebellious barons; and, it is said, even empowered his agents to make charters of the estates of several particulars. The utmost success attended these negotiations in an age when Europe abounded with a warlike and poor nobility; with younger brothers, for whom there was no provision in regular armies, who seldom entered into the church, and never applied themselves to commerce; and when every considerable family was surrounded by an innumerable multitude of retainers and dependants, idle, and greedy of war and pillage. The crusade had universally diffused a spirit of adventure; and if any adventure had the pope's approbation, it was sure to have a number of followers.

John waited the effect of his measures. He kept up no longer the solemn mockery of a court, in which a degraded king must always have been the lowest object. He retired to the Isle of Wight: his only companions were sailors and fishermen, among whom he became extremely popular.[25] Never was he more to be dreaded than in this sullen retreat, whilst the barons amused themselves by idle jests, and vain conjectures on his conduct. Such was the strange want of foresight in that barbarous age, and such the total neglect of design in their affairs, that the barons, when they had got the charter, which was weakened even by the force by which it was obtained and the great power which it granted, set no watch upon the king; seemed to have no intelligence of the great and open machinations which were carrying on against them, and had made no sort of dispositions for their defence. They spent their time in tournaments and bear-baitings, and other diversions suited to the fierce rusticity of their manners. At length the storm broke forth, and found them

utterly unprovided. The papal excommunication, the indignation of their prince, and a vast army of lawless and bold adventurers, were poured down at once upon their heads. Such
numbers were engaged in this enterprise, that forty thousand are
said to have perished at sea.[26] Yet a number still remained
sufficient to compose two great armies; one of which, with the
enraged king at its head, ravaged without mercy the north of
England; whilst the other turned all the west to a like scene of
blood and desolation. The memory of Stephen's wars[27] was
renewed with every image of horror, misery, and crime. The
barons, dispersed and trembling in their castles, waited who
should fall the next victim. They had no army able to keep the
field. The archbishop, on whom they had great reliance, was suspended from his functions. There was no hope even from submission; the king could not fulfil his engagements to his foreign
troops at a cheaper rate than the utter ruin of his barons. In these
circumstances of despair they resolved to have recourse to Philip,
the ancient enemy of their country. Throwing off all allegiance
to John, they agreed to accept Lewis,[28] the son of that monarch,
as their king. Philip had once more an opportunity of bringing
the crown of England into his family, and he readily embraced
it. He immediately sent his son into England with seven hundred
ships, and slighted the menaces and excommunications of the
pope to attain the same object for which he had formerly armed
to support and execute them. The affairs of the barons assumed
quite a new face by this reinforcement, and their rise was as sudden and striking as their fall. The foreign army of King John,
without discipline, pay, or order, ruined and wasted in the midst
of its successes, was little able to oppose the natural force of the
country, called forth and recruited by so considerable a succour.
Besides, the French troops who served under John, and made
a great part of his army, immediately went over to the enemy,
unwilling to serve against their sovereign in a cause which now
began to look desperate. The son of the king of France was
acknowledged in London, and received the homage of all ranks
of men. John, thus deserted, had no other ally than the pope,
who indeed served him to the utmost of his power; but with
arms to which the circumstances of the time alone can give any
force. He excommunicated Lewis and his adherents; he laid England under an interdict; he threatened the king of France himself

AD 1216

with the same sentence; but Philip continued firm, and the interdict had little effect in England. Cardinal Langton, by his remarkable address, by his interest in the sacred college, and his prudent
submissions, had been restored to the exercise of his office; but,
steady to the cause he had first espoused, he made use of the
recovery of his authority to carry on his old designs against the
king and the pope. He celebrated divine service in spite of the
interdict; and by his influence and example taught others to despise it. The king, thus deserted, and now only solicitous for his
personal safety, rambled, or rather fled, from place to place at the
head of a small party. He was in great danger in passing a marsh
in Norfolk, in which he lost the greatest part of his baggage and
his most valuable effects. With difficulty he escaped to the
monastery of Swinestead; where, violently agitated by grief and
disappointments, his late fatigue and the use of an improper diet
threw him into a fever, of which he died in a few days at Newark,
not without suspicion of poison, after a reign, or rather a struggle
to reign, for eighteen years, the most turbulent and calamitous
both to king and people of any that are recorded in the English
history.

It may not be improper to pause here for a few moments, and
to consider a little more minutely the causes which had produced
the grand revolution in favour of liberty, by which this reign was
distinguished; and to draw all the circumstances which led to this
remarkable event into a single point of view. Since the death of
Edward the Confessor only two princes succeeded to the crown
upon undisputed titles. William the Conqueror established his
by force of arms. His successors were obliged to court the people
by yielding many of the possessions and many of the prerogatives
of the Crown; but they supported a dubious title by a vigorous
administration; and recovered by their policy in the course of
their reign what the necessity of their affairs obliged them to
relinquish for the establishment of their power. Thus was the
nation kept continually fluctuating between freedom and servitude. But the principles of freedom were predominant, though
the thing itself was not yet fully formed. The continual struggle
of the clergy for the ecclesiastical liberties laid open at the same
time the natural claims of the people; and the clergy were obliged
to show some respect for those claims, in order to add strength
to their own party. The concessions which Henry the Second

made to the ecclesiastics on the death of Becket, which were afterwards confirmed by Richard the First, gave a grievous blow to the authority of the Crown; as thereby an order of so much power and influence triumphed over it in many essential points. The latter of these princes brought it very low by the whole tenor of his conduct. Always abroad, the royal authority was felt in its full vigour, without being supported by the dignity, or softened by the graciousness, of the royal presence. Always in war, he considered his dominions only as a resource for his armies. The demesnes of the Crown were squandered. Every office in the state was made vile by being sold. Excessive grants, followed by violent and arbitrary resumptions, tore to pieces the whole contexture of the government. The civil tumults which arose in that king's absence showed that the king's lieutenants at least might be disobeyed with impunity.

Then came John to the Crown. The arbitrary taxes which he imposed very early in his reign, which offended even more by the improper use made of them than their irregularity, irritated the people extremely, and joined with all the preceding causes to make his government contemptible. Henry the Second, during his contests with the church, had the address to preserve the barons in his interests. Afterwards, when the barons had joined in the rebellion of his children, this wise prince found means to secure the bishops and ecclesiastics. But John drew upon himself at once the hatred of all orders of his subjects. His struggle with the pope weakened him; his submission to the pope weakened him yet more. The loss of his foreign territories, besides what he lost along with them in reputation, made him entirely dependent upon England; whereas his predecessors made one part of their territories subservient to the preservation of their authority in another, where it was endangered. Add to all these causes the personal character of the king, in which there was nothing uniform or sincere, and which introduced the like unsteadiness into all his government. He was indolent, yet restless, in his disposition; fond of working by violent methods, without any vigour; boastful, but continually betraying his fears; showing, on all occasions, such a desire of peace as hindered him from ever enjoying it. Having no spirit of order, he never looked forward; content by any temporary expedient to extricate himself from a present difficulty. Rash, arrogant, perfidious, irreligious, unquiet, he made a tolerable head of a party, but a bad king; and had talents fit to disturb another's government, not to support his own. A most striking contrast presents itself between the conduct and fortune of John and his adversary Philip. Philip came to the Crown when many of the provinces of France, by being in the hands of too powerful vassals, were in a manner dismembered from the kingdom; the royal authority was very low in what remained. He reunited to the Crown a country as valuable as what belonged to it before; he reduced his subjects of all orders to a stricter obedience than they had given to his predecessors. He withstood the papal usurpation, and yet used it as an instrument in his designs; whilst John, who inherited a great territory, and an entire prerogative, by his vices and weakness gave up his independency to the pope, his prerogative to his subjects, and a large part of his dominions to the king of France.

ON PARTIES

1757

AT A TIME when every body laments our ill success or complains so bitterly of those mismanagements which have produced them: may it not seem a little odd that nobody has enquired into their real Cause[,] that nobody has looked further than some personal mismanagements which often themselves take their Rise from a Complication of other things.

To learn the real cause perhaps we should [examine] what is & what has been the State of Parties.

After the Restoration their Equality obliged both Whig & Tory[1] to some moderation. The former did not love the Regal Power, their Designs were much the same as formerly. They meditated new restrictions on Royalty & new Reformations in Religion. The latter grew more in love with regal Power than ever & would certainly notwithstanding any Palliatives have let it extend to every thing but Religion. K[ing] James[,] fatally for him[,] brought it to this last Proof & then sunk under a junction of both Parties united in the only Point, where they were capable of an Union.

On the Revolution the Tory party began to lose its Scheme from the Nature of its new Engagements but they kept the Spirit of it which could only exert itself in shewing its Discontent to the new Establishment. This Party must always be considered as not the same with the Jacobite[2] which was a real & considerable one & joined with the other as they agreed in distressing the common adversary the Whigs.

From this time we must consider the Design of the Whigs to be the support of themselves, the great Design of all Parties, & the perpetual exclusion of the abdicated family.[3] They became friends to Royalty which they never had been before, because they no otherwise could exclude the old Royal family which they hated, & the Tories became Enemies to it because it was inconsistent with their Principles to have the new.

These were the Designs of each party at the accession of the present family royal.

The Jacobite interest was what really kept Life in both Partys, they gave a real Design to what was only Speculation in the Tories, & the Whigs had thereby a real ground to oppose them.

But a long Exclusion, frequent Disappointments, numerous Desertions, an odious Cause, Court Influence & two unsuccessful wars has absolutely annihilated that Party.[4] The Tory party could not subsist without it, their shaking off their old Prince, & both their Submission & their opposition to those who successively came in his place left them without Scheme or Principle & the Destruction of the Jacobites completed their Ruin. With out these how could the Whigs subsist? Their resisting Principle & their Practice of Submission has left the notion of Whiggistry as a party no better than a jest.

There never can be any Party properly so called where the Constitution is simple & unmixed: Factions there may be & are undoubtedly: as the factions of the Green & Blue in the Decay of the Roman Empire & those of Caesar & Pompey in the Decay of the Commonwealth after a pure Democracy had been establisht. Such were the Partisans of Anthony & Octavian & such truly might the York & Lancaster[5] be considered with ourselves. But to form a Party there must be as an object[,] the Real Aggrandisement of some of the Powers which form the Political Constitution of every state. Now as there is nothing further from the Nature of Man than any sort of moderation nor is it to be imagined that any body will rest satisfied with any Definite portion of Power[,] the Constituent Parts will each have its Party & it is absolutely necessary that it should. This keeps matters even. There is a watchful Eye on every side & the result of the workings of opposite Ambition whilst any sort of Equality subsists creates the Appearance at least of something like moderate Counsels. But where this Complexity does not afford food for Party, all Division[s] must be factions: Cabals fomented by Ambition swelled up by popular madness & nothing more. Hence it is that Party is always useful, faction always pernicious[,] which has hardly been enough considered.

Holland in its Original Constitution had no thing to bind its Democracy but the Authority of the Prince of Orange.[6] For I look upon the Dutch Nobility as nothing; they were neither rich nor Numerous. It was the house of Orange[']s Authority which from the beginning was the food of the Partys & gave them activity. I look upon the Republican Party [as] entirely Abolished. The Oligarchy it is that only can contend with the family of Orange, but it has not the Authority & reverence of Nobility nor the Affections of the People. Upon what grounds then does it stand? It has been tottering & only perhaps waits the Maturity of the Prince of Orange to give it the final stroke.

We have at the present no Party properly so called among us[,] but have we no Divisions? We have[,] but they are mere factions: without any Design[,] with out any principle[,] but only a junction of People intreaguing for their own Interest. For it is a rule confirmed by a too constant & too woeful Experience that there can be no Body of People united by a bond strong enough to hold them together, or animated by a Principle vigorous enough to give them Activity upon a mere abstract notion of [the] publick. & when they have not some general Scheme & some fixed object they must be mere factions fomented & kept up by Discontent[,] by Envy, by a Spirit of Sedition on one side, & by Ambition on the other. Such are our Divisions. Such were in Rome the factions of Marius & Sylla[,][7] of Caesar & Pompey. Such must all [those] be who have no common Standard to resort to. For let any body point out to me what the Principle of our opposition really is. Let any body shew me, suppose the Managers of the Party were dead or converted[,] what the scheme those who would continue it could have [i.e. be]. In our antient Parties, except in some of the tories[,] the meanest Man knew very well what scheme he adopted[,] what End he aimed at, what principles of Government he espoused.

It might be imagined we should be considerable gainers by this Extinction of Party but this is very problematical. It is certain no free Government ever was without parties: whilst these were something balanced[,] the freedom & the Consequences of it[,] the Spirit[,] the Dignity[,] the Power of these states remained[,] but when one Party was wholly swallowed up in the other[,] then the Nation, not better united than before, but divided upon no principle[,] came to a speedy & often terrible Destruction.

In Athens there long subsisted the Oligarchick & Democratick Parties. The former was the term of Popular Dislike, & as such we find their orators objecting it to each other much in the same manner [as] Jacobite is bandied about in our Disputes.

In all the free Estates of Greece & indeed in those of Italy too a Contention was kept up between the Nobility & the Plebeians which often endangered these states it is true, but it was what preserved the vigour of their Constitution, & they fell as soon as one Party had wholly destroyed the other. In every Constitution there are powers which are to balance. There ought to be parties which may nearly balance too.

I have observed that we have no Parties for what restraint on the Crown should we desire? Or what can the Court desire of the People which it has not? I need not say which of the Scales has preponderated. We are very obviously grown in effect whatever Appearances may be, into a perfect Democracy. The Power of the Crown is not mentioned, for we must distinguish between the Crown & the Court: those whom we see urge every thing so violently for the latter do not desire[,] nay they would un-doubtedly oppose[,] any Design for setting the Crown upon such an Independent footing that it might chuse what persons it should employ. There never was any thing further from the Intention of the leading Men. They are not grown great at Court by court favour but by popular Influence, by their Interest in forming or their address in managing the assemblies of the People, far from bowing to the throne they know they are neces-sary to it. They are those great Demagogue[s] to whom all the established Powers must pay Court. To ascertain the Degree of Power any man has in great Britain, you must enquire, how many Boroughs he can influence. How is he versed in the Business of the house? Of what Powers of Oratory? Of what Arts in managing a Debate? Point me out the first Man in any of these particulars & I will shew you our first Minister or one that must be so shortly. It is not the Caprice of a monarch, it is not the Trickery of a Court, it is not the Intreagues & caballing of the Women that raises a Man to that Degree with us, but the Powers & Arts I have mentioned.

The Court then is no other than a Combination of the great Officers of the State become such by popular Influence & Authority.

The Court Party is composed of the Officers under those & the Expectants.

The Country Party, of those who oppose because they are turned out, of those who want to come in, & those of some small remains too pitiful almost to be mentioned of the Jacobites. What is the Consequence to the Nation? The Minister as he holds all his Power in the Grace & favour of the People is obliged to Court them by all means. If he is to nominate an officer to Command in the Army[,] in the Marine or in the finances, in vain shall the

Ability of a Candidate plead. The Authority of his Master is of no avail. His own private Inclination[s] are not to be consulted here: he must flatter those to whom he is to owe his Support & must sacrifice the safety of the nation, his own Desires & his Master[']s Honour to the support of an Interest to which he must owe his Continuance in the Place that enables him in any Manner to act in his Publick Capacity.

Let us suppose a Minister of the very best Intentions, thus circumstanced. Suppose him deeply sensible of that Corruption that wastes & cankers to the very Vitals of the state. Suppose him touched at the Idleness[,] Dissipation & Luxury that drains the wealthiest Counties. Let his Indignation be roused at the Profaneness & Indolence of the lower order which has been the forerunner of the Dissolution of all Governments. NB. then to consider the immediate effects of an attempt for a reformation & shew its impossibility.

CONSIDERATIONS ON
A MILITIA

MARCH 1757

AT PRESENT WE have a standing Army.[1] At present we have no militia.[2] Whilst things stand on their present footing we know upon what Ground we stand. We know that for 60 years past we have subsisted happily & gloriously for ourselves, usefully for our neighbours, & with Terror to our Enemys, that we had honour abroad & liberty at home & that we have compassed all these great Ends without the assistance of a militia.

But when we adopt this new System we do it without Experience of its good effects & we cannot positively know with how many & how dangerous Evils it may be pregnant. Some of them we can point out even now. When Men already in a good Condition, think of innovating in any Respect, they have a Course of which they know the advantages, so as to push them to their Utmost. They leave a Course of which they know the disadvantages, so as to know the best Methods of contending against them: they leave this for another the good of which is uncertain & many of whose Evil Consequences lying in the womb of time [']tis impossible to know. How fatal they may prove when produced in the face of Day, & how far beyond all the Powers of the Constitution to overcome. We leave a certain good health in hopes of gaining a better habit of Body by the assistance of Physick.

To consider this Matter properly let us view our Army as it now stands, & the Militia as it is proposed to be. But first I must observe that all fears for our Liberty from our Army[,] even all the pretended fears of those who had Ends to answer in being alarmed[,] are in a manner vanished[.] They who were the most sanguine for this new Scheme of a Militia do not at all propose that we should lay by the standing Army: a Plain demonstration this, that any danger to Liberty from our Army is allowed on all hands to be Chimerical & whoever considers what our Standing Army is & how it is constituted must be convinced that it is to the last degree so. Our Army is paid by the Parliament: on the Parliament it depends for its Existence, from the Parliament the Matter & Substance is derived: the ordering and managing it (which is only the form) is the well understood Prerogative of the Crown. Our Army exactly resembles our Laws. Our Laws are made, their Body is formed by the Parliament, the Crown inspires them with Life, supports [and] executes them. Our Army therefore may be said to be in every Sense a legal Army. It is not the Army of the Commons, or the Army of the Lords, or the Army of the King. It is the Army of the Constitution. In the civil Government the Power of making Peace or War as well as the intire conduct of the latter is left in the hands of the Crown. & the wisdom of our Constitution as thought, & Experience has fully shewn, that the Power of granting money religiously preserved to the Parliament was a Check sufficient to prevent any Abuse of this Power. By this means a mutual & necessary Dependence is preserved among the Orders of the State, for if the whole of any compleat act of supreme Power was left in any distinct Branch of the Constitution, that Branch would be so far Absolute, & independent of the others, & the Balance of the Constitution would be so far reversed.

In the present Establishment of our Military the Power of the Crown is the same as in the civil. The Check to prevent the Abuse of this Power is the same, & the salutary Consequences are in every respect the same. There is no Argument by which You can evince the Wisdom which appears in the forming of our Constitution that may not be used with equal strength to shew the Wise foundation upon which we have established our Army which is [in] every way the Counterpart of our Constitution. And therefore the best adapted to strengthen[,] support, & co-operate with it. & it was not till our Constitution was poised upon its proper Base, that is, since the Revolution that we have had these Parliamentary Armys. The Use of which we never for a moment since have laid aside tho they have been constantly opposed chiefly by those who wished ill to the Revolution.

I do not know any Body of Men in the Kingdom who have more reason from their particular Interest to wish well to the Constitution, & to the Liberties of their Country than the Officers of our Army. & after all the Interest of men is that motive which can be relied on with the most certainty, for influencing their Conduct, at least it must be politically considered in this light.

Many if not most of the Officers own the Posts which they actually hold, & must lay a great Part of their hopes of advancement on a Parliamentary Interest. Many of them are themselves Members of the one or the other house[,] & many more are nearly connected to such as are by Blood or by other very close ties. This shews how little they understood the Genius of our Constitution or how little they regarded it, who would have thrust out of the house of Commons all Officers of the Army, & all other Persons who hold Places under the Crown. The Pretence was popular & plausible, it must be owned. But the Design was ill laid. In all Governments the officers of the Crown, a numerous, powerful & wealthy body & exercising all the common functions of Government, must necessarily have great weight & Credit & Influence. If you detach these from the Body of the Constitution & create for them a separate & independent Interest, You turn all that Credit, Weight & Influence against all Orders in the State except that one which has the disposal of offices. & thus instead of a well connected[,] harmonious System of Government you introduce a jarring Mixture of discordant Powers.

But as things now stand & as they must stand whilst our present Constitution & Army continue nothing less than the most unaccountable Madness can ever make our Corps of Officers revolt from the sure means of Interest which they have from personal Authority or personal connections, to become dependent upon the precarious Will of any Man or any set of Men.

But can this be said of the militia that is proposed? The Officers of this are not to depend for their advancement upon this or upon that form of Government[,] upon the Liberties or upon the Servitude of the People, but upon their own fortunes in the Country: their Pay in any rank is nothing: & therefore an Army independent of [and] unconnected with the Constitution is created. They are to have no attachment either to the King or to the Parliament by any tie of Interest & having no sure Bias they may be thrown on this side or that, as faction or if possible some worse motive may chance to influence them. Where are to be seen in this new scheme those mutual constitutional checks that counteract one another[?] Those Counterpoises which hang upon every part of our Government, which are opposed to the Violence of Prerogative on the one side, & to the unbridled Licentiousness of freedom on the other: & which if any material part of our Government should want, the safety of the whole would unquestionably be in Danger. The Militia has no shadow of these. But the Officers of the Army are connected not only by their general principles as Englishmen, but by their very Interest as officers of the Army to the Constitution as it is now established.

It was not till the Revolution had explained & fixt our Constitution that these Parliamentary standing Armies were settled, but ever since, they have been uniformly opposed, it must be owned by some good men misled by false representations of things: but for much the greater part by those who hated the Constitution as it became established, & those means which they saw but too effectually secured it: they therefore made two Arguments walk constantly hand in hand through their Designs. First they urge in Season & out of Season, that the regular Army should be laid aside, & a militia be substituted in its Place. For this in Spite of all their subterfuges & concessions is their real drift. They know how incompatible two such forms must necessarily be, & that one must in time come wholly to thrust out the other. & they have reason to hope, that it is the Militia which must prevail: as that Body is to be equally numerous in time of War & Peace. Whilst its existence will always serve as a plausible Argument for bringing down the standing Army by continual Reductions.

And secondly they urge with equal Violence, that we should preserve no sort of Connection with the Continent because they know that the Providence of our Whig Ancestors, connected them to us, & us to them by the closest & strongest ties. They observed that those who were ill inclined to our Liberties at home, had always kept up the closest Connections with those who were Enemies to the freedom & Peace of Europe: & therefore the thing itself pointed out to them that they ought to unite themselves firmly to those who must find it the Interest of their own Independence & freedom to preserve ours inviolate. Therefore our Ancestors thought it no Shame to secure our Constitution & the Protestant Succession not only by the Walls & Bastions of Laws at home, but to cover it by the Dykes & outworks of Alliances & Guarantees of those Powers abroad who had the same cause. But what firmness could those alliances have, if we in our turn had not always an Army at hand ready to serve & assist them, & ourselves? But had they left every thing to a Militia, no where to be compared to regular troops, but never by their Constitution to be sent any-where abroad & that this militia & a regular Army could never subsist together has been I think already shewn sufficiently, & I hope we shall never have from Experience a better Argument against it.

I know that in other Countries a Militia & a Standing Army in some sort subsist together. But I know too that the Militia is drowned in the splendor of the Standing Army, which in number, in Discipline, in the Nobility and Consideration of its Officers, in the favour of the Crown, in every thing outshines it infinitely. They act in intire Subordination to the regular Army which is recruited from them, they are only to be considered as a sort of seminary for their Army & not as an independent Body supported by a Party in the state to the exclusion of the other: In vain is the Army of Sweden objected to us. Who does not see at the first Glance, that neither is the Army of Sweden at all like [our] proposed Militia, nor is the Constitution of Sweden the same with that of Great Britain.

Now let us consider the Militia in an other light as they are more or less fit to defend their Country without endeavouring its Liberty or its Peace.

The feudal Armies & the Militia which rose out of their ruins served formerly two purposes. They defended the Kingdom against foreign attacks, & they defended occasionally the Constitution against the attack of internal Enemies.

They were very fit for the former of these purposes at a time when Courage & Impetuosity stood in the place of Military Skill, when Militia was opposed to Militia, & Europe had not seen Armys so prodigious in Numbers, so powerful in Discipline, or headed by Commanders so finished in the Schools of a nice & various Experience as we behold at this Day.

Again feudal Armys, & the Militia were useful, perhaps necessary when the Constitution, but ill understood, was worse protected. When the people were utterly unacquainted with the Art of contriving pacific methods or any systematical Policy which might be a Wall to their Liberties & preclude the Necessity of taking up Arms on every real or pretended Infringement on their privileges.

For a Liberty which was neither well defined nor supported by any proper orders in the Constitution of the Government could only have been supported by Arms; but this is a bad Method not only from the Irregularity of the means, but from the Insufficiency to compass the Ends which they were designed to answer, for during the whole time that we relyed upon those Methods we knew nothing but Bondage: whilst we had any repose, or quitting that repose, a Liberty (if it deserved that name) which lost all its sweetness by the Violence, & confusion which attended it.

Parliaments were formerly Medicines in our Constitution, seldom used, violent in their operations, & not lasting in their Effects. They are now its regular, its constant nourishment. They enter fully into its habit. Our Liberty is defended by the force of civil Institutions, all the several parts of the Constitution are so linked together, so dependent upon each other, that it is not possible by Artifice or by the force that any distinct Member of it could exert to disunite them. So that a Military check though perhaps necessary at times of Rudeness & Violence is improper & even unnatural where a Government is poised by its own proper weight. I insist the rather on this Argument, because I have heard some suggestions, as if a fear from this use of a Militia had some Influence upon those who opposed it, & truly if there be any Grounds for a fear of that nature there cannot be a better reason for supposing it unless people prefer Confusion to order, Violence to justice, & the uncertain Die of War to a constitutional & systematick method of defending their Liberties.

Another colour allied to the former is thrown upon the Conduct of those who oppose a Militia. It is said they are afraid of putting Arms into the hands of the people. If they are so may it not be with very good Reason?

The antient commonwealths who knew the value of their Freedom as well at least as we do never permitted their People to carry arms within their Cities, because they knew that from their form of Government, & from the high spirit which it inspired, they were more liable to tumult & Disorders, than of Arbitrary Power: they thought that the people whilst the Constitution lasted oppose none but constitutional Methods to any Grievances, & they never put Arms into their hands but when they sent them with the Commission of the State against their Enemies. A Country where people are rude & simple & where Pasturage & Agriculture is their sole Employ, most may be perhaps safely entrusted with Arms because being poor they have not any mutinous Spirit & being dispersed they have not those frequent opportunities of Cabal & inflaming each other.

But the People of great Cities & towns who have had considerable Manufactures & an extensive trade & who were at the same time encouraged by their privileges & immunities & the right of protecting themselves have been always of so mutinous & turbulent a spirit that having caused infinite & frequent Dangers to their Government they have finally destroyed themselves.

Whilst Paris remained unbound by a strong Military force her mutinies were frequent & violent to the last degree, she has often besieged & has often forced her kings to fly. How furious & ungovernable was the city of Ghent whilst it remained the capital of a great State & was full of Wealth, & of men employed in Manufactures! In earlier times Constantinople filled with Men of the same sort scarce permitted any Emperor to reign a Year. It were well if all those Cities had only exerted this spirit nobly in Defence of their lawful Principles. But it was quite otherwise: false pretences, Vulgar notions, the popular Arts of Ambitious Men much more frequently & powerfully roused that Spirit than any honourable & national Design, & the whole ended in the Slavery, Ruin or the total subversion of those Cities. What those Cities were formerly every part of Great Britain is now. By the distribution of trade, it may be all considered as one great manufacturing City, where the People being close together, the fire of Sedition may easily catch from one to another until it spreads over the kingdom [as] in effect we see that it does. In our Manufacturing towns the people are almost constantly engaged in seditious Cabals or open risings. Upon every Appearance of Want tho proceeding solely from the Inclemency of the Season, the Populace rises every where committing a thousand outrages, though this want happens but seldom & is nothing near so pressing as what all our neighbouring Countries so frequently experience. How easy would it be at such a time when the poor are clamorous for Bread, & the Manufacturers discontented with their Masters, how easy would it be then to give the people[']s fluctuating Minds some dangerous turn, to confound natural with political Evils to animate them with hopes of Gain & Plunder to seduce their Minds with Specious Ideas of what they might expect under an other Government, & uniting with them the already disaffected part of the people to persuade all to run to their churches to seize their Arms, & to overturn in a moment that Glorious fabrick of Government which had cost their Ancestors such Expence of Study to form [and] of Labour to raise up, of Blood to cement & of treasure to secure.

From THOUGHTS ON THE CAUSE OF THE PRESENT DISCONTENTS

1770

Hoc vero occultum, intestinum, domesticum malum, non modo non existit, verum etiam opprimit antequam perspicere atque explorare potueris.

CICERO[1]

IT IS AN undertaking of some degree of delicacy to examine into the cause of public disorders. If a man happens not to succeed in such an inquiry, he will be thought weak and visionary; if he touches the true grievance, there is a danger that he may come near to persons of weight and consequence, who will rather be exasperated at the discovery of their errors, than thankful for the occasion of correcting them. If he should be obliged to blame the favourites of the people, he will be considered as the tool of power; if he censures those in power, he will be looked on as an instrument of faction. But in all exertions of duty something is to be hazarded. In cases of tumult and disorder, our law has invested every man, in some sort, with the authority of a magistrate. When the affairs of the nation are distracted, private people are, by the spirit of that law, justified in stepping a little out of their ordinary sphere. They enjoy a privilege, of somewhat more dignity and effect, than that of idle lamentation over the calamities of their country. They may look into them narrowly; they may reason upon them liberally; and if they should be so fortunate as to discover the true source of the mischief, and to suggest any probable method of removing it, though they may displease the rulers for the day, they are certainly of service to the cause of government. Government is deeply interested in everything which, even through the medium of some temporary uneasiness, may tend finally to compose the minds of the subject, and to conciliate their affections. I have nothing to do here with the abstract value of the voice of the people. But as long as reputation, the most precious possession of every individual, and as long as opinion, the great support of the state, depend entirely upon that voice, it can never be considered as a thing of little consequence either to individuals or to governments. Nations are not primarily ruled by laws; less by violence. Whatever original energy may be supposed either in force or regulation, the operation of both is, in truth, merely instrumental. Nations are governed by the same methods, and on the same principles, by which an individual without authority is often able to govern those who are his equals or his superiors; by a knowledge of their temper, and by a judicious management of it; I mean, – when public affairs are steadily and quietly conducted; not when government is nothing but a continued scuffle between the magistrate and the multitude; in which sometimes the one and sometimes the other is uppermost; in which they alternately yield and prevail, in a series of contemptible victories and scandalous submissions. The temper of the people amongst whom he presides ought therefore to be the first study of a statesman. And the knowledge of this temper it is by no means impossible for him to attain, if he has not an interest in being ignorant of what it is his duty to learn.

To complain of the age we live in, to murmur at the present possessors of power, to lament the past, to conceive extravagant hopes of the future, are the common dispositions of the greatest part of mankind; indeed the necessary effects of the ignorance and levity of the vulgar. Such complaints and humours have existed, in all times; yet as all times have *not* been alike, true political sagacity manifests itself in distinguishing that complaint which only characterises the general infirmity of human nature, from those which are symptoms of the particular distemperature of our own air and season.

Nobody, I believe, will consider it merely as the language of spleen or disappointment, if I say, that there is something particularly alarming in the present conjuncture. There is hardly a man, in or out of power, who holds any other language. That government is at once dreaded and contemned; that the laws are despoiled of all their respected and salutary terrors; that their inaction is a subject of ridicule, and their exertion of abhorrence; that rank, and office, and title, and all the solemn plausibilities of the world, have lost their reverence and effect; that our foreign politics are as much deranged as our domestic economy; that our dependencies are slackened in their affection, and loosened from their obedience; that we know neither how to yield nor how to enforce; that hardly anything above or below, abroad or at home, is sound and entire; but that disconnexion and confusion, in offices, in parties, in families, in parliament, in the nation, prevail beyond the disorders of any former time: these are facts universally admitted and lamented.

This state of things is the more extraordinary, because the great parties[2] which formerly divided and agitated the kingdom are known to be in a manner entirely dissolved. No great external calamity has visited the nation; no pestilence or famine. We do not labour at present under any scheme of taxation new or oppressive in the quantity or in the mode. Nor are we engaged in an unsuccessful war; in which our misfortunes might easily pervert our judgment; and our minds, sore from the loss of national glory, might feel every blow of fortune as a crime in government.

It is impossible that the cause of this strange distemper should not sometimes become a subject of discourse. It is a compliment due, and which I willingly pay, to those who administer our affairs, to take notice in the first place of their speculation. Our ministers are of opinion, that the increase of our trade and manufactures, that our growth by colonisation and by conquest, have concurred to accumulate immense wealth in the hands of some individuals; and this again being dispersed among the people, has rendered them universally proud, ferocious, and ungovernable; that the insolence of some from their enormous wealth, and the boldness of others from a guilty poverty, have rendered them capable of the most atrocious attempts; so that they have trampled upon all subordination, and violently borne down the unarmed laws of a free government; barriers too feeble against the fury of a populace so fierce and licentious as ours. They contend, that no adequate provocation has been given for so spreading a discontent; our affairs having been conducted throughout with remarkable temper and consummate wisdom. The wicked industry of some libellers, joined to the intrigues of a few disappointed politicians, have, in their opinion, been able to produce this unnatural ferment in the nation.

Nothing indeed can be more unnatural than the present convulsions of this country, if the above account be a true one. I confess I shall assent to it with great reluctance, and only on the compulsion of the clearest and firmest proofs; because their account resolves itself into this short but discouraging proposition, "That we have a very good ministry, but that we are a very bad people;" that we set ourselves to bite the hand that feeds us; that with a malignant insanity we oppose the measures, and ungratefully vilify the persons, of those whose sole object is our own peace and prosperity. If a few puny libellers, acting under a knot of factious politicians, without virtue, parts, or character, (such they are constantly represented by these gentlemen,) are sufficient to excite this disturbance, very perverse must be the disposition of that people, amongst whom such a disturbance can be excited by such means. It is besides no small aggravation of the public misfortune, that the disease, on this hypothesis, appears to be without remedy. If the wealth of the nation be the cause of its turbulence, I imagine it is not proposed to introduce poverty, as a constable to keep the peace. If our dominions abroad are the roots which feed all this rank luxuriance of sedition, it is not intended to cut them off in order to famish the fruit. If our liberty has enfeebled the executive power, there is no design, I hope, to call in the aid of despotism, to fill up the deficiencies of law. Whatever may be intended, these things are not yet professed. We seem therefore to be driven to absolute despair; for we have no other materials to work upon, but those out of which God has been pleased to form the inhabitants of this island. If these be radically and essentially vicious, all that can be said is that those men are very unhappy, to whose fortune or duty it falls to administer the affairs of this untoward people. I hear it indeed sometimes asserted, that a steady perseverance in the present measures, and a rigorous punishment of those who oppose them, will in course of time infallibly put an end to these disorders. But this, in my opinion, is said without much observation of our present disposition, and without any knowledge at all of the general nature of mankind. If the matter of which this nation is composed be so very fermentable as these gentlemen describe it, leaven never will be wanting to work it up, as long as discontent, revenge, and ambition have existence in the world. Particular punishments are the cure for accidental distempers in the state; they inflame rather than allay those heats which arise from the settled mismanagement of the government or from a natural indisposition in the people. It is of the utmost moment not to make mistakes in the use of strong measures; and firmness is then only a virtue when it accompanies the most perfect wisdom. In truth, inconstancy is a sort of natural corrective of folly and ignorance.

I am not one of those who think that the people are never in the wrong. They have been so, frequently and outrageously, both in other countries and in this. But I do say, that in all disputes between them and their rulers, the presumption is at least upon a par in favour of the people. Experience may perhaps justify me in going further. When popular discontents have been very prevalent, it may well be affirmed and supported, that there has been generally something found amiss in the constitution, or in the conduct of government. The people have no interest in disorder. When they do wrong, it is their error, and not their crime. But with the governing part of the state, it is far otherwise. They certainly may act ill by design, as well as by mistake. *"Les révolutions qui arrivent dans les grands états ne sont point un effect du hazard, ni du caprice des peuples. Rien ne révolte les grands d'un royaume comme un gouvernement foible et dérangé. Pour la populace, ce n'est jamais par envie d'attaquer qu'elle se soulève, mais par impatience de souffrir."* These are the words of a great man; of a minister of state; and a zealous assertor of monarchy. They are applied to the *system of favouritism* which was adopted by Henry the Third of France, and to the dreadful consequences it produced. What he says of revolutions, is equally true of all great disturbances. If this presumption in favour of the subjects against the trustees of power be not the more probable, I am sure it is the more comfortable speculation; because it is more easy to change an administration than to reform a people.

Upon a supposition, therefore, that, in the opening of the cause, the presumptions stand equally balanced between the parties, there seems sufficient ground to entitle any person to a fair hearing, who attempts some other scheme beside that easy one which is fashionable in some fashionable companies, to account for the present discontents. It is not to be argued that we endure no grievance, because our grievances are not of the same sort with those under which we laboured formerly; not precisely those which we bore from the Tudors, or vindicated on the Stuarts. A great change has taken place in the affairs of this country. For in the silent lapse of events as material alterations have been insensibly brought about in the policy and character of governments and nations, as those which have been marked by the tumult of public revolutions.

It is very rare indeed for men to be wrong in their feelings concerning public misconduct; as rare to be right in their speculation upon the cause of it. I have constantly observed, that the generality of people are fifty years, at least, behind-hand in their

* Mem. de Sully,[1] tom. i. p. 133.

politics. There are but very few, who are capable of comparing and digesting what passes before their eyes at different times and occasions, so as to form the whole into a distinct system. But in books everything is settled for them, without the exertion of any considerable diligence or sagacity. For which reason men are wise with but little reflection, and good with little self-denial, in the business of all times except their own. We are very uncorrupt and tolerably enlightened judges of the transactions of past ages; where no passions deceive, and where the whole train of circumstances, from the trifling cause to the tragical event, is set in an orderly series before us. Few are the partisans of departed tyranny; and to be a Whig on the business of an hundred years ago, is very consistent with every advantage of present servility. This retrospective wisdom, and historical patriotism, are things of wonderful convenience; and serve admirably to reconcile the old quarrel between speculation and practice. Many a stern republican, after gorging himself with a full feast of admiration of the Grecian commonwealths and of our true Saxon constitution, and discharging all the splendid bile of his virtuous indignation on King John and King James, sits down perfectly satisfied to the coarsest work and homeliest job of the day he lives in. I believe there was no professed admirer of Henry the Eighth among the instruments of the Last King James; nor in the court of Henry the Eighth was there, I dare say, to be found a single advocate for the favourites of Richard the Second.[4]

No complaisance to our court, or to our age, can make me believe nature to be so changed, but that public liberty will be among us, as among our ancestors, obnoxious to some person or other; and that opportunities will be furnished for attempting, at least, some alteration to the prejudice of our constitution. These attempts will naturally vary in their mode, according to times and circumstances. For ambition, though it has ever the same general views, has not at all times the same means, nor the same particular objects. A great deal of the furniture of ancient tyranny is worn to rags; the rest is entirely out of fashion. Besides, there are few statesmen so very clumsy and awkward in their business, as to fall into the identical snare which has proved fatal to their predecessors. When an arbitrary imposition is attempted upon the subject, undoubtedly it will not bear on its forehead the name of *Ship-money*. There is no danger that an extension of the *Forest laws*[5] should be the chosen mode of

oppression in this age. And when we hear any instance of ministerial rapacity, to the prejudice of the rights of private life, it will
certainly not be the exaction of two hundred pullets, from a
woman of fashion, for leave to lie with her own husband.*

Every age has its own manners, and its politics dependent
upon them; and the same attempts will not be made against a
constitution fully formed and matured, that were used to destroy
it in the cradle, or to resist its growth during its infancy.

Against the being of parliament, I am satisfied, no designs have
ever been entertained since the revolution. Every one must perceive, that it is strongly the interest of the court, to have some
second cause interposed between the ministers and the people.
The gentlemen of the House of Commons have an interest
equally strong, in sustaining the part of that intermediate cause.
However they may hire out the *usufruct* of their voices, they never
will part with the *fee and inheritance.*[6] Accordingly those, who
have been of the most known devotion to the will and pleasure
of a court, have, at the same time, been most forward in asserting
a high authority in the House of Commons. When they knew
who were to use that authority, and how it was to be employed,
they thought it never could be carried too far. It must be always
the wish of an unconstitutional statesman, that a House of
Commons, who are entirely dependent upon him, should have
every right of the people entirely dependent upon their pleasure.
It was soon discovered that the forms of a free, and the ends of an
arbitrary, government, were things not altogether incompatible.

The power of the crown, almost dead and rotten as Prerogative, has grown up anew, with much more strength, and far less
odium, under the name of Influence. An influence, which operated without noise and without violence; an influence, which
converted the very antagonist into the instrument of power;
which contained in itself a perpetual principle of growth and
renovation; and which the distresses and the prosperity of the
country equally tended to augment, was an admirable substitute
for a prerogative, that, being only the offspring of antiquated
prejudices, had moulded in its original stamina irresistible principles of decay and dissolution. The ignorance of the people is a
bottom but for a temporary system; the interest of active men in

---

* "Uxor Hugonis de Nevill dat Domino Regi ducentas Gallinas, eo quod possit jacere
una nocte cum Domino suo Hugone de Nevill." Maddox, Hist. Exch. c. xiii, p. 326.[7]

the state is a foundation perpetual and infallible. However, some circumstances, arising, it must be confessed, in a great degree from accident, prevented the effects of this influence for a long time from breaking out in a manner capable of exciting any serious apprehensions. Although government was strong and flourished exceedingly, the court had drawn far less advantage than one would imagine from this great source of power.

At the Revolution,[8] the crown, deprived, for the ends of the Revolution itself, of many prerogatives, was found too weak to struggle against all the difficulties which pressed so new and unsettled a government.[9] The court was obliged therefore to delegate a part of its powers to men of such interest as could support, and of such fidelity as would adhere to, its establishment. Such men were able to draw in a greater number to a concurrence in the common defence. This connexion, necessary at first, continued long after convenient; and properly conducted might indeed, in all situations, be an useful instrument of government. At the same time, through the intervention of men of popular weight and character, the people possessed a security for their just proportion of importance in the state. But as the title to the crown grew stronger by long possession, and by the constant increase of its influence, these helps have of late seemed to certain persons no better than encumbrances. The powerful managers for government were not sufficiently submissive to the pleasure of the possessors of immediate and personal favour, sometimes from a confidence in their own strength natural and acquired; sometimes from a fear of offending their friends, and weakening that lead in the country, which gave them a consideration independent of the court. Men acted as if the court could receive, as well as confer, an obligation. The influence of government, thus divided in appearance between the court and the leaders of parties, became in many cases an accession rather to the popular than to the royal scale; and some part of that influence, which would otherwise have been possessed as in a sort of mortmain[10] and unalienable domain, returned again to the great ocean from whence it arose, and circulated among the people. This method, therefore, of governing by men of great natural interest or great acquired consideration, was viewed in a very invidious light by the true lovers of absolute monarchy. It is the nature of despotism to abhor power held by any means but its own momentary pleasure; and to annihilate all intermediate situations between boundless strength on its own part, and total debility on the part of the people.

To get rid of all this intermediate and independent impor-tance, and *to secure to the court the unlimited and uncontrolled use of its own vast influence, under the sole direction of its own private favour,* has for some years past been the great object of policy. If this were compassed, the influence of the crown must of course produce all the effects which the most sanguine partisans of the court could possibly desire. Government might then be carried on without any concurrence on the part of the people; without any attention to the dignity of the greater, or to the affections of the lower sorts. A new project was therefore devised by a certain set of intriguing men, totally different from the system of administration which had prevailed since the accession of the House of Brunswick.[11] This project, I have heard, was first conceived by some persons in the court of Frederic Prince of Wales.[12]

The earliest attempt in the execution of this design was to set up for minister, a person, in rank indeed respectable, and very ample in fortune; but who, to the moment of this vast and sudden elevation, was little known or considered in the kingdom.[13] To him the whole nation was to yield an immediate and implicit sub-mission. But whether it was from want of firmness to bear up against the first opposition; or that things were not yet fully ripened, or that this method was not found the most eligible; that idea was soon abandoned. The instrumental part of the project was a little altered, to accommodate it to the time, and to bring things more gradually and more surely to the one great end proposed.

The first part of the reformed plan was to draw *a line which should separate the court from the ministry.* Hitherto these names had been looked upon as synonymous; but for the future, court and administration were to be considered as things totally distinct. By this operation, two systems of administration were to be formed; one which should be in the real secret and confidence; the other merely ostensible to perform the official and executory duties of government. The latter were alone to be responsible; whilst the real advisers, who enjoyed all the power, were effec-tually removed from all the danger.

Secondly, *A party under these leaders was to be formed in favour of the court against the ministry:*[14] this party was to have a large share in the emoluments of government, and to hold it totally separate from, and independent of, ostensible administration.

The third point, and that on which the success of the whole scheme ultimately depended, was *to bring parliament to an acquiescence in this project*. Parliament was therefore to be taught by degrees a total indifference to the persons, rank, influence, abilities, connexions, and character of the ministers of the crown. By means of a discipline, on which I shall say more hereafter, that body was to be habituated to the most opposite interests, and the most discordant politics. All connexions and dependencies among subjects were to be entirely dissolved. As, hitherto, business had gone through the hands of leaders of Whigs or Tories, men of talents to conciliate the people, and to engage their confidence; now the method was to be altered; and the lead was to be given to men of no sort of consideration or credit in the country. This want of natural importance was to be their very title to delegated power. Members of parliament were to be hardened into an insensibility, to pride as well as to duty. Those high and haughty sentiments, which are the great support of independence, were to be let down gradually. Points of honour and precedence were no more to be regarded in parliamentary decorum, than in a Turkish army. It was to be avowed, as a constitutional maxim, that the king might appoint one of his footmen, or one of your footmen, for minister; and that he ought to be, and that he would be, well followed as the first name for rank or wisdom in the nation. Thus parliament was to look on, as if perfectly unconcerned, while a cabal of the closet and back-stairs was substituted in the place of a national administration.

With such a degree of acquiescence, any measure of any court might well be deemed thoroughly secure. The capital objects, and by much the most flattering characteristics, of arbitrary power, would be obtained. Everything would be drawn from its holdings in the country to the personal favour and inclination of the prince. This favour would be the sole introduction to power, and the only tenure by which it was to be held: so that no person looking towards another, and all looking towards the court, it was impossible but that the motive which solely influenced every man's hopes must come in time to govern every man's conduct; till at last the servility became universal, in spite of the dead letter of any laws or institutions whatsoever.

How it should happen that any man could be tempted to venture upon such a project of government, may at first view appear surprising. But the fact is, that opportunities very inviting to such an attempt have offered; and the scheme itself was not destitute of some arguments, not wholly unplausible, to recommend it. These opportunities and these arguments, the use that has been made of both, the plan for carrying this new scheme of government into execution, and the effects which it has produced, are in my opinion worthy of our serious consideration.

His Majesty[15] came to the throne of these kingdoms with more advantages than any of his predecessors since the Revolution. Fourth in descent, and third in succession of his royal family, even the zealots of hereditary right, in him, saw something to flatter their favourite prejudices; and to justify a transfer of their attachments, without a change in their principles. The person and cause of the Pretender[16] were become contemptible; his title disowned throughout Europe; his party disbanded in England. His Majesty came indeed to the inheritance of a mighty war;[17] but, victorious in every part of the globe, peace was always in his power, not to negotiate, but to dictate. No foreign habitudes or attachments withdrew him from the cultivation of his power at home. His revenue for the civil establishment, fixed (as it was then thought) at a large, but definite sum, was ample without being invidious. His influence, by additions from conquest, by an augmentation of debt, by an increase of military and naval establishment, much strengthened and extended. And coming to the throne in the prime and full vigour of youth, as from affection there was a strong dislike, so from dread there seemed to be a general averseness, from giving anything like offence to a monarch, against whose resentment opposition could not look for a refuge in any sort of reversionary hope.[18]

These singular advantages inspired his Majesty only with a more ardent desire to preserve unimpaired the spirit of that national freedom to which he owed a situation so full of glory. But to others it suggested sentiments of a very different nature. They thought they now beheld an opportunity (by a certain sort of statesmen never long undiscovered or employed) of drawing to themselves, by the aggrandisement of a court faction, a degree of power which they could never hope to derive from natural influence or from honourable service; and which it was impossible they could hold with the least security, whilst the system of administration rested upon its former bottom. In order to facilitate the execution of their design, it was necessary to make many alterations in political arrangement, and a signal change in the opinions, habits, and connexions of the greatest part of those who at that time acted in public.

In the first place, they proceeded gradually, but not slowly, to destroy everything of strength which did not derive its principal nourishment from the immediate pleasure of the court. The greatest weight of popular opinion and party connexion were then with the Duke of Newcastle and Mr. Pitt.[19] Neither of these held their importance by the *new tenure* of the court; they were not therefore thought to be so proper as others for the services which were required by that tenure. It happened very favourably for the new system, that under a forced coalition there rankled an incurable alienation and disgust between the parties which composed the administration. Mr. Pitt was first attacked. Not satisfied with removing him from power, they endeavoured by various artifices to ruin his character. The other party seemed rather pleased to get rid of so oppressive a support; not perceiving that their own fall was prepared by his, and involved in it. Many other reasons prevented them from daring to look their true situation in the face. To the great Whig families it was extremely disagreeable, and seemed almost unnatural, to oppose the administration of a prince of the House of Brunswick. Day after day they hesitated, and doubted, and lingered, expecting that other counsels would take place; and were slow to be persuaded, that all which had been done by the cabal was the effect not of humour, but of system. It was more strongly and evidently the interest of the new court faction, to get rid of the great Whig connexions, than to destroy Mr. Pitt. The power of that gentleman was vast indeed and merited; but it was in a great degree personal, and therefore transient. Theirs was rooted in the country. For, with a good deal less of popularity, they possessed a far more natural and fixed influence. Long possession of government; vast property; obligations of favours given and received; connexion of office; ties of blood, of alliance, of friendship; (things at that time supposed of some force;) the name of Whig, dear to the majority of the people; the zeal early begun and steadily continued to the royal family: all these together formed a body of power in the nation, which was criminal and devoted. The great ruling principle of the cabal, and that which animated and harmonised all their proceedings, how various soever they may have been, was to signify to the world, that the court would proceed upon its own proper forces only; and that the pretence of bringing any other into its service was an affront to it, and not a support. Therefore when the chiefs were removed, in order to go to the root, the whole party was put under a proscription, so general and severe as to take their hard-earned bread from the lowest officers, in a manner which had never been known before, even in general revolutions. But it was thought necessary effectually to destroy all dependencies but one; and to show an example of the firmness and rigour with which the new system was to be supported.

Thus for the time were pulled down, in the persons of the Whig leaders and of Mr. Pitt, (in spite of the services of the one at the accession of the royal family, and the recent services of the other in the war,) the *two only securities for the importance of the people; power arising from popularity; and power arising from connexion.* Here and there indeed a few individuals were left standing, who gave security for their total estrangement from the odious principles of party connexion and personal attachment; and it must be confessed that most of them have religiously kept their faith. Such a change could not however be made without a mighty shock to government.

To reconcile the minds of the people to all these movements, principles correspondent to them had been preached up with great zeal. Every one must remember that the cabal set out with the most astonishing prudery, both moral and political. Those, who in a few months after soused over head and ears into the deepest and dirtiest pits of corruption, cried out violently against the indirect practices in the electing and managing of parliaments, which had formerly prevailed. This marvellous abhorrence which the court had suddenly taken to all influence, was not only circulated in conversation through the kingdom, but pompously announced to the public, with many other extraordinary things, in a pamphlet* which had all the appearance of a manifesto pro-paratory to some considerable enterprise. Throughout it was a satire, though in terms managed and decent enough, on the politics of the former reign. It was indeed written with no small art and address.

In this piece appeared the first dawning of the new system; there first appeared the idea (then only in speculation) of *separating the court from the administration*; of carrying everything from

* Sentiments of an Honest Man.[20]

national connexion to personal regards; and of forming a regular party for that purpose, under the name of *king's men*.

To recommend this system to the people, a perspective view of the court, gorgeously painted, and finely illuminated from within, was exhibited to the gaping multitude. Party was to be totally done away, with all its evil works. Corruption was to be cast down from court, as *Atè*[21] was from heaven. Power was thenceforward to be the chosen residence of public spirit; and no one was to be supposed under any sinister influence, except those who had the misfortune to be in disgrace at court, which was to stand in lieu of all vices and all corruptions. A scheme of perfection to be realised in a monarchy far beyond the visionary republic of Plato. The whole scenery was exactly disposed to captivate those good souls, whose credulous morality is so invaluable a treasure to crafty politicians. Indeed there was wherewithal to charm everybody, except those few who are not much pleased with professions of supernatural virtue, who know of what stuff such professions are made, for what purposes they are designed, and in what they are sure constantly to end. Many innocent gentlemen, who had been talking prose all their lives without knowing anything of the matter, began at last to open their eyes upon their own merits, and to attribute their not having been lords of the treasury and lords of trade many years before, merely to the prevalence of party, and to the ministerial power, which had frustrated the good intentions of the court in favour of their abilities. Now was the time to unlock the sealed fountain of royal bounty, which had been infamously monopolised and huckstered, and to let it flow at large upon the whole people. The time was come, to restore royalty to its original splendour. *Mettre le Roy hors de page*,[22] became a sort of watchword. And it was constantly in the mouths of all the runners of the court, that nothing could preserve the balance of the constitution from being overturned by the rabble, or by a faction of the nobility, but to free the sovereign effectually from that ministerial tyranny under which the royal dignity had been oppressed in the person of his Majesty's grandfather.

These were some of the many artifices used to reconcile the people to the great change which was made in the persons who composed the ministry, and the still greater which was made and avowed in its constitution. As to individuals, other methods were employed with them; in order so thoroughly to disunite every party, and even every family, that *no concert, order, or effect, might appear in any future opposition.* And in this manner an administration without connexion with the people, or with one another, was first put in possession of government. What good consequences followed from it, we have all seen; whether with regard to virtue, public or private; to the ease and happiness of the sovereign; or to the real strength of government. But as so much stress was then laid on the necessity of this new project, it will not be amiss to take a view of the effects of this royal servitude and vile durance, which was so deplored in the reign of the late monarch, and was so carefully to be avoided in the reign of his successor. The effects were these.

In times full of doubt and danger to his person and family, George II maintained the dignity of his crown connected with the liberty of his people, not only unimpaired, but improved, for the space of thirty-three years. He overcame a dangerous rebellion, abetted by foreign force, and raging in the heart of his kingdoms; and thereby destroyed the seeds of all future rebellion that could arise upon the same principle. He carried the glory, the power, the commerce of England, to a height unknown even to this renowned nation in the times of its greatest prosperity: and he left his succession resting on the true and only true foundations of all national and all regal greatness; affection at home, reputation abroad, trust in allies, terror in rival nations. The most ardent lover of his country cannot wish for Great Britain a happier fate than to continue as she was then left. A people, emulous as we are in affection to our present sovereign, know not how to form a prayer to heaven for a greater blessing upon his virtues, or a higher state of felicity and glory, than that he should live, and should reign, and, when Providence ordains it, should die, exactly like his illustrious predecessors.

A great prince may be obliged (though such a thing cannot happen very often) to sacrifice his private inclination to his public interest. A wise prince will not think that such a restraint implies a condition of servility; and truly, if such was the condition of the last reign, and the effects were also such as we have described, we ought, no less for the sake of the sovereign whom we love, than for our own, to hear arguments convincing indeed, before we depart from the maxims of that reign, or fly in the face of this great body of strong and recent experience.

* * *

In such a strait the wisest may well be perplexed, and the boldest staggered. The circumstances are in a great measure new. We have hardly any land-marks from the wisdom of our ancestors to guide us. At best we can only follow the spirit of their proceeding in other cases. I know the diligence with which my observations on our public disorders have been made; I am very sure of the integrity of the motives on which they are published: I cannot be equally confident in any plan for the absolute cure of those disorders, or for their certain future prevention. My aim is to bring this matter into more public discussion. Let the sagacity of others work upon it. It is not uncommon for medical writers to describe histories of diseases very accurately, on whose cure they can say but very little.

The first ideas which generally suggest themselves, for the cure of parliamentary disorders, are, to shorten the duration of parliaments; and to disqualify all, or a great number, of placemen from a seat in the House of Commons. Whatever efficacy there may be in those remedies, I am sure in the present state of things it is impossible to apply them. A restoration of the right of free election is a preliminary indispensable to every other reformation. What alterations ought afterwards to be made in the constitution, is a matter of deep and difficult research.

If I wrote merely to please the popular palate, it would indeed be as little troublesome to me as to another, to extol these remedies, so famous in speculation, but to which their greatest admirers have never attempted seriously to resort in practice. I confess, then, that I have no sort of reliance upon either a triennial parliament, or a place-bill.[23] With regard to the former, perhaps, it might rather serve to counteract, than to promote, the ends that are proposed by it. To say nothing of the horrible disorders among the people attending frequent elections, I should be fearful of committing, every three years, the independent gentlemen of the country into a contest with the treasury. It is easy to see which of the contending parties would be ruined first. Whoever has taken a careful view of public proceedings, so as to endeavour to ground his speculations on his experience, must have observed how prodigiously greater the power of ministry is in the first and last session of a parliament, than it is in the intermediate periods, when members sit a little firm on their seats. The persons of the greatest parliamentary experience, with whom I have conversed, did constantly, in canvassing the fate of questions, allow something to the court side, upon account of the elections depending or imminent. The evil complained of, if it exists in the present state of things, would hardly be removed by a triennial parliament: for, unless the influence of government in elections can be entirely taken away, the more frequently they return, the more they will harass private independence; the more generally men will be compelled to fly to the settled systematic interest of government, and to the resources of a boundless civil list. Certainly something may be done, and ought to be done, towards lessening that influence in elections; and this will be necessary upon a plan either of longer or shorter duration of parliament. But nothing can so perfectly remove the evil, as not to render such contentions, too frequently repeated, utterly ruinous, first to independence of fortune, and then to independence of spirit. As I am only giving an opinion on this point, and not at all debating it in an adverse line, I hope I may be excused in another observation. With great truth I may aver, that I never remember to have talked on this subject with any man much conversant with public business, who considered short parliaments as a real improvement of the constitution. Gentlemen, warm in a popular cause, are ready enough to attribute all the declarations of such persons to corrupt motives. But the habit of affairs, if, on one hand, it tends to corrupt the mind, furnishes it, on the other, with the means of better information. The authority of such persons will always have some weight. It may stand upon a par with the speculations of those who are less practised in business; and who, with perhaps purer intentions, have not so effectual means of judging. It is besides an effect of vulgar and puerile malignity to imagine, that every statesman is of course corrupt; and that his opinion, upon every constitutional point, is solely formed upon some sinister interest.

The next favourite remedy is a place-bill. The same principle guides in both; I mean, the opinion which is entertained by many, of the infallibility of laws and regulations, in the cure of public distempers. Without being as unreasonably doubtful as many are unwisely confident, I will only say, that this also is a matter very well worthy of serious and mature reflection. It is not easy to foresee, what the effect would be of disconnecting

with parliament the greatest part of those who hold civil employments, and of such mighty and important bodies as the military
and naval establishments. It were better, perhaps, that they should
have a corrupt interest in the forms of the constitution, than
that they should have none at all. This is a question altogether
different from the disqualification of a particular description of
revenue officers from seats in parliament; or, perhaps, of all the
lower sorts of them from votes in elections. In the former case,
only the few are affected; in the latter, only the inconsiderable.
But a great official, a great professional, a great military and naval
interest, all necessarily comprehending many people of the first
weight, ability, wealth, and spirit, has been gradually formed in
the kingdom. These new interests must be let into a share of
representation, else possibly they may be inclined to destroy
those institutions of which they are not permitted to partake.
This is not a thing to be trifled with; nor is it every well-meaning
man that is fit to put his hands to it. Many other serious considerations occur. I do not open them here, because they are not
directly to my purpose; proposing only to give the reader some
taste of the difficulties that attend all capital changes in the constitution; just to hint the uncertainty, to say no worse, of being able
to prevent the court, as long as it has the means of influence
abundantly in its power, of applying that influence to parliament;
and perhaps, if the public method were precluded, of doing it
in some worse and more dangerous method. Underhand and
oblique ways would be studied. The science of evasion, already
tolerably understood, would then be brought to the greatest perfection. It is no inconsiderable part of wisdom, to know how
much of an evil ought to be tolerated; lest, by attempting a degree
of purity impracticable in degenerate times and manners, instead
of cutting off the subsisting ill practices, new corruptions might
be produced for the concealment and security of the old. It were
better, undoubtedly, that no influence at all could affect the mind
of a member of parliament. But of all modes of influence, in my
opinion, a place under the government is the least disgraceful to
the man who holds it, and by far the most safe to the country.
I would not shut out that sort of influence which is open and
visible, which is connected with the dignity and the service of
the state, when it is not in my power to prevent the influence of
contracts, of subscriptions, of direct bribery, and those innumerable methods of clandestine corruption, which are abundantly in

the hands of the court, and which will be applied as long as these means of corruption, and the disposition to be corrupted, have existence amongst us. Our constitution stands on a nice equipoise, with steep precipices and deep waters upon all sides of it. In removing it from a dangerous leaning towards one side, there may be a risk of oversetting it on the other. Every project of a material change in a government so complicated as ours, combined at the same time with external circumstances still more complicated, is a matter full of difficulties; in which a considerate man will not be too ready to decide; a prudent man too ready to undertake; or an honest man too ready to promise. They do not respect the public nor themselves, who engage for more than they are sure that they ought to attempt, or that they are able to perform. These are my sentiments, weak perhaps, but honest and unbiassed; and submitted entirely to the opinion of grave men, well affected to the constitution of their country, and of experience in what may best promote or hurt it.

Indeed, in the situation in which we stand, with an immense revenue, an enormous debt, mighty establishments, government itself a great banker and a great merchant, I see no other way for the preservation of a decent attention to public interest in the representatives, but *the interposition of the body of the people itself*, whenever it shall appear, by some flagrant and notorious act, by some capital innovation, that these representatives are going to over-leap the fences of the law, and to introduce an arbitrary power. This interposition is a most unpleasant remedy. But, if it be a legal remedy, it is intended on some occasion to be used; to be used then only, when it is evident that nothing else can hold the constitution to its true principles.

The distempers of monarchy were the great subjects of apprehension and redress, in the last century; in this, the distempers of parliament. It is not in parliament alone that the remedy for parliamentary disorders can be completed; hardly indeed can it begin there. Until a confidence in government is re-established, the people ought to be excited to a more strict and detailed attention to the conduct of their representatives. Standards for judging more systematically upon their conduct ought to be settled in the meetings of counties and corporations. Frequent and correct lists of the voters in all important questions ought to be procured.

By such means something may be done. By such means it may appear who those are, that, by an indiscriminate support of all administrations, have totally banished all integrity and confidence out of public proceedings; have confounded the best men with the worst; and weakened and dissolved, instead of strengthening and compacting, the general frame of government. If any person is more concerned for government and order, than for the liberties of his country, even he is equally concerned to put an end to this course of indiscriminate support. It is this blind and undistinguishing support, that feeds the spring of those very disorders, by which he is frightened into the arms of the faction which contains in itself the source of all disorders, by enfeebling all the visible and regular authority of the state. The distemper is increased by his injudicious and preposterous endeavours, or pretences, for the cure of it.

An exterior administration, chosen for its impotency, or after it is chosen purposely rendered impotent, in order to be rendered subservient, will not be obeyed. The laws themselves will not be respected, when those who execute them are despised: and they will be despised, when their power is not immediate from the crown, or natural in the kingdom. Never were ministers better supported in parliament. Parliamentary support comes and goes with office, totally regardless of the man, or the merit. Is government strengthened? It grows weaker and weaker. The popular torrent gains upon it every hour. Let us learn from our experience. It is not support that is wanting to government, but reformation. When ministry rests upon public opinion, it is not indeed built upon a rock of adamant; it has, however, some stability. But when it stands upon private humour, its structure is of stubble, and its foundation is on quicksand. I repeat it again – He that supports every administration subverts all government. The reason is this: The whole business in which a court usually takes an interest goes on at present equally well, in whatever hands, whether high or low, wise or foolish, scandalous or reputable; there is nothing therefore to hold it firm to any one body of men, or to any one consistent scheme of politics. Nothing interposes, to prevent the full operation of all the caprices and all the passions of a court upon the servants of the public. The system of administration is open to continual shocks and changes, upon the principles of the meanest cabal, and the most contemptible intrigue. Nothing can be solid and permanent. All good men at length fly with horror from such a service. Men of rank and ability, with the spirit which ought to animate such men in a free state, while they decline the jurisdiction of dark cabal on their actions and their fortunes, will, for both, cheerfully put themselves upon their country. They will trust an inquisitive and distinguishing parliament; because it does inquire, and does distinguish. If they act well, they know that, in such a parliament, they will be supported against any intrigue; if they act ill, they know that no intrigue can protect them. This situation, however awful, is honourable. But in one hour and in the self-same assembly, without any assigned or assignable cause, to be precipitated from the highest authority to the most marked neglect, possibly into the greatest peril of life and reputation, is a situation full of danger, and destitute of honour. It will be shunned equally by every man of prudence, and every man of spirit.

Such are the consequences of the division of court from the administration; and of the division of public men among themselves. By the former of these, lawful government is undone; by the latter, all opposition to lawless power is rendered impotent. Government may in a great measure be restored, if any considerable bodies of men have honesty and resolution enough never to accept administration, unless this garrison of *king's men*, which is stationed, as in a citadel, to control and enslave it, be entirely broken and disbanded, and every work they have thrown up be levelled with the ground. The disposition of public men to keep this corps together, and to act under it, or to co-operate with it, is a touch-stone by which every administration ought in future to be tried. There has not been one which has not sufficiently experienced the utter incompatibility of that faction with the public peace, and with all the ends of good government: since, if they opposed it, they soon lost every power of serving the crown; if they submitted to it, they lost all the esteem of their country. Until ministers give to the public a full proof of their entire alienation from that system, however plausible their pretences, we may be sure they are more intent on the emoluments than the duties of office. If they refuse to give this proof, we know of what stuff they are made. In this particular, it ought to be the electors' business to look to their representatives. The electors ought to esteem it no less culpable in their member to give a single vote in parliament to such an administration, than to take an office under it; to endure it, than to act in it. The notorious infidelity and versatility of members of parliament, in their opinions of men and things, ought in a particular manner to be considered by the electors in the inquiry which is recommended to them. This is one of the principal holdings of that destructive system, which has endeavoured to unhinge all the virtuous, honourable, and useful connexions in the kingdom.

This cabal has, with great success, propagated a doctrine which serves for a colour to those acts of treachery; and whilst it receives any degree of countenance, it will be utterly senseless to look for a vigorous opposition to the court party. The doctrine is this: That all political connexions are in their nature factious, and as such ought to be dissipated and destroyed; and that the rule for forming administrations is mere personal ability, rated by the judgment of this cabal upon it, and taken by draughts from every division and denomination of public men. This decree was solemnly promulgated by the head of the court corps, the Earl of Bute[24] himself, in a speech which he made, in the year 1766, against the then administration, the only administration which he has ever been known directly and publicly to oppose.

It is indeed in no way wonderful, that such persons should make such declarations. That connexion and faction are equivalent terms, is an opinion which has been carefully inculcated at all times by unconstitutional statesmen. The reason is evident. Whilst men are linked together, they easily and speedily communicate the alarm of any evil design. They are enabled to fathom it with common counsel, and to oppose it with united strength. Whereas, when they lie dispersed, without concert, order, or discipline, communication is uncertain, counsel difficult, and resistance impracticable. Where men are not acquainted with each other's principles, nor experienced in each other's talents, nor at all practised in their mutual habitudes and dispositions by joint efforts in business; no personal confidence, no friendship, no common interest, subsisting among them; it is evidently impossible that they can act a public part with uniformity, perseverance, or efficacy. In a connexion, the most inconsiderable man, by adding to the weight of the whole, has his value, and his use; out of it, the greatest talents are wholly unserviceable to the public. No man, who is not inflamed by vain-glory into enthusiasm, can flatter himself that his single, unsupported, desultory, unsystematic endeavours, are of power to defeat the subtle designs and united cabals of ambitious citizens. When bad men combine, the good must associate; else they will fall, one by one, an unpitied sacrifice in a contemptible struggle.

It is not enough in a situation of trust in the commonwealth, that a man means well to his country; it is not enough that in his single person he never did an evil act, but always voted according to his conscience, and ever harangued against every design which he apprehended to be prejudicial to the interests of his country. This innoxious and ineffectual character, that seems formed upon a plan of apology and disculpation, falls miserably short of the mark of public duty. That duty demands and requires, that what is right should not only be made known, but made prevalent; that what is evil should not only be detected, but defeated. When the public man omits to put himself in a situation of doing his duty with effect, it is an omission that frustrates the purposes of his trust almost as much as if he had formally betrayed it. It is surely no very rational account of a man's life, that he has always acted right; but has taken special care to act in such a manner that his endeavours could not possibly be productive of any consequence.

I do not wonder that the behaviour of many parties should have made persons of tender and scrupulous virtue somewhat out of humour with all sorts of connexion in politics. I admit that people frequently acquire in such confederacies a narrow, bigoted, and proscriptive spirit; that they are apt to sink the idea of the general good in this circumscribed and partial interest. But, where duty renders a critical situation a necessary one, it is our business to keep free from the evils attendant upon it; and not to fly from the situation itself. If a fortress is seated in an unwholesome air, an officer of the garrison is obliged to be attentive to his health, but he must not desert his station. Every profession, not excepting the glorious one of a soldier, or the sacred one of a priest, is liable to its own particular vices; which, however, form no argument against those ways of life; nor are the vices themselves inevitable to every individual in those professions. Of such a nature are connexions in politics; essentially necessary for the full performance of our public duty, accidentally liable to degenerate into faction. Commonwealths are made of families, free commonwealths of parties also; and we may as well affirm, that our natural regards and ties of blood tend inevitably to make men bad citizens, as that the bonds of our party weaken those by which we are held to our country.

Some legislators went so far as to make neutrality in party a crime against the state. I do not know whether this might not have been rather to overstrain the principle. Certain it is, the best patriots in the greatest commonwealths have always commended and promoted such connexions. *Idem sentire de republicâ*,[25] was with them a principal ground of friendship and attachment; nor do I know any other capable of forming firmer, dearer, more pleasing, more honourable, and more virtuous habitudes. The Romans carried this principle a great way. Even the holding of offices together, the disposition of which arose from chance, not selection, gave rise to a relation which continued for life. It was called *necessitudo sortis*;[26] and it was looked upon with a sacred reverence. Breaches of any of these kinds of civil relation were considered as acts of the most distinguished turpitude. The whole people was distributed into political societies, in which they acted in support of such interests in the state as they severally affected. For it was then thought no crime, to endeavour by every honest means to advance to superiority and power those of your own sentiments and opinions. This wise people was far from imagining that those connexions had no tie, and obliged to no duty; but that men might quit them without shame, upon every call of interest. They believed private honour to be the great foundation of public trust; that friendship was no mean step towards patriotism; that he who, in the common intercourse of life, showed he regarded somebody besides himself, when he came to act in a public situation, might probably consult some other interests than his own. Never may we become *plus sages que les sages*,[27] as the French comedian has happily expressed it, wiser than all the wise and good men who have lived before us. It was their wish, to see public and private virtues, not dissonant and jarring, and mutually destructive, but harmoniously combined, growing out of one another in a noble and orderly gradation, reciprocally supporting and supported. In one of the most fortunate periods of our history this country was governed by a *connexion*; I mean the great connexion of Whigs in the reign of Queen Anne.[28] They were complimented upon the principle of this connexion by a poet who was in high esteem with them. Addison,[29] who knew their sentiments, could not praise them for what they considered as no proper subject of commendation. As a poet who knew his business, he could not applaud them for a thing which in general estimation was not highly reputable. Addressing himself to Britain,

"Thy favourites grow not up by fortune's sport,
Or from the crimes or follies of a court.
On the firm basis of desert they rise,
From long-tried faith, and friendship's holy ties."

The Whigs of those days believed that the only proper method of rising into power was through hard essays of practised friendship and experimented fidelity. At that time it was not imagined, that patriotism was a bloody idol, which required the sacrifice of children and parents, or dearest connexions in private life, and of all the virtues that rise from those relations. They were not of that ingenious paradoxical morality, to imagine that a spirit of moderation was properly shown in patiently bearing the sufferings of your friends; or that disinterestedness was clearly manifested at the expense of other people's fortune. They believed that no men could act with effect, who did not act in concert; that no men could act in concert, who did not act with confidence; that no men could act with confidence, who were not bound together by common opinions, common affections, and common interests.

These wise men, for such I must call Lord Sunderland, Lord Godolphin, Lord Somers, and Lord Marlborough,[30] were too well principled in these maxims upon which the whole fabric of public strength is built, to be blown off their ground by the breath of every childish talker. They were not afraid that they should be called an ambitious Junto; or that their resolution to stand or fall together should, by placemen, be interpreted into a scuffle for places.

Party is a body of men united, for promoting by their joint endeavours the national interest, upon some particular principle in which they are all agreed. For my part, I find it impossible to conceive, that any one believes in his own politics, or thinks them to be of any weight, who refuses to adopt the means of having them reduced into practice. It is the business of the speculative philosopher to mark the proper ends of government. It is the business of the politician, who is the philosopher in action, to find out proper means towards those ends, and to employ them with effect. Therefore every honourable connexion will avow it is their first purpose, to pursue every just method to put the men who hold their opinions into such a condition as may enable them to carry their common plans into execution, with all the power and authority of the state. As this power is attached to certain situations, it is their duty to contend for these situations. Without a proscription of others, they are bound to give to their own party the preference in all things; and by no means, for private considerations, to accept any offers of power in which the whole body is not included; nor to suffer themselves to be led, or to be controlled, or to be overbalanced, in office or in council, by those who contradict the very fundamental principles on which their party is formed, and even those upon which every fair connexion must stand. Such a generous contention for power, on such manly and honourable maxims, will easily be distinguished from the mean and interested struggle for place and emolument. The very style of such persons will serve to discriminate them from those numberless impostors, who have deluded the ignorant with professions incompatible with human practice, and have afterwards incensed them by practices below the level of vulgar rectitude.

It is an advantage to all narrow wisdom and narrow morals, that their maxims have a plausible air; and, on a cursory view, appear equal to first principles. They are light and portable. They are as current as copper coin; and about as valuable. They serve equally the first capacities and the lowest; and they are, at least, as useful to the worst men as the best. Of this stamp is the cant of *Not men but measures*;[31] a sort of charm by which many people get loose from every honourable engagement. When I see a man acting this desultory and disconnected part, with as much detriment to his own fortune as prejudice to the cause of any party, I am not persuaded that he is right; but I am ready to believe he is in earnest. I respect virtue in all its situations; even when it is found in the unsuitable company of weakness. I lament to see qualities, rare and valuable, squandered away without any public utility. But when a gentleman with great visible emoluments abandons the party in which he has long acted, and tells you, it is because he proceeds upon his own judgment; that he acts on the merits of the several measures as they arise; and that he is obliged to follow his own conscience, and not that of others; he gives reasons which it is impossible to controvert, and discovers a character which it is impossible to mistake. What shall we think of him who never differed from a certain set of men until the moment they lost their power, and who never agreed with them in a single instance afterwards? Would not such a coincidence of interest and opinion be rather fortunate? Would it not be an extraordinary cast upon the dice, that a man's connexions should degenerate into faction, precisely at the critical moment when they lose their power, or he accepts a place? When people desert their connexions, the desertion is a manifest *fact*, upon which a direct simple issue lies, triable by plain men. Whether a *measure* of government be right or wrong, is *no matter of fact*, but a mere affair of opinion, on which men may, as they do, dispute and wrangle without end. But whether the individual *thinks* the measure right or wrong, is a point at still a greater distance from the reach of all human decision. It is therefore very convenient to politicians, not to put the judgment of their conduct on overt acts, cognisable in any ordinary court, but upon such matter as can be triable only in that secret tribunal, where they are sure of being heard with favour, or where at worst the sentence will be only private whipping.

I believe the reader would wish to find no substance in a doctrine which has a tendency to destroy all test of character as deduced from conduct. He will therefore excuse my adding something more, towards the further clearing up a point, which the great convenience of obscurity to dishonesty has been able to cover with some degree of darkness and doubt.

In order to throw an odium on political connexion, these politicians suppose it a necessary incident to it, that you are blindly to follow the opinions of your party, when in direct opposition to your own clear ideas; a degree of servitude that no worthy man could bear the thought of submitting to; and such as, I believe, no connexions (except some court factions) ever could be so senselessly tyrannical as to impose. Men thinking freely, will, in particular instances, think differently. But still as the greater part of the measures which arise in the course of public business are related to, or dependent on, some great *leading general principles in government*, a man must be peculiarly unfortunate in the choice of his political company if he does not agree with them at least nine times in ten. If he does not concur in these general principles upon which the party is founded, and which necessarily draw on a concurrence in their application, he ought from the beginning to have chosen some other, more conformable to his opinions. When the question is in its nature doubtful, or not very material, the modesty which becomes an individual, and (in spite of our court moralists) that partiality which becomes a well-chosen friendship, will frequently bring on an acquiescence in the general sentiment. Thus the disagreement will naturally be rare; it will be only enough to indulge freedom, without violating concord, or disturbing arrangement. And this is all that ever was required for a character of the greatest uniformity and steadiness in connexion. How men can proceed without any connexion at all, is to me utterly incomprehensible. Of what sort of materials must that man be made, how must he be tempered and put together, who can sit whole years in parliament, with five hundred and fifty of his fellow-citizens, amidst the storm of such tempestuous passions, in the sharp conflict of so many wits, and tempers, and characters, in the agitation of such mighty questions, in the discussion of such vast and ponderous interests, without seeing any one sort of men, whose character, conduct, or disposition, would lead him to associate himself with them, to aid and be aided, in any one system of public utility?

I remember an old scholastic aphorism, which says, "that the man who lives wholly detached from others, must be either an angel or a devil." When I see in any of these detached gentlemen of our times the angelic purity, power, and beneficence, I shall admit them to be angels. In the mean time we are born only to be men. We shall do enough if we form ourselves to be good ones. It is therefore our business carefully to cultivate in our minds, to rear to the most perfect vigour and maturity, every sort of generous and honest feeling that belongs to our nature. To bring the dispositions that are lovely in private life into the service and conduct of the commonwealth; so to be patriots, as not to forget we are gentlemen. To cultivate friendships, and to incur enmities. To have both strong, but both selected: in the one, to be placable; in the other, immoveable. To model our principles to our duties and our situation. To be fully persuaded, that all virtue which is impracticable is spurious; and rather to run the risk of falling into faults in a course which leads us to act with effect and energy, than to loiter out our days without blame and without use. Public life is a situation of power and energy; he trespasses against his duty who sleeps upon his watch, as well as he that goes over to the enemy.

There is, however, a time for all things. It is not every conjuncture which calls with equal force upon the activity of honest men;

but critical exigencies now and then arise; and I am mistaken, if this be not one of them. Men will see the necessity of honest combination; but they may see it when it is too late. They may embody, when it will be ruinous to themselves, and of no advantage to the country; when, for want of such a timely union as may enable them to oppose in favour of the laws, with the laws on their side, they may at length find themselves under the necessity of conspiring, instead of consulting. The law, for which they stand, may become a weapon in the hands of its bitterest enemies; and they will be cast, at length, into that miserable alternative, between slavery and civil confusion, which no good man can look upon without horror; an alternative in which it is impossible he should take either part, with a conscience perfectly at repose. To keep that situation of guilt and remorse at the utmost distance is, therefore, our first obligation. Early activity may prevent late and fruitless violence. As yet we work in the light. The scheme of the enemies of public tranquillity has disarranged, it has not destroyed us.

If the reader believes that there really exists such a faction as I have described; a faction ruling by the private inclinations of a court, against the general sense of the people; and that this faction, whilst it pursues a scheme for undermining all the foundations of our freedom, weakens (for the present at least) all the powers of executory government, rendering us abroad contemptible, and at home distracted; he will believe also, that nothing but a firm combination of public men against this body, and that, too, supported by the hearty concurrence of the people at large, can possibly get the better of it. The people will see the necessity of restoring public men to an attention to the public opinion, and of restoring the constitution to its original principles. Above all, they will endeavour to keep the House of Commons from assuming a character which does not belong to it. They will endeavour to keep that House, for its existence, for its powers, and its privileges, as independent of every other, and as dependent upon themselves, as possible. This servitude is to a House of Commons (like obedience to the Divine law) "perfect freedom." For if they once quit this natural, rational, and liberal obedience, having deserted the only proper foundation of their power, they must seek a support in an abject and unnatural dependence somewhere else. When, through the medium of this just connexion with their constituents, the genuine dignity of the

House of Commons is restored, it will begin to think of casting
from it, with scorn, as badges of servility, all the false ornaments
of illegal power, with which it has been, for some time, disgraced.
It will begin to think of its old office of CONTROL. It will not
suffer that last of evils to predominate in the country; men without popular confidence, public opinion, natural connexion, or
mutual trust, invested with all the powers of government.

When they have learned this lesson themselves, they will be
willing and able to teach the court, that it is the true interest of the
prince to have but one administration; and that one composed of
those who recommend themselves to their sovereign through the
opinion of their country, and not by their obsequiousness to a
favourite. Such men will serve their sovereign with affection and
fidelity; because his choice of them, upon such principles, is a
compliment to their virtue. They will be able to serve him effectually; because they will add the weight of the country to the
force of the executory power. They will be able to serve their
king with dignity; because they will never abuse his name to the
gratification of their private spleen or avarice. This, with allowances for human frailty, may probably be the general character
of a ministry, which thinks itself accountable to the House of
Commons, when the House of Commons thinks itself accountable to its constituents. If other ideas should prevail, things must
remain in their present confusion; until they are hurried into all
the rage of civil violence; or until they sink into the dead repose
of despotism.

SPEECH ON THE
MIDDLESEX ELECTION*

7 FEBRUARY 1771

MR. SPEAKER,

IN EVERY COMPLICATED constitution (and every free constitution is complicated) cases will arise, when the several orders of the state will clash with one another; and disputes will arise about the limits of their several rights and privileges. It may be almost impossible to reconcile them.

Carry the principle on by which you expelled Mr. Wilkes,[1] there is not a man in the House, hardly a man in the nation, who may not be disqualified. That this House should have no power of expulsion, is a hard saying. That this House should have a general discretionary power of disqualification is a dangerous saying. That the people should not choose their own representative, is a saying that shakes the constitution. That this House should name the representative, is a saying which, followed by practice, subverts the constitution.[2] They have the right of electing, you have a right of expelling; they of choosing, you of judging, and only of judging, of the choice. What bounds shall be set to the freedom of that choice? Their right is prior to ours, we all originate there. They are the mortal enemies of the House of Commons, who would persuade them to think or to act as if they were a self-originated magistracy, independent of the people, and unconnected with their opinions and feelings. Under a pretence of exalting the dignity, they undermine the very foundations of this House. When the question is asked *here*, What disturbs the people, whence all this clamour? we apply to the treasury-bench, and they tell us it is from the efforts of libellers, and the wickedness of the people:– a worn-out ministerial pretence. If abroad the people are deceived by popular, within we are deluded by ministerial, cant. The question amounts to this, whether you mean to be a legal tribunal, or an arbitrary and despotic assembly. I see, and I feel, the delicacy and difficulty of the ground upon which we stand in this question. I could wish,

* This motion, which was for leave to bring in a bill to ascertain the rights of the electors in respect to the eligibility of persons to serve in parliament, was rejected by a majority of 167 against 103.

indeed, that they who advise the Crown had not left parliament in this very ungraceful distress, in which they can neither retract with dignity nor persist with justice. Another parliament might have satisfied the people without lowering themselves. But our situation is not in our own choice; our conduct in that situation is all that is in our own option. The substance of the question is, to put bounds to your own power by the rules and principles of law. This is, I am sensible, a difficult thing to the corrupt, grasping, and ambitious part of human nature. But the very difficulty argues and enforces the necessity of it. First, because the greater the power the more dangerous the abuse. Since the revolution, at least, the power of the nation has all flowed with a full tide into the House of Commons. Secondly, because the House of Commons, as it is the most powerful, is the most corruptible part of the whole constitution. Our public wounds cannot be concealed; to be cured, they must be laid open. The public does think we are a corrupt body. In our *legislative capacity* we are, in most instances, esteemed a very wise body. In our judicial, we have no credit, no character at, all. Our judgments stink in the nostrils of the people. They think us to be not only without virtue, but without shame. Therefore the greatness of our power, and the great and just opinion of our corruptibility and our corruption, render it necessary to fix some bound, to plant some landmark, which we are never to exceed. That is what the bill proposes. First, on this head, I lay it down as a fundamental rule in the law and constitution of this country, that this House has not by itself alone a legislative authority in any case whatsoever. I know that the contrary was the doctrine of the usurping House of Commons, which threw down the fences and bulwarks of law, which annihilated first the Lords, then the Crown, then its constituents.[3] But the first thing that was done on the restoration of the Constitution was to settle this point. Secondly, I lay it down as a rule, that the power of occasional incapacitation, on discretionary grounds, is a legislative power. In order to establish this principle, if it should not be sufficiently proved by being stated, tell me what are the criteria, the characteristics, by which you distinguish between a legislative and a juridical act. It will be necessary to state, shortly, the difference between a legislative and a juridical act. A legislative act has no reference to any rule but these two, original justice and discretionary application. Therefore it can give rights; rights where no rights existed before; and it can take away rights where they were before established. For the law which binds all others does not and cannot bind the law-maker; he, and he alone, is above the law. But a judge, a person exercising a judicial capacity, is neither to apply to original justice, nor to a discretionary application of it. He goes to justice and discretion only at second-hand, and through the medium of some superiors. He is to work neither upon his opinion of the one nor of the other; but upon a fixed rule, of which he has not the making, but singly and solely the *application* to the case.

The power assumed by the House neither is, nor can be, judicial power exercised according to known law. The properties of law are, first, that it should be known; secondly, that it should be fixed, and not occasional. First, this power cannot be according to the first property of law; because no man does or can know it, nor do you yourselves know upon what grounds you will vote the incapacity of any man. No man in Westminster Hall, or in any court upon earth, will say that is law upon which, if a man going to his counsel should say to him, 'What is my tenure in law of this estate?' he would answer, 'Truly, Sir, I know not; the court has no rule but its own discretion: they will determine.' It is not a fixed law – because you profess you vary it according to the occasion, exercise it according to your discretion; no man can call for it as a right. It is argued that the incapacity is not originally voted, but a consequence of a power of expulsion: but if you expel, not upon legal, but upon arbitrary, that is, upon discretionary, grounds, and the incapacity is *ex vi termini*[4] and inclusively comprehended in the expulsion, is not the incapacity voted in the expulsion? Are they not convertible terms? And, if incapacity is voted to be inherent in expulsion, if expulsion be arbitrary, incapacity is arbitrary also. I have therefore shown that the power of incapacitation is a legislative power; I have shown that legislative power does not belong to the House of Commons; and therefore it follows that the House of Commons has not a power of incapacitation.

I know not the origin of the House of Commons, but am very sure that it did not create itself; the electors were prior to the elected; whose rights originated either from the people at large, or from some other form of legislature, which never could intend for the chosen a power of superseding the choosers.

If you have not a power of declaring an incapacity simply by the mere act of declaring it, it is evident to the most ordinary reason, you cannot have a right of expulsion, inferring, or rather including, an incapacity, For as the law, when it gives any direct right, gives also as necessary incidents all the means of acquiring the possession of that right; so where it does not give a right directly, it refuses all the means by which such a right may by any mediums be exercised, or, in effect, be indirectly acquired. Else it is very obvious that the intention of the law in refusing that right might be entirely frustrated, and the whole power of the legislature baffled. If there be no certain, invariable rule of eligibility, it were better to get simplicity, if certainty is not to be had; and to resolve all the franchises of the subject into this one short proposition – the will and pleasure of the House of Commons.

The argument drawn from the courts of law applying the principles of law to new cases as they emerge is altogether frivolous, inapplicable, and arises from a total ignorance of the bounds between civil and criminal jurisdiction, and of the separate maxims that govern these two provinces of law, that are eternally separate. Undoubtedly the courts of law, where a new case comes before them, as they do every hour, then, that there may be no defect in justice, call in similar principles, and the example of the nearest determination, and do everything to draw the law to as near a conformity to general equity and right reason as they can bring it with its being a fixed principle. *Boni judicis est ampliare justitiam* – that is, to make open and liberal justice. But in criminal matters this parity of reason, and these analogies, ever have been, and ever ought to be, shunned.

Whatever is incident to a court of judicature is necessary to the House of Commons, as judging in elections. But a power of making incapacities is not necessary to a court of judicature – therefore a power of making incapacities is not necessary to the House of Commons.

Incapacity, declared by whatever authority, stands upon two principles. First, an incapacity arising from the supposed incongruity of two duties in the commonwealth. Secondly, an incapacity arising from unfitness by infirmity of nature or the criminality of conduct. As to the first class of incapacities, they have no *hardship* annexed to them. The persons so incapacitated are paid by one dignity for what they abandon in another, and, for the most part, the situation arises from their own choice. But as to the second, arising from an unfitness not fixed by nature, but superinduced by some positive acts, or arising from honourable motives, such as an occasional personal disability, of all things it ought to be defined by the fixed rule of law – what Lord Coke[5] calls the golden metwand of the law,[6] and not by the crooked cord of discretion. Whatever is general is better borne. We take our common lot with men of the same description. But to be selected and marked out by a particular brand of unworthiness among our fellow-citizens, is a lot of all others the hardest to be borne; and consequently is of all others that act which ought only to be trusted to the legislature, as not only *legislative* in its nature, but of all parts of legislature the most odious. The question is over, if this is shown not to be a legislative act. But what is very usual and natural, is to corrupt judicature into legislature. On this point it is proper to inquire whether a court of judicature, which decides without appeal, has it as a necessary incident of such judicature, that whatever it decides is *de jure* law. Nobody will, I hope, assert this, because the direct consequence would be the entire extinction of the difference between true and false judgments. For if the judgment makes the law, and not the law directs the judgment, it is impossible there should be such a thing as an illegal judgment given.

But instead of standing upon this ground, they introduce another question, wholly foreign to it, whether it ought not to be submitted to as if it were law. And then the question is, – by the constitution of this country, what degree of submission is due to the authoritative acts of a limited power? This question of submission, determine it how you please, has nothing to do in this discussion and in this House. Here it is not how long the people are bound to tolerate the illegality of our judgments, but whether we have a right to substitute our occasional opinion in the place of law; so as to deprive the citizen of his franchise.

SPEECH AT THE CONCLUSION
OF THE POLL AT BRISTOL

3 NOVEMBER 1774

GENTLEMEN,

I CANNOT AVOID sympathising strongly with the feelings of the gentleman who has received the same honour that you have conferred on me.[1] If he, who was bred and passed his whole life amongst you; if he, who through the easy gradations of acquaintance, friendship, and esteem, has obtained the honour, which seems of itself, naturally and almost insensibly, to meet with those, who, by the even tenour of pleasing manners and social virtues, slide into the love and confidence of their fellow-citizens; – if he cannot speak but with great emotion on this subject, surrounded as he is on all sides with his old friends; you will have the goodness to excuse me, if my real, unaffected embarrassment prevents me from expressing my gratitude to you as I ought.

I was brought hither under the disadvantage of being un-known, even by sight, to any of you. No previous canvass was made for me. I was put in nomination after the poll was opened. I did not appear until it was far advanced. If, under all these accu-mulated disadvantages, your good opinion has carried me to this happy point of success; you will pardon me, if I can only say to you collectively, as I said to you individually, simply, and plainly, I thank you – I am obliged to you – I am not insensible of your kindness.

This is all that I am able to say for the inestimable favour you have conferred upon me. But I cannot be satisfied, without say-ing a little more in defence of the right you have to confer such a favour. The person that appeared here as counsel for the candi-date,[2] who so long and so earnestly solicited your votes, thinks proper to deny, that a very great part of you have any votes to give. He fixes a standard period of time in his own imagination, not what the law defines, but merely what the convenience of his client suggests, by which he would cut off, at one stroke, all those freedoms which are the dearest privileges of your corpora-tion; which the common law authorises; which your magistrates are compelled to grant; which come duly authenticated into this court; and are saved in the clearest words, and with the most religious care and tenderness, in that very act of parliament, which was made to regulate the elections by freemen, and to prevent all possible abuses in making them.

I do not intend to argue the matter here. My learned counsel has supported your cause with his usual ability; the worthy sheriffs have acted with their usual equity, and I have no doubt, that the same equity, which dictates the return, will guide the final determination. I had the honour, in conjunction with many far wiser men, to contribute a very small assistance, but, however, some assistance, to the forming the judicature which is to try such questions. It would be unnatural in me to doubt the justice of that court, in the trial of my own cause, to which I have been so active to give jurisdiction over every other.

I assure the worthy freemen, and this corporation, that, if the gentleman perseveres in the intentions which his present warmth dictates to him, I will attend their cause with diligence, and I hope with effect. For, if I know anything of myself, it is not my own interest in it, but my full conviction, that induces me to tell you – *I think there is not a shadow of doubt in the case.*

I do not imagine that you find me rash in declaring myself, or very forward in troubling you. From the beginning to the end of the election, I have kept silence in all matters of discussion. I have never asked a question of a voter on the other side, or supported a doubtful vote on my own. I respected the abilities of my managers; I relied on the candour of the court. I think the worthy sheriffs will bear me witness, that I have never once made an attempt to impose upon their reason, to surprise their justice, or to ruffle their temper. I stood on the hustings (except when I gave my thanks to those who favoured me with their votes) less like a candidate, than an unconcerned spectator of a public proceeding. But here the face of things is altered. Here is an attempt for a general *massacre* of suffrages; an attempt, by a promiscuous carnage of *friends* and *foes,* to exterminate above two thousand votes, including *seven hundred polled for the gentleman himself, who now complains,* and who would destroy the friends whom he has obtained, only because he cannot obtain as many of them as he wishes.

How he will be permitted, in another place, to stultify and disable himself, and to plead against his own acts, is another question. The law will decide it. I shall only speak of it as it concerns the propriety of public conduct in this city. I do not pretend to lay down rules of decorum for other gentlemen. They are best judges of the mode of proceeding that will recommend them to the favour of their fellow-citizens. But I confess I should look rather awkward, if I had been the *very first to produce the new copies of freedom*, if I had persisted in producing them to the last; if I had ransacked, with the most unremitting industry and the most penetrating research, the remotest corners of the kingdom to discover them; if I were then, all at once, to turn short, and declare, that I had been sporting all this while with the right of election; and that I had been drawing out a poll, upon no sort of rational grounds, which disturbed the peace of my fellow-citizens for a month together – I really, for my part, should appear awkward under such circumstances.

It would be still more awkward in me, if I were gravely to look the sheriffs in the face, and to tell them, they were not to determine my cause on my own principles; not to make the return upon those votes upon which I had rested my election. Such would be my appearance to the court and magistrates.

But how should I appear to the *voters* themselves? If I had gone round to the citizens entitled to freedom, and squeezed them by the hand – "Sir, I humbly beg your vote – I shall be eternally thankful – may I hope for the honour of your support? – Well! – come – we shall see you at the council-house." – If I were then to deliver them to my managers, pack them into tallies, vote them off in court, and when I heard from the bar – "Such a one only! and such a one for ever! – he's my man!" – "Thank you, good Sir – Hah! my worthy friend! thank you kindly – that's an honest fellow – how is your good family?" – Whilst these words were hardly out of my mouth, if I should have wheeled round at once, and told them – "Get you gone, you pack of worthless fellows! you have no votes – you are usurpers! you are intruders on the rights of real freemen! I will have nothing to do with you! you ought never to have been produced at this election, and the sheriffs ought not to have admitted you to poll."

Gentlemen, I should make a strange figure if my conduct had been of this sort. I am not so old an acquaintance of yours as the worthy gentleman. Indeed I could not have ventured on such kind of freedoms with you. But I am bound, and I will endeavour, to have justice done to the rights of freemen; even though I should, at the same time, be obliged to vindicate the former* part of my antagonist's conduct against his own present inclinations.

I owe myself, in all things, to *all* the freemen of this city. My particular friends have a demand on me that I should not deceive their expectations. Never was cause or man supported with more constancy, more activity, more spirit. I have been supported with a zeal indeed and heartiness in my friends, which (if their object had been at all proportioned to their endeavours) could never be sufficiently commended. They supported me upon the most liberal principles. They wished that the members for Bristol should be chosen for the city, and for their country at large, and not for themselves.

So far they are not disappointed. If I possess nothing else, I am sure I possess the temper that is fit for your service. I know nothing of Bristol, but by the favours I have received, and the virtues I have seen exerted in it.

I shall ever retain, what I now feel, the most perfect and grateful attachment to my friends – and I have no enmities; no resentment. I never can consider fidelity to engagements, and constancy in friendships, but with the highest approbation; even when those noble qualities are employed against my own pretensions. The gentleman, who is not so fortunate as I have been in this contest, enjoys, in this respect, a consolation full of honour both to himself and to his friends. They have certainly left nothing undone for his service.

As for the trifling petulance, which the rage of party stirs up in little minds, though it should show itself even in this court, it has not made the slightest impression on me. The highest flight of such clamorous birds is winged in an inferior reign of the air. We hear them, and we look upon them, just as you, gentlemen, when you enjoy the serene air on your lofty rocks, look down upon the gulls that skim the mud of your river, when it is exhausted of its tide.

I am sorry I cannot conclude without saying a word on a topic touched upon by my worthy colleague. I wish that topic had been passed by at a time when I have so little leisure to discuss it. But since he has thought proper to throw it out, I owe you a clear explanation of my poor sentiments on that subject.

---

* Mr. Brickdale opened his poll, it seems, with a tally of those very kind of freemen, and voted many hundreds of them.

He tells you that "the topic of instructions has occasioned much altercation and uneasiness in this city;" and he expresses himself (if I understand him rightly) in favour of the coercive authority of such instructions.

Certainly, gentlemen, it ought to be the happiness and glory of a representative to live in the strictest union, the closest correspondence, and the most unreserved communication with his constituents. Their wishes ought to have great weight with him; their opinion, high respect; their business, unremitted attention. It is his duty to sacrifice his repose, his pleasures, his satisfactions, to theirs; and above all, ever, and in all cases, to prefer their interest to his own. But his unbiassed opinion, his mature judgment, his enlightened conscience, he ought not to sacrifice to you, to any man, or to any set of men living. These he does not derive from your pleasure; no, nor from the law and the constitution. They are a trust from Providence, for the abuse of which he is deeply answerable. Your representative owes you, not his industry only, but his judgment; and he betrays, instead of serving you, if he sacrifices it to your opinion.

My worthy colleague says, his will ought to be subservient to yours. If that be all, the thing is innocent. If government were a matter of will upon any side, yours, without question, ought to be superior. But government and legislation are matters of reason and judgment, and not of inclination; and what sort of reason is that, in which the determination precedes the discussion; in which one set of men deliberate, and another decide; and where those who form the conclusion are perhaps three hundred miles distant from those who hear the arguments?

To deliver an opinion, is the right of all men; that of constituents is a weighty and respectable opinion, which a representative ought always to rejoice to hear; and which he ought always most seriously to consider. But *authoritative* instructions; *mandates* issued, which the member is bound blindly and implicitly to obey, to vote, and to argue for, though contrary to the clearest conviction of his judgment and conscience, – these are things utterly unknown to the laws of this land, and which arise from a fundamental mistake of the whole order and tenor of our constitution.

Parliament is not a *congress* of ambassadors from different and hostile interests; which interests each must maintain, as an agent and advocate, against other agents and advocates; but parliament is a *deliberative* assembly of *one* nation, with *one* interest, that of the whole; where, not local purposes, not local prejudices, ought to guide, but the general good, resulting from the general reason of the whole. You choose a member indeed; but when you have chosen him, he is not member of Bristol, but he is a member of *parliament*. If the local constituent should have an interest, or should form an hasty opinion, evidently opposite to the real good of the rest of the community, the member for that place ought to be as far, as any other, from any endeavour to give it effect. I beg pardon for saying so much on this subject. I have been unwillingly drawn into it; but I shall ever use a respectful frankness of communication with you. Your faithful friend, your devoted servant, I shall be to the end of my life: a flatterer you do not wish for. On this point of instructions, however, I think it scarcely possible we ever can have any sort of difference. Perhaps I may give you too much, rather than too little, trouble.

From the first hour I was encouraged to court your favour, to this happy day of obtaining it, I have never promised you anything but humble and persevering endeavours to do my duty. The weight of that duty, I confess, makes me tremble: and whoever well considers what it is, of all things in the world, will fly from what has the least likeness to a positive and precipitate engagement. To be a good member of parliament is, let me tell you, no easy task; especially at this time, when there is so strong a disposition to run into the perilous extremes of servile compliance or wild popularity To unite circumspection with vigour, is absolutely necessary; but it is extremely difficult. We are now members for a rich commercial *city*; this city, however, is but a part of a rich commercial *nation*, the interests of which are various, multiform, and intricate. We are members for that great nation, which however is itself but part of a great *empire*, extended by our virtue and our fortune to the farthest limits of the east and of the west. All these wide-spread interests must be considered; must be compared; must be reconciled, if possible. We are members for a *free* country; and surely we all know, that the machine of a free constitution is no simple thing; but as intricate and as delicate as it is valuable. We are members in a great and ancient *monarchy*; and we must preserve religiously the true legal rights of the sovereign, which form the key-stone that binds together the noble and well-constructed arch of our empire and our constitution. A constitution made up of balanced powers must ever be a critical thing. As such I mean to touch that part of it which comes within my reach. I know my inability, and I wish for support from every quarter. In particular I shall aim at the friendship, and shall cultivate the best correspondence, of the worthy colleague you have given me.

I trouble you no further than once more to thank you all; you, gentlemen, for your favours; the candidates, for their temperate and polite behaviour; and the sheriffs, for a conduct which may give a model for all who are in public stations.

SPEECH ON CONCILIATION
WITH AMERICA

22 MARCH 1775

SIR,

I HOPE THAT, notwithstanding the austerity of the Chair, your good-nature will incline you to some degree of indulgence towards human frailty. You will not think it unnatural, that those who have an object depending, which strongly engages their hopes and fears, should be somewhat inclined to superstition. As I came into the House full of anxiety about the event of my motion, I found, to my infinite surprise, that the grand penal bill, by which he had passed sentence on the trade and sustenance of America, is to be returned to us from the other House.* I do confess, I could not help looking on this event as a fortunate omen. I look upon it as a sort of providential favour; by which we are put once more in possession of our deliberative capacity, upon a business so very questionable in its nature, so very un-certain in its issue. By the return of this bill, which seemed to have taken its flight for ever, we are at this very instant nearly as free to choose a plan for our American government as we were on the first day of the session. If, Sir, we incline to the side of conciliation, we are not at all embarrassed (unless we please to make ourselves so) by any incongruous mixture of coercion and restraint. We are therefore called upon, as it were by a superior warning voice, again to attend to America; to attend to the whole of it together; and to review the subject with an unusual degree of care and calmness.

Surely it is an awful subject; or there is none so on this side of the grave. When I first had the honour of a seat in this House, the affairs of that continent pressed themselves upon us, as the most important and most delicate object of parliamentary atten-tion. My little share in this great deliberation oppressed me.

* The Act to restrain the trade and commerce of the provinces of Massachusetts Bay and New Hampshire, and colonies of Connecticut and Rhode Island, and Provid-ence Plantation, in North America, to Great Britain, Ireland, and the British Islands in the West Indies; and to prohibit such provinces and colonies from carrying on any fishery on the banks of Newfoundland, and other places therein mentioned, under certain conditions and limitations.

I found myself a partaker in a very high trust; and having no sort of reason to rely on the strength of my natural abilities for the proper execution of that trust, I was obliged to take more than common pains to instruct myself in everything which relates to our colonies. I was not less under the necessity of forming some fixed ideas concerning the general policy of the British empire. Something of this sort seemed to be indispensable; in order, amidst so vast a fluctuation of passions and opinions, to concentre my thoughts; to ballast my conduct; to preserve me from being blown about by every wind of fashionable doctrine. I really did not think it safe, or manly, to have fresh principles to seek upon every fresh mail which should arrive from America.

At that period I had the fortune to find myself in perfect concurrence with a large majority in this House. Bowing under that high authority, and penetrated with the sharpness and strength of that early impression, I have continued ever since, without the least deviation, in my original sentiments. Whether this be owing to an obstinate perseverance in error, or to a religious adherence to what appears to me truth and reason, it is in your equity to judge.

Sir, Parliament having an enlarged view of objects, made, during this interval, more frequent changes in their sentiments and their conduct, than could be justified in a particular person upon the contracted scale of private information. But though I do not hazard anything approaching to censure on the motives of former parliaments to all those alterations, one fact is undoubted, – that under them the state of America has been kept in continual agitation. Everything administered as remedy to the public complaint, if it did not produce, was at least followed by, an heightening of the distemper; until by a variety of experiments, that important country has been brought into her present situation; – a situation which I will not miscall, which I dare not name; which I scarcely know how to comprehend in the terms of any description.

In this posture, Sir, things stood at the beginning of the session. About that time, a worthy member* of great parliamentary experience, who, in the year 1766, filled the chair of the American committee with much ability, took me aside; and lamenting the present aspect of our politics, told me, things were come to

* Mr. Rose Fuller.[1]

such a pass, that our former methods of proceeding in the House would be no longer tolerated. That the public tribunal (never too indulgent to a long and unsuccessful opposition) would now scrutinise our conduct with unusual severity. That the very vicissitudes and shiftings of ministerial measures, instead of convicting their authors of inconstancy and want of system, would be taken as an occasion of charging us with a predetermined discontent, which nothing could satisfy; whilst we accused every measure of vigour as cruel, and every proposal of lenity as weak and irresolute. The public, he said, would not have patience to see us play the game out with our adversaries: we must produce our hand. It would be expected, that those who for many years had been active in such affairs should show, that they had formed some clear and decided idea of the principles of colony government; and were capable of drawing out something like a platform of the ground which might be laid for future and permanent tranquillity.

I felt the truth of what my hon. friend represented; but I felt my situation too. His application might have been made with far greater propriety to many other gentlemen. No man was indeed ever better disposed, or worse qualified, for such an undertaking, than myself. Though I gave so far in to his opinion, that I immediately threw my thoughts into a sort of parliamentary form, I was by no means equally ready to produce them. It generally argues some degree of natural impotence of mind, or some want of knowledge of the world, to hazard plans of government except from a seat of authority. Propositions are made, not only ineffectually, but somewhat disreputably, when the minds of men are not properly disposed for their reception; and for my part, I am not ambitious of ridicule; not absolutely a candidate for disgrace.

Besides, Sir, to speak the plain truth, I have in general no very exalted opinion of the virtue of paper government; nor of any politics in which the plan is to be wholly separated from the execution. But when I saw that anger and violence prevailed every day more and more; and that things were hastening towards an incurable alienation of our colonies; I confess my caution gave way. I felt this, as one of those few moments in which decorum yields to a higher duty. Public calamity is a mighty leveller; and there are occasions when any, even the slightest, chance of doing good, must be laid hold on, even by the most inconsiderable person.

To restore order and repose to an empire so great and so

distracted as ours, is, merely in the attempt, an undertaking that would ennoble the flights of the highest genius, and obtain pardon for the efforts of the meanest understanding. Struggling a good while with these thoughts, by degrees I felt myself more firm. I derived, at length, some confidence from what in other circumstances usually produces timidity. I grew less anxious, even from the idea of my own insignificance. For, judging of what you are by what you ought to be, I persuaded myself that you would not reject a reasonable proposition because it had nothing but its reason to recommend it. On the other hand, being totally destitute of all shadow of influence, natural or adventitious, I was very sure, that, if my proposition were futile or dangerous; if it were weakly conceived, or improperly timed, there was nothing exterior to it, of power to awe, dazzle, or delude you. You will see it just as it is: and you will treat it just as it deserves.

The proposition is peace. Not peace through the medium of war; not peace to be hunted through the labyrinth of intricate and endless negotiations; not peace to arise out of universal discord, fomented from principle, in all parts of the empire; not peace to depend on the juridical determination of perplexing questions, or the precise marking the shadowy boundaries of a complex government. It is simple peace; sought in its natural course, and in its ordinary haunts. – It is peace sought in the spirit of peace; and laid in principles purely pacific. I propose, by removing the ground of the difference, and by restoring the *former unsuspecting confidence of the colonies in the mother country*, to give permanent satisfaction to your people; and (far from a scheme of ruling by discord) to reconcile them to each other in the same act, and by the bond of the very same interest which reconciles them to British government.

My idea is nothing more. Refined policy ever has been the parent of confusion; and ever will be so, as long as the world endures. Plain good intention, which is as easily discovered at the first view, as fraud is surely detected at last, is, let me say, of no mean force in the government of mankind. Genuine simplicity of heart is an healing and cementing principle. My plan, therefore, being formed upon the most simple grounds imaginable, may disappoint some people, when they hear it. It has nothing to recommend it to the pruriency of curious ears. There is nothing at all new and captivating in it. It has nothing of the splendour of the project, which has been lately laid upon your table by the noble lord in the blue riband.* It does not propose to fill your lobby with squabbling colony agents, who will require the interposition of your mace, at every instant, to keep the peace amongst them. It does not institute a magnificent auction of finance, where captivated provinces come to general ransom by bidding against each other, until you knock down the hammer, and determine a proportion of payments beyond all the powers of algebra to equalise and settle.

The plan which I shall presume to suggest, derives, however, one great advantage from the proposition and registry of that noble lord's project. The idea of conciliation is admissible. First, the House, in accepting the resolution moved by the noble lord, has admitted, notwithstanding the menacing front of our address, notwithstanding our heavy bill of pains and penalties – that we do not think ourselves precluded from all ideas of free grace and bounty.

The House has gone further; it has declared conciliation admissible, *previous* to any submission on the part of America. It has even shot a good deal beyond that mark, and has admitted, that the complaints of our former mode of exerting the right of taxation were not wholly unfounded. That right thus exerted is allowed to have had something reprehensible in it; something unwise, or something grievous; since, in the midst of our heat and resentment, we, of ourselves, have proposed a capital altera-tion; and, in order to get rid of what seemed so very exception-able, have instituted a mode that is altogether new; one that is, indeed, wholly alien from all the ancient methods and forms of parliament.

* "That when the governor, council, or assembly, or general court, of any of his Majesty's provinces or colonies in America, shall *propose* to make provision, *according to the condition, circumstances,* and *situation,* of such province or colony, for contributing their *proportion* to the *common defence,* (such *proportion* to be raised under the authority of the general court, or general assembly, of such province or colony, and disposable by parliament,) and shall engage to make provision also for the support of the civil government, and the administration of justice, in such province or colony, it will be proper, *if such proposal shall be approved by his Majesty, and the two Houses of Parliament,* and for so long as such provision shall be made accordingly, to forbear, *in respect of such province or colony,* to levy any duty, tax, or assessment, or to impose any further duty, tax, or assessment, except such duties as it may be expedient to continue to levy or impose, for the regulation of commerce; the nett produce of the duties last mentioned to be carried to the account of such province or colony respectively." – Resolution moved by Lord North[2] in the committee; and agreed to by the House, 27th Feb., 1775.

The *principle* of this proceeding is large enough for my purpose. The means proposed by the noble lord for carrying his ideas into execution, I think, indeed, are very indifferently suited to the end; and this I shall endeavour to show you before I sit down. But, for the present, I take my ground on the admitted principle. I mean to give peace. Peace implies reconciliation; and, where there has been a material dispute, reconciliation does in a manner always imply concession on the one part or on the other. In this state of things I make no difficulty in affirming that the proposal ought to originate from us. Great and acknowledged force is not impaired, either in effect or in opinion, by an unwillingness to exert itself. The superior power may offer peace with honour and with safety. Such an offer from such a power will be attributed to magnanimity. But the concessions of the weak are the concessions of fear. When such a one is disarmed, he is wholly at the mercy of his superior; and he loses for ever that time and those chances, which, as they happen to all men, are the strength and resources of all inferior power.

The capital leading questions on which you must this day decide, are these two: First, whether you ought to concede; and secondly, what your concession ought to be. On the first of these questions we have gained (as I have just taken the liberty of observing to you) some ground. But I am sensible that a good deal more is still to be done. Indeed, Sir, to enable us to determine both on the one and the other of these great questions with a firm and precise judgment, I think it may be necessary to consider distinctly the true nature and the peculiar circumstances of the object which we have before us. Because after all our struggle, whether we will or not, we must govern America according to that nature, and to those circumstances; and not according to our own imaginations; nor according to abstract ideas of right; by no means according to mere general theories of government, the resort to which appears to me, in our present situation, no better than arrant trifling. I shall therefore endeavour, with your leave, to lay before you some of the most material of these circumstances in as full and as clear a manner as I am able to state them.

The first thing that we have to consider with regard to the nature of the object is – the number of people in the colonies. I have taken for some years a good deal of pains on that point. I can by no calculation justify myself in placing the number below two millions of inhabitants of our own European blood

and colour; besides at least 500,000 others, who form no inconsiderable part of the strength and opulence of the whole. This,
Sir, is, I believe, about the true number. There is no occasion to
exaggerate, where plain truth is of so much weight and importance. But whether I put the present numbers too high or too
low, is a matter of little moment. Such is the strength with which
population shoots in that part of the world, that state the numbers
as high as we will, whilst the dispute continues, the exaggeration
ends. Whilst we are discussing any given magnitude, they are
grown to it. Whilst we spend our time in deliberating on the
mode of governing two millions, we shall find we have millions
more to manage. Your children do not grow faster from infancy
to manhood, than they spread from families to communities, and
from villages to nations.

I put this consideration of the present and the growing
numbers in the front of our deliberation; because, Sir, this consideration will make it evident to a blunter discernment than
yours, that no partial, narrow, contracted, pinched, occasional
system will be at all suitable to such an object. It will show you,
that it is not to be considered as one of those *minima* which are
out of the eye and consideration of the law; not a paltry excres-
cence of the state; not a mean dependent, who may be neglected
with little damage, and provoked with little danger. It will prove
that some degree of care and caution is required in the handling
such an object; it will show that you ought not, in reason, to trifle
with so large a mass of the interests and feelings of the human
race. You could at no time do so without guilt; and be assured
you will not be able to do it long with impunity.

But the population of this country, the great and growing
population, though a very important consideration, will lose
much of its weight, if not combined with other circumstances.
The commerce of your colonies is out of all proportion beyond
the numbers of the people. This ground of their commerce
indeed has been trod some days ago, and with great ability, by a
distinguished person,* at your bar. This gentleman, after thirty-
five years – it is so long since he first appeared at the same place
to plead for the commerce of Great Britain – has come again
before you to plead the same cause, without any other effect of

* Mr. Glover.[3]

time, than, that to the fire of imagination and extent of erudition, which even then marked him as one of the first literary characters of his age, he has added a consummate knowledge in the commercial interest of his country, formed by a long course of enlightened and discriminating experience.

Sir, I should be inexcusable in coming after such a person with any detail, if a great part of the members who now fill the House had not the misfortune to be absent when he appeared at your bar. Besides, Sir, I propose to take the matter at periods of time somewhat different from his. There is, if I mistake not, a point of view, from whence if you will look at this subject, it is impossible that it should not make an impression upon you.

I have in my hand two accounts; one a comparative state of the export trade of England to its colonies, as it stood in the year 1704, and as it stood in the year 1772. The other a state of the export trade of this country to its colonies alone, as it stood in 1772, compared with the whole trade of England to all parts of the world (the colonies included) in the year 1704. They are from good vouchers; the latter period from the accounts on your table, the earlier from an original manuscript of Davenant, who first established the inspector-general's office, which has been ever since his time so abundant a source of parliamentary information.

The export trade to the colonies consists of three great branches. The African, which, terminating almost wholly in the colonies, must be put to the account of their commerce; the West Indian; and the North American. All these are so interwoven, that the attempt to separate them, would tear to pieces the contexture of the whole; and if not entirely destroy, would very much depreciate the value of all the parts. I therefore consider these three denominations to be, what in effect they are, one trade.

The trade to the colonies, taken on the export side, at the beginning of this century, that is, in the year 1704, stood thus:

Exports to North America, and the West Indies £483,265
To Africa 86,665

£569,930

In the year 1772, which I take as a middle year between the highest and lowest of those lately laid on your table, the account was as follows:

To North America, and the West Indies..........£4,791,734
To Africa... 866,398
To which if you add the export trade from
    Scotland, which had in 1704 no existence ...   364,000
                                     £6,022,132

From five hundred and odd thousand, it has grown to six millions. It has increased no less than twelve-fold. This is the state of the colony trade, as compared with itself at these two periods, within this century; – and this is matter for meditation. But this is not all. Examine my second account. See how the export trade to the colonies alone in 1772 stood in the other point of view, that is, as compared to the whole trade of England in 1704.

The whole export trade of England, including
    that to the colonies, in 1704 ....£6,509,000
Export to the colonies alone, in 1772 6,024,000

                            Difference   £ 485,000

The trade with America alone is now within less than £500,000 of being equal to what this great commercial nation, England, carried on at the beginning of this century with the whole world! If I had taken the largest year of those on your table, it would rather have exceeded. But, it will be said, is not this American trade an unnatural protuberance, that has drawn the juices from the rest of the body? The reverse. It is the very food that has nourished every other part into its present magnitude. Our general trade has been greatly augmented, and augmented more or less in almost every part to which it ever extended; but with this material difference, that of the six millions which in the beginning of the century constituted the whole mass of our export commerce, the colony trade was but one twelfth part; it is now (as a part of sixteen millions) considerably more than a third of the whole. This is the relative proportion of the importance of the colonies at these two periods: and all reasoning concerning our mode of treating them must have this proportion as its basis, or it is a reasoning weak, rotten, and sophistical.

Mr. Speaker, I cannot prevail on myself to hurry over this great consideration. It is good for us to be here. We stand where we have an immense view of what is, and what is past. Clouds, indeed, and darkness rest upon the future. Let us, however, before we descend from this noble eminence, reflect that this growth of our national prosperity has happened within the short period of the life of man. It has happened within sixty-eight years. There are those alive whose memory might touch the two extremities. For instance, my Lord Bathurst[4] might remember all the stages of the progress. He was in 1704 of an age at least to be made to comprehend such things. He was then old enough *acta parentum jam legere, et quæ sit poterit cognoscere virtus*[5] – Suppose, Sir, that the angel of this auspicious youth, foreseeing the many virtues, which made him one of the most amiable, as he is one of the most fortunate, men of his age, had opened to him in vision, that when, in the fourth generation, the third prince of the House of Brunswick had sat twelve years on the throne of that nation, which (by the happy issue of moderate and healing councils) was to be made Great Britain, he should see his son, Lord Chancellor of England, turn back the current of hereditary dignity to its fountain, and raise him to a higher rank of peerage, whilst he enriched the family with a new one – If amidst these bright and happy scenes of domestic honour and prosperity, that angel should have drawn up the curtain, and unfolded the rising glories of his country, and whilst he was gazing with admiration on the then commercial grandeur of England, the genius should point out to him a little speck, scarce visible in the mass of the national interest, a small seminal principle, rather than a formed body, and should tell him – "Young man, there is America – which at this day serves for little more than to amuse you with stories of savage men, and uncouth manners; yet shall, before you taste of death, show itself equal to the whole of that commerce which now attracts the envy of the world. Whatever England has been growing to by a progressive increase of improvement, brought in by varieties of people, by succession of civilising conquests and civilising settlements in a series of seventeen hundred years, you shall see as much added to her by America in the course of a single life!" If this state of his country had been foretold to him, would it not require all the sanguine credulity of youth, and all the fervid glow of enthusiasm, to make him believe it? Fortunate man, he has lived to see it! Fortunate indeed, if he lives to see nothing that shall vary the prospect, and cloud the setting of his day!

Excuse me, Sir, if turning from such thoughts I resume this

comparative view once more. You have seen it on a large scale; look at it on a small one. I will point out to your attention a particular instance of it in the single province of Pennsylvania. In the year 1704, that province called for £11,459 in value of your commodities, native and foreign. This was the whole. What did it demand in 1772? Why nearly fifty times as much; for in that year the export to Pennsylvania was £507,909, nearly equal to the export to all the colonies together in the first period.

I choose, Sir, to enter into these minute and particular details; because generalities, which in all other cases are apt to heighten and raise the subject, have here a tendency to sink it. When we speak of the commerce with our colonies, fiction lags after truth; invention is unfruitful, and imagination cold and barren.

So far, Sir, as to the importance of the object in view of its commerce, as concerned in the exports from England. If I were to detail the imports, I could show how many enjoyments they procure, which deceive the burthen of life; how many materials which invigorate the springs of national industry, and extend and animate every part of our foreign and domestic commerce. This would be a curious subject indeed – but I must prescribe bounds to myself in a matter so vast and various.

I pass therefore to the colonies in another point of view, their agriculture. This they have prosecuted with such a spirit, that, besides feeding plentifully their own growing multitude, their annual export of grain, comprehending rice, has some years ago exceeded a million in value. Of their last harvest, I am persuaded they will export much more. At the beginning of the century some of these colonies imported corn from the mother country. For some time past, the Old World has been fed from the New. The scarcity which you have felt would have been a desolating famine, if this child of your old age, with a true filial piety, with a Roman charity, had not put the full breast of its youthful exuberance to the mouth of its exhausted parent.

As to the wealth which the colonies have drawn from the sea by their fisheries, you had all that matter fully opened at your bar. You surely thought these acquisitions of value, for they seemed even to excite your envy; and yet the spirit by which that enterprising employment has been exercised, ought rather, in my opinion, to have raised your esteem and admiration. And pray, Sir, what in the world is equal to it? Pass by the other parts, and look at the manner in which the people of New England have of late carried on the whale fishery. Whilst we follow them among the tumbling mountains of ice, and behold them penetrating into the deepest frozen recesses of Hudson's Bay and Davis's Straits, whilst we are looking for them beneath the arctic circle, we hear that they have pierced into the opposite region of polar cold, that they are at the antipodes, and engaged under the frozen serpent of the south. Falkland Island, which seemed too remote and romantic an object for the grasp of national ambition, is but a stage and resting-place in the progress of their victorious industry. Nor is the equinoctial heat more discouraging to them, than the accumulated winter of both the poles. We know that whilst some of them draw the line and strike the harpoon on the coast of Africa, others run the longitude, and pursue their gigantic game along the coast of Brazil. No sea but what is vexed by their fisheries. No climate that is not witness to their toils. Neither the perseverance of Holland, nor the activity of France, nor the dexterous and firm sagacity of English enterprise, ever carried this most perilous mode of hard industry to the extent to which it has been pushed by this recent people; a people who are still, as it were, but in the gristle, and not yet hardened into the bone of manhood. When I contemplate these things; when I know that the colonies in general owe little or nothing to any care of ours, and that they are not squeezed into this happy form by the constraints of watchful and suspicious government, but that, through a wise and salutary neglect, a generous nature has been suffered to take her own way to perfection; when I reflect upon these effects, when I see how profitable they have been to us, I feel all the pride of power sink, and all presumption in the wisdom of human contrivances melt and die away within me. My rigour relents. I pardon something to the spirit of liberty.

I am sensible, Sir, that all which I have asserted in my detail, is admitted in the gross; but that quite a different conclusion is drawn from it. America, gentlemen say, is a noble object. It is an object well worth fighting for. Certainly it is, if fighting a people be the best way of gaining them. Gentlemen in this respect will be led to their choice of means by their complexions and their habits. Those who understand the military art, will of course have some predilection for it. Those who wield the thunder of the state, may have more confidence in the efficacy of arms. But I confess, possibly for want of this knowledge, my opinion is much more in favour of prudent management, than of force;

considering force not as an odious, but a feeble instrument, for preserving a people so numerous, so active, so growing, so spirited as this, in a profitable and subordinate connexion with us.

First, Sir, permit me to observe, that the use of force alone is but *temporary*. It may subdue for a moment; but it does not remove the necessity of subduing again: and a nation is not governed, which is perpetually to be conquered.

My next objection is its *uncertainty*. Terror is not always the effect of force; and an armament is not a victory. If you do not succeed, you are without resource; for, conciliation failing, force remains; but, force failing, no further hope of reconciliation is left. Power and authority are sometimes bought by kindness; but they can never be begged as alms by an impoverished and defeated violence.

A further objection to force is, that you *impair the object* by your very endeavours to preserve it. The thing you fought for is not the thing which you recover; but depreciated, sunk, wasted, and consumed in the contest. Nothing less will content me, than *whole America*. I do not choose to consume its strength along with our own; because in all parts it is the British strength that I consume. I do not choose to be caught by a foreign enemy at the end of this exhausting conflict; and still less in the midst of it. I may escape; but I can make no insurance against such an event. Let me add, that I do not choose wholly to break the American spirit; because it is the spirit that has made the country.

Lastly, we have no sort of *experience* in favour of force as an instrument in the rule of our colonies. Their growth and their utility has been owing to methods altogether different. Our ancient indulgence has been said to be pursued to a fault. It may be so. But we know if feeling is evidence, that our fault was more tolerable than our attempt to mend it; and our sin far more salutary than our penitence.

These, Sir, are my reasons for not entertaining that high opinion of untried force, by which many gentlemen, for whose sentiments in other particulars I have great respect, seem to be so greatly captivated. But there is still behind a third consideration concerning this object, which serves to determine my opinion on the sort of policy which ought to be pursued in the management of America, even more than its population and its commerce, I mean its *temper and character*.

In this character of the Americans, a love of freedom is

the predominating feature which marks and distinguishes the whole: and as an ardent is always a jealous affection, your colonies become suspicious, restive, and untractable, whenever they see the least attempt to wrest from them by force, or shuffle from them by chicane, what they think the only advantage worth living for. This fierce spirit of liberty is stronger in the English colonies probably than in any other people of the earth; and this from a great variety of powerful causes; which, to understand the true temper of their minds, and the direction which this spirit takes, it will not be amiss to lay open somewhat more largely.

First, the people of the colonies are descendants of Englishmen. England, Sir, is a nation, which still I hope respects, and formerly adored, her freedom. The colonists emigrated from you when this part of your character was most predominant; and they took this bias and direction the moment they parted from your hands. They are therefore not only devoted to liberty, but to liberty according to English ideas, and on English principles. Abstract liberty, like other mere abstractions, is not to be found. Liberty inheres in some sensible object; and every nation has formed to itself some favourite point, which by way of eminence becomes the criterion of their happiness. It happened, you know, Sir, that the great contests for freedom in this country were from the earliest times chiefly upon the question of taxing. Most of the contests in the ancient commonwealths turned primarily on the right of election of magistrates; or on the balance among the several orders of the state. The question of money was not with them so immediate. But in England it was otherwise. On this point of taxes the ablest pens, and most eloquent tongues, have been exercised; the greatest spirits have acted and suffered. In order to give the fullest satisfaction concerning the importance of this point, it was not only necessary for those who in argument defended the excellence of the English constitution, to insist on this privilege of granting money as a dry point of fact, and to prove, that the right had been acknowledged in ancient parchments, and blind usages, to reside in a certain body called a House of Commons. They went much farther; they attempted to prove, and they succeeded, that in theory it ought to be so, from the particular nature of a House of Commons, as an immediate representative of the people; whether the old records had delivered this oracle or not. They took infinite pains to inculcate, as a fundamental principle, that in all monarchies the people must in

effect themselves, mediately or immediately, possess the power
of granting their own money, or no shadow of liberty could
subsist. The colonies draw from you, as with their life-blood,
these ideas and principles. Their love of liberty, as with you, fixed
and attached on this specific point of taxing. Liberty might be
safe, or might be endangered, in twenty other particulars, without their being much pleased or alarmed. Here they felt its pulse;
and as they found that beat, they thought themselves sick or
sound. I do not say whether they were right or wrong in applying
your general arguments to their own case. It is not easy indeed
to make a monopoly of theorems and corollaries. The fact is, that
they did thus apply those general arguments; and your mode of
governing them, whether through lenity or indolence, through
wisdom or mistake, confirmed them in the imagination, that
they, as well as you, had an interest in these common principles.

They were further confirmed in this pleasing error by the form
of their provincial legislative assemblies. Their governments
are popular in a high degree; some are merely popular; in all, the
popular representative is the most weighty; and this share of the
people in their ordinary government never fails to inspire them
with lofty sentiments, and with a strong aversion from whatever
tends to deprive them of their chief importance.

If anything were wanting to this necessary operation of the
form of government, religion would have given it a complete
effect. Religion, always a principle of energy, in this new people
is no way worn out or impaired; and their mode of professing it
is also one main cause of this free spirit. The people are Protestants; and of that kind which is the most adverse to all implicit
submission of mind and opinion. This is a persuasion not only
favourable to liberty, but built upon it. I do not think, Sir, that
the reason of this averseness in the dissenting churches, from all
that looks like absolute government, is so much to be sought in
their religious tenets, as in their history. Every one knows that
the Roman Catholic religion is at least coeval with most of the
governments where it prevails; that it has generally gone hand
in hand with them, and received great favour and every kind of
support from authority. The Church of England too was formed
from her cradle under the nursing care of regular government.
But the dissenting interests have sprung up in direct opposition
to all the ordinary powers of the world; and could justify that
opposition only on a strong claim to natural liberty. Their very

existence depended on the powerful and unremitted assertion of that claim. All Protestantism, even the most cold and passive, is a sort of dissent. But the religion most prevalent in our northern colonies is a refinement on the principle of resistance; it is the dissidence of dissent, and the Protestantism of the Protestant religion. This religion, under a variety of denominations agreeing in nothing but in the communion of the spirit of liberty, is predominant in most of the northern provinces; where the Church of England, notwithstanding its legal rights, is in reality no more than a sort of private sect, not composing most probably the tenth of the people. The colonists left England when this spirit was high, and in the emigrants was the highest of all; and even that stream of foreigners, which has been constantly flowing into these colonies, has, for the greatest part, been composed of dissenters from the establishments of their several countries, and have brought with them a temper and character far from alien to that of the people with whom they mixed.

Sir, I can perceive by their manner, that some gentlemen object to the latitude of this description; because in the southern colonies the Church of England forms a large body, and has a regular establishment. It is certainly true. There is, however, a circumstance attending these colonies, which, in my opinion, fully counterbalances this difference, and makes the spirit of liberty still more high and haughty than in those to the northward. It is, that in Virginia and the Carolinas they have a vast multitude of slaves. Where this is the case in any part of the world, those who are free, are by far the most proud and jealous of their freedom. Freedom is to them not only an enjoyment, but a kind of rank and privilege. Not seeing there, that freedom, as in countries where it is a common blessing, and as broad and general as the air, may be united with much abject toil, with great misery, with all the exterior of servitude, liberty looks, amongst them, like something that is more noble and liberal. I do not mean, Sir, to commend the superior morality of this sentiment, which has at least as much pride as virtue in it; but I cannot alter the nature of man. The fact is so; and these people of the southern colonies are much more strongly, and with a higher and more stubborn spirit, attached to liberty, than those to the northward. Such were all the ancient commonwealths; such were our Gothic ancestors; such in our days were the Poles; and such will be all masters of slaves, who are not slaves themselves. In such a people,

the haughtiness of domination combines with the spirit of freedom, fortifies it, and renders it invincible.

Permit me, Sir, to add another circumstance in our colonies,
which contributes no mean part towards the growth and effect
of this untractable spirit. I mean their education. In no country
perhaps in the world is the law so general a study. The profession
itself is numerous and powerful; and in most provinces it takes
the lead. The greater number of the deputies sent to the congress
were lawyers. But all who read, and most do read, endeavour to
obtain some smattering in that science. I have been told by an
eminent bookseller, that in no branch of his business, after tracts
of popular devotion, were so many books as those on the law
exported to the plantations. The colonists have now fallen into
the way of printing them for their own use. I hear that they have
sold nearly as many of Blackstone's Commentaries[6] in America
as in England. General Gage[7] marks out this disposition very particularly in a letter on your table. He states, that all the people in
his government are lawyers, or smatterers in law; and that in
Boston they have been enabled, by successful chicane, wholly to
evade many parts of one of your capital penal constitutions. The
smartness of debate will say, that this knowledge ought to teach
them more clearly the rights of legislature, their obligations to
obedience, and the penalties of rebellion. All this is mighty well.
But my honourable and learned friend* on the floor, who condescends to mark what I say for animadversion, will disdain that
ground. He has heard, as well as I, that when great honours and
great emoluments do not win over this knowledge to the service
of the state, it is a formidable adversary to government. If the
spirit be not tamed and broken by these happy methods, it is stubborn and litigious. *Abeunt studia in mores.*[8] This study renders men
acute, inquisitive, dexterous, prompt in attack, ready in defence,
full of resources. In other countries, the people, more simple, and
of a less mercurial cast, judge of an ill principle in government
only by an actual grievance; here they anticipate the evil, and
judge of the pressure of the grievance by the badness of the principle. They augur misgovernment at a distance; and sniff the
approach of tyranny in every tainted breeze.

The last cause of this disobedient spirit in the colonies is hardly
less powerful than the rest, as it is not merely moral, but laid deep

* The Attorney-general.

in the natural constitution of things. Three thousand miles of ocean lie between you and them. No contrivance can prevent the effect of this distance in weakening government. Seas roll, and months pass, between the order and the execution; and the want of a speedy explanation of a single point is enough to defeat a whole system. You have, indeed, winged ministers of vengeance, who carry your bolts in their pounces to the remotest verge of the sea. But there a power steps in, that limits the arrogance of raging passions and furious elements, and says, "So far shalt thou go, and no farther." Who are you, that should fret and rage, and bite the chains of nature? – Nothing worse happens to you than does to all nations who have extensive empire; and it happens in all the forms into which empire can be thrown. In large bodies, the circulation of power must be less vigorous at the extremities. Nature has said it. The Turk cannot govern Egypt, and Arabia, and Curdistan, as he governs Thrace; nor has he the same dominion in Crimea and Algiers, which he has at Brusa and Smyrna. Despotism itself is obliged to truck and huckster. The Sultan gets such obedience as he can. He governs with a loose rein, that he may govern at all; and the whole of the force and vigour of his authority in his centre is derived from a prudent relaxation in all his borders. Spain, in her provinces, is, perhaps, not so well obeyed as you are in yours. She complies too; she submits; she watches times. This is the immutable condition, the eternal law, of extensive and detached empire.

Then, Sir, from these six capital sources; of descent; of form of government; of religion in the northern provinces; of manners in the southern; of education; of the remoteness of situation from the first mover of government; from all these causes a fierce spirit of liberty has grown up. It has grown with the growth of the people in your colonies, and increased with the increase of their wealth; a spirit, that unhappily meeting with an exercise of power in England, which, however lawful, is not reconcilable to any ideas of liberty, much less with theirs, has kindled this flame that is ready to consume us.

I do not mean to commend either the spirit in this excess, or the moral causes which produce it. Perhaps a more smooth and accommodating spirit of freedom in them would be more acceptable to us. Perhaps ideas of liberty might be desired, more reconcilable with an arbitrary and boundless authority. Perhaps we might wish the colonists to be persuaded, that their liberty is more secure when held in trust for them by us (as their guardians during a perpetual minority) than with any part of it in their own hands. The question is, not whether their spirit deserves praise or blame, but – what, in the name of God, shall we do with it? You have before you the object, such as it is, with all its glories, with all its imperfections on its head. You see the magnitude; the importance; the temper; the habits; the disorders. By all these considerations we are strongly urged to determine something concerning it. We are called upon to fix some rule and line for our future conduct, which may give a little stability to our politics, and prevent the return of such unhappy deliberations as the present. Every such return will bring the matter before us in a still more untractable form. For, what astonishing and incredible things have we not seen already! What monsters have not been generated from this unnatural contention! Whilst every principle of authority and resistance has been pushed, upon both sides, as far as it would go, there is nothing so solid and certain, either in reasoning or in practice, that has not been shaken. Until very lately, all authority in America seemed to be nothing but an emanation from yours. Even the popular part of the colony constitution derived all its activity, and its first vital movement, from the pleasure of the crown. We thought, Sir, that the utmost which the discontented colonists could do, was to disturb authority; we never dreamt they could of themselves supply it; knowing in general what an operose business it is to establish a government absolutely new. But having, for our purposes in this contention, resolved, that none but an obedient assembly should sit; the humours of the people there, finding all passage through the legal channel stopped, with great violence broke out another way. Some provinces have tried their experiment, as we have tried ours; and theirs has succeeded. They have formed a government sufficient for its purposes, without the bustle of a revolution, or the troublesome formality of an election. Evident necessity, and tacit consent, have done the business in an instant. So well they have done it, that Lord Dunmore[9] (the account is among the fragments on your table) tells you, that the new institution is infinitely better obeyed than the ancient government ever was in its most fortunate periods. Obedience is what makes government, and not the names by which it is called; not the name of governor, as formerly, or committee, as at present. This new government has originated directly from the people; and was not transmitted through any of the ordinary artificial media of a positive constitution. It was not a manufacture ready formed, and transmitted to them in that condition from England. The evil arising from hence is this; that the colonists having once found the possibility of enjoying the advantages of order in the midst of a struggle for liberty, such struggles will not henceforward seem so terrible to the settled and sober part of mankind as they had appeared before the trial.

Pursuing the same plan of punishing by the denial of the exercise of government to still greater lengths, we wholly abrogated the ancient government of Massachusetts. We were confident that the first feeling, if not the very prospect of anarchy, would instantly enforce a complete submission. The experiment was tried. A new, strange, unexpected face of things appeared. Anarchy is found tolerable. A vast province has now subsisted, and subsisted in a considerable degree of health and vigour, for near a twelvemonth, without governor, without public council, without judges, without executive magistrates. How long it will continue in this state, or what may arise out of this unheard-of situation, how can the wisest of us conjecture? Our late experience has taught us that many of those fundamental principles, formerly believed infallible, are either not of the importance they were imagined to be; or that we have not at all adverted to some other far more important and far more powerful principles, which entirely overrule those we had considered as omnipotent. I am much against any further experiments, which tend to put to the proof any more of these allowed opinions, which contribute so much to the public tranquillity. In effect, we suffer as much at home by this loosening of all ties, and this concussion of all established opinions, as we do abroad. For, in order to prove that the Americans have no right to their liberties, we are every day endeavouring to subvert the maxims which preserve the whole spirit of our own. To prove that the Americans ought not to be free, we are obliged to depreciate the value of freedom itself; and we never seem to gain a paltry advantage over them in debate, without attacking some of those principles, or deriding some of those feelings, for which our ancestors have shed their blood.

But, Sir, in wishing to put an end to pernicious experiments, I do not mean to preclude the fullest inquiry. Far from it. Far from deciding on a sudden or partial view, I would patiently go round and round the subject, and survey it minutely in every possible aspect. Sir, if I were capable of engaging you to an equal attention, I would state, that, as far as I am capable of discerning, there are but three ways of proceeding relative to this stubborn spirit, which prevails in your colonies, and disturbs your government. These are – To change that spirit, as inconvenient, by removing the causes. To prosecute it as criminal. Or, to comply with it as necessary. I would not be guilty of an imperfect enumeration; I can think of but these three. Another has indeed been started, that of giving up the colonies; but it met so slight a reception, that I do not think myself obliged to dwell a great while upon it. It is nothing but a little sally of anger, like the frowardness of peevish children, who, when they cannot get all they would have, are resolved to take nothing.

The first of these plans, to change the spirit as inconvenient, by removing the causes, I think is the most like a systematic proceeding. It is radical in its principle; but is attended with great difficulties, some of them little short, as I conceive, of impossibilities. This will appear by examining into the plans which have been proposed.

As the growing population in the colonies is evidently one cause of their resistance, it was last session mentioned in both Houses, by men of weight, and received not without applause, that in order to check this evil, it would be proper for the crown to make no further grants of land. But to this scheme there are two objections. The first, that there is already so much unsettled land in private hands, as to afford room for an immense future population, although the crown not only withheld its grants, but annihilated its soil. If this be the case, then the only effect of this avarice of desolation, this hoarding of a royal wilderness, would be to raise the value of the possessions in the hands of the great private monopolists, without any adequate check to the growing and alarming mischief of population.

But if you stopped your grants, what would be the consequence? The people would occupy without grants. They have already so occupied in many places. You cannot station garrisons in every part of these deserts. If you drive the people from one place, they will carry on their annual tillage, and remove with their flocks and herds to another. Many of the people in the back settlements are already little attached to particular situations. Already they have topped the Appalachian mountains. From thence they behold before them an immense plain, one vast, rich, level meadow; a square of five hundred miles. Over this they would wander without a possibility of restraint; they would change their manners with the habits of their life; would soon forget a government by which they were disowned; would become hordes of English Tartars; and pouring down upon your unfortified frontiers a fierce and irresistible cavalry, become masters of your governors and your counsellors, your collectors and comptrollers, and of all the slaves that adhered to them. Such would, and, in no long time, must be, the effect of attempting to forbid as a crime, and to suppress as an evil, the command and blessing of Providence, "Increase and multiply." Such would be the happy result of an endeavour to keep as a lair of wild beasts, that earth, which God, by an express charter, has given to the children of men. Far different, and surely much wiser, has been our policy hitherto. Hitherto we have invited our people, by every kind of bounty, to fixed establishments. We have invited the husbandman to look to authority for his title. We have taught him piously to believe in the mysterious virtue of wax and parchment. We have thrown each tract of land, as it was peopled, into districts; that the ruling power should never be wholly out of sight. We have settled all we could; and we have carefully attended every settlement with government.

Adhering, Sir, as I do, to this policy, as well as for the reasons I have just given, I think this new project of hedging-in population to be neither prudent nor practicable.

To impoverish the colonies in general, and in particular to arrest the noble course of their marine enterprises, would be a more easy task. I freely confess it. We have shown a disposition to a system of this kind; a disposition even to continue the restraint after the offence; looking on ourselves as rivals to our colonies, and persuaded that of course we must gain all that they shall lose. Much mischief we may certainly do. The power inadequate to all other things is often more than sufficient for this. I do not look on the direct and immediate power of the colonies to resist our violence as very formidable. In this, however, I may be mistaken. But when I consider, that we have colonies for no purpose but to be serviceable to us, it seems to my poor understanding a little preposterous, to make them unserviceable, in order to keep them obedient. It is, in truth, nothing more than the old, and, as I thought, exploded problem of tyranny, which proposes to beggar its subjects into submission. But remember, when you have completed your system of impoverishment, that nature still proceeds in her ordinary course; that discontent will increase with misery; and that there are critical moments in the fortune of all states, when they who are too weak to contribute to your prosperity, may be strong enough to complete your ruin. *Spoliatis arma supersunt.*[10]

The temper and character which prevail in our colonies are, I am afraid, unalterable by any human art. We cannot, I fear, falsify the pedigree of this fierce people, and persuade them that they are not sprung from a nation in whose veins the blood of freedom circulates. The language in which they would hear you tell them this tale would detect the imposition; your speech would betray you. An Englishman is the unfittest person on earth to argue another Englishman into slavery.

I think it is nearly as little in our power to change their republican religion, as their free descent; or to substitute the Roman Catholic, as a penalty; or the Church of England, as an improvement. The mode of inquisition and dragooning is going out of fashion in the Old World; and I should not confide much to their efficacy in the New. The education of the Americans is also on the same unalterable bottom with their religion. You cannot persuade them to burn their books of curious science; to banish their lawyers from their courts of laws; or to quench the lights of their assemblies, by refusing to choose those persons who are best read in their privileges. It would be no less impractible to think of wholly annihilating the popular assemblies, in which these lawyers sit. The army, by which we must govern in their place, would be far more chargeable to us; not quite so effectual; and perhaps, in the end, full as difficult to be kept in obedience.

With regard to the high aristocratic spirit of Virginia and the southern colonies, it has been proposed, I know, to reduce it, by declaring a general enfranchisement of their slaves. This project has had its advocates and panegyrists; yet I never could argue myself into any opinion of it. Slaves are often much attached to their masters. A general wild offer of liberty would not always be accepted. History furnishes few instances of it. It is sometimes as hard to persuade slaves to be free, as it is to compel freemen to be slaves; and in this auspicious scheme, we should have both these pleasing tasks on our hands at once. But when we talk of enfranchisement, do we not perceive that the American master may enfranchise too; and arm servile hands in defence of freedom? A measure to which other people have had recourse more than once, and not without success, in a desperate situation of their affairs.

Slaves as these unfortunate black people are, and dull as all men are from slavery, must they not a little suspect the offer of freedom from that very nation which has sold them to their present masters? from that nation, one of whose causes of quarrel with those masters is their refusal to deal any more in that inhuman traffic? An offer of freedom from England would come rather oddly, shipped to them in an African vessel, which is refused an entry into the ports of Virginia or Carolina, with a cargo of three Angola negroes. It would be curious to see the Guinea captain attempting at the same instant to publish his proclamation of liberty, and to advertise his sale of slaves.

But let us suppose all these moral difficulties got over. The ocean remains. You cannot pump this dry; and as long as it continues in its present bed, so long all the causes which weaken authority by distance will continue. "Ye gods, annihilate but space and time, and make two lovers happy!" – was a pious and passionate prayer; – but just as reasonable, as many of the serious wishes of very grave and solemn politicians.

If then, Sir, it seems almost desperate to think of any alterative course, for changing the moral causes (and not quite easy to remove the natural) which produce prejudices irreconcilable to the late exercise of our authority; but that the spirit infallibly will continue; and, continuing, will produce such effects as now embarrass us; the second mode under consideration is, to prosecute that spirit in its overt acts, as *criminal*.

At this proposition I must pause a moment. The thing seems a great deal too big for my ideas of jurisprudence. It should seem to my way of conceiving such matters, that there is a very wide difference in reason and policy, between the mode of proceeding on their regular conduct of scattered individuals, or even of bands of men, who disturb order within the state, and the civil dissensions which may, from time to time, on great questions, agitate the several communities which compose a great empire. It looks to me to be narrow and pedantic, to apply the ordinary ideas of criminal justice to this great public contest. I do not know the method of drawing up an indictment against a whole people. I cannot insult and ridicule the feelings of millions of my fellow-creatures, as Sir Edward Coke insulted one excellent individual (Sir Walter Raleigh) at the bar.[11] I hope I am not ripe to pass sentence on the gravest public bodies, intrusted with magistracies of great authority and dignity, and charged with the safety of their fellow-citizens, upon the very same title that I am. I really think, that for wise men this is not judicious; for sober men, not decent; for minds tinctured with humanity, not mild and merciful.

Perhaps, Sir, I am mistaken in my idea of an empire, as distinguished from a single state or kingdom. But my idea of it is this; that an empire is the aggregate of many states under one common head; whether this head be a monarch, or a presiding republic. It does, in such constitutions, frequently happen (and nothing but the dismal, cold, dead uniformity of servitude can prevent its happening) that the subordinate parts have many local privileges and immunities. Between these privileges and the supreme common authority the line may be extremely nice. Of course disputes, often, too, very bitter disputes, and much ill blood, will arise. But though every privilege is an exemption (in the case) from the ordinary exercise of the supreme authority, it is no denial of it. The claim of a privilege seems rather, *ex vi termini,*[12] to imply a superior power. For to talk of the privileges of a state, or of a person, who has no superior, is hardly any better than speaking nonsense. Now, in such unfortunate quarrels among the component parts of a great political union of communities, I can scarcely conceive anything more completely imprudent, than for the head of the empire to insist, that, if any privilege is pleaded against his will, or his acts, his whole authority is denied; instantly to proclaim rebellion, to beat to arms, and to put the offending provinces under the ban. Will not this, Sir, very soon teach the provinces to make no distinctions on their part? Will it not teach them that the government, against which a claim of liberty is tantamount to high treason, is a government to which submission is equivalent to slavery? It may not always be quite convenient to impress dependent communities with such an idea.

We are indeed, in all disputes with the colonies, by the necessity of things, the judge. It is true, Sir. But I confess, that the character of judge in my own cause is a thing that frightens me. Instead of filling me with pride, I am exceedingly humbled by it. I cannot proceed with a stern, assured, judicial confidence, until I find myself in something more like a judicial character. I must have these hesitations as long as I am compelled to recollect, that, in my little reading upon such contests as these, the sense of mankind has, at least, as often decided against the superior as the subordinate power. Sir, let me add too, that the opinion of my having some abstract right in my favour, would not put me much at my ease in passing sentence; unless I could be sure, that there were no rights which, in their exercise under certain circumstances, were not the most odious of all wrongs, and the most vexatious of all injustice. Sir, these considerations have great weight with me, when I find things so circumstanced, that I see the same party, at once a civil litigant against me in point of right, and a culprit before me; while I sit as a criminal judge, on acts of his, whose moral quality is to be decided upon the merits of that very litigation. Men are every now and then put, by the complexity of human affairs, into strange situations; but justice is the same, let the judge be in what situation he will.

There is, Sir, also a circumstance which convinces me, that this mode of criminal proceeding is not (at least in the present stage of our contest) altogether expedient; which is nothing less than the conduct of those very persons who have seemed to adopt that mode, by lately declaring a rebellion in Massachusetts Bay, as they had formerly addressed to have traitors brought hither, under an act of Henry the Eighth, for trial. For though rebellion is declared, it is not proceeded against as such; nor have any steps been taken towards the apprehension or conviction of any individual offender, either on our late or our former address; but modes of public coercion have been adopted, and such as have much more resemblance to a sort of qualified hostility towards an independent power than the punishment of rebellious subjects. All this seems rather inconsistent; but it shows how difficult it is to apply these juridical ideas to our present case.

In this situation, let us seriously and coolly ponder. What is it we have got by all our menaces, which have been many and ferocious? What advantage have we derived from the penal laws we have passed, and which, for the time, have been severe and numerous? What advances have we made towards our object, by the sending of a force, which, by land and sea, is no contemptible strength? Has the disorder abated? Nothing less. – When I see things in this situation, after such confident hopes, bold promises, and active exertions, I cannot, for my life, avoid a suspicion, that the plan itself is not correctly right.

If then the removal of the causes of this spirit of American liberty be, for the greater part, or rather entirely, impracticable; if the ideas of criminal process be inapplicable, or if applicable, are in the highest degree inexpedient; what way yet remains? No way is open, but the third and last – to comply with the American spirit as necessary; or, if you please, to submit to it as a necessary evil.

If we adopt this mode; if we mean to conciliate and concede; let us see of what nature the concession ought to be: to ascertain the nature of our concession, we must look at their complaint. The colonies complain, that they have not the characteristic mark and seal of British freedom. They complain, that they are taxed in a parliament in which they are not represented. If you mean to satisfy them at all, you must satisfy them with regard to this complaint. If you mean to please any people, you must give them the boon which they ask; not what you may think better for them, but of a kind totally different. Such an act may be a wise regulation, but it is no concession: whereas our present theme is the mode of giving satisfaction.

Sir, I think you must perceive, that I am resolved this day to have nothing at all to do with the question of the right of taxation. Some gentlemen startle – but it is true; I put it totally out of the question. It is less than nothing in my consideration. I do not indeed wonder, nor will you, Sir, that gentlemen of profound learning are fond of displaying it on this profound subject. But my consideration is narrow, confined, and wholly limited to the policy of the question. I do not examine, whether the giving away a man's money be a power excepted and reserved out of the general trust of government; and how far all mankind, in all forms of polity, are entitled to an exercise of that right by the charter of nature. Or whether, on the contrary, a right of taxation is necessarily involved in the general principle of legislation, and inseparable from the ordinary supreme power. These are deep questions, where great names militate against each other; where reason is perplexed; and an appeal to authorities only thickens the confusion. For high and reverend authorities lift up their heads on both sides; and there is no sure footing in the middle. This point is the *great Serbonian bog, betwixt Damiata and Mount Casius old, where armies whole have sunk.*[13] I do not intend to be overwhelmed in that bog, though in such respectable company. The question with me is, not whether you have a right to render your people miserable; but whether it is not your interest to make them happy. It is not, what a lawyer tells me I *may* do; but what humanity, reason, and justice tell me I ought to do. Is a politic act the worse for being a generous one? Is no concession proper, but that which is made from your want of right to keep what you grant? Or does it lessen the grace or dignity of relaxing in the exercise of an odious claim, because you have your evidence-room full of titles, and your magazines stuffed with arms to enforce them? What signify all those titles, and all those arms? Of what avail are they, when the reason of the thing tells me, that the assertion of my title is the loss of my suit; and that I could do nothing but wound myself by the use of my own weapons?

Such is stedfastly my opinion of the absolute necessity of keeping up the concord of this empire by a unity of spirit, though in a diversity of operations, that, if I were sure the colonists had, at their leaving this country, sealed a regular compact of servitude; that they had solemnly abjured all the rights of citizens; that they had made a vow to renounce all ideas of liberty for them and their posterity to all generations; yet I should hold myself obliged to conform to the temper I found universally prevalent in my own day, and to govern two millions of men, impatient of servitude, on the principles of freedom. I am not determining a point of law; I am restoring tranquillity; and the general character and situation of a people must determine what sort of government is fitted for them. That point nothing else can or ought to determine.

My idea, therefore, without considering whether we yield as matter of right, or grant as matter of favour, is *to admit the people of our colonies into an interest in the constitution*; and, by recording that admission in the journals of parliament, to give them as strong an assurance as the nature of the thing will admit, that we mean for ever to adhere to that solemn declaration of systematic indulgence.

Some years ago, the repeal of a revenue act, upon its understood principle, might have served to show, that we intended an unconditional abatement of the exercise of a taxing power. Such a measure was then sufficient to remove all suspicion, and to give perfect content. But unfortunate events, since that time, may make something further necessary; and not more necessary for the satisfaction of the colonies, than for the dignity and consistency of our own future proceedings.

I have taken a very incorrect measure of the disposition of the House, if this proposal in itself would be received with dislike.

I think, Sir, we have few American financiers. But our misfortune is, we are too acute; we are too exquisite in our conjectures of the future, for men oppressed with such great and present evils. The more moderate among the opposers of parliamentary concession freely confess, that they hope no good from taxation; but they apprehend the colonists have further views; and if this point were conceded, they would instantly attack the trade laws. These gentlemen are convinced, that this was the intention from the beginning; and the quarrel of the Americans with taxation was no more than a cloak and cover to this design. Such has been the language even of a gentleman* of real moderation, and of a natural temper well adjusted to fair and equal government. I am, however, Sir, not a little surprised at this kind of discourse, whenever I hear it; and I am the more surprised, on account of the arguments which I constantly find in company with it, and which are often urged from the same mouths, and on the same day.

For instance, when we allege, that it is against reason to tax a people under so many restraints in trade as the Americans, the noble lord† in the blue riband shall tell you, that the restraints on trade are futile and useless; of no advantage to us, and of no burthen to those on whom they are imposed; that the trade to America is not secured by the acts of navigation, but by the natural and irresistible advantage of a commercial preference.

Such is the merit of the trade laws in this posture of the debate. But when strong internal circumstances are urged against the taxes; when the scheme is dissected; when experience and the nature of things are brought to prove, and do prove, the utter impossibility of obtaining an effective revenue from the colonies; when these things are pressed, or rather press themselves, so as to drive the advocates of colony taxes to a clear admission of the futility of the scheme; then, Sir, the sleeping trade laws revive from their trance; and this useless taxation is to be kept sacred, not for its own sake, but as a counter-guard and security of the laws of trade.

Then, Sir, you keep up revenue laws which are mischievous, in order to preserve trade laws that are useless. Such is the wisdom of our plan in both its members. They are separately given up as of no value; and yet one is always to be defended for the sake of

* Mr. Rice.[14]
† Lord North.

the other. But I cannot agree with the noble lord, nor with the pamphlet from whence he seems to have borrowed these ideas, concerning the inutility of the trade laws. For, without idolising them, I am sure they are still, in many ways, of great use to us: and in former times they have been of the greatest. They do confine, and they do greatly narrow, the market for the Americans. But my perfect conviction of this does not help me in the least to discern how the revenue laws form any security whatsoever to the commercial regulations; or that these commercial regulations are the true ground of the quarrel; or that the giving way, in any one instance of authority, is to lose all that may remain unconceded.

One fact is clear and indisputable. The public and avowed origin of this quarrel was on taxation. This quarrel has indeed brought on new disputes on new questions; but certainly the least bitter, and the fewest of all, on the trade laws. To judge which of the two be the real, radical cause of quarrel, we have to see whether the commercial dispute did, in order of time, precede the dispute on taxation? There is not a shadow of evidence for it. Next, to enable us to judge whether at this moment a dislike to the trade laws be the real cause of quarrel, it is absolutely necessary to put the taxes out of the question by a repeal. See how the Americans act in this position, and then you will be able to discern correctly what is the true object of the controversy, or whether any controversy at all will remain. Unless you consent to remove this cause of difference, it is impossible, with decency, to assert that the dispute is not upon what it is avowed to be. And I would, Sir, recommend to your serious consideration, whether it be prudent to form a rule for punishing people, not on their own acts, but on your conjectures? Surely it is preposterous at the very best. It is not justifying your anger, by their misconduct; but it is converting your ill-will into their delinquency.

But the colonies will go further. – Alas! alas! when will this speculating against fact and reason end? – What will quiet these panic fears which we entertain of the hostile effect of a conciliatory conduct? Is it true, that no case can exist, in which it is proper for the sovereign to accede to the desires of his discontented subjects? Is there anything peculiar in this case, to make a rule for itself? Is all authority of course lost, when it is not pushed to the extreme? Is it a certain maxim, that the fewer causes of dissatisfaction are left by government, the more the subject will be inclined to resist and rebel?

All these objections being in fact no more than suspicions, conjectures, divinations, formed in defiance of fact and experience; they did not, Sir, discourage me from entertaining the idea of a conciliatory concession, founded on the principles which I have just stated.

In forming a plan for this purpose, I endeavoured to put myself in that frame of mind which was the most natural, and the most reasonable; and which was certainly the most probable means of securing me from all error. I set out with a perfect distrust of my own abilities; a total renunciation of every speculation of my own; and with a profound reverence for the wisdom of our ancestors, who have left us the inheritance of so happy a constitution, and so flourishing an empire, and what is a thousand times more valuable, the treasury of the maxims and principles which formed the one, and obtained the other.

During the reigns of the kings of Spain of the Austrian family, whenever they were at a loss in the Spanish councils, it was common for their statesmen to say, that they ought to consult the genius of Philip the Second. The genius of Philip the Second might mislead them; and the issue of their affairs showed, that they had not chosen the most perfect standard. But, Sir, I am sure that I shall not be misled, when, in a case of constitutional difficulty, I consult the genius of the English constitution. Consulting at that oracle (it was with all due humility and piety) I found four capital examples in a similar case before me; those of Ireland, Wales, Chester, and Durham.

Ireland, before the English conquest, though never governed by a despotic power, had no parliament. How the English parliament itself was at that time modelled according to the present form, is disputed among antiquarians. But we have all the reason in the world to be assured that a form of parliament, such as England then enjoyed, she instantly communicated to Ireland; and we are equally sure that almost every successive improvement in constitutional liberty, as fast as it was made here, was transmitted thither. The feudal baronage, and the feudal knighthood, the roots of our primitive constitution, were early transplanted into that soil; and grew and flourished there. Magna Charta, if it did not give us originally the House of Commons, gave us at least a House of Commons of weight and consequence.

But your ancestors did not churlishly sit down alone to the feast of Magna Charta. Ireland was made immediately a partaker. This benefit of English laws and liberties, I confess, was not at first extended to *all* Ireland. Mark the consequence. English authority and English liberties had exactly the same boundaries. Your standard could never be advanced an inch before your privileges. Sir John Davis[15] shows beyond a doubt, that the refusal of a general communication of these rights was the true cause why Ireland was five hundred years in subduing; and after the vain projects of a military government, attempted in the reign of Queen Elizabeth, it was soon discovered, that nothing could make that country English, in civility and allegiance, but your laws and your forms of legislature. It was not English arms, but the English constitution, that conquered Ireland. From that time, Ireland has ever had a general parliament, as she had before a par-tial parliament. You changed the people; you altered the religion; but you never touched the form or the vital substance of free government in that kingdom. You deposed kings; you restored them; you altered the succession to theirs, as well as to your own crown; but you never altered their constitution; the principle of which was respected by usurpation; restored with the restoration of monarchy, and established, I trust, for ever, by the glorious Revolution.[16] This has made Ireland the great and flourishing kingdom that it is; and from a disgrace and a burthen intolerable to this nation, has rendered her a principal part of our strength and ornament. This country cannot be said to have ever formally taxed her. The irregular things done in the confusion of mighty troubles, and on the hinge of great revolution, even if all were done that is said to have been done, form no example. If they have any effect in argument, they make an exception to prove the rule. None of your own liberties could stand a moment if the casual deviations from them, at such times, were suffered to be used as proofs of their nullity. By the lucrative amount of such casual breaches in the constitution, judge what the stated and fixed rule of supply has been in that kingdom. Your Irish pen-sioners would starve if they had no other fund to live on than taxes granted by English authority. Turn your eyes to those popular grants from whence all your great supplies are come; and learn to respect that only source of public wealth in the British empire.

My next example is Wales. This country was said to be reduced by Henry the Third. It was said more truly to be so by Edward the First. But though then conquered, it was not looked upon as any part of the realm of England. Its old constitution, whatever that might have been, was destroyed; and no good one was substituted in its place. The care of that tract was put into the hands of lords marchers – a form of government of a very singular kind; a strange heterogeneous monster, something between hostility and government; perhaps it has a sort of resemblance, according to the modes of those times, to that of commander-in-chief at present, to whom all civil power is granted as secondary. The manners of the Welsh nation followed the genius of the government; the people were ferocious, restive, savage, and uncultivated; sometimes composed, never pacified. Wales, within itself, was in perpetual disorder; and it kept the frontier of England in perpetual alarm. Benefits from it to the state there were none. Wales was only known to England by incursion and invasion.

Sir, during that state of things, parliament was not idle. They attempted to subdue the fierce spirit of the Welsh by all sorts of rigorous laws. They prohibited by statute the sending all sorts of arms into Wales, as you prohibit by proclamation (with something more of doubt on the legality) the sending arms to America. They disarmed the Welsh by statute, as you attempted (but still with more question on the legality) to disarm New England by an instruction. They made an act to drag offenders from Wales into England for trial, as you have done (but with more hardship) with regard to America. By another act, where one of the parties was an Englishman, they ordained, that his trial should be always by English. They made acts to restrain trade, as you do; and they prevented the Welsh from the use of fairs and markets, as you do the Americans from fisheries and foreign ports. In short, when the statute book was not quite so much swelled as it is now, you find no less than fifteen acts of penal regulation on the subject of Wales.

Here we rub our hands – A fine body of precedents for the authority of parliament and the use of it!– I admit it fully; and pray add likewise to these precedents, that all the while, Wales rid this kingdom like an *incubus*; that it was an unprofitable and oppressive burthen; and that an Englishman travelling in that country could not go six yards from the high road without being murdered.

The march of the human mind is slow. Sir, it was not, until

after two hundred years, discovered, that, by an eternal law, Providence had decreed vexation to violence, and poverty to rapine. Your ancestors did however at length open their eyes to the ill husbandry of injustice. They found that the tyranny of a free people could of all tyrannies the least be endured; and that laws made against a whole nation were not the most effectual methods for securing its obedience. Accordingly, in the twenty-seventh year of Henry VIII the course was entirely altered. With a preamble stating the entire and perfect rights of the crown of England, it gave to the Welsh all the rights and privileges of English subjects. A political order was established; the military power gave way to the civil; the marches were turned into counties. But that a nation should have a right to English liberties, and yet no share at all in the fundamental security of these liberties – the grant of their own property – seemed a thing so incongruous, that, eight years after, that is, in the thirty-fifth of that reign, a complete and not ill-proportioned representation by counties and boroughs was bestowed upon Wales, by act of parliament. From that moment, as by a charm, the tumults subsided, obedience was restored, peace, order and civilisation followed in the train of liberty. – When the day-star of the English constitution had arisen in their hearts, all was harmony within and without –

> – Simul alba nautis
>   Stella refulsit,
> Defluit saxis agitatus humor;
> Concidunt venti, fugiúntque nubes,
> Et minax (quòd sic voluere) ponto
>   Unda recumbit.[17]

The very same year the county palatine of Chester received the same relief from its oppressions, and the same remedy to its disorders. Before this time Chester was little less distempered than Wales. The inhabitants, without rights themselves, were the fittest to destroy the rights of others; and from thence Richard II drew the standing army of archers, with which for a time he oppressed England. The people of Chester applied to parliament in a petition penned as I shall read to you:

"To the king our sovereign lord, in most humble wise shown unto your excellent Majesty, the inhabitants of your Grace's county palatine of Chester; That where the said county palatine of Chester is and hath been always hitherto exempt, excluded and separated out and from your high court of parliament, to have any knights and burgesses within the said court; by reason whereof the said inhabitants have hitherto sustained manifold disherisons, losses, and damages, as well in their lands, goods, and bodies, as in the good, civil, and politic governance and maintenance of the commonwealth of their said country: (2.) And forasmuch as the said inhabitants have always hitherto been bound by the acts and statutes made and ordained by your said Highness, and your most noble progenitors, by authority of the said court, as far forth as other counties, cities, and boroughs have been, that have had their knights and burgesses within your said court of parliament, and yet have had neither knight no burgess there for the said county palatine; the said inhabitants, for lack thereof, have been oftentimes touched and grieved with acts and statutes made within the said court, as well derogatory unto the most ancient jurisdictions, liberties, and privileges of your said county palatine, as prejudicial unto the commonwealth, quietness, rest, and peace of your Grace's most bounden subjects inhabiting within the same."

What did parliament with this audacious address? – Reject it as a libel? Treat it as an affront to government? Spurn it as a derogation from the rights of legislature? Did they toss it over the table? Did they burn it by the hands of the common hangman? They took the petition of grievance, all rugged as it was, without softening or temperament, unpurged of the original bitterness and indignation of complaint; they made it the very preamble to their act of redress; and consecrated its principle to all ages in the sanctuary of legislation.

Here is my third example. It was attended with the success of the two former. Chester, civilised as well as Wales, has demonstrated that freedom, and not servitude, is the cure of anarchy; as religion, and not atheism, is the true remedy for superstition. Sir, this pattern of Chester was followed in the reign of Charles II with regard to the county palatine of Durham, which is my fourth example. This county had long lain out of the pale of free legislation. So scrupulously was the example of Chester followed, that the style of the preamble is nearly the same with that of the Chester act; and, without affecting the abstract extent of the authority of parliament, it recognises the equity of not suffering any considerable district, in which the British subjects may act as a body, to be taxed without their own voice in the grant.

Now if the doctrines of policy contained in these preambles, and the force of these examples in the acts of parliament, avail anything, what can be said against applying them with regard to America? Are not the people of America as much Englishmen as the Welsh? The preamble of the act of Henry VIII says, the Welsh speak a language no way resembling that of his Majesty's English subjects. Are the Americans not as numerous? If we may trust the learned and accurate Judge Barrington's[18] account of North Wales, and take that as a standard to measure the rest, there is no comparison. The people cannot amount to above 200,000; not a tenth part of the number in the colonies. Is America in rebellion? Wales was hardly ever free from it. Have you attempted to govern America by penal statutes? You made fifteen for Wales. But your legislative authority is perfect with regard to America; was it less perfect in Wales, Chester, and Durham? But America is virtually represented. What! does the electric force of virtual representation more easily pass over the Atlantic, than pervade Wales, which lies in your neighbourhood; or than Chester and Durham, surrounded by abundance of representation that is actual and palpable? But, Sir, your ancestors thought this sort of virtual representation, however ample, to be totally insufficient for the freedom of the inhabitants of territories that are so near, and comparatively so inconsiderable. How then can I think it sufficient for those which are infinitely greater, and infinitely more remote?

You will now, Sir, perhaps imagine, that I am on the point of proposing to you a scheme for a representation of the colonies in parliament. Perhaps I might be inclined to entertain some such thought; but a great flood stops me in my course. *Opposuit natura* – I cannot remove the eternal barriers of the creation. The thing, in that mode, I do not know to be possible. As I meddle with no theory, I do not absolutely assert the impracticability of such a representation. But I do not see my way to it; and those who have been more confident have not been more successful. However, the arm of public benevolence is not shortened; and there are often several means to the same end. What nature has disjoined in one way, wisdom may unite in another. When we cannot give the benefit as we would wish, let us not refuse it altogether. If we cannot give the principal, let us find a substitute. But how? Where? What substitute?

Fortunately I am not obliged for the ways and means of this

substitute to tax my own unproductive invention. I am not even obliged to go to the rich treasury of the fertile framers of imaginary commonwealths; not to the Republic of Plato; not to the Utopia of More; not to the Oceana of Harrington.[19] It is before me – it is at my feet, *and the rude swain treads daily on it with his clouted shoon*. I only wish you to recognise, for the theory, the ancient constitutional policy of this kingdom with regard to representation, as that policy has been declared in acts of parliament; and, as to the practice, to return to that mode which an uniform experience has marked out to you, as best; and in which you walked with security, advantage, and honour, until the year 1763.

My resolutions therefore mean to establish the equity and justice of a taxation of America, by *grant*, and not by *imposition*. To mark the *legal competency* of the colony assemblies for the support of their government in peace, and for public aids in time of war. To acknowledge that this legal competency has had a *dutiful and beneficial exercise*; and that experience has shown the *benefit of their grants*, and the *futility of parliamentary taxation as a method of supply*.

These solid truths compose six fundamental propositions. There are three more resolutions corollary to these. If you admit the first set, you can hardly reject the others. But if you admit the first, I shall be far from solicitous whether you accept or refuse the last. I think these six massive pillars will be of strength sufficient to support the temple of British concord. I have no more doubt than I entertain of my existence, that, if you admitted these, you would command an immediate peace; and, with but tolerable future management, a lasting obedience in America. I am not arrogant in this confident assurance. The propositions are all mere matters of fact; and if they are such facts as draw irresistible conclusions even in the stating, this is the power of truth, and not any management of mine.

Sir, I shall open the whole plan to you, together with such observations on the motions as may tend to illustrate them where they may want explanation. The first is a resolution – "That the colonies and plantations of Great Britain in North America, consisting of fourteen separate governments, and containing two millions and upwards of free inhabitants, have not had the liberty and privilege of electing and sending any knights and burgesses, or others, to represent them in the high court of parliament." –

This is a plain matter of fact, necessary to be laid down, and (excepting the description) it is laid down in the language of the constitution; it is taken nearly *verbatim* from acts of parliament.

The second is like unto the first – "That the said colonies and plantations have been liable to, and bounden by, several subsidies, payments, rates, and taxes, given and granted by parliament, though the said colonies and plantations have not their knights and burgesses, in the said high court of parliament, of their own election, to represent the condition of their country; by lack whereof they have been oftentimes touched and grieved by subsidies given, granted, and assented to, in the said court, in a manner prejudicial to the commonwealth, quietness, rest, and peace of the subjects inhabiting within the same."

Is this description too hot, or too cold, too strong, or too weak? Does it arrogate too much to the supreme legislature? Does it lean too much to the claims of the people? If it runs into any of these errors, the fault is not mine. It is the language of your own ancient acts of parliament.

> *Non meus hic sermo, sed quæ præcepit Ofellus,*
> *Rusticus, abnormis sapiens.*[20]

It is the genuine produce of the ancient, rustic, manly, home-bred sense of this country. – I did not dare to rub off a particle of the venerable rust that rather adorns and preserves, than destroys, the metal. It would be a profanation to touch with a tool the stones which construct the sacred altar of peace. I would not violate with modern polish the ingenuous and noble roughness of these truly constitutional materials. Above all things, I was resolved not to be guilty of tampering: the odious vice of restless and unstable minds. I put my foot in the tracks of our forefathers, where I can neither wander nor stumble. Determining to fix articles of peace, I was resolved not to be wise beyond what was written; I was resolved to use nothing else than the form of sound words; to let others abound in their own sense; and carefully to abstain from all expressions of my own. What the law has said, I say. In all things else I am silent. I have no organ but for her words. This, if it be not ingenious, I am sure is safe.

There are indeed words expressive of grievance in this second resolution, which those who are resolved always to be in the right will deny to contain matter of fact, as applied to the present case; although parliament thought them true, with regard to the counties of Chester and Durham. They will deny that the Americans were ever "touched and grieved" with the taxes. If they consider nothing in taxes but their weight as pecuniary impositions, there might be some pretence for this denial. But men may be sorely touched and deeply grieved in their privileges, as well as in their purses. Men may lose little in property by the act which takes away all their freedom. When a man is robbed of a trifle on the highway, it is not the two-pence lost that constitutes the capital outrage. This is not confined to privileges. Even ancient indulgences withdrawn, without offence on the part of those who enjoyed such favours, operate as grievances. But were the Americans then not touched and grieved by the taxes, in some measure, merely as taxes? If so, why were they almost all either wholly repealed or exceedingly reduced? Were they not touched and grieved even by the regulating duties of the sixth of George II? Else why were the duties first reduced to one third in 1764, and afterwards to a third of that third in the year 1766? Were they not touched and grieved by the stamp act?[21] I shall say they were, until that tax is revived. Were they not touched and grieved by the duties of 1767, which were likewise repealed, and which Lord Hillsborough[22] tells you (for the ministry) were laid contrary to the true principle of commerce? Is not the assurance given by that noble person to the colonies of a resolution to lay no more taxes on them, an admission that taxes would touch and grieve them? Is not the resolution of the noble lord in the blue riband, now standing on your journals, the strongest of all proofs that parliamentary subsidies really touched and grieved them? Else why all these changes, modifications, repeals, assurances, and resolutions?

The next proposition is – "That, from the distance of the said colonies, and from other circumstances, no method hath hitherto been devised for procuring a representation in parliament for the said colonies." This is an assertion of a fact. I go no further on the paper; though, in my private judgment, an useful representation is impossible; I am sure it is not desired by them; nor ought it perhaps by us; but I abstain from opinions.

The fourth resolution is – "That each of the said colonies hath within itself a body, chosen in part, or in the whole, by the freemen, freeholders, or other free inhabitants thereof, commonly called the General Assembly, or General Court; with powers legally to raise, levy, and assess, according to the several usage of such colonies, duties and taxes towards defraying all sorts of public services."

This competence in the colony assemblies is certain. It is proved by the whole tenor of their acts of supply in all the assemblies, in which the constant style of granting is, "an aid to his Majesty;" and acts granting to the crown have regularly for near a century passed the public offices without dispute. Those who have been pleased paradoxically to deny this right, holding that none but the British parliament can grant to the crown, are wished to look to what is done, not only in the colonies, but in Ireland, in one uniform unbroken tenor every session. Sir, I am surprised that this doctrine should come from some of the law servants of the crown. I say, that if the crown could be responsible, his Majesty – but certainly the ministers, and even these law officers themselves, through whose hands the acts pass biennially in Ireland, or annually in the colonies, are in an habitual course of committing impeachable offences. What habitual offenders have been all presidents of the council, all secretaries of state, all first lords of trade, all attornies and all solicitors general! However, they are safe; as no one impeaches them; and there is no ground of charge against them, except in their own unfounded theories.

The fifth resolution is also a resolution of fact – "That the said general assemblies, general courts, or other bodies legally qualified as aforesaid, have at sundry times freely granted several large subsidies and public aids for his Majesty's service, according to their abilities, when required thereto by letter from one of his Majesty's principal secretaries of state; and that their right to grant the same, and their cheerfulness and sufficiency in the said grants, have been at sundry times acknowledged by parliament." To say nothing of their great expenses in the Indian wars; and not to take their exertion in foreign ones, so high as the supplies in the year 1695; not to go back to their public contributions in the year 1710; I shall begin to travel only where the journals give me light; resolving to deal in nothing but fact, authenticated by parliamentary record; and to build myself wholly on that solid basis.

On the 4th of April, 1748,* a committee of this House came to the following resolution:

* Journals of the House, vol. xxv.

"Resolved,

"That it is the opinion of this committee, *That it is just and reasonable* that the several provinces and colonies of Massachusetts Bay, New Hampshire, Connecticut, and Rhode Island, be reimbursed the expenses they have been at in taking and securing to the crown of Great Britain the island of Cape Breton and its dependencies."

These expenses were immense for such colonies. They were above £200,000 sterling; money first raised and advanced on their public credit.

On the 28th of January, 1756,[*] a message from the king came to us, to this effect – "His Majesty, being sensible of the zeal and vigour with which his faithful subjects of certain colonies in North America have exerted themselves in defence of his Majesty's just rights and possessions, recommends it to this House to take the same into their consideration, and to enable his Majesty to give them such assistance as may be a *proper reward and encouragement.*"

On the 3rd of February, 1756,[†] the House came to a suitable resolution, expressed in words nearly the same as those of the message: but with the further addition, that the money then voted was as an *encouragement* to the colonies to exert themselves with vigour. It will not be necessary to go through all the testimonies which your own records have given to the truth of my resolutions, I will only refer you to the places in the journals:

Vol. xxvii. – 16th and 19th May, 1757.
Vol. xxviii. – June 1st, 1758 – April 26th and 30th, 1759
         – March 26th and 31st, and April 28th, 1760
         – Jan. 9th and 20th, 1761.
Vol. xxix. – Jan. 22nd and 26th, 1762 – March 14th and 17th, 1763.

Sir, here is the repeated acknowledgment of parliament, that the colonies not only gave, but gave to satiety. This nation has formally acknowledged two things; first, that the colonies had gone beyond their abilities, parliament having thought it necessary to reimburse them; secondly, that they had acted legally and

[*] Journals of the House, vol. xxvii.
[†] Ibid., vol. xxvii.

laudably in their grants of money, and their maintenance of troops, since the compensation is expressly given as reward and encouragement. Reward is not bestowed for acts that are un-lawful; and encouragement is not held out to things that deserve reprehension. My resolution therefore does nothing more than collect into one proposition, what is scattered through your journals. I give you nothing but your own; and you cannot refuse in the gross, what you have so often acknowledged in detail. The admission of this, which will be so honourable to them and to you, will, indeed, be mortal to all the miserable stories, by which the passions of the misguided people have been engaged in an unhappy system. The people heard, indeed, from the beginning of these disputes, one thing continually dinned in their ears, that reason and justice demanded, that the Americans, who paid no taxes, should be compelled to contribute. How did that fact, of their paying nothing, stand, when the taxing system began? When Mr. Grenville[23] began to form his system of American revenue, he stated in this House, that the colonies were then in debt two million six hundred thousand pounds sterling money; and was of opinion they would discharge that debt in four years. On this state, those untaxed people were actually subject to the payment of taxes to the amount of six hundred and fifty thousand a year. In fact, however, Mr. Grenville was mistaken. The funds given for sinking the debt did not prove quite so ample as both the colonies and he expected. The calculation was too sanguine; the reduction was not completed till some years after, and at different times in different colonies. However, the taxes after the war continued too great to bear any addition, with prudence or propriety; and when the burthens imposed in consequence of former requisitions were discharged, our tone became too high to resort again to requisition. No colony, since that time, ever has had any requisition whatsoever made to it.

We see the sense of the crown, and the sense of parliament, on the productive nature of a *revenue by grant*. Now search the same journals for the produce of the *revenue by imposition* – Where is it? – let us know the volume and the page – what is the gross, what is the net produce? – to what service is it applied? – how have you appropriated its surplus? – What, can none of the many skilful index-makers that we are now employing, find any trace of it? – Well, let them and that rest together. – But are the journals, which say nothing of the revenue, as silent on the discontent? – Oh no! a child may find it. It is the melancholy burthen and blot of every page.

I think then I am, from those journals, justified in the sixth and last resolution, which is – "That it hath been found by experience, that the manner of granting the said supplies and aids, by the said general assemblies, hath been more agreeable to the said colonies, and more beneficial, and conducive to the public service, than the mode of giving and granting aids in parliament, to be raised and paid in the said colonies." This makes the whole of the fundamental part of the plan. The conclusion is irresistible. You cannot say, that you were driven by any necessity to an exercise of the utmost rights of legislature. You cannot assert, that you took on yourselves the task of imposing colony taxes, from the want of another legal body, that is competent to the purpose of supplying the exigencies of the state without wounding the prejudices of the people. Neither is it true that the body so qualified, and having that competence, had neglected the duty.

The question now, on all this accumulated matter, is; – whether you will choose to abide by a profitable experience, or a mischievous theory; whether you choose to build on imagination, or fact; whether you prefer enjoyment, or hope; satisfaction in your subjects, or discontent?

If these propositions are accepted, everything which has been made to enforce a contrary system, must, I take it for granted, fall along with it. On that ground, I have drawn the following resolution, which, when it comes to be moved, will naturally be divided in a proper manner: "That it may be proper to repeal an act, made in the seventh year of the reign of his present Majesty, intituled, An act for granting certain duties in the British colonies and plantations in America; for allowing a drawback of the duties of customs upon the exportation from this kingdom, of coffee and cocoa-nuts of the produce of the said colonies or plantations; for discontinuing the drawbacks payable on China earthenware exported to America; and for more effectually preventing the clandestine running of goods in the said colonies and plantations. – And that it may be proper to repeal an act, made in the fourteenth year of the reign of his present Majesty, intituled, An act to discontinue, in such manner, and for such time, as are therein mentioned, the landing and discharging, lading or shipping, of goods, wares, and merchandise, at the town and within the harbour of Boston, in the province of Massachusetts Bay, in

North America. – And that it may be proper to repeal an act, made in the fourteenth year of the reign of his present Majesty, intituled, An act for the impartial administration of justice, in the cases of persons questioned for any acts done by them, in the, execution of the law, or for the suppression of riots and tumults, in the province of Massachusetts Bay, in New England. – And that it may be proper to repeal an act, made in the fourteenth year of the reign of his present Majesty, intituled, An act for the better regulating the government of the province of Massachu-setts Bay, in New England. – And, also, that it may be proper to explain and amend an act, made in the thirty-fifth year of the reign of King Henry the Eighth, intituled, An act for the trial of treasons committed out of the king's dominions.''

I wish, Sir, to repeal the Boston Port Bill, because (indepen-dently of the dangerous precedent of suspending the rights of the subject during the king's pleasure) it was passed, as I apprehend, with less regularity, and on more partial principles, than it ought. The corporation of Boston was not heard before it was con-demned. Other towns, full as guilty as she was, have not had their ports blocked up. Even the restraining bill of the present session does not go to the length of the Boston Port Act. The same ideas of prudence, which induced you not to extend equal punishment to equal guilt, even when you were punishing, induced me, who mean not to chastise, but to reconcile, to be satisfied with the punishment already partially inflicted.

Ideas of prudence and accommodation to circumstances, prevent you from taking away the charters of Connecticut and Rhode Island, as you have taken away that of Massachusetts colony, though the crown has far less power in the two former provinces than it enjoyed in the latter; and though the abuses have been full as great, and as flagrant, in the exempted as in the punished. The same reasons of prudence and accommodation have weight with me in restoring the charter of Massachusetts Bay. Besides, Sir, the act which changes the charter of Massachu-setts is in many particulars so exceptionable, that if I did not wish absolutely to repeal, I would by all means desire to alter it; as several of its provisions tend to the subversion of all public and private justice. Such, among others, is the power in the governor to change the sheriff at his pleasure; and to make a new returning officer for every special cause. It is shameful to behold such a regulation standing among English laws.

The act for bringing persons accused of committing murder under the orders of government to England for trial is but temporary. That act has calculated the probable duration of our quarrel with the colonies; and is accommodated to that supposed duration. I would hasten the happy moment of reconciliation; and therefore must, on my principle, get rid of that most justly obnoxious act.

The act of Henry the Eighth, for the trial of treasons, I do not mean to take away, but to confine it to its proper bounds and original intention; to make it expressly for trial of treasons (and the greatest treasons may be committed) in places where the jurisdiction of the crown does not extend.

Having guarded the privileges of local legislature, I would next secure to the colonies a fair and unbiassed judicature; for which purpose, Sir, I propose the following resolution: "That, from the time when the general assembly or general court of any colony or plantation in North America, shall have appointed by act of assembly, duly confirmed, a settled salary to the offices of the chief justice and other judges of the superior court, it may be proper that the said chief justice and other judges of the superior courts of such colony, shall hold his and their office and offices during their good behaviour; and shall not be removed therefrom, but when the said removal shall be adjudged by his Majesty in council, upon a hearing on complaint from the general assembly, or on a complaint from the governor, or council, or the house of representatives severally, or of the colony in which the said chief justice and other judges have exercised the said offices."

The next resolution relates to the courts of admiralty.

It is this: – "That it may be proper to regulate the courts of admiralty, or vice-admiralty, authorised by the fifteenth chapter of the fourth of George the Third, in such a manner as to make the same more commodious to those who sue, or are sued, in the said courts, and to provide for the more decent maintenance of the judges in the same."

These courts I do not wish to take away; they are in themselves proper establishments. This court is one of the capital securities of the act of navigation. The extent of its jurisdiction, indeed, has been increased; but this is altogether as proper, and is indeed on many accounts more eligible, where new powers were wanted, than a court absolutely new. But courts incommodiously situated, in effect, deny justice; and a court, partaking in the fruits of its own condemnation, is a robber. The congress complain, and complain justly, of this grievance.*

These are the three consequential propositions. I have thought of two or three more; but they come rather too near detail, and to the province of executive government; which I wish parliament always to superintend, never to assume. If the first six are granted, congruity will carry the latter three. If not, the things that remain unrepealed will be, I hope, rather unseemly encumbrances on the building, than very materially detrimental to its strength and stability.

Here, Sir, I should close; but I plainly perceive some objections remain, which I ought, if possible, to remove. The first will be, that, in resorting to the doctrine of our ancestors, as contained in the preamble to the Chester act, I prove too much; that the grievance from a want of representation, stated in that preamble, goes to the whole of legislation as well as to taxation. And that the colonies, grounding themselves upon that doctrine, will apply it to all parts of legislative authority.

To this objection, with all possible deference and humility, and wishing as little as any man living to impair the smallest particle of our supreme authority, I answer, that *the words are the words of parliament, and not mine*; and, that all false and inconclusive inferences, drawn from them, are not mine; for I heartily disclaim any such inference. I have chosen the words of an act of parliament, which Mr. Grenville, surely a tolerably zealous and very judicious advocate for the sovereignty of parliament, formerly moved to have read at your table in confirmation of his tenets. It is true, that Lord Chatham[24] considered these preambles as declaring strongly in favour of his opinions. He was a no less powerful advocate for the privileges of the Americans. Ought I not from hence to presume, that these preambles are as favourable as possible to both, when properly understood; favourable both to the rights of parliament, and to the privilege of the dependencies of this crown? But, Sir, the object of grievance in my resolution I have not taken from the Chester, but from the Durham act, which confines the hardship of want of representation to the case of subsidies; and which therefore falls in exactly

*The Solicitor-general informed Mr. B. when the resolutions were separately moved, that the grievance of the judges partaking of the profits of the seizure had been redressed by office; accordingly the resolution was amended.

with the case of the colonies. But whether the unrepresented counties were *de jure*, or *de facto*, bound, the preambles do not accurately distinguish, nor indeed was it necessary; for, whether *de jure*, or *de facto*, the legislature thought the exercise of the power of taxing, as of right, or as of fact without right, equally a grievance, and equally oppressive.

I do not know that the colonies have, in any general way, or in any cool hour, gone much beyond the demand of immunity in relation to taxes. It is not fair to judge of the temper or dispositions of any man, or any set of men, when they are composed and at rest, from their conduct, or their expressions, in a state of disturbance and irritation. It is besides a very great mistake to imagine, that mankind follow up practically any speculative principle, either of government or of freedom, as far as it will go in argument and logical illation. We Englishmen stop very short of the principles upon which we support any given part of our constitution; or even the whole of it together. I could easily, if I had not already tired you, give you very striking and convincing instances of it. This is nothing but what is natural and proper. All government, indeed every human benefit and enjoyment, every virtue, and every prudent act, is founded on compromise and barter. We balance inconveniences; we give and take; we remit some rights that we may enjoy others; and we choose rather to be happy citizens than subtle disputants. As we must give away some natural liberty, to enjoy civil advantages; so we must sacrifice some civil liberties, for the advantages to be derived from the communion and fellowship of a great empire. But, in all fair dealings, the thing bought must bear some proportion to the purchase paid. None will barter away the immediate jewel of his soul. Though a great house is apt to make slaves haughty, yet it is purchasing a part of the artificial importance of a great empire too dear, to pay for it all essential rights, and all the intrinsic dignity of human nature. None of us who would not risk his life rather than fall under a government purely arbitrary. But although there are some amongst us who think our constitution wants many improvements, to make it a complete system of liberty; perhaps none who are of that opinion would think it right to aim at such improvement, by disturbing his country, and risking everything that is dear to him. In every arduous enterprise, we consider what we are to lose as well as what we are to gain;

and the more and better stake of liberty every people possess, the less they will hazard in a vain attempt to make it more. These are *the cords of man.* Man acts from adequate motives relative to his interest; and not on metaphysical speculations. Aristotle, the great master of reasoning, cautions us, and with great weight and propriety, against this species of delusive geometrical accuracy in moral arguments, as the most fallacious of all sophistry.

The Americans will have no interest contrary to the grandeur and glory of England, when they are not oppressed by the weight of it; and they will rather be inclined to respect the acts of a superintending legislature, when they see them the acts of that power, which is itself the security, not the rival, of their secondary importance. In this assurance, my mind most perfectly acquiesces: and I confess, I feel not the least alarm from the discontents which are to arise from putting people at their ease; nor do I apprehend the destruction of this empire, from giving, by an act of free grace and indulgence, to two millions of my fellow-citizens some share of those rights, upon which I have always been taught to value myself.

It is said, indeed, that this power of granting, vested in American assemblies, would dissolve the unity of the empire; which was preserved entire, although Wales, and Chester, and Durham were added to it. Truly, Mr. Speaker, I do not know what this unity means; nor has it ever been heard of, that I know, in the constitutional policy of this country. The very idea of subordination of parts, excludes this notion of simple and undivided unity. England is the head; but she is not the head and the members too. Ireland has ever had from the beginning a separate, but not an independent, legislature; which, far from distracting, promoted the union of the whole. Everything was sweetly and harmoniously disposed through both islands for the conservation of English dominion, and the communication of English liberties. I do not see that the same principles might not be carried into twenty islands, and with the same good effect. This is my model with regard to America, as far as the internal circumstances of the two countries are the same. I know no other unity of this empire, than I can draw from its example during these periods, when it seemed to my poor understanding more united than it is now, or than it is likely to be by the present methods.

But since I speak of these methods, I recollect, Mr. Speaker,

almost too late, that I promised, before I finished, to say something of the proposition of the noble lord* on the floor, which
has been so lately received, and stands on your journals. I must
be deeply concerned, whenever it is my misfortune to continue
a difference with the majority of this House. But as the reasons
for that difference are my apology for thus troubling you, suffer
me to state them in a very few words. I shall compress them into
as small a body as I possibly can, having already debated that
matter at large, when the question was before the committee.

First, then, I cannot admit that proposition of a ransom by
auction; – because it is a mere project. It is a thing new; unheard
of; supported by no experience; justified by no analogy; without
example of our ancestors, or root in the constitution.

It is neither regular parliamentary taxation, nor colony grant.
Experimentum in corpore vili,[25] is a good rule, which will ever make
me adverse to any trial of experiments on what is certainly the
most valuable of all subjects, the peace of this empire.

Secondly, it is an experiment which must be fatal in the end
to our constitution. For what is it but a scheme for taxing the
colonies in the antechamber of the noble lord and his successors?
To settle the quotas and proportions in this House, is clearly
impossible. You, Sir, may flatter yourself you shall sit a state
auctioneer, with your hammer in your hand, and knock down
to each colony as it bids. But to settle (on the plan laid down by
the noble lord) the true proportional payment for four or five and
twenty governments, according to the absolute and the relative
wealth of each, and according to the British proportion of wealth
and burthen, is a wild and chimerical notion. This new taxation
must therefore come in by the back-door of the constitution.
Each quota must be brought to this House ready formed; you
can neither add nor alter. You must register it. You can do nothing further. For on what grounds can you deliberate either before
or after the proposition? You cannot hear the counsel for all these
provinces, quarrelling each on its own quantity of payment, and
its proportion to others. If you should attempt it, the committee
of provincial ways and means, or by whatever other name it will
delight to be called, must swallow up all the time of parliament.

Thirdly, it does not give satisfaction to the complaint of the
colonies. They complain, that they are taxed without their

* Lord North.

consent; you answer, that you will fix the sum at which they shall be taxed. That is, you give them the very grievance for the remedy. You tell them indeed, that you will leave the mode to themselves. I really beg pardon: it gives me pain to mention it; but you must be sensible that you will not perform this part of the compact. For, suppose the colonies were to lay the duties, which furnished their contingent, upon the importation of your manufactures; you know you would never suffer such a tax to be laid. You know, too, that you would not suffer many other modes of taxation. So that, when you come to explain yourself, it will be found, that you will neither leave to themselves the quantum nor the mode; nor indeed anything. The whole is delusion from one end to the other.

Fourthly, this method of ransom by auction, unless it be *universally* accepted, will plunge you into great and inextricable difficulties. In what year of our Lord are the proportions of payments to be settled? To say nothing of the impossibility that colony agents should have general powers of taxing the colonies at their discretion; consider, I implore you, that the communication by special messages, and orders between these agents and their constituents on each variation of the case, when the parties come to contend together, and to dispute on their relative proportions, will be a matter of delay, perplexity, and confusion that never can have an end.

If all the colonies do not appear at the outcry, what is the condition of those assemblies, who offer by themselves or their agents, to tax themselves up to your ideas of their proportion? The refractory colonies, who refuse all composition, will remain taxed only to your old impositions, which, however grievous in principle, are trifling as to production. The obedient colonies in this scheme are heavily taxed; the refractory remain unburthened. What will you do? Will you lay new and heavier taxes by parliament on the disobedient? Pray consider in what way you can do it. You are perfectly convinced, that, in the way of taxing, you can do nothing but at the ports. Now suppose it is Virginia that refuses to appear at your auction, while Maryland and North Carolina bid handsomely for their ransom, and are taxed to your quota, how will you put these colonies on a par? Will you tax the tobacco of Virginia? If you do, you give its death-wound to your English revenue at home, and to one of the very greatest articles of your own foreign trade. If you tax the import of that rebellious colony, what do you tax but your own manufactures, or the goods of some other obedient and already well-taxed colony? Who has said one word on this labyrinth of detail, which bewilders you more and more as you enter into it? Who has presented, who can present you with a clue, to lead you out of it? I think, Sir, it is impossible, that you should not recollect that the colony bounds are so implicated in one another, (you know it by your other experiments in the bill for prohibiting the New England fishery,) that you can lay no possible restraints on almost any of them which may not be presently eluded, if you do not confound the innocent with the guilty, and burthen those whom, upon every principle, you ought to exonerate. He must be grossly ignorant of America, who thinks that, without falling into this confusion of all rules of equity and policy, you can restrain any single colony, especially Virginia and Maryland, the central and most important of them all.

Let it also be considered, that, either in the present confusion you settle a permanent contingent, which will and must be trifling; and then you have no effectual revenue: or you change the quota at every exigency; and then on every new repartition you will have a new quarrel.

Reflect besides, that when you have fixed a quota for every colony, you have not provided for prompt and punctual payment. Suppose one, two, five, ten years' arrears. You cannot issue a treasury extent against the failing colony. You must make new Boston Port Bills, new restraining laws, new acts for dragging men to England for trial. You must send out new fleets, new armies. All is to begin again. From this day forward the empire is never to know an hour's tranquillity. An intestine fire will be kept alive in the bowels of the colonies, which one time or other must consume this whole empire. I allow indeed that the empire of Germany raises her revenue and her troops by quotas and contingents; but the revenue of the empire, and the army of the empire, is the worst revenue and the worst army in the world.

Instead of a standing revenue, you will therefore have a perpetual quarrel. Indeed the noble lord, who proposed this project of a ransom by auction, seemed himself to be of that opinion. His project was rather designed for breaking the union of the colonies, than for establishing a revenue. He confessed, he apprehended that his proposal would not be to *their taste*. I say, this scheme of disunion seems to be at the bottom of the project; for

I will not suspect that the noble lord meant nothing but merely to delude the nation by an airy phantom which he never intended to realise. But whatever his views may be; as I propose the peace and union of the colonies as the very foundation of my plan, it cannot accord with one whose foundation is perpetual discord.

Compare the two. This I offer to give you is plain and simple. The other full of perplexed and intricate mazes. This is mild; that harsh. This is found by experience effectual for its purposes; the other is a new project. This is universal; the other calculated for certain colonies only. This is immediate in its conciliatory operation; the other remote, contingent, full of hazard. Mine is what becomes the dignity of a ruling people; gratuitous, unconditional, and not held out as matter of bargain and sale. I have done my duty in proposing it to you. I have indeed tired you by a long discourse; but this is the misfortune of those to whose influence nothing will be conceded, and who must win every inch of their ground by argument. You have heard me with goodness. May you decide with wisdom! For my part, I feel my mind greatly disburthened by what I have done to-day. I have been the less fearful of trying your patience, because on this subject I mean to spare it altogether in future. I have this comfort, that in every stage of the American affairs, I have steadily opposed the measures that have produced the confusion, and may bring on the destruction, of this empire. I now go so far as to risk a proposal of my own. If I cannot give peace to my country, I give it to my conscience.

But what (says the financier) is peace to us without money? Your plan gives us no revenue. No! But it does – For it secures to the subject the power of REFUSAL; the first of all revenues. Experience is a cheat, and fact a liar, if this power in the subject of proportioning his grant, or of not granting at all, has not been found the richest mine of revenue ever discovered by the skill or by the fortune of man. It does not indeed vote you £152,750:11:2¾ths, nor any other paltry limited sum. – But it gives the strong box itself, the fund, the bank, from whence only revenues can arise amongst a people sensible of freedom: *Posita luditur arca.*[26] Cannot you in England; cannot you at this time of day; cannot you, a House of Commons, trust to the principle which has raised so mighty a revenue, and accumulated a debt of near 140 millions in this country? Is this principle to be true in England, and false everywhere else? Is it not true in Ireland?

Has it not hitherto been true in the colonies? (Why should you presume, that, in any country, a body duly constituted for any function, will neglect to perform its duty, and abdicate its trust? Such a presumption would go against all governments in all modes. But, in truth, this dread of penury of supply, from a free assembly, has no foundation in nature. For first observe, that, besides the desire which all men have naturally of supporting the honour of their own government, that sense of dignity, and that security to property, which ever attends freedom, has a tendency to increase the stock of the free community. Most may be taken where most is accumulated. And what is the soil or climate where experience has not uniformly proved, that the voluntary flow of heaped-up plenty, bursting from the weight of its own rich luxuriance, has ever run with a more copious stream of revenue, than could be squeezed from the dry husks of oppressed indigence, by the straining of all the politic machinery in the world.

Next we know, that parties must ever exist in a free country. We know too, that the emulations of such parties, their contradictions, their reciprocal necessities, their hopes, and their fears, must send them all in their turns to him that holds the balance of the state. The parties are the gamesters; but government keeps the table, and is sure to be the winner in the end. When this game is played, I really think it is more to be feared that the people will be exhausted, than that government will not be supplied. Whereas, whatever is got by acts of absolute power ill obeyed, because odious, or by contracts ill kept, because constrained, will be narrow, feeble, uncertain, and precarious. "*Ease would retract vows made in pain, as violent and void.*"[27]

I, for one, protest against compounding our demands: I declare against compounding for a poor limited sum, the immense, overgrowing, eternal debt, which is due to generous government from protected freedom. And so may I speed in the great object I propose to you, as I think it would not only be an act of injustice, but would be the worst economy in the world, to compel the colonies to a sum certain, either in the way of ransom, or in the way of compulsory compact.

But to clear up my ideas on this subject – a revenue from America transmitted hither – do not delude yourselves – you never can receive it – No, not a shilling. We have experience that from remote countries it is not to be expected. If, when you attempted to extract revenue from Bengal,[28] you were obliged to return in loan what you had taken in imposition; what can you expect from North America? For certainly, if ever there was a country qualified to produce wealth, it is India; or an institution fit for the transmission, it is the East India Company. America has none of these aptitudes. If America gives you taxable objects, on which you lay your duties here, and gives you, at the same time, a surplus by a foreign sale of her commodities to pay the duties on these objects, which you tax at home, she has performed her part to the British revenue. But with regard to her own internal establishments; she may, I doubt not she will, contribute in moderation. I say in moderation; for she ought not to be permitted to exhaust herself. She ought to be reserved to a war; the weight of which, with the enemies that we are most likely to have, must be considerable in her quarter of the globe. There she may serve you, and serve you essentially.

For that service, for all service, whether of revenue, trade or empire, my trust is in her interest in the British constitution. My hold of the colonies is in the close affection which grows from common names, from kindred blood, from similar privileges, and equal protection. These are ties, which, though light as air, are as strong as links of iron. Let the colonies always keep the idea of their civil rights associated with your government; – they will cling and grapple to you; and no force under heaven will be of power to tear them from their allegiance. But let it be once understood, that your government may be one thing, and their privileges another; that these two things may exist without any mutual relation; the cement is gone; the cohesion is loosened; and everything hastens to decay and dissolution. As long as you have the wisdom to keep the sovereign authority of this country as the sanctuary of liberty, the sacred temple consecrated to our common faith, wherever the chosen race and sons of England worship freedom, they will turn their faces towards you. The more they multiply, the more friends you will have; the more ardently they love liberty, the more perfect will be their obedience. Slavery they can have anywhere. It is a weed that grows in every soil. They may have it from Spain, they may have it from Prussia. But, until you become lost to all feeling of your true interest and your natural dignity, freedom they can have from none but you. This is the commodity of price, of which you have the monopoly. This is the true act of navigation, which binds to you the commerce of the colonies, and through them secures to you the wealth of the world. Deny them this participation of freedom, and you break that sole bond, which originally made, and must still preserve, the unity of the empire. Do not entertain so weak an imagination, as that your registers and your bonds, your affidavits and your sufferances, your cockets and your clearances, are what form the great securities of your commerce. Do not dream that your letters of office, and your instructions, and your suspending clauses, are the things that hold together the great contexture of the mysterious whole. These things do not make your government. Dead instruments, passive tools as they are, it is the spirit of the English communion that gives all their life and efficacy to them. It is the spirit of the English constitution, which, infused through the mighty mass, pervades, feeds, unites, invigorates, vivifies every part of the empire, even down to the minutest member.

Is it not the same virtue which does everything for us here in England? Do you imagine then, that it is the land tax act which raises your revenue? that it is the annual vote in the committee of supply which gives you your army? or that it is the mutiny bill which inspires it with bravery and discipline? No! surely no! It is the love of the people; it is their attachment to their government, from the sense of the deep stake they have in such a glorious institution, which gives you your army and your navy, and infuses into both that liberal obedience, without which your army would be a base rabble, and your navy nothing but rotten timber.

All this, I know well enough, will sound wild and chimerical to the profane herd of those vulgar and mechanical politicians, who have no place among us; a sort of people who think that nothing exists but what is gross and material; and who therefore, far from being qualified to be directors of the great movement of empire, are not fit to turn a wheel in the machine. But to men truly initiated and rightly taught, these ruling and master principles, which, in the opinion of such men as I have mentioned, have no substantial existence, are in truth everything, and all in all. Magnanimity in politics is not seldom the truest wisdom; and a great empire and little minds go ill together. If we are conscious of our situation, and glow with zeal to fill our place as becomes our station and ourselves, we ought to auspicate all our public proceedings on America with the old warning of the church, *Sursum corda!*[29] We ought to elevate our minds to the greatness of that trust to which the order of Providence has called us. By adverting to the dignity of this high calling, our ancestors have turned a savage wilderness into a glorious empire; and have made the most extensive, and the only honourable conquests, not by destroying, but by promoting the wealth, the number, the happiness of the human race. Let us get an American revenue as we have got an American empire. English privileges have made it all that it is; English privileges alone will make it all it can be.

In full confidence of this unalterable truth, I now (*quod felix faustumque sit*)[30] lay the first stone of the temple of peace; and I move you,

"That the colonies and plantations of Great Britain in North America, consisting of fourteen separate governments, and containing two millions and upwards of free inhabitants, have not had the liberty and privilege of electing and sending any knights and burgesses, or others, to represent them in the high court of parliament."

Upon this resolution, the previous question was put, and carried; – for the previous question 270, against it 78.

As the propositions were opened separately in the body of the speech, the reader perhaps may wish to see the whole of them together, in the form in which they were moved for.

"Moved,
"That the colonies and plantations of Great Britain in North America, consisting of fourteen separate governments, and containing two millions and upwards of free inhabitants, have not had the liberty and privilege of electing and sending any knights and burgesses, or others, to represent them in the high court of parliament."

"That the said colonies and plantations have been made liable to, and bounden by, several subsidies, payments, rates, and taxes, given and granted by parliament; though the said colonies and plantations have not their knights and burgesses, in the said high court of parliament, of their own election, to represent the condition of their country; *by lack whereof, they have been oftentimes touched and grieved by subsidies given, granted, and assented to, in the said court, in a manner prejudicial to the commonwealth, quietness, rest, and peace, of the subjects inhabiting within the same.*"

"That, from the distance of the said colonies, and from other circumstances, no method hath hitherto been devised for procuring a representation in parliament for the said colonies."

"That each of the said colonies hath within itself a body, chosen, in part or in the whole, by the freemen, freeholders, or other free inhabitants thereof, commonly called the general assembly, or general court; with powers legally to raise, levy, and assess, according to the several usage of such colonies, duties and taxes towards defraying all sorts of public services."*

"That the said general assemblies, general courts, or other bodies, legally qualified as aforesaid, have at sundry tunes freely granted several large subsidies and public aids for his Majesty's service, according to their abilities, when required thereto by letter from one of his Majesty's principal secretaries of state; and that their right to grant the same, and their cheerfulness and sufficiency in the said grants, have been at sundry times acknowledged by parliament."

"That it hath been found by experience, that the manner of granting the said supplies and aids, by the said general assemblies, hath been more agreeable to the inhabitants of the said colonies, and more beneficial and conducive to the public service, than the mode of giving and granting aids and subsidies in parliament to be raised and paid in the said colonies."

"That it may be proper to repeal an act, made in the seventh year of the reign of his present Majesty, intituled, An act for granting certain duties in the British colonies and plantations in America; for allowing a drawback of the duties of customs, upon the exportation from this kingdom, of coffee and cocoa-nuts, of the produce of the said colonies or plantations; for discontinuing the drawbacks payable on China earthenware exported to America; and for more effectually preventing the clandestine running of goods in the said colonies and plantations."

"That it may be proper to repeal an act, made in the fourteenth year of the reign of his present Majesty, intituled, An act to discontinue, in such manner, and for such time, as therein mentioned, the landing and discharging, lading or shipping of

---

* The first four motions and the last had the previous question put on them. The others were negatived.

The words in *Italics* were, by an amendment that was carried, left out of the motion; which will appear in the journals, though it is not the practice to insert such amendments in the votes.

goods, wares, and merchandise, at the town, and within the harbour, of Boston, in the province of Massachusetts Bay, in North America."

"That it may be proper to repeal an act, made in the fourteenth year of the reign of his present Majesty, intituled, An act for the impartial administration of justice, in cases of persons questioned for any acts done by them in the execution of the law, or for the suppression of riots and tumults, in the province of Massachusetts Bay, in New England."

"That it is proper to repeal an act, made in the fourteenth year of the reign of his present Majesty, intituled, An act for the better regulating the government of the province of Massachusetts Bay, in New England."

"That it is proper to explain and amend an act made in the thirty-fifth year of the reign of King Henry VIII, intituled, An act for the trial of treasons committed out of the king's dominions."

"That, from the time when the general assembly, or general court, of any colony or plantation, in North America, shall have appointed, by act of assembly duly confirmed, a settled salary to the offices of the chief justice and judges of the superior courts, it may be proper that the said chief justice and other judges of the superior courts of such colony shall hold his and their office and offices during their good behaviour; and shall not be removed therefrom, but when the said removal shall be adjudged by his Majesty in council, upon a hearing on complaint from the general assembly, or on a complaint from the governor, or council, or the house of representatives, severally, of the colony in which the said chief justice and other judges have exercised the said office."

"That it may be proper to regulate the courts of admiralty, or vice-admiralty, authorised by the fifteenth chapter of the fourth of George III, in such a manner, as to make the same more commodious to those who sue, or are sued, in the said courts; *and to provide for the more decent maintenance of the judges of the same.*"

LETTER TO THE SHERIFFS
OF BRISTOL

3 APRIL 1777

GENTLEMEN,

I HAVE THE honour of sending you the two last acts[1] which have
been passed with regard to the troubles in America. These acts
are similar to all the rest which have been made on the same
subject. They operate by the same principle; and they are
derived from the very same policy. I think they complete the
number of this sort of statutes to nine. It affords no matter for
very pleasing reflection to observe that our subjects diminish as
our laws increase.

If I have the misfortune of differing with some of my fellow-
citizens on this great and arduous subject, it is no small consolation to me that I do not differ from you. With you I am perfectly
united. We are heartily agreed in our detestation of a civil war.
We have ever expressed the most unqualified disapprobation of
all the steps which have led to it, and of all those which tend to
prolong it. And I have no doubt that we feel exactly the same
emotions of grief and shame in all its miserable consequences;
whether they appear, on the one side or the other, in the shape
of victories or defeats, of captures made from the English on the
continent, or from the English in these islands; of legislative
regulations which subvert the liberties of our brethren, or which
undermine our own.

Of the first of these statutes (that for the letter of marque) I shall
say little. Exceptionable as it may be, and as I think it is in some
particulars, it seems the natural, perhaps necessary, result of the
measures we have taken, and the situation we are in. The other
(for a partial suspension of the *Habeas Corpus*)[2] appears to me of
a much deeper malignity. During its progress through the House
of Commons, it has been amended, so as to express, more distinctly than at first it did, the avowed sentiments of those who
framed it: and the main ground of my exception to it is, because
it does express, and does carry into execution, purposes which
appear to me so contradictory to all the principles, not only of
the constitutional policy of Great Britain, but even of that species

of hostile justice, which no asperity of war wholly extinguishes in the minds of a civilised people.

It seems to have in view two capital objects; the first, to enable administration to confine, as long as it shall think proper, those whom that act is pleased to qualify by the name of *pirates*. Those so qualified I understand to be the commanders and mariners of such privateers and ships of war belonging to the colonies, as in the course of this unhappy contest may fall into the hands of the crown. They are therefore to be detained in prison, under the criminal description of piracy, to a future trial and ignominious punishment, whenever circumstances shall make it convenient to execute vengeance on them, under the colour of that odious and infamous offence.

To this first purpose of the law I have no small dislike; because the act does not (as all laws and all equitable transactions ought to do) fairly describe its object. The persons who make a naval war upon us, in consequence of the present troubles, may be rebels; but to call and treat them as pirates, is confounding, not only the natural distinction of things, but the order of crimes: which, whether by putting them from a higher part of the scale to the lower, or from the lower to the higher, is never done without dangerously disordering the whole frame of jurisprudence. Though piracy may be, in the eye of the law, a *less* offence than treason; yet as both are, in effect, punished with the same death, the same forfeiture, and the same corruption of blood, I never would take from any fellow-creature whatever any sort of advantage which he may derive to his safety from the pity of mankind, or to his reputation from their general feelings, by degrading his offence, when I cannot soften his punishment. The general sense of mankind tells me, that those offences, which may possibly arise from mistaken virtue, are not in the class of infamous actions. Lord Coke,[3] the oracle of the English law, conforms to that general sense where he says, that "those things which are of the highest criminality may be of the least disgrace." The act prepares a sort of masked proceeding, not honourable to the justice of the kingdom, and by no means necessary for its safety. I cannot enter into it. If Lord Balmerino,[4] in the last rebellion, had driven off the cattle of twenty clans, I should have thought it would have been a scandalous and low juggle, utterly unworthy of the manliness of an English judicature, to have tried him for felony as a stealer of cows.

Besides, I must honestly tell you, that I could not vote for, or countenance in any way, a statute, which stigmatises with the crime of piracy these men, whom an act of parliament had previously put out of the protection of the law. When the legislature of this kingdom had ordered all their ships and goods, for the mere new-created offence of exercising trade, to be divided as a spoil among the seamen of the navy, – to consider the necessary reprisal of an unhappy, proscribed, interdicted people, as the crime of piracy, would have appeared, in any other legislature than ours, a strain of the most insulting and most unnatural cruelty and injustice. I assure you I never remember to have heard of anything like it in any time or country.

The second professed purpose of the act is, to detain in England for trial those who shall commit high treason in America.

That you may be enabled to enter into the true spirit of the present law, it is necessary, gentlemen, to apprise you, that there is an act, made so long ago as in the reign of Henry the Eighth, before the existence or thought of any English colonies in America, for the trial in this kingdom of treasons committed out of the realm. In the year 1769, parliament thought proper to acquaint the crown with their construction of that act in a formal address, wherein they entreated his Majesty to cause persons, charged with high treason in America, to be brought into this kingdom for trial. By this act of Henry the Eighth, *so construed and so applied*, almost all that is substantial and beneficial in a trial by jury is taken away from the subject in the colonies. This is however saying too little; for to try a man under that act is, in effect, to condemn him unheard. A person is brought hither in the dungeon of a ship's hold; thence he is vomited into a dungeon on land; loaded with irons, unfurnished with money, unsupported by friends, three thousand miles from all means of calling upon or confronting evidence, where no one local circumstance that tends to detect perjury, can possibly be judged of; – such a person may be executed according to form, but he can never be tried according to justice.

I therefore could never reconcile myself to the bill I send you; which is expressly provided to remove all inconveniences from the establishment of a mode of trial, which has ever appeared to me most unjust and most unconstitutional. Far from removing the difficulties which impede the execution of so mischievous a project, I would heap new difficulties upon it, if it were in my power. All the ancient, honest, juridical principles and institutions of England are so many clogs to check and retard the headlong course of violence and oppression. They were invented for this one good purpose, that what was not just should not be convenient. Convinced of this, I would leave things as I found them. The old, cool-headed, general law, is as good as any deviation dictated by present heat.

I could see no fair, justifiable expedience pleaded to favour this new suspension of the liberty of the subject. If the English in the colonies can support the independency, to which they have been unfortunately driven, I suppose nobody has such a fanatical zeal for the criminal justice of Henry the Eighth, that he will contend for executions which must be retaliated tenfold on his own friends; or who has conceived so strange an idea of English dignity, as to think the defeats in America compensated by the triumphs at Tyburn.[5] If, on the contrary, the colonies are reduced to the obedience of the crown, there must be, under that authority, tribunals in the country itself, fully competent to administer justice on all offenders. But if there are not, and that we must suppose a thing so humiliating to our government, as with all this vast continent should unanimously concur in thinking, that no ill fortune can convert resistance to the royal authority into a criminal act, we may call the effect of our victory peace, or obedience, or what we will; but the war is not ended; the hostile mind continues in full vigour, and it continues under a worse form. If your peace be nothing more than a sullen pause from arms; if their quiet be nothing but the meditation of revenge, where smitten pride smarting from its wounds festers into new rancour; neither the act of Henry the Eighth, nor its handmaid of this reign, will answer any wise end of policy or justice. For if the bloody fields, which they saw and felt, are not sufficient to subdue the reason of America, (to use the expressive phrase of a great lord in office,) it is not the judicial slaughter, which is made in another hemisphere against their universal sense of justice, that will ever reconcile them to the British government.

I take it for granted, gentlemen, that we sympathise in a proper horror of all punishment further than as it serves for an example. To whom then does the example of an execution in England for this American rebellion apply? Remember, you are told every day, that the present is a contest between the two countries; and that we in England are at war for *our own* dignity against our rebellious children. Is this true? If it be, it is surely among such rebellious children that examples for disobedience should be made, to be in any degree instructive: for whoever thought of teaching parents their duty by an example from the punishment of an undutiful son? As well might the execution of a fugitive negro in the plantations be considered as a lesson to teach masters humanity to their slaves. Such executions may indeed satiate our revenge; they may harden our hearts, and puff us up with pride and arrogance. Alas! this is not instruction!

If anything can be drawn from such examples by a parity of the case, it is to show how deep their crime and how heavy their punishment will be, who shall at any time dare to resist a distant power actually disposing of their property, without their voice or consent to the disposition; and overturning their franchises without charge or hearing. God forbid that England should ever read this lesson written in the blood of *any* of her offspring!

War is at present carried on between the king's natural and foreign troops on one side, and the English in America on the other, upon the usual footing of other wars; and accordingly an exchange of prisoners has been regularly made from the beginning. If notwithstanding this hitherto equal procedure, upon some prospect of ending the war with success, (which however may be delusive,) administration prepares to act against those as *traitors* who remain in their hands at the end of the troubles, in my opinion we shall exhibit to the world as indecent a piece of injustice as ever civil fury has produced. If the prisoners, who have been exchanged, have not by that exchange been *virtually pardoned*, the cartel (whether avowed or understood) is a cruel fraud; for you have received the life of a man, and you ought to return a life for it, or there is no parity of fairness in the transaction.

If, on the other hand, we admit, that they who are actually exchanged are pardoned, but contend that you may justly reserve for vengeance those who remain unexchanged; then this unpleasant and unhandsome consequence will follow; that you judge of the delinquency of men merely by the time of their guilt, and not by the heinousness of it; and you make fortune and accidents, and not the moral qualities of human action, the rule of your justice.

These strange incongruities must ever perplex those who confound the unhappiness of civil dissensions with the crime of treason. Whenever a rebellion really and truly exists, which is as easily known in fact as it is difficult to define in words, government has not entered into such military conventions; but has ever declined all intermediate treaty, which should put rebels in possession of the law of nations with regard to war. Commanders would receive no benefits at their hands, because they could make no return for them. Who has ever heard of capitulation, and parole of honour, and exchange of prisoners, in the late rebellions in this kingdom? The answer to all demands of that sort was, "We can engage for nothing; you are at the king's pleasure." We ought to remember, that if our present enemies be, in reality and truth, rebels, the king's generals have no right to release them upon any conditions whatsoever; and they are themselves answerable to the law, and as much in want of a pardon for doing so, as the rebels whom they release.

Lawyers, I know, cannot make the distinction for which I contend; because they have their strict rule to go by. But legislators ought to do what lawyers cannot; for they have no other rules to bind them, but the great principles of reason and equity, and the general sense of mankind. These they are bound to obey and follow; and rather to enlarge and enlighten law by the liberality of legislative reason, than to fetter and bind their higher capacity by the narrow constructions of subordinate, artificial justice. If we had adverted to this, we never could consider the convulsions of a great empire, not disturbed by a little disseminated faction, but divided by whole communities and provinces, and entire legal representatives of a people, as fit matter of discussion under a commission of Oyer and Terminer.[6] It is as opposite to reason and prudence, as it is to humanity and justice.

This act, proceeding on these principles, that is, preparing to end the present troubles by a trial of one sort of hostility under the name of piracy, and of another by the name of treason, and executing the act of Henry the Eighth according to a new and unconstitutional interpretation, I have thought evil and dangerous, even though the instruments of effecting such purposes had been merely of a neutral quality.

But it really appears to me, that the means which this act employs are, at least, as exceptionable as the end. Permit me to open myself a little upon this subject, because it is of importance to me, when I am obliged to submit to the power without acquiescing in the reason of an act of legislature, that I should justify my dissent by such arguments as may be supposed to have weight with a sober man.

The main operative regulation of the act is to suspend the common law, and the statute *Habeas Corpus*, (the sole securities either for liberty or justice,) with regard to all those who have been out of the realm, or on the high seas, within a given time. The rest of the people, as I understand, are to continue as they stood before.

I confess, gentlemen, that this appears to me as bad in the principle, and far worse in its consequence, than an universal suspension of the *Habeas Corpus* act; and the limiting qualification, instead of taking out the sting, does in my humble opinion sharpen and envenom it to a greater degree. Liberty, if I understand it at all, is a *general* principle, and the clear right of all the subjects within the realm, or of none. Partial freedom seems to me a most invidious mode of slavery. But, unfortunately, it is the kind of slavery the most easily admitted in times of civil discord; for parties are but too apt to forget their own future safety in their desire of sacrificing their enemies. People without much difficulty admit the entrance of that injustice of which they are not to be the immediate victims. In times of high proceeding it is never the faction of the predominant power that is in danger: for no tyranny chastises its own instruments. It is the obnoxious and the suspected who want the protection of law; and there is nothing to bridle the partial violence of state factions, but this; "that whenever an act is made for a cessation of law and justice, the whole people should be universally subjected to the same suspension of their franchises." The alarm of such a proceeding would then be universal. It would operate as a sort of *Call of the nation*. It would become every man's immediate and instant concern to be made very sensible of the *absolute necessity* of this total eclipse of liberty. They would more carefully advert to every renewal, and more powerfully resist it. These great determined measures are not commonly so dangerous to freedom. They are marked with too strong lines to slide into use. No plea, nor pretence, of *inconvenience or evil example* (which must in their nature be daily and ordinary incidents) can be admitted as a reason for such mighty operations. But the true danger is, when liberty is nibbled away, for expedients, and by parts. The *Habeas Corpus* act supposes, contrary to the genius of most other laws, that the lawful magistrate may see particular men with a malignant eye, and it provides for that identical case. But when men, in particular descriptions, marked out by the magistrate himself, are delivered over by parliament to this possible malignity, it is not the *Habeas Corpus* that is occasionally suspended, but its spirit that is mistaken, and its principle that is subverted. Indeed nothing is security to any individual but the common interest of all.

This act, therefore, has this distinguished evil in it, that it is the first partial suspension of the *Habeas Corpus* that has been made. The precedent, which is always of very great importance, is now established. For the first time a distinction is made among the people within this realm. Before this act, every man putting his foot on English ground, every stranger owing only a local and temporary allegiance, even negro slaves who had been sold in the colonies and under an act of parliament, became as free as every other man who breathed the same air with them.[7] Now a line is drawn, which may be advanced farther and farther at pleasure, on the same argument of mere expedience, on which it was first described. There is no equality among us; we are not fellow-citizens, if the mariner, who lands on the quay, does not rest on as firm legal ground as the merchant who sits in his counting-house. Other laws may injure the community, this dissolves it. As things now stand, every man in the West Indies, every one inhabitant of three unoffending provinces on the continent, every person coming from the East Indies, every gentleman who has travelled for his health or education, every mariner who has navigated the seas, is, for no other offence, under a temporary proscription. Let any of these facts (now become presumptions of guilt) be proved against him, and the bare suspicion of the crown puts him out of the law. It is even by no means clear to me, whether the negative proof does not lie upon the person apprehended on suspicion, to the subversion of all justice.

I have not debated against this bill in its progress through the House; because it would have been vain to oppose, and impossible to correct it.[8] It is some time since I have been clearly convinced, that in the present state of things all opposition to any measures proposed by ministers, where the name of America appears, is vain and frivolous. You may be sure that I do not speak of my opposition, which in all circumstances must be so; but that of men of the greatest wisdom and authority in the nation. Everything proposed against America is supposed of course to be in favour of Great Britain. Good and ill success are equally admitted as reasons for persevering in the present methods. Several very prudent, and very well-intentioned, persons were of opinion, that during the prevalence of such dispositions, all struggle rather inflamed than lessened the distemper of the public councils. Finding such resistance to be considered as factious by most within-doors, and by very many without, I cannot conscientiously support what is against my opinion, nor prudently contend with what I know is irresistible. Preserving my principles unshaken, I reserve my activity for rational endeavours; and I hope that my past conduct has given sufficient evidence that if I am a single day from my place, it is not owing to indolence or love of dissipation. The slightest hope of doing good is sufficient to recall me to what I quitted with regret. In declaring for some time my usual strict attendance, I do not in the least condemn the spirit of those gentlemen, who, with a just confidence in their abilities, (in which I claim a sort of share from my love and admiration of them,) were of opinion that their exertions in this desperate case might be of some service. They thought, that by contracting the sphere of its application, they might lessen the malignity of an evil principle. Perhaps they were in the right. But when my opinion was so very clearly to the contrary, for the reasons I have just stated, I am sure *my* attendance would have been ridiculous.

I must add in further explanation of my conduct, that, far from softening the features of such a principle, and thereby removing any part of the popular odium or natural terrors attending it, I should be sorry that anything framed in contradiction to the spirit of our constitution did not instantly produce, in fact, the grossest of the evils with which it was pregnant in its nature. It is by lying dormant a long time, being at first very rarely exercised, that arbitrary power steals upon a people. On the next unconstitutional act, all the fashionable world will be ready to say – Your prophecies are ridiculous, your fears are vain, you see how little of the mischiefs which you formerly foreboded are come to pass. Thus, by degrees, that artful softening of all arbitrary power, the alleged infrequency or narrow extent of its operation, will be received as a sort of aphorism – and Mr. *Hume*[9] will not be singular in telling us that the felicity of mankind is no more disturbed by it, than by earthquakes or thunder, or the other more unusual accidents of nature.

The act of which I speak is among the fruits of the American war; a war in my humble opinion productive of many mischiefs, of a kind which distinguish it from all others. Not only our policy is deranged, and our empire distracted, but our laws and our legislative spirit appear to have been totally perverted by it. We have made war on our colonies, not by arms only, but by laws. As hostility and law are not very concordant ideas, every step we have taken in this business has been made by trampling on some maxim of justice, or some capital principle of wise government. What precedents were established, and what principles over-turned, (I will not say of English privilege, but of general justice,) in the Boston Port, the Massachusetts Charter, the Military Bill, and all that long array of hostile acts of parliament, by which the war with America has been begun and supported! Had the principles of any of these acts been first exerted on English ground, they would probably have expired as soon as they touched it. But by being removed from our persons, they have rooted in our laws, and the latest posterity will taste the fruits of them.

Nor is it the worst effect of this unnatural contention, that our *laws* are corrupted. Whilst *manners* remain entire, they will correct the vices of law, and soften it at length to their own temper. But we have to lament, that in most of the late proceedings we see very few traces of that generosity, humanity, and dignity of mind, which formerly characterised this nation. War suspends the rules of moral obligation, and what is long suspended is in danger of being totally abrogated. Civil wars strike deepest of all into the manners of the people. They vitiate their politics; they corrupt their morals; they pervert even the natural taste and relish of equity and justice. By teaching us to consider our fellow-citizens in a hostile light, the whole body of our nation becomes gradually less dear to us. The very names of affection and kindred, which were the bond of charity whilst we agreed, become new incentives to hatred and rage, when the communion of our country is dissolved. We may flatter ourselves that we shall not fall into this misfortune. But we have no charter of exemption, that I know of, from the ordinary frailties of our nature.

What but that blindness of heart which arises from the phrensy of civil contention, could have made any persons conceive the present situation of the British affairs as an object of triumph to themselves, or of congratulation to their sovereign? Nothing surely could be more lamentable to those who remember the flourishing days of this kingdom, than to see the insane joy of several unhappy people, amidst the sad spectacle which our affairs and conduct exhibit to the scorn of Europe. We behold (and it seems some people rejoice in beholding) our native land, which used to sit the envied arbiter of all her neighbours, reduced to a servile dependence on their mercy; acquiescing in assurances of friendship which she does not trust; complaining of hostilities which she dares not resent; deficient to her allies; lofty to her subjects, and submissive to her enemies; whilst the liberal government of this free nation is supported by the hireling sword of German boors and vassals; and three millions of the subjects of Great Britain are seeking for protection to English privileges in the arms of France!

These circumstances appear to me more like shocking prodigies, than natural changes in human affairs. Men of firmer minds may see them without staggering or astonishment. – Some may think them matters of congratulation and complimentary addresses; but I trust your candour will be so indulgent to my weakness, as not to have the worse opinion of me for my declining to participate in this joy, and my rejecting all share whatsoever in such a triumph. I am too old, too stiff in my inveterate partialities, to be ready at all the fashionable evolutions of opinion. I scarcely know how to adapt my mind to the feelings with which the court gazettes mean to impress the people. It is not instantly that I can be brought to rejoice, when I hear of the slaughter and captivity of long lists of those names which have been familiar to my ears from my infancy, and to rejoice that they have fallen under the sword of strangers, whose barbarous appellations I scarcely know how to pronounce. The glory acquired at the White Plains by Colonel Raille has no charms for me; and I fairly acknowledge, that I have not yet learned to delight in finding Fort Kniphausen in the heart of the British dominions.[10]

It might be some consolation for the loss of our old regards, if our reason were enlightened in proportion as our honest prejudices are removed. Wanting feelings for the honour of our country, we might then in cold blood be brought to think a little of our interests as individual citizens, and our private conscience as moral agents.

Indeed our affairs are in a bad condition. I do assure those gentlemen who have prayed for war, and have obtained the blessing they have sought, that they are at this instant in very great straits. The abused wealth of this country continues a little longer to feel its distemper. As yet they, and their German allies of twenty hireling states, have contended only with the unprepared strength of our own infant colonies. But America is not sub- dued. Not one unattacked village which was originally adverse throughout that vast continent, has yet submitted from love or terror. You have the ground you encamp on; and you have no more. The cantonments of your troops and your dominions are exactly of the same extent. You spread devastation, but you do not enlarge the sphere of authority.

The events of this war are of so much greater magnitude than those who either wished or feared it ever looked for, that this alone ought to fill every considerate mind with anxiety and diffidence. Wise men often tremble at the very things which fill the thoughtless with security. For many reasons I do not choose to expose to public view all the particulars of the state in which you stood with regard to foreign powers, during the whole course of the last year. Whether you are yet wholly out of danger from them, is more than I know, or than your rulers can divine. But even if I were certain of my safety, I could not easily forgive those who had brought me into the most dreadful perils, because by accidents, unforeseen by them or me, I have escaped.

Believe me, gentlemen, the way still before you is intricate, dark, and full of perplexed and treacherous mazes. Those who think they have the clue may lead us out of this labyrinth. We may trust them as amply as we think proper; but as they have most certainly a call for all the reason which their stock can furnish, why should we think it proper to disturb its operation by inflaming their passions? I may be unable to lend an helping hand to those who direct the state; but I should be ashamed to make myself one of a noisy multitude to halloo and hearten them into doubtful and dangerous courses. A conscientious man would be cautious how he dealt in blood. He would feel some apprehension at being called to a tremendous account for engag- ing so deep a play, without any sort of knowledge of the game. It is no excuse for presumptuous ignorance, that it is directed by insolent passion. The poorest being that crawls on earth, contending to save itself from injustice and oppression, is an object respectable in the eyes of God and man. But I cannot conceive any existence under heaven, (which, in the depths of its wisdom, tolerates all sorts of things,) that is more truly odious and disgusting, than an impotent, helpless creature, without civil wisdom or military skill, without a consciousness of any other qualification for power but his servility to it, bloated with pride and arrogance, calling for battles which he is not to fight, contending for a violent dominion which he can never exercise, and satisfied to be himself mean and miserable, in order to render others contemptible and wretched.

If you and I find our talents not of the great and ruling kind, our conduct, at least, is conformable to our faculties. No man's life pays the forfeit of our rashness. No desolate widow weeps tears of blood over our ignorance. Scrupulous and sober in our well-grounded distrust of ourselves, we would keep in the port of peace and security; and perhaps in recommending to others something of the same diffidence, we should show ourselves more charitable in their welfare, than injurious to their abilities.

There are many circumstances in the zeal shown for civil war, which seem to discover but little of real magnanimity. The addressers offer their own persons, and they are satisfied with hiring Germans. They promise their private fortunes, and they mortgage their country. They have all the merit of volunteers, without risk of person or charge of contribution; and when the unfeeling arm of a foreign soldiery pours out their kindred blood like water, they exult and triumph as if they themselves had performed some notable exploit. I am really ashamed of the fashionable language which has been held for some time past; which, to say the best of it, is full of levity. You know that I allude to the general cry against the cowardice of the Americans, as if we despised them for not making the king's soldiery purchase the advantage they have obtained at a dearer rate. It is not, gentlemen, it is not to respect the dispensations of Providence, nor to provide any decent retreat in the mutability of human affairs. It leaves no medium between insolent victory and infamous defeat. It tends to alienate our minds farther and farther from our natural regards, and to make an eternal rent and schism in the British nation. Those who do not wish for such a separation, would not dissolve that cement of reciprocal esteem and regard, which can alone bind together the parts of this great fabric. It ought to be our wish, as it is our duty, not only to forbear this style of outrage ourselves, but to make every one as sensible as we can of the impropriety and unworthiness of the tempers which give rise to it, and which designing men are labouring with such malignant industry to diffuse amongst us. It is our business to counteract them, if possible; if possible, to awake our natural regards; and to revive the old partiality to the English name. Without something of this kind I do not see how it is ever practicable really to reconcile with those, whose affection, after all, must be the surest hold of our government; and which is a thousand times more worth to us, than the mercenary zeal of all the circles of Germany.

I can well conceive a country completely overrun, and miserably wasted, without approaching in the least to settlement. In my apprehension, as long as English government is attempted to be supported over Englishmen by the sword alone, things will thus continue. I anticipate in my mind the moment of the final triumph of foreign military force. When that hour arrives, (for it may arrive,) then it is, that all this mass of weakness and violence will appear in its full light. If we should be expelled from America, the delusion of the partisans of military government might still continue. They might still feed their imaginations with the possible good consequences which might have attended success. Nobody could prove the contrary by facts. But in case the sword should do all that the sword can do, the success of their arms and the defeat of their policy will be one and the same thing. You will never see any revenue from America. Some increase of the means of corruption, without ease of the public burthens, is the very best that can happen. Is it for this that we are at war; and in such a war?

As to the difficulties of laying once more the foundations of that government, which, for the sake of conquering what was our own, has been voluntarily and wantonly pulled down by a court faction here, I tremble to look at them. Has any of these gentlemen, who are so eager to govern all mankind, showed himself possessed of the first qualification towards government, some knowledge of the object, and of the difficulties which occur in the task they have undertaken?

I assure you, that, on the most prosperous issue of your arms, you will not be where you stood, when you called in war to supply the defects of your political establishment. Nor would any disorder or disobedience to government which could arise from the most abject concession on our part, ever equal those which will be felt, after the most triumphant violence. You have got all the intermediate evils of war into the bargain.

I think I know America. If I do not, my ignorance is incurable, for I have spared no pains to understand it and I do most solemnly assure those of my constituents who put any sort of confidence in my industry and integrity, that every thing that has been done there has arisen from a total misconception of the object; that our means of originally holding America, that our means of reconciling with it after quarrel, of recovering it after separation, of keeping it after victory, did depend, and must depend in their several stages and periods, upon a total renunciation of that unconditional submission, which has taken such possession of the minds of violent men. The whole of those maxims, upon which we have made and continued this war, must be abandoned. Nothing indeed (for I would not deceive you) can place us in our former situation. That hope must be laid aside. But there is a difference between bad and the worst of all. Terms relative to the cause of the war ought to be offered by the authority of parliament. An arrangement at home promising some security for them ought to be made. By doing this, without the least impairing of our strength, we add to the credit of our moderation, which, in itself, is always strength more or less.

I know many have been taught to think, that moderation, in a case like this, is a sort of treason; and that all arguments for it are sufficiently answered by railing at rebels and rebellion, and by charging all the present or future miseries, which we may suffer, on the resistance of our brethren. But I would wish them, in this grave matter, and if peace is not wholly removed from their hearts, to consider seriously, first, that to criminate and recriminate never yet was the road to reconciliation, in any difference amongst men. In the next place, it would be right to reflect, that the American English (whom they may abuse, if they think it honourable to revile the absent) can, as things now stand, neither be provoked at our railing, nor bettered by our instruction. All communication is cut off between us, but this we know with certainty, that, though we cannot reclaim them, we may reform ourselves. If measures of peace are necessary, they must begin somewhere; and a conciliatory temper must precede and prepare every plan of reconciliation. Nor do I conceive that we suffer anything by thus regulating our own minds. We are not disarmed by being disencumbered of our passions. Declaiming on rebellion never added a bayonet, or a charge of powder, to your military force; but I am afraid that it has been the means of taking up many muskets against you.

This outrageous language, which has been encouraged and kept alive by every art, has already done incredible mischief. For a long time, even amidst the desolations of war, and the insults of hostile laws daily accumulated on one another, the American leaders seem to have had the greatest difficulty in bringing up their people to a declaration of total independence. But the court gazette accomplished what the abettors of independence had attempted in vain.[11] When that disingenuous compilation, and strange medley of railing and flattery, was adduced as a proof of the united sentiments of the people of Great Britain, there was a great change throughout all America. The tide of popular affection, which had still set towards the parent country, begun immediately to turn, and to flow with great rapidity in a contrary course. Far from concealing these wild declarations of enmity, the author of the celebrated pamphlet, which prepared the minds of the people for independence, insists largely on the multitude and the spirit of these addresses; and he draws an argument from them, which (if the fact was as he supposes) must be irresistible.[12] For I never knew a writer on the theory of government so partial to authority as not to allow, that the hostile mind of the rulers to their people did fully justify a change of government; nor can any reason whatever be given, why one people should voluntarily yield any degree of pre-eminence to another, but on a supposition of great affection and benevolence towards them. Unfortunately your rulers, trusting to other things, took no notice of this great principle of connexion. From the beginning of this affair, they have done all they could to alienate your minds from your own kindred; and if they could excite hatred enough in one of the parties towards the other, they seemed to be of opinion that they had gone half the way towards reconciling the quarrel.

I know it is said, that your kindness is only alienated on account of their resistance; and therefore if the colonies surrender at discretion, all sort of regard, and even much indulgence, is meant towards them in future. But can those who are partisans for continuing a war to enforce such a surrender be responsible (after all that has passed) for such a future use of a power, that is bound by no compacts, and restrained by no terror? Will they tell us what they call indulgences? Do they not at this instant call the present war, and all its horrors, a lenient and merciful proceeding?

No conqueror, that I ever heard of, has *professed* to make a cruel, harsh, and insolent use of his conquest. No! The man of the most declared pride scarcely dares to trust his own heart with this dreadful secret of ambition. But it will appear in its time; and no man, who professes to reduce another to the insolent mercy of a foreign arm, ever had any sort of good-will towards him. The profession of kindness, with that sword in his hand, and that demand of surrender, is one of the most provoking acts of his hostility. I shall be told, that all this is lenient as against rebellious adversaries. But are the leaders of their faction more lenient to those who submit? Lord Howe and General Howe[13] have powers, under an act of parliament, to restore to the king's peace and to free trade any men, or district, which shall submit. Is this done? We have been over and over informed by the authorised gazette, that the city of New York, and the countries of Staten and Long Island, have submitted voluntarily and cheerfully, and that many are very full of zeal to the cause of administration. Were they instantly restored to trade? Are they yet restored to it? Is not the benignity of two commissioners, naturally most humane and generous men, some way fettered by instructions, equally against their dispositions and spirit of parliamentary faith; when Mr. Tryon,[14] vaunting of the fidelity of the city in which he is governor, is obliged to apply to ministry for leave to protect the king's loyal subjects, and to grant to them (not the disputed rights and privileges of freedom) but the common rights of men, by the name of *graces*? Why do not the commissioners restore them on the spot? Were they not named as commissioners for that express purpose? But we see well enough to what the whole leads. The trade of America is to be dealt out in *private indulgences and graces*; that is, in jobs to recompense the incendiaries of war. They will be informed of the proper time in which to send out their merchandise. From a national, the American trade is to be turned into a personal monopoly: and one set of merchants are to be rewarded for the pretended zeal, of which another set are the dupes; and thus, between craft and credulity, the voice of reason is stifled; and all the misconduct, all the calamities of the war are covered and continued.

If I had not lived long enough to be little surprised at anything, I should have been in some degree astonished at the continued rage of several gentlemen, who, not satisfied with carrying fire and sword into America, are animated nearly with the same fury against those neighbours of theirs, whose only crime it is, that they have charitably and humanely wished them to entertain more reasonable sentiments, and not always to sacrifice their interest to their passion. All this rage against unresisting dissent convinces me, that, at bottom, they are far from satisfied they are in the right. For what is it they would have? A war? They certainly have at this moment the blessing of something that is very like one; and if the war they enjoy at present be not sufficiently hot and extensive, they may shortly have it as warm and as spreading as their hearts can desire. Is it the force of the kingdom they call for? They have it already; and if they choose to fight their battles in their own person, nobody prevents their setting sail to America in the next transports. Do they think, that the service is stinted for want of liberal supplies? Indeed they complain without reason. The table of the House of Commons will glut them, let their appetite for expense be never so keen. And I assure them further, that those who think with them in the House of Commons are full as easy in the control, as they are liberal in the vote, of these expenses. If this be not supply or confidence sufficient, let them open their own private purse-strings, and give, from what is left to them, as largely and with as little care as they think proper.

Tolerated in their passions, let them learn not to persecute the moderation of their fellow-citizens. If all the world joined them in a full cry against rebellion, and were as hotly inflamed against the whole theory and enjoyment of freedom, as those who are the most factious for servitude, it could not in my opinion answer any one end whatsoever in this contest. The leaders of this war could not hire (to gratify their friends) one German more than they do; or inspire him with less feeling for the persons, or less value for the privileges, of their revolted brethren. If we all adopted their sentiments to a man, their allies, the savage Indians, could not be more ferocious than they are: they could not murder one more helpless woman or child, or with more exquisite refinements of cruelty torment to death one more of their English flesh and blood, than they do already. The public money is given to purchase this alliance; – and they have their bargain.

They are continually boasting of unanimity; or calling for it. But before this unanimity can be matter either of wish or congratulation, we ought to be pretty sure that we are engaged in a rational pursuit. Phrensy does not become a slighter distemper on account of the number of those who may be infected with it. Delusion and weakness produce not one mischief the less, because they are universal. I declare, that I cannot discern the least advantage which could accrue to us, if we were able to persuade our colonies that they had not a single friend in Great Britain. On the contrary, if the affections and opinions of mankind be not exploded as principles of connexion, I conceive it would be happy for us if they were taught to believe, that there was even a formed American party in England, to whom they could always look for support! Happy would it be for us, if, in all tempers, they might turn their eyes to the parent state; so that their very turbulence and sedition should find vent in no other place than this. I believe there is not a man (except those who prefer the interest of some paltry faction to the very being of their country) who would not wish that the Americans should from time to time carry many points, and even some of them not quite reasonable, by the aid of any denomination of men here, rather than they should be driven to seek for protection against the fury of foreign mercenaries, and the waste of savages, in the arms of France.

When any community is subordinately connected with another, the great danger of the connexion is the extreme pride and self-complacency of the superior, which in all matters of controversy will probably decide in its own favour. It is a powerful corrective to such a very rational cause of fear, if the inferior body can be made to believe, that the party inclination, or political views, of several in the principal state, will induce them in some degree to counteract this blind and tyrannical partiality. There is no danger that any one acquiring consideration or power in the presiding state should carry this learning to the inferior too far. The fault of human nature is not of that sort. Power, in whatever hands, is rarely guilty of too strict limitations on itself. But one great advantage to the support of authority attends such an amicable and protecting connexion, that those who have conferred favours obtain influence; and from the foresight of future events can persuade men, who have received obligations, sometimes to return them. Thus by the mediation of those healing principles, (call them good or evil,) troublesome discussions are brought to some sort of adjustment; and every hot controversy is not a civil war.

But, if the colonies (to bring the general matter home to us) could see, that, in Great Britain, the mass of the people is melted into its government, and that every dispute with the ministry must of necessity be always a quarrel with the nation; they can stand no longer in the equal and friendly relation of fellow-citizens to the subjects of this kingdom. Humble as this relation may appear to some, when it is once broken, a strong tie is dissolved. Other sort of connexions will be sought. For, there are very few in the world, who will not prefer a useful ally to an insolent master.

Such discord has been the effect of the unanimity into which so many have of late been seduced or bullied, or into the appearance of which they have sunk through mere despair. They have been told that their dissent from violent measures is an encouragement to rebellion. Men of great presumption and little knowledge will hold a language which is contradicted by the whole course of history. *General* rebellions and revolts of a whole people never were *encouraged*, now or at any time. They are always *provoked*. But if this unheard-of doctrine of the encouragement of rebellion were true, if it were true that an assurance of the friendship of numbers in this country towards the colonies could become an encouragement to them to break off all connexion with it, what is the inference? Does anybody seriously maintain, that, charged with my share of the public councils, I am obliged not to resist projects which I think mischievous, lest men who suffer should be encouraged to resist? The very tendency of such projects to produce rebellion is one of the chief reasons against them. Shall that reason not be given? Is it then a rule, that no man in this nation shall open his mouth in favour of the colonies, shall defend their rights, or complain of their sufferings? Or when war finally breaks out, no man shall express his desires of peace? Has this been the law of our past, or is it to be the terms of our future connexion? Even looking no farther than ourselves, can it be true loyalty to any government, or true patriotism towards any country, to degrade their solemn councils into servile drawing-rooms, to flatter their pride and passions, rather than to enlighten their reason, and to prevent them from being cautioned against violence lest others should be encouraged to resistance? By such acquiescence great kings and mighty nations have been undone; and if any are at this day in a perilous situation from resisting truth, and listening to flattery, it would rather become them to reform the errors under which they suffer, than to reproach those who forewarned them of their danger.

But the rebels looked for assistance from this country. They did so, in the beginning of this controversy, most certainly; and they sought it by earnest supplications to government, which dignity rejected, and by a suspension of commerce, which the wealth of this nation enabled you to despise. When they found that neither prayers nor menaces had any sort of weight, but that a firm resolution was taken to reduce them to unconditional obedience by a military force, they came to the last extremity. Despairing of us, they trusted in themselves. Not strong enough themselves, they sought succour in France. In proportion as all encouragement here lessened, their distance from this country increased. The encouragement is over; the alienation is complete.

In order to produce this favourite unanimity in delusion, and to prevent all possibility of a return to our ancient happy concord, arguments for our continuance in this course are drawn from the wretched situation itself into which we have been betrayed. It is said, that being at war with the colonies, whatever our sentiments might have been before, all ties between us are now dissolved; and all the policy we have left is to strengthen the hands of government to reduce them. On the principle of this argument, the more mischiefs we suffer from any administration, the more our trust in it is to be confirmed. Let them but once get us into a war, and then their power is safe, and an act of oblivion passed for all their misconduct.

But is it really true, that government is always to be strengthened with the instruments of war, but never furnished with the means of peace? In former times, ministers, I allow, have been sometimes driven by the popular voice to assert by arms the national honour against foreign powers. But the wisdom of the nation has been far more clear, when those ministers have been compelled to consult its interests by treaty. We all know that the sense of the nation obliged the court of King Charles the Second to abandon the *Dutch war*; a war next to the present the most impolitic which we ever carried on. The good people of England considered Holland as a sort of dependency on this kingdom; they dreaded to drive it to the protection, or subject it to the power of France, by their own inconsiderate hostility. They paid but little respect to the court jargon of that day; nor were they inflamed by the pretended rivalship of the Dutch in trade; by their massacre at Amboyna,[15] acted on the stage to provoke the public vengeance; nor by declamations against the ingratitude of the United Provinces for the benefits England had conferred upon them in their infant state. They were not moved from their evident interest by all these arts; nor was it enough to tell them, they were at war; that they must go through with it; and that the cause of the dispute was lost in the consequences. The people of England were then, as they are now, called upon to make government strong. They thought it a great deal better to make it wise and honest.

When I was amongst my constituents at the last summer assizes, I remember that men of all descriptions did then express a very strong desire for peace, and no slight hopes of attaining it from the commission sent out by my Lord Howe. And it is not a little remarkable, that, in proportion as every person showed a zeal for the court measures, he was then earnest in circulating an opinion of the extent of the supposed powers of that commission. When I told them that Lord Howe had no powers to treat, or to promise satisfaction on any point whatsoever of the controversy, I was hardly credited; so strong and general was the desire of terminating this war by the method of accommodation. As far as I could discover, this was the temper then prevalent through the kingdom. The king's forces, it must be observed, had at that time been obliged to evacuate Boston. The superiority of the former campaign rested wholly with the colonists. If such powers of treaty were to be wished, whilst success was very doubtful, how came they to be less so, since his Majesty's arms have been crowned with many considerable advantages? Have these successes induced us to alter our mind; as thinking the season of victory not the time for treating with honour or advantage? Whatever changes have happened in the national character, it can scarcely be our wish, that terms of accommodation never should be proposed to our enemy, except when they must be attributed solely to our fears. It has happened, let me say unfortunately, that we read of his Majesty's commission for making peace, and his troops evacuating his last town in the thirteen colonies, at the same hour and in the same gazette. It was still more unfortunate, that no commission went to America to settle the troubles there, until several months after an act had been passed to put the colonies out of the protection of this government, and to divide their trading property, without a possibility of restitution, as spoil among the seamen of the navy. The most abject submission on the part of the colonies could not redeem them. There was no man on that whole continent, or within three thousand miles of it, qualified by law to follow allegiance with protection, or submission with pardon. A proceeding of this kind has no example in history. Independency, and independency with an enmity, (which putting ourselves out of the question, would be called natural and much provoked,) was the inevitable consequence. How this came to pass, the nation may be one day in an humour to inquire.

All the attempts made this session to give fuller powers of peace to the commanders in America, were stifled by the fatal confidence of victory, and the wild hopes of unconditional submission. There was a moment favourable to the king's arms, when if any powers of concession had existed on the other side of the Atlantic, even after all our errors, peace in all probability might have been restored. But calamity is unhappily the usual season of reflection; and the pride of men will not often suffer reason to have any scope until it can be no longer of service.

I have always wished, that as the dispute had its apparent origin from things done in parliament, and as the acts passed there had provoked the war, that the foundations of peace should be laid in parliament also. I have been astonished to find, that those, whose zeal for the dignity of our body was so hot as to light up the flames of civil war, should even publicly declare, that these delicate points ought to be wholly left to the crown. Poorly as I may be thought affected to the authority of parliament, I shall never admit that our constitutional rights can ever become a matter of ministerial negotiation.

I am charged with being an American. If warm affection towards those over whom I claim any share of authority be a crime, I am guilty of this charge. But I do assure you, (and they who know me publicly and privately will bear witness to me,) that if ever one man lived more zealous than another for the supremacy of parliament, and the rights of this imperial crown, it was myself. Many others indeed might be more knowing in the extent of the foundation of these rights. I do not pretend to be an antiquary, a lawyer, or qualified for the chair of professor in metaphysics. I never ventured to put your solid interests upon speculative grounds. My having constantly declined to do so has been attributed to my incapacity for such disquisitions; and I am inclined to believe it is partly the cause. I never shall be ashamed to confess, that where I am ignorant I am diffident. I am indeed not very solicitous to clear myself of this imputed incapacity;

because men, even less conversant than I am in this kind of subtleties, and placed in stations to which I ought not to aspire, have, by the mere force of civil discretion, often conducted the affairs of great nations with distinguished felicity and glory.

When I first came into a public trust, I found your parliament in possession of an unlimited legislative power over the colonies. I could not open the statute book without seeing the actual exercise of it, more or less, in all cases whatsoever. This possession passed with me for a title. It does so in all human affairs. No man examines into the defects of his title to his paternal estate, or to his established government. Indeed common sense taught me, that a legislative authority, not actually limited by the express terms of its foundation or by its own subsequent acts, cannot have its powers parcelled out by argumentative distinctions, so as to enable us to say, that here they can, and there they cannot, bind. Nobody was so obliging as to produce to me any record of such distinctions, by compact or otherwise, either at the successive formation of the several colonies, or during the existence of any of them. If any gentlemen were able to see how one power could be given up (merely on abstract reasoning) without giving up the rest, I can only say, that they saw farther than I could; nor did I ever presume to condemn any one for being clear-sighted, when I was blind. I praise the penetration and learning; and hope that their practice has been correspondent to their theory.

I had indeed very earnest wishes to keep the whole body of this authority perfect and entire as I found it: and to keep it so, not for our advantage solely; but principally for the sake of those, on whose account all just authority exists; I mean the people to be governed. For I thought I saw, that many cases might well happen, in which the exercise of every power comprehended in the broadest idea of legislature, might become, in its time and circumstances, not a little expedient for the peace and union of the colonies amongst themselves, as well as for their perfect harmony with Great Britain. Thinking so, (perhaps erroneously,) but being honestly of that opinion, I was at the same time very sure, that the authority, of which I was so jealous, could not under the actual circumstances of our plantations be at all preserved in any of its members, but by the greatest reserve in its application; particularly in those delicate points, in which the feelings of mankind are the most irritable. They who thought otherwise, have found a few more difficulties in their work than (I hope) they were thoroughly aware of, when they undertook the present business. I must beg leave to observe, that it is not only the invidious branch of taxation that will be resisted, but that no other given part of legislative rights can be exercised, without regard to the general opinion of those who are to be governed. That general opinion is the vehicle and organ of legislative omnipotence. Without this, it may be a theory to entertain the mind, but it is nothing in the direction of affairs. The completeness of the legislative authority of parliament *over this kingdom* is not questioned; and yet many things indubitably included in the abstract idea of that power, and which carry no absolute injustice in themselves, yet being contrary to the opinions and feelings of the people, can as little be exercised, as if parliament in that case had been possessed of no right at all. I see no abstract reason, which can be given, why the same power, which made and repealed the high-commission court and the star-chamber,[16] might not revive them again; and these courts, warned by their former fate, might possibly exercise their powers with some degree of justice. But the madness would be as unquestionable, as the competence of that parliament which should attempt such things. If anything can be supposed out of the power of human legislature, it is religion: I admit, however, that the established religion of this country has been three or four times altered by act of parliament; and therefore that a statute binds even in that case. But we may very safely affirm, that, notwithstanding this apparent omnipotence, it would be now found as impossible for king and parliament to alter the established religion of this country, as it was to King James alone, when he attempted to make such an alteration without a parliament. In effect, to follow, not to force the public inclination; to give a direction, a form, a technical dress, and a specific sanction, to the general sense of the community, is the true end of legislature.

It is so with regard to the exercise of all the powers which our constitution knows in any of its parts, and indeed to the substantial existence of any of the parts themselves. The king's negative to bills is one of the most indisputed of the royal prerogatives; and it extends to all cases whatsoever. I am far from certain, that if several laws which I know had fallen under the stroke of that sceptre, that the public would have had a very heavy loss. But it is not the *propriety* of the exercise which is in question. The exercise itself is wisely forborne. Its repose may be the preservation of its

existence; and its existence may be the means of saving the constitution itself, on an occasion worthy of bringing it forth. As the
disputants, whose accurate and logical reasonings have brought
us into our present condition, think it absurd, that powers or
members of any constitution should exist, rarely or never to be
exercised, I hope I shall be excused in mentioning another
instance, that is material. We know, that the convocation of the
clergy[17] had formerly been called, and sat with nearly as much
regularity to business as parliament itself. It is now called for form
only. It sits for the purpose of making some polite ecclesiastical
compliments to the king; and, when that grace is said, retires and
is heard of no more. It is however *a part of the constitution*, and may
be called out into act and energy, whenever there is occasion; and
whenever those, who conjure up that spirit, will choose to abide
the consequences. It is wise to permit its legal existence; it is
much wiser to continue it a legal existence only. So truly has prudence (constituted as the god of this lower world) the entire
dominion over every exercise of power committed into its hands;
and yet I have lived to see prudence and conformity to circumstances wholly set at nought in our late controversies, and treated
as if they were the most contemptible and irrational of all things.
I have heard it a hundred times very gravely alleged, that in order
to keep power in wind, it was necessary, by preference, to exert
it in those very points in which it was most likely to be resisted,
and the least likely to be productive of any advantage.

These were the considerations, gentlemen, which led me early
to think, that, in the comprehensive dominion which the Divine
Providence had put into our hands, instead of troubling our
understandings with speculations concerning the unity of empire,
and the identity or distinction of legislative powers, and inflaming our passions with the heat and pride of controversy, it was
our duty, in all soberness, to conform our government to the
character and circumstances of the several people who composed
this mighty and strangely diversified mass. I never was wild
enough to conceive, that one method would serve for the whole;
that the natives of Hindostan and those of Virginia could be
ordered in the same manner; or that the Cutchery court[18] and
the grand jury of Salem could be regulated on a similar plan. I was
persuaded that government was a practical thing, made for the
happiness of mankind, and not to furnish out a spectacle of
uniformity, to gratify the schemes of visionary politicians. Our

business was to rule, not to wrangle; and it would have been a poor compensation that we had triumphed in a dispute, whilst we lost an empire.

If there be one fact in the world perfectly clear it is this: "That the disposition of the people of America is wholly averse to any other than a free government;" and this is indication enough to any honest statesman, how he ought to adapt whatever power he finds in his hands to their case. If any ask me what a free government is, I answer, that, for any practical purpose, it is what the people think so; and that they, and not I, are the natural, lawful, and competent judges of this matter. If they practically allow me a greater degree of authority over them than is consistent with any correct ideas of perfect freedom, I ought to thank them for so great a trust, and not to endeavour to prove from thence, that they have reasoned amiss, and that having gone so far, by analogy, they must hereafter have no enjoyment but by my pleasure.

If we had seen this done by any others, we should have concluded them far gone in madness. It is melancholy as well as ridiculous, to observe the kind of reasoning with which the public has been amused, in order to divert our minds from the common sense of our American policy. There are people, who have split and anatomised the doctrine of free government, as if it were an abstract question concerning metaphysical liberty and necessity; and not a matter of moral prudence and natural feeling. They have disputed, whether liberty be a positive or a negative idea; whether it does not consist in being governed by laws, without considering what are the laws, or who are the makers; whether man has any rights by nature; and whether all the property he enjoys be not the alms of his government, and his life itself their favour and indulgence. Others, corrupting religion, as these have perverted philosophy, contend, that Christians are redeemed into captivity; and the blood of the Saviour of mankind has been shed to make them the slaves of a few proud and insolent sinners. These shocking extremes provoking to extremes of another kind, speculations are let loose as destructive to all authority, as the former are to all freedom; and every government is called tyranny and usurpation which is not formed on their fancies. In this manner the stirrers-up of this contention, not satisfied with distracting our dependencies and filling them with blood and slaughter, are corrupting our understandings: they are endeavouring to tear up, along with practical liberty, all the foundations of human society, all equity and justice, religion and order.

Civil freedom, gentlemen, is not, as many have endeavoured to persuade you, a thing that lies hid in the depth of abstruse science. It is a blessing and a benefit, not an abstract speculation; and all the just reasoning that can be upon it is of so coarse a texture, as perfectly to suit the ordinary capacities of those who are to enjoy, and of those who are to defend it. Far from any resemblance to those propositions in geometry and metaphysics, which admit no medium, but must be true or false in all their latitude; social and civil freedom, like all other things in common life, are variously mixed and modified, enjoyed in very different degrees, and shaped into an infinite diversity of forms, according to the temper and circumstances of every community. The *extreme* of liberty (which is its abstract perfection, but its real fault) obtains nowhere, nor ought to obtain anywhere. Because extremes, as we all know, in every point which relates either to our duties or satisfactions in life, are destructive both to virtue and enjoyment. Liberty too must be limited in order to be possessed. The degree of restraint it is impossible in any case to settle precisely. But it ought to be the constant aim of every wise public council, to find out by cautious experiments, and rational, cool endeavours, with how little, not how much, of this restraint, the community can subsist. For liberty is a good to be improved, and not an evil to be lessened. It is not only a private blessing of the first order, but the vital spring and energy of the state itself, which has just so much life and vigour as there is liberty in it. But whether liberty be advantageous or not, (for I know it is a fashion to decry the very principle,) none will dispute that peace is a blessing; and peace must in the course of human affairs be frequently bought by some indulgence and toleration at least to liberty. For as the sabbath (though of Divine institution) was made for man, not man for the sabbath, government, which can claim no higher origin or authority, in its exercise at least, ought to conform to the exigences of the time, and the temper and character of the people, with whom it is concerned; and not always to attempt violently to bend the people to their theories of subjection. The bulk of mankind on their part are not excessively curious concerning any theories, whilst they are really happy; and one sure symptom of an ill-conducted state is the propensity of the people to resort to them.

But when subjects, by a long course of such ill conduct, are once thoroughly inflamed, and the state itself violently distempered, the people must have some satisfaction to their feelings more solid than a sophistical speculation on law and government. Such was our situation; and such a satisfaction was necessary to prevent recourse to arms; it was necessary towards laying them down; it will be necessary to prevent the taking them up again and again. Of what nature this satisfaction ought to be, I wish it had been the disposition of parliament seriously to consider. It was certainly a deliberation that called for the exertion of all their wisdom.

I am, and ever have been, deeply sensible of the difficulty of reconciling the strong presiding power, that is so useful towards the conservation of a vast, disconnected, infinitely diversified empire, with that liberty and safety of the provinces, which they must enjoy, (in opinion and practice at least,) or they will not be provinces at all. I know, and have long felt, the difficulty of reconciling the unwieldy haughtiness of a great ruling nation, habituated to command, pampered by enormous wealth, and confident from a long course of prosperity and victory, to the high spirit of free dependencies, animated with the first glow and activity of juvenile heat, and assuming to themselves, as their birthright, some part of that very pride which oppresses them. They who perceive no difficulty in reconciling these tempers, (which however to make peace must some way or other be reconciled,) are much above my capacity, or much below the magnitude of the business. Of one thing I am perfectly clear, that it is not by deciding the suit, but by compromising the difference, that peace can be restored or kept. They who would put an end to such quarrels, by declaring roundly in favour of the whole demands of either party, have mistaken, in my humble opinion, the office of a mediator.

The war is now of full two years' standing; the controversy, of many more. In different periods of the dispute different methods of reconciliation were to be pursued. I mean to trouble you with a short state of things at the most important of these periods, in order to give you a more distinct idea of our policy with regard to this most delicate of all objects. The colonies were from the beginning subject to the legislature of Great Britain, on principles which they never examined; and we permitted to them many local privileges, without asking how they agreed with that legislative authority. Modes of administration were formed in an insensible and very unsystematic manner. But they gradually adapted themselves to the varying condition of things. – What was first a single kingdom, stretched into an empire; and an imperial superintendency, of some kind or other, became necessary. Parliament, from a mere representative of the people, and a guardian of popular privileges for its own immediate constituents, grew into a mighty sovereign. Instead of being a control on the crown on its own behalf, it communicated a sort of strength to the royal authority; which was wanted for the conservation of a new object, but which could not be safely trusted to the crown alone. On the other hand, the colonies, advancing by equal steps, and governed by the same necessity, had formed within themselves, either by royal instruction or royal charter, assemblies so exceedingly resembling a parliament, in all their forms, functions, and powers, that it was impossible they should not imbibe some opinion of a similar authority.

At the first designation of these assemblies, they were probably not intended for anything more, (nor perhaps did they think themselves much higher,) than the municipal corporations within this island, to which some at present love to compare them. But nothing in progression can rest on its original plan. We may as well think of rocking a grown man in the cradle of an infant. Therefore as the colonies prospered and increased to a numerous and mighty people, spreading over a very great tract of the globe; it was natural that they should attribute to assemblies, so respectable in their formal constitution, some part of the dignity of the the nations which they represented. No longer tied to by-laws, these assemblies made acts of all sorts and in all cases whatsoever. They levied money, not for parochial purposes, but upon regular grants to the crown, following all the rules and principles of a parliament to which they approached every day more and more nearly. Those who think themselves wiser than Providence, and stronger than the course of nature, may complain of all this variation, on the one side or the other, as their several humours and prejudices may lead them. But things could not be otherwise; and English colonies must be had on these terms, or not had at all. In the mean time, neither party felt any inconvenience from this double legislature, to which they had been formed by imperceptible habits, and old custom, the great support of all the governments in the world. Though these two legislatures were sometimes found perhaps performing the very same functions, they did not very grossly or systematically clash. In all likelihood this arose from mere neglect; possibly from the natural operation of things, which, left to themselves, generally fall into their proper order. But whatever was the cause, it is certain that a regular revenue, by the authority of parliament, for the support of civil and military establishments, seems not to have been thought of until the colonies were too proud to submit, too strong to be forced, too enlightened not to see all the consequences which must arise from such a system.

If ever this scheme of taxation was to be pushed against the inclinations of the people, it was evident that discussions must arise, which would let loose all the elements that composed this double constitution; would show how much each of their members had departed from its original principles; and would discover contradictions in each legislature, as well to its own first principles as to its relation to the other, very difficult, if not absolutely impossible, to be reconciled.

Therefore at the first fatal opening of this contest, the wisest course seemed to be to put an end as soon as possible to the immediate causes of the dispute; and to quiet a discussion, not easily settled upon clear principles, and arising from claims, which pride would permit neither party to abandon, by resorting as nearly as possible to the old, successful course. A mere repeal of the obnoxious tax, with a declaration of the legislative authority of this kingdom, was then fully sufficient to procure peace to *both sides*. Man is a creature of habit, and, the first breach being of very short continuance, the colonies fell back exactly into their ancient state. The congress has used an expression with regard to this pacification, which appears to me truly significant. After the repeal of the stamp act, "the colonies fell," says this assembly, "into their ancient state of *unsuspecting confidence in the mother country.*" This unsuspecting confidence is the true centre of gravity amongst mankind, about which all the parts are at rest. It is this *unsuspecting confidence* that removes all difficulties, and reconciles all the contradictions which occur in the complexity of all ancient, puzzled, political establishments. Happy are the rulers which have the secret of preserving it!

The whole empire has reason to remember, with eternal gratitude, the wisdom and temper of that man and his excellent associates, who, to recover this confidence, formed a plan of pacification in 1766.[19] That plan, being built upon the nature of man, and the circumstances and habits of the two countries, and not on any visionary speculations, perfectly answered its end, as long as it was thought proper to adhere to it. Without giving a rude shock to the dignity (well or ill understood) of this parliament, they gave perfect content to our dependencies. Had it not been for the mediatorial spirit and talents of that great man, between such clashing pretensions and passions, we should then have rushed headlong (I know what I say) into the calamities of that civil war, in which, by departing from his system, we are at length involved; and we should have been precipitated into that war, at a time when circumstances both at home and abroad were far, very far, more unfavourable unto us than they were at the breaking out of the present troubles.

I had the happiness of giving my first votes in parliament for their pacification. I was one of those almost unanimous members, who, in the necessary concessions of parliament, would as much as possible have preserved its authority, and respected its honour.[20] I could not at once tear from my heart prejudices which were dear to me, and which bore a resemblance to virtue. I had then, and I have still, my partialities. What parliament gave up, I wished to be given as of grace, and favour, and affection, and not as a restitution of stolen goods. High dignity relented as it was soothed; and a benignity from old acknowledged greatness had its full effect on our dependencies. Our unlimited declaration of legislative authority produced not a single murmur. If this undefined power has become odious since that time, and full of horror to the colonies, it is because the *unsuspicious confidence* is lost, and the parental affection, in the bosom of whose boundless authority they reposed their privileges, is become estranged and hostile.

It will be asked, if such was then my opinion of the mode of pacification, how I came to be the very person who moved, not only for a repeal of all the late coercive statutes, but for mutilating, by a positive law, the entireness of the legislative power of parliament, and cutting off from it the whole right of taxation? I answer, because a different state of things requires a different conduct. When the dispute had gone to these last extremities, (which no man laboured more to prevent than I did,) the concessions which had satisfied in the beginning, could satisfy no longer; because the violation of tacit faith required explicit security. The same cause which has introduced all formal compacts and covenants among men made it necessary. I mean habits of soreness, jealousy, and distrust. I parted with it, as with a limb; but as a limb to save the body; and I would have parted with more, if more had been necessary; anything rather than a fruitless, hopeless, unnatural civil war. This mode of yielding would, it is said, give way to independency, without a war. I am persuaded from the nature of things, and from every information, that it would have had a directly contrary effect. But if it had this effect, I confess that I should prefer independency without war, to independency with it; and I have so much trust in the inclinations and prejudices of mankind, and so little in anything else, that I should expect ten times more benefit to this kingdom from the affection of America, though under a separate establishment, than from her perfect submission to the crown and parliament, accompanied with her terror, disgust, and abhorrence. Bodies tied together by so unnatural a bond of union as mutual hatred, are only connected to their ruin.

One hundred and ten respectable members of parliament voted for that concession. Many not present, when the motion was made, were of the sentiments of those who voted. I knew it would then have made peace. I am not without hopes that it would do so at present if it were adopted. No benefit, no revenue, could be lost by it; something might possibly be gained by its consequences. For be fully assured, that, of all the phantoms that ever deluded the fond hopes of a credulous world, a parliamentary revenue in the colonies is the most perfectly chimerical. Your breaking them to any subjection, far from relieving your burthens, (the pretext for this war,) will never pay that military force which will be kept up to the destruction of their liberties and yours. I risk nothing in this prophecy.

Gentlemen, you have my opinion on the present state of public affairs. Mean as they may be in themselves, your partiality has made them of some importance. Without troubling myself to inquire whether I am under a formal obligation to it, I have a pleasure in accounting for my conduct to my constituents. I feel warmly on this subject, and I express myself as I feel. If I presume to blame any public proceeding, I cannot be supposed to be personal. Would to God I could be suspected of it. My fault might be greater, but the public calamity would be less extensive. If my conduct has not been able to make any impression on the warm part of that ancient and powerful party, with whose support I was not honoured at my election; on my side, my respect, regard, and duty to them is not at all lessened. I owe the gentlemen who compose it my most humble service in everything. I hope that whenever any of them were pleased to command me, that they found me perfectly equal in my obedience. But flattery and friendship are very diffent things; and to mislead is not to serve them. I cannot purchase the favour of any man by concealing from him what I think his ruin. By the favour of my fellow-citizens, I am the representative of an honest, well-ordered, virtuous city; of a people, who preserve more of the original English simplicity, and purity of manners, than perhaps any other. You possess among you several men and magistrates of large and cultivated understandings; fit for any employment in any sphere. I do, to the best of my power, act so as to make myself worthy of so honourable a choice. If I were ready, on any call of my own vanity or interest, or to answer any election purpose, to forsake principles, (whatever they are,) which I had formed at a mature age, on full reflection, and which had been confirmed by long experience, I should forfeit the only thing which makes you pardon so many errors and imperfections in me. Not that I think it fit for any one to rely too much on his own understanding; or to be filled with a presumption, not becoming a Christian man, in his own personal stability and rectitude.

I hope I am far from that vain confidence, which almost always fails in trial. I know my weakness in all respects, as much at least as any enemy I have; and I attempt to take security against it. The only method which has ever been found effectual to preserve any man against the corruption of nature and example, is an habit of life and communication of counsels with the most virtuous and public-spirited men of the age you live in. Such a society cannot be kept without advantage, or deserted without shame. For this rule of conduct I may be called in reproach a *party man*; but I am little affected with such aspersions. In the way which they call party, I worship the constitution of your fathers; and I shall never blush for my political company. All reverence to honour, all idea of what it is, will be lost out of the world, before it can be imputed as a fault to any man, that he has been closely connected with those incomparable persons, living and dead, with whom for eleven years I have constantly thought and acted. If I have wandered out of the paths of rectitude into those of interested faction, it was in company with the Saviles, the Dowdeswells, the Wentworths, the Bentincks; with the Lenoxes, the Manchesters, the Keppels, the Saunderses;[21] with the temperate, permanent, hereditary virtue of the whole House of Cavendish;[22] names, among which, some have extended your fame and empire in arms, and all have fought the battle of your liberties in fields not less glorious. – These, and many more like these, grafting public principles on private honour, have redeemed the present age, and would have adorned the most splendid period in your history. Where could any man, conscious of his own inability to act alone, and willing to act as he ought to do, have arranged himself better? If any one thinks this kind of society to be taken up as the best method of gratifying low, personal pride, or ambitious interest, he is mistaken; and he knows nothing of the world.

Preferring this connexion, I do not mean to detract in the slightest degree from others. There are some of those, whom I admire at something of a greater distance, with whom I have had the happiness also perfectly to agree, in almost all the particulars, in which I have differed with some successive administrations; and they are such, as it never can be reputable to any government to reckon among its enemies. I hope there are none of you corrupted with the doctrine taught by wicked men for the worst purposes, and received by the malignant credulity of envy and ignorance, which is, that the men who act upon the public stage are all alike; all equally corrupt; all influenced by no other views than the sordid lure of salary and pension. The thing I know by experience to be false. Never expecting to find perfection in men, and not looking for Divine attributes in created beings, in my commerce with my contemporaries, I have found much human virtue. I have seen not a little public spirit; a real subordination of interest to duty; and a decent and regulated sensibility to honest fame and reputation. The age unquestionably produces (whether in a greater or less number than former times, I know not) daring profligates, and insidious hypocrites. What then? Am I not to avail myself of whatever good is to be found in the world, because of the mixture of evil that will always be in it? The smallness of the quantity in currency only heightens the value. They who raise suspicions on the good on account of the behaviour of ill men, are of the party of the latter. The common cant is no justification for taking this party. I have been deceived, say they, by *Titius* and *Mœvius*;[23] I have been the dupe of this pretender or of that mountebank; and I can trust appearances no longer. But my credulity and want of discernment cannot, as I conceive, amount to a fair presumption against any man's integrity. A conscientious person would rather doubt his own judgment, than condemn his species. He would say, I have observed without attention, or judged upon erroneous maxims; I trusted to profession, when I ought to have attended to conduct. Such a man will grow wise, not malignant, by his acquaintance with the world. But he that accuses all mankind of corruption, ought to remember that he is sure to convict only one. In truth I should, much rather admit those, whom at any time I have disrelished the most, to be patterns of perfection, than seek a consolation to my own unworthiness, in a general communion of depravity with all about me.

That this ill-natured doctrine should be preached by the missionaries of a court, I do not wonder. It answers their purpose. But that it should be heard among those who pretend to be strong assertors of liberty, is not only surprising, but hardly natural. This moral levelling is a *servile principle*. It leads to practical passive obedience far better than all the doctrines which the pliant accommodation of theology to power has ever produced. It cuts up by the roots, not only all idea of forcible resistance, but even of civil opposition. It disposes men to an abject submission, not by opinion, which may be shaken by argument or altered by passion, but by the strong ties of public and private interest. For if all men who act in a public situation are equally selfish, corrupt, and venal, what reason can be given for desiring any sort of change, which, besides the evils which must attend all changes, can be productive of no possible advantage? The active men in the state are true samples of the mass. If they are universally depraved, the commonwealth itself is not sound. We may amuse ourselves with talking as much as we please of the virtue of middle or humble life; that is, we may place our confidence in the virtue of those who have never been tried. But if the persons who are continually emerging out of that sphere, be no better than those whom birth has placed above it, what hopes are there in the remainder of the body, which is to furnish the perpetual succession of the state? All who have ever written on government are unanimous, that among a people generally corrupt, liberty cannot long exist. And indeed how is it possible? when those who are to make the laws, to guard, to enforce, or to obey them, are, by a tacit confederacy of manners, indisposed to the spirit of all generous and noble institutions.

I am aware that the age is not what we all wish. But I am sure, that the only means of checking its precipitate degeneracy, is heartily to concur with whatever is the best in our time: and to have some more correct standard of judging what that best is, than the transient and uncertain favour of a court. If once we are able to find, and can prevail on ourselves to strengthen, an union of such men, whatever accidentally becomes indisposed to ill-exercised power, even by the ordinary operation of human passions, must join with that society, and cannot long be joined without in some degree assimilating to it. Virtue will catch as well as vice by contact; and the public stock of honest, manly principle will daily accumulate. We are not too nicely to scrutin-ise motives as long as action is irreproachable. It is enough (and for a worthy man perhaps too much) to deal out its infamy to convicted guilt and declared apostasy.

This, gentlemen, has been from the beginning the rule of my conduct; and I mean to continue it, as long as such a body as I have described can by any possibility be kept together; for I should think it the most dreadful of all offences, not only towards the present generation, but to all the future, if I were to do anything which could make the minutest breach in this great conservatory of free principles. Those who perhaps have the same intentions, but are separated by some little political animosities, will I hope discern at last, how little conducive it is to any rational purpose, to lower its reputation. For my part, gentlemen, from much experience, from no little thinking, and from comparing a great variety of things, I am thoroughly persuaded, that the last hopes of preserving the spirit of the English constitution, or of reuniting the dissipated members of the English race upon a common plan of tranquillity and liberty, does entirely depend on their firm and lasting union; and above all, on their keeping themselves from that despair, which is so very apt to fall on those, whom a violence of character and a mixture of ambitious views do not support through a long, painful, and unsuccessful struggle.

There never, gentlemen, was a period in which the stedfast-ness of some men has been put to so sore a trial. It is not very difficult for well-formed minds to abandon their interest; but the separation of fame and virtue is a harsh divorce. Liberty is in danger of being made unpopular to Englishmen. Contending for an imaginary power, we begin to acquire the spirit of domination, and to lose the relish of honest equality. The principles of our forefathers become suspected to us, because we see them animating the present opposition of our children. The faults which grow out of the luxuriance of freedom appear much more shocking to us than the base vices which are generated from the rankness of servitude. Accordingly the least resistance to power appears more inexcusable in our eyes than the greatest abuses of authority. All dread of a standing military force is looked upon as a superstitious panic. All shame of calling in foreigners and savages in a civil contest is worn off. We grow indifferent to the consequences inevitable to ourselves from the plan of ruling half the empire by a mercenary sword. We are taught to believe, that a desire of domineering over our countrymen is love to our country; that those who hate civil war abate rebellion, and that the amiable and conciliatory virtues of lenity, moderation, and tenderness to the privileges of those who depend on this kingdom, are a sort of treason to the state.

It is impossible that we should remain long in a situation, which breeds such notions and dispositions, without some great alteration in the national character. Those ingenuous and feeling minds who are so fortified against all other things, and so unarmed to whatever approaches in the shape of disgrace, finding these principles, which they considered as sure means of honour, to be grown into disrepute, will retire disheartened and disgusted. Those of a more robust make, the bold, able, ambitious men, who pay some of their court to power through the people, and substitute the voice of transient opinion in the place of true glory, will give in to the general mode; and those superior understandings which ought to correct vulgar prejudice, will confirm and aggravate its errors. Many things have been long operating towards a gradual change in our prnciples. But this American war has done more in a very few years, than all the other causes could have effected in a century. It is therefore not on its own separate account, but because of its attendant circumstances, that I consider its continuance, or its ending in any way but that of an honourable and liberal accommodation, as the greatest evils which can befall us. For that reason I have troubled you with this long letter. For that reason I entreat you again and again, neither to be persuaded, shamed, or frighted out of the principles that have hitherto led so many of you to abhor the war, its cause, and its consequences. Let us not be among the first who renounce the maxims of our forefathers.

I have the honour to be,

GENTLEMEN,

Your most obedient and faithful humble servant,

EDMUND BURKE

Beaconsfield, April 3, 1777

P.S. You may communicate this letter in any manner you think proper to my constituents.

SPEECH ON
ECONOMICAL REFORM

11 FEBRUARY 1780

MR. SPEAKER,

I RISE, IN ACQUITTAL of my engagement to the House, in obedience to the strong and just requisition of my constituents, and, I am persuaded, in conformity to the unanimous wishes of the whole nation, to submit to the wisdom of parliament, "A Plan of reform in the constitution of several parts of the public economy."

I have endeavoured, that this plan should include, in its execution, a considerable reduction of improper expense; that it should effect a conversion of unprofitable titles into a productive estate; that it should lead to, and indeed almost compel, a provident administration of such sums of public money as must remain under discretionary trusts; that it should render the incurring debts on the civil establishment (which must ultimately affect national strength and national credit) so very difficult, as to become next to impracticable.

But what, I confess, was uppermost with me, what I bent the whole force of my mind to, was the reduction of that corrupt influence, which is itself the perennial spring of all prodigality, and of all disorder; which loads us, more than millions of debt; which takes away vigour from our arms, wisdom from our councils, and every shadow of authority and credit from the most venerable parts of our constitution.

Sir, I assure you, very solemnly, and with a very clear conscience, that nothing in the world has led me to such an undertaking, but my zeal for the honour of this House, and the settled, habitual, systematic affection I bear to the cause and to the principles of government.

I enter perfectly into the nature and consequences of my attempt; and I advance to it with a tremor that shakes me to the inmost fibre of my frame. I feel that I engage in a business, in itself most ungracious, totally wide of the course of prudent conduct; and, I really think, the most completely adverse that can be imagined to the natural turn and temper of my own mind. I know, that all parsimony is of a quality approaching to unkindness; and that (on some person or other) every reform must operate as a sort of punishment. Indeed the whole class of the severe and restrictive virtues are at a market almost too high for humanity. What is worse, there are very few of those virtues which are not capable of being imitated, and even outdone, in many of their most striking effects, by the worst of vices. Malignity and envy will carve much more deeply, and finish much more sharply, in the work of retrenchment, than frugality and providence. I do not, therefore, wonder, that gentlemen have kept away from such a task, as well from good-nature as from prudence. Private feeling might, indeed, be overborne by legislative reason; and a man of a long-sighted and strong-nerved humanity might bring himself, not so much to consider from whom he takes a superfluous enjoyment, as for whom in the end he may preserve the absolute necessaries of life.

But it is much more easy to reconcile this measure to human-ity, than to bring it to any agreement with prudence. I do not mean that little, selfish, pitiful, bastard thing, which sometimes goes by the name of a family in which it is not legitimate, and to which it is a disgrace; – I mean even that public and enlarged prudence, which, apprehensive of being disabled from rendering acceptable services to the world, withholds itself from those that are invidious. Gentlemen who are, with me, verging towards the decline of life, and are apt to form their ideas of kings from kings of former times, might dread the anger of a reigning prince: – they who are more provident of the future, or by being young are more interested in it, might tremble at the resentment of the successor; they might see a long, dull, dreary, unvaried visto of despair and exclusion, for half a century, before them. This is no pleasant prospect at the outset of a political journey.

Besides this, Sir, the private enemies to be made in all attempts of this kind are innumerable; and their enmity will be the more bitter, and the more dangerous too, because a sense of dignity will oblige them to conceal the cause of their resent-ment. Very few men of great families and extensive connexions, but will feel the smart of a cutting reform, in some close relation, some bosom friend, some pleasant acquaintance, some dear, protected dependent. Emolument is taken from some; patron-age from others; objects of pursuit from all. Men, forced into an involuntary independence, will abhor the authors of a blessing which in their eyes has so very near a resemblance to a curse.

When officers are removed and the offices remain, you may set the gratitude of some against the anger of others; you may oppose the friends you oblige against the enemies you provoke. But services of the present sort create no attachments. The individual good felt in a public benefit is comparatively so small, comes round through such an involved labyrinth of intricate and tedious revolutions; whilst a present, personal detriment is so heavy where it falls, and so instant in its operation, that the cold commendation of a public advantage never was, and never will be, a match for the quick sensibility of a private loss: and you may depend upon it, Sir, that when many people have an interest in railing, sooner or later, they will bring a considerable degree of unpopularity upon any measure. So that, for the present at least, the reformation will operate against the reformers; and revenge (as against them at the least) will produce all the effects of corruption.

This, Sir, is almost always the case, where the plan has complete success. But how stands the matter in the mere attempt? Nothing, you know, is more common than for men to wish, and call loudly too, for a reformation, who, when it arrives, do by no means like the severity of its aspect. Reformation is one of those pieces which must be put at some distance in order to please. Its greatest favourers love it better in the abstract than in the substance. When any old prejudice of their own, or any interest that they value, is touched, they become scrupulous, they become captious, and every man has his separate exception. Some pluck out the black hairs, some the grey; one point must be given up to one, another point must be yielded to another; nothing is suffered to prevail upon its own principle; the whole is so frittered down, and disjointed, that scarcely a trace of the original scheme remains! Thus, between the resistance of power, and the unsystematical process of popularity, the undertaker and the undertaking are both exposed, and the poor reformer is hissed off the stage both by friends and foes.

Observe, Sir, that the apology for my undertaking (an apology which, though long, is no longer than necessary) is not grounded on my want of the fullest sense of the difficult and invidious nature of the task I undertake. I risk odium if I succeed, and contempt if I fail. My excuse must rest in my own and your conviction of the absolute, urgent *necessity* there is that something of the kind should be done. If there is any sacrifice to be made, either of estimation or of fortune, the smallest is the best. Commanders-in-chief are not to be put upon the forlorn hope. But, indeed, it is necessary that the attempt should be made. It is necessary from our own political circumstances; it is necessary from the operations of the enemy; it is necessary from the demands of the people, whose desires, when they do not militate with the stable and eternal rules of justice and reason, (rules which are above us and above them,) ought to be as a law to a House of Commons.

As to our circumstances, I do not mean to aggravate the difficulties of them by the strength of any colouring whatsoever. On the contrary, I observe, and observe with pleasure, that our affairs rather wear a more promising aspect than they did on the opening of this session. We have had some leading successes. But those who rate them at the highest (higher a great deal indeed than I dare to do) are of opinion, that, upon the ground of such advantages, we cannot at this time hope to make any treaty of peace, which would not be ruinous and completely disgraceful. In such an anxious state of things, if dawnings of success serve to animate our diligence, they are good; if they tend to increase our presumption, they are worse than defeats. The state of our affairs shall then be as promising as any one may choose to conceive it: it is, however, but promising. We must recollect, that, with but half of our natural strength, we are at war against confederated powers, who have singly threatened us with ruin; we must recollect, that, whilst we are left naked on one side, our other flank is uncovered by any alliance; that, whilst we are weighing and balancing our successes against our losses, we are accumulating debt to the amount of at least fourteen millions in the year. That loss is certain.

I have no wish to deny, that our successes are as brilliant as any one chooses to make them; our resources too may, for me, be as unfathomable as they are represented. Indeed, they are just what-ever the people possess, and will submit to pay. Taxing is an easy business. Any projector can contrive new impositions; any bungler can add to the old. But is it altogether wise to have no other bounds to your impositions, than the patience of those who are to bear them?

All I claim upon the subject of your resources is this, that they are not likely to be increased by wasting them. – I think I shall be permitted to assume, that a system of frugality will not lessen your riches, whatever they may be; – I believe it will not be hotly disputed, that those resources which lie heavy on the subject, ought not to be objects of preference; that they ought not to be the *very first choice*, to an honest representative of the people.

This is all, Sir, that I shall say upon our circumstances and our resources; I mean to say a little more on the operations of the enemy, because this matter seems to me very natural in our present deliberation. When I look to the other side of the water, I cannot help recollecting what Pyrrhus[1] said on reconnoitring the Roman camp, "These barbarians have nothing barbarous in their discipline." When I look, as I have pretty carefully looked, into the proceedings of the French king, I am sorry to say it, I see nothing of the character and genius of arbitrary finance; none of the bold frauds of bankrupt power; none of the wild struggles, and plunges, of despotism in distress; – no lopping off from the capital of debt; – no suspension of interest; – no robbery under the name of loan; – no raising the value, no debasing the substance, of the coin. I see neither Louis the Fourteenth nor Louis the Fifteenth. On the contrary, I behold with astonishment, rising before me, by the very hands of arbitrary power, and in the very midst of war and confusion, a regular methodical system of public credit: I behold a fabric laid on the natural and solid foundations of trust and confidence among men; and rising, by fair gradations, order over order, according to the just rules of symmetry and art. What a reverse of things! Principle, method, regularity, economy, frugality, justice to individuals, and care of the people, are the resources with which France makes war upon Great Britain. God avert the omen! But if we should see any genius in war and politics arise in France to second what is done in the bureau! – I turn my eyes from the consequences.

The noble lord in the blue riband,[2] last year, treated all this with contempt. He never could conceive it possible that the French minister of finance could go through that year with a loan of but seventeen hundred thousand pounds; and that he should be able to fund that loan without any tax. The second year, however, opens the very same scene. A small loan, a loan of no more than two millions five hundred thousand pounds, is to carry our enemies through the service of this year also. No tax is raised to fund that debt; no tax is raised for the current services. I am credibly informed that there is no anticipation whatsoever.

Compensations* are correctly made. Old debts continue to be sunk as in the time of profound peace. Even payments, which their treasury had been authorised to suspend during the time of war, are not suspended.

A general reform, executed through every *department of the revenue*, creates an annual income of more than half a million, whilst it facilitates and simplifies all the functions of administration. The king's *household* – at the remotest avenues to which all reformation has been hitherto stopped, – that household, which has been the strong-hold of prodigality, the virgin fortress which was never before attacked – has been not only not defended, but it has, even in the forms, been surrendered by the king to the economy of his minister. No capitulation; no reserve. Economy has entered in triumph into the public splendour of the monarch, into his private amusements, into the appointments of his nearest and highest relations. Economy and public spirit have made a beneficent and an honest spoil; they have plundered from extravagance and luxury, for the use of substantial service, a revenue of near four hundred thousand pounds. The reform of the finances, joined to this reform of the court, gives to the public nine hundred thousand pounds a year and upwards.

The minister who does these things is a great man – but the king who desires that they should be done is a far greater. We must do justice to our enemies – these are the acts of a patriot king. I am not in dread of the vast armies of France: I am not in dread of the gallant spirit of its brave and numerous nobility: I am not alarmed even at the great navy which has been so miraculously created. All these things Louis the Fourteenth had before. With all these things, the French monarchy has more than once fallen prostrate at the feet of the public faith of Great Britain. It was the want of public credit which disabled France from recovering after her defeats, or recovering even from her victories and triumphs. It was a prodigal court, it was an ill-ordered revenue, that sapped the foundations of all her greatness. Credit cannot exist under the arm of necessity. Necessity strikes at credit, I allow, with a heavier and quicker blow under an arbitrary monarchy, than under a limited and balanced government; but still necessity and credit are natural enemies, and cannot be long

---

* This term comprehends various retributions made to persons whose offices are taken away, or who, in any other way, suffer by the new arangements that are made.

reconciled in any situation. From necessity and corruption, a free state may lose the spirit of that complex constitution which is the foundation of confidence. On the other hand, I am far from being sure, that a monarchy, when once it is properly regulated, may not for a long time furnish a foundation for credit upon the solidity of its maxims, though it affords no ground of trust in its institutions. I am afraid I see in England, and in France, something like a beginning of both these things. I wish I may be found in a mistake.

This very short and very imperfect state of what is now going on in France (the last circumstances of which I received in about eight days after the registry of the edict*) I do not, Sir, lay before you for any invidious purpose. It is in order to excite in us the spirit of a noble emulation. – Let the nations make war upon each other (since we must make war) not with a low and vulgar malignity, but by a competition of virtues. This is the only way by which both parties can gain by war. The French have imitated us; let us, through them, imitate ourselves; ourselves in our better and happier days. If public frugality, under whatever men, or in whatever mode of government, is national strength, it is a strength which our enemies are in possession of before us.

Sir, I am well aware that the state and the result of the French economy which I have laid before you, are even now lightly treated by some, who ought never to speak but from information. Pains have not been spared to represent them as impositions on the public. Let me tell you, Sir, that the creation of a navy, and a two years' war without taxing, are a very singular species of imposture. But be it so. For what end does Neckar[3] carry on this delusion? Is it to lower the estimation of the crown he serves, and to render his own administration contemptible? No! no! He is conscious that the sense of mankind is so clear and decided in favour of economy, and of the weight and value of its resources, that he turns himself to every species of fraud and artifice to obtain the mere reputation of it. Men do not affect a conduct that tends to their discredit. Let us, then, get the better of Monsieur Neckar in his own way – let us do in reality what he does only in pretence – let us turn his French tinsel into English gold. Is then the mere opinion and appearance of frugality and good management of such use to France, and is the substance to be

* Edict, registered 29th January, 1780.

so mischievous to England? Is the very constitution of nature so altered by a sea of twenty miles, that economy should give power on the continent, and that profusion should give it here? For God's sake let not this be the only fashion of France which we refuse to copy.

To the last kind of necessity, the desires of the people, I have but a very few words to say. The ministers seem to contest this point; and affect to doubt whether the people do really desire a plan of economy in the civil government. Sir, this is too ridiculous. It is impossible that they should not desire it. It is impossible that a prodigality, which draws its resources from their indigence, should be pleasing to them. Little factions of pensioners, and their dependents, may talk another language. But the voice of nature is against them; and it will be heard. The people of England will not, they cannot take it kindly, that representatives should refuse to their constituents, what an absolute sovereign voluntarily offers to his subjects. The expression of the petitions is, that "*before any new burthens are laid upon this country, effectual measures be taken by this House to inquire into and correct the gross abuses in the expenditure of public money.*"[4]

This has been treated by the noble lord in the blue riband, as a wild, factious language. It happens, however, that the people in their address to us, use almost word for word the same terms as the king of France uses in addressing himself to his people; and it differs only, as it falls short of the French king's idea of what is due to his subjects. "To convince," says he, "our faithful subjects of *the desire we entertain not to recur to new impositions*, until we have first exhausted all the resources which order and economy can possibly supply," &c., &c.

These desires of the people of England, which come far short of the voluntary concessions of the king of France, are moderate indeed. They only contend that we should interweave some economy with the taxes with which we have chosen to begin the war. They request not that you should rely upon economy exclusively, but that you should give it rank and precedence, in the order of the ways and means of this single session.

But if it were possible, that the desires of our constituents, desires which are at once so natural, and so very much tempered and subdued, should have no weight with a House of Commons, which has its eye elsewhere; I would turn my eyes to the very quarter to which theirs are directed. I would reason this matter with the House, on the mere policy of the question; and I would undertake to prove, that an early dereliction of abuse is the direct interest of government; of government taken abstractedly from its duties, and considered merely as a system intending its own conservation.

If there is any one eminent criterion, which, above all the rest, distinguishes a wise government from an administration weak and improvident, it is this; – "well to know the best time and manner of yielding what it is impossible to keep." There have been, Sir, and there are, many who choose to chicane with their situation, rather than be instructed by it. Those gentlemen argue against every desire of reformation, upon the principles of a criminal prosecution. It is enough for them to justify their adherence to a pernicious system, that it is not of their contrivance; that it is an inheritance of absurdity, derived to them from their ancestors; that they can make out a long and unbroken pedigree of mismanagers that have gone before them. They are proud of the antiquity of their house; and they defend their errors, as if they were defending their inheritance: afraid of derogating from their nobility; and carefully avoiding a sort of blot in their scutcheon, which they think would degrade them for ever.

It was thus that the unfortunate Charles the First defended himself on the practice of the Stuart who went before him, and of all the Tudors; his partisans might have gone to the Plantagenets. – They might have found bad examples enough, both abroad and at home, that could have shown an ancient and illustrious descent. But there is a time when men will not suffer bad things because their ancestors have suffered worse. There is a time, when the hoary head of inveterate abuse will neither draw reverence, nor obtain protection. If the noble lord in the blue riband pleads "*not guilty*" to the charges brought against the present system of public economy, it is not possible to give a fair verdict by which he will not stand acquitted. But pleading is not our present business. His plea or his traverse may be allowed as an answer to a charge, when a charge is made. But if he puts himself in the way to obstruct reformation, then the faults of his office instantly become his own. Instead of a public officer in an abusive department, whose province is an object to be regulated, he becomes a criminal who is to be punished. I do most seriously put it to administration, to consider the wisdom of a timely reform. Early reformations are amicable arrangements with a friend in power; late reformations are terms imposed upon a conquered enemy: early reformations are made in cool blood; late reformations are made under a state of inflammation. In that state of things the people behold in government nothing that is respectable. They see the abuse, and they will see nothing else – They fall into the temper of a furious populace provoked at the disorder of a house of ill fame; they never attempt to correct or regulate; they go to work by the shortest way – They abate the nuisance, they pull down the house.

This is my opinion with regard to the true interest of government. But as it is the interest of government that reformation should be early, it is the interest of the people that it should be temperate. It is their interest, because a temperate reform is permanent; and because it has a principle of growth. Whenever we improve, it is right to leave room for a further improvement. It is right to consider, to look about us, to examine the effect of what we have done. – Then we can proceed with confidence, because we can proceed with intelligence. Whereas in hot reformations, in what men, more zealous than considerate, call *making clear work*, the whole is generally so crude, so harsh, so indigested; mixed with so much imprudence, and so much injustice; so contrary to the whole course of human nature and human institutions, that the very people who are most eager for it are among the first to grow disgusted at what they have done. Then some part of the abdicated grievance is recalled from its exile in order to become a corrective of the correction. Then the abuse assumes all the credit and popularity of a reform. The very idea of purity and disinterestedness in politics falls into disrepute, and is considered as a vision of hot and inexperienced men; and thus disorders become incurable, not by the virulence of their own quality, but by the unapt and violent nature of the remedies. A great part, therefore, of my idea of reform is meant to operate gradually; some benefits will come at a nearer, some at a more remote period. We must no more make haste to be rich by parsimony, than by intemperate acquisition.

In my opinion, it is our duty when we have the desires of the people before us, to pursue them, not in the spirit of literal obedience, which may militate with their very principle, much less to treat them with a peevish and contentious litigation, as if we were adverse parties in a suit. It would, Sir, be most dishonourable for a faithful representative of the commons to take advantage of an inartificial expression of the people's wishes, in order to frustrate their attainment of what they have an undoubted right to expect. We are under infinite obligations to our constituents, who have raised us to so distinguished a trust, and have imparted such a degree of sanctity to common characters. We ought to walk before them with purity, plainness, and integrity of heart; with filial love, and not with slavish fear, which is always a low and trickling thing. For my own part, in what I have meditated upon that subject, I cannot indeed take upon me to say I have the honour *to follow* the sense of the people. The truth is, *I met it on the way*, while I was pursuing their interest according to my own ideas. I am happy beyond expression to find that my intentions have so far coincided with theirs, that I have not had cause to be in the least scrupulous to sign their petition, conceiving it to express my own opinions, as nearly as general terms can express the object of particular arrangements.

I am therefore satisfied to act as a fair mediator between government and the people, endeavouring to form a plan which should have both an early and a temperate operation. I mean, that it should be substantial; that it should be systematic. That it should rather strike at the first cause of prodigality and corrupt influence, than attempt to follow them in all their effects.

It was to fulfil the first of these objects (the proposal of something substantial) that I found myself obliged, at the outset, to reject a plan proposed by an honourable and attentive member of parliament,* with very good intentions on his part, about a year or two ago. Sir, the plan I speak of was the tax of 25 *per cent*, moved upon places and pensions during the continuance of the American war. – Nothing, Sir, could have met my ideas more than such a tax if it was considered as a practical satire on that war, and as a penalty upon those who led us into it; but in any other view it appeared to me very liable to objections. I considered the scheme as neither substantial, nor permanent, nor systematical, nor likely to be a corrective of evil influence. I have always thought employments a very proper subject of regulation, but a very ill-chosen subject for a tax. An equal tax upon property is reasonable; because the object is of the same quality throughout. The species is the same, it differs only in its quantity: but a tax upon salaries is totally of a different nature; there can be no

* Thomas Gilbert, Esq., member for Lichfield.[5]

equality, and consequently no justice, in taxing them by the hundred in the gross.

We have, Sir, on our establishment, several offices which perform real service – We have also places that provide large rewards for no service at all. We have stations which are made for the public decorum; made for preserving the grace and majesty of a great people – We have likewise expensive formalities, which tend rather to the disgrace than the ornament of the state and the court. This, Sir, is the real condition of our establishments. To fall with the same severity on objects so perfectly dissimilar, is the very reverse of a reformation. I mean a reformation framed, as all serious things ought to be, in number, weight, and measure. – Suppose, for instance, that two men received a salary of £800 a year each. – In the office of one there is nothing at all to be done; in the other, the occupier is oppressed by its duties. – Strike off 25 *per cent* from these two offices, you take from one man £200, which in justice he ought to have, and you give in effect to the other £600, which he ought not to receive. The public robs the former, and the latter robs the public; and this mode of mutual robbery is the only way in which the office and the public can make up their accounts.

But the balance, in settling the account of this double injustice, is much against the state. The result is short. You purchase a saving of two hundred pounds, by a profusion of six. Besides, Sir, whilst you leave a supply of unsecured money behind, wholly at the discretion of ministers, they make up the tax to such places as they wish to favour, or in such new places as they may choose to create. Thus the civil list becomes oppressed with debt; and the public is obliged to repay, and to repay with a heavy interest, what it has taken by an injudicious tax. Such has been the effect of the taxes hitherto laid on pensions and employments, and it is no encouragement to recur again to the same expedient.

In effect, such a scheme is not calculated to produce, but to prevent, reformation. It holds out a shadow of present gain to a greedy and necessitous public, to divert their attention from those abuses, which in reality are the great causes of their wants. It is a composition to stay inquiry; it is a fine paid by mismanagement, for the renewal of its lease. What is worse, it is a fine paid by industry and merit, for an indemnity to the idle and the worthless. But I shall say no more upon this topic, because (whatever may be given out to the contrary) I know that the noble lord in the blue riband perfectly agrees with me in these sentiments.

After all that I have said on this subject, I am so sensible that it is our duty to try everything which may contribute to the relief of the nation, that I do not attempt wholly to reprobate the idea even of a tax. Whenever, Sir, the encumbrance of useless office (which lies no less a dead weight upon the service of the state, than upon its revenues) shall be removed; – when the remaining offices shall be classed according to the just proportion of their rewards and services, so as to admit the application of an equal rule to their taxation; when the discretionary power over the civil list cash shall be so regulated, that a minister shall no longer have the means of repaying with a private, what is taken by a public, hand – if after all these preliminary regulations, it should be thought that a tax on places is an object worthy of the public attention, I shall be very ready to lend my hand to a reduction of their emoluments.

Having thus, Sir, not so much absolutely rejected, as postponed, the plan of a taxation of office, – my next business was to find something which might be really substantial and effectual. I am quite clear, that if we do not go to the very origin and first ruling cause of grievances, we do nothing. What does it signify to turn abuses out of one door, if we are to let them in at another? What does it signify to promote economy upon a measure, and to suffer it to be subverted in the principle? Our ministers are far from being wholly to blame for the present ill order which prevails. Whilst institutions directly repugnant to good management are suffered to remain, no effectual or lasting reform *can* be introduced.

I therefore thought it necessary, as soon as I conceived thoughts of submitting to you some plan of reform, to take a comprehensive view of the state of this country; to make a sort of survey of its jurisdictions, its estates, and its establishments. Something, in every one of them, seemed to me to stand in the way of all economy in their administration, and prevented every possibility of methodising the system. But being, as I ought to be, doubtful of myself, I was resolved not to proceed in an *arbitrary* manner, in any particular which tended to change the settled state of things, or in any degree to affect the fortune or situation, the interest or the importance, of any individual. By an arbitrary proceeding, I mean one conducted by the private opinions, tastes, or feelings, of the man who attempts to regulate. These private measures are not standards of the exchequer, nor balances of the sanctuary. General principles cannot be debauched or corrupted by interest or caprice; and by those principles I was resolved to work.

Sir, before I proceed further, I will lay these principles fairly before you, that afterwards you may be in a condition to judge whether every object of regulation, as I propose it, comes fairly under its rule. This will exceedingly shorten all discussion between us, if we are perfectly in earnest in establishing a system of good management. I therefore lay down to myself seven fundamental rules; they might indeed be reduced to two or three simple maxims; but they would be too general, and their application to the several heads of the business before us would not be so distinct and visible. I conceive then,

First, That all jurisdictions, which furnish more matter of expense, more temptation to oppression, or more means and instruments of corrupt influence, than advantage to justice or political administration, ought to be abolished.

Secondly, That all public estates which are more subservient to the purposes of vexing, overawing, and influencing those who hold under them, and to the expense of perception and management, than of benefit to the revenue, ought, upon every principle both of revenue and of freedom, to be disposed of.

Thirdly, That all offices which bring more charge than proportional advantage to the state; that all offices which may be ingrafted on others, uniting and simplifying their duties, ought in the first case to be taken away; and in the second, to be consolidated.

Fourthly, That all such offices ought to be abolished, as obstruct the prospect of the general superintendent of finance; which destroy his superintendency, which disable him from foreseeing and providing for charges as they may occur; from preventing expense in its origin, checking it in its progress, or securing its application to its proper purposes. A minister, under whom expenses can be made without his knowledge, can never say what it is that he can spend, or what it is that he can save.

Fifthly, That it is proper to establish an invariable order in all payments; which will prevent partiality; which will give preference to services, not according to the importunity of the demandant, but the rank and order of their utility or their justice.

Sixthly, That it is right to reduce every establishment, and every part of an establishment, (as nearly as possible,) to certainty; the life of all order and good management.

Seventhly, That all subordinate treasuries, as the nurseries of mismanagement, and as naturally drawing to themselves as much money as they can, keeping it as long as they can, and accounting for it as late as they can, ought to be dissolved. They have a tendency to perplex and distract the public accounts, and to excite a suspicion of government even beyond the extent of their abuse.

Under the authority and with the guidance of those principles, I proceed; wishing that nothing in any establishment may be changed, where I am not able to make a strong, direct, and solid application of those principles, or of some one of them. An economical constitution is a necessary basis for an economical administration.

First, with regard to the sovereign jurisdictions, I must observe, Sir, that whoever takes a view of this kingdom in a cursory manner will imagine, that he beholds a solid, compacted, uniform system of monarchy; in which all inferior jurisdictions are but as rays diverging from one centre. But on examining it more nearly you find much eccentricity and confusion. It is not a monarchy in strictness. But, as in the Saxon times this country was an heptarchy, it is now a strange sort of *pentarchy.* It is divided into five several distinct principalities, besides the supreme. There is indeed this difference from the Saxon times, that as in the itinerant exhibitions of the stage, for want of a complete company, they are obliged to throw a variety of parts on their chief performer; so our sovereign condescends himself to act not only the principal, but all the subordinate, parts in the play. He condescends to dissipate the royal character, and to trifle with those light, subordinate, lacquered sceptres in those hands that sustain the ball representing the world, or which wield the trident that commands the ocean. Cross a brook, and you lose the king of England; but you have some comfort in coming again under his Majesty, though "shorn of his beams," and no more than Prince of Wales. Go to the north, and you find him dwindled to a Duke of Lancaster; turn to the west of that north, and he pops upon you in the humble character of Earl of Chester. Travel a few miles on, the Earl of Chester disappears; and the king surprises you again as Count Palatine of Lancaster. If you travel beyond Mount Edgecombe, you find him once more in his incognito, and he is Duke of Cornwall. So that, quite fatigued and satiated with this dull variety, you are infinitely refreshed when you return to the sphere of his proper splendour, and behold your amiable sovereign in his true, simple, undisguised, native character of majesty.

In every one of these five principalities, duchies, palatinates, there is a regular establishment of considerable expense, and most domineering influence. As his Majesty submits to appear in this state of subordination to himself, his loyal peers and faithful commons attend his royal transformations; and are not so nice as to refuse to nibble at those crumbs of emoluments, which console their petty metamorphoses. Thus every one of those principalities has the apparatus of a kingdom, for the jurisdiction over a few private estates; and the formality and charge of the exchequer of Great Britain, for collecting the rents of a country 'squire. Cornwall is the best of them; but, when you compare the charge with the receipt, you will find that it furnishes no exception to the general rule. The duchy and county palatine of Lancaster do not yield, as I have reason to believe, on an average of twenty years, four thousand pounds a year clear to the crown. As to Wales, and the county palatine of Chester, I have my doubts whether their productive exchequer yields any returns at all. Yet one may say, that this revenue is more faithfully applied to its purposes than any of the rest; as it exists for the sole purpose of multiplying offices and extending influence.

An attempt was lately made to improve this branch of local influence, and to transfer it to the fund of general corruption. I have on the seat behind me, the constitution of Mr. John Probert;[6] a knight-errant dubbed by the noble lord in the blue riband, and sent to search for revenues and adventures upon the mountains of Wales. The commission is remarkable; and the event not less so. The commission sets forth, that "Upon a report of the *deputy auditor* (for there is a deputy auditor) of the principality of Wales, it appeared, that his Majesty's land revenues in the said principalities *are greatly diminished*;" – and "that upon a *report* of the *surveyor-general* of his Majesty's land revenues, upon a *memorial* of the auditor of his Majesty's revenues *within the said principality*, that his mines and forests have produced very *little profit either to the public revenue or to individuals*;" – and therefore they appoint Mr. Probert, with a pension of three hundred pounds a year from the said principality, to try whether he can make anything more of that very *little* which is stated to be so *greatly* diminished. *"A beggarly account of empty boxes."* And yet, Sir, you will remark – that this diminution from littleness (which serves only to prove the infinite divisibility of matter) was not for want of the tender and officious care (as we see) of surveyors-general and surveyors-particular; of auditors and deputy auditors; not for want of memorials, and remonstrances, and reports, and commissions, and constitutions, and inquisitions, and pensions.

Probert, thus armed, and accoutred – and paid, proceeded on his adventure; but he was no sooner arrived on the confines of Wales, than all Wales was in arms to meet him. That nation is brave and full of spirit. Since the invasion of King Edward, and the massacre of the bards,[7] there never was such a tumult, and alarm, and uproar, through the region of *Prestatyn. Snowden* shook to its base; *Cader Idris* was loosened from its foundations. The fury of litigious war blew her horn on the mountains. The rocks poured down their goatherds, and the deep caverns vomited out their miners. Everything above ground, and everything under ground, was in arms.

In short, Sir, to alight from my Welsh Pegasus, and to come to level ground; the *Preux Chevalier* Probert went to look for revenue like his masters upon other occasions; and, like his masters, he found rebellion. But we were grown cautious by experience. A civil war of paper might end in a more serious war; for now remonstrance met remonstrance, and memorial was opposed to memorial. The wise Britons thought it more reasonable that the poor, wasted, decrepit revenue of the principality should die a natural than a violent death. In truth, Sir, the attempt was no less an affront upon the understanding of that respectable people, than it was an attack on their property. They chose rather that their ancient, moss-grown castles should moulder into decay, under the silent touches of time, and the slow formality of an oblivious and drowsy exchequer, than that they should be battered down all at once, by the lively efforts of a pensioned engineer. As it is the fortune of the noble lord, to whom the auspices of this campaign belonged, frequently to provoke resistance, so it is his rule and nature to yield to that resistance *in all cases whatsoever.*

He was true to himself on this occasion. He submitted with spirit to the spirited remonstrances of the Welsh. Mr. Probert gave up his adventure, and keeps his pension – and so ends "the famous history of the revenue adventures of the bold baron North, and the good knight Probert, upon the mountains of Venodotia."

In such a state is the exchequer of Wales at present, that upon the report of the treasury itself, its *little* revenue is *greatly* diminished; and we see, by the whole of this strange transaction, that an attempt to improve it produces resistance; the resistance produces submission; and the whole ends in pension.*

It is nearly the same with the revenues of the duchy of Lancaster. To do nothing with them is extinction; to improve them is oppression. Indeed the whole of the estates, which support these minor principalities, is made up, not of revenues, and rents, and profitable fines, but of claims, of pretensions, of vexations, of litigations. They are exchequers of unfrequent receipt, and constant charge; a system of finances not fit for an economist who would be rich; not fit for a prince who would govern his subjects with equity and justice.

It is not only between prince and subject, that these mock jurisdictions, and mimic revenues, produce great mischief. They excite among the people a spirit of informing and delating; a spirit of supplanting and undermining one another. So that many, in such circumstances, conceive it advantageous to them rather to continue subject to vexation themselves, than to give up the means and chance of vexing others. It is exceedingly common for men to contract their love to their country into an attachment to its petty subdivisions; and they sometimes even cling to their provincial abuses, as if they were franchises and local privileges. Accordingly, in places where there is much of this kind of estate, persons will be always found, who would rather trust to their talents in recommending themselves to power for the renewal of their interests, than to encumber their purses, though never so lightly, in order to transmit independence to their posterity. It is a great mistake, that the desire of securing property is universal among mankind. Gaming is a principle inherent in human

---

* Here Lord North shook his head, and told those who sat near him, that Mr. Probert's pension was to depend on his success. It may be so. Mr. Probert's pension was, however, no essential part of the question; nor did Mr. B. care whether he still possessed it or not. His point was, to show the folly of attempting an improvement of the Welsh revenue under its present establishment.

nature. It belongs to us all. I would therefore break those tables: I would furnish no evil occupation for that spirit. I would make every man look everywhere, except to the intrigue of a court, for the improvement of his circumstances, or the security of his fortune. I have in my eye a very strong case in the duchy of Lancaster (which lately occupied Westminster Hall and the House of Lords) as my voucher for many of these reflections.*

For what plausible reason are these principalities suffered to exist? When a government is rendered complex (which in itself is no desirable thing) it ought to be for some political end which cannot be answered otherwise. Subdivisions in government are only admissible in favour of the dignity of inferior princes, and high nobility; or for the support of an aristocratic confederacy under some head; or for the conservation of the franchises of the people in some privileged province. For the two former of these ends, such are the subdivisions in favour of the electoral and other princes in the empire; for the latter of these purposes, are the jurisdictions of the imperial cities and the Hanse towns.[8] For the latter of these ends are also the countries of the States [Pais d'Etats] and certain cities and orders in France. These are all regulations with an object, and some of them with a very good object. But how are the principles of any of these subdivisions applicable in the case before us?

Do they answer any purpose to the king? The principality of Wales was given by patent to Edward the Black Prince,[9] on the ground on which it has since stood. – Lord Coke sagaciously observes upon it, "That in the charter of creating the Black Prince Edward prince of Wales, there is a great mystery – for less than an estate of inheritance so great a prince could not have, and an absolute estate of inheritance in so great a principality as Wales (this principality being so dear to him) he should not have; and therefore it was made, sibi et heredibus suis regibus Angliæ,[10] that by his decease, or attaining to the crown, it might be extinguished in the crown."

For the sake of this foolish mystery, of what a great prince could not have less, and should not have so much, of a principality which was too dear to be given, and too great to be kept – and for no other cause that ever I could find – this form and shadow of a

* Case of Richard Lee, Esq. appellant, against George Venables Lord Vernon, respondent, in the year 1776.

principality, without any substance, has been maintained. That you may judge in this instance (and it serves for the rest) of the difference between a great and a little economy, you will please to recollect, Sir, that Wales may be about the tenth part of England in size and population; and certainly not an hundredth part in opulence. Twelve judges perform the whole of the business, both of the stationary and the itinerant justice of this kingdom; but for Wales there are eight judges. There is in Wales an exchequer, as well as in all the duchies, according to the very best and most authentic absurdity of form. There are, in all of them, a hundred more difficult trifles and laborious fooleries, which serve no other purpose than to keep alive corrupt hope and servile dependence.

These principalities are so far from contributing to the ease of the king, to his wealth, or his dignity, that they render both his supreme and his subordinate authority perfectly ridiculous. It was but the other day, that that pert, factious fellow, the Duke of Lancaster, presumed to fly in the face of his liege lord, our gracious sovereign; and, *associating* with a parcel of lawyers as factious as himself, to the destruction of *all law and order*, and in *committees leading directly to rebellion* – presumed to go to law with the king. The object is neither your business nor mine. Which of the parties got the better, I really forget. I think it was (as it ought to be) the king. The material point is, that the suit cost about fifteen thousand pounds. But as the Duke of Lancaster is but a sort of *Duke Humphrey*,[11] and not worth a groat, our sovereign was obliged to pay the costs of both. Indeed this art of converting a great monarch into a little prince, this royal masquerading, is a very dangerous and expensive amusement; and one of the king's *menus plaisirs*, which ought to be reformed. This duchy, which is not worth four thousand pounds a year at best to revenue, is worth forty or fifty thousand to *influence*.

The duchy of Lancaster and the county palatine of Lancaster answered, I admit, some purpose in their original creation. They tended to make a subject imitate a prince. When Henry the Fourth from that stair ascended the throne, high-minded as he was, he was not willing to kick away the ladder. To prevent that principality from being extinguished in the crown, he severed it by act of parliament. He had a motive, such as it was: he thought his title to the crown unsound, and his possession insecure. He therefore managed a retreat in his duchy; which Lord Coke calls

(I do not know why) *par multis regnis*.[12] He flattered himself that it was practicable to make a projecting point half-way down, to break his fall from the precipice of royalty; as if it were possible for one who had lost a kingdom to keep anything else. However, it is evident that he thought so. When Henry the Fifth united, by act of parliament, the estates of his mother to the duchy, he had the same predilection with his father to the root of his family honours, and the same policy in enlarging the sphere of a possible retreat from the slippery royalty of the two great crowns he held. All this was changed by Edward the Fourth. He had no such family partialities, and his policy was the reverse of that of Henry the Fourth and Henry the Fifth. He accordingly again united the duchy of Lancaster to the crown. But when Henry the Seventh, who chose to consider himself as of the house of Lancaster, came to the throne, he brought with him the old pretensions and the old politics of that house. A new act of parliament, a second time, dissevered the duchy of Lancaster from the crown; and in that line things continued until the subversion of the monarchy, when principalities and powers fell along with the throne. The duchy of Lancaster must have been extinguished, if Cromwell,[13] who began to form ideas of aggrandising his house, and raising the several branches of it, had not caused the duchy to be again separated from the commonwealth, by an act of the parliament of those times.

What partiality, what objects of the politics of the house of Lancaster, or of Cromwell, has his present Majesty or his Majesty's family? What power have they within any of these principalities, which they have not within their kingdom? In what manner is the dignity of the nobility concerned in these principalities? What rights have the subject there, which they have not at least equally in every other part of the nation? These distinctions exist for no good end to the king, to the nobility, or to the people. They ought not to exist at all. If the crown (contrary to its nature, but most conformably to the whole tenor of the advice that has been lately given) should so far forget its dignity as to contend, that these jurisdictions and revenues are estates of private property, I am rather for acting as if that groundless claim were of some weight, than for giving up that essential part of the reform. I would value the clear income, and give a clear annuity to the crown, taken on the medium produce for twenty years.

If the crown has any favourite name or title, if the subject has any matter of local accommodation within any of these jurisdictions, it is meant to preserve them; and to improve them, if any improvement can be suggested. As to the crown reversions or titles upon the property of the people there, it is proposed to convert them from a snare to their independence into a relief from their burthens. I propose, therefore, to unite all the five principalities to the crown, and to its ordinary jurisdiction, – to abolish all those offices that produce an useless and chargeable separation from the body of the people, – to compensate those who do not hold their offices (if any such there are) at the pleasure of the crown, – to extinguish vexatious titles by an act of short limitation, – to sell those unprofitable estates which support useless jurisdictions, and to turn the tenant-right into a fee, on such moderate terms as will be better for the state than its present right, and which it is impossible for any rational tenant to refuse.

As to the duchies, their judicial economy may be provided for without charge. They have only to fall of course into the common county administration. A commission, more or less made or omitted, settles the matter fully. As to Wales, it has been proposed to add a judge to the several courts of Westminster Hall; and it has been considered as an improvement in itself. For my part, I cannot pretend to speak upon it with clearness or with decision; but certainly this arrangement would be more than sufficient for Wales. My original thought was to suppress five of the eight judges; and to leave the chief justice of Chester, with the two senior judges; and, to facilitate the business, to throw the twelve counties into six districts, holding the sessions alternately in the counties of which each district shall be composed. But on this I shall be more clear, when I come to the particular bill.

Sir, the House will now see whether, in praying for judgment against the minor principalities, I do not act in conformity to the laws that I had laid to myself, of getting rid of every jurisdiction more subservient to oppression and expense, than to any end of justice or honest policy; of abolishing offices more expensive than useful; of combining duties improperly separated; of changing revenues, more vexatious than productive, into ready money; of suppressing offices which stand in the way of economy; and of cutting off lurking subordinate treasuries. Dispute the rules; controvert the application; or give your hands to this salutary measure.

Most of the same rules will be found applicable to my second object – *the landed estate of the crown*. A landed estate is certainly the very worst which the crown can possess. All minute and dispersed possessions, possessions that are often of indeterminate value, and which require a continued personal attendance, are of a nature more proper for private management than public administration. They are fitter for the care of a frugal land steward than of an office in the state. Whatever they may possibly have been in other times, or in other countries, they are not of magnitude enough with us, to occupy a public department, nor to provide for a public object. They are already given up to parliament, and the gift is not of great value. Common prudence dictates, even in the management of private affairs, that all dispersed and chargeable estates should be sacrificed to the relief of estates more compact and better circumstanced.

If it be objected, that these lands at present would sell at a low market; this is answered, by showing that money is at a high price. The one balances the other. Lands sell at the current rate; and nothing can sell for more. But be the price what it may, a great object is always answered, whenever any property is transferred from hands that are not fit for that property, to those that are. The buyer and seller must mutually profit by such a bargain; and, what rarely happens in matters of revenue, the relief of the subject will go hand in hand with the profit of the exchequer.

As to the *forest lands*, in which the crown has (where they are not granted or prescriptively held) the *dominion* of the *soil*, and the *vert* and *venison*, that is to say, the timber and the game; and in which the people have a variety of rights, in common of herbage, and other commons, according to the usage of the several forests; – I propose to have those rights of the crown valued as manorial rights are valued on an enclosure; and a defined portion of land to be given for them; which land is to be sold for the public benefit.

As to the timber, I propose a survey of the whole. What is useless for the naval purposes of the kingdom, I would condemn, and dispose of for the security of what may be useful; and to enclose such other parts as may be most fit to furnish a perpetual supply; wholly extinguishing, for a very obvious reason, all right of *venison* in those parts.

The forests *rights* which extend over the lands and possessions of others, being of no profit to the crown, and a grievance, as far as it goes, to the subject; these I propose to extinguish without charge to the proprietors. The several commons are to be allotted and compensated for, upon ideas which I shall hereafter explain. They are nearly the same with the principles upon which you have acted in private enclosures. I shall never quit precedents where I find them applicable. For those regulations and compensations, and for every other part of the detail, you will be so indulgent as to give me credit for the present.

The revenue to be obtained from the sale of the forest lands and rights will not be so considerable, I believe, as many people have imagined; and I conceive it would be unwise to screw it up to the utmost, or even to suffer bidders to enhance, according to their eagerness, the purchase of objects, wherein the expense of that purchase may weaken the capital to be employed in their cultivation. This, I am well aware, might give room for partiality in the disposal. In my opinion it would be the lesser evil of the two. But I really conceive, that a rule of fair preference might be established, which would take away all sort of unjust and corrupt partiality. The principal revenue, which I propose to draw from these uncultivated wastes, is to spring from the improvement and population of the kingdom; which never can happen without producing an improvement more advantageous to the revenues of the crown, than the rents of the best landed estates which it can hold. I believe, Sir, it will hardly be necessary for me to add, that in this sale I naturally except all the houses, gardens, and parks, belonging to the crown, and such one forest, as shall be chosen by his Majesty, as best accommodated to his pleasures.

By means of this part of the reform, will fall the expensive office of *surveyor-general*, with all the influence that attends it. By this will fall *two chief justices in Eyre*,[14] with all their train of dependents. You need be under no apprehension, Sir, that your office is to be touched in its emoluments; they are yours by law; and they are but a moderate part of the compensation which is given to you for the ability with which you execute an office of quite another sort of importance; it is far from overpaying your diligence; or more than sufficient for sustaining the high rank you stand in, as the first gentleman of England. As to the duties of your chief justiceship, they are very different from those for which you have received the office. Your dignity is too high for a jurisdiction over wild beasts; and your learning and talents too valuable to be wasted as chief justice of a desert. I cannot reconcile it to myself that you, Sir, should be stuck up as a useless piece of antiquity.

I have now disposed of the unprofitable landed estates of the crown, and thrown them into the mass of private property; by which they will come, through the course of circulation, and through the political secretions of the state, into our better understood and better ordered revenues.

I come next to the great supreme body of the civil government itself. I approach it with that awe and reverence with which a young physician approaches to the cure of the disorders of his parent. Disorders, Sir, and infirmities, there are – such disorders, that all attempts towards method, prudence, and frugality, will be perfectly vain, whilst a system of confusion remains, which is not only alien, but adverse to all economy; a system, which is not only prodigal in its very essence, but causes everything else which belongs to it to be prodigally conducted.

It is impossible, Sir, for any person to be an economist, where no order in payments is established; it is impossible for a man to be an economist, who is not able to take a comparative view of his means, and of his expenses, for the year which lies before him; it is impossible for a man to be an economist, under whom various officers in their several departments may spend, – even just what they please, – and often with an emulation of expense, as contributing to the importance, if not profit, of their several departments. Thus much is certain; that neither the present, nor any other first lord of the treasury, has been ever able to take a survey, or to make even a tolerable guess, of the expenses of government for any one year; so as to enable him with the least degree of certainty, or even probability, to bring his affairs within compass. Whatever scheme may be formed upon them must be made on a calculation of chances. As things are circumstanced, the first lord of the treasury cannot make an estimate. I am sure I serve the king, and I am sure I assist administration, by putting economy at least in their power. We must *class services*; we must (as far as their nature admits) *appropriate* funds; or everything, however reformed, will fall again into the old confusion.

Coming upon this ground of the civil list, the first thing in dignity and charge that attracts our notice, is the *royal household*. This establishment, in my opinion, is exceedingly abusive in its constitution. It is formed upon manners and customs that have long since expired. In the first place it is formed, in many

respects, upon *feudal principles*. In the feudal times, it was not uncommon, even among subjects, for the lowest offices to be held
by considerable persons; persons as unfit by their incapacity, as
improper from their rank, to occupy such employments. They
were held by patent, sometimes for life, and sometimes by inheritance. If my memory does not deceive me, a person of no slight
consideration held the office of patent hereditary cook to an Earl
of Warwick – The Earl of Warwick's soups, I fear, were not the
better for the dignity of his kitchen. I think it was an Earl of
Gloucester, who officiated as steward of the household to the
Archbishops of Canterbury. Instances of the same kind may in
some degree be found in the Northumberland house-book, and
other family records. There was some reason in ancient necessities for these ancient customs. Protection was wanted; and the
domestic tie, though not the highest, was the closest.

The king's household has not only several strong traces of
this *feudality*, but it is formed also upon the principles of a *body
corporate*; it has its own magistrates, courts, and by-laws. This
might be necessary in the ancient times, in order to have a government within itself, capable of regulating the vast and often
unruly multitude which composed and attended it. This was the
origin of the ancient court called the *Green Cloth* – composed of
the marshal, treasurer, and other great officers of the household,
with certain clerks. The rich subjects of the kingdom who had
formerly the same establishments (only on a reduced scale) have
since altered their economy; and turned the course of their
expense from the maintenance of vast establishments within
their walls, to the employment of a great variety of independent
trades abroad. Their influence is lessened; but a mode of accommodation, and a style of splendour, suited to the manners of the
times, has been increased. Royalty itself has insensibly followed;
and the royal household has been carried away by the resistless
tide of manners: but with this very material difference; – private
men have got rid of the establishments along with the reasons of
them; whereas the royal household has lost all that was stately and
venerable in the antique manners, without retrenching anything
of the cumbrous charge of a Gothic establishment. It is shrunk
into the polished littleness of modern elegance and personal
accommodation; it has evaporated from the gross concrete into
an essence and rectified spirit of expense, where you have tuns
of ancient pomp in a vial of modern luxury.

But when the reason of old establishments is gone, it is absurd to preserve nothing but the burthen of them. This is superstitiously to embalm a carcass not worth an ounce of the gums that are used to preserve it. It is to burn precious oils in the tomb; it is to offer meat and drink to the dead, – not so much an honour to the deceased, as a disgrace to the survivors. Our palaces are vast inhospitable halls. There the bleak winds, there "Boreas, and Eurus, and Canrus, and Argestes loud,"[15] howling through the vacant lobbies, and clattering the doors of deserted guard-rooms, appal the imagination, and conjure up the grim spectres of departed tyrants – the Saxon, the Norman, and the Dane; the stern Edwards and fierce Henries – who stalk from desolation to desolation, through the dreary vacuity and melancholy succession of chill and comfortless chambers. When this tumult subsides, a dead and still more frightful silence would reign in this desert, if every now and then the tacking of hammers did not announce, that those constant attendants upon all courts in all ages, Jobs, were still alive; for whose sake alone it is, that any trace of ancient grandeur is suffered to remain. These palaces are a true emblem of some governments; the inhabitants are decayed, but the governors and magistrates still flourish. They put me in mind of *Old Sarum*,[16] where the representatives, more in number than the constituents, only serve to inform us, that this was once a place of trade, and sounding with "the busy hum of men," though now you can only trace the streets by the colour of the corn; and its sole manufacture is in members of parliament.

These old establishments were formed also on a third principle, still more adverse to the living economy of the age. They were formed, Sir, on the principle of *purveyance*, and *receipt in kind*. In former days, when the household was vast, and the supply scanty and precarious, the royal purveyors, sallying forth from under the Gothic portcullis, to purchase provision with power and prerogative instead of money, brought home the plunder of a hundred markets, and all that could be seized from a flying and hiding country, and deposited their spoil in a hundred caverns, with each its keeper. There every commodity, received in its rawest condition, went through all the process which fitted it for use. This inconvenient receipt produced an economy suited only to itself. It multiplied offices beyond all measure; buttery, pantry, and all that rabble of places, which, though profitable to the holders, and expensive to the state, are almost too mean to mention.

All this might be, and I believe was, necessary at first; for it is remarkable, that *purveyance*, after its regulation had been the subject of a long line of statutes, (not fewer, I think, than twenty-six,) was wholly taken away by the twelfth of Charles the Second; yet in the next year of the same reign, it was found necessary to revive it by a special act of parliament, for the sake of the king's journies. This, Sir, is curious; and what would hardly be expected in so reduced a court as that of Charles the Second, and in so improved a country as England might then be thought. But so it was. In our time, one well-filled and well-covered stage-coach requires more accommodation than a royal progress; and every district, at an hour's warning, can supply an army.

I do not say, Sir, that all these establishments, whose principle is gone, have been systematically kept up for influence solely: neglect had its share. But this I am sure of, that a consideration of influence has hindered any one from attempting to pull them down. For the purposes of influence, and for those purposes only, are retained half at least of the household establishments. No revenue, no, not a royal revenue, can exist under the accumulated charge of ancient establishment, modern luxury, and parliamentary political corruption.

If therefore we aim at regulating this household, the question will be, whether we ought to economise by *detail* or by *principle*? The example we have had of the success of an attempt to economise by detail, and under establishments adverse to the attempt, may tend to decide this question.

At the beginning of his Majesty's reign Lord Talbot[17] came to the administration of a great department in the household. I believe no man ever entered into his Majesty's service, or into the service of any prince, with a more clear integrity, or with more zeal and affection for the interest of his master; and, I must add, with abilities for a still higher service. Economy was then announced as a maxim of the reign. This noble lord, therefore, made several attempts towards a reform. In the year 1777, when the king's civil list debts came last to be paid, he explained very fully the success of his undertaking. He told the House of Lords, that he had attempted to reduce the charges of the king's tables, and his kitchen. – The thing, Sir, was not below him. He knew that there is nothing interesting in the concerns of men, whom we love and honour, that is beneath our attention. – "Love," says one of our old poets, "esteems no office mean;" and with still more spirit, "entire affection scorneth nicer hands."[18] Frugality, Sir, is founded on the principle, that all riches have limits. A royal household, grown enormous, even in the meanest departments, may weaken and perhaps destroy all energy in the highest offices of the state. The gorging a royal kitchen may stint and famish the negotiations of a kingdom. Therefore the object was worthy of his, was worthy of any man's, attention.

In consequence of this noble lord's resolution, (as he told the other House,) he reduced several tables, and put the persons entitled to them upon board wages, much to their own satisfaction. But unluckily, subsequent duties requiring constant attendance, it was not possible to prevent their being fed where they were employed – and thus this first step towards economy doubled the expense.

There was another disaster far more doleful than this. I shall state it, as the cause of that misfortune lies at the bottom of almost all our prodigality. Lord Talbot attempted to reform the kitchen; but such, as he well observed, is the consequence of having duty done by one person, whilst another enjoys the emoluments, that he found himself frustrated in all his designs. On that rock his whole adventure split – His whole scheme of economy was dashed to pieces; his department became more expensive than ever; – the civil list debt accumulated – Why? It was truly from a cause, which, though perfectly adequate to the effect, one would not have instantly guessed; – It was because the *turnspit in the king's kitchen was a member of parliament*.* The king's domestic servants were all undone; his tradesmen remained unpaid, and became bankrupt – *because the turnspit of the king's kitchen was a member of parliament*. His Majesty's slumbers were interrupted, his pillow was stuffed with thorns, and his peace of mind entirely broken – *because the king's turnspit was a member of parliament*. The judges were unpaid; the justice of the kingdom bent and gave way; the foreign ministers remained inactive and unprovided; the system of Europe was dissolved; the chain of our alliances was broken; all the wheels of government at home and abroad were stopped – *because the king's turnspit was a member of parliament*.

Such, Sir, was the situation of affairs, and such the cause of that situation, when his Majesty came a second time to parliament,

* Vide Lord Talbot's speech in Almond's Parliamentary Register, vol. vii p. 79, of the proceedings of the Lords.

to desire the payment of those debts which the employment of its members in various offices, visible and invisible, had occasioned. I believe that a like fate will attend every attempt at economy by detail, under similar circumstances, and in every department. A complex, operose office of account and control is, in itself, and even if members of parliament had nothing to do with it, the most prodigal of all things. The most audacious robberies, or the most subtle frauds, would never venture upon such a waste, as an over-careful, detailed guard against them would infallibly produce. In our establishments, we frequently see an office of account, of a hundred pounds a year expense, and another office of an equal expense, to control that office; and the whole upon a matter that is not worth twenty shillings.

To avoid, therefore, this minute care which produces the consequences of the most extensive neglect, and to oblige members of parliament to attend to public cares, and not to the servile offices of domestic management, I propose, Sir, to *economise by principle*, that is, I propose to put affairs into that train which experience points out as the most effectual, from the nature of things, and from the constitution of the human mind. In all dealings where it is possible, the principles of radical economy prescribe three things; first, undertaking by the great; secondly, engaging with persons of skill in the subject matter; thirdly, engaging with those who shall have an immediate and direct interest in the proper execution of the business.

To avoid frittering and crumbling down the attention by a blind, unsystematic observance of every trifle, it has ever been found the best way to do all things which are great in the total amount, and minute in the component parts, by a *general contract*. The principles of trade have so pervaded every species of dealing, from the highest to the lowest objects; all transactions are got so much into system, that we may, at a moment's warning, and to a farthing value, be informed at what rate any service may be supplied. No dealing is exempt from the possibility of fraud. But by a contract on a matter certain, you have this advantage – you are sure to know the utmost *extent* of the fraud to which you are subject. By a contract with a person in *his own trade*, you are sure you shall not suffer by *want of skill*. By a *short* contract you are sure of making it the interest of the contractor to exert that skill for the satisfaction of his employers.

I mean to derogate nothing from the diligence or integrity of the present, or of any former, board of Green Cloth.[19] But what skill can members of parliament obtain in that low kind of province? What pleasure can they have in the execution of that kind of duty? And, if they should neglect it, how does it affect their interest, when we know that it is their vote in parliament, and not their diligence in cookery or catering, that recommends them to their office, or keeps them in it?

I therefore propose, that the king's tables (to whatever number of tables, or covers to each, he shall think proper to command) should be classed by the steward of the household, and should be contracted for, according to their rank, by the head or cover; – that the estimate and circumstance of the contract should be carried to the treasury to be approved; and that its faithful and satisfactory performance should be reported there previously to any payment; that there, and there only, should the payment be made. I propose, that men should be contracted with only in their proper trade; and that no member of parliament should be capable of such contract. By this plan, almost all the infinite offices under the lord steward may be spared; to the extreme simplification, and to the far better execution, of every one of his functions. The king of Prussia is so served. He is a great and eminent (though indeed a very rare) instance of the possibility of uniting, in a mind of vigour and compass, an attention to minute objects with the largest views, and the most complicated plans. His tables are served by contract, and by the head. Let me say, that no prince can be ashamed to imitate the king of Prussia; and particularly to learn in his school, when the problem is – "The best manner of reconciling the state of a court with the support of war?" Other courts, I understand, have followed him with effect, and to their satisfaction.

The same clue of principle leads us through the labyrinth of the other departments. What, Sir, is there in the office of *the great wardrobe* (which has the care of the king's furniture) that may not be executed by the *lord chamberlain himself*? He has an honourable appointment; he has time sufficient to attend to the duty; and he has the vice-chamberlain to assist him. Why should not he deal also by contract for all things belonging to this office, and carry his estimates first, and his report of the execution in its proper time, for payment, directly to the board of treasury itself? By a simple operation (containing in it a treble control) the expenses of a department, which for naked walls, or walls hung with cobwebs, has in a few years cost the crown £150,000, may at length hope for regulation. But, Sir, the office and its business are at variance. As it stands, it serves not to furnish the palace with its hangings, but the parliament with its dependent members.

To what end, Sir, does the office of *removing wardrobe* serve at all? Why should a *jewel office* exist for the sole purpose of taxing the king's gifts of plate? Its object falls naturally within the *chamberlain's* province; and ought to be under his care and inspection without any fee. Why should an office of the *robes* exist, when that of *groom of the stole* is a sinecure, and that this is a proper object of his department?

All these encumbrances, which are themselves nuisances, produce other encumbrances and other nuisances. For the payment of these useless establishments, there are no less than *three useless treasurers*; two to hold a purse, and one to play with a stick. The treasurer of the household is a mere name. The cofferer and the treasurer of the chamber receive and pay great sums, which it is not at all necessary *they* should either receive or pay. All the proper officers, servants, and tradesmen, may be enrolled in their several departments, and paid in proper classes and times with great simplicity and order, at the exchequer, and by direction from the treasury.

The *board of works*, which in the seven years preceding 1777, has cost towards £400,000;* and (if I recollect rightly) has not cost less in proportion from the beginning of the reign, is under the very same description of all the other ill-contrived establishments, and calls for the very same reform. We are to seek for the visible signs of all this expense. – For all this expense, we do not see a building of the size and importance of a pigeon-house. Buckingham House was reprised by a bargain with the public for one hundred thousand pounds; – and the small house at Windsor has been, if I mistake not, undertaken since that account was brought before us. The good works of that board of works, are as carefully concealed as other good works ought to be; they are perfectly invisible. But though it is the perfection of charity to be concealed, it is, Sir, the property and glory of magnificence to appear and stand forward to the eye.

That board, which ought to be a concern of builders and such like, and of none else, is turned into a junto of members of

* More exactly, £378,616 10s. 1¾d.

parliament. That office too has a *treasury* and a paymaster of its own; and, lest the arduous affairs of that important exchequer should be too fatiguing, that paymaster has a deputy to partake of his profits and relieve his cares. I do not believe, that, either now or in former times, the chief managers of that board have made any profit of its abuse. It is, however, no good reason that an abusive establishment should subsist, because it is of as little private as of public advantage. But this establishment has the grand radical fault, the original sin, that pervades and perverts all our establishments; – the apparatus is not fitted to the object, nor the workmen to the work. Expenses are incurred on the private opinion of an inferior establishment, without consulting the principal; who can alone determine the proportion which it ought to bear to the other establishments of the state, in the order of their relative importance.

I propose, therefore, along with the rest, to pull down this whole ill-contrived scaffolding, which obstructs, rather than forwards, our public works; to take away its treasury; to put the whole into the hands of a real builder, who shall not be a member of parliament; and to oblige him, by a previous estimate and final payment, to appear twice at the treasury before the public can be loaded. The king's gardens are to come under a similar regulation.

The *mint*, though not a department of the household, has the same vices. It is a great expense to the nation, chiefly for the sake of members of parliament. It has its officers of parade and dignity. It has its treasury too. It is a sort of corporate body; and formerly was a body of great importance; as much so on the then scale of things, and the then order of business, as the bank is at this day. It was the great centre of money transactions and remittances for our own, and for other nations; until King Charles the First, among other arbitrary projects, dictated by despotic necessity, made him withhold the money that lay there for remittance. That blow (and happily too) the mint never recovered. Now it is no bank; no remittance-shop. The mint, Sir, is a *manufacture*, and it is nothing else; and it ought to be undertaken upon the principles of a manufacture; that is, for the best and cheapest execution, by a contract upon proper securities, and under proper regulations.

The *artillery* is a far greater object; it is a military concern; but having an affinity and kindred in its defects with the establishments I am now speaking of, I think it best to speak of it along with them. It is, I conceive, an establishment, not well suited to its martial, though exceedingly well calculated for its parliamentary, purposes. – Here there is a *treasury*, as in all the other inferior departments of government. Here the military is subordinate to the civil, and the naval confounded with the land service. The object indeed is much the same in both. But, when the detail is examined, it will be found that they had better be separated. For a reform of this office, I propose to restore things to what (all considerations taken together) is their natural order; to restore them to their just proportion, and to their just distribution. I propose, in this military concern, to render the civil subordinate to the military; and this will annihilate the greatest part of the expense, and all the influence belonging to the office. I propose to send the military branch to the army, and the naval to the admiralty: and I intend to perfect and accomplish the whole detail (where it becomes too minute and complicated for legislature, and requires exact, official, military, and mechanical knowledge) by a commission of competent officers in both departments. I propose to execute by contract, what by contract can be executed; and to bring, as much as possible, all estimates to be previously approved, and finally to be paid by the treasury.

Thus by following the course of nature, and not the purposes of politics, or the accumulated patch-work of occasional accommodation, this vast expensive department may be methodised; its service proportioned to its necessities, and its payments subjected to the inspection of the superior minister of finance; who is to judge of it on the result of the total collected exigences of the state. This last is a reigning principle through my whole plan; and it is a principle which I hope may hereafter be applied to other plans.

By these regulations taken together – besides the three subordinate treasuries in the lesser principalities, five other subordinate treasuries are suppressed. There is taken away the whole *establishment of detail* in the household; – the *treasurer*; the *comptroller* (for a comptroller is hardly necessary where there is no treasurer); the *cofferer of the household*; the *treasurer of the chamber*; the *master of the household*; the whole *board of Green Cloth*; – and a vast number of subordinate offices in the department of the *steward of the household*; – the whole establishment of the *great wardrobe*; – the *removing wardrobe*; – the *jewel office*; – the *robes*; –

the *board of works*; almost the whole charge of the *civil branch* of the *board of ordnance* are taken away. All these arrangements together will be found to relieve the nation from a vast weight of influence, without distressing, but rather by forwarding every public service. When something of this kind is done, then the public may begin to breathe. Under other governments, a question of expense is only a question of economy, and it is nothing more; with us, in every question of expense, there is always a mixture of constitutional considerations.

It is, Sir, because I wish to keep this business of subordinate treasuries as much as I can together, that I brought the *ordnance office* before you, though it is properly a military department. For the same reason I will now trouble you with my thoughts and propositions upon two of the greatest *under treasuries*, I mean the office of *paymaster of the land forces*, or *treasurer of the army*, and that of the *treasurer of the navy*. The former of these has long been a great object of public suspicion and uneasiness. Envy too has had its share in the obloquy which is cast upon this office. But I am sure that it has no share at all in the reflections I shall make upon it, or in the reformations that I shall propose. I do not grudge to the honourable gentleman, who at present holds the office, any of the effects of his talents, his merit, or his fortune. He is respectable in all these particulars. I follow the constitution of the office without persecuting its holder. It is necessary in all matters of public complaint, where men frequently feel right and argue wrong, to separate prejudice from reason; and to be very sure, in attempting the redress of a grievance, that we hit upon its real seat, and its true nature. Where there is an abuse of office, the first thing that occurs in heat is to censure the officer. Our natural disposition leads all our inquiries rather to persons than to things. But this prejudice is to be corrected by maturer thinking.

Sir, the profits of the *pay-office* (as an office) are not too great, in my opinion, for its duties, and for the rank of the person who has generally held it. He has been generally a person of the highest rank; that is to say, a person of eminence and consideration in this House. The great and the invidious profits of the pay-office are from the *bank* that is held in it. According to the present course of the office, and according to the present mode of accounting there, this bank must necessarily exist somewhere. Money is a productive thing; and when the usual time of its demand can be tolerably calculated, it may, with prudence, be safely laid out to the profit of the holder. It is on this calculation that the business of banking proceeds. But no profit can be derived from the use of money, which does not make it the interest of the holder to delay his account. The process of the exchequer colludes with this interest. Is this collusion from its want of rigour and strictness, and great regularity of form? The reverse is true. They have in the exchequer brought rigour and formalism to their ultimate perfection. The process against accountants is so rigorous, and in a manner so unjust, that correctives must, from time to time, be applied to it. These correctives being discretionary, upon the case, and generally remitted by the barons to the lords of the treasury, as the best judges of the reasons for respite, hearings are had; delays are produced; and thus the extreme of rigour in office (as usual in all human affairs) leads to the extreme of laxity. What with the interested delay of the officer; the ill-conceived exactness of the court; the applications for dispensations from that exactness; the revival of rigorous process, after the expiration of the time; and the new rigours producing new applications, and new enlargements of time, such delays happen in the public accounts, that they can scarcely ever be closed.

Besides, Sir, they have a rule in the exchequer, which, I believe, they have founded upon a very ancient statute, that of the 51st of Henry III, by which it is provided, "That when a sheriff or bailiff hath began his account, none other shall be received to account until he that was first appointed hath clearly accounted, and that the sum has been received." * Whether this clause of that statute be the ground of that absurd practice, I am not quite able to ascertain. But it has very generally prevailed, though I am told that of late they have began to relax from it. In consequence of forms adverse to substantial account, we have a long succession of paymasters and their representatives, who have never been admitted to account, although perfectly ready to do so.

As the extent of our wars has scattered the accountants under the paymaster into every part of the globe, the grand and sure paymaster, Death, in all his shapes, calls these accountants to another reckoning. Death, indeed, domineers over everything but the forms of the exchequer. Over these he has no power. They are impassive and immortal. The audit of the exchequer,

* Et quant viscount ou bailliff ait commence de accompter, nul autre ne seit resceu de acconter tanque le primer qe soit assis, eit peraccompte, et qe la somme soit resceu. Stat. 5, ann. dom. 1266.

more severe than the audit to which the accountants are gone, demands proofs which in the nature of things are difficult, sometimes impossible to be had. In this respect too, rigour, as usual, defeats itself. Then, the exchequer never gives a particular receipt, or clears a man of his account as far as it goes. A final acquittance (or a *quietus*, as they term it) is scarcely ever to be obtained. Terrors and ghosts of unlaid accountants haunt the houses of their children from generation to generation. Families, in the course of succession, fall into minorities; the inheritance comes into the hands of females; and very perplexed affairs are often delivered over into the hands of negligent guardians and faithless stewards. So that the demand remains, when the advantage of the money is gone; if ever any advantage at all has been made of it. This is a cause of infinite distress to families; and becomes a source of influence to an extent that can scarcely be imagined, but by those who have taken some pains to trace it. The mildness of government, in the employment of useless and dangerous powers, furnishes no reason for their continuance.

As things stand, can you in justice (except perhaps in that over-perfect kind of justice which has obtained, by its merits, the title of the opposite vice*) insist, that any man should, by the course of his office, keep a *bank* from whence he is to derive no advantage? That a man should be subject to demands below, and be in a manner refused an acquittance above; that he should transmit an original sin, an inheritance of vexation, to his posterity, without a power of compensating himself in some way or other, for so perilous a situation? We know, that if the paymaster should deny himself the advantages of his bank, the public, as things stand, is not the richer for it by a single shilling. This I thought it necessary to say, as to the offensive magnitude of the profits of this office; that we may proceed in reformation on the principles of reason, and not on the feelings of envy.

The treasurer of the navy is, *mutatis mutandis*, in the same circumstances. Indeed all accountants are. Instead of the present mode, which is troublesome to the officer, and unprofitable to the public, I propose to substitute something more effectual than rigour, which is the worst exactor in the world. I mean to remove the very temptations to delay; to facilitate the account; and to transfer this bank, now of private emolument, to the public. The

* Summum jus summa injuria.[20]

crown will suffer no wrong at least from the pay-offices; and
its terrors will no longer reign over the families of those who
hold, or have held them. I propose that these offices should be
no longer *banks* or *treasuries*, but mere *offices of administration*. –
I propose, first, that the present paymaster and the treasurer of
the navy should carry into the exchequer the whole body of the
vouchers for what they have paid over to deputy paymasters, to
regimental agents, or to any of those to whom they have and
ought to have paid money. I propose that those vouchers shall
be admitted as actual payments in their accounts; and that the
persons to whom the money has been paid shall then stand
charged in the exchequer in their place. After this process, they
shall be debited or charged for nothing but the money balance
that remains in their hands.

I am conscious, Sir, that if this balance (which they could not
expect to be so suddenly demanded by any usual process of the
exchequer) should now be exacted all at once, not only their ruin,
but a ruin of others to an extent which I do not like to think of,
but which I can well conceive, and which you may well conceive,
might be the consequence. I told you, Sir, when I promised
before the holidays to bring in this plan, that I never would suffer
any man, or description of men, to suffer from errors that naturally have grown out of the abusive constitution of those offices
which I propose to regulate. If I cannot reform with equity, I will
not reform at all.

For the regulation of past accounts, I shall therefore propose
such a mode, as men, temperate and prudent, make use of in the
management of their private affairs, when their accounts are various, perplexed, and of long standing. I would therefore, after their
example, divide the public debts into three sorts; good, bad, and
doubtful. In looking over the public accounts, I should never
dream of the blind mode of the exchequer, which regards things
in the abstract, and knows no difference in the quality of its debts,
or the circumstances of its debtors. By this means, it fatigues itself;
it vexes others; it often crushes the poor; it lets the rich escape; or,
in a fit of mercy or carelessness, declines all means of recovering its
just demands. Content with the eternity of its claims, it enjoys its
epicurean divinity with epicurean languor. But it is proper that
all sorts of accounts should be closed some time or other – by payment; by composition; or by oblivion. *Expedit reipublicæ ut sit finis*

litium.[21] Constantly taking along with me, that an extreme rigour is sure to arm everything against it, and at length to relax into a supine neglect, I propose, Sir, that even the best, soundest, and the most recent debts, should be put into instalments, for the mutual benefit of the accountant and the public.

In proportion, however, as I am tender of the past, I would be provident of the future. All money that was formerly impressed to the two great *pay-offices*, I would have impressed in future to the *bank of England*. These offices should, in future, receive no more than cash sufficient for small payments. Their other payments ought to be made by drafts on the bank, expressing the service. A check account from both offices, of drafts and receipts, should be annually made up in the exchequer; charging the bank in account with the cash-balance, but not demanding the payment until there is an order from the treasury, in consequence of a vote of parliament.

As I did not, Sir, deny to the paymaster the natural profits of the bank that was in his hands; so neither would I to the bank of England. A share of that profit might be derived to the public in various ways. My favourite mode is this; that, in compensation for the use of this money, the bank may take upon themselves, first, *the charge of the mint*; to which they are already, by their charter, obliged to bring in a great deal of bullion annually to be coined.

In the next place, I mean that they should take upon themselves the charge of *remittances to our troops abroad*. This is a species of dealing from which, by the same charter, they are not debarred. One and a quarter *per cent* will be saved instantly thereby to the public, on very large sums of money. This will be at once a matter of economy, and a considerable reduction of influence, by taking away a private contract of an expensive nature, if the bank, which is a great corporation, and of course receives the least profits from the money in their custody, should of itself refuse, or be persuaded to refuse, this offer upon those terms, I can speak with some confidence, that one at least, if not both parts of the condition would be received, and gratefully received, by several bankers of eminence. There is no banker who will not be at least as good security as any paymaster of the forces, or any treasurer of the navy, that have ever been bankers to the public: as rich at least as my Lord Chatham, or my Lord Holland,[22] or either of the honourable gentlemen who now hold the offices, were at the time that they entered into them; or as ever the whole establishment of the *mint* has been at any period.

These, Sir, are the outlines of the plan I mean to follow, in suppressing these two large subordinate treasuries. I now come to another subordinate treasury; I mean, that of the *paymaster of the pensions*; for which purpose I re-enter the limits of the civil establishment. – I departed from those limits in pursuit of a principle; and, following the same game in its doubles, I am brought into those limits again. That treasury, and that office, I mean to take away; and to transfer the payment of every name, mode, and denomination of pensions, to the *exchequer*. The present course of diversifying the same object can answer no good purpose; whatever its use may be to purposes of another kind. There are also other lists of pensions; and I mean that they should all be hereafter paid at one and the same place. The whole of the new consolidated list I mean to reduce to £60,000 a year, which sum I intend it shall never exceed. I think that sum will fully answer as a reward for all real merit, and a provision for all real public charity that is ever like to be placed upon the list. If any merit of an extraordinary nature should emerge before that reduction is completed, I have left it open for an address of either House of Parliament to provide for the case. To all other demands, it must be answered, with regret, but with firmness, "the public is poor."

I do not propose, as I told you before Christmas, to take away any pension. I know that the public seem to call for a reduction of such of them as shall appear unmerited. As a censorial act, and punishment of an abuse, it might answer some purpose. But this can make no part of *my* plan. I mean to proceed by bill; and I cannot stop for such an inquiry. I know some gentlemen may blame me. It is with great submission to better judgments that I recommend it to consideration; that a critical retrospective examination of the pension list, upon the principle of merit, can never serve for my basis. – It cannot answer, according to my plan, any effectual purpose of economy or of future permanent reformation. The process in any way will be entangled and difficult; and it will be infinitely slow: there is a danger that if we turn our line of march, now directed towards the grand object, into this more laborious than useful detail of operations, we shall never arrive at our end.

The king, Sir, has been by the constitution appointed sole judge of the merit for which a pension is to be given. We have a right, undoubtedly, to canvass this, as we have to canvass every act of government. But there is a material difference between an office to be reformed, and a pension taken away for demerit. In the former case, no charge is implied against the holder; in the latter, his character is slurred, as well as his lawful emolument affected. The former process is against the thing; the second against the person. The pensioner certainly, if he pleases, has a right to stand on his own defence; to plead his possession; and to bottom his title in the competency of the crown to give him what he holds. Possessed and on the defensive as he is, he will not be obliged to prove his special merit, in order to justify the act of legal discretion, now turned into his property, according to his tenure. The very act, he will contend, is a legal presumption, and an implication of his merit. If this be so, from the natural force of all legal presumption, he would put us to the difficult proof, that he has no merit at all. But other questions would arise in the course of such an inquiry; that is, questions of the merit when weighed against the proportion of the reward; then the difficulty will be much greater.

The difficulty will not, Sir, I am afraid, be much less, if we pass to the person really guilty, in the question of an unmerited pension; the minister himself. I admit that when called to account for the execution of a trust, he might fairly be obliged to prove the affirmative; and to state the merit for which the pension is given; though on the pensioner himself such a process would be hard. If in this examination we proceed methodically, and so as to avoid all suspicion of partiality and prejudice, we must take the pensions in order of time, or merely alphabetically. The very first pension to which we come in either of these ways may appear the most grossly unmerited of any. But the minister may very possibly show that he knows nothing of the putting on this pension – that it was prior in time to his administration – that the minister who laid it on is dead: and then we are thrown back upon the pensioner himself, and plunged into all our former difficulties. Abuses, and gross ones, I doubt not, would appear; and to the correction of which I would readily give my hand; but, when I consider that pensions have not generally been affected by the revolutions of ministry, as I know not where such inquiries would stop, and as an absence of merit is a negative and loose thing, one might be led to derange the order of families, founded on the probable continuance of their kind of income. I might hurt children; I might injure creditors. I really think it the more prudent course, not to follow the letter of the petitions. If we fix this mode of inquiry as a basis, we shall, I fear, end as parliament has often ended under similar circumstances. There will be great delay; much confusion; much inequality in our proceedings. But what presses me most of all is this; that though we should strike off all the unmerited pensions, while the power of the crown remains unlimited, the very same undeserving persons might afterwards return to the very same list; or, if they did not, other persons, meriting as little as they do, might be put upon it to an undefinable amount. This I think is the pinch of the grievance.

For these reasons, Sir, I am obliged to waive this mode of proceeding as any part of my plan. In a plan of reformation, it would be one of my maxims, that, when I know of an establishment which may be subservient to useful purposes, and which, at the same time, from its discretionary nature, is liable to a very great perversion from those purposes, *I would limit the quantity of the power that might be so abused.* For I am sure, that, in all such cases, the rewards of merit will have very narrow bounds; and that partial or corrupt favour will be infinite. This principle is not arbitrary; but the limitation of the specific quantity must be so in some measure. I therefore state £60,000, leaving it open to the House to enlarge or contract the sum as they shall see, on examination, that the discretion I use is scanty or liberal. The whole amount of the pensions of all denominations, which have been laid before us, amount, for a period of seven years, to considerably more than £100,000 a year. To what the other lists amount, I know not. That will be seen hereafter. But from those that do appear, a saving will accrue to the public, at one time or other, of £40,000 a year, and we had better, in my opinion, let it fall in naturally, than tear it crude and unripe from the stalk.*

There is a great deal of uneasiness among the people, upon an article which I must class under the head of pensions. I mean the

---

* It was supposed by the lord advocate, in a subsequent debate, that Mr. Burke, because he objected to an inquiry into the pension list for the purpose of economy and relief of the public, would have it withheld from the judgment of parliament for all purposes whatsoever. This learned gentleman certainly misunderstood him. His plan shows that he wished the whole list to be easily accessible; and he knows that the public eye is of itself a great guard against abuse.

great patent offices in the exchequer. They are in reality and substance no other than pensions, and in no other light shall I consider them. They are sinecures. They are always executed by deputy. The duty of the principal is as nothing. They differ however from the pensions on the list, in some particular. They are held for life. I think, with the public, that the profits of those places are grown enormous; the magnitude of those profits, and the nature of them, both call for reformation. The nature of their profits, which grow out of the public distress, is itself invidious and grievous. But I fear that reform cannot be immediate. I find myself under a restriction. These places, and others of the same kind, which are held for life, have been considered as property. They have been given as a provision for children; they have been the subject of family settlements; they have been the security of creditors. What the law respects shall be sacred to me. If the barriers of law should be broken down, upon ideas of convenience, even of public convenience, we shall have no longer anything certain among us. If the discretion of power is once let loose upon property, we can be at no loss to determine whose power, and what discretion, it is that will prevail at last. It would be wise to attend upon the order of things; and not to attempt to outrun the slow, but smooth and even, course of nature. There are occasions, I admit, of public necessity, so vast, so clear, so evident, that they supersede all laws. Law, being only made for the benefit of the community, cannot in any one of its parts resist a demand which may comprehend the total of the public interest. To be sure, no law can set itself up against the cause and reason of all law. But such a case very rarely happens; and this most certainly is not such a case. The mere time of the reform is by no means worth the sacrifice of a principle of law. Individuals pass like shadows; but the commonwealth is fixed and stable. The difference, therefore, of today and tomorrow, which to private people is immense, to the state is nothing. At any rate, it is better, if possible, to reconcile our economy with our laws, than to set them at variance; a quarrel which in the end must be destructive to both.

My idea, therefore, is to reduce those officers to fixed salaries, as the present lives and reversions shall successively fall. I mean that the office of the great auditor (the auditor of the receipt) shall be reduced to £3000 a year; and the auditors of the imprest, and the rest of the principal officers, to fixed appointments of £1500 a year each. It will not be difficult to calculate the value of this fall of lives to the public, when we shall have obtained a just account of the present income of those places; and we shall obtain that account with great facility, if the present possessors are not alarmed with any apprehension of danger to their freehold office.

I know too, that it will be demanded of me, how it comes, that since I admit these offices to be no better than pensions, I choose, after the principle of law had been satisfied, to retain them at all? To this, Sir, I answer, that conceiving it to be a fundamental part of the constitution of this country, and of the reason of state in every country, that there must be means of rewarding public service, those means will be incomplete, and indeed wholly insufficient for that purpose, if there should be no further reward for that service, than the daily wages it receives during the pleasure of the crown.

Whoever seriously considers the excellent argument of Lord Somers,[23] in the banker's case, will see he bottoms himself upon the very same maxim which I do; and one of his principal grounds of doctrine for the alienability of the domain in England,* contrary to the maxim of the law in France, he lays in the constitutional policy of furnishing a permanent reward to public service; of making that reward the origin of families; and the foundation of wealth as well as of honours. It is indeed the only genuine, unadulterated origin of nobility. It is a great principle in government; a principle at the very foundation of the whole structure. The other judges who held the same doctrine went beyond Lord Somers with regard to the remedy, which they thought was given by law against the crown, upon the grant of pensions. Indeed no man knows, when he cuts off the incitements to a virtuous ambition, and the just rewards of public service, what infinite mischief he may do his country, through all generations. Such saving to the public may prove the worst mode of robbing it. The crown, which has in its hands the trust of the daily pay for national service, ought to have in its hands also the means for the repose of public labour, and the fixed settlement of acknowledged merit. There is a time, when the weather-beaten vessels of the state ought to come into harbour. They must at length have a retreat from the malice of rivals, from the perfidy of political friends, and the inconstancy of the people. Many of the persons, who in all times have filled the great offices

* Before the statute of Queen Anne, which limited the alienation of land.

of state, have been younger brothers, who had originally little, if any, fortune. These offices do not furnish the means of amassing wealth. There ought to be some power in the crown of granting pensions out of the reach of its own caprices. An entail of dependence is a bad reward of merit.

I would, therefore, leave to the crown the possibility of conferring some favours which, whilst they are received as a reward, do not operate as corruption. When men receive obligations from the crown, through the pious hands of fathers, or of connexions as venerable as the paternal, the dependencies which arise from thence are the obligations of gratitude, and not the fetters of servility. Such ties originate in virtue, and they promote it. They continue men in those habitudes of friendship, those political connexions, and those political principles, in which they began life. They are antidotes against a corrupt levity, instead of causes of it. What an unseemly spectacle would it afford, what a disgrace would it be to the commonwealth that suffered such things, to see the hopeful son of a meritorious minister begging his bread at the door of that treasury, from whence his father dispensed the economy of an empire, and promoted the happiness and glory of his country! Why should he be obliged to prostrate his honour, and to submit his principles at the levee of some proud favourite, shouldered and thrust aside by every impudent pretender, on the very spot where a few days before he saw himself adored? – obliged to cringe to the author of the calamities of his house, and to kiss the hands that are red with his father's blood? – No, Sir, these things are unfit – they are intolerable.

Sir, I shall be asked, why I do not choose to destroy those offices which are pensions, and appoint pensions under the direct title in their stead? I allow that in some cases it leads to abuse; to have things appointed for one purpose and applied to another. I have no great objection to such a change: but I do not think it quite prudent for me to propose it. If I should take away the present establishment, the burthen of proof rests upon me, that so many pensions, and no more, and to such an amount each, and no more, are necessary for the public service. This is what I can never prove; for it is a thing incapable of definition. I do not like to take away an object that I think answers my purpose, in hopes of getting it back again in a better shape. People will bear an old establishment when its excess is corrected, who will revolt at a new one. I do not think these office-pensions to be more in number than sufficient: but on that point the House will exercise its discretion. As to abuse, I am convinced that very few trusts in the ordinary course of administration have admitted less abuse than this. Efficient ministers have been their own paymasters. It is true. But their very partiality has operated as a kind of justice; and still it was service that was paid. When we look over this exchequer list, we find it filled with the descendants of the Walpoles, of the Pelhams, of the Townshends;[24] names to whom this country owes its liberties; and to whom his Majesty owes his crown. It was in one of these lines, that the immense and envied employment he now holds came to a certain duke,* who is now probably sitting quietly at a very good dinner directly under us, and acting *high life below stairs*, whilst we, his masters, are filling our mouths with unsubstantial sounds, and talking of hungry economy over his head. But he is the elder branch of an ancient and decayed house, joined to and repaired by the reward of services done by another. I respect the original title, and the first purchase of merited wealth and honour through all its descents, through all its transfers, and all its assignments. May such fountains never be dried up! May they ever flow with their original purity, and refresh and fructify the commonwealth, for ages!

Sir, I think myself bound to give you my reasons as clearly, and as fully, for stopping in the course of reformation, as for proceeding in it. My limits are the rules of law; the rules of policy; and the service of the state. This is the reason why I am not able to intermeddle with another article, which seems to be a specific object in several of the petitions; I mean the reduction of exorbitant emoluments to efficient offices. If I knew of any real, efficient office, which did possess exorbitant emoluments, I should be extremely desirous of reducing them. Others may know of them; I do not. I am not possessed of an exact common measure between real service and its reward. I am very sure, that states do sometimes receive services, which is hardly in their power to reward according to their worth. If I were to give my judgment with regard to this country, I do not think the great efficient offices of the state to be overpaid. The service of the public is a thing which cannot be put to auction, and struck down to those who will agree to execute it the cheapest. When the proportion between reward and service is our object, we must always

* Duke of Newcastle,[25] whose dining-room is under the House of Commons.

consider of what nature the service is, and what sort of men they are that must perform it. What is just payment for one kind of labour, and full encouragement for one kind of talents, is fraud and discouragement to others. Many of the great offices have much duty to do, and much expense of representation to maintain. A secretary of state, for instance, must not appear sordid in the eyes of the ministers of other nations; neither ought our ministers abroad to appear contemptible in the courts where they reside. In all offices of duty, there is, almost necessarily, a great neglect of all domestic affairs. A person in high office can rarely take a view of his family-house. If he sees that the state takes no detriment, the state must see that his affairs should take as little.

I will even go so far as to affirm, that if men were willing to serve in such situations without salary, they ought not to be permitted to do it. Ordinary service must be secured by the motives to ordinary integrity. I do not hesitate to say, that that state, which lays its foundation in rare and heroic virtues, will be sure to have its superstructure in the basest profligacy and corruption. An honourable and fair profit is the best security against avarice and rapacity; as in all things else, a lawful and regulated enjoyment is the best security against debauchery and excess. For as wealth is power, so all power will infallibly draw wealth to itself by some means or other; and when men are left no way of ascertaining their profits but by their means of obtaining them, those means will be increased to infinity. This is true in all the parts of administration, as well as in the whole. If any individual were to decline his appointments, it might give an unfair advantage to ostentatious ambition over unpretending service; it might breed invidious comparisons; it might tend to destroy whatever little unity and agreement may be found among ministers. And, after all, when an ambitious man had run down his competitors by a fallacious show of disinterestedness, and fixed himself in power by that means, what security is there that he would not change his course, and claim as an indemnity ten times more than he has given up?

This rule, like every other, may admit its exceptions. When a great man has some one great object in view to be achieved in a given time, it may be absolutely necessary for him to walk out of all the common roads, and, if his fortune permits it, to hold himself out as a splendid example. I am told, that something of this kind is now doing in a country near us. But this is for a short race;

the training for a heat or two, and not the proper preparation for the regular stages of a methodical journey. I am speaking of establishments, and not of men.

It may be expected, Sir, that when I am giving my reasons why I limit myself in the reduction of employments, or of their profits, I should say something of those which seem of eminent inutility in the state; I mean the number of officers who, by their places, are attendant on the person of the king. Considering the commonwealth merely as such, and considering those officers only as relative to the direct purposes of the state, I admit that they are of no use at all. But there are many things in the constitution of establishments, which appear of little value on the first view, which, in a secondary and oblique manner, produce very material advantages. It was on full consideration that I determined not to lessen any of the offices of honour about the crown, in their number, or their emoluments. These emoluments, except in one or two cases, do not much more than answer the charge of attendance. Men of condition naturally love to be about a court; and women of condition love it much more. But there is in all regular attendance so much of constraint, that if it were a mere charge, without any compensation, you would soon have the court deserted by all the nobility of the kingdom.

Sir, the most serious mischiefs would follow from such a desertion. Kings are naturally lovers of low company. They are so elevated above all the rest of mankind, that they must look upon all their subjects as on a level. They are rather apt to hate than to love their nobility, on account of the occasional resistance to their will, which will be made by their virtue, their petulance, or their pride. It must indeed be admitted, that many of the nobility are as perfectly willing to act the part of flatterers, tale-bearers, parasites, pimps, and buffoons, as any of the lowest and vilest of mankind can possibly be. But they are not properly qualified for this object of their ambition. The want of a regular education, and early habits, and some lurking remains of their dignity, will never permit them to become a match for an Italian eunuch, a mountebank, a fiddler, a player, or any regular practitioner of that tribe. The Roman emperors, almost from the beginning, threw themselves into such hands; and the mischief increased every day till the decline and final ruin of the empire. It is therefore of very great importance (provided the thing is not overdone) to contrive such an establishment as must, almost whether a prince will or not, bring into daily and hourly offices about his person a great number of his first nobility; and it is rather an useful prejudice that gives them a pride in such a servitude. Though they are not much the better for a court, a court will be much the better for them. I have therefore not attempted to reform any of the offices of honour about the king's person.

There are, indeed, two offices in his stables which are sine-cures. By the change of manners, and indeed by the nature of the thing, they must be so; I mean the several keepers of buck-hounds, stag-hounds, fox-hounds, and harriers. They answer no purpose of utility or of splendour. These I propose to abolish. It is not proper that great noblemen should be keepers of dogs, though they were the king's dogs. In every part of my scheme, I have endeavoured that no primary, and that even no secondary, service of the state should suffer by its frugality. I mean to touch no offices but such as I am perfectly sure are either of no use at all, or not of any use in the least assignable proportion to the burthen with which they load the revenues of the kingdom, and to the influence with which they oppress the freedom of parlia-mentary deliberation; for which reason there are but two offices which are properly state offices, that I have a desire to reform.

The first of them is the new office of *third secretary of state*, which is commonly called *secretary of state for the colonies*.

We know that all the correspondence of the colonies had been, until within a few years, carried on by the southern secre-tary of state; and that this department has not been shunned upon account of the weight of its duties; but, on the contrary, much sought on account of its patronage. Indeed he must be poorly acquainted with the history of office, who does not know how very lightly the American functions have always leaned on the shoulders of the ministerial *Atlas*,[26] who has upheld that side of the sphere. Undoubtedly, great temper and judgment were requisite in the management of the colony politics; but the official detail was a trifle. Since the new appointment, a train of unfortunate accidents has brought before us almost the whole correspondence of this favourite secretary's office, since the first day of its establishment. I will say nothing of its auspicious foundation; of the quality of its correspondence; or of the effects that have ensued from it. I speak merely of its *quantity*; which we know would have been little or no addition to the trouble of whatever office had its hands the fullest. But what has been the real condition of the old office of secretary of state? Have their velvet bags, and their red boxes, been so full, that nothing more could possibly be crammed into them?

A correspondence of a curious nature has been lately published.* In that correspondence, Sir, we find the opinion of a noble person, who is thought to be the grand manufacturer of administrations;[27] and therefore the best judge of the quality of his work. He was of opinion, that there was but one man of diligence and industry in the whole administration – it was the late Earl of Suffolk.[28] The noble lord lamented very justly, that this statesman, of so much mental vigour, was almost wholly disabled from the exertion of it, by his bodily infirmities. Lord Suffolk, dead to the state long before he was dead to nature, at last paid his tribute to the common treasury to which we must all be taxed. But so little want was found even of his intentional industry, that the office, vacant in reality to its duties long before, continued vacant even in nomination and appointment for a year after his death. The whole of the laborious and arduous correspondence of this empire rested solely upon the activity and energy of Lord Weymouth.[29]

It is therefore demonstrable, since one diligent man was fully equal to the duties of the two offices, that two diligent men will be equal to the duty of three. The business of the new office, which I shall propose to you to suppress, is by no means too much to be returned to either of the secretaries which remain. If this dust in the balance should be thought too heavy, it may be divided between them both; North America (whether free or reduced) to the northern secretary, the West Indies to the southern. It is not necessary that I should say more upon the inutility of this office. It is burning daylight. But before I have done, I shall just remark, that the history of this office is too recent to suffer us to forget, that it was made for the mere convenience of the arrangements of political intrigue, and not for the service of the state; that it was made, in order to give a colour to an exorbitant increase of the civil list; and in the same act to bring a new accession to the loaded compost heap of corrupt influence.

There is, Sir, another office which was not long since closely connected with this of the American secretary; but has been lately separated from it for the very same purpose for which it

---

* Letters between Dr. Addington and Sir James Wright.

had been conjoined; I mean the sole purpose of all the separations and all the conjunctions that have been lately made – a job. I speak, Sir, of the *board of trade and plantations*. This board is a sort of temperate bed of influence; a sort of gently ripening hot-house, where eight members of parliament receive salaries of a thousand a year, for a certain given time, in order to mature, at a proper season, a claim to two thousand, granted for doing less, and on the credit of having toiled so long in that inferior, laborious department.

I have known that board, off and on, for a great number of years. Both of its pretended objects have been much the objects of my study, if I have a right to call any pursuits of mine by so respectable a name. I can assure the House, and I hope they will not think that I risk my little credit lightly, that, without meaning to convey the least reflection upon any one of its members past or present, – it is a board which, if not mischievous, is of no use at all.

You will be convinced, Sir, that I am not mistaken, if you reflect how generally it is true, that commerce, the principal object of that office, flourishes most when it is left to itself. Interest, the great guide of commerce, is not a blind one. It is very well able to find its own way; and its necessities are its best laws. But if it were possible, in the nature of things, that the young should direct the old, and the inexperienced instruct the knowing; if a board in the state was the best tutor for the counting-house; if the desk ought to read lectures to the anvil, and the pen to usurp the place of the shuttle – yet in any matter of regulation, we know that board must act with as little authority as skill. The prerogative of the crown is utterly inadequate to the object; because all regulations are, in their nature, restrictive of some liberty. In the reign, indeed, of *Charles the First*, the council, or committees of council, were never a moment unoccupied with affairs of trade. But even where they had no ill intention (which was sometimes the case) trade and manufacture suffered infinitely from their injudicious tampering. But since that period, whenever regulation is wanting (for I do not deny that sometimes it may be wanting) parliament constantly sits; and parliament alone is competent to such regulation. We want no instructions from boards of trade, or from any other board; and God forbid we should give the least attention to their reports. Parliamentary inquiry is the only mode of obtaining parliamentary information. There is more real knowledge to be obtained by attending the detail of business in the committees above-stairs, than ever did come, or ever will come, from any board in this kingdom, or from all of them together. An assiduous member of parliament will not be the worse instructed there, for not being paid a thousand a year for learning his lesson. And now that I speak of the committees above-stairs, I must say, that having till lately attended them a good deal, I have observed that no description of members give so little attendance, either to communicate or to obtain instruction upon matters of commerce, as the honourable members of the grave board of trade. I really do not recollect that I have ever seen one of them in that sort of business. Possibly some members may have better memories; and may call to mind some job that may have accidentally brought one or other of them, at one time or other, to attend a matter of commerce.

This board, Sir, has had both its original formation, and its regeneration, in a job. In a job it was conceived, and in a job its mother brought it forth. It made one among those showy and specious impositions, which one of the experiment-making administrations of *Charles the Second* held out to delude the people, and to be substituted in the place of the real service which they might expect from a parliament annually sitting. It was intended, also, to corrupt that body whenever it should be permitted to sit. It was projected in the year 1668, and it continued in a tottering and rickety childhood for about three or four years; for it died in the year 1673, a babe of as little hopes as ever swelled the bills of mortality in the article of convulsed or over-laid children, who have hardly stepped over the threshold of life.

It was buried with little ceremony; and never more thought of until the reign of *King William*, when in the strange vicissitude of neglect and rigour, of good and ill success, that attended his wars in the year 1695, the trade was distressed beyond all example of former sufferings, by the piracies of the French cruisers. This suffering incensed, and, as it should seem, very justly incensed, the House of Commons. In this ferment they struck, not only at the administration, but at the very constitution of the executive government. They attempted to form in parliament a board for the protection of trade; which, as they planned it, was to draw to itself a great part, if not the whole, of the functions and powers, both of the admiralty and of the treasury; and thus, by a parliamentary delegation of office and officers, they threatened absolutely to separate these departments from the whole system of the executive government, and of course to vest the most leading and essential of its attributes in this board. As the executive government was in a manner convicted of a dereliction of its functions, it was with infinite difficulty that this blow was warded off in that session. There was a threat to renew the same attempt in the next. To prevent the effect of this manœuvre, the court opposed another manœuvre to it; and, in the year 1696, called into life this board of trade, which had slept since 1673.

This, in a few words, is the history of the regeneration of the board of trade. It has perfectly answered its purposes. It was intended to quiet the minds of the people, and to compose the ferment that was then strongly working in parliament. The courtiers were too happy to be able to substitute a board, which they knew would be useless, in the place of one that they feared would be dangerous. Thus the board of trade was reproduced in a job; and perhaps it is the only instance of a public body, which has never degenerated; but to this hour preserves all the health and vigour of its primitive institution.

This board of trade and plantations has not been of any use to the colonies, as colonies; so little of use, that the flourishing settlements of New England, of Virginia, and of Maryland, and all our wealthy colonies in the West Indies, were of a date prior to the first board of Charles the Second. Pennsylvania and Carolina were settled during its dark quarter, in the interval between the extinction of the first and the formation of the second board. Two colonies alone owe their origin to that board. Georgia, which, till lately, has made a very slow progress; and never did make any progress at all, until it wholly got rid of all the regulations which the board of trade had moulded into its original constitution. That colony has cost the nation very great sums of money; whereas the colonies which have had the fortune of not being godfathered by the board of trade never cost the nation a shilling, except what has been so properly spent in losing them. But the colony of Georgia, weak as it was, carried with it to the last hour, and carries even in its present dead, pallid visage, the perfect resemblance of its parents. It always had, and it now has, an *establishment* paid by the public of England, for the sake of the influence of the crown; that colony having never been able or willing to take upon itself the expense of its proper government, or its own appropriated jobs.

The province of Nova Scotia was the youngest and the favourite child of the board. Good God! what sums the nursing of that ill-thriven, hard-visaged, and ill-favoured brat has cost to this wittol nation! Sir, this colony has stood us in a sum of not less than seven hundred thousand pounds. To this day it has made no repayment – It does not even support those offices of expense, which are miscalled its government; the whole of that job still lies upon the patient, callous shoulders of the people of England.

Sir, I am going to state a fact to you, that will serve to set in full sunshine the real value of formality, and official superintendence. There was, in the province of Nova Scotia, one little neglected corner, the country of the *neutral French*; which having the good fortune to escape the fostering care of both France and England, and to have been shut out from the protection and regulation of councils of commerce and of boards of trade, did in silence, without notice, and without assistance, increase to a considerable degree. But it seems our nation had more skill and ability in destroying than in settling a colony. In the last war we did, in my opinion, most inhumanly, and upon pretences that in the eye of an honest man are not worth a farthing, root out this poor inno-cent, deserving people, whom our utter inability to govern, or to reconcile, gave us no sort of right to extirpate. Whatever the merits of that extirpation might have been, it was on the foot-steps of a neglected people, it was on the fund of unconstrained poverty, it was on the acquisitions of unregulated industry, that anything which deserves the name of a colony in that province has been formed. It has been formed by overflowings from the exuberant population of New England, and by emigration from other parts of Nova Scotia of fugitives from the protection of the board of trade.

But if all of these things were not more than sufficient to prove to you the inutility of that expensive establishment, I would desire you to recollect, Sir, that those, who may be very ready to defend it, are very cautious how they employ it; cautious how they employ it even in appearance and pretence. They are afraid they should lose the benefit of its influence in parliament, if they seemed to keep it up for any other purpose. If ever there were commercial points of great weight, and most closely connected with our dependencies, they are those which have been agitated and decided in parliament since I came into it. Which of the innumerable regulations since made had their origin or their improvement in the board of trade? Did any of the several East India bills, which have been successively produced since 1767, originate there? Did any one dream of referring them, or any part of them, thither? Was anybody so ridiculous as even to think of it? If ever there was an occasion on which the board was fit to be consulted, it was with regard to the acts that were preludes to the American war, or attendant on its commencement: those acts were full of commercial regulations, such as they were – the intercourse bill; the prohibitory bill; the fishery bill. If the board was not concerned in such things, in what particular was it thought fit that it should be concerned? In the course of all these bills through the House, I observed the members of that board to be remarkably cautious of intermeddling. They understood decorum better – they know that matters of trade and plantations are no business of theirs.

There were two very recent occasions, which, if the idea of any use for the board had not been extinguished by prescription, appeared loudly to call for their interference.

When commissioners were sent to pay his Majesty's and our dutiful respects to the congress of the United States, a part of their powers under the commission were, it seems, of a commercial nature. They were authorised, in the most ample and undefined manner, to form a commercial treaty with America on the spot. This was no trivial object. As the formation of such a treaty would necessarily have been no less than the breaking up of our whole commercial system, and the giving it an entirely new form; one would imagine, that the board of trade would have sat day and night to model propositions, which, on our side, might serve as a basis to that treaty. No such thing. Their learned leisure was not in the least interrupted, though one of the members of the board was a commissioner, and might, in mere compliment to his office, have been supposed to make a show of deliberation on the subject. But he knew that his colleagues would have thought he laughed in their faces, had he attempted to bring anything the most distantly relating to commerce or colonies before *them*. A noble person, engaged in the same commission, and sent to learn his commercial rudiments in New York, (then under the operation of an act for the universal prohibition of trade,) was soon after put at the head of that board. This contempt from the present ministers of all the pretended functions of that board, and their manner of breathing into its very soul, of inspiring it with its animating and presiding principle, puts an end to all dispute concerning their opinion of the clay it was made of. But I will give them heaped measure.

It was but the other day, that the noble lord in the blue riband carried up to the House of Peers two acts, altering I think much for the better, but altering in a great degree, our whole commercial system. Those acts, I mean, for giving a free trade to Ireland in woollens, and in all things else, with independent nations, and giving them an equal trade to our own colonies. Here too the novelty of this great, but arduous and critical, improvement of system, would make you conceive that the anxious solicitude of the noble lord in the blue riband would have wholly destroyed the plan of summer recreation of that board, by references to examine, compare, and digest matters for parliament. – You would imagine, that Irish commissioners of customs, and English commissioners of customs, and commissioners of excise, that merchants and manufacturers of every denomination, had daily crowded their outer rooms. *Nil horum*.[30] The perpetual virtual adjournment, and the unbroken sitting vacation of that board, was no more disturbed by the Irish than by the plantation commerce, or any other commerce. The same matter made a large part of the business which occupied the House for two sessions before; and as our ministers were not then mellowed by the mild, emollient, and engaging blandishments of our dear sister, into all the tenderness of unqualified surrender, the bounds and limits of a restrained benefit naturally required much detailed management and positive regulation. But neither the qualified propositions which were received, nor those other qualified propositions which were rejected by ministers, were the least concern of theirs, nor were they ever thought of in the business.

It is therefore, Sir, on the opinion of parliament, on the opinion of the ministers, and even on their own opinion of their inutility, that I shall propose to you to *suppress the board of trade and plantations*; and to recommit all its business to the council from whence it was very improvidently taken; and which business (whatever it might be) was much better done, and without any expense; and indeed where in effect it may all come at last. Almost all that deserves the name of business there, is the reference of the plantation acts to the opinion of gentlemen of the law. But all this may be done, as the Irish business of the same nature has always been done, by the council, and with a reference to the attorney and solicitor-general.

There are some regulations in the household, relative to officers of the yeomen of the guards, and the officers and band of gentlemen pensioners, which I shall likewise submit to your consideration, for the purpose of regulating establishments, which at present are much abused.

I have now finished all that for the present I shall trouble you with on the *plan of reduction*. I mean next to propose to you the *plan of arrangement*, by which I mean to appropriate and fix the civil list money to its several services according to their nature; for I am thoroughly sensible, that if a discretion, wholly arbitrary, can be exercised over the civil list revenue, although the most effectual method may be taken to prevent the inferior departments from exceeding their bounds, the plan of reformation will still be left very imperfect. It will not, in my opinion, be safe to permit an entirely arbitrary discretion even in the first lord of the treasury himself: it will not be safe to leave with him a power of diverting the public money from its proper objects, of paying it in an irregular course, or of inverting perhaps the order of time, dictated by the proportion of value, which ought to regulate his application of payment to service.

I am sensible too, that the very operation of a plan of economy, which tends to exonerate the civil list of expensive establishments, may in some sort defeat the capital end we have in view; the independence of parliament; and that in removing the public and ostensible means of influence, we may increase the fund of private corruption. I have thought of some methods to prevent an abuse of surplus cash under discretionary application; I mean the heads of *secret service, special service, various payments*, and the like; which I hope will answer, and which in due time I shall lay before you. Where I am unable to limit the quantity of the sums to be applied, by reason of the uncertain quantity of the service, I endeavour to confine it to its *line*; to secure an indefinite application to the definite service to which it belongs; not to stop the progress of expense in its line, but to confine it to that line in which it professes to move.

But that part of my plan, Sir, upon which I principally rest, that on which I rely for the purpose of binding up and securing the whole, is to establish a fixed and invariable order in all its payments, which it shall not be permitted to the first lord of the treasury, upon any pretence whatsoever, to depart from. I therefore divide the civil list payment into *nine* classes, putting each class forward according to the importance or justice of the demand, and to the inability of the persons entitled to enforce their pretensions; that is, to put those first who have the most efficient offices, or claim the justest debts; and, at the same time, from the character of that description of men, from the retiredness or the remoteness of their situation, or from their want of weight and power to enforce their pretensions, or from their being entirely subject to the power of a minister, without any reciprocal power of awing, ought to be the most considered, and are the most likely to be neglected; all these I place in the highest classes: I place in the lowest those whose functions are of the least importance, but whose persons or rank are often of the greatest power and influence.

In the first class, I place the *judges*, as of the first importance. It is the public justice that holds the community together; the ease, therefore, and independence of the judges ought to supersede all other considerations, and they ought to be the very last to feel the necessities of the state, or to be obliged either to court or bully a minister for their right; they ought to be as *weak solicitors on their own demands*, as strenuous assertors of the rights and liberties of others. The judges are, or ought to be, of a reserved and retired character, and wholly unconnected with the political world.

In the second class, I place the foreign ministers. The judges are the links of our connexions with one another; the foreign ministers are the links of our connexion with other nations. They are not upon the spot to demand payment, and are therefore the most likely to be, as in fact they have sometimes been, entirely neglected, to the great disgrace, and perhaps the great detriment, of the nation.

In the third class, I would bring all the tradesmen who supply the crown by contract, or otherwise.

In the fourth class, I place all the domestic servants of the king, and all persons in efficient offices, whose salaries do not exceed two hundred pounds a year.

In the fifth, upon account of honour, which ought to give place to nothing but charity and rigid justice, I would place the pensions and allowances of his Majesty's royal family, comprehending of course the queen, together with the stated allowance of the privy purse.

In the sixth class, I place those efficient offices of duty, whose salaries may exceed the sum of two hundred pounds a year.

In the seventh class, that mixed mass, the whole pension list.

In the eighth, the offices of honour about the king.

In the ninth, and the last of all, the salaries and pensions of the first lord of the treasury himself, the chancellor of the exchequer, and the other commissioners of the treasury.

If by any possible mismanagement of that part of the revenue which is left at discretion, or by any other mode of prodigality, cash should be deficient for the payment of the lowest classes, I propose that the amount of those salaries, where the deficiency may happen to fall, shall not be carried as debt to the account of the succeeding year, but that it shall be entirely lapsed, sunk, and lost; so that government will be enabled to start in the race of every new year wholly unloaded, fresh in wind and in vigour. Hereafter, no civil list debt can ever come upon the public. And those who do not consider this as saving, because it is not a certain sum, do not ground their calculations of the future on their experience of the past.

I know of no mode of preserving the effectual execution of any duty, but to make it the direct interest of the executive officer that it shall be faithfully reformed. Assuming, then, that the present vast allowance to the civil list is perfectly adequate to all its purposes, if there should be any failure, it must be from the mismanagement or neglect of the first commissioner of the treasury; since, upon the proposed plan, there can be no expense of any consequence, which he is not himself previously to authorise, and finally to control. It is therefore just, as well as politic, that the loss should attach upon the delinquency.

If the failure from the delinquency should be very considerable, it will fall on the class directly above the first lord of the treasury, as well as upon himself and his board. It will fall, as it ought to fall, upon offices of no primary importance in the state; but then it will fall upon persons, whom it will be a matter of no slight importance for a minister to provoke – it will fall upon persons of the first rank and consequence in the kingdom; upon those who are nearest to the king, and frequently have a more interior credit with him than the minister himself. It will fall upon masters of the horse, upon lord chamberlains, upon lord stewards, upon grooms of the stole, and lords of the bedchamber. The household troops form an army, who will be ready to mutiny for want of pay, and whose mutiny will be *really* dreadful to a commander-in-chief. A rebellion of the thirteen lords of the bedchamber would be far more terrible to a minister, and would probably affect his power more to the quick, than a revolt of thirteen colonies. What an uproar such an event would create at court! What *petitions*, and *committees*, and *associations*, would it not produce! Bless me! what a clattering of white sticks and yellow sticks would be about his head – what a storm of gold keys would fly about the ears of the minister – what a shower of Georges, and Thistles, and medals, and collars of S.S. would assail him at his first entrance into the antechamber, after an insolvent Christmas quarter! A tumult which could not be appeased by all the harmony of the new-year's ode.[31] Rebellion it is certain there would be; and rebellion may not now indeed be so critical an event to those who engage in it, since its price is so correctly ascertained at just a thousand pounds.

Sir, this classing, in my opinion, is a serious and solid security for the performance of a minister's duty. Lord Coke says, that the staff was put into the treasurer's hand to enable him to support himself when there was no money in the exchequer, and to beat away importunate solicitors. The method, which I propose, would hinder him from the necessity of such a broken staff to lean on, or such a miserable weapon for repulsing the demands of worthless suitors, who, the noble lord in the blue riband knows, will bear many hard blows on the head, and many other indignities, before they are driven from the treasury. In this plan, he is furnished with an answer to all their importunity; an answer far more conclusive, than if he had knocked them down with his staff – "Sir, (or my Lord,) you are calling for my own salary – Sir, you are calling for the appointments of my colleagues who sit about me in office – Sir, you are going to excite a mutiny at court against me – you are going to estrange his Majesty's confidence from me, through the chamberlain, or the master of the horse, or the groom of the stole."

As things now stand, every man, in proportion to his consequence at court, tends to add to the expense of the civil list, by all manner of jobs, if not for himself, yet for his dependents. When the new plan is established, those, who are now suitors for jobs, will become the most strenuous opposers of them. They will have a common interest with the minister in public economy. Every class, as it stands low, will become security for the payment of the preceding class; and thus the persons, whose insignificant services defraud those that are useful, would then become interested in their payment. Then the powerful, instead of oppressing, would be obliged to support the weak; and idleness would become concerned in the reward of industry. The whole fabric of the civil economy would become compact and connected in all its parts; it would be formed into a well-organised body, where every member contributes to the support of the whole; and where even the lazy stomach secures the rigour of the active arm.

This plan, I really flatter myself, is laid, not in official formality, nor in airy speculation, but in real life, and in human nature, in what "comes home (as Bacon says)[32] to the business and bosoms of men." You have now, Sir, before you, the whole of my scheme, as far as I have digested it into a form, that might be in any respect worthy of your consideration – I intend to lay it before you in five bills.* The plan consists, indeed, of many parts; but they stand upon a few plain principles. It is a plan which takes nothing from the civil list without discharging it of a burthen equal to the sum carried to the public service. It weakens no one function necessary to government; but on the contrary, by appropriating supply to service, it gives it greater vigour. It provides the means of order and foresight to a minister of finance, which may always keep all the objects of his office, and their state, condition, and relations, distinctly before him. It brings forward accounts without hurrying and distressing the accountants: whilst it provides for public convenience, it regards private rights. It extinguishes secret corruption almost to the possibility of its existence. It destroys direct and visible influence equal to the offices of at least fifty members of parliament. Lastly, it prevents the provision for his Majesty's children from being diverted to the political purposes of his minister.

These are the points on which I rely for the merit of the plan: I pursue economy in a secondary view, and only as it is connected with these great objects. I am persuaded, that even for supply this scheme will be far from unfruitful, if it be executed to the extent I propose it. I think it will give to the public, at its periods, two or three hundred thousand pounds a year; if not, it will give them a system of economy, which is itself a great revenue. It gives me no little pride and satisfaction, to find that the principles of my

* Titles of the bills read.

proceedings are, in many respects, the very same with those which are now pursued in the plans of the French minister of finance. I am sure, that I lay before you a scheme easy and practicable in all its parts. I know it is common at once to applaud and to reject all attempts of this nature. I know it is common for men to say, that such and such things are perfectly right – very desirable; but that, unfortunately, they are not practicable. Oh! no, Sir, no. Those things which are not practicable, are not desirable. There is nothing in the world really beneficial, that does not lie within the reach of an informed understanding and a well-directed pursuit. There is nothing that God has judged good for us, that he has not given us the means to accomplish, both in the natural and the moral world. If we cry, like children, for the moon, like children, we must cry on.

We must follow the nature of our affairs, and conform ourselves to our situation. If we do, our objects are plain and compassable. Why should we resolve to do nothing, because what I propose to you may not be the exact demand of the petition; when we are far from resolved to comply even with what evidently is so? Does this sort of chicanery become us? The people are the masters. They have only to express their wants at large and in gross. We are the expert artists; we are the skilful workmen, to shape their desires into perfect form, and to fit the utensil to the use. They are the sufferers, they tell the symptoms of the complaint; but we know the exact seat of the disease, and how to apply the remedy according to the rules of art. How shocking would it be to see us pervert our skill into a sinister and servile dexterity, for the purpose of evading our duty, and defrauding our employers, who are our natural lords, of the object of their just expectations. I think the whole not only practicable, but practicable in a very short time. If we are in earnest about it, and if we exert that industry, and those talents, in forwarding the work, which, I am afraid, may be exerted in impeding it – I engage, that the whole may be put in complete execution within a year. For my own part, I have very little to recommend me for this or for any task, but a kind of earnest and anxious perseverance of mind, which, with all its good and all its evil effects, is moulded into my constitution. I faithfully engage to the House, if they choose to appoint me to any part in the execution of this work, which (when they have made it theirs by the improvements of their wisdom) will be worthy of the able assistance they may give me, that by night and by day, in town or in country, at the desk or in the forest, I will, without regard to convenience, ease, or pleasure, devote myself to their service, not expecting or admitting any reward whatsoever. I owe to this country my labour, which is my all: and I owe to it ten times more industry, if ten times more I could exert. After all, I shall be an unprofitable servant.

At the same time, if I am able, and if I shall be permitted, I will lend an humble, helping hand to any other good work which is going on. I have not, Sir, the frantic presumption to suppose, that this plan contains in it the whole of what the public has a right to expect, in the great work of reformation they call for. Indeed it falls infinitely short of it. It falls short even of my own ideas. I have some thoughts, not yet fully ripened, relative to a reform in the customs and excise, as well as in some other branches of financial administration. There are other things too, which form essential parts in a great plan for the purpose of restoring the independence of parliament. The contractors bill of last year it is fit to revive; and I rejoice that it is in better hands than mine. The bill for suspending the votes of custom-house officers, brought into parliament several years ago, by one of our worthiest and wisest members,* (would to God we could along with the plan revive the person who designed it). But a man of very real integrity, honour, and ability, will be found to take his place, and to carry his idea into full execution. You all see how necessary it is to review our military expenses for some years past, and, if possible, to bind up and close that bleeding artery of profusion: but that business also, I have reason to hope, will be undertaken by abilities that are fully adequate to it. Something must be devised (if possible) to check the ruinous expense of elections.

Sir, all or most of these things must be done. Every one must take his part.

If we should be able by dexterity, or power, or intrigue, to disappoint the expectations of our constituents, what will it avail us? We shall never be strong or artful enough to parry, or to put by, the irresistible demands of our situation. That situation calls upon us, and upon our constituents too, with a voice which *will* be heard. I am sure no man is more zealously attached than I am to the privileges of this House, particularly in regard to the exclusive management of money. The lords have no right to

* W. Dowdeswell, Esq.,[33] chancellor of the exchequer, 1765.

the disposition, in any sense, of the public purse; but they have gone further in self-denial* than our utmost jealousy could have required. A power of examining accounts, to censure, correct, and punish, we never, that I know of, have thought of denying to the House of Lords. It is something more than a century since we voted that body useless: they have now voted themselves so. The whole hope of reformation is at length cast upon *us*: and let us not deceive the nation, which does us the honour to hope everything from our virtue. If *all* the nation are not equally forward to press this duty upon us, yet be assured, that they all equally expect we should perform it. The respectful silence of those who wait upon your pleasure ought to be as powerful with you, as the call of those who require your service as their right. Some, without doors, affect to feel hurt for your dignity, because they suppose that menaces are held out to you. Justify their good opinion, by showing that no menaces are necessary to stimulate you to your duty. – But, Sir, whilst we may sympathise with them, in one point, who sympathise with us in another, we ought to attend no less to those who approach us like men, and who, in the guise of petitioners, speak to us in the tone of a concealed authority. It is not wise to force them to speak out more plainly, what they plainly mean. – But the petitioners are violent. Be it so. Those, who are least anxious about your conduct, are not those that love you most. Moderate affection, and satiated enjoyment, are cold and respectful; but an ardent and injured passion is tempered up with wrath, and grief, and shame, and conscious worth, and the maddening sense of violated right. A jealous love lights his torch from the firebrands of the furies. – They who call upon you to belong *wholly* to the people, are those who wish you to return to your *proper* home; to the sphere of your duty, to the post of your honour, to the mansion-house of all genuine, serene, and solid satisfaction. We have furnished to the people of England (indeed we have) some real cause of jealousy. Let us leave that sort of company which, if it does not destroy our innocence, pollutes our honour; let us free ourselves at once from everything that can increase their suspicions, and inflame their just resentment; let us cast away from us, with a generous scorn, all the love-tokens and symbols that we have

* Rejection of Lord Shelburne's motion in the House of Lords.[34]

been vain and light enough to accept; – all the bracelets, and snuff-boxes, and miniature pictures, and hair devices, and all the other adulterous trinkets that are the pledges of our alienation, and the monuments of our shame. Let us return to our legitimate home, and all jars and all quarrels will be lost in embraces. Let the commons in parliament assembled be one and the same thing with the commons at large. The distinctions that are made to so separate us are unnatural and wicked contrivances. Let us identify, let us incorporate, ourselves with the people. Let us cut all the cables and snap the chains which tie us to an unfaithful shore, and enter the friendly harbour, that shoots far out into the main its moles and jettees to receive us. – "War with the world, and peace with our constituents." Be this our motto, and our principle. Then, indeed, we shall be truly great. Respecting ourselves, we shall be respected by the world. At present all is troubled, and cloudy, and distracted, and full of anger and turbulence, both abroad and at home; but the air may be cleared by this storm, and light and fertility may follow it. Let us give a faithful pledge to the people that we honour, indeed, the crown; but that we *belong* to them; that we are their auxiliaries and not their task-masters; the fellow-labourers in the same vineyard, not lording over their rights, but helpers of their joy: that to tax them is a grievance to ourselves; but to cut off from our enjoyments to forward theirs, is the highest gratification we are capable of receiving. I feel with comfort, that we are all warmed with these sentiments, and while we are thus warm, I wish we may go directly and with a cheerful heart to this salutary work.

Sir, I move for leave to bring in a bill, "For the better regulation of his Majesty's civil establishments, and of certain public offices; for the limitation of pensions, and the suppression of sundry useless, expensive, and inconvenient places; and for applying the monies saved thereby to the public service."*

Lord North stated, that there was a difference between this bill for regulating the establishments, and some of the others, as they affected the ancient patrimony of the crown; and therefore wished them to be postponed, till the king's consent could be obtained. This distinction was strongly controverted; but when

---

* The motion was seconded by Mr. Fox.

it was insisted on as a point of decorum *only*, it was agreed to postpone them to another day. Accordingly, on the Monday following, viz. February 14, leave was given, on the motion of Mr.
Burke, without opposition, to bring in,

1st, "A bill for the sale of the forests and other crown lands,
rents, and hereditaments, with certain exceptions; *and for applying
the produce thereof to the public service*; and for securing, ascertaining,
and satisfying, *tenant-rights*, and common and other rights."

2nd, "A bill for the more perfectly uniting to the crown the
principality of Wales, and the county palatine of Chester, and for
the more commodious administration of justice within the same;
as also for abolishing certain offices now appertaining thereto; *for
quieting dormant claims, ascertaining and securing tenant-rights*; and
for the sale of all forest lands, and other lands, tenements, and
hereditaments, held by his Majesty in right of the said principality, or county palatine of Chester, *and for applying the produce
thereof to the public service.*"

3rd, "A bill for uniting to the crown the duchy and county
palatine of Lancaster; for the suppression of unnecessary offices
now belonging thereto; for the *ascertainment and security of tenant
and other rights*; and for the sale of all rents, lands, tenements, and
hereditaments, and forests, within the said duchy, and county
palatine, or either of them; *and for applying the produce thereof to the
public service.*" – *And it was ordered that* Mr. Burke, Mr. Fox, Lord
John Cavendish, Sir George Savile, Colonel Barrè, Mr. Thomas
Townshend, Mr. Byng, Mr. Dunning, Sir Joseph Mawbey,
Mr. Recorder of London, Sir Robert Clayton, Mr. Frederick
Montagu, the Earl of Upper Ossory, Sir William Guise, and
Mr. Gilbert, *do prepare and bring in the same.*

At the same time, Mr. Burke moved for leave to bring in –
4th, "A bill for uniting the duchy of Cornwall to the crown; for
the suppression of certain unnecessary offices now belonging
thereto; for the *ascertainment and security of tenant and other rights*;
and for the sale of certain rents, lands, and tenements, within or
belonging to the said duchy; *and for applying the produce thereof to
the public service.*"

But some objections being made by the surveyor-general of
the duchy, concerning the rights of the prince of Wales, now
in his minority, and Lord North remaining perfectly silent, Mr.
Burke, at length, though he strongly contended against the principle of the objection, consented to withdraw this last motion
for the *present*, to be renewed upon an early occasion.

SPEECH ON A BILL FOR SHORTENING THE DURATION OF PARLIAMENTS

8 MAY 1780

IT IS ALWAYS to be lamented when men are driven to search into the foundations of the commonwealth. It is certainly necessary to resort to the theory of your government whenever you propose any alteration in the frame of it, whether that alteration means the revival of some former antiquated and forsaken constitution of state, or the introduction of some new improvement in the commonwealth. The object of our deliberation is to promote the good purposes for which elections have been instituted, and to prevent their inconveniences. If we thought frequent elections attended with no inconvenience, or with but a trifling inconvenience, the strong overruling principle of the constitution would sweep us like a torrent towards them. But your remedy is to be suited to your disease – your present disease, and to your whole disease. That man thinks much too highly, and therefore he thinks weakly and delusively, of any contrivance of human wisdom, who believes that it can make any sort of approach to perfection. There is not, there never was, a principle of government under heaven, that does not, in the very pursuit of the good it proposes, naturally and inevitably lead into some inconvenience, which makes it absolutely necessary to counterwork and weaken the application of that first principle itself; and to abandon something of the extent of the advantage you proposed by it, in order to prevent also the inconveniences which have arisen from the instrument of all the good you had in view.

To govern according to the sense and agreeably to the interests of the people, is a great and glorious object of government. This object cannot be obtained but through the medium of popular election; and popular election is a mighty evil. It is such, and so great an evil, that though there are few nations whose monarchs were not originally elective, very few are now elected. They are the distempers of elections that have destroyed all free states. To cure these distempers is difficult, if not impossible; the only thing, therefore, left to save the commonwealth is to prevent their return too frequently. The objects in view are, to have parliaments as frequent as they can be without distracting them in the prosecution of public business; on one hand to secure their dependence upon the people; on the other to give them that quiet in their minds, and that ease in their fortunes, as to enable them to perform the most arduous and most painful duty in the world with spirit, with efficiency, with independency, and with experience, as real public counsellors, not as the canvassers at a perpetual election. It is wise to compass as many good ends as possibly you can, and, seeing there are inconveniences on both sides, with benefits on both, to give up a part of the benefit to soften the inconvenience. The perfect cure is impracticable, because the disorder is dear to those from whom alone the cure can possibly be derived. The utmost to be done is to palliate, to mitigate, to respite, to put off the evil day of the constitution to its latest possible hour, and may it be a very late one!

This bill, I fear, would precipitate one of two consequences, I know not which most likely, or which most dangerous; either that the Crown, by its constant stated power, influence, and revenue, would wear out all opposition in elections, or that a violent and furious popular spirit would arise. I must see, to satisfy me, the remedies; I must see, from their operation in the cure of the old evil, and in the cure of those new evils which are inseparable from all remedies, how they balance each other, and what is the total result. The excellence of mathematics and metaphysics is to have but one thing before you; but he forms the best judgment in all moral disquisitions, who has the greatest number and variety of considerations in one view before him, and can take them in with the best possible consideration of the middle results of all.

We of the opposition, who are not friends to the bill, give this pledge at least of our integrity and sincerity to the people, that in our situation of systematic opposition to the present ministers, in which all our hope of rendering it effectual depends upon popular interest and favour, we will not flatter them by a surrender of our uninfluenced judgment and opinion; we give a security, that, if ever we should be in another situation, no flattery to any other sort of power and influence would induce us to act against the true interests of the people.

All are agreed that parliaments should not be perpetual; the only question is, what is the most convenient time for their duration? On which there are three opinions.[1] We are agreed, too, that the term ought not to be chosen most likely in its operation to spread corruption, and to augment the already overgrown influence of the Crown. On these principles I mean to debate the question. It is easy to pretend a zeal for liberty. Those who think themselves not likely to be encumbered with the performance of their promises, either from their known inability, or total indifference about the performance, never fail to entertain the most lofty ideas. They are certainly the most specious, and they cost them neither reflection to frame, nor pains to modify, nor management to support. The task is of another nature to those who mean to promise nothing that it is not in their intention, or may possibly be in their power, to perform; to those who are bound and principled no more to delude the understandings than to violate the liberty of their fellow-subjects. Faithful watchmen we ought to be over the rights and privileges of the people. But our duty, if we are qualified for it as we ought, is to give them information, and not to receive it from them; we are not to go to school to them to learn the principles of law and government. In doing so, we should not dutifully serve, but we should basely and scandalously betray, the people, who are not capable of this service by nature, nor in any instance called to it by the constitution. I reverentially look up to the opinion of the people, and with an awe that is almost superstitious. I should be ashamed to show my face before them if I changed my ground, as they cried up or cried down men, or things, or opinions; if I wavered and shifted about with every change, and joined in it, or opposed, as best answered any low interest or passion; if I held them up hopes which I knew I never intended, or promised what I well knew I could not perform. Of all these things they are perfect sovereign judges, without appeal; but as to the detail of particular measures, or to any general schemes of policy, they have neither enough of speculation in the closet, nor of experience in business, to decide upon it. They can well see whether we are tools of a court, or their honest servants. Of that they can well judge; and I wish that they always exercised their judgment; but of the particular merits of a measure I have other standards.

That the frequency of elections proposed by this bill has a tendency to increase the power and consideration of the electors, not lessen corruptibility, I do most readily allow; so far it is desirable; this is what it has, I will tell you now what it has not. 1st, It has no sort of tendency to increase their integrity and public spirit, unless an increase of power has an operation upon voters in elections that it has in no other situation in the world, and upon no other part of mankind. 2nd, This bill has no tendency to limit the quantity of influence in the Crown, to render its operation more difficult, or to counteract that operation, which it cannot prevent, in any way whatsoever. It has its full weight, its full range, and its uncontrolled operation on the electors exactly as it had before. 3rd, Nor, thirdly, does it abate the interest or inclination of ministers to apply that influence to the electors; on the contrary, it renders it much more necessary to them, if they seek to have a majority in parliament, to increase the means of that influence, and redouble their diligence, and to sharpen dexterity in the application. The whole effect of the bill is therefore the removing the application of some part of the influence from the elected to the electors, and further to strengthen and extend a court interest already great and powerful in boroughs, here to fix their magazines and places of arms, and thus to make them the principal, not the secondary, theatre of their manœuvres for securing a determined majority in parliament.

I believe nobody will deny that the electors are corruptible. They are men; it is saying nothing worse of them; many of them are but ill informed in their minds, many feeble in their circumstances, easily over-reached, easily seduced. If they are many, the wages of corruption are the lower; and would to God it were not rather a contemptible and hypocritical adulation than a charitable sentiment to say that there is already no debauchery, no corruption, no bribery, no perjury, no blind fury, and interested faction among the electors in many parts of this kingdom; nor is it surprising, or at all blameable in that class of private men, when they see their neighbours aggrandised, and themselves poor and virtuous without that *eclat* or dignity which attends men in higher situations.

But admit it were true, that the great mass of the electors were too vast an object for court influence to grasp, or extend to, and that in despair they must abandon it; he must be very ignorant of the state of every popular interest who does not know, that in all the corporations, all the open boroughs, indeed in every district of the kingdom, there is some leading man, some agitator, some wealthy merchant, or considerable manufacturer, some active attorney, some popular preacher, some money-lender, &c.

&c., who is followed by the whole flock. This is the style of all free countries.

> – *Multum in Fabiâ valet hic, valet ille Velinâ;*
> *Cuilibet hic fasces dabit eripietque curule.*[2]

These spirits, each of which informs and governs his own little orb, are neither so many, nor so little powerful, nor so incorruptible, but that a minister may, as he does frequently, find means of gaining them, and through them all their followers. To establish, therefore, a very general influence among electors will no more be found an impracticable project, than to gain an undue influence over members of parliament. Therefore I am apprehensive, that this bill, though it shifts the place of the disorder, does by no means relieve the constitution. I went through almost every contested election in the beginning of this parliament, and acted as a manager in very many of them; by which, though as at a school of pretty severe and rugged discipline, I came to have some degree of instruction concerning the means by which parliamentary interests are in general procured and supported.

Theory, I know, would suppose, that every general election is to the representative a day of judgment, in which he appears before his constituents to account for the use of the talent with which they intrusted him, and for the improvement he has made of it for the public advantage. It would be so, if every corruptible representative were to find an enlightened and incorruptible constituent. But the practice and knowledge of the world will not suffer us to be ignorant, that the constitution on paper is one thing, and in fact and experience is another. We must know, that the candidate, instead of trusting at his election to the testimony of his behaviour in parliament, must bring the testimony of a large sum of money, the capacity of liberal expense in entertainments, the power of serving and obliging the rulers of corporations, of winning over the popular leaders of political clubs, associations, and neighbourhoods. It is ten thousand times more necessary to show himself a man of power, than a man of integrity, in almost all the elections with which I have been acquainted. Elections, therefore, become a matter of heavy expense; and, if contests are frequent, to many they will become a matter of an expense totally ruinous, which no fortunes can bear; but least of all the landed fortunes, encumbered as they often, indeed as they mostly, are with debts, with portions, with jointures; and tied up in the hands of the possessor by the limitations of settlement. It is a material, it is in my opinion a lasting, consideration in all the questions concerning election. Let no one think the charges of elections a trivial matter.

The charge, therefore, of elections ought never to be lost sight of in a question concerning their frequency; because the grand object you seek is independence. Independence of mind will ever be more or less influenced by independence of fortune; and if, every three years, the exhausting sluices of entertainments, drinkings, open houses, to say nothing of bribery, are to be periodically drawn up and renewed; – if government-favours, for which now, in some shape or other, the whole race of men are candidates, are to be called for upon every occasion, I see that private fortunes will be trashed away, and every, even to the least, trace of independence borne down by the torrent. I do not seriously think this constitution, even to the wrecks of it, could survive five triennial elections. If you are to fight the battle, you must put on the armour of the ministry; you must call in the public, to the aid of private, money. The expense of the last election has been computed (and I am persuaded that it has not been over-rated) at £1,500,000; – three shillings in the pound more in the land tax. About the close of the last parliament, and the beginning of this, several agents for boroughs went about, and I remember well that it was in every one of their mouths – "Sir, your election will cost you three thousand pounds if you are independent; but if the ministry supports you it may be done for two, and perhaps for less;" and, indeed, the thing spoke itself. Where a living was to be got for one, a commission in the army for another, a lift in the navy for a third, and custom-house offices scattered about without measure or number, who doubts but money may be saved? The treasury may even add money; but indeed it is superfluous. A gentleman of two thousand a year who meets another of the same fortune fights with equal arms; but if to one of the candidates you add a thousand a year in places for himself, and a power of giving away as much among others, one must, or there is no truth in arithmetical demonstration, ruin his adversary, if he is to meet him and to fight with him every third year. It will be said, I do not allow for the operation of character; but I do; and I know it will have its weight in most elections; perhaps it may be decisive in some. But there are few in which it will prevent great expenses.

The destruction of independent fortunes will be the consequence on the part of the candidate. What will be the consequence of triennial corruption, triennial drunkenness, triennial idleness, triennial law-suits, litigations, prosecutions, triennial phrensy, of society dissolved, industry interrupted, ruined; of those personal hatreds that will never be suffered to soften; those animosities and feuds which will be rendered immortal; those quarrels which are never to be appeased; morals vitiated and gangrened to the vitals? I think no stable and useful advantages were ever made by the money got at elections by the voter, but all he gets is doubly lost to the public; it is money given to diminish the general stock of the community, which is in the industry of the subject. I am sure that it is a good while before he or his family settle again to their business. Their heads will never cool; the temptations of elections will be for ever glittering before their eyes. They will all grow politicians; every one, quitting his business, will choose to enrich himself by his vote. They will all take the gauging-rod; new places will be made for them; they will run to the custom-house quay; their looms and ploughs will be deserted.

So was Rome destroyed by the disorders of continual elections, though those of Rome were sober disorders. They had nothing but faction, bribery, bread, and stage plays, to debauch them. We have the inflammation of liquor super-added, a fury hotter than any of them. There the contest was only between citizen and citizen; here you have the contests of ambitious citizens on one side, supported by the Crown, to oppose to the efforts (let it be so) of private and unsupported ambition on the other. Yet Rome was destroyed by the frequency and charge of elections, and the monstrous expense of an unremitted courtship to the people. I think, therefore, the independent candidate and elector may each be destroyed by it; the whole body of the community be an infinite sufferer; and a vicious ministry the only gainer. Gentlemen, I know, feel the weight of this argument; they agree that this would be the consequence of more frequent elections, if things were to continue as they are. But they think the greatness and frequency of the evil would itself be a remedy for it; that, sitting but for a short time, the member would not find it worth while to make such vast expenses, while the fear of their constituents will hold them the more effectually to their duty.

To this I answer, that experience is full against them. This is no new thing; we have had triennial parliaments; at no period of time were seats more eagerly contested. The expenses of elections ran higher, taking the state of all charges, than they do now. The expense of entertainments was such, that an act, equally severe and ineffectual, was made against it; every monument of the time bears witness of the expense, and most of the acts against corruption in elections were then made; all the writers talked of it and lamented it. Will any one think that a corporation will be contented with a bowl of punch or a piece of beef the less, because elections are every three, instead of every seven, years? Will they change their wine for ale, because they are to get more ale three years hence? Don't think it. Will they make fewer demands for the advantages of patronage in favours and offices, because their member is brought more under their power? We have not only our own historical experience in England upon the subject, but we have the experience co-existing with us in Ireland; where, since their parliament has been shortened, the expense of elections has been so far from being lowered, that it has been very near doubled. Formerly they sat for the king's life; the ordinary charge of a seat in parliament was then £1500. They now sit eight years, four sessions; it is now £2500, and upwards. The spirit of *emulation* has also been extremely increased, and all who are acquainted with the tone of that country have no doubt that the spirit is still growing; that new candidates will take the field; that the contests will be more violent, and the expenses of elections larger than ever.

It never can be otherwise. A seat in this House, for good purposes, for bad purposes, for no purposes at all, (except the mere consideration derived from being concerned in the public counsels,) will ever be a first-rate object of ambition in England. Ambition is no exact calculator. Avarice itself does not calculate strictly, when it games. One thing is certain, that in this political game the great lottery of power is that into which men will purchase with millions of chances against them. In Turkey, where the place, where the fortune, where the head itself, are so insecure, that scarcely any have died in their beds for ages, so that the bow-string is the natural death of bashaws, yet in no country is power and distinction (precarious enough, God knows, in all!) sought for with such boundless avidity, as if the value of place was enhanced by the danger and insecurity of its tenure. Nothing will ever make a seat in this House not an object of desire to numbers by any means or at any charge, but the depriving it of all power and all dignity; this would do it. This is the true and only nostrum for that purpose. But a House of Commons without power and without dignity, either in itself or in its members, is no House of Commons for the purposes of this constitution.

But they will be afraid to act ill, if they know that the day of their account is always near. I wish it were true; but it is not; here again we have experience, and experience is against us. The distemper of this age is a poverty of spirit and of genius; it is trifling, it is futile, worse than ignorant, superficially taught; with the politics and morals of girls at a boarding-school, rather than of men and statesmen; but it is not yet desperately wicked, or so scandalously venal as in former times. Did not a triennial parliament give up the national dignity, approve the peace of Utrecht,[3] and almost give up everything else in taking every step to defeat the Protestant succession?[4] Was not the constitution saved by those who had no election at all to go to, the Lords, because the court applied to electors, and by various means carried them from their true interests; so that the Tory ministry had a majority without an application to a single member? Now as to the conduct of the members, it was then far from pure and independent. Bribery was infinitely more flagrant. A predecessor of yours, Mr. Speaker, put the question of his own expulsion for bribery. Sir William Musgrave[5] was a wise man; a grave man; an independent man; a man of good fortune and good family; however, he carried on while in opposition a traffic, a shameful traffic, with the ministry. Bishop Burnet[6] knew of £6000 which he had received at one payment. I believe the payment of sums in hard money, naked bribery, is rare amongst us. It was then far from uncommon.

A triennial was near ruining, a septennial parliament saved, your constitution; nor perhaps have you ever known a more flourishing period for the union of national prosperity, dignity, and liberty, than the sixty years you have passed under that constitution of parliament.

The shortness of time in which they are to reap the profits of iniquity is far from checking the avidity of corrupt men; it renders them infinitely more ravenous. They rush violently and precipitately on their object; they lose all regard to decorum. The moments of profits are precious; never are men so wicked as during a general mortality. It was so in the great plague at

Athens;[7] every symptom of which (and this its worst symptom amongst the rest) is so finely related by a great historian of antiquity. It was so in the plague of London[8] in 1665. It appears in soldiers, sailors, &c. Whoever would contrive to render the life of man much shorter than it is, would, I am satisfied, find the surest receipt for increasing the wickedness of our nature.

Thus, in my opinion, the shortness of a triennial sitting would have the following ill effects; it would make the member more shamelessly and shockingly corrupt; it would increase his dependence on those who could best support him at his election; it would rack and tear to pieces the fortunes of those who stood upon their own fortunes and their private interest; it would make the electors infinitely more venal; and it would make the whole body of the people, who are, whether they have votes or not, concerned in elections, more lawless, more idle, more debauched; it would utterly destroy the sobriety, the industry, the integrity, the simplicity of all the people; and undermine, I am much afraid, the deepest and best-laid foundations of the commonwealth.

Those who have spoken and written upon this subject without-doors do not so much deny the probable existence of these inconveniences, in their measure, as they trust for prevention to remedies of various sorts, which they propose. First, a place bill; but if this will not do, as they fear it will not, then they say we will have a rotation, and a certain number of you shall be rendered incapable of being elected for ten years. Then for the electors, they shall ballot; the members of parliament also shall decide by ballot; a fifth project is the change of the present legal representation of the kingdom. On all this I shall observe, that it will be very unsuitable to your wisdom to adopt the project of a bill, to which there are objections insuperable by anything in the bill itself, upon the hope that those objections may be removed by subsequent projects; every one of which is full of difficulties of its own, and which are all of them very essential alterations in the constitution. This seems very irregular and unusual. If anything should make this a very doubtful measure, what can make it more so than that, in the opinion of its advocates, it would aggravate all our old inconveniences in such a manner as to require a total alteration in the constitution of the kingdom? If the remedies are proper in triennial, they will not be less so in septennial, elections; let us try them first; see how the House relishes them; see how they will operate in the nation; and then, having felt your way and prepared against these inconveniences.

The honourable gentleman sees that I respect the principle upon which he goes, as well as his intentions and his abilities. He will believe that I do not differ from him wantonly, and on trivial grounds. He is very sure that it was not his embracing one way, which determined me to take the other. *I* have not, in newspapers, to derogate from his fair fame with the nation, printed the first rude sketch of his bill with ungenerous and invidious comments. *I* have not, in conversations industriously circulated about the town, and talked on the benches of this House, attributed his conduct to motives low and unworthy, and as groundless as they are injurious. *I* do not affect to be frightened with his proposition, as if some hideous spectre had started from hell, which was to be sent back again by every form of exorcism, and every kind of incantation. *I* invoke no Acheron[9] to overwhelm him in the whirlpools of its muddy gulf. *I* do not tell the respectable mover and seconder, by a perversion of their sense and expressions, that their proposition halts between the ridiculous and the dangerous. *I* am not one of those who start up, three at a time, and fall upon and strike at him with so much eagerness, that our daggers hack one another in his sides. My honourable friend has not brought down a spirited imp of chivalry to win the first achievement and blazon of arms on his milk-white shield in a field listed against him; nor brought out the generous offspring of lions, and said to them – Not against that side of the forest, beware of that – here is the prey where you are to fasten your paws; and seasoning his unpractised jaws with blood, tell him – This is the milk for which you are to thirst hereafter. *We* furnish at his expense no holiday, nor suspend hell, that a crafty Ixion[10] may have rest from his wheel; nor give the common adversary, if he be a common adversary, reason to say, I would have put in my word to oppose, but the eagerness of your allies in your social war was such, that I could not break in upon you. I hope he sees and feels, and that every member sees and feels along with him, the difference between amicable dissent and civil discord.

SKETCH OF THE NEGRO CODE[1]

1780

DEAR SIR,

I SHOULD HAVE been punctual in sending you the sketch I promised of my old African Code, if some friends from London had not come in upon me last Saturday, and engaged me till noon this day; I send this pacquet by one of them, who is still here. If what I send be, as under present circumstances it must be, imperfect, you will excuse it, as being done near twelve years ago.[2] About four years since I made an abstract of it, upon which I cannot at present lay my hands; but I hope the marginal heads[3] will in some measure supply it.

If the African trade could be considered with regard to itself only, and as a single object, I should think the utter abolition to be, on the whole, more advisable, than any scheme of regulation and reform. Rather than suffer it to continue as it is, I heartily wish it at an end. What has been lately done, has been done by a popular spirit, which seldom calls for, and indeed very rarely relishes, a system made up of a great variety of parts, and which is to operate its effect in a great length of time. The people like short methods; the consequences of which they sometimes have reason to repent of. Abolition is but a single act. To prove the nature of the trade, and to expose it properly, required, indeed, a vast collection of materials, which have been laboriously collected, and compiled with great judgment. It required also much perseverance and address to excite the spirit, which has been excited without-doors, and which has carried it through.[4] The greatest eloquence ever displayed in the House has been employed to second the efforts which have been made abroad. All this, however, leads but to one single resolve. When this was done, all was done. I speak of absolute and immediate abolition, the point which the first motions went to, and which is in effect still pressed; though in this session, according to order, it cannot take effect. A *remote,* and a *gradual* abolition, though they may be connected, are not the same thing. The idea of the House seems to me, if I rightly comprehend it, that the two things are to be combined; that is to say, that the trade is gradually to decline, and to cease entirely at a determinate period. To make the abolition gradual, the regulations must operate as a strong discouragement. But it is much to be feared, that a trade continued and discouraged, and with a sentence of death passed upon it, will perpetuate much ill blood between those who struggle for the abolition, and those who contend for an effectual continuance.

At the time when I formed the plan which I have the honour to transmit to you, an abolition of the slave trade would have appeared a very chimerical project. My plan, therefore, supposes the continued existence of that commerce. Taking for my basis that I had an incurable evil to deal with, I cast about how I should make it as small an evil as possible, and draw out of it some collateral good.

In turning the matter over in my mind at that time, and since, I never was able to consider the African trade upon a ground disconnected with the employment of negroes in the West Indies, and distinct from their condition in the plantations whereon they serve. I conceived that the true origin of the trade was not in the place it was begun at, but at the place of its final destination. I therefore was, and I still am, of opinion, that the whole work ought to be taken up together; and that a gradual abolition of slavery in the West Indies ought to go hand in hand with anything which should be done with regard to its supply from the coast of Africa. I could not trust a cessation of the demand for this supply to the mere operation of any abstract principle, (such as, that if their supply was cut off, the planters would encourage and produce an effectual population,) knowing that nothing can be more uncertain than the operation of general principles, if they are not embodied in specific regulations. I am very apprehensive that so long as the slavery continues some means for its supply will be found. If so, I am persuaded that it is better to allow the evil, in order to correct it, than by endeavouring to forbid, what we cannot be able wholly to prevent, to leave it under an illegal, and therefore an unreformed, existence. It is not that my plan does not lead to the extinction of the slave trade; but it is through a very slow progress, the chief effect of which is to be operated in our own plantations by rendering, in a length of time, all foreign supply unnecessary. It was my wish, whilst the slavery continued, and the consequent commerce, to take such measures as to civilize the coast of Africa by the trade, which now renders it more barbarous; and to lead by degrees to a more reputable, and, possibly, a more profitable, connection with it, than we maintain at present.

I am sure that you will consider, as a mark of my confidence in yours and Mr Pitt's honour and generosity, that I venture to put into your hands a scheme composed of many and intricate combinations, without a full explanatory preface, or any attendant notes, to point out the principles upon which I proceeded in every regulation, which I have proposed towards the civilization and gradual manumission of negroes in the two hemispheres. I confess, I trust infinitely more (according to the sound principles of those, who ever have at any time meliorated the state of mankind) to the effect and influence of religion, than to all the rest of the regulations put together.

Whenever, in my proposed reformation, we take our *point of departure* from a state of slavery, we must precede the donation of freedom by disposing the minds of the objects to a disposition to receive it without danger to themselves or to us. The process of bringing *free* savages to order and civilization is very different. When a state of slavery is that upon which we are to work, the very means which lead to liberty must partake of compulsion. The minds of men being crippled with that restraint can do nothing for themselves; everything must be done for them. The regulations can owe little to consent. Everything must be the creature of power. Hence it is, that regulations must be multiplied; particularly as you have two parties to deal with. The Planter you must at once restrain and support; and you must control, at the same time that you ease, the servant. This necessarily makes the work a matter of care, labour, and expense. It becomes in its nature complex. But I think neither the object impracticable nor the expense intolerable; and I am fully convinced, that the cause of humanity would be far more benefited by the continuance of the trade and servitude, regulated and reformed, than by the total destruction of both or either. What I propose, however, is but a beginning of a course of measures, which an experience of the effects of the evil and the reform will enable the Legislature hereafter to supply and correct.

I need not observe to you, that the forms are often neglected, penalties not provided, &c. &c. &c. But all this is merely mechanical, and what a couple of days' application would set to rights.

I have seen what has been done by the West Indian assemblies. It is arrant trifling. They have done little; and what they have done is good for nothing; for it is totally destitute of an *executory* principle. This is the point, to which I have applied my whole diligence. It is easy enough to say what shall be done: – to cause it to be done, – *Hic labor, hoc opus.*[5]

I ought not to apologize for letting this scheme lie beyond the period of the *Horatian* keeping[6] – I ought much more to entreat an excuse for producing it now. Its whole value (if it has any) is the coherence and mutual dependency of parts in the scheme; separately they can be of little or no use.

> I have the honour to be, with very great respect and regard,
> Dear Sir,
> Your most faithful and
> obedient humble Servant,
> EDMUND BURKE.

Beaconsfield,
Easter-Monday night, 1792

This constitution consists of four principal members.

I. The rules for qualifying a ship for the African trade.

II. The mode of carrying on the trade upon the coast of Africa, which includes a plan for introducing civilization in that part of the world.

III. What is to be observed from the time of shipping negroes to the sale in the West India islands.

IV. The regulations relative to the state and condition of slaves in the West Indies, their manumission, &c.

Whereas it is expedient, and conformable to the principles of true religion and morality, and to the rules of sound policy, to put an end to all traffic in the persons of men, and to the detention of their said persons in a state of slavery, as soon as the same may be effected without producing great inconveniences in the sudden change of practices of such long standing; and, during the time of the continuance of the said practices, it is desirable and expedient, by proper regulations, to lessen the inconveniences and evils attendant on the said traffic and state of servitude, until both shall be gradually done away:

And whereas the objects of the said trade, and consequential servitude, and the grievances resulting therefrom, come under the principal heads following, the regulations ought thereto to be severally applied; that is to say, that provision should be made by the said regulations,

1st   For duly qualifying ships for the said traffic;

2d   For the mode and conditions of permitting the said trade to be carried on upon the coast of Africa;

3d   For the treatment of the negroes in their passage to the West India islands;

4th   For the government of the negroes, which are or shall be employed in his Majesty's colonies and plantations in the West Indies:

Be it therefore enacted, that every ship or trading vessel which is intended for the negro trade, with the name of the owner or owners thereof, shall be entered and registered as ships trading to the West Indies are by law to be registered, with the further provisions following:

1. The said entry and register shall contain an account of the greatest number of negroes, of all descriptions, which are proposed to be taken into the said ship or trading vessel; and the said ship, before she is permitted to be entered outwards, shall be surveyed by a ship-carpenter to be appointed by the collector of the port from which the said vessel is to depart, and by a surgeon, also appointed by the collector, who hath been conversant in the service of the said trade, but not at the time actually engaged or covenanted therein; and the said carpenter and surgeon shall report to the collector, or, in his absence, to the next principal officer of the port, upon oath, (which oath the said collector or principal officer is hereby empowered to administer,) her measurement, and what she contains in builder's tonnage, and that she has —— feet of grated port-holes between the decks, and that she is otherwise fitly found as a good transport-vessel.

2. And be it enacted, that no ship employed in the said trade shall upon any pretence take in more negroes than one grown man or woman for one ton and half of builder's tonnage, nor more than one boy or girl for one ton.

3. That the said ship or other vessel shall lay in, in proportion to the ship's company of the said vessel, and the number of negroes registered, a full and sufficient store of sound provision, so as to be secure against all probable delays and accidents; namely, salted beef, pork, salt-fish, butter, cheese, biscuit, flour, rice, oatmeal, and white peas; but no horse beans, or other inferiour

provisions; and the said ship shall be properly provided with water-casks or jars, in proportion to the intended number of the said negroes; and the said ship shall be also provided with a proper and sufficient stock of coals or fire-wood.

4. And every ship, entered as aforesaid, shall take out a coarse shirt, and a pair of trowsers, or petticoat, for each negro intended to be taken aboard; as also a mat, or coarse mattress, or hammock, for the use of the said negroes.

The proportions of provision, fuel and clothing, to be regulated by the table annexed to this Act.

5. And be it enacted, that no ship shall be permitted to proceed on the said voyage or adventure, until the searcher of the port, from whence the said vessel shall sail, or such person as he shall appoint to act for him, shall report to the collector that he hath inspected the said stores, and that the ship is accommodated and provided in the manner hereby directed.

6. And be it enacted, that no guns be exported to the coast of Africa, in the said or any other trade, unless the same be duly marked with the maker's name on the barrels before they are put into the stocks, and vouched by an inspector in the place where the same are made to be without fraud, and sufficient and merchantable arms.

7. And be it enacted, that before any ship as aforesaid shall proceed on her voyage, the owner or owners, or an attorney by them named, if the owners are more than two, and the master, shall severally give bond, the owners by themselves, the master for himself, that the said master shall duly conform himself in all things to the regulations in this Act contained, so far as the same regards his part in executing and conforming to the same.

II. And whereas, in providing for the second object of this Act, that is to say, for the trade on the coast of Africa, it is first prudent not only to provide against the manifold abuses to which a trade of that nature is liable, but that the same may be accompanied, as far as it is possible, with such advantages to the natives as may tend to the civilizing them, and enabling them to enrich themselves by means more desirable, and to carry on hereafter a trade more advantageous and honourable to all parties:

And whereas religion, order, morality and virtue are the elemental principles, and the knowledge of letters, arts and handicraft trades, the chief means of such civilization and improvement; for the better attainment of the said good purposes,

1. Be it hereby enacted, that the coast of Africa, on which the said trade for negroes may be carried on, shall be and is hereby divided into marts or staples as hereafter follows [here name the marts]. And be it enacted, that it shall not be lawful for the master of any ship to purchase any negro or negroes, but at one of the said marts or staples.

2. That the directors of the African Company[7] shall appoint, where not already appointed, a governor, with three counsellors, at each of the said marts, with a salary of —— to the governor, and of —— to each of the said counsellors. The said governor, or in his absence or illness the senior counsellor, shall and is hereby empowered to act as a justice of the peace, and they, or either of them, are authorized, ordered, and directed, to provide for the peace of the settlement, and the good regulation of their station and stations severally, according to the rules of justice, to the directions of this Act, and the instructions they shall receive from time to time from the said African Company: and the said African Company is hereby authorized to prepare instructions, with the assent of the lords of his Majesty's privy council, which shall be binding in all things not contrary to this Act, or to the laws of England, on the said governors and counsellors, and every of them, and on all persons acting in commission with them under this Act, and on all persons residing within the jurisdiction of the magistrates of the said mart.

3. And be it enacted, that the lord high admiral, or commissioners for executing his office, shall appoint one or more, as they shall see convenient, of his Majesty's ships or sloops of war, under the command severally of a post captain, or master and commander, to each mart, as a naval station.

4. And be it enacted, that the lord high treasurer, or the commissioners for executing his office, shall name two inspectors of the said trade at every mart, who shall provide for the execution of this Act, according to the directions thereof, so far as shall relate to them; and it is hereby provided and enacted, that as cases of sudden emergency may arise, the said governour or first counsellor and the first commander of his Majesty's ship or ships on the said station, and the said inspectors, or the majority of them, the governour having a double or casting vote, shall have power

and authority to make such occasional rules and orders relating to the said trade as shall not be contrary to the instructions of the African Company, and which shall be valid until the same are revoked by the said African Company.

5. That the said African Company is hereby authorized to purchase, if the same may conveniently be done, with the consent of the privy council, any lands adjoining to the fort or principal mart aforesaid, not exceeding —— acres, and to make allotments of the same. No allotment to one person to exceed (on pain of forfeiture) —— acres.

6. That the African Company shall, at each fort, or mart, cause to be erected, in a convenient place, and at a moderate cost, the estimate of which shall be approved by the treasury, one church, and one school-house, and one hospital; and shall appoint one principal chaplain, with a curate or assistant in holy orders, both of whom shall be recommended by the lord bishop of London; and the said chaplain, or his assistant, shall perform divine service, and administer the sacraments, according to the usage of the Church of England, or to such mode, not contrary thereto, as to the said bishop shall seem more suitable to the circumstances of the people. And the said principal chaplain shall be the third member in the council, and shall be entitled to receive from the directors of the said African Company a salary of——, and his assistant a salary of——, and he shall have power to appoint one sober and discreet person, white or black, to be his clerk and catechist at a salary of——.

7. And be it enacted, that the African Company shall appoint one sufficient schoolmaster, who shall be approved by the bishop of London, and who shall be capable of teaching writing, arithmetic, surveying, and mensuration, at a salary of —— And the said African Company is hereby authorized to provide, for each settlement, a carpenter and blacksmith, with such encouragement as to them shall seem expedient; who shall take each two apprentices from amongst the natives, to instruct them in the several trades; the African Company allowing them, as a fee for each apprentice, ——. And the said African Company shall appoint one surgeon, and one surgeon's mate, who are to be approved on examination at Surgeons' Hall, to each fort or mart, with a salary of—— for the surgeon, and—— for his mate and the said surgeon shall take one native apprentice, at a fee to be settled by the African Company.

8. And be it enacted, that the said catechist, schoolmaster, sur-geon, and surgeon's mate, as well as the tradesmen in the com-pany's service, shall be obedient to the orders they shall from time to time receive from the governor and council of each fort; and if they, or any of them, or any other person, in whatever station, shall appear, on complaint and proof to the majority of the com-missioners, to lead a disorderly and debauched life, or use any profane or impious discourses, to the danger of defeating the purposes of this institution, and to the scandal of the natives, who are to be led, by all due means, into a respect for our holy religion, and a desire of partaking of the benefits thereof, they are author-ized and directed to suspend the said person from his office, or the exercise of his trade, and to send him to England (but without any hard confinement, except in case of resistance) with a com-plaint, with inquiry and proofs adjoined, to the African Company.

9. And be it enacted, that the bishop of London for the time being shall have full authority to remove the said chaplain, for such causes as to him shall seem reasonable.

10. That no governor, counsellor, inspector, chaplain, sur-geon, or schoolmaster, shall be concerned, or have any share, dir-ectly or indirectly, in the negro trade, on pain of ——.

11. Be it enacted, that the said governour and council shall keep a journal of all their proceedings, and a book, in which copies of all their correspondence shall be entered, and they shall transmit copies of the said journals and letter-book, and their books of accounts, to the African Company, who, within —— of their receipt thereof, shall communicate the same to one of his Majesty's principal secretaries of state.

12. And be it enacted, that the said chaplain, or principal min-ister, shall correspond with the bishop of London, and faithfully and diligently transmit to him an account of whatever hath been done for the advancement of religion, morality and learning, amongst the natives.

13. And be it enacted, that no negro shall be conclusively sold until he shall be attested by the two inspectors and chaplain; or in case of the illness of any of them, by one inspector, and the governor, or one of the council; who are hereby authorized and directed, by the best means in their power, to examine into the circumstances and condition of the persons exposed to sale.

14. And, for the better direction of the said Inspectors, no

persons are to be sold, who, to the best judgment of the said inspectors, shall be above thirty-five years of age, or who shall appear, on examination, stolen or carried away, by the dealers, by surprise; nor any person, who is able to read in the Arabian or any other book; nor any woman who shall appear to be advanced three months in pregnancy; nor any person distorted or feeble, unless the said persons are consenting to such sale; or any person afflicted with a grievous or contagious distemper. But if any person so offered is only lightly disordered, the said person may be sold; but must be kept in the hospital of the mart, and shall not be shipped until completely cured.

15. Be it enacted, that no black or European factor or trader into the interior country, or on the coast, (the masters of English ships only excepted, for whose good conduct provision is otherwise herein made,) shall be permitted to buy or sell in any of the said marts, unless he be approved by the governor of the mart in which he is to deal, or, in his absence or disability, by the senior counsellor for the time being, and obtaining a licence from such governor or counsellor; and the said traders and factors shall, severally or jointly, as they shall be concerned, before they shall obtain the said licence, be bound in a recognizance, with such surety for his or their good behaviour, as to the said governor shall seem the best that can be obtained.

16. Be it enacted, that the said governor, or other authority aforesaid, shall examine, as by duty of office, into the conduct of all such traders and factors, and shall receive and publicly hear (with the assistance of the council and inspectors aforesaid, and of the commodore, captain, or other principal commander of one of his Majesty's ships on the said station, or as many of the same as can be assembled, two whereof, with the governor, are hereby enabled to act) all complaints against them, or any of them; and if any black or white trader or factor, (other than in this Act excepted,) either on inquisition of office, or on complaint, shall be convicted by a majority of the said commissioners present of stealing or taking by surprise any person or persons whatsoever, whether free, or the slaves of others, without the consent of their masters; or of wilfully and maliciously killing or maiming any person; or of any cruelty, (necessary restraint only excepted) or of firing houses, or destroying goods, the said trader or factor shall be deemed to have forfeited his recognizance, and his surety to have forfeited his; and the said trader or factor, so

convicted, shall be for ever disabled from dealing in any of the said marts, unless the offence shall not be that of murder, maiming, arson, or stealing or surprising the person, and shall appear to the commissioners aforesaid to merit only, besides the penalty of his bond, a suspension for one year: and the said trader or factor, so convicted of murder, maiming, arson, stealing or surprising the person, shall, if a native, be delivered over to the prince to whom he belongs, to execute further justice on him. But it is hereby provided and enacted, that if any European shall be convicted of any of the said offences, he shall be sent to Europe, together with the evidence against him; and on the warrant of the said commissioners, the keeper of any of his Majesty's jails in London, Bristol, Liverpool, or Glasgow, shall receive him, until he be delivered according to due course of law, as if the said offences had been committed within the cities and towns aforesaid.

17. Be it further enacted, that if the said governor, &c. shall be satisfied that any person or persons are exposed to sale, who have been stolen or surprised as aforesaid, or are not within the qualifications of sale in this Act described, they are hereby authorized and required, if it can be done, to send the persons so exposed to sale to their original habitation or settlement, in the manner they shall deem best for their security (the reasonable charges whereof shall be allowed to the said governor by the African Company,) unless the said persons choose to sell themselves; and then, and in that case, their value in money and goods, at their pleasure, shall be secured to them, and be applicable to their use, without any dominion over the same of any purchaser, or of any master, to whom they may in any colony or plantation be sold, and which shall always be in some of his Majesty's colonies and plantations only. And the master of the ship, in which such person shall embark, shall give bond for the faithful execution of his part of the trust at the island where he shall break bulk.

18. Be it further enacted, that besides the hospitals on shore, one or more hospital-ships shall be employed at each of the said chief marts, wherein slaves taken ill in the trading ships shall be accommodated until they shall be cured; and then the owner may reclaim, and shall receive them, paying the charges, which shall be settled by regulation to be made by the authority in this Act enabled to provide such regulations.

III. And whereas it is necessary that regulations be made to prevent abuses in the passage from Africa to the West Indies;

1. Be it further enacted, that the commander or lieutenant of the king's ship on each station shall have authority, as often as he shall see occasion, attended with one other of his officers, and his surgeon or mate, to enter into and inspect every trading ship, in order to provide for the due execution of this Act, and of any ordinances made in virtue thereof and conformable thereto, by the authorities herein constituted and appointed: and the said officer and officers are hereby required to examine every trading ship before she sails, and to stop the sailing of the said ship, for the breach of the said rules and ordinances, until the governor in council shall order and direct otherwise; and the master of the said ship shall not presume, under the penalty of —— to be recovered in the courts of the West Indies, to sail without a certificate from the commander aforesaid, and one of the inspectors in this Act appointed, that the vessel is provided with stores and other accommodation sufficient for her voyage, and has not a greater number of slaves on board than by the provisions of this Act is allowed.

2. And be it enacted, that the governor and council, with the assistance of the said naval commander, shall have power to give such special written instructions, for the health, discipline, and care of the said slaves, during their passage, as to them shall seem good.

3. And be it further enacted, that each slave, at entering the said ship, is to receive some present, not exceeding in value ——, to be provided according to the instructions aforesaid; and musical instruments, according to the fashion of the country, are to be provided.

4. And be it further enacted, that the negroes on board the transports, and the seamen who navigate the same, are to receive their daily allowance, according to the table hereunto annexed, together with a certain quantity of spirits to be mixed with their water. And it is enacted, that the table is to be fixed, and continue for one week after sailing, in some conspicuous part of the said ship, for the seamen's inspection of the same.

5. And be it enacted, that the captain of each trading vessel shall be enabled, and is required, to divide the slaves in his ship into crews of not less than ten nor more than twenty persons each, and to appoint one negro man to have such authority

severally over each crew, as according to his judgment, with the advice of the mate and surgeon, he and they shall see good to commit to them, and to allow to each of them some compensation, in extraordinary diet and presents, not exceeding [ten shillings.]

6. And be it enacted, that any European officer or seaman, having unlawful communication with any woman slave, shall, if an officer, pay five pounds to the use of the said woman, on landing her from the said ship, to be stopped out of his wages; or, if a seaman, forty shillings; the said penalties to be recovered on the testimony of the woman so abused, and one other.

7. And be it enacted, that all and every commander of a vessel or vessels employed in slave trade, having received certificates from the port of the outfit, and from the proper officers in Africa and the West Indies, of their having conformed to the regulations of this Act, and of their not having lost more than one in thirty of their slaves by death, shall be entitled to a bounty or premium of [ten pounds.]

IV. And whereas the condition of persons in a state of slavery is such that they are utterly unable to take advantage of any remedy which the laws may provide for their protection, and the amendment of their condition, and have not the proper means of pursuing any process for the same, but are and must be under guardianship; and whereas it is not fitting that they should be under the sole guardianship of their masters, or their attornies and overseers, to whom their grievances, whenever they suffer any, must ordinarily be owing;

1. Be it therefore enacted, that his Majesty's attorney-general for the time being successively shall, by his office, exercise the trust and employment of protector of negroes within the island, in which he is or shall be attorney-general to his Majesty, his heirs and successors: and that the said attorney-general, protector of negroes, is hereby authorized to hear any complaint on the part of any negro or negroes, and inquire into the same, or to institute an inquiry *ex officio* into any abuses, and to call before him and examine witnesses upon oath, relative to the subject matter of the said official inquiry or complaint; and it is hereby enacted and declared, that the said attorney-general, protector of negroes, is hereby authorized and empowered, at his discretion, to file an information *ex officio* for any offences committed

against the provisions of this Act, or for any misdemeanors or wrongs against the said negroes, or any of them.

2. And it is further enacted, that in all trials of such informations the said protector of negroes may and is hereby authorized to challenge, peremptorily, a number not exceeding —— of the jury, who shall be impannelled to try the charge in the said information contained.

3. And be it enacted, that the said attorney-general, protector of negroes, shall appoint inspectors, not exceeding the number of ——, at his discretion; and the said inspectors shall be placed in convenient districts in each island severally, or shall twice in the year make a circuit in the same, according to the direction which they shall receive from the protector of negroes aforesaid; and the inspectors shall, and they are hereby required, twice in the year, to report in writing to the protector aforesaid the state and condition of the negroes in their districts, or on their circuit severally, the number, sex, age, and occupation of the said negroes on each plantation; and the overseer, or chief manager on each plantation is hereby required to furnish an account thereof, within [ten days] after the demand of the said inspectors, and to permit the inspector or inspectors aforesaid to examine into the same; and the said inspectors shall set forth, in the said report, the distempers to which the negroes are most liable, in the several parts of the island.

4. And be it enacted, that the said protector of negroes, by and with the consent of the governor and chief judge of each island, shall form instructions, by which the said inspectors shall discharge their trust in the manner the least capable of exciting any unreasonable hopes in the said negroes, or of weakening the proper authority of the overseer, and shall transmit them to one of his Majesty's principal secretaries of state; and when sent back with his approbation, the same shall become the rule for the conduct of the said inspectors.

5. And be it enacted, that the said attorney-general, protector of negroes, shall appoint an office for registering all proceedings relative to the duty of his place, as protector of negroes, and shall appoint his chief clerk to be registrar, with a salary not exceeding ——.

6. And be it enacted, that no negroes shall be landed for sale in any but the ports following; that is to say, ——; and the collector of each of the said ports severally shall, within —— days

after the arrival of any ship transporting negroes, report the same to the protector of negroes, or to one of his inspectors; and the said protector is hereby authorized and required to examine, or cause to be examined by one of his inspectors, with the assistance of the said collector, or his deputy, and a surgeon to be called in on the occasion, the state of the said ship and negroes; and upon what shall appear to them, the said protector of negroes, and the said collector and surgeon, to be a sufficient proof, either as arising from their own inspection, or sufficient information on a summary process, of any contravention of this Act, or cruelty to the negroes, or other malversation of the said captain, or any of his officers, the said protector shall impose a fine on him or them, not exceeding ———; which shall not, however, weaken or invalidate any penalty growing from the bond of the said master or his owners. And it is hereby provided, that if the said master, or any of his officers, shall find himself aggrieved by the said fine, he may, within ——— days, appeal to the chief judge, if the court shall be sitting, or to the governor, who shall and are required to hear the said parties, and on hearing are to annul or confirm the same.

7. And be it enacted, that no sale of negroes shall be made but in the presence of an inspector, and all negroes shall be sold severally, or in known and ascertained lots, and not otherwise; and a paper containing the state and description of each negro severally sold, and of each lot, shall be taken and registered in the office aforesaid; and if on inspection or information it shall be found that any negroes shall have, in the same ship, or any other at the same time examined, a wife, an husband, a brother, sister, or child, the person, or persons so related, shall not be sold separately at that or any future sale.

8. And be it enacted, that each and every of his Majesty's islands and plantations, in which negroes are used in cultivation, shall be, by the governor and the protector of negroes for the time being, divided into districts, allowing as much as convenience will admit to the present division into parishes, and subdividing them, where necessary, into districts, according to the number of negroes. And the said governor and protector of negroes shall cause in each district a church to be built in a convenient place, and a cemetery annexed, and an house for the residence of a clergyman, with ——— acres of land annexed; and they are hereby authorized to treat for the necessary ground with the

proprietor, who is hereby obliged to sell and dispose of the same to the said use; and in case of dispute concerning the value, the same to be settled by a jury as in like cases is accustomed.

9. And be it enacted, that in each of the said districts shall be established a presbyter of the Church of England, as by law established, who shall appoint under him one clerk, who shall be a free negro, when such properly qualified can be found, (otherwise a white man,) with a salary, in each case, of——; and the said minister and clerk, both or one, shall instruct the said negroes in the Church catechism, or such other as shall be provided by the authority in this Act named: and the said minister shall baptize, as he shall think fit, all negroes not baptized, and not belonging to dissenters from the Church of England.

10. And the principal overseer of each plantation is hereby required to deliver annually unto the minister a list of all the negroes upon his plantation, distinguishing their sex and age, and shall, under a penalty of ——, cause all the negroes under his care, above the age of —— years, to attend divine service once on every Sunday, except in case of sickness, infirmity, or other necessary cause to be given at the time; and shall, by himself or one of those who are under him, provide for the orderly behavior of the negroes under him, and cause them to return to his plantation when divine service, or administration of sacraments, or catechism, is ended.

11. And be it enacted, that the minister shall have power to punish any negro for disorderly conduct during divine service, by a punishment not exceeding [ten] blows, to be given in one day, and for one offence, which the overseer, or his under agent or agents, is hereby directed, according to the orders of the said minister, effectually to inflict, whenever the same shall be ordered.

12. And be it enacted, that no spirituous liquors of any kind shall be sold, except in towns, within —— miles distant of any church, nor within any district during divine service, and an hour preceding, and an hour following, the same; and the minister of each parish shall and is hereby authorized to act as a justice of the peace in enforcing the said regulation.

13. And be it enacted, that every minister shall keep a register of births, burials, and marriages, of all negroes and mulattoes in his district.

14. And be it enacted, that the ministers of the several districts

shall meet annually, on the —— day of ——, in a synod of the island, to which they belong; and the said synod shall have for its president such person as the bishop of London shall appoint for his commissary; and the said synod or general assembly is hereby authorized, by a majority of voices, to make regulations, which regulations shall be transmitted by the said president or commissary to the bishop of London; and when returned by the bishop of London approved of, then, and not before, the said regulations shall be held in force to bind the said clergy, their assistants, clerks, and schoolmasters only, and no other persons.

15. And be it enacted, that the said president shall collect matter in the said assembly, and shall make a report of the state of religion and morals in the several parishes from whence the synod is deputed, and shall transmit the same, once in the year, in duplicate, through the governor and protector of negroes, to the bishop of London.

16. And be it enacted and declared, that the bishop of London for the time being shall be patron to all and every the said cures in this Act directed, and the said Bishop is hereby required to provide for the due filling thereof, and is to receive from the fund in this Act provided, for the due execution of this Act, a sum not exceeding —— for each of the said ministers, for his outfit and passage.

17. And be it enacted, that on misbehaviour, and on complaint from the said synod, and on hearing the party accused in a plain and summary manner, it shall and may be lawful for the bishop of London to suspend or to remove any minister from his cure, as his said offences shall appear to merit.

18. And be it enacted, that for every two districts a school shall be established for young negroes to be taught three days in the week, and to be detained from their owner four hours in each day: the number not to be more or fewer than twenty males in each district, who shall be chosen, and vacancies filled, by the minister of the district; and the said minister shall pay to the owner of the said boy, and shall be allowed the same in his accounts at the synod, to the age of twelve years old, three-pence by the day; and for every boy, from twelve years old to fifteen, five-pence by the day.

19. And it is enacted, that if the president of the synod aforesaid shall certify to the protector of negroes, that any boys in the said schools (provided that the number in no one year shall

exceed one in the island of Jamaica, and one in two years in the islands of Barbadoes, Antigua, and Grenada, and one in four years in any of the other islands) do show a remarkable aptitude for learning, the said protector is hereby authorized and directed to purchase the said boy at the best rate, at which boys of that age and strength have been sold within the year; and the said negro so purchased shall be under the entire guardianship of the said protector of negroes, who shall send him to the bishop of London, for his further education in England, and may charge in his accounts for the expense of transporting him to England: and the bishop of London shall provide for the education of such of the said negroes as he shall think proper subjects, until the age of twenty-four years, and shall order those, who shall fall short of expectation after one year, to be bound apprentice to some handicraft trade; and when his apprenticeship is finished, the lord mayor of London is hereby authorized and directed to receive the said negro from his master, and to transmit him to the island from which he came in the West Indies, to be there as a free negro; subject, however, to the direction of the protector of negroes, relatively to his behavior and employment.

20. And it is hereby enacted and provided, that any planter or owner of negroes, not being of the Church of England, and not choosing to send his negroes to attend divine service in manner by this Act directed, shall give, jointly or severally, as the case shall require, security to the protector of negroes, that a competent minister of some Christian church or congregation shall be provided for the due instruction of the negroes, and for their performing divine service according to the description of the religion of the master or masters, in some church or house thereto allotted, in the manner and with the regulations in this Act prescribed with regard to the exercise of religion according to the Church of England.

Provided always, that the marriages of the said negroes belonging to dissenters shall be celebrated only in the church of the said district, and that a register of the births shall be transmitted to the minister of the said district.

21. And whereas a state of matrimony, and the government of a family, is a principal means of forming men to a fitness for freedom, and to become good citizens; Be it enacted, that all negro men and women, above eighteen years of age for the man, and sixteen for the woman, who have cohabited together for

twelve months or upwards, or shall cohabit for the same time, and have a child or children, shall be deemed to all intents and purposes to be married; and either of the parties is authorized to require of the ministers of the district, to be married in the face of the church.

22. And be it enacted, that from and after the —— of ——, all negro men in an healthy condition, and so reported to be, in case the same is denied, by a surgeon and by an inspector of negroes, and being twenty-one year's old or upwards, until fifty, and not being before married, shall, on requisition of the inspectors, be provided by their masters or overseers with a woman not having children living, and not exceeding the age of the man; nor in any case exceeding the age of twenty-five years; and such persons shall be married publicly in the face of the church.

23. And be it enacted, that if any negro shall refuse a competent marriage tendered to him, and shall not demand another specifically, such as it may be in his master's power to provide, the master or overseer shall be authorized to constrain him by an increase of work, or a lessening of allowance.

24. And be it enacted, that the minister in each district shall have, with the assent of the inspector, full power and authority to punish all acts of adultery, unlawful concubinage, and fornication, amongst negroes, on hearing and a summary process, by ordering a number of blows, not exceeding —— for each offence; and if any white person shall be proved, on information in the supreme court to be exhibited by the protector of negroes, to have committed adultery with any negro woman, or to have corrupted any negro woman under sixteen years of age, he shall be fined in the sum of ——, and shall be for ever disabled from serving the office of overseer of negroes, or being attorney to any plantation.

25. And be it enacted, that no slaves shall be compelled to do any work for their masters for [three] days after their marriage.

26. And be it enacted, that no woman shall be obliged to field-work, or any other laborious work, for one month before her delivery, or for six weeks afterwards.

27. And be it enacted, that no husband and wife shall be sold separately, if originally belonging to the same master, nor shall any children, under sixteen, be sold separately from their parents, or one parent, if one be living.

28. And be it enacted, that if an husband and wife, which

before their intermarriage belonged to different owners, shall be sold, they shall not be sold at such a distance as to prevent mutual help and cohabitation; and of this distance the minister shall judge, and his certificate of the inconvenient distance shall be valid, so as to make such sale unlawful, and to render the same null and void.

29. And be it enacted, that no negro shall be compelled to work for his owner at field-work, or any service relative to a plantation, or to work at any handicraft trade, from eleven o'clock on Saturday forenoon until the usual working hour on Monday morning.

30. And whereas habits of industry and sobriety, and the means of acquiring and preserving property, are proper and reasonable preparatives to freedom, and will secure against an abuse of the same; Be it enacted, that every negro man, who shall have served ten years, and is thirty years of age, and is married, and has had two children born of any marriage, shall obtain the whole of Saturday for himself and his wife, and for his own bene-fit; and after thirty-seven years of age, the whole of Friday for himself and his wife; provided that in both cases the minister of the district, and the inspector of negroes, shall certify that they know nothing against his peaceable, orderly, and industrious behavior.

31. And be it enacted, that the master of every plantation shall provide the materials of a good and substantial hut for each mar-ried field negro; and if his plantation shall exceed —— acres, he shall allot to the same a portion of land not less than ——: and the said hut and land shall remain and stand annexed to the said negro, for his natural life, or during his bondage; but the same shall not be alienated without the consent of the owners.

32. And be it enacted, that it shall not be lawful for the owner of any negro, by himself or any other, to take from him any land, house, cattle, goods, or money, acquired by the said negro, whether by purchase, donation, or testament, whether the same has been derived from the owner of the said negro, or any other.

33. And be it enacted, that if the said negro shall die possessed of any lands, goods, or chattels, and dies without leaving a wife or issue, it shall be lawful for the said negro to devise or bequeath the same by his last will; but in case the said negro shall die intestate, and leave a wife and children, the same shall be distri-buted amongst them, according to the usage under the statute,

commonly called the Statute of Distributions. But if the negro shall die intestate without wife or children, then and in that case his estate shall go to the fund provided for the better execution of this Act.

34. And be it enacted, that no negro, who is married, and hath resided upon any plantation for twelve months, shall be sold either privately, or by the decree of any court, but along with the plantation, on which he hath resided, unless he should himself request to be separated therefrom.

35. And be it enacted, that no blows or stripes, exceeding thirteen, shall be inflicted for one offence upon any negro, without the order of one of his Majesty's justices of peace.

36. And it is enacted, that it shall be lawful for the protector of negroes, as often as on complaint and hearing he shall be of opinion that any negro hath been cruelly and inhumanly treated, or when it shall be made to appear to him that an overseer hath any particular malice, to order, at the desire of the suffering party, the said negro to be sold to another master.

37. And be it enacted, that, in all cases of injury to member or life, the offences against a negro shall be deemed and taken to all intents and purposes as if the same were perpetrated against any of his Majesty's subjects; and the protector of negroes, on complaint, or if he shall receive credible information thereof, shall cause an indictment to be presented for the same; and in case of suspicion of any murder of a negro, an inquest by the coroner, or officer acting as such, shall, if practicable, be held into the same.

38. And in order to a gradual manumission of slaves, as they shall seem fitted to fill the offices of freemen, Be it enacted, that every negro slave, being thirty years of age and upwards, and who has had three children born to him in lawful matrimony, and who hath received a certificate from the minister of his district, or any other Christian teacher, of his regularity in the duties of religion, and of his orderly and good behaviour, may purchase, at rates to be fixed by two justices of peace, the freedom of himself, or his wife or children, or of any of them separately, valuing the wife and children, if purchased into liberty by the father of the family, at half only of their marketable values; provided that the said father shall bind himself in a penalty of —— for the good behavior of his children.

39. And be it enacted, that it shall be lawful for the protector

of negroes to purchase the freedom of any negro, who shall appear to him to excel in any mechanical art, or other knowledge or practice deemed liberal, and the value shall be settled by a jury.

40. And be it enacted, that the protector of negroes shall be and is authorized and required to act as a magistrate for the coercion of all idle, disobedient, or disorderly free negroes, and he shall by office prosecute them for the offences of idleness, drunkenness, quarrelling, gaming, or vagrancy, in the supreme court, or cause them to be prosecuted before one justice of peace, as the case may require.

41. And be it enacted, that if any free negro hath been twice convicted for any of the said misdemeanors, and is judged by the said protector of negroes, calling to his assistance two justices of the peace, to be incorrigibly idle, dissolute and vicious, it shall be lawful, by the order of the said protector and two justices of peace, to sell the said free negro into slavery: the purchase-money to be paid to the person so remanded into servitude, or kept in hand by the protector and governor for the benefit of his family.

42. And be it enacted, that the governor in each colony shall be assistant to the execution of this Act, and shall receive the reports of the protector, and such other accounts, as he shall judge material, relative thereto, and shall transmit the same annually to one of his Majesty's principal secretaries of state.

FIRST SPEECH ON THE SEIZURE AND CONFISCATION OF PRIVATE PROPERTY IN THE ISLAND OF ST. EUSTATIUS[1]

14 MAY 1781

MR. BURKE ROSE, and drew the attention of the House to the very important question of the Seizure and Confiscation of Private Property on the late capture of the island of St. Eustatius. The hon. gentleman began with stating the very great consequence of the question on which they were about to enter. The eyes of Europe would be on the conduct of the British legislature in the present instance, and it would be exceedingly necessary to be cautious and grave, to be cool and impartial in their deliberations; perhaps the fate of Britain would depend on the decision of that question; for it ought to be remembered, that we stood in a new situation: we were engaged in a most calamitous war, in which we had many enemies and no friends. It was a situation unprecedented in the history of Britain, and called for all the wisdom and all the prudence of the government. We ought not, by instituting a scheme of inhuman plunder and unjust oppression, to make more enemies, or to incense and provoke those with whom we are already involved. We ought, instead of pushing war to its extremes, to endeavour, by every means in our power, to moderate its horrors, and to commit no other depredations than such as were necessary to public success, or contributed to national glory. Private emolument ought not to be received as an excuse for rapacity. By such civil regards, the resentments of our enemies might be softened; their enmity might be subdued, and their minds be brought to a favourable inclination towards peace. Or neutral nations, perceiving that, even in a struggle for our existence, we did not deviate from honour, might be brought to applaud the dignity of our sentiments as a people, and assist us in the conflict. But a contrary behaviour on our part was likely to provoke them to unite against us, and make the protection of human nature from plunder and robbery a common cause. They would not stand unconcerned spectators of the renovation of that system of havoc which it had been the pride of civilised Europe to execrate and explode.

The hon. gentleman called back to the recollection of the House the terms of the Manifesto[2] published by Great Britain on the commencement of hostilities with the Dutch. That Manifesto was published on the 20th of December; the terms and language of which threatened no inhuman cruelty, no uncommon severity; but, on the contrary, seemed rather to portend the short variance of old allies, in which all their old friendship and affection would operate rather as the softener than the inflamer of the common calamities of war. It breathed expressions of kindness and long-suffering, and the menaces which it held out seemed to be torn by constraint from a heart bleeding under the affliction of unwilling strife. The harbinger was so gentle, that it was not to be feared that the war would be shocking. It was expected by men of both countries as no more than a temporary rupture, flowing from the rash petulance of the parties, and which their mutual good sense would in the coolness of deliberation suddenly heal. The proclamations, with respect to letters of marque, &c. which followed the Manifesto, warranted the same expectations. There was no predatory system threatened, nor powers granted of an unusual nature. The hon. gentleman proved this by reading the various passages in these state-papers, containing the language of the court, and the powers granted in the commencement of the war.

He now came to the transactions in the West Indies. The rapidity of the expedition against the island of St. Eustatius was a matter which begot suspicions, that the orders of government to the commanders on that station had not waited for the event of the declaration of hostilities; or else the circumstances of the affairs were proofs of the vigilance and wisdom of our government, and of the promptitude, alacrity, and conduct of our commanders. But, in order to the due consideration of this very important question, it was necessary that all the circumstances of the situation and the time, of the prospect, and the event should be attended to. First then, it was on the close of a most melancholy and general disaster, which happened in that part of the world; a hurricane[3] which had involved all the islands in common suffering and common distress. When all that extensive branch of islands and settlements had been visited by the scourge of Providence, as a correction of their vices, or an humbler of their pride. At such a time it might have been expected that the deadly serpents of war would for a time have been hushed into a calm in that quarter of the world: their stores of poison being exhausted, and wanting the recruit and fructification which the rich earth was accustomed to bestow, that they would have remained for a time mutual spectators as they were mutual sufferers, and would not have increased the stock of their distress, by adscititious calamities. The hurricane seemed the particular visitation of Heaven, as if the Deity had meant thereby to check the fury of mankind against each other, and reconcile them by the sense of their common necessities. Surely, when human pride was levelled in the dust, and we saw what worms we were beneath the hand of Omnipotence, it became us to crawl from our holes with a feeling of brotherly love to each other; to abate a little of our rancour; and not add the devastations of war to those of the hurricane. But it was not so with Great Britain; for even when the stern breast of rebellion melted with generous sympathy, and Dr. Franklin[4] issued express orders that provision-ships should pass to the British as well as to the other islands without impediment or injury; even this was thought the fit and proper moment by our commanders for an expedition to St. Vincent's for the recovery of that island. An expedition under-taken with so little knowledge of the state of defence in which the island stood, that after the troops were debarked, and had reconnoitred the works and the garrison, they found it conveni-ent to retreat without attempting the object of their expedition.

At this time, too, it was, that, in obedience to the orders of ministers, the expedition was undertaken against St. Eustatius. This island was different from all others. It seemed to have been shot up from the ocean by some convulsion; the chimney of a volcano, rocky and barren. It had no produce. Its extent was but 30 miles. It seemed to be but a late production of nature, a sort of *lusus naturæ*,[5] hastily framed, neither shapen nor organised, and differing in qualities from all other. Its proprietors had, in the spirit of commerce, made it an emporium for all the world; a mart, a magazine for all the nations of the earth. It had no fortifications for its defence; no garrison, no martial spirit, nor military regulations. Its inhabitants were a mixed body of all nations and climates; not reduced to any species of military duty or military discipline. Its utility was its defence. The universality of its use, the constant neutrality of its nature, which made it advantageous to all the nations of the world, was its security and its safe-guard. It had risen, like another Tyre,[6] upon the waves, to communicate to all countries and climates the conveniencies and the necessaries of life. Its wealth was prodigious, arising from its industry, and the nature of its commerce. At the time of this expedition there were only 55 soldiers in the garrison, if such a place deserves the name of a garrison. There was, indeed, a build-ing which, by courtesy and in compliment, might be called a fort. These soldiers, too, were of the worst description, for out of these there were only 12 men of colour. Against this island then, so circumstanced and so defended, the British commanders went with 14 ships of the line, and several frigates, and a body of 3,000 land forces on board. They had heard of no war being com-menced. They had received no intimation of hostilities being begun or designed. But thus unprepared, naked and defenceless, they were summoned to surrender at discretion within an hour. That time, however short in point of precedent, was on this occa-sion not only sufficient, but ample. It was needless to hesitate where they could not resist. It required but little discussion or debate to resolve on what was to be done. The Dutch com-mander yielded up the dominion, the territory, the public prop-erty, and every thing that belonged to the United States,[7] to the British commanders without any stipulation, relying totally on the discretion, the mercy, and the clemency of the conquerors.

What was the discretion and the mercy of the conquerors? A general confiscation of all the property found upon the island, public and private, Dutch and British; without discrimination, without regard to friend or foe, to the subjects of neutral powers, or to the subjects of our own state; the wealth of the opulent, the goods of the merchant, the utensils of the artisan, the necessaries of the poor were seized on, and a sentence of general beggary pronounced in one moment upon a whole people. A cruelty unheard of in Europe for many years, and such as he would venture to proclaim was a most unjustifiable, outrageous, and un-principled violation of the laws of nations! It was accompanied, too, with cruelties, almost unheard of in the history of those barbarous times, when war was pushed to all its extremes of rigour, and when the sword and the firebrand were in concert. All the property had not only been condemned to one general indiscriminate confiscation, but the warehouses were locked up, and access was denied to the proprietors, by which they might

have an opportunity of ascertaining the amount of their commodities, and securing their property by labels, or by inventories.
Thus deprived of their merchandises, and all the honest profits
of their labours, there remained, however, this ground of hope,
that by explaining the nature of their misfortune to their correspondents in the neighbouring islands, or in Europe, they might
procure a loan to form a new stock with, and by industry retrieve
their misfortunes; but the next step was to seize on their books;
by which they were divested of this last refuge of hope. All their
circumstances were laid open; their weak side exposed; and the
places pointed out, by which malice or enmity might attack them
with success. Was there known till that moment a more complete
act of tyranny than this? It was unparalleled in the annals of
conquest, but it was surpassed by what followed; for, the next act
was to seize upon all their letters also, and their private papers.
It was not enough that the secrets of their trade and their
weaknesses should be laid open, but also that the secrets of
their families should be discovered; the private calamities, to
which all are more or less incident, and all anxious to conceal,
and to suffer unknown, were exposed; and their miseries aggravated, by becoming a matter perhaps of derision and merriment
to insulting plunderers.

It would have been conceived, that farther than this even
inventive tyranny could not proceed; but it proceeded in this
instance as much beyond the reach of common oppression as it
did of common credulity. If the facts were not ascertained
beyond a possibility of doubt, he could not have believed that
such acts were perpetrated at such a day by British soldiers. The
merchants and inhabitants plundered and robbed of all that they
possessed in the world, and of all the hopes that they had of
having their property restored; involved in all the calamities of
want and wretchedness, thought it at least reasonable to exact
that, destitute as they were of all the means of sustenance, and
actually starving, upon application, a part at least of their own
provisions might be remitted to them. They presented an application to the quarter-master-general for this purpose; and what
was the sublime, the generous answer which the gentleman
returned? "Not a mouthful," was exactly his expression. Notwithstanding this answer, they made another application, in the
confidence that so just a request would be ultimately complied
with; still the answer was, "Not a mouthful." They presented a

third representation, and they received still the same reply, "Not a mouthful, not a mouthful, if you were starving." Nor was this the extent of the oppression on the one hand, or of the suffering on the other. Their cash was seized upon; and thus effectually deprived of every thing but the liberty of drawing out a miserable existence, they had recourse to an expedient suggested by necessity, of making use of their former credit with their correspondents in the neighbouring islands, by drawing upon them for a temporary supply. Of this resource they were also deprived; for a proclamation was issued preventing the issuing of such bills; nay, to such a length did the cruelty of this persecution go, that a bill which was found among the papers of a considerable trader in the island, drawn upon government, but not signed nor indorsed, was brought to the unhappy man, and he was forced, absolutely forced, to sign and indorse it, to his injury, if not to his ruin. After all these stages of unheard-of oppression had been successfully gone through, there wanted no more but an attack upon the persons of the unhappy people to finish the scene. He blushed, he said, to relate the sequel for the honour of humanity, of this enlightened age, and still more of the Christian character. The persecution was begun with the people, whom of all others it ought to be the care and the wish of human nations to protect, the Jews.[8] Having no fixed settlement in any part of the world, no kingdom nor country in which they have a government, a community, and a system of laws, they are thrown upon the benevolence of nations, and claim protection and civility from their weakness, as well as from their utility. They were a people, who by shunning the profession of any, could give no well-founded jealousy to any state. If they have contracted some vices, they are such as naturally arise from their dispersed, wandering, and proscribed state. It was an observation as old as Homer, and confirmed by the experience of all ages, that in a state of servitude the human mind loses half its value. From the east to the west, from one end of the world to the other, they are scattered and connected; the links of communication, in the mercantile chain; or, to borrow a phrase from electricity, the conductors by which credit was transmitted through the world. Their abandoned state, and their defenceless situation calls most forcibly for the protection of civilised nations. If Dutchmen are injured and attacked, the Dutch have a nation, a government, and armies to redress or revenge their cause. If Britons are injured, Britons have armies and laws, the laws of nations, (or at least they once had the laws of nations,) to fly to for protection and justice. But the Jews have no such power, and no such friend to depend on. Humanity then must become their protector and ally. Did they find it in the British conquerors of St. Eustatius? No. On the contrary, a resolution was taken to banish this unhappy people from the island. They suffered in common with the rest of the inhabitants, the loss of their merchandise, their bills, their houses, and their provisions; and after this they were ordered to quit the island; and only one day was given them for preparation; they petitioned, they remonstrated against so hard a sentence, but in vain; it was irrevocable. They asked to what part of the world they were to be transported? The answer was, that they should not be informed. Must they take their property along with them? No. Must they not then take with them their wives and children? No. The only information they could obtain was, that they must prepare to depart the island the next day; and without their families, the very last comfort of wretchedness; – they must appear the next day at an appointed place to embark. The next day they did appear to the number of 101, the whole that were upon the island. They were confined in a weigh-house, a place, in some respects, similar to a turnpike-house, but strongly guarded; and orders were given that they should be stripped, and all the linings of their clothes ripped up, that every shilling of money which they might attempt to conceal and carry off should be discovered and taken from them. This order was carried into rigid execution, and money, to the amount of 8,000*l.* was taken from these poor, miserable outcasts; and thus deprived of the fruits of their assiduity, and the comfort of their age, thirty of them were embarked on board the Shrewsbury, and carried to St. Kitt's. The rest, after being confined for three days unheard of, and unknown, were set at liberty to return to their families, that they might be melancholy spectators of the sale of their own property. He mentioned some particular instances of aggravated cruelty inflicted on the Jews while they remained in the weigh-house. One of these poor wretches had sewed up 200 Johannes in his coat, and the money was discovered; he was immediately turned from among the rest; and set apart for punishment, for having endeavoured to conceal some little remains of the wreck of his fortune. Two more Jews had been detected also in a breach of the order for delivering up all their money. Upon one of them were found 900 Johannes. This poor man's case was peculiarly severe, his name was Pollock. He had formerly lived on Rhode Island; and, because he had imported tea contrary to the command of the Americans, he was stripped of all he was worth, and driven out of the island; his brother shared in his misfortunes, but did not survive them; his death increased the cares of the survivor, as he got an additional family, in his brother's children, to provide for. Another Jew married his sister; and, both of them following the British army, had for their loyalty some lands given them, along with some other American refugees, on Long Island, by sir William Howe:[9] they built a kind of a fort there to defend themselves; but it was soon after attacked and carried by the Americans; and not a man who defended it escaped either death or captivity; the Jew's brother-in-law fell during the attack; he survived; and had then the family of his deceased brother and brother-in-law, his mother and sister, to support; he settled at St. Eustatius, where he maintained his numerous family, and had made some money, when he and his family were once more ruined, by the commanders of a British force, to whose cause he was so attached; and in whose cause he had lost two brothers, and his property twice. Another Jew, named Vertram, was treated with as much severity, nor had the commanders any pretext from his profession, for confiscating his property; he sold no warlike or naval stores to the enemy; he dealt simply in China wares; brittle emblems of the tenure he was to have in them! an order was given, and he was left a beggar.

These cruelties were soon followed by others as dreadful. The persecution was not confined to the Hebrew nation. Another proclamation was issued, ordering all the Americans, without distinction, to depart the island. Those who had retired from their native country, that they might avoid taking a share in the dispute with Great Britain, as well as those who might have come there for the purpose of assisting America, were doomed to instantaneous banishment. The next was a proclamation, ordering all the French inhabitants to depart. The next was a proclamation ordering all the inhabitants, late citizens of Amsterdam, to depart; and, last of all, a proclamation, ordering all foreigners of every kind, and all but the settled inhabitants of the island, to depart. The hon. gentleman animadverted with indignation on all those shameful proceedings, and said they were not suggestions of imagination, they were not exaggerated by any factious spirit; they were proved, by the authority of the St. Christopher's Gazette,[10] immediately on the issue of the transactions, with the authentication of the government there. The facts would also be proved by affidavits, if required.

He now gave a particular relation of the conduct of the assembly and inhabitants of St. Kitt's on these melancholy oppressions. The transported beggars of St. Eustatius came there, presenting before them miserable objects of distress and pity. The calamities were beyond the relief of private donation. Visited as they had been by the hand of Providence, they had hardly wherewithal to supply their own necessities; but out of the little that was left, they generously condescended, out of the common stock, to bestow a something. The hon. gentleman gave an account of the several steps which they had taken for the recovery of their own property and that of the other sufferers. The British subjects in St. Eustatius might well claim respect and protection from British commanders, but they met only with insult and rapacity. The legislature of St. Christopher's took the matter up, being astonished at the unprecedented length to which the British commanders had proceeded; and after drawing up a strong remonstrance on the subject, sent it by Mr. Moore, and other gentlemen of the committee of the island of St. Christopher's, to the island of St. Eustatius. On their arrival, they were admitted to an interview with the admiral and general, in the great cabin of the Sandwich, where sir George Rodney[11] asked Mr. Moore if he did not bring a remonstrance. On which he produced it, and after sir George had read a small part of it, he said, he could not possibly give any answer to it then; but, after he had considered it, that he should have an answer. Mr. Burke said, that the next day Mr. Moore and the other gentlemen were admitted on shore to an interview with sir George and the general; where a conversation passed, of which Mr. Burke read an attested copy, having been committed to paper immediately after the interview, and sworn to by the gentlemen of the St. Christopher committee; the conversation was various. The admiral gave as a reason for the confiscation of the property, that they used St. Eustatius only as a deposit for their goods, and that they meant to supply the enemies of their country. And when it was answered to this, that they conceived, by the Grenada Act, the Tobacco Act, and the Cotton Act,[12] they were justified in the commerce which they legally carried on at this place; that it was a commerce not only justified by British Acts, but encouraged by the British government: they were told in reply, that those Acts were foolish and idle; that they had been procured by factious men, for partial and pernicious ends. He could not but observe, that it was a very contemptuous treatment of the legislature of this kingdom, for any officer whatsoever, to pronounce Acts, which it was his duty to see enforced, impolitic; and to say that they had been obtained by factious persons, and for partial views. The persons who had brought in the Grenada, Tobacco, and Cotton, Acts, were lord Beauchamp [13] and sir Grey Cooper:[14] the gentlemen on the other side of the House, would not surely call those two members factious persons; and as the object they had in view, was the augmentation of the revenue, it could not be said that they had acted for partial ends. The committee agreed upon the security which these Acts held out to the merchants, whose stores the commanders had seized on, and said, that as the goods were legally stored under the sanction of the British legislature, they ought to be delivered up to the owners. Sir George replied, that he and the general did not come there to hear acts of parliament explained, but to obey his Majesty's orders. On Mr. Moore's mentioning the possibility of retaliation from the French, sir George said, they dared not retaliate, and after other conversation told them, that if they or any other persons thought themselves aggrieved, they might go to law for redress. No other interview took place, though a second remonstrance and petition was drawn up in St. Christopher's, and sent to St. Eustatius; but Mr. Glanville, the Solicitor General, by whom it was written and carried, could not procure an interview; but to the excellent remonstrance which he presented, received only an answer, that they had no time to attend to the memorial. Mr. Glanville's reply to some of those arguments was extremely ingenious and strong. Mr. Burke thought it a production worthy of any solicitor general in the world. He particularly retorted upon the admiral, by saying, that if it was illegal in the merchants to send their property for sale to St. Eustatius, the naval officers had equally transgressed the law by selling their prizes there.

Having done this, the hon. gentleman came to examine the proceedings, and entered largely into the investigation of that right which a conqueror attains to the property of the vanquished by the laws of nations. These were the two questions to which he wished to draw the attention of the House. Under these circumstances, or even without all the aggravations of cruelty that had taken place, he declared that the general confiscation of the private property found upon the island was contrary to the law of nations, and to that system of war which civilised states had of late, by their consent and practice, thought proper to introduce. Perhaps it might be said, there was no positive law of nations, no general established laws framed, and settled by acts in which every nation had a voice. There was not indeed any law of nations, established like the laws of Britain in black letter, by statute and record; but there was a law of nations as firm, as clear, as manifest, as obligatory, as indispensable. First, it was a maxim generally established and agreed to, that the rights of war were not unlimited. If they were unlimited, it would be ridiculous to say that there were laws of war; for as confessedly a law existed to regulate the practice of states in hostility with each other, if the rights of war were unbounded, it would follow, that the law placed limits to infinity. But this being the established maxim, he had it in his power to prove that there were certain limited and defined rights of war recognised by civilised states, and practised in enlightened Europe. First, he could prove that they were established by reason, in which they had their origin and rise; next, by the convention of parties; thirdly, by the authorities of writers, who took the laws and maxims not from their own invention and ideas, but from the consent and sense of ages; and lastly, from the evidence of precedent.

The hon. gentleman went largely into this description and proof of the rights of civilised war. From the authority of reason he formed general opinions and sentiments, entertained and rendered maxims by consent and use; "that a king conquered, to acquire dominion, not plunder; that a state does not go to war with individuals, but with a state; and in the case of conquest does not take possession of the private property, but of the public property of the state conquered." By this maxim the calamities of war are mitigated. They are not felt so severely by the private individual, by the citizen, and the husbandman, the manufacturer, and the merchant. This law, therefore, directs that the private property of individuals, in a territory surrendering at discretion, is not only to be spared, but to be secured. The very essence of war presumes offence, and offence reciprocity. But when surrendered upon summons at discretion, and without resistance, there is no reciprocity; and consequently there is not the essence of war. When men surrender, they are intitled to protection. There is a virtual compact in conquest, by which protection arises out of, and accompanies allegiance. Can the king of Great Britain seize upon the property of his subjects at his will and pleasure? No; nor can he in the instant of conquest seize on the goods and effects of the conquered. Not only the king of Great Britain, but every monarch, however despotic, is bound down by the very essence of his tenure to observe this obligation. For in all governments there is a trust reposed. "Shew me a government," said the hon. gentleman, "and I will shew you a trust;" there must be a care where there is a dominion; and a king must abandon that trust, he must give up his royalty and his government, when he seizes upon the property of the subject; he must dethrone himself from the just dominion, when he becomes the unjust plunderer of his people; and when he thus departs from the character and the dignity and the office of a king, to take up that of a robber and a spoiler, there is a sword in every hand to execute upon him the vengeance of human nature. The king, who should receive the surrender of a people, thereby admitting them within the pale of his government, and after-wards strip them of their property, must, in so doing, forfeit his royal authority, and be considered only as a robber. It was ridiculous to suppose for a moment, that the subject could lose his effects, and all the benefit of regal protection, and yet be bound by the duty of allegiance; or that a monarch could retain that character when the whole property of the state was vested in himself: he might then be called lord of the soil, or sole possessor of it; but he could not arrogate the title of king. This is a principle inspired by the Divine Author of all good; it is felt in the heart; it is recognised by reason; it is established by consent. The rights of war were not thus limited by the learning of the schools, by the light of philosophy, by the disquisitions of councils, by the debates of legislatures, or by the sense of delegated assemblies. It originated in necessity, in reason, and in the field. The soldiers themselves introduced it; and being taught by necessity, which in all cases is the best tutor, they adopted, and they exercised it, without having the assistance of lucubration. He now stated, that by the convention of parties, this law of nations was established and confirmed. Private property was exempted from the confis-cation which followed public property on the issue of a conquest. A distinction was made in this virtual convention between property found afloat, and found ashore. For what reason that seized on shipboard was mutually agreed to be confiscated, he could not tell. The time was not far distant when even that inhuman species of war would be abolished; but certainly the convention made a difference between the goods found ashore and those found afloat.

He called upon the House, and defied them even to mention one instance, beside the present, of a general and indiscriminate confiscation that had occurred within the last fifty years on any conquest or surrender by discretion. There was no such thing. This was the instance that had occurred to stain and disgrace the age, and the country, and the cause. As to the authority of books, he thought them the weakest part of the argument, although they had collected the wisdom of ages, and had connected, with that of their authors, sagacity, judgment, and sense. He quoted Vattel[15] as being the latest and best, and whose testimony he preferred; because, being a modern writer, he expressed the sense of the day in which we live. As to the testimony of precedent, not one instance had occurred for the last fifty years. The last precedent of a surrender at discretion he considered as the best to be adduced. The case of Grenada was the latest. There the island surrendered at discretion, but not without resistance, like St. Eustatia. The conquest was contested, and was won with a profusion of blood. What was the consequence there? The count D'Estaing,[16] though a man by no means remarkable for the weakness of his nature, did not venture to make a general confiscation of the private property of the inhabitants, or to go to the lengths of cruelty and oppression lately practised at St. Eustatius. He indeed went farther than he ought, in framing certain regulations of a severe nature against the estates of absentees, and to other objects: but on an application to the French king, he gave full and ample redress; he countermanded the orders of D'Estaing, and secured to every merchant, planter, and inhabitant, the full and quiet possession of their property.

The hon. gentleman having, in a variety of most beautiful and forcible arguments, inforced the doctrine of the law of nations, with respect to the security which ought to have been given to the private property of the Dutch in that island, came to speak to the question of the confiscation of British property in that island. In this he answered very fully all that had been suggested by the commanders upon that station, in justification of their conduct, that they made St. Eustatius a deposit, for the supply of the enemy. If this was true with respect to the inhabitants in general, it was a good cause for going to war; but it was a doctrine universally established, that when war is once declared and instituted, the belligerent powers are to treat one another, as having mutually justice on their side, until the final issue is known. So that though the perfidiousness of the Dutch might be a just cause for going to war, it was no excuse for aggravating the horrors of it. Every war presumed an offence on the one part, and when the cause was referred to this mode of decision, it was to be considered as *sub judice*, during which time both parties were intitled to the same treatment; for it was a first principle in the law of nations, as laid down by every writer, that to expound the rights of war, we must conceive each party to have justice on its side, and every thing preceding the commencement of hostilities must be forgotten in that exposition. To make the island of St. Eustatius a deposit was no crime. In the spirit of merchandise, it could not be a deposit, without also being a market. The merchant does not carry his goods to a place to lay them up, but to sell them; and it was the known, established, and admitted principle of St. Eustatius to be a mart for all the world, and consequently equally advantageous to us as to the enemy. We had thrown open Dominica upon the same principle. That had been taken from us, and the moment that we procured a new Dominica, we threw away its advantages. But if it was a fault to send goods to St. Eustatius, and there to sell them, it was a fault for which the legislature of this country were answerable, and not the merchants; for they had encouraged them to the trade. They had passed positive Acts, inculcating in the most express terms this traffic, in which Acts, the Grenada-Act, the Tobacco-Act, the Cotton-Act, the general good of this country was consulted; the revenues were enlarged, the manufacturers promoted, and the merchants enriched. These were the Acts declared by our commanders to have originated in faction, for bad ends. It was by them, however, that ministers had been enabled to say that the commerce of this country, and the manufactures of this country, had not suffered by the war. But this species of traffic had been recognised by his Majesty's ministers in every possible manner. Nay, on this very principle of sharing the advantages in common with the enemy, to be reaped by the establishment of a neutral mart, the minister had but the very last week defended the proclamation for giving up the rights of Britain to chastise her enemies, or fight her cause in the Baltic.[17] The merchants of Britain traded to St. Eustatius under positive acts of parliament; and if the traffic was improper or pernicious, only parliament should be blamed. "But they supplied the enemies of their country;" so did the very men who confiscated their property and deprived them of their rights. They advertised it at a public auction, and invited all the neutral islands to come and purchase it; nay, for the convenience of these neutral powers, advertised that small vessels would be sold also to carry it off the island. It was accordingly transported to French and American settlements, and also to the Danish islands of St. Croix and St. Thomas; from which the Americans, French, and Spaniards, might be supplied. It was treachery in the merchants to sell their property to the enemy; it was right in the commanders in chief to do so. The act of confiscation changed the nature of the market. The hon. gentleman dwelt with great energy on this part of the conduct of the commanders in chief. He said, the whole property had been sold for one fourth part of its value, by which means the enemy had been supplied by government at a much cheaper rate than they otherwise could have been, and a whole people ruined besides.

But if the enemies of Great Britain were supplied from St. Eustatius with stores, it was an advantage that was not exclusively theirs; they enjoyed it in common with the English and the rest of the world; we likewise got supplies from it; and in 1778 our windward islands would have been starved if they had not been relieved from St. Eustatius. If the Dutch had supplied the enemy with stores, and had refused to sell them to us, then perhaps we might have had cause to complain: but they had formed an alliance with ready money, let it come from whom it might; and nothing was ever withheld from any one who called for supplies with ready money in their hands. It was known that the Dutch at St. Eustatius had, for money, furnished us with cordage, provisions, ammunition, and even men, for an expedition against the Spaniards; and that they also defeated that expedition, by selling for ready money also to the Spaniards, the very same kind of commodities, men only excepted. The island therefore was a common blessing; and as it was opened to us by acts of parliament, our commanders in chief ought to have felt themselves bound by a double tie not to confiscate the private property; and it was reasonable to presume that they would not have done it, if they had not had positive orders from ministers at home for all that they had done. He also was exceedingly severe on the observation of the commanders, "that the British subjects might have redress in our courts of law." What! when they had no marks to distinguish their property, no possibility of ascertaining its value, or of watching its sale! What! when they were robbed of their last shilling, and deprived of all the means by which the prosecutions could be carried on! By the exultations from the treasury-bench, when that passage of his letter was read, it was to be concluded that ministers applauded such an answer to their complaints. True it was, they might recover their property by law, but at the same time those men should be punished who drove them to the necessity of doing so. It would be a strange justification, should the crown lay hands on all the property in this country, to tell the parties injured, the courts are open to you. But how were many of the sufferers to prosecute the offenders? stripped as they were of their possessions, how were they to pay the expences of a law-suit, while their antagonists might combat with their own money. He mentioned the case of a gentle-woman, who at the recommendation of a lady, not more dis-tinguished for her rank than for her benevolence, he had endeavoured to serve in the city. This lady had many children, and had been married to an Englishman, who had acted as a cap-tain of a Dutch trader, and had been absent 16 years; during all which time he had made his family frequent remittances, and about two years ago had sent his wife word that after three more trips, he intended to make up his savings, and come and end his days with her and his children in peace and comfort. It happened that for sixteen months she got no tidings of him; and lately, to her astonishment and despair, not only discovered that he was dead, but that his property amounted to something more than 8,000*l.* which was in the island of St. Eustatius, when that island was captured, and the whole of it was seized and confiscated; so that she and her children were reduced to a state of absolute beggary, without in any wise meriting so severe a misfortune. Mr. Burke heightened the pathos of this affecting case, and put it home to the bosoms of the House, in a manner that could not but rouse and excite the pity and compassion of every gentleman present; but she must go to law, destitute of the common neces-saries of life; she must go to law with the rich conquerors of

St. Eustatius, armed with all the plunder which they had seized, and backed by the powers and interest of government. The poor unhappy lady was also deprived of the certificates of her fortune, prevented from proving her property; for these conquerors wisely took care that the books, inventories, and vouchers, should go along with the property, and not remain to be brought up against them in the day of restitution.

The admiral's ideas concerning the retaliation of France, he reprehended severely: "She would not dare to do it." What was this but provoking the enemy to exercise that power already in their hands, by revoking the immunity granted to our fellow-subjects in Grenada; the inhabitants of that island would then have to curse the injustice of our government, but could not reasonably complain of their conquerors. He instanced the case of Mr. Simon, an old gentleman of 90, whose credit formerly stood highest at the Exchange, who now saw himself cut off from a profitable trade, by which he used to clear 18,000*l.* a year. He had been brought over in his infancy to escape from the persecuting tyranny of Louis the 14th, but he had lived to see tyranny change sides, and to see himself ruined by the severity of the English government, at the very time that Louis the 16th was setting the brightest examples of humanity and justice.

It was not extraordinary that a man sitting on a great gun in a ship's cabin, should hold language like that of admiral Rodney; for however much he respected his naval character, his judgment as a lawyer could not be expected to have any consequence, but to see ministers of this country echoing and applauding such maxims was strange indeed. But indeed, he did not want the testimony of sir Samuel Hood[18] to convince him that it was not sir George Rodney that had been the author of these shameful proceedings, but his Majesty's ministers. The hon. gentleman spoke of the whole plan, which they had adopted and pursued, as infamous and unbecoming to the last degree: from the unsuccessful attempt on St. Vincent's to the destructive overthrow of St. Eustatius. An order from a noble lord, formerly secretary of state for the American department, and now again employed in another department by his Majesty, had driven the Caribbees[19] to desperation; and this attempt upon the island at such a time, had renewed all their antipathy to the English; the retreat of our commanders having deprived them of an opportunity to be revenged upon our soldiers, they turned their rage against the

British inhabitants, who then resided there, under the protection of the French; and such was the sense the Caribbees entertained of the infamy of an attack upon the island, immediately after the visitation of heaven, that they would have sacrificed to their resentment all the British on the island, if the French commandant had not, by the most strenuous exertions, screened them from the fury of the savages. Defeated in our hopes against St. Vincent's, our commanders expected, that they might have been able to reduce Martinique and Guadaloupe by famine, in consequence of the destruction of provisions by the late hurricanes; but we lost the opportunity of shewing that we were inhuman, and had not the satisfaction of starving either of these islands into a surrender.

Their attempt on St. Eustatius had been more successful, and it seemed to fill ministers, as well as officers, with transport, that they had been able to conquer a people that did not resist, and plunder them when they surrendered to their mercy. The hon. gentleman concluded with a solemn appeal to the House, whether it was fit that the legislature of Great Britain should be the first to plunge Europe into all the horrors of barbarity, and institute a system of devastation, which would not only bring disgrace, but in all probability ruin upon ourselves. He wished to bring the matter properly before the House, that they might be fully possessed of the facts before they proceeded to a decision: for he sincerely wished them to be deliberate, to be impartial, to be disinterested. It was a question as important as any that had ever come before them, for it was from their conduct that Europe was to learn the system of Great Britain, and by which they were to be forced to regulate their own; he therefore moved,[20]

"That an humble Address be presented to his Majesty, that he will be graciously pleased to give directions, that there be laid before this House, copies of all proclamations, memorials, orders, and instructions, and of all official correspondence, from and to any of his Majesty's ministers, relative to the disposition of the property belonging to the States General and to individuals, inhabiting or interested in the places or territories taken from the said states General in the West Indies."

From SPEECH ON FOX'S
EAST-INDIA BILL[1]

1 DECEMBER 1783

MR. SPEAKER,

I THANK YOU for pointing to me. I really wished much to engage your attention in an early stage of the debate. I have been long very deeply, though perhaps ineffectually, engaged in the preliminary inquiries, which have continued without intermission for some years. Though I have felt, with some degree of sensibility, the natural and inevitable impressions of the several matters of fact, as they have been successively disclosed, I have not at any time attempted to trouble you on the merits of the subject; and very little on any of the points which incidentally arose in the course of our proceedings. But I should be sorry to be found totally silent upon this day. Our inquiries are now come to their final issue: – It is now to be determined whether the three years of laborious parliamentary research, whether the twenty years of patient Indian suffering, are to produce a substantial reform in our Eastern administration; or whether our knowledge of the grievances has abated our zeal for the correction of them, and our very inquiry into the evil was only a pretext to elude the remedy, which is demanded from us by humanity, by justice, and by every principle of true policy. Depend upon it, this business cannot be indifferent to our fame. It will turn out a matter of great disgrace, or great glory, to the whole British nation. We are on a conspicuous stage, and the world marks our demeanour.

I am therefore a little concerned to perceive the spirit and temper in which the debate has been all along pursued upon one side of the House. The declamation of the gentlemen who oppose the bill has been abundant and vehement; but they have been reserved and even silent about the fitness or unfitness of the plan to attain the direct object it has in view. By some gentlemen it is taken up (by way of exercise I presume) as a point of law on a question of private property, and corporate franchise: by others it is regarded as the petty intrigue of a faction at court, and argued merely as it tends to set this man a little higher, or that a little lower, in situation and power. All the void has been filled with invectives against coalition; with allusions to the loss of America;

with the activity and inactivity of ministers. The total silence of these gentlemen concerning the interest and well-being of the people of India, and concerning the interest which this nation has in the commerce and revenues of that country, is a strong indication of the value which they set upon these objects.

It has been a little painful to me to observe the intrusion into this important debate of such company as *quo warranto*,[2] and *mandamus*,[3] and *certiorari*;[4] as if we were on a trial about mayors and aldermen, and capital burgesses; or engaged in a suit concerning the borough of Penryn, or Saltash, or St. Ives, or St. Mawes. Gentlemen have argued with as much heat and passion, as if the first things in the world were at stake; and their topics are such as belong only to matter of the lowest and meanest litigation. It is not right, it is not worthy of us, in this manner to depreciate the value, to degrade the majesty, of this grave deliberation of policy and empire.

For my part, I have thought myself bound, when a matter of this extraordinary weight came before me, not to consider (as some gentlemen are so fond of doing) whether the bill originated from a secretary of state for the home department,[5] or from a secretary for the foreign, from a minister of influence, or a minister of the people; from Jacob, or from Esau.* I asked myself, and I asked myself nothing else, what part of it was fit for a member of parliament, who has supplied a mediocrity of talents by the extreme of diligence, and who has thought himself obliged, by the research of years, to wind himself into the inmost recesses and labyrinths of the Indian detail, what part, I say, it became such a member of parliament to take, when a minister of state, in conformity to a recommendation from the throne, has brought before us a system for the better government of the territory and commerce of the East. In this light, and in this only, I will trouble you with my sentiments.

It is not only agreed, but demanded, by the right honourable gentleman,† and by those who act with him, that a *whole* system ought to be produced; that it ought not to be an *half measure*; that it ought to be no *palliative*; but a legislative provision, vigorous, substantial, and effective. – I believe that no man who understands the subject can doubt for a moment, that those must be

---

* An allusion made by Mr. Powis.[6]

† Mr. Pitt.[7]

the conditions of anything deserving the name of a reform in the Indian government; that anything short of them would not only be delusive, but, in this matter, which admits no medium, noxious in the extreme.

To all the conditions proposed by his adversaries the mover of the bill perfectly agrees; and on his performance of them he rests his cause. On the other hand, not the least objection has been taken, with regard to the efficiency, the vigour, or the completeness of the scheme. I am therefore warranted to assume, as a thing admitted, that the bills accomplish what both sides of the House demand as essential. The end is completely answered, so far as the direct and immediate object is concerned.

But though there are no direct, yet there are various collateral, objections made; objections from the effects which this plan of reform for Indian administration may have on the privileges of great public bodies in England; from its probable influence on the constitutional rights, or on the freedom and integrity, of the several branches of the legislature.

Before I answer these objections, I must beg leave to observe, that if we are not able to contrive some method of governing India *well*, which will not of necessity become the means of governing Great Britain *ill*, a ground is laid for their eternal separation; but none for sacrificing the people of that country to our constitution. I am however far from being persuaded that any such incompatibility of interest does at all exist. On the contrary, I am certain that every means, effectual to preserve India from oppression, is a guard to preserve the British constitution from its worst corruption. To show this, I will consider the objections, which I think are four:

1st, That the bill is an attack on the chartered rights of men.

2dly, That it increases the influence of the crown.

3dly, That it does *not* increase, but diminishes, the influence of the crown, in order to promote the interests of certain ministers and their party.

4thly, That it deeply affects the national credit.

As to the first of these objections; I must observe that the phrase of "the chartered rights *of men*;" is full of affectation; and very unusual in the discussion of privileges conferred by charters of the present description. But it is not difficult to discover what end that ambiguous mode of expression, so often reiterated, is meant to answer.

The rights of *men*, that is to say, the natural rights of mankind, are indeed sacred things; and if any public measure is proved mischievously to affect them, the objection ought to be fatal to that measure, even if no charter at all could be set up against it. If these natural rights are further affirmed and declared by express covenants, if they are clearly defined and secured against chicane, against power, and authority, by written instruments and positive engagements, they are in a still better condition: they partake not only of the sanctity of the object so secured, but of that solemn public faith itself, which secures an object of such importance. Indeed this formal recognition, by the sovereign power, of an original right in the subject, can never be subverted, but by rooting up the holding, radical principles of government, and even of society itself. The charters, which we call by distinction *great*, are public instruments of this nature; I mean the charters of King John and King Henry the Third.[8] The things secured by these instruments may, without any deceitful ambiguity, be very fitly called the *chartered rights of men*.

These charters have made the very name of a charter dear to the heart of every Englishman. – But, Sir, there may be, and there are charters, not only different in nature, but formed on principles the *very reverse* of those of the great charter. Of this kind is the charter of the East-India Company. *Magna Charta* is a charter to restrain power, and to destroy monopoly. The East-India charter is a charter to establish monopoly, and to create power. Political power and commercial monopoly are *not* the rights of men; and the rights to them derived from charters, it is fallacious and sophistical to call "the chartered rights of men." These chartered rights (to speak of such charters and of their effects in terms of the greatest possible moderation) do at least suspend the natural rights of mankind at large; and in their very frame and constitution are liable to fall into a direct violation of them.

It is a charter of this latter description (that is to say, a charter of power and monopoly) which is affected by the bill before you. The bill, Sir, does, without question, affect it; it does affect it essentially and substantially. But having stated to you of what description the chartered rights are which this bill touches, I feel no difficulty at all in acknowledging the existence of those chartered rights in their fullest extent. They belong to the Company in the surest manner; and they are secured to that body by every sort of public sanction. They are stamped by the faith of the king;

they are stamped by the faith of parliament; they have been bought for money, for money honestly and fairly paid; they have been bought for valuable consideration, over and over again.

I therefore freely admit to the East-India Company their claim to exclude their fellow-subjects from the commerce of half the globe. I admit their claim to administer an annual territorial revenue of seven millions sterling; to command an army of sixty thousand men; and to dispose (under the control of a sovereign, imperial discretion, and with the due observance of the natural and local law) of the lives and fortunes of thirty millions of their fellow-creatures. All this they possess by charter, and by acts of parliament, (in my opinion,) without a shadow of controversy.

Those who carry the rights and claims of the Company the furthest, do not contend for more than this; and all this I freely grant. But granting all this, they must grant to me in my turn, that all political power which is set over men, and that all privilege claimed or exercised in exclusion of them, being wholly artificial, and for so much a derogation from the natural equality of mankind at large, ought to be some way or other exercised ultimately for their benefit.

If this is true with regard to every species of political dominion, and every description of commercial privilege, none of which can be original, self-derived rights, or grants for the mere private benefit of the holders, then such rights, or privileges, or whatever else you choose to call them, are all in the strictest sense a *trust*; and it is of the very essence of every trust to be rendered *accountable*; and even totally to cease, when it substantially varies from the purposes for which alone it could have a lawful existence.

This I conceive, Sir, to be true of trusts of power vested in the highest hands, and of such as seem to hold of no human creature. But about the application of this principle to subordinate, *derivative* trusts, I do not see how a controversy can be maintained. To whom then would I make the East-India Company accountable? Why, to parliament, to be sure; to parliament, from which their trust was derived; to parliament, which alone is capable of comprehending the magnitude of its object, and its abuse; and alone capable of an effectual legislative remedy. The very charter, which is held out to exclude parliament from correcting malversation with regard to the high trust vested in the Company, is the very thing which at once gives a title and imposes on us a duty to interfere with effect, wherever power and authority originating from ourselves are perverted from their purposes, and become instruments of wrong and violence.

If parliament, Sir, had nothing to do with this charter, we might have some sort of Epicurean excuse to stand aloof, in-different spectators of what passes in the Company's name in India and in London. But if we are the very cause of the evil, we are in a special manner engaged to the redress; and for us passively to bear with oppressions committed under the sanction of our own authority, is in truth and reason for this House to be an active accomplice in the abuse.

That the power, notoriously, grossly abused, has been bought from us, is very certain. But this circumstance, which is urged against the bill, becomes an additional motive for our inter-ference; lest we should be thought to have sold the blood of millions of men, for the base consideration of money. We sold, I admit, all that we had to sell; that is, our authority, not our control. We had not a right to make a market of our duties.

I ground myself therefore on this principle – that if the abuse is proved, the contract is broken; and we re-enter into all our rights; that is, into the exercise of all our duties. Our own author-ity is indeed as much a trust originally, as the Company's authority is a trust derivatively; and it is the use we make of the resumed power that must justify or condemn us in the resump-tion of it. When we have perfected the plan laid before us by the right honourable mover, the world will then see what it is we destroy, and what it is we create. By that test we stand or fall; and by that test I trust that it will be found in the issue, that we are going to supersede a charter abused to the full extent of all the powers which it could abuse, and exercised in the plenitude of despotism, tyranny, and corruption; and that in one and the same plan, we provide a real chartered security for the *rights of men*, cruelly violated under that charter.

This bill, and those connected with it, are intended to form the *Magna Charta* of Hindostan. Whatever the treaty of West-phalia[9] is to the liberty of the princes and free cities of the empire, and to the three religions there professed – Whatever the great charter, the statute of tallege,[10] the petition of right, and the declaration of right, are to Great Britain, these bills are to the people of India. Of this benefit, I am certain, their condition is capable; and when I know that they are capable of more, my vote shall most assuredly be for our giving to the full extent of their capacity of receiving; and no charter of dominion shall stand as a bar in my way to their charter of safety and protection.

The strong admission I have made of the Company's rights (I am conscious of it) binds me to do a great deal. I do not presume to condemn those who argue *a priori*, against the propriety of leaving such extensive political powers in the hands of a company of merchants. I know much is, and much more may be, said against such a system. But, with my particular ideas and sentiments, I cannot go that way to work. I feel an insuperable reluctance in giving my hand to destroy any established institution of government, upon a theory, however plausible it may be. My experience in life teaches me nothing clear upon the subject. I have known merchants with the sentiments and the abilities of great statesmen; and I have seen persons in the rank of statesmen, with the conceptions and characters of pedlars. Indeed, my observation has furnished me with nothing that is to be found in any habits of life or education, which tends wholly to disqualify men for the functions of government, but that by which the power of exercising those functions is very frequently obtained, I mean a spirit and habits of low cabal and intrigue; which I have never, in one instance, seen united with a capacity for sound and manly policy.

To justify us in taking the administration of their affairs out of the hands of the East-India Company, on my principles, I must see several conditions. 1st, The object affected by the abuse should be great and important. 2nd, The abuse affecting this great object ought to be a great abuse. 3rd, It ought to be habitual, and not accidental. 4th, It ought to be utterly incurable in the body as it now stands constituted. All this ought to be made as visible to me as the light of the sun, before I should strike off an atom of their charter. A right honourable gentleman* has said, and said I think but once, and that very slightly, (whatever his original demand for a plan might seem to require,) that "there are abuses in the Company's government." If that were all, the scheme of the mover of this bill, the scheme of his learned friend, and his own scheme of reformation, (if he has any,) are all equally needless. There are, and must be, abuses in all governments. It amounts to no more than a nugatory proposition. But before I consider of what nature these abuses are, of which the gentleman speaks so

* Mr. Pitt.

very lightly, permit me to recall to your recollection the map of the country which this abused chartered right affects. This I shall do, that you may judge whether in that map I can discover anything like the first of my conditions; that is, Whether the object affected by the abuse of the East-India Company's power be of importance sufficiently to justify the measure and means of reform applied to it in this bill.

[...]

When I accuse the court of directors of this habitual treachery, in the use of reward and punishment, I do not mean to include all the individuals in that court. There have been, Sir, very frequently, men of the greatest integrity and virtue amongst them; and the contrariety in the declarations and conduct of that court has arisen, I take it, from this: − That the honest directors have, by the force of matter of fact on the records, carried the reprobation of the evil measures of the servants in India. This could not be prevented, whilst these records stared them in the face; nor were the delinquents, either here or there, very solicitous about their reputation, as long as they were able to secure their power. The agreement of their partisans to censure them, blunted for a while the edge of a severe proceeding. It obtained for them a character of impartiality, which enabled them to recommend, with some sort of grace, what will always carry a plausible appearance, those treacherous expedients, called moderate measures. Whilst these were under discussion, new matter of complaint came over, which seemed to antiquate the first. The same circle was here trod round once more; and thus through years they proceeded in a compromise of censure for punishment; until, by shame and despair, one after another, almost every man, who preferred his duty to the Company to the interests of their servants, has been driven from that court.

This, Sir, has been their conduct; and it has been the result of the alteration which was insensibly made in their constitution. The change was made insensibly; but it is now strong and adult, and as public and declared as it is fixed beyond all power of reformation. So that there is none who hears me, that is not as certain as I am, that the Company, in the sense in which it was formerly understood, has no existence. The question is not, what injury you may do to the proprietors of India stock; for there

are no such men to be injured. If the active, ruling part of the
Company, who form the general court, who fill the offices, and
direct the measures, (the rest tell for nothing,) were persons who
held their stock as a means of their subsistence, who in the part
they took were only concerned in the government of India for
the rise or fall of their dividend, it would be indeed a defective
plan of policy. The interest of the people who are governed by
them would not be their primary object; perhaps a very small
part of their consideration at all. But then they might well be
depended on, and perhaps more than persons in other respects
preferable, for preventing the peculation of their servants to their
own prejudice. Such a body would not easily have left their trade
as a spoil to the avarice of those who received their wages. But
now things are totally reversed. The stock is of no value, whether
it be the qualification of a director or proprietor; and it is impossible that it should. A director's qualification may be worth about
two thousand five hundred pounds – and the interest, at eight
per cent, is about one hundred and sixty pounds a year. Of what
value is that, whether it rise to ten, or fall to six, or to nothing,
to him whose son, before he is in Bengal two months, and before
he descends the steps of the council-chamber, sells the grant of
a single contract for forty thousand pounds? Accordingly the
stock is bought up in qualifications. The vote is not to protect
the stock, but the stock is bought to acquire the vote; and the
end of the vote is to cover and support, against justice, some man
of power who has made an obnoxious fortune in India; or to
maintain in power those who are actually employing it in the
acquisition of such a fortune; and to avail themselves in return of
his patronage, that he may shower the spoils of the East, "barbaric
pearl and gold," on them, their families, and dependents. So that
all the relations of the Company are not only changed, but
inverted. The servants in India are not appointed by the directors, but the directors are chosen by them. The trade is carried
on with their capitals. To them the revenues of the country are
mortgaged. The seat of the supreme power is in Calcutta. The
house in Leadenhall Street is nothing more than a 'change for
their agents, factors, and deputies to meet in, to take care of their
affairs, and support their interests; and this so avowedly, that we
see the known agents of the delinquent servants marshalling and
disciplining their forces, and the prime spokesmen in all their
assemblies.

Everything has followed in this order, and according to the natural train of events. I will close what I have to say on the incorrigible condition of the Company, by stating to you a few facts that will leave no doubt of the obstinacy of that corporation, and of their strength too, in resisting the reformation of their servants. By these facts you will be enabled to discover the sole grounds upon which they are tenacious of their charter. It is now more than two years that, upon account of the gross abuses and ruinous situation of the Company's affairs, (which occasioned the cry of the whole world long before it was taken up here,) we instituted two committees to inquire into the mismanagements by which the Company's affairs had been brought to the brink of ruin. These inquiries had been pursued with unremitting diligence; and a great body of facts was collected and printed for general information. In the result of those inquiries, although the committees consisted of very different descriptions, they were unanimous. They joined in censuring the conduct of the Indian administration, and enforcing the responsibility upon two men, whom this House, in consequence of these reports, declared it to be the duty of the directors to remove from their stations, and recall to Great Britain, "*because they had acted in a manner repugnant to the honour and policy of this nation, and thereby brought great calamities on India, and enormous expenses on the East-India Company.*"

Here was no attempt on the charter. Here was no question of their privileges. To vindicate their own honour, to support their own interests, to enforce obedience to their own orders; these were the sole object of the monitory resolution of this House. But as soon as the general court could assemble, they assembled to demonstrate who they really were. Regardless of the proceedings of this House, they ordered the directors not to carry into effect any resolution they might come to for the removal of Mr. Hastings[11] and Mr. Hornby.[12] The directors, still retaining some shadow of respect to this House, instituted an inquiry themselves, which continued from June to October; and, after an attentive perusal and full consideration of papers, resolved to take steps for removing the persons who had been the objects of our resolution; but not without a violent struggle against evidence. Seven directors went so far as to enter a protest against the vote of their court. Upon this the general court takes the alarm; it reassembles; it orders the directors to rescind their resolution, that is, not to recall Mr. Hastings and Mr. Hornby, and to despise the resolution of the House of Commons. Without so much as the pretence of looking into a single paper, without the formality of instituting any committee of inquiry, they superseded all the labours of their own directors, and of this House.

It will naturally occur to ask, how it was possible that they should not attempt some sort of examination into facts, as a colour for their resistance to a public authority, proceeding so very deliberately; and exerted, apparently at least, in favour of their own? The answer, and the only answer which can be given, is, that they were afraid that their true relation should be mistaken. They were afraid that their patrons and masters in India should attribute their support of them to an opinion of their cause, and not to an attachment to their power. They were afraid it should be suspected, that they did not mean blindly to support them in the use they made of that power. They determined to show that they at least were set against reformation; that they were firmly resolved to bring the territories, the trade, and the stock of the Company, to ruin, rather than be wanting in fidelity to their nominal servants and real masters, in the ways they took to their private fortunes.

Even since the beginning of this session, the same act of audacity was repeated, with the same circumstances of contempt of all the decorum of inquiry on their part, and of all the proceedings of this House. They again made it a request to their favourite, and your culprit, to keep his post; and thanked and applauded him, without calling for a paper which could afford light into the merit or demerit of the transaction, and without giving themselves a moment's time to consider, or even to understand, the articles of the Maratta peace.[13] The fact is, that for a long time there was a struggle, a faint one indeed, between the Company and their servants. But it is a struggle no longer. For some time the superiority has been decided. The interests abroad are become the settled preponderating weight, both in the court of proprietors and the court of directors. Even the attempt you have made, to inquire into their practices and to reform abuses, has raised and piqued them to a far more regular and steady support. The Company has made a common cause, and identified themselves, with the destroyers of India. They have taken on themselves all that mass of enormity; they are supporting what you have reprobated; those you condemn they applaud; those you order home to answer for their conduct, they request to stay, and thereby encourage to proceed in their practices. Thus the servants of the East-India Company triumph, and the representatives of the people of Great Britain are defeated.

I therefore conclude, what you all conclude, that this body, being totally perverted from the purposes of its institution, is utterly incorrigible; and because they are incorrigible, both in conduct and constitution, power ought to be taken out of their hands; just on the same principles on which have been made all the just changes and revolutions of government that have taken place since the beginning of the world.

I will now say a few words to the general principle of the plan which is set up against that of my right honourable friend. It is to re-commit the government of India to the court of directors. Those, who would commit the reformation of India to the destroyers of it, are the enemies to that reformation. They would make a distinction between directors and proprietors, which, in the present state of things, does not, cannot exist. But a right honourable gentleman says, he would keep the present government of India in the court of directors; and would, to curb them, provide salutary regulations; – wonderful! That is, he would appoint the old offenders to correct the old offences; and he would render the vicious and the foolish wise and virtuous, by salutary regulations. He would appoint the wolf as guardian of the sheep; but he has invented a curious muzzle, by which this protecting wolf shall not be able to open his jaws above an inch or two at the utmost. Thus his work is finished. But I tell the right honourable gentleman, that controlled depravity is not innocence; and that it is not the labour of delinquency in chains that will correct abuses. Will these gentlemen of the direction animadvert on the partners of their own guilt? Never did a serious plan of amending any old tyrannical establishment propose the authors and abettors of the abuses as the reformers of them. If the undone people of India see their old oppressors in confirmed power, even by the reformation, they will expect nothing but what they will certainly feel, a continuance, or rather an aggravation, of all their former sufferings. They look to the seat of power, and to the persons who fill it; and they despise those gentlemen's regulations as much as the gentlemen do who talk of them.

But there is a cure for everything. Take away, say they, the court of proprietors, and the court of directors will do their duty.

Yes; as they have done it hitherto. That the evils in India have solely arisen from the court of proprietors, is grossly false. In many of them, the directors were heartily concurring; in most of them, they were encouraging, and sometimes commanding; in all, they were conniving.

But who are to choose this well-regulated and reforming court of directors? – Why, the very proprietors who are excluded from all management, for the abuse of their power. They will choose, undoubtedly, out of themselves, men like themselves; and those who are most forward in resisting your authority, those who are most engaged in faction or interests with the delinquents abroad, will be the objects of their selection. But gentlemen say, that when this choice is made, the proprietors are not to interfere in the measures of the directors, whilst those directors are busy in the control of their common patrons and masters in India. No, indeed, I believe they will not desire to interfere. They will choose those whom they know may be trusted, safely trusted, to act in strict conformity to their common principles, manners, measures, interests, and connexions. They will want neither monitor nor control. It is not easy to choose men to act in conformity to a public interest against their private: but a sure dependence may be had on those who are chosen to forward their private interest, at the expense of the public. But if the directors should slip, and deviate into rectitude, the punishment is in the hands of the general court, and it will surely be remembered to them at their next election.

If the government of India wants no reformation; but gentlemen are amusing themselves with a theory, conceiving a more democratic or aristocratic mode of government for these dependencies, or if they are in a dispute only about patronage; the dispute is with me of so little concern, that I should not take the pains to utter an affirmative or negative to any proposition in it. If it be only for a theoretical amusement that they are to propose a bill; the thing is at best frivolous and unnecessary. But if the Company's government is not only full of abuse, but is one of the most corrupt and destructive tyrannies that probably ever existed in the world, (as I am sure it is,) what a cruel mockery would it be in me, and in those who think like me, to propose this kind of remedy for this kind of evil!

I now come to the third objection, That this bill will increase the influence of the crown. An honourable gentleman has demanded of me, whether I was in earnest when I proposed to this House a plan for the reduction of that influence. Indeed, Sir, I was much, very much, in earnest. My heart was deeply concerned in it; and I hope the public has not lost the effect of it. How far my judgment was right, for what concerned personal favour and consequence to myself, I shall not presume to determine; nor is its effect upon me of any moment. But as to this bill, whether it increases the influence of the crown, or not, is a question I should be ashamed to ask. If I am not able to correct a system of oppression and tyranny, that goes to the utter ruin of thirty millions of my fellow-creatures and fellow-subjects, but by some increase to the influence of the crown, I am ready here to declare that I, who have been active to reduce it, shall be at least as active and strenuous to restore it again. I am no lover of names; I contend for the substance of good and protecting government, let it come from what quarter it will.

But I am not obliged to have recourse to this expedient. Much, very much the contrary. I am sure that the influence of the crown will by no means aid a reformation of this kind; which can neither be originated nor supported, but by the uncorrupt public virtue of the representatives of the people of England. Let it once get into the ordinary course of administration, and to me all hopes of reformation are gone. I am far from knowing or believing, that this bill will increase the influence of the crown. We all know, that the crown has ever had some influence in the court of directors; and that it has been extremely increased by the Acts of 1773 and 1780. The gentlemen who, as a part of their reformation, propose "a more active control on the part of the crown," which is to put the directors under a secretary of state, especially named for that purpose, must know that their project will increase it further. But that old influence has had, and the new will have, incurable inconveniences, which cannot happen under the parliamentary establishment proposed in this bill. An honourable gentleman,* not now in his place, but who is well acquainted with the India Company, and by no means a friend to this bill, has told you that a ministerial influence has always been predominant in that body; and that to make the directors pliant to their purposes, ministers generally caused persons meanly qualified to be chosen directors. According to his idea,

* Governor Johnstone.

to secure subserviency, they submitted the Company's affairs to the direction of incapacity. This was to ruin the Company, in order to govern it. This was certainly influence in the very worst form in which it could appear. At best it was clandestine and irresponsible. Whether this was done so much upon system as that gentleman supposes, I greatly doubt. But such in effect the operation of government on that court unquestionably was; and such, under a similar constitution, it will be for ever. Ministers must be wholly removed from the management of the affairs of India, or they will have an influence in its patronage. The thing is inevitable. Their scheme of a new secretary of state, "with a more vigorous control," is not much better than a repetition of the measure which we know by experience will not do. Since the year 1773 and the year 1780, the Company has been under the control of the secretary of state's office, and we had then three secretaries of state. If more than this is done, then they annihilate the direction which they pretend to support; and they augment the influence of the crown, of whose growth they affect so great a horror. But in truth this scheme of reconciling a direction really and truly deliberative, with an office really and substantially controlling, is a sort of machinery that can be kept in order but a very short time. Either the directors will dwindle into clerks, or the secretary of state, as hitherto has been the course, will leave everything to them, often through design, often through neglect. If both should affect activity, collision, procrastination, delay, and, in the end, utter confusion, must ensue.

But, Sir, there is one kind of influence far greater than that of the nomination to office. This gentlemen in opposition have totally overlooked, although it now exists in its full vigour; and it will do so, upon their scheme, in at least as much force as it does now. That influence this bill cuts up by the roots: I mean the *influence of protection*. I shall explain myself: – The office given to a young man going to India is of trifling consequence. But he that goes out an insignificant boy, in a few years returns a great Nabob. Mr. Hastings says he has two hundred and fifty of that kind of raw materials, who expect to be speedily manufactured into the merchantable quality I mention. One of these gentlemen, suppose, returns hither, laden with odium and with riches. When he comes to England, he comes as to a prison, or as to a sanctuary; and either is ready for him, according to his demeanour. What is the influence in the grant of any place in India, to that which is acquired by the protection or compromise with such guilt, and with the command of such riches, under the dominion of the hopes and fears which power is able to hold out to every man in that condition? That man's whole fortune, half a million perhaps, becomes an instrument of influence, without a shilling of charge to the civil list; and the influx of fortunes which stand in need of this protection is continual. It works both ways; it influences the delinquent, and it may corrupt the minister. Compare the influence acquired by appointing, for instance, even a governor-general, and that obtained by protecting him. I shall push this no further. But I wish gentlemen to roll it a little in their own minds.

The bill before you cuts off this source of influence. Its design and main scope is to regulate the administration of India upon the principles of a court of judicature; and to exclude, as far as human prudence can exclude, all possibility of a corrupt partiality, in appointing to office, or supporting in office, or covering from inquiry and punishment, any person who has abused or shall abuse his authority. At the board, as appointed and regulated by this bill, reward and punishment cannot be shifted and reversed by a whisper. That comission becomes fatal to cabal, to intrigue, and to secret representation, those instruments of the ruin of India. He that cuts off the means of premature fortune, and the power of protecting it when acquired, strikes a deadly blow at the great fund, the bank, the capital stock of Indian influence, which cannot be vested anywhere, or in any hands, without most dangerous consequences to the public.

The third and contradictory objection is, That this bill does not increase the influence of the crown. On the contrary, That the just power of the crown will be lessened, and transferred to the use of a party, by giving the patronage of India to a commission nominated by parliament, and independent of the crown. The contradiction is glaring, and it has been too well exposed to make it necessary for me to insist upon it. But passing the contradiction, and taking it without any relation, of all objections that is the most extraordinary. Do not gentlemen know, that the crown has not at present the grant of a single office under the Company, civil or military, at home or abroad? So far as the crown is concerned, it is certainly rather a gainer; for the vacant offices in the new commission are to be filled up by the king.

It is argued as a part of the bill, derogatory to the prerogatives of the crown, that the commissioners named in the bill are to continue for a short term of years, too short in my opinion; and because, during that time, they are not at the mercy of every predominant faction of the court. Does not this objection lie against the present directors; none of whom are named by the crown, and a proportion of whom hold for this very term of four years? Did it not lie against the governor-general and council named in the act of 1773 – who were invested by name, as the present commissioners are to be appointed in the body of the act of parliament, who were to hold their places for a term of years, and were not removable at the discretion of the crown? Did it not lie against the re-appointment, in the year 1780, upon the very same terms? Yet at none of these times, whatever other objections the scheme might be liable to, was it supposed to be a derogation to the just prerogative of the crown, that a commission created by act of parliament should have its members named by the authority which called it into existence? This is not the disposal by parliament of any office derived from the authority of the crown, or now disposable by that authority. It is so far from being anything new, violent, or alarming, that I do not recollect, in any parliamentary commission, down to the commissioners of the land-tax, that it has ever been otherwise.

The objection of the tenure for four years is an objection to all places that are not held during pleasure; but in that objection I pronounce the gentlemen, from my knowledge of their complexion and of their principles, to be perfectly in earnest. The party (say these gentlemen) of the minister who proposes this scheme will be rendered powerful by it; for he will name his party friends to the commission. This objection against party is a party objection; and in this too these gentlemen are perfectly serious. They see that if, by any intrigue, they should succeed to office, they will lose the *clandestine* patronage, the true instrument of clandestine influence, enjoyed in the name of subservient directors, and of wealthy, trembling, Indian delinquents. But as often as they are beaten off this ground, they return to it again. The minister will name his friends, and persons of his own party. – Whom should he name? Should he name his adversaries? Should he name those whom he cannot trust? Should he name those to execute his plans, who are the declared enemies to the principles of his reform? His character is here at stake. If he proposes for his own ends (but he never will propose) such names as, from their want of rank, fortune, character, ability, or knowledge, are likely to betray or to fall short of their trust, he is in an independent House of Commons which has, by its own virtue, destroyed the instruments of parliamentary subservience. This House of Commons would not endure the sound of such names. He would perish by the means which he is supposed to pursue for the security of his power. The first pledge he must give of his sincerity in this great reform will be in the confidence which ought to be reposed in those names.

For my part, Sir, in this business I put all indirect considerations wholly out of mind. My sole question, on each clause of the bill, amounts to this : – Is the measure proposed required by the necessities of India? I cannot consent totally to lose sight of the real wants of the people who are the objects of it, and to hunt after every matter of party squabble that may be started on the several provisions. On the question of the duration of the commission I am clear and decided. Can I, can any one who has taken the smallest trouble to be informed concerning the affairs of India, amuse himself with so strange an imagination, as that the habitual despotism and oppression, that the monopolies, the peculations, the universal destruction of all the legal authority of this kingdom, which have been for twenty years maturing to their present enormity, combined with the distance of the scene, the boldness and artifice of delinquents, their combination, their excessive wealth, and the faction they have made in England, can be fully corrected in a shorter term than four years? None has hazarded such an assertion – None, who has a regard for his reputation, will hazard it.

Sir, the gentlemen, whoever they are, who shall be appointed to this commission, have an undertaking of magnitude on their hands, and their stability must not only be, but it must be thought, real; – and who is it will believe, that anything short of an establishment made, supported, and fixed in its duration, with all the authority of parliament, can be thought secure of a reasonable stability? The plan of my honourable friend is the reverse of that of reforming by the authors of the abuse. The best we could expect from them is, that they should not continue their ancient, pernicious activity. To those we could think of nothing but applying *control*; as we are sure that even a regard to their reputation (if any such thing exists in them) would oblige them to cover, to conceal, to suppress, and consequently to prevent, all cure of the grievances of India. For what can be discovered, which is not to their disgrace? Every attempt to correct an abuse would be a satire on their former administration. Every man they should pretend to call to an account would be found their instrument, or their accomplice. They can never see a beneficial regulation, but with a view to defeat it. The shorter the tenure of such persons, the better would be the chance of some amendment.

But the system of the bill is different. It calls in persons in nowise concerned with any act censured by parliament; persons generated with, and for, the reform, of which they are themselves the most essential part. To these the chief regulations in the bill are helps, not fetters; they are authorities to support, not regulations to restrain them. From these we look for much more than innocence. From these we expect zeal, firmness, and unremitted activity. Their duty, their character, binds them to proceedings of vigour; and they ought to have a tenure in their office which precludes all fear, whilst they are acting up to the purposes of their trust; a tenure without which none will undertake plans that require a series and system of acts. When they know that they cannot be whispered out of their duty, that their public conduct cannot be censured without a public discussion, that the schemes which they have begun will not be committed to those who will have an interest and credit in defeating and disgracing them, then we may entertain hopes. The tenure is for four years, or during their good behaviour. That good behaviour is as long as they are true to the principles of the bill; and the judgment is in either House of Parliament. This is the tenure of your judges; and the valuable principle of the bill is to make a judicial administration for India. It is to give confidence in the execution of a duty, which requires as much perseverance and fortitude, as can fall to the lot of any that is born of woman.

As to the gain by party, from the right honourable gentleman's bill, let it be shown, that this supposed party advantage is pernicious to its object, and the objection is of weight: but until this is done, and this has not been attempted, I shall consider the sole objection, from its tendency to promote the interest of a party, as altogether contemptible. The kingdom is divided into parties, and it ever has been so divided, and it ever will be so divided; and if no system for relieving the subjects of this kingdom from oppression, and snatching its affairs from ruin, can be adopted, until it is demonstrated that no party can derive an advantage from it, no good can ever be done in this country. If party is to derive an advantage from the reform of India, (which is more than I know, or believe,) it ought to be that party which alone, in this kingdom, has its reputation, nay its very being, pledged to the protection and preservation of that part of the empire. Great fear is expressed, that the commissioners named in this bill will show some regard to a minister out of place. To men made like the objectors, this must appear criminal. Let it however be remembered by others, that if the commissioners should be his friends, they cannot be his slaves. But dependents are not in a condition to adhere to friends, nor to principles, nor to any uniform line of conduct. They may begin censors, and be obliged to end accomplices. They may be even put under the direction of those whom they were appointed to punish.

The fourth and last objection is, that the bill will hurt public credit. I do not know whether this requires an answer. But if it does, look to your foundations. The sinking fund is the pillar of credit in this country; and let it not be forgotten, that the distresses, owing to the mismanagement of the East-India Company, have already taken a million from that fund by the non-payment of duties. The bills drawn upon the Company, which are about four millions, cannot be accepted without the consent of the treasury. The treasury, acting under a parliamentary trust and authority, pledges the public for these millions. If they pledge the public, the public must have a security in its hands for the management of this interest, or the national credit is gone. For otherwise it is not only the East-India Company, which is a great interest, that is undone, but, clinging to the security of all your funds, it drags down the rest, and the whole fabric perishes in one ruin. If this bill does not provide a direction of integrity and of ability competent to that trust, the objection is fatal. If it does, public credit must depend on the support of the bill.

It has been said, if you violate this charter, what security has the charter of the bank, in which public credit is so deeply concerned, and even the charter of London, in which the rights of so many subjects are involved? I answer, In the like case they have no security at all – No – no security at all. If the bank should, by every species of mismanagement, fall into a state similar to that of the East India Company; if it should be oppressed with demands it could not answer, engagements which it could not perform, and with bills for which it could not procure payment;

no charter should protect the mismanagement from correction, and such public grievances from redress. If the city of London had the means and will of destroying an empire, and of cruelly oppressing and tyrannising over millions of men as good as themselves, the charter of the city of London should prove no sanction to such tyranny and such oppression. Charters are kept, when their purposes are maintained: they are violated, when the privilege is supported against its end and its object.

Now, Sir, I have finished all I proposed to say, as my reasons for giving my vote to this bill. If I am wrong, it is not for want of pains to know what is right. This pledge, at least, of my rectitude I have given to my country.

And now, having done my duty to the bill, let me say a word to the author. I should leave him to his own noble sentiments, if the unworthy and illiberal language with which he has been treated, beyond all example of parliamentary liberty, did not make a few words necessary; not so much in justice to him, as to my own feelings. I must say then, that it will be a distinction honourable to the age, that the rescue of the greatest number of the human race that ever were so grievously oppressed, from the greatest tyranny that was ever exercised, has fallen to the lot of abilities and dispositions equal to the task; that it has fallen to one who has the enlargement to comprehend, the spirit to undertake, and the eloquence to support, so great a measure of hazardous benevolence. His spirit is not owing to his ignorance of the state of men and things; he well knows what snares are spread about his path, from personal animosity, from court intrigues, and possibly from popular delusion. But he has put to hazard his ease, his security, his interest, his power, even his darling popularity, for the benefit of a people whom he has never seen. This is the road that all heroes have trod before him. He is traduced and abused for his supposed motives. He will remember, that obloquy is a necessary ingredient in the composition of all true glory. He will remember, that it was not only in the Roman customs, but it is in the nature and constitution of things, that calumny and abuse are essential parts of triumph. These thoughts will support a mind, which only exists for honour, under the burthen of temporary reproach. He is doing indeed a great good; such as rarely falls to the lot, and almost as rarely coincides with the desires, of any man. Let him use his time. Let him give the whole length of the reins to his benevolence. He is now on a great eminence, where the eyes of mankind are turned to him. He may live long, he may do much. But here is the summit. He never can exceed what he does this day.

He has faults; but they are faults that, though they may in a small degree tarnish the lustre, and sometimes impede the march, of his abilities, have nothing in them to extinguish the fire of great virtues. In those faults, there is no mixture of deceit, of hypocrisy, of pride, of ferocity, of complexional despotism, or want of feeling for the distresses of mankind. His are faults which might exist in a descendant of Henry the Fourth of France,[14] as they did exist in that father of his country. Henry the Fourth wished that he might live to see a fowl in the pot of every peasant in his kingdom. That sentiment of homely benevolence was worth all the splendid sayings that are recorded of kings. But he wished perhaps for more than could be obtained, and the goodness of the man exceeded the power of the king. But this gentleman, a subject, may this day say this at least, with truth, that he secures the rice in his pot to every man in India. A poet of antiquity thought it one of the first distinctions to a prince whom he meant to celebrate, that through a long succession of generations, he had been the progenitor of an able and virtuous citizen, who by force of the arts of peace, had corrected governments of oppression, and suppressed wars of rapine.

> *Indole proh quanta juvenis, quantumque daturus*
> *Ausoniæ populis, ventura in spæcula civem.*
> *Ille super Gangem, super exauditus et Indos,*
> *Implebit terras voce; et furialia bella*
> *Fulmine compescet linguæ.*—[15]

This was what was said of the predecessor of the only person to whose eloquence it does not wrong that of the mover of this bill to be compared. But the Ganges and the Indus are the patrimony of the fame of my honourable friend, and not of Cicero. I confess, I anticipate with joy the reward of those, whose whole consequence, power, and authority, exist only for the benefit of mankind; and I carry my mind to all the people, and all the names and descriptions, that, relieved by this bill, will bless the labours of this parliament, and the confidence which the best House of Commons has given to him who the best deserves it. The little cavils of party will not be heard, where freedom and happiness will be felt. There is not a tongue, a nation, or religion in India, which will not bless the presiding care and manly beneficence of this House, and of him who proposes to you this great work. Your names will never be separated before the throne of the Divine Goodness, in whatever language, or with whatever rites, pardon is asked for sin, and reward for those who imitate the Godhead in his universal bounty to his creatures. These honours you deserve, and they will surely be paid, when all the jargon of influence, and party, and patronage, are swept into oblivion.

I have spoken what I think, and what I feel, of the mover of this bill. An honourable friend of mine, speaking of his merits, was charged with having made a studied panegyric. I don't know what his was. Mine, I am sure, is a studied panegyric; the fruit of much meditation; the result of the observation of near twenty years. For my own part, I am happy that I have lived to see this day; I feel myself overpaid for the labours of eighteen years, when, at this late period, I am able to take my share, by one humble vote, in destroying a tyranny that exists to the disgrace of this nation, and the destruction of so large a part of the human species.

INSCRIPTION ON THE TOMB
OF LORD ROCKINGHAM[1]

1784

CHARLES WATSON WENTWORTH

MARQUISS OF ROCKINGHAM. Earl of Malton,
Viscount Higham of Higham Ferrers,
Baron of Rockingham, Malton, Wath, and
Harrowden and Baronet, in Great Britain.
Earl and Baron of Malton in the
Kingdom of Ireland. Lord Lieutenant and
Custos Rotulorum of the West Riding
of Yorkshire, City of York, and County
of the same, Custos Rotulorum of the
North Riding, and Vice Admiral of the
Maritime Parts thereof. High Steward
of Kingston upon Hull, Knight of the
Garter, and first Commissioner of the
Board of Treasury.
Born May 24th. 1730, died July 1st. 1782.

2

A man worthy to be held in remembrance: because
he did not live for himself. His Abilities, Industry and
Influence were employed, without interruption, to
the last hour of his life, to give stability to the
liberties of his country; security to its landed
property; increase to its commerce; independence to
its publick councils, and concord to its empire.
These were his Ends.

For the attainment of those ends, his policy
consisted in Sincerity, Fidelity, Directness, and
Constancy. His virtues were his arts. In opposition,
he respected the principles of government. In
administration, he provided for the liberties of the
people. He employed his moments of power in
realising every thing which he had proposed in a
popular situation; the distinguishing mark of his

publick conduct. Reserved in profession, sure in
performance, he laid the foundation of a solid
confidence.

He far exceeded all other statesmen in the art
of drawing together, without the seduction of
self-interest, the concurrence and co-operation of
various dispositions and abilities of men, whom he
assimilated to his character, and associated in his
labours: for it was his aim through his life to convert
party connexion, and personal friendship, (which
others had rendered subservient only to temporary
views, and the purposes of ambition) into a lasting
depository for his principles; that their energy should not
depend upon his life, nor fluctuate with the intrigues of a
court, or with capricious fashions among the people; but
that by securing a succession in support of his maxims, the
British constitution might be preserved, according to its true
genius, on antient foundations, and institutions of tried utility.

The virtues of his private life, and those which he exerted in
the service of the state, were not, in him, seperate principles.
His private virtues, without any change in their character,
expanded with the occasion into enlarged publick affections.
The very same tender, benevolent, feeling, liberal mind, which,
in the internal relations of life, conciliated the genuine love
of those who see men as they are, rendered him an inflexible
Patriot. He was devoted to the cause of Freedom, not because
he was haughty and intractable, but because he was
beneficent and humane.

A sober, unaffected, unpresuming piety, the basis of all
sure morality, gave truth and permanence to his Virtues.

He died at a fortunate time, before he could feel, by a decisive
proof, that virtue like his must be nourished from his own
substance only, and cannot be assured of any external support.

Let his successors, who daily behold this monument,
consider that it was not built to entertain the eye, but to
instruct the mind. Let them reflect, that their conduct
will make it their Glory, or their Reproach. Let them feel,
that similarity of Manners, not proximity of Blood, gives
them an interest in this Statue.

REMEMBER. RESEMBLE. PERSEVERE.

ANGELS, whose guardian care is ENGLAND, spread
Your shadowing wings o'er Patriot WENTWORTH dead:
With sacred awe his hallow'd ashes keep,
Where Commerce, Science, Honor, Friendship weep,
The pious Heir, the deeply sorrowing Wife,
All the soft ties which bless'd his virtuous life.
Gentle, Intrepid, Generous, Mild, & Just:
These heartfelt titles grac'd his honor'd dust.
No fields of blood, by laurels ill repaid,
No plunder'd provinces disturb his shade:
But white-rob'd Peace compos'd his closing eyes,
And join'd with soft Humanity her sighs:
They mourn their Patron gone, their Friend no more,
And ENGLAND'S tears his short-liv'd power deplore.

SPEECH ON THE REFORM OF THE REPRESENTATION OF THE COMMONS IN PARLIAMENT

16 JUNE 1784

MR. SPEAKER,

WE HAVE NOW discovered, at the close of the eighteenth century, that the constitution of England, which for a series of ages had been the proud distinction of this country, always the admiration, and sometimes the envy, of the wise and learned in every other Nation, – we have discovered, that this boasted constitution, in the most boasted part of it, is a gross imposition upon the understanding of mankind, an insult to their feelings, and acting by contrivances destructive to the best and most valuable interests of the people. Our political architects have taken a survey of the fabric of the British constitution. It is singular that they report nothing against the Crown, nothing against the Lords; but in the House of Commons everything is unsound; it is ruinous in every part. It is infested by the dry rot, and ready to tumble about our ears without their immediate help. You know by the faults they find what are their ideas of the alteration. As all government stands upon opinion, they know that the way utterly to destroy it is to remove that opinion, to take away all reverence, all confidence from it; and then, at the first blast of publick discontent and popular tumult, it tumbles to the ground.

In considering this question, they who oppose it oppose it on different grounds: one is in the nature of a previous question; that some alterations may be expedient, but that this is not the time for making them. The other is, that no essential alterations are at all wanting: and that neither *now* nor at *any* time is it prudent or safe to be meddling with the fundamental principles, and ancient tried usages of our constitution – that our representation is as nearly perfect as the necessary imperfection of human affairs and of human creatures will suffer it to be; and that it is a subject of prudent and honest use and thankful enjoyment, and not of captious criticism and rash experiment.

On the other side, there are two parties who proceed on two grounds, in my opinion, as they state them, utterly irreconcileable. The one is juridical, the other political. The one is in the nature of a claim of right, on the supposed rights of man as man; this party desire the decision of a suit. The other ground, as far as I can divine what it directly means, is, that the representation is not so politically framed as to answer the theory of its institution. As to the claim of *right,* the meanest petitioner, the most gross and ignorant, is as good as the best; in some respects his claim is more favourable on account of his ignorance; his weakness, his poverty, and distress, only add to his titles; he sues in *forma pauperis;*[1] he ought to be a favourite of the court. But when the *other* ground is taken, when the question is political, when a new constitution is to be made on a sound theory of government, then the presumptuous pride of didactic ignorance is to be excluded from the counsel in this high and arduous matter, which often bids defiance to the experience of the wisest. The first claims a personal representation, the latter rejects it with scorn and fervour. The language of the first party is plain and intelligible; they who plead an absolute right cannot be satisfied with anything short of personal representation, because all *natural* rights must be the rights of individuals; as by *nature* there is no such thing as politic or corporate personality; all these ideas are mere fictions of law, they are creatures of voluntary institution; men as men are individuals, and nothing else. They, therefore, who reject the principle of natural and personal representation, are essentially and eternally at variance with those, who claim it. As to the first sort of reformers, it is ridiculous to talk to them of the British constitution upon any or upon all of its bases; for they lay it down that every man ought to govern himself, and that where he cannot go himself he must send his representative; that all other government is usurpation; and is so far from having a claim to our obedience, it is not only our right, but our duty, to resist it. Nine-tenths of the reformers argue thus, that is, on the natural right. It is impossible not to make some reflection on the nature of this claim, or avoid a comparison between the extent of the principle and the present object of the demand. If this claim be founded, it is clear to what it goes. The House of Commons, in that light, undoubtedly is no representative of the people, as a collection of individuals. Nobody pretends it, nobody can justify such an assertion. When you come to examine into this claim of right, founded on the right of self-government in each individual, you find the thing demanded infinitely short of the principle of the demand. What! one *third* only of the legislature,[2] and of the government no share at all? What sort of treaty of partition is this for those who have an inherent right to the whole? Give them all they ask, and your grant is still a cheat; for how comes only a third to be their younger children's fortune in this settlement? How came they neither to have the choice of kings, or lords, or judges, or generals, or admirals, or bishops, or priests, or ministers, or justices of peace? Why, what have you to answer in favour of the prior rights of the Crown and peerage but this – Our constitution is a prescriptive constitution; it is a constitution whose sole authority is that it has existed time out of mind. It is settled in these *two* portions against one, legislatively; and in the whole of the judicature, the whole of the federal capacity, of the executive, the prudential, and the financial administration, in one alone. Nor was your House of Lords and the prerogatives of the Crown settled on any adjudication in favour of natural rights, for they could never be so partitioned. Your king, your lords, your judges, your juries, grand and little, all are prescriptive; and what proves it is the disputes not yet concluded, and never near becoming so, when any of them first originated. Prescription[3] is the most solid of all titles, not only to property, but, which is to secure that property, to government. They harmonise with each other, and give mutual aid to one another. It is accompanied with another ground of authority in the constitution of the human mind, – presumption. It is a presumption in favour of any settled scheme of government against any untried project, that a nation has long existed and flourished under it. It is a better presumption even of the *choice* of a nation, far better than any sudden and temporary arrangement by actual election. Because a nation is not an idea only of local extent, and individual momentary aggregation; but it is an idea of continuity, which extends in time as well as in numbers and in space. And this is a choice not of one day, or one set of people, not a tumultuary and giddy choice; it is a deliberate election of ages and of generations; it is a constitution made by what is ten thousand times better than choice, it is made by the peculiar circumstances, occasions, tempers, dispositions, and moral, civil, and social habitudes of the people, which disclose themselves only in a long space of time. It is a vestment, which accommodates itself to the body. Nor is prescription of government formed upon blind, unmeaning prejudices – for man is a most unwise and a most wise being. The individual is foolish;

the multitude, for the moment, is foolish, when they act without deliberation; but the species is wise, and, when time is given to it, as a species it almost always acts right.

The reason for the Crown as it is, for the Lords as they are, is my reason for the Commons as they are, the electors as they are. Now, if the Crown and the Lords, and the Judicatures, are all prescriptive, so is the House of Commons of the very same origin and of no other. We and our electors have their powers and privileges both made and circumscribed by prescription, as much to the full as the other parts; and as such we have always claimed them, and on no other title. The House of Commons is a legislative body corporate by prescription, not made upon any given theory, but existing prescriptively – just like the rest. This prescription has made it essentially what it is, – an aggregate collection of three parts, knights, citizens, burgesses. The question is whether this has been always so, since the House of Commons has taken its present shape and circumstances, and has been an essential operative part of the constitution; which, I take it, it has been for at least five hundred years.

This I resolve to myself in the affirmative: and then another question arises, whether this House stands firm upon its ancient foundations, and is not, by time and accidents, so declined from its perpendicular, as to want the hand of the wise and experienced architects of the day to set it upright again, and to prop and buttress it up for duration; – whether it continues true to the principles upon which it has hitherto stood; – whether this be *de facto* the constitution of the House of Commons, as it has been since the time that the House of Commons has, without dispute, become a necessary and an efficient part of the British constitution? To ask whether a thing which has always been the same stands to its usual principle, seems to me to be perfectly absurd; for how do you know the principles but from the construction? and if that remains the same, the principles remain the same. It is true, that to say your constitution is what it has been is no sufficient defence for those who say it is a bad constitution. It is an answer to those who say that it is a degenerate constitution. To those who say it is a bad one I answer, look to its effects. In all moral machinery the moral results are its test.

On what grounds do we go to restore our constitution to what it has been at one given period, or to reform and reconstruct it upon principles more conformable to a sound theory of government? A prescriptive government, such as ours, never was the work of any legislator, never was made upon any foregone theory. It seems to me a preposterous way of reasoning, and a perfect confusion of ideas, to take the theories which learned and speculative men have made from that government, and then, supposing it made on those theories, which were made from it, to accuse the government as not corresponding with them. I do not vilify theory and speculation – no, because that would be to vilify reason itself. *Neque decipitur ratio, neque decipit unquam.*[4] No; whenever I speak against theory, I mean always a weak, erroneous, fallacious, unfounded, or imperfect theory; and one of the ways of discovering that it is a false theory is by comparing it with practice. This is the true touchstone of all theories which regard man and the affairs of men – does it suit his nature in general – does it suit his nature as modified by his habits?

The more frequently this affair is discussed, the stronger the case appears to the sense and the feelings of mankind. I have no more doubt than I entertain of my existence that this very thing, which is stated as a horrible thing, is the means of the preservation of our constitution whilst it lasts; of curing it of many of the disorders which, attending every species of institution, would attend the principle of an exact local representation, or a representation on the principle of numbers. If you reject personal representation, you are pushed upon expedience; and then what they wish us to do is to prefer their speculations on that subject to the happy experience of this country of a growing liberty and a growing prosperity for five hundred years. Whatever respect I have for their talents, this, for one, I will not do. Then what is the standard of expedience? Expedience is that which is good for the community, and good for every individual in it. Now this expedience is the *desideratum* to be sought either without the experience of means or with that experience. If without, as in case of the fabrication of a new commonwealth, I will hear the learned arguing what promises to be expedient: but if we are to judge of a commonwealth actually existing, the first thing I inquire is, what has been *found* expedient or inexpedient? And I will not take their *promise* rather than the *performance* of the constitution.

* * *[5] But no, this was not the cause of the discontents. I went through most of the northern parts – the Yorkshire election was then raging; the year before, through most of the western counties – Bath, Bristol, Gloucester; – not one word, either in

the towns or country, on the subject of representation; much on the receipt tax, something on Mr. Fox's ambition;[6] much greater apprehension of danger from thence than from want of representation. One would think that the ballast of the ship was shifted with us, and that our constitution had the gunnel under water. But can you fairly and distinctly point out what one evil or grievance has happened which you can refer to the representative not following the opinion of his constituents? What one symptom do we find of this inequality? But it is not an arithmetical inequality with which we ought to trouble ourselves. If there be a moral, a political equality, this is the *desideratum* in our constitution, and in every constitution in the world. Moral inequality is as between places and between classes. Now, I ask, what advantage do you find that the places which abound in representation possess over others, in which it is more scanty, in security for freedom, in security for justice, or in any one of those means of procuring temporal prosperity and eternal happiness, the ends for which society was formed? Are the local interests of Cornwall and Wiltshire, for instance, their roads, canals, their prisons, their police, better than Yorkshire, Warwickshire, or Staffordshire? Warwick has members; is Warwick, or Stafford, more opulent, happy, or free than Newcastle, or than Birmingham? Is Wiltshire the pampered favourite, whilst Yorkshire, like the child of a bond-woman, is turned out to the desert? This is like the unhappy persons who live, if they can be said to live, in the statical chair;[7] who are ever feeling their pulse, and who do not judge of health by the aptitude of the body to perform its functions, but by their ideas of what ought to be the true balance between the several secretions. Is a committee of Cornwall, &c. thronged, and the others deserted? No. You have an equal representation, because you have men equally interested in the prosperity of the whole who are involved in the general interest and the general sympathy; and, perhaps, these places, furnishing a superfluity of public agents and administrators, (whether in strictness they are representatives or not I do not mean to inquire, but they are agents and administrators,) will stand clearer of local interests, passions, prejudices, and cabals, than the others, and therefore preserve the balance of the parts, and with a more general view, and a more steady hand, than the rest. * * * * *

In every political proposal we must not leave out of the question the political views and object of the proposer; and these we discover, not by what he says, but by the principles he lays down. I mean, says he, a moderate and temperate reform; that is, I mean to do as little good as possible. If the constitution be what you represent it, and there be no danger in the change, you do wrong not to make the reform commensurate to the abuse. Fine reformer indeed! generous donor! What is the cause of this parsimony of the liberty which you dole out to the people? Why all this limitation in giving blessings and benefits to mankind? You admit that there is an extreme in liberty, which may be infinitely noxious to those who are to receive it, and which in the end will leave them no liberty at all. I think so too; they know it, and they feel it. The question is, then, what is the standard of that extreme? What that gentleman, and the associations,[8] or some parts of their phalanxes, think proper? Then our liberties are in their pleasure; it depends on their arbitrary will how far I shall be free. I will have none of that freedom. If, therefore, the standard of moderation be sought for, I will seek for it. Where? Not in their fancies, nor in my own; I will seek for it where I know it is to be found, – in the constitution I actually enjoy. Here it says to an encroaching prerogative, – Your sceptre has its length, you cannot add a hair to your head, or a gem to your crown, but what an eternal law has given to it. Here it says to an overweening peerage, – Your pride finds banks that it cannot overflow: here to a tumultuous and giddy people, – There is a bound to the raging of the sea. Our constitution is like our island, which uses and restrains its subject sea; in vain the waves roar. In that constitution I know, and exultingly I feel, both that I am free and that I am not free dangerously to myself or to others. I know that no power on earth, acting as I ought to do, can touch my life, my liberty, or my property. I have that inward and dignified consciousness of my own security and independence which constitutes, and is the only thing which does constitute, the proud and comfortable sentiment of freedom in the human breast. I know too, and I bless God for, my safe mediocrity; I know that if I possessed all the talents of the gentlemen on the side of the House I sit and on the other, I cannot by royal favour, or by popular delusion, or by oligarchical cabal, elevate myself above a certain very limited point, so as to endanger my own fall, or the ruin of my country. I know there is an order that keeps things fast in their place; it is made to us, and we are made to it. Why not ask another wife, other children, another body, another mind?

The great object of most of these reformers is to prepare the destruction of the constitution by disgracing and discrediting the House of Commons. For they think, prudently in my opinion, that if they can persuade the nation that the House of Commons is so constituted as not to secure the public liberty; not to have a proper connexion with the public interests; so constituted as not either actually or virtually to be the representative of the people; it will be easy to prove, that a government composed of a monarchy, an oligarchy chosen by the Crown, and such a House of Commons, – whatever good can be in such a system can by no means be a system of free government.

The constitution of England is never to have a quietus; it is to be continually vilified, attacked, reproached, resisted. Instead of being the hope and sure anchor in all storms, instead of being the means of redress to all grievances, itself is the grand grievance of the nation, our shame instead of our glory. If the only specific plan proposed, – individual personal representation, – is directly rejected by the person who is looked on as the great support of this business, then the only way of considering it is a question of convenience. An honourable gentleman prefers the individual to the present. He therefore himself sees no middle term whatsoever, and therefore prefers of what he sees, the individual; this is the only thing distinct and sensible that has been advocated. He has, then, a scheme, which is the individual representation; he is not at a loss, not inconsistent, – which scheme the other right honourable gentleman reprobates. Now what does this go to, but to lead directly to anarchy? For to discredit the only government which he either possesses or can project, what is this but to destroy all government? and this is anarchy. My right honourable friend, in supporting this motion, disgraces his friends and justifies his enemies, in order to blacken the constitution of his country, even of that House of Commons which supported him. There is a difference between a moral or political exposure of a public evil, relative to the administration of government, whether in men or systems, and a declaration of defects, real or supposed, in the fundamental constitution of your country. The first may be cured in the individual by the motives of religion, virtue, honour, fear, shame, or interest. Men may be made to abandon also false systems, by exposing their absurdity or mischievous tendency to their own better thoughts, or to the contempt or indignation of the public; and after all, if they should exist, and exist uncorrected, they only disgrace individuals as fugitive opinions. But it is quite otherwise with the frame and constitution of the state; if that is disgraced, patriotism is destroyed in its very source. No man has ever willingly obeyed, much less was desirous of defending with his blood, a mischievous and absurd scheme of government. Our first, our dearest, most comprehensive relation, our country, is gone.

It suggests melancholy reflections, in consequence of the strange course we have long held, that we are now no longer quarrelling about the character or about the conduct of men, or the tenor of measures; but we are grown out of humour with the English constitution itself; this is become the object of the animosity of Englishmen. This constitution in former days used to be the admiration and the envy of the world; it was the pattern for politicians; the theme of the eloquent; the meditation of the philosopher in every part of the world. As to Englishmen, it was their pride, their consolation. By it they lived, for it they were ready to die. Its defects, if it had any, were partly covered by partiality, and partly borne by prudence. Now all its excellencies are forgot, its faults are now forcibly dragged into day, exaggerated by every artifice of representation. It is despised and rejected of men; and every device and invention of ingenuity, or idleness, set up in opposition or in preference to it. It is to this humour, and it is to the measures growing out of it, that I set myself (I hope not alone) in the most determined opposition. Never before did we at any time in this country meet upon the theory of our frame of government, to sit in judgment on the constitution of our country, to call it as a delinquent before us, and to accuse it of every defect and every vice; to see whether it, an object of our veneration, even our adoration, did or did not accord with a pre-conceived scheme in the minds of certain gentlemen. Cast your eyes on the journals of parliament. It is for fear of losing the inestimable treasure we have, that I do not venture to game it out of my hands for the vain hope of improving it. I look with filial reverence on the constitution of my country, and never will cut it in pieces, and put it into the kettle of any magician, in order to boil it, with the puddle of their compounds, into youth and vigour. On the contrary, I will drive away such pretenders; I will nurse its venerable age, and with lenient arts extend a parent's breath.

From SPEECH IN OPENING THE IMPEACHMENT OF WARREN HASTINGS

MY LORDS,

THE GENTLEMEN WHO have it in command to support the impeachment against Mr. Hastings,[1] have directed me to open the cause with a general view of the grounds upon which the Commons have proceeded in their charge against him. They have directed me to accompany this with another general view of the extent, the magnitude, the nature, the tendency, and the effect of the crimes which they allege to have been by him committed. They have also directed me to give an explanation (with their aid I may be enabled to give it) of such circumstances preceding the crimes charged on Mr. Hastings, or concomitant with them, as may tend to elucidate whatever may be found obscure in the articles as they stand. To these they wished me to add a few illustrative remarks on the laws, customs, opinions, and manners of the people concerned, and who are the objects of the crimes we charge on Mr. Hastings.

The several articles, as they appear before you, will be opened by other gentlemen with more particularity, with more distinctness, and, without doubt, with infinitely more ability, when they come to apply the evidence which naturally belongs to each article of this accusation. This, my lords, is the plan which we mean to pursue on the great charge which is now to abide your judgment.

My lords, I must look upon it as an auspicious circumstance to this cause, in which the honour of the kingdom and the fate of many nations are involved, that, from the first commencement of our parliamentary process to this the hour of solemn trial, not the smallest difference of opinion has arisen between the two Houses.

My lords, there are persons who, looking rather upon what was to be found in our records and histories than what was to be expected from the public justice, had formed hopes consolatory to themselves and dishonourable to us. They flattered themselves that the corruptions of India would escape amidst the dissensions of parliament. They are disappointed. They will be disappointed in all the rest of their expectations, which they have formed upon everything except the merits of their cause. The Commons will not have the melancholy unsocial glory of having acted a solitary part in a noble but imperfect work. What the greatest inquest of the nation has begun, its highest tribunal will accomplish. At length justice will be done to India. It is true that your lordships will have your full share in this great achievement; but the Commons have always considered, that whatever honour is divided with you is doubled on themselves.

My lords, I must confess, that amidst these encouraging prospects the Commons do not approach your bar without awe and anxiety. The magnitude of the interests which we have in charge will reconcile some degree of solicitude for the event with the undoubting confidence with which we repose ourselves upon your lordships' justice. For we are men, my lords; and men are so made, that it is not only the greatness of danger, but the value of the adventure, which measures the degree of our concern in every undertaking. I solemnly assure your lordships, that no standard is sufficient to estimate the value which the Commons set upon the event of the cause they now bring before you. My lords, the business of this day is not the business of this man – it is not solely whether the prisoner at the bar be found innocent or guilty; but whether millions of mankind shall be made miserable or happy.

Your lordships will see in the progress of this cause, that there is not only a long-connected, systematic series of misdemeanours, but an equally connected system of maxims and principles invented to justify them. Upon both of these you must judge. According to the judgment that you shall give upon the past transactions in India, inseparably connected as they are with the principles which support them, the whole character of your future government in that distant empire is to be unalterably decided. It will take its perpetual tenour, it will receive its final impression, from the stamp of this very hour.

It is not only the interest of India, now the most considerable part of the British empire, which is concerned, but the credit and honour of the British nation itself will be decided by this decision. We are to decide by this judgment, whether the crimes of individuals are to be turned into public guilt and national ignominy; or whether this nation will convert the very offences which have thrown a transient shade upon its government, into something that will reflect a permanent lustre upon the honour, justice, and humanity of this kingdom.

My lords, there is another consideration, which augments the solicitude of the Commons, equal to those other two great interests I have stated, those of our empire and our national character; something that, if possible, comes more home to the hearts and feelings of every Englishman: I mean, the interests of our constitution itself, which is deeply involved in the event of this cause. The future use, and the whole effect, if not the very existence, of the process of an impeachment of high crimes and misdemeanours before the peers of this kingdom, upon the charge of the Commons, will very much be decided by your judgment in this cause. This tribunal will be found (I hope it will always be found) too great for petty causes; if it should at the same time be found incompetent to one of the greatest, – that is, if little offences, from their minuteness, escape you, and the greatest, from their magnitude, oppress you, – it is impossible that this form of trial should not, in the end, vanish out of the constitution. For we must not deceive ourselves; whatever does not stand with credit cannot stand long. And if the constitution should be deprived, I do not mean in form, but virtually, of this resource, it is virtually deprived of everything else that is valuable in it. For this process is the cement which binds the whole together; this is the individuating principle, that makes England what England is. In this court it is, that no subject, in no part of the empire, can fail of competent and proportionable justice: here it is that we provide for that which is the substantial excellence of our constitution; I mean, the great circulation of responsibility, by which (excepting the supreme power) no man, in no circumstance, can escape the account which he owes to the laws of his country. It is by this process that magistracy, which tries and controls all other things, is itself tried and controlled. Other constitutions are satisfied with making good subjects; this is a security for good governors. It is by this tribunal that statesmen who abuse their power, are accused by statesmen, and tried by statesmen, not upon the niceties of a narrow jurisprudence, but upon the enlarged and solid principles of state morality. It is here that those who by the abuse of power have violated the spirit of law, can never hope for protection from any of its forms: – it is here that those who have refused to conform themselves to its perfections, can never hope to escape through any of its defects. It ought, therefore, my lords, to become our common care to guard this your precious deposit, rare in its use, but powerful in its effect, with a religious vigilance, and never to suffer it to be either discredited or antiquated. For this great end your lordships are invested with great and plenary powers: but you do not suspend, you do not supersede, you do not annihilate, any subordinate jurisdiction; on the contrary, you are auxiliary and supplemental to them all.

Whether it is owing to the felicity of our times, less fertile in great offences than those which have gone before us, or whether it is from a sluggish apathy which has dulled and enervated the public justice, I am not called upon to determine; but, whatever may be the cause, it is now sixty-three years since any impeachment, grounded upon abuse of authority and misdemeanour in office, has come before this tribunal. The last is that of Lord Macclesfield,[2] which happened in the year 1725. So that the oldest process known to the constitution of this country has, upon its revival, some appearance of novelty. At this time, when all Europe is in a state of, perhaps, contagious fermentation, – when antiquity has lost all its reverence and all its effect on the minds of men, at the same time that novelty is still attended with the suspicions that always will be attached to whatever is new, – we have been anxiously careful, in a business which seems to combine the objections both to what is antiquated and what is novel, so to conduct ourselves that nothing in the revival of this great parliamentary process shall afford a pretext for its future disuse.

My lords, strongly impressed as they are with these sentiments, the Commons have conducted themselves with singular care and caution. Without losing the spirit and zeal of a public prosecution, they have comported themselves with such moderation, temper, and decorum, as would not have ill become the final judgment, if with them rested the final judgment, of this great cause.

With very few intermissions, the affairs of India have constantly engaged the attention of the Commons for more than fourteen years. We may safely affirm, we have tried every mode of legislative provision, before we had recourse to anything of penal process. It was in the year 1774 we framed an act of parliament for remedy to the then existing disorders in India, such as the then information before us enabled us to enact. Finding that the act of parliament did not answer all the ends that were expected from it, we had, in the year 1782, recourse to a body of monitory resolutions. Neither had we the expected fruit from them. When, therefore, we found that our inquiries and our reports, our laws and our admonitions, were alike despised; that enormities increased in proportion as they were forbidden, detected, and exposed; when we found that guilt stalked with an erect and upright front, and that legal authority seemed to skulk and hide its head like outlawed guilt; when we found that some of those very persons who were appointed by parliament to assert the authority of the laws of this kingdom, were the most forward, the most bold, and the most active in the conspiracy for their destruction; then it was time for the justice of the nation to recollect itself. To have forborne longer would not have been patience, but collusion; it would have been participation with guilt; it would have been to make ourselves accomplices with the criminal.

We found it was impossible to evade painful duty without betraying a sacred trust. Having, therefore, resolved upon the last and only resource, a penal prosecution, it was our next business to act in a manner worthy of our long deliberation. In all points we proceeded with selection. We have chosen (we trust it will so appear to your lordships) such a cime, and such a criminal, and such a body of evidence, and such a mode of process, as would have recommended this course of justice to posterity, even if it had not been supported by an example in the practice of our forefathers.

First, to speak of the process: we are to inform your lordships, that, besides that long previous deliberation of fourteen years, we examined, as a preliminary to this proceeding, every circumstance which could prove favourable to parties apparently delinquent, before we finally resolved to prosecute. There was no precedent to be found in the journals, favourable to persons in Mr. Hastings's circumstances, that was not applied to. Many measures utterly unknown to former parliamentary proceedings, and which, indeed, seemed in some degree to enfeeble them, but which were all to the advantage of those that were to be prosecuted, were adopted, for the first time, upon this occasion. – In an early stage of the proceeding, the criminal desired to be heard. He was heard; and he produced before the bar of the House that insolent and unbecoming paper which lies upon our table. It was deliberately given in by his own hand, and signed with his own name. The Commons, however, passed by everything offensive in that paper with a magnanimity that became them. They considered nothing in it but the facts that the defendant alleged, and the principles he maintained; and after a deliberation, not short of judicial, we proceeded with confidence to your bar.

So far as to the process; which, though I mentioned last in the line and order in which I stated the objects of our selection, I thought it best to despatch first.

As to the crime which we chose, we first considered well what it was in its nature, under all the circumstances which attended it. We weighed it with all its extenuations, and with all its aggravations. On that review we are warranted to assert, that the crimes with which we charge the prisoner at the bar are substantial crimes; that they are no errors or mistakes, such as wise and good men might possibly fall into; which may even produce very pernicious effects, without being in fact great offences. The Commons are too liberal not to allow for the difficulties of a great and arduous public situation. They know too well the domineering neccessities, which frequently occur in all great affairs. They know the exigency of a pressing occasion, which in its precipitate career bears everything down before it, which does not give time to the mind to recollect its faculties, to reinforce its reason, and to have recourse to fixed principles, but, by compelling an instant and tumultuous decision, too often obliges men to decide in a manner that calm judgment would certainly have rejected. We know, as we are to be served by men, that the persons who serve us must be tried as men, and with a very large allowance indeed to human infirmity and human error. This, my lords, we knew, and we weighed before we came before you. But the crimes which we charge in these articles, are not lapses, defects, errors, of common human frailty, which, as we know and feel, we can allow for. We charge this offender with no crimes that have not arisen from passions which it is criminal to harbour; with no offences that have not their root in avarice, rapacity, pride, insolence, ferocity, treachery, cruelty, malignity of temper; in short, in nothing that does not argue a total extinction of all moral principle, that does not manifest an inveterate blackness of heart, died in grain with malice, vitiated, corrupted, gangrened to the very core. If we do not plant his crimes in those vices which the breast of man is made to abhor, and the spirit of all laws human and divine to interdict, we desire no longer to be heard upon this occasion. Let everything that can be pleaded on the ground of surprise or error, upon those grounds be pleaded with success: we give up the whole of those predicaments. We urge no crimes that were not crimes of forethought. We charge him with nothing that he did not commit upon deliberation; that he did not commit against advice, supplication, and remonstrance; that he did not commit against the direct command of lawful authority; that he did not commit after reproof and reprimand, the reproof and reprimand of those who are authorised by the laws to reprove and reprimand him. The crimes of Mr. Hastings are crimes not only in themselves, but aggravated by being crimes of contumacy. They were crimes not against forms, but against those eternal laws of justice, which are our rule and our birthright. His offences are, not in formal, technical language, but in reality, in substance, and effect, *high* crimes and high misdemeanours.

So far as to the crimes. As to the criminal, we have chosen him on the same principle on which we selected the crimes. We have not chosen to bring before you a poor, puny, trembling delinquent, misled, perhaps, by those who ought to have taught him better, but who have afterwards oppressed him by their power, as they had first corrupted him by their example. Instances there have been many, wherein the punishment of minor offences, in inferior persons, has been made the means of screening crimes of a high order, and in men of high description. Our course is different. We have not brought before you an obscure offender, who, when his insignificance and weakness are weighed against the power of the prosecution, gives even to public justice something of the appearance of oppression; no, my lords, we have brought before you the first man of India in rank, authority, and station. We have brought before you the chief of the tribe, the head of the whole body of eastern offenders; a captain-general of iniquity, under whom all the fraud, all the peculation, all the tyranny, in India, are embodied, disciplined, arrayed, and paid. This is the person, my lords, that we bring before you. We have brought before you such a person, that, if you strike at him with the firm and decided arm of justice, you will not have need of a great many more examples. You strike at the whole corps, if you strike at the head.

So far as to the crime: so far as to the criminal. Now, my lords, I shall say a few words relative to the evidence which we have brought to support such a charge, and which ought to be equal in weight to the charge itself. It is chiefly evidence of record, officially signed by the criminal himself in many instances. We have brought before you his own letters, authenticated by his own hand. On these we chiefly rely. But we shall likewise bring before you living witnesses, competent to speak to the points to which they are brought.

When you consider the late enormous power of the prisoner; when you consider his criminal, indefatigable assiduity in the destruction of all recorded evidence; when you consider the influence he has over almost all living testimony; when you consider the distance of the scene of action, – I believe your lordships, and I believe the world, will be astonished that so much, so clear, so solid, and so conclusive evidence of all kinds has been obtained against him. I have no doubt that in nine instances in ten the evidence is such as would satisfy the narrow precision supposed to prevail, and to a degree rightly to prevail, in all subordinate power and delegated jurisdiction. But your lordships will maintain, what we assert and claim as the right of the subjects of Great Britain, – that you are not bound by any rules of evidence, or any other rules whatever, except those of natural, immutable, and substantial justice.

God forbid the Commons should desire that anything should be received as proof from them, which is not by nature adapted to prove the thing in question. If they should make such a request, they would aim at overturning the very principles of that justice to which they resort. They would give the nation an evil example, that would rebound back on themselves, and bring destruction upon their own heads, and on those of all their posterity.

On the other hand, I have too much confidence in the learning with which you will be advised, and the liberality and nobleness of the sentiments with which you are born, to suspect that you would, by any abuse of the forms, and a technical course of proceeding, deny justice to so great a part of the world that claims it at your hands. Your lordships always had an ample power, and almost unlimited jurisdiction; you have now a boundless object. It is not from this district, or from that parish, not from this city, or the other province, that relief is now applied for: exiled and undone princes, extensive tribes, suffering nations, infinite descriptions of men, different in language, in manners, and in rites – men, separated by every barrier of nature from you, by the providence of God are blended in one common cause, and are now become suppliants at your bar. For the honour of this nation, in vindication of this mysterious providence, let it be known that no rule formed upon municipal maxims (if any such rule exists) will prevent the course of that imperial justice which you owe to the people that call to you from all parts of a great disjointed world. For, situated as this kingdom is, an object, thank God, of envy to the rest of the nations; its conduct in that high and elevated situation will undoubtedly be scrutinised with a severity as great as its power is invidious.

It is well known, that enormous wealth has poured into this country from India through a thousand channels, public and concealed; and it is no particular derogation from our honour to suppose a possibility of being corrupted by that by which other empires have been corrupted, and assemblies almost as respectable and venerable as your lordships have been directly or indirectly vitiated. Forty millions of money at least have within our memory been brought from India into England. In this case the most sacred judicature ought to look to its reputation. Without offence we may venture to suggest, that the best way to secure reputation is not by a proud defiance of public opinion, but by guiding our actions in such a manner as that public opinion may in the end be securely defied by having been previously respected and dreaded. No direct false judgment is apprehended from the tribunals of this country. But it is feared that partiality may lurk and nestle in the abuse of our forms of proceeding. It is necessary, therefore, that nothing in that proceeding should appear to mark the slightest trace, should betray the faintest odour, of chicane. God forbid that when you try the most serious of all causes, that when you try the cause of Asia in the presence of Europe, there should be the least suspicion that a narrow partiality utterly destructive of justice should so guide us, that a British subject in power should appear in substance to possess rights which are denied to the humble allies, to the attached dependants of this kingdom, who by their distance have a double demand upon your protection, and who by an implicit (I hope not a weak and useless) trust in you have stripped themselves of every other resource under heaven.

I do not say this from any fear, doubt, or hesitation, concerning what your lordships will finally do — none in the world; but I cannot shut my ears to the rumours which you all know to be disseminated abroad. The abusers of power may have a chance to cover themselves by those fences and intrenchments which

were made to secure the liberties of the people against men of
that very description. But God forbid it should be bruited from
Pekin to Paris, that the laws of England are for the rich and the
powerful, but to the poor, the miserable, and defenceless they
afford no resource at all. God forbid it should be said, no nation
is equal to the English in *substantial* violence and in *formal* justice,
– that in this kingdom we feel ourselves competent to confer the
most extravagant and inordinate powers upon public ministers,
but that we are deficient, poor, helpless, lame, and impotent in
the means of calling them to account for their use of them. An
opinion has been insidiously circulated through this kingdom,
and through foreign nations too, that in order to cover our
participation in guilt, and our common interest in the plunder
of the East, we have invented a set of scholastic distinctions,
abhorrent to the common sense and unpropitious to the common
necessities of mankind, by which we are to deny ourselves the
knowledge of what the rest of the world knows, and what so
great a part of the world both knows and feels. I do not deprecate
any appearance which may give countenance to this aspersion
from suspicion that any corrupt motive can influence this court;
I deprecate it from knowing that hitherto we have moved within
the narrow circle of municipal justice. I am afraid that, from the
habits acquired by moving within a circumscribed sphere, we
may be induced rather to endeavour at forcing nature into that
municipal circle, than to enlarge the circle of national justice to
the necessities of the empire we have obtained.

This is the only thing which does create any doubt or difficulty
in the minds of sober people. But there are those who will not
judge so equitably. Where two motives, neither of them perfectly
justifiable, may be assigned, the worst has the chance of being
preferred. If, from any appearance of chicane in the court, justice
should fail, all men will say, better there were no tribunals at all.
In my humble opinion, it would be better a thousand times to
give all complainants the short answer the Dey of Algiers[3] gave
a British ambassador representing certain grievances suffered by
the British merchants, – "My friend" (as the story is related
by Dr. Shawe),[4] "do not you know that my subjects are a band of
robbers, and that I am their captain?" – better it would be a
thousand times, and a thousand thousand times more manly, than
a hypocritical process, which, under a pretended reverence to
punctilious ceremonies and observances of law, abandons

mankind, without help and resource, to all the desolating consequences of arbitrary power. The conduct and event of this
cause will put an end to such doubts, wherever they may be
entertained. Your lordships will exercise the great plenary powers
with which you are invested in a manner that will do honour
to the protecting justice of this kingdom, that will completely
avenge the great people who are subjected to it. You will not
suffer your proceedings to be squared by any rules, but by their
necessities, and by that law of a common nature which cements
them to us and us to them. The reports to the contrary have been
spread abroad with uncommon industry, but they will be speedily
refuted by the humanity, simplicity, dignity, and nobleness of
your lordships' justice.

[. . .]

19 FEBRUARY 1788[5]

MY LORDS, YOU have heard the proceedings of the court before
which Gunga Govin Sing[6] thought proper to appeal, in consequence of the power and protection of Mr. Hastings being
understood to exist after he left India, and authenticated by his
last parting deed. Your lordships will judge by that last act of
Mr. Hastings what the rest of his whole life was.

My lords, I do not mean now to go further than just to remind
your lordships of this, that Mr. Hastings's government was one
whole system of oppression, of robbery of individuals, of destruction of the public, and of supersession of the whole system
of the English government, in order to vest in the worst of the
natives all the powers that could possibly exist in any government, in order to defeat the ends which all governments ought
in common to have in view. Thus, my lords, I show you, at one
point of view, what you are to expect from him in all the rest.
I have, I think, made out as clear as can be to your lordships, so
far as it was necessary to go, that his bribery and peculation was
not occasional, but habitual; that it was not urged upon him at
the moment, but was regular and systematic. I have shown to
your lordships the operation of such a system on the revenues.

My lords, Mr. Hastings pleads one constant merit to justify
those acts; namely, that they produce an increase of the public
revenue; and accordingly he never sells to any of those wicked
agents any trusts whatever in the country, that you do not hear

that it will considerably tend to the increase of the revenue. – Your lordships will see, when he sold to wicked men the province of Bahar, in the same way in which Debi Sing had this province of Dinagepore, that consequences of a horrid and atrocious nature (though not to so great an extent) followed from it. I will just beg leave to state to your lordships, that the kingdom of Bahar is annexed to the kingdom of Bengal; that this kingdom was governed by another provincial council; that he turned out that provincial council, and sold that government to two wicked men, – one of no fortune at all, and the other of a very suspicious fortune; one a total bankrupt, the other justly excommunicated for his wickedness in his country, and then in prison for misdemeanours in a subordinate situation of government.

Mr. Hastings destroyed the council that imprisoned him, and, instead of putting one of the best and most reputable of the natives to govern it, he takes out of prison this excommunicated wretch, hated by God and man, – this bankrupt, this man of evil and desperate character, this mismanager of the public revenue in an inferior station; and, as he had given Bengal to Gunga Govin Sing,[6] he gave this province to Rajahs Kelleram and Cullian Sing.[7]

It was done upon this principle, that they would increase and very much better the revenue. These men seemed to be as strange instruments for improving a revenue as ever were chosen, I suppose, since the world began. Perhaps their merit was giving a bribe of £40,000 to Mr. Hastings. How he disposed of it I don't know. He says, I disposed of it to the public, and it was in a case of emergency. You will see in the course of this business the falsehood of that pretence; for you will see, though the obligation is given for it as a round sum of money, that the payment was not accomplished till a year after; that therefore it could not answer any immediate exigence of the Company. Did it answer in an increase of the revenue? – The very reverse. Those persons who had given this bribe of £40,000, at the end of that year were found £80,000 in debt to the Company. The Company always loses when Mr. Hastings takes a bribe; and when he proposes an increase of the revenue, the Company loses often double. But I hope and trust your lordships will consider this idea of a monstrous rise of rent, given by men of desperate fortunes and characters, to be one of the grievances, instead of one of the advantages, of this system.

It has been necessary to lay these facts before you (and I have stated them to your lordships far short of their reality, partly through my infirmity, and partly on account of the odiousness of the task of going through things that disgrace human nature), that you may be enabled fully to enter into the dreadful consequences which attend a system of bribery and corruption in a governor-general. On a transient view bribery is rather a subject of disgust than horror, – the sordid practice of a venal, mean, and abject mind; and the effect of the crime seems to end with the act. It looks to be no more than the corrupt transfer of property from one person to another; at worst a theft. But it will appear in a very different light, when you regard the consideration for which the bribe is given; namely, that a governor-general, claiming an arbitrary power in himself, for that consideration delivers up the properties, the liberties, and the lives of a whole people to the arbitrary discretion of any wicked and rapacious person, who will be sure to make good from their blood the purchase he has paid for his power over them. It is possible that a man may pay a bribe merely to redeem himself from some evil. It is bad, however, to live under a power whose violence has no restraint except in its avarice. But no man ever paid a bribe for a power to charge and tax others, but with a view to oppress them. No man ever paid a bribe for the handling of the public money, but to peculate from it. When once such offices become thus privately and corruptly venal, the very worst men will be chosen (as Mr. Hastings has in fact constantly chosen the very worst), because none but those who do not scruple the use of any means are capable, consistently with profit, to discharge at once the rigid demands of a severe public revenue and the private bribes of a rapacious chief magistrate. Not only the worst men will be thus chosen, but they will be restrained by no dread whatsoever in the execution of their worst oppressions. Their protection is sure. The authority that is to restrain, to control, to punish them, is previously engaged; he has his retaining fee for the support of their crimes. Mr. Hastings never dared, because he could not, arrest oppression in its course, without drying up the source of his own corrupt emolument. Mr. Hastings never dared, after the fact, to punish extortion in others, because he could not, without risking the discovery of bribery in himself. The same corruption, the same oppression, and the same impunity will reign through all the subordinate gradations.

A fair revenue may be collected without the aid of wicked, violent, and unjust instruments. But when once the line of just and legal demand is transgressed, such instruments are of absolute necessity; and they comport themselves accordingly. When we know that men must be well paid (and they ought to be well paid) for the performance of honourable duty, can we think that men will be found to commit wicked, rapacious, and oppressive acts with fidelity and disinterestedness, for the sole emolument of dishonest employers? No; they must have their full share of the prey, and the greater share as they are the nearer and more necessary instruments of the general extortion. We must not therefore flatter ourselves, when Mr. Hastings takes £40,000 in bribes for Dinagepore and its annexed provinces, that from the people nothing more than £40,000 is extorted. I speak within compass, four times forty must be levied on the people; and these violent sales, fraudulent purchases, confiscations, inhuman and unutterable tortures, imprisonment, irons, whips, fines, general despair, general insurrection, the massacre of the officers of revenue by the people, the massacre of the people by the soldiery, and the total waste and destruction of the finest provinces in India, are things of course, and all a necessary consequence involved in the very substance of Mr. Hastings's bribery.

I, therefore, charge Mr. Hastings with having destroyed, for private purposes, the whole system of government by the six provincial councils, which he had no right to destroy.

I charge him with having delegated to others that power which the act of parliament had directed him to preserve unalienably in himself.

I charge him with having formed a committee to be mere instruments and tools, at the enormous expense of £62,000 per annum.

I charge him with having appointed a person their dewan, to whom these Englishmen were to be subservient tools; whose name, to his own knowledge, was by the general voice of India, by the general recorded voice of the Company, by recorded official transactions, by everything that can make a man known, abhorred, and detested, stamped with infamy; and with giving him the whole power which he had thus separated from the council-general and from the provincial councils.

I charge him with taking bribes of Gunga Govin Sing.

I charge him with not having done that bribe service which fidelity even in iniquity requires at the hands of the worst of men.

I charge him with having robbed those people of whom he took the bribes.

I charge him with having fraudulently alienated the fortunes of widows.

I charge him with having, without right, title, or purchase, taken the lands of orphans, and given them to wicked persons under him.

I charge him with having removed the natural guardians of a minor Rajah, and with having given that trust to a stranger, Debi Sing,[8] whose wickedness was known to himself and all the world; and by whom the Rajah, his family and dependants were cruelly oppressed.

I charge him with having committed to the management of Debi Sing three great provinces; and thereby, with having wasted the country, ruined the landed interest, cruelly harassed the peasants, burnt their houses, seized their crops, tortured and degraded their persons, and destroyed the honour of the whole female race of that country.

In the name of the Commons of England, I charge all this villany upon Warren Hastings, in this last moment of my application to you.

My lords, what is it that we want here to a great act of national justice? Do we want a cause, my lords? You have the cause of oppressed princes, of undone women of the first rank, of desolated provinces, and of wasted kingdoms.

Do you want a criminal, my lords? When was there so much iniquity ever laid to the charge of any one? – No, my lords, you must not look to punish any other such delinquent from India. – Warren Hastings has not left substance enough in India to nourish such another delinquent.

My lords, is it a prosecutor you want? – You have before you the Commons of Great Britain as prosecutors; and, I believe, my lords, that the sun in his beneficent progress round the world does not behold a more glorious sight than that of men, separated from a remote people by the material bounds and barriers of nature, united by the bond of a social and moral community; – all the Commons of England resenting, as their own, the indignities and cruelties that are offered to all the people of India.

Do we want a tribunal? My lords, no example of antiquity, nothing in the modern world, nothing in the range of human imagination, can supply us with a tribunal like this. My lords, here we see virtually in the mind's eye that sacred majesty of the crown, under whose authority you sit, and whose power you exercise. We see in that invisible authority, what we all feel in reality and life, the beneficent powers and protecting justice of his Majesty. We have here the heir-apparent to the crown, such as the fond wishes of the people of England wish an heir-apparent of the crown to be. We have here all the branches of the royal family in a situation between majesty and subjection, between the sovereign and the subject, – offering a pledge in that situation for the support of the rights of the crown and the liberties of the people, both which extremities they touch. My lords, we have a great hereditary peerage here; those who have their own honour, the honour of their ancestors, and of their posterity, to guard; and who will justify, as they have always justified, that provision in the constitution by which justice is made an hereditary office. My lords, we have here a new nobility, who have risen and exalted themselves by various merits, by great military services, which have extended the fame of this country from the rising to the setting sun: we have those who by various civil merits and various civil talents have been exalted to a situation which they well deserve, and in which they will justify the favour of their sovereign, and the good opinion of their fellow-subjects, and make them rejoice to see those virtuous characters, that were the other day upon a level with them, now exalted above them in rank, but feeling with them in sympathy what they felt in common with them before. We have persons exalted from the practice of the law, from the place in which they administered high though subordinate justice, to a seat here, to enlighten with their knowledge and to strengthen with their votes those principles which have distinguished the courts in which they have presided.

My lords, you have here also the lights of our religion; you have the bishops of England. My lords, you have that true image of the primitive church in its ancient form, in its ancient ordinances, purified from the superstitions and the vices which a long succession of ages will bring upon the best institutions. You have the representatives of that religion which says that their God is love, that the very vital spirit of their institution is charity; a religion which so much hates oppression, that when the God whom we adore appeared in human form, he did not appear in a form of greatness and majesty, but in sympathy with the lowest of the people, – and thereby made it a firm and ruling principle, that their welfare was the object of all government; since the person, who was the Master of Nature, chose to appear himself in a subordinate situation. These are the considerations which influence them, which animate them, and will animate them, against all oppression; knowing, that He who is called first among them, and first among us all, both of the flock that is fed and of those who feed it, made Himself "the servant of all."

My lords, these are the securities which we have in all the constituent parts of the body of this House. We know them, we reckon, we rest upon them, and commit safely the interests of India and of humanity into your hands. Therefore, it is with confidence that, ordered by the Commons,

I impeach Warren Hastings, Esq., of high crimes and misdemeanours.

I impeach him in the name of the Commons of Great Britain in parliament assembled, whose parliamentary trust he has betrayed.

I impeach him in the name of all the Commons of Great Britain, whose national character he has dishonoured.

I impeach him in the name of the people in India, whose laws, rights, and liberties he has subverted, whose properties he has destroyed, whose country he has laid waste and desolate.

I impeach him in the name and by virtue of those eternal laws of justice which he has violated.

I impeach him in the name of human nature itself, which he has cruelly outraged, injured, and oppressed in both sexes, in every age, rank, situation, and condition of life.

From SPEECH ON THE SLAVE TRADE

12 MAY 1789

MR BURKE SAID, he did not mean to detain the committee[1] but for a very few minutes. He was not able, even if he had been inclined to it; but as from his other parliamentary duties he might not have it in his power to attend the business in its progress, he would take that opportunity of stating his opinion upon the subject. In the first place, he thought the House, the nation, and all Europe, under very great and serious obligations to the hon. gentleman,[2] for having brought the subject forward in a manner the most masterly, impressive, and eloquent. Principles so admirable, laid down with so much order and force, were equal to any thing he had ever heard of in modern oratory; and perhaps were not excelled by any thing to be met with in Demosthenes.[3] A trade begun with savage war, prosecuted with unheard-of cruelty, continued during the mid passage with the most loathsome imprisonment, and ending in perpetual exile and unremitting slavery, was a trade so horrid in all its circumstances, that it was impossible a single argument could be adduced in its favour. On the score of prudence nothing could be said in defence of it, nor could it be justified by necessity, and no case of inhumanity could be justified, but upon necessity; but no such necessity could be made out strong enough to bear out such a traffick. It was the duty of that House, therefore, to put an end to it. If it were said, that the interest of individuals required that it should continue, that argument ought not to be listened to. Supposing a rich man had a capital to a considerable amount lying by him, and every one, he observed, who had a large capital was a rich man; all capitals required active motion, it was their nature not to remain passive and unemployed; but if a large capital were employed in a traffic disgraceful to the nation, and shocking to humanity, it was the duty of that House to change its application, and instead of suffering it to be ill-employed, to direct it to be employed in some trade, at once advantageous in its end, respectable in its nature, and useful to mankind. Nor was it any argument to say the capital was already engaged in the slave-trade; for, from its active principle, when taken out of that trade, it would soon find employment in another channel. This had been the case with the merchants and ship-owners of Liverpool, during the American War; the African trade was then almost wholly lost, and yet the ship-owners of Liverpool had their ships employed, either as transports in the service of government, or in other ways. – After descanting on this point for some time, with great soundness of reasoning, Mr. Burke said, he could have wished that the business might have come to a conclusion at once, without voting the propositions that had been read to them. He was not over fond of abstract propositions. They were seldom necessary, and often caused great difficulty and embarrassment. There was, besides, no occasion whatever to assign detailed reasons for a vote, which, upon the face of it, sufficiently justified the House in coming to it. If the propositions should happen to be made, and not be carried in that House or in the other, such a complication of mischiefs might follow, as would cause them heartily to lament that they ever were voted. If the ultimate Resolution should happen to be lost, he declared he was afraid the propositions would pass as waste paper. – He reminded the committee, that it was necessary to look farther than the present moment, and to ask themselves, if they had fortified their minds sufficiently to bear the consequences of the step they were that night about to take. When they abandoned the slave-trade, the Spaniards, and some other foreign powers, might possibly take it up, and clandestinely supply our West-India islands with slaves. Had they virtue enough to see that, to bear the idea of another country reaping profits they had laid down, and to abstain from that envy natural to competitors in trade, so as to keep their virtue, steadily to pursue their purpose, and firmly to adhere to their determination? If so, let them thankfully proceed to vote the immediate abolition of the trade. But if they should repent of their virtue, (and he had experienced miserable instances of such repentance) all hopes of future reformation would be lost; they would go back to a trade they had abandoned, with redoubled attachment, and would adhere to it with a degree of avidity and shameless ardour, to their own humiliation, and to the degradation and disgrace of the nation in the eyes of all Europe. These were considerations well worth adverting to, before they took a decisive step in a business, in which they ought not to move with any other determination than to abide the consequence at all hazards. If they had virtue enough to act in that manner, they would do themselves immortal honour, and would see the abolition of the most shameful trade, that ever the hardened heart of man could bear. Viewing the traffic and all the circumstances of it, with the horror that the full view of it which the hon. gentleman had that day displayed, could not fail to excite in the breast of every man not dead to sensibility, he blamed not the hon. gentleman for knocking at every door, and appealing to every passion; well knowing, as the hon. gentleman had forcibly and correctly said, that mankind were governed by their sympathies. There were other passions, however, to be regarded; men were always ready to obey their sympathies when it cost them nothing. Were they prepared to pay the price of their virtue? The hon. gentleman had said, the West India planters would have a compensation adequate to the loss incurred by the abolition of the slave trade. He believed they would; but how they would have instant compensation for what they would lose, he could not conceive. In proportion to their loss, their virtue would be greater. – Having put this very forcibly, Mr. Burke took notice of the testimony of admiral Barrington,[4] who had said, he envied the condition of the negroes in the West-India islands. The hon. admiral, he should rather suppose, meant, that as he had fought so often and so bravely for his country, he was determined to fight again, rather than suffer his countrymen to be made slaves. If, however, he was to be taken literally, his sensation could only be accounted for by his having seen the negroes in the hour of their sports, when a sense of the misery of their condition was neither felt by themselves, nor visible to others. Mr. Burke reasoned on this with infinite knowledge of human nature, great nicety of discernment, and great truth of observation. Nothing, he said, made a happy slave, but a degraded man. In proportion as the mind grew callous to its degradation, and all sense of manly pride was lost, the slave felt comfort, in fact, he was no longer a man. If he were to define a man, Mr. Burke declared, he would say with Shakspeare,

> "Man is a being, holding large discourse,
> "Looking before and after."

A slave was incapable of either looking before or after. Mr. Burke took notice of the reference which Mr. Wilberforce had made to the evidence delivered at the bar with so much ability by the late Mr. Glover,[5] (the author of Leonidas), a gentleman who had fortified the learned world with works, that would preserve his reputation to future ages. That gentleman, he said, had told them at their bar the probable mischiefs that the American war would draw on their trade, and because, by a happy coincidence of circumstances, that mischief had not ensued to its full predicated extent, was the evidence of Mr. Glover to be despised and ridiculed, and was such a man to be treated as a false prophet? After dwelling upon this for some time, Mr. Burke said he would conclude as he had begun, with giving his hearty and sincere thanks to the hon. gentleman for his speech, and though he might not entirely approve of his mode of proceeding, he was ready to let him pursue his own course, be that what it might, and to give him every possible support.

Mr. Pitt said, that he could not help expressing his approbation of the right hon. gentleman's sentiments, with almost every one of which he cordially concurred; and when he differed at all, it was only as to those sentiments which the right hon. gentleman had stated with respect to the mode of proceeding, and the propriety of coming to the several distinct propositions, which were the grounds of the ultimate vote for an unqualified abolition of the slave trade. He returned his hon. friend, therefore, his sincere thanks for the manner in which he had brought the subject before the House, not merely in regard to the masterly, forcible, and perspicuous mode of argument which he had pursued respecting it, but particularly for having chosen the only way in which it could be made obvious to the world, that they were warranted in every ground of fact and of reason, in coming to that vote, which he trusted would be the end of their proceeding. He was satisfied, that no argument reconcileable to any idea of justice, could be given for continuing the trade in question; and he was perfectly clear that his opinion, at least the principles on which it was founded in his own mind, were unalterable; yet he was ready to hear all the arguments that could be offered by those who entertained different sentiments: being from all the attention he had been able to pay the subject, firmly persuaded that nothing but the obscurity of general notions, unfathomed and unexamined, could have hitherto prevented all mankind (those immediately interested in the question alone excepted) from agreeing in one and the same opinion on the subject. The real grounds of the proceeding, which he doubted not but that House would adopt, were stated distinctly in the propositions,

which when put point by point would be found to be such as no
people could venture to say No to, if they were not equally deaf
to the language of reason and of undeniable fact. Let those propositions once be put upon the Journals of that House and it was
almost impossible for them to fail. Persuaded as he was of the
policy as well as humanity of the measure, could he have ever
entertained any doubt of its success, still that would not have
deterred him from persisting in its purpose. As to the mode by
which the abolition of the slave trade was to be ultimately carried
into effect, they were not at present to discuss it; but he trusted
that it would not be found the means of inviting foreign powers
to supply our islands with slaves by a clandestine trade, because,
after a debt founded on the immutable principles of justice was
found to be due, it was impossible but that the country had means
to have it paid; and when once they had come to a resolution
to abolish the slave trade, they were not to be prevented by any
fears of other nations being tempted by the profit resulting from
a commerce, which upon grounds of humanity and national
honour they had abandoned, to carry it on in an illicit manner.
Should that be the case, the language must be, that Great Britain
had resources to enable her to protect her islands, and prevent
that traffic being clandestinely carried on with them, which she
had thought it for her own honour and character to abandon.
It was their duty, and it should be their ambition, to take the
lead in a business of so much national importance, and so much
national credit; and he declared, he could not but have great
confidence that foreign nations would be inclined to share the
honour, and that if they were ready and willing to do so, they
ought on their part, for the sake of the general good that would
result from such a measure being universally taken, to forego the
honour in their favour, and to be contented to follow as their
imitators in so excellent a work. If they were disposed to set about
it in earnest, foreign nations might be invited to concur with
them, either by negociation immediately to be commenced, or
by the effect that the propositions being put upon their journals
would in all probability produce.

REFLECTIONS ON THE
REVOLUTION IN FRANCE

1790

IT MAY NOT be unnecessary to inform the reader, that the following Reflections had their origin in a correspondence between the Author and a very young gentleman at Paris,[1] who did him the honour of desiring his opinion upon the important transactions, which then, and ever since, have so much occupied the attention of all men. An answer was written some time in the month of October, 1789; but it was kept back upon prudential considerations. That letter is alluded to in the beginning of the following sheets. It has been since forwarded to the person to whom it was addressed. The reasons for the delay in sending it were assigned in a short letter to the same gentleman. This produced on his part a new and pressing application for the Author's sentiments.

The Author began a second and more full discussion of the subject. This he had some thoughts of publishing early in the last spring; but, the matter gaining upon him, he found that what he had undertaken not only far exceeded the measure of a letter, but that its importance required rather a more detailed consideration than at that time he had any leisure to bestow upon it. However, having thrown down his first thoughts in the form of a letter, and, indeed, when he sat down to write, having intended it for a private letter, he found it difficult to change the form of address, when his sentiments had grown into a greater extent, and had received another direction. A different plan, he is sensible, might be more favourable to a commodious division and distribution of his matter.

DEAR SIR,

You are pleased to call again, and with some earnestness, for my thoughts on the late proceedings in France. I will not give you reason to imagine that I think my sentiments of such value as to wish myself to be solicited about them. They are of too little consequence to be very anxiously either communicated or withheld. It was from attention to you, and to you only, that I hesitated at the time when you first desired to receive them. In the first letter I had the honour to write to you, and which at length I send, I wrote neither for, nor from, any description of men; nor shall I in this. My errors, if any, are my own. My reputation alone is to answer for them.

You see, Sir, by the long letter I have transmitted to you, that though I do most heartily wish that France may be animated by a spirit of rational liberty, and that I think you bound, in all honest policy, to provide a permanent body in which that spirit may reside, and an effectual organ by which it may act, it is my misfortune to entertain great doubts concerning several material points in your late transactions.

You imagined, when you wrote last, that I might possibly be reckoned among the approvers of certain proceedings in France, from the solemn public seal of sanction they have received from two clubs of gentlemen in London, called the Constitutional Society, and the Revolution Society.[2]

I certainly have the honour to belong to more clubs than one, in which the constitution of this kingdom, and the principles of the glorious Revolution, are held in high reverence; and I reckon myself among the most forward in my zeal for maintaining that constitution and those principles in their utmost purity and vigour. It is because I do so that I think it necessary for me that there should be no mistake. Those who cultivate the memory of our Revolution, and those who are attached to the constitution of this kingdom, will take good care how they are involved with persons, who under the pretext of zeal towards the Revolution and constitution too frequently wander from their true principles; and are ready on every occasion to depart from the firm but cautious and deliberate spirit which produced the one, and which presides in the other. Before I proceed to answer the more material particulars in your letter, I shall beg leave to give you such information as I have been able to obtain of the two clubs which have thought proper, as bodies, to interfere in the concerns of France; first assuring you, that I am not, and that I have never been, a member of either of those societies.

The first, calling itself the Constitutional Society, or Society for Constitutional Information, or by some such title, is, I believe, of seven or eight years standing. The institution of this society appears to be of a charitable, and so far of a laudable nature: it was intended for the circulation, at the expense of the members, of many books, which few others would be at the expense of buying; and which might lie on the hands of the booksellers, to the great loss of an useful body of men. Whether the books, so charitably circulated, were ever as charitably read, is more than I know. Possibly several of them have been exported to France; and, like goods not in request here, may with you have found a market. I have heard much talk of the lights to be drawn from books that are sent from hence. What improvements they have had in their passage (as it is said some liquors are meliorated by crossing the sea) I cannot tell: but I never heard a man of common judgment, or the least degree of information, speak a word in praise of the greater part of the publications circulated by that society; nor have their proceedings been accounted, except by some of themselves, as of any serious consequence.

Your National Assembly seems to entertain much the same opinion that I do of this poor charitable club. As a nation, you reserved the whole stock of your eloquent acknowledgments for the Revolution Society; when their fellows in the Constitutional were, in equity, entitled to some share. Since you have selected the Revolution Society as the great object of your national thanks and praises, you will think me excusable in making its late conduct the subject of my observations. The National Assembly of France[3] has given importance to these gentlemen by adopting them: and they return the favour, by acting as a committee in England for extending the principles of the National Assembly. Henceforward we must consider them as a kind of privileged persons; as no inconsiderable members in the diplomatic body. This is one among the revolutions which have given splendour to obscurity, and distinction to undiscerned merit. Until very lately I do not recollect to have heard of this club. I am quite sure that it never occupied a moment of my thoughts; nor, I believe, those of any person out of their own set. I find, upon inquiry, that on the anniversary of the Revolution in 1688, a club of dissenters, but of what denomination I know not, have long had the custom of hearing a sermon in one of their churches; and that afterwards they spent the day cheerfully, as other clubs do, at the tavern. But I never heard that any public measure, or political system, much less that the merits of the constitution of any foreign nation, had been the subject of a formal proceeding at their festivals; until, to my inexpressible surprise, I found them in a sort of public capacity, by a congratulatory address, giving an authoritative sanction to the proceedings of the National Assembly in France.

In the ancient principles and conduct of the club, so far at least as they were declared, I see nothing to which I could take exception. I think it very probable, that for some purpose, new members may have entered among them; and that some truly Christian politicians, who love to dispense benefits, but are careful to conceal the hand which distributes the dole, may have made them the instruments of their pious designs. Whatever I may have reason to suspect concerning private management, I shall speak of nothing as of a certainty but what is public.

For one, I should be sorry to be thought, directly or indirectly, concerned in their proceedings. I certainly take my full share, along with the rest of the world, in my individual and private capacity, in speculating on what has been done, or is doing, on the public stage, in any place ancient or modern; in the republic of Rome, or the republic of Paris; but having no general apostolical mission, being a citizen of a particular state, and being bound up, in a considerable degree, by its public will, I should think it at least improper and irregular for me to open a formal public correspondence with the actual government of a foreign nation, without the express authority of the government under which I live.

I should be still more unwilling to enter into that correspondence under anything like an equivocal description, which to many, unacquainted with our usages, might make the address, in which I joined, appear as the act of persons in some sort of corporate capacity, acknowledged by the laws of this kingdom, and authorised to speak the sense of some part of it. On account of the ambiguity and uncertainty of unauthorised general descriptions, and of the deceit which may be practised under them, and not from mere formality, the House of Commons would reject the most sneaking petition for the most trifling object, under that mode of signature to which you have thrown open the folding doors of your presence chamber, and have ushered into your National Assembly with as much ceremony and parade, and with as great a bustle of applause, as if you had been visited by the whole representative majesty of the whole English nation. If what this society has thought proper to send forth had been a piece of argument, it would have signified little whose argument it was. It would be neither the more nor the less convincing on account of the party it came from. But this is only a vote and resolution. It stands solely on authority; and in this case it is the mere authority of individuals, few of whom appear.

Their signatures ought, in my opinion, to have been annexed to their instrument. The world would then have the means of knowing how many they are; who they are; and of what value their opinions may be, from their personal abilities, from their knowledge, their experience, or their lead and authority in this state. To me, who am but a plain man, the proceeding looks a little too refined, and too ingenious; it has too much the air of a political stratagem, adopted for the sake of giving, under a high-sounding name, an importance to the public declarations of this club, which, when the matter came to be closely inspected, they did not altogether so well deserve. It is a policy that has very much the complexion of a fraud.

I flatter myself that I love a manly, moral, regulated liberty as well as any gentleman of that society, be he who he will; and perhaps I have given as good proofs of my attachment to that cause, in the whole course of my public conduct. I think I envy liberty as little as they do, to any other nation. But I cannot stand forward, and give praise or blame to anything which relates to human actions, and human concerns, on a simple view of the object, as it stands stripped of every relation, in all the nakedness and solitude of metaphysical abstraction. Circumstances (which with some gentlemen pass for nothing) give in reality to every political principle its distinguishing colour and discriminating effect. The circumstances are what render every civil and political scheme beneficial or noxious to mankind. Abstractedly speaking, government, as well as liberty, is good; yet could I, in common sense, ten years ago, have felicitated France on her enjoyment of a government (for she then had a government) without inquiry what the nature of that government was, or how it was adminis-tered? Can I now congratulate the same nation upon its freedom? Is it because liberty in the abstract may be classed amongst the blessings of mankind, that I am seriously to felicitate a mad-man, who has escaped from the protecting restraint and wholesome darkness of his cell, on his restoration to the enjoyment of light and liberty? Am I to congratulate a highwayman and murderer, who has broke prison, upon the recovery of his natural rights? This would be to act over again the scene of the criminals condemned to the galleys, and their heroic deliverer, the meta-physic knight of the sorrowful countenance.

When I see the spirit of liberty in action, I see a strong principle at work; and this, for a while, is all I can possibly know of it. The wild *gas*, the fixed air, is plainly broke loose: but we ought to suspend our judgment until the first effervescence is a little subsided, till the liquor is cleared, and until we see something deeper than the agitation of a troubled and frothy surface. I must be tolerably sure, before I venture publicly to congratulate men upon a blessing, that they have really received one. Flattery corrupts both the receiver and the giver; and adulation is not of more service to the people than to kings. I should therefore suspend my congratulations on the new liberty of France, until I was informed how it had been combined with government; with public force; with the discipline and obedience of armies; with the collection of an effective and well-distributed revenue; with morality and religion; with the solidity of property; with peace and order; with civil and social manners. All these (in their way) are good things too; and, without them, liberty is not a benefit whilst it lasts, and is not likely to continue long. The effect of liberty to individuals is, that they may do what they please: we ought to see what it will please them to do, before we risk congratulations, which may be soon turned into complaints. Prudence would dictate this in the case of separate, insulated, private men; but liberty, when men act in bodies, is *power*. Considerate people, before they declare themselves, will observe the use which is made of *power*; and particularly of so trying a thing as *new* power in *new* persons, of whose principles, tempers, and dispositions they have little or no experience, and in situations, where those who appear the most stirring in the scene may possibly not be the real movers.

All these considerations however were below the transcendental dignity of the Revolution Society. Whilst I continued in the country, from whence I had the honour of writing to you, I had but an imperfect idea of their transactions. On my coming to town, I sent for an account of their proceedings, which had been published by their authority, containing a sermon of Dr. Price, with the Duke de Rochefaucault's and the Archbishop of Aix's[4] letter, and several other documents annexed. The whole of that publication, with the manifest design of connecting the affairs of France with those of England, by drawing us into an imitation of the conduct of the National Assembly, gave me a considerable degree of uneasiness. The effect of that conduct upon the power, credit, prosperity, and tranquillity of France, became every day more evident. The form of constitution to be settled, for its future polity, became more clear. We are now in a condition to discern, with tolerable exactness, the true nature of the object held up to our imitation. If the prudence of reserve and decorum dictates silence in some circumstances, in others prudence of a higher order may justify us in speaking our thoughts. The beginnings of confusion with us in England are at present feeble enough; but, with you, we have seen an infancy, still more feeble, growing by moments into a strength to heap mountains upon mountains, and to wage war with heaven itself. Whenever our neighbour's house is on fire, it cannot be amiss for the engines to play a little on our own. Better to be despised for too anxious apprehensions, than ruined by too confident a security.

Solicitous chiefly for the peace of my own country, but by no means unconcerned for yours, I wish to communicate more largely what was at first intended only for your private satisfaction. I shall still keep your affairs in my eye, and continue to address myself to you. Indulging myself in the freedom of epistolary intercourse, I beg leave to throw out my thoughts, and express my feelings, just as they arise in my mind, with very little attention to formal method. I set out with the proceedings of the Revolution Society; but I shall not confine myself to them. Is it possible I should? It appears to me as if I were in a great crisis, not of the affairs of France alone, but of all Europe, perhaps of more than Europe. All circumstances taken together, the French Revolution is the most astonishing that has hitherto happened in the world. The most wonderful things are brought about in many instances by means the most absurd and ridiculous; in the most ridiculous modes; and, apparently, by the most contemptible instruments. Everything seems out of nature in this strange chaos of levity and ferocity, and of all sorts of crimes jumbled together with all sorts of follies. In viewing this monstrous tragicomic scene, the most opposite passions necessarily succeed, and sometimes mix with each other in the mind; alternate contempt and indignation; alternate laughter and tears; alternate scorn and horror.

It cannot however be denied, that to some this strange scene appeared in quite another point of view. Into them it inspired no other sentiments than those of exultation and rapture. They saw nothing in what has been done in France, but a firm and temperate exertion of freedom; so consistent, on the whole, with morals and with piety as to make it deserving not only of the secular applause of dashing Machiavelian politicians, but to render it a fit theme for all the devout effusions of sacred eloquence.

On the forenoon of the 4th of November last, Doctor Richard Price, a non-conforming minister of eminence, preached at the dissenting meeting-house of the Old Jewry, to his club or society, a very extraordinary miscellaneous sermon, in which there are some good moral and religious sentiments, and not ill expressed, mixed up in a sort of porridge of various political opinions and reflections; but the Revolution in France is the grand ingredient in the cauldron. I consider the address transmitted by the Revolution Society to the National Assembly, through Earl Stanhope,[5] as originating in the principles of the sermon, and as a corollary from them. It was moved by the preacher of that discourse. It was passed by those who came reeking from the effect of the sermon, without any censure or qualification, expressed or implied. If, however, any of the gentlemen concerned shall wish to separate the sermon from the resolution, they know how to acknowledge the one, and to disavow the other. They may do it: I cannot.

For my part, I looked on that sermon as the public declaration of a man much connected with literary caballers, and intriguing philosophers; with political theologians, and theological politicians, both at home and abroad. I know they set him up as a sort of oracle; because, with the best intentions in the world, he naturally *philippises*,[6] and chants his prophetic song in exact unison with their designs.

That sermon is in a strain which I believe has not been heard in this kingdom, in any of the pulpits which are tolerated or encouraged in it, since the year 1648; when a predecessor of Dr. Price, the Rev. Hugh Peters,[7] made the vault of the king's own chapel at St. James's ring with the honour and privilege of the saints, who, with the "high praises of God in their mouths, and a *two*-edged sword in their hands, were to execute judgment on the heathen, and punishments upon the *people*; to bind their *kings* with chains, and their *nobles* with fetters of iron."* Few harangues from the pulpit, except in the days of your league[8] in France, or in the days of our solemn league and covenant in England, have ever breathed less of the spirit of moderation than this lecture in the Old Jewry. Supposing, however, that something like moderation were visible in this political sermon; yet

* Psalm cxlix.

politics and the pulpit are terms that have little agreement. No sound ought to be heard in the church but the healing voice of Christian charity. The cause of civil liberty and civil govern-ment gains as little as that of religion by this confusion of duties. Those who quit their proper character, to assume what does not belong to them, are, for the greater part, ignorant both of the character they leave, and of the character they assume. Wholly unacquainted with the world in which they are so fond of meddling, and inexperienced in all its affairs, on which they pronounce with so much confidence, they have nothing of poli-tics but the passions they excite. Surely the church is a place where one day's truce ought to be allowed to the dissensions and animosities of mankind.

This pulpit style, revived after so long a discontinuance, had to me the air of novelty, and of a novelty not wholly without danger. I do not charge this danger equally to every part of the discourse. The hint given to a noble and reverend lay-divine,[9] who is supposed high in office in one of our universities,* and other lay-divines "of *rank* and literature," may be proper and seasonable, though somewhat new. If the noble *Seekers*[10] should find nothing to satisfy their pious fancies in the old staple of the national church, or in all the rich variety to be found in the well-assorted warehouses of the dissenting congregations, Dr. Price advises them to improve upon non-conformity; and to set up, each of them, a separate meeting-house upon his own particular principles.† It is somewhat remarkable that this reverend divine should be so earnest for setting up new churches, and so per-fectly indifferent concerning the doctrine which may be taught in them. His zeal is of a curious character. It is not for the propa-gation of his own opinions, but of any opinions. It is not for the diffusion of truth, but for the spreading of contradiction. Let the noble teachers but dissent, it is no matter from whom or from what. This great point once secured, it is taken for granted their religion will be rational and manly. I doubt whether reli-gion would reap all the benefits which the calculating divine

---

* Discourse on the Love of our Country, Nov. 4th, 1789, by Dr. Richard Price, 3rd edition, p. 17 and 18.

† "Those who dislike that mode of worship which is prescribed by public authority, ought, if they can find *no* worship *out* of the church which they approve, *to set up a separate worship for themselves*; and by doing this, and giving an example of a rational and manly worship, men of *weight* from their *rank* and literature may do the greatest service to society and the world." – P. 18 Dr. Price's Sermon.

computes from this "great company of great preachers." It would certainly be a valuable addition of nondescripts to the ample collection of known classes, genera and species, which at present beautify the *hortus siccus*[11] of dissent. A sermon from a noble duke, or a noble marquis, or a noble earl, or baron bold, would certainly increase and diversify the amusements of this town, which begins to grow satiated with the uniform round of its vapid dissipations. I should only stipulate that these new *Mess-Johns*[12] in robes and coronets should keep some sort of bounds in the democratic and levelling principles which are expected from their titled pulpits. The new evangelists will, I dare say, disappoint the hopes that are conceived of them. They will not become, literally as well as figuratively, polemic divines, nor be disposed so to drill their congregations, that they may, as in former blessed times, preach their doctrines to regiments of dragoons and corps of infantry and artillery. Such arrangements, however favourable to the cause of compulsory freedom, civil and religious, may not be equally conducive to the national tranquillity. These few restrictions I hope are no great stretches of intolerance, no very violent exertions of despotism.

But I may say of our preacher, "*utinam nugis tota illa dedisset tempora sævitiæ.*"[13] – All things in this his fulminating bull are not of so innoxious a tendency. His doctrines affect our constitution in its vital parts. He tells the Revolution Society in this political sermon, that his Majesty "is almost the *only* lawful king in the world, because the *only* one who owes his crown to the *choice of his people.*" As to the kings of *the world*, all of whom (except one) this arch-pontiff of the *rights of men*, with all the plenitude, and with more than the boldness, of the papal deposing power in its meridian fervour of the twelfth century, puts into one sweeping clause of ban and anathema, and proclaims usurpers by circles of longitude and latitude, over the whole globe, it behoves them to consider how they admit into their territories these apostolic missionaries, who are to tell their subjects they are not lawful kings. That is their concern. It is ours, as a domestic interest of some moment, seriously to consider the solidity of the *only* principle upon which these gentlemen acknowledge a king of Great Britain to be entitled to their allegiance.

This doctrine, as applied to the prince now on the British throne, either is nonsense, and therefore neither true nor false,

or it affirms a most unfounded, dangerous, illegal, and unconstitutional position. According to this spiritual doctor of politics, if
his Majesty does not owe his crown to the choice of his people,
he is no *lawful king*. Now nothing can be more untrue than that
the crown of this kingdom is so held by his Majesty. Therefore
if you follow their rule, the king of Great Britain, who most
certainly does not owe his high office to any form of popular
election, is in no respect better than the rest of the gang of
usurpers, who reign, or rather rob, all over the face of this
our miserable world, without any sort of right or title to the allegiance of their people. The policy of this general doctrine, so
qualified, is evident enough. The propagators of this political
gospel are in hopes that their abstract principle (their principle
that a popular choice is necessary to the legal existence of the
sovereign magistracy) would be overlooked, whilst the king of
Great Britain was not affected by it. In the mean time the ears
of their congregations would be gradually habituated to it, as if
it were a first principle admitted without dispute. For the present
it would only operate as a theory, pickled in the preserving juices
of pulpit eloquence, and laid by for future use. *Condo et compono
quæ mox depromere possim.*[14] By this policy, whilst our government
is soothed with a reservation in its favour, to which it has no
claim, the security, which it has in common with all governments, so far as opinion is security, is taken away.

Thus these politicians proceed, whilst little notice is taken of
their doctrines; but when they come to be examined upon the
plain meaning of their words, and the direct tendency of their
doctrines, then equivocations and slippery constructions come
into play. When they say the king owes his crown to the choice
of his people, and is therefore the only lawful sovereign in the
world, they will perhaps tell us they mean to say no more than
that some of the king's predecessors have been called to the
throne by some sort of choice; and therefore he owes his crown
to the choice of his people. Thus, by a miserable subterfuge, they
hope to render their proposition safe, by rendering it nugatory.
They are welcome to the asylum they seek for their offence, since
they take refuge in their folly. For, if you admit this interpretation, how does their idea of election differ from our idea of
inheritance? And how does the settlement of the crown in the
Brunswick line[15] derived from James the First come to legalise

our monarchy, rather than that of any of the neighbouring countries? At some time or other, to be sure, all the beginners of
dynasties were chosen by those who called them to govern.
There is ground enough for the opinion that all the kingdoms of
Europe were, at a remote period, elective, with more or fewer
limitations in the objects of choice. But whatever kings might
have been here, or elsewhere, a thousand years ago, or in whatever manner the ruling dynasties of England or France may have
begun, the king of Great Britain is, at this day, king by a fixed rule
of succession, according to the laws of his country; and whilst the
legal conditions of the compact of sovereignty are performed by
him, (as they are performed,) he holds his crown in contempt of
the choice of the Revolution Society, who have not a single vote
for a king amongst them, either individually or collectively;
though I make no doubt they would soon erect themselves into
an electoral college, if things were ripe to give effect to their
claim. His Majesty's heirs and successors, each in his time and
order, will come to the crown with the same contempt of their
choice with which his Majesty has succeeded to that he wears.

Whatever may be the success of evasion in explaining away
the gross error of *fact*, which supposes that his Majesty (though
he holds it in concurrence with the wishes) owes his crown to
the choice of his people, yet nothing can evade their full explicit
declaration, concerning the principle of a right in the people
to choose; which right is directly maintained, and tenaciously
adhered to. All the oblique insinuations concerning election
bottom in this proposition, and are referable to it. Lest the foundation of the king's exclusive legal title should pass for a mere
rant of adulatory freedom, the political divine proceeds dog-
matically to assert,* that, by the principles of the Revolution, the
people of England have acquired three fundamental rights, all
which, with him, compose one system, and lie together in one
short sentence; namely, that we have acquired a right,

1. "To choose our own governors."
2. "To cashier them for misconduct."
3. "To frame a government for ourselves."

This new, and hitherto unheard-of, bill of rights, though made
in the name of the whole people, belongs to those gentlemen
and their faction only. The body of the people of England have

---

* P. 34, Discourse on the Love of our Country, by Dr. Price.

no share in it. They utterly disclaim it. They will resist the practical assertion of it with their lives and fortunes. They are bound
to do so by the laws of their country, made at the time of that
very Revolution which is appealed to in favour of the fictitious
rights claimed by the Society which abuses its name.

These gentlemen of the Old Jewry, in all their reasonings on
the Revolution of 1688, have a Revolution which happened in
England about forty years before, and the late French Revolution, so much before their eyes, and in their hearts, that they are
constantly confounding all the three together. It is necessary that
we should separate what they confound. We must recall their
erring fancies to the *acts* of the Revolution which we revere, for
the discovery of its true *principles*. If the *principles* of the Revolution of 1688 are anywhere to be found, it is in the statute called
the *Declaration of Right*.[16] In that most wise, sober, and considerate declaration, drawn up by great lawyers and great statesmen,
and not by warm and inexperienced enthusiasts, not one word
is said, nor one suggestion made, of a general right "to choose
our own *governors*; to cashier them for misconduct; and to *form* a
government for *ourselves*."

This Declaration of Right (the act of the 1st of William and
Mary, sess. 2, ch. 2) is the corner-stone of our constitution, as
reinforced, explained, improved, and in its fundamental principles for ever settled. It is called "An Act for declaring the rights
and liberties of the subject, and for *settling* the *succession* of the
crown." You will observe, that these rights and this succession
are declared in one body, and bound indissolubly together.

A few years after this period, a second opportunity offered for
asserting a right of election to the crown. On the prospect of a
total failure of issue from King William, and from the Princess,
afterwards Queen Anne, the consideration of the settlement of
the crown, and of a further security for the liberties of the people,
again came before the legislature. Did they this second time make
any provision for legalising the crown on the spurious revolution
principles of the Old Jewry? No. They followed the principles
which prevailed in the Declaration of Right; indicating with
more precision the persons who were to inherit in the Protestant
line. This act also incorporated, by the same policy, our liberties,
and an hereditary succession in the same act. Instead of a right to
choose our own governors, they declared that the *succession* in
that line (the Protestant line drawn from James the First) was

absolutely necessary "for the peace, quiet, and security of the
realm," and that it was equally urgent on them "to maintain a
certainty in the succession thereof, to which the subjects may safely
have recourse for their protection." Both these acts, in which are
heard the unerring, unambiguous oracles of revolution policy,
instead of countenancing the delusive, gipsy predictions of a
"right to choose our governors," prove to a demonstration how
totally adverse the wisdom of the nation was from turning a case
of necessity into a rule of law.

Unquestionably there was at the Revolution, in the person
of King William, a small and a temporary deviation from the
strict order of a regular hereditary succession; but it is against all
genuine principles of jurisprudence to draw a principle from a
law made in a special case, and regarding an individual person.
Privilegium non transit in exemplum.[17] If ever there was a time
favourable for establishing the principle, that a king of popular
choice was the only legal king, without all doubt it was at the
Revolution. Its not being done at that time is a proof that the
nation was of opinion it ought not to be done at any time. There
is no person so completely ignorant of our history as not to know,
that the majority in parliament of both parties were so little disposed to anything resembling that principle, that at first they
were determined to place the vacant crown, not on the head of
the Prince of Orange, but on that of his wife Mary, daughter of
King James, the eldest born of the issue of that king, which they
acknowledged as undoubtedly his.[18] It would be to repeat a very
trite story, to recall to your memory all those circumstances
which demonstrated that their accepting King William was not
properly a *choice*; but to all those who did not wish, in effect, to
recall King James, or to deluge their country in blood, and again
to bring their religion, laws, and liberties into the peril they had
just escaped, it was an act of *necessity*, in the strictest moral sense
in which necessity can be taken.

In the very act, in which for a time, and in a single case, parliament departed from the strict order of inheritance, in favour of
a prince, who, though not next, was however very near, in the
line of succession, it is curious to observe how Lord Somers,[19]
who drew the bill called the Declaration of Right, has
comported himself on that delicate occasion. It is curious to
observe with what address this temporary solution of continuity
is kept from the eye; whilst all that could be found in this act of

necessity to countenance the idea of an hereditary succession is brought forward, and fostered, and made the most of, by this great man, and by the legislature who followed him. Quitting the dry, imperative style of an act of parliament, he makes the Lords and Commons fall to a pious, legislative ejaculation, and declare, that they consider it "as a marvellous providence, and merciful goodness of God to this nation, to preserve their said Majesties' *royal* persons, most happily to reign over us *on the throne of their ancestors*, for which, from the bottom of their hearts, they return their humblest thanks and praises." – The legislature plainly had in view the act of recognition of the first of Queen Elizabeth, chap. 3rd, and of that of James the First, chap. 1st, both acts strongly declaratory of the inheritable nature of the crown, and in many parts they follow, with a nearly literal precision, the words and even the form of thanksgiving which is found in these old declaratory statutes.

The two Houses, in the act of King William, did not thank God that they had found a fair opportunity to assert a right to choose their own governors, much less to make an election the *only lawful* title to the crown. Their having been in a condition to avoid the very appearance of it, as much as possible, was by them considered as a providential escape. They threw a politic, well-wrought veil over every circumstance tending to weaken the rights, which in the meliorated order of succession they meant to perpetuate; or which might furnish a precedent for any future departure from what they had then settled for ever. Accordingly, that they might not relax the nerves of their monarchy, and that they might preserve a close conformity to the practice of their ancestors, as it appeared in the declaratory statutes of Queen Mary* and Queen Elizabeth, in the next clause they vest, by recognition, in their Majesties, *all* the legal prerogatives of the crown, declaring, "that in them they are most *fully*, rightfully, and *entirely* invested, incorporated, united, and annexed." In the clause which follows, for preventing questions, by reason of any pretended titles to the crown, they declare, (observing also in this the traditionary language, along with the traditionary policy of the nation, and repeating as from a rubric the language of the preceding acts of Elizabeth and James,) that on the preserving "a *certainty* in the SUCCESSION thereof, the

* 1st Mary, sess. 3, ch. 1.

unity, peace, and tranquillity of this nation doth, under God, wholly depend."

They knew that a doubtful title of succession would but too much resemble an election; and that an election would be utterly destructive of the "unity, peace, and tranquillity of this nation," which they thought to be considerations of some moment. To provide for these objects, and therefore to exclude for ever the Old Jewry doctrine of "a right to choose our own governors," they follow with a clause containing a most solemn pledge, taken from the preceding act of Queen Elizabeth, as solemn a pledge as ever was or can be given in favour of an hereditary succession, and as solemn a renunciation as could be made of the principles by this Society imputed to them. "The Lords spiritual and temporal, and Commons, do, in the name of all the people aforesaid, most humbly and faithfully submit *themselves, their heirs and posterities for ever*; and do faithfully promise that they will stand to, maintain, and defend their said Majesties, and also the *limitation of the crown*, herein specified and contained, to the utmost of their powers," &c. &c.

So far is it from being true, that we acquired a right by the Revolution to elect our kings, that if we had possessed it before, the English nation did at that time most solemnly renounce and abdicate it, for themselves, and for all their posterity for ever. These gentlemen may value themselves as much as they please on their Whig principles; but I never desire to be thought a better Whig than Lord Somers; or to understand the principles of the Revolution better than those by whom it was brought about; or to read in the Declaration of Right any mysteries unknown to those whose penetrating style has engraved in our ordinances, and in our hearts, the words and spirit of that immortal law.

It is true, that, aided with the powers derived from force and opportunity, the nation was at that time, in some sense, free to take what course it pleased for filling the throne; but only free to do so upon the same grounds on which they might have wholly abolished their monarchy, and every other part of their constitution. However, they did not think such bold changes within their commission. It is indeed difficult, perhaps impossible, to give limits to the mere *abstract* competence of the supreme power, such as was exercised by parliament at that time; but the limits of a *moral* competence, subjecting, even in powers more indisputably sovereign, occasional will to permanent reason, and to the steady maxims of faith, justice, and fixed fundamental policy, are perfectly intelligible, and perfectly binding upon those who exercise any authority, under any name, or under any title, in the state. The House of Lords, for instance, is not morally competent to dissolve the House of Commons; no, nor even to dissolve itself, nor to abdicate, if it would, its portion in the legislature of the kingdom. Though a king may abdicate for his own person, he cannot abdicate for the monarchy. By as strong, or by a stronger reason, the House of Commons cannot renounce its share of authority. The engagement and pact of society, which generally goes by the name of the constitution, forbids such invasion and such surrender. The constituent parts of a state are obliged to hold their public faith with each other, and with all those who derive any serious interest under their engagements, as much as the whole state is bound to keep its faith with separate communities. Otherwise competence and power would soon be confounded, and no law be left but the will of a prevailing force. On this principle the succession of the crown has always been what it now is, an hereditary succession by law: in the old line it was a succession by the common law; in the new by the statute law, operating on the principles of the common law, not changing the substance, but regulating the mode, and describing the persons. Both these descriptions of law are of the same force, and are derived from an equal authority, emanating from the common agreement and original compact of the state, *communi sponsione reipublicæ*,[20] and as such are equally binding on king and people too, as long as the terms are observed, and they continue the same body politic.

It is far from impossible to reconcile, if we do not suffer ourselves to be entangled in the mazes of metaphysic sophistry, the use both of a fixed rule and an occasional deviation; the sacredness of an hereditary principle of succession in our government, with a power of change in its application in cases of extreme emergency. Even in that extremity, (if we take the measure of our rights by our exercise of them at the Revolution,) the change is to be confined to the peccant part only; to the part which produced the necessary deviation; and even then it is to be effected without a decomposition of the whole civil and political mass, for the purpose of originating a new civil order out of the first elements of society.

A state without the means of some change is without the

means of its conservation. Without such means it might even risk
the loss of that part of the constitution which it wished the most
religiously to preserve. The two principles of conservation and
correction operated strongly at the two critical periods of the
Restoration and Revolution, when England found itself without
a king. At both those periods the nation had lost the bond of
union in their ancient edifice; they did not, however, dissolve
the whole fabric. On the contrary, in both cases they regenerated
the deficient part of the old constitution through the parts which
were not impaired. They kept these old parts exactly as they
were, that the part recovered might be suited to them. They acted
by the ancient organised states in the shape of their old organisation, and not by the organic *moleculæ* of a disbanded people.
At no time, perhaps, did the sovereign legislature manifest a more
tender regard to that fundamental principle of British constitutional policy, than at the time of the Revolution, when it deviated from the direct line of hereditary succession. The crown was
carried somewhat out of the line in which it had before moved;
but the new line was derived from the same stock. It was still a
line of hereditary descent; still an hereditary descent in the same
blood, though an hereditary descent qualified with Protestantism. When the legislature altered the direction, but kept the
principle, they showed that they held it inviolable.

On this principle, the law of inheritance had admitted some
amendment in the old time, and long before the era of the
Revolution. Some time after the conquest great questions arose
upon the legal principles of hereditary descent. It became a
matter of doubt, whether the heir *per capita* or the heir *per stirpes*[21]
was to succeed; but whether the heir *per capita* gave way when
the heirdom *per stirpes* took place, or the Catholic heir when the
Protestant was preferred, the inheritable principle survived with
a sort of immortality through all transmigrations – *multosque per
annos stat fortuna domus, et avi numerantur avorum.*[22] This is the
spirit of our constitution, not only in its settled course, but in all
its revolutions. Whoever came in, or however he came in,
whether he obtained the crown by law, or by force, the hereditary succession was either continued or adopted.

The gentlemen of the Society for Revolutions see nothing
in that of 1688 but the deviation from the constitution; and
they take the deviation from the principle for the principle. They
have little regard to the obvious consequences of their doctrine,

though they must see, that it leaves positive authority in very few of the positive institutions of this country. When such an unwarrantable maxim is once established, that no throne is lawful but the elective, no one act of the princes who preceded this era of fictitious election can be valid. Do these theorists mean to imitate some of their predecessors, who dragged the bodies of our ancient sovereigns out of the quiet of their tombs? Do they mean to attaint and disable backwards all the kings that have reigned before the Revolution, and consequently to stain the throne of England with the blot of a continual usurpation? Do they mean to invalidate, annul, or to call into question, together with the titles of the whole line of our kings, that great body of our statute law which passed under those whom they treat as usurpers? to annul laws of inestimable value to our liberties – of as great value at least as any which have passed at or since the period of the Revolution? If kings, who did not owe their crown to the choice of their people, had no title to make laws, what will become of the statute *de tallagio non concedendo*? – of the *petition of right*? – of the act of *habeas corpus*?[23] Do these new doctors of the rights of men presume to assert, that King James the Second, who came to the crown as next of blood, according to the rules of a then unqualified succession, was not to all intents and purposes a lawful king of England, before he had done any of those acts which were justly construed into an abdication of his crown? If he was not, much trouble in parliament might have been saved at the period these gentlemen commemorate. But King James was a bad king with a good title, and not an usurper. The princes who succeeded according to the act of parliament which settled the crown on the Electress Sophia and on her descendants, being Protestants, came in as much by a title of inheritance as King James did. He came in according to the law, as it stood at his accession to the crown; and the princes of the House of Brunswick came to the inheritance of the crown, not by election, but by the law, as it stood at their several accessions of Protestant descent and inheritance, as I hope I have shown sufficiently.

The law, by which this royal family is specifically destined to the succession, is the act of the 12th and 13th of King William. The terms of this act bind "us and our *heirs*, and our *posterity*, to them, their *heirs*, and their *posterity*," being Protestants, to the end of time, in the same words as the Declaration of Right had bound us to the heirs of King William and Queen Mary.

It therefore secures both an hereditary crown and an hereditary allegiance. On what ground, except the constitutional policy of forming an establishment to secure that kind of succession which is to preclude a choice of the people for ever, could the legislature have fastidiously rejected the fair and abundant choice which our country presented to them, and searched in strange lands for a foreign princess, from whose womb the line of our future rulers were to derive their title to govern millions of men through a series of ages?

The Princess Sophia[24] was named in the act of settlement of the 12th and 13th of King William, for a *stock* and root of *inheritance* to our kings, and not for her merits as a temporary administratrix of a power, which she might not, and in fact did not, herself ever exercise. She was adopted for one reason, and for one only, because, says the act, "the most excellent Princess Sophia, Electress and Duchess Dowager of Hanover, is *daughter* of the most excellent Princess Elizabeth, late Queen of Bohemia, *daughter* of our late *sovereign lord* King James the First, of happy memory, and is hereby declared to be the next in *succession* in the Protestant line," &c. &c.; "and the crown shall continue to the *heirs* of her body, being Protestants." This limitation was made by parliament, that through the Princess Sophia an inheritable line not only was to be continued in future, but (what they thought very material) that through her it was to be connected with the old stock of inheritance in King James the First; in order that the monarchy might preserve an unbroken unity through all ages, and might be preserved (with safety to our religion) in the old approved mode by descent, in which, if our liberties had been once endangered, they had often, through all storms and struggles of prerogative and privilege, been preserved. They did well. No experience has taught us, that in any other course or method than that of an *hereditary crown* our liberties can be regularly perpetuated and preserved sacred as our *hereditary right*. An irregular, convulsive movement may be necessary to throw off an irregular, convulsive disease. But the course of succession is the healthy habit of the British constitution. Was it that the legislature wanted, at the act for the limitation of the crown in the Hanoverian line, drawn through the female descendants of James the First, a due sense of the inconveniences of having two or three, or possibly more, foreigners in succession to the British throne? No! – they had a due sense of the evils which might happen from such foreign rule, and more than a due sense of them. But a more decisive proof cannot be given of the full conviction of the British nation, that the principles of the Revolution did not authorise them to elect kings at their pleasure, and without any attention to the ancient fundamental principles of our government, than their continuing to adopt a plan of hereditary Protestant succession in the old line, with all the dangers and all the inconveniences of its being a foreign line full before their eyes, and operating with the utmost force upon their minds.

A few years ago I should be ashamed to overload a matter, so capable of supporting itself, by the then unnecessary support of any argument; but this seditious, unconstitutional doctrine is now publicly taught, avowed, and printed. The dislike I feel to revolutions, the signals for which have so often been given from pulpits; the spirit of change that is gone abroad; the total contempt which prevails with you, and may come to prevail with us, of all ancient institutions, when set in opposition to a present sense of convenience, or to the bent of a present inclination: all these considerations make it not unadvisable, in my opinion, to call back our attention to the true principles of our own domestic laws; that you, my French friend, should begin to know, and that we should continue to cherish them. We ought not, on either side of the water, to suffer ourselves to be imposed upon by the counterfeit wares which some persons, by a double fraud, export to you in illicit bottoms, as raw commodities of British growth, though wholly alien to our soil, in order afterwards to smuggle them back again into this country, manufactured after the newest Paris fashion of an improved liberty.

The people of England will not ape the fashions they have never tried, nor go back to those which they have found mischievous on trial. They look upon the legal hereditary succession of their crown as among their rights, not as among their wrongs; as a benefit, not as a grievance; as a security for their liberty, not as a badge of servitude. They look on the frame of their commonwealth, *such as it stands*, to be of inestimable value; and they conceive the undisturbed succession of the crown to be a pledge of the stability and perpetuity of all the other members of our constitution.

I shall beg leave, before I go any further, to take notice of some paltry artifices, which the abettors of election, as the only lawful

title to the crown, are ready to employ, in order to render the
support of the just principles of our constitution a task somewhat
invidious. These sophisters substitute a fictitious cause, and
feigned personages, in whose favour they suppose you engaged,
whenever you defend the inheritable nature of the crown. It is
common with them to dispute as if they were in a conflict with
some of those exploded fanatics of slavery, who formerly maintained, what I believe no creature now maintains, "that the
crown is held by divine hereditary and indefeasible right." –
These old fanatics of single arbitrary power dogmatised as if hereditary royalty was the only lawful government in the world, just
as our new fanatics of popular arbitrary power maintain that a
popular election is the sole lawful source of authority. The old
prerogative enthusiasts, it is true, did speculate foolishly, and perhaps impiously too, as if monarchy had more of a divine sanction
than any other mode of government; and as if a right to govern
by inheritance were in strictness *indefeasible* in every person, who
should be found in the succession to a throne, and under every
circumstance, which no civil or political right can be. But an
absurd opinion concerning the king's hereditary right to the
crown does not prejudice one that is rational, and bottomed
upon solid principles of law and policy. If all the absurd theories
of lawyers and divines were to vitiate the objects in which they
are conversant, we should have no law and no religion left in the
world. But an absurd theory on one side of a question forms no
justification for alleging a false fact, or promulgating mischievous
maxims, on the other.

The second claim of the Revolution Society is "a right of
cashiering their governors for *misconduct.*" Perhaps the apprehensions our ancestors entertained of forming such a precedent as
that "of cashiering for misconduct," was the cause that the
declaration of the act, which implied the abdication of King
James, was, if it had any fault, rather too guarded, and too
circumstantial.* But all this guard, and all this accumulation of
circumstances, serves to show the spirit of caution which predominated in the national councils in a situation in which men

---

* "That King James the Second, having endeavoured to *subvert the constitution* of the
kingdom by breaking the *original contract* between king and people, and, by the advice
of Jesuits, and other wicked persons, having violated the *fundamental* laws, and *having
withdrawn himself out of the kingdom*, hath *abdicated* the government, and the throne is
thereby *vacant.*"

irritated by oppression, and elevated by a triumph over it, are apt to abandon themselves to violent and extreme courses: it shows the anxiety of the great men who influenced the conduct of affairs at that great event to make the Revolution a parent of settlement, and not a nursery of future revolutions.

No government could stand a moment, if it could be blown down with anything so loose and indefinite as an opinion of "*misconduct*." They who led at the Revolution grounded the virtual abdication of King James upon no such light and uncertain principle. They charged him with nothing less than a design, confirmed by a multitude of illegal overt acts, to *subvert the Protestant church and state*, and their *fundamental*, unquestionable laws and liberties: they charged him with having broken the *original contract* between king and people. This was more than *misconduct*. A grave and overruling necessity obliged them to take the step they took, and took with infinite reluctance, as under that most rigorous of all laws. Their trust for the future preservation of the constitution was not in future revolutions. The grand policy of all their regulations was to render it almost impracticable for any future sovereign to compel the states of the kingdom to have again recourse to those violent remedies. They left the crown what, in the eye and estimation of law, it had ever been, perfectly irresponsible. In order to lighten the crown still further, they aggravated responsibility on ministers of state. By the statute of the 1st of King William, sess. 2nd, called "*the act for declaring the rights and liberties of the subject, and for settling the succession to the crown*," they enacted, that the ministers should serve the crown on the terms of that declaration. They secured soon after the *frequent meetings of parliament*, by which the whole government would be under the constant inspection and active control of the popular representative and of the magnates of the kingdom. In the next great constitutional act, that of the 12th and 13th of King William, for the further limitation of the crown, and *better* securing the rights and liberties of the subject, they provided, "that no pardon under the great seal of England should be pleadable to an impeachment by the Commons in parliament."[25] The rule laid down for government in the Declaration of Right, the constant inspection of parliament, the practical claim of impeachment, they thought infinitely a better security not only for their constitutional liberty, but against the vices of administration, than the reservation of a right so difficult in the practice,

so uncertain in the issue, and often so mischievous in the consequences, as that of "cashiering their governors."

Dr. Price, in his sermon,* condemns very properly the practice of gross, adulatory addresses to kings. Instead of this fulsome
style, he proposes that his Majesty should be told, on occasions
of congratulation, that "he is to consider himself as more
properly the servant than the sovereign of his people." For a
compliment, this new form of address does not seem to be very
soothing. Those who are servants in name, as well as in effect,
do not like to be told of their situation, their duty, and their
obligations. The slave, in the old play, tells his master, "*Hæc com-
memoratio est quasi exprobatio.*"[26] It is not pleasant as compliment;
it is not wholesome as instruction. After all, if the king were to
bring himself to echo this new kind of address, to adopt it in
terms, and even to take the appellation of Servant of the People
as his royal style, how either he or we should be much mended
by it, I cannot imagine. I have seen very assuming letters, signed,
Your most obedient, humble servant. The proudest denomination that ever was endured on earth took a title of still greater
humility than that which is now proposed for sovereigns by the
Apostle of Liberty. Kings and nations were trampled upon by
the foot of one calling himself "the Servant of Servants;" and
mandates for deposing sovereigns were sealed with the signet of
"the Fisherman."[27]

I should have considered all this as no more than a sort of flip-
pant, vain discourse, in which, as in an unsavoury fume, several
persons suffer the spirit of liberty to evaporate, if it were not
plainly in support of the idea, and a part of the scheme, of
"cashiering kings for misconduct." In that light it is worth some
observation.

Kings, in one sense, are undoubtedly the servants of the
people, because their power has no other rational end than
that of the general advantage; but it is not true that they are, in
the ordinary sense, (by our constitution at least,) anything like
servants; the essence of whose situation is to obey the commands
of some other, and to be removable at pleasure. But the king of
Great Britain obeys no other person; all other persons are individually, and collectively too, under him, and owe to him a legal
obedience. The law, which knows neither to flatter nor to insult,

* P. 22–24.

calls this high magistrate, not our servant, as this humble divine calls him, but "*our sovereign Lord the king;*" and we, on our parts, have learned to speak only the primitive language of the law, and not the confused jargon of their Babylonian pulpits.

As he is not to obey us, but as we are to obey the law in him, our constitution has made no sort of provision towards rendering him, as a servant, in any degree responsible. Our constitution knows nothing of a magistrate like the *Justicia* of Arragon;[28] nor of any court legally appointed, nor of any process legally settled, for submitting the king to the responsibility belonging to all servants. In this he is not distinguished from the Commons and the Lords; who, in their several public capacities, can never be called to an account for their conduct; although the Revolution Society chooses to assert, in direct opposition to one of the wisest and most beautiful parts of our constitution, that "a king is no more than the first servant of the public, created by it, *and responsible to it.*"

Ill would our ancestors at the Revolution have deserved their fame for wisdom, if they had found no security for their freedom, but in rendering their government feeble in its operations and precarious in its tenure; if they had been able to contrive no better remedy against arbitrary power than civil confusion. Let these gentlemen state who that *representative* public is to whom they will affirm the king, as a servant, to be responsible. It will be then time enough for me to produce to them the positive statute law which affirms that he is not.

The ceremony of cashiering kings, of which these gentlemen talk so much at their ease, can rarely, if ever, be performed without force. It then becomes a case of war, and not of constitution. Laws are commanded to hold their tongues amongst arms; and tribunals fall to the ground with the peace they are no longer able to uphold. The Revolution of 1688 was obtained by a just war, in the only case in which any war, and much more a civil war, can be just. "Justa bella quibus *necessaria.*"[29] The question of dethroning, or, if these gentlemen like the phrase better, "cashiering kings," will always be, as it has always been, an extraordinary question of state, and wholly out of the law; a question (like all other questions of state) of dispositions, and of means, and of probable consequences, rather than of positive rights. As it was not made for common abuses, so it is not to be agitated by common minds. The speculative line of demarcation, where obedience ought to end, and resistance must begin, is faint, obscure, and not easily definable. It is not a single act, or a single event, which determines it. Governments must be abused and deranged indeed, before it can be thought of; and the prospect of the future must be as bad as the experience of the past. When things are in that lamentable condition, the nature of the disease is to indicate the remedy to those whom nature has qualified to administer in extremities this critical, ambiguous, bitter potion to a distempered state. Times, and occasions, and provocations, will teach their own lessons. The wise will determine from the gravity of the case; the irritable, from sensibility to oppression; the high-minded, from disdain and indignation at abusive power in unworthy hands; the brave and bold, from the love of honourable danger in a generous cause: but, with or without right, a revolution will be the very last resource of the thinking and the good.

The third head of right, asserted by the pulpit of the Old Jewry, namely, the "right to form a government for ourselves," has, at least, as little countenance from anything done at the Revolution, either in precedent or principle, as the two first of their claims. The Revolution was made to preserve our *ancient*, indisputable laws and liberties, and that *ancient* constitution of government which is our only security for law and liberty. If you are desirous of knowing the spirit of our constitution, and the policy which predominated in that great period which has secured it to this hour, pray look for both in our histories, in our records, in our acts of parliament, and journals of parliament, and not in the sermons of the Old Jewry, and the after-dinner toasts of the Revolution Society. In the former you will find other ideas and another language. Such a claim is as ill-suited to our temper and wishes as it is unsupported by any appearance of authority. The very idea of the fabrication of a new government is enough to fill us with disgust and horror. We wished at the period of the Revolution, and do now wish, to derive all we possess as *an inheritance from our forefathers*. Upon that body and stock of inheritance we have taken care not to inoculate any scion alien to the nature of the original plant. All the reformations we have hitherto made have proceeded upon the principle of reverence to antiquity; and I hope, nay I am persuaded, that all those which possibly may be made hereafter, will be carefully formed upon analogical precedent, authority, and example.

Our oldest reformation is that of Magna Charta.[30] You will see that Sir Edward Coke,[31] that great oracle of our law, and indeed all the great men who follow him, to Blackstone,*[32] are industrious to prove the pedigree of our liberties. They endeavour to prove, that the ancient charter, the Magna Charta of King John, was connected with another positive charter from Henry I,[33] and that both the one and the other were nothing more than a reaffirmance of the still more ancient standing law of the kingdom. In the matter of fact, for the greater part, these authors appear to be in the right; perhaps not always; but if the lawyers mistake in some particulars, it proves my position still the more strongly; because it demonstrates the powerful prepossession towards antiquity, with which the minds of all our lawyers and legislators, and of all the people whom they wish to influence, have been always filled; and the stationary policy of this kingdom in considering their most sacred rights and franchises as an *inheritance*.

In the famous law of the 3rd of Charles I, called the *Petition of Right*,[34] the parliament says to the king, "Your subjects have *inherited* this freedom," claiming their franchises not on abstract principles "as the rights of men," but as the rights of Englishmen, and as a patrimony derived from their forefathers. Selden,[35] and the other profoundly learned men, who drew this Petition of Right, were as well acquainted, at least, with all the general theories concerning the "rights of men," as any of the discoursers in our pulpits, or on your tribune; full as well as Dr. Price, or as the Abbé Sieyes.[36] But, for reasons worthy of that practical wisdom which superseded their theoretic science, they preferred this positive, recorded, *hereditary* title to all which can be dear to the man and the citizen, to that vague speculative right, which exposed their sure inheritance to be scrambled for and torn to pieces by every wild, litigious spirit.

The same policy pervades all the laws which have since been made for the preservation of our liberties. In the 1st of William and Mary, in the famous statute, called the Declaration of Right, the two Houses utter not a syllable of "a right to frame a government for themselves." You will see, that their whole care was to secure the religion, laws, and liberties, that had been long possessed, and had been lately endangered. "Taking[†] into their most serious consideration the *best* means for making such an

---

* See Blackstone's Magna Charta, printed at Oxford, 1759.
† 1 W. and M.

establishment, that their religion, laws, and liberties might not be in danger of being again subverted," they auspicate all their proceedings, by stating as some of those *best* means, "in the *first place*" to do "as their *ancestors in like cases have usually* done for vindicating their *ancient* rights and liberties, to *declare*;" – and then they pray the king and queen, "that it may be *declared* and enacted, that *all and singular* the rights and liberties *asserted and declared*, are the true *ancient* and indubitable rights and liberties of the people of this kingdom."

You will observe, that from Magna Charta to the Declaration of Right, it has been the uniform policy of our constitution to claim and assert our liberties, as an *entailed inheritance* derived to us from our forefathers, and to be transmitted to our posterity; as an estate specially belonging to the people of this kingdom, without any reference whatever to any other more general or prior right. By this means our constitution preserves a unity in so great a diversity of its parts. We have an inheritable crown; an inheritable peerage; and a House of Commons and a people inheriting privileges, franchises, and liberties, from a long line of ancestors.

This policy appears to me to be the result of profound reflection; or rather the happy effect of following nature, which is wisdom without reflection, and above it. A spirit of innovation is generally the result of a selfish temper, and confined views. People will not look forward to posterity, who never look backward to their ancestors. Besides, the people of England well know, that the idea of inheritance furnishes a sure principle of conservation, and a sure principle of transmission; without at all excluding a principle of improvement. It leaves acquisition free; but it secures what it acquires. Whatever advantages are obtained by a state proceeding on these maxims, are locked fast as in a sort of family settlement; grasped as in a kind of mortmain[37] for ever. By a constitutional policy, working after the pattern of nature, we receive, we hold, we transmit our government and our privileges, in the same manner in which we enjoy and transmit our property and our lives. The institutions of policy, the goods of fortune, the gifts of providence, are handed down to us, and from us, in the same course and order. Our political system is placed in a just correspondence and symmetry with the order of the world, and with the mode of existence decreed to a permanent body composed of transitory parts; wherein, by the disposition

of a stupendous wisdom, moulding together the great mysterious incorporation of the human race, the whole, at one time,
is never old, or middle-aged, or young, but, in a condition of
unchangeable constancy, moves on through the varied tenor of
perpetual decay, fall, renovation, and progression. Thus, by
preserving the method of nature in the conduct of the state, in
what we improve, we are never wholly new; in what we retain,
we are never wholly obsolete. By adhering in this manner and
on those principles to our forefathers, we are guided not by the
superstition of antiquarians, but by the spirit of philosophic
analogy. In this choice of inheritance we have given to our frame
of polity the image of a relation in blood; binding up the constitution of our country with our dearest domestic ties; adopting
our fundamental laws into the bosom of our family affections;
keeping inseparable, and cherishing with the warmth of all their
combined and mutually reflected charities, our state, our
hearths, our sepulchres, and our altars.

Through the same plan of a conformity to nature in our artificial institutions, and by calling in the aid of her unerring and
powerful instincts, to fortify the fallible and feeble contrivances
of our reason, we have derived several other, and those no small
benefits, from considering our liberties in the light of an inheritance. Always acting as if in the presence of canonised forefathers,
the spirit of freedom, leading in itself to misrule and excess, is
tempered with an awful gravity. This idea of a liberal descent
inspires us with a sense of habitual native dignity, which prevents
that upstart insolence almost inevitably adhering to and disgracing those who are the first acquirers of any distinction. By this
means our liberty becomes a noble freedom. It carries an imposing and majestic aspect. It has a pedigree and illustrating ancestors.
It has its bearings and its ensigns armorial. It has its gallery of portraits; its monumental inscriptions; its records, evidences, and
titles. We procure reverence to our civil institutions on the principle upon which nature teaches us to revere individual men; on
account of their age, and on account of those from whom they are
descended. All your sophisters cannot produce anything better
adapted to preserve a rational and manly freedom than the course
that we have pursued, who have chosen our nature rather than
our speculations, our breasts rather than our inventions, for the
great conservatories and magazines of our rights and privileges.

You might, if you pleased, have profited of our example,

and have given to your recovered freedom a correspondent dignity. Your privileges, though discontinued, were not lost to memory. Your constitution, it is true, whilst you were out of possession, suffered waste and dilapidation; but you possessed in some parts the walls, and, in all, the foundations, of a noble and venerable castle. You might have repaired those walls; you might have built on those old foundations. Your constitution was suspended before it was perfected; but you had the elements of a constitution very nearly as good as could be wished. In your old states[38] you possessed that variety of parts corresponding with the various descriptions of which your community was happily composed; you had all that combination, and all that opposition of interests, you had that action and counteraction, which, in the natural and in the political world, from the reciprocal struggle of discordant powers, draws out the harmony of the universe. These opposed and conflicting interests, which you considered as so great a blemish in your old and in our present constitution, interpose a salutary check to all precipitate resolutions. They render deliberation a matter not of choice, but of necessity; they make all change a subject of *compromise*, which naturally begets moderation; they produce *temperaments* preventing the sore evil of harsh, crude, unqualified reformations; and rendering all the headlong exertions of arbitrary power, in the few or in the many, for ever impracticable. Through that diversity of members and interests, general liberty had as many securities as there were separate views in the several orders; whilst by pressing down the whole by the weight of a real monarchy, the separate parts would have been prevented from warping, and starting from their allotted places.

You had all these advantages in your ancient states; but you chose to act as if you had never been moulded into civil society, and had everything to begin anew. You began ill, because you began by despising everything that belonged to you. You set up your trade without a capital. If the last generations of your country appeared without much lustre in your eyes, you might have passed them by, and derived your claims from a more early race of ancestors. Under a pious predilection for those ancestors, your imaginations would have realised in them a standard of virtue and wisdom, beyond the vulgar practice of the hour: and you would have risen with the example to whose imitation you aspired. Respecting your forefathers, you would have been taught to respect yourselves. You would not have chosen to consider the French as a people of yesterday, as a nation of low-born servile wretches until the emancipating year of 1789. In order to furnish, at the expense of your honour, an excuse to your apologists here for several enormities of yours, you would not have been content to be represented as a gang of Maroon slaves,[39] suddenly broke loose from the house of bondage, and therefore to be pardoned for your abuse of the liberty to which you were not accustomed, and ill fitted. Would it not, my worthy friend, have been wiser to have you thought, what I, for one, always thought you, a generous and gallant nation, long misled to your disadvantage by your high and romantic sentiments of fidelity, honour, and loyalty; that events had been unfavourable to you, but that you were not enslaved through any illiberal or servile disposition; that in your most devoted submission, you were actuated by a principle of public spirit, and that it was your country you worshipped, in the person of your king? Had you made it to be understood, that in the delusion of this amiable error you had gone further than your wise ancestors; that you were resolved to resume your ancient privileges, whilst you preserved the spirit of your ancient and your recent loyalty and honour; or if, diffident of yourselves, and not clearly discerning the almost obliterated constitution of your ancestors, you had looked to your neighbours in this land, who had kept alive the ancient principles and models of the old common law of Europe meliorated and adapted to its present state – by following wise examples you would have given new examples of wisdom to the world. You would have rendered the cause of liberty venerable in the eyes of every worthy mind in every nation. You would have shamed despotism from the earth, by showing that freedom was not only reconcilable, but, as when well disciplined it is, auxiliary to law. You would have had an unoppressive but a productive revenue. You would have had a flourishing commerce to feed it. You would have had a free constitution; a potent monarchy; a disciplined army; a reformed and venerated clergy; a mitigated but spirited nobility, to lead your virtue, not to overlay it; you would have had a liberal order of commons, to emulate and to recruit that nobility; you would have had a protected, satisfied, laborious, and obedient people, taught to seek and to recognise the happiness that is to be found by virtue in all conditions; in which consists the true moral equality of mankind, and not in that monstrous fiction, which, by inspiring false ideas and vain expectations into men destined to travel in the obscure walk of laborious life, serves only to aggravate and embitter that real inequality, which it never can remove; and which the order of civil life establishes as much for the benefit of those whom it must leave in an humble state, as those whom it is able to exalt to a condition more splendid, but not more happy. You had a smooth and easy career of felicity and glory laid open to you, beyond anything recorded in the history of the world; but you have shown that difficulty is good for man.

Compute your gains: see what is got by those extravagant and presumptuous speculations which have taught your leaders to despise all their predecessors, and all their contemporaries, and even to despise themselves, until the moment in which they became truly despicable. By following those false lights, France has bought undisguised calamities at a higher price than any nation has purchased the most unequivocal blessings! France has bought poverty by crime! France has not sacrificed her virtue to her interest, but she has abandoned her interest, that she might prostitute her virtue. All other nations have begun the fabric of a new government, or the reformation of an old, by establishing originally, or by enforcing with greater exactness, some rites or other of religion. All other people have laid the foundations of civil freedom in severer manners, and a system of a more austere and masculine morality. France, when she let loose the reins of regal authority, doubled the licence of a ferocious dissoluteness in manners, and of an insolent irreligion in opinions and practices; and has extended through all ranks of life, as if she were communicating some privilege, or laying open some secluded benefit, all the unhappy corruptions that usually were the disease of wealth and power. This is one of the new principles of equality in France.

France, by the perfidy of her leaders, has utterly disgraced the tone of lenient council in the cabinets of princes, and disarmed it of its most potent topics. She has sanctified the dark, suspicious maxims of tyrannous distrust; and taught kings to tremble at (what will hereafter be called) the delusive plausibilities of moral politicians. Sovereigns will consider those, who advise them to place an unlimited confidence in their people, as subverters of their thrones; as traitors who aim at their destruction, by leading their easy good-nature, under specious pretences, to admit combinations of bold and faithless men into a participation of their power. This alone (if there were nothing else) is an irreparable calamity to you and to mankind. Remember that your parliament of Paris[40] told your king, that, in calling the states together, he had nothing to fear but the prodigal excess of their zeal in providing for the support of the throne. It is right that these men should hide their heads. It is right that they should bear their part in the ruin which their counsel has brought on their sovereign and their country. Such sanguine declarations tend to lull authority asleep; to encourage it rashly to engage in perilous adventures of untried policy; to neglect those provisions, preparations, and precautions, which distinguish benevolence from imbecility; and without which no man can answer for the salutary effect of any abstract plan of government or of freedom. For want of these, they have seen the medicine of the state corrupted into its poison. They have seen the French rebel against a mild and lawful monarch, with more fury, outrage, and insult, than ever any people has been known to rise against the most illegal usurper, or the most sanguinary tyrant. Their resistance was made to concession; their revolt was from protection; their blow was aimed at a hand holding out graces, favours, and immunities.

This was unnatural. The rest is in order. They have found their punishment in their success. Laws overturned; tribunals subverted; industry without vigour; commerce expiring; the revenue unpaid, yet the people impoverished; a church pillaged, and a state not relieved; civil and military anarchy made the constitution of the kingdom; everything human and divine sacrificed to the idol of public credit, and national bankruptcy the consequence; and, to crown all, the paper securities of new, precarious, tottering power, the discredited paper securities of impoverished fraud and beggared rapine, held out as a currency for the support of an empire, in lieu of the two great recognised species that represent the lasting, conventional credit of mankind, which disappeared and hid themselves in the earth from whence they came, when the principle of property, whose creatures and representatives they are, was systematically subverted.

Were all these dreadful things necessary? Were they the inevitable results of the desperate struggle of determined patriots, compelled to wade through blood and tumult, to the quiet shore of a tranquil and prosperous liberty? No! nothing like it. The fresh ruins of France, which shock our feelings wherever we can turn our eyes, are not the devastation of civil war; they are the sad but instructive monuments of rash and ignorant counsel in time of profound peace. They are the display of inconsiderate and presumptuous, because unresisted and irresistible, authority. The persons who have thus squandered away the precious treasure of their crimes, the persons who have made this prodigal and wild waste of public evils, (the last stake reserved for the ultimate ransom of the state,) have met in their progress with little, or rather with no opposition at all. Their whole march was more like a triumphal procession, than the progress of a war. Their pioneers have gone before them, and demolished and laid everything level at their feet. Not one drop of *their* blood have they shed in the cause of the country they have ruined. They have made no sacrifices to their projects of greater consequence than their shoe-buckles,[41] whilst they were imprisoning their king, murdering their fellow-citizens, and bathing in tears, and plunging in poverty and distress, thousands of worthy men and worthy families. Their cruelty has not even been the base result of fear. It has been the effect of their sense of perfect safety, in authorising treasons, robberies, rapes, assassinations, slaughters, and burnings, throughout their harassed land. But the cause of all was plain from the beginning.

This unforced choice, this fond election of evil, would appear perfectly unaccountable, if we did not consider the composition of the National Assembly: I do not mean its formal constitution, which, as it now stands, is exceptionable enough, but the materials of which, in a great measure, it is composed, which is of ten thousand times greater consequence than all the formalities in the world. If we were to know nothing of this assembly but by its title and function, no colours could paint to the imagination anything more venerable. In that light the mind of an inquirer, subdued by such an awful image as that of the virtue and wisdom of a whole people collected into a focus, would pause and hesitate in condemning things even of the very worst aspect. Instead of blameable, they would appear only mysterious. But no name, no power, no function, no artificial institution whatsoever, can make the men of whom any system of authority is composed, any other than God, and nature, and education, and their habits of life have made them. Capacities beyond these the people have not to give. Virtue and wisdom may be the objects of their choice; but their choice confers neither the one nor the other on those upon whom they lay their ordaining hands. They have not the engagement of nature, they have not the promise of revelation, for any such powers.

After I had read over the list of the persons and descriptions elected into the *Tiers Etat*,[42] nothing which they afterwards did could appear astonishing. Among them, indeed, I saw some of known rank; some of shining talents; but of any practical experience in the state, not one man was to be found. The best were only men of theory. But whatever the distinguished few may have been, it is the substance and mass of the body which constitutes its character, and must finally determine its direction. In all bodies, those who will lead, must also, in a considerable degree, follow. They must conform their propositions to the taste, talent, and disposition, of those whom they wish to conduct: therefore, if an assembly is viciously or feebly composed in a very great part of it, nothing but such a supreme degree of virtue as very rarely appears in the world, and for that reason cannot enter into calculation, will prevent the men of talent disseminated through it from becoming only the expert instruments of absurd projects! If, what is the more likely event, instead of that unusual degree of virtue, they should be actuated by sinister ambition, and a lust of meretricious glory, then the feeble part of the assembly, to whom at first they conform, becomes in its turn the dupe and instrument of their designs. In this political traffic, the leaders will be obliged to bow to the ignorance of their followers, and the followers to become subservient to the worst designs of their leaders.

To secure any degree of sobriety in the propositions made by the leaders in any public assembly, they ought to respect, in some degree perhaps to fear, those whom they conduct. To be led any otherwise than blindly, the followers must be qualified, if not for actors, at least for judges; they must also be judges of natural weight and authority. Nothing can secure a steady and moderate conduct in such assemblies, but that the body of them should be respectably composed, in point of condition in life, of permanent property, of education, and of such habits as enlarge and liberalise the understanding.

In the calling of the states-general[43] of France, the first thing that struck me, was a great departure from the ancient course. I found the representation for the third estate composed of six hundred persons. They were equal in number to the representatives of both the other orders. If the orders were to act separately, the number would not, beyond the consideration of the expense, be of much moment. But when it became apparent that the three orders were to be melted down into one, the policy and necessary effect of this numerous representation became obvious. A very small desertion from either of the other two orders must throw the power of both into the hands of the third. In fact, the whole power of the state was soon resolved into that body.[44] Its due composition became therefore of infinitely the greater importance.

Judge, Sir, of my surprise, when I found that a very great proportion of the assembly (a majority, I believe, of the members who attended) was composed of practitioners in the law.[45] It was composed, not of distinguished magistrates, who had given pledges to their country of their science, prudence, and integrity; not of leading advocates, the glory of the bar; not of renowned professors in universities; – but for the far greater part, as it must in such a number, of the inferior, unlearned, mechanical, merely instrumental members of the profession. There were distinguished exceptions; but the general composition was of obscure provincial advocates, of stewards of petty local jurisdictions, country attornies, notaries, and the whole train of the ministers of municipal litigation, the fomenters and conductors of the petty war of village vexation. From the moment I read the list, I saw distinctly, and very nearly as it has happened, all that was to follow.

The degree of estimation in which any profession is held becomes the standard of the estimation in which the professors hold themselves. Whatever the personal merits of many individual lawyers might have been, and in many it was undoubtedly very considerable, in that military kingdom no part of the profession had been much regarded, except the highest of all, who often united to their professional offices great family splendour, and were invested with great power and authority. These certainly were highly respected, and even with no small degree of awe. The next rank was not much esteemed; the mechanical part was in a very low degree of repute.

Whenever the supreme authority is vested in a body so composed, it must evidently produce the consequences of supreme authority placed in the hands of men not taught habitually to respect themselves; who had no previous fortune in character at stake; who could not be expected to bear with moderation, or to conduct with discretion, a power, which they themselves, more than any others, must be surprised to find in their hands.

Who could flatter himself that these men, suddenly, and, as it were, by enchantment, snatched from the humblest rank of subordination, would not be intoxicated with their unprepared greatness? Who could conceive that men, who are habitually meddling, daring, subtle, active, of litigious dispositions and unquiet minds would easily fall back into their old condition of obscure contention, and laborious, low, and unprofitable chicane? Who could doubt but that, at any expense to the state, of which they understood nothing, they must pursue their private interests which they understood but too well? It was not an event depending on chance, or contingency. It was inevitable; it was necessary; it was planted in the nature of things. They must *join* (if their capacity did not permit them to *lead*) in any project which could procure to them a *litigious constitution*; which could lay open to them those innumerable lucrative jobs, which follow in the train of all great convulsions and revolutions in the state, and particularly in all great and violent permutations of property. Was it to be expected that they would attend to the stability of property, whose existence had always depended upon whatever rendered property questionable, ambiguous, and insecure? Their objects would be enlarged with their elevation, but their disposition and habits, and mode of accomplishing their designs, must remain the same.

Well! but these men were to be tempered and restrained by other descriptions, of more sober and more enlarged understandings. Were they then to be awed by the super-eminent authority and awful dignity of a handful of country clowns,[46] who have seats in that assembly, some of whom are said not to be able to read and write? and by not a greater number of traders, who, though somewhat more instructed, and more conspicuous in the order of society, had never known anything beyond their counting-house. No! both these descriptions were more formed to be overborne and swayed by the intrigues and artifices of lawyers, than to become their counterpoise. With such a dangerous disproportion, the whole must needs be governed by them. To the faculty of law was joined a pretty considerable proportion of the faculty of medicine. This faculty had not, any more than that of the law, possessed in France its just estimation. Its professors, therefore, must have the qualities of men not habituated to sentiments of dignity. But supposing they had ranked as they ought to do, and as with us they do actually, the sides of sick beds are not the academies for forming statesmen and legislators. Then came the dealers in stocks and funds, who must be eager, at any expense, to change their ideal paper wealth for the more solid substance of land. To these were joined men of other descriptions, from whom as little knowledge of, or attention to, the interests of a great state was to be expected, and as little regard to the stability of any institution; men formed to be instruments, not controls. Such in general was the composition of the *Tiers Etat* in the National Assembly; in which was scarcely to be perceived the slightest traces of what we call the natural landed interest of the country.

We know that the British House of Commons, without shutting its doors to any merit in any class, is, by the sure operation of adequate causes, filled with everything illustrious in rank, in descent, in hereditary and in acquired opulence, in cultivated talents, in military, civil, naval, and politic distinction, that the country can afford. But supposing, what hardly can be supposed as a case, that the House of Commons should be composed in the same manner with the *Tiers Etat* in France, would this dominion of chicane be borne with patience, or even conceived without horror? God forbid I should insinuate anything derogatory to that profession, which is another priesthood, administrating the rights of sacred justice. But whilst I revere men in the functions which belong to them, and would do as much as one man can do to prevent their exclusion from any, I cannot, to flatter them, give the lie to nature. They are good and useful in the composition; they must be mischievous if they preponderate so as virtually to become the whole. Their very excellence in their peculiar functions may be far from a qualification for others. It cannot escape observation, that when men are too much confined to professional and faculty habits, and as it were inveterate in the recurrent employment of that narrow circle, they are rather disabled than qualified for whatever depends on the knowledge of mankind, on experience in mixed affairs, on a comprehensive, connected view of the various, complicated, external and internal interests, which go to the formation of that multifarious thing called a state.

After all, if the House of Commons were to have a wholly professional and faculty composition, what is the power of the House of Commons, circumscribed and shut in by the immoveable barriers of laws, usages, positive rules of doctrine and practice, counterpoised by the House of Lords, and every moment of its existence at the discretion of the crown to continue, prorogue, or dissolve us? The power of the House of Commons, direct or indirect, is indeed great; and long may it be able to preserve its greatness, and the spirit belonging to true greatness, at the full; and it will do so, as long as it can keep the breakers of law in India from becoming the makers of law for England.[47] The power, however, of the House of Commons, when least diminished, is as a drop of water in the ocean, compared to that residing in a settled majority of your National Assembly. That assembly, since the destruction of the orders, has no fundamental law, no strict convention, no respected usage to restrain it. Instead of finding themselves obliged to conform to a fixed constitution, they have a power to make a constitution which shall conform to their designs. Nothing in heaven or upon earth can serve as a control on them. What ought to be the heads, the hearts, the dispositions, that are qualified, or that dare, not only to make laws under a fixed constitution, but at one heat to strike out a totally new constitution for a great kingdom, and in every part of it, from the monarch on the throne to the vestry of a parish? But – *"fools rush in where angels fear to tread."* In such a state of unbounded power for undefined and undefinable purposes, the evil of a moral and almost physical inaptitude of the man to the function must be the greatest we can conceive to happen in the management of human affairs.

Having considered the composition of the third estate as it stood in its original frame, I took a view of the representatives of the clergy. There too it appeared, that full as little regard was had to the general security of property, or to the aptitude of the deputies for their public purposes, in the principles of their election. That election was so contrived, as to send a very large proportion of mere country curates[48] to the great and arduous work of new-modelling a state; men who never had seen the state so much as in a picture; men who knew nothing of the world beyond the bounds of an obscure village; who, immersed in hopeless poverty, could regard all property, whether secular or ecclesiastical, with no other eye than that of envy; among whom must be many who, for the smallest hope of the meanest dividend in plunder, would readily join in any attempts upon a body of wealth, in which they could hardly look to have any share, except in a general scramble. Instead of balancing the power of the active chicaners in the other assembly, these curates must necessarily become the active coadjutors, or at best the passive instruments, of those by whom they had been habitually guided in their petty village concerns. They too could hardly be the most conscientious of their kind, who presuming upon their incompetent understanding, could intrigue for a trust which led them from their natural relation to their flocks, and their natural spheres of action, to undertake the regeneration of kingdoms. This preponderating weight, being added to the force of the body of chicane in the *Tiers Etat*, completed that momentum of ignorance, rashness, presumption, and lust of plunder, which nothing has been able to resist.

To observing men it must have appeared from the beginning, that the majority of the Third Estate, in conjunction with such a deputation from the clergy as I have described, whilst it pursued the destruction of the nobility, would inevitably become subservient to the worst designs of individuals in that class. In the spoil and humiliation of their own order these individuals would possess a sure fund for the pay of their new followers. To squander away the objects which made the happiness of their fellows, would be to them no sacrifice at all. Turbulent, discontented men of quality, in proportion as they are puffed up with personal pride and arrogance, generally despise their own order. One of the first symptoms they discover of a selfish and mischievous ambition, is a profligate disregard of a dignity which they partake with others. To be attached to the subdivision, to love the little platoon we belong to in society, is the first principle (the germ as it were) of public affections. It is the first link in the series by which we proceed towards a love to our country, and to mankind. The interest of that portion of social arrangement is a trust in the hands of all those who compose it; and as none but bad men would justify it in abuse, none but traitors[49] would barter it away for their own personal advantage.

There were in the time of our civil troubles in England, (I do not know whether you have any such in your assembly in France,) several persons, like the then Earl of Holland,[50] who by themselves or their families had brought an odium on the throne, by the prodigal dispensation of its bounties towards them, who afterwards joined in the rebellions arising from the discontents of which they were themselves the cause; men who helped to subvert that throne to which they owed, some of them, their existence, others all that power which they employed to ruin their benefactor. If any bounds are set to the rapacious demands of that sort of people, or that others are permitted to partake in the objects they would engross, revenge and envy soon fill up the craving void that is left in their avarice. Confounded by the complication of distempered passions, their reason is disturbed; their views become vast and perplexed; to others inexplicable; to themselves uncertain. They find, on all sides, bounds to their unprincipled ambition in any fixed order of things. But in the fog and haze of confusion all is enlarged, and appears without any limit.

When men of rank sacrifice all ideas of dignity to an ambition without a distinct object, and work with low instruments and for low ends, the whole composition becomes low and base. Does not something like this now appear in France? Does it not produce something ignoble and inglorious? a kind of meanness in all the prevalent policy? a tendency in all that is done to lower along with individuals all the dignity and importance of the state? Other revolutions have been conducted by persons, who, whilst they attempted or affected changes in the commonwealth, sanctified their ambition by advancing the dignity of the people whose peace they troubled. They had long views. They aimed at the rule, not at the destruction, of their country. They were men of great civil and great military talents, and if the terror, the ornament of their age. They were not like Jew brokers, contending with each other who could best remedy with fraudulent circulation and depreciated paper the wretchedness and ruin brought on their country by their degenerate councils. The compliment made to one of the great bad men of the old stamp (Cromwell) by his kinsman, a favourite poet of that time, shows what it was he proposed, and what indeed to a great degree he accomplished, in the success of his ambition:

> "Still as *you* rise, the *state* exalted too,
> Finds no distemper whilst 'tis changed by *you*;
> Changed like the world's great scene, when without noise
> The rising sun night's *vulgar* lights destroys."[51]

These disturbers were not so much like men usurping power, as asserting their natural place in society. Their rising was to illuminate and beautify the world. Their conquest over their competitors was by outshining them. The hand that, like a destroying angel, smote the country, communicated to it the force and energy under which it suffered. I do not say, (God forbid,) I do not say, that the virtues of such men were to be taken as a balance to their crimes: but they were some corrective to their effects. Such was, as I said, our Cromwell. Such were your whole race of Guises, Condés, and Colignis.[52] Such the Richelieus,[53] who in more quiet times acted in the spirit of a civil war. Such, as better men, and in a less dubious cause, were your Henry the Fourth and your Sully,[54] though nursed in civil confusions, and not wholly without some of their taint. It is a thing to be wondered at, to see how very soon France, when she had a moment to respire, recovered and emerged from the longest and most dreadful civil war that ever was known in any nation. Why? Because among all their massacres, they had not slain the *mind* in their country. A conscious dignity, a noble pride, a generous sense of glory and emulation, was not extinguished. On the contrary, it was kindled and inflamed. The organs also of the state, however shattered, existed. All the prizes of honour and virtue, all the rewards, all the distinctions remained. But your present confusion, like a palsy, has attacked the fountain of life itself. Every person in your country, in a situation to be actuated by a principle of honour, is disgraced and degraded, and can entertain no sensation of life, except in a mortified and humiliated indignation. But this generation will quickly pass away. The next generation of the nobility will resemble the artificers and clowns, and money-jobbers, usurers, and Jews,[55] who will be always their fellows, sometimes their masters. Believe me, Sir, those who attempt to level, never equalise. In all societies, consisting of various descriptions of citizens, some description must be uppermost. The levellers therefore only change and pervert the natural order of things; they load the edifice of society, by setting up in the air what the solidity of the structure requires to be on the ground. The association of tailors and carpenters, of which the republic (of Paris, for instance) is composed, cannot be equal to the situation, into which, by the worst of usurpations, an usurpation on the prerogatives of nature, you attempt to force them.

The Chancellor of France at the opening of the states, said, in a tone of oratorical flourish, that all occupations were honourable. If he meant only, that no honest employment was disgraceful, he would not have gone beyond the truth. But in asserting that anything is honourable, we imply some distinction in its favour. The occupation of a hair-dresser, or of a working tallow-chandler, cannot be a matter of honour to any person — to say nothing of a number of other more servile employments. Such descriptions of men ought not to suffer oppression from the state; but the state suffers oppression, if such as they, either individually or collectively, are permitted to rule. In this you think you are combating prejudice, but you are at war with nature.*

I do not, my dear Sir, conceive you to be of that sophistical, captious spirit, or of that uncandid dulness, as to require, for every general observation or sentiment, an explicit detail of the correctives and exceptions, which reason will presume to be included in all the general propositions which come from reasonable men. You do not imagine, that I wish to confine power, authority, and distinction to blood, and names, and titles. No, Sir. There is no qualification for government but virtue and wisdom, actual or presumptive. Wherever they are actually found, they have, in whatever state, condition, profession, or trade, the passport of Heaven to human place and honour. Woe to the country which would madly and impiously reject the service of the talents and virtues, civil, military, or religious, that are given to grace and to serve it; and would condemn to obscurity everything formed to diffuse lustre and glory around a state! Woe to that country too, that, passing into the opposite extreme, considers a low education, a mean contracted view of things, a sordid, mercenary occupation, as a preferable title to command! Everything ought to be open; but not indifferently to every man. No rotation; no appointment by lot; no mode of election operating in the spirit of sortition, or rotation, can be generally good in a government conversant in extensive objects. Because they have no tendency, direct or indirect, to select the man with a view to the duty, or

---

* Ecclesiasticus, chap. xxxviii. verse 24, 25. "The wisdom of a learned man cometh by opportunity of leisure: and he that hath little business shall become wise." – "How can he get wisdom that holdeth the plough, and that glorieth in the goad; that driveth oxen; and is occupied in their labours; and whose talk is of bullocks?"

Ver. 27. "So every carpenter and work-master that laboureth night and day," &c.

Ver. 33. "They shall not be sought for in public counsel, nor sit high in the congregation: they shall not sit on the judge's seat, nor understand the sentence of judgment; they cannot declare justice and judgment, and they shall not be found where parables are spoken."

Ver. 34. "But they will maintain the state of the world."

I do not determine whether this book be canonical, as the Gallican church (till lately) has considered it, or apocryphal, as here it is taken. I am sure it contains a great deal of sense and truth.

to accommodate the one to the other. I do not hesitate to say, that the road to eminence and power, from obscure condition, ought not to be made too easy, nor a thing too much of course. If rare merit be the rarest of all rare things, it ought to pass through some sort of probation. The temple of honour ought to be seated on an eminence. If it be opened through virtue, let it be remembered too, that virtue is never tried but by some difficulty and some struggle.

Nothing is a due and adequate representation of a state, that does not represent its ability, as well as its property. But as ability is a vigorous and active principle, and as property is sluggish, inert, and timid, it never can be safe from the invasions of ability, unless it be, out of all proportion, predominant in the representation. It must be represented too in great masses of accumulation, or it is not rightly protected. The characteristic essence of property, formed out of the combined principles of its acquisition and conservation, is to be *unequal*. The great masses therefore which excite envy, and tempt rapacity, must be put out of the possibility of danger. Then they form a natural rampart about the lesser properties in all their gradations. The same quantity of property, which is by the natural course of things divided among many, has not the same operation. Its defensive power is weakened as it is diffused. In this diffusion each man's portion is less than what, in the eagerness of his desires, he may flatter himself to obtain by dissipating the accumulations of others. The plunder of the few would indeed give but a share inconceivably small in the distribution to the many. But the many are not capable of making this calculation; and those who lead them to rapine never intend this distribution.

The power of perpetuating our property in our families is one of the most valuable and interesting circumstances belonging to it, and that which tends the most to the perpetuation of society itself. It makes our weakness subservient to our virtue; it grafts benevolence even upon avarice. The possessors of family wealth, and of the distinction which attends hereditary possession, (as most concerned in it,) are the natural securities for this transmission. With us the House of Peers is formed upon this principle. It is wholly composed of hereditary property and hereditary distinction; and made therefore the third of the legislature; and, in the last event, the sole judge of all property in all its subdivisions. The House of Commons too, though not necessarily, yet in fact,

is always so composed, in the far greater part. Let those large proprietors be what they will, and they have their chance of being
amongst the best, they are, at the very worst, the ballast in the
vessel of the commonwealth. For though hereditary wealth, and
the rank which goes with it, are too much idolised by creeping
sycophants, and the blind, abject admirers of power, they are too
rashly slighted in shallow speculations of the petulant, assuming,
short-sighted coxcombs of philosophy. Some decent, regulated
pre-eminence, some preference (not exclusive appropriation)
given to birth, is neither unnatural, nor unjust, nor impolitic.

It is said, that twenty-four millions ought to prevail over two
hundred thousand. True; if the constitution of a kingdom be a
problem of arithmetic. This sort of discourse does well enough
with the lamp-post for its second:[56] to men who may reason
calmly, it is ridiculous. The will of the many, and their interest,
must very often differ; and great will be the difference when they
make an evil choice. A government of five hundred country
attornies and obscure curates is not good for twenty-four millions of men, though it were chosen by eight and forty millions;
nor is it the better for being guided by a dozen of persons of quality, who have betrayed their trust in order to obtain that power.
At present, you seem in everything to have strayed out of the
high road of nature. The property of France does not govern it.
Of course property is destroyed, and rational liberty has no existence. All you have got for the present is a paper circulation, and
a stock-jobbing constitution: and, as to the future, do you seriously think that the territory of France, upon the republican system of eighty-three independent municipalities, (to say nothing
of the parts that compose them,) can ever be governed as one
body, or can ever be set in motion by the impulse of one mind?
When the National Assembly has completed its work, it will have
accomplished its ruin. These commonwealths will not long bear
a state of subjection to the republic of Paris. They will not bear
that this one body should monopolise the captivity of the king,
and the dominion over the assembly calling itself national. Each
will keep its own portion of the spoil of the church to itself; and
it will not suffer either that spoil, or the more just fruits of their
industry, or the natural produce of their soil, to be sent to swell
the insolence, or pamper the luxury, of the mechanics of Paris.
In this they will see none of the equality, under the pretence of
which they have been tempted to throw off their allegiance to

their sovereign, as well as the ancient constitution of their country. There can be no capital city in such a constitution as they have lately made. They have forgot, that when they framed democratic governments, they had virtually dismembered their country. The person, whom they persevere in calling king, has not power left to him by the hundredth part sufficient to hold together this collection of republics. The republic of Paris will endeavour indeed to complete the debauchery of the army, and illegally to perpetuate the assembly, without resort to its constituents, as the means of continuing its despotism. It will make efforts, by becoming the heart of a boundless paper circulation, to draw everything to itself; but in vain. All this policy in the end will appear as feeble as it is now violent.

If this be your actual situation, compared to the situation to which you were called, as it were by the voice of God and man, I cannot find it in my heart to congratulate you on the choice you have made, or the success which has attended your endeavours. I can as little recommend to any other nation a conduct grounded on such principles, and productive of such effects. That I must leave to those who can see farther into your affairs than I am able to do, and who best know how far your actions are favourable to their designs. The gentlemen of the Revolution Society, who were so early in their congratulations, appear to be strongly of opinion that there is some scheme of politics relative to this country, in which your proceedings may, in some way, be useful. For your Dr. Price, who seems to have speculated himself into no small degree of fervour upon this subject, addresses his auditory in the following very remarkable words: "I cannot conclude without recalling *particularly* to your recollection a consideration which I have *more than once alluded to*, and which probably your thoughts have *been all along anticipating*; a consideration with which my *mind is impressed more than I can express*. I mean the consideration of the *favourableness of the present times to all exertions in the cause of liberty*."

It is plain that the mind of this *political* preacher was at the time big with some extraordinary design; and it is very probable that the thoughts of his audience, who understood him better than I do, did all along run before him in his reflection, and in the whole train of consequences to which it led.

Before I read that sermon, I really thought I had lived in a free country; and it was an error I cherished, because it gave me a greater liking to the country I lived in. I was indeed aware, that a jealous, ever-waking vigilance, to guard the treasure of our liberty, not only from invasion, but from decay and corruption, was our best wisdom, and our first duty. However, I considered that treasure rather as a possession to be secured, than as a prize to be contended for. I did not discern how the present time came to be so very favourable to all *exertions* in the cause of freedom. The present time differs from any other only by the circumstance of what is doing in France. If the example of that nation is to have an influence on this, I can easily conceive why some of their proceedings which have an unpleasant aspect, and are not quite reconcilable to humanity, generosity, good faith, and justice, are palliated with so much milky good-nature towards the actors, and borne with so much heroic fortitude towards the sufferers. It is certainly not prudent to discredit the authority of an example we mean to follow. But allowing this, we are led to a very natural question; – What is that cause of liberty, and what are those exertions in its favour, to which the example of France is so singularly auspicious? Is our monarchy to be annihilated, with all the laws, all the tribunals, and all the ancient corporations of the kingdom? Is every land-mark of the country to be done away in favour of a geometrical and arithmetical constitution? Is the House of Lords to be voted useless? Is episcopacy to be abolished? Are the church lands to be sold to Jews and jobbers; or given to bribe new-invented municipal republics into a participation in sacrilege? Are all the taxes to be voted grievances, and the revenue reduced to a patriotic contribution, or patriotic presents? Are silver shoe-buckles to be substituted in the place of the land tax and the malt tax, for the support of the naval strength of this kingdom? Are all orders, ranks, and distinctions to be confounded, that out of universal anarchy, joined to national bankruptcy, three or four thousand democracies should be formed into eighty-three, and that they may all, by some sort of unknown attractive power, be organised into one? For this great end is the army to be seduced from its discipline and its fidelity, first by every kind of debauch-ery, and then by the terrible precedent of a donative in the increase of pay? Are the curates to be seduced from their bishops, by hold-ing out to them the delusive hope of a dole out of the spoils of their own order? Are the citizens of London to be drawn from their allegiance by feeding them at the expense of their fellow-subjects? Is a compulsory paper currency to be substituted in the place of the legal coin of this kingdom? Is what remains of the plundered stock of public revenue to be employed in the wild project of maintaining two armies to watch over and to fight with each other? If these are the ends and means of the Revolution Society, I admit they are well assorted; and France may furnish them for both with precedents in point.

I see that your example is held out to shame us. I know that we are supposed a dull, sluggish race, rendered passive by finding our situation tolerable, and prevented by a mediocrity of freedom from ever attaining to its full perfection. Your leaders in France began by affecting to admire, almost to adore, the British constitution; but as they advanced, they came to look upon it with a sovereign contempt. The friends of your National Assembly amongst us have full as mean an opinion of what was formerly thought the glory of their country. The Revolution Society has discovered that the English nation is not free. They are convinced that the inequality in our representation is a "defect in our constitution *so gross and palpable*, as to make it excellent chiefly in *form* and *theory*." * That a representation in the legislature of a kingdom is not only the basis of all constitutional liberty in it, but of "*all legitimate government*; that without it a *government* is nothing but an *usurpation*;" – that "when the representation is *partial*, the kingdom possesses liberty only *partially*; and if extremely partial; it gives only a *semblance*; and if not only extremely partial, but corruptly chosen, it becomes a *nuisance*." Dr. Price considers this inadequacy of representation as our *fundamental grievance*; and though, as to the corruption of this semblance of representation, he hopes it is not yet arrived to its full perfection of depravity, he fears that "nothing will be done towards gaining for us this *essential blessing*, until some *great abuse of power* again provokes our resentment, or some *great calamity* again alarms our fears, or perhaps till the acquisition of a *pure and equal representation by other countries*, whilst we are *mocked* with the *shadow*, kindles our shame." To this he subjoins a note in these words: "A representation chosen chiefly by the treasury, and a *few* thousands of the *dregs* of the people, who are generally paid for their votes."

You will smile here at the consistency of those democratists, who, when they are not on their guard, treat the humbler part of the community with the greatest contempt, whilst, at the

* Discourse on the Love of our Country, 3rd edit. p. 39.

same time, they pretend to make them the depositories of all power. It would require a long discourse to point out to you the many fallacies that lurk in the generality and equivocal nature of the terms "inadequate representation." I shall only say here, in justice to that old-fashioned constitution, under which we have long prospered, that our representation has been found perfectly adequate to all the purposes for which a representation of the people can be desired or devised. I defy the enemies of our constitution to show the contrary. To detail the particulars in which it is found so well to promote its ends, would demand a treatise on our practical constitution. I state here the doctrine of the Revolutionists, only that you and others may see what an opinion these gentlemen entertain of the constitution of their country, and why they seem to think that some great abuse of power, or some great calamity, as giving a chance for the blessing of a constitution according to their ideas, would be much palliated to their feelings; you see *why they* are so much enamoured of your fair and equal representation, which being once obtained, the same effects might follow. You see they consider our House of Commons as only "a semblance," "a form," "a theory," "a shadow," "a mockery," perhaps "a nuisance."

These gentlemen value themselves on being systematic; and not without reason. They must therefore look on this gross and palpable defect of representation, this fundamental grievance, (so they call it,) as a thing not only vicious in itself, but as rendering our whole government absolutely *illegitimate*, and not at all better than a downright *usurpation*. Another revolution, to get rid of this illegitimate and usurped government, would of course be perfectly justifiable, if not absolutely necessary. Indeed their principle, if you observe it with any attention, goes much further than to an alteration in the election of the House of Commons; for, if popular representation, or choice, is necessary to the *legitimacy* of all government, the House of Lords is, at one stroke, bastardised and corrupted in blood. That House is no representative of the people at all, even in "semblance or in form." The case of the crown is altogether as bad. In vain the crown may endeavour to screen itself against these gentlemen by the authority of the establishment made on the Revolution. The Revolution which is resorted to for a title, on their system, wants a title itself. The Revolution is built, according to their theory, upon a basis not more solid than our present formalities, as it was made by a House of Lords, not representing any one but themselves; and by a House of Commons exactly such as the present, that is, as they term it, by a mere "shadow and mockery" of representation.

Something they must destroy, or they seem to themselves to exist for no purpose. One set is for destroying the civil power through the ecclesiastical; another, for demolishing the ecclesiastic through the civil. They are aware that the worst consequences might happen to the public in accomplishing this double ruin of church and state; but they are so heated with their theories, that they give more than hints, that this ruin, with all the mischiefs that must lead to it and attend it, and which to themselves appear quite certain, would not be unacceptable to them, or very remote from their wishes. A man[57] amongst them of great authority, and certainly of great talents, speaking of a supposed alliance between church and state, says, "perhaps *we must wait for the fall of the civil powers* before this most unnatural alliance be broken. Calamitous no doubt will that time be. But what convulsion in the political world ought to be a subject of lamentation, if it be attended with so desirable an effect?" You see with what a steady eye these gentlemen are prepared to view the greatest calamities which can befall their country.

It is no wonder therefore, that with these ideas of everything in their constitution and government at home, either in church or state, as illegitimate and usurped, or at best as a vain mockery, they look abroad with an eager and passionate enthusiasm. Whilst they are possessed by these notions, it is vain to talk to them of the practice of their ancestors, the fundamental laws of their country, the fixed form of a constitution, whose merits are confirmed by the solid test of long experience, and an increasing public strength and national prosperity. They despise experience as the wisdom of unlettered men; and as for the rest, they have wrought under-ground a mine that will blow up, at one grand explosion, all examples of antiquity, all precedents, charters, and acts of parliament. They have "the rights of men." Against these there can be no prescription; against these no agreement is binding: these admit no temperament, and no compromise: anything withheld from their full demand is so much of fraud and injustice. Against these their rights of men let no government look for security in the length of its continuance, or in the justice and lenity of its administration. The objections of these speculatists, if its forms do not quadrate with their theories, are as valid against such an old and beneficent government, as against the most violent tyranny, or the greenest usurpation. They are always at issue with governments, not on a question of abuse, but a question of competency, and a question of title. I have nothing to say to the clumsy subtilty of their political metaphysics. Let them be their amusement in the schools. – "Illa *se jactat in aula – Æolus, et clauso ventorum carcere regnet*."[58] – But let them not break prison to burst like a *Levanter*, to sweep the earth with their hurricane, and to break up the fountains of the great deep to overwhelm us.

Far am I from denying in theory, full as far is my heart from withholding in practice, (if I were of power to give or to withhold,) the *real* rights of men. In denying their false claims of right, I do not mean to injure those which are real, and are such as their pretended rights would totally destroy. If civil society be made for the advantage of man, all the advantages for which it is made become his right. It is an institution of beneficence; and law itself is only beneficence acting by a rule. Men have a right to live by that rule; they have a right to do justice, as between their fellows, whether their fellows are in public function or in ordinary occupation. They have a right to the fruits of their industry; and to the means of making their industry fruitful. They have a right to the acquisitions of their parents; to the nourishment and improvement of their offspring; to instruction in life, and to consolation in death. Whatever each man can separately do, without trespassing upon others, he has a right to do for himself; and he has a right to a fair portion of all which society, with all its combinations of skill and force, can do in his favour. In this partnership all men have equal rights; but not to equal things. He that has but five shillings in the partnership, has as good a right to it, as he that has five hundred pounds has to his larger proportion. But he has not a right to an equal dividend in the product of the joint stock; and as to the share of power, authority, and direction which each individual ought to have in the management of the state, that I must deny to be amongst the direct original rights of man in civil society; for I have in my contemplation the civil social man, and no other. It is a thing to be settled by convention.

If civil society be the offspring of convention, that convention must be its law. That convention must limit and modify all the descriptions of constitution which are formed under it. Every sort of legislative, judicial, or executory power are its creatures. They can have no being in any other state of things; and how can any man claim under the conventions of civil society, rights which do not so much as suppose its existence? rights which are absolutely repugnant to it? One of the first motives to civil society, and which becomes one of its fundamental rules, is, *that no man should be judge in his own cause*. By this each person has at once divested himself of the first fundamental right of uncovenanted man, that is, to judge for himself, and to assert his own cause. He abdicates all right to be his own governor. He inclusively, in a great measure, abandons the right of self-defence, the first law of nature. Men cannot enjoy the rights of an uncivil and of a civil state together. That he may obtain justice, he gives up his right of determining what it is in points the most essential to him. That he may secure some liberty, he makes a surrender in trust of the whole of it.

Government is not made in virtue of natural rights, which may and do exist in total independence of it; and exist in much greater clearness, and in a much greater degree of abstract perfection: but their abstract perfection is their practical defect. By having a right to everything they want everything. Government is a contrivance of human wisdom to provide for human *wants*. Men have a right that these wants should be provided for by this wisdom. Among these wants is to be reckoned the want, out of civil society, of a sufficient restraint upon their passions. Society requires not only that the passions of individuals should be subjected, but that even in the mass and body, as well as in the individuals, the inclinations of men should frequently be thwarted, their will controlled, and their passions brought into subjection. This can only be done *by a power out of themselves*; and not, in the exercise of its function, subject to that will and to those passions which it is its office to bridle and subdue. In this sense the restraints on men, as well as their liberties, are to be reckoned among their rights. But as the liberties and the restrictions vary with times and circumstances, and admit of infinite modifications, they cannot be settled upon any abstract rule; and nothing is so foolish as to discuss them upon that principle.

The moment you abate anything from the full rights of men, each to govern himself, and suffer any artificial, positive limitation upon those rights, from that moment the whole organisation of government becomes a consideration of convenience. This it is which makes the constitution of a state, and the due distribution of its powers, a matter of the most delicate and complicated skill. It requires a deep knowledge of human nature and human necessities, and of the things which facilitate or obstruct the various ends, which are to be pursued by the mechanism of civil institutions. The state is to have recruits to its strength, and remedies to its distempers. What is the use of discussing a man's abstract right to food or medicine? The question is upon the method of procuring and administering them. In that deliberation I shall always advise to call in the aid of the farmer and the physician, rather than the professor of metaphysics.

The science of constructing a commonwealth, or renovating it, or reforming it, is, like every other experimental science, not to be taught *à priori*. Nor is it a short experience that can instruct us in that practical science; because the real effects of moral causes are not always immediate; but that which in the first instance is prejudicial may be excellent in its remoter operation; and its excellence may arise even from the ill effects it produces in the beginning. The reverse also happens: and very plausible schemes, with very pleasing commencements, have often shameful and lamentable conclusions. In states there are often some obscure and almost latent causes, things which appear at first view of little moment, on which a very great part of its prosperity or adversity may most essentially depend. The science of government being therefore so practical in itself, and intended for such practical purposes, a matter which requires experience, and even more experience than any person can gain in his whole life, however sagacious and observing he may be, it is with infinite caution that any man ought to venture upon pulling down an edifice, which has answered in any tolerable degree for ages the common purposes of society, or on building it up again, without having models and patterns of approved utility before his eyes.

These metaphysic rights entering into common life, like rays of light which pierce into a dense medium, are, by the laws of nature, refracted from their straight line. Indeed in the gross and complicated mass of human passions and concerns, the primitive rights of men undergo such a variety of refractions and reflections, that it becomes absurd to talk of them as if they continued in the simplicity of their original direction. The nature of man is intricate; the objects of society are of the greatest possible complexity: and therefore no simple disposition or direction of power can be suitable either to man's nature, or to the quality of his affairs. When I hear the simplicity of contrivance aimed at and boasted of in any new political constitutions, I am at no loss to decide that the artificers are grossly ignorant of their trade, or totally negligent of their duty. The simple governments are fundamentally defective, to say no worse of them. If you were to contemplate society in but one point of view, all these simple modes of polity are infinitely captivating. In effect each would answer its single end much more perfectly than the more complex is able to attain all its complex purposes. But it is better that the whole should be imperfectly and anomalously answered, than that, while some parts are provided for with great exactness, others might be totally neglected, or perhaps materially injured, by the over-care of a favourite member.

The pretended rights of these theorists are all extremes: and in proportion as they are metaphysically true, they are morally and politically false. The rights of men are in a sort of *middle*, incapable of definition, but not impossible to be discerned. The rights of men in governments are their advantages; and these are often in balances between differences of good; in compromises sometimes between good and evil, and sometimes between evil and evil. Political reason is a computing principle; adding, subtracting, multiplying, and dividing, morally and not metaphysically, or mathematically, true moral denominations.

By these theorists the right of the people is almost always sophistically confounded with their power. The body of the community, whenever it can come to act, can meet with no effectual resistance; but till power and right are the same, the whole body of them has no right inconsistent with virtue, and the first of all virtues, prudence. Men have no right to what is not reasonable, and to what is not for their benefit; for though a pleasant writer said, *Liceat perire poetis*, when one of them, in cold blood, is said to have leaped into the flames of a volcanic revolution, *Ardentem frigidus Ætnam insiluit*,[59] I consider such a frolic rather as an unjustifiable poetic licence, than as one of the franchises of Parnassus;[60] and whether he were poet, or divine, or politician, that chose to exercise this kind of right, I think that more wise, because more charitable, thoughts would urge me rather to save the man, than to preserve his brazen slippers as the monuments of his folly.

The kind of anniversary sermons to which a great part of what I write refers, if men are not shamed out of their present course, in commemorating the fact, will cheat many out of the principles, and deprive them of the benefits, of the revolution they commemorate. I confess to you, Sir, I never liked this continual talk of resistance, and revolution, or the practice of making the extreme medicine of the constitution its daily bread. It renders the habit of society dangerously valetudinary: it is taking periodical doses of mercury sublimate, and swallowing down repeated provocatives of cantharides[61] to our love of liberty.

This distemper of remedy, grown habitual, relates and wears out, by a vulgar and prostituted use, the spring of that spirit which is to be exerted on great occasions. It was in the most patient period of Roman servitude that themes of tyrannicide made the ordinary exercise of boys at school – *cum perimit sævos classis numerosa tyrannos.*[62] In the ordinary state of things, it produces in a country like ours the worst effects, even on the cause of that liberty which it abuses with the dissoluteness of an extravagant speculation. Almost all the high-bred republicans of my time have, after a short space, become the most decided, thorough-paced courtiers; they soon left the business of a tedious, moderate, but practical resistance, to those of us whom, in the pride and intoxication of their theories, they have slighted as not much better than Tories. Hypocrisy, of course, delights in the most sublime speculations; for, never intending to go beyond speculation, it costs nothing to have it magnificent. But even in cases where rather levity than fraud was to be suspected in these ranting speculations, the issue has been much the same. These professors, finding their extreme principles not applicable to cases which call only for a qualified, or, as I may say, civil and legal resistance, in such cases employ no resistance at all. It is with them a war or a revolution, or it is nothing. Finding their schemes of politics not adapted to the state of the world in which they live, they often come to think lightly of all public principle; and are ready, on their part, to abandon for a very trivial interest what they find of very trivial value. Some indeed are of more steady and persevering natures; but these are eager politicians out of parliament, who have little to tempt them to abandon their favourite projects. They have some change in the church or state, or both, constantly in their view. When that is the case, they are always bad citizens, and perfectly unsure connexions. For, considering their speculative designs as of infinite value, and the actual arrangement of the state as of no estimation, they are at best indifferent about it. They see no merit in the good, and no fault in the vicious, management of public affairs, they rather rejoice in the latter, as more propitious to revolution. They see no merit or demerit in any man, or any action, or any political principle, any further than as they may forward or retard their design of change: they therefore take up, one day, the most violent and stretched prerogative, and another time the wildest democratic ideas of freedom, and pass from the one to the other without any sort of regard to cause, to person, or to party.

In France you are now in the crisis of a revolution, and in the transit from one form of government to another – you cannot see that character of men exactly in the same situation in which we see it in this country. With us it is militant; with you it is triumphant; and you know how it can act when its power is commensurate to its will. I would not be supposed to confine those observations to any description of men, or to comprehend all men of any description within them – No! far from it. I am as incapable of that injustice, as I am of keeping terms with those who profess principles of extremities; and who, under the name of religion, teach little else than wild and dangerous politics. The worst of these politics of revolution is this: they temper and harden the breast, in order to prepare it for the desperate strokes which are sometimes used in extreme occasions. But as these occasions may never arrive, the mind receives a gratuitous taint; and the moral sentiments suffer not a little, when no political purpose is served by the depravation. This sort of people are so taken up with their theories about the rights of man, that they have totally forgotten his nature. Without opening one new avenue to the understanding, they have succeeded in stopping up those that lead to the heart. They have perverted in themselves, and in those that attend to them, all the well-placed sympathies of the human breast.

This famous sermon of the Old Jewry breathes nothing but this spirit through all the political part. Plots, massacres, assassinations, seem to some people a trivial price for obtaining a revolution. A cheap, bloodless reformation, a guiltless liberty, appear flat and vapid to their taste. There must be a great change of scene; there must be a magnificent stage effect; there must be a grand spectacle to rouse the imagination, grown torpid with the lazy enjoyment of sixty years' security, and the still unanimating repose of public prosperity. The preacher found them all in the French Revolution. This inspires a juvenile warmth through his whole frame. His enthusiasm kindles as he advances; and when he arrives at his peroration it is in a full blaze. Then viewing, from the Pisgah[63] of his pulpit, the free, moral, happy, flourishing, and glorious state of France, as in a bird's-eye landscape of a promised land, he breaks out into the following rapture:

"What an eventful period is this! I am *thankful* that I have lived to it; I could almost say, *Lord, now lettest thou thy servant depart in peace, for mine eyes have seen thy salvation.* – I have lived to see a *diffusion* of knowledge, which has undermined superstition and error. – I have lived to see *the rights of men* better understood than ever; and nations panting for liberty which seemed to have lost the idea of it. – I have lived to see *thirty millions of people*, indignant and resolute, spurning at slavery, and demanding liberty with an irresistible voice. *Their king led in triumph, and an arbitrary monarch surrendering himself to his subjects.*" *

Before I proceed further, I have to remark, that Dr. Price seems rather to overvalue the great acquisitions of light which he has obtained and diffused in this age. The last century appears to me to have been quite as much enlightened. It had, though in a different place, a triumph as memorable as that of Dr. Price; and some of the great preachers of that period partook of it as eagerly as he has done in the triumph of France. On the trial of the Rev. Hugh Peters for high treason, it was deposed, that when King Charles was brought to London for his trial, the Apostle of Liberty in that day conducted the *triumph*. "I saw," says the witness, "his Majesty in the coach with six horses, and Peters riding before the king, *triumphing*." Dr. Price, when he talks as if he had made a discovery, only follows a precedent; for, after the commencement of the king's trial, this precursor, the same Dr. Peters, concluding a long prayer at the Royal Chapel at White-hall, (he had very triumphantly chosen his place,) said, "I have prayed and preached these twenty years; and now I may say with old Simeon, *Lord, now lettest thou thy servant depart in peace, for mine eyes have seen thy salvation.*" † Peters had not the fruits of his prayer; for he neither departed so soon as he wished, nor in

---

* Another of these reverend gentlemen, who was witness to some of the spectacles which Paris has lately exhibited, expresses himself thus – "*A king dragged in submissive triumph by his conquering subjects*, is one of those appearances of grandeur which seldom rise in the prospect of human affairs, and which, during the remainder of my life, I shall think of with wonder and gratification." These gentlemen agree marvellously in their feelings.

† State Trials, vol. ii. p. 360, 363.

peace. He became (what I heartily hope none of his followers may be in this country) himself a sacrifice to the triumph which he led as pontiff. They dealt at the Restoration, perhaps, too hardly with this poor good man. But we owe it to his memory and his sufferings, that he had as much illumination, and as much zeal, and had as effectually undermined all *the superstition and error* which might impede the great business he was engaged in, as any who follow and repeat after him, in this age, which would assume to itself an exclusive title to the knowledge of the rights of men, and all the glorious consequences of that knowledge.

After this sally of the preacher of the Old Jewry, which differs only in place and time, but agrees perfectly with the spirit and letter of the rapture of 1648, the Revolution Society, the fabricators of governments, the heroic band of *cashierers* of *monarchs*, electors of sovereigns, and leaders of kings in triumph, strutting with a proud consciousness of the diffusion of knowledge, of which every member had obtained so large a share in the donative, were in haste to make a generous diffusion of the knowledge they had thus gratuitously received. To make this bountiful communication, they adjourned from the church in the Old Jewry to the London Tavern; where the same Dr. Price, in whom the fumes of his oracular tripod were not entirely evaporated, moved and carried the resolution, or address of congratulation, transmitted by Lord Stanhope to the National Assembly of France.

I find a preacher of the gospel profaning the beautiful and prophetic ejaculation, commonly called "*nunc dimittis*,"[64] made on the first presentation of our Saviour in the temple, and applying it, with an inhuman and unnatural rapture, to the most horrid, atrocious, and afflicting spectacle that perhaps ever was exhibited to the pity and indignation of mankind. This "*leading in triumph*," a thing in its best form unmanly and irreligious, which fills our preacher with such unhallowed transports, must shock, I believe, the moral taste of every well-born mind. Several English were the stupified and indignant spectators of that triumph. It was (unless we have been strangely deceived) a spectacle more resembling a procession of American savages, entering into Onondaga,[65] after some of their murders called victories, and leading into hovels hung round with scalps, their captives, overpowered with the scoffs and buffets of women as ferocious as themselves, much more than it resembled the triumphal pomp of a civilised, martial nation; — if a civilised nation, or any men who had a sense of generosity, were capable of a personal triumph over the fallen and afflicted.

This, my dear Sir, was not the triumph of France. I must believe that, as a nation, it overwhelmed you with shame and horror. I must believe that the National Assembly find themselves in a state of the greatest humiliation in not being able to punish the authors of this triumph, or the actors in it; and that they are in a situation in which any inquiry they may make upon the subject must be destitute even of the appearance of liberty or impartiality. The apology of that assembly is found in their situation; but when we approve what they *must* bear, it is in us the degenerate choice of a vitiated mind.

With a compelled appearance of deliberation, they vote under the dominion of a stern necessity. They sit in the heart, as it were, of a foreign republic: they have their residence in a city whose constitution has emanated neither from the charter of their king, nor from their legislative power. There they are surrounded by an army[66] not raised either by the authority of their crown, or by their command; and which, if they should order to dissolve itself, would instantly dissolve them. There they sit, after a gang of assassins[67] had driven away some hundreds of the members; whilst those who held the same moderate principles, with more patience or better hope, continued every day exposed to outrageous insults and murderous threats. There a majority, sometimes real, sometimes pretended, captive itself, compels a captive king to issue as royal edicts, at third hand, the polluted nonsense of their most licentious and giddy coffee-houses. It is notorious, that all their measures are decided before they are debated. It is beyond doubt, that under the terror of the bayonet, and the lamp-post, and the torch to their houses, they are obliged to adopt all the crude and desperate measures suggested by clubs composed of a monstrous medley of all conditions, tongues, and nations. Among these are found persons, in comparison of whom Catiline would be thought scrupulous, and Cethegus[68] a man of sobriety and moderation. Nor is it in these clubs alone that the public measures are deformed into monsters. They undergo a previous distortion in academies, intended as so many seminaries for these clubs, which are set up in all the places of public resort. In these meetings of all sorts, every counsel, in proportion as it is daring, and violent, and perfidious, is taken for the mark of superior genius. Humanity and compassion are ridiculed as the fruits of superstition and ignorance. Tenderness to individuals is considered as treason to the public. Liberty is always to be estimated perfect as property is rendered insecure. Amidst assassination, massacre, and confiscation, perpetrated or meditated, they are forming plans for the good order of future society. Embracing in their arms the carcases of base criminals, and promoting their relations on the title of their offences, they drive hundreds of virtuous persons to the same end, by forcing them to subsist by beggary or by crime.

The assembly, their organ, acts before them the farce of deliberation with as little decency as liberty. They act like the comedians of a fair before a riotous audience; they act amidst the tumultuous cries of a mixed mob of ferocious men, and of women lost to shame, who, according to their insolent fancies, direct, control, applaud, explode them; and sometimes mix and take their seats amongst them; domineering over them with a strange mixture of servile petulance and proud, presumptuous authority. As they have inverted order in all things, the gallery is in the place of the house. This assembly, which overthrows kings and kingdoms, has not even the physiognomy and aspect of a grave legislative body – *nec color imperii, nec frons ulla senatûs.*[69] They have a power given to them, like that of the evil principle, to subvert and destroy; but none to construct, except such machines as may be fitted for further subversion and further destruction.

Who is it that admires, and from the heart is attached to, national representative assemblies, but must turn with horror and disgust from such a profane burlesque, and abominable per-version of that sacred institute? Lovers of monarchy, lovers of republics, must alike abhor it. The members of your assembly must themselves groan under the tyranny of which they have all the shame, none of the direction, and little of the profit. I am sure many of the members who compose even the majority of that body must feel as I do, notwithstanding the applauses of the Revolution Society. Miserable king! miserable assembly! How must that assembly be silently scandalised with those of their members, who could call a day which seemed to blot the sun out of heaven, *"un beau jour!"* * How must they be inwardly indig-nant at hearing others, who thought fit to declare to them, "that

* 6th of October, 1789.

the vessel of the state would fly forward in her course towards regeneration with more speed than ever,"[70] from the stiff gale of treason and murder, which preceded our preacher's triumph! What must they have felt, whilst, with outward patience, and inward indignation, they heard of the slaughter of innocent gentlemen in their houses, that "the blood spilled was not the most pure!"[71] What must they have felt, when they were besieged by complaints of disorders which shook their country to its foundations, at being compelled coolly to tell the complainants, that they were under the protection of the law, and that they would address the king (the captive king) to cause the laws to be enforced for their protection; when the enslaved ministers of that captive king had formally notified to them, that there were neither law, nor authority, nor power left to protect! What must they have felt at being obliged, as a felicitation on the present new year, to request their captive king to forget the stormy period of the last, on account of the great good which *he* was likely to produce to his people; to the complete attainment of which good they adjourned the practical demonstrations of their loyalty, assuring him of their obedience, when he should no longer possess any authority to command!

This address was made with much good nature and affection, to be sure. But among the revolutions in France must be reckoned a considerable revolution in their ideas of politeness. In England we are said to learn manners as second-hand from your side of the water, and that we dress our behaviour in the frippery of France. If so, we are still in the old cut; and have not so far conformed to the new Parisian mode of good breeding, as to think it quite in the most refined strain of delicate compliment (whether in condolence or congratulation) to say, to the most humiliated creature that crawls upon the earth, that great public benefits are derived from the murder of his servants, the attempted assassination of himself and of his wife, and the mortification, disgrace, and degradation, that he has personally suffered. It is a topic of consolation which our ordinary of Newgate would be too humane to use to a criminal at the foot of the gallows. I should have thought that the hangman of Paris, now that he is liberalised by the vote of the National Assembly, and is allowed his rank and arms in the herald's college of the rights of men, would be too generous, too gallant a man, too full of the sense of his new dignity, to employ that cutting consolation to any of the persons whom the *leze nation*[72] might bring under the administration of his *executive power*.

A man is fallen indeed, when he is thus flattered. The anodyne draught of oblivion, thus drugged, is well calculated to preserve a galling wakefulness, and to feed the living ulcer of a corroding memory. Thus to administer the opiate potion of amnesty, pow-dered with all the ingredients of scorn and contempt, is to hold to his lips, instead of "the balm of hurt minds," the cup of human misery full to the brim, and to force him to drink it to the dregs.

Yielding to reasons, at least as forcible as those which were so delicately urged in the compliment on the new year, the king of France will probably endeavour to forget these events and that compliment. But history, who keeps a durable record of all our acts, and exercises her awful censure over the proceedings of all sorts of sovereigns, will not forget either those events, or the era of this liberal refinement in the intercourse of mankind. History will record, that on the morning of the 6th of October, 1789, the king and queen of France, after a day of confusion, alarm, dismay, and slaughter, lay down, under the pledged security of public faith, to indulge nature in a few hours of respite, and troubled, melancholy repose. From this sleep the queen was first startled by the voice of the sentinel[73] at her door, who cried out to her to save herself by flight – that this was the last proof of fidelity he could give – that they were upon him, and he was dead. Instantly he was cut down. A band of cruel ruffians and assassins, reeking with his blood, rushed into the chamber of the queen, and pierced with a hundred strokes of bayonets and poniards the bed, from whence this persecuted woman had but just time to fly almost naked, and, through ways unknown to the murderers, had escaped to seek refuge at the feet of a king and husband, not secure of his own life for a moment.[74]

This king, to say no more of him, and this queen, and their infant children, (who once would have been the pride and hope of a great and generous people,) were then forced to abandon the sanctuary of the most splendid palace in the world, which they left swimming in blood, polluted by massacre, and strewed with scattered limbs and mutilated carcases. Thence they were con-ducted into the capital of their kingdom. Two had been selected from the unprovoked, unresisted, promiscuous slaughter, which was made of the gentlemen of birth and family who composed the king's body guard. These two gentlemen, with all the parade of an execution of justice, were cruelly and publicly dragged to the block, and beheaded in the great court of the palace. Their heads were stuck upon spears, and led the procession; whilst the royal captives who followed in the train were slowly moved along, amidst the horrid yells, and shrilling screams, and frantic dances, and infamous contumelies, and all the unutterable abominations of the furies of hell, in the abused shape of the vilest of women. After they had been made to taste, drop by drop, more than the bitterness of death, in the slow torture of a journey of twelve miles, protracted to six hours, they were, under a guard, composed of those very soldiers who had thus conducted them through this famous triumph, lodged in one of the old palaces of Paris, now converted into a bastile for kings.

Is this a triumph to be consecrated at altars? to be commemorated with grateful thanksgiving? to be offered to the divine humanity with fervent prayer and enthusiastic ejaculation? – These Theban and Thracian orgies,[75] acted in France, and applauded only in the Old Jewry, I assure you, kindle prophetic enthusiasm in the minds but of very few people in this kingdom: although a saint and apostle, who may have revelations of his own, and who has so completely vanquished all the mean superstitions of the heart, may incline to think it pious and decorous to compare it with the entrance into the world of the Prince of Peace, proclaimed in a holy temple by a venerable sage, and not long before not worse announced by the voice of angels to the quiet innocence of shepherds.

At first I was at a loss to account for this fit of unguarded transport. I knew, indeed, that the sufferings of monarchs make a delicious repast to some sort of palates. There were reflections which might serve to keep this appetite within some bounds of temperance. But when I took one circumstance into my consideration, I was obliged to confess, that much allowance ought to be made for the society, and that the temptation was too strong for common discretion; I mean, the circumstance of the Io Pæan[76] of the triumph, the animating cry which called "for *all* the BISHOPS to be hanged on the lamp-posts," * might well have brought forth a burst of enthusiasm on the foreseen consequences of this happy day. I allow to so much enthusiasm some little deviation from prudence. I allow this prophet to break forth into

* Tous les Evêques à la lanterne.

hymns of joy and thanksgiving on an event which appears like the precursor of the Millenium, and the projected fifth monarchy,[77] in the destruction of all church establishments. There was, however, (as in all human affairs there is,) in the midst of this joy, something to exercise the patience of these worthy gentlemen, and to try the long-suffering of their faith. The actual murder of the king and queen, and their child, was wanting to the other auspicious circumstances of this *"beautiful day."* The actual murder of the bishops, though called for by so many holy ejaculations, was also wanting. A group of regicide and sacrilegious slaughter, was indeed boldly sketched, but it was only sketched. It unhappily was left unfinished, in this great history-piece of the massacre of innocents. What hardy pencil of a great master, from the school of the rights of men, will finish it, is to be seen hereafter. The age has not yet the complete benefit of that diffusion of knowledge that has undermined superstition and error; and the king of France wants another object or two to consign to oblivion, in consideration of all the good which is to arise from his own sufferings, and the patriotic crimes of an enlightened age.*

* It is proper here to refer to a letter written upon this subject by an eye-witness. That eye-witness was one of the most honest, intelligent, and eloquent members of the National Assembly, one of the most active and zealous reformers of the state. He was obliged to secede from the assembly; and he afterwards became a voluntary exile, on account of the horrors of this pious triumph, and the dispositions of men, who, profiting of crimes, if not causing them, have taken the lead in public affairs.

Extract of M. de Lally Tollendal's Second Letter to a Friend[78]

"Parlons du parti que j'ai pris; il est bien justifié dans ma conscience – Ni cette ville coupable, ni cette assemblée plus coupable encore, ne meritoient que je me justifie; mais j'ai à cœur que vous, et les personnes qui pensent comme vous, ne me condamnent pas. – Ma santé, je vous jure, me rendoit mes fonctions impossibles; mais même en les mettant de côté il a été au-dessus de mes forces de supporter plus longtems l'horreur que me causoit ce sang, – ces têtes – cette reine *presque égorgée,* – ce roi, – amené *sclave,* – entrant à Paris, au milieu de ses assassins, et précédé des têtes de ses malheureux grades – ces perfides janissaires, ces assassins, ces femmes cannibales, ce cri de TOUS LES ÉVÊQUES À LA LANTERNE, dans le moment où le roi entre sa capitale avec deux évêques de son conseil dans sa voiture – un *coup de fusil,* que j'ai vu tirer dans un *des carosses de la reine.* M. Bailly appellant cela *un beau jour,* – l'assemblée afant déclaré froidement le matin, qu'il n'étoit pas de sa dignité d'aller toute entière environner le roi – M. Mirabeau disant impunément dans cette assemblée que le vaisseau de l'état, loins d'être arrêté dans sa course, s'élanceroit avec plus de rapidité que jamais vers sa régénération – M. Barnave, riant avec lui, quand des flots de sang couloient autour de nous – le vertueux Mounier† échappant par miracle à vingt assassins, qui avoient voulu faire de sa tête un trophée de plus: Voilà ce qui me fit jurer de ne plus mettre le pied *dans cette caverne d'Antropophages* [the National Assembly] où je n'avois plus de force d'élever la voix, où depuis six semaines je l'avois élevée en vain.

Although this work of our new light and knowledge did not go to the length that in all probability it was intended it should be carried, yet I must think that such treatment of any human creatures must be shocking to any but those who are made for accomplishing revolutions. But I cannot stop here. Influenced by the inborn feelings of my nature, and not being illuminated by a single ray of this new-sprung modern light, I confess to you, Sir, that the exalted rank of the persons suffering, and particularly the sex, the beauty, and the amiable qualities of the descendant of so many kings and emperors, with the tender age of royal infants, insensible only through infancy and innocence of the cruel outrages to which their parents were exposed, instead of being a subject of exultation, adds not a little to my sensibility on that most melancholy occasion.

I hear that the august person, who was the principal object of our preacher's triumph, though he supported himself, felt much on that shameful occasion. As a man, it became him to feel for his wife and his children, and the faithful guards of his person, that were massacred in cold blood about him; as a prince, it became him to feel for the strange and frightful transformation of his civilised subjects, and to be more grieved for them than solicitous for himself. It derogates little from his fortitude, while it adds infinitely to the honour of his humanity. I am very sorry to say it, very sorry indeed, that such personages are in a situation in which it is not becoming in us to praise the virtues of the great.

"Moi, Mounier, et tous les honnètes gens, ont pensé que le dernier effort à faire pour le bien étoit d'en sortir. Aucune idée de crainte ne s'est approchée de moi. Je rougirois de m'en défendre. J'avois encore reçû sur la route de la part de ce peuple, moins coupable que ceux qui l'ont enivré de fureur, des acclamations, et des applaudissements, dont d'autres auroient été flattés, et qui m'ont fait frémir. C'est à l'indignation, c'est à l'horreur, c'est aux convulsions physiques, que le seul aspect du sang me fait éprouver que j'ai cédé. On brave une seul mort; on la brave plusieurs fois, quand elle peut être utile. Mais aucune puissance sous le Ciel, mais aucune opinion publique ou privée n'ont le droit de me condamner à souffrir inutilement mille supplices par minute, et à perir de désespoir, de rage, au milieu des *triomphes*, du crime que je n'ai pu arrêter. Ils me proscriront, ils confisqueront mes biens. Je laboureai la terre, et je ne les verrai plus. – Voilà ma justification. Vous pourrez la lire, la montrer, la laisser copier; tant pis pour ceux qui ne la comprendront pas; ce ne sera alors moi qui auroit en tort de la leur donner."

This military man had not so good nerves as the peaceable gentleman of the Old Jewry. – See Mons. Mounier's narrative of these transactions; a man also of honour, and virtue, and talents, and therefore a fugitive.

† N.B. Mr. Mounier was then speaker of the National Assembly. He has since been obliged to live in exile, though one of the firmest assertors of liberty.

I hear, and I rejoice to hear, that the great lady, the other object of the triumph, has borne that day, (one is interested that beings made for suffering should suffer well,) and that she bears all the succeeding days, that she bears the imprisonment of her husband, and her own captivity, and the exile of her friends, and the insulting adulation of addresses, and the whole weight of her accumulated wrongs, with a serene patience, in a manner suited to her rank and race, and becoming the offspring of a sovereign distinguished for her piety and her courage: that, like her, she has lofty sentiments; that she feels with the dignity of a Roman matron; that in the last extremity she will save herself from the last disgrace; and that, if she must fall, she will fall by no ignoble hand.

It is now sixteen or seventeen years since I saw the queen of France, then the dauphiness, at Versailles; and surely never lighted on this orb, which she hardly seemed to touch, a more delightful vision. I saw her just above the horizon, decorating and cheering the elevated sphere she just began to move in, – glittering like the morning-star, full of life, and splendour, and joy. Oh! what a revolution! and what a heart must I have to contemplate without emotion that elevation and that fall! Little did I dream when she added titles of veneration to those of enthusiastic, distant, respectful love, that she should ever be obliged to carry the sharp antidote against disgrace concealed in that bosom; little did I dream that I should have lived to see such disasters fallen upon her in a nation of gallant men, in a nation of men of honour, and of cavaliers. I thought ten thousand swords must have leaped from their scabbards to avenge even a look that threatened her with insult. But the age of chivalry is gone. That of sophisters, economists, and calculators, has succeeded; and the glory of Europe is extinguished for ever. Never, never more shall we behold that generous loyalty to rank and sex, that proud submission, that dignified obedience, that subordination of the heart, which kept alive, even in servitude itself, the spirit of an exalted freedom. The unbought grace of life, the cheap defence of nations, the nurse of manly sentiment and heroic enterprise, is gone! It is gone, that sensibility of principle, that chastity of honour, which felt a stain like a wound, which inspired courage whilst it mitigated ferocity, which ennobled whatever it touched, and under which vice itself lost half its evil, by losing all its grossness.

This mixed system of opinion and sentiment had its origin in the ancient chivalry; and the principle, though varied in its appearance by the varying state of human affairs, subsisted and influenced through a long succession of generations, even to the time we live in. If it should ever be totally extinguished, the loss I fear will be great. It is this which has given its character to modern Europe. It is this which has distinguished it under all its forms of government, and distinguished it to its advantage, from the states of Asia, and possibly from those states which flourished in the most brilliant periods of the antique world. It was this, which, without confounding ranks, had produced a noble equality, and handed it down through all the gradations of social life. It was this opinion which mitigated kings into companions, and raised private men to be fellows with kings. Without force or opposition, it subdued the fierceness of pride and power; it obliged sovereigns to submit to the soft collar of social esteem, compelled stern authority to submit to elegance, and gave a dominating vanquisher of laws to be subdued by manners.

But now all is to be changed. All the pleasing illusions, which made power gentle and obedience liberal, which harmonised the different shades of life, and which, by a bland assimilation, incorporated into politics the sentiments which beautify and soften private society, are to be dissolved by this new conquering empire of light and reason. All the decent drapery of life is to be rudely torn off. All the super-added ideas, furnished from the wardrobe of a moral imagination, which the heart owns, and the understanding ratifies, as necessary to cover the defects of our naked, shivering nature, and to raise it to dignity in our own estimation, are to be exploded as a ridiculous, absurd, and anti-quated fashion.

On this scheme of things, a king is but a man, a queen is but a woman; a woman is but an animal, and an animal not of the highest order. All homage paid to the sex in general as such, and without distinct views, is to be regarded as romance and folly. Regicide, and parricide, and sacrilege, are but fictions of superstition, corrupting jurisprudence by destroying its simplicity. The murder of a king, or a queen, or a bishop, or a father, are only common homicide; and if the people are by any chance, or in any way, gainers by it, a sort of homicide much the most pardonable, and into which we ought not to make too severe a scrutiny.

On the scheme of this barbarous philosophy, which is the off-spring of cold hearts and muddy understandings, and which is as void of solid wisdom as it is destitute of all taste and elegance, laws are to be supported only by their own terrors, and by the concern which each individual may find in them from his own private speculations, or can spare to them from his own private interests. In the groves of *their* academy, at the end of every vista, you see nothing but the gallows. Nothing is left which engages the affections on the part of the commonwealth. On the principles of this mechanic philosophy, our institutions can never be embodied, if I may use the expression, in persons; so as to create in us love, veneration, admiration, or attachment. But that sort of reason which banishes the affections is incapable of filling their place. These public affections, combined with manners, are required sometimes as supplements, sometimes as correctives, always as aids to law. The precept given by a wise man, as well as a great critic, for the construction of poems, is equally true as to states: − *Non satis est pulchra esse poemata, dulcia sunto.*[79] There ought to be a system of manners in every nation, which a well-formed mind would be disposed to relish. To make us love our country, our country ought to be lovely.

But power, of some kind or other, will survive the shock in which manners and opinions perish; and it will find other and worse means for its support. The usurpation which, in order to subvert ancient institutions, has destroyed ancient principles, will hold power by arts similar to those by which it has acquired it. When the old feudal and chivalrous spirit of *fealty*, which, by freeing kings from fear, freed both kings and subjects from the precautions of tyranny, shall be extinct in the minds of men, plots and assassinations will be anticipated by preventive murder and preventive confiscation, and that long roll of grim and bloody maxims, which form the political code of all power, not standing on its own honour, and the honour of those who are to obey it. Kings will be tyrants from policy, when subjects are rebels from principle.

When ancient opinions and rules of life are taken away, the loss cannot possibly be estimated. From that moment we have no compass to govern us; nor can we know distinctly to what port we steer. Europe, undoubtedly, taken in a mass, was in a flourishing condition the day on which your revolution was completed. How much of that prosperous state was owing to the spirit of our old manners and opinions is not easy to say; but as such causes cannot be indifferent in their operation, we must presume, that, on the whole, their operation was beneficial.

We are but too apt to consider things in the state in which we find them, without sufficiently adverting to the causes by which they have been produced, and possibly may be upheld. Nothing is more certain, than that our manners, our civilisation, and all the good things which are connected with manners and with civilisation, have, in this European world of ours, depended for ages upon two principles; and were indeed the result of both combined; I mean the spirit of a gentleman, and the spirit of religion. The nobility and the clergy, the one by profession, the other by patronage, kept learning in existence, even in the midst of arms and confusions, and whilst governments were rather in their causes, than formed. Learning paid back what it received to nobility and to priesthood; and paid it with usury, by enlarging their ideas, and by furnishing their minds. Happy if they had all continued to know their indissoluble union, and their proper place! Happy if learning, not debauched by ambition, had been satisfied to continue the instructor, and not aspired to be the master! Along with its natural protectors and guardians, learning will be cast into the mire, and trodden down under the hoofs of a swinish multitude.*

If, as I suspect, modern letters owe more than they are always willing to own to ancient manners, so do other interests which we value full as much as they are worth. Even commerce, and trade, and manufacture, the gods of our economical politicians, are themselves perhaps but creatures; are themselves but effects, which, as first causes, we choose to worship. They certainly grew under the same shade in which learning flourished. They too may decay with their natural protecting principles. With you, for the present at least, they all threaten to disappear together. Where trade and manufactures are wanting to a people, and the spirit of nobility and religion remains, sentiment supplies, and not always ill supplies, their place; but if commerce and the arts should be lost in an experiment to try how well a state may stand without these old fundamental principles, what sort of a thing must be a nation of gross, stupid, ferocious, and, at the same time, poor and sordid, barbarians, destitute of religion, honour, or manly pride, possessing nothing at present, and hoping for nothing hereafter?

* See the fate of Bailly and Condorcet,[80] supposed to be here particularly alluded to. Compare the circumstances of the trial and execution of the former with this prediction. [1803]

I wish you may not be going fast, and by the shortest cut, to that horrible and disgustful situation. Already there appears a poverty of conception, a coarseness and vulgarity, in all the proceedings of the Assembly and of all their instructors. Their liberty is not liberal. Their science is presumptuous ignorance. Their humanity is savage and brutal.

It is not clear, whether in England we learned those grand and decorous principles and manners, of which considerable traces yet remain, from you, or whether you took them from us. But to you, I think, we trace them best. You seem to me to be – *gentis incunabula nostræ*.[81] France has always more or less influenced manners in England; and when your fountain is choked up and polluted, the stream will not run long, or not run clear, with us, or perhaps with any nation. This gives all Europe, in my opinion, but too close and connected a concern in what is done in France. Excuse me, therefore, if I have dwelt too long on the atrocious spectacle of the 6th of October, 1789, or have given too much scope to the reflections which have arisen in my mind on occasion of the most important of all revolutions, which may be dated from that day, I mean a revolution in sentiments, manners, and moral opinions. As things now stand, with everything respectable destroyed without us, and an attempt to destroy within us every principle of respect, one is almost forced to apologise for harbouring the common feelings of men.

Why do I feel so differently from the Reverend Dr. Price, and those of his lay flock who will choose to adopt the sentiments of his discourse? – For this plain reason – because it is *natural* I should; because we are so made, as to be affected at such spectacles with melancholy sentiments upon the unstable condition of mortal prosperity, and the tremendous uncertainty of human greatness; because in those natural feelings we learn great lessons; because in events like these our passions instruct our reason; because when kings are hurled from their thrones by the Supreme Director of this great drama, and become the objects of insult to the base, and of pity to the good, we behold such disasters in the moral, as we should behold a miracle in the physical, order of things. We are alarmed into reflection; our minds (as it has long since been observed) are purified by terror and pity; our weak, unthinking pride is humbled under the dispensations of a mysterious wisdom. Some tears might be drawn from me, if such a spectacle were exhibited on the stage. I should be truly ashamed of finding in myself that superficial, theatric sense of painted distress, whilst I could exult over it in real life. With such a perverted mind, I could never venture to show my face at a tragedy. People would think the tears that Garrick formerly, or that Siddons[82] not long since, have extorted from me, were the tears of hypocrisy; I should know them to be the tears of folly.

Indeed the theatre is a better school of moral sentiments than churches, where the feelings of humanity are thus outraged. Poets who have to deal with an audience not yet graduated in the school of the rights of men, and who must apply themselves to the moral constitution of the heart, would not dare to produce such a triumph as a matter of exultation. There, where men follow their natural impulses, they would not bear the odious maxims of a Machiavelian policy, whether applied to the attainment of monarchical or democratic tyranny. They would reject them on the modern, as they once did on the ancient stage, where they could not bear even the hypothetical proposition of such wickedness in the mouth of a personated tyrant, though suitable to the character he sustained. No theatric audience in Athens would bear what has been borne, in the midst of the real tragedy of this triumphal day; a principal actor weighing, as it were in scales hung in a shop of horrors, – so much actual crime against so much contingent advantage, – and after putting in and out weights, declaring that the balance was on the side of the advantages. They would not bear to see the crimes of new democracy posted as in a ledger against the crimes of old despotism, and the book-keepers of politics finding democracy still in debt, but by no means unable or unwilling to pay the balance. In the theatre, the first intuitive glance, without any elaborate process of reasoning, will show, that this method of political computation would justify every extent of crime. They would see, that on these principles, even where the very worst acts were not perpetrated, it was owing rather to the fortune of the conspirators, than to their parsimony in the expenditure of treachery and blood. They would soon see, that criminal means once tolerated are soon preferred. They present a shorter cut to the object than through the highway of the moral virtues. Justifying perfidy and murder for public benefit, public benefit would soon become the pretext, and perfidy and murder the end; until rapacity, malice, revenge, and fear more dreadful than revenge, could satiate their insatiable appetites. Such must be the consequences of losing, in the splendour of these triumphs of the rights of men, all natural sense of wrong and right.

But the reverend pastor exults in this "leading in triumph," because truly Louis the Sixteenth was "an arbitrary monarch;" that is, in other words, neither more nor less than because he was Louis the Sixteenth, and because he had the misfortune to be born king of France, with the prerogatives of which, a long line of ancestors, and a long acquiescence of the people, without any act of his, had put him in possession. A misfortune it has indeed turned out to him, that he was born king of France. But misfortune is not crime, nor is indiscretion always the greatest guilt. I shall never think that a prince, the acts of whose whole reign was a series of concessions to his subjects, who was willing to relax his authority, to remit his prerogatives, to call his people to a share of freedom, not known, perhaps not desired, by their ancestors; such a prince, though he should be subjected to the common frailties attached to men and to princes, though he should have once thought it necessary to provide force against the desperate designs manifestly carrying on against his person, and the remnants of his authority; though all this should be taken into consideration, I shall be led with great difficulty to think he deserves the cruel and insulting triumph of Paris and of Dr. Price. I tremble for the cause of liberty, from such an example to kings. I tremble for the cause of humanity, in the unpunished outrages of the most wicked of mankind. But there are some people of that low and degenerate fashion of mind, that they look up with a sort of complacent awe and admiration to kings, who know to keep firm in their seat, to hold a strict hand over their subjects, to assert their prerogative, and, by the awakened vigilance of a severe despotism, to guard against the very first approaches of freedom. Against such as these they never elevate their voice. Deserters from principle, listed with fortune, they never see any good in suffering virtue, nor any crime in prosperous usurpation.

If it could have been made clear to me, that the king and queen of France (those I mean who were such before the triumph) were inexorable and cruel tyrants, that they had formed a deliberate scheme for massacring the National Assembly, (I think I have seen something like the latter insinuated in certain publications,) I should think their captivity just. If this be true, much more ought to have been done, but done, in my opinion, in another manner. The punishment of real tyrants is a noble and awful act of justice; and it has with truth been said to be consolatory to the human mind. But if I were to punish a wicked king, I should regard the dignity in avenging the crime. Justice is grave and decorous, and in its punishments rather seems to submit to a necessity, than to make a choice. Had Nero, or Agrippina, or Louis the Eleventh, or Charles the Ninth, been the subject; if Charles the Twelfth of Sweden, after the murder of Patkul, or his predecessor Christina, after the murder of Monaldeschi,[83] had fallen into your hands, Sir, or into mine, I am sure our conduct would have been different.

If the French king, or king of the French, (or by whatever name he is known in the new vocabulary of your constitution,) has in his own person, and that of his queen, really deserved these unavowed, but unavenged, murderous attempts, and those frequent indignities more cruel than murder, such a person would ill deserve even that subordinate executory trust, which I understand is to be placed in him; nor is he fit to be called chief in a nation which he has outraged and oppressed. A worse choice for such an office in a new commonwealth, than that of a deposed tyrant, could not possibly be made. But to degrade and insult a man as the worst of criminals, and afterwards to trust him in your highest concerns, as a faithful, honest, and zealous servant, is not consistent with reasoning, nor prudent in policy, nor safe in practice. Those who could make such an appointment must be guilty of a more flagrant breach of trust than any they have yet committed against the people. As this is the only crime in which your leading politicians could have acted inconsistently, I conclude that there is no sort of ground for these horrid insinuations. I think no better of all the other calumnies.

In England, we give no credit to them. We are generous enemies: we are faithful allies. We spurn from us with disgust and indignation the slanders of those who bring us their anecdotes with the attestation of the flower-de-luce[84] on their shoulder. We have Lord George Gordon[85] fast in Newgate; and neither his being a public proselyte to Judaism, nor his having, in his zeal against catholic priests and all sorts of ecclesiastics, raised a mob (excuse the term, it is still in use here) which pulled down all our prisons, have preserved to him a liberty, of which he did not render himself worthy by a virtuous use of it. We have rebuilt Newgate, and tenanted the mansion. We have prisons almost as strong as the

Bastile, for those who dare to libel the queens of France. In this spiritual retreat, let the noble libeller remain. Let him there meditate on his Thalmud, until he learns a conduct more becoming his birth and parts, and not so disgraceful to the ancient religion to which he has become a proselyte; or until some persons from your side of the water, to please your new Hebrew brethren, shall ransom him. He may then be enabled to purchase, with the old hoards of the synagogue, and a very small poundage on the long compound interest of the thirty pieces of silver, (Dr. Price has shown us what miracles compound interest will perform in 1790 years,) the lands which are lately discovered to have been usurped by the Gallican church.[86] Send us your Popish archbishop of Paris, and we will send you our Protestant Rabbin. We shall treat the person you send us in exchange like a gentleman and an honest man, as he is; but pray let him bring with him the fund of his hospitality, bounty, and charity; and, depend upon it, we shall never confiscate a shilling of that honourable and pious fund, nor think of enriching the treasury with the spoils of the poor-box.

To tell you the truth, my dear Sir, I think the honour of our nation to be somewhat concerned in the disclaimer of the proceedings of this society of the Old Jewry and the London Tavern. I have no man's proxy. I speak only for myself, when I disclaim, as I do with all possible earnestness, all communion with the actors in that triumph, or with the admirers of it. When I assert anything else, as concerning the people of England, I speak from observation, not from authority; but I speak from the experience I have had in a pretty extensive and mixed communication with the inhabitants of this kingdom, of all descriptions and ranks, and after a course of attentive observation, began early in life, and continued for nearly forty years. I have often been astonished, considering that we are divided from you but by a slender dyke of about twenty-four miles, and that the mutual intercourse between the two countries has lately been very great, to find how little you seem to know of us. I suspect that this is owing to your forming a judgment of this nation from certain publications, which do, very erroneously, if they do at all, represent the opinions and dispositions generally prevalent in England. The vanity, restlessness, petulance, and spirit of intrigue, of several petty cabals, who attempt to hide their total want of consequence in bustle and noise, and puffing, and mutual quotation of each other, makes you imagine that our contemptuous neglect of their abilities is a mark of general acquiescence in their opinions. No such thing, I assure you. Because half a dozen grasshoppers under a fern make the field ring with their importunate chink, whilst thousands of great cattle, reposed beneath the shadow of the British oak, chew the cud and are silent, pray do not imagine that those who make the noise are the only inhabitants of the field; that, of course, they are many in number; or that, after all, they are other than the little, shrivelled, meagre, hopping, though loud and troublesome, insects of the hour.

I almost venture to affirm, that not one in a hundred amongst us participates in the "triumph" of the Revolution Society. If the king and queen of France, and their children, were to fall into our hands by the chance of war, in the most acrimonious of all hostilities, (I deprecate such an event, I deprecate such hostility,) they would be treated with another sort of triumphal entry into London. We formerly have had a king of France in that situation; you have read how he was treated by the victor in the field;[87] and in what manner he was afterwards received in England. Four hundred years have gone over us; but I believe we are not materially changed since that period. Thanks to our sullen resistance to innovation, thanks to the cold sluggishness of our national character, we still bear the stamp of our forefathers. We have not (as I conceive) lost the generosity and dignity of thinking of the fourteenth century; nor as yet have we subtilised ourselves into savages. We are not the converts of Rousseau; we are not the disciples of Voltaire; Helvetius[88] has made no progress amongst us. Atheists are not our preachers; madmen are not our lawgivers. We know that we have made no discoveries, and we think that no discoveries are to be made, in morality; nor many in the great principles of government, nor in the ideas of liberty, which were understood long before we were born, altogether as well as they will be after the grave has heaped its mould upon our presumption, and the silent tomb shall have imposed its law on our pert loquacity. In England we have not yet been completely embowelled of our natural entrails; we still feel within us, and we cherish and cultivate, those inbred sentiments which are the faithful guardians, the active monitors of our duty, the true supporters of all liberal and manly morals. We have not been drawn and trussed, in order that we may be filled, like stuffed birds in a museum, with chaff and rags and paltry blurred shreds of paper about the rights of man. We preserve the whole of our feelings still native and entire, unsophisticated by pedantry and infidelity. We have real hearts of flesh and blood beating in our bosoms. We fear God; we look up with awe to kings; with affection to parliaments; with duty to magistrates; with reverence to priests; and with respect to nobility.* Why? Because when such ideas are brought before our minds, it is *natural* to be so affected; because all other feelings are false and spurious, and tend to corrupt our minds, to vitiate our primary morals, to render us unfit for rational liberty; and by teaching us a servile, licentious, and abandoned insolence, to be our low sport for a few holidays, to make us perfectly fit for, and justly deserving of, slavery, through the whole course of our lives.

You see, Sir, that in this enlightened age I am bold enough to confess, that we are generally men of untaught feelings; that instead of casting away all our old prejudices, we cherish them to a very considerable degree, and, to take more shame to ourselves, we cherish them because they are prejudices; and the longer they have lasted, and the more generally they have prevailed, the more we cherish them. We are afraid to put men to live and trade each on his own private stock of reason; because we suspect that this stock in each man is small, and that the individuals would do better to avail themselves of the general bank and capital of nations and of ages. Many of our men of speculation, instead of exploding general prejudices, employ their sagacity to discover the latent wisdom which prevails in them. If they find what they seek, and they seldom fail, they think it more wise to continue the prejudice, with the reason involved, than to cast away the coat of prejudice, and to leave nothing but the naked reason; because prejudice, with its reason, has a motive to give action to that reason, and an affection which will give it permanence. Prejudice is of ready application in the emergency; it previously engages the mind in a steady course of wisdom and virtue, and does not leave the man hesitating in the moment of decision, sceptical, puzzled, and unresolved.

* The English are, I conceive, misrepresented in a letter published in one of the papers, by a gentleman thought to be a dissenting minister. – When writing to Dr. Price of the spirit which prevails at Paris, he says, "The spirit of the people in this place has abolished all the proud *distinctions* which the king and nobles had usurped in their minds; whether they talk of *the king, the noble, or the priest, their whole language is that of the most enlightened and liberal amongst the English.*" If this gentleman means to confine the terms *enlightened and liberal* to one set of men in England, it may be true. It is not generally so.

Prejudice renders a man's virtue his habit; and not a series of unconnected acts. Through just prejudice, his duty becomes a part of his nature.

Your literary men, and your politicians, and so do the whole clan of the enlightened among us, essentially differ in these points. They have no respect for the wisdom of others; but they pay it off by a very full measure of confidence in their own. With them it is a sufficient motive to destroy an old scheme of things, because it is an old one. As to the new, they are in no sort of fear with regard to the duration of a building run up in haste; because duration is no object to those who think little or nothing has been done before their time, and who place all their hopes in discovery. They conceive, very systematically, that all things which give perpetuity are mischievous, and therefore they are at inexpiable war with all establishments. They think that government may vary like modes of dress, and with as little ill effect: that there needs no principle of attachment, except a sense of present conveniency, to any constitution of the state. They always speak as if they were of opinion that there is a singular species of compact between them and their magistrates, which binds the magistrate, but which has nothing reciprocal in it, but that the majesty of the people has a right to dissolve it without any reason, but its will. Their attachment to their country itself is only so far as it agrees with some of their fleeting projects; it begins and ends with that scheme of polity which falls in with their momentary opinion.

These doctrines, or rather sentiments, seem prevalent with your new statesmen. But they are wholly different from those on which we have always acted in this country.

I hear it is sometimes given out in France, that what is doing among you is after the example of England. I beg leave to affirm, that scarcely anything done with you has originated from the practice or the prevalent opinions of this people, either in the act or in the spirit of the proceeding. Let me add, that we are as unwilling to learn these lessons from France, as we are sure that we never taught them to that nation. The cabals here, who take a sort of share in your transactions, as yet consist of but a handful of people. If unfortunately by their intrigues, their sermons, their publications, and by a confidence derived from an expected union with the counsels and forces of the French nation, they should draw considerable numbers into their faction, and in consequence should seriously attempt anything here in imitation of what has been done with you, the event, I dare venture to prophesy, will be, that, with some trouble to their country, they will soon accomplish their own destruction. This people refused to change their law in remote ages from respect to the infallibility of popes; and they will not now alter it from a pious implicit faith in the dogmatism of philosophers; though the former was armed with the anathema and crusade, and though the latter should act with the libel and the lamp-iron.

Formerly your affairs were your own concern only. We felt for them as men; but we kept aloof from them, because we were not citizens of France. But when we see the model held up to ourselves, we must feel as Englishmen, and feeling, we must provide as Englishmen. Your affairs, in spite of us, are made a part of our interest; so far at least as to keep at a distance your panacea, or your plague. If it be a panacea, we do not want it. We know the consequences of unnecessary physic. If it be a plague, it is such a plague that the precautions of the most severe quarantine ought to be established against it.

I hear on all hands that a cabal, calling itself philosophic, receives the glory of many of the late proceedings; and that their opinions and systems are the true actuating spirit of the whole of them. I have heard of no party in England, literary or political, at any time, known by such a description. It is not with you composed of those men, is it? whom the vulgar, in their blunt, homely style, commonly call atheists and infidels? If it be, I admit that we too have had writers of that description, who made some noise in their day. At present they repose in lasting oblivion. Who, born within the last forty years, has read one word of Collins, and Toland, and Tindal, and Chubb, and Morgan, and that whole race who called themselves Freethinkers? Who now reads Bolingbroke?[89] Who ever read him through? Ask the booksellers of London what is become of all these lights of the world. In as few years their few successors will go to the family vault of "all the Capulets." But whatever they were, or are, with us, they were and are wholly unconnected individuals. With us they kept the common nature of their kind, and were not gregarious. They never acted in corps, or were known as a faction in the state, nor presumed to influence in that name or character, or for the purposes of such a faction, on any of our public concerns. Whether they ought so to exist, and so be permitted to act, is another question. As such cabals have not existed in England, so neither has the spirit of them had any influence in establishing the original frame of our constitution, or in any one of the several reparations and improvements it has undergone. The whole has been done under the auspices, and is confirmed by the sanctions, of religion and piety. The whole has emanated from the simplicity of our national character, and from a sort of native plainness and directness of understanding, which for a long time characterised those men who have successively obtained authority amongst us. This disposition still remains; at least in the great body of the people.

We know, and what is better, we feel inwardly, that religion is the basis of civil society, and the source of all good and of all comfort.* In England we are so convinced of this, that there is no rust of superstition, with which the accumulated absurdity of the human mind might have crusted it over in the course of ages, that ninety-nine in a hundred of the people of England would not prefer to impiety. We shall never be such fools as to call in an enemy to the substance of any system to remove its corruptions, to supply its defects, or to perfect its construction. If our religious tenets should ever want a further elucidation, we shall not call on atheism to explain them. We shall not light up our temple from that unhallowed fire. It will be illuminated with other lights. It will be perfumed with other incense, than the infectious stuff which is imported by the smugglers of adulterated metaphysics. If our ecclesiastical establishment should want a revision, it is not avarice or rapacity, public or private, that we shall employ for the audit, or receipt, or application of its consecrated revenue. Violently condemning neither the Greek nor the Armenian, nor, since heats are subsided, the Roman system of religion, we prefer the Protestant; not because we think it has less of the Christian religion in it, but because, in our judgment, it has more. We are Protestants, not from indifference, but from zeal.

We know, and it is our pride to know, that man is by his constitution a religious animal; that atheism is against, not only our

---

* Sit igitur hoc ab initio persuasum civibus, dominos esse omnium rerum ac moderatores, deos; eaque, quæ gerantur, eorum geri vi, ditione, ac numine; eosdemque optime de genere hominum mereri; et qualis quisque sit, quid agat, quid in se admittat, qua mente, qua pietate colat religiones intueri; piorum et impiorum habere rationem. His enim rebus imbutæ mentes haud sane abhorrebunt ab utili et à vera sententia. Cic. de Legibus 1. 2.[90]

reason, but our instincts; and that it cannot prevail long. But if, in the moment of riot, and in a drunken delirium from the hot spirit drawn out of the alembic of hell, which in France is now so furiously boiling, we should uncover our nakedness, by throwing off that Christian religion which has hitherto been our boast and comfort, and one great source of civilisation amongst us, and amongst many other nations, we are apprehensive (being well aware that the mind will not endure a void) that some uncouth, pernicious, and degrading superstition might take place of it.

For that reason, before we take from our establishment the natural, human means of estimation, and give it up to contempt, as you have done, and in doing it have incurred the penalties you well deserve to suffer, we desire that some other may be presented to us in the place of it. We shall then form our judgment.

On these ideas, instead of quarrelling with establishments, as some do, who have made a philosophy and a religion of their hostility to such institutions, we cleave closely to them. We are resolved to keep an established church, an established monarchy, an established aristocracy, and an established democracy, each in the degree it exists, and in no greater. I shall show you presently how much of each of these we possess.

It has been the misfortune (not, as these gentlemen think it, the glory) of this age, that everything is to be discussed, as if the constitution of our country were to be always a subject rather of altercation, than enjoyment. For this reason, as well as for the satisfaction of those among you (if any such you have among you) who may wish to profit of examples, I venture to trouble you with a few thoughts upon each of these establishments. I do not think they were unwise in ancient Rome, who, when they wished to new-model their laws, set commissioners to examine the best constituted republics within their reach.

First, I beg leave to speak of our church establishment, which is the first of our prejudices, not a prejudice destitute of reason, but involving in it profound and extensive wisdom. I speak of it first. It is first, and last, and midst in our minds. For, taking ground on that religious system, of which we are now in possession, we continue to act on the early received and uniformly continued sense of mankind. That sense not only, like a wise architect, hath built up the august fabric of states, but like a provident proprietor, to preserve the structure from profanation and ruin, as a sacred temple purged from all the impurities of fraud, and violence, and injustice, and tyranny, hath solemnly and for ever consecrated the commonwealth, and all that officiate in it. This consecration is made, that all who administer in the government of men, in which they stand in the person of God himself, should have high and worthy notions of their function and destination; that their hope should be full of immortality; that they should not look to the paltry pelf of the moment, nor to the temporary and transient praise of the vulgar, but to a solid, permanent existence, in the permanent part of their nature, and to a permanent fame and glory, in the example they leave as a rich inheritance to the world.

Such sublime principles ought to be infused into persons of exalted situations; and religious establishments provided, that may continually revive and enforce them. Every sort of moral, every sort of civil, every sort of politic institution, aiding the rational and natural ties that connect the human understanding and affections to the divine, are not more than necessary, in order to build up that wonderful structure, Man; whose prerogative it is, to be in a great degree a creature of his own making; and who, when made as he ought to be made, is destined to hold no trivial place in the creation. But whenever man is put over men, as the better nature ought ever to preside, in that case more particularly, he should as nearly as possible be approximated to his perfection.

The consecration of the state, by a state religious establishment, is necessary also to operate with a wholesome awe upon free citizens; because, in order to secure their freedom, they must enjoy some determinate portion of power. To them therefore a religion connected with the state, and with their duty towards it, becomes even more necessary than in such societies, where the people, by the terms of their subjection, are confined to private sentiments, and the management of their own family concerns. All persons possessing any portion of power ought to be strongly and awfully impressed with an idea that they act in trust and that they are to account for their conduct in that trust to the one great Master, Author, and Founder of society.

This principle ought even to be more strongly impressed upon the minds of those who compose the collective sovereignty, than upon those of single princes. Without instruments, these princes can do nothing. Whoever uses instruments, in finding helps, finds also impediments. Their power is therefore by no means complete; nor are they safe in extreme abuse. Such persons, however elevated by flattery, arrogance, and self-opinion, must be sensible, that, whether covered or not by positive law, in some way or other they are accountable even here for the abuse of their trust. If they are not cut off by a rebellion of their people, they may be strangled by the very janissaries[91] kept for their security against all other rebellion. Thus we have seen the king of France sold by his soldiers for an increase of pay. But where popular authority is absolute and unrestrained, the people have an infinitely greater, because a far better founded, confidence in their own power. They are themselves, in a great measure, their own instruments. They are nearer to their objects. Besides, they are less under responsibility to one of the greatest controlling powers on earth, the sense of fame and estimation. The share of infamy, that is likely to fall to the lot of each individual in public acts, is small indeed; the operation of opinion being in the inverse ratio to the number of those who abuse power. Their own approbation of their own acts has to them the appearance of a public judgment in their favour. A perfect democracy is therefore the most shameless thing in the world. As it is the most shameless, it is also the most fearless. No man apprehends in his person that he can be made subject to punishment. Certainly the people at large never ought: for as all punishments are for example towards the conservation of the people at large, the people at large can never become the subject of punishment by any human hand.* It is therefore of infinite importance that they should not be suffered to imagine that their will, any more than that of kings, is the standard of right and wrong. They ought to be persuaded that they are full as little entitled, and far less qualified with safety to themselves, to use any arbitrary power whatsoever; that therefore they are not, under a false show of liberty, but in truth, to exercise an unnatural, inverted domination, tyrannically to exact, from those who officiate in the state, not an entire devotion to their interest, which is their right, but an abject submission to their occasional will; extinguishing thereby, in all those who serve them, all moral principle, all sense of dignity, all use of judgment, and all consistency of character; whilst by the very same process they give themselves up a proper, a suitable, but a most contemptible prey to the servile ambition of popular sycophants, or courtly flatterers.

When the people have emptied themselves of all the lust of

* Quicquid multis peccatur inultem.[92]

selfish will, which without religion it is utterly impossible they ever should, when they are conscious that they exercise, and exercise perhaps in a higher link of the order of delegation, the power, which to be legitimate must be according to that eternal, immutable law, in which will and reason are the same, they will be more careful how they place power in base and incapable hands. In their nomination to office, they will not appoint to the exercise of authority, as to a pitiful job, but as to a holy function; not according to their sordid, selfish interest, nor to their wanton caprice, nor to their arbitrary will; but they will confer that power (which any man may well tremble to give or to receive) on those only, in whom they may discern that predominant pro-portion of active virtue and wisdom, taken together and fitted to the charge, such, as in the great and inevitable mixed mass of human imperfections and infirmities, is to be found.

When they are habitually convinced that no evil can be accept-able, either in the act or the permission, to him whose essence is good, they will be better able to extirpate out of the minds of all magistrates, civil, ecclesiastical, or military, anything that bears the least resemblance to a proud and lawless domination.

But one of the first and most leading principles on which the commonwealth and the laws are consecrated, is lest the temporary possessors and life-renters in it, unmindful of what they have received from their ancestors, or of what is due to their posterity, should act as if they were the entire masters; that they should not think it among their rights to cut off the entail, or commit waste on the inheritance, by destroying at their pleasure the whole original fabric of their society; hazarding to leave to those who come after them a ruin instead of an habitation – and teaching these successors as little to respect their contrivances, as they had themselves respected the institutions of their forefathers. By this unprincipled facility of changing the state as often, and as much, and in as many ways, as there are floating fancies or fashions, the whole chain and continuity of the commonwealth would be broken. No one generation could link with the other. Men would become little better than the flies of a summer.

And first of all, the science of jurisprudence, the pride of the human intellect, which, with all its defects, redundancies, and errors, is the collected reason of ages, combining the principles of original justice with the infinite variety of human concerns, as a heap of old exploded errors, would be no longer studied.

Personal self-sufficiency and arrogance (the certain attendants upon all those who have never experienced a wisdom greater than their own) would usurp the tribunal. Of course no certain laws, establishing invariable grounds of hope and fear, would keep the actions of men in a certain course, or direct them to a certain end. Nothing stable in the modes of holding property, or exercising function, could form a solid ground on which any parent could speculate in the education of his offspring, or in a choice for their future establishment in the world. No principles would be early worked into the habits. As soon as the most able instructor had completed his laborious course of institution, instead of sending forth his pupil, accomplished in a virtuous discipline, fitted to procure him attention and respect, in his place in society, he would find everything altered; and that he had turned out a poor creature to the contempt and derision of the world, ignorant of the true grounds of estimation. Who would insure a tender and delicate sense of honour to beat almost with the first pulses of the heart, when no man could know what would be the test of honour in a nation, continually varying the standard of its coin? No part of life would retain its acquisitions. Barbarism with regard to science and literature, unskilfulness with regard to arts and manufactures, would infallibly succeed to the want of a steady education and settled principle; and thus the commonwealth itself would, in a few generations, crumble away, be disconnected into the dust and powder of individuality, and at length dispersed to all the winds of heaven.

To avoid therefore the evils of inconstancy and versatility, ten thousand times worse than those of obstinacy and the blindest prejudice, we have consecrated the state, that no man should approach to look into its defects or corruptions but with due caution; that he should never dream of beginning its reformation by its subversion; that he should approach to the faults of the state as to the wounds of a father, with pious awe and trembling solicitude. By this wise prejudice we are taught to look with horror on those children of their country, who are prompt rashly to hack that aged parent in pieces, and put him into the kettle of magicians, in hopes that by their poisonous weeds, and wild incantations, they may regenerate the paternal constitution, and renovate their father's life.

Society is indeed a contract. Subordinate contracts for objects of mere occasional interest may be dissolved at pleasure – but the state ought not to be considered as nothing better than a partnership agreement in a trade of pepper and coffee, calico or tobacco, or some other such low concern, to be taken up for a little temporary interest, and to be dissolved by the fancy of the parties. It is to be looked on with other reverence; because it is not a partnership in things subservient only to the gross animal existence of a temporary and perishable nature. It is a partnership in all science; a partnership in all art; a partnership in every virtue, and in all perfection. As the ends of such a partnership cannot be obtained in many generations, it becomes a partnership not only between those who are living, but between those who are living, those who are dead, and those who are to be born. Each contract of each particular state is but a clause in the great primæval contract of eternal society, linking the lower with the higher natures, connecting the visible and invisible world, according to a fixed compact sanctioned by the inviolable oath which holds all physical and all moral natures, each in their appointed place. This law is not subject to the will of those, who by an obligation above them, and infinitely superior, are bound to submit their will to that law. The municipal corporations of that universal kingdom are not morally at liberty at their pleasure, and on their speculations of a contingent improvement, wholly to separate and tear asunder the bands of their subordinate community, and to dissolve it into an unsocial, uncivil, unconnected chaos of elementary principles. It is the first and supreme necessity only, a necessity that is not chosen, but chooses, a necessity paramount to deliberation, that admits no discussion, and demands no evidence, which alone can justify a resort to anarchy. This necessity is no exception to the rule; because this necessity itself is a part too of that moral and physical disposition of things, to which man must be obedient by consent or force: but if that which is only submission to necessity should be made the object of choice, the law is broken, nature is disobeyed, and the rebellious are outlawed, cast forth, and exiled, from this world of reason, and order, and peace, and virtue, and fruitful penitence, into the antagonist world of madness, discord, vice, confusion, and unavailing sorrow.

These, my dear Sir, are, were, and, I think, long will be, the sentiments of not the least learned and reflecting part of this kingdom. They, who are included in this description, form their opinions on such grounds as such persons ought to form them.

The less inquiring receive them from an authority, which those whom Providence dooms to live on trust need not be ashamed to rely on. These two sorts of men move in the same direction, though in a different place. They both move with the order of the universe. They all know or feel this great ancient truth: "Quod illi principi et præpotenti Deo qui omnem hunc mundum regit, nihil eorum quæ quidem fiant in terris acceptius quam concilia et cœtus hominum jure sociati quæ civitates appellantur."[93] They take this tenet of the head and heart, not from the great name which it immediately bears, nor from the greater from whence it is derived; but from that which alone can give true weight and sanction to any learned opinion, the common nature and common relation of men. Persuaded that all things ought to be done with reference, and referring all to the point of reference to which all should be directed, they think themselves bound, not only as individuals in the sanctuary of the heart, or as congregated in that personal capacity, to renew the memory of their high origin and cast; but also in their corporate character to perform their national homage to the institutor, and author, and protector of civil society; without which civil society man could not by any possibility arrive at the perfection of which his nature is capable, nor even make a remote and faint approach to it. They conceive that He who gave our nature to be perfected by our virtue, willed also the necessary means of its perfection. – He willed therefore the state – He willed its connexion with the source and original archetype of all perfection. They who are convinced of this his will, which is the law of laws, and the sovereign of sovereigns, cannot think it reprehensible that this our corporate fealty and homage, that this our recognition of a signiory paramount, I had almost said this oblation of the state itself, as a worthy offering on the high altar of universal praise, should be performed as all public, solemn acts are performed, in buildings, in music, in decoration, in speech, in the dignity of persons, according to the customs of mankind, taught by their nature; this is, with modest splendour and unassuming state, with mild majesty and sober pomp. For those purposes they think some part of the wealth of the country is as usefully employed as it can be in fomenting the luxury of individuals. It is the public ornament. It is the public consolation. It nourishes the public hope. The poorest man finds his own importance and dignity in it, whilst the wealth and pride of individuals at every moment makes the man of humble rank and fortune sensible of his inferiority, and degrades and vilifies his condition. It is for the man in humble life, and to raise his nature, and to put him in mind of a state in which the privileges of opulence will cease, when he will be equal by nature, and may be more than equal by virtue, that this portion of the general wealth of his country is employed and sanctified.

I assure you I do not aim at singularity. I give you opinions which have been accepted amongst us, from very early times to this moment, with a continued and general approbation, and which indeed are so worked into my mind, that I am unable to distinguish what I have learned from others from the results of my own meditation.

It is on some such principles that the majority of the people of England, far from thinking a religious national establishment unlawful, hardly think it lawful to be without one. In France you are wholly mistaken if you do not believe us above all other things attached to it, and beyond all other nations; and when this people has acted unwisely and unjustifiably in its favour, (as in some instances they have done most certainly,) in their very errors you will at least discover their zeal.

This principle runs through the whole system of their polity. They do not consider their church establishment as convenient, but as essential to their state; not as a thing heterogeneous and separable; something added for accommodation; what they may either keep or lay aside, according to their temporary ideas of convenience. They consider it as the foundation of their whole constitution, with which, and with every part of which, it holds an indissoluble union. Church and state are ideas inseparable in their minds, and scarcely is the one ever mentioned without mentioning the other.

Our education is so formed as to confirm and fix this impression. Our education is in a manner wholly in the hands of ecclesiastics, and in all stages from infancy to manhood. Even when our youth, leaving schools and universities, enter that most important period of life which begins to link experience and study together, and when with that view they visit other countries, instead of old domestics whom we have seen as governors to principal men from other parts, three-fourths of those who go abroad with our young nobility and gentlemen are ecclesiastics; not as austere masters, nor as mere followers; but as friends and

companions of a graver character, and not seldom persons as well
born as themselves. With them, as relations, they most constantly
keep up a close connexion through life. By this connexion we
conceive that we attach our gentlemen to the church; and we
liberalise the church by an intercourse with the leading characters of the country.

So tenacious are we of the old ecclesiastical modes and fashions of institution, that very little alteration has been made in
them since the fourteenth or fifteenth century: adhering in this
particular, as in all things else, to our old settled maxim, never
entirely nor at once to depart from antiquity. We found these
old institutions, on the whole, favourable to morality and discipline; and we thought they were susceptible of amendment,
without altering the ground. We thought that they were capable
of receiving and meliorating, and above all of preserving, the
accessions of science and literature, as the order of Providence
should successively produce them. And after all, with this Gothic
and monkish education (for such it is in the ground-work) we
may put in our claim to as ample and as early a share in all the
improvements in science, in arts, and in literature, which have
illuminated and adorned the modern world, as any other nation
in Europe: we think one main cause of this improvement was
our not despising the patrimony of knowledge which was left
us by our forefathers.

It is from our attachment to a church establishment, that the
English nation did not think it wise to intrust that great, fundamental interest of the whole to what they trust no part of their
civil or military public service, that is, to the unsteady and precarious contribution of individuals. They go further. They certainly
never have suffered, and never will suffer, the fixed estate of the
church to be converted into a pension, to depend on the treasury,
and to be delayed, withheld, or perhaps to be extinguished, by
fiscal difficulties: which difficulties may sometimes be pretended
for political purposes, and are in fact often brought on by the
extravagance, negligence, and rapacity of politicians. The people
of England think that they have constitutional motives, as well as
religious, against any project of turning their independent clergy
into ecclesiastical pensioners of state. They tremble for their
liberty, from the influence of clergy dependent on the crown;
they tremble for the public tranquillity from the disorders of a
factious clergy, if it were made to depend upon any other than

the crown. They therefore made their church, like their king and their nobility, independent.

From the united considerations of religion and constitutional policy, from their opinion of a duty to make sure provision for the consolation of the feeble and the instruction of the ignorant, they have incorporated and identified the estate of the church with the mass of *private property*, of which the state is not the proprietor, either for use or dominion, but the guardian only and the regulator. They have ordained that the provision of this establishment might be as stable as the earth on which it stands, and should not fluctuate with the Euripus[94] of funds and actions.

The men of England, the men, I mean, of light and leading in England, whose wisdom (if they have any) is open and direct, would be ashamed, as of a silly, deceitful trick, to profess any religion in name, which, by their proceedings, they appear to contemn. If by their conduct (the only language that rarely lies) they seemed to regard the great ruling principle of the moral and the natural world, as a mere invention to keep the vulgar in obedience, they apprehend that by such a conduct they would defeat the politic purpose they have in view. They would find it difficult to make others believe in a system to which they manifestly give no credit themselves. The Christian statesmen of this land would indeed first provide for the *multitude*; because it is the *multitude*; and is therefore, as such, the first object in the ecclesiastical institution, and in all institutions. They have been taught, that the circumstance of the gospel's being preached to the poor, was one of the great tests of its true mission. They think, therefore, that those do not believe it, who do not take care it should be preached to the poor. But as they know that charity is not confined to any one description, but ought to apply itself to all men who have wants, they are not deprived of a due and anxious sensation of pity to the distresses of the miserable great. They are not repelled through a fastidious delicacy, at the stench of their arrogance and presumption, from a medicinal attention to their mental blotches and running sores. They are sensible, that religious instruction is of more consequence to them than to any others; from the greatness of the temptation to which they are exposed; from the important consequences that attend their faults; from the contagion of their ill example; from the necessity of bowing down the stubborn neck of their pride and ambition to the yoke of moderation and virtue; from a consideration of the fat stupidity and gross ignorance concerning what imports men most to know, which prevails at courts, and at the head of armies, and in senates, as much as at the loom and in the field.

The English people are satisfied, that to the great the consolations of religion are as necessary as its instructions. They too are among the unhappy. They feel personal pain, and domestic sorrow. In these they have no privilege, but are subject to pay their full contingent to the contributions levied on mortality. They want this sovereign balm under their gnawing cares and anxieties, which, being less conversant about the limited wants of animal life, range without limit, and are diversified by infinite combinations, in the wild and unbounded regions of imagination. Some charitable dole is wanting to these, our often very unhappy brethren, to fill the gloomy void that reigns in minds which have nothing on earth to hope or fear; something to relieve in the killing languor and over-laboured lassitude of those who have nothing to do; something to excite an appetite to existence in the palled satiety which attends on all pleasures which may be bought, where nature is not left to her own process, where even desire is anticipated, and therefore fruition defeated by meditated schemes and contrivances of delight; and no interval, no obstacle, is interposed between the wish and the accomplishment.

The people of England know how little influence the teachers of religion are likely to have with the wealthy and powerful of long standing, and how much less with the newly fortunate, if they appear in a manner no way assorted to those with whom they must associate, and over whom they must even exercise, in some cases, something like an authority. What must they think of that body of teachers, if they see it in no part above the establishment of their domestic servants? If the poverty were voluntary, there might be some difference. Strong instances of self-denial operate powerfully on our minds; and a man who has no wants has obtained great freedom, and firmness, and even dignity. But as the mass of any description of men are but men, and their poverty cannot be voluntary, that disrespect, which attends upon all lay poverty, will not depart from the ecclesiastical. Our provident constitution has therefore taken care that those who are to instruct presumptuous ignorance, those who are to be censors over insolent vice, should neither incur their contempt, nor live upon their alms; nor will it tempt the rich to a neglect of the true medicine of their minds. For these reasons, whilst we provide first for the poor, and with a parental solicitude, we have not relegated religion (like something we were ashamed to show) to obscure municipalities, or rustic villages. No! we will have her to exalt her mitred front in courts and parliaments. We will have her mixed throughout the whole mass of life, and blended with all the classes of society. The people of England will show to the haughty potentates of the world, and to their talking sophisters, that a free, a generous, an informed nation honours the high magistrates of its church; that it will not suffer the insolence of wealth and titles, or any other species of proud pretension, to look down with scorn upon what they look up to with reverence; nor presume to trample on that acquired personal nobility, which they intend always to be, and which often is, the fruit, not the reward, (for what can be the reward?) of learning, piety, and virtue. They can see, without pain or grudging, an archbishop precede a duke. They can see a bishop of Durham, or a bishop of Winchester, in possession of ten thousand pounds a year; and cannot conceive why it is in worse hands than estates to the like amount in the hands of this earl, or that squire; although it may be true, that so many dogs and horses are not kept by the former, and fed with the victuals which ought to nourish the children of the people. It is true, the whole church revenue is not always employed, and to every shilling, in charity; nor perhaps ought it; but something is generally so employed. It is better to cherish virtue and humanity, by leaving much to free will, even with some loss to the object, than to attempt to make men mere machines and instruments of a political benevolence. The world on the whole will gain by a liberty, without which virtue cannot exist.

When once the commonwealth has established the estates of the church as property, it can, consistently, hear nothing of the more or the less. Too much and too little are treason against property. What evil can arise from the quantity in any hand, whilst the supreme authority has the full, sovereign superintendence over this, as over all property, to prevent every species of abuse; and, whenever it notably deviates, to give to it a direction agreeable to the purposes of its institution.

In England most of us conceive that it is envy and malignity towards those who are often the beginners of their own fortune, and not a love of the self-denial and mortification of the ancient church, that makes some look askance at the distinctions, and honours, and revenues, which, taken from no person, are set apart for virtue. The ears of the people of England are distinguishing. They hear these men speak broad. Their tongue betrays them. Their language is in the *patois* of fraud; in the cant and gibberish of hypocrisy. The people of England must think so, when these praters affect to carry back the clergy to that primitive, evangelic poverty, which, in the spirit, ought always to exist in them, (and in us too, however we may like it,) but in the thing must be varied, when the relation of that body to the state is altered; when manners, when modes of life, when indeed the whole order of human affairs, has undergone a total revolution. We shall believe those reformers then to be honest enthusiasts, not, as now we think them, cheats and deceivers, when we see them throwing their own goods into common, and submitting their own persons to the austere discipline of the early church.

With these ideas rooted in their minds, the Commons of Great Britain, in the national emergencies, will never seek their resource from the confiscation of the estates of the church and poor. Sacrilege and proscription are not among the ways and means of our committee of supply. The Jews in Change Alley have not yet dared to hint their hopes of a mortgage on the revenues belonging to the see of Canterbury. I am not afraid that I shall be disavowed, when I assure you, that there is not *one* public man in this kingdom, whom you would wish to quote, no not one, of any party or description, who does not reprobate the dishonest, perfidious, and cruel confiscation which the National Assembly has been compelled to make of that property, which it was their first duty to protect.

It is with the exultation of a little national pride I tell you, that those amongst us who have wished to pledge the societies of Paris in the cup of their abominations have been disappointed. The robbery of your church has proved a security to the possessions of ours. It has roused the people. They see with horror and alarm that enormous and shameless act of proscription. It has opened, and will more and more open, their eyes upon the selfish enlargement of mind, and the narrow liberality of sentiment, of insidious men, which, commencing in close hypocrisy and fraud, have ended in open violence and rapine. At home we behold similar beginnings. We are on our guard against similar conclusions.

I hope we shall never be so totally lost to all sense of the duties imposed upon us by the law of social union, as, upon any pretext of public service, to confiscate the goods of a single unoffending citizen. Who but a tyrant (a name expressive of everything which can vitiate and degrade human nature) could think of seizing on the property of men, unaccused, unheard, untried, by whole descriptions, by hundreds and thousands together? Who, that had not lost every trace of humanity, could think of casting down men of exalted rank and sacred function, some of them of an age to call at once for reverence and compassion, of casting them down from the highest situation in the commonwealth, wherein they were maintained by their own landed property, to a state of indigence, depression, and contempt?

The confiscators truly have made some allowance to their victims from the scraps and fragments of their own tables, from which they have been so harshly driven, and which have been so bountifully spread for a feast to the harpies of usury. But to drive men from independence to live on alms, is itself great cruelty. That which might be a tolerable condition to men in one state of life, and not habituated to other things, may, when all these circumstances are altered, be a dreadful revolution; and one to which a virtuous mind would feel pain in condemning any guilt, except that which would demand the life of the offender. But to many minds this punishment of *degradation* and *infamy* is worse than death. Undoubtedly it is an infinite aggravation of this cruel suffering, that the persons who were taught a double prejudice in favour of religion, by education, and by the place they held in the administration of its functions, are to receive the remnants of their property as alms from the profane and impious hands of those who had plundered them of all the rest; to receive (if they are at all to receive) not from the charitable contributions of the faithful, but from the insolent tenderness of known and avowed atheism, the maintenance of religion, measured out to them on the standard of the contempt in which it is held; and for the purpose of rendering those who receive the allowance vile, and of no estimation, in the eyes of mankind.

But this act of seizure of property, it seems, is a judgment in law, and not a confiscation. They have, it seems, found out in the academies of the *Palais Royal*, and the *Jacobins*,[95] that certain men had no right to the possessions which they held under law, usage, the decisions of courts, and the accumulated prescription of a thousand years. They say that ecclesiastics are fictitious persons, creatures of the state, whom at pleasure they may destroy, and of course limit and modify in every particular; that the goods they possess are not properly theirs, but belong to the state which created the fiction; and we are therefore not to trouble ourselves with what they may suffer in their natural feelings and natural persons, on account of what is done towards them in this their constructive character. Of what import is it under what names you injure men, and deprive them of the just emoluments of a profession, in which they were not only permitted but encouraged by the state to engage; and upon the supposed certainty of which emoluments they had formed the plan of their lives, contracted debts, and led multitudes to an entire dependence upon them?

You do not imagine, Sir, that I am going to compliment this miserable distinction of persons with any long discussion. The arguments of tyranny are as contemptible as its force is dreadful. Had not your confiscators, by their early crimes, obtained a power which secures indemnity to all the crimes of which they have since been guilty, or that they can commit, it is not the syllogism of the logician, but the lash of the executioner, that would have refuted a sophistry which becomes an accomplice of theft and murder. The sophistic tyrants of Paris are loud in their declamations against the departed regal tyrants, who in former ages have vexed the world. They are thus bold, because they are safe from the dungeons and iron cages of their old masters. Shall we be more tender of the tyrants of our own time, when we see them acting worse tragedies under our eyes? shall we not use the same liberty that they do, when we can use it with the same safety? when to speak honest truth only requires a contempt of the opinions of those whose actions we abhor?

This outrage on all the rights of property was at first covered with what, on the system of their conduct, was the most astonishing of all pretexts – a regard to national faith. The enemies to property at first pretended a most tender, delicate, and scrupulous anxiety for keeping the king's engagements with the public creditor. These professors of the rights of men are so busy in teaching others, that they have not leisure to learn anything themselves; otherwise they would have known, that it is to the property of the citizen, and not to the demands of the creditor of the state, that the first and original faith of civil society is pledged. The claim of the citizen is prior in time, paramount in title, superior in equity. The fortunes of individuals, whether

possessed by acquisition, or by descent, or in virtue of a participation in the goods of some community, were no part of the
creditor's security, expressed or implied. They never so much as
entered into his head when he made his bargain. He well knew
that the public, whether represented by a monarch or by a senate,
can pledge nothing but the public estate; and it can have no
public estate, except in what it derives from a just and proportioned imposition upon the citizens at large. This was engaged,
and nothing else could be engaged, to the public creditor. No
man can mortgage his injustice as a pawn for his fidelity.

It is impossible to avoid some observation on the contradictions caused by the extreme rigour and the extreme laxity of this
new public faith, which influenced in this transaction, and which
influenced not according to the nature of the obligation, but to
the description of the persons to whom it was engaged. No acts
of the old government of the kings of France are held valid in the
National Assembly, except his pecuniary engagements; acts of all
others of the most ambiguous legality. The rest of the acts of
that royal government are considered in so odious a light, that to
have a claim under its authority is looked on as a sort of crime.
A pension, given as a reward for service to the state, is surely as
good a ground of property, as any security for money advanced
to the state. It is better; for money is paid, and well paid, to obtain
that service. We have however seen multitudes of people under
this description in France, who never had been deprived of their
allowances by the most arbitrary ministers, in the most arbitrary
times, by this assembly of the rights of men, robbed without
mercy. They were told, in answer to their claim to the bread
earned with their blood, that their services had not been rendered
to the country that now exists.

This laxity of public faith is not confined to those unfortunate
persons. The Assembly, with perfect consistency it must be
owned, is engaged in a respectable deliberation how far it is
bound by the treaties made with other nations under the former
government, and their committee is to report which of them
they ought to ratify, and which not. By this means they have put
the external fidelity of this virgin state on a par with its internal.

It is not easy to conceive upon what rational principle the royal
government should not, of the two, rather have possessed the
power of rewarding service, and making treaties, in virtue of its
prerogative, than that of pledging to creditors the revenue of the

state, actual and possible. The treasure of the nation, of all things, has been the least allowed to the prerogative of the king of France, or to the prerogative of any king in Europe. To mortgage the public revenue implies the sovereign dominion, in the fullest sense, over the public purse. It goes far beyond the trust even of a temporary and occasional taxation. The acts however of that dangerous power (the distinctive mark of a boundless despotism) have been alone held sacred. Whence arose this preference given by a democratic assembly to a body of property deriving its title from the most critical and obnoxious of all the exertions of monarchical authority? Reason can furnish nothing to reconcile inconsistency; nor can partial favour be accounted for upon equitable principles. But the contradiction and partiality which admit no justification, are not the less without an adequate cause; and that cause I do not think it difficult to discover.

By the vast debt of France a great monied interest has insensibly grown up, and with it a great power. By the ancient usages which prevailed in that kingdom, the general circulation of property, and in particular the mutual convertibility of land into money, and of money into land, had always been a matter of difficulty. Family settlements, rather more general and more strict than they are in England, the *jus retractus*,[96] the great mass of landed property held by the crown, and, by a maxim of the French law, held unalienably, the vast estates of the ecclesiastic corporations, – all these had kept the landed and monied interests more separated in France, less miscible, and the owners of the two distinct species of property not so well disposed to each other as they are in this country.

The monied property was long looked on with rather an evil eye by the people. They saw it connected with their distresses, and aggravating them. It was no less envied by the old landed interests, partly for the same reasons that rendered it obnoxious to the people, but much more so as it eclipsed, by the splendour of an ostentatious luxury, the unendowed pedigrees and naked titles of several among the nobility. Even when the nobility, which represented the more permanent landed interest, united themselves by marriage (which sometimes was the case) with the other description, the wealth which saved the family from ruin, was supposed to contaminate and degrade it. Thus the enmities and heart-burnings of these parties were increased even by the usual means by which discord is made to cease and quarrels are turned into friendship. In the mean time, the pride of the wealthy men, not noble or newly noble, increased with its cause. They felt with resentment an inferiority, the grounds of which they did not acknowledge. There was no measure to which they were not willing to lend themselves, in order to be revenged of the outrages of this rival pride, and to exalt their wealth to what they considered as its natural rank and estimation. They struck at the nobility through the crown and the church. They attacked them particularly on the side on which they thought them the most vulnerable, that is, the possessions of the church, which, through the patronage of the crown, generally devolved upon the nobility. The bishoprics, and the great commendatory abbeys, were, with few exceptions, held by that order.

In this state of real, though not always perceived, warfare between the noble ancient landed interest and the new monied interest, the greatest because the most applicable strength was in the hands of the latter. The monied interest is in its nature more ready for any adventure; and its possessors more disposed to new enterprises of any kind. Being of a recent acquisition, it falls in more naturally with any novelties. It is therefore the kind of wealth which will be resorted to by all who wish for change.

Along with the monied interest, a new description of men had grown up, with whom that interest soon formed a close and marked union; I mean the political men of letters. Men of letters, fond of distinguishing themselves, are rarely averse to innovation. Since the decline of the life and greatness of Louis the Fourteenth, they were not so much cultivated either by him, or by the regent,[97] or the successors to the crown, nor were they engaged to the court by favours and emoluments so systematically as during the splendid period of that ostentatious and not impolitic reign. What they lost in the old court protection, they endeavoured to make up by joining in a sort of incorporation of their own; to which the two academies of France,[98] and afterwards the vast undertaking of the Encyclopædia,[99] carried on by a society of these gentlemen, did not a little contribute.

The literary cabal had some years ago formed something like a regular plan for the destruction of the Christian religion. This object they pursued with a degree of zeal which hitherto had been discovered only in the propagators of some system of piety. They were possessed with a spirit of proselytism in the most fanatical degree; and from thence, by an easy progress, with the spirit of persecution according to their means.* What was not to be done towards their great end by any direct or immediate act, might be wrought by a longer process through the medium of opinion. To command that opinion, the first step is to establish a dominion over those who direct it. They contrived to possess themselves, with great method and perseverance, of all the avenues to literary fame. Many of them indeed stood high in the ranks of literature and science. The world had done them justice; and in favour of general talents forgave the evil tendency of their peculiar principles. This was true liberality; which they returned by endeavouring to confine the reputation of sense, learning, and taste to themselves or their followers. I will venture to say that this narrow, exclusive spirit has not been less prejudicial to literature and to taste, than to morals and true philosophy. These atheistical fathers have a bigotry of their own; and they have learnt to talk against monks with the spirit of a monk. But in some things they are men of the world. The resources of intrigue are called in to supply the defects of argument and wit. To this system of literary monopoly was joined an unremitting industry to blacken and discredit in every way, and by every means, all those who did not hold to their faction. To those who have observed the spirit of their conduct, it has long been clear that nothing was wanted but the power of carrying the intolerance of the tongue and of the pen into a persecution which would strike at property, liberty, and life.

The desultory and faint persecution carried on against them, more from compliance with form and decency, than with serious resentment, neither weakened their strength, nor relaxed their efforts. The issue of the whole was, that, what with opposition, and what with success, a violent and malignant zeal, of a kind hitherto unknown in the world, had taken an entire possession of their minds, and rendered their whole conversation, which otherwise would have been pleasing and instructive, perfectly disgusting. A spirit of cabal, intrigue, and proselytism, pervaded all their thoughts, words, and actions. And, as controversial zeal soon turns its thoughts on force, they began to insinuate themselves into a correspondence with foreign princes; in hopes,

* This (down to the end of the first sentence in the next paragraph) and some other parts here and there, were inserted, on his reading the manuscript, by my lost Son.

through their authority, which at first they flattered, they might bring about the changes they had in view. To them it was indifferent whether these changes were to be accomplished by the thunderbolt of despotism, or by the earthquake of popular commotion. The correspondence between this cabal and the late king of Prussia[100] will throw no small light upon the spirit of all their proceedings.* For the same purpose for which they intrigued with princes, they cultivated, in a distinguished manner, the monied interest of France; and partly through the means furnished by those whose peculiar offices gave them the most extensive and certain means of communication, they carefully occupied all the avenues to opinion.

Writers, especially when they act in a body, and with one direction, have great influence on the public mind; the alliance, therefore, of these writers with the monied interest† had no small effect in removing the popular odium and envy which attended that species of wealth. These writers, like the propagators of all novelties, pretended to a great zeal for the poor, and the lower orders, whilst in their satires they rendered hateful, by every exaggeration, the faults of courts, of nobility, and of priesthood. They became a sort of demagogues. They served as a link to unite, in favour of one object, obnoxious wealth to restless and desperate poverty.

As these two kinds of men appear principal leaders in all the late transactions, their junction and politics will serve to account, not upon any principles of law or of policy, but as a cause, for the general fury with which all the landed property of ecclesiastical corporations has been attacked; and the great care which, contrary to their pretended principles, has been taken, of a monied interest originating from the authority of the crown. All the envy against wealth and power was artificially directed against other descriptions of riches. On what other principle than that which I have stated can we account for an appearance so extraordinary and unnatural as that of the ecclesiastical possessions, which had stood so many successions of ages and shocks of civil violences, and were girded at once by justice, and by prejudice, being applied to the payment of debts, comparatively recent, invidious, and contracted by a decried and subverted government?

* I do not choose to shock the feeling of the moral reader with any quotation of their vulgar, base, and profane language.
† Their connexion with Turgot[101] and almost all the people of the finance.

Was the public estate a sufficient stake for the public debts? Assume that it was not, and that a loss *must* be incurred some- where – When the only estate lawfully possessed, and which the contracting parties had in contemplation at the time in which their bargain was made, happens to fail, who according to the principles of natural and legal equity, ought to be the sufferer? Certainly it ought to be either the party who trusted, or the party who persuaded him to trust; or both; and not third parties who had no concern with the transaction. Upon any insolvency they ought to suffer who are weak enough to lend upon bad security, or they who fraudulently held out a security that was not valid. Laws are acquainted with no other rules of decision. But by the new institute of the rights of men, the only persons, who in equity ought to suffer, are the only persons who are to be saved harmless: those are to answer the debt who neither were lenders nor borrowers, mortgagers nor mortgagees.

What had the clergy to do with these transactions? What had they to do with any public engagement further than the extent of their own debt? To that, to be sure, their estates were bound to the last acre. Nothing can lead more to the true spirit of the Assembly, which fits for public confiscation, with its new equity, and its new morality, than an attention to their proceeding with regard to this debt of the clergy. The body of confiscators, true to that monied interest for which they were false to every other, have found the clergy competent to incur a legal debt. Of course they declared them legally entitled to the property which their power of incurring the debt and mortgaging the estate implied; recognising the rights of those persecuted citizens, in the very act in which they were thus grossly violated.

If, as I said, any persons are to make good deficiencies to the public creditor, besides the public at large, they must be those who managed the agreement. Why therefore are not the estates of all the comptrollers-general[102] confiscated?* Why not those of the long succession of ministers, financiers, and bankers who have been enriched whilst the nation was impoverished by their dealings and their counsels? Why is not the estate of M. Laborde[103] declared forfeited rather than of the archbishop of Paris, who has had nothing to do in the creation or in the jobbing of the public funds? Or, if you must confiscate old landed estates

* All have been confiscated in their turn.

in favour of the money-jobbers, why is the penalty confined to one description? I do not know whether the expenses of the Duke de Choiseul[104] have left anything of the infinite sums which he had derived from the bounty of his master, during the transactions of a reign which contributed largely by every species of prodigality in war and peace, to the present debt of France. If any such remains, why is not this confiscated? I remember to have been in Paris during the time of the old government. I was there just after the Duke d'Aiguillon[105] had been snatched (as it was generally thought) from the block by the hand of a protecting despotism. He was a minister, and had some concern in the affairs of that prodigal period. Why do I not see his estate delivered up to the municipalities in which it is situated? The noble family of Noailles[106] have long been servants (meritorious servants I admit) to the crown of France, and have had of course some share in its bounties. Why do I hear nothing of the application of their estates to the public debt? Why is the estate of the Duke de Rochefoucault more sacred than that of the Cardinal de Rochefoucault?[107] The former is, I doubt not, a worthy person; and (if it were not a sort of profaneness to talk of the use, as affecting the title to property) he makes a good use of his revenues; but it is no disrespect to him to say, what authentic information well warrants me in saying, that the use made of a property equally valid, by his brother* the cardinal archbishop of Rouen, was far more laudable and far more public-spirited. Can one hear of the proscription of such persons, and the confiscation of their effects, without indignation and horror? He is not a man who does not feel such emotions on such occasions. He does not deserve the name of a free-man who will not express them.

Few barbarous conquerors have ever made so terrible a revolution in property. None of the heads of the Roman factions, when they established "*crudelem illam hastam*"[108] in all their auctions of rapine, have ever set up to sale the goods of the conquered citizen to such an enormous amount. It must be allowed in favour of those tyrants of antiquity, that what was done by them could hardly be said to be done in cold blood. Their passions were inflamed, their tempers soured, their understandings confused, with the spirit of revenge, with the innumerable reciprocated and recent inflictions and retaliations of blood and rapine. They were

---

* Not his brother, nor any near relation; but this mistake does not affect the argument.

driven beyond all bounds of moderation by the apprehension of the return of power with the return of property, to the families of those they had injured beyond all hope of forgiveness.

These Roman confiscators, who were yet only in the elements of tyranny, and were not instructed in the rights of men to exercise all sorts of cruelties on each other without provocation, thought it necessary to spread a sort of colour over their injustice. They considered the vanquished party as composed of traitors who had borne arms, or otherwise had acted with hostility, against the commonwealth. They regarded them as persons who had forfeited their property by their crimes. With you, in your improved state of the human mind, there was no such formality. You seized upon five millions sterling of annual rent, and turned forty or fifty thousand human creatures out of their houses, because "such was your pleasure." The tyrant Harry the Eighth of England, as he was not better enlightened than the Roman Mariuses and Syllas,[109] and had not studied in your new schools, did not know what an effectual instrument of despotism was to be found in that grand magazine of offensive weapons, the rights of men. When he resolved to rob the abbeys, as the club of the Jacobins have robbed all the ecclesiastics, he began by setting on foot a commission to examine into the crimes and abuses which prevailed in those communities. As it might be expected, his commission reported truths, exaggerations, and falsehoods. But truly or falsely, it reported abuses and offences. However, as abuses might be corrected, as every crime of persons does not infer a forfeiture with regard to communities, and as property, in that dark age, was not discovered to be a creature of prejudice, all those abuses (and there were enow of them) were hardly thought sufficient ground for such a confiscation as it was for his purpose to make. He therefore procured the formal surrender of these estates. All these operose proceedings were adopted by one of the most decided tyrants in the rolls of history, as necessary preliminaries, before he could venture, by bribing the members of his two servile houses with a share of the spoil, and holding out to them an eternal immunity from taxation, to demand a confirmation of his iniquitous proceedings by an act of parliament. Had fate reserved him to our times, four technical terms would have done his business, and saved him all this trouble; he needed nothing more than one short form of incantation – "*Philosophy, Light, Liberality, the Rights of Men.*"

I can say nothing in praise of those acts of tyranny, which no voice has hitherto ever commended under any of their false colours; yet in these false colours nil homage was paid by despotism to justice. The power which was above all fear and all remorse was not set above all shame. Whilst shame keeps its watch, virtue is not wholly extinguished in the heart; nor will moderation be utterly exiled from the minds of tyrants.

I believe every honest man sympathises in his reflections with our political poet on that occasion, and will pray to avert the omen whenever these acts of rapacious despotism present themselves to his view or his imagination:

> – "May no such storm
> Fall on our times, where ruin must reform.
> Tell me (my Muse) what monstrous dire offence,
> What crimes could any Christian king incense
> To such a rage? Was 't luxury, or lust?
> Was *he* so temperate, so chaste, so just?
> Were these their crimes? they were his own much more,
> But wealth is crime enough to him that's poor."*

* The rest of the passage is this –

> "Who having spent the treasures of his crown,
> Condemns their luxury to feed his own.
> And yet this act, to varnish o'er the shame
> Of sacrilege, must bear devotion's name.
> No crime so bold, but would be understood
> A real, or at least a seeming good;
> Who fears not to do ill, yet fears the name,
> And, free from conscience, is a slave to fame.
> Thus he the church at once protects, and spoils;
> But princes' swords are sharper than their styles.
> And thus to th' ages past he makes amends,
> Their charity destroys, their faith defends.
> Then did religion in a lazy cell,
> In empty, aëry contemplation dwell;
> And, like the block, unmoved lay; but ours,
> As much too active, like the stork devours.
> Is there no temperate region can be known,
> Betwixt their frigid and our torrid zone?
> Could we not wake from that lethargic dream,
> But to be restless in a worse extreme?
> And for that lethargy was there no cure,
> But to be cast into a calenture;
> Can knowledge have no bound, but must advance
> So far, to make us wish for ignorance?
> And rather in the dark to grope our way,
> Than, led by a false guide, to err by day?"

This same wealth, which is at all times treason and *lese nation* to indigent and rapacious despotism, under all modes of polity, was your temptation to violate property, law, and religion, united in one object. But was the state of France so wretched and undone, that no other resource but rapine remained to preserve its existence? On this point I wish to receive some information. When the states met, was the condition of the finances of France such, that, after economising on principles of justice and mercy through all departments, no fair repartition of burthens upon all the orders could possibly restore them? If such an equal imposition would have been sufficient, you well know it might easily have been made. M. Necker,[110] in the budget which he laid before the orders assembled at Versailles, made a detailed exposition of the state of the French nation.*

If we give credit to him, it was not necessary to have recourse to any new impositions whatsoever, to put the receipts of France on a balance with its expenses. He stated the permanent charges of all descriptions, including the interest of a new loan of four hundred millions, at 531,444,000 livres; the fixed revenue at 475,294,000, making the deficiency 56,150,000, or short of £2,200,000 sterling. But to balance it, he brought forward savings and improvements of revenue (considered as entirely certain) to rather more than the amount of that deficiency; and he concludes with these emphatical words, (p. 39,) "Quel pays, Messieurs, que celui, où, *sans impôts* et avec de simples objets *inapperçus*, on peut faire disparoître un deficit qui a fait tant de bruit en Europe." As to the reimbursement, the sinking of debt, and the other great objects of public credit and political arrangement indicated in Mons. Necker's speech, no doubt could be entertained, but that a very moderate and proportioned assessment on the citizens without distinction would have provided for all of them to the fullest extent of their demand.

> Who sees these dismal heaps, but would demand,
> What barbarous invader sacked the land?
> But when he hears, no Goth, no Turk did bring
> This desolation, but a Christian king;
> When nothing, but the name of zeal, appears
> 'Twixt our best actions and the worst of theirs,
> What does he think our sacrilege would spare,
> When such th' effects of our devotion are?"
>
> COOPER'S HILL, by Sir JOHN DENHAM

* Rapport de Mons, le Directeur-Général des Finances, fait par ordre du Roi à Versailles. Mai 5, 1789.

If this representation of Mons. Necker was false, then the Assembly are in the highest degree culpable for having forced the king to accept as his minister, and since the king's deposition, for having employed, as *their* minister, a man who had been capable of abusing so notoriously the confidence of his master and their own; in a matter too of the highest moment, and directly appertaining to his particular office. But if the representation was exact, (as having always, along with you, conceived a high degree of respect for M. Necker, I make no doubt it was,) then what can be said in favour of those, who, instead of moderate, reasonable, and general contribution, have in cold blood, and impelled by no necessity, had recourse to a partial and cruel confiscation?

Was that contribution refused on a pretext of privilege, either on the part of the clergy, or on that of the nobility? No, certainly. As to the clergy, they even ran before the wishes of the third order. Previous to the meeting of the states, they had in all their instructions expressly directed their deputies to renounce every immunity, which put them upon a footing distinct from the condition of their fellow-subjects. In this renunciation the clergy were even more explicit than the nobility.

But let us suppose that the deficiency had remained at the fifty-six millions, (or £2,200,000 sterling,) as at first stated by M. Necker. Let us allow that all the resources he opposed to that deficiency were impudent and groundless fictions; and that the Assembly (or their lords of articles* at the Jacobins) were from thence justified in laying the whole burthen of that deficiency on the clergy, – yet allowing all this, a necessity of £2,200,000 sterling will not support a confiscation to the amount of five millions. The imposition of £2,200,000 on the clergy, as partial, would have been oppressive and unjust, but it would not have been altogether ruinous to those on whom it was imposed; and therefore it would not have answered the real purpose of the managers.

Perhaps persons unacquainted with the state of France, on hearing the clergy and the noblesse were privileged in point of taxation, may be led to imagine, that, previous to the Revolution, these bodies had contributed nothing to the state. This is a

---

* In the constitution of Scotland, during the Stuart reigns, a committee sat for preparing bills; and none could pass, but those previously approved by them. This committee was called lords of articles.

great mistake. They certainly did not contribute equally with each other, nor either of them equally with the commons. They both however contributed largely. Neither nobility nor clergy enjoyed any exemption from the excise on consumable commodities, from duties of custom, or from any of the other numerous *indirect* impositions, which in France, as well as here, make so very large a proportion of all payments to the public. The noblesse paid the capitation. They paid also a land-tax, called the twentieth penny, to the height sometimes of three, sometimes of four, shillings in the pound; both of them *direct* impositions of no light nature, and no trivial produce. The clergy of the provinces annexed by conquest to France, (which in extent make about an eighth part of the whole, but in wealth a much larger proportion,) paid likewise to the capitation and the twentieth penny, at the rate paid by the nobility. The clergy in the old provinces did not pay the capitation; but they had redeemed themselves at the expense of about 24 millions, or a little more than a million sterling. They were exempted from the twentieths: but then they made free gifts; they contracted debts for the state; and they were subject to some other charges, the whole computed at about a thirteenth part of their clear income. They ought to have paid annually about forty thousand pounds more, to put them on a par with the contribution of the nobility.

When the terrors of this tremendous proscription hung over the clergy, they made an offer of a contribution, through the archbishop of Aix, which, for its extravagance, ought not to have been accepted. But it was evidently and obviously more advantageous to the public creditor, than anything which could rationally be promised by the confiscation. Why was it not accepted? The reason is plain – There was no desire that the church should be brought to serve the state. The service of the state was made a pretext to destroy the church. In their way to the destruction of the church they would not scruple to destroy their country: and they have destroyed it. One great end in the project would have been defeated, if the plan of extortion had been adopted in lieu of the scheme of confiscation. The new landed interest connected with the new republic, and connected with it for its very being, could not have been created. This was among the reasons why that extravagant ransom was not accepted.

The madness of the project of confiscation, on the plan that was first pretended, soon became apparent. To bring this unwieldy mass of landed property, enlarged by the confiscation of all the vast landed domain of the crown, at once into market, was obviously to defeat the profits proposed by the confiscation, by depreciating the value of those lands, and indeed of all the landed estates throughout France. Such a sudden diversion of all its circulating money from trade to land, must be an additional mischief. What step was taken? Did the Assembly, on becoming sensible of the inevitable ill effects of their projected sale, revert to the offers of the clergy? No distress could oblige them to travel in a course which was disgraced by any appearance of justice. Giving over all hopes from a general immediate sale, another project seems to have succeeded. They proposed to take stock in exchange for the church lands. In that project great difficulties arose in equalising the objects to be exchanged. Other obstacles also presented themselves, which threw them back again upon some project of sale. The municipalities had taken an alarm. They would not hear of transferring the whole plunder of the kingdom to the stock-holders in Paris. Many of those municipalities had been (upon system) reduced to the most deplorable indigence. Money was nowhere to be seen. They were therefore led to the point that was so ardently desired. They panted for a currency of any kind which might revive their perishing industry. The municipalities were then to be admitted to a share in the spoil, which evidently rendered the first scheme (if ever it had been seriously entertained) altogether impracticable. Public exigencies pressed upon all sides. The minister of finance reiterated his call for supply with a most urgent, anxious, and boding voice. Thus pressed on all sides, instead of the first plan of converting their bankers into bishops and abbots, instead of paying the old debt, they contracted a new debt, at 3 per cent, creating a new paper currency, founded on an eventual sale of the church lands. They issued this paper currency to satisfy in the first instance chiefly the demands made upon them by the *bank of discount*, the great machine, or paper-mill, of their fictitious wealth.

The spoil of the church was now become the only resource of all their operations in finance, the vital principle of all their politics, the sole security for the existence of their power. It was necessary by all, even the most violent means, to put every individual on the same bottom, and to bind the nation in one guilty interest to uphold this act, and the authority of those by whom it was done. In order to force the most reluctant into a participation of their pillage, they rendered their paper circulation compulsory in all payments. Those who consider the general tendency of their schemes to this one object as a centre, and a centre from which afterwards all their measures radiate, will not think that I dwell too long upon this part of the proceedings of the National Assembly.

To cut off all appearance of connexion between the crown and public justice, and to bring the whole under implicit obedience to the dictators in Paris, the old independent judicature of the parliaments, with all its merits, and all its faults, was wholly abolished. Whilst the parliaments existed, it was evident that the people might some time or other come to resort to them, and rally under the standard of their ancient laws. It became however a matter of consideration that the magistrates and officers, in the courts now abolished, *had purchased their places* at a very high rate, for which, as well as for the duty they performed, they received but a very low return of interest. Simple confiscation is a boon only for the clergy; – to the lawyers some appearances of equity are to be observed; and they are to receive compensation to an immense amount. Their compensation becomes part of the national debt, for the liquidation of which there is the one exhaustless fund. The lawyers are to obtain their compensation in the new church paper, which is to march with the new principles of judicature and legislature. The dismissed magistrates are to take their share of martyrdom with the ecclesiastics, or to receive their own property from such a fund, and in such a manner, as all those, who have been seasoned with the ancient principles of jurisprudence, and had been the sworn guardians of property, must look upon with horror. Even the clergy are to receive their miserable allowance out of the depreciated paper, which is stamped with the indelible character of sacrilege, and with the symbols of their own ruin, or they must starve. So violent an outrage upon credit, property, and liberty, as this compulsory paper currency, has seldom been exhibited by the alliance of bankruptcy and tyranny, at any time, or in any nation.

In the course of all these operations, at length comes out the grand *arcanum*; – that in reality, and in a fair sense, the lands of the church (so far as anything certain can be gathered from their proceedings) are not to be sold at all. By the late resolutions of the National Assembly, they are indeed to be delivered to the highest bidder. But it is to be observed, that *a certain portion only*

of the purchase money is to be laid down. A period of twelve years
is to be given for the payment of the rest. The philosophic
purchasers are therefore, on payment of a sort of fine, to be put
instantly into possession of the estate. It becomes in some respects
a sort of gift to them; to be held on the feudal tenure of zeal to
the new establishment. This project is evidently to let in a body
of purchasers without money. The consequence will be, that
these purchasers, or rather grantees, will pay, not only from the
rents as they accrue, which might as well be received by the state,
but from the spoil of the materials of buildings, from waste in
woods, and from whatever money, by hands habituated to the
gripings of usury, they can wring from the miserable peasant. He
is to be delivered over to the mercenary and arbitrary discretion
of men, who will be stimulated to every species of extortion by
the growing demands on the growing profits of an estate held
under the precarious settlement of a new political system.

When all the frauds, impostures, violences, rapines, burnings,
murders, confiscations, compulsory paper currencies, and every
description of tyranny and cruelty employed to bring about and
to uphold this Revolution, have their natural effect, that is, to
shock the moral sentiments of all virtuous and sober minds, the
abettors of this philosophic system immediately strain their
throats in a declamation against the old monarchical government
of France. When they have rendered that deposed power sufficiently black, they then proceed in argument, as if all those who
disapprove of their new abuses must of course be partisans of the
old; that those who reprobate their crude and violent schemes of
liberty ought to be treated as advocates for servitude. I admit that
their necessities do compel them to this base and contemptible
fraud. Nothing can reconcile men to their proceedings and projects, but the supposition that there is no third option between
them and some tyranny as odious as can be furnished by the
records of history, or by the invention of poets. This prattling of
theirs hardly deserves the name of sophistry. It is nothing but
plain impudence. Have these gentlemen never heard, in the
whole circle of the worlds of theory and practice, of anything
between the despotism of the monarch and the despotism of the
multitude? Have they never heard of a monarchy directed by
laws, controlled and balanced by the great hereditary wealth
and herediary dignity of a nation; and both again controlled by
a judicious check from the reason and feeling of the people at

large, acting by a suitable and permanent organ? Is it then impossible that a man may be found, who, without criminal ill intention, or pitiable absurdity, shall prefer such a mixed and tempered government to either of the extremes; and who may repute that nation to be destitute of all wisdom and of all virtue, which, having in its choice to obtain such a government with ease, *or rather to confirm it when actually possessed*, thought proper to commit a thousand crimes, and to subject their country to a thousand evils, in order to avoid it? Is it then a truth so universally acknowledged, that a pure democracy is the only tolerable form into which human society can be thrown, that a man is not permitted to hesitate about its merits, without the suspicion of being a friend to tyranny, that is, of being a foe to mankind?

I do not know under what description to class the present ruling authority in France. It affects to be a pure democracy, though I think it in a direct train of becoming shortly a mischievous and ignoble oligarchy. But for the present I admit it to be a contrivance of the nature and effect of what it pretends to. I reprobate no form of government merely upon abstract principles. There may be situations in which the purely democratic form will become necessary. There may be some (very few, and very particularly circumstanced) where it would be clearly desirable. This I do not take to be the case of France, or of any other great country. Until now, we have seen no examples of considerable democracies. The ancients were better acquainted with them. Not being wholly unread in the authors, who had seen the most of those constitutions, and who best understood them, I cannot help concurring with their opinion, that an absolute democracy, no more than absolute monarchy, is to be reckoned among the legitimate forms of government. They think it rather the corruption and degeneracy, than the sound constitution of a republic. If I recollect rightly, Aristotle observes, that a democracy has many striking points of resemblance with a tyranny.* Of this I am certain, that in a democracy, the majority of the citizens is

---

* When I wrote this I quoted from memory, after many years had elapsed from my reading the passage. A learned friend has found it, and it is as follows:

τὸ ἦθος τὸ αὐτό, καὶ ἄμφω δεσποτικὰ τῶν βελτιόνων, καὶ τὰ ψηφίσματα ὥσπερ ἐκεῖ τὰ ἐπιτάγματα, καὶ ὁ δημαγωγὸς καὶ ὁ κόλαξ οἱ αὐτοὶ καὶ ἀνάλογον. καὶ μάλιστα δ᾽ ἑκάτεροι παρ᾽ ἑκατέροις ἰσχύουσιν, οἱ μὲν κόλακες παρὰ τοῖς τυράννοις

"The ethical character is the same; both exercise despotism over the better class of citizens; and decrees are in the one, what ordinances and arrêts are in the other: the

capable of exercising the most cruel oppressions upon the minority, whenever strong divisions prevail in that kind of polity, as they often must; and that oppression of the minority will extend to far greater numbers, and will be carried on with much greater fury, than can almost ever be apprehended from the dominion of a single sceptre. In such a popular persecution, individual sufferers are in a much more deplorable condition than in any other. Under a cruel prince they have the balmy compassion of mankind to assuage the smart of their wounds; they have the plaudits of the people to animate their generous constancy under their sufferings: but those who are subjected to wrong under multitudes, are deprived of all external consolation. They seem deserted by mankind, overpowered by a conspiracy of their whole species.

But admitting democracy not to have that inevitable tendency to party tyranny, which I suppose it to have, and admitting it to possess as much good in it when unmixed, as I am sure it possesses when compounded with other forms; does monarchy, on its part, contain nothing at all to recommend it? I do not often quote Bolingbroke, nor have his works in general left any permanent impression on my mind. He is a presumptuous and a superficial writer. But he has one observation, which, in my opinion, is not without depth and solidity. He says, that he prefers a monarchy to other governments; because you can better ingraft any description of republic on a monarchy than anything of monarchy upon the republican forms. I think him perfectly in the right. The fact is so historically; and it agrees well with the speculation.

I know how easy a topic it is to dwell on the faults of departed greatness. By a revolution in the state, the fawning sycophant of yesterday is converted into the austere critic of the present hour. But steady, independent minds, when they have an object of so serious a concern to mankind as government under their contemplation, will disdain to assume the part of satirists and declaimers. They will judge of human institutions as they do of human characters. They will sort out the good from the evil, which is mixed in mortal institutions, as it is in mortal men.

Your government in France, though usually, and I think justly,

---

demagogue too, and the court favourite, are not unfrequently the same identical men, and always bear a close analogy; and these have the principal power, each in their respective forms of government, favourites with the absolute monarch, and demagogues with a people such as I have described." Arist. Politic. lib. iv. cap. 4.

reputed the best of the unqualified or ill-qualified monarchies, was still full of abuses. These abuses accumulated in a length of time, as they must accumulate in every monarchy not under the constant inspection of a popular representative. I am no stranger to the faults and defects of the subverted government of France; and I think I am not inclined by nature or policy to make a panegyric upon anything which is a just and natural object of censure. But the question is not now of the vices of that monarchy, but of its existence. Is it then true, that the French government was such as to be incapable or undeserving of reform; so that it was of absolute necessity that the whole fabric should be at once pulled down, and the area cleared for the erection of a theoretic, experimental edifice in its place? All France was of a different opinion in the beginning of the year 1789. The instructions to the representatives to the states-general, from every district in that kingdom, were filled with projects for the reformation of that government, without the remotest suggestion of a design to destroy it. Had such a design been then even insinuated, I believe there would have been but one voice, and that voice for rejecting it with scorn and horror. Men have been sometimes led by degrees, sometimes hurried, into things of which, if they could have seen the whole together, they never would have permitted the most remote approach. When those instructions were given, there was no question but that abuses existed, and that they demanded a reform; nor is there now. In the interval between the instructions and the Revolution, things changed their shape; and, in consequence of that change, the true question at present is, Whether those who would have reformed, or those who have destroyed, are in the right?

To hear some men speak of the late monarchy of France, you would imagine that they were talking of Persia bleeding under the ferocious sword of Tahmas Kouli Khân;[111] or at least describing the barbarous anarchic despotism of Turkey, where the finest countries in the most genial climates in the world are wasted by peace more than any countries have been worried by war; where arts are unknown, where manufactures languish, where science is extinguished, where agriculture decays, where the human race itself melts away and perishes under the eye of the observer. Was this the case of France? I have no way of determining the question but by a reference to facts. Facts do not support this resemblance. Along with much evil, there is some good in monarchy itself; and some corrective to its evil from religion, from laws, from manners, from opinions, the French monarchy must have received; which rendered it (though by no means a free, and therefore by no means a good, constitution) a despotism rather in appearance than in reality.

Among the standards upon which the effects of government on any country are to be estimated, I must consider the state of its population as not the least certain. No country in which population flourishes, and is in progressive improvement, can be under a *very* mischievous government. About sixty years ago, the Intendants of the generalities of France[112] made, with other matters, a report of the population of their several districts. I have not the books, which are very voluminous, by me, nor do I know where to procure them, (I am obliged to speak by memory, and therefore the less positively,) but I think the population of France was by them, even at that period, estimated at twenty-two millions of souls. At the end of the last century it had been generally calculated at eighteen. On either of these estimations, France was not ill peopled. M. Necker, who is an authority for his own time at least equal to the Intendants for theirs, reckons, and upon apparently sure principles, the people of France, in the year 1780, at twenty-four millions six hundred and seventy thousand. But was this the probable ultimate term under the old establishment? Dr. Price is of opinion, that the growth of population in France was by no means at its *acmé* in that year. I certainly defer to Dr. Price's authority a good deal more in these speculations, than I do in his general politics. This gentleman, taking ground on M. Necker's data, is very confident that since the period of that minister's calculation, the French population has increased rapidly; so rapidly, that in the year 1789 he will not consent to rate the people of that kingdom at a lower number than thirty millions. After abating much (and much I think ought to be abated) from the sanguine calculation of Dr. Price, I have no doubt that the population of France did increase considerably during this later period: but supposing that it increased to nothing more than will be sufficient to complete the twenty-four millions six hundred and seventy thousand to twenty-five millions, still a population of twenty-five millions, and that in an increasing progress, on a space of about twenty-seven thousand square leagues, is immense. It is, for instance, a good deal more than the proportionable population of this island, or even than that of England, the best peopled part of the united kingdom.

It is not universally true, that France is a fertile country. Considerable tracts of it are barren, and labour under other natural disadvantages. In the portions of that territory where things are more favourable, as far as I am able to discover, the numbers of the people correspond to the indulgence of nature.* The Generality of Lisle (this I admit is the strongest example) upon an extent of four hundred and four leagues and a half, about ten years ago, contained seven hundred and thirty-four thousand six hundred souls, which is one thousand seven hundred and seventy-two inhabitants to each square league. The middle term for the rest of France is about nine hundred inhabitants to the same admeasurement.

I do not attribute this population to the deposed government; because I do not like to compliment the contrivances of men with what is due in a great degree to the bounty of Providence. But that decried government could not have obstructed, most probably it favoured, the operation of those causes, (whatever they were,) whether of nature in the soil, or habits of industry among the people, which has produced so large a number of the species throughout that whole kingdom, and exhibited in some particular places such prodigies of population. I never will suppose that fabric of a state to be the worst of all political institutions, which, by experience, is found to contain a principle favourable (however latent it may be) to the increase of mankind.

The wealth of a country is another, and no contemptible standard, by which we may judge whether, on the whole, a government be protecting or destructive. France far exceeds England in the multitude of her people; but I apprehend that her comparative wealth is much inferior to ours; that it is not so equal in the distribution, nor so ready in the circulation. I believe the difference in the form of the two governments to be amongst the causes of this advantage on the side of England. I speak of England, not of the whole British dominions; which, if compared with those of France, will, in some degree, weaken the comparative rate of wealth upon our side. But that wealth, which will not endure a comparison with the riches of England, may constitute a very respectable degree of opulence. M. Necker's

---

* De l'Administration des Finances de la France, par Mons. Necker.

book, published in 1785,* contains an accurate and interesting collection of facts relative to public economy and to political arithmetic; and his speculations on the subject are in general wise and liberal. In that work he gives an idea of the state of France, very remote from the portrait of a country whose government was a perfect grievance, an absolute evil, admitting no cure but through the violent and uncertain remedy of a total revolution. He affirms, that from the year 1726 to the year 1784, there was coined at the mint of France, in the species of gold and silver, to the amount of about one hundred millions of pounds sterling.†

It is impossible that M. Necker should be mistaken in the amount of the bullion which has been coined in the mint. It is a matter of official record. The reasonings of this able financier, concerning the quantity of gold and silver which remained for circulation, when he wrote in 1785, that is, about four years before the deposition and imprisonment of the French king, are not of equal certainty; but they are laid on grounds so apparently solid, that it is not easy to refuse a considerable degree of assent to his calculation. He calculates the *numeraire*, or what we call *specie*, then actually existing in France, at about eighty-eight millions of the same English money. A great accumulation of wealth for one country, large as that country is! M. Necker was so far from considering this influx of wealth as likely to cease, when he wrote in 1785, that he presumes upon a future annual increase of two per cent upon the money brought into France during the periods from which he computed.

Some adequate cause must have originally introduced all the money coined at its mint into that kingdom; and some cause as operative must have kept at home, or returned into its bosom, such a vast flood of treasure as M. Necker calculates to remain for domestic circulation. Suppose any reasonable deductions from M. Necker's computation, the remainder must still amount to an immense sum. Causes thus powerful to acquire, and to retain, cannot be found in discouraged industry, insecure property, and a positively destructive government. Indeed, when I consider the face of the kingdom of France; the multitude and opulence of her cities; the useful magnificence of her spacious high roads and bridges; the opportunity of her artificial canals

---

* De l'Administration des Finances de la France, par Mons. Necker.
† Vol. iii. chap. 8 and chap. 9.

and navigations opening the conveniences of maritime communication through a solid continent of so immense an extent; when I turn my eyes to the stupendous works of her ports and harbours, and to her whole naval apparatus, whether for war or trade; when I bring before my view the number of her fortifications, constructed with so bold and masterly a skill, and made and maintained at so prodigious a charge, presenting an armed front and impenetrable barrier to her enemies upon every side; when I recollect how very small a part of that extensive region is without cultivation, and to what complete perfection the culture of many of the best productions of the earth have been brought in France; when I reflect on the excellence of her manufactures and fabrics, second to none but ours, and in some particulars not second; when I contemplate the grand foundations of charity, public and private; when I survey the state of all the arts that beautify and polish life; when I reckon the men she has bred for extending her fame in war, her able statesmen, the multitude of her profound lawyers and theologians, her philosophers, her critics, her historians and antiquaries, her poets and her orators, sacred and profane; I behold in all this something which awes and commands the imagination, which checks the mind on the brink of precipitate and Indiscriminate censure, and which demands that we should very seriously examine, what and how great are the latent vices that could authorise us at once to level so spacious a fabric with the ground. I do not recognise in this view of things, the despotism of Turkey. Nor do I discern the character of a government, that has been, on the whole, so oppressive, or so corrupt, or so negligent, as to be utterly unfit *for all reformation*. I must think such a government well deserved to have its excellencies heightened, its faults corrected, and its capacities improved into a British constitution.

Whoever has examined into the proceedings of that deposed government for several years back, cannot fail to have observed, amidst the inconstancy and fluctuation natural to courts, an earnest endeavour towards the prosperity and improvement of the country; he must admit, that it had long been employed, in some instances wholly to remove, in many considerably to correct, the abusive practices and usages that had prevailed in the state; and that even the unlimited power of the sovereign over the persons of his subjects, inconsistent, as undoubtedly it was, with law and liberty, had yet been every day growing more mitigated in the exercise. So far from refusing itself to reformation, that government was open, with a censurable degree of facility, to all sorts of projects and projectors on the subject. Rather too much countenance was given to the spirit of innovation, which soon was turned against those who fostered it, and ended in their ruin. It is but cold, and no very flattering, justice to that fallen monarchy, to say, that, for many years, it trespassed more by levity and want of judgment in several of its schemes, than from any defect in diligence or in public spirit. To compare the government of France for the last fifteen or sixteen years with wise and well-constituted establishments during that, or during any period, is not to act with fairness. But if in point of prodigality in the expenditure of money, or in point of rigour in the exercise of power, it be compared with any of the former reigns, I believe candid judges will give little credit to the good intentions of those who dwell perpetually on the donations to favourites, or on the expenses of the court, or on the horrors of the Bastile, in the reign of Louis the Sixteenth.*

Whether the system, if it deserves such a name, now built on the ruins of that ancient monarchy, will be able to give a better account of the population and wealth of the country, which it has taken under its care, is a matter very doubtful. Instead of improving by the change, I apprehend that a long series of years must be told, before it can recover in any degree the effects of this philosophic revolution, and before the nation can be replaced on its former footing. If Dr. Price should think fit, a few years hence, to favour us with an estimate of the population of France, he will hardly be able to make up his tale of thirty millions of souls, as computed in 1789, or the Assembly's computation of twenty-six millions of that year; or even M. Necker's twenty-five millions in 1780. I hear that there are considerable emigrations from France; and that many, quitting that voluptuous climate, and that seductive *Circean* liberty, have taken refuge in the frozen regions, and under the British despotism, of Canada.

In the present disappearance of coin, no person could think it the same country, in which the present minister of the finances has been able to discover fourscore millions sterling in specie.

* The world is obliged to M. de Calonne[113] for the pains he has taken to refute the scandalous exaggerations relative to some of the royal expenses, and to detect the fallacious account given of pensions, for the wicked purpose of provoking the populace to all sorts of crimes.

From its general aspect one would conclude that it had been for some time past under the special direction of the learned academicians of Laputa and Balnibarbi.* Already the population of Paris has so declined, that M. Necker stated to the National Assembly the provision to be made for its subsistence at a fifth less than what had formerly been found requisite.† It is said (and I have never heard it contradicted) that a hundred thousand people are out of employment in that city, though it is become the seat of the imprisoned court and National Assembly. Nothing, I am credibly informed, can exceed the shocking and disgusting spectacle of mendicancy displayed in that capital. Indeed the votes of the National Assembly leave no doubt of the fact. They have lately appointed a standing committee of mendicancy. They are contriving at once a vigorous police on this subject, and, for the first time, the imposition of a tax to maintain the poor, for whose present relief great sums appear on the face of the public accounts of the year.‡ In the mean time the leaders of the legislative clubs and coffee-houses are intoxicated with admiration at their own wisdom and ability. They speak with the most sovereign contempt of the rest of the world. They tell the people, to comfort them in the rags with which they have

---

* See Gulliver's Travels for the idea of countries governed by philosophers.

† M. de Calonne states the falling off of the population of Paris as far more considerable; and it may be so, since the period of M. Necker's calculation.

‡ Travaux de charité pour subvenir au manque	Livres.	£	s.	d.
de travail à Paris et dans les provinces	3,866,920 —	161,121	13	4
Destruction de vagabondage et de la mendicité	1,671,417 —	69,642	7	6
Primes pour l'importation de grains	5,671,907 —	236,329	9	2
Dépenses relatives aux subsistances, déduction				
fait des récouvrements qui ont eu lieu	39,871,790 —	1,661,324	11	8

Total   Liv. 51,082,034 — £2,128,418   1   8

When I sent this book to the press, I entertained some doubt concerning the nature and extent of the last article in the above accounts, which is only under a general head, without any detail. Since then I have seen M. de Calonne's work. I must think it a great loss to me that I had not that advantage earlier. M. de Calonne thinks this article to be on account of general subsistence; but as he is not able to comprehend how so great a loss as upwards of £1,661,000 sterling could be sustained on the difference between the price and the sale of grain, he seems to attribute this enormous head of charge to secret expenses of the Revolution. I cannot say anything positively on that subject. The reader is capable of judging, by the aggregate of these immense charges, on the state and condition of France; and the system of public economy adopted in that nation. These articles of account produced no inquiry or discussion in the National Assembly.

clothed them, that they are a nation of philosophers; and, sometimes, by all the arts of quackish parade, by show, tumult, and
bustle, sometimes by the alarms of plots and invasions, they
attempt to drown the cries of indigence, and to divert the eyes of
the observer from the ruin and wretchedness of the state. A brave
people will certainly prefer liberty accompanied with a virtuous
poverty to a depraved and wealthy servitude. But before the price
of comfort and opulence is paid, one ought to be pretty sure it is
real liberty which is purchased, and that she is to be purchased at
no other price. I shall always, however, consider that liberty as
very equivocal in her appearance, which has not wisdom and
justice for her companions; and does not lead prosperity and
plenty in her train.

The advocates for this Revolution, not satisfied with exaggerating the vices of their ancient government, strike at the fame
of their country itself, by painting almost all that could have
attracted the attention of strangers, I mean their nobility and
their clergy, as objects of horror. If this were only a libel, there
had not been much in it. But it has practical consequences. Had
your nobility and gentry, who formed the great body of your
landed men, and the whole of your military officers, resembled
those of Germany, at the period when the Hanse-towns were
necessitated to confederate against the nobles in defence of their
property – had they been like the *Orsini* and *Vitelli* in Italy,
who used to sally from their fortified dens to rob the trader and
traveller – had they been such as the *Mamelukes* in Egypt, or the
Nayres[114] on the coast of Malabar, I do admit, that too critical an
inquiry might not be advisable into the means of freeing the
world from such a nuisance. The statues of Equity and Mercy
might be veiled for a moment. The tenderest minds, confounded
with the dreadful exigence in which morality submits to the
suspension of its own rules in favour of its own principles, might
turn aside whilst fraud and violence were accomplishing the
destruction of a pretended nobility which disgraced, whilst it
persecuted, human nature. The persons most abhorrent from
blood, and treason, and arbitrary confiscation, might remain
silent spectators of this civil war between the vices.

But did the privileged nobility who met under the king's
precept at Versailles, in 1789, or their constituents, deserve to be
looked on as the *Nayres* or *Mamelukes* of this age, or as the *Orsini*
and *Vitelli* of ancient times? If I had then asked the question

I should have passed for a madman. What have they since done that they were to be driven into exile, that their persons should be hunted about, mangled, and tortured, their families dispersed, their houses laid in ashes, and that their order should be abolished, and the memory of it, if possible, extinguished, by ordaining them to change the very names by which they were usually known? Read their instructions to their representatives. They breathe the spirit of liberty as warmly, and they recommend reformation as strongly, as any other order. Their privileges relative to contribution were voluntarily surrendered;[115] as the king, from the beginning, surrendered all pretence to a right of taxation. Upon a free constitution there was but one opinion in France. The absolute monarchy was at an end. It breathed its last, without a groan, without struggle, without convulsion. All the struggle, all the dissension, arose afterwards upon the preference of a despotic democracy to a government of reciprocal control. The triumph of the victorious party was over the principles of a British constitution.

I have observed the affectation, which for many years past, has prevailed in Paris even to a degree perfectly childish, of idolising the memory of your Henry the Fourth.[116] If anything could put one out of humour with that ornament to the kingly character, it would be this overdone style of insidious panegyric. The persons who have worked this engine the most busily, are those who have ended their panegyrics in dethroning his successor and descendant; a man, as good-natured, at the least, as Henry the Fourth; altogether as fond of his people; and who has done infinitely more to correct the ancient vices of the state than that great monarch did, or we are sure he ever meant to do. Well it is for his panegyrists that they have not him to deal with. For Henry of Navarre was a resolute, active, and politic prince. He possessed indeed great humanity and mildness; but a humanity and mildness that never stood in the way of his interests. He never sought to be loved without putting himself first in a condition to be feared. He used soft language with determined conduct. He asserted and maintained his authority in the gross, and distributed his acts of concession only in the detail. He spent the income of his prerogative nobly; but he took care not to break in upon the capital; never abandoning for a moment any of the claims which he made under the fundamental laws, nor sparing to shed the blood of those who opposed him, often in the field, sometimes upon the scaffold. Because he knew how to make his virtues respected by the ungrateful, he has merited the praises of those, whom, if they had lived in his time, he would have shut up in the Bastile, and brought to punishment along with the regicides whom he hanged after he had famished Paris into a surrender.

If these panegyrists are in earnest in their admiration of Henry the Fourth, they must remember, that they cannot think more highly of him than he did of the noblesse of France; whose virtue, honour, courage, patriotism, and loyalty were his constant theme.

But the nobility of France are degenerated since the days of Henry the Fourth. This is possible. But it is more than I can believe to be true in any great degree. I do not pretend to know France as correctly as some others; but I have endeavoured through my whole life to make myself acquainted with human nature; otherwise I should be unfit to take even my humble part in the service of mankind. In that study I could not pass by a vast portion of our nature, as it appeared modified in a country but twenty-four miles from the shore of this island. On my best observation, compared with my best inquiries, I found your nobility for the greater part composed of men of high spirit, and of a delicate sense of honour, both with regard to themselves individually, and with regard to their whole corps, over whom they kept, beyond what is common in other countries, a censorial eye. They were tolerably well bred; very officious, humane, and hospitable; in their conversation frank and open; with a good military tone; and reasonably tinctured with literature, particularly of the authors in their own language. Many had pretensions far above this description. I speak of those who were generally met with.

As to their behaviour to the inferior classes, they appeared to me to comport themselves towards them with good-nature, and with something more nearly approaching to familiarity, than is generally practised with us in the intercourse between the higher and lower ranks of life. To strike any person, even in the most abject condition, was a thing in a manner unknown, and would be highly disgraceful. Instances of other ill-treatment of the humble part of the community were rare: and as to attacks made upon the property or the personal liberty of the commons, I never heard of any whatsoever from *them*; nor, whilst the laws were in vigour under the ancient government, would such tyranny in subjects have been permitted. As men of landed estates, I had no fault to find with their conduct, though much to reprehend, and much to wish changed, in many of the old tenures. Where the letting of their land was by rent, I could not discover that their agreements with their farmers were oppressive; nor when they were in partnership with the farmer, as often was the case, have I heard that they had taken the lion's share. The proportions seemed not inequitable. There might be exceptions; but certainly they were exceptions only. I have no reason to believe that in these respects the landed noblesse of France were worse than the landed gentry of this country; certainly in no respect more vexatious than the landholders, not noble, of their own nation. In cities the nobility had no manner of power; in the country very little. You know, Sir, that much of the civil government, and the police in the most essential parts, was not in the hands of that nobility which presents itself first to our consideration. The revenue, the system and collection of which were the most grievous parts of the French government, was not administered by the men of the sword; nor were they answerable for the vices of its principle, or the vexations, where any such existed, in its management.

Denying, as I am well warranted to do, that the nobility had any considerable share in the oppression of the people, in cases in which real oppression existed, I am ready to admit that they were not without considerable faults and errors. A foolish imitation of the worst part of the manners of England, which impaired their natural character, without substituting in its place what perhaps they meant to copy, has certainly rendered them worse than formerly they were. Habitual dissoluteness of manners continued beyond the pardonable period of life, was more common amongst them than it is with us; and it reigned with the less hope of remedy, though possibly with something of less mischief, by being covered with more exterior decorum. They countenanced too much that licentious philosophy which has helped to bring on their ruin. There was another error amongst them more fatal. Those of the commons, who approached to or exceeded many of the nobility in point of wealth, were not fully admitted to the rank and estimation which wealth, in reason and good policy, ought to bestow in every country; though I think not equally with that of other nobility. The two kinds of aristocracy were too punctiliously kept asunder; less so, however, than in Germany and some other nations.

This separation, as I have already taken the liberty of suggesting to you, I conceive to be one principal cause of the destruction of the old nobility. The military, particularly, was too exclusively reserved for men of family. But, after all, this was an error of opinion, which a conflicting opinion would have rectified. A permanent assembly, in which the commons had their share of power, would soon abolish whatever was too invidious and insulting in these distinctions; and even the faults in the morals of the nobility would have been probably corrected, by the greater varieties of occupation and pursuit to which a constitution by orders would have given rise.

All this violent cry against the nobility I take to be a mere work of art. To be honoured and even privileged by the laws, opinions, and inveterate usages of our country, growing out of the prejudice of ages, has nothing to provoke horror and indignation in any man. Even to be too tenacious of those privileges is not absolutely a crime. The strong struggle in every individual to preserve possession of what he has found to belong to him, and to distinguish him, is one of the securities against injustice and despotism implanted in our nature. It operates as an instinct to secure property, and to preserve communities in a settled state. What is there to shock in this? Nobility is a graceful ornament to the civil order. It is the Corinthian capital of polished society. *Omnes boni nobilitati semper favemus,*[117] was the saying of a wise and good man. It is indeed one sign of a liberal and benevolent mind to incline to it with some sort of partial propensity. He feels no ennobling principle in his own heart, who wishes to level all the artificial institutions which have been adopted for giving a body to opinion, and permanence to fugitive esteem. It is a sour, malignant, envious disposition, without taste for the reality, or for any image or representation of virtue, that sees with joy the unmerited fall of what had long flourished in splendour and in honour. I do not like to see anything destroyed; any void produced in society; any ruin on the face of the land. It was therefore with no disappointment or dissatisfaction that my inquiries and observations did not present to me any incorrigible vices in the noblesse of France, or any abuse which could not be removed by a reform very short of abolition. Your noblesse did not deserve punishment: but to degrade is to punish.

It was with the same satisfaction I found that the result of my inquiry concerning your clergy was not dissimilar. It is no soothing news to my ears, that great bodies of men are incurably corrupt. It is not with much credulity I listen to any, when they speak evil of those whom they are going to plunder. I rather suspect that vices are feigned or exaggerated, when profit is looked for in their punishment. An enemy is a bad witness; a robber is a worse. Vices and abuses there were undoubtedly in that order, and must be. It was an old establishment, and not frequently revised. But I saw no crimes in the individuals that merited confiscation of their substance, nor those cruel insults and degradations, and that unnatural persecution, which have been substituted in the place of meliorating regulation.

If there had been any just cause for this new religious persecution, the atheistic libellers, who act as trumpeters to animate the populace to plunder, do not love any body so much as not to dwell with complacence on the vices of the existing clergy. This they have not done. They find themselves obliged to rake into the histories of former ages (which they have ransacked with a malignant and profligate industry), for every instance of oppression and persecution which has been made by that body or in its favour, in order to justify, upon very iniquitous, because very illogical, principles of retaliation, their own persecutions, and their own cruelties. After destroying all other genealogies and family distinctions, they invent a sort of pedigree of crimes. It is not very just to chastise men for the offences of their natural ancestors: but to take the fiction of ancestry in a corporate succession, as a ground for punishing men who have no relation to guilty acts, except in names and general descriptions, is a sort of refinement in injustice belonging to the philosophy of this enlightened age. The Assembly punishes men, many, if not most, of whom abhor the violent conduct of ecclesiastics in former times as much as their present persecutors can do, and who would be as loud and as strong in the expression of that sense, if they were not well aware of the purposes for which all this declamation is employed.

Corporate bodies are immortal for the good of the members, but not for their punishment. Nations themselves are such corporations. As well might we in England think of waging inexpiable war upon all Frenchmen for the evils which they have brought upon us in the several periods of our mutual hostilities. You might, on your part, think yourselves justified in falling upon all Englishmen on account of the unparalleled calamities brought on the people of France by the unjust invasions of our Henries and our Edwards. Indeed we should be mutually justified in this exterminatory war upon each other, full as much as you are in the unprovoked persecution of your present countrymen, on account of the conduct of men of the same name in other times.

We do not draw the moral lessons we might from history. On the contrary, without care it may be used to vitiate our minds and to destroy our happiness. In history a great volume is unrolled for our instruction, drawing the materials of future wisdom from the past errors and infirmities of mankind. It may, in the perversion, serve for a magazine, furnishing offensive and defensive weapons for parties in church and state, and supplying the means of keeping alive, or reviving, dissensions and animosities, and adding fuel to civil fury. History consists, for the greater part, of the miseries brought upon the world by pride, ambition, avarice, revenge, lust, sedition, hypocrisy, ungoverned zeal, and all the train of disorderly appetites, which shake the public with the same

> – "troublous storms that toss
> The private state, and render life unsweet."

These vices are the *causes* of those storms. Religion, morals, laws, prerogatives, privileges, liberties, rights of men, are the *pretexts*. The pretexts are always found in some specious appearance of a real good. You would not secure men from tyranny and sedition, by rooting out of the mind the principles to which these fraudulent pretexts apply? If you did, you would root out everything that is valuable in the human breast. As these are the pretexts, so the ordinary actors and instruments in great public evils are kings, priests, magistrates, senates, parliaments, national assemblies, judges, and captains. You would not cure the evil by resolving, that there should be no more monarchs, nor ministers of state, nor of the gospel; no interpreters of law; no general officers; no public councils. You might change the names. The things in some shape must remain. A certain *quantum* of power must always exist in the community, in some hands, and under some appellation. Wise men will apply their remedies to vices, not to names; to the causes of evil which are permanent, not to the occasional organs by which they act, and the transitory modes in which they appear. Otherwise you will be wise historically, a fool in practice. Seldom have two ages the same fashion in their pretexts and the same modes of mischief. Wickedness is a little more inventive. Whilst you are discussing fashion, the fashion is gone by. The very same vice assumes a new body. The spirit transmigrates; and, far from losing its principle of life by the change of its appearance, it is renovated in its new organs with a fresh vigour of a juvenile activity. It walks abroad, it continues its ravages, whilst you are gibbeting the carcase, or demolishing the tomb. You are terrifying yourselves with ghosts and apparitions, whilst your house is the haunt of robbers. It is thus with all those, who, attending only to the shell and husk of history, think they are waging war with intolerance, pride, and cruelty, whilst, under colour of abhorring the ill principles of antiquated parties, they are authorising and feeding the same odious vices in different factions, and perhaps in worse.

Your citizens of Paris formerly had lent themselves as the ready instruments to slaughter the followers of Calvin, at the infamous massacre of St. Bartholomew.[118] What should we say to those who could think of retaliating on the Parisians of this day the abominations and horrors of that time? They are indeed brought to abhor *that* massacre. Ferocious as they are, it is not difficult to make them dislike it; because the politicians and fashionable teachers have no interest in giving their passions exactly the same direction. Still however they find it their interest to keep the same savage dispositions alive. It was but the other day that they caused this very massacre to be acted on the stage for the diversion of the descendants of those who committed it. In this tragic farce they produced the cardinal of Lorraine in his robes of function, ordering general slaughter. Was this spectacle intended to make the Parisians abhor persecution, and loathe the effusion of blood? – No; it was to teach them to persecute their own pastors; it was to excite them, by raising a disgust and horror of their clergy, to an alacrity in hunting down to destruction an order, which, if it ought to exist at all, ought to exist not only in safety, but in reverence. It was to stimulate their cannibal appetites (which one would think had been gorged sufficiently) by variety and seasoning; and to quicken them to an alertness in new murders and massacres, if it should suit the purpose of the Guises[119] of the day. An assembly, in which sat a multitude of priests and prelates, was obliged to suffer this indignity at its door. The author was not sent to the galleys, nor the players to the house of correction. Not long after this exhibition, those players came forward to the Assembly to claim the rites of that very religion which they had dared to expose, and to show their prostituted faces in the senate, whilst the archbishop of Paris, whose function was known to his people only by his prayers and benedictions, and his wealth only by his alms, is forced to abandon his house, and to fly from his flock, (as from ravenous wolves,) because, truly, in the sixteenth century, the cardinal of Lorraine was a rebel and a murderer.*

Such is the effect of the perversion of history, by those, who, for the same nefarious purposes, have perverted every other part of learning. But those who will stand upon that elevation of reason, which places centuries under our eye, and brings things to the true point of comparison, which obscures little names, and effaces the colours of little parties, and to which nothing can ascend but the spirit and moral quality of human actions, will say to the teachers of the Palais Royal, – The cardinal of Lorraine was the murderer of the sixteenth century, you have the glory of being the murderers in the eighteenth; and this is the only difference between you. But history in the nineteenth century, better understood, and better employed, will, I trust, teach a civilised posterity to abhor the misdeeds of both these barbarous ages. It will teach future priests and magistrates not to retaliate upon the speculative and inactive atheists of future times, the enormities committed by the present practical zealots and furious fanatics of that wretched error, which, in its quiescent state, is more than punished, whenever it is embraced. It will teach posterity not to make war upon either religion or philosophy, for the abuse which the hypocrites of both have made of the two most valuable blessings conferred upon us by the bounty of the universal Patron, who in all things eminently favours and protects the race of man.

If your clergy, or any clergy, should show themselves vicious beyond the fair bounds allowed to human infirmity, and to those professional faults which can hardly be separated from professional virtues, though their vices never can countenance the exercise of oppression, I do admit, that they would naturally have the effect of abating very much of our indignation against the tyrants who exceed measure and justice in their punishment.

---

* This is on a supposition of the truth of this story, but he was not in France at the time. One name serves as well as another. [1803]

I can allow in clergymen, through all their divisions, some ten-
aciousness of their own opinion, some overflowings of zeal for
its propagation, some predilection to their own state and office,
some attachment to the interest of their own corps, some preference to those who listen with docility to their doctrines, beyond
those who scorn and deride them. I allow all this, because I am
a man who have to deal with men, and who would not, through
a violence of toleration, run into the greatest of all intolerance.
I must bear with infirmities until they fester into crimes.

Undoubtedly, the natural progress of the passions, from frailty
to vice, ought to be prevented by a watchful eye and a firm hand.
But is it true that the body of your clergy had past those limits of
a just allowance? From the general style of your late publications
of all sorts, one would be led to believe that your clergy in France
were a sort of monsters; an horrible composition of superstition,
ignorance, sloth, fraud, avarice, and tyranny. But is this true? Is it
true, that the lapse of time, the cessation of conflicting interests,
the woeful experience of the evils resulting from party rage, have
had no sort of influence gradually to meliorate their minds? Is it
true, that they were daily renewing invasions on the civil power,
troubling the domestic quiet of their country, and rendering the
operations of its government feeble and precarious? Is it true,
that the clergy of our time have pressed down the laity with an
iron hand, and were, in all places, lighting up the fires of a savage
persecution? Did they by every fraud endeavour to increase their
estates? Did they use to exceed the due demands on estates that
were their own? Or, rigidly screwing up right into wrong, did
they convert a legal claim into a vexatious extortion? When not
possessed of power, were they filled with the vices of those who
envy it? Were they inflamed with a violent, litigious spirit of
controversy? Goaded on with the ambition of intellectual sovereignty, were they ready to fly in the face of all magistracy, to fire
churches, to massacre the priests of other descriptions, to pull
down altars, and to make their way over the ruins of subverted
governments to an empire of doctrine, sometimes flattering,
sometimes forcing, the consciences of men from the jurisdiction
of public institutions into a submission to their personal authority, beginning with a claim of liberty, and ending with an abuse
of power?

These, or some of these, were the vices objected, and not
wholly without foundation, to several of the churchmen of

former times, who belonged to the two great parties, which then divided and distracted Europe.

If there was in France, as in other countries there visibly is, a great abatement, rather than any increase of these vices, instead of loading the present clergy with the crimes of other men, and the odious character of other times, in common equity they ought to be praised, encouraged, and supported, in their departure from a spirit which disgraced their predecessors, and for having assumed a temper of mind and manners more suitable to their sacred function.

When my occasions took me into France, towards the close of the late reign, the clergy, under all their forms, engaged a considerable part of my curiosity. So far from finding (except from one set of men, not then very numerous, though very active) the complaints and discontents against that body, which some publications had given me reason to expect, I perceived little or no public or private uneasiness on their account. On further examination, I found the clergy, in general, persons of moderate minds and decorous manners; I include the seculars, and the regulars of both sexes. I had not the good fortune to know a great many of the parochial clergy: but in general I received a perfectly good account of their morals, and of their attention to their duties. With some of the higher clergy I had a personal acquaintance; and of the rest in that class, a very good means of information. They were, almost all of them, persons of noble birth. They resembled others of their own rank; and where there was any difference, it was in their favour. They were more fully educated than the military noblesse; so as by no means to disgrace their profession by ignorance, or by want of fitness for the exercise of their authority. They seemed to me, beyond the clerical character, liberal and open; with the hearts of gentlemen, and men of honour; neither insolent nor servile in their manners and conduct. They seemed to me rather a superior class; a set of men, amongst whom you would not be surprised to find a *Fenelon*.[120] I saw among the clergy in Paris (many of the description are not to be met with anywhere) men of great learning and candour; and I had reason to believe, that this description was not confined to Paris. What I found in other places, I know was accidental; and therefore to be presumed a fair sample. I spent a few days in a provincial town, where, in the absence of the bishop, I passed my evenings with three clergymen, his vicars-general, persons

who would have done honour to any church. They were all well
informed; two of them of deep, general, and extensive erudition,
ancient and modern, oriental and western; particularly in their
own profession. They had a more extensive knowledge of our
English divines than I expected; and they entered into the genius
of those writers with a critical accuracy. One of these gentlemen
is since dead, the Abbé *Morangis*. I pay this tribute, without
reluctance, to the memory of that noble, reverend, learned, and
excellent person; and I should do the same, with equal cheerfulness, to the merits of the others, who I believe are still living,
if I did not fear to hurt those whom I am unable to serve.

Some of these ecclesiastics of rank are, by all titles, persons
deserving of general respect. They are deserving of gratitude from
me, and from many English. If this letter should ever come into
their hands, I hope they will believe there are those of our nation
who feel for their unmerited fall, and for the cruel confiscation
of their fortunes, with no common sensibility. What I say of them
is a testimony, as far as one feeble voice can go, which I owe to
truth. Whenever the question of this unnatural persecution is
concerned, I will pay it. No one shall prevent me from being just
and grateful. The time is fitted for the duty; and it is particularly
becoming to show our justice and gratitude, when those, who
have deserved well of us and of mankind, are labouring under
popular obloquy, and the persecutions of oppressive power.

You had before your Revolution about an hundred and
twenty bishops.[121] A few of them were men of eminent sanctity,
and charity without limit. When we talk of the heroic, of course
we talk of rare virtue. I believe the instances of eminent depravity
may be as rare amongst them as those of transcendent goodness.
Examples of avarice and of licentiousness may be picked out, I do
not question it, by those who delight in the investigation which
leads to such discoveries. A man as old as I am will not be astonished that several, in every description, do not lead that perfect
life of self-denial, with regard to wealth or to pleasure, which is
wished for by all, by some expected, but by none exacted with
more rigour, than by those who are the most attentive to their
own interests, or the most indulgent to their own passions. When
I was in France, I am certain that the number of vicious prelates
was not great. Certain individuals among them, not distinguishable for the regularity of their lives, made some amends for
their want of the severe virtues, in their possession of the liberal;

and were endowed with qualities which made them useful in the church and state. I am told, that, with few exceptions, Louis the Sixteenth had been more attentive to character, in his promotions to that rank, than his immediate predecessor; and I believe (as some spirit of reform has prevailed through the whole reign) that it may be true. But the present ruling power has shown a disposition only to plunder the church. It has punished *all* prelates; which is to favour the vicious, at least in point of reputation. It has made a degrading pensionary establishment, to which no man of liberal ideas or liberal condition will destine his children. It must settle into the lowest classes of the people. As with you the inferior clergy are not numerous enough for their duties; as these duties are, beyond measure, minute and toilsome, as you have left no middle classes of clergy at their ease, in future nothing of science or erudition can exist in the Gallican church. To complete the project, without the least attention to the rights of patrons, the Assembly has provided in future an elective clergy; an arrangement which will drive out of the clerical profession all men of sobriety; all who can pretend to independence in their function or their conduct; and which will throw the whole direction of the public mind into the hands of a set of licentious, bold, crafty, factious, flattering wretches, of such condition and such habits of life as will make their contemptible pensions (in comparison of which the stipend of an exciseman is lucrative and honourable) an object of low and illiberal intrigue. Those officers, whom they still call bishops, are to be elected to a provision comparatively mean, through the same arts, (that is, electioneering arts,) by men of all religious tenets that are known or can be invented. The new lawgivers have not ascertained anything whatsoever concerning their qualifications, relative either to doctrine or to morals; no more than they have done with regard to the subordinate clergy: nor does it appear but that both the higher and the lower may, at their discretion, practise or preach any mode of religion or irreligion that they please. I do not yet see what the jurisdiction of bishops over their subordinates is to be, or whether they are to have any jurisdiction at all.

In short, Sir, it seems to me, that this new ecclesiastical establishment is intended only to be temporary, and preparatory to the utter abolition, under any of its forms, of the Christian religion, whenever the minds of men are prepared for this last stroke against it, by the accomplishment of the plan for bringing its ministers into universal contempt. They who will not believe, that the philosophical fanatics, who guide in these matters, have long entertained such a design, are utterly ignorant of their character and proceedings. These enthusiasts do not scruple to avow their opinion, that a state can subsist without any religion better than with one; and that they are able to supply the place of any good which may be in it, by a project of their own – namely, by a sort of education they have imagined, founded in a knowledge of the physical wants of men; progressively carried to an enlightened self-interest, which, when well understood, they tell us, will identify with an interest more enlarged and public. The scheme of this education has been long known. Of late they distinguish it (as they have got an entirely new nomenclature of technical terms) by the name of a *Civic Education*.

I hope their partisans in England (to whom I rather attribute very inconsiderate conduct, than the ultimate object in this detestable design) will succeed neither in the pillage of the ecclesiastics, nor in the introduction of a principle of popular election to our bishoprics and parochial cures. This, in the present condition of the world, would be the last corruption of the church; the utter ruin of the clerical character; the most dangerous shock that the state ever received through a misunderstood arrangement of religion. I know well enough that the bishoprics and cures, under kingly and seignoral patronage, as now they are in England, and as they have been lately in France, are sometimes acquired by unworthy methods; but the other mode of ecclesiastical canvass subjects them infinitely more surely and more generally to all the evil arts of low ambition, which, operating on and through greater numbers, will produce mischief in proportion.

Those of you, who have robbed the clergy, think that they shall easily reconcile their conduct to all Protestant nations; because the clergy, whom they have thus plundered, degraded, and given over to mockery and scorn, are of the Roman Catholic, that is, of *their own* pretended persuasion. I have no doubt that some miserable bigots will be found here, as well as elsewhere, who hate sects and parties different from their own, more than they love the substance of religion; and who are more angry with those who differ from them in their particular plans and systems, than displeased with those who attack the foundation of our common hope. These men will write and speak on the subject in the manner that is to be expected from their temper and character. Burnet[122] says, that, when he was in France, in the year 1683, "the method which carried over the men of the finest parts to Popery was this – they brought themselves to doubt of the whole Christian religion. When that was once done, it seemed a more indifferent thing of what side or form they continued outwardly." If this was then the ecclesiastical policy of France, it is what they have since but too much reason to repent of. They preferred atheism to a form of religion not agreeable to their ideas. They succeeded in destroying that form; and atheism has succeeded in destroying them. I can readily give credit to Burnet's story; because I have observed too much of a similar spirit (for a little of it is "much too much") amongst ourselves. The humour, however, is not general.

The teachers who reformed our religion in England bore no sort of resemblance to your present reforming doctors in Paris. Perhaps they were (like those whom they opposed) rather more than could be wished under the influence of a party spirit; but they were more sincere believers; men of the most fervent and exalted piety; ready to die (as some of them did die) like true heroes in defence of their particular ideas of Christianity; as they would with equal fortitude, and more cheerfully, for that stock of general truth, for the branches of which they contended with their blood. These men would have disavowed with horror those wretches who claimed a fellowship with them upon no other titles than those of their having pillaged the persons with whom they maintained controversies, and their having despised the common religion, for the purity of which they exerted themselves with a zeal, which unequivocally bespoke their highest reverence for the substance of that system which they wished to reform. Many of their descendants have retained the same zeal, but (as less engaged in conflict) with more moderation. They do not forget that justice and mercy are substantial parts of religion. Impious men do not recommend themselves to their communion by iniquity and cruelty towards any description of their fellow-creatures.

We hear these new teachers continually boasting of their spirit of toleration. That those persons should tolerate all opinions, who think none to be of estimation, is a matter of small merit. Equal neglect is not impartial kindness. The species of benevolence, which arises from contempt, is no true charity. There are in England abundance of men who tolerate in the true spirit of toleration. They think the dogmas of religion, though in different degrees, are all of moment: and that amongst them there is, as amongst all things of value, a just ground of preference. They favour, therefore, and they tolerate. They tolerate, not because they despise opinions, but because they respect justice. They would reverently and affectionately protect all religions, because they love and venerate the great principle upon which they all agree, and the great object to which they are all directed. They begin more and more plainly to discern, that we have all a common cause, as against a common enemy. They will not be so misled by the spirit of faction, as not to distinguish what is done in favour of their subdivision, from those acts of hostility, which, through some particular description, are aimed at the whole corps, in which they themselves, under another denomination, are included. It is impossible for me to say what may be the character of every description of men amongst us. But I speak for the greater part; and for them, I must tell you, that sacrilege is no part of their doctrine of good works; that, so far fron calling you into their fellowship on such title, if your professors are admitted to their communion, they must carefully conceal their doctrine of the lawfulness of the proscription of innocent men; and that they must make restitution of all stolen goods whatsoever. Till then they are none of ours.

You may suppose that we do not approve your confiscation of the revenues of bishops, and deans, and chapters, and parochial clergy possessing independent estates arising from land, because we have the same sort of establishment in England. That objection, you will say, cannot hold as to the confiscation of the goods of monks and nuns, and the abolition of their order. It is true that this particular part of your general confiscation does not affect England, as a precedent in point: but the reason implies, and it goes a great way. The long parliament[123] confiscated the lands of deans and chapters in England on the same ideas upon which your assembly set to sale the lands of the monastic orders. But it is in the principle of injustice that the danger lies, and not in the description of persons on whom it is first exercised. I see, in a country very near us, a course of policy pursued, which sets justice, the common concern of mankind, at defiance. With the National Assembly of France, possession is nothing, law and usage are nothing. I see the National Assembly openly reprobate the doctrine of prescription, which one of the greatest of their own lawyers* tells us, with great truth, is a part of the law of nature. He tells us, that the positive ascertainment of its limits, and its security from invasion, were among the causes for which civil society itself has been instituted. If prescription be once shaken, no species of property is secure, when it once becomes an object large enough to tempt the cupidity of indigent power. I see a practice perfectly correspondent to their contempt of this great fundamental part of natural law. I see the confiscators begin with bishops, and chapters, and monasteries; but I do not see them end there. I see the princes of the blood, who, by the oldest usages of that kingdom, held large landed estates, (hardly with the compliment of a debate,) deprived of their possessions, and, in lieu of their stable, independent property, reduced to the hope of some precarious, charitable pension, at the pleasure of an assembly, which of course will pay little regard to the rights of pensioners at pleasure, when it despises those of legal proprie- tors. Flushed with the insolence of their first inglorious victories, and pressed by the distresses caused by their lust of unhallowed lucre, disappointed but not discouraged, they have at length ventured completely to subvert all property of all descriptions throughout the extent of a great kingdom. They have compelled all men, in all transactions of commerce, in the disposal of lands, in civil dealing, and through the whole communion of life, to accept as perfect payment and good and lawful tender, the sym- bols of their speculations on a projected sale of their plunder. What vestiges of liberty or property have they left? The tenant- right of a cabbage-garden, a year's interest in a hovel, the good- will of an ale-house or a baker's shop, the very shadow of a constructive property, are more ceremoniously treated in our parliament, than with you the oldest and most valuable landed possessions, in the hands of the most respectable personages, or than the whole body of the monied and commercial interest of your country. We entertain a high opinion of the legislative authority; but we have never dreamt that parliaments had any right whatever to violate property, to overrule prescription, or to force a currency of their own fiction in the place of that which is real, and recognised by the law of nations. But you, who began with refusing to submit to the most moderate restraints, have

* Domat.[124]

ended by establishing an unheard-of despotism. I find the ground upon which your confiscators go is this; that indeed their proceedings could not be supported in a court of justice; but that the rules of prescription cannot bind a legislative assembly.* So that this legislative assembly of a free nation sits, not for the security, but for the destruction, of property, and not of property only, but of every rule and maxim which can give it stability, and of those instruments which can alone give it circulation.

When the Anabaptists of Munster,[125] in the sixteenth century, had filled Germany with confusion, by their system of levelling, and their wild opinions concerning property, to what country in Europe did not the progress of their fury furnish just cause of alarm? Of all things, wisdom is the most terrified with epidemical fanaticism, because of all enemies it is that against which she is the least able to furnish any kind of resource. We cannot be ignorant of the spirit of atheistical fanaticism, that is inspired by a multitude of writings, dispersed with incredible assiduity and expense, and by sermons delivered in all the streets and places of public resort in Paris. These writings and sermons have filled the populace with a black and savage atrocity of mind, which supersedes in them the common feelings of nature, a well as all sentiments of morality and religion; insomuch that these wretches are induced to bear with a sullen patience the intolerable distresses brought upon them by the violent convulsions and permutations that have been made in property.† The spirit of proselytism

---

* Speech of Mr. Camus,[126] published by order of the National Assembly.

† Whether the following description is strictly true, I know not; but it is what the publishers would have pass for true in order to animate others. In a letter from Toul, given in one of their papers, is the following passage concerning the people of that district: "Dans la Révolution actuelle, ils ont résisté à toutes les *séductions du bigotisme, aux persécutions, et aux tracasseries* des ennemis de la Révolution. *Oubliant leurs plus grânds intérêts* pour rendre hommage aux vues d'ordre général qui ont déterminé l'Assemblée Nationale, ils voient, *sans se plaindre*, supprimer cette foule d'établissemens ecclésiastiques par lesquels *ils subsistoient*; et même, en perdant leur siège épiscopal, la seul de toutes ses ressources qui pouvoit, ou plutôt *qui devoit, en toute équité*, leur être conservée; condamnés *à la plus effrayante misère*, sans avoir *été ni pu être entendus, ils ne murmurent point*, ils restent fidèles aux principe du plus pur patriotisme; ils sont encore prêts à *verser leur sang* pour le maintien de la Constitution, qui va réduire leur ville *à la plus déplorable nullité*." These people are not supposed to have endured those sufferings and injustices in a struggle for liberty, for the same account states truly that they had been always free; their patience in beggary and ruin, and their suffering, without remonstrance, the most flagrant and confessed injustice, if strictly true, can be nothing but the effect of this dire fanaticism. A great multitude all over France is in the same condition and the same temper.

attends this spirit of fanaticism. They have societies to cabal and correspond at home and abroad for the propagation of their tenets. The republic of Berne, one of the happiest, the most prosperous, and the best governed countries upon earth, is one of the great objects, at the destruction of which they aim. I am told they have in some measure succeeded in sowing there the seeds of discontent. They are busy throughout Germany. Spain and Italy have not been untried. England is not left out of the comprehensive scheme of their malignant charity: and in England we find those who stretch out their arms to them, who recommend their example from more than one pulpit, and who choose in more than one periodical meeting, publicly to correspond with them, to applaud them, and to hold them up as objects for imitation; who receive from them tokens of confraternity, and standards consecrated amidst their rights and mysteries;* who suggest to them leagues of perpetual amity, at the very time when the power, to which our constitution has exclusively delegated the federative capacity of this kingdom, may find it expedient to make war upon them.

It is not the confiscation of our church property from this example in France that I dread, though I think this would be no trifling evil. The great source of my solicitude is, lest it should ever be considered in England as the policy of a state to seek a resource in confiscations of any kind; or that any one description of citizens should be brought to regard any of the others as their proper prey.† Nations are wading deeper and deeper into an ocean of boundless debt. Public debts, which at first were a security to governments, by interesting many in the public tranquillity,

---

* See the proceedings of the confederation at *Nantz*.

† "Si plures sunt ii quibus improbe datum est, quam illi quibus injuste ademptum est, idcirco plus etiam valent? Non enim numero hæc judicantur sed pondere. Quam autem habet æquitatem, ut agrum multis annis, aut etiam sæculis ante possessum, qui nullum habuit habeat; qui autem habuit amittat? Ac, propter hoc injuriæ genus, Lacedæmonii Lysandrum Ephorum expulerunt: Agin regem (quod nunquam antea apud eos acciderat) necaverunt: exque eo tempore tantæ discordiæ secutæ sunt, ut et tyranni existerint, et optimates exterminarentur, et preclarissime constituta respublica dilaberetur. Nec vero solum ipsa cecidit, sed etiam reliquam Græciam evertit contagionibus malorum, quæ a Lacedæmoniis profectæ manarunt latius." – After speaking of the conduct of the model of true patriots, Aratus of Sicyon, which was in a very different spirit, he says, "Sic par est agere cum civibus; non ut bis jam vidimus, hastam in foro ponere et bona civium voci subjicere præconis. At ille Græcus (id quod fuit sapientis et præstantis viri) omnibus consulendum esse putavit: eaque est summa ratio et sapientia boni civis, commode civium non divellere, sed omnes cadem æquitate continere." – Cic. Off. 1. 2.[127]

are likely in their excess to become the means of their subversion. If governments provide for these debts by heavy impositions, they perish by becoming odious to the people. If they do not provide for them they will be undone by the efforts of the most dangerous of all parties; I mean an extensive, discontented monied interest, injured and not destroyed. The men who compose this interest look for their security, in the first instance, to the fidelity of government; in the second, to its power. If they find the old governments effete, worn out, and with their springs relaxed, so as not to be of sufficient vigour for their purposes, they may seek new ones that shall be possessed of more energy; and this energy will be derived, not from an acquisition of resources, but from a contempt of justice. Revolutions are favourable to confiscation; and it is impossible to know under what obnoxious names the next confiscations will be authorised. I am sure that the principles predominant in France extend to very many persons, and descriptions of persons, in all countries who think their innoxious indolence their security. This kind of innocence in proprietors may be argued into inutility; and inutility into an unfitness for their estates. Many parts of Europe are in open disorder. In many others there is a hollow murmuring under ground; a confused movement is felt, that threatens a general earthquake in the political world. Already confederacies and correspondencies of the most extraordinary nature are forming, in several countries.* In such a state of things we ought to hold ourselves upon our guard. In all mutations (if mutations must be) the circumstance which will serve most to blunt the edge of their mischief, and to promote what good may be in them, is, that they should find us with our minds tenacious of justice, and tender of property.

But it will be argued, that this confiscation in France ought not to alarm other nations. They say it is not made from wanton rapacity; that it is a great measure of national policy, adopted to remove an extensive, inveterate, superstitious mischief. It is with the greatest difficulty that I am able to separate policy from justice. Justice itself is the great standing policy of civil society; and any eminent departure from it, under any circumstances, lies under the suspicion of being no policy at all.

---

* See two books entitled, Enige Originalschriften des Illummatenordens – System und Folgen des Illuminatenordens. Munchen, 1787.[128]

When men are encouraged to go into a certain mode of life by the existing laws, and protected in that mode as in a lawful occupation – when they have accommodated all their ideas and all their habits to it – when the law had long made their adherence to its rules a ground of reputation, and their departure from them a ground of disgrace and even of penalty – I am sure it is unjust in legislature, by an arbitrary act, to offer a sudden violence to their minds and their feelings; forcibly to degrade them from their state and condition, and to stigmatise with shame and infamy that character, and those customs, which before had been made the measure of their happiness and honour. If to this be added an expulsion from their habitations, and a confiscation of all their goods, I am not sagacious enough to discover how this despotic sport, made of the feelings, consciences, prejudices, and properties of men, can be discriminated from the rankest tyranny.

If the injustice of the course pursued in France be clear, the policy of the measure, that is, the public benefit to be expected from it, ought to be at least as evident, and at least as important. To a man who acts under the influence of no passion, who has nothing in view in his projects but the public good, a great difference will immediately strike him between what policy would dictate on the original introduction of such institutions, and on a question of their total abolition, where they have cast their roots wide and deep, and where, by long habit, things more valuable than themselves are so adapted to them, and in a manner interwoven with them, that the one cannot be destroyed without notably impairing the other. He might be embarrassed if the case were really such as sophisters represent it in their paltry style of debating. But in this, as in most questions of state, there is a middle. There is something else than the mere alternative of absolute destruction, or unreformed existence. *Spartam nactus es; hanc exorna.*[129] This is, in my opinion, a rule of profound sense, and ought never to depart from the mind of an honest reformer. I cannot conceive how any man can have brought himself to that pitch of presumption, to consider his country as nothing but *carte blanche*, upon which he may scribble whatever he pleases. A man full of warm, speculative benevolence may wish his society otherwise constituted than he finds it; but a good patriot, and a true politician, always considers how he shall make the most of the existing materials of his country. A disposition to preserve, and an ability to improve, taken together, would be my standard

of a statesman. Everything else is vulgar in the conception, perilous in the execution.

There are moments in the fortune of states, when particular
men are called to make improvements, by great mental exertion.
In those moments, even when they seem to enjoy the confidence
of their prince and country, and to be invested with full authority, they have not always apt instruments. A politician, to do
great things, looks for a *power*, what our workmen call a *purchase*;
and if he finds that power, in politics as in mechanics, he cannot
be at a loss to apply it. In the monastic institutions, in my opinion, was found a great *power* for the mechanism of politic benevolence. There were revenues with a public direction; there were
men wholly set apart and dedicated to public purposes, without
any other than public ties and public principles; men without
the possibility of converting the estate of the community into a
private fortune; men denied to self-interests, whose avarice is for
some community; men to whom personal poverty is honour,
and implicit obedience stands in the place of freedom. In vain
shall a man look to the possibility of making such things when
he wants them. The winds blow as they list. These institutions
are the products of enthusiasm; they are the instruments of wisdom. Wisdom cannot create materials; they are the gifts of
nature or of chance; her pride is in the use. The perennial existence of bodies corporate and their fortunes are things particularly suited to a man who has long views; who meditates designs
that require time in fashioning, and which propose duration
when they are accomplished. He is not deserving to rank high,
or even to be mentioned in the order of great statesmen, who,
having obtained the command and direction of such a power
as existed in the wealth, the discipline, and the habits of such
corporations, as those which you have rashly destroyed, cannot
find any way of converting it to the great and lasting benefit of
his country. On the view of this subject, a thousand uses suggest
themselves to a contriving mind. To destroy any power, growing
wild from the rank productive force of the human mind, is
almost tantamount, in the moral world, to the destruction of the
apparently active properties of bodies in the material. It would
be like the attempt to destroy (if it were in our competence to
destroy) the expansive force of fixed air in nitre, or the power of
steam, or of electricity, or of magnetism. These energies always
existed in nature, and they were always discernible. They

seemed, some of them unserviceable, some noxious, some no better than a sport to children; until contemplative ability, combining with practice skill, tamed their wild nature, subdued them to use, and rendered them at once the most powerful and the most tractable agents, in subservience to the great views and designs of men. Did fifty thousand persons, whose mental and whose bodily labour you might direct, and so many hundred thousand a year of a revenue, which was neither lazy nor super-stitious, appear too big for your abilities to wield? Had you no way of using the men but by converting monks into pen-sioners?[130] Had you no way of turning the revenue to account, but through the improvident resource of a spendthrift sale? If you were thus destitute of mental funds, the proceeding is in its natural course. Your politicians do not understand their trade; and therefore they sell their tools.

But the institutions savour of superstition in their very prin-ciple; and they nourish it by a permanent and standing influence. This I do not mean to dispute; but this ought not to hinder you from deriving from superstition itself any resources which may thence be furnished for the public advantage. You derive benefits from many dispositions and many passions of the human mind, which are of as doubtful a colour, in the moral eye, as superstition itself. It was your business to correct and mitigate everything which was noxious in this passion, as in all the passions. But is superstition the greatest of all possible vices? In its possible excess I think it becomes a very great evil. It is, however, a moral sub-ject; and of course admits of all degrees and all modifications. Superstition is the religion of feeble minds; and they must be tolerated in an intermixture of it, in some trifling or some enthu-siastic shape or other, else you will deprive weak minds of a resource found necessary to the strongest. The body of all true religion consists, to be sure, in obedience to the will of the Sover-eign of the world; in a confidence in his declarations; and in imitation of his perfections. The rest is our own. It may be preju-dicial to the great end; it may be auxiliary. Wise men, who as such are not *admirers*, (not admirers at least of the *Munera Terræ*,)[131] are not violently attached to these things, nor do they violently hate them. Wisdom is not the most severe corrector of folly. They are the rival follies, which mutually wage so unrelenting a war; and which make so cruel a use of their advantages, as they can happen to engage the immoderate vulgar, on the one side, or the other,

in their quarrels. Prudence would be neuter; but if, in the contention between fond attachment and fierce antipathy concerning things in their nature not made to produce such heats, a
prudent man were obliged to make a choice of what errors and
excesses of enthusiasm he would condemn or bear, perhaps he
would think the superstition which builds, to be more tolerable
than that which demolishes – that which adorns a country, than
that which deforms it – that which endows, than that which
plunders – that which disposes to mistaken beneficence, than
that which stimulates to real injustice – that which leads a man
to refuse to himself lawful pleasures, than that which snatches
from others the scanty subsistence of their self-denial. Such,
I think, is very nearly the state of the question between the
ancient founders of monkish superstition, and the superstition of
the pretended philosophers of the hour.

For the present I postpone all consideration of the supposed
public profit of the sale, which however I conceive to be perfectly
delusive. I shall here only consider it as a transfer of property. On
the policy of that transfer I shall trouble you with a few thoughts.

In every prosperous community something more is produced
than goes to the immediate support of the producer. This surplus
forms the income of the landed capitalist. It will be spent by a
proprietor who does not labour. But this idleness is itself the
spring of labour; this repose the spur to industry. The only concern of the state is, that the capital taken in rent from the land,
should be returned again to the industry from whence it came;
and that its expenditure should be with the least possible detriment to the morals of those who expend it, and to those of the
people to whom it is returned.

In all the views of receipt, expenditure, and personal employment, a sober legislator would carefully compare the possessor
whom he was recommended to expel, with the stranger who
was proposed to fill his place. Before the inconveniencies are
incurred which *must* attend all violent revolutions in property
through extensive confiscation, we ought to have some rational
assurance that the purchasers of the confiscated property will be
in a considerable degree more laborious, more virtuous, more
sober, less disposed to extort an unreasonable proportion of the
gains of the labourer, or to consume on themselves a larger share
than is fit for the measure of an individual; or that they should
be qualified to dispense the surplus in a more steady and equal

mode, so as to answer the purposes of a politic expenditure, than the old possessors, call those possessors bishops, or canons, or commendatory abbots, or monks, or what you please. The monks are lazy. Be it so. Suppose them no otherwise employed than by singing in the choir. They are as usefully employed as those who neither sing nor say. As usefully even as those who sing upon the stage. They are as usefully employed as if they worked from dawn to dark in the innumerable servile, degrading, unseemly, unmanly, and often most unwholesome and pestiferous occupations, to which by the social economy so many wretches are inevitably doomed. If it were not generally pernicious to disturb the natural course of things, and to impede, in any degree, the great wheel of circulation which is turned by the strangely-directed labour of these unhappy people, I should be infinitely more inclined forcibly to rescue them from their miserable industry, than violently to disturb the tranquil repose of monastic quietude. Humanity, and perhaps policy, might better justify me in the one than in the other. It is a subject on which I have often reflected, and never reflected without feeling from it. I am sure that no consideration, except the necessity of submitting to the yoke of luxury, and the despotism of fancy, who in their own imperious way will distribute the surplus product of the soil, can justify the toleration of such trades and employments in a well-regulated state. But for this purpose of distribution, it seems to me, that the idle expenses of monks are quite as well directed as the idle expenses of us lay-loiterers.

When the advantages of the possession and of the project are on a par, there is no motive for a change. But in the present case, perhaps, they are not upon a par, and the difference is in favour of the possession. It does not appear to me, that the expenses of those whom you are going to expel, do in fact take a course so directly and so generally leading to vitiate and degrade and render miserable those through whom they pass, as the expenses of those favourites whom you are intruding into their houses. Why should the expenditure of a great landed property, which is a dispersion of the surplus product of the soil, appear intolerable to you or to me, when it takes its course through the accumulation of vast libraries, which are the history of the force and weakness of the human mind; through great collections of ancient records, medals, and coins, which attest and explain laws and customs; through paintings and statues, that, by imitating nature, seem to extend the limits of creation; through grand monuments of the dead, which continue the regards and connexions of life beyond the grave; through collections of the specimens of nature, which become a representative assembly of all the classes and families of the world, that by disposition facilitate, and, by exciting curiosity, open the avenues to science? If by great permanent establishments, all these objects of expense are better secured from the inconstant sport of personal caprice and personal extravagance, are they worse than if the same tastes prevailed in scattered individuals? Does not the sweat of the mason and carpenter, who toil in order to partake the sweat of the peasant, flow as pleasantly and as salubriously, in the construction and repair of the majestic edifices of religion, as in the painted booths and sordid sties of vice and luxury; as honourably and as profitably in repairing those sacred works, which grow hoary with innumerable years, as on the momentary receptacles of transient voluptuousness; in opera-houses, and brothels, and gaming-houses, and club-houses, and obelisks in the Champ de Mars? Is the surplus product of the olive and the vine worse employed in the frugal sustenance of persons, whom the fictions of a pious imagination raise to dignity by construing in the service of God, than in pampering the innumerable multitude of those who are degraded by being made useless domestics, subservient to the pride of man? Are the decorations of temples an expenditure less worthy a wise man, than ribbons, and laces, and national cockades, and petit maisons, and petit soupers, and all the innumerable fopperies and follies, in which opulence sports away the burthen of its superfluity?

We tolerate even these; not from love of them, but for fear of worse. We tolerate them, because property and liberty, to a degree, require that toleration. But why proscribe the other, and surely, in every point of view, the more laudable use of estates? Why, through the violation of all property, through an outrage upon every principle of liberty, forcibly carry them from the better to the worse?

This comparison between the new individuals and the old corps is made upon a supposition that no reform could be made in the latter. But, in a question of reformation, I always consider corporate bodies, whether sole or consisting of many, to be much more susceptible of a public direction by the power of the state, in the use of their property, and in the regulation of modes and habits of life in their members, than private citizens ever can be, or perhaps ought to be: and this seems to me a very material consideration for those who undertake anything which merits the name of a politic enterprise. – So far as to the estates of monasteries.

With regard to the estates possessed by bishops and canons, and commendatory abbots, I cannot find out for what reason some landed estates may not be held otherwise than by inheritance. Can any philosophic spoiler undertake to demonstrate the positive or the comparative evil of having a certain, and that too a large, portion of landed property, passing in succession through persons whose title to it is, always in theory, and often in fact, an eminent degree of piety, morals, and learning; a property, which, by its destination, in their turn, and on the score of merit, gives to the noblest families renovation and support, to the lowest the means of dignity and elevation; a property, the tenure of which is the performance of some duty, (whatever value you may choose to set upon that duty,) and the character of whose proprietors demands, at least, an exterior decorum, and gravity of manners; who are to exercise a generous but temperate hospitality; part of whose income they are to consider as a trust for charity; and who, even when they fail in their trust, when they slide from their character, and degenerate into a mere common secular nobleman or gentleman, are in no respect worse than those who may succeed them in their forfeited possessions? Is it better that estates should be held by those who have no duty, than by those who have one? – by those whose character and destination point to virtues, than by those who have no rule and direction in the expenditure of their estates but their own will and appetite? Nor are these estates held altogether in the character or with the evils supposed inherent in mortmain. They pass from hand to hand with a more rapid circulation than any other. No excess is good; and therefore too great a proportion of landed property may be held officially for life: but it does not seem to me of material injury to any commonwealth, that there should exist some estates that have a chance of being acquired by other means than the previous acquisition of money.

This letter is grown to a great length, though it is indeed short with regard to the infinite extent of the subject. Various avocations have from time to time called my mind from the subject. I was not sorry to give myself leisure to observe whether, in the proceedings of the National Assembly, I might not find reasons to change or to qualify some of my first sentiments. Everything has confirmed me more strongly in my first opinions. It was my original purpose to take a view of the principles of the National Assembly with regard to the great and fundamental establishments; and to compare the whole of what you have substituted in the place of what you have destroyed, with the several members of our British constitution. But this plan is of a greater extent than at first I computed, and I find that you have little desire to take the advantage of any examples. At present I must content myself with some remarks upon your establishments; reserving for another time what I proposed to say concerning the spirit of our British monarchy, aristocracy, and democracy, as practically they exist.

I have taken a view of what has been done by the governing power in France. I have certainly spoke of it with freedom. Those whose principle it is to despise the ancient, permanent sense of mankind, and to set up a scheme of society on new principles, must naturally expect that such of us, who think better of the judgment of the human race than of theirs, should consider both them and their devices, as men and schemes upon their trial. They must take it for granted that we attend much to their reason, but not at all to their authority. They have not one of the great influencing prejudices of mankind in their favour. They avow their hostility to opinion. Of course they must expect no support from that influence, which, with every other authority, they have deposed from the seat of its jurisdiction.

I can never consider this Assembly as anything else than a voluntary association of men, who have availed themselves of circumstances to seize upon the power of the state. They have not the sanction and authority of the character under which they first met. They have assumed another of a very different nature; and have completely altered and inverted all the relations in which they originally stood. They do not hold the authority they exercise under any constitutional law of the state. They have departed from the instructions of the people by whom they were sent; which instructions, as the Assembly did not act in virtue of any ancient usage or settled law, were the sole source of their authority. The most considerable of their acts have not been done by great majorities; and in this sort of near divisions, which carry only the constructive authority of the whole, strangers will consider reasons as well as resolutions.

If they had set up this new, experimental government, as a necessary substitute for an expelled tyranny, mankind would anticipate the time of prescription, which, through long usage, mellows into legality governments that were violent in their commencement. All those who have affections which lead them to the conservation of civil order would recognise, even in its cradle, the child as legitimate, which has been produced from those principles of cogent expediency to which all just governments owe their birth, and on which they justify their continuance. But they will be late and reluctant in giving any sort of countenance to the operations of a power, which has derived its birth from no law and no necessity; but which on the contrary has had its origin in those vices and sinister practices by which the social union is often disturbed and sometimes destroyed. This Assembly has hardly a year's prescription. We have their own word for it that they have made a revolution. To make a revolution is a measure which, *prima fronte*, requires an apology. To make a revolution is to subvert the ancient state of our country; and no common reasons are called for to justify so violent a proceeding. The sense of mankind authorises us to examine into the mode of acquiring new power, and to criticise on the use that is made of it, with less awe and reverence than that which is usually conceded to a settled and recognised authority.

In obtaining and securing their power, the Assembly proceeds upon principles the most opposite to those which appear to direct them in the use of it. An observation on this difference will let us into the true spirit of their conduct. Everything which they have done, or continue to do, in order to obtain and keep their power, is by the most common arts. They proceed exactly as their ancestors of ambition have done before them. – Trace them through all their artifices, frauds, and violences, you can find nothing at all that is new. They follow precedents and examples with the punctilious exactness of a pleader. They never depart an iota from the authentic formulas of tyranny and usurpation. But in all the regulations relative to the public good, the spirit has been the very reverse of this. There they commit the whole to the mercy of untried speculations; they abandon the dearest interests of the public to those loose theories, to which none of them would choose to trust the slightest of his private concerns. They make this difference, because in their desire of obtaining and securing power they are thoroughly in earnest; there they travel in the beaten road. The public interests, because about them they have no real solicitude, they abandon wholly to chance: I say to chance, because their schemes have nothing in experience to prove their tendency beneficial.

We must always see with a pity not unmixed with respect, the errors of those who are timid and doubtful of themselves with regard to points wherein the happiness of mankind is concerned. But in these gentlemen there is nothing of the tender, parental solicitude, which fears to cut up the infant for the sake of an experiment. In the vastness of their promises, and the confidence of their predictions, they far outdo all the boasting of empirics. The arrogance of their pretensions in a manner provokes and challenges us to an inquiry into their foundation.

I am convinced that there are men of considerable parts among the popular leaders in the National Assembly. Some of them display eloquence in their speeches and their writings. This cannot be without powerful and cultivated talents. But eloquence may exist without a proportionable degree of wisdom. When I speak of ability, I am obliged to distinguish. What they have done towards the support of their system bespeaks no ordinary men. In the system itself, taken as the scheme of a republic constructed for procuring the prosperity and security of the citizen, and for promoting the strength and grandeur of the state, I confess myself unable to find out anything which displays, in a single instance, the work of a comprehensive and disposing mind, or even the provisions of a vulgar prudence. Their purpose everywhere seems to have been to evade and slip aside from *difficulty*. This it has been the glory of the great masters in all the arts to confront, and to overcome; and when they had overcome the first difficulty, to turn it into an instrument for new conquests over new difficulties; thus to enable them to extend the empire of their science; and even to push forward, beyond the reach of their original thoughts, the land-marks of the human understanding itself. Difficulty is a severe instructor, set over us by the supreme ordinance of a parental Guardian and Legislator, who knows us better than we know ourselves, as he loves us better too. *Pater ipse colendi haud facilem esse viam voluit.*[132] He that wrestles with us strengthens our nerves, and sharpens our skill. Our antagonist is our helper. This amicable conflict with difficulty obliges us to an intimate acquaintance with our object, and compels us to consider it in all its relations. It will not suffer us to be superficial. It is the want of nerves of understanding for such a task, it is the degenerate fondness for tricking short-cuts, and little fallacious facilities, that has in so many parts of the world created governments with arbitrary powers. They have created the late arbitrary monarchy of France. They have created the arbitrary republic of Paris. With them defects in wisdom are to be supplied by the plenitude of force. They get nothing by it. Commencing their labours on a principle of sloth, they have the common fortune of slothful men. The difficulties, which they rather had eluded than escaped, meet them again in their course; they multiply and thicken on them; they are involved, through a labyrinth of confused detail, in an industry without limit, and without direction; and, in conclusion, the whole of their work becomes feeble, vicious, and insecure.

It is this inability to wrestle with difficulty which has obliged the arbitrary Assembly of France to commence their schemes of reform with abolition and total destruction.* But is it in destroying and pulling down that skill is displayed? Your mob can do this as well at least as your assemblies. The shallowest understanding, the rudest hand, is more than equal to that task. Rage and phrensy will pull down more in half an hour, than prudence, deliberation, and foresight can build up in a hundred years. The errors and defects of old establishments are visible and palpable. It calls for little ability to point them out; and where absolute power is given, it requires but a word wholly to abolish the vice and the establishment together. The same lazy but restless disposition, which loves sloth and hates quiet, directs the politicians, when they come to work for supplying the place of what they have destroyed. To make everything the reverse of what they have seen is quite as easy as to destroy. No difficulties occur in what has never been tried. Criticism is almost baffled in discovering

---

* A leading member of the Assembly, M. Rabaud de St. Etienne, has expressed the principle of all their proceedings as clearly as possible – Nothing can be more simple: – "*Tous les établissemens en France couronnent le malheur du peuple: pour le rendre heureux il faut le rénouveler; changer ses idées; changer ses loix; changer ses mœurs; . . . changer les hommes; changer les choses; changer les mots . . . tout détruire; oui, tout détruire; puisque tout est à recréer.*" This gentleman was chosen president in an assembly not sitting at the *Quinze-vingt*, or the *Petits Maisons*;[133] and composed of persons giving themselves out to be rational beings; but neither his ideas, language, or conduct, differ in the smallest degree from the discourses, opinions, and actions of those within and without the Assembly, who direct the operations of the machine now at work in France.

the defects of what has not existed; and eager enthusiasm and cheating hope have all the wide field of imagination, in which they may expatiate with little or no opposition.

At once to preserve and to reform is quite another thing. When the useful parts of an old establishment are kept, and what is superadded is to be fitted to what is retained, a vigorous mind, steady, persevering attention, various powers of comparison and combination, and the resources of an understanding fruitful in expedients, are to be exercised; they are to be exercised in a continued conflict with the combined force of opposite vices, with the obstinacy that rejects all improvement, and the levity that is fatigued and disgusted with everything of which it is in possession. But you may object – "A process of this kind is slow. It is not fit for an assembly, which glories in performing in a few months the work of ages. Such a mode of reforming, possibly, might take up many years." Without question it might; and it ought. It is one of the excellencies of a method in which time is amongst the assistants, that its operation is slow, and in some cases almost imperceptible. If circumspection and caution are a part of wisdom, when we work only upon inanimate matter, surely they become a part of duty too, when the subject of our demolition and construction is not brick and timber, but sentient beings, by the sudden alteration of whose state, condition, and habits, multitudes may be rendered miserable. But it seems as if it were the prevalent opinion in Paris, that an unfeeling heart, and an undoubting confidence, are the sole qualifications for a perfect legislator. Far different are my ideas of that high office. The true lawgiver ought to have a heart full of sensibility. He ought to love and respect his kind, and to fear himself. It may be allowed to his temperament to catch his ultimate object with an intuitive glance; but his movements towards it ought to be deliberate. Political arrangement, as it is a work for social ends, is to be only wrought by social means. There mind must conspire with mind. Time is required to produce that union of minds which alone can produce all the good we aim at. Our patience will achieve more than our force. If I might venture to appeal to what is so much out of fashion in Paris, I mean to experience, I should tell you, that in my course I have known, and, according to my measure, have co-operated with great men; and I have never yet seen any plan which has not been mended by the observations of those who were much inferior in understanding to the person who took the lead in the business. By a slow but well-sustained progress, the effect of each step is watched; the good or ill success of the first gives light to us in the second; and so, from light to light, we are conducted with safety through the whole series. We see that the parts or the system do not clash. The evils latent in the most promising contrivances are provided for as they arise. One advantage is as little as possible sacrificed to another. We compensate, we reconcile, we balance. We are enabled to unite into a consistent whole the various anomalies and contending principles that are found in the minds and affairs of men. From hence arises, not an excellence in simplicity, but one far superior, an excellence in composition. Where the great interests of mankind are concerned through a long succession of generations, that succession ought to be admitted into some share in the councils which are so deeply to affect them. If justice requires this, the work itself requires the aid of more minds than one age can furnish. It is from this view of things that the best legislators have been often satisfied with the establishment of some sure, solid, and ruling principle in government; a power like that which some of the philosophers have called a plastic nature; and having fixed the principle, they have left it afterwards to its own operation.

To proceed in this manner, that is, to proceed with a presiding principle, and a prolific energy, is with me the criterion of profound wisdom. What your politicians think the marks of a bold, hardy genius, are only proofs of a deplorable want of ability. By their violent haste and their defiance of the process of nature, they are delivered over blindly to every projector and adventurer, to every alchymist and empiric. They despair of turning to account anything that is common. Diet is nothing in their system of remedy. The worst of it is, that this their despair of curing common distempers by regular methods, arises not only from defect of comprehension, but, I fear, from some malignity of disposition. Your legislators seem to have taken their opinions of all professions, ranks, and offices, from the declamations and buffooneries of satirists; who would themselves be astonished if they were held to the letter of their own descriptions. By listening only to these, your leaders regard all things only on the side of their vices and faults, and view those vices and faults under every colour of exaggeration. It is undoubtedly true, though it may seem paradoxical; but in general, those who are habitually employed in finding and displaying faults, are unqualified for

the work of reformation: because their minds are not only unfurnished with patterns of the fair and good, but by habit they
come to take no delight in the contemplation of those things.
By hating vices too much, they come to love men too little.
It is therefore not wonderful, that they should be indisposed
and unable to serve them. From hence arises the complexional
disposition of some of your guides to pull everything in pieces.
At this malicious game they display the whole of their *quadri-
manous* activity. As to the rest, the paradoxes of eloquent writers,
brought forth purely as a sport of fancy, to try their talents, to
rouse attention and excite surprise, are taken up by these gentlemen, not in the spirit of the original authors, as means of cultivating their taste and improving their style. These paradoxes
become with them serious grounds of action, upon which they
proceed in regulating the most important concerns of the state.
Cicero ludicrously describes Cato[134] as endeavouring to act, in
the commonwealth, upon the school paradoxes, which exercised
the wits of the junior students in the Stoic philosophy.[135] If this
was true of Cato, these gentlemen copy after him in the manner
of some persons who lived about his time – *pede nudo Catonem*.[136]
Mr. Hume told me that he had from Rousseau[137] himself the
secret of his principles of composition. That acute though
eccentric observer had perceived, that to strike and interest the
public, the marvellous must be produced; that the marvellous of
the heathen mythology had long since lost its effects; that giants,
magicians, fairies, and heroes of romance which succeeded, had
exhausted the portion of credulity which belonged to their age;
that now nothing was left to the writer but that species of the
marvellous which might still be produced, and with as great an
effect as ever, though in another way; that is, the marvellous in
life, in manners, in characters, and in extraordinary situations,
giving rise to new and unlooked-for strokes in politics and
morals. I believe, that were Rousseau alive, and in one of his
lucid intervals, he would be shocked at the practical phrensy of
his scholars, who in their paradoxes are servile imitators, and
even in their incredulity discover an implicit faith.

Men who undertake considerable things, even in a regular way,
ought to give us ground to presume ability. But the physician of
the state, who, not satisfied with the cure of distempers, under-
takes to regenerate constitutions, ought to show uncommon
powers. Some very unusual appearances of wisdom ought to

display themselves on the face of the designs of those, who appeal to no practice, and who copy after no model. Has any such been manifested? I shall take a view (it shall for the subject be a very short one) of what the Assembly has done, with regard, first, to the constitution of the legislature; in the next place, to that of the executive power; then to that of the judicature; afterwards to the model of the army; and conclude with the system of finance; to see whether we can discover in any part of their schemes the portentous ability, which may justify these bold undertakers in the superiority which they assume over mankind.

It is in the model of the sovereign and presiding part of this new republic, that we should expect their grand display. Here they were to prove their title to their proud demands. For the plan itself at large, and for the reasons on which it is grounded, I refer to the journals of the Assembly of the 29th of September, 1789, and to the subsequent proceedings which have made any alterations in the plan. So far as in a matter somewhat confused I can see light, the system remains substantially as it has been originally framed. My few remarks will be such as regard its spirit, its tendency, and its fitness for framing a popular commonwealth, which they profess theirs to be, suited to the ends for which any commonwealth, and particularly such a commonwealth, is made. At the same time, I mean to consider its consistency with itself and its own principles.

Old establishments are tried by their effects. If the people are happy, united, wealthy, and powerful, we presume the rest. We conclude that to be good from whence good is derived. In old establishments various correctives have been found for their aberrations from theory. Indeed they are the results of various necessities and expediences. They are not often constructed after any theory; theories are rather drawn from them. In them we often see the end best obtained, where the means seem not perfectly reconcilable to what we may fancy was the original scheme. The means taught by experience may be better suited to political ends than those contrived in the original project. They again react upon the primitive constitution, and sometimes improve the design itself, from which they seem to have departed. I think all this might be curiously exemplified in the British Constitution. At worst, the errors and deviations of every kind in reckoning are found and computed and the ship proceeds in her course. This is the case of old establishments; but in a new and merely theoretic system, it is expected that every contrivance shall appear, on the face of it, to answer its ends; especially where the projectors are no way embarrassed with an endeavour to accommodate the new building to an old one, either in the walls or on the foundations.

The French builders, clearing away as mere rubbish whatever they found, and, like their ornamental gardeners, forming everything into an exact level, propose to rest the whole local and general legislature on three bases of three different kinds; one geometrical, one arithmetical, and the third financial; the first of which they call the *basis of territory*; the second, the *basis of population*; and the third, the *basis of contribution*. For the accomplishment of the first of these purposes, they divide the area of their country into eighty-three pieces, regularly square, of eighteen leagues by eighteen. These large divisions are called *Departments*. These they portion, proceeding by square measurement, into seventeen hundred and twenty districts, called *Communes*. These again they subdivide, still proceeding by square measurement, into smaller districts called *Cantons*,[138] making in all 6400.

At first view this geometrical basis of theirs presents not much to admire or to blame. It calls for no great legislative talents. Nothing more than an accurate land surveyor, with his chain, sight, and theodolite, is requisite for such a plan as this. In the old divisions of the country, various accidents at various times, and the ebb and flow of various properties and jurisdictions, settled their bounds. These bounds were not made upon any fixed system undoubtedly. They were subject to some inconveniences: but they were inconveniences for which use had found remedies, and habit had supplied accommodation and patience. In this new pavement of square within square, and this organisation, and semi-organisation, made on the system of Empedocles and Buffon,[139] and not upon any politic principle, it is impossible that innumerable local inconveniences, to which men are not habituated, must not arise. But these I pass over, because it requires an accurate knowledge of the country, which I do not possess, to specify them.

When these state surveyors came to take a view of their work of measurement, they soon found, that in politics the most fallacious of all things was geometrical demonstration. They had then recourse to another basis (or rather buttress) to support the building, which tottered on that false foundation. It was evident, that the goodness of the soil, the number of the people, their wealth, and the largeness of their contribution, made such infinite variations between square and square, as to render mensuration a ridiculous standard of power in the commonwealth, and equality in geometry the most unequal of all measures in the distribution of men. However, they could not give it up. But dividing their political and civil representation into three parts, they allotted one of those parts to the square measurement, without a single fact or calculation to ascertain whether this territorial proportion of representation was fairly assigned, and ought upon any principle really to be a third. Having however given to geometry this portion (of a third for her dower) out of compliment, I suppose, to that sublime science, they left the other two to be scuffled for between the other parts, population and contribution.

When they came to provide for population, they were not able to proceed quite so smoothly as they had done in the field of their geometry. Here their arithmetic came to bear upon their juridical metaphysics. Had they stuck to their metaphysic principles, the arithmetical process would be simple indeed. Men, with them, are strictly equal, and are entitled to equal rights in their own government. Each head, on this system, would have its vote, and every man would vote directly for the person who was to represent him in the legislature. "But soft – by regular degrees, not yet."[140] This metaphysic principle, to which law, custom, usage, policy, reason, were to yield, is to yield itself to their pleasure. There must be many degrees, and some stages, before the representative can come in contact with his constituent. Indeed, as we shall soon see, these two persons are to have no sort of communion with each other. First, the voters in the *Canton*, who compose what they call *primary assemblies*, are to have a *qualification*. What! a qualification on the indefeasible rights of men? Yes; but it shall be a very small qualification. Our injustice shall be very little oppressive; only the local valuation of three days' labour paid to the public. Why, this is not much, I readily admit, for anything but the utter subversion of your equalising principle. As a qualification it might as well be let alone; for it answers no one purpose for which qualifications are established; and, on your ideas, it excludes from a vote the man of all others whose natural equality stands the most in need of protection and defence: I mean the man who has nothing else but his natural equality to guard him. You order him to buy the right, which you before told him nature had given to him gratuitously at his birth, and of which no authority on earth could lawfully deprive him. With regard to the person who cannot come up to your market, a tyrannous aristocracy, as against him, is established at the very outset, by you who pretend to be its sworn foe.

The gradation proceeds. These primary assemblies of the *Canton* elect deputies to the *Commune*; one for every two hundred qualified inhabitants. Here is the first medium put between the primary elector and the representative legislator; and here a new turnpike is fixed for taxing the rights of men with a second qualification: for none can be elected into the *Commune* who does not pay the amount of ten days' labour. Nor have we yet done. There is still to be another gradation.* These *Communes*, chosen by the *Canton*, choose to the *Department*; and the deputies of the *Department* choose their deputies to the *National Assembly*. Here is a third barrier of a senseless qualification. Every deputy to the National Assembly must pay, in direct contribution, to the value of a *mark of silver*. Of all these qualifying barriers we must think alike; that they are impotent to secure independence; strong only to destroy the rights of men.

In all this process, which in its fundamental elements affects to consider only *population* upon a principle of natural right, there is a manifest attention to *property*; which, however just and reasonable on other schemes, is on theirs perfectly unsupportable.

When they come to their third basis, that of *Contribution*, we find that they have more completely lost sight of their rights of men. This last basis rests *entirely* on property. A principle totally different from the equality of men, and utterly irreconcilable to it, is thereby admitted; but no sooner is this principle admitted, than (as usual) it is subverted; and it is not subverted (as we shall presently see) to approximate the inequality of riches to the level of nature. The additional share in the third portion of representation (a portion reserved exclusively for the higher contribution) is made to regard the *district* only, and not the individuals in it

---

* The Assembly, in executing the plan of their committee, made some alterations. They have struck out one stage in these gradations; this removes a part of the objection; but the main objection, namely, that in their scheme the first constituent voter has no connexion with the representative legislator, remains in all its force. There are other alterations, some possibly for the better, some certainly for the worse; but to the author the merit or demerit of these smaller alterations appears to be of no moment, where the scheme itself is fundamentally vicious and absurd.

who pay. It is easy to perceive, by the course of their reasonings, how much they were embarrassed by their contradictory ideas of the rights of men and the privileges of riches. The committee of constitution do as good as admit that they are wholly irreconcilable. "The relation with regard to the contributions, is without doubt *null* (say they) when the question is on the balance of the political rights as between individual and individual; without which *personal equality would be destroyed*, and *an aristocracy of the rich* would be established. But this inconvenience entirely disappears when the proportional relation of the contribution is only considered in the *great masses*, and is solely between province and province; it serves in that case only to form a just reciprocal proportion between the cities, without affecting the personal rights of the citizens."

Here the principle of *contribution*, as taken between man and man, is reprobated as *null*, and destructive to equality: and as pernicious too; because it leads to the establishment of an *aristocracy of the rich*. However, it must not be abandoned. And the way of getting rid of the difficulty is to establish the inequality as between department and department, leaving all the individuals in each department upon an exact par. Observe, that this parity between individuals had been before destroyed, when the qualifications within the departments were settled; nor does it seem a matter of great importance whether the equality of men be injured by masses or individually. An individual is not of the same importance in a mass represented by a few, as in a mass represented by many. It would be too much to tell a man jealous of his equality, that the elector has the same franchise who votes for three members as he who votes for ten.

Now take it in the other point of view, and let us suppose their principle of representation according to contribution, that is, according to riches, to be well imagined, and to be a necessary basis for their republic. In this their third basis they assume, that riches ought to be respected, and that justice and policy require that they should entitle men, in some mode or other, to a larger share in the administration of public affairs; it is now to be seen how the Assembly provides for the pre-eminence, or even for the security, of the rich, by conferring, in virtue of their opulence, that larger measure of power to their district which is denied to them personally. I readily admit (indeed I should lay it down as a fundamental principle) that in a republican government, which has a democratic basis, the rich do require an additional security above what is necessary to them in monarchies. They are subject to envy, and through envy to oppression. On the present scheme it is impossible to divine what advantage they derive from the aristocratic preference upon which the unequal representation of the masses is founded. The rich cannot feel it, either as a support to dignity, or as security to fortune: for the aristocratic mass is generated from purely democratic principles; and the preference given to it in the general representation has no sort of reference to, or connexion with, the persons, upon account of whose property this superiority of the mass is established. If the contrivers of this scheme meant any sort of favour to the rich, in consequence of their contribution, they ought to have conferred the privilege either on the individual rich, or on some class formed of rich persons (as historians represent Servius Tullius[141] to have done in the early constitution of Rome); because the contest between the rich and the poor is not a struggle between corporation and corporation, but a contest between men and men; a competition not between districts, but between descriptions. It would answer its purpose better if the scheme were inverted; that the votes of the masses were rendered equal; and that the votes within each mass were proportioned to property.

Let us suppose one man in a district (it is an easy supposition) to contribute as much as an hundred of his neighbours. Against these he has but one vote. If there were but one representative for the mass, his poor neighbours would outvote him by an hundred to one for that single representative. Bad enough. But amends are to be made him. How? The district, in virtue of his wealth, is to choose, say ten members instead of one: that is to say, by paying a very large contribution he has the happiness of being outvoted, an hundred to one, by the poor, for ten representatives, instead of being outvoted exactly in the same proportion for a single member. In truth, instead of benefiting by this superior quantity of representation, the rich man is subjected to an additional hardship. The increase of representation within his province sets up nine persons more, and as many more than nine as there may be democratic candidates, to cabal and intrigue, and to flatter the people at his expense and to his oppression. An interest is by this means held out to multitudes of the inferior sort, in obtaining a salary of eighteen livres a day, (to them a vast object,) besides the pleasure of a residence in Paris, and their share in the government of the kingdom. The more the objects of ambition are multiplied and become democratic, just in that proportion the rich are endangered.

Thus it must fare between the poor and the rich in the province deemed aristocratic, which in its internal relation is the very reverse of that character. In its external relation, that is, its relation to the other provinces, I cannot see how the unequal representation, which is given to masses on account of wealth, becomes the means of preserving the equipoise and the tranquillity of the commonwealth. For if it be one of the objects to secure the weak from being crushed by the strong, (as in all society undoubtedly it is,) how are the smaller and poorer of these masses to be saved from the tyranny of the more wealthy? Is it by adding to the wealthy further and more systematical means of oppressing them? When we come to a balance of representation between corporate bodies, provincial interests, emulations, and jealousies are full as likely to arise among them as among individuals; and their divisions are likely to produce a much hotter spirit of dissension, and something leading much more nearly to a war.

I see that these aristocratic masses are made upon what is called the principle of direct contribution. Nothing can be a more unequal standard than this. The indirect contribution, that which arises from duties on consumption, is in truth a better standard, and follows and discovers wealth more naturally than this of direct contribution. It is difficult indeed to fix a standard of local preference on account of the one, or of the other, or of both, because some provinces may pay the more of either or of both, on account of causes not intrinsic, but originating from those very districts over whom they have obtained a preference in consequence of their ostensible contribution. If the masses were independent, sovereign bodies, who were to provide for a federative treasury by distinct contingents, and that the revenue had not (as it has) many impositions running through the whole, which affect men individually, and not corporately, and which, by their nature, confound all territorial limits, something might be said for the basis of contribution as founded on masses. But of all things, this representation, to be measured by contribution, is the most difficult to settle upon principles of equity in a country, which considers its districts as members of a whole. For a great city, such as Bourdeaux, or Paris, appears to pay a vast body of duties, almost out of all assignable proportion to other places, and its mass is considered accordingly. But are these cities the true contributors in that proportion? No. The consumers of the commodities imported into Bourdeaux, who are scattered through all France, pay the import duties of Bourdeaux. The produce of the vintage in Guienne and Languedoc give to that city the means of its contribution growing out of an export commerce. The landholders who spend their estates in Paris, and are thereby the creators of that city, contribute for Paris from the provinces out of which their revenues arise. Very nearly the same arguments will apply to the representative share given on account of *direct* contribution: because the direct contribution must be assessed on wealth real or presumed; and that local wealth will itself arise from causes not local, and which therefore in equity ought not to produce a local preference.

It is very remarkable, that in this fundamental regulation, which settles the representation of the mass upon the direct contribution, they have not yet settled how that direct contribution shall be laid, and how apportioned. Perhaps there is some latent policy towards the continuance of the present Assembly in this strange procedure. However, until they do this, they can have no certain constitution. It must depend at last upon the system of taxation, and must vary with every variation in that system. As they have contrived matters, their taxation does not so much depend on their constitution, as their constitution on their taxation. This must introduce great confusion among the masses; as the variable qualification for votes within the district must, if ever real contested elections take place, cause infinite internal controversies.

To compare together the three bases, not on their political reason, but on the ideas on which the Assembly works, and to try its consistency with itself, we cannot avoid observing, that the principle which the committee call the basis of *population*, does not begin to operate from the same point with the two other principles called the bases of *territory* and of *contribution*, which are both of an aristocratic nature. The consequence is, that, where all three begin to operate together, there is the most absurd inequality produced by the operation of the former on the two latter principles. Every canton contains four square leagues, and is estimated to contain, on the average, 4000 inhabitants, or 680 voters in the *primary assemblies*, which vary in numbers with the population of the canton, and send *one deputy* to the *commune* for every 200 voters. *Nine cantons* make a *commune*.

Now let us take *a canton* containing *a sea-port town of trade*, or *a great manufacturing town*. Let us suppose the population of this canton to be 12,700 inhabitants, or 2193 voters, forming *three primary assemblies*, and sending *ten deputies* to the *commune*.

Oppose to this *one* canton *two* others of the remaining eight in the same commune. These we may suppose to have their fair population of 4000 inhabitants and 680 voters each, or 8000 inhabitants and 1360 voters, both together. These will form only *two primary assemblies*, and send only *six* deputies to the *commune*.

When the assembly of the *commune* comes to vote on the *basis of territory*, which principle is first admitted to operate in that assembly, the *single canton*, which has *half* the territory of the *other two*, will have *ten* voices to *six* in the election of *three deputies* to the assembly of the department, chosen on the express ground of a representation of territory. This inequality, striking as it is, will be yet highly aggravated, if we suppose, as we fairly may, the *several* other cantons of the *commune* to fall proportionably short of the average population, as much as the *principal canton* exceeds it.

Now as to *the basis of contribution*, which also is a principle admitted first to operate in the assembly of the *commune*. Let us again take *one* canton, such as is stated above. If the whole of the direct contributions paid by a great trading or manufacturing town be divided equally among the inhabitants, each individual will be found to pay much more than an individual living in the country according to the same average. The whole paid by the inhabitants of the former will be more than the whole paid by the inhabitants of the latter – we may fairly assume one-third more. Then the 12,700 inhabitants, or 2193 voters of the canton, will pay as much as 19,050 inhabitants, or 3289 voters of the *other cantons*, which are nearly the estimated proportion of inhabitants and voters of *five* other cantons. Now the 2193 voters will, as I before said, send only *ten* deputies to the assembly; the 3289 voters will send *sixteen*. Thus, for an *equal* share in the contribution of the whole *commune*, there will be a difference of *sixteen* voices to *ten* in voting for deputies to be chosen on the principle of representing the general contribution of the whole *commune*.

By the same mode of computation we shall find 15,875

inhabitants, or 2741 voters of the *other* cantons, who pay *one-sixth* LESS to the contribution of the whole *commune*, will have *three* voices MORE than the 12,700 inhabitants, or 2193 voters of the *one* canton.

Such is the fantastical and unjust inequality between mass and mass, in this curious repartition of the rights of representation arising out of *territory* and *contribution*. The qualifications which these confer are in truth negative qualifications, that give a right in an inverse proportion to the possession of them.

In this whole contrivance of the three bases, consider it in any light you please, I do not see a variety of objects reconciled in one consistent whole, but several contradictory principles reluctantly and irreconcilably brought and held together by your philosophers, like wild beasts shut up in a cage, to claw and bite each other to their mutual destruction.

I am afraid I have gone too far into their way of considering the formation of a constitution. They have much, but bad, metaphysics; much, but bad, geometry; much, but false, proportionate arithmetic; but if it were all as exact as metaphysics, geometry, and arithmetic ought to be, and if their schemes were perfectly consistent in all their parts, it would make only a more fair and sightly vision. It is remarkable, that, in a great arrangement of mankind, not one reference whatsoever is to be found to anything moral or anything politic; nothing that relates to the concerns, the actions, the passions, the interests of men. *Hominem non sapiunt.*[142]

You see I only consider this constitution as electoral, and leading by steps to the National Assembly. I do not enter into the internal government of the departments, and their genealogy through the communes and cantons. These local governments are, in the original plan, to be as nearly as possible composed in the same manner and on the same principles with the elective assemblies. They are each of them bodies perfectly compact and rounded in themselves.

You cannot but perceive in this scheme, that it has a direct and immediate tendency to sever France into a variety of republics, and to render them totally independent of each other without any direct constitutional means of coherence, connexion, or subordination, except what may be derived from their acquiescence in the determinations of the general congress of the ambassadors from each independent republic. Such in reality is the National

Assembly, and such governments I admit do exist in the world, though in forms infinitely more suitable to the local and habitual circumstances of their people. But such associations, rather than bodies politic, have generally been the effect of necessity, not choice; and I believe the present French power is the very first body of citizens, who, having obtained full authority to do with their country what they pleased, have chosen to dissever it in this barbarous manner.

It is impossible not to observe, that, in the spirit of this geometrical distribution, and arithmetical arrangement, these pretended citizens treat France exactly like a country of conquest. Acting as conquerors, they have imitated the policy of the harshest of that harsh race. The policy of such barbarous victors, who contemn a subdued people, and insult their feelings, has ever been, as much as in them lay, to destroy all vestiges of the ancient country, in religion, in polity, in laws, and in manners; to confound all territorial limits; to produce a general poverty; to put up their properties to auction; to crush their princes, nobles, and pontiffs; to lay low everything which had lifted its head above the level, or which could serve to combine or rally, in their distresses, the disbanded people, under the standard of old opinion. They have made France free in the manner in which those sincere friends to the rights of mankind, the Romans, freed Greece, Macedon, and other nations. They destroyed the bonds of their union, under colour of providing for the independence of each of their cities.

When the members who compose these new bodies of cantons, communes, and departments, arrangements purposely produced through the medium of confusion, begin to act, they will find themselves in a great measure strangers to one another. The electors and elected throughout, especially in the rural *cantons*, will be frequently without any civil habitudes or connexions, or any of that natural discipline which is the soul of a true republic. Magistrates and collectors of revenue are now no longer acquainted with their districts, bishops with their dioceses, or curates with their parishes. These new colonies of the rights of men bear a strong resemblance to that sort of military colonies which Tacitus[143] has observed upon in the declining policy of Rome. In better and wiser days (whatever course they took with foreign nations) they were careful to make the elements of methodical subordination and settlement to be coeval; and even to lay the foundations of civil discipline in the military.* But, when all the good arts had fallen into ruin, they proceeded, as your Assembly does, upon the equality of men, and with as little judgment, and as little care for those things which make a republic tolerable or durable. But in this, as well as almost every instance, your new commonwealth is born, and bred, and fed, in those corruptions which mark degenerated and worn-out republics. Your child comes into the world with the symptoms of death; the *facies Hippocratica*[144] forms the character of its physiognomy, and the prognostic of its fate.

The legislators who framed the ancient republics knew that their business was too arduous to be accomplished with no better apparatus than the metaphysics of an undergraduate, and the mathematics and arithmetic of an exciseman. They had to do with men, and they were obliged to study human nature. They had to do with citizens, and they were obliged to study the effects of those habits which are communicated by the circumstances of civil life. They were sensible that the operation of this second nature on the first produced a new combination; and thence arose many diversities amongst men, according to their birth, their education, their professions, the periods of their lives, their residence in towns or in the country, their several ways of acquiring and of fixing property, and according to the quality of the property itself, all which rendered them as it were so many different species of animals. From hence they thought themselves obliged to dispose their citizens into such classes, and to place them in such situations in the state, as their peculiar habits might qualify them to fill, and to allot to them such appropriated privileges as might secure to them what their specific occasions required, and which might furnish to each description such force as might protect it in the conflict caused by the diversity of interests, that must exist, and must contend, in all complex society: for the legislator would have been ashamed, that the coarse husbandman should well know how to assort and to use his sheep, horses, and oxen, and should have enough of common

---

* Non, ut olim, universæ legiones deducebantur cum tribunis, et centurionibus, et sui cujusque ordinis militibus, ut consensu et caritate rempublicam afficerent; sed ignoti inter se, diversis manipulis, sine rectore, sine affectibus mutuis, quasi ex alio genere mortalium, repente in unum collecti, numerus magis quam colonia.[145] Tac. Annal. l. 14, sect. 27. All this will be still more applicable to the unconnected, rotatory, biennial national assemblies in this absurd and senseless constitution.

sense, not to abstract and equalise them all into animals, without providing for each kind an appropriate food, care, and employment; whilst he, the economist, disposer, and shepherd of his own kindred, subliming himself into an airy metaphysician, was resolved to know nothing of his flocks but as men in general. It is for this reason that Montesquieu[146] observed very justly, that in their classification of the citizens, the great legislators of antiquity made the greatest display of their powers, and even soared above themselves. It is here that your modern legislators have gone deep into the negative series, and sunk even below their own nothing. As the first sort of legislators attended to the different kinds of citizens, and combined them into one commonwealth, the others, the metaphysical and alchemistical legislators, have taken the direct contrary course. They have attempted to confound all sorts of citizens, as well as they could, into one homogeneous mass; and then they divided this their amalgama into a number of incoherent republics. They reduce men to loose counters, merely for the sake of simple telling, and not to figures whose power is to arise from their place in the table. The elements of their own metaphysics might have taught them better lessons. The troll of their categorical table might have informed them that there was something else in the intellectual world besides *substance* and *quantity*. They might learn from the catechism of metaphysics that there were eight heads more,* in every complex deliberation, which they have never thought of; though these, of all the ten, are the subjects on which the skill of man can operate anything at all.

So far from this able disposition of some of the old republican legislators, which follows with a solicitous accuracy the moral conditions and propensities of men, they have levelled and crushed together all the orders which they found, even under the coarse unartificial arrangement of the monarchy, in which mode of government the classing of the citizens is not of so much importance as in a republic. It is true, however, that every such classification, if properly ordered, is good in all forms of government; and composes a strong barrier against the excesses of despotism, as well as it is the necessary means of giving effect and permanence to a republic. For want of something of this kind, if the present project of a republic should fail, all securities to a

* Qualitas, Relatio, Actio, Passio, Ubi, Quando, Situs, Habitus.[147]

moderated freedom fail along with it; all the indirect restraints which mitigate despotism are removed; insomuch that if monarchy should ever again obtain an entire ascendency in France, under this or under any other dynasty, it will probably be, if not voluntarily tempered, at setting out, by the wise and virtuous counsels of the prince, the most completely arbitrary power that has ever appeared on earth. This is to play a most desperate game.

The confusion which attends on all such proceedings, they even declare to be one of their objects, and they hope to secure their constitution by a terror of a return of those evils which attended their making it. "By this," say they, "its destruction will become difficult to authority, which cannot break it up without the entire disorganisation of the whole state." They presume, that if this authority should ever come to the same degree of power that they have acquired, it would make a more moderate and chastised use of it, and would piously tremble entirely to disorganise the state in the savage manner that they have done. They expect, from the virtues of returning despotism, the security which is to be enjoyed by the offspring of their popular vices.

I wish, Sir, that you and my readers would give an attentive perusal to the work of M. de Calonne, on this subject. It is indeed not only an eloquent, but an able and instructive, performance. I confine myself to what he says relative to the constitution of the new state, and to the condition of the revenue. As to the disputes of this minister with his rivals, I do not wish to pronounce upon them. As little do I mean to hazard any opinion concerning his ways and means, financial or political, for taking his country out of its present disgraceful and deplorable situation of servitude, anarchy, bankruptcy, and beggary. I cannot speculate quite so sanguinely as he does: but he is a Frenchman, and has a closer duty, relative to those objects, and better means of judging of them, than I can have. I wish that the formal avowal which he refers to, made by one of the principal leaders in the Assembly, concerning the tendency of their scheme to bring France not only from a monarchy to a republic, but from a republic to a mere confederacy, may be very particularly attended to. It adds new force to my observations: and indeed M. de Calonne's work supplies my deficiencies by many new and striking arguments on most of the subjects of this letter.*

* See l'Etat de la France, p. 363.

It is this resolution, to break their country into separate republics, which has driven them into the greatest number of their difficulties and contradictions. If it were not for this, all the questions of exact equality, and these balances, never to be settled, of individual rights, population, and contribution, would be wholly useless. The representation, though derived from parts, would be a duty which equally regarded the whole. Each deputy to the Assembly would be the representative of France, and of all its descriptions, of the many and of the few, of the rich and of the poor, of the great districts and of the small. All these districts would themselves be subordinate to some standing authority, existing independently of them, an authority in which their representation, and everything that belongs to it, originated, and to which it was pointed. This standing, unalterable, fundamental government would make, and it is the only thing which could make, that territory truly and properly a whole. With us, when we elect popular representatives, we send them to a council, in which each man individually is a subject, and submitted to a government complete in all its ordinary functions. With you the elective Assembly is the sovereign, and the sole sovereign; all the members are therefore integral parts of this sole sovereignty. But with us it is totally different. With us the representative, separated from the other parts, can have no action and no existence. The government is the point of reference of the several members and districts of our representation. This is the centre of our unity. This government of reference is a trustee for the whole, and not for the parts. So is the other branch of our public council, I mean the House of Lords. With us the king and the lords are several and joint securities for the equality of each district, each province, each city. When did you hear in Great Britain of any province suffering from the inequality of its representation; what district from having no representation at all? Not only our monarchy and our peerage secure the equality on which our unity depends, but it is the spirit of the House of Commons itself. The very inequality of representation, which is so foolishly complained of, is perhaps the very thing which prevents us from thinking or acting as members for districts. Cornwall elects as many members as all Scotland. But is Cornwall better taken care of than Scotland? Few trouble their heads about any of your bases, out of some giddy clubs. Most of those who wish for any change, upon any plausible grounds, desire it on different ideas.

Your new constitution is the very reverse of ours in its principle; and I am astonished how any persons could dream of holding out anything done in it, as an example for Great Britain. With you there is little, or rather no, connexion between the last representative and the first constituent. The member who goes to the National Assembly is not chosen by the people, nor accountable to them. There are three elections before he is chosen: two sets of magistracy intervene between him and the primary assembly, so as to render him, as I have said, an ambassador of a state, and not the representative of the people within a state. By this the whole spirit of the election is changed; nor can any corrective, which your constitution-mongers have devised, render him anything else than what he is. The very attempt to do it would inevitably introduce a confusion, if possible, more horrid than the present. There is no way to make a connexion between the original constituent and the representative, but by the circuitous means which may lead the candidate to apply in the first instance to the primary electors, in order that by their authoritative instructions (and something more perhaps) these primary electors may force the two succeeding bodies of electors to make a choice agreeable to their wishes. But this would plainly subvert the whole scheme. It would be to plunge them back into that tumult and confusion of popular election, which, by their interposed gradation of elections, they mean to avoid, and at length to risk the whole fortune of the state with those who have the least knowledge of it, and the least interest in it. This is a perpetual dilemma, into which they are thrown by the vicious, weak, and contradictory principles they have chosen. Unless the people break up and level this gradation, it is plain that they do not at all substantially elect to the Assembly; indeed they elect as little in appearance as reality.

What is it we all seek for in an election? To answer its real purposes, you must first possess the means of knowing the fitness of your man; and then you must retain some hold upon him by personal obligation or dependence. For what end are these primary electors complimented, or rather mocked, with a choice? They can never know anything of the qualities of him that is to serve them, nor has he any obligation whatsoever to them. Of all the powers unfit to be delegated by those who have any real means of judging, that most peculiarly unfit is what relates to a *personal* choice. In case of abuse, that body of primary electors never can call the representative to an account for his conduct. He is too far removed from them in the chain of representation. If he acts improperly at the end of his two years' lease, it does not concern him for two years' more. By the new French constitution the best and the wisest representatives go equally with the worst into this *Limbus Patrum*.[148] Their bottoms are supposed foul, and they must go into dock to be refitted. Every man who has served in an assembly is ineligible for two years after. Just as these magistrates begin to learn their trade, like chimney-sweepers, they are disqualified for exercising it. Superficial, new, petulant acquisition, and interrupted, dronish, broken, ill recollection, is to be the destined character of all your future governors. Your constitution has too much of jealousy to have much of sense in it. You consider the breach of trust in the representative so principally, that you do not at all regard the question of his fitness to execute it.

This purgatory interval is not unfavourable to a faithless representative, who may be as good a canvasser as he was a bad governor. In this time he may cabal himself into a superiority over the wisest and most virtuous. As, in the end, all the members of this elective constitution are equally fugitive, and exist only for the election, they may be no longer the same persons who had chosen him, to whom he is to be responsible when he solicits for a renewal of his trust. To call all the secondary electors of the *Commune* to account, is ridiculous, impracticable, and unjust; they may themselves have been deceived in their choice, as the third set of electors, those of the *Department*, may be in theirs. In your elections responsibility cannot exist.

Finding no sort of principle of coherence with each other in the nature and constitution of the several new republics of France, I considered what cement the legislators had provided for them from any extraneous materials. Their confederations, their *spectacles*, their civic feasts, and their enthusiasm, I take no notice of; they are nothing but mere tricks; but tracing their policy through their actions, I think I can distinguish the arrangements by which they propose to hold these republics together. The first, is the *confiscation*, with the compulsory paper currency annexed to it; the second, is the supreme power of the city of Paris; the third, is the general army of the state. Of this last I shall reserve what I have to say, until I come to consider the army as a head by itself.

As to the operation of the first (the confiscation and paper currency) merely as a cement, I cannot deny that these, the one depending on the other, may for some time compose some sort of cement, if their madness and folly in the management, and in the tempering of the parts together, does not produce a repulsion in the very outset. But allowing to the scheme some coherence and some duration, it appears to me, that if, after a while, the confiscation should not be found sufficient to support the paper coinage, (as I am morally certain it will not,) then, instead of cementing, it will add infinitely to the dissociation, distraction, and confusion of these confederate republics, both with relation to each other, and to the several parts within themselves. But if the confiscation should so far succeed as to sink the paper currency, the cement is gone with the circulation. In the mean time its binding force will be very uncertain, and it will straiten or relax with every variation in the credit of the paper.

One thing only is certain in this scheme, which is an effect seemingly collateral, but direct, I have no doubt, in the minds of those who conduct this business, that is, its effect in producing an *Oligarchy* in every one of the republics. A paper circulation, not founded on any real money deposited or engaged for, amounting already to four-and-forty millions of English money, and this currency by force substituted in the place of the coin of the kingdom, becoming thereby the substance of its revenue, as well as the medium of all its commercial and civil intercourse, must put the whole of what power, authority, and influence is left, in any form whatsoever it may assume, into the hands of the managers and conductors of this circulation.

In England we feel the influence of the bank; though it is only the centre of a voluntary dealing. He knows little indeed of the influence of money upon mankind, who does not see the force of the management of a monied concern, which is so much more extensive, and in its nature so much more depending on the managers, than any of ours. But this is not merely a money concern. There is another member in the system inseparably connected with this money management. It consists in the means of drawing out at discretion portions of the confiscated lands for sale; and carrying on a process of continual transmutation of paper into land, and land into paper. When we follow this process in its effects, we may conceive something of the intensity of the force with which this system must operate. By this means the spirit of money-jobbing and speculation goes into the mass of land itself, and incorporates with it. By this kind of operation, that species of property becomes (as it were) volatilised; it assumes an unnatural and monstrous activity, and thereby throws into the hands of the several managers, principal and subordinate, Parisian and provincial, all the representative of money, and perhaps a full tenth part of all the land in France, which has now acquired the worst and most pernicious part of the evil of a paper circulation, the greatest possible uncertainty in its value. They have reversed the Latonian kindness to the landed property of Delos. They have sent theirs to be blown about, like the light fragments of a wreck, *oras et littora circum.*[149]

The new dealers, being all habitually adventurers, and without any fixed habits or local predilections, will purchase to job out again, as the market of paper, or of money, or of land, shall present an advantage. For though a holy bishop[150] thinks that agriculture will derive great advantages from the *"enlightened"* usurers who are to purchase the church confiscations, I, who am not a good, but an old farmer, with great humility beg leave to tell his late lordship, that usury is not a tutor of agriculture; and if the word "enlightened" be understood according to the new dictionary, as it always is in your new schools, I cannot conceive how a man's not believing in God can teach him to cultivate the earth with the least of any additional skill or encouragement. "Diis immortalibus sero,"[151] said an old Roman, when he held one handle of the plough, whilst Death held the other. Though you were to join in the commission all the directors of the two academies to the directors of the *Caisse d'Escompte,*[152] one old, experienced peasant is worth them all. I have got more information upon a curious and interesting branch of husbandry, in one short conversation with an old Carthusian monk, than I have derived from all the Bank directors that I have ever conversed with. However, there is no cause for apprehension from the meddling of money-dealers with rural economy. These gentlemen are too wise in their generation. At first, perhaps, their tender and susceptible imaginations may be captivated with the innocent and unprofitable delights of a pastoral life; but in a little time they will find that agriculture is a trade much more laborious, and much less lucrative, than that which they had left. After making its panegyric, they will turn their backs on it like their great precursor and prototype. They may, like him, begin by singing *"Beatus ille"* —[153] but what will be the end?

Hæc ubi locutus fænerator Alphius,
Jam jam futurus rusticus
Omnem relegit idibus pecuniam;
Quærit calendis ponere.

They will cultivate the *Caisse d'Eglise*,[154] under the sacred auspices of this prelate, with much more profit than its vineyards and
its corn-fields. They will employ their talents according to their
habits and their interests. They will not follow the plough whilst
they can direct treasuries, and govern provinces.

Your legislators, in everything new, are the very first who have
founded a commonwealth upon gaming, and infused this spirit
into it as its vital breath. The great object in these politics is to
metamorphose France from a great kingdom into one great play-
table; to turn its inhabitants into a nation of gamesters; to make
speculation as extensive as life; to mix it with all its concerns; and
to divert the whole of the hopes and fears of the people from
their usual channels into the impulses, passions, and superstitions
of those who live on chances. They loudly proclaim their opinion, that this their present system of a republic cannot possibly
exist without this kind of gaming fund; and that the very thread
of its life is spun out of the staple of these speculations. The old
gaming in funds was mischievous enough undoubtedly; but it
was so only to individuals. Even when it had its greatest extent,
in the Mississippi and South Sea,[155] it affected but few, comparatively; where it extends further, as in lotteries, the spirit has but
a single object. But where the law, which in most circumstances
forbids, and in none countenances, gaming, is itself debauched,
so as to reverse its nature and policy, and expressly to force the
subject to this destructive table, by bringing the spirit and symbols of gaming into the minutest matters, and engaging everybody in it, and in everything, a more dreadful epidemic
distemper of that kind is spread than yet has appeared in the
world. With you a man can neither earn nor buy his dinner without a speculation. What he receives in the morning will not have
the same value at night. What he is compelled to take as pay for
an old debt will not be received as the same when he comes to
pay a debt contracted by himself; nor will it be the same when
by prompt payment he would avoid contracting any debt at all.
Industry must wither away. Economy must be driven from your
country. Careful provision will have no existence. Who will

labour without knowing the amount of his pay? Who will study to increase what none can estimate? Who will accumulate, when he does not know the value of what he saves? If you abstract it from its uses in gaming, to accumulate your paper wealth would be not the providence of a man, but the distempered instinct of a jackdaw.

The truly melancholy part of the policy of systematically making a nation of gamesters is this, that though all are forced to play, few can understand the game; and fewer still are in a condition to avail themselves of the knowledge. The many must be the dupes of the few who conduct the machine of these speculations. What effect it must have on the country people is visible. The townsman can calculate from day to day; not so the inhabitant of the country. When the peasant first brings his corn to market, the magistrate in the towns obliges him to take the assign at at par; when he goes to the shop with his money, he finds it seven per cent the worse for crossing the way. This market he will not readily resort to again. The towns-people will be inflamed; they will force the country people to bring their corn. Resistance will begin, and the murders of Paris and St. Denis may be renewed through all France.

What signifies the empty compliment paid to the country, by giving it, perhaps, more than its share in the theory of your representation? Where have you placed the real power over monied and landed circulation? Where have you placed the means of raising and falling the value of every man's freehold? Those, whose operations can take from, or add ten per cent to, the possessions of every man in France, must be the masters of every man in France. The whole of the power obtained by this revolution will settle in the towns among the burghers, and the monied directors who lead them. The landed gentleman, the yeoman, and the peasant, have, none of them, habits, or inclinations, or experience, which can lead them to any share in this the sole source of power and influence now left in France. The very nature of a country life, the very nature of landed property, in all the occupations, and all the pleasures they afford, render combination and arrangement (the sole way of procuring and exerting influence) in a manner impossible amongst country people. Combine them by all the art you can, and all the industry, they are always dissolving into individuality. Anything in the nature of incorporation is almost impracticable amongst them.

Hope, fear, alarm, jealousy, the ephemerous tale that does its business and dies in a day, all these things, which are the reins and spurs by which leaders check or urge the minds of followers, are not easily employed, or hardly at all, amongst scattered people. They assemble, they arm, they act, with the utmost difficulty, and at the greatest charge. Their efforts, if ever they can be commenced, cannot be sustained. They cannot proceed systematically. If the country gentlemen attempt an influence through the mere income of their property, what is it to that of those who have ten times their income to sell, and who can ruin their property by bringing their plunder to meet it at market? If the landed man wishes to mortgage, he falls the value of his land, and raises the value of assignats.[156] He augments the power of his enemy by the very means he must take to contend with him. The country gentleman therefore, the officer by sea and land, the man of liberal views and habits, attached to no profession, will be as completely excluded from the government of his country as if he were legislatively proscribed. It is obvious, that in the towns, all the things which conspire against the country gentleman combine in favour of the money manager and director. In towns combination is natural. The habits of burghers, their occupations, their diversion, their business, their idleness, continually bring them into mutual contact. Their virtues and their vices are sociable; they are always in garrison; and they come embodied and half disciplined into the hands of those who mean to form them for civil or military action.

All these considerations leave no doubt on my mind, that, if this monster of a constitution can continue, France will be wholly governed by the agitators in corporations, by societies in the towns formed of directors of assignats, and trustees for the sale of church lands, attornies, agents, money-jobbers, speculators, and adventurers, composing an ignoble oligarchy, founded on the destruction of the crown, the church, the nobility, and the people. Here end all the deceitful dreams and visions of the equality and rights of men. In "the Serbonian bog"[157] of this base oligarchy they are all absorbed, sunk, and lost for ever.

Though human eyes cannot trace them, one would be tempted to think some great offences in France must cry to heaven, which has thought fit to punish it with a subjection to a vile and inglorious domination, in which no comfort or compensation is to be found in any even of those false splendours, which, playing about other tyrannies, prevent mankind from feeling themselves dishonoured even whilst they are oppressed. I must confess I am touched with a sorrow, mixed with some indignation, at the conduct of a few men, once of great rank, and still of great character, who, deluded with specious names, have engaged in a business too deep for the line of their understanding to fathom; who have lent their fair reputation, and the authority of their high-sounding names, to the designs of men with whom they could not be acquainted; and have thereby made their very virtues operate to the ruin of their country.

So far as to the first cementing principle.

The second material of cement for their new republic is the superiority of the city of Paris: and this I admit is strongly connected with the other cementing principle of paper circulation and confiscation. It is in this part of the project we must look for the cause of the destruction of all the old bounds of provinces and jurisdictions, ecclesiastical and secular, and the dissolution of all ancient combinations of things, as well as the formation of so many small unconnected republics. The power of the city of Paris is evidently one great spring of all their politics. It is through the power of Paris, now become the centre and focus of jobbing, that the leaders of this faction direct, or rather command, the whole legislative and the whole executive government. Everything therefore must be done which can confirm the authority of that city over the other republics. Paris is compact; she has an enormous strength, wholly disproportioned to the force of any of the square republics; and this strength is collected and condensed within a narrow compass. Paris has a natural and easy connexion of its parts, which will not be affected by any scheme of a geometrical constitution, nor does it much signify, whether its proportion of representation be more or less, since it has the whole draft of fishes in its drag-net. The other divisions of the kingdom being hackled and torn to pieces, and separated from all their habitual means, and even principles of union, cannot, for some time at least, confederate against her. Nothing was to be left in all the subordinate members, but weakness, disconnexion, and confusion. To confirm this part of the plan, the Assembly has lately come to a resolution, that no two of their republics shall have the same commander-in-chief.

To a person who takes a view of the whole, the strength of Paris, thus formed, will appear a system of general weakness. It is boasted that the geometrical policy has been adopted, that all local ideas should be sunk, and that the people should no longer be Gascons, Picards, Bretons, Normans; but Frenchmen, with one country, one heart, and one Assembly. But instead of being all Frenchmen, the greater likelihood is, that the inhabitants of that region will shortly have no country. No man ever was attached by a sense of pride, partiality, or real affection, to a description of square measurement. He never will glory in belonging to the Chequer No. 71, or to any other badge-ticket. We begin our public affections in our families. No cold relation is a zealous citizen. We pass on to our neighbourhoods, and our habitual provincial connexions. These are inns and resting-places. Such divisions of our country as have been formed by habit, and not by a sudden jerk of authority, were so many little images of the great country in which the heart found something which it could fill. The love to the whole is not extinguished by this subordinate partiality. Perhaps it is a sort of elemental train-ing to those higher and more large regards, by which alone men come to be affected, as with their own concern, in the prosperity of a kingdom so extensive as that of France. In that general terri-tory itself, as in the old name of provinces, the citizens are interested from old prejudices and unreasoned habits, and not on account of the geometric properties of its figure. The power and pre-eminence of Paris does certainly press down and hold these republics together as long as it lasts. But, for the reasons I have already given you, I think it cannot last very long.

Passing from the civil creating and the civil cementing prin-ciples of this constitution, to the National Assembly, which is to appear and act as sovereign, we see a body in its constitution with every possible power, and no possible external control. We see a body without fundamental laws, without established maxims, without respected rules of proceeding, which nothing can keep firm to any system whatsoever. Their idea of their powers is always taken at the utmost stretch of legislative competency, and their examples for common cases from the exceptions of the most urgent necessity. The future is to be in most respects like the present Assembly; but, by the mode of the new elections and the tendency of the new circulations, it will be purged of the small degree of internal control existing in a minority chosen originally from various interests, and preserving something of their spirit. If possible, the next Assembly must be worse than the present. The present, by destroying and altering everything, will leave to their successors apparently nothing popular to do. They will be roused by emulation and example to enterprises the boldest and the most absurd. To suppose such an assembly sitting in perfect quietude is ridiculous.

Your all-sufficient legislators, in their hurry to do everything at once, have forgot one thing that seems essential, and which I believe never has been before, in the theory or the practice, omitted by any projector of a republic. They have forgot to constitute a *senate*, or something of that nature and character. Never, before this time, was heard of a body politic composed of one legislative and active assembly, and its executive officers, without such a council; without something to which foreign states might connect themselves; something to which, in the ordinary detail of government, the people could look up; something which might give a bias, and steadiness, and preserve something like consistency in the proceedings of state. Such a body kings generally have as a council. A monarchy may exist without it; but it seems to be in the very essence of a republican government. It holds a sort of middle place between the supreme power exercised by the people, or immediately delegated from them, and the mere executive. Of this there are no traces in your constitution; and, in providing nothing of this kind, your Solons and Numas[158] have, as much as in anything else, discovered a sovereign incapacity.

Let us now turn our eyes to what they have done towards the formation of an executive power. For this they have chosen a degraded king. This their first executive officer is to be a machine, without any sort of deliberative discretion in any one act of his function. At best he is but a channel to convey to the National Assembly such matter as it may import that body to know. If he had been made the exclusive channel, the power would not have been without its importance; though infinitely perilous to those who would choose to exercise it. But public intelligence and statement of facts may pass to the Assembly with equal authenticity, through any other conveyance. As to the means, therefore, of giving a direction to measures by the statement of an authorised reporter, this office of intelligence is as nothing.

To consider the French scheme of an executive officer, in its two natural divisions of civil and political. – In the first it must be observed, that, according to the new constitution, the higher parts of judicature, in either of its lines, are not in the king. The king of France is not the fountain of justice. The judges, neither the original nor the appellate, are of his nomination. He neither proposes the candidates, nor has a negative on the choice. He is not even the public prosecutor. He serves only as a notary to authenticate the choice made of the judges in the several districts. By his officers he is to execute their sentence. When we look into the true nature of his authority, he appears to be nothing more than a chief of bumbailiffs, serjeants at mace, catchpoles, jailers, and hangmen. It is impossible to place anything called royalty in a more degrading point of view. A thousand times better had it been for the dignity of this unhappy prince, that he had nothing at all to do with the administration of justice, deprived as he is of all that is venerable, and all that is consolatory, in that function, without power of originating any process; without a power of suspension, mitigation, or pardon. Everything in justice that is vile and odious is thrown upon him. It was not for nothing that the Assembly has been at such pains to remove the stigma from certain offices, when they are resolved to place the person who had lately been their king in a situation but one degree above the executioner, and in an office nearly of the same quality. It is not in nature, that, situated as the king of the French now is, he can respect himself, or can be respected by others.

View this new executive officer on the side of his political capacity, as he acts under the orders of the National Assembly. To execute laws is a royal office; to execute orders is not to be a king. However, a political executive magistracy, though merely such, is a great trust. It is a trust indeed that has much depending upon its faithful and diligent performance, both in the person presiding in it and in all its subordinates. Means of performing this duty ought to be given by regulation; and dispositions towards it ought to be infused by the circumstances attendant on the trust. It ought to be environed with dignity, authority, and consideration, and it ought to lead to glory. The office of execution is an office of exertion. It is not from impotence we are to expect the tasks of power. What sort of person is a king to command executory service, who has no means whatsoever to reward it? Not in a permanent office; not in a grant of land; no, not in a pension of fifty pounds a year; not in the vainest and most trivial title. In France the king is no more the fountain of honour than he is the fountain of justice. All rewards, all distinctions, are in other hands. Those who serve the king can be actuated by no natural motive but fear; by a fear of everything except their master. His functions of internal coercion are as odious as those which he exercises in the department of justice. If relief is to be given to any municipality, the Assembly gives it. If troops are to be sent to reduce them to obedience to the Assembly, the king is to execute the order; and upon every occasion he is to be spattered over with the blood of his people. He has no negative; yet his name and authority is used to enforce every harsh decree. Nay, he must concur in the butchery of those who shall attempt to free him from his imprisonment, or show the slightest attachment to his person or to his ancient authority.

Executive magistracy ought to be constituted in such a manner, that those who compose it should be disposed to love and to venerate those whom they are bound to obey. A purposed neglect, or, what is worse, a literal but perverse and malignant obedience, must be the ruin of the wisest counsels. In vain will the law attempt to anticipate or to follow such studied neglects and fraudulent attentions. To make them act zealously is not in the competence of law. Kings, even such as are truly kings, may and ought to bear the freedom of subjects that are obnoxious to them. They may too, without derogating from themselves, bear even the authority of such persons, if it promotes their service. Louis the Thirteenth mortally hated the Cardinal de Richelieu;[159] but his support of that minister against his rivals was the source of all the glory of his reign, and the solid foundation of his throne itself. Louis the Fourteenth, when come to the throne, did not love the Cardinal Mazarin; but for his interests he preserved him in power. When old, he detested Louvois;[160] but for years, whilst he faithfully served his greatness, he endured his person. When George the Second took Mr. Pitt,[161] who certainly was not agreeable to him, into his councils, he did nothing which could humble a wise sovereign. But these ministers, who were chosen by affairs, not by affections, acted in the name of, and in trust for, kings; and not as their avowed, constitutional, and ostensible masters. I think it impossible that any king, when he has recovered his first terrors, can cordially infuse vivacity and vigour into measures which he knows to be dictated by those, who, he must be persuaded, are in the highest degree ill affected to his person. Will any ministers, who serve such a king (or whatever he may be called) with but a decent appearance of respect, cordially obey the orders of those whom but the other day in his name they had committed to the Bastile? will they obey the orders of those whom, whilst they were exercising despotic justice upon them, they conceived they were treating with levity; and from whom, in a prison, they thought they had provided an asylum? If you expect such obedience, amongst your other innovations and regenerations, you ought to make a revolution in nature, and provide a new constitution for the human mind. Otherwise, your supreme government cannot harmonise with its executory system. There are cases in which we cannot take up with names and abstractions. You may call half a dozen leading individuals, whom we have reason to fear and hate, the nation. It makes no other difference, than to make us fear and hate them the more. If it had been thought justifiable and expedient to make such a revolution by such means, and through such persons, as you have made yours, it would have been more wise to have completed the business of the fifth and sixth of October. The new executive officer would then owe his situation to those who are his creators as well as his masters; and he might be bound in interest, in the society of crime, and (if in crimes there could be virtues) in gratitude, to serve those who had promoted him to a place of great lucre and great sensual indulgence; and of something more; for more he must have received from those who certainly would not have limited an aggrandised creature, as they have done a submitting antagonist.

A king circumstanced as the present, if he is totally stupified by his misfortunes, so as to think it not the necessity, but the premium and privilege, of life, to eat and sleep, without any regard to glory, can never be fit for the office. If he feels as men commonly feel, he must be sensible, that an office so circumstanced is one in which he can obtain no fame or reputation. He has no generous interest that can excite him to action. At best, his conduct will be passive and defensive. To inferior people such an office might be matter of honour. But to be raised to it, and to descend to it, are different things, and suggest different sentiments. Does he *really* name the ministers? They will have a sympathy with him. Are they forced upon him? The whole business between them and the nominal king will be mutual counteraction. In all other countries, the office of ministers of state is of the highest dignity. In France it is full of peril, and incapable of glory. Rivals however they will have in their nothingness, whilst shallow ambition exists in the world, or the desire of a miserable salary is an incentive to short-sighted avarice. Those competitors of the ministers are enabled by your constitution to attack them in their vital parts, whilst they have not the means of repelling their charges in any other than the degrading character of culprits. The ministers of state in France are the only persons in that country who are incapable of a share in the national councils. What ministers! What councils! What a nation! – But they are responsible. It is a poor service that is to be had from responsibility. The elevation of mind to be derived from fear will never make a nation glorious. Responsibility prevents crimes. It makes all attempts against the laws dangerous. But for a principle of active and zealous service, none but idiots could think of it. Is the conduct of a war to be trusted to a man who may abhor its principle; who, in every step he may take to render it successful, confirms the power of those by whom he is oppressed? Will foreign states seriously treat with him who has no prerogative of peace or war; no, not so much as in a single vote by himself or his ministers, or by any one whom he can possibly influence? A state of contempt is not a state for a prince: better get rid of him at once.

I know it will be said that these humours in the court and executive government will continue only through this generation; and that the king has been brought to declare the dauphin shall be educated in a conformity to his situation. If he is made to conform to his situation, he will have no education at all. His training must be worse even than that of an arbitrary monarch. If he reads – whether he reads or not, some good or evil genius will tell him his ancestors were kings. Thenceforward his object must be to assert himself, and to avenge his parents. This you will say is not his duty. That may be; but it is nature; and whilst you pique nature against you, you do unwisely to trust to duty. In this futile scheme of polity, the state nurses in its bosom, for the present, a source of weakness, perplexity, counteraction, inefficiency, and decay; and it prepares the means of its final ruin. In short, I see nothing in the executive force (I cannot call it authority) that has even an appearance of vigour, or that has the smallest degree of just correspondence or symmetry, or amicable relation with the supreme power, either as it now exists, or as it is planned for the future government.

You have settled, by an economy as perverted as the policy, two* establishments of government; one real, one fictitious. Both maintained at a vast expense; but the fictitious at, I think, the greatest. Such a machine as the latter is not worth the grease of its wheels. The expense is exorbitant; and neither the show nor the use deserve the tenth part of the charge. Oh! but I don't do justice to the talents of the legislators: I don't allow, as I ought to do, for necessity. Their scheme of executive force was not their choice. This pageant must be kept. The people would not consent to part with it. Right; I understand you. You do, in spite of your grand theories, to which you would have heaven and earth to bend, you do know how to conform yourselves to the nature and circumstances of things. But when you were obliged to conform thus far to circumstances, you ought to have carried your submission farther, and to have made, what you were obliged to take, a proper instrument, and useful to its end. That was in your power. For instance, among many others, it was in your power to leave to your king the right of peace and war. What! to leave to the executive magistrate the most dangerous of all prerogatives? I know none more dangerous; nor any one more necessary to be so trusted. I do not say that this prerogative ought to be trusted to your king, unless he enjoyed other auxiliary trusts along with it, which he does not now hold. But, if he did possess them, hazardous as they are undoubtedly, advantages would arise from such a constitution, more than compensating the risk. There is no other way of keeping the several potentates of Europe from intriguing distinctly and personally with the members of your Assembly, from intermeddling in all your concerns, and fomenting, in the heart of your country, the most pernicious of all factions; factions in the interest and under the direction of foreign powers. From that worst of evils, thank God, we are still free. Your skill, if you had any, would be well employed to find out indirect correctives and controls upon this perilous trust. If you did not like those which in England we have chosen, your leaders might have exerted their abilities in contriving better. If it were necessary to exemplify the consequences of such an executive government as yours, in the management of great affairs, I should refer you to the late reports of M. de Montmorin[162] to the National Assembly, and all the other proceedings relative to the

* In reality three, to reckon the provincial republican establishments.

differences between Great Britain and Spain. It would be treating your understanding with disrespect to point them out to you.

I hear that the persons who are called ministers have signified an intention of resigning their places. I am rather astonished that they have not resigned long since. For the universe I would not have stood in the situation in which they have been for this last twelve-month. They wished well, I take it for granted, to the Revolution. Let this fact be as it may, they could not, placed as they were upon an eminence, though an eminence of humiliation, but be the first to see collectively, and to feel each in his own department, the evils which have been produced by that revolution. In every step which they took, or forbore to take, they must have felt the degraded situation of their country, and their utter incapacity of serving it. They are in a species of subordinate servitude, in which no men before them were ever seen. Without confidence from their sovereign, on whom they were forced, or from the Assembly who forced them upon him, all the noble functions of their office are executed by committees of the Assembly, without any regard whatsoever to their personal or their official authority. They are to execute, without power; they are to be responsible, without discretion; they are to deliberate, without choice. In their puzzled situation, under two sovereigns, over neither of whom they have any influence, they must act in such a manner as (in effect, whatever they may intend) sometimes to betray the one, sometimes the other, and always to betray themselves. Such has been their situation; such must be the situation of those who succeed them. I have much respect, and many good wishes, for M. Necker. I am obliged to him for attentions. I thought when his enemies had driven him from Versailles, that his exile was a subject of most serious congratulation – *sed multæ urbes et publica vota vicerunt.*[163] He is now sitting on the ruins of the finances, and of the monarchy of France.

A great deal more might be observed on the strange constitution of the executory part of the new government, but fatigue must give bounds to the discussion of subjects, which in themselves have hardly any limits.

As little genius and talent am I able to perceive in the plan of judicature formed by the National Assembly. According to their invariable course, the framers of your constitution have begun with the utter abolition of the parliaments. These venerable bodies, like the rest of the old government, stood in need of reform, even though there could be no change made in the monarchy. They required several more alterations to adapt them to the system of a free constitution. But they had particulars in their constitution, and those not a few which deserved approbation from the wise. They possessed one fundamental excellence; they were independent. The most doubtful circumstance attendant on their office, that of its being vendible, contributed however to this independency of character. They held for life. Indeed they may be said to have held by inheritance. Appointed by the monarch, they were considered as nearly out of his power. The most determined exertions of that authority against them only showed their radical independence. They composed permanent bodies politic, constituted to resist arbitrary innovation; and from that corporate constitution, and from most of their forms, they were well calculated to afford both certainty and stability to the laws. They had been a safe asylum to secure these laws, in all the revolutions of humour and opinion. They had saved that sacred deposit of the country during the reigns of arbitrary princes, and the struggles of arbitrary factions. They kept alive the memory and record of the constitution. They were the great security to private property; which might be said (when personal liberty had no existence) to be, in fact, as well guarded in France as in any other country. Whatever is supreme in a state, ought to have, as much as possible, its judicial authority so constituted as not only not to depend upon it, but in some sort to balance it. It ought to give a security to its justice against its power. It ought to make its judicature, as it were, something exterior to the state.

These parliaments had furnished, not the best certainly, but some considerable corrective to the excesses and vices of the monarchy. Such an independent judicature was ten times more necessary when a democracy became the absolute power of the country. In that constitution, elective, temporary, local judges, such as you have contrived, exercising their dependent functions in a narrow society, must be the worst of all tribunals. In them it will be vain to look for any appearance of justice towards strangers, towards the obnoxious rich, towards the minority of routed parties, towards all those who in the election have supported unsuccessful candidates. It will be impossible to keep the new tribunals clear of the worst spirit of faction. All contrivances by ballot we know experimentally to be vain and childish to prevent a discovery of inclinations. Where they may the best answer the purposes of concealment, they answer to produce suspicion, and this is a still more mischievous cause of partiality.

If the parliaments had been preserved, instead of being dissolved at so ruinous a change to the nation, they might have served in this new commonwealth, perhaps not precisely the same, (I do not mean an exact parallel,) but nearly the same, purposes as the court and senate of Areopagus[164] did in Athens; that is, as one of the balances and correctives to the evils of a light and unjust democracy. Every one knows that this tribunal was the great stay of that state; every one knows with what care it was upheld, and with what a religious awe it was consecrated. The parliaments were not wholly free from faction, I admit; but this evil was exterior and accidental, and not so much the vice of their constitution itself, as it must be in your new contrivance of sexennial elective judicatories. Several English commend the abolition of the old tribunals, as supposing that they determined everything by bribery and corruption. But they have stood the test of monarchic and republican scrutiny. The court was well disposed to prove corruption on those bodies when they were dissolved in 1771. – Those who have again dissolved them would have done the same if they could – but both inquisitions having failed, I conclude, that gross pecuniary corruption must have been rather rare amongst them.

It would have been prudent, along with the parliaments, to preserve their ancient power of registering, and of remonstrating at least, upon all the decrees of the National Assembly, as they did upon those which passed in the time of the monarchy. It would be a means of squaring the occasional decrees of a democracy to some principles of general jurisprudence. The vice of the ancient democracies, and one cause of their ruin, was, that they ruled, as you do, by occasional decrees, *psephismata*.[165] This practice soon broke in upon the tenour and consistency of the laws; it abated the respect of the people towards them; and totally destroyed them in the end.

Your vesting the power of remonstrance, which, in the time of the monarchy, existed in the parliament of Paris, in your principal executive officer, whom, in spite of common sense, you persevere in calling king, is the height of absurdity. You ought never to suffer remonstrance from him who is to execute. This is to understand neither council nor execution; neither authority nor obedience. The person whom you call king, ought not to have this power, or he ought to have more.

Your present arrangement is strictly judicial. Instead of imitating your monarchy, and seating your judges on a bench of independence, your object is to reduce them to the most blind obedience. As you have changed all things, you have invented new principles of order. You first appoint judges, who, I suppose, are to determine according to law, and then you let them know, that, at some time or other, you intend to give them some law by which they are to determine. Any studies which they have made (if any they have made) are to be useless to them. But to supply these studies, they are to be sworn to obey all the rules, orders, and instructions which from time to time they are to receive from the National Assembly. These if they submit to, they leave no ground of law to the subject. They become complete and most dangerous instruments in the hands of the governing power, which, in the midst of a cause, or on the prospect of it, may wholly change the rule of decision. If these orders of the National Assembly come to be contrary to the will of the people, who locally choose those judges, such confusion must happen as is terrible to think of. For the judges owe their places to the local authority; and the commands they are sworn to obey come from those who have no share in their appointment. In the mean time they have the example of the court of *Chatelet*[166] to encourage and guide them in the exercise of their functions. That court is to try criminals sent to it by the National Assembly, or brought before it by other courses of delation. They sit under a guard to save their own lives. They know not by what law they judge, nor under what authority they act, nor by what tenure they hold. It is thought that they are sometimes obliged to condemn at peril of their lives. This is not perhaps certain, nor can it be ascertained; but when they acquit, we know they have seen the persons whom they discharge, with perfect impunity to the actors, hanged at the door of their court.

The Assembly indeed promises that they will form a body of law, which shall be short, simple, clear, and so forth. That is, by their short laws, they will leave much to the discretion of the judge; whilst they have exploded the authority of all the learning which could make judicial discretion (a thing perilous at best) deserving the appellation of a *sound* discretion.

It is curious to observe, that the administrative bodies are carefully exempted from the jurisdiction of these new tribunals.

That is, those persons are exempted from the power of the laws, who ought to be the most entirely submitted to them. Those who execute public pecuniary trusts, ought of all men to be the most strictly held to their duty. One would have thought that it must have been among your earliest cares, if you did not mean that those administrative bodies should be real, sovereign, independent states, to form an awful tribunal, like your late parliaments, or like our king's bench, where all corporate officers might obtain protection in the legal exercise of their functions, and would find coercion if they trespassed against their legal duty. But the cause of the exemption is plain. These administrative bodies are the great instruments of the present leaders in their progress through democracy to oligarchy. They must therefore be put above the law. It will be said, that the legal tribunals which you have made are unfit to coerce them. They are undoubtedly. They are unfit for any rational purpose. It will be said too, that the administrative bodies will be accountable to the general assembly. This I fear is talking without much consideration of the nature of that assembly, or of these corporations. However, to be subject to the pleasure of that assembly, is not to be subject to law either for protection or for constraint.

This establishment of judges as yet wants something to its completion. It is to be crowned by a new tribunal. This is to be a grand state judicature; and it is to judge of crimes committed against the nation, that is, against the power of the Assembly. It seems as if they had something in their view of the nature of the high court of justice erected in England during the time of the great usurpation. As they have not yet finished this part of the scheme, it is impossible to form a right judgment upon it. However, if great care is not taken to form it in a spirit very different from that which has guided them in their proceedings relative to state offences, this tribunal, subservient to their inquisition, *the committee of research,*[167] will extinguish the last sparks of liberty in France, and settle the most dreadful and arbitrary tyranny ever known in any nation. If they wish to give to this tribunal any appearance of liberty and justice, they must not evoke from or send to it the causes relative to their own members, at their pleasure. They must also remove the seat of that tribunal out of the republic of Paris.*

---

* For further elucidations upon the subject of all these judicatures, and of the committee of research, see M. de Calonne's work.

Has more wisdom been displayed in the constitution of your army than what is discoverable in your plan of judicature? The able arrangement of this part is the more difficult, and requires the greater skill and attention, not only as a great concern in itself, but as it is the third cementing principle in the new body of republics, which you call the French nation. Truly it is not easy to divine what that army may become at last. You have voted a very large one, and on good appointments, at least fully equal to your apparent means of payment. But what is the principle of its discipline? or whom is it to obey? You have got the wolf by the ears, and I wish you joy of the happy position in which you have chosen to place yourselves, and in which you are well circumstanced for a free deliberation, relatively to that army, or to anything else.

The minister and secretary of state for the war department is M. de la Tour du Pin.[168] This gentleman, like his colleagues in administration, is a most zealous assertor of the Revolution, and a sanguine admirer of the new constitution, which originated in that event. His statement of facts, relative to the military of France, is important, not only from his official and personal authority, but because it displays very clearly the actual condition of the army in France, and because it throws light on the principles upon which the Assembly proceeds, in the administration of this critical object. It may enable us to form some judgment, how far it may be expedient in this country to imitate the martial policy of France.

M. de la Tour du Pin, on the fourth of last June, comes to give an account of the state of his department, as it exists under the auspices of the National Assembly. No man knows it so well; no man can express it better. Addressing himself to the National Assembly, he says, "His Majesty has *this day* sent me to apprise you of the multiplied disorders of which *every day* he receives the most distressing intelligence. The army (le corps militaire) threatens to fall into the most turbulent anarchy. Entire regiments have dared to violate at once the respect due to the laws, to the king, to the order established by your decrees, and to the oaths which they have taken with the most awful solemnity. Compelled by my duty to give you information of these excesses, my heart bleeds when I consider who they are that have committed them. Those, against whom it is not in my power to withhold the most grievous complaints, are a part of that very soldiery which to this day have been so full of honour and loyalty, and with whom, for fifty years, I have lived the comrade and the friend.

"What incomprehensible spirit of delirium and delusion has all at once led them astray? Whilst you are indefatigable in establishing uniformity in the empire, and moulding the whole into one coherent and consistent body; whilst the French are taught by you, at once the respect which the laws owe to the rights of man, and that which the citizens owe to the laws, the administration of the army presents nothing but disturbance and confusion. I see in more than one corps the bonds of discipline relaxed or broken; the most unheard-of pretensions avowed directly and without any disguise; the ordinances without force; the chiefs without authority; the military chest and the colours carried off; the authority of the king himself [*risum teneatis?*][169] proudly defied; the officers despised, degraded, threatened, driven away, and some of them prisoners in the midst of their corps, dragging on a precarious life in the bosom of disgust and humiliation. To fill up the measure of all these horrors, the commandants of places have had their throats cut, under the eyes, and almost in the arms, of their own soldiers.

"These evils are great; but they are not the worst consequences which may be produced by such military insurrection. Sooner or later they may menace the nation itself. *The nature of things requires* that the army should never act but as *an instrument*. The moment that, erecting itself into a deliberative body, it shall act according to its own resolutions, the *government, be it what it may, will immediately degenerate into a military democracy*; a species of political monster, which has always ended by devouring those who have produced it.

"After all this, who must not be alarmed at the irregular consultations, and turbulent committees, formed in some regiments by the common soldiers and non-commissioned officers, without the knowledge, or even in contempt of the authority, of their superiors; although the presence and concurrence of those superiors could give no authority to such monstrous democratic assemblies [comices]."

It is not necessary to add much to this finished picture: finished as far as its canvass admits; but as I apprehend, not taking in the whole of the nature and complexity of the disorders of this military democracy, which, the minister at war truly and wisely observes, wherever it exists, must be the true constitution of the state, by whatever formal appellation it may pass. For, though he informs the Assembly that the more considerable part of the army have not cast off their obedience, but are still attached to their duty, yet those travellers, who have seen the corps whose conduct is the best, rather observe in them the absence of mutiny, than the existence of discipline.

I cannot help pausing here for a moment, to reflect upon the expressions of surprise which this minister has let fall, relative to the excesses he relates. To him the departure of the troops from their ancient principles of loyalty and honour seems quite inconceivable. Surely those to whom he addresses himself know the causes of it but too well. They know the doctrines which they have preached, the degrees which they have passed, the practices which they have countenanced. The soldiers remember the 6th of October. They recollect the French guards. They have not forgotten the taking of the king's castles in Paris and Marseilles. That the governors in both places were murdered with impunity, is a fact that has not passed out of their minds. They do not abandon the principles laid down so ostentatiously and laboriously of the equality of men. They cannot shut their eyes to the degradation of the whole noblesse of France, and the suppression of the very idea of a gentleman. The total abolition of titles and distinctions is not lost upon them. But M. de la Tour du Pin is astonished at their disloyalty, when the doctors of the Assembly have taught them at the same time the respect due to laws. It is easy to judge which of the two sorts of lessons men with arms in their hands are likely to learn. As to the authority of the king, we may collect from the minister himself (if any argument on that head were not quite superfluous) that it is not of more consideration with these troops, than it is with everybody else. "The king," says he, "has over and over again repeated his orders to put a stop to these excesses: but, in so terrible a crisis, *your* [the Assembly's] concurrence is become indispensably necessary to prevent the evils which menace the state. You unite to the force of the legislative power, *that of opinion* still more important." To be sure the army can have no opinion of the power or authority of the king. Perhaps the soldier has by this time learned, that the Assembly itself does not enjoy a much greater degree of liberty than that royal figure.

It is now to be seen what has been proposed in this exigency, one of the greatest that can happen in a state. The minister requests the Assembly to array itself in all its terrors, and to call forth all its majesty. He desires that the grave and severe principles announced by them may give vigour to the king's proclamation. After this we should have looked for courts civil and martial; breaking of some corps, decimating of others, and all the terrible means which necessity has employed in such cases to arrest the progress of the most terrible of all evils; particularly, one might expect, that a serious inquiry would be made into the murder of commandants in the view of their soldiers. Not one word of all this, or of anything like it. After they had been told that the soldiery trampled upon the decrees of the Assembly promulgated by the king, the Assembly pass new decrees; and they authorise the king to make new proclamations. After the secretary at war had stated that the regiments had paid no regard to oaths *prêtés avec la plus imposante solemnité*[170] – they propose – what? More oaths. They renew decrees and proclamations as they experience their insufficiency, and they multiply oaths in proportion as they weaken, in the minds of men, the sanctions of religion. I hope that handy abridgments of the excellent sermons of Voltaire, d'Alembert, Diderot, and Helvetius, on the Immortality of the Soul, on a particular superintending Providence, and on a Future State of Rewards and Punishments, are sent down to the soldiers along with their civic oaths. Of this I have no doubt; as I understand that a certain description of reading makes no inconsiderable part of their military exercises, and that they are full as well supplied with the ammunition of pamphlets as of cartridges.

To prevent the mischiefs arising from conspiracies, irregular consultations, seditious committees, and monstrous democratic assemblies ["comitia, comices"][171] of the soldiers, and all the disorders arising from idleness, luxury, dissipation, and insubordination, I believe the most astonishing means have been used that ever occurred to men, even in all the inventions of this prolific age. It is no less than this: – The king has promulgated in circular letters to all the regiments his direct authority and encouragement, that the several corps should join themselves with the clubs and confederations in the several municipalities, and mix with them in their feasts and civic entertainments! This jolly discipline, it seems, is to soften the ferocity of their minds; to reconcile them to their bottle companions of other descriptions,

and to merge particular conspiracies in more general associations.* That this remedy would be pleasing to the soldiers, as
they are described by M. de la Tour du Pin, I can readily believe;
and that, however mutinous otherwise, they will dutifully submit themselves to *these* royal proclamations. But I should question whether all this civic swearing, clubbing, and feasting,
would dispose them, more than at present they are disposed, to
an obedience to their officers; or teach them better to submit
to the austere rules of military discipline. It will make them
admirable citizens after the French mode, but not quite so good
soldiers after any mode. A doubt might well arise, whether the
conversations at these good tables would fit them a great deal
the better for the character of *mere instruments*, which this veteran
officer and statesman justly observes the nature of things always
requires an army to be.

Concerning the likelihood of this improvement in discipline,
by the free conversation of the soldiers with municipal festive
societies, which is thus officially encouraged by royal authority
and sanction, we may judge by the state of the municipalities
themselves, furnished to us by the war minister in this very
speech. He conceives good hopes of the success of his endeavours towards restoring order *for the present* from the good disposition of certain regiments; but he finds something cloudy
with regard to the future. As to preventing the return of confusion, "for this, the administration (says he) cannot be answerable
to you, as long as they see the municipalities arrogate to themselves an authority over the troops, which your institutions have
reserved wholly to the monarch. You have fixed the limits of
the military authority and the municipal authority. You have
bounded the action, which you have permitted to the latter
over the former, to the right of requisition; but never did the
letter or the spirit of your decrees authorise the commons in
these municipalities to break the officers, to try them, to give
orders to the soldiers, to drive them from the posts committed
to their guard, to stop them in their marches ordered by the

* Comme sa majesté y a reconnu, non une système d'associations particulières, mais
une réunion de volontés de tous les François pour la liberté et la prospérité communes, ainsi pour le maintien de l'ordre publique; il a pensé qu'il convenoit que
chaque régiment prit part à ces fêtes civiques pour multiplier les rapports et referrer
les liens d'union entre les citoyens et les troupes. – Lest I should not be credited,
I insert the words, authorising the troops to feast with the popular confederacies.[172]

king, or, in a word, to enslave the troops to the caprice of each of the cities, or even market towns, through which they are to pass."

Such is the character and disposition of the municipal society which is to reclaim the soldiery, to bring them back to the true principles of military subordination, and to render them machines in the hands of the supreme power of the country! Such are the distempers of the French troops! Such is their cure! As the army is, so is the navy. The municipalities supersede the orders of the Assembly, and the seamen in their turn supersede the orders of the municipalities. From my heart I pity the condition of a respectable servant of the public, like this war minister, obliged in his old age to pledge the Assembly in their civic cups, and to enter with a hoary head into all the fantastic vagaries of these juvenile politicians. Such schemes are not like propositions coming from a man of fifty years' wear and tear amongst mankind. They seem rather such as ought to be expected from those grand compounders in politics, who shorten the road to their degrees in the state; and have a certain inward fanatical assurance and illumination upon all subjects; upon the credit of which one of their doctors has thought fit, with great applause, and greater success, to caution the Assembly not to attend to old men, or to any persons who valued themselves upon their experience. I suppose all the ministers of state must qualify, and take this test; wholly abjuring the errors and heresies of experience and observation. Every man has his own relish. But I think if I could not attain to the wisdom, I would at least preserve something of the stiff and peremptory dignity of age. These gentlemen deal in regeneration: but at any price I should hardly yield my rigid fibres to be regenerated by them; nor begin, in my grand climacteric, to squall in their new accents, or to stammer, in my second cradle, the elemental sounds of their barbarous metaphysics.* *Si isti mihi largiantur ut repueriscam, et in eorum cunis vagiam, valde recusem!*[173]

The imbecility of any part of the puerile and pedantic system, which they call a constitution, cannot be laid open without discovering the utter insufficiency and mischief of every other part with which it comes in contact, or that bears any the remotest relation to it. You cannot propose a remedy for the incompetence

* This war minister has since quitted the school, and resigned his office.

of the crown, without displaying the debility of the Assembly. You cannot deliberate on the confusion of the army of the state, without disclosing the worse disorders of the armed municipalities. The military lays open the civil, and the civil betrays the military, anarchy. I wish everybody carefully to peruse the eloquent speech (such it is) of Mons. de la Tour du Pin. He attributes the salvation of the municipalities to the good behaviour of some of the troops. These troops are to preserve the well-disposed part of those municipalities, which is confessed to be the weakest, from the pillage of the worst disposed, which is the strongest. But the municipalities affect a sovereignty, and will command those troops which are necessary for their protection. Indeed they must command them or court them. The municipalities, by the necessity of their situation, and by the republican powers they have obtained, must, with relation to the military, be the masters, or the servants, or the confederates, or each successively; or they must make a jumble of all together, according to circumstances. What government is there to coerce the army but the municipality, or the municipality but the army? To preserve concord where authority is extinguished, at the hazard of all consequences, the Assembly attempts to cure the distempers by the distempers themselves; and they hope to preserve themselves from a purely military democracy, by giving it a debauched interest in the municipal.

If the soldiers once come to mix for any time in the municipal clubs, cabals, and confederacies, an elective attraction will draw them to the lowest and most desperate part. With them will be their habits, affections, and sympathies. The military conspiracies, which are to be remedied by civic confederacies; the rebellious municipalities, which are to be rendered obedient by furnishing them with the means of seducing the very armies of the state that are to keep them in order; all these chimeras of a monstrous and portentous policy must aggravate the confusion from which they have arisen. There must be blood. The want of common judgment manifested in the construction of all their descriptions of forces, and in all their kinds of civil and judicial authorities, will make it flow. Disorders may be quieted in one time and in one part. They will break out in others; because the evil is radical and intrinsic. All these schemes of mixing mutinous soldiers with seditious citizens must weaken still more and more the military connexion of soldiers with their officers, as well as add military and mutinous audacity to turbulent artificers and peasants. To secure a real army, the officer should be first and last in the eye of the soldier; first and last in his attention, observance, and esteem. Officers it seems there are to be, whose chief qualification must be temper and patience. They are to manage their troops by electioneering arts. They must bear themselves as candidates, not as commanders. But as by such means power may be occasionally in their hands, the authority by which they are to be nominated becomes of high importance.

What you may do finally does not appear; nor is it of much moment, whilst the strange and contradictory relation between your army and all the parts of your republic, a well as the puzzled relation of those parts to each other and to the whole, remain as they are. You seem to have given the provisional nomination of the officers, in the first instance, to the king, with a reserve of approbation by the National Assembly. Men who have an interest to pursue are extremely sagacious in discovering the true seat of power. They must soon perceive that those, who can negative indefinitely, in reality appoint. The officers must therefore look to their intrigues in that Assembly, as the sole, certain road to promotion. Still, however, by your new constitution they must begin their solicitation at court. This double negotiation for military rank seems to me a contrivance as well adapted, as if it were studied for no other end, to promote faction in the Assembly itself, relative to this vast military patronage; and then to poison the corps of officers with factions of a nature still more dangerous to the safety of government, upon any bottom on which it can be placed, and destructive in the end to the efficiency of the army itself. Those officers, who lose the promotions intended for them by the crown, must become of a faction opposite to that of the Assembly which has rejected their claims, and must nourish discontents in the heart of the army against the ruling powers. Those officers, on the other hand, who, by carrying their point through an interest in the Assembly, feel themselves to be at best only second in the good-will of the crown, though first in that of the Assembly, must slight an authority which would not advance and could not retard their promotion. If to avoid these evils you will have no other rule for command or promotion than seniority, you will have an army of formality; at the same time it will become more independent, and more of a military republic. Not they, but the king is the

machine. A king is not to be deposed by halves. If he is not everything in the command of an army, he is nothing. What is the
effect of a power placed nominally at the head of the army, who
to that army is no object of gratitude, or of fear? Such a cipher is
not fit for the administration of an object, of all things the most
delicate, the supreme command of military men. They must be
constrained (and their inclinations lead them to what their
necessities require) by a real, vigorous, effective, decided, personal authority. The authority of the Assembly itself suffers by
passing through such a debilitating channel as they have chosen.
The army will not long look to an assembly acting through the
organ of false show, and palpable imposition. They will not
seriously yield obedience to a prisoner. They will either despise
a pageant, or they will pity a captive king. This relation of your
army to the crown will, if I am not greatly mistaken, become a
serious dilemma in your politics.

It is besides to be considered, whether an assembly like yours,
even supposing that it was in possesson of another sort of organ
through which its orders were to pass, is fit for promoting the
obedience and discipline of an army. It is known, that armies
have hitherto yielded a very precarious and uncertain obedience
to any senate, or popular authority; and they will least of all yield
it to an assembly which is only to have a continuance of two
years. The officers must totally lose the characteristic disposition
of military men, if they see with perfect submission and due
admiration, the dominion of pleaders; especially when they find
that they have a new court to pay to an endless succession of those
pleaders; whose military policy, and the genius of whose command, (if they should have any,) must be as uncertain as their
duration is transient. In the weakness of one kind of authority,
and in the fluctuation of all, the officers of an army will remain
for some time mutinous and full of faction, until some popular
general, who understands the art of conciliating the soldiery, and
who possesses the true spirit of command, shall draw the eyes
of all men upon himself. Armies will obey him on his personal
account. There is no other way of securing military obedience
in this state of things. But the moment in which that event shall
happen, the person who really commands the army is your
master; the master (that is little) of your king, the master of your
Assembly, the master of your whole republic.[174]

How came the Assembly by their present power over the

army? Chiefly, to be sure, by debauching the soldiers from their officers. They have begun by a most terrible operation. They have touched the central point, about which the particles that compose armies are at repose. They have destroyed the principle of obedience in the great, essential, critical link between the officer and the soldier, just where the chain of military sub-ordination commences and on which the whole of that system depends. The soldier is told he is a citizen, and has the rights of man and citizen. The right of a man, he is told, is to be his own governor, and to be ruled only by those to whom he delegates that self-government. It is very natural he should think that he ought most of all to have his choice where he is to yield the great-est degree of obedience. He will therefore, in all probability, systematically do, what he does at present occasionally; that is, he will exercise at least a negative in the choice of his officers. At present the officers are known at best to be only permissive, and on their good behaviour. In fact, there have been many instances in which they have been cashiered by their corps. Here is a second negative on the choice of the king; a negative as effectual at least as the other of the Assembly. The soldiers know already that it has been a question, not ill received in the National Assembly, whether they ought not to have the direct choice of their officers, or some proportion of them? When such matters are in deliberation it is no extravagant supposition that they will incline to the opinion most favourable to their pretensions. They will not bear to be deemed the army of an imprisoned king, whilst another army in the same country, with whom too they are to feast and confederate, is to be considered as the free army of a free constitution. They will cast their eyes on the other and more permanent army; I mean the municipal. That corps, they well know, does actually elect its own officers. They may not be able to discern the grounds of distinction on which they are not to elect a Marquis de la Fayette[175] (or what is his new name?) of their own. If this election of a commander-in-chief be a part of the rights of men, why not of theirs? They see elective justices of peace, elective judges, elective curates, elective bishops, elec-tive municipalities, and elective commanders of the Parisian army. – Why should they alone be excluded? Are the brave troops of France the only men in that nation who are not the fit judges of military merit, and of the qualifications necessary for a commander-in-chief? Are they paid by the state, and do they therefore lose the rights of men? They are a part of that nation themselves, and contribute to that pay. And is not the king, is not the National Assembly, and are not all who elect the National Assembly, likewise paid? Instead of seeing all these forfeit their rights by their receiving a salary, they perceive that in all these cases a salary is given for the exercise of those rights. All your resolutions, all your proceedings, all your debates, all the works of your doctors in religion and politics, have industriously been put into their hands; and you expect that they will apply to their own case just as much of your doctrines and examples as suits your pleasure.

Everything depends upon the army in such a government as yours; for you have industriously destroyed all the opinions, and prejudices, and, as far as in you lay, all the instincts which support government. Therefore the moment any difference arises between your National Assembly and any part of the nation, you must have recourse to force. Nothing else is left to you; or rather you have left nothing else to yourselves. You see, by the report of your war minister, that the distribution of the army is in a great measure made with a view of internal coercion.* You must rule by an army; and you have infused into that army by which you rule, as well as into the whole body of the nation, principles which after a time must disable you in the use you resolve to make of it. The king is to call out troops to act against his people, when the world has been told, and the assertion is still ringing in our ears, that troops ought not to fire on citizens. The colonies assert to themselves an independent constitution and a free trade. They must be constrained by troops. In what chapter of your code of the rights of men are they able to read, that it is a part of the rights of men to have their commerce monopolised and restrained for the benefit of others? As the colonists rise on you,[176] the negroes rise on them. Troops again – Massacre, torture, hanging! These are your rights of men! These are the fruits of metaphysic declarations wantonly made, and shamefully retracted! It was but the other day, that the farmers of land in one of your provinces refused to pay some sorts of rents to the lord of the soil. In consequence of this, you decree, that the country people shall pay all rents and dues, except those which as grievances you have abolished; and if they refuse, then you order the king to march

* Courier François, 30th July, 1790. Assemblée Nationale, Numero 210.

troops against them.[177] You lay down metaphysic propositions which infer universal consequences, and then you attempt to limit logic by despotism. The leaders of the present system tell them of their rights, as men, to take fortresses, to murder guards, to seize on kings without the least appearance of authority even from the Assembly, whilst, as the sovereign legislative body, that Assembly was sitting in the name of the nation – and yet these leaders presume to order out the troops which have acted in these very disorders, to coerce those who shall judge on the principles, and follow the examples, which have been guaranteed by their own approbation.

The leaders teach the people to abhor and reject all feudality as the barbarism of tyranny, and they tell them afterwards how much of that barbarous tyranny they are to bear with patience. As they are prodigal of light with regard to grievances, so the people find them sparing in the extreme with regard to redress. They know that not only certain quit-rents and personal duties, which you have permitted them to redeem, (but have furnished no money for the redemption,) are as nothing to those burthens for which you have made no provision at all. They know, that almost the whole system of landed property in its origin is feudal; that it is the distribution of the possessions of the original proprietors, made by a barbarous conqueror to his barbarous instruments; and that the most grievous effects of the conquest are the land rents of every kind, as without question they are.

The peasants, in all probability, are the descendants of these ancient proprietors, Romans or Gauls. But if they fail, in any degree, in the titles which they make on the principles of anti-quaries and lawyers, they retreat into the citadel of the rights of men. There they find that men are equal; and the earth, the kind and equal mother of all, ought not to be monopolised to foster the pride and luxury of any men, who by nature are no better than themselves, and who, if they do not labour for their bread, are worse. They find, that by the laws of nature the occupant and subduer of the soil is the true proprietor; that there is no prescription against nature; and that the agreements (where any there are) which have been made with the landlords, during the time of slavery, are only the effect of duresse and force; and that when the people re-entered into the rights of men, those agreements were made as void, as everything else which had been settled under the prevalence of the old feudal and aristocratic tyranny. They will tell you that they see no difference between an idler with a hat and a national cockade, and an idler in a cowl, or in a rochet.[178] If you ground the title to rents on succession and prescription, they tell you from the speech of M. *Camus*, published by the National Assembly for their information, that things ill begun cannot avail themselves of prescription; that the title of these lords was vicious in its origin; and that force is at least as bad as fraud. As to the title by succession, they will tell you, that the succession of those who have cultivated the soil is the true pedigree of property, and not rotten parchments and silly substitutions; that the lords have enjoyed their usurpation too long; and that if they allow to these lay monks any charitable pension, they ought to be thankful to the bounty of the true proprietor, who is so generous towards a false claimant to his goods.

When the peasants give you back that coin of sophistic reason, on which you have set your image and superscription, you cry it down as base money, and tell them you will pay for the future with French guards, and dragoons, and hussars. You hold up, to chastise them, the second-hand authority of a king, who is only the instrument of destroying, without any power of protecting either the people or his own person. Through him it seems you will make yourselves obeyed. They answer, You have taught us that there are no gentlemen; and which of your principles teach us to bow to kings whom we have not elected? We know, without your teaching, that lands were given for the support of feudal dignities, feudal titles, and feudal offices. When you took down the cause as a grievance, why should the more grievous effect remain? As there are now no hereditary honours, and no distinguished families, why are we taxed to maintain what you tell us ought not to exist? You have sent down our old aristocratic landlords in no other character, and with no other title, but that of exactors under your authority. Have you endeavoured to make these your rent-gatherers respectable to us? No. You have sent them to us with their arms reversed, their shields broken, their impresses defaced; and so displumed, degraded, and metamorphosed, such unfeathered two-legged things, that we no longer know them. They are strangers to us. They do not even go by the names of our ancient lords. Physically they may be the same men; though we are not quite sure of that, on your new philosophic doctrines of personal identity. In all other respects they are totally changed. We do not see why we have not as good a right to refuse them their rents as you have to abrogate all their honours, titles, and distinctions. This we have never commissioned you to do; and it is one instance, among many indeed, of your assumption of undelegated power. We see the burghers of Paris, through their clubs, their mobs, and their national guards, directing you at their pleasure, and giving that as law to you, which, under your authority, is transmitted as law to us. Through you, these burghers dispose of the lives and fortunes of us all. Why should not you attend as much to the desires of the laborious husbandman with regard to our rent, by which we are affected in the most serious manner, as you do to the demands of these insolent burghers, relative to distinctions and titles of honour, by which neither they nor we are affected at all? But we find you pay more regard to their fancies than to our necessities. Is it among the rights of man to pay tribute to his equals? Before this measure of yours, we might have thought we were not perfectly equal. We might have entertained some old, habitual, unmeaning prepossession in favour of those landlords; but we cannot conceive with what other view than that of destroying all respect to them, you could have made the law that degrades them. You have forbidden us to treat them with any of the old formalities of respect, and now you send troops to sabre and to bayonet us into a submission to fear and force, which you did not suffer us to yield to the mild authority of opinion.

The ground of some of these arguments is horrid and ridiculous to all rational ears; but to the politicians of metaphysics who have opened schools for sophistry, and made establishments for anarchy, it is solid and conclusive. It is obvious, that on a mere consideration of the right, the leaders in the Assembly would not in the least have scrupled to abrogate the rents along with the titles and family ensigns. It would be only to follow up the principle of their reasonings, and to complete the analogy of their conduct. But they had newly possessed themselves of a great body of landed property by confiscation. They had this commodity at market; and the market would have been wholly destroyed, if they were to permit the husbandmen to riot in the speculations with which they so freely intoxicated themselves. The only security which property enjoys in any one of its descriptions, is from the interests of their rapacity with regard to some other. They have left nothing but their own arbitrary pleasure to determine what property is to be protected and what subverted.

Neither have they left any principle by which any of their municipalities can be bound to obedience; or even conscientiously obliged not to separate from the whole to become independent, or to connect itself with some other state. The people of Lyons, it seems, have refused lately to pay taxes. Why should they not? What lawful authority is there left to exact them? The king imposed some of them. The old states, methodised by orders, settled the more ancient. They may say to the Assembly, Who are you, that are not our kings, nor the states we have elected, nor sit on the principles on which we have elected you? And who are we, that when we see the gabelles,[179] which you have ordered to be paid, wholly shaken off, when we see the act of disobedience afterwards ratified by yourselves, who are we, that we are not to judge what taxes we ought or ought not to pay, and who are not to avail ourselves of the same powers, the validity of which you have approved in others? To this the answer is, We will send troops. The last reason of kings is always the first with your Assembly. This military aid may serve for a time, whilst the impression of the increase of pay remains, and the vanity of being umpires in all disputes is flattered. But this weapon will snap short, unfaithful to the hand that employs it. The Assembly keep a school, where, systematically, and with unremitting perseverance, they teach principles, and form regulations, destructive to all spirit of subordination, civil and military – and then they expect that they shall hold in obedience an anarchic people by an anarchic army.

The municipal army which, according to their new policy, is to balance this national army, if considered in itself only, is of a constitution much more simple, and in every respect less exceptionable. It is a mere democratic body, unconnected with the crown or the kingdom; armed, and trained, and officered at the pleasure of the districts to which the corps severally belong; and the personal service of the individuals, who compose, or the fine in lieu of personal service, are directed by the same authority.*

* I see by M. Necker's account, that the national guards of Paris have received, over and above the money levied within their own city, about £145,000 sterling out of the public treasure. Whether this be an actual payment for the nine months of their existence, or an estimate of their yearly charge, I do not clearly perceive. It is of no great importance, as certainly they may take whatever they please.

Nothing is more uniform. If, however, considered in any relation to the crown, to the National Assembly, to the public tribunals, or to the other army, or considered in a view to any coherence or connexion between its parts, it seems a monster, and can hardly fail to terminate its perplexed movements in some great national calamity. It is a worse preservative of a general constitution, than the systasis of Crete, or the confederation of Poland,[180] or any other ill-devised corrective which has yet been imagined, in the necessities produced by an ill-constructed system of government.

Having concluded my few remarks on the constitution of the supreme power, the executive, the judicature, the military, and on the reciprocal relation of all these establishments, I shall say something of the ability showed by your legislators with regard to the revenue.

In their proceedings relative to this object, if possible, still fewer traces appear of political judgment or financial resource. When the states met, it seemed to be the great object to improve the system of revenue, to enlarge its collection, to cleanse it of oppression and vexation, and to establish it on the most solid footing. Great were the expectations entertained on that head throughout Europe. It was by this grand arrangement that France was to stand or fall; and this became, in my opinion, very properly, the test by which the skill and patriotism of those who ruled in that Assembly would be tried. The revenue of the state is the state. In effect all depends upon it, whether for support or for reformation. The dignity of every occupation wholly depends upon the quantity and the kind of virtue that may be exerted in it. As all great qualities of the mind which operate in public, and are not merely suffering and passive, require force for their display, I had almost said for their unequivocal existence, the revenue, which is the spring of all power, becomes in its administration the sphere of every active virtue. Public virtue, being of a nature magnificent and splendid, instituted for great things, and conversant about great concerns, requires abundant scope and room, and cannot spread and grow under confinement, and in circumstances straitened, narrow, and sordid. Through the revenue alone the body politic can act in its true genius and character, and therefore it will display just as much of its collective virtue, and as much of that virtue which may characterise those who move it, and are, as it were, its life and guiding principle, as it is possessed of a just revenue. For from hence not only magnanimity, and liberality, and beneficence, and fortitude, and providence, and the tutelary protection of all good arts, derive their food, and the growth of their organs, but continence, and self-denial, and labour, and vigilance, and frugality, and whatever else there is in which the mind shows itself above the appetite, are nowhere more in their proper element than in the provision and distribution of the public wealth. It is therefore not without reason that the science of speculative and practical finance, which must take to its aid so many auxiliary branches of knowledge, stands high in the estimation not only of the ordinary sort, but of the wisest and best men; and as this science has grown with the progress of its object, the prosperity and improvement of nations has generally increased with the increase of their revenues; and they will both continue to grow and flourish, as long as the balance between what is left to strengthen the efforts of individuals, and what is collected for the common efforts of the state, bear to each other a due reciprocal proportion, and are kept in a close correspondence and communication. And perhaps it may be owing to the greatness of revenues, and to the urgency of state necessities, that old abuses in the constitution of finances are discovered, and their true nature and rational theory comes to be more perfectly understood; insomuch, that a smaller revenue might have been more distressing in one period than a far greater is found to be in another; the proportionate wealth even remaining the same. In this state of things, the French Assembly found something in their revenues to preserve, to secure, and wisely to administer, as well as to abrogate and alter. Though their proud assumption might justify the severest tests, yet in trying their abilities on their financial proceedings, I would only consider what is the plain, obvious duty of a common finance minister, and try them upon that, and not upon models of ideal perfection.

The objects of a financier are, then, to secure an ample revenue; to impose it with judgment and equality; to employ it economically; and, when necessity obliges him to make use of credit, to secure its foundations in that instance, and for ever, by the clearness and candour of his proceedings, the exactness of his calculations, and the solidity of his funds. On these heads we may take a short and distinct view of the merits and abilities of those in the National Assembly, who have taken to themselves the management of this arduous concern. Far from any increase of revenue in their hands, I find, by a report of M. Vernier,[181] from the committee of finances, of the second of August last, that the amount of the national revenue, as compared with its produce before the Revolution, was diminished by the sum of two hundred millions, or *eight millions sterling* of the annual income, considerably more than one-third of the whole.

If this be the result of great ability, never surely was ability displayed in a more distinguished manner, or with so powerful an effect. No common folly, no vulgar incapacity, no ordinary official negligence, even no official crime, no corruption, no peculation, hardly any direct hostility which we have seen in the modern world, could in so short a time have made so complete an overthrow of the finances, and with them, of the strength of a great kingdom. – *Cedò qui vestram rempublicam tantam amisistis tam cito?*[182]

The sophisters and declaimers, as soon as the Assembly met, began with decrying the ancient constitution of the revenue in many of its most essential branches, such as the public monopoly of salt. They charged it, as truly as unwisely, with being ill-contrived, oppressive, and partial. This representation they were not satisfied to make use of in speeches preliminary to some plan of reform; they declared it in a solemn resolution or public sentence, as it were judicially, passed upon it; and this they dispersed throughout the nation. At the time they passed the decree, with the same gravity they ordered the same absurd, oppressive, and partial tax to be paid, until they could find a revenue to replace it. The consequence was inevitable. The provinces which had been always exempted from this salt monopoly, some of whom were charged with other contributions, perhaps equivalent, were totally disinclined to bear any part of the burthen, which by an equal distribution was to redeem the others. As to the Assembly, occupied as it was with the declaration and violation of the rights of men, and with their arrangements for general confusion, it had neither leisure nor capacity to contrive, nor authority to enforce, any plan of any kind relative to the replacing the tax or equalising it, or compensating the provinces, or for conducting their minds to any scheme of accommodation with the other districts which were to be relieved.

The people of the salt provinces, impatient under taxes, damned by the authority which had directed their payment, very soon found their patience exhausted. They thought themselves as skilful in demolishing as the Assembly could be. They relieved themselves by throwing off the whole burthen. Animated by this example, each district, or part of a district, judging of its own grievance by its own feeling, and of its remedy by its own opinion, did as it pleased with other taxes.

We are next to see how they have conducted themselves in contriving equal impositions, proportioned to the means of the citizens, and the least likely to lean heavy on the active capital employed in the generation of that private wealth, from whence the public fortune must be derived. By suffering the several districts, and several of the individuals in each district, to judge of what part of the old revenue they might withhold, instead of better principles of equality, a new inequality was introduced of the most oppressive kind. Payments were regulated by dispositions. The parts of the kingdom which were the most submissive, the most orderly, or the most affectionate to the commonwealth, bore the whole burthen of the state. Nothing turns out to be so oppressive and unjust as a feeble government. To fill up all the deficiencies in the old impositions, and the new deficiencies of every kind which were to be expected, what remained to a state without authority? The National Assembly called for a voluntary benevolence; for a fourth part of the income of all the citizens, to be estimated on the honour of those who were to pay.[183] They obtained something more than could be rationally calculated, but what was far indeed from answerable to their real necessities, and much less to their fond expectations. Rational people could have hoped for little from this their tax in the disguise of a benevolence; a tax weak, ineffective, and unequal; a tax by which luxury, avarice, and selfishness were screened, and the load thrown upon productive capital, upon integrity, generosity, and public spirit – a tax of regulation upon virtue. At length the mask is thrown off, and they are now trying means (with little success) of exacting their benevolence by force.

This benevolence, the ricketty offspring of weakness, was to be supported by another resource, the twin brother of the same prolific imbecility. The patriotic donations were to make good the failure of the patriotic contribution. John Doe was to become security for Richard Roe.[184] By this scheme they took things of much price from the giver, comparatively of small value to the receiver; they ruined several trades; they pillaged the crown of its ornaments, the churches of their plate, and the people of their personal decorations. The invention of these juvenile pretenders to liberty was in reality nothing more than a servile imitation of one of the poorest resources of doting despotism. They took an old huge full-bottomed periwig out of the wardrobe of the antiquated frippery of Louis the Fourteenth, to cover the premature baldness of the National Assembly. They produced this old-fashioned formal folly, though it had been so abundantly exposed in the Memoirs of the Duke de St. Simon,[185] if to reasonable men it had wanted any arguments to display its mischief and insufficiency. A device of the same kind was tried in my memory by Louis the Fifteenth, but it answered at no time. However, the necessities of ruinous wars were some excuse for desperate projects. The deliberations of calamity are rarely wise. But here was a season for disposition and providence. It was in a time of profound peace, then enjoyed for five years, and promising a much longer continuance, that they had recourse to this desperate trifling. They were sure to lose more reputation by sporting, in their serious situation, with these toys and playthings of finance, which have filled half their journals, than could possibly be compensated by the poor temporary supply which they afforded. It seemed as if those who adopted such projects were wholly ignorant of their circumstances, or wholly unequal to their necessities. Whatever virtue may be in these devices, it is obvious that neither the patriotic gifts, nor the patriotic contribution, can ever be resorted to again. The resources of public folly are soon exhausted. The whole indeed of their scheme of revenue is to make, by any artifice, an appearance of a full reservoir for the hour, whilst at the same time they cut off the springs and living fountains of perennial supply. The account not long since furnished by M. Necker was meant, without question, to be favourable. He gives a flattering view of the means of getting through the year; but he expresses, as it is natural he should, some apprehension for that which was to succeed. On this last prognostic, instead of entering into the grounds of this apprehension, in order, by a proper foresight, to prevent the prognosticated evil, M. Necker receives a sort of friendly reprimand from the president of the Assembly.

As to their other schemes of taxation, it is impossible to say anything of them with certainty; because they have not yet had their operation: but nobody is so sanguine as to imagine they will fill up any perceptible part of the wide gaping breach which their incapacity has made in their revenues. At present the state of their treasury sinks every day more and more in cash, and swells more and more in fictitious representation. When so little within or without is now found but paper, the representative not of opulence but of want, the creature not of credit but of power, they imagine that our flourishing state in England is owing to that bank-paper, and not the bank-paper to the flourishing condition of our commerce, to the solidity of our credit, and to the total exclusion of all idea of power from any part of the transaction. They forget that, in England, not one shilling of paper-money of any description is received but of choice; that the whole has had its origin in cash actually deposited; and that it is convertible at pleasure, in an instant, and without the smallest loss, into cash again. Our paper is of value in commerce, because in law it is of none. It is powerful on 'Change,[186] because in Westminster Hall it is impotent. In payment of a debt of twenty shillings, a creditor may refuse all the paper of the bank of England. Nor is there amongst us a single public security, of any quality or nature whatsoever, that is enforced by authority. In fact it might be easily shown, that our paper wealth, instead of lessening the real coin, has a tendency to increase it; instead of being a substitute for money, it only facilitates its entry, its exit, and its circulation; that it is the symbol of prosperity, and not the badge of distress. Never was a scarcity of cash, and an exuberance of paper, a subject of complaint in this nation.

Well! but a lessening of prodigal expenses, and the economy which has been introduced by the virtuous and sapient Assembly, make amends for the losses sustained in the receipt of revenue. In this at least they have fulfilled the duty of a financier. – Have those, who say so, looked at the expenses of the National Assembly itself? of the municipalities? of the city of Paris? of the increased pay of the two armies? of the new police? of the new judicatures? Have they even carefully compared the present pension list with the former? These politicians have been cruel, not economical. Comparing the expenses of the former prodigal government and its relation to the then revenues with the expenses of this new system as opposed to the state of its new treasury, I believe the present will be found beyond all comparison more chargeable.*

It remains only to consider the proofs of financial ability, furnished by the present French managers when they are to raise supplies on credit. Here I am a little at a stand; for credit, properly speaking, they have none. The credit of the ancient government was not indeed the best; but they could always, on some terms, command money, not only at home, but from most of the countries of Europe where a surplus capital was accumulated; and the credit of that government was improving daily. The establishment of a system of liberty would of course be supposed to give it new strength: and so it would actually have done, if a system of liberty had been established. What offers has their government of pretended liberty had from Holland, from Hamburgh, from Switzerland, from Genoa, from England, for a dealing in their paper? Why should these nations of commerce and economy enter into any pecuniary dealings with a people, who attempt to reverse the very nature of things; amongst whom they see the debtor prescribing at the point of the bayonet, the medium of his solvency to the creditor; discharging one of his engagements with another; turning his very penury into his resource; and paying his interest with his rags?

Their fanatical confidence in the omnipotence of church plunder has induced these philosophers to overlook all care of the public estate, just as the dream of the philosopher's stone induces dupes, under the more plausible delusion of the hermetic art, to neglect all rational means of improving their fortunes. With these philosophic financiers, this universal medicine made of church mummy[187] is to cure all the evils of the state. These gentlemen perhaps do not believe a great deal in the miracles of piety;

* The reader will observe, that I have but lightly touched (my plan demanded nothing more) on the condition of the French finances, as connected with the demands upon them. If I had intended to do otherwise, the materials in my hands for such a task are not altogether perfect. On this subject I refer the reader to M. de Calonne's work; and the tremendous display that he has made of the havoc and devastation in the public estate, and in all the affairs of France, caused by the presumptuous good intentions of ignorance and incapacity. Such effects those causes will always produce. Looking over that account with a pretty strict eye, and, with perhaps too much rigour, deducting everything which may be placed to the account of a financier out of place, who might be supposed by his enemies desirous of making the most of his cause, I believe it will be found, that a more salutary lesson of caution against the daring spirit of innovators, than what has been supplied at the expense of France, never was at any time furnished to mankind.

but it cannot be questioned, that they have an undoubting faith in the prodigies of sacrilege. Is there a debt which presses them? – Issue *assignats*. Are compensations to be made, or a maintenance decreed to those whom they have robbed of their freehold in their office, or expelled from their profession? – *Assignats*. Is a fleet to be fitted out? – *Assignats*. If sixteen millions sterling of these *assignats*, forced on the people, leave the wants of the state as urgent as ever – issue, says one, thirty millions sterling of *assignats* – says another, issue fourscore millions more of *assignats*. The only difference among their financial factions is on the greater or the lesser quantity of *assignats* to be imposed on the public sufferance. They are all professors of *assignats*. Even those, whose natural good sense and knowledge of commerce, not obliterated by philosophy, furnish decisive arguments against this delusion, conclude their arguments, by proposing the emission of *assignats*. I suppose they must talk of *assignats*, as no other language would be understood. All experience of their inefficacy does not in the least discourage them. Are the old *assignats* depreciated at market? – What is the remedy? Issue new *assignats*. – *Mais si maladia, opiniatria, non vult se garire, quid illi facere? assignare – postea assignare; ensuita assignare.*[188] The word is a trifle altered. The Latin of your present doctors may be better than that of your old comedy; their wisdom and the variety of their resources are the same. They have not more notes in their song than the cuckoo; though, far from the softness of that harbinger of summer and plenty, their voice is as harsh and as ominous as that of the raven.

Who but the most desperate adventurers in philosophy and finance could at all have thought of destroying the settled revenue of the state, the sole security for the public credit, in the hope of rebuilding it with the materials of confiscated property? If, however, an excessive zeal for the state should have led a pious and venerable prelate[189] (by anticipation a father of the church*) to pillage his own order, and, for the good of the church and people, to take upon himself the place of grand financier of confiscation, and comptroller-general of sacrilege, he and his coadjutors were, in my opinion, bound to show, by their subsequent conduct, that they knew something of the office they assumed. When they had resolved to appropriate to the *Fisc*,[190] a certain portion of the lauded property of their conquered country, it was

---

* La Bruyère of Bossuet.[191]

their business to render their bank a real fund of credit, as far as such a bank was capable of becoming so.

To establish a current circulating credit upon any *Land-bank*, under any circumstances whatsoever, has hitherto proved difficult at the very least. The attempt has commonly ended in bankruptcy. But when the Assembly were led, through a contempt of moral, to a defiance of economical, principles, it might at least have been expected, that nothing would be omitted on their part to lessen this difficulty, to prevent any aggravation of this bankruptcy. It might be expected, that, to render your *Land-bank* tolerable, every means would be adopted that could display openness and candour in the statement of the security; everything which could aid the recovery of the demand. To take things in their most favourable point of view, your condition was that of a man of a large landed estate, which he wished to dispose of for the discharge of a debt, and the supply of certain services. Not being able instantly to sell, you wished to mortgage. What would a man of fair intentions, and a commonly clear understanding, do in such circumstances? Ought he not first to ascertain the gross value of the estate; the charges of its management and disposition; the encumbrances perpetual and temporary of all kinds that affect it; then, striking a net surplus, to calculate the just value of the security? When that surplus (the only security to the creditor) had been clearly ascertained, and properly vested in the hands of trustees; then he would indicate the parcels to be sold, and the time and conditions of sale; after this, he would admit the public creditor, if he chose it, to subscribe his stock into this new fund; or he might receive proposals for an *assignat* from those who would advance money to purchase this species of security.

This would be to proceed like men of business, methodically and rationally; and on the only principles of public and private credit that have an existence. The dealer would then know exactly what he purchased; and the only doubt which could hang upon his mind would be, the dread of the resumption of the spoil, which one day might be made (perhaps with an addition of punishment) from the sacrilegious gripe of those execrable wretches who could become purchasers at the auction of their innocent fellow-citizens.

An open and exact statement of the clear value of the property, and of the time, the circumstances, and the place of sale, were all necessary, to efface as much as possible the stigma that has hitherto been branded on every kind of *Land-bank*. It became necessary on another principle, that is, on account of a pledge of faith previously given on that subject, that their future fidelity in a slippery concern might be established by their adherence to their first engagement. When they had finally determined on a state resource from church booty, they came, on the 14th of April, 1790, to a solemn resolution on the subject; and pledged themselves to their country, "that in the statement of the public charges for each year, there should be brought to account a sum sufficient for defraying the expenses of the R. C. A. religion, the support of the ministers at the altars, the relief of the poor, the pensions to the ecclesiastics, secular as well as regular, of the one and of the other sex, *in order that the estates and goods which are at the disposal of the nation may be disengaged of all charges, and employed by the representatives, or the legislative body, to the great and most pressing exigences of the state.*" They further engaged, on the same day, that the sum necessary for the year 1791 should be forthwith determined.

In this resolution they admit it their duty to show distinctly the expense of the above objects, which, by other resolutions, they had before engaged should be first in the order of provision. They admit that they ought to show the estate clear and dis-engaged of all charges, and that they should show it immediately. Have they done this immediately, or at any time? Have they ever furnished a rent-roll of the immovable estates, or given in an inventory of the movable effects, which they confiscate to their assignats? In what manner they can fulfil their engagements of holding out to public service, "an estate disengaged of all charges," without authenticating the value of the estate, or the quantum of the charges, I leave it to their English admirers to explain. Instantly upon this assurance, and previously to any one step towards making it good, they issue, on the credit of so hand-some a declaration, sixteen millions sterling of their paper. This was manly. Who, after this masterly stroke, can doubt of their abilities in finance? – But then, before any other emission of these financial *indulgences*, they took care at least to make good their original promise! – If such estimate, either of the value of the estate or the amount of the encumbrances, has been made, it has escaped me. I never heard of it.

At length they have spoken out, and they have made a full dis-covery of their abominable fraud, in holding out the church lands as a security for any debts, or any service whatsoever. They rob only to enable them to cheat; but in a very short time they defeat the ends both of the robbery and the fraud, by making out accounts for other purposes, which blow up their whole apparatus of force and of deception. I am obliged to M. de Calonne for his reference to the document which proves this extraordinary fact; it had by some means escaped me. Indeed it was not necessary to make out my assertion as to the breach of faith on the declaration of the 14th of April, 1790. By a report of their committee it now appears, that the charge of keeping up the reduced ecclesiastical establishments, and other expenses attendant on religion, and maintaining the religious of both sexes, retained or pensioned, and the other concomitant expenses of the same nature, which they have brought upon themselves by this convulsion in property, exceeds the income of the estates acquired by it in the enormous sum of two millions sterling annually; besides a debt of seven millions and upwards. These are the calculating powers of imposture! This is the finance of philosophy! This is the result of all the delusions held out to engage a miserable people in rebellion, murder, and sacrilege, and to make them prompt and zealous instruments in the ruin of their country! Never did a state, in any case, enrich itself by the confiscations of the citizens. This new experiment has succeeded like all the rest. Every honest mind, every true lover of liberty and humanity, must rejoice to find that injustice is not always good policy, nor rapine the high road to riches. I subjoin with pleasure, in a note, the able and spirited observations of M. de Calonne on this subject.*

* "Ce n'est point à l'assemblée entière que je m'adresse ici; je ne parle qu'à ceux qui l'égarent, en lui cachant sous des gazes séduisantes le but où ils l'entraînent. C'est à eux que je dis: votre objet, vous n'en disconviendrez pas, c'est d'ôter tout espoir au clergé, et de consommer sa ruine; c'est-là, est ne vous soupçonnant d'aucune combinaison de cupidité, d'aucun regard sur le jeu des effets publics, c'est-là ce qu'on doit croire que vous avez en vue dans la terrible opération que vous proposez; c'est ce qui doit en être le fruit. Mais le peuple que vous y intéressez, quel avantage peut-il y trouver? En vous servant sans cesse de lui, que faites vous pour lui? Rien, absolument rien; et, au contraire, vous faites ce qui ne conduit qu'à l'accabler de nouvelles charges. Vous avez rejeté, à son préjudice, une offre de 400 millions, dont l'acceptation pouvoit devenir un moyen de soulagement en sa faveur; et à cette ressource, aussi profitable que legitime, vous avez substitué une injustice ruineuse, qui, de votre propre aveu, charge le trésor public, et par conséquent le peuple, d'un surcroît de dépense annuelle de 50 millions au moins, et d'un remboursement de 150 millions.

"Malheureux peuple! voilà ce que vous vaut en dernier résultat l'expropriation de l'Eglise, et la dureté des décrets taxateurs du traitement des ministres d'une religion

In order to persuade the world of the bottomless resource of ecclesiastical confiscation, the Assembly have proceeded to other confiscations of estates in offices, which could not be done with any common colour without being compensated out of this grand confiscation of landed property. They have thrown upon this fund, which was to show a surplus disengaged of all charges, a new charge; namely, the compensation to the whole body of the disbanded judicature; and of all suppressed offices and estates; a charge which I cannot ascertain, but which unquestionably amounts to many French millions. Another of the new charges is an annuity of four hundred and eighty thousand pounds sterling, to be paid (if they choose to keep faith) by daily payments, for the interest of the first assignats. Have they ever given themselves the trouble to state fairly the expense of the management; of the church lands in the hands of the municipalities, to whose care, skill, and diligence, and that of their legion of unknown under-agents, they have chosen to commit the charge of the forfeited estates, and the consequence of which had been so ably pointed out by the bishop of Nancy?[192]

But it is unnecessary to dwell on these obvious heads of encumbrance. Have they made out any clear state of the grand encumbrance of all, I mean the whole of the general and municipal establishments of all sorts, and compared it with the regular income by revenue? Every deficiency in these becomes a charge on the confiscated estate, before the creditor can plant his cabbages on an acre of church property. There is no other prop than this confiscation to keep the whole state from tumbling to the ground. In this situation they have purposely covered all, that they ought industriously to have cleared, with a thick fog; and then, blindfold themselves, like bulls that shut their eyes when they push, they drive, by the point of the bayonets, their slaves, blindfolded indeed no worse than their lords, to take their fictions for currencies, and to swallow down paper pills by thirty-four millions sterling at a dose. Then they proudly lay in their claim to a future credit, on failure of all their past engagements, and at a time when (if in such a matter anything can be clear) it is clear that the surplus estates will never answer even the first of their mortgages, I mean that of the four hundred millions (or

---

bienfaisante; et désormais ils seront à votre charge: leurs charités soulageoient les pauvres; et vous allez être imposés pour subvenir à leur entretien!" – *De l'Etat de la France*, p. 81. See also p. 92, and the following pages.

sixteen millions sterling) of *assignats*. In all this procedure I can discern neither the solid sense of plain dealing, nor the subtle dexterity of ingenious fraud. The objections within the Assembly to pulling up the flood-gates for this inundation of fraud are unanswered; but they are thoroughly refuted by an hundred thousand financiers in the street. These are the numbers by which the metaphysic arithmeticians compute. These are the grand calculations on which a philosophical public credit is founded in France. They cannot raise supplies; but they can raise mobs. Let them rejoice in the applauses of the club at Dundee,[193] for their wisdom and patriotism in having thus applied the plunder of the citizens to the service of the state. I hear of no address upon this subject from the directors of the bank of England; though their approbation would be of a *little* more weight in the scale of credit than that of the club at Dundee. But, to do justice to the club, I believe the gentlemen who compose it to be wiser than they appear; that they will be less liberal of their money than of their addresses; and that they would not give a dog's-ear of their most rumpled and ragged Scotch paper for twenty of your fairest assignats.

Early in this year the Assembly issued paper to the amount of sixteen millions sterling: what must have been the state into which the Assembly has brought your affairs, that the relief afforded by so vast a supply has been hardly perceptible? This paper also felt an almost immediate depreciation of five per cent, which in a little time came to about seven. The effect of these assignats on the receipt of the revenue is remarkable. M. Necker found that the collectors of the revenue, who received in coin, paid the treasury in *assignats*. The collectors made seven per cent by thus receiving in money, and accounting in depreciated paper. It was not very difficult to foresee, that this must be inevitable. It was, however, not the less embarrassing. M. Necker was obliged (I believe, for a considerable part, in the market of London) to buy gold and silver for the mint, which amounted to about twelve thousand pounds above the value of the commodity gained. That minister was of opinion, that whatever their secret nutritive virtue might be, the state could not live upon *assignats* alone; that some real silver was necessary, particularly for the satisfaction of those who, having iron in their hands, were not likely to distinguish themselves for patience, when they should perceive that, whilst an increase of pay was held out to them in

real money, it was again to be fraudulently drawn back by depreciated paper. The minister, in this very natural distress, applied
to the Assembly, that they should order the collectors to pay in
specie what in specie they had received. It could not escape him,
that if the treasury paid three per cent for the use of a currency,
which should be returned seven per cent worse than the minister
issued it, such a dealing could not very greatly tend to enrich the
public. The Assembly took no notice of his recommendation.
They were in this dilemma – If they continued to receive the
assignats, cash must become an alien to their treasury: if the treasury should refuse those paper *amulets*, or should discountenance
them in any degree, they must destroy the credit of their sole
resource. They seem then to have made their option; and to have
given some sort of credit to their paper by taking it themselves;
at the same time in their speeches they made a sort of swaggering
declaration, something, I rather think, above legislative competence; that is, that there is no difference in value between metallic
money and their assignats. This was a good, stout, proof article
of faith, pronounced under an anathema, by the venerable fathers
of this philosophic synod. *Credat* who will – certainly not
Judæus Apella.[194]

A noble indignation rises in the minds of your popular leaders,
on bearing the magic lantern in their show of finance compared
to the fraudulent exhibitions of Mr. Law.[195] They cannot bear to
hear the sands of his Mississippi compared with the rock of the
church, on which they build their system. Pray let them suppress
this glorious spirit, until they show to the world what piece of
solid ground there is for their assignats, which they have not
pre-occupied by other charges. They do injustice to that great,
mother fraud, to compare it with their degenerate imitation. It is
not true that Law built solely on a speculation concerning the
Mississippi. He added the East India trade; he added the African
trade; he added the farms of all the farmed revenue of France. All
these together unquestionably could not support the structure
which the public enthusiasm, not he, chose to build upon these
bases. But these were, however, in comparison, generous delusions. They supposed, and they aimed at, an increase of the
commerce of France. They opened to it the whole range of
the two hemispheres. They did not think of feeding France from
its own substance. A grand imagination found in this flight of
commerce something to captivate. It was wherewithal to dazzle

the eye of an eagle. It was not made to entice the smell of a mole, nuzzling and burying himself in his mother earth, as yours is. Men were not then quite shrunk from their natural dimensions by a degrading and sordid philosophy, and fitted for low and vulgar deceptions. Above all, remember, that, in imposing on the imagination, the then managers of the system made a compliment to the freedom of men. In their fraud there was no mixture of force. This was reserved to our time, to quench the little glimmerings of reason which might break in upon the solid darkness of this enlightened age.

On recollection, I have said nothing of a scheme of finance which may be urged in favour of the abilities of these gentlemen, and which has been introduced with great pomp, though not yet finally adopted, in the National Assembly. It comes with something solid in aid of the credit of the paper circulation; and much has been said of its utility and its elegance. I mean the project for coining into money the bells of the suppressed churches. This is their alchymy. There are some follies which baffle argument; which go beyond ridicule; and which excite no feeling in us but disgust; and therefore I say no more upon it.

It is as little worth remarking any further upon all their drawing and re-drawing, on their circulation for putting off the evil day, on the play between the treasury and the *Caisse d'Escompte*, and on all these old, exploded contrivances of mercantile fraud, now exalted into policy of state. The revenue will not be trifled with. The prattling about the rights of men will not be accepted in payment for a biscuit or a pound of gunpowder. Here then the metaphysicians descend from their airy speculations, and faithfully follow examples. What examples? The examples of bankrupts. But defeated, baffled, disgraced, when their breath, their strength, their inventions, their fancies desert them, their confidence still maintains its ground. In the manifest failure of their abilities, they take credit for their benevolence. When the revenue disappears in their hands, they have the presumption, in some of their late proceedings, to value *themselves* on the relief given to the people. They did not relieve the people. If they entertained such intentions, why did they order the obnoxious taxes to be paid? The people relieved themselves in spite of the Assembly.

But waving all discussion on the parties who may claim the merit of this fallacious relief, has there been, in effect, any relief to the people in any form? Mr. Bailly, one of the grand agents of paper circulation, lets you into the nature of this relief. His speech to the National Assembly contained a high and laboured panegyric on the inhabitants of Paris, for the constancy and unbroken resolution with which they have borne their distress and misery. A fine picture of public felicity! What! great courage and unconquerable firmness of mind to endure benefits, and sustain redress? One would think from the speech of this learned lord mayor, that the Parisians, for this twelvemonth past, had been suffering the straits of some dreadful blockade; that Henry the Fourth had been stopping up the avenues to their supply, and Sully thundering with his ordnance at the gates of Paris; where in reality they are besieged by no other enemies than their own madness and folly, their own credulity and perverseness. But Mr. Bailly will sooner thaw the eternal ice of his Atlantic regions, than restore the central heat to Paris, whilst it remains "smitten with the cold, dry, petrific mace"[196] of a false and unfeeling philosophy. Some time after this speech, that is, on the thirteenth of last August, the same magistrate, giving an account of his government at the bar of the same Assembly, expresses himself as follows: "in the month of July, 1789," [the period of everlasting commemoration,] "the finances of the city of Paris were *yet* in good order; the expenditure was counterbalanced by the receipt, and she had at that time a million" [forty thousand pounds sterling] "in bank. The expenses which she has been constrained to incur, *subsequent to the Revolution*, amount to 2,500,000 livres. From these expenses, and the great falling off in the product of *the free gifts*, not only a momentary, but a *total*, want of money has taken place." This is the Paris, upon whose nourishment, in the course of the last year, such immense sums, drawn from the vitals of all France, have been expended. As long as Paris stands in the place of ancient Rome, so long she will be maintained by the subject provinces. It is an evil inevitably attendant on the dominion of sovereign democratic republics. As it happened in Rome, it may survive that republican domination which gave rise to it. In that case despotism itself must submit to the vices of popularity. Rome, under her emperors, united the evils of both systems; and this unnatural combination was one great cause of her ruin.

To tell the people that they are relieved by the dilapidation of their public estate, is a cruel and insolent imposition. Statesmen, before they valued themselves on the relief given to the people by the destruction of their revenue, ought first to have carefully attended to the solution of this problem: – Whether it be more advantageous to the people to pay considerably, and to gain in proportion; or to gain little or nothing, and to be disburthened of all contribution? My mind is made up to decide in favour of the first proposition. Experience is with me, and, I believe, the best opinions also. To keep a balance between the power of acquisition on the part of the subject, and the demands he is to answer on the part of the state, is the fundamental part of the skill of a true politician. The means of acquisition are prior in time and in arrangement. Good order is the foundation of all good things. To be enabled to acquire, the people, without being servile, must be tractable and obedient. The magistrate must have his reverence, the laws their authority. The body of the people must not find the principles of natural subordination by art rooted out of their minds. They must respect that property of which they cannot partake. They must labour to obtain what by labour can be obtained; and when they find, as they commonly do, the success disproportioned to the endeavour, they must be taught their consolation in the final proportions of eternal justice. Of this consolation whoever deprives them, deadens their industry, and strikes at the root of all acquisition as of all conservation. He that does this is the cruel oppressor, the merciless enemy of the poor and wretched; at the same time that by his wicked speculations he exposes the fruits of successful industry, and the accumulations of fortune, to the plunder of the negligent, the disappointed, and the unprosperous.

Too many of the financiers by profession are apt to see nothing in revenue but banks, and circulations, and annuities on lives, and tontines,[197] and perpetual rents, and all the small wares of the shop. In a settled order of the state, these things are not to be slighted, nor is the skill in them to be held of trivial estimation. They are good, but then only good, when they assume the effects of that settled order, and are built upon it. But when men think that these beggarly contrivances may supply a resource for the evils which result from breaking up the foundations of public order, and from causing or suffering the principles of property to be subverted, they will, in the ruin of their country, leave a melancholy and lasting monument of the effect of preposterous politics, and presumptuous, short-sighted, narrow-minded wisdom.

The effects of the incapacity shown by the popular leaders in all the great members of the commonwealth are to be covered with the "all-atoning name" of liberty. In some people I see great liberty indeed; in many, if not in the most, an oppressive, degrading servitude. But what is liberty without wisdom, and without virtue? It is the greatest of all possible evils; for it is folly, vice, and madness without tuition or restraint. Those who know what virtuous liberty is, cannot bear to see it disgraced by incapable heads, on account of their having high-sounding words in their mouths. Grand, swelling sentiments of liberty I am sure I do not despise. They warm the heart; they enlarge and liberalise our minds; they animate our courage in a time of conflict. Old as I am, I read the fine raptures of Lucan and Corneille[198] with pleasure. Neither do I wholly condemn the little arts and devices of popularity. They facilitate the carrying of many points of moment; they keep the people together; they refresh the mind in its exertions; and they diffuse occasional gaiety over the severe brow of moral freedom. Every politician ought to sacrifice to the graces; and to join compliance with reason. But in such an undertaking as that in France, all these subsidiary sentiments and artifices are of little avail. To make a government requires no great prudence. Settle the seat of power; teach obedience: and the work is done. To give freedom is still more easy. It is not necessary to guide; it only requires to let go the rein. But to form a *free government*; that is, to temper together these opposite elements of liberty and restraint in one consistent work, requires much thought, deep reflection, a sagacious, powerful, and combining mind. This I do not find in those who take the lead in the National Assembly. Perhaps they are not so miserably deficient as they appear. I rather believe it. It would put them below the common level of human understanding. But when the leaders choose to make themselves bidders at an auction of popularity, their talents, in the construction of the state, will be of no service. They will become flatterers instead of legislators; the instruments, not the guides, of the people. If any of them should happen to propose a scheme of liberty, soberly limited, and defined with proper qualifications, he will be immediately outbid by his competitors, who will produce something more splendidly popular. Suspicions will be raised of his fidelity to his cause. Moderation will be stigmatised as the virtue of cowards; and compromise as the prudence of traitors; until, in hopes of preserving the credit which may enable him to temper, and moderate, on some occasions, the popular leader is obliged to become active in propagating doctrines, and establishing powers, that will afterwards defeat any sober purpose at which he ultimately might have aimed.

But am I so unreasonable as to see nothing at all that deserves commendation in the indefatigable labours of this assembly? I do not deny that, among an infinite number of acts of violence and folly, some good may have been done. They who destroy every-thing certainly will remove some grievance. They who make everything new, have a chance that they may establish something beneficial. To give them credit for what they have done in virtue of the authority they have usurped, or which can excuse them in the crimes by which that authority has been acquired, it must appear, that the same things could not have been accomplished without producing such a revolution. Most assuredly they might; because almost every one of the regulations made by them, which is not very equivocal, was either in the cession of the king, voluntarily made at the meeting of the states, or in the concur-rent instructions to the orders. Some usages have been abolished on just grounds; but they were such, that if they had stood as they were to all eternity, they would little detract from the happiness and prosperity of any state. The improvements of the National Assembly are superficial, their errors fundamental.

Whatever they are, I wish my countrymen rather to recom-mend to our neighbours the example of the British constitution, than to take models from them for the improvement of our own. In the former they have got an invaluable treasure. They are not, I think, without some causes of apprehension and complaint; but these they do not owe to their constitution, but to their own conduct. I think our happy situation owing to our constitution; but owing to the whole of it, and not to any part singly; owing in a great measure to what we have left standing in our several reviews and reformations, as well as to what we have altered or superadded. Our people will find employment enough for a truly patriotic, free, and independent spirit, in guarding what they possess from violation. I would not exclude alteration neither; but even when I changed, it should be to preserve. I should be led to my remedy by a great grievance. In what I did, I should follow the example of our ancestors. I would make the reparation as nearly as possible in the style of the building. A politic caution, a guarded circumspection, a moral rather than a complexional timidity, were among the ruling principles of our forefathers in their most decided conduct. Not being illuminated with the light of which the gentlemen of France tell us they have got so abundant a share, they acted under a strong impression of the ignorance and fallibility of mankind. He that had made them thus fallible, rewarded them for having in their conduct attended to their nature. Let us imitate their caution, if we wish to deserve their fortune, or to retain their bequests. Let us add, if we please, but let us preserve what they have left; and standing on the firm ground of the British constitution, let us be satisfied to admire, rather than attempt to follow in their desperate flights, the aëronauts of France.

I have told you candidly my sentiments. I think they are not likely to alter yours. I do not know that they ought. You are young; you cannot guide, but must follow the fortune of your country. But hereafter they may be of some use to you, in some future form which your commonwealth may take. In the present it can hardly remain; but before its final settlement it may be obliged to pass, as one of our poets says, "through great varieties of untried being,"[199] and in all its transmigrations to be purified by fire and blood.

I have little to recommend my opinions but long observation and much impartiality. They come from one who has been no tool of power, no flatterer of greatness; and who in his last acts does not wish to belie the tenour of his life. They come from one, almost the whole of whose public exertion has been a struggle for the liberty of others; from one in whose breast no anger durable or vehement has ever been kindled, but by what he considered as tyranny; and who snatches from his share in the endeavours which are used by good men to discredit opulent oppression, the hours he has employed on your affairs; and who in so doing persuades himself he has not departed from his usual office: they come from one who desires honours, distinctions, and emoluments, but little; and who expects them not at all; who has no contempt for fame, and no fear of obloquy; who shuns contention, though he will hazard an opinion: from one who wishes to preserve consistency, but who would preserve consistency by varying his means to secure the unity of his end; and, when the equipoise of the vessel in which he sails may be endangered by overloading it upon one side, is desirous of carrying the small weight of his reasons to that which may preserve its equipoise.

LETTER TO A MEMBER OF
THE NATIONAL ASSEMBLY[1]

1791

SIR,

I HAD THE honour to receive your letter of the 17th of November last; in which, with some exceptions, you are pleased to consider favourably the letter I have written on the affairs of France. I shall ever accept any mark of approbation attended with instruction with more pleasure than general and unqualified praises. The latter can serve only to flatter our vanity; the former, whilst it encourages us to proceed, may help to improve us in our progress.

Some of the errors you point out to me in my printed letter are really such. One only I find to be material. It is corrected in the edition which I take the liberty of sending to you. As to the cavils which may be made on some part of my remarks, with regard to the *gradations* in your new constitution, you observe justly that they do not affect the substance of my objections. Whether there be a round more or less in the ladder of representation, by which your workmen ascend from their parochial tyranny to their federal anarchy, when the whole scale is false, appears to me of little or no importance.

I published my thoughts on that constitution, that my countrymen might be enabled to estimate the wisdom of the plans which were held out to their imitation. I conceived that the true character of those plans would be best collected from the committee appointed to prepare them. I thought that the scheme of their building would be better comprehended in the design of the architects than in the execution of the masons. It was not worth my reader's while to occupy himself with the alterations by which bungling practice corrects absurd theory. Such an investigation would be endless: because every day's past experience of impracticability has driven, and every day's future experience will drive, those men to new devices as exceptionable as the old; and, which are no otherwise worthy of observation than as they give a daily proof of the delusion of their promises, and the falsehood of their professions. Had I followed all these changes, my letter would have been only a gazette of their wanderings; a journal of their march from error to error, through a dry dreary desert, unguided by the lights of heaven, or by the contrivance which wisdom has invented to supply their place.

I am unalterably persuaded, that the attempt to oppress, degrade, impoverish, confiscate, and extinguish the original gentlemen and landed property of a whole nation, cannot be justified under any form it may assume. I am satisfied beyond a doubt, that the project of turning a great empire into a vestry, or into a collection of vestries, and of governing it in the spirit of a parochial administration, is senseless, and absurd, in any mode, or with any qualifications. I can never be convinced, that the scheme of placing the highest powers of the state in church-wardens and constables, and other such officers, guided by the prudence of litigious attornies and Jew brokers, and set in action by shameless women of the lowest condition, by keepers of hotels, taverns, and brothels, by pert apprentices, by clerks, shop-boys, hairdressers, fiddlers, and dancers on the stage, (who, in such a commonwealth as yours, will in future overbear, as already they have overborne, the sober incapacity of dull, uninstructed men, of useful but laborious occupations,) can never be put into any shape, that must not be both disgraceful and destructive. The whole of this project, even if it were what it pretends to be, and was not, in reality, the dominion, through that disgraceful medium, of half a dozen, or perhape fewer, intriguing politi-cians, is so mean, so low-minded, so stupid a contrivace, in point of wisdom, as well as so perfectly detestable for its wickedness, that I must always consider the correctives, which might make it in any degree practicable, to be so many new objections to it.

In that wretched state of things, some are afraid that the authors of your miseries may be led to precipitate their further designs, by the hints they may receive from the very arguments used to expose the absurdity of their system, to mark the in-congruity of its parts, and its inconsistency with their own principles; and that your masters may be led to render their schemes more consistent, by rendering them more mischievous. Excuse the liberty which your indulgence authorises me to take, when I observe to you, that such apprehensions as these would prevent all exertion of our faculties in this great cause of mankind.

A rash recourse to *forrce* is not to be justified in a state of real weakness. Such attempts bring on disgrace; and, in their failure, discountenance and discourage more rational endeavours. But *reason* is to be hazarded, though it may be perverted, by craft and sophistry; for reason can suffer no loss nor shame, nor can it impede any useful plan of future policy. In the unavoidable uncertainty, as to the effect, which attends on every measure of human prudence, nothing seems a surer antidote to the poison of fraud than its detection. It is true the fraud may be swallowed after this discovery; and perhaps even swallowed the more greedily for being a detected fraud. Men sometimes make a point of honour not to be disabused; and they had rather fall into an hundred errors than confess one. But after all, – when neither our principles nor our disposition, nor, perhaps, our talents, enable us to encounter delusion with delusion, we must use our best reason to those that ought to be reasonable creatures, and to take our chance for the event. We cannot act on these anomalies in the minds of men. I do not conceive that the persons who have contrived these things can be made much the better or the worse for anything which can be said to them. *They* are reason proof. Here and there, some men, who were at first carried away by wild, good intentions, may be led, when their first fervours are abated, to join in a sober survey of the schemes into which they had been deluded. To those only (and I am sorry to say they are not likely to make a large description) we apply with any hope. I may speak it upon an assurance almost approaching to absolute knowledge, that nothing has been done that has not been contrived from the beginning, even before the states had assembled. *Nulla nova mihi res inopinave surgit.*[2] They are the same men and the same designs that they were from the first, though varied in their appearance. It was the very same animal that at first crawled about in the shape of a caterpillar, that you now see rise into the air, and expand his wings to the sun.

Proceeding, therefore, as we are obliged to proceed, that is, upon an hypothesis that we address rational men, can false political principles be more effectually exposed, than by demonstrating that they lead to consequences directly inconsistent with and subversive of the arrangements grounded upon them? If this kind of demonstration is not permitted, the process of reasoning called *deductio ad absurdum*,[3] which even the severity of geometry does not reject, could not be employed at all in legislative discussions. One of our strongest weapons against folly acting with authority would be lost.

You know, Sir, that even the virtuous efforts of you patriots to prevent the ruin of your country have had this very turn given to them. It has been said here, and in France too, that the reigning usurpers would not have carried their tyranny to such destructive lengths, if they had not been stimulated and provoked to it by the acrimony of your opposition. There is a dilemma to which every opposition to successful iniquity must, in the nature of things, be liable. If you lie still, you are considered as an accomplice in the measures in which you silently acquiesce. If you resist, you are accused of provoking irritable power to new excesses. The conduct of a losing party never appears right: at least it never can possess the only infallible criterion of wisdom to vulgar judgments – success.

The indulgence of a sort of undefined hope, an obscure confidence, that some lurking remains of virtue, some degree of shame, might exist in the breasts of the oppressors of France, has been among the causes which have helped to bring on the common ruin of king and people. There is no safety for honest men, but by believing all possible evil of evil men, and by acting with promptitude, decision, and steadiness on that belief. I well remember at every epocha of this wonderful history, in every scene of this tragic business, that when your sophistic usurpers were laying down mischievous principles, and even applying them in direct resolutions, it was the fashion to say, that they never intended to execute those declarations in their rigour. This made men careless in their opposition, and remiss in early precaution. By holding out this fallacious hope, the impostors deluded sometimes one description of men, and sometimes another, so that no means of resistance were provided against them, when they came to execute in cruelty what they had planned in fraud.

There are cases in which a man would be ashamed not to have been imposed on. There is a confidence necessary to human intercourse, and without which men are often more injured by their own suspicions than they could be by the perfidy of others. But when men whom we *know* to be wicked impose upon us, we are something worse than dupes. When we know them, their fair pretences become new motives for distrust. There is one case indeed, in which it would be madness not to give the fullest credit to the most deceitful of men, that is, when they make declarations of hostility against us.

I find that some persons entertain other hopes, which I confess appear more specious than those by which at first so many were deluded and disarmed. They flatter themselves that the extreme misery brought upon the people by their folly will at last open the eyes of the multitude, if not of their leaders. Much the contrary, I fear. As to the leaders in this system of imposture, – you know, that cheats and deceivers never can repent. The fraudulent have no resource but in fraud. They have no other goods in their magazine. They have no virtue or wisdom in their minds, to which, in a disappointment concerning the profitable effects of fraud and cunning, they can retreat. The wearing out of an old serves only to put them upon the invention of a new delusion. Unluckily too, the credulity of dupes is as inexhaustible as the invention of knaves. They never give people possession; but they always keep them in hope. Your state doctors do not so much as pretend that any good whatsoever has hitherto been derived from their operations, or that the public has prospered in any one instance, under their management. The nation is sick, very sick, by their medicines. But the *charlatan* tells them that what is passed cannot be helped; – they have taken the draught, and they must wait its operation with patience; – that the first effects indeed are unpleasant, but that the very sickness is a proof that the dose is of no sluggish operation; – that sickness is inevitable in all constitutional revolutions; – that the body must pass through pain to ease; – that the prescriber is not an empiric who proceeds by vulgar experience, but one who grounds his practice* on the sure rules of art, which cannot possibly fail. You have read, Sir, the last manifesto, or mountebank's bill, of the National Assembly. You see their presumption in their promises is not lessened by all their failures in the performance. Compare this last address of the Assembly and the present state of your affairs with the early engagements of that body; engagements which, not content with declaring, they solemnly deposed upon oath; swearing lustily, that if they were supported they would make their country glorious and happy; and then judge whether those who can write such things, or those who can bear to read them, are of *themselves* to be brought to any reasonable course of thought or action.

* It is said in the last quackish address of the National Assembly to the people of France, that they have not formed their arrangements upon vulgar practice; but on a theory which cannot fail; or something to that effect.

As to the people at large, when once these miserable sheep have broken the fold, and have got themselves loose, not from the restraint, but from the protection, of all the principles of natural authority and legitimate subordination, they become the natural prey of impostors. When they have once tasted of the flattery of knaves, they can no longer endure reason, which appears to them only in the form of censure and reproach. Great distress has never hitherto taught, and whilst the world lasts it never will teach, wise lessons to any part of mankind. Men are as much blinded by the extremes of misery as by the extremes of prosperity. Desperate situations produce desperate counsels and desperate measures. The people of France, almost generally, have been taught to look for other resources than those which can be derived from order, frugality, and industry. They are generally armed; and they are made to expect much from the use of arms. *Nihil non arrogant armis.*[4] Besides this, the retrograde order of society has something flattering to the dispositions of mankind. The life of adventurers, gamesters, gipsies, beggars, and robbers is not unpleasant. It requires restraint to keep men from falling into that habit. The shifting tides of fear and hope, the flight and pursuit, the peril and escape, the alternate famine and feasts of the savage and the thief, after a time, render all course of slow, steady, progressive, unvaried occupation, and the prospect only of a limited mediocrity at the end of long labour, to the last degree tame, languid, and insipid. Those who have been once intoxicated with power, and have derived any kind of emolument from it, even though but for one year, never can willingly abandon it. They may be distressed in the midst of all their power; but they will never look to anything but power for their relief. When did distress ever oblige a prince to abdicate his authority? And what effect will it have upon those who are made to believe themselves a people of princes?

The more active and stirring part of the lower orders having got government, and the distribution of plunder, into their hands, they will use its resources in each municipality to form a body of inherents. These rulers, and their adherents, will be strong enough to overpower the discontents of those who have not been able to assert their share of the spoil. The unfortunate adventurers in the cheating lottery of plunder will probably be the least sagacious, or the most inactive and irresolute, of the gang. If, on disappointment, they should dare to stir, they will soon be suppressed as rebels and mutineers by their brother rebels. Scantily fed for a while with the offal of plunder, they will drop off by degrees; they will be driven out of sight and out of thought; and they will be left to perish obscurely, like rats, in holes and corners.

From the forced repentance of invalid mutineers and disbanded thieves, you can hope for no resource. Government itself, which ought to constrain the more bold and dexterous of these robbers, is their accomplice. Its arms, its treasures, its all are in their hands. Judicature, which above all things should awe them, is their creature and their instrument. Nothing seems to me to render your internal situation more desperate than this one circumstance of the state of your judicature. Many days are not passed since we have seen a set of men brought forth by your rulers for a most critical function. Your rulers brought forth a set of men, steaming from the sweat and drudgery, and all black with the smoke and soot, of the forge of confiscation and robbery – *ardentis massæ fuligine lippos*,[5] a set of men brought forth from the trade of hammering arms of proof, offensive and defensive, in aid of the enterprises, and for the subsequent protection, of housebreakers, murderers, traitors, and malefactors; men, who had their minds seasoned with theories perfectly conformable to their practice, and who had always laughed at possession and prescription, and defied all the fundamental maxims of jurisprudence. To the horror and stupefaction of all the honest part of this nation, and indeed of all nations who are spectators, we have seen, on the credit of those very practices and principles, and to carry them further into effect, these very men placed on the sacred seat of justice in the capital city of your late kingdom. We see that in future you are to be destroyed with more form and regularity. This is not peace; it is only the introduction of a sort of discipline in their hostility. Their tyranny is complete in their justice; and their lanterne[6] is not half so dreadful as their court.

One would think that out of common decency they would have given you men who had not been in the habit of trampling upon law and justice in the Assembly, neutral men, or men apparently neutral, for judges, who are to dispose of your lives and fortunes.

Cromwell, when he attempted to legalise his power, and to settle his conquered country in a state of order, did not look for dispensers of justice in the instruments of his usurpation. Quite the contrary. He sought out, with great solicitude and selection, and even from the party most opposite to his designs, men of weight and decorum of character; men unstained with the violence of the times, and with hands not fouled with confiscation and sacrilege: for he chose a *Hale*[7] for his chief justice, though he absolutely refused to take civic oaths, or to make any acknowledgment whatsoever of the legality of his government. Cromwell told this great lawyer, that since he did not approve his title, all he required of him was, to administer, in a manner agreeable to his pure sentiments and unspotted character, that justice without which human society cannot subsist: that it was not his particular government, but civil order itself, which, as a judge, he wished him to support. Cromwell knew how to separate the institutions expedient to his usurpation from the administration of the public justice of his country. For Cromwell was a man in whom ambition had not wholly suppressed, but only suspended, the sentiments of religion, and the love (as far as it could consist with his designs) of fair and honourable reputation. Accordingly, we are indebted to this act of his for the preservation of our laws, which some senseless assertors of the rights of men were then on the point of entirely erasing, as relics of feudality and barbarism. Besides, he gave in the appointment of that man, to that age, and to all posterity, the most brilliant example of sincere and fervent piety, exact justice, and profound jurisprudence.* But these are not the things in which your philosophic usurpers choose to follow Cromwell.

One would think, that after an honest and necessary revolution (if they had a mind that theirs should pass for such) your masters would have imitated the virtuous policy of those who have been at the head of revolutions of that glorious character. Burnet[8] tells us, that nothing tended to reconcile the English nation to the government of King William so much as the care he took to fill the vacant bishoprics with men who had attracted the public esteem by their learning, eloquence, and piety, and, above all, by their known moderation in the state. With you, in your purifying revolution, whom have you chosen to regulate the church? M. Mirabeau[9] is a fine speaker, – and a fine writer, – and a fine – a very fine man; – but really nothing gave more

* See Burnet's Life of Hale.

surprise to everybody here, than to find him the supreme head of your ecclesiastical affairs. The rest is of course. Your Assembly addresses a manifesto to France, in which they tell the people, with an insulting irony, that they have brought the church to its primitive condition. In one respect their declaration is undoubtedly true; for they have brought it to a state of poverty and persecution. What can be hoped for after this? Have not men, (if they deserve the name,) under this new hope and head of the church, been made bishops for no other merit than having acted as instruments of atheists; for no other merit than having thrown the children's bread to dogs; and in order to gorge the whole gang of usurers, pedlars, and itinerant Jew-discounters at the corners of streets, starved the poor of their Christian flocks, and their own brother pastors? Have not such men been made bishops to administer in temples, in which (if the patriotic donations have not already stripped them of their vessels) the churchwardens ought to take security for the altar plate, and not so much as to trust the chalice in their sacrilegious hands, so long as Jews have assignats on ecclesiastic plunder, to exchange for the silver stolen from churches?

I am told, that the very sons of such Jew-jobbers have been made bishops; persons not to be suspected of any sort of *Christian* superstition, fit colleagues to the holy prelate of Autun[10] and bred at the feet of that Gamaliel.[11] We know who it was that drove the money-changers out of the temple. We see too who it is that brings them in again. We have in London very respectable persons of the Jewish nation, whom we will keep; but we have of the same tribe others of a very different description, – housebreakers, and receivers of stolen goods, and forgers of paper currency, more than we can conveniently hang. These we can spare to France, to fill the new episcopal thrones; men well versed in swearing; and who will scruple no oath which the fertile genius of any of your reformers can devise.

In matters so ridiculous, it is hard to be grave. On a view of their consequences, it is almost inhuman to treat them lightly. To what a state of savage, stupid, servile insensibility must your people be reduced, who can endure such proceedings in their church, their state, and their judicature, even for a moment! But the deluded people of France are like other madmen, who, to a miracle, bear hunger, and thirst, and cold, and confinement, and the chains and lash of their keeper, whilst all the while they support themselves by the imagination that they are generals of armies, prophets, kings, and emperors. As to a change of mind in these men, who consider infamy as honour, degradation as preferment, bondage to low tyrants as liberty, and the practical scorn and contumely of the upstart masters as marks of respect and homage, I look upon it as absolutely impracticable. These madmen, to be cured, must first, like other madmen, be subdued. The sound part of the community, which I believe to be large, but by no means the largest part, has been taken by surprise, and is disjointed, terrified, and disarmed. That sound part of the community must first be put into a better condition, before it can do anything in the way of deliberation or persuasion. This must be an act of power, as well as of wisdom; of power, in the hands of firm, determined patriots, who can distinguish the misled from traitors, who will regulate the state (if such should be their fortune) with a discriminating, manly, and provident mercy; men who are purged of the surfeit and indigestion of systems, if ever they have been admitted into the habit of their minds; men who will lay the foundation of a real reform, in effacing every vestige of that philosophy which pretends to have made discoveries in the *terra australis*[12] of morality; men who will fix the state upon these bases of morals and politics, which are our old, and immemorial, and, I hope, will be our eternal, possession.

This power, to such men, must come from *without*. It may be given to you in pity; for surely no nation ever called so pathetically on the compassion of all its neighbours. It may be given by those neighbours on motives of safety to themselves. Never shall I think any country in Europe to be secure, whilst there is established, in the very centre of it, a state (if so it may be called) founded on principles of anarchy, and which is, in reality, a college of armed fanatics, for the propagation of the principles of assassination, robbery, rebellion, fraud, faction, oppression, and impiety. *Mahomet*, hid,[13] as for a time he was, in the bottom of the sands of Arabia, had his spirit and character been discovered, would have been an object of precaution to provident minds. What if he had erected his fanatic standard for the destruction of the Christian religion in *luce Asiæ*,[14] in the midst of the then noon-day splendour of the then civilised world? The princes of Europe, in the beginning of this century, did well not to suffer the monarchy of France to swallow up the others. They ought not now, in my opinion, to suffer all the monarchies and commonwealths to be swallowed up in the gulf of this polluted anarchy. They may be tolerably safe at present, because the comparative power of France for the present is little. But times and occasions make dangers. Intestine troubles may arise in other countries. There is a power always on the watch, qualified and disposed to profit of every conjuncture, to establish its own principles and modes of mischief, wherever it can hope for success. What mercy would these usurpers have on other sovereigns, and on other nations, when they treat their own king with such unparalleled indignities, and so cruelly oppress their own countrymen?

The king of Prussia, in concurrence with us, nobly interfered to save Holland from confusion.[15] The same power, joined with the rescued Holland and with Great Britain, has put the emperor in the possession of the Netherlands; and secured, under that prince, from all arbitrary innovation, the ancient hereditary constitution of those provinces. The chamber of Wetzler has restored the bishop of Liege,[16] unjustly dispossessed by the rebellion of his subjects. The king of Prussia was bound by no treaty, nor alliance of blood, nor had any particular reasons for thinking the emperor's government would be more mischievous or more oppressive to human nature than that of the Turk: yet on mere motives of policy that prince has interposed with the threat of all his force, to snatch even the Turk from the pounces of the imperial eagle. If this is done in favour of a barbarous nation, with a barbarous neglect of police, fatal to the human race, in favour of a nation, by principle in eternal enmity with the Christian name; a nation which will not so much as give the salutation of peace (Salam) to any of us; nor make any pact with any Christian nation beyond a truce; – if this be done in favour of the Turk, shall it be thought either impolitic, or unjust, or uncharitable, to employ the same power to rescue from captivity a virtuous monarch (by the courtesy of Europe considered as Most Christian) who, after an intermission of one hundred and seventy-five years, had called together the states of his kingdom to reform abuses, to establish a free government, and to strengthen his throne; a monarch, who at very outset, without force, even without solicitation, had given to his people such a Magna Charta of privileges as never was given by any king to any subjects? – Is it to be tamely borne by kings who love their subjects, or by subjects who love their kings, that this monarch, in the midst of these gracious acts, was insolently and cruelly torn from his palace by a gang of traitors and assassins, and kept in close prison to this very hour, whilst his royal name and sacred character were used for the total ruin of those whom the laws had appointed him to protect?

The only offence of this unhappy monarch towards his people was his attempt, under a monarchy, to give them a free constitution. For this, by an example hitherto unheard-of in the world, he has been deposed. It might well disgrace sovereigns to take part with a deposed tyrant. It would suppose in them a vicious sympathy. But not to make a common cause with a just prince, dethroned by traitors and rebels, who proscribe, plunder, confiscate, and in every way cruelly oppress their fellow-citizens, in my opinion is to forget what is due to the honour and to the rights of all virtuous and legal government.

I think the king of France to be as much an object both of policy and compassion as the Grand Seignior[17] or his states. I do not conceive that the total annihilation of France (if that could be effected) is a desirable thing to Europe; or even to this its rival nation. Provident patriots did not think it good for Rome that even Carthage should be quite destroyed; and he was a wise Greek, wise for the general Grecian interests, as well as a brave Lacedæmonian enemy,[18] and generous conqueror, who did not wish, by the destruction of Athens, to pluck out the other eye of Greece.

However, Sir, what I have here said of the interference of foreign princes is only the opinion of a private individual; who is neither the representative of any state, nor the organ of any party; but who thinks himself bound to express his own sentiments with freedom and energy in a crisis of such importance to the whole human race.

I am not apprehensive that in speaking freely on the subject of the king and queen of France, I shall accelerate (as you fear) the execution of traitorous designs against them. You are of opinion, Sir, that the usurpers may, and that they will, gladly lay hold of any pretext to throw off the very name of a king: – assuredly I do not wish ill to your king; but better for him not to live (he does not reign) than to live the passive instrument of tyranny and usurpation.

I certainly meant to show, to the best of my power, that the existence of such an executive officer, in such a system of republic as theirs, is absurd in the highest degree. But in demonstrating this – to *them*, at least, I can have made no discovery. They only held out the royal name to catch those Frenchmen to whom the name of king is still venerable. They calculate the duration of that sentiment; and when they find it nearly expiring, they will not trouble themselves with excuses for extinguishing the name, as they have the thing. They used it as a sort of navel-string to nourish their unnatural offspring from the bowels of royalty itself. Now that the monster can purvey for its own subsistence, it will only carry the mark about it, as a token of its having torn the womb it came from. Tyrants seldom want pretexts. Fraud is the ready minister of injustice; and whilst the currency of false pretence and sophistic reasoning was expedient to their designs, they were under no necessity of drawing upon me to furnish them with that coin. But pretexts and sophisms have had their day, and have done their work. The usurpation no longer seeks plausibility. It trusts to power.

Nothing that I can say, or that you can say, will hasten them, by a single hour, in the execution of a design which they have long since entertained. In spite of their solemn declarations, their soothing addresses, and the multiplied oaths which they have taken and forced others to take, they will assassinate the king when his name will no longer be necessary to their designs; but not a moment sooner. They will probably first assassinate the queen, whenever the renewed menace of such an assassination loses its effect upon the anxious mind of an affectionate husband. At present, the advantage which they derive from the daily threats against her life is her only security for preserving it. They keep their sovereign alive for the purpose of exhibiting him, like some wild beast at a fair; as if they had a Bajazet[19] in a cage. They choose to make monarchy contemptible by exposing it to derision in the person of the most benevolent of their kings.

In my opinion their insolence appears more odious even than their crimes. The horrors of the 5th and 6th of October were less detestable than the festival of the 14th of July. There are situations (God forbid I should think that of the 5th and 6th of October one of them) in which the best men may be confounded with the worst, and in the darkness and confusion, in the press and medley of such extremities, it may not be so easy to discriminate the one from the other. The necessities created, even by ill designs, have their excuse. They may be forgotten by others when the guilty themselves do not choose to cherish their recollection, and by ruminating their offences, nourish themselves through the example of their past, to the perpetration of future, crimes. It is in the relaxation of security, it is in the expansion of prosperity, it is in the hour of dilatation of the heart, and of its softening into festivity and pleasure, that the real character of men is discerned. If there is any good in them, it appears then or never. Even wolves and tigers, when gorged with their prey, are safe and gentle. It is at such times that noble minds give all the reins to their good nature. They indulge their genius even to intemperance, in kindness to the afflicted, in generosity to the conquered; forbearing insults, forgiving injuries, over-paying benefits. Full of dignity themselves, they respect dignity in all, but they feel it sacred in the unhappy. But it is then, and basking in the sunshine of unmerited fortune, that low, sordid, ungenerous, and reptile souls swell with their hoarded poisons; it is then that they display their odious splendour, and shine out in the full lustre of their native villany and baseness. It is in that season that no man of sense or honour can be mistaken for one of them. It was in such a season, for them of political ease and security, though their people were but just emerged from actual famine, and were ready to be plunged into the gulf of penury and beggary, that your philosophic lords chose, with an ostentatious pomp and luxury, to feast an incredible number of idle and thoughtless people, collected, with art and pains, from all quarters of the world. They constructed a vast amphitheatre in which they raised a species of pillory.* On this pillory they set their lawful king and queen, with an insulting figure over their heads. There they exposed these objects of pity and respect to all good minds to the derision of an unthinking and unprincipled multitude, degenerated even from the versatile tenderness which marks the irregular and capricious feelings of the populace. That their cruel insult might have nothing wanting to complete it, they chose the anniversary of that day in which they exposed the life of their prince to the most imminent dangers and the vilest indignities, just following the instant when the assassins, whom they had hired without owning, first openly took up arms against their king, corrupted his guard, surprised his castle, butchered

---

* The pillory (carcan) in England is generally made very high, like that raised for exposing the king of France.

some of the poor invalids of his garrison, murdered his governor, and, like wild beasts, tore to pieces the chief magistrate of his capital city, on account of his fidelity to his service.

Till the justice of the world is awakened, such as these will go on, without admonition, and without provocation, to every extremity. Those who have made the exhibition of the 14th of July are capable of every evil. They do not commit crimes for their designs; but they form designs that they may commit crimes. It is not their necessity, but their nature, that impels them. They are modern philosophers; which when you say of them you express everything that is ignoble, savage, and hard-hearted.

Besides the sure tokens which are given by the spirit of their particular arrangements, there are some characteristic lineaments in the general policy of your tumultuous despotism, which, in my opinion, indicate, beyond a doubt, that no revolution what-soever *in their disposition* is to be expected. I mean their scheme of educating the rising generation, the principles which they intend to instil, and the sympathies which they wish to form in the mind, at the season in which it is the most susceptible. Instead of forming their young minds to that docility, to that modesty, which are the grace and charm of youth, to an admiration of fam-ous examples, and to an averseness to anything which approaches to pride, petulance, and self-conceit, (distempers to which that time of life is of itself sufficiently liable,) they artificially foment these evil dispositions, and even form them into springs of action. Nothing ought to be more weighed than the nature of books recommended by public authority. So recommended, they soon form the character of the age. Uncertain indeed is the efficacy, limited indeed is the extent, of a virtuous institution. But if edu-cation takes in *vice* as any part of its system, there is no doubt but that it will operate with abundant energy, and to an extent indefinite. The magistrate, who in favour of freedom thinks him-self obliged to suffer all sorts of publications, is under a stricter duty than any other well to consider what sort of writers he shall authorise; and shall recommend by the strongest of all sanctions, that is, by public honours and rewards. He ought to be cautious how he recommends authors of mixed or ambiguous morality. He ought to be fearful of putting into the hands of youth writers indulgent to the peculiarities of their own complexion, lest they should teach the humours of the professor, rather than the prin-ciples of the science. He ought, above all, to be cautious in recommending any writer who has carried marks of a deranged understanding; for where there is no sound reason there can be no real virtue; and madness is ever vicious and malignant.

The Assembly proceeds on maxims the very reverse of these. The Assembly recommends to its youth a study of the bold experimenters of morality. Everybody knows that there is a great dispute amongst their leaders, which of them is the best resemblance of Rousseau. In truth, they all resemble him. His blood they transfuse into their minds and into their manners. Him they study; him they meditate; him they turn over in all the time they can spare from the laborious mischief of the day, or the debauches of the night. Rousseau is their canon of holy writ; in his life he is their canon of *Polycletus*;[20] he is their standard figure of perfection. To this man and this writer, as a pattern to authors and to Frenchmen, the founderies of Paris are now running for statues, with the kettles of their poor and the bells of their churches. If an author had written like a great genius on geometry, though his practical and speculative morals were vicious in the extreme, it might appear, that in voting the statue, they honoured only the geometrician. But Rousseau is a moralist, or he is nothing. It is impossible, therefore, putting the circumstances together, to mistake their design in choosing the author, with whom they have begun to recommend a course of studies.

Their great problem is to find a substitute for all the principles which hitherto have been employed to regulate the human will and action. They find dispositions in the mind of such force and quality as may fit men, far better than the old morality, for the purposes of such a state as theirs, and may go much further in supporting their power, and destroying their enemies. They have therefore chosen a selfish, flattering, seductive, ostentatious vice, in the place of plain duty. True humility, the basis of the Christian system, is the low, but deep and firm, foundation of all real virtue. But this, as very painful in the practice, and little imposing in the appearance, they have totally discarded. Their object is to merge all natural and all social sentiment in inordinate vanity. In a small degree, and conversant in little things, vanity is of little moment. When full grown, it is the worst of vices, and the occasional mimic of them all. It makes the whole man false. It leaves nothing sincere or trustworthy about him. His best qualities are poisoned and perverted by it, and operate exactly as the worst. When your lords had many writers as immoral as the object of their statue (such as Voltaire and others) they chose Rousseau; because in him that peculiar vice, which they wished to erect into ruling virtue, was by far the most conspicuous.

We have had the great professor and founder of *the philosophy of vanity* in England. As I had good opportunities of knowing his proceedings almost from day to day, he left no doubt on my mind that he entertained no principle either to influence his heart, or to guide his understanding, but *vanity*. With this vice he was possessed to a degree little short of madness. It is from the same deranged, eccentric vanity, that this, the insane *Socrates* of the National Assembly, was impelled to publish a mad confession of his mad faults, and to attempt a new sort of glory from bringing hardily to light the obscure and vulgar vices, which we know may sometimes be blended with eminent talents. He has not observed on the nature of vanity who does not know that it is omnivorous; that it has no choice in its food; that it is fond to talk even of its own faults and vices, as what will excite surprise and draw attention, and what will pass at worst for openness and candour.

It was this abuse and perversion, which vanity makes even of hypocrisy, that has driven Rousseau to record a life not so much as chequered, or spotted here and there, with virtues, or even distinguished by a single good action. It is such a life he chooses to offer to the attention of mankind. It is such a life that, with a wild defiance, he flings in the face of his Creator, whom he acknowledges only to brave. Your Assembly, knowing how much more powerful example is found than precept, has chosen this man (by his own account without a single virtue) for a model. To him they erect their first statue. From him they commence their series of honours and distinctions.

It is that new invented virtue, which your masters canonise, that led their moral hero constantly to exhaust the stores of his powerful rhetoric in the expression of universal benevolence; whilst his heart was incapable of harbouring one spark of common parental affection. Benevolence to the whole species, and want of feeling for every individual with whom the professors come in contact, form the character of the new philosophy. Setting up for an unsocial independence, this their hero of vanity refuses the just price of common labour, as well as the tribute which opulence owes to genius, and which, when paid, honours the giver and the receiver: and then he pleads his beggary as an excuse for his crimes. He melts with tenderness for those only who touch him by the remotest relation, and then, without one natural pang, casts away, as a sort of offal and excrement, the spawn of his disgustful amours, and sends his children to the hospital of foundlings. The bear loves, licks, and forms her young; but bears are not philosophers. Vanity, however, finds its account in reversing the train of our natural feelings. Thousands admire the sentimental writer; the affectionate father is hardly known in his parish.

Under this philosophic instructor in the *ethics of vanity*, they have attempted in France a regeneration of the moral constitution of man. Statesmen, like your present rulers, exist by everything which is spurious, fictitious, and false; by everything which takes the man from his house, and sets him on a stage; which makes him up an artificial creature, with painted, theatric sentiments, fit to be seen by the glare of candle-light, and formed to be contemplated at a due distance. Vanity is too apt to prevail in all of us, and in all countries. To the improvement of Frenchmen it seems not absolutely necessary that it should be taught upon system. But it is plain that the present rebellion was its legitimate offspring, and it is piously fed by that rebellion with a daily dole.

If the system of institution recommended by the Assembly be false and theatric, it is because their system of government is of the same character. To that, and to that alone, it is strictly conformable. To understand either, we must connect the morals with the politics of the legislators. Your practical philosophers, systematic in everything, have wisely begun at the source. As the relation between parents and children is the first amongst the elements of vulgar, natural morality;* they erect statues to a wild, ferocious, low-minded, hard-hearted father, of fine general feelings; a lover of his kind, but a hater of his kindred. Your masters reject the duties of this vulgar relation, as contrary to liberty; as not founded in the social compact; and not binding according to the rights of men; because the relation is not, of course, the result of *free election*; never so on the side of the children, not always on the part of the parents.

---

* Filiola tua te delectari lætor et probari tibi στοργην φυσικην esse την προς τα τεκνα: etenim, si hæc non est, nulla potest homini esse ad hominem naturæ adjunctio: qua sublata vitæ societas tollitur. Valete Patron (Rousseau) et tui condiscipuli! (L'Assemblée Nationale.) — Cic. Ep. ad Atticum.

The next relation which they regenerate by their statues to Rousseau, is that which is next in sanctity to that of a father. They differ from those old-fashioned thinkers, who considered pedagogues as sober and venerable characters, and allied to the parental. The moralists of the dark times, *preceptorum sancti voluere parentis esse loco.*[21] In this age of light, they teach the people that preceptors ought to be in the place of gallants. They systematically corrupt a very corruptible race, (for some time a growing nuisance amongst you,) a set of pert, petulant literators, to whom, instead of their proper, but severe, unostentatious duties, they assign the brilliant part of men of wit and pleasure, of gay, young, military sparks, and danglers at toilets. They call on the rising generation in France to take a sympathy in the adventures and fortunes, and they endeavour to engage their sensibility on the side of pedagogues, who betray the most awful family trusts, and vitiate their female pupils. They teach the people that the debauchers of virgins, almost in the arms of their parents, may be safe inmates in the houses, and even fit guardians of the honour, of those husbands who succeed legally to the office which the young literators had pre-occupied, without asking leave of law or conscience.

Thus they dispose of all the family relations of parents and children, husbands and wives. Through this same instructor, by whom they corrupt the morals, they corrupt the taste. Taste and elegance, though they are reckoned only among the smaller and secondary morals, yet are of no mean importance in the regulation of life. A moral taste is not of force to turn vice into virtue; but it recommends virtue with something like the blandishments of pleasure; and it infinitely abates the evils of vice. Rousseau, a writer of great force and vivacity, is totally destitute of taste in any sense of the word. Your masters, who are his scholars, conceive that all refinement has an aristocratic character. The last age had exhausted all its powers in giving a grace and nobleness to our natural appetites, and in raising them into a higher class and order than seemed justly to belong to them. Through Rousseau, your masters are resolved to destroy these aristocratic prejudices. The passion called love has so general and powerful an influence; it makes so much of the entertainment, and indeed so much of the occupation, of that part of life which decides the character for ever, that the mode and the principles on which it engages the sympathy, and strikes the imagination,

become of the utmost importance to the morals and manners of
every society. Your rulers were well aware of this; and in their
system of changing your manners to accommodate them to their
politics, they found nothing so convenient as Rousseau.
Through him they teach men to love after the fashion of philosophers; that is, they teach to men, to Frenchmen, a love without
gallantry; a love without anything of that fine flower of youth-
fulness and gentility, which places it, if not among the virtues,
among the ornaments of life. Instead of this passion, naturally
allied to grace and manners, they infuse into their youth an unfashioned, indelicate, sour, gloomy, ferocious medley of pedantry
and lewdness; of metaphysical speculations blended with the
coarsest sensuality. Such is the general morality of the passions
to be found in their famous philosopher, in his famous work of
philosophic gallantry the *Nouvelle Eloise.*[22]

When the fence from the gallantry of preceptors is broken
down, and your families are no longer protected by decent pride,
and salutary domestic prejudice, there is but one step to a frightful corruption. The rulers in the National Assembly are in good
hopes that the females of the first families in France may become
an easy prey to dancing-masters, fiddlers, pattern-drawers,
friseurs, and valets de chambre, and other active citizens of that
description, who having the entry into your houses, and being
half domesticated by their situation, may be blended with you by
regular and irregular relations. By a law they have made these
people your equals. By adopting the sentiments of Rousseau
they have made them your rivals. In this manner these great legislators complete their plan of levelling, and establish their rights
of men on a sure foundation.

I am certain that the writings of Rousseau lead directly to this
kind of shameful evil. I have often wondered how he comes to
be so much more admired and followed on the continent than
he is here. Perhaps a secret charm in the language may have its
share in this extraordinary difference. We certainly perceive, and
to a degree we feel, in this writer, a style glowing, animated,
enthusiastic; at the same time that we find it lax, diffuse, and not
in the best taste of composition; all the members of the piece
being pretty equally laboured and expanded, without any due
selection or subordination of parts. He is generally too much on
the stretch, and his manner has little variety. We cannot rest upon

any of his works, though they contain observations which occasionally discover a considerable insight into human nature. But his doctrines, on the whole, are so inapplicable to real life and manners, that we never dream of drawing from them any rule for laws or conduct, or for fortifying or illustrating anything by a reference to his opinions. They have with us the fate of older paradoxes,

> Cum ventum ad verum est sensus moresque *repugnant*,
> *Atque ipsa utilitas justi prope mater et æqui.*[23]

Perhaps bold speculations are more acceptable because more new to you than to us, who have been long since satiated with them. We continue, as in the two last ages, to read, more generally than I believe is now done on the continent, the authors of sound antiquity. These occupy our minds. They give us another taste and turn; and will not suffer us to be more than transiently amused with paradoxical morality. It is not that I consider this writer as wholly destitute of just notions. Amongst his irregularities, it must be reckoned that he is sometimes moral, and moral in a very sublime strain. But the *general spirit and tendency* of his works is mischievous; and the more mischievous for this mixture: for perfect depravity of sentiment is not reconcilable with eloquence; and the mind (though corruptible, not complexionally vicious) would reject, and throw off with disgust, a lesson of pure and unmixed evil. These writers make even virtue a pander to vice.

However, I less consider the author than the system of the Assembly in perverting morality through his means. This I confess makes me nearly despair of any attempt upon the minds of their followers, through reason, honour, or conscience. The great object of your tyrants is to destroy the gentlemen of France; and for that purpose they destroy, to the best of their power, all the effect of those relations which may render considerable men powerful, or even safe. To destroy that order, they vitiate the whole community. That no means may exist of confederating against their tyranny, by the false sympathies of this Nouvelle Eloise they endeavour to subvert those principles of domestic trust and fidelity, which form the discipline of social life. They propagate principles by which every servant may think it, if not his duty, at least his privilege, to betray his master. By these principles, every considerable father of a family loses the sanctuary of his house. *Debet sua cuique domus esse perfugium tutissimum,*[24] says the law, which your legislators have taken so much pains first to decry, then to repeal. They destroy all the tranquillity and security of domestic life; turning the asylum of the house into a gloomy prison, where the father of the family must drag out a miserable existence, endangered in proportion to the apparent means of his safety; where he is worse than solitary in a crowd of domestics, and more apprehensive from his servants and inmates, than from the hired, blood-thirsty mob without-doors, who are ready to pull him to the lanterne.

It is thus, and for the same end, that they endeavour to destroy that tribunal of conscience which exists independently of edicts and decrees. Your despots govern by terror. They know that he who fears God fears nothing else: and therefore they eradicate from the mind, through their Voltaire, their Helvetius,[25] and the rest of that infamous gang, that only sort of fear which generates true courage. Their object is, that their fellow-citizens may be under the dominion of no awe, but that of their committee of research, and of their lanterne.

Having found the advantage of assassination in the formation of their tyranny, it is the grand resource in which they trust for the support of it. Whoever opposes any of their proceedings, or is suspected of a design to oppose them, is to answer it with his life, or the lives of his wife and children. This infamous, cruel, and cowardly practice of assassination they have the impudence to call *merciful*. They boast that they have operated their usurpation rather by terror than by force; and that a few seasonable murders have prevented the bloodshed of many battles. There is no doubt they will extend these acts of mercy whenever they see an occasion. Dreadful, however, will be the consequences of their attempt to avoid the evils of war by the merciful policy of murder. If, by effectual punishment of the guilty, they do not wholly disavow that practice, and the threat of it too, as any part of their policy; if ever a foreign prince enters into France, he must enter it as into a country of assassins. The mode of civilised war will not be practised; nor are the French who act on the present system entitled to expect it. They, whose known policy is to assassinate every citizen whom they suspect to be discontented by their tyranny, and to corrupt the soldiery of every open enemy, must look for no modified hostility. All war, which is not battle, will be military execution. This will beget acts of retaliation from you; and every retaliation will beget a new revenge. The hell-hounds of war, on all sides, will be uncoupled and unmuzzled. The new school of murder and barbarism, set up in Paris, having destroyed (so far as in it lies) all the other manners and principles which have hitherto civilised Europe, will destroy also the mode of civilised war, which, more than anything else, has distinguished the Christian world. Such is the approaching golden age, which the Virgil* of your Assembly has sung to his Pollios![26]

In such a situation of your political, your civil, and your social morals and manners, how can you be hurt by the freedom of any discussion? Caution is for those who have something to lose. What I have said, to justify myself in not apprehending any ill consequence from a free discussion of the absurd consequences which flow from the relation of the lawful king to the usurped constitution, will apply to my vindication with regard to the exposure I have made of the state of the army under the same sophistic usurpation. The present tyrants want no arguments to prove, what they must daily feel, that no good army can exist on their principles. They are in no want of a monitor to suggest to them the policy of getting rid of the army, as well as of the king, whenever they are in a condition to effect that measure. What hopes may be entertained of your army for the restoration of your liberties, I know not. At present, yielding obedience to the pretended orders of a king, who, they are perfectly apprised, has no will, and who never can issue a mandate which is not intended, in the first operation, or in its certain consequences, for his own destruction, your army seems to make one of the principal links in the chain of that servitude of anarchy, by which a cruel usurpation holds an undone people at once in bondage and confusion.

You ask me what I think of the conduct of General Monk.[27] How this affects your case I cannot tell. I doubt whether you possess, in France, any persons of a capacity to serve the French monarchy in the same manner in which Monk served the monarchy of England. The army which Monk commanded had been formed by Cromwell to a perfection of discipline which perhaps has never been exceeded. That army was besides of an excellent composition. The soldiers were men of extraordinary piety after their mode, of the greatest regularity, and even severity of manners; brave in the field, but modest, quiet, and orderly in

---

* Mirabeau's speech concerning universal peace.

their quarters; men who abhorred the idea of assassinating their officers or any other persons; and who (they at least who served in this island) were firmly attached to those generals by whom they were well treated and ably commanded. Such an army, once gained, might be depended on. I doubt much, if you could now find a Monk, whether a Monk could find in France such an army.

I certainly agree with you, that in all probability we owe our whole constitution to the restoration of the English monarchy. The state of things from which Monk relieved England, was however by no means, at that time, so deplorable, in any sense, as yours is now, and under the present sway is likely to continue. Cromwell had delivered England from anarchy. His government, though military and despotic, had been regular and orderly. Under the iron, and under the yoke, the soil yielded its produce. After his death, the evils of anarchy were rather dreaded than felt. Every man was yet safe in his house and in his property. But it must be admitted, that Monk freed this nation from great and just apprehensions both of future anarchy and of probable tyranny in some form or other. The king whom he gave us was indeed the very reverse of your benignant sovereign, who, in reward for his attempt to bestow liberty on his subjects, languishes himself in prison. The person given to us by Monk was a man without any sense of his duty as a prince, without any regard to the dignity of his crown; without any love to his people; dissolute, false, venal, and destitute of any positive good quality whatsoever, except a pleasant temper, and the manners of a gentleman. Yet the restoration of our monarchy, even in the person of such a prince, was everything to us; for without monarchy in England, most certainly we never can enjoy either peace or liberty. It was under this conviction that the very regular step, which we took on the Revolution of 1688, was to fill the throne with a real king; and even before it could be done in due form, the chiefs of the nation did not attempt themselves to exercise authority so much as by *interim*. They instantly requested the Prince of Orange to take the government on himself. The throne was not effectively vacant for an hour.

Your fundamental laws, as well as ours, suppose a monarchy. Your zeal, Sir, in standing so firmly for it as you have done, shows not only a sacred respect for your honour and fidelity, but a well-informed attachment to the real welfare and true liberties of your country. I have expressed myself ill, if I have given you cause to imagine that I prefer the conduct of those who have retired from this warfare, to your behaviour, who, with a courage and constancy almost supernatural, have struggled against tyranny. and kept the field to the last. You see I have corrected the exceptionable part in the edition which I now send you. Indeed, in such terrible extremities as yours, it is not easy to say, in a political view, what line of conduct is the most advisable. In that state of things, I cannot bring myself severely to condemn persons who are wholly unable to bear so much as the sight of those men in the throne of legislation, who are only fit to be the objects of criminal justice. If fatigue, if disgust, if unsurmountable nausea drive them away from such spectacles, *ubi miseriarum pars non minima erat, videre et aspici,*[28] I cannot blame them. He must have a heart of adamant who could hear a set of traitors, puffed up with unexpected and undeserved power, obtained by an ignoble, unmanly, and perfidious rebellion, treating their honest fellow-citizens as *rebels*, because they refused to bind themselves, through their conscience, against the dictates of conscience itself, and had declined to swear an active compliance with their own ruin. How could a man of common flesh and blood endure, that those, who but the other day had skulked unobserved in their antechambers, scornfully insulting men, illustrious in their rank, sacred in their function, and venerable in their character, now in decline of life, and swimming on the wrecks of their fortunes, that those miscreants should tell such men scornfully and outrageously, after they had robbed them of all their property, that it is more than enough if they are allowed what will keep them from absolute famine, and that, for the rest, they must let their grey hairs fall over the plough, to make out a scanty subsistence with the labour of their hands! Last, and worst, who could endure to hear this unnatural, insolent, and savage despotism called liberty? If, at this distance, sitting by my fire, I cannot read their decrees and speeches without indignation, shall I condemn those who have fled from the actual sight and hearing of all these horrors? No, no! mankind has no title to demand that we should be slaves to their guilt and insolence; or that we should serve them in spite of themselves. Minds, sore with the poignant sense of insulted virtue, filled with high disdain against the pride of triumphant baseness, often have it not in their choice to stand their ground. Their complexion (which might defy the rack) cannot go through such a trial. Something very high must fortify

men to that proof. But when I am driven to comparison, surely
I cannot hesitate for a moment to prefer to such men as are common, those heroes, who, in the midst of despair, perform all the
tasks of hope; who subdue their feelings to their duties; who,
in the cause of humanity, liberty, and honour, abandon all the
satisfactions of life, and every day incur a fresh risk of life itself.
Do me the justice to believe that I never can prefer any fastidious
virtue (virtue still) to the unconquered perseverance, to the
affectionate patience, of those who watch day and night by the
bed-side of their delirious country, who, for their love to that
dear and venerable name, bear all the disgusts and all the buffets
they receive from their frantic mother. Sir, I do look on you as
true martyrs; I regard you as soldiers who act far more in the spirit
of our Commander-in-chief, and the Captain of our salvation,
than those who have left you; though I must first bolt myself very
thoroughly, and know that I could do better, before I can censure
them. I assure you, Sir, that when I consider your unconquerable
fidelity to your sovereign, and to your country; the courage, fortitude, magnanimity, and long-suffering of yourself, and the
Abbé Maury,[29] and of M. Cazales,[30] and of many worthy persons
of all orders, in your Assembly, I forget, in the lustre of these great
qualities, that on your side has been displayed an eloquence so
rational, manly, and convincing, that no time or country, perhaps, has ever excelled. But your talents disappear in my admiration of your virtues.

As to M. Mounier and M. Lally,[31] I have always wished to do
justice to their parts, and their eloquence, and the general purity
of their motives. Indeed I saw very well, from the beginning, the
mischiefs which, with all these talents and good intentions, they
would do their country, through their confidence in systems. But
their distemper was an epidemic malady. They were young and
inexperienced; and when will young and inexperienced men
learn caution and distrust of themselves? And when will men,
young or old, if suddenly raised to far higher power than that
which absolute kings and emperors commonly enjoy, learn
anything like moderation? Monarchs in general respect some
settled order of things, which they find it difficult to move from
its basis, and to which they are obliged to conform, even when
there are no positive limitations to their power. These gentlemen
conceived that they were chosen to new-model the state, and
even the whole order of civil society itself. No wonder that

they entertained dangerous visions, when the king's ministers, trustees for the sacred deposit of the monarchy, were so infected with the contagion of project and system, (I can hardly think it black premeditated treachery,) that they publicly advertised for plans and schemes of government, as if they were to provide for the rebuilding of an hospital that had been burned down. What was this, but to unchain the fury of rash speculation amongst a people of itself but too apt to be guided by a heated imagination, and a wild spirit of adventure?

The fault of M. Mounier and M. Lally was very great; but it was very general. If those gentlemen stopped when they came to the brink of the gulf of guilt and public misery, that yawned before them in the abyss of these dark and bottomless specula-tions, I forgive their first error: in that they were involved with many. Their repentance was their own.

They who consider Mounier and Lally as deserters, must regard themselves as murderers and as traitors: for from what else than murder and treason did they desert? For my part, I honour them for not having carried mistake into crime. If, indeed, I thought that they were not cured by experience; that they were not made sensible that those, who would reform a state, ought to assume some actual constitution of government which is to be reformed; if they are not at length satisfied that it is become a necessary preliminary to liberty in France, to commence by the re-establishment of order and property of *every* kind, and, through the re-establishment of their monarchy, of every one of the old habitual distinctions and classes of the state; if they do not see that these classes are not to be confounded in order to be afterwards revived and separated; if they are not convinced that the scheme of parochial and club governments takes up the state at the wrong end, and is a low and senseless contrivance, (as making the sole constitution of a supreme power,) I should then allow that their early rashness ought to be remembered to the last moment of their lives.

You gently reprehend me, because, in holding out the picture of your disastrous situation, I suggest no plan for a remedy. Alas! Sir, the proposition of plans, without an attention to circum-stances, is the very cause of all your misfortunes; and never shall you find me aggravating, by the infusion of any speculations of mine, the evils which have arisen from the speculations of others. Your malady, in this respect, is a disorder of repletion. You seem to think that my keeping back my poor ideas may arise from an indifference to the welfare of a foreign, and, sometimes, an hostile nation. No, Sir, I faithfully assure you, my reserve is owing to no such causes. Is this letter, swelled to a second book, a mark of national antipathy, or even of national indifference? I should act altogether in the spirit of the same caution, in a similar state of our own domestic affairs. If I were to venture any advice, in any case, it would be my best. The sacred duty of an adviser (one of the most inviolable that exists) would lead me, towards a real enemy, to act as if my best friend were the party concerned. But I dare not risk a speculation with no better view of your affairs than at present I can command; my caution is not from disregard, but from solicitude for your welfare. It is suggested solely from my dread of becoming the author of inconsiderate counsel.

It is not, that, as this strange series of actions has passed before my eyes, I have not indulged my mind in a great variety of political speculations concerning them. But compelled by no such positive duty as does not permit me to evade an opinion; called upon by no ruling power, without authority as I am, and without confidence, I should ill answer my own ideas of what would become myself, or what would be serviceable to others, if I were, as a volunteer, to obtrude any project of mine upon a nation, to whose circumstances I could not be sure it might be applicable.

Permit me to say, that if I were as confident, as I ought to be diffident, in my own loose, general ideas, I never should venture to broach them, if but at twenty leagues distance from the centre of your affairs. I must see with mine own eyes, I must, in a manner, touch with my own hands, not only the fixed but the momentary circumstances, before I could venture to suggest any political project whatsoever. I must know the power and disposition to accept, to execute, to persevere. I must see all the aids, and all the obstacles. I must see the means of correcting the plan, where correctives would be wanted. I must see the things; I must see the men. Without a concurrence and adaptation of these to the design, the very best speculative projects might become not only useless but mischievous. Plans must be made for men. We cannot think of making men and binding nature to our designs. People at a distance must judge ill of men. They do not always answer to their reputation when you approach them. Nay, the perspective varies, and shows them quite otherwise than you thought them. At a distance, if we judge uncertainly of men, we must judge worse of *opportunities*, which continually vary their shapes and colours, and pass away like clouds. The Eastern politicians never do anything without the opinion of the astrologers on the *fortunate moment*. They are in the right if they do no better; for the opinion of fortune is something towards commanding it. Statesmen of a more judicious prescience look for the fortunate moment too; but they seek it, not in the conjunctions and oppositions of planets, but in the conjunctions and oppositions of men and things. These form their almanack.

To illustrate the mischief of a wise plan, without any attention to means and circumstances, it is not necessary to go farther than to your recent history. In the condition in which France was found three years ago, what better system could be proposed, what less, even savouring of wild theory, what fitter to provide for all the exigencies, whilst it reformed all the abuses, of government, than the convention of the states-general? I think nothing better could be imagined. But I have censured, and do still presume to censure, your parliament of Paris for not having suggested to the king, that this proper measure was of all measures the most critical and arduous; one in which the utmost circumspection and the greatest number of precautions were the most absolutely necessary. The very confession that a government wants either amendment in its conformation, or relief to great distress, causes it to lose half its reputation, and as great a proportion of its strength as depends upon that reputation. It was therefore necessary, first to put government out of danger, whilst at its own desire it suffered such an operation, as a general reform at the hands of those who were much more filled with a sense of the disease, than provided with rational means of a cure.

It may be said, that this care, and these precautions, were more naturally the duty of the king's ministers, than that of the parliament. They were so; but every man must answer in his estimation for the advice he gives, when he puts the conduct of his measure into hands who he does not know will execute his plans according to his ideas. Three or four ministers were not to be trusted with the being of the French monarchy, of all the orders, and of all the distinctions, and all the property of the kingdom. What must be the prudence of those who could think, in the then known temper of the people of Paris, of assembling the states at a place situated as Versailles?

The parliament of Paris did worse than to inspire this blind confidence into the king. For, as if names were things, they took no notice of (indeed they rather countenanced) the deviations which were manifest in the execution, from the true ancient principles of the plan which they recommended. These deviations (as guardians of the ancient laws, usages, and constitution of the kingdom) the parliament of Paris ought not to have suffered, without the strongest remonstrances to the throne. It ought to have sounded the alarm to the whole nation, as it had often done on things of infinitely less importance. Under pretence of resuscitating the ancient constitution, the parliament saw one of the strongest acts of innovation, and the most leading in its consequences, carried into effect before their eyes; and an innovation through the medium of despotism; that is, they suffered the king's ministers to new-model the whole representation of the *tiers état*,[32] and, in a great measure, that of the clergy too, and to destroy the ancient proportions of the orders. These changes, unquestionably, the king had no right to make; and here the parliaments failed in their duty, and, along with their country, have perished by this failure.

What a number of faults have led to this multitude of misfortunes, and almost all from this one source, – that of considering certain general maxims, without attending to circumstances, to times, to places, to conjunctures, and to actors! If we do not attend scrupulously to all these, the medicine of to-day becomes the poison of to-morrow. If any measure was in the abstract better than another, it was to call the states – *ea visa salus morientibus una.*[33] – Certainly it had the appearance. – But see the consequences of not attending to critical moments, of not regarding the symptoms which discriminate diseases, and which distinguish constitutions, complexions, and humours:

> *Mox erat hoc ipsum exitio; furiisque refecti,*
> *Ardebant; ipsique suos, jam morte sub ægra,*
> *Discissos nudis laniabant dentibus artus.*[34]

Thus the potion which was given to strengthen the constitution, to heal divisions, and to compose the minds of men, became the source of debility, phrensy, discord, and utter dissolution.

In this, perhaps, I have answered, I think, another of your questions – Whether the British constitution is adapted to your circumstances? When I praised the British constitution, and wished it to be well studied, I did not mean that its exterior form and positive arrangement should become a model for you, or for any people, servilely to copy. I meant to recommend the *principles* from which it has grown, and the policy on which it has been progressively improved out of elements common to you and to us. I am sure it is no visionary theory of mine. It is not an advice that subjects you to the hazard of any experiment. I believed the ancient principles to be wise in all cases of a large empire that would be free. I thought you possessed our principles in your old forms, in as great a perfection as we did originally. If your states agreed (as I think they did) with your circumstances, they were best for you. As you had a constitution formed upon principles similar to ours, my idea was, that you might have improved them as we have done, conforming them to the state and exigencies of the times, and the condition of property in your country; having the conservation of that property, and the substantial basis of your monarchy, as principal objects in all your reforms.

I do not advise a House of Lords to you. Your ancient course by representatives of the noblesse (in your circumstances) appears to me rather a better institution. I know that, with you, a set of men of rank have betrayed their constituents, their honour, their trust, their king, and their country, and levelled themselves with their footmen, that through this degradation they might afterwards put themselves above their natural equals. Some of these persons have entertained a project, that, in reward of this their black perfidy and corruption, they may be chosen to give rise to a new order, and to establish thamselves into a House of Lords. Do you think that, under the name of a British constitution, I mean to recommend to you such lords, made of such kind of stuff? I do not however include in this description all of those who are fond of this scheme.

If you were now to form such a House of Peers, it would bear, in my opinion, but little resemblance to ours in its origin, character, or the purposes which it might answer, at the same time that it would destroy your true natural nobility: but if you are not in a condition to frame a House of Lords, still less are you capable, in my opinion, of framing anything which virtually and substantially could be answerable (for the purposes of a stable, regular government) to our House of Commons. That House is, within itself, a much more subtle and artificial combination of parts and powers, than people are generally aware of. What knits it to the other members of the constitution; what fits it to be at once the great support and the great control of government; what makes it of such admirable service to that monarchy which, if it limits, it secures and strengthens, would require a long discourse, belonging to the leisure of a contemplative man, not to one whose duty it is to join in communicating practically to the people the blessings of such a constitution.

Your *tiers état* was not in effect and substance a House of Commons. You stood in absolute need of something else to supply the manifest defects in such a body as your *tiers état*. On a sober and dispassionate view of your old constitution, as connected with all the present circumstances, I was fully persuaded, that the crown, standing as things have stood, (and are likely to stand, if you are to have any monarchy at all,) was and is capable, alone and by itself, of holding a just balance between the two orders, and at the same time of effecting the interior and exterior purposes of a protecting government. I, whose leading principle it is, in a reformation of the state, to make use of existing materials, am of opinion, that the representation of the clergy, as a separate order, was an institution which touched all the orders more nearly than any of them touched the other; that it was well fitted to connect them; and to hold a place in any wise, monarchical commonwealth. If I refer you to your original constitution, and think it, as I do, substantially a good one, I do not amuse you in this, more than in other things, with any inventions of mine. A certain intemperance of intellect is the disease of the time, and the source of all its other diseases. I will keep myself as untainted by it as I can. Your architects build without a foundation. I would readily lend a helping hand to any superstructure, when once this is effectually secured – but first I would say,[35] δος που στω.

You think, Sir, and you may think rightly, upon the first view of the theory, that to provide for the exigencies of an empire, so situated and so related as that of France, its king ought to be invested with powers very much superior to those which the king of England possesses under the letter of our constitution. Every degree of power necessary to the state, and not destructive to the rational and moral freedom of individuals, to that personal liberty, and personal security, which contribute so much to the vigour, the prosperity, the happiness, and the dignity of a nation – every degree of power which does not suppose the total absence of all control and all responsibility on the part of ministers, – a king of France, in common sense, ought to possess. But whether the exact measure of authority, assigned by the letter of the law to the king of Great Britain, can answer to the exterior or interior purposes of the French monarchy, is a point which I cannot venture to judge upon. Here, both in the power given, and its limitations, we have always cautiously felt our way. The parts of our constitution have gradually, and almost insensibly, in a long course of time, accommodated themselves to each other, and to their common, as well as to their separate, purposes. But this adaptation of contending parts, as it has not been in ours, so it can never be in yours, or in any country, the effect of a single instantaneous regulation, and no sound heads could ever think of doing it in that manner.

I believe, Sir, that many on the continent altogether mistake the condition of a king of Great Britain. He is a real king, and not an executive officer. If he will not trouble himself with contemptible details, nor wish to degrade himself by becoming a party in little squabbles, I am far from sure, that a king of Great Britain, in whatever concerns him as a king, or indeed as a rational man, who combines his public interest with his personal satisfaction, does not possess a more real, solid, extensive power, than the king of France was possessed of before this miserable Revolution. The direct power of the king of England is considerable. His indirect, and far more certain power, is great indeed. He stands in need of nothing towards dignity; of nothing towards splendour; of nothing towards authority; of nothing at all towards consideration abroad. When was it that a king of England wanted wherewithal to make him respected, courted, or perhaps even feared, in every state of Europe?

I am constantly of opinion, that your states, in three orders, on the footing on which they stood in 1614, were capable of being brought into a proper and harmonious combination with royal authority. This constitution by estates, was the natural and only just representation of France. It grew out of the habitual conditions, relations, and reciprocal claims of men. It grew out of the circumstances of the country, and out of the state of property. The wretched scheme of your present masters is not to fit the constitution to the people, but wholly to destroy conditions, to dissolve relations, to change the state of the nation, and to subvert property, in order to fit their country to their theory of a constitution.

Until you make out practically that great work, a combination of opposing forces, "a work of labour long, and endless praise,"[36] the utmost caution ought to have been used in the reduction of the royal power, which alone was capable of holding together the comparatively heterogeneous mass of your states. But, at this day, all these considerations are unseasonable. To what end should we discuss the limitations of royal power? Your king is in prison. Why speculate on the measure and standard of liberty? I doubt much, very much indeed, whether France is at all ripe for liberty on any standard. Men are qualified for civil liberty in exact proportion to their disposition to put moral chains upon their own appetites; in proportion as their love to justice is above their rapacity; in proportion as their soundness and sobriety of understanding is above their vanity and presumption; in proportion as they are more disposed to listen to the counsels of the wise and good, in preference to the flattery of knaves. Society cannot exist unless a controlling power upon will and appetite be placed somewhere, and the less of it there is within, the more there must be without. It is ordained in the eternal constitution of things, that men of intemperate minds cannot be free. Their passions forge their fetters.

This sentence the prevalent part of your countrymen execute on themselves. They possessed not long since, what was next to freedom, a mild paternal monarchy. They despised it for its weakness. They were offered a well-poised, free constitution. It did not suit their taste nor their temper. They carved for themselves; they flew out, murdered, robbed, and rebelled. They have succeeded, and put over their country an insolent tyranny made up of cruel and inexorable masters, and that too of a description hitherto not known in the world. The powers and policies by which they have succeeded are not those of great statesmen, or great military commanders, but the practices of incendiaries, assassins, housebreakers, robbers, spreaders of false news, forgers of false orders from authority, and other delinquencies, of which ordinary justice takes cognisance. Accordingly the spirit of their rule is exactly correspondent to the means by which they obtained it. They act more in the manner of thieves who have got possession of a house, than of conquerors who have subdued a nation.

Opposed to these in appearance, but in appearance only, is another band, who call themselves the *moderate*. These, if I conceive rightly of their conduct, are a set of men who approve heartily of the whole new constitution, but wish to lay heavily on the most atrocious of those crimes, by which this fine constitution of theirs has been obtained. They are a sort of people who affect to proceed as if they thought that men may deceive without fraud, rob without injustice, and overturn everything without violence. They are men who would usurp the government of their country with decency and moderation. In fact, they are nothing more or better, than men engaged in desperate designs, with feeble minds. They are not honest; they are only ineffectual and unsystematic in their iniquity. They are persons who want not the dispositions, but the energy and vigour, that is necessary for great evil machinations. They find that in such designs they fall at best into a secondary rank, and others take the place and lead in usurpation, which they are not qualified to obtain or to hold. They envy to their companions the natural fruit of their crimes; they join to run them down with the hue and cry of mankind, which pursues their common offences; and then hope to mount into their places on the credit of the sobriety with which they show themselves disposed to carry on what may seem most plausible in the mischievous projects they pursue in common. But these men are naturally despised by those who have heads to know, and hearts that are able to go through, the necessary demands of bold wicked enterprises. They are naturally classed below the latter description, and will only be used by them as inferior instruments. They will be only the Fairfaxes[37] of your Cromwells. If they mean honestly, why do they not strengthen the arms of honest men, to support their ancient, legal, wise, and free government, given to them in the spring of 1788, against the inventions of craft, and the theories of ignorance and folly? If they do not, they must continue the scorn of both parties; sometimes the tool, sometimes the encumbrance, of that, whose views they approve, whose conduct they decry. These people are only made to be the sport of tyrants. They never can obtain or communicate freedom.

You ask me too, whether we have a committee of research.[38] No, Sir, – God forbid! It is the necessary instrument of tyranny and usurpation; and therefore I do not wonder that it has had an early establishment under your present lords. We do not want it.

Excuse my length. I have been somewhat occupied since I was honoured with your letter; and I should not have been able to answer it at all, but for the holidays, which have given me means of enjoying the leisure of the country. I am called to duties which I am neither able nor willing to evade. I must soon return to my old conflict with the corruptions and oppressions which have prevailed in our eastern dominions. I must turn myself wholly from those of France.

In England we *cannot* work so hard as Frenchmen. Frequent relaxation is necessary to us. You are naturally more intense in your application. I did not know this part of your national character, until I went into France in 1773. At present, this your disposition to labour is rather increased than lessened. In your Assembly you do not allow yourselves a recess even on Sundays. We have two days in the week, besides the festivals; and besides five or six months of the summer and autumn. This continued, unremitted effort of the members of your Assembly, I take to be one among the causes of the mischief they have done. They who always labour can have no true judgment. You never give yourselves time to cool. You can never survey, from its proper point of sight, the work you have finished, before you decree its final execution. You can never plan the future by the past. You never go into the country, soberly and dispassionately to observe the effect of your measures on their objects. You cannot feel distinctly how far the people are rendered better and improved, or more miserable and depraved, by what you have done. You cannot see with your own eyes the sufferings and afflictions you cause. You know them but at a distance, on the statements of those who always flatter the reigning power, and who, amidst their representations of the grievances, inflame your minds against those who are oppressed. These are amongst the effects of unremitted labour, when men exhaust their attention, burn out their candles, and are left in the dark. – *Malo meorum negligentiam, quam istorum obscuram diligentiam.*

I have the honour, &c.

(Signed) EDMUND BURKE

Beaconsfield, January 19th, 1791.

From AN APPEAL FROM THE
NEW TO THE OLD WHIGS

1791

AT MR. BURKE'S time of life, and in his dispositions, *petere hon-estam missionem*[1] was all he had to do with his political associates. This boon they have not chosen to grant him. With many expressions of good-will, in effect they tell him he has loaded the stage too long. They conceive it, though a harsh, yet a necessary office, in full parliament to declare to the present age, and to as late a posterity, as shall take any concern in the proceedings of our day, that by one book he has disgraced the whole tenour of his life. Thus they dismiss their old partner of the war. He is advised to retire, whilst they continue to serve the public upon wiser principles, and under better auspices.

Whether Diogenes the Cynic[2] was a true philosopher, cannot easily be determined. He has written nothing. But the sayings of his which are handed down by others are lively; and may be easily and aptly applied on many occasions by those whose wit is not so perfect as their memory. This Diogenes (as every one will recollect) was citizen of a little bleak town situated on the coast of the Euxine, and exposed to all the buffets of that unhospitable sea. He lived at a great distance from those weather-beaten walls, in ease and indolence, and in the midst of literary leisure, when he was informed that his townsmen had condemned him to be banished from Sinope; he answered coolly, "And I condemn them to live in Sinope."

The gentlemen of a party in which Mr. Burke has always acted, in passing upon him the sentence of retirement, have done nothing more than to confirm the sentence which he had long before passed upon himself. When that retreat was choice, which the tribunal of his peers inflict as punishment, it is plain he does not think their sentence intolerably severe. Whether they, who are to continue in the Sinope which shortly he is to leave, will spend the long years which, I hope, remain to them, in a manner more to their satisfaction, than he shall slide down, in silence and obscurity, the slope of his declining days, is best known to Him who measures out years, and days, and fortunes.

The quality of the sentence does not however decide on the

justice of it. Angry friendship is sometimes as bad as calm enmity. For this reason the cold neutrality of abstract justice is, to a good and clear cause, a more desirable thing than an affection liable to be any way disturbed. When the trial is by friends, if the decision should happen to be favourable, the honour of the acquittal is lessened; if adverse, the condemnation is exceedingly embittered. It is aggravated by coming from lips professing friendship, and pronouncing judgment with sorrow and reluctance. Taking in the whole view of life, it is more safe to live under the jurisdiction of severe but steady reason, than under the empire of indulgent but capricious passion. It is certainly well for Mr. Burke that there are impartial men in the world. To them I address myself, pending the appeal which on his part is made from the living to the dead, from the modern Whigs to the antient.

The gentlemen, who, in the name of the party, have passed sentence on Mr. Burke's book, in the light of literary criticism, are judges above all challenge. He did not indeed flatter himself, that as a writer he could claim the approbation of men whose talents, in his judgment and in the public judgment, approach to prodigies; if ever such persons should be disposed to estimate the merit of a composition upon the standard of their own ability.

In their critical censure, though Mr. Burke may find himself humbled by it as a writer, as a man, and as an Englishman, he finds matter not only of consolation, but of pride. He proposed to convey to a foreign people, not his own ideas, but the prevalent opinions and sentiments of a nation, renowned for wisdom, and celebrated in all ages for a well-understood and well-regulated love of freedom. This was the avowed purpose of the far greater part of his work. As that work has not been ill received, and as his critics will not only admit but contend, that this reception could not be owing to any excellence in the composition capable of perverting the public judgment, it is clear that he is not disavowed by the nation whose sentiments he had undertaken to describe. His representation is authenticated by the verdict of his country. Had his piece, as a work of skill, been thought worthy of commendation, some doubt might have been entertained of the cause of his success. But the matter stands exactly as he wishes it. He is more happy to have his fidelity in representation recognised by the body of the people, than if he were to be ranked in point of ability (and higher he could not be ranked) with those whose critical censure he has had the misfortune to incur.

It is not from this part of their decision which the author wishes an appeal. There are things which touch him more nearly. To abandon them would argue, not diffidence in his abilities, but treachery to his cause. Had his work been recognised as a pattern for dextrous argument and powerful eloquence, yet if it tended to establish maxims, or to inspire sentiments, adverse to the wise and free constitution of this kingdom, he would only have cause to lament, that it possessed qualities fitted to perpetuate the memory of his offence. Oblivion would be the only means of his escaping the reproaches of posterity. But, after receiving the common allowance due to the common weakness of man, he wishes to owe no part of the indulgence of the world to its forget-fulness. He is at issue with the party before the present, and, if ever he can reach it, before the coming, generation.

The author, several months previous to his publication, well knew, that two gentlemen, both of them possessed of the most distinguished abilities, and of a most decisive authority in the party, had differed with him in one of the most material points relative to the French Revolution; that is, in their opinion of the behaviour of the French soldiery, and its revolt from its officers. At the time of their public declaration on this subject, he did not imagine the opinion of these two gentlemen had extended a great way beyond themselves. He was however well aware of the probability, that persons of their just credit and influence would at length dispose the greater number to an agreement with their sentiments; and perhaps might induce the whole body to a tacit acquiescence in their declarations, under a natural, and not always an improper dislike of showing a difference with those who lead their party. I will not deny, that in general this conduct in parties is defensible; but within what limits the practice is to be circumscribed, and with what exceptions the doctrine which supports it is to be received, it is not my present purpose to define. The present question has nothing to do with their motives; it only regards the public expression of their sentiments.

The author is compelled, however reluctantly, to receive the sentence pronounced upon him in the House of Commons as that of the party. It proceeded from the mouth of him who must be regarded as its authentic organ.[3] In a discussion which continued for two days, no one gentleman of the opposition interposed a negative, or even a doubt, in favour of him or of his opinions. If an idea consonant to the doctrine of his book, or favourable to his conduct, lurks in the minds of any persons in that description, it is to be considered only as a peculiarity which they indulge to their own private liberty of thinking. The author cannot reckon upon it. It has nothing to do with them as members of a party. In their public capacity, in everything that meets the public ear, or public eye, the body must be considered as unanimous.

They must have been animated with a very warm zeal against those opinions, because they were under no *necessity* of acting as they did, from any just cause of apprehension that the errors of this writer should be taken for theirs. They might disapprove; it was not necessary they should *disavow* him, as they have done in the whole, and in all the parts of his book; because neither in the whole, nor in any of the parts, were they, directly, or by any implication, involved. The author was known indeed to have been warmly, strenuously, and affectionately, against all allure- ments of ambition, and all possibility of alienation from pride, or personal picque, or peevish jealousy, attached to the Whig party. With one of them he has had a long friendship, which he must ever remember with a melancholy pleasure. To the great, real, and amiable virtues, and to the unequalled abilities, of that gentleman, he shall always join with his country in paying a just tribute of applause. There are others in that party for whom, without any shade of sorrow, he bears as high a degree of love as can enter into the human heart; and as much veneration as ought to be paid to human creatures; because he firmly believes, that they are endowed with as many and as great virtues, as the nature of man is capable of producing, joined to great clearness of intel- lect, to a just judgment, to a wonderful temper, and to true wis- dom. His sentiments with regard to them can never vary, without subjecting him to the just indignation of mankind, who are bound, and are generally disposed, to look up with reverence to the best patterns of their species, and such as give a dignity to the nature of which we all participate. For the whole of the party he has high respect. Upon a view indeed of the composition of all parties, he finds great satisfaction. It is, that in leaving the service of his country, he leaves parliament without all comparison richer in abilities than he found it. Very solid and very brilliant talents distinguish the ministerial benches. The opposite rows are a sort of seminary of genius, and have brought forth such and so great talents as never before (amongst us at least) have appeared together. If their owners are disposed to serve their country (he trusts they are,) they are in a condition to render it services of the highest importance. If, through mistake or passion, they are led to contribute to its ruin, we shall at least have a consolation denied to the ruined country that adjoins us – we shall not be destroyed by men of mean or secondary capacities.

All these considerations of party attachment, of personal regard, and of personal admiration, rendered the Author of the Reflections extremely cautious, lest the slightest suspicion should arise of his having undertaken to express the sentiments even of a single man of that description. His words at the outset of his Reflections are these:

"In the first letter I had the honour to write to you, and which at length I send, I wrote neither *for*, nor *from* any description of men; nor shall I in this. My errors, if any, are *my own*. My reputation *alone* is to answer for them." In another place, he says "I have *no man's* proxy. I speak *only* from *myself*; when I disclaim, as I do, with all possible earnestness, all communion with the actors in that triumph, or with the admirers of it. When I assert anything else, as concerning the people of England, I speak from observation, *not from authority.*"

To say then, that the book did not contain the sentiments of their party, is not to contradict the author, or to clear themselves. If the party had denied his doctrines to be the current opinions of the majority in the nation, they would have put the question on its true issue. There, I hope and believe, his censurers will find on the trial, that the author is as faithful a representative of the general sentiment of the people of England, as any person amongst them can be of the ideas of his own party.

The French Revolution can have no connexion with the objects of any parties in England formed before the period of that event, unless they choose to imitate any of its acts, or to consolidate any principles of that Revolution with their own opinions. The French Revolution is no part of their original contract. The matter, standing by itself, is an open subject of political discussion, like all the other revolutions (and there are many) which have been attempted or accomplished in our age. But if any considerable number of British subjects, taking a factious interest in the proceedings of France, begin publicly to incorporate themselves for the subversion of nothing short of the *whole* constitution of this kingdom; to incorporate themselves for the utter overthrow of the body of its laws, civil and ecclesiastical, and with them of the whole system of its manners, in favour of the new constitution, and of the modern usages, of the French nation, I think no party principle could bind the author not to express his sentiments strongly against such a faction. On the contrary, he was perhaps bound to mark his dissent, when the leaders of the party were daily going out of their way to make public declarations in parliament, which, notwithstanding the purity of their intentions, had a tendency to encourage ill-designing men in their practices against our constitution.

The members of this faction leave no doubt of the nature and the extent of the mischief they mean to produce. They declare it openly and decisively. Their intentions are not left equivocal. They are put out of all dispute by the thanks which formally, and as it were officially, they issue, in order to recommend and to promote the circulation of the most atrocious and treasonable libels against all the hitherto cherished objects of the love and veneration of this people. Is it contrary to the duty of a good subject, to reprobate such proceedings? Is it alien to the office of a good member of parliament, when such practices increase, and when the audacity of the conspirators grows with their impunity, to point out in his place their evil tendency to the happy constitution which he is chosen to guard? Is it wrong, in any sense, to render the people of England sensible how much they must suffer if unfortunately such a wicked faction should become possessed in this country of the same power which their allies in the very next to us have so perfidiously usurped, and so outrageously abused? Is it inhuman to prevent, if possible, the spilling of *their* blood, or imprudent to guard against the effusion of *our own*? Is it contrary to any of the honest principles of party, or repugnant to any of the known duties of friendship, for any senator, respectfully, and amicably, to caution his brother members against countenancing, by inconsiderate expressions, a sort of proceeding which it is impossible they should deliberately approve?

He had undertaken to demonstrate, by arguments which he thought could not be refuted, and by documents, which he was sure could not be denied, that no comparison was to be made between the British government, and the French usurpation. That they who endeavoured madly to compare them, were by no means making the comparison of one good system with another good system, which varied only in local and circumstantial differences; much less, that they were holding out to us a superior pattern of legal liberty, which we might substitute in the place of our old, and, as they describe it, superannuated constitution. He meant to demonstrate, that the French scheme was not a comparative good, but a positive evil. That the question did not at all turn, as it had been stated, on a parallel between a monarchy and a republic. He denied that the present scheme of things in France did at all deserve the respectable name of a republic: he had therefore no comparison between monarchies and republics to make. That what was done in France was a wild attempt to methodise anarchy; to perpetuate and fix disorder. That it was a foul, impious, monstrous thing, wholly out of the course of moral nature. He undertook to prove, that it was generated in treachery, fraud, falsehood, hypocrisy, and unprovoked murder. He offered to make out, that those who have led in that business, had conducted themselves with the utmost perfidy to their colleagues in function, and with the most flagrant perjury both towards their king and their constituents; to the one of whom the Assembly had sworn fealty, and to the other, when under no sort of violence or constraint, they had sworn a full obedience to instructions. That, by the terror of assassination, they had driven away a very great number of the members, so as to produce a false appearance of a majority. That this fictitious majority had fabricated a constitution, which as it now stands, is a tyranny far beyond any example that can be found in the civilised European world of our age; that therefore the lovers of it must be lovers, not of liberty, but, if they really understand its nature, of the lowest and basest of all servitude.

He proposed to prove, that the present state of things in France is not a transient evil, productive, as some have too favourably represented it, of a lasting good; but that the present evil is only the means of producing future, and (if that were possible) worse evils. That it is not an undigested, imperfect, and crude scheme of liberty, which may gradually be mellowed and ripened into an orderly and social freedom; but that it is so fundamentally wrong, as to be utterly incapable of correcting itself by any length of time, or of being formed into any mode of polity, of which a member of the House of Commons could publicly declare his approbation.

If it had been permitted to Mr. Burke, he would have shown distinctly, and in detail, that what the Assembly calling itself

National, had held out as a large and liberal toleration, is in reality a cruel and insidious religious persecution; infinitely more bitter than any which had been heard of within this century. That it had a feature in it worse than the old persecutions. That the old persecutors acted, or pretended to act, from zeal towards some system of piety and virtue: they gave strong preferences to their own; and if they drove people from one religion, they provided for them another, in which men might take refuge and expect consolation. That their new persecution is not against a variety in conscience, but against all conscience. That it professes contempt towards its object; and whilst it treats all religion with scorn, is not so much as neutral about the modes: it unites the opposite evils of intolerance and of indifference.

He could have proved, that it is so far from rejecting tests, (as unaccountably had been asserted,) that the Assembly had imposed tests of a peculiar hardship, arising from a cruel and premeditated pecuniary fraud: tests against old principles, sanctioned by the laws, and binding upon the conscience. That these tests were not imposed as titles to some new honour or some new benefit, but to enable men to hold a poor compensation for their legal estates, of which they had been unjustly deprived; and, as they had before been reduced from affluence to indigence; so, on refusal to swear against their conscience, they are now driven from indigence to famine, and treated with every possible degree of outrage, insult, and inhumanity. That these tests, which their imposers well knew would not be taken, were intended for the very purpose of cheating their miserable victims out of the compensation which the tyrannic impostors of the Assembly had previously and purposely rendered the public unable to pay. That thus their ultimate violence arose from their original fraud.

He would have shown that the universal peace and concord amongst nations, which these common enemies to mankind had held out with the same fraudulent ends and pretences with which they had uniformly conducted every part of their proceeding, was a coarse and clumsy deception, unworthy to be proposed as an example, by an informed and sagacious British senator, to any other country. That far from peace and good-will to men, they meditated war against all other governments; and proposed systematically to excite in them all the very worst kind of seditions, in order to lead to their common destruction. That they had discovered, in the few instances in which they have hitherto had the power of discovering it, (as at Avignon, and in the Comtat, at Cavailhon and at Carpentras,)[4] in what a savage manner they mean to conduct the seditions and wars they have planned against their neighbours for the sake of putting themselves at the head of a confederation of republics as wild and as mischievous as their own. He would have shown in what manner that wicked scheme was carried on in those places, without being directly either owned or disclaimed, in hopes that the undone people should at length be obliged to fly to their tyrannic protection, as some sort of refuge from their barbarous and treacherous hostility. He would have shown from those examples, that neither this nor any other society could be in safety as long as such a public enemy was in a condition to continue directly or indirectly such practices against its peace. That Great Britain was a principal object of their machinations; and that they had begun by establishing correspondences, communications, and a sort of federal union with the factious here. That no practical enjoyment of a thing so imperfect and precarious, as human happiness must be, even under the very best of governments, could be a security for the existence of these governments, during the prevalence of the principles of France, propagated from that grand school of every disorder and every vice.

He was prepared to show the madness of their declaration of the pretended rights of man; the childish futility of some of their maxims; the gross and stupid absurdity, and the palpable falsity of others; and the mischievous tendency of all such declarations to the well-being of men and of citizens, and to the safety and prosperity of every just commonwealth. He was prepared to show that, in their conduct, the Assembly had directly violated not only every sound principle of government, but every one, without exception, of their own false or futile maxims; and indeed every rule they had pretended to lay down for their own direction.

In a word, he was ready to show, that those who could, after such a full and fair exposure, continue to countenance the French insanity, were not mistaken politicians, but bad men; but he thought that in this case, as in many others, ignorance had been the cause of admiration.

These are strong assertions. They required strong proofs. The member who laid down these positions was and is ready to give, in his place, to each position decisive evidence, correspondent to the nature and quality of the several allegations.

In order to judge on the propriety of the interruption given
to Mr. Burke, in his speech in the committee of the Quebec bill,[5]
it is necessary to inquire, first, whether, on general principles, he
ought to have been suffered to prove his allegations? Secondly,
whether the time he had chosen was so very unseasonable as to
make his exercise of a parliamentary right productive of ill effects
on his friends or his country? Thirdly, whether the opinions
delivered in his book, and which he had begun to expatiate upon
that day were in contradiction to his former principles, and
inconsistent with the general tenor of his public conduct?

They who have made eloquent panegyrics on the French
Revolution, and who think a free discussion so very advantageous in every case, and under every circumstance, ought not,
in my opinion, to have prevented their eulogies from being tried
on the test of facts. If their panegyric had been answered with an
invective (bating the difference in point of eloquence) the one
would have been as good as the other; that is, they would both
of them have been good for nothing. The panegyric and the
satire ought to be suffered to go to trial; and that which shrinks
from it must be contented to stand at best as a mere declamation.

I do not think Mr. Burke was wrong in the course he took.
That which seemed to be recommended to him by Mr. Pitt, was
rather to extol the English constitution, than to attack the
French. I do not determine what would be best for Mr. Pitt to
do in his situation. I do not deny that *he* may have good reasons
for his reserve. Perhaps they might have been as good for a similar
reserve on the part of Mr. Fox, if his zeal had suffered him to
listen to them. But there were no motives of ministerial prudence, or of that prudence which ought to guide a man perhaps
on the eve of being minister, to restrain the author of the
Reflections. He is in no office under the crown; he is not the
organ of any party.

The excellencies of the British constitution had already exercised and exhausted the talents of the best thinkers, and the
most eloquent writers and speakers, that the world ever saw.
But in the present case a system declared to be far better, and
which certainly is much newer, (to restless and unstable minds
no small recommendation,) was held out to the admiration of the
good people of England. In that case, it was surely proper for
those, who had far other thoughts of the French constitution,
to scrutinise that plan which has been recommended to our

imitation by active and zealous factions, at home and abroad. Our complexion is such, that we are palled with enjoyment, and stimulated with hope; that we become less sensible to a long-possessed benefit, from the very circumstance that it is become habitual. Specious, untried, ambiguous prospects of new advantage, recommend themselves to the spirit of adventure, which more or less prevails in every mind. From this temper, men and factions, and nations too, have sacrificed the good, of which they had been in assured possession, in favour of wild and irrational expectations. What should hinder Mr. Burke, if he thought this temper likely, at one time or other, to prevail in our country, from exposing to a multitude, eager to game, the false calculations of this lottery of fraud.

I allow, as I ought to do, for the effusions which come from a *general* zeal for liberty. This is to be indulged, and even to be encouraged, as long as the *question is general*. An orator, above all men, ought to be allowed a full and free use of the praise of liberty. A common-place in favour of slavery and tyranny, delivered to a popular assembly, would indeed be a bold defiance to all the principles of rhetoric. But in a question whether any particular constitution is or is not a plan of rational liberty, this kind of rhetorical flourish in favour of freedom in general is surely a little out of its place. It is virtually a begging of the question. It is a song of triumph, before the battle.

"But Mr. Fox does not make the panegyric of the new constitution; it is the destruction only of the absolute monarchy he commends." When that nameless thing, which has been lately set up in France was described as "the most stupendous and glorious edifice of liberty, which had been erected on the foundation of human integrity in any time or country," it might at first have led the hearer into an opinion, that the construction of the new fabric was an object of admiration, as well as the demolition of the old. Mr. Fox, however, has explained himself; and it would be too like that captious and cavilling spirit, which I so perfectly detest, if I were to pin down the language of an eloquent and ardent mind to the punctilious exactness of a pleader. Then Mr. Fox did not mean to applaud that monstrous thing, which, by the courtesy of France, they call a constitution. I easily believe it. Far from meriting the praises of a great genius like Mr. Fox, it cannot be approved by any man of common sense, or common information. He cannot admire the change of one piece of barbarism for another, and a worse. He cannot rejoice at the destruction of a monarchy, mitigated by manners, respectful to laws and usages, and attentive, perhaps but too attentive, to public opinion, in favour of the tyranny of a licentious, ferocious, and savage multitude, without laws, manners, or morals, and which so far from respecting the general sense of mankind, insolently endeavours to alter all the principles and opinions, which have hitherto guided and contained the world, and to force them into a conformity to their views and actions. His mind is made to better things.

That a man should rejoice and triumph in the destruction of an absolute monarchy; that in such an event he should overlook the captivity, disgrace, and degradation of an unfortunate prince, and the continual danger to a life which exists only to be endangered; that he should overlook the utter ruin of whole orders and classes of men, extending itself directly, or in its nearest consequences, to at least a million of our kind, and to at least the temporary wretchedness of a whole community, I do not deny to be in some sort natural: because when people see a political object, which they ardently desire, but in one point of view, they are apt extremely to palliate, or underrate the evils which may arise in obtaining it. This is no reflection on the humanity of those persons. Their good nature I am the last man in the world to dispute. It only shows that they are not sufficiently informed, or sufficiently considerate. When they come to reflect seriously on the transaction, they will think themselves bound to examine what the object is that has been acquired by all this havoc. They will hardly assert that the destruction of an absolute monarchy is a thing good in itself, without any sort of reference to the antecedent state of things, or to consequences which result from the change; without any consideration whether under its ancient rule a country was to a considerable degree flourishing and populous, highly cultivated, and highly commercial; and whether, under that domination, though personal liberty had been precarious and insecure, property at least was ever violated. They cannot take the moral sympathies of the human mind along with them, in abstractions separated from the good or evil condition of the state, from the quality of actions, and the character of the actors. None of us love absolute and uncontrolled monarchy; but we could not rejoice at the sufferings of a Marcus Aurelius,[6] or a Trajan,[7] who were absolute monarchs, as we do when Nero[8] is condemned by the senate to be punished *more majorum*:[9] nor when that monster was obliged to fly with his wife Sporus, and to drink puddle, were men affected in the same manner, as when the venerable Galba,[10] with all his faults and errors, was murdered by a revolted mercenary soldiery. With such things before our eyes our feelings contradict our theories; and when this is the case, the feelings are true, and the theory is false. What I contend for is, that in commending the destruction of an absolute monarchy, *all the circumstances* ought not to be wholly overlooked, as "considerations fit only for shallow and superficial minds" – the words of Mr. Fox, or to that effect.

The subversion of a government, to deserve any praise, must be considered but as a step preparatory to the formation of something better, either in the scheme of the government itself, or in the persons who administer it, or in both. These events cannot in reason be separated. For instance, when we praise our Revolution of 1688, though the nation, in that act, was on the defensive, and was justified in incurring all the evils of a defensive war, we do not rest there. We always combine with the subversion of the old government the happy settlement which followed. When we estimate that revolution, we mean to comprehend in our calculation both the value of the thing parted with, and the value of the thing received in exchange.

The burthen of proof lies heavily on those who tear to pieces the whole frame and contexture of their country, that they could find no other way of settling a government fit to obtain its rational ends, except that which they have pursued by means unfavourable to all the present happiness of millions of people, and to the utter ruin of several hundreds of thousands. In their political arrangements, men have no right to put the well-being of the present generation wholly out of the question. Perhaps the only moral trust with any certainty in our hands, is the care of our own time. With regard to futurity, we are to treat it like a ward. We are not so to attempt an improvement of his fortune, as to put the capital of his estate to any hazard.

It is not worth our while to discuss, like sophisters, whether, in no case, some evil, for the sake of some benefit, is to be tolerated. Nothing universal can be rationally affirmed on any moral or any political subject. Pure metaphysical abstraction does not belong to these matters. The lines of morality are not like the ideal lines of mathematics. They are broad and deep as well as long. They

admit of exceptions; they demand modifications. These exceptions and modifications are not made by the process of logic, but
by the rules of prudence. Prudence is not only the first in rank
of the virtues political and moral, but she is the director, the regulator, the standard of them all. Metaphysics cannot live without
definition; but prudence is cautious how she defines. Our courts
cannot be more fearful in suffering fictitious cases to be brought
before them for eliciting their determination on a point of law,
than prudent moralists are in putting extreme and hazardous
cases of conscience upon emergencies not existing. Without
attempting therefore to define, what never can be defined, the
case of a revolution in government, this, I think, may be safely
affirmed, that a sore and pressing evil is to be removed, and that
a good, great in its amount, and unequivocal in its nature, must
be probable almost to certainty, before the inestimable price of
our own morals, and the well-being of a number of our fellow-
citizens, is paid for a revolution. If ever we ought to be economists even to parsimony, it is in the voluntary production of evil.
Every revolution contains in it something of evil.

It must always be, to those who are the greatest amateurs, or
even professors of revolutions, a matter very hard to prove, that
the late French government was so bad, that nothing worse in
the infinite devices of men could come in its place. They who
have brought France to its present condition ought to prove also,
by something better than prattling about the Bastile, that their
subverted government was as incapable as the present certainly
is, of all improvement and correction. How dare they to say so
who have never made that experiment? They are experimentors
by their trade. They have made a hundred others, infinitely more
hazardous.

The English admirers of the forty-eight thousand republics
which form the French federation, praise them not for what they
are, but for what they are to become. They do not talk as politicians but as prophets. But in whatever character they choose to
found panegyric on prediction, it will be thought a little singular
to praise any work, not for its own merits, but for the merits of
something else which may succeed to it. When any political
institution is praised, in spite of great and prominent faults of
every kind, and in all its parts, it must be supposed to have something excellent in its fundamental principles. It must be shown
that it is right though imperfect; that it is not only by possibility

susceptible of improvement, but that it contains in it a principle tending to its melioration.

Before they attempt to show this progression of their favourite work, from absolute pravity to finished perfection, they will find themselves engaged in a civil war with those whose cause they maintain. What! alter our sublime constitution, the glory of France, the envy of the world, the pattern for mankind, the master-piece of legislation, the collected and concentrated glory of this enlightened age! Have we not produced it ready made and ready armed, mature in its birth, a perfect goddess of wisdom and of war, hammered by our blacksmith midwives out of the brain of Jupiter himself? Have we not sworn our devout, profane, believing, infidel people, to an allegiance to this goddess, even before she had burst the *dura mater*,[11] and as yet existed only in embryo? Have we not solemnly declared this constitution unalterable by any future legislature? Have we not bound it on posterity for ever, though our abettors have declared that no one generation is competent to bind another? Have we not obliged the members of every future assembly to qualify themselves for their seats by swearing to its conservation?

Indeed the French constitution always must be (if a change is not made in all their principles and fundamental arrangements) a government wholly by popular representation. It must be this or nothing. The French faction considers as a usurpation, as an atrocious violation of the indefeasible rights of man, every other description of government. Take it or leave it; there is no medium. Let the irrefragable doctors fight out their own controversy in their own way, and with their own weapons; and when they are tired, let them commence a treaty of peace. Let the plenipotentiary sophisters of England settle with the diplomatic sophisters of France, in what manner right is to be corrected by an infusion of wrong, and how truth may be rendered more true by a due intermixture of falsehood. [. . .]

These are the notions which, under the idea of Whig principles, several persons, and among them persons of no mean mark, have associated themselves to propagate. I will not attempt in the smallest degree to refute them. This will probably be done (if such writings shall be thought to deserve any other than the refutation of criminal justice) by others, who may think with Mr. Burke. He has performed his part.

I do not wish to enter very much at large into the discussions

which diverge and ramify in all ways from this productive subject. But there is one topic upon which I hope I shall be excused
in going a little beyond my design. The factions, now so busy
amongst us, in order to divest men of all love for their country,
and to remove from their minds all duty with regard to the state,
endeavour to propagate an opinion, that the *people*, in forming
their commonwealth, have by no means parted with their power
over it. This is an impregnable citadel, to which these gentlemen
retreat whenever they are pushed by the battery of laws and
usages, and positive conventions. Indeed it is such and of so great
force, that all they have done in defending their outworks, is so
much time and labour thrown away. Discuss any of their schemes
– their answer is – It is the act of the *people*, and that is sufficient.
Are we to deny to a *majority* of the people the right of altering
even the whole frame of their society, if such should be their
pleasure? They may change it, say they, from a monarchy to a
republic to-day, and to-morrow back again from a republic to
a monarchy; and so backward and forward as often as they like.
They are masters of the commonwealth; because in substance
they are themselves the commonwealth. The French Revolution, say they, was the act of the majority of the people; and if the
majority of any other people, the people of England for instance,
wish to make the same change, they have the same right.

Just the same undoubtedly. That is, none at all. Neither the
few nor the many have a right to act merely by their will, in any
matter connected with duty, trust, engagement, or obligation.
The constitution of a country being once settled upon some
compact, tacit or expressed, there is no power existing of force
to alter it, without the breach of the covenant, or the consent of
all the parties. Such is the nature of a contract. And the votes of
a majority of the people, whatever their infamous flatterers may
teach in order to corrupt their minds, cannot alter the moral any
more than they can alter the physical essence of things. The
people are not to be taught to think lightly of their engagements
to their governors; else they teach governors to think lightly of
their engagements towards them. In that kind of game in the end
the people are sure to be losers. To flatter them into a contempt
of faith, truth, and justice, is to ruin them; for in these virtues
consist their whole safety. To flatter any man, or any part of mankind, in any description, by asserting, that in engagements he or

they are free, whilst any other human creature is bound, is ultimately to vest the rule of morality in the pleasure of those who ought to be rigidly submitted to it; to subject the sovereign reason of the world to the caprices of weak and giddy men.

But, as no one of us men can dispense with public or private faith, or with any other tie of moral obligation, so neither can any number of us. The number engaged in crimes, instead of turning them into laudable acts, only augments the quantity and the intensity of the guilt. I am well aware, that men love to hear of their power, but have an extreme disrelish to be told of their duty. This is of course; because every duty is a limitation of some power. Indeed arbitrary power is so much to the depraved taste of the vulgar, of the vulgar of every description, that almost all the dissensions which lacerate the commonwealth, are not concerning the manner in which it is to be exercised, but concerning the hands in which it is to be placed. Somewhere they are resolved to have it. Whether they desire it to be vested in the many or the few, depends with most men upon the chance which they imagine they themselves may have of partaking in the exercise of that arbitrary sway, in the one mode or in the other.

It is not necessary to teach men to thirst after power. But it is very expedient that by moral instruction they should be taught, and by their civil constitutions they should be compelled, to put many restrictions upon the immoderate exercise of it, and the inordinate desire. The best method of obtaining these two great points forms the important, but at the same time the difficult, problem to the true statesman. He thinks of the place in which political power is to be lodged, with no other attention, than as it may render the more or the less practicable its salutary restraint, and its prudent direction. For this reason no legislator, at any period of the world, has willingly placed the seat of active power in the hands of the multitude; because there it admits of no control, no regulation, no steady direction whatsoever. The people are the natural control on authority; but to exercise and to control together is contradictory and impossible.

As the exorbitant exercise of power cannot, under popular sway, be effectually restrained, the other great object of political arrangement, the means of abating an excessive desire of it, is in such a state still worse provided for. The democratic commonwealth is the foodful nurse of ambition. Under the other forms it meets with many restraints. Whenever, in states which have had a democratic basis, the legislators have endeavoured to put restraints upon ambition, their methods were as violent, as in the end they were ineffectual: as violent indeed as any the most jealous despotism could invent. The ostracism could not very long save itself, and much less the state which it was meant to guard, from the attempts of ambition, one of the natural inbred, incurable distempers of a powerful democracy.

But to return from this short digression, which however is not wholly foreign to the question of the effect of the will of the majority upon the form or the existence of their society. I cannot too often recommend it to the serious consideration of all men, who think civil society to be within the province of moral juris-diction, that if we owe to it any duty, it is not subject to our will. Duties are not voluntary. Duty and will are even contradictory terms. Now though civil society might be at first a voluntary act, (which in many cases it undoubtedly was,) its continuance is under a permanent standing covenant, co-existing with the soci-ety; and it attaches upon every individual of that society, without any formal act of his own. This is warranted by the general prac-tice, arising out of the general sense of mankind. Men without their choice derive benefits from that association; without their choice they are subjected to duties in consequence of these benefits; and without their choice they enter into a virtual obligation as binding as any that is actual. Look through the whole of life and the whole system of duties. Much the strongest moral obligations are such as were never the results of our option. I allow, that if no supreme ruler exists, wise to form, and potent to enforce, the moral law, there is no sanction to any contract, virtual or even actual, against the will of prevalent power. On that hypothesis, let any set of men be strong enough to set their duties at defiance, and they cease to be duties any longer. We have but this one appeal against irresistible power –

> Si genus humanum et mortalia temnitis arma,
> At sperate Deos memores fandi atque nefandi.[12]

Taking it for granted that I do not write to the disciples of the Parisian philosophy, I may assume, that the awful Author of our being is the Author of our place in the order of existence; and that having disposed and marshalled us by a divine tactic, not according to our will, but according to his, he has, in and by that disposition, virtually subjected us to act the part which belongs to the place assigned us. We have obligations to mankind at large, which are not in consequence of any special voluntary pact. They arise from the relation of man to man, and the relation of man to God, which relations are not matters of choice. On the contrary, the force of all the pacts which we enter into with any particular person, or number of persons amongst mankind, depends upon those prior obligations. In some cases the subordinate relations are voluntary, in others they are necessary – but the duties are all compulsive. When we marry, the choice is voluntary, but the duties are not matter of choice. They are dictated by the nature of the situation. Dark and inscrutable are the ways by which we come into the world. The instincts which give rise to this mysterious process of nature are not of our making. But out of physical causes, unknown to us, perhaps unknowable, arise moral duties, which, as we are able perfectly to comprehend, we are bound indispensably to perform. Parents may not be consenting to their moral relation; but consenting or not, they are bound to a long train of burthensome duties towards those with whom they have never made a convention of any sort. Children are not consenting to their relation, but their relation, without their actual consent, binds them to its duties; or rather it implies their consent because the presumed consent of every rational creature is in unison with the predisposed order of things. Men come in that manner into a community with the social state of their parents, endowed with all the benefits, loaded with all the duties of their situation. If the social ties and ligaments, spun out of those physical relations which are the elements of the commonwealth, in most cases begin, and always continue, independently of our will; so, without any stipulation, on our, part, are we bound by that relation called our country, which comprehends (as it has been well said) "all the charities of all."* Nor are we left without powerful instincts to make this duty as dear and grateful to us, as it is awful and coercive. Our country is not a thing of mere physical locality. It consists, in a great measure, in the ancient order into which we are born. We may have the same geographical situation, but another country; as we may have the same country in another soil. The place that determines our duty to our country is a social, civil relation.

* Omnes omnium charitates patria una complectitur. Cic.

These are the opinions of the author whose cause I defend. I lay them down not to enforce them upon others by disputation, but as an account of his proceedings. On them he acts; and from them he is convinced that neither he, nor any man, or number of men, have a right (except what necessity, which is out of and above all rule, rather imposes than bestows) to free themselves from that primary engagement into which every man born into a community as much contracts by his being born into it, as he contracts an obligation to certain parents by his having been derived from their bodies. The place of every man determines his duty. If you ask, *Quem te Deus esse jussit?* You will be answered when you resolve this other question, *Humana qua parte locatus es in re?**

I admit, indeed, that in morals, as in all things else, difficulties will sometimes occur. Duties will sometimes cross one another. Then questions will arise, which of them is to be placed in subordination; which of them may be entirely superseded? These doubts give rise to that part of moral science called *casuistry*; which, though necessary to be well studied by those who would become expert in that learning, who aim at becoming what, I think, Cicero somewhere calls, *artifices officiorum*;[13] it requires a very solid and discriminating judgment, great modesty and caution, and much sobriety of mind in the handling; else there is a danger that it may totally subvert those offices which it is its object only to methodise and reconcile. Duties, at their extreme bounds, are drawn very fine, so as to become almost evanescent. In that state some shade of doubt will always rest on these questions, when they are pursued with great subtilty. But the very habit of stating these extreme cases is not very laudable or safe: because, in general, it is not right to turn our duties into doubts. They are imposed to govern our conduct, not to exercise our ingenuity; and therefore, our opinions about them ought not to be in a state of fluctuation, but steady, sure, and resolved.

Amongst these nice and therefore dangerous points of casuistry may be reckoned the question so much agitated in the

---

* A few lines in Persius contain a good summary of all the objects of moral investigation, and hint the result of our inquiry; there human will has no place.

Quid *sumus?* et quidnam *victuri gignimur?* ordo
Quis *datus?* et *metæ* quis mollis flexus et unde?
Quis modus argento? Quid *fas optare?* Quid asper
Utile nummus habet? *Patriæ charisque propinquis*
Quantum elargiri *debet?*—Quem te Deus esse
Jussit?—et humana qua parte *locatus es* in re?[14]

present hour – Whether, after the people have discharged themselves of their original power by an habitual delegation, no occasion can possibly occur which may justify their resumption of it?
This question, in this latitude, is very hard to affirm or deny: but
I am satisfied that no occasion can justify such a resumption,
which would not equally authorise a dispensation with any other
moral duty, perhaps with all of them together. However, if in
general it be not easy to determine concerning the lawfulness of
such devious proceedings, which must be ever on the edge of
crimes, it is far from difficult to foresee the perilous consequences
of the resuscitation of such a power in the people. The practical
consequences of any political tenet go a great way in deciding
upon its value. Political problems do not primarily concern truth
or falsehood. They relate to good or evil. What in the result is
likely to produce evil, is politically false: that which is productive
of good, politically is true.

Believing it therefore a question at least arduous in the theory,
and in the practice very critical, it would become us to ascertain,
as well as we can, what form it is that our incantations are about
to call up from darkness and the sleep of ages. When the supreme
authority of the people is in question, before we attempt to
extend or to confine it, we ought to fix in our minds, with some
degree of distinctness, an idea of what it is we mean when we say
the PEOPLE.

In a state of *rude* nature there is no such thing as a people.
A number of men in themselves have no collective capacity. The
idea of a people is the idea of a corporation. It is wholly artificial;
and made, like all other legal fictions, by common agreement.
What the particular nature of that agreement was, is collected
from the form into which the particular society has been cast.
Any other is not *their* covenant. When men, therefore, break up
the original compact or agreement which gives its corporate
form and capacity to a state, they are no longer a people; they
have no longer a corporate existence; they have no longer a legal
coactive force to bind within, nor a claim to be recognised
abroad. They are a number of vague, loose individuals, and nothing more. With them all is to begin again. Alas! they little know
how many a weary step is to be taken before they can form themselves into a mass, which has a true, politic personality.

We hear much from men, who have not acquired their hardi-
ness of assertion from the profundity of their thinking, about the

omnipotence of a *majority*, in such a dissolution of an ancient society as hath taken place in France. But amongst men so disbanded, there can be no such thing as majority or minority; or power in any one person to bind another. The power of acting by a majority, which the gentlemen theorists seem to assume so readily, after they have violated the contract out of which it has arisen, (if at all it existed,) must be grounded on two assumptions; first, that of an incorporation produced by unanimity; and secondly, an unanimous agreement, that the act of a mere majority (say of one) shall pass with them and with others as the act of the whole.

We are so little affected by things which are habitual, that we consider this idea of the decision of a *majority* as if it were a law of our original nature: but such constructive whole, residing in a part only, is one of the most violent fictions of positive law, that ever has been or can be made on the principles of artificial incorporation. Out of civil society nature knows nothing of it; nor are men, even when arranged according to civil order, otherwise than by very long training, brought at all to submit to it. The mind is brought far more easily to acquiesce in the proceedings of one man, or a few, who act under a general procuration for the state, than in the vote of a victorious majority in councils, in which every man has his share in the deliberation. For there the beaten party are exasperated and soured by the previous contention, and mortified by the conclusive defeat. This mode of decision, where wills may be so nearly equal, where, according to circumstances, the smaller number may be the stronger force, and where apparent reason may be all upon one side, and on the other little else than impetuous appetite; all this must be the result of a very particular and special convention, confirmed afterwards by long habits of obedience, by a sort of discipline in society, and by a strong hand, vested with stationary permanent power, to enforce this sort of constructive general will. What organ it is that shall declare the corporate mind is so much a matter of positive arrangement, that several states, for the validity of several of their acts, have required a proportion of voices much greater than that of a mere majority. These proportions are so entirely governed by convention, that in some cases the minority decides. The laws in many countries to *condemn* require more than a mere majority; less than an equal number to *acquit*. In our judicial trials we require unanimity either to condemn or to absolve. In some incorporations one man speaks for the whole; in others, a few. Until the other day, in the constitution of Poland, unanimity was required to give validity to any act of their great national council or diet. This approaches much more nearly to rude nature than the institutions of any other country. Such, indeed, every commonwealth must be, without a positive law to recognise in a certain number the will of the entire body.

If men dissolve their ancient incorporation, in order to regenerate their community, in that state of things each man has a right, if he pleases, to remain an individual. Any number of individuals, who can agree upon it, have an undoubted right to form themselves into a state apart and wholly independent. If any of these is forced into the fellowship of another, this is conquest and not compact. On every principle, which supposes society to be in virtue of a free covenant, this compulsive incorporation must be null and void.

As a people can have no right to a corporate capacity without universal consent, so neither have they a right to hold exclusively any lands in the name and title of a corporation. On the scheme of the present rulers in our neighbouring country, regenerated as they are, they have no more right to the territory called France than I have. I have a right to pitch my tent in any unoccupied place I can find for it; and I may apply to my own maintenance any part of their unoccupied soil. I may purchase the house or vineyard of any individual proprietor who refuses his consent (and most proprietors have, as far as they dared, refused it) to the new incorporation. I stand in his independent place. Who are these insolent men calling themselves the French nation, that would monopolise this fair domain of nature? Is it because they speak a certain jargon? Is it their mode of chattering, to me unintelligible, that forms their title to my land? Who are they who claim by prescription and descent from certain gangs of banditti called Franks, and Burgundians, and Visigoths, of whom I may have never heard, and ninety-nine out of an hundred of themselves certainly never have heard; whilst at the very time they tell me, that prescription and long possession form no title to property? Who are they that presume to assert that the land which I purchased of the individual, a natural person, and not a fiction of state, belongs to them, who in the very capacity in which they make their claim can exist only as an imaginary being, and in virtue of the very prescription which they reject and disown?

This mode of arguing might be pushed into all the detail, so as to leave no sort of doubt, that on their principles, and on the sort of footing on which they have thought proper to place themselves, the crowd of men, on the other side of the channel, who have the impudence to call themselves a people, can never be the lawful exclusive possessors of the soil. By what they call reasoning without prejudice, they leave not one stone upon another in the fabric of human society. They subvert all the authority which they hold, as well as all that which they have destroyed.

As in the abstract, it is perfectly clear, that, out of a state of civil society, majority and minority are relations which can have no existence; and that, in civil society, its own specific conventions in each corporation determine what it is that constitutes the people, so as to make their act the signification of the general will: to come to particulars, it is equally clear, that neither in France nor in England has the original or any subsequent compact of the state, expressed or implied, constituted *a majority of men, told by the head,* to be the acting people of their several communities. And I see as little of policy or utility, as there is of right, in laying down a principle that a majority of men told by the head are to be considered as the people, and that as such their will is to be law. What policy can there be found in arrangements made in defiance of every political principle? To enable men to act with the weight and character of a people, and to answer the ends for which they are incorporated into that capacity, we must suppose them (by means immediate or consequential) to be in that state of habitual social discipline, in which the wiser, the more expert, and the more opulent conduct, and by conducting enlighten and protect the weaker, the less knowing, and the less provided with the goods of fortune. When the multitude are not under this discipline, they can scarcely be said to be in civil society. Give once a certain constitution of things, which produces a variety of conditions and circumstances in a state, and there is in nature and reason a principle which, for their own benefit, postpones, not the interest, but the judgment, of those who are *numero plures,* to those who are *virtute et honore majores.*[15] Numbers in a state (supposing, which is not the case in France, that a state does exist) are always of consideration – but they are not the whole consideration. It is in things more serious than a play, that it may be truly said, *satis est equitem mihi plaudere.*[16]

A true natural aristocracy is not a separate interest in the state, or separable from it. It is an essential integrant part of any large people rightly constituted. It is formed out of a class of legitimate presumptions, which, taken as generalities, must be admitted for actual truths. To be bred in a place of estimation; to see nothing low and sordid from one's infancy; to be taught to respect one's self; to be habituated to the censorial inspection of the public eye; to look early to public opinion; to stand upon such elevated ground as to be enabled to take a large view of the wide-spread and infinitely diversified combinations of men and affairs in a large society; to have leisure to read, to reflect, to converse; to be enabled to draw the court and attention of the wise and learned wherever they are to be found; – to be habituated in armies to command and to obey; to be taught to despise danger in the pursuit of honour and duty; to be formed to the greatest degree of vigilance, foresight, and circumspection, in a state of things in which no fault is committed with impunity, and the slightest mistakes draw on the most ruinous consequences – to be led to a guarded and regulated conduct, from a sense that you are considered as an instructor of your fellow-citizens in their highest concerns, and that you act as a reconciler between God and man – to be employed as an administrator of law and justice, and to be thereby amongst the first benefactors to mankind – to be a professor of high science, or of liberal and ingenuous art – to be amongst rich traders, who from their success are presumed to have sharp and vigorous understandings, and to possess the virtues of diligence, order, constancy, and regularity, and to have cultivated an habitual regard to commutative justice – these are the circumstances of men, that form what I should call a *natural* aristocracy, without which there is no nation.

The state of civil society, which necessarily generates this aristocracy, is a state of nature; and much more truly so than a savage and incoherent mode of life. For man is by nature reasonable; and he is never perfectly in his natural state, but when he is placed where reason may be best cultivated, and most predominates. Art is man's nature. We are as much, at least, in a state of nature in formed manhood, as in immature and helpless infancy. Men, qualified in the manner I have just described, form in nature, as she operates in the common modification of society, the leading, guiding, and governing part. It is the soul to the body, without which the man does not exist. To give therefore no more importance, in the social order, to such descriptions of men, than that of so many units, is an horrible usurpation.

When great multitudes act together, under that discipline of nature, I recognise the PEOPLE. I acknowledge something that perhaps equals, and ought always to guide, the sovereignty of convention. In all things the voice of this grand chorus of national harmony ought to have a mighty and decisive influence. But when you disturb this harmony; when you break up this beautiful order, this array of truth and nature, as well as of habit and prejudice; when you separate the common sort of men from their proper chieftains, so as to form them into an adverse army, I no longer know that venerable object called the People in such a disbanded race of deserters and vagabonds. For a while they may be terrible indeed; but in such a manner as wild beasts are terrible. The mind owes to them no sort of submission. They are, as they have always been reputed, rebels. They may lawfully be fought with, and brought under, whenever an advantage offers. Those who attempt by outrage and violence to deprive men of any advantage which they hold under the laws, and to destroy the natural order of life, proclaim war against them.

We have read in history of that furious insurrection of the common people in France called the *Jacquerie*;[17] for this is not the first time that the people have been enlightened into treason, murder, and rapine. Its object was to extirpate the gentry. The *Captal de Buche*,[18] a famous soldier of those days, dishonoured the name of a gentleman and of a man by taking, for their cruelties, a cruel vengeance on these deluded wretches: it was, however, his right and his duty to make war upon them, and afterwards, in moderation, to bring them to punishment for their rebellion; though in the sense of the French Revolution, and of some of our clubs, they were the *people*; and were truly so, if you will call by that appellation *any majority of men told by the head*.

At a time not very remote from the same period (for these humours never have affected one of the nations without some influence on the other) happened several risings of the lower commons in England. These insurgents were certainly the majority of the inhabitants of the counties in which they resided; and Cade, Ket, and Straw,[19] at the head of their national guards, and fomented by certain traitors of high rank, did no more than

exert, according to the doctrines of ours and the Parisian societies, the sovereign power inherent in the majority.

We call the time of those events a dark age. Indeed we are
too indulgent to our own proficiency. The Abbé John Ball
understood the rights of man as well as the Abbé Gregoire.[20] That
reverend patriarch of sedition, and prototype of our modern
preachers, was of opinion with the National Assembly, that all the
evils which have fallen upon men had been caused by an ignorance of their "having been born and continued equal as to their
rights." Had the populace been able to repeat that profound
maxim all would have gone perfectly well with them. No tyranny,
no vexation, no oppression, no care, no sorrow, could have
existed in the world. This would have cured them like a charm
for the tooth-ache. But the lowest wretches, in their most ignorant state, were able at all times to talk such stuff; and yet at all times
have they suffered many evils and many oppressions, both before
and since the republication by the National Assembly of this spell
of healing potency and virtue. The enlightened Dr. Ball, when
he wished to rekindle the lights and fires of his audience on this
point, chose for the text the following couplet:

> When Adam delved and Eve span,
> Who was then the gentleman?[21]

Of this sapient maxim, however, I do not give him for the
inventor. It seems to have been handed down by tradition, and
had certainly become proverbial; but whether then composed,
or only applied, thus much must be admitted, that in learning,
sense, energy, and comprehensiveness, it is fully equal to all the
modern dissertations on the equality of mankind; and it has one
advantage over them, – that it is in rhyme.

There is no doubt, but that this great teacher of the rights of
man decorated his discourse on this valuable text, with lemmas,
theorems, scholia, corollaries, and all the apparatus of science,
which was furnished in as great plenty and perfection out of the
dogmatic and polemic magazines, the old horse-armoury, of the
schoolmen, among whom the Rev. Dr. Ball was bred, as they can
be supplied from the new arsenal at Hackney. It was, no doubt,
disposed with all the adjutancy of definition and division, in
which (I speak it with submission) the old marshals were as able as
the modern martinets. Neither can we deny that the philosophic
auditory, when they had once obtained this knowledge, could

never return to their former ignorance; or after so instructive a lecture be in the same state of mind as if they had never heard it. But these poor people, who were not to be envied for their knowledge, but pitied for their delusion, were not reasoned (that was impossible) but beaten out of their lights. With their teacher they were delivered over to the lawyers; who wrote in their blood the statutes of the land as harshly, and in the same sort of ink, as they and their teachers had written the rights of man.

Our doctors of the day are not so fond of quoting the opinions of this ancient sage as they are of imitating his conduct; first, because it might appear, that they are not as great inventors as they would be thought; and next, because, unfortunately for his fame, he was not successful. It is a remark, liable to as few exceptions as any generality can be, that they who applaud prosperous folly, and adore triumphant guilt, have never been known to succour or even to pity human weakness or offence when they become subject to human vicissitude, and meet with punishment instead of obtaining power. Abating for their want of sensibility to the sufferings of their associates, they are not so much in the wrong: for madness and wickedness are things foul and deformed in themselves; and stand in need of all the coverings and trappings of fortune to recommend them to the multitude. Nothing can be more loathsome in their naked nature.

Aberrations like these, whether ancient or modern, unsuccessful or prosperous, are things of passage. They furnish no argument for supposing a *multitude told by the head to be the people*. Such a multitude can have no sort of title to alter the seat of power in the society, in which it ever ought to be the obedient, and not the ruling or presiding part. What power may belong to the whole mass, in which mass, the natural *aristocracy*, or what by convention is appointed to represent and strengthen it, acts in its proper place, with its proper weight, and without being subjected to violence, is a deeper question. But in that case, and with that concurrence, I should have much doubt whether any rash or desperate changes in the state, such as we have seen in France, could ever be effected.

I have said, that in all political questions the consequences of any assumed rights are of great moment in deciding upon their validity. In this point of view let us a little scrutinise the effects of a right in the mere majority of the inhabitants of any country of superseding and altering their government *at pleasure*.

The sum total of every people is composed of its units. Every individual must have a right to originate what afterwards is to become the act of the majority. Whatever he may lawfully originate, he may lawfully endeavour to accomplish. He has a right therefore in his own particular to break the ties and engagements which bind him to the country in which he lives; and he has a right to make as many converts to his opinions, and to obtain as many associates in his designs, as he can procure: for how can you know the dispositions of the majority to destroy their government, but by tampering with some part of the body? You must begin by a secret conspiracy, that you may end with a national confederation. The mere pleasure of the beginning must be the sole guide; since the mere pleasure of others must be the sole ultimate sanction, as well as the sole actuating principle in every part of the progress. Thus, arbitrary will, (the last corruption of ruling power,) step by step, poisons the heart of every citizen. If the undertaker fails, he has the misfortune of a rebel, but not the guilt. By such doctrines, all love to our country, all pious veneration and attachment to its laws and customs, are obliterated from our minds; and nothing can result from this opinion, when grown into a principle, and animated by discontent, ambition, or enthusiasm, but a series of conspiracies and seditions, sometimes ruinous to their authors, always noxious to the state. No sense of duty can prevent any man from being a leader or a follower in such enterprises. Nothing restrains the tempter; nothing guards the tempted. Nor is the new state, fabricated by such arts, safer than the old. What can prevent the mere will of any person, who hopes to unite the wills of others to his own, from an attempt wholly to overturn it? It wants nothing but a disposition to trouble the established order, to give a title to the enterprise.

When you combine this principle of the right to change a fixed and tolerable constitution of things at pleasure, with the theory and practice of the French Assembly, the political, civil, and moral irregularity are if possible aggravated. The Assembly have found another road, and a far more commodious, to the destruction of an old government, and the legitimate formation of a new one, than through the previous will of the majority of what they call the people. Get, say they, the possession of power by any means you can into your hands; and then a subsequent consent (what they call an *address of adhesion*) makes your authority as much the act of the people as if they had conferred upon you originally that kind and degree of power, which, without their permission, you had seized upon. This is to give a direct sanction to fraud, hypocrisy, perjury, and the breach of the most sacred trusts that can exist between man and man. What can sound with such horrid discordance in the moral ear, as this position. That a delegate with limited powers may break his sworn engagements to his constituents, assume an authority, never committed to him, to alter all things at his pleasure; and then, if he can persuade a large number of men to flatter him in the power he has usurped, that he is absolved in his own conscience, and ought to stand acquitted in the eyes of mankind? On this scheme the maker of the experiment must begin with a determined perjury. That point is certain. He must take his chance for the expiatory addresses. This is to make the success of villainy the standard of innocence.

Without drawing on, therefore, very shocking consequences, neither by previous consent, nor by subsequent ratification of a *mere reckoned majority*, can any set of men attempt to dissolve the state at their pleasure. To apply this to our present subject. When the several orders, in their several bailages,[22] had met in the year 1789, such of them, I mean, as had met peaceably and constitutionally, to choose and to instruct their representatives, so organised, and so acting, (because they were organised and were acting according to the conventions which made them a people,) they were the *people* of France. They had a legal and a natural capacity to be considered as that people. But, observe, whilst they were in this state, that is, whilst they were a people, in no one of their instructions did they charge or even hint at any of those things, which have drawn upon the usurping Assembly, and their adherents, the detestation of the rational and thinking part of mankind. I will venture to affirm, without the least apprehension of being contradicted by any person who knows the then state of France, that if any one of the changes were proposed, which form the fundamental parts of their Revolution, and compose its most distinguishing acts, it would not have had one vote in twenty thousand in any order. Their instructions purported the direct contrary to all those famous proceedings, which are defended as the acts of the people. Had such proceedings been expected, the great probability is, that the people would then have risen, as to a man, to prevent them. The whole organisation of the Assembly was altered, the whole frame of the kingdom was changed, before these things could be done. It is long to tell, by what evil arts of the conspirators, and by what extreme weakness and want of steadiness in the lawful government, this equal usurpation on the rights of the prince and people, having first cheated, and then offered violence to both, has been able to triumph, and to employ with success the forged signature of an imprisoned sovereign, and the spurious voice of dictated addresses, to a subsequent ratification of things that had never received any previous sanction, general or particular, expressed or implied, from the nation, (in whatever sense that word is taken,) or from any part of it.

After the weighty and respectable part of the people had been murdered, or driven by the menaces of murder from their houses, or were dispersed in exile into every country in Europe; after the soldiery had been debauched from their officers; after property had lost its weight and consideration, along with its security; after voluntary clubs and associations of factious and unprincipled men were substituted in the place of all the legal corporations of the kingdom arbitrarily dissolved; after freedom had been banished from those popular meetings, whose sole recommendation is freedom; – after it had come to that pass, that no dissent dared to appear in any of them, but at the certain price of life; after even dissent had been anticipated, and assassination became as quick as suspicion; – such pretended ratification by addresses could be no act of what any lover of the people would choose to call by their name. It is that voice which every successful usurpation, as well as this before us, may easily procure, even without making (as these tyrants have made) donatives from the spoil of one part of the citizens to corrupt the other.

The pretended *rights of man*, which have made this havoc, cannot be the rights of the people. For to be a people, and to have these rights, are things incompatible. The one supposes the presence, the other the absence, of a state of civil society. The very foundation of the French commonwealth is false and self-destructive; nor can its principles be adopted in any country, without the certainty of bringing it to the very same condition in which France is found. Attempts are made to introduce them into every nation in Europe. This nation, as possessing the greatest influence, they wish most to corrupt, as by that means they are assured the contagion must become general. I hope, therefore, I shall be excused, if I endeavour to show, as shortly as the matter will admit, the danger of giving to them, either avowedly or tacitly, the smallest countenance.

There are times and circumstances, in which not to speak out is at least to connive. Many think it enough for them, that the principles propagated by these clubs and societies, enemies to their country and its constitution, are not owned by the *modern Whigs in parliament*, who are so warm in condemnation of Mr. Burke and his book, and of course of all the principles of the ancient constitutional Whigs of this kingdom. Certainly they are not owned. But are they condemned with the same zeal as Mr. Burke and his book are condemned? Are they condemned at all? Are they rejected or discountenanced in any way whatsoever? Is any man who would fairly examine into the demeanour and principles of those societies, and that too very moderately, and in the way rather of admonition than of punishment, is such a man even decently treated? Is he not reproached, as if, in condemning such principles, he had belied the conduct of his whole life, suggesting that his life had been governed by principles similar to those which he now reprobates? The French system is in the mean time, by many active agents out of doors, rapturously praised; the British constitution is coldly tolerated. But these constitutions are different, both in the foundation and in the whole superstructure; and it is plain, that you cannot build up the one but on the ruins of the other. After all, if the French be a superior system of liberty, why should we not adopt it? To what end are our praises? Is excellence held out to us only that we should not copy after it? And what is there in the manners of the people, or in the climate of France, which renders that species of republic fitted for them, and unsuitable to us? A strong and marked difference between the two nations ought to be shown, before we can admit a constant affected panegyric, a standing annual commemoration, to be without any tendency to an example.

But the leaders of party will not go the length of the doctrines taught by the seditious clubs. I am sure they do not mean to do so. God forbid! Perhaps even those who are directly carrying on the work of this pernicious foreign faction, do not all of them intend to produce all the mischiefs which must inevitably follow from their having any success in their proceedings. As to leaders in parties, nothing is more common than to see them blindly led. The world is governed by go-betweens. These go-betweens influence the persons with whom they carry on the intercourse, by stating their own sense to each of them as the sense of the other; and thus they reciprocally master both sides. It is first buzzed about the ears of leaders, "that their friends without-doors are very eager for some measure, or very warm about some opinion – that you must not be too rigid with them. They are useful persons, and zealous in the cause. They may be a little wrong; but the spirit of liberty must not be damped; and by the influence you obtain from some degree of concurrence with them at present, you may be enabled to set them right hereafter."

Thus the leaders are at first drawn to a connivance with sentiments and proceedings, often totally different from their serious and deliberate notions. But their acquiescence answers every purpose.

With no better than such powers, the go-betweens assume a new representative character. What at best was but an acquiescence, is magnified into an authority, and thence into a desire on the part of the leaders; and it is carried down as such to the subordinate members of parties. By this artifice they in their turn are led into measures which at first, perhaps, few of them wished at all, or at least did not desire vehemently or systematically.

There is in all parties, between the principal leaders in parliament, and the lowest followers out of doors, a middle sort of men; a sort of equestrian order, who, by the spirit of that middle situation, are the fittest for preventing things from running to excess. But indecision, though a vice of a totally different character, is the natural accomplice of violence. The irresolution and timidity of those, who compose this middle order, often prevent the effect of their controlling situation. The fear of differing with the authority of leaders on the one hand, and of contradicting the desires of the multitude on the other, induces them to give a careless and passive assent to measures in which they never were consulted: and thus things proceed, by a sort of activity of inertness, until whole bodies, leaders, middle men, and followers, are all hurried, with every appearance, and with many of the effects, of unanimity, into schemes of politics, in the substance of which no two of them were ever fully agreed, and the origin and authors of which, in this circular mode of communication, none of them find it possible to trace. In my experience I have seen much of this in affairs, which, though trifling in comparison to the present, were yet of some importance to parties;

and I have known them suffer by it. The sober part give their sanction, at first through inattention and levity; at last they give it through necessity. A violent spirit is raised, which the presiding minds, after a time, find it impracticable to stop at their pleasure, to control, to regulate, or even to direct.

This shows, in my opinion, how very quick and awakened all men ought to be, who are looked up to by the public, and who deserve that confidence, to prevent a surprise on their opinions, when dogmas are spread, and projects pursued, by which the foundations of society may be affected. Before they listen even to moderate alterations in the government of their country, they ought to take care that principles are not propagated for that purpose, which are too big for their object. Doctrines limited in their present application, and wide in their general principles, are never meant to be confined to what they at first pretend. If I were to form a prognostic of the effect of the present machinations on the people, from their sense of any grievance they suffer under this constitution, my mind would be at ease. But there is a wide difference between the multitude, when they act against their government from a sense of grievance, or from zeal for some opinions. When men are thoroughly possessed with that zeal, it is difficult to calculate its force. It is certain, that its power is by no means in exact proportion to its reasonableness. It must always have been discoverable by persons of reflection, but it is now obvious to the world, that a theory concerning government may become as much a cause of fanaticism as a *dogma* in religion. There is a boundary to men's passions when they act from feeling; none when they are under the influence of imagination. Remove a grievance, and, when men act from feeling, you go a great way towards quieting a commotion. But the good or bad conduct of a government, the protection men have enjoyed, or the oppression they have suffered under it, are of no sort of moment, when a faction, proceeding upon speculative grounds, is thoroughly heated against its form. When a man is, from system, furious against monarchy or episcopacy, the good conduct of the monarch or the bishop has no other effect than further to irritate the adversary. He is provoked at it as furnishing a plea for preserving the thing which he wishes to destroy. His mind will be heated as much by the sight of a sceptre, a mace, or a verge, as if he had been daily bruised and wounded by these symbols of authority. Mere spectacles, mere names, will become sufficient causes to stimulate the people to war and tumult.

Some gentlemen are not terrified by the facility with which government has been overturned in France. The people of France, they say, had nothing to lose in the destruction of a bad constitution; but, though not the best possible, we have still a good stake in ours, which will hinder us from desperate risks. Is this any security at all against those who seem to persuade themselves, and who labour to persuade others, that our constitution is an usurpation in its origin, unwise in its contrivance, mischievous in its effects, contrary to the rights of man, and in all its parts a perfect nuisance? What motive has any rational man, who thinks in that manner, to spill his blood, or even to risk a shilling of his fortune, or to waste a moment of his leisure, to preserve it? If he has any duty relative to it, his duty is to destroy it. A constitution on sufferance is a constitution condemned. Sentence is already passed upon it. The execution is only delayed. On the principles of these gentlemen it neither has, nor ought to have, any security. So far as regards them, it is left naked, without friends, partisans, assertors, or protectors.

Let us examine into the value of this security upon the principles of those who are more sober; of those who think, indeed, the French constitution better, or at least as good, as the British, without going to all the lengths of the warmer politicians in reprobating their own. Their security amounts in reality to nothing more than this; – that the difference between their republican system and the British limited monarchy is not worth a civil war. This opinion, I admit, will prevent people not very enterprising in their nature, from an active undertaking against the British constitution. But it is the poorest defensive principle that ever was infused into the mind of man against the attempts of those who will enterprise. It will tend totally to remove from their minds that very terror of a civil war which is held out as our sole security. They who think so well of the French constitution, certainly will not be the persons to carry on a war to prevent their obtaining a great benefit, or at worst a fair exchange. They will not go to battle in favour of a cause in which their defeat might be more advantageous to the public than their victory. They must at least tacitly abet those who endeavour to make converts to a sound opinion; they must discountenance those who would oppose its propagation. In proportion as by these means the enterprising party is strengthened, the dread of a struggle is lessened. See what an encouragement this is to the enemies of the constitution! A few assassinations, and a very great destruction of property, we know they consider as no real obstacles in the way of a grand political change. And they will hope, that here, if anti-monarchical opinions gain ground, as they have done in France, they may, as in France, accomplish a revolution without a war.

They who think so well of the French constitution cannot be seriously alarmed by any progress made by its partisans. Provisions for security are not to be received from those who think that there is no danger. No! there is no plan of security to be listened to but from those who entertain the same fears with ourselves; from those who think that the thing to be secured is a great blessing; and the thing against which we would secure it a great mischief. Every person of a different opinion must be careless about security.

I believe the author of the Reflections, whether he fears the designs of that set of people with reason or not, cannot prevail on himself to despise them. He cannot despise them for their numbers, which, though small, compared with the sound part of the community, are not inconsiderable: he cannot look with contempt on their influence, their activity, or the kind of talents and tempers which they possess, exactly calculated for the work they have in hand, and the minds they chiefly apply to. Do we not see their most considerable and accredited ministers, and several of their party of weight and importance, active in spreading mischievous opinions, in giving sanction to seditious writings, in promoting seditious anniversaries? and what part of their description has disowned them or their proceedings? When men, circumstanced as these are, publicly declare such admiration of a foreign constitution, and such contempt of our own, it would be, in the author of the Reflections, thinking as he does of the French constitution, infamously to cheat the rest of the nation to their ruin, to say there is no danger.

In estimating danger, we are obliged to take into our calculation the character and disposition of the enemy into whose hands we may chance to fall. The genius of this faction is easily discerned, by observing with what a very different eye they have viewed the late foreign revolutions. Two have passed before them. That of France and that of Poland. The state of Poland was such, that there could scarcely exist two opinions, but that a reformation of its constitution, even at some expense of blood, might be seen without much disapprobation. No confusion could be feared in such an enterprise; because the establishment to be reformed was itself a state of confusion. A king without authority; nobles without union or subordination; a people without arts, industry, commerce, or liberty; no order within; no defence without; no effective public force, but a foreign force, which entered a naked country at will, and disposed of everything at pleasure. Here was a state of things which seemed to invite, and might perhaps justify, bold enterprise and desperate experiment. But in what manner was this chaos brought into order? The means were as striking to the imagination, as satisfactory to the reason, and soothing to the moral sentiments. In contemplating that change, humanity has everything to rejoice and to glory in; nothing to be ashamed of, nothing to suffer. So far as it has gone, it probably is the most pure and defecated public good which ever has been conferred on mankind. We have seen anarchy and servitude at once removed; a throne strengthened for the protection of the people, without trenching on their liberties; all foreign cabal banished, by changing the crown from elective to hereditary; and what was a matter of pleasing wonder, we have seen a reigning king, from an heroic love to his country, exerting himself with all the toil, the dexterity, the management, the intrigue, in favour of a family of strangers, with which ambitious men labour for the aggrandisement of their own. Ten millions of men in a way of being freed gradually, and therefore safely to themselves and the state, not from civil or political chains, which, bad as they are, only fetter the mind, but from substantial personal bondage. Inhabitants of cities, before without privileges, placed in the consideration which belongs to that improved and connecting situation of social life. One of the most proud, numerous, and fierce bodies of nobility and gentry ever known in the world, arranged only in the foremost rank of free and generous citizens. Not one man incurred loss, or suffered degradation. All, from the king to the day-labourer, were improved in their condition. Everything was kept in its place and order; but in that place and order everything was bettered. To add to this happy wonder, (this unheard-of conjunction of wisdom and fortune,) not one drop of blood was spilled; no treachery; no outrage; no system of slander more

cruel than the sword; no studied insults on religion, morals, or
manners; no spoil; no confiscation; no citizen beggared; none
imprisoned; none exiled; the whole was effected with a policy,
a discretion, an unanimity and secresy, such as have never been
before known on any occasion; but such wonderful conduct was
reserved for this glorious conspiracy in favour of the true and
genuine rights and interests of men. Happy people, if they know
to proceed as they have begun! Happy prince, worthy to begin
with splendour, or to close with glory, a race of patriots and of
kings: and to leave

> A name, which every wind to heaven would bear,
> Which men to speak, and angels joy to hear.[23]

To finish all – this great good, as in the instant it is, contains in it
the seeds of all further improvement; and may be considered as
in a regular progress, because founded on similar principles,
towards the stable excellence of a British constitution.

Here was a matter for congratulation and for festive remembrance through ages. Here moralists and divines might indeed
relax in their temperance to exhilarate their humanity. But mark
the character of our faction. All their enthusiasm is kept for the
French Revolution. They cannot pretend that France had stood
so much in need of a change as Poland. They cannot pretend
that Poland has not obtained a better system of liberty, or of
government, than it enjoyed before. They cannot assert, that the
Polish Revolution cost more dearly than that of France to the
interests and feelings of multitudes of men. But the cold and
subordinate light in which they look upon the one, and the pains
they take to preach up the other of these Revolutions, leave us
no choice in fixing on their motives. Both Revolutions profess
liberty as their object; but in obtaining this object the one proceeds from anarchy to order: the other from order to anarchy.
The first secures its liberty by establishing its throne; the other
builds its freedom on the subversion of its monarchy. In the one
their means are unstained by crimes, and their settlement favours
morality. In the other, vice and confusion are in the very essence
of their pursuit and of their enjoyment. The circumstances in
which these two events differ, must cause the difference we
make in their comparative estimation. These turn the scale with
the societies in favour of France. *Ferrum est quod amant.*[24] The
frauds, the violences, the sacrileges, the havoc and ruin of

families, the dispersion and exile of the pride and flower of a great country, the disorder, the confusion, the anarchy, the violation of property, the cruel murders, the inhuman confiscations, and in the end the insolent domination of bloody, ferocious, and senseless clubs. These are the things which they love and admire. What men admire and love, they would surely act. Let us see what is done in France; and then let us undervalue any the slightest danger of falling into the hands of such a merciless and savage faction!

"But the leaders of the factious societies are too wild to succeed in this their undertaking." I hope so. But supposing them wild and absurd, is there no danger but from wise and reflecting men? Perhaps the greatest mischiefs that have happened in the world, have happened from persons as wild as those we think the wildest. In truth, they are the fittest beginners of all great changes. Why encourage men in a mischievous proceeding, because their absurdity may disappoint their malice? "But noticing them may give them consequence." Certainly. But they are noticed; and they are noticed, not with reproof, but with that kind of countenance which is given by an *apparent* concurrence (not a *real* one, I am convinced) of a great party, in the praises of the object which they hold out to imitation.

But I hear a language still more extraordinary, and indeed of such a nature as must suppose, or leave, us at their mercy. It is this – "You know their promptitude in writing, and their diligence in caballing; to write, speak, or act against them, will only stimulate them to new efforts." – This way of considering the principle of their conduct pays but a poor compliment to these gentlemen. They pretend that their doctrines are infinitely beneficial to mankind: but it seems they would keep them to themselves, if they were not greatly provoked. They are benevolent from spite. Their oracles are like those of *Proteus*,[25] (whom some people think they resemble in many particulars,) who never would give his responses unless you used him as ill as possible. These cats, it seems, would not give out their electrical light without having their backs well rubbed. But this is not to do them perfect justice. They are sufficiently communicative. Had they been quiet, the propriety of any agitation of topics on the origin and primary rights of government, in opposition to their private sentiments, might possibly be doubted. But, as it is notorious, that they were proceeding as fast, and as far, as time and circumstances would admit, both in their discussions and cabals – as it is not to be denied, that they had opened a correspondence with a foreign faction, the most wicked the world ever saw, and established anniversaries to commemorate the most monstrous, cruel, and perfidious of all the proceedings of that faction – the question is, whether their conduct was to be regarded in silence, lest our interference should render them outrageous? Then let them deal as they please with the constitution. Let the lady be passive, lest the ravisher should be driven to force. Resistance will only increase his desires. Yes, truly, if the resistance be feigned and feeble. But they who are wedded to the constitution will not act the part of wittols. They will drive such seducers from the house on the first appearance of their love-letters and offered assignations. But if the author of the Reflections, though a vigilant, was not a discreet guardian of the constitution, let them who have the same regard to it, show themselves as vigilant and more skilful in repelling the attacks of seduction or violence. Their freedom from jealousy is equivocal, and may arise as well from indifference to the object, as from confidence in her virtue.

On their principle, it is the resistance, and not the assault, which produces the danger. I admit, indeed, that if we estimated the danger by the value of the writings, it would be little worthy of our attention: contemptible these writings are in every sense. But they are not the cause, they are the disgusting symptoms, of a frightful distemper. They are not otherwise of consequence than as they show the evil habit of the bodies from whence they come. In that light the meanest of them is a serious thing. If however I should under-rate them; and if the truth is, that they are not the result, but the cause of the disorders I speak of, surely those who circulate operative poisons, and give, to whatever force they have by their nature, the further operation of their authority and adoption, are to be censured, watched, and, if possible, repressed.

At what distance the direct danger from such factions may be, it is not easy to fix. An adaptation of circumstances to designs and principles is necessary. But these cannot be wanting for any long time in the ordinary course of sublunary affairs. Great discontents frequently arise in the best constituted governments, from causes which no human wisdom can foresee, and no human power can prevent. They occur at uncertain periods, but at periods which are not commonly far asunder. Governments of all kinds are administered only by men; and great mistakes, tending to inflame these discontents, may concur. The indecision of those who happen to rule at the critical time, their supine neglect, or their precipitate and ill-judged attention, may aggravate the public misfortunes. In such a state of things, the principles, now only sown, will shoot out and vegetate in full luxuriance. In such circumstances the minds of the people become sore and ulcerated. They are put out of humour with all public men, and all public parties; they are fatigued with their dissensions; they are irritated at their coalitions; they are made easily to believe, (what much pains are taken to make them believe,) that all oppositions are factious, and all courtiers base and servile. From their disgust at men, they are soon led to quarrel with their frame of government, which they presume gives nourishment to the vices, real or supposed, of those who administer in it. Mistaking malignity for sagacity, they are soon led to cast off all hope from a good administration of affairs, and come to think that all reformation depends, not on a change of actors, but upon an alteration in the machinery. Then will be felt the full effect of encouraging doctrines which tend to make the citizens despise their constitution. Then will be felt the plenitude of the mischief of teaching the people to believe, that all ancient institutions are the results of ignorance; and that all prescriptive government is in its nature usurpation. Then will be felt, in all its energy, the danger of encouraging a spirit of litigation in persons of that immature and imperfect state of knowledge which serves to render them susceptible of doubts, but incapable of their solution. Then will be felt, in all its aggravation, the pernicious consequence of destroying all docility in the minds of those who are not formed for finding their own way in the labyrinths of political theory, and are made to reject the clue, and to disdain the guide. Then will be felt, and too late will be acknowledged, the ruin which follows the disjoining of religion from the state; the separation of morality from policy; and the giving conscience no concern and no coactive or coercive force in the most material of all the social ties, the principle of our obligations to government.

I know too, that besides this vain, contradictory, and self-destructive security, which some men derive from the habitual attachment of the people to this constitution, whilst they suffer it with a sort of sportive acquiescence to be brought into contempt before their faces, they have other grounds for removing all apprehension from their minds. They are of opinion, that there are too many men of great hereditary estates and influence in the kingdom, to suffer the establishment of the levelling system which has taken place in France. This is very true, if in order to guide the power, which now attends their property, these men possess the wisdom which is involved in early fear. But if through a supine security, to which such fortunes are peculiarly liable, they neglect the use of their influence in the season of their power, on the first derangement of society, the nerves of their strength will be cut. Their estates, instead of being the means of their security, will become the very causes of their danger. Instead of bestowing influence they will excite rapacity. They will be looked to as a prey.

Such will be the impotent condition of those men of great hereditary estates, who indeed dislike the designs that are carried on, but whose dislike is rather that of spectators, than of parties that may be concerned in the catastrophe of the piece. But riches do not in all cases secure even an inert and passive resistance. There are always, in that description, men whose fortunes, when their minds are once vitiated by passion or by evil principle, are by no means a security from their actually taking their part against the public tranquillity. We see to what low and despicable passions of all kinds many men in that class are ready to sacrifice the patrimonial estates, which might be perpetuated in their families with splendour, and with the fame of hereditary benefactors to mankind from generation to generation. Do we not see how lightly people treat their fortunes when under the influence of the passion of gaming? The game of ambition or resentment will be played by many of the rich and great, as desperately, and with as much blindness to the consequences, as any other game. Was he a man of no rank or fortune, who first set on foot the disturbances which have ruined France? Passion blinded him to the consequences, so far as they concerned himself; and as to the consequences with regard to others, they were no part of his consideration, nor ever will be with those who bear any resemblance to that virtuous patriot and lover of the rights of man.

There is also a time of insecurity, when interests of all sorts become objects of speculation. Then it is, that their very attachment to wealth and importance will induce several persons of opulence to lift themselves, and even to take a lead with the party which they think most likely to prevail, in order to obtain to themselves consideration in some new order or disorder of things. They may be led to act in this manner, that they may secure some portion of their own property, and perhaps to become partakers of the spoil of their own order. Those who speculate on change, always make a great number among people of rank and fortune, as well as amongst the low and the indigent.

What security against all this? – All human securities are liable to uncertainty. But if any thing bids fair for the prevention of so great a calamity, it must consist in the use of the ordinary means of just influence in society, whilst those means continue un-impaired. The public judgment ought to receive a proper direc-tion. All weighty men may have their share in so good a work. As yet, notwithstanding the strutting and lying independence of a braggart philosophy, nature maintains her rights, and great names have great prevalence. Two such men as Mr. Pitt and Mr. Fox, adding to their authority in a point in which they concur, even by their disunion in everything else, might frown these wicked opinions out of the kingdom. But if the influence of either of them, or the influence of men like them, should, against their serious intentions, be otherwise perverted, they may coun-tenance opinions which (as I have said before, and could wish over and over again to press) they may in vain attempt to control. In their theory, these doctrines admit no limit, no qualification whatsoever. No man can say how far he will go, who joins with those who are avowedly going to the utmost extremities. What security is there for stopping short at all in these wild conceits? Why, neither more nor less than this – that the moral sentiments of some few amongst them do put some check on their savage theories. But let us take care. The moral sentiments, so nearly connected with early prejudice as to be almost one and the same thing, will assuredly not live long under a discipline, which has for its basis the destruction of all prejudices, and the making the mind proof against all dread of consequences flowing from the pretended truths that are taught by their philosophy.

In this school the moral sentiments must grow weaker and weaker every day. The more cautious of these teachers, in laying down their maxims, draw as much of the conclusion as suits, not with their premises, but with their policy. They trust the rest to the sagacity of their pupils. Others, and these are the most vaunted for their spirit, not only lay down the same premises, but boldly draw the conclusions to the destruction of our whole constitution in church and state. But are these conclusions truly drawn? Yes, most certainly. Their principles are wild and wicked. But let justice be done even to phrensy and villainy. These teachers are perfectly systematic. No man who assumes their grounds can tolerate the British constitution in church or state. These teachers profess to scorn all mediocrity; to engage for perfection; to proceed by the simplest and shortest course. They build their politics, not on convenience, but on truth; and they profess to conduct men to certain happiness by the assertion of their undoubted rights. With them there is no compromise. All other governments are usurpations, which justify and even demand resistance.

Their principles always go to the extreme. They who go with the principles of the ancient Whigs, which are those contained in Mr. Burke's book, never can go too far. They may indeed stop short of some hazardous and ambiguous excellence, which they will be taught to postpone to any reasonable degree of good they may actually possess. The opinions maintained in that book never can lead to an extreme, because their foundation is laid in an opposition to extremes. The foundation of government is there laid, not in imaginary rights of men, (which at best is a confusion of judicial with civil principles,) but in political convenience, and in human nature; either as that nature is universal, or as it is modified by local habits and social aptitudes. The foundation of government (those who have read that book will recollect) is laid in a provision for our wants, and in a conformity to our duties; it is to purvey for the one; it is to enforce the other. These doctrines do of themselves gravitate to a middle point, or to some point near a middle. They suppose indeed a certain portion of liberty to be essential to all good government; but they infer that this liberty is to be blended into the government; to harmonise with its forms and its rules; and to be made subordinate to its end. Those who are not with that book are with its opposite. For there is no medium besides the medium itself. That medium is not such, because it is found there; but it is found there, because it is conformable to truth and nature. In this we do not follow the author; but we and the author travel together upon the same safe and middle path.

The theory contained in his book is not to furnish principles for making a new constitution, but for illustrating the principles of a constitution already made. It is a theory drawn from the *fact* of our government. They who oppose it are bound to show, that his theory militates with that fact. Otherwise, their quarrel is not with his book, but with the constitution of their country. The whole scheme of our mixed constitution is to prevent any one of its principles from being carried as far, as, taken by itself, and theoretically, it would go. Allow that to be the true policy of the British system, then most of the faults with which that system stands charged will appear to be, not imperfections into which it has inadvertently fallen, but excellencies which it has studiously sought. To avoid the perfections of extreme, all its several parts are so constituted, as not alone to answer their own several ends, but also each to limit and control the others: insomuch, that take which of the principles you please – you will find its operation checked and stopped at a certain point. The whole movement stands still rather than that any part should proceed beyond its boundary. From thence it results, that in the British constitution, there is a perpetual treaty and compromise going on, sometimes openly, sometimes with less observation. To him who contemplates the British constitution, as to him who contemplates the subordinate material world, it will always be a matter of his most curious investigation, to discover the secret of this mutual limitation.

> – Finita *potestas denique* cuique
> Quanam sit ratione, atque alte terminus haerens?[26]

They who have acted, as in France they have done, upon a scheme wholly different, and who aim at the abstract and unlimited perfection of power in the popular part, can be of no service to us in any of our political arrangements. They who in their headlong career have overpassed the goal, can furnish no example to those who aim to go no further. The temerity of such speculators is no more an example than the timidity of others. The one sort scorns the right; the other fears it; both miss it. But those, who by violence go beyond the barrier, are without question the most mischievous; because to go beyond it they overturn and destroy it. To say they have spirit, is to say nothing in their praise. The untempered spirit of madness, blindness, immorality, and impiety, deserves no commendation. He that sets his house on fire because his fingers are frost-bitten, can never be a fit instructor in the method of providing our habitations with a cheerful and salutary warmth. We want no foreign examples to rekindle in us the flame of liberty. The example of our own ancestors is abundantly sufficient to maintain the spirit of freedom in its full vigour, and to qualify it in all its exertions. The example of a wise, moral, well-natured, and well-tempered spirit of freedom, is that alone which can be useful to us, or in the least degree reputable or safe. Our fabric is so constituted; one part of it bears so much on the other, the parts are so made for one another, and for nothing else, that to introduce any foreign matter into it, is to destroy it.

What has been said of the Roman empire, is at least as true of the British constitution – "*Octingentorum annorum fortuna, disciplinaque, compages haec coaluit; quae convelli sine convellentium exitio non potest.*"[27] – This British constitution has not been struck out at an heat by a set of presumptuous men, like the assembly of pettifoggers run mad in Paris.

> "'Tis not the hasty product of a day,
> But the well-ripen'd fruit of wise delay."[28]

It is the result of the thoughts of many minds, in many ages. It is no simple, no superficial thing, nor to be estimated by superficial understandings. An ignorant man, who is not fool enough to meddle with his clock, is however sufficiently confident to think he can safely take to pieces, and put together at his pleasure, a moral machine of another guise, importance, and complexity, composed of far other wheels, and springs, and balances, and counteracting and co-operating powers. Men little think how immorally they act in rashly meddling with what they do not understand. Their delusive good intention is no sort of excuse for their presumption. They who truly mean well must be fearful of acting ill. The British constitution may have its advantages pointed out to wise and reflecting minds; but it is of too high an order of excellence to be adapted to those which are common. It takes in too many views, it makes too many combinations, to be so much as comprehended by shallow and superficial understandings. Profound thinkers will know it in its reason and spirit. The less inquiring will recognise it in their feelings and their experience. They will thank God they have a standard, which, in the most essential point of this great concern, will put them on a par with the most wise and knowing.

If we do not take to our aid the foregone studies of men reputed intelligent and learned, we shall be always beginners. But men must learn somewhere; and the new teachers mean no more than what they effect, as far as they succeed, that is, to deprive men of the benefit of the collected wisdom of mankind, and to make them blind disciples of their own particular presumption. Talk to these deluded creatures (all the disciples and most of the masters) who are taught to think themselves so newly fitted up and furnished, and you will find nothing in their houses but the refuse of *Knaves Acre*;[29] nothing but the rotten stuff, worn out in the service of delusion and sedition in all ages, and which being newly furbished up, patched, and varnished, serves well enough for those who being unacquainted with the conflict which has always been maintained between the sense and the nonsense of mankind, know nothing of the former existence and the ancient refutation of the same follies. It is nearly two thousand years since it has been observed, that these devices of ambition, avarice, and turbulence, were antiquated. They are, indeed, the most ancient of all common-places; common-places, sometimes of good and necessary causes; more frequently of the worst, but which decide upon neither. – *Eadem semper causa, libido et avaritia, et mutandarum rerum amor.* – *Ceterum libertas et speciosa nomina pretexuntur; nec quisquam alienum servitium, et dominationem sibi concupivit, ut non eadem ista vocabula usurparet.*[30]

Rational and experienced men tolerably well know, and have always known, how to distinguish between true and false liberty; and between the genuine adherence and the false pretence to what is true. But none, except those who are profoundly studied, can comprehend the elaborate contrivance of a fabric fitted to unite private and public liberty with public force, with order, with peace, with justice, and, above all, with the institutions formed for bestowing permanence and stability, through ages, upon this invaluable whole.

Place, for instance, before your eyes, such a man as Montesquieu.[31] Think of a genius not born in every country, or every time; a man gifted by nature with a penetrating aquiline eye; with a judgment prepared with the most extensive erudition; with an herculean robustness of mind, and nerves not to be broken with labour; a man who could spend twenty years in one pursuit. Think of a man, like the universal patriarch in Milton,[32] (who had drawn up before him in his prophetic vision the whole series of the generations which were to issue from his loins,) a man capable of placing in review, after having brought together from

the east, the west, the north, and the south, from the coarseness
of the rudest barbarism to the most refined and subtle civilisation,
all the schemes of government which had ever prevailed amongst
mankind, weighing, measuring, collating, and comparing them
all, joining fact with theory, and calling into council, upon all
this infinite assemblage of things, all the speculations which have
fatigued the understandings of profound reasoners in all times! –
Let us then consider, that all these were but so many preparatory
steps to qualify a man, and such a man, tinctured with no national
prejudice, with no domestic affection, to admire, and to hold out
to the admiration of mankind, the constitution of England! And
shall we Englishmen revoke to such a suit? Shall we, when so
much more than he has produced remains still to be understood
and admired, instead of keeping ourselves in the schools of real
science, choose for our teachers men incapable of being taught,
whose only claim to know is, that they have never doubted; from
whom we can learn nothing but their own indocility; who
would teach us to scorn what in the silence of our hearts we
ought to adore.

Different from them are all the great critics. They have taught
us one essential rule. I think the excellent and philosophic artist,
a true judge, as well as a perfect follower of nature, Sir Joshua
Reynolds[33] has somewhere applied it, or something like it, in his
own profession. It is this, that if ever we should find ourselves
disposed not to admire those writers or artists, Livy and Virgil
for instance, Raphael or Michael Angelo, whom all the learned
had admired, not to follow our own fancies, but to study them
until we know how and what we ought to admire; and if we
cannot arrive at this combination of admiration with knowledge,
rather to believe that we are dull, than that the rest of the world
has been imposed on. It is as good a rule, at least, with regard to
this admired constitution. We ought to understand it according
to our measure; and to venerate where we are not able presently
to comprehend.

Such admirers were our fathers to whom we owe this splendid
inheritance. Let us improve it with zeal, but with fear. Let us
follow our ancestors, men not without a rational, though without an exclusive, confidence in themselves; who, by respecting
the reason of others, who, by looking backward as well as forward, by the modesty as well as by the energy of their minds,
went on, insensibly drawing this constitution nearer and nearer

to its perfection, by never departing from its fundamental principles, nor introducing any amendment which had not a subsisting root in the laws, constitution, and usages of the kingdom. Let those who have the trust of political or of natural authority ever keep watch against the desperate enterprises of innovation: let even their benevolence be fortified and armed. They have before their eyes the example of a monarch, insulted, degraded, confined, deposed; his family dispersed, scattered, imprisoned; his wife insulted to his face like the vilest of the sex, by the vilest of all populace; himself three times dragged by these wretches in an infamous triumph; his children torn from him, in violation of the first right of nature, and given into the tuition of the most desperate and impious of the leaders of desperate and impious clubs; his revenues dilapidated and plundered; his magistrates murdered; his clergy proscribed, persecuted, famished; his nobility degraded in their rank, undone in their fortunes, fugitives in their persons; his armies corrupted and ruined; his whole people impoverished, disunited, dissolved; whilst through the bars of his prison, and amidst the bayonets of his keepers, he hears the tumult of two conflicting factions, equally wicked and abandoned, who agree in principles, in dispositions, and in objects, but who tear each other to pieces about the most effectual means of obtaining their common end; the one contending to preserve for a while his name and his person, the more easily to destroy the royal authority – the other clamouring to cut off the name, the person, and the monarchy together, by one sacrilegious execution. All this accumulation of calamity, the greatest that ever fell upon one man, has fallen upon his head, because he had left his virtues unguarded by caution; because he was not taught that where power is concerned, he who will confer benefits must take security against ingratitude.

I have stated the calamities which have fallen upon a great prince and nation, because they were not alarmed at the approach of danger, and because, what commonly happens to men surprised, they lost all resource when they were caught in it. When I speak of danger, I certainly mean to address myself to those who consider the prevalence of the new Whig doctrines as an evil.

The Whigs of this day have before them, in this Appeal, their constitutional ancestors; they have the doctors of the modern school. They will choose for themselves. The author of the Reflections has chosen for himself. If a new order is coming on, and all the political opinions must pass away as dreams, which our ancestors have worshipped as revelations, I say for him, that he would rather be the last (as certainly he is the least) of that race of men, than the first and greatest of those who have coined to themselves Whig principles from a French die, unknown to the impress of our fathers in the constitution.

LETTER TO SIR HERCULES
LANGRISHE[1]

3 JANUARY 1792

MY DEAR SIR,

YOUR REMEMBRANCE OF ME, with sentiments of so much kindness, has given me the most sincere satisfaction. It perfectly agrees with the friendly and hospitable reception which my son and I received from you, some time since, when, after an absence of twenty-two years, I had the happiness of embracing you, among my few surviving friends.

I really imagined that I should not again interest myself in any public business. I had, to the best of my moderate faculties, paid my club to the society, which I was born in some way or other to serve; and I thought I had a right to put on my night-gown and slippers, and wish a cheerful evening to the good company I must leave behind. But if our resolutions of vigour and exertion are so often broken or procrastinated in the execution, I think we may be excused, if we are not very punctual in fulfilling our engagements to indolence and inactivity. I have indeed no power of action; and am almost a cripple, even with regard to thinking: but you descend with force into the stagnant pool; and you cause such a fermentation, as to cure at least one impotent creature of his lameness, though it cannot enable him either to run or to wrestle.

You see by the paper* I take that I am likely to be long with malice prepense. You have brought under my view a subject, always difficult, at present critical. — It has filled my thoughts, which I wish to lay open to you with the clearness and simplicity which your friendship demands from me. I thank you for the communication of your ideas. I should be still more pleased if they had been more your own. What you hint, I believe to be the case; that if you had not deferred to the judgment of others, our opinions would not differ more materially at this day, than they did when we used to confer on the same subject, so many years ago. If I still persevere in my old opinions, it is no small comfort to me, that it is not with regard to doctrines properly yours that I discover my indocility.

* This letter is written on folio sheets.

The case, upon which your letter of the 10th of December turns, is hardly before me with precision enough, to enable me to form any very certain judgment upon it. It seems to be some plan of further indulgence proposed for the Catholics of Ireland. You observe, that your "general principles are not changed, but that *times and circumstances are altered.*" I perfectly agree with you, that times and circumstances, considered with reference to the public, ought very much to govern our conduct; though I am far from slighting, when applied with discretion to those circumstances, general principles, and maxims of policy. I cannot help observing, however, that you have said rather less upon the inapplicability of your own old principles to the *circumstances* that are likely to influence your conduct against these principles, than of the general maxims of state, which I can very readily believe not to have great weight with you personally.

In my present state of imperfect information, you will pardon the errors into which I may easily fall. The principles you lay down are, "that the Roman Catholics should enjoy everything *under* the state, but should not be *the state itself.*" And you add, "that when you exclude them from being *a part of the state,* you rather conform to the spirit of the age, than to any abstract doctrine;" but you consider the constitution as already established – that our state is Protestant. "It was declared so at the Revolution. It was so provided in the acts for settling the succession of the crown; – the king's coronation oath was enjoined, in order to keep it so. The king, as first magistrate of the state, is obliged to take the oath of abjuration,* and to subscribe the declaration; and, by laws subsequent, every other magistrate and member of the state, legislative and executive, are bound under the same obligation."

As to the plan to which these maxims are applied, I cannot speak, as I told you, positively about it. Because, neither from your letter, nor from any information I have been able to collect, do I find anything settled, either on the part of the Roman Catholics themselves, or on that of any persons who may wish to conduct their affairs in parliament. But if I have leave to conjecture, something is in agitation towards admitting them, under *certain qualifications,* to have some share in the election of members of parliament. This I understand is the scheme of those who are

* A small error of fact as to the abjuration oath; but of no importance in the argument.

entitled to come within your description of persons of consideration, property, and character; and firmly attached to the king and
constitution, as by "law established, with a grateful sense of your
former concessions, and a patient reliance on the benignity of
parliament, for the further mitigation of the laws that still affect
them." – As to the low, thoughtless, wild, and profligate, who
have joined themselves with those of other professions, but of
the same character; you are not to imagine, that, for a moment,
I can suppose them to be met with anything else than the manly
and enlightened energy of a firm government, supported by the
united efforts of all virtuous men, if ever their proceedings
should become so considerable as to demand its notice. I really
think that such associations should be crushed in their very
commencement.[2]

Setting, therefore, this case out of the question, it becomes an
object of very serious consideration whether, because wicked
men of *various* descriptions are engaged in seditious courses, the
rational, sober, and valuable part of *one* description should not
be indulged in their sober and rational expectations? You, who
have looked deeply into the spirit of the Popery laws,[3] must be
perfectly sensible, that a great part of the present mischief, which
we abhor in common, (if it at all exists,) has arisen from them.
Their declared object was to reduce the Catholics of Ireland to a
miserable populace, without property, without estimation, without education. The professed object was to deprive the few men
who, in spite of those laws, might hold or obtain any property
amongst them, of all sort of influence or authority over the rest.
They divided the nation into two distinct bodies, without
common interest, sympathy, or connexion. One of these bodies
was to possess *all* the franchises, *all* the property, *all* the education:
the other was to be composed of drawers of water and cutters of
turf for them. Are we to be astonished, when, by the efforts of
so much violence in conquest, and so much policy in regulation,
continued without intermission for nearly an hundred years, we
had reduced them to a mob; that whenever they came to act at
all, many of them would act exactly like a mob, without temper,
measure, or foresight? Surely it might be just now a matter of
temperate discussion, whether you ought not to apply a remedy
to the real cause of the evil. If the disorder you speak of be real
and considerable, you ought to raise an aristocratic interest; that
is, an interest of property and education amongst them; and to

strengthen, by every prudent means, the authority and influence of men of that description. It will deserve your best thoughts, to examine whether this can be done without giving such persons the means of demonstrating to the rest, that something more is to be got by their temperate conduct, than can be expected from the wild and senseless projects[4] of those who do not belong to their body, who have no interest in their well being, and only wish to make them the dupes of their turbulent ambition.

If the absurd persons[5] you mention find no way of providing for liberty, but by overturning this happy constitution, and introducing a frantic democracy, let us take care how we prevent better people from any rational expectations of partaking in the benefit of that constitution *as it stands*. The maxims you establish cut the matter short. They have no sort of connexion with the good or the ill behaviour of the persons who seek relief, or with the proper or improper means by which they seek it. They form a perpetual bar to all pleas, and to all expectations.

You begin by asserting, that "the Catholics ought to enjoy all things *under* the state, but that they ought not to *be the state*." A position which, I believe, in the latter part of it, and in the latitude there expressed, no man of common sense has ever thought proper to dispute; because the contrary implies, that the state ought to be in them *exclusively*. But before you have finished the line, you express yourself as if the other member of your proposition, namely, that "they ought not to be *a part* of the state," were necessarily included in your first – Whereas I conceive it to be as different as a part is from the whole; that is, just as different as possible. I know, indeed, that it is common with those who talk very differently from you, that is, with heat and animosity, to confound those things, and to argue the admission of the Catholics into any, however minute and subordinate, parts of the state, as a surrender into their hands of the whole government of the kingdom. To them I have nothing at all to say.

Wishing to proceed with a deliberative spirit and temper in so very serious a question, I shall attempt to analyse, as well as I can, the principles you lay down, in order to fit them for the grasp of an understanding so little comprehensive as mine. – "State" – "Protestant" – "Revolution." These are terms, which, if not well explained, may lead us into many errors. In the word *State*, I conceive there is much ambiguity. The state is sometimes used to signify *the whole commonwealth*, comprehending all its orders, with the several privileges belonging to each. Sometimes it signifies only *the higher and ruling part* of the commonwealth; which we commonly call *the Government*. In the first sense, to be under the state, but not the state itself, *nor any part of it*, that is, to be nothing at all in the commonwealth, is a situation perfectly intelligible: but to those who fill that situation, not very pleasant, when it is understood. It is a state of *civil servitude* by the very force of the definition. *Servorum non est respublica*,[6] is a very old and a very true maxim. This servitude, which makes men *subject* to a state without being *citizens*, may be more or less tolerable from many circumstances: but these circumstances, more or less favourable, do not alter the nature of the thing. The mildness by which absolute masters exercise their dominion, leaves them masters still. We may talk a little presently of the manner in which the majority of the people of Ireland (the Catholics) are affected by this situation; which at present undoubtedly is theirs, and which you are of opinion ought so to continue for ever.

In the other sense of the word *State*, by which is understood the *Supreme Government* only, I must observe this upon the question: that to exclude whole classes of men entirely from this *part* of government, cannot be considered as *absolute slavery*. It only implies a lower and degraded state of citizenship; such is (with more or less strictness) the condition of all countries in which an hereditary nobility possess the exclusive rule. This may be no bad mode of government; provided that the personal authority of individual nobles be kept in due bounds, that their cabals and factions are guarded against with a severe vigilance, and that the people (who have no share in granting their own money) are subjected to but light impositions, and are otherwise treated with attention, and with indulgence to their humours and prejudices.

The republic of Venice is one of those which strictly confines all the great functions and offices, such as are truly *state*-functions and *state*-offices, to those who, by hereditary right or admission, are noble Venetians. But there are many offices, and some of them not mean nor unprofitable, (that of chancellor is one,) which are reserved for the *Cittadini*. Of these all citizens of Venice are capable. The inhabitants of the *Terra firma*, who are mere subjects of conquest, that is, as you express it, under the state, but "not a part of it," are not, however, subjects in so very rigorous a sense as not to be capable of numberless subordinate employments. It is indeed one of the advantages attending the narrow bottom of their aristocracy, (narrow as compared with their acquired dominions, otherwise broad enough,) that an exclusion from such employments cannot possibly be made amongst their subjects. There are, besides, advantages in states so constituted, by which those who are considered as of an inferior race, are indemnified for their exclusion from the government and from noble employments. In all these countries, either by express law, or by usage more operative, the noble casts are almost universally, in their turn, excluded from commerce, manufacture, farming of land, and in general from all lucrative civil professions. The nobles have the monopoly of honour. The plebeians a monopoly of all the means of acquiring wealth. Thus some sort of a balance is formed, among conditions; a sort of compensation is furnished to those, who, in a *limited sense*, are excluded from the government of the state.

Between the extreme of *a total exclusion*, to which your maxim goes, and *an universal unmodified capacity*, to which the fanatics pretend, there are many different degrees and stages, and a great variety of temperaments, upon which prudence may give full scope to its exertions. For you know that the decisions of prudence (contrary to the system of the insane reasoners) differ from those of judicature; and that almost all the former are determined on the more or the less, the earlier or the later, and on a balance of advantage and inconvenience, of good and evil.

In all considerations which turn upon the question of vesting or continuing the state solely and exclusively in some one description of citizens, prudent legislators will consider, how far the *general form and principles of their commonwealth render it fit to be cast into an oligarchical shape, or to remain always in it*. We know that the government of Ireland (the same as the British) is not in its constitution *wholly* aristocratical; and, as it is not such in its form, so neither is it in its spirit. If it had been inveterately aristocratical, exclusions might be more patiently submitted to. The lot of one plebeian would be the lot of all; and an habitual reverence and admiration of certain families might make the people content to see government wholly in hands to whom it seemed naturally to belong. But our constitution has *a plebeian member*, which forms an essential integrant part of it. A plebeian oligarchy is a monster: and no people, not absolutely domestic or predial slaves, will long endure it. The Protestants of Ireland are not *alone* sufficiently the people to form a democracy; and they are *too numerous* to answer the ends and purposes of an *aristocracy*. Admiration, that first source of obedience, can be only the claim or the imposture of the few. I hold it to be absolutely impossible for two millions of plebeians, composing certainly a very clear and decided majority in that class, to become so far in love with six or seven hundred thousand of their fellow-citizens, (to all outward appearance plebeians like themselves, and many of them tradesmen, servants, and otherwise inferior to some of them,) as to see with satisfaction, or even with patience, an exclusive power vested in them, by which *constitutionally* they become the absolute masters; and, by the *manners* derived from their circumstances, must be capable of exercising upon them, daily and hourly, an insulting and vexatious superiority. Neither are the majority of the Irish indemnified (as in some aristocracies) for this state of humiliating vassalage, (often inverting the nature of things and relations,) by having the lower walks of industry wholly abandoned to them. They are rivalled, to say the least of the matter, in every laborious and lucrative course of life; while every franchise, every honour, every trust, every place down to the very lowest and least confidential, (besides whole professions,) is reserved for the master cast.

Our constitution is not made for great, general, and proscriptive exclusions; sooner or later it will destroy them, or they will destroy the constitution. In our constitution there has always been a difference made between *a franchise* and *an office*, and between the capacity for the one and for the other. Franchises were supposed to belong to the *subject*, as *a subject*, and not *as a member of the governing part of the state*. The policy of government has considered them as things very different; for whilst parliament excluded by the test acts[7] (and for a while these test acts were not a dead letter, as now they are in England) Protestant dissenters from all civil and military employments, they *never touched their right of voting for members of parliament or sitting in either House*; a point I state, not as approving or condemning, with regard to them, the measure of exclusion from employments, but to prove that the distinction has been admitted in legislature, as, in truth, it is founded in reason.

I will not here examine, whether the principles of the British [the Irish] constitution be wise or not. I must assume that they are; and that those, who partake the franchises which make it, partake of a benefit. They who are excluded from votes (under proper qualifications inherent in the constitution that gives them) are excluded, not from the *state*, but from the *British constitution*. They cannot by any possibility, whilst they hear its praises continually rung in their ears, and are present at the declaration which is so generally and so bravely made by those who possess the privilege – that the best blood in their veins ought to be shed, to preserve their share in it; they, the disfranchised part, cannot, I say, think themselves in a *happy* state, to be utterly excluded from all its direct and all its consequential advantages. The popular part of the constitution must be to them by far the most odious part of it. To them it is not *an actual*, and, if possible, still less a *virtual*, representation. It is indeed the direct contrary. It is power unlimited, placed in the hands of *an adverse* description, *because it is an adverse description*. And if they who compose the privileged body have not an interest, they must but too frequently have motives of pride, passion, petulance, peevish jealousy, or tyrannic suspicion, to urge them to treat the excluded people with contempt and rigour.

This is not a mere theory; though whilst men are men, it is a theory that cannot be false. I do not desire to revive all the particulars in my memory; I wish them to sleep for ever; but it is impossible I should wholly forget what happened in some parts of Ireland, with very few and short intermissions, from the year 1761 to the year 1766, both inclusive. In a country of miserable police, passing from the extremes of laxity to the extremes of rigour, among a neglected, and therefore disorderly, populace – if any disturbance or sedition, from any grievance real or imaginary, happened to arise, it was presently perverted from its true nature, often criminal enough in itself to draw upon it a severe, appropriate punishment; it was metamorphosed into a conspiracy against the state, and prosecuted as such. Amongst the Catholics, as being by far the most numerous and the most wretched, all sorts of offenders against the laws must commonly be found. The punishment of low people for the offences usual among low people would warrant no inference against any description of religion or of politics. Men of consideration from their age, their profession, or their character; men of proprietary landed estates, substantial renters, opulent merchants, physicians, and titular bishops; could not easily be suspected of riot in open day, or of nocturnal assemblies for the purpose of pulling down hedges, making breaches in park walls, firing barns, maiming cattle, and outrages of a similar nature, which characterise the disorders of an oppressed or a licentious populace. But when the evidence, given on the trial for such misdemeanours, qualified them as overt acts of high treason, and when witnesses were found (such witnesses as they were) to depose to the taking of oaths of allegiance by the rioters to the king of France, to their being paid by his money, and embodied and exercised under his officers, to overturn the state for the purposes of that potentate; in that case, the rioters might (if the witness was believed) be supposed only the troops and persons more reputable, the leaders and commanders in such a rebellion. All classes in the obnoxious description, who could not be suspected of the lower crime of riot, might be involved in the odium, in the suspicion, and sometimes in the punishment, of a higher and far more criminal species of offence. These proceedings did not arise from any one of the Popery laws since repealed,[8] but from this circumstance, that when it answered the purposes of an election party, or a malevolent person of influence, to forge such plots, the people had no protection. The people of that description have no hold on the gentlemen who aspire to be popular representatives. The candidates neither love, nor respect, nor fear them, individually or collectively. I do not think this evil (an evil amongst a thousand others) at this day entirely over; for I conceive I have lately seen some indication of a disposition perfectly similar to the old one; that is, a disposition to carry the imputation of crimes from persons to descriptions, and wholly to alter the character and quality of the offences themselves.

This universal exclusion seems to me a serious evil – because many collateral oppressions, besides what I have just now stated, have arisen from it. In things of this nature, it would not be either easy or proper to quote chapter and verse; but I have great reason to believe, particularly since the octennial act,[9] that several have refused at all to let their lands to Roman Catholics; because it would so far disable them from promoting such interests in counties as they were inclined to favour.[10] They who consider also the state of all sorts of tradesmen, shopkeepers, and particularly publicans, in towns, must soon discern the disadvantages under which those labour who have no votes. It cannot be otherwise, whilst the spirit of elections, and the tendencies of human nature, continue as they are. If property be artificially separated from franchise, the franchise must in some way or other, and in some proportion, naturally attract property to it. Many are the collateral disadvantages amongst a *privileged* people, which must attend on those who have *no* privileges.

Among the rich each individual, with or without a franchise, is of importance; the poor and the middling are no otherwise so, than as they obtain some collective capacity and can be aggregated to some corps. If legal ways are not found, illegal will be resorted to; and seditious clubs and confederacies, such as no man living holds in greater horror than I do, will grow and flourish in spite, I am afraid, of anything which can be done to prevent the evil. Lawful enjoyment is the surest method to prevent unlawful gratification. Where there is property, there will be less theft; where there is marriage, there will always be less fornication.

I have said enough of the question of state, *as it affects the people merely as such*. But it is complicated with a political question relative to religion, to which it is very necessary I should say something; because the term *Protestant*, which you apply, is too general for the conclusions which one of your accurate understanding would wish to draw from it; and because a great deal of argument will depend on the use that is made of that term.

It is *not* a fundamental part of the settlement at the Revolution, that the state should be Protestant without *any qualification of the term*. With a qualification it is unquestionably true; not in all its latitude. With the qualification, it was true before the Revolution. Our predecessors in legislation were not so irrational (not to say impious) as to form an operose ecclesiastical establishment, and even to render the state itself in some degree subservient to it, when their religion (if such it might be called) was nothing but a mere *negation* of some other – without any positive idea either of doctrine, discipline, worship, or morals, in the scheme which they professed themselves, and which they imposed upon others, even under penalties and incapacities – No! No! This never could have been done even by reasonable atheists. They who think religion of no importance to the state, have abandoned it to the conscience, or caprice, of the individual; they make no provision for it whatsoever, but leave every club to make, or not, a voluntary contribution towards its support, according to their fancies. This would be consistent. The other always appeared to me to be a monster of contradiction and

absurdity. It was for that reason, that, some years ago, I strenuously opposed the clergy who petitioned, to the number of about
three hundred, to be freed from the subscription to the Thirty-
nine Articles,[11] without proposing to substitute any other in their
place. There never has been a religion of the state, (the few years
of the parliament only excepted,) but that of *the episcopal church
of England*; the episcopal church of England, before the
Reformation, connected with the see of Rome, since then, disconnected and protesting against some of her doctrines, and
against the whole of her authority, as binding in our national
church: nor did the fundamental laws of this kingdom (in Ireland
it has been the same) ever know, at any period, any other church
as an object of establishment; or in that light, any other Protestant
religion. Nay, our Protestant *toleration* itself[12] at the Revolution,
and until within a few years, required a signature of thirty-six,
and a part of the thirty-seventh, out of the Thirty-nine Articles.
So little idea had they at the Revolution of *establishing* Protestantism indefinitely, that they did not indefinitely tolerate it
under that name. I do not mean to praise that strictness, where
nothing more than merely religious toleration is concerned. Toleration, being a part of moral and political prudence, ought to
be tender and large. A tolerant government ought not to be too
scrupulous in its investigations; but may bear without blame, not
only very ill-grounded doctrines, but even many things that are
positively vices, where they are *adulta et prævalida*.[13] The good of
the commonwealth is the rule which rides over the rest; and to
this every other must completely submit.

The church of Scotland knows as little of Protestantism
undefined, as the church of England and Ireland do. She has by the
articles of union secured to herself the perpetual establishment of
the Confession of Faith,[14] and the *Presbyterian* church government.
In England, even during the troubled interregnum, it was not
thought fit to establish a *negative* religion; but the parliament
settled the *presbyterian*, as the church *discipline*; the *Directory*,[15] as
the rule of public *worship*; and the *Westminster Catechism*, as the
institute of *faith*. This is to show, that at no time was the Protestant religion, *undefined*, established here or anywhere else, as
I believe. I am sure that when the three religions were established
in Germany, they were expressly characterised and declared to
be the *Evangelic*, the *Reformed*, and the *Catholic*; each of which

has its confession of faith and its settled discipline; so that you always may know the best and the worst of them, to enable you to make the most of what is good, and to correct, or to qualify, or to guard against whatever may seem evil or dangerous.

As to the coronation oath, to which you allude, as opposite to admitting a Roman Catholic to the use of any franchise whatsoever, I cannot think that the king would be perjured if he gave his assent to any regulation which parliament might think fit to make with regard to that affair. The king is bound by law, as clearly specified in several acts of parliament, to be in communion with the church of England. It is a part of the tenure by which he holds his crown; and though no provision was made till the Revolution, which could be called positive and valid in law, to ascertain this great principle, I have always considered it as in fact fundamental, that the king of England should be of the Christian religion, according to the national legal church for the time being. I conceive it was so before the Reformation. Since the Reformation it became doubly necessary; because the king is the head of that church; in some sort an ecclesiastical person; and it would be incongruous and absurd, to have the head of the church of one faith, and the members of another. The king may *inherit* the crown as a *Protestant*, but he cannot *hold it*, according to law, without being a Protestant *of the church of England.*[16]

Before we take it for granted, that the king is bound by his coronation oath not to admit any of his Catholic subjects to the rights and liberties, which ought to belong to them as Englishmen, (not as religionists,) or to settle the conditions or proportions of such admission by an act of parliament, I wish you to place before your eyes that oath itself, as it is settled in the act of William and Mary.

"Will you to the utmost of your power maintain – The laws of God, the true profession of the gospel – and the Protestant reformed religion *as it is established by law.* – And will you preserve unto *bishops* and clergy, and the churches committed to *their* charge, all such rights and privileges as by law do, or shall appertain to them, or any of them. – All this I promise to do."

Here are the coronation engagements of the king. In them I do not find one word to preclude his Majesty from consenting to any arrangement which parliament may make with regard to the civil privileges of any part of his subjects.

It may not be amiss, on account of the light which it will throw on this discussion, to look a little more narrowly into the matter of that oath – in order to discover how far it has hitherto operated, or how far in future it ought to operate, as a bar to any proceedings of the crown and parliament in favour of those, against whom it may be supposed that the king has engaged to support the Protestant church of England, in the two kingdoms, in which it is established by law. First, the king swears he will maintain, to the utmost of his power, "the laws of God." I suppose it means the natural moral laws. – Secondly, he swears to maintain "the true profession of the gospel." By which I suppose is understood *affirmatively* the Christian religion. – Thirdly, that he will maintain "the Protestant reformed religion." This leaves me no power of supposition or conjecture; for that Protestant reformed religion is defined and described by the subsequent words, "established by law," and in this instance, to define it beyond all possibility of doubt, he "swears to maintain the bishops and clergy, and the churches committed to their charge," in their rights present and future.

The oath as effectually prevents the king from doing any thing to the prejudice of the church in favour of sectaries, Jews, Mahometans, or plain avowed infidels; as if he should do the same thing in favour of the Catholics. You will see, that it is the same Protestant church, so described, that the king is to maintain and communicate with, according to the act of settlement of the 12th and 13th of William III. The act of the 5th of Anne, made in prospect of the Union, is entitled, "An act for securing the church of England as by law established." It meant to guard the church implicitly against any other mode of Protestant religion which might creep in by means of the Union. It proves beyond all doubt, that the legislature did not mean to guard the church on one part only, and to leave it defenceless and exposed upon every other. This church, in that act, is declared to be "fundamental and essential" for ever, in the constitution of the united kingdom, so far as England is concerned; and I suppose as the law stands, even since the independence, it is so in Ireland.[17]

All this shows, that the religion which the king is bound to maintain has a positive part in it as well as a negative; and that the positive part of it (in which we are in perfect agreement with the Catholics and with the church of Scotland) is infinitely the most valuable and essential. Such an agreement we had with Protestant dissenters in England, of those descriptions who came under the toleration act of King William and Queen Mary; an act coeval with the Revolution; and which ought, on the principles of the gentlemen who oppose the relief to the Catholics, to have been held sacred and unalterable. Whether we agree with the present Protestant dissenters in the points at the Revolution held essential and fundamental among Christians, or in any other fundamental, at present it is impossible for us to know; because, at their own very earnest desire, we have repealed the toleration act of William and Mary, and discharged them from the signature required by that act; and because, for the far greater part, they publicly declare against all manner of confessions of faith, even the *consensus*.

For reasons forcible enough at all times, but at this time particularly forcible with me, I dwell a little the longer upon this matter, and take the more pains, to put us both in mind that it was not settled at the Revolution, that the state should be Protestant, in the latitude of the term, but in a defined and limited sense only, and that in that sense only the king is sworn to maintain it. To suppose that the king has sworn with his utmost power to maintain what it is wholly out of his power to discover, or which, if he could discover, he might discover to consist of things directly contradictory to each other, some of them perhaps impious, blasphemous, and seditious upon principle, would be not only a gross, but a most mischievous, absurdity. If mere dissent from the church of Rome be a merit, he that dissents the most perfectly is the most meritorious. In many points we hold strongly with that church. He that dissents throughout with that church will dissent with the church of England, and then it will be a part of his merit that he dissents with ourselves: – a whimsical species of merit for any set of men to establish. We quarrel to extremity with those, who we know agree with us in many things, but we are to be so malicious even in the principle of our friendships, that we are to cherish in our bosom those who accord with us in nothing, because, whilst they despise ourselves, they abhor, even more than we do, those with whom we have some disagreement. A man is certainly the most perfect Protestant, who protests against the whole Christian religion. Whether a person's having no Christian religion be a title to favour, in exclusion to the largest description of Christians who hold all the doctrines of Christianity, though holding along with them some errors and some superfluities, is rather more than any man, who has not become recreant and apostate from his baptism, will, I believe, choose to affirm. The countenance given from a spirit of controversy to that negative religion may, by degrees, encourage light and unthinking people to a total indifference to everything positive in matters of doctrine; and, in the end, of practice too. If continued, it would play the game of that sort of active, proselytising, and persecuting atheism, which is the disgrace and calamity of our time, and which we see to be as capable of subverting a government, as any mode can be of misguided zeal for better things.

Now let us fairly see what course has been taken relative to those, against whom, in part at least, the king has sworn to maintain a church, *positive in its doctrine and its discipline*. The first thing done, even when the oath was fresh in the mouth of the sovereigns, was to give a toleration to Protestant dissenters, *whose doctrines they ascertained*. As to the mere civil privileges which the dissenters held as subjects before the Revolution, these were not touched at all. The laws have fully permitted, in a qualification for all offices, to such dissenters, *an occasional conformity*; a thing I believe singular, where tests are admitted. The act called the Test Act itself, is, with regard to them, grown to be hardly anything more than a dead letter. Whenever the dissenters cease by their conduct to give any alarm to the government, in church and state, I think it very probable that even this matter, rather disgustful, than inconvenient to them, may be removed, or at least so modified as to distinguish the qualification to those offices which really *guide the state*, from those which are *merely instrumental*; or that some other and better tests may be put in their place.

So far as to England. In Ireland you have outrun us. Without waiting for an English example, you have totally, and without any modification whatsoever, repealed the test as to Protestant dissenters.[18] Not having the repealing act by me, I ought not to say positively that there is no exception in it; but if it be what I suppose it is, you know very well, that a Jew in religion, or a Mahometan, or even *a public, declared atheist*, and blasphemer, is perfectly qualified to be lord-lieutenant, a lord justice, or even keeper of the king's conscience; and by virtue of his office (if with you it be as it is with us) administrator to a great part of the ecclesiastical patronage of the crown.

Now let us deal a little fairly. We must admit, that Protestant dissent was one of the quarters from which danger was apprehended at the Revolution, and against which a part of the coronation oath was peculiarly directed. By this unqualified repeal, you certainly did not mean to deny that it was the duty of the crown to preserve the church against Protestant dissenters; or taking this to be the true sense of the two revolution acts of King William, and of the previous and subsequent union acts of Queen Anne, you did not declare by this most unqualified repeal, by which you broke down all the barriers, not invented indeed, but carefully preserved at the Revolution; you did not then and by that proceeding declare, that you had advised the king to perjury towards God, and perfidy towards the church. No! far, very far from it! you never would have done it, if you did not think it could be done with perfect repose to the royal conscience, and perfect safety to the national established religion. You did this upon a full consideration of the circumstances of your country. Now if circumstances required it, why should it be contrary to the king's oath, his parliament judging on those circumstances, to restore to his Catholic people, in such measure, and with such modifications as the public wisdom shall think proper to add, *some part* in these franchises which they formerly had held without limitation at all, and which, upon no sort of urgent reason at the time, they were deprived of? If such means can with any probability be shown, from circumstances, rather to add strength to our mixed ecclesiastical and secular constitution, than to weaken it; surely they are means infinitely to be preferred to penalties, incapacities, and proscriptions continued from generation to generation. They are perfectly consistent with the other parts of the coronation oath, in which the king swears to maintain "the laws of God and the true profession of the gospel, and to govern the people according to the statutes in parliament agreed upon, and the laws and customs of the realm." In consenting to such a statute, the crown would act at least as agreeably to the laws of God, and to the true profession of the gospel, and to the laws and customs of the kingdom, as George I did when he passed the statute which took from the body of the people everything which, to that hour, and even after the monstrous acts of the 2nd and 8th of Anne,[19] (the objects of our common hatred,) they still enjoyed inviolate.

It is hard to distinguish with the least degree of accuracy, what

laws are fundamental, and what not. However, there is a distinction between them authorised by the writers on jurisprudence,
and recognised in some of our statutes. I admit the acts of King
William and Queen Anne to be fundamental, but they are not
the only fundamental laws. The law called *Magna Charta*, by
which it is provided, that "no man shall be disseised of his liberties and free customs but by the judgment of his peers, or the
laws of the land," (meaning clearly for some proved crime tried
and adjudged,) I take to be a *fundamental law*. Now, although this
Magna Charta, or some of the statutes establishing it, provide that
law shall be perpetual, and all statutes contrary to it shall be void,
yet I cannot go so far as to deny the authority of statutes made in
defiance of Magna Charta and all its principles. This however
I will say, that it is a very venerable law, made by very wise and
learned men, and that the legislature, in their attempt to perpetuate it, even against the authority of future parliaments, have
shown their judgment that it is *fundamental* on the same grounds,
and in the same manner, as the act of the fifth of Anne has considered and declared the establishment of the church of England to
be fundamental. Magna Charta, which secured these franchises
to the subjects, regarded the rights of freeholders in counties to
be as much a fundamental part of the constitution, as the establishment of the church of England was thought either at that
time, or in the act of King William, or in the act of Queen Anne.

The churchmen, who led in that transaction, certainly took
care of the material interest of which they were the natural guardians. It is the first article of Magna Charta, "that the church of
England shall be free," &c. &c. But at that period churchmen,
and barons, and knights, took care of the franchises and free
customs of the people too. Those franchises are part of the constitution itself, and inseparable from it. It would be a very strange
thing if there should not only exist anomalies in our laws, a thing
not easy to prevent, but, that the fundamental parts of the
constitution should be perpetually and irreconcilably at variance
with each other. I cannot persuade myself that the lovers of our
church are not as able to find effectual ways of reconciling its
safety with the franchises of the people, as the ecclesiastics of the
thirteenth century were able to do; I cannot conceive how anything worse can be said of the Protestant religion of the church
of England than this, that wherever it is judged proper to give it
a legal establishment, it becomes necessary to deprive the body

of the people, if they adhere to their old opinions, of "their liberties and of all their free customs," and to reduce them to a state of *civil* servitude.

There is no man on earth, I believe, more willing than I am, to lay it down as a fundamental of the constitution, that the church of England should be united and even identified with it; but, allowing this, I cannot allow that all *laws of regulation*, made from time to time, in support of that fundamental law, are, of course, equally fundamental and equally unchangeable. This would be to confound all the branches of legislation and of jurisprudence. – The *crown* and the personal safety of the monarch are *fundamentals* in our constitution: yet I hope that no man regrets, that the rabble of statutes got together during the reign of Henry the Eighth, by which treasons are multiplied with so prolific an energy, have been all repealed in a body; although they were all, or most of them, made in support of things truly fundamental in our constitution. So were several of the acts by which the crown exercised its supremacy; such as the act of Elizabeth for making the *high commission courts*, and the like; as well as things made treason in the time of Charles II. None of this species of *secondary and subsidiary laws* have been held fundamental. They have yielded to circumstances: particularly where they were thought, even in their consequences, or obliquely, to affect other fundamentals. How much more, certainly, ought they to give way, when, as in our case, they affect, not here and there, in some particular point or in their consequence, but universally, collectively, and directly, the fundamental franchises of a people, equal to the whole inhabitants of several respectable kingdoms and states; equal to the subjects of the kings of Sardinia or of Denmark; equal to those of the United Netherlands; and more than are to be found in all the states of Switzerland. This way of proscribing men by whole nations as it were, from all the benefits of the constitution to which they were born, I never can believe to be politic or expedient, much less necessary for the existence of any state or church in the world. Whenever I shall be convinced, which will be late and reluctantly, that the safety of the church is utterly inconsistent with all the civil rights whatsoever of the far larger part of the inhabitants of our country, I shall be extremely sorry for it; because I shall think the church to be truly in danger. It is putting things into the position of an ugly alternative, into which I hope in God they never will be put.

I have said most of what occurs to me on the topics you touch upon, relative to the religion of the king, and his coronation oath. I shall conclude the observations which I wished to submit to you on this point, by assuring you, that I think you the most remote that can be conceived from the metaphysicians of our times, who are the most foolish of men, and who, dealing in universals and essences, see no difference between more and less; and who of course would think that the reason of the law which obliged the king to be a communicant of the church of England would be as valid to exclude a Catholic from being an exciseman, or to deprive a man who has five hundred a year, under that description, from voting on a par with a factitious Protestant dissenting freeholder of forty shillings.

Recollect, my dear friend, that it was a fundamental principle in the French monarchy, whilst it stood, that the state should be Catholic; yet the edict of Nantz[20] gave, not a full ecclesiastical, but a complete civil *establishment*, with places of which only they were capable, to the Calvinists of France; and there were very few employments indeed of which they were not capable. The world praised the Cardinal de Richelieu, who took the first opportunity to strip them of their fortified places and cautionary towns. The same world held and does hold in execration (so far as that business is concerned) the memory of Louis the Fourteenth, for the total repeal of that favourable edict; though the talk of "fundamental laws, established religion, religion of the prince, safety to the state," &c. &c., was then as largely held, and with as bitter a revival of the animosities of the civil confusions during the struggles between the parties, as now they can be in Ireland.

Perhaps there are persons who think that the same reasons do not hold when the religious relation of the sovereign and subject is changed; but they who have their shop full of false weights and measures, and who imagine that the adding or taking away the name of Protestant or Papist, Guelph or Ghibelline,[21] alters all the principles of equity, policy, and prudence, leave us no common data upon which we can reason. I therefore pass by all this, which on you will make no impression, to come to what seems to be a serious consideration in your mind; I mean the dread you express of "reviewing, for the purpose of altering, the *principles of the Revolution.*" This is an interesting topic; on which I will, as fully as your leisure and mine permits, lay before you the ideas I have formed.

First, I cannot possibly confound in my mind all the things which were done at the Revolution, with the *principles* of the Revolution. As in most great changes, many things were done from the necessities of the time, well or ill understood, from passion or from vengeance, which were not only not perfectly agreeable to its principles, but in the most direct contradiction to them. I shall not think that the *deprivation of some millions of people of all the rights of citizens, and all interest in the constitution, in and to which they were born*, was a thing conformable to the declared principles of the Revolution. This I am sure is true relatively to England, (where the operation of these *anti-principles* comparatively were of little extent,) and some of our late laws, in repealing acts made immediately after the Revolution, admit that some things then done were not done in the true spirit of the Revolution. But the Revolution operated differently in England and Ireland, in many, and these essential, particulars. Supposing the principles to have been altogether the same in both kingdoms, by the application of those principles to very different objects, the whole spirit of the system was changed, not to say reversed. In England it was the struggle of the *great body* of the people for the establishment of their liberties against the efforts of a very *small faction*, who would have oppressed them. In Ireland it was the establishment of the power of the smaller number, at the expense of the civil liberties and properties of the far greater part; and at the expense of the political liberties of the whole. It was, to say the truth, not a revolution, but a conquest; which is not to say a great deal in its favour. To insist on everything done in Ireland at the Revolution, would be to insist on the severe and jealous policy of a conqueror, in the crude settlement of his new acquisition, as a *permanent* rule for its future government. This, no power, in no country that ever I heard of, has done or professed to do – except in Ireland; where it is done, and possibly by some people will be professed. Time has, by degrees, in all other places and periods, blended and coalited the conquered with the conquerors. So, after some time, and after one of the most rigid conquests that we read of in history, the Normans softened into the English. I wish you to turn your recollection to the fine speech of Cerealis[22] to the Gauls, made to dissuade them from revolt. Speaking of the Romans, – "*Nos* quamvis toties lacessiti, jure victoriæ id solum vobis addidimus, quo pacem tueremur: nam neque quies gentium sine armis; neque arma sine stipendiis;

neque stipendia sine tributis, haberi queant. *Cætera in communi sita sunt*: ipsi plerumque nostris exercitibus *presidetis*: ipsi has aliasque provincias *regitas: nil separatum clausumve* − Proinde pacem et urbem, quam *victores victique eodem jure obtinemus*, amate, colite."[23] You will consider, whether the arguments used by that Roman to these Gauls, would apply to the case in Ireland; and whether you could use so plausible a preamble to any severe warning you may think it proper to hold out to those, who should resort to sedition, instead of supplication, to obtain any object that they may pursue with the governing power.

For a much longer period than that which had sufficed to blend the Romans with the nation to which of all others they were the most adverse, the Protestants settled in Ireland, consider themselves in no other light than that of a sort of a colonial garrison, to keep the natives in subjection to the other state of Great Britain. The whole spirit of the Revolution in Ireland, was that of not the mildest conqueror. In truth, the spirit of those proceedings did not commence at that æra, nor was religion of any kind their primary object. What was done, was not in the spirit of a contest between two religious factions; but between two adverse nations. The statutes of Kilkenny[24] show, that the spirit of the Popery laws, and some even of their actual provisions, as applied between Englishry and Irishry, had existed in that harassed country before the words Protestant and Papist were heard of in the world. If we read Baron Finglass, Spenser, and Sir John Davis,[25] we cannot miss the true genius and policy of the English government there before the Revolution, as well as during the whole reign of Queen Elizabeth. Sir John Davis boasts of the benefits received by the natives, by extending to them the English law, and turning the whole kingdom into shire ground. But the appearance of things alone was changed. The original scheme was never deviated from for a single hour. Unheard-of confiscations were made in the northern parts, upon grounds of plots and conspiracies, never proved upon their supposed authors. The war of chicane succeeded to the war of arms and of hostile statutes; and a regular series of operations was carried on, particularly from Chichester's time,[26] in the ordinary courts of justice, and by special commissions and inquisitions; first under pretence of tenures, and then of titles in the crown, for the purpose of the total extirpation of the interest of the natives in their own soil − until this species of subtle ravage, being carried to the last excess of oppression and insolence under Lord Strafford,[27] it kindled the flames of that rebellion which broke out in 1641. By the issue of that war, by the turn which the Earl of Clarendon[28] gave to things at the Restoration, and by the total reduction of the kingdom of Ireland in 1691, the ruin of the native Irish, and, in a great measure too, of the first races of the English, was completely accomplished. The new English interest was settled with as solid a stability as anything in human affairs can look for. All the penal laws of that unparalleled code of oppression, which were made after the last event, were manifestly the effects of national hatred and scorn towards a conquered people; whom the victors delighted to trample upon, and were not at all afraid to provoke. They were not the effect of their fears, but of their security. They who carried on this system looked to the irresistible force of Great Britain for their support in their acts of power. They were quite certain, that no complaints of the natives would be heard on this side of the water, with any other sentiments than those of contempt and indignation. Their cries served only to augment their torture. Machines which could answer their purposes so well must be of an excellent contrivance. Indeed, in England, the double name of the complainants, Irish and Papist, (it would be hard to say which singly was the most odious,) shut up the hearts of every one against them. Whilst that temper prevailed, and it prevailed in all its force to a time within our memory, every measure was pleasing and popular, just in proportion as it tended to harass and ruin a set of people who were looked upon as enemies to God and man; and, indeed, as a race of bigoted savages who were a disgrace to human nature itself.

However, as the English in Ireland began to be domiciliated, they began also to recollect that they had a country. The *English interest*, at first by faint and almost insensible degrees, but at length openly and avowedly, became an *independent Irish interest*; full as independent as it could ever have been, if it had continued in the persons of the native Irish; and it was maintained with more skill, and more consistency, than probably it would have been in theirs. With their views, the *Anglo-Irish* changed their maxims – it was necessary to demonstrate to the whole people, that there was something, at least, of a common interest, combined with the independency, which was to become the object of common exertions. The mildness of government produced the first relaxation towards the Irish; the necessities, and, in part too, the temper that predominated at this great change, produced the second and the most important of these relaxations. English government, and Irish legislature, felt jointly the propriety of this measure. The Irish parliament and nation became independent.

The true revolution to you, that which most intrinsically and substantially resembled the English Revolution of 1688, was the Irish Revolution of 1782.[29] The Irish parliament of 1782 bore little resemblance to that which sat in that kingdom, after the period of the first of these revolutions. It bore a much nearer resemblance to that which sat under King James. The change of the parliament in 1782 from the character of the parliament which, as a token of its indignation, had burned all the journals[30] indiscriminately of the former parliament in the council-chamber, was very visible. The address of King William's parliament, the parliament which assembled after the Revolution, amongst other causes of complaint, (many of them sufficiently just,) complains of the repeal by their predecessors of Poyning's law;[31] no absolute idol with the parliament of 1782.

Great Britain, finding the Anglo-Irish highly animated with a spirit, which had indeed shown itself before, though with little energy and many interruptions, and therefore suffered a multitude of uniform precedents to be established against it, acted, in my opinion, with the greatest temperance and wisdom. She saw that the disposition of the *leading part* of the nation would not permit them to act any longer the part of a *garrison*. She saw that true policy did not require that they ever should have appeared in that character; or if it had done so formerly, the reasons had now ceased to operate. She saw that the Irish of her race were resolved to build their constitution and their politics upon another bottom. With those things under her view, she instantly complied with the whole of your demands, without any reservation whatsoever. She surrendered that boundless superiority, for the preservation of which, and the acquisition, she had supported the English colonies in Ireland for so long a time, and at so vast an expense (according to the standard of those ages) of her blood and treasure.

When we bring before us the matter which history affords for our selection, it is not improper to examine the spirit of the several precedents, which are candidates for our choice. Might it not be as well for your statesmen, on the other side of the water, to take an example from this latter, and surely more conciliatory, revolution, as a pattern for your conduct towards your own fellow-citizens, than from that of 1688, when a paramount sovereignty over both you and them was more loftily claimed, and more sternly exerted, than at any former, or at any subsequent period? Great Britain, in 1782, rose above the vulgar ideas of policy, the ordinary jealousies of state, and all the sentiments of national pride and national ambition. If she had been more disposed than, I thank God for it, she was, to listen to the suggestions of passion, than to the dictates of prudence; she might have urged the principles, the maxims, the policy, the practice of the Revolution, against the demands of the leading description in Ireland, with full as much plausibility, and full as good a grace, as any amongst them can possibly do, against the supplications of so vast and extensive a description of their own people.

A good deal too, if the spirit of domination and exclusion had prevailed in England, might have been excepted against some of the means then employed in Ireland, whilst her claims were in agitation. They were, at least, as much out of ordinary course, as those which are now objected against admitting your people to any of the benefits of an English constitution. Most certainly, neither with you, nor here, was any one ignorant of what was at that time said, written, and done. But on all sides we separated the means from the end: and we separated the cause of the moderate and rational, from the ill-intentioned and seditious; which on such occasions are so frequently apt to march together. At that time, on your part, you were not afraid to review what was done at the Revolution of 1688; and what had been continued during the subsequent flourishing period of the British empire. The change then made was a great and fundamental alteration. In the execution, it was an operose business on both sides of the water. It required the repeal of several laws, the modification of many, and a new course to be given to an infinite number of legislative, judicial, and official practices and usages in both kingdoms. This did not frighten any of us. You are now asked to give, in some moderate measure, to your fellow-citizens, what Great Britain gave to you, without any measure at all. Yet, notwithstanding all the difficulties at the time, and the apprehensions which some very well meaning people entertained, through the admirable temper in which this revolution (or restoration in the nature of a revolution) was conducted in both kingdoms, it has hitherto produced no inconvenience to either; and I trust, with the continuance of the same temper, that it never will. I think that this small, inconsiderable change (relative to an exclusive statute not made at the Revolution) for restoring the people to the benefits from which the green soreness of a civil war had not excluded them, will be productive of no sort of mischief whatsoever. Compare what was done in 1782, with what is wished in 1792; consider the spirit of what has been done at the several periods of reformation; and weigh maturely, whether it be exactly true that conciliatory concessions are of good policy only in discussions between nations; but that among descriptions in the same nation, they must always be irrational and dangerous. What have you suffered in your peace, your prosperity, or, in what ought ever to be dear to a nation, your glory, by the last act by which you took the property of that people under the protection of the *laws*? What reason have you to dread the consequences of admitting the people possessing that property to some share in the protection of the *constitution*?

I do not mean to trouble you with anything to remove the objections, I will not call them arguments, against this measure, taken from a ferocious hatred to all that numerous description of Christians. It would be to pay a poor compliment to your understanding or your heart. Neither *your* religion, nor *your* politics, consists "in odd perverse antipathies." You are not resolved to persevere in proscribing from the constitution so many millions of your countrymen, because, in contradiction to experience and to common sense, you think proper to imagine, that their principles are subversive of common human society. To that I shall only say, that whosoever has a temper which can be gratified by indulging himself in these good-natured fancies ought to do a great deal more. For an exclusion from the privileges of British subjects is not a cure for so terrible a distemper of the human mind, as they are pleased to suppose in their countrymen. I rather conceive a participation in those privileges to be itself a remedy for some mental disorders.

As little shall I detain you with matters that can as little obtain admission into a mind like yours; such as the fear, or pretence of fear, that, in spite of your own power, and the trifling power of

Great Britain, you may be conquered by the pope; or that this commodious bugbear (who is of infinitely more use to those who pretend to fear, than to those who love him) will absolve his Majesty's subjects from their allegiance, and send over the Cardinal of York[32] to rule you as his viceroy; or that, by the plenitude of his power, he will take that fierce tyrant, the king of the French, out of his jail, and arm that nation (which on all occasions treats his Holiness so very politely) with his bulls and pardons, to invade poor old Ireland, to reduce you to Popery and slavery, and to force the free-born, naked feet of your people into the wooden shoes of that arbitrary monarch. I do not believe that discourses of this kind, are held, or that anything like them will be held, by any who walk about without a keeper. Yet, I confess, that on occasions of this nature, I am the most afraid of the weakest reasonings; because they discover the strongest passions. These things will never be brought out in indefinite propositions. They would not prevent pity towards any persons; they would only cause it for those who were capable of talking in such a strain. But I know, and am sure, that such ideas as no man will distinctly produce to another, or hardly venture to bring in any plain shape to his own mind – he will utter in obscure, ill-explained doubts, jealousies, surmises, fears, and apprehensions; and that, in such a fog, they will appear to have a good deal of size, and will make an impression; when, if they were clearly brought forth and defined, they would meet with nothing but scorn and derision.

There is another way of taking an objection to this concession, which I admit to be something more plausible, and worthy of a more attentive examination. It is, that this numerous class of people is mutinous, disorderly, prone to sedition, and easy to be wrought upon by the insidious arts of wicked and designing men; that, conscious of this, the sober, rational, and wealthy part of that body, who are totally of another character, do by no means desire any participation for themselves, or for any one else of their description, in the franchises of the British constitution.

I have great doubt of the exactness of any part of this observation. But let us admit that the body of the Catholics are prone to sedition, (of which, as I have said, I entertain much doubt,) is it possible that any fair observer, or fair reasoner, can think of confining this description to them only? I believe it to be possible for men to be mutinous and seditious who feel no grievance; but I believe no man will assert seriously, that, when people are of a turbulent spirit, the best way to keep them in order, is to furnish them with something substantial to complain of.

You separate very properly the sober, rational, and substantial part of their description from the rest. You give, as you ought to do, weight only to the former. What I have always thought of the matter is this – that the most poor, illiterate, and uninformed creatures upon earth are judges of a *practical* oppression. It is a matter of feeling; and as such persons generally have felt most of it, and are not of an over-lively sensibility, they are the best judges of it. But for the *real cause*, or the *appropriate remedy*, they ought never to be called into council about the one or the other. They ought to be totally shut out; because their reason is weak; because, when once roused, their passions are ungoverned; because they want information; because the smallness of the property, which individually they possess, renders them less attentive to the consequence of the measures they adopt in affairs of moment. When I find a great cry amongst the people who speculate little, I think myself called seriously to examine into it, and to separate the real cause from the ill effects of the passion it may excite; and the bad use which artful men may make of an irritation of the popular mind. Here we must be aided by persons of a contrary character; we must not listen to the desperate or the furious; but it is therefore necessary for us to distinguish who are the *really* indigent, and the *really* intemperate. As to the persons who desire this part in the constitution, I have no reason to imagine that they are men who have nothing to lose and much to look for in public confusion. The popular meeting, from which apprehensions have been entertained, has assembled. I have accidentally had conversation with two friends of mine, who know something of the gentleman who was put into the chair upon that occasion; one of them has had money transactions with him; the other, from curiosity, has been to see his concerns; they both tell me he is a man of some property;[33] but you must be the best judge of this, who by your office are likely to know his transactions. Many of the others are certainly persons of fortune; and all, or most, fathers of families, men in respectable ways of life, and some of them far from contemptible, either for their information, or for the abilities which they have shown in the discussion of their interests. What such men think it for their advantage to acquire, ought not, *prima facie*, to be considered as rash or heady, or incompatible with the public safety or welfare.

I admit, that men of the best fortunes and reputations, and of the best talents and education too, may, by accident, show themselves furious and intemperate in their desires. This is a great misfortune when it happens; for the first presumptions are undoubtedly in their favour. We have two standards of judging in this case of the sanity and sobriety of any proceedings; of unequal certainty indeed, but neither of them to be neglected: the first is by the value of the object sought, the next is by the means through which it is pursued.

The object pursued by the Catholics is, I understand, and have all along reasoned as if it were so, in some degree or measure to be again admitted to the franchises of the constitution. Men are considered as under some derangement of their intellects, when they see good and evil in a different light from other men; when they choose nauseous and unwholesome food; and reject such as to the rest of the world seems pleasant, and is known to be nutritive. I have always considered the British constitution, not to be a thing in itself so vicious, as that none but men of deranged understanding, and turbulent tempers, could desire a share in it: on the contrary, I should think very indifferently of the understanding and temper of any body of men, who did not wish to partake of this great and acknowledged benefit. I cannot think quite so favourably either of the sense or temper of those, if any such there are, who would voluntarily persuade their brethren that the object is not fit for them, or they for the object. Whatever may be my thoughts concerning them, I am quite sure, that they who hold such language must forfeit all credit with the rest. This is infallible – If they conceive any opinion of their judgment, they cannot possibly think them their friends. There is, indeed, one supposition, which would reconcile the conduct of such gentlemen to sound reason, and to the purest affection towards their fellow-sufferers; it is, that they act under the impression of a well-grounded fear for the general interest. If they should be told, and should believe the story, that if they dare attempt to make their condition better, they will infallibly make it worse – that if they aim at obtaining liberty, they will have their slavery doubled – that their endeavour to put themselves upon anything which approaches towards an equitable footing with their fellow-subjects will be considered as an indication of a seditious and rebellious disposition – such a view of things ought perfectly to restore the gentlemen, who so anxiously dissuade their countrymen from wishing a participation with the privileged part of the people, to the good opinion of their fellows. But what is to them a very full justification, is not quite so honourable to that power from whose maxims and temper so good a ground of rational terror is furnished. I think arguments of this kind will never be used by the friends of a government which I greatly respect; or by any of the leaders of an opposition whom I have the honour to know, and the sense to admire. I remember Polybius tells us, that, during his captivity in Italy as a Peloponnesian hostage – he solicited old Cato[34] to intercede with the senate for his release, and that of his countrymen: this old politician told him that he had better continue in his present condition, however irksome, than apply again to that formidable authority for their relief; that he ought to imitate the wisdom of his countryman Ulysses, who, when he was once out of the den of the Cyclops, had too much sense to venture again into the same cavern. But I conceive too high an opinion of the Irish legislature to think that they are to their fellow-citizens, what the grand oppressors of mankind were to a people whom the fortune of war had subjected to their power. For though Cato could use such a parallel with regard to his senate, I should really think it nothing short of impious, to compare an Irish parliament to a den of Cyclops. I hope the people, both here and with you, will always apply to the House of Commons with becoming modesty; but at the same time with minds unembarrassed with any sort of terror.

As to the means which the Catholics employ to obtain this object, so worthy of sober and rational minds: I do admit that such means may be used in the pursuit of it, as may make it proper for the legislature, in this case, to defer their compliance until the demandants are brought to a proper sense of their duty. A concession in which the governing power of our country loses its dignity, is dearly bought even by him who obtains his object. All the people have a deep interest in the dignity of parliament. But as the refusal of franchises which are drawn out of the first vital stamina of the British constitution is a very serious thing, we ought to be very sure, that the manner and spirit of the application is offensive and dangerous indeed, before we ultimately reject all applications of this nature. The mode of application, I hear, is by petition. It is the manner in which all the sovereign powers in the world are approached; and I never heard (except in the case of James the Second) that any prince considered this manner of supplication to be contrary to the humility of a subject, or to the respect due to the person or authority of the sovereign. This rule, and a corresponding practice, are observed, from the Grand Seignior, down to the most petty prince or republic in Europe.

You have sent me several papers, some in print, some in manuscript. I think I had seen all of them, except the formula of association. I confess they appear to me to contain matter mischievous, and capable of giving alarm, if the spirit in which they are written should be found to make any considerable progress. But I am at a loss to know how to apply them, as objections to the case now before us. When I find that the *general committee*, which acts for the Roman Catholics in Dublin, prefers the association proposed in the written draft you have sent me,[35] to a respectful application in parliament, I shall think the persons who sign such a paper to be unworthy of any privilege which may be thought fit to be granted; and that such men ought, *by name*, to be excepted from any benefit under the constitution to which they offer this violence. But I do not find that this form of a seditious league has been signed by any person whatsoever, either on the part of the supposed projectors, or on the part of those whom it is calculated to seduce. I do not find, on inquiry, that such a thing was mentioned, or even remotely alluded to, in the general meeting of the Catholics, from which so much violence was apprehended. I have considered the other publications, signed by individuals, on the part of certain societies – I may mistake, for I have not the honour of knowing them personally, but I take Mr. Butler and Mr. Tandy[36] not to be Catholics, but members of the established church. Not *one* that I recollect of these publications which you and I equally dislike appears to be written by persons of that persuasion. Now, if, whilst a man is dutifully soliciting a favour from parliament, any person should choose, in an improper manner, to show his inclination towards the cause depending; and if that *must* destroy the cause of the petitioner; then, not only the petitioner, but the legislature itself, is in the power of any weak friend or artful enemy, that the supplicant or that the parliament may have. A man must be judged by his own actions only. Certain Protestant dissenters make seditious propositions to the Catholics, which it does not appear that they have yet accepted. It would be strange that the tempter should escape all punishment, and that he, who, under circumstances full of seduction and full of provocation, has resisted the temptation, should incur the penalty. You know, that, with regard to the dissenters, who are *stated* to be the chief movers in the vile scheme of altering the principles of election to a right of voting by the head, you are not able (if you ought even to wish such a thing) to deprive them of any part of the franchises and privileges which they hold on a footing of perfect equality with yourselves. *They* may do what they please with constitutional impunity; but the others cannot even listen with civility to an invitation from them to an ill-judged scheme of liberty, without forfeiting, for ever, all hopes of any of those liberties which we admit to be sober and rational.

It is known, I believe, that the greater, as well as the sounder, part of our excluded countrymen have not adopted the wild ideas, and wilder engagements, which have been held out to them; but have rather chosen to hope small and safe concessions from the legal power, than boundless objects from trouble and confusion. This mode of action seems to me to mark men of sobriety, and to distinguish them from those who are intemperate, from circumstance or from nature. But why do they not instantly disclaim and disavow those who make such advances to them? In this, too, in my opinion, they show themselves no less sober and circumspect. In the present moment, nothing short of insanity could induce them to take such a step. Pray consider the circumstances. Disclaim, says somebody, all union with the dissenters: – right – But, when this your injunction is obeyed, shall I obtain the object which I solicit from *you*? – Oh, no, nothing at all like it! – But, in punishing us by an exclusion from the constitution through the great gate, for having been invited to enter into it by a postern, will you punish by deprivation of their privileges, or mulct in any other way, those who have tempted us? – Far from it – we mean to preserve all *their* liberties and immunities, as *our* life-blood. We mean to cultivate *them*, as brethren whom we love and respect – with *you* we have no fellowship. We can bear with patience their enmity to ourselves; but their friendship with you we will not endure. But mark it well! All our quarrels with *them* are always to be revenged upon you. Formerly, it is notorious, that we should have resented with the highest indignation, your presuming to show any ill-will to them. You must not suffer them, now, to show any good-will to you. Know – and take it once for all – that it is, and ever has been, and ever will be, a fundamental maxim in our politics, that you are not to have any part, or shadow, or name of interest whatever in our state. That we look upon you as under an irreversible outlawry from our constitution – as perpetual and unalliable aliens.

Such, my dear Sir, is the plain nature of the argument drawn from the revolution maxims, enforced by a supposed disposition in the Catholics to unite with the dissenters. Such it is, though it were clothed in never such bland and civil forms, and wrapped up, as a poet says, in a thousand "artful folds of sacred lawn."[37] For my own part, I do not know in what manner to shape such arguments, so as to obtain admission for them into a rational understanding. Everying of this kind is to be reduced, at last, to threats of power. – I cannot say *væ victis*,[38] and then throw the sword into the scale. I have no sword; and if I had, in this case most certainly I would not use it as a make-weight in political reasoning.

Observe, on these principles, the difference between the procedure of the parliament and the dissenters, towards the people in question. One employs courtship, the other force. The dissenters offer bribes, the parliament nothing but the *front negatif* of a stern and forbidding authority. A man may be very wrong in his ideas of what is good for him. But no man affronts me, nor can therefore justify my affronting him, by offering to make me as happy as himself, according to his own ideas of happiness. This the dissenters do to the Catholics. You are on the different extremes. The dissenters offer, with regard to constitutional rights and civil advantages of all sorts, *everything* – you refuse *everything*. With them there is boundless though not very assured, hope; with you, a very sure and very unqualified despair. The terms of alliance, from the dissenters, offer a representation of the Commons chosen out of the people by the head. This is absurdly and dangerously large, in my opinion; and that scheme of electon is known to have been, at all times, perfectly odious to me. But I cannot think it right of course to punish the Irish Roman Catholics by an universal exclusion, because others, whom you would not punish at all, propose an universal admission. I cannot dissemble to myself, that, in this very kingdom, many persons who are not in the situation of the Irish Catholics, but who, on the contrary, enjoy the full benefit of the constitution as it stands, and some of whom, from the effect of their fortunes, enjoy it in a large measure, had some years ago associated to procure great and undefined changes (they considered them as reforms) in the popular part of the constitution. Our friend, the late Mr. Flood,[39] (no slight man,) proposed in his place, and in my hearing, a representation not much less extensive than this, for England; in which every house was to be inhabited by a voter – *in addition* to all the actual votes by other titles (some of the corporate) which we know do not require a house, or a shed. Can I forget that a person of the very highest rank,[40] of very large fortune, and of the first class of ability, brought a bill into the House of Lords, in the head–quarters of aristocracy, containing identically the same project, for the supposed adoption of which by a club or two, it is thought right to extinguish all hopes in the Roman Catholics of Ireland? I cannot say it was very eagerly embraced or very warmly pursued. But the Lords neither did disavow the bill, nor treat it with any disregard, nor express any sort of disapprobation of its noble author, who has never lost, with king or people, the least degree of the respect and consideration which so justly belongs to him.

I am not at all enamoured, as I have told you, with this plan of representation; as little do I relish any bandings or associations for procuring it. But if the question was to be put to you and me – *universal* popular representation, or *none at all for us and ours* – we should find ourselves in a very awkward position. I do not like this kind of dilemmas, especially when they are practical.

Then, since our oldest fundamental laws follow, or rather couple, freehold with franchise; since no principle of the Revolution shakes these liberties; since the oldest and one of the best monuments of the constitution demands for the Irish the privilege which they supplicate; since the principles of the Revolution coincide with the declarations of the Great Charter; since the practice of the Revolution, in this point, did not contradict its principles; since, from that event, twenty-five years had elapsed, before a domineering party, on a party principle, had ventured to disfranchise, without any proof whatsoever of abuse, the greater part of the community; since the king's coronation oath does not stand in his way to the performance of his duty to all his subjects; since you have given to all other dissenters these privileges without limit, which are hitherto withheld, without any limitation whatsoever, from the Catholics; since no nation in the world has ever been known to exclude so great a body of men (not born slaves) from the civil state, and all the benefits of its constitution; the whole question comes before parliament as a matter for its prudence. I do not put the thing on a question of right. That discretion, which, in judicature, is well said by Lord Coke[41] to be a crooked cord, in legislature is a golden rule. Supplicants ought not to appear too much in the character of litigants. If the subject think so highly and reverently of the sovereign authority, as not to claim anything of right, so that it may seem to be independent of the power and free choice of its government; and if the sovereign, on his part, considers the advantages of the subjects as their right, and all their reasonable wishes as so many claims; in the fortunate conjunction of these mutual dispositions are laid the foundations of a happy and prosperous commonwealth. For my own part, desiring of all things that the authority of the legislature under which I was born, and which I cherish, not only with a dutiful awe, but with a partial and cordial affection, to be maintained in the utmost possible respect, I never will suffer myself to suppose, that, at bottom, their discretion will be found to be at variance with their justice.

The whole being at discretion, I beg leave just to suggest some matters for your consideration – Whether the government in church or state is likely to be more secure by continuing causes of grounded discontent, to a very great number (say two millions) of the subjects? or, Whether the constitution, combined and balance as it is, will be rendered more solid, by depriving so large a part of the people of all concern, or interest, or share, in its representation, actual or *virtual*? I here mean to lay an emphasis on the word *virtual*. Virtual representation is that in which there is a communion of interests, and a sympathy in feelings and desires, between those who act in the name of any description of people, and the people in whose name they act, though the trustees are not actually chosen by them. This is virtual representation. Such a representation I think to be, in many cases, even better than the actual. It possesses most of its advantages, and is free from many of its inconveniences; it corrects the irregularities in the literal representation, when the shifting current of human

affairs, or the acting of public interests in different ways, carry it
obliquely from its first line of direction. The people may err in
their choice; but common interest and common sentiment are
rarely mistaken. But this sort of virtual representation cannot
have a long or sure existence, if it has not a substratum in the
actual. The member must have some relation to the constituent.
As things stand, the Catholic, as a Catholic, and belonging to a
description, has no *virtual* relation to the representative; but the
contrary. There is a relation in mutual obligation. Gratitude may
not always have a very lasting power; but the frequent recurrence
of an application for favours will revive and refresh it, and will
necessarily produce some degree of mutual attention. It will produce, at least, acquaintance. The several descriptions of people
will not be kept so much apart as they now are, as if they were
not only separate nations, but separate species. The stigma and
reproach, the hideous mask, will be taken off, and men will see
each other as they are. Sure I am, that there have been thousands
in Ireland, who have never conversed with a Roman Catholic in
their whole lives, unless they happened to talk to their gardener's
workmen, or to ask their way, when they had lost it, in their
sports; or at best, who had known them only as footmen, or other
domestics, of the second and third order: and so averse were they,
some time ago, to have them near their persons, that they would
not employ even those who could never find their way beyond
the stable. I well remember a great, and in many respects a good,
man, who advertised for a blacksmith; but at the same time
added, he must be a Protestant. It is impossible that such a state
of things, though natural goodness in many persons will undoubtedly make exceptions, must not produce alienation on the
one side, and pride and insolence on the other.

Reduced to a question of discretion, and that discretion exercised solely upon what will appear best for the conservation of
the state on its present basis, I should recommend it to your
serious thoughts, whether the narrowing of the foundation is
always the best way to secure the building? The body of disfranchised men will not be perfectly satisfied to remain always
in that state. If they are not satisfied, you have two millions of
subjects in your bosom, full of uneasiness; not that they cannot
overturn the act of settlement, and put themselves and you under
an arbitrary master; or that they are not permitted to spawn a
hydra of wild republics, on principles of a pretended natural

equality in man; but, because you will not suffer them to enjoy
the ancient, fundamental, tried advantages of a British constitution: that you will not permit them to profit of the protection of
a common father, or the freedom of common citizens; and that
the only reason which can be assigned for this disfranchisement
has a tendency more deeply to ulcerate their minds, than the act
of exclusion itself. What the consequence of such feelings must
be, it is for you to look to. To warn, is not to menace.

I am far from asserting, that men will not excite disturbances
without just cause. I know that such an assertion is not true. But,
neither is it true that disturbances have never just complaints for
their origin. I am sure that it is hardly prudent to furnish them
with such causes of complaint, as every man who thinks the
British constitution a benefit may think at least colourable and
plausible.

Several are in dread of the manœuvres of certain persons
among the dissenters, who turn this ill humour to their own ill
purposes. You know, better than I can, how much these proceedings of certain among the dissenters are to be feared. You are to
weigh, with the temper which is natural to you, whether it may
be for the safety of our establishment, that the Catholics should
be ultimately persuaded that they have no hope to enter into the
constitution, but through the dissenters.

Think, whether this be the way to prevent or dissolve factious
combinations against the church, or the state. Reflect seriously
on the possible consequences of keeping, in the heart of your
country, a bank of discontent, every hour accumulating, upon
which every description of seditious men may draw at pleasure.
They, whose principles of faction would dispose them to the
establishment of an arbitrary monarchy, will find a nation of men
who have no sort of interest in freedom; but who will have an
interest in that equality of justice or favour, with which a wise
despot must view all his subjects who do not attack the foundations of his power. Love of liberty itself may, in such men,
become the means of establishing an arbitrary domination. On
the other hand, they who wish for a democratic republic, will
find a set of men who have no choice between civil servitude
and the entire ruin of a mixed constitution.

Suppose the people of Ireland divided into three parts; of these
(I speak within compass) two are Catholic. Of the remaining

third, one half is composed of dissenters. There is no natural union between those descriptions. It may be produced. If the two parts Catholic be driven into a close confederacy with half the third part of Protestants, with a view to a change in the constitution in church or state, or both; and you rest the whole of their security on a handful of gentlemen, clergy, and their dependants; compute the strength *you have in Ireland*, to oppose to grounded discontent, to capricious innovation, to blind popular fury, and to ambitious, turbulent intrigue.

You mention that the minds of some gentlemen are a good deal heated: and that it is often said, that, rather than submit to such persons having a share in their franchises, they would throw up their independence, and precipitate an union with Great Britain.[42] I have heard a discussion concerning such an union amongst all sorts of men ever since I remember anything. For my own part, I have never been able to bring my mind to anything clear and decisive upon the subject. There cannot be a more arduous question. As far as I can form an opinion, it would not be for the mutual advantage of the two kingdoms. Persons, however, more able than I am, think otherwise. But, whatever the merits of this union may be, to make it a *menace*, it must be shown to be an *evil*; and an evil more particularly to those who are threatened with it, than to those who hold it out as a terror. I really do not see how this threat of an union can operate, or that the Catholics are more likely to be losers by that measure than the churchmen.

The humours of the people, and of politicians too, are so variable in themselves, and are so much under the occasional influence of some leading men, that it is impossible to know what turn the public mind here would take on such an event. There is but one thing certain concerning it. Great divisions and vehement passions would precede this union, both on the measure itself and on its terms; and particularly this very question of a share in the representation for the Catholics, from whence the project of an union originated, would form a principal part in the discussion; and in the temper in which some gentlemen seem inclined to throw themselves, by a sort of high, indignant passion, into the scheme, those points would not be deliberated with all possible calmness.

From my best observation, I should greatly doubt, whether,

in the end, these gentlemen would obtain their object, so as to make the exclusion of two millions of their countrymen a fundamental article in the union. The demand would be of a nature quite unprecedented. You might obtain the union: and yet a gentleman, who, under the new union establishment, would aspire to the honour of representing his county, might possibly be as much obliged, as he may fear to be under the old separate establishment, to the unsupportable mortification of asking his neighbours, who have a different opinion concerning the elements in the sacrament, for their votes.

I believe, nay, I am sure, that the people of Great Britain, with or without an union, might be depended upon, in cases of any real danger, to aid the government of Ireland, with the same cordiality as they would support their own, against any wicked attempts to shake the security of the happy constitution in church and state. But before Great Britain engages in any quarrel, the *cause of the dispute* would certainly be a part of her consideration. If confusions should arise in that kingdom, from too steady an attachment to a proscriptive, monopolising system, and from the resolution of regarding the franchise, and in it the security of the subject, as belonging rather to religious opinions than to civil qualification and civil conduct, I doubt whether you might quite certainly reckon on obtaining an aid of force from hence, for the support of that system. We might extend your distractions to this country, by taking part in them. England will be indisposed, I suspect, to send an army for the conquest of Ireland. What was done in 1782 is a decisive proof of her sentiments of justice and moderation. She will not be fond of making another American war in Ireland. The principles of such a war would but too much resemble the former one. The well-disposed and the ill-disposed in England would (for different reasons perhaps) be equally averse to such an enterprise. The confiscations, the public auctions, the private grants, the plantations, the transplantations, which formerly animated so many adventurers, even among sober citizens, to such Irish expeditions, and which possibly might have animated some of them to the American, can have no existence in the case that we suppose.

Let us form a supposition, (no foolish or ungrounded supposition,) that in an age when men are infinitely more disposed to heat themselves with political than religious controversies, the former should entirely prevail, as we see that in some places they have prevailed, over the latter; and that the Catholics of Ireland, from the courtship paid them on the one hand, and the high tone of refusal on the other, should, in order to enter into all the rights of subjects, all become Protestant dissenters; and as the others do, take all your oaths. They would all obtain their civil objects; and the change, for anything I know to the contrary, (in the dark as I am about the Protestant dissenting tenets,) might be of use to the health of their souls. But, what security our constitution, in church or state, could derive from that event, I cannot possibly discern. Depend upon it, it is as true as nature is true, that if you force them out of the religion of habit, education, or opinion, it is not to yours they will ever go. Shaken in their minds, they will go to that where the dogmas are fewest; where they are the most uncertain; where they lead them the least to a consideration of what they have abandoned. They will go to that uniformly democratic system, to whose first movements they owed their emancipation. I recommend you seriously to turn this in your mind. Believe that it requires your best and maturest thoughts. Take what course you please – union or no union; whether the people remain Catholics or become Protestant dissenters, sure it is, that the present state of monopoly *cannot* continue.

If England were animated, as I think she is not, with her former spirit of domination, and with the strong theological hatred which she once cherished for that description of her fellow-Christians and fellow-subjects; I am yet convinced, that after the fullest success in a ruinous struggle, you would be obliged to abandon that monopoly. We were obliged to do this, even when everything promised success in the American business. If you should make this experiment at last, under the pressure of any necessity, you never can do it well. But if, instead of falling into a passion, the leading gentlemen of the country themselves should undertake the business cheerfully, and with hearty affection towards it, great advantages would follow. What is forced, cannot be modified: but here you may measure your concessions.

It is a consideration of great moment, that you make the desired admission without altering the system of your representation in the smallest degree, or in any part. You may leave that deliberation of a parliamentary change or reform, if ever you should think fit to engage in it, uncomplicated and unembarrassed with the other question. Whereas, if they are mixed and confounded, as some people attempt to mix and confound them, no one can answer for the effects on the constitution itself.

There is another advantage in taking up this business singly, and by an arrangement for the single object. It is that you may proceed by *degrees*. We must all obey the great law of change. It is the most powerful law of nature, and the means perhaps of its conservation. All we can do, and that human wisdom can do, is to provide that the change shall proceed by insensible degrees. This has all the benefits which may be in change, without any of the inconveniences of mutation. Everything is provided for as it arrives. This mode will, on the one hand, prevent the *unfixing old interests at once*: a thing which is apt to breed a black and sullen discontent in those who are at once dispossessed of all their influence and consideration. This gradual course, on the other side, will prevent men, long under depression, from being intoxicated with a large draught of new power, which they always abuse with a licentious insolence. But wishing, as I do, the change to be gradual and cautious, I would, in my first steps, lean rather to the side of enlargement than restriction.

It is one excellence of our constitution, that all our rights of provincial election regard rather property than person. It is another, that the rights which approach more nearly to the personal are most of them corporate, and suppose a restrained and strict education of seven years in some useful occupation. In both cases the practice may have slid from the principle. The standard of qualification in both cases may be so low, or not so judiciously chosen, as in some degree to frustrate the end. But all this is for your prudence in the case before you. You may raise, a step or two, the qualification of the Catholic voters. But if you were, tomorrow, to put the Catholic freeholder on the footing of the most favoured forty-shilling Protestant dissenter, you know that such is the actual state of Ireland, this would not make a sensible alteration in almost any *one* election in the kingdom. The effect in their favour, even defensively, would be infinitely slow. But it would be healing; it would be satisfactory and protecting. The stigma would be removed. By admitting settled, permanent substance in lieu of the numbers, you would avoid the great danger of our time, that of setting up number against property. The numbers ought never to be neglected; because (besides what is due to them as men) collectively, though not individually, they have great property: they ought to have therefore protection:

they ought to have security: they ought to have even consideration: but they ought not to predominate.

My dear Sir, I have nearly done; I meant to write you a long
letter; I have written a long dissertation. I might have done it
earlier and better, I might have been more forcible and more
clear, if I had not been interrupted as I have been; and this obliges
me not to write to you in my own hand. Though my hand but
signs it, my heart goes with what I have written. Since I could
think at all, those have been my thoughts. You know that thirty-
two years ago they were as fully matured in my mind as they are
now. A letter of mine to Lord Kenmare,[43] though not by my
desire, and full of lesser mistakes, has been printed in Dublin. It
was written ten or twelve years ago, at the time when I began the
employment, which I have not yet finished, in favour of another
distressed people,[44] injured by those who have vanquished them,
or stolen a dominion over them. It contained my sentiments
then; you will see how far they accord with my sentiments now.
Time has more and more confirmed me in them all. The present
circumstances fix them deeper in my mind.

I voted last session, if a particular vote could be distinguished,
in unanimity, for an establishment of the church of England
conjointly with the establishment which was made some years
before by act of parliament, of the Roman Catholic, in the
French conquered country of Canada.[45] At the time of making
this English ecclesiastical establishment, we did not think it
necessary for its safety, to destroy the former Gallican church settlement. In our first act we settled a government altogether monarchical, or nearly so. In that system, the Canadian Catholics
were far from being deprived of the advantages or distinctions,
of any kind, which they enjoyed under their former monarchy.
It is true, that some people, and amongst them one eminent
divine, predicted at that time, that by this step we should lose our
dominions in America. He foretold that the pope would send his
indulgences hither; that the Canadians would fall in with France;
would declare independence, and draw or force our colonies into
the same design. The independence happened according to his
prediction; but in directly the reverse order. All our English
Protestant colonies revolted. They joined themselves to France:
and it so happened that Popish Canada was the only place which
preserved its fidelity; the only place in which France got no footing; the only peopled colony which now remains to Great

Britain. Vain are all the prognostics taken from ideas and passions, which survive the state of things which gave rise to them. When last year we gave a popular representation to the same Canada, by the choice of the landholders, and an aristocratic representation, at the choice of the crown, neither was the choice of the crown, nor the election of the landholders, limited by a consideration of religion. We had no dread for the Protestant church, which we settled there, because we permitted the French Catholics, in the utmost latitude of the description, to be free subjects. They are good subjects, I have no doubt; but I will not allow that any French Canadian Catholics are better men or better citizens than the Irish of the same communion. Passing from the extremity of the west to the extremity almost of the east; I have been many years (now entering into the twelfth) employed in supporting the rights, privileges, laws, and immunities, of a very remote people. I have not as yet been able to finish my task. I have struggled through much discouragement and much opposition, much obloquy, much calumny, for a people with whom I have no tie, but the common bond of mankind. In this I have not been left alone. We did not fly from our undertaking, because the people are Mahometans or Pagans, and that a great majority of the Christians amongst them are Papists. Some gentlemen in Ireland, I dare say, have good reasons for what they may do, which do not occur to me. I do not presume to condemn them: but thinking and acting as I have done, towards these remote nations, I should not know how to show my face, here or in Ireland, if I should say that all the Pagans, all the Mussulmen, and even all the Papists, (since they must form the highest stage in the climax of evil,) are worthy of a liberal and honourable condition, except those of one of the descriptions, which forms the majority of the inhabitants of the country in which you and I were born. If such are the Catholics of Ireland, – ill-natured and unjust people, from our own data, may be inclined not to think better of the Protestants of a soil, which is supposed to infuse into its sects a kind of venom unknown in other places.

You hated the old system as early as I did. Your first juvenile lance was broken against that giant. I think you were even the first who attacked the grim phantom. You have an exceedingly good understanding, very good humour, and the best heart in the world. The dictates of that temper and that heart, as well as the policy pointed out by that understanding, led you to abhor the old code. You abhorred it, as I did, for its vicious perfection. For I must do it justice: it was a complete system, full of coherence and consistency; well digested and well composed in all its parts. It was a machine of wise and elaborate contrivance; and as well fitted for the oppression, impoverishment, and degradation of a people, and the debasement, in them, of human nature itself, as ever proceeded from the perverted ingenuity of man. It is a thing humiliating enough, that we are doubtful of the effect of the medicines we compound. We are sure of our poisons. My opinion ever was, (in which I heartily agreed with those that admired the old code,) that it was so constructed, that if there was once a breach in any essential part of it, the ruin of the whole, or nearly of the whole, was, at some time or other, a certainty. For that reason I honour, and shall for ever honour and love you, and those who first caused it to stagger, crack, and gape. – Others may finish; the beginners have the glory; and, take what part you please at this hour,[46] (I think you will take the best,) your first services will never be forgotten by a grateful country. Adieu! Present my best regards to those I know, and as many as I know in our country, I honour. There never was so much ability, nor, I believe, virtue, in it. They have a task worthy of both. I doubt not they will perform it, for the stability of the church and state, and for the union and the separation of the people: for the union of the honest and peaceable of all sects; for their separation from all that is ill-intentioned and seditious in any of them.

BEACONSFIELD, 3 JANUARY 1792

LETTER TO RICHARD BURKE

POST 19 FEBRUARY 1792

MY DEAR SON,

WE ARE ALL again assembled in town, to finish the last, but the most laborious, of the tasks which have been imposed upon me during my parliamentary service. We are as well as at our time of life we can expect to be. We have, indeed, some moments of anxiety about you. You are engaged in an undertaking similar in its principle to mine.[1] You are engaged in the relief of an oppressed people. In that service you must necessarily excite the same sort of passions in those who have exercised, and who wish to continue, that oppression that I have had to struggle with in this long labour. As your father has done, you must make enemies of many of the rich, of the proud, and of the powerful. I and you began in the same way. I must confess, that, if our place was of our choice, I could wish it had been your lot to begin the career of your life with an endeavour to render some more moderate, and less invidious, service to the public. But being engaged in a great and critical work, I have not the least hesitation about your having hitherto done your duty as becomes you. If I had not an assurance not to be shaken from the character of your mind, I should be satisfied on that point by the cry that is raised against you. If you had behaved, as they call it, discreetly, that is, faintly and treacherously, in the execution of your trust, you would have had, for a while, the good word of all sorts of men, even of many of those whose cause you had betrayed; and whilst your favour lasted you might have coined that false reputation into a true and solid interest to yourself. This you are well apprised of; and you do not refuse to travel that beaten road from an ignorance, but from a contempt, of the objects it leads to.

When you choose an arduous and slippery path, God forbid that any weak feelings of my declining age, which calls for soothings and supports, and which can have none but from you, should make me wish that you should abandon what you are about, or should trifle with it. In this House we submit, though with troubled minds, to that order which has connected all great duties with toils and with perils, which has conducted the road to glory through the regions of obloquy and reproach, and which will never suffer the disparaging alliance of spurious, false, and fugitive praise with genuine and permanent reputation. We know that the Power, which has settled that order, and subjected you to it by placing you in the situation you are in, is able to bring you out of it with credit and with safety. His will be done. All must come right. You may open the way with pain, and under reproach. Others will pursue it with ease and with applause.

I am sorry to find that pride and passion, and that sort of zeal for religion which never shows any wonderful heat but when it afflicts and mortifies our neighbour, will not let the ruling description perceive, that the privilege for which your clients contend is very nearly as much for the benefit of those who refuse it, as those who ask it. I am not to examine into the charges that are daily made on the administration of Ireland. I am not qualified to say how much in them is cold truth, and how much rhetorical exaggeration. Allowing some foundation to the complaint, it is to no purpose that these people allege that their government is a job in its administration. I am sure it is a job in its constitution; nor is it possible a scheme of polity which, in total exclusion of the body of the community, confines (with little or no regard to their rank or condition in life) to a certain set of favoured citizens the rights which formerly belonged to the whole, should not, by the operation of the same selfish and narrow principles, teach the persons who administer in that government to prefer their own particular, but well understood, private interest to the false and ill calculated private interest of the monopolising company they belong to. Eminent characters, to be sure, overrule places and circumstances. I have nothing to say to that virtue, which shoots up in full force by the native vigour of the seminal principle, in spite of the adverse soil and climate that it grows in. But, speaking of things in their ordinary course, in a country of monopoly there *can* be no patriotism. There may be a party spirit – but public spirit there can be none. As to a spirit of liberty, still less can it exist, or anything like it. A liberty made up of penalties! a liberty made up of incapacities! a liberty made up of exclusion and proscription, continued for ages, of four-fifths, perhaps, of the inhabitants of all ranks and fortunes! In what does such liberty differ from the description of the most shocking kind of servitude?

But, it will be said, in that country some people are free – why this is the very description of despotism! *Partial freedom is privilege and prerogative, and not liberty*. Liberty, such as deserves the name, is an honest, equitable, diffusive, and impartial principle. It is a great and enlarged virtue, and not a sordid, selfish, and illiberal vice. It is the portion of the mass of the citizens; and not the haughty licence of some potent individual, or some predominant faction.

If anything ought to be despotic in a country, it is its government; because there is no cause of constant operation to make its yoke unequal. But the dominion of a party must continually, steadily, and by its very essence, lean upon the prostrate description. A constitution formed so as to enable a party to overrule its very government, and to overpower the people too, answers the purposes neither of government nor of freedom. It compels that power which ought, and often would be disposed, *equally* to protect the subjects, to fail in its trust, to counteract its purposes, and to become no better than the instrument of the wrongs of a faction. Some degree of influence must exist in all governments. But a government which has no interest to please the body of the people, and can neither support them, nor with safety call for their support, nor is of power to sway the domineering faction, can only exist by corruption; and, taught by that monopolising party which usurps the title and qualities of the public, to consider the body of the people as out of the constitution, they will consider those who are in it in the light in which they choose to consider themselves. The whole relation of government and of freedom will be a battle, or a traffic.

This system in its real nature, and under its proper appellations, is odious and unnatural, especially when a constitution is admitted which not only, as all constitutions do profess, has a regard to the good of the multitude, but in its theory makes profession of their power also. But of late this scheme of theirs has been new christened – *honestum nomen imponitur vitio*.[2] A word has been lately struck in the mint of the Castle of Dublin;[3] thence it was conveyed to the Tholsel, or city-hall, where, having passed the touch of the corporation,[4] so respectably stamped and vouched, it soon became current in parliament, and was carried back by the Speaker of the House of Commons in great pomp, as an offering of homage from whence it came. The word is *Ascendency*. It is not absolutely new. But the sense in which I have hitherto seen it used was to signify an influence obtained over the minds of some other person by love and reverence, or by superior management and dexterity. It had, therefore, to this its promotion no more than a moral, not a civil or political, use. But I admit it is capable of being so applied; and if the Lord Mayor of Dublin, and the Speaker of the Irish parliament, who recommend the preservation of the Protestant ascendency, mean to employ the word in that sense, that is, if they understand by it the preservation of the influence of that description of gentlemen over the Catholics by means of an authority derived from their wisdom and virtue, and from an opinion they raise in that people of a pious regard and affection for their freedom and happiness, it is impossible not to commend their adoption of so apt a term into the family of politics. It may be truly said to enrich the language. Even if the Lord Mayor and Speaker mean to insinuate that this influence is to be obtained and held by flattering their people, by managing them, by skilfully adapting themselves to the humours and passions of those whom they would govern, he must be a very untoward critic who would cavil even at this use of the word, though such cajoleries would perhaps be more prudently practised than professed. These are all meanings laudable, or at least tolerable. But when we look a little more narrowly, and compare it with the plan to which it owes its present technical application, I find it has strayed far from its original sense. It goes much further than the privilege allowed by Horace. It is more than *parcè detortum*.[5] This Protestant ascendency means nothing less than an influence obtained by virtue, by love, or even by artifice and seduction; full as little an influence derived from the means by which ministers have obtained an influence, which might be called, without straining, an *ascendency* in public assemblies in England, that is, by a liberal distribution of places and pensions, and other graces of government. This last is wide indeed of the signification of the word. New *ascendency* is the old mastership. It is neither more nor less than the resolution of one set of people in Ireland to consider themselves as the sole citizens in the commonwealth; and to keep a dominion over the rest by reducing them to absolute slavery under a military power; and, thus fortified in their power, to divide the public estate, which is the result of general contribution, as a military booty solely amongst themselves.

The poor word ascendency, so soft and melodious in its sound, so lenitive and emollient in its first usage, is now employed to cover to the world the most rigid, and perhaps not the most wise, of all plans of policy. The word is large enough in its comprehension. I cannot conceive what mode of oppression in civil life, or what mode of religious persecution, may not come within the methods of preserving an *ascendency*. In plain old English, as they apply it, it signifies *pride and dominion* on the one part of the relation, and on the other *subserviency and contempt* – and it signifies nothing else. The old words are as fit to be set to music as the new; but use has long since affixed to them their true signification, and they sound, as the other will, harshly and odiously to the moral and intelligent ears of mankind.

This ascendency, by being a *Protestant* ascendency, does not better it from the combination of a note or two more in this anti-harmonic scale. If Protestant ascendency means the proscription from citizenship of by far the major part of the people of any country, then Protestant ascendency is a bad thing; and it ought to have no existence. But there is a deeper evil. By the use that is so frequently made of the term, and the policy which is in-grafted on it, the name Protestant becomes nothing more or better than the name of a persecuting faction, with a relation of some sort of theological hostility to others, but without any sort of ascertained tenets of its own, upon the ground of which it persecutes other men; for the patrons of this Protestant ascendency neither do, nor can, by anything positive, define or describe what they mean by the word Protestant. It is defined, as Cowley[6] defines wit, not by what it is, but by what it is not. It is not the Christian religion as professed in the churches holding communion with Rome, the majority of Christians; that is all which in the latitude of the term is known about its signification. This makes such persecutors ten times worse than any of that description that hitherto have been known in the world. The old persecutors, whether Pagan or Christian, whether Arian or Orthodox, whether Catholics, Anglicans, or Calvinists, actually were, or at least had the decorum to pretend to be, strong dogmatists. They pretended that their religious maxims were clear and ascertained, and so useful, that they were bound, for the eternal benefit of mankind, to defend or diffuse them, though by any sacrifices of the temporal good of those who were the objects of their system of experiment.

The bottom of this theory of persecution is false. It is not permitted to us to sacrifice the temporal good of any body of men to our own ideas of the truth and falsehood of any religious opinions. By making men miserable in this life they counteract one of the great ends of charity; which is, inasmuch as in us lies, to make men happy in every period of their existence, and most in what most depends upon us. But give to these old persecutors their mistaken principle, in their reasoning they are consistent, and in their tempers they may be even kind and good-natured. But whenever a faction would render millions of mankind miserable, – some millions of the race co-existent with themselves, and many millions in their succession, without knowing, or so much as pretending to ascertain, the doctrines of their own school, (in which there is much of the lash and nothing of the lesson,) the errors which the persons in such a faction fall into are not those that are natural to human imbecility, nor is the least mixture of mistaken kindness to mankind an ingredient in the severities they inflict. The whole is nothing but pure and perfect malice. It is, indeed, a perfection in that kind belonging to beings of a higher order than man, and to them we ought to leave it.

This kind of persecutors, without zeal, without charity, know well enough that religion, to pass by all questions of the truth or falsehood of any of its particular systems, (a matter I abandon to the theologians on all sides,) is a source of great comfort to us mortals in this our short but tedious journey through the world. They know that to enjoy this consolation men must believe their religion upon some principle or other, whether of education, habit, theory, or authority. When men are driven from any of those principles on which they have received religion, without embracing with the same assurance and cordiality some other system, a dreadful void is left in their minds, and a terrible shock is given to their morals. They lose their guide, their comfort, their hope. None but the most cruel and hard-hearted of men, who had banished all natural tenderness from their minds, such as those beings of iron, the atheists, could bring themselves to any persecution like this. Strange it is, but so it is, that men, driven by force from their habits in one mode of religion, have, by contrary habits, under the same force, often quietly settled in another. They suborn their reason to declare in favour of their necessity. Man and his conscience cannot always be at war. If the first races have not been able to make a pacification between the conscience and the convenience, their descendants come generally to submit to the violence of the laws, without violence to their minds. As things stood formerly, they possessed a *positive* scheme of direction, and of consolation. In this men may acquiesce. The harsh methods in use with the old class of persecutors were to make converts, not apostates only. If they perversely hated other sects and factions, they loved their own inordinately. But in this Protestant persecution there is anything but benevolence at work. What do the Irish statutes? They do not make a conformity to the *established* religion, and to its doctrines and practices, the condition of getting out of servitude. No such thing. Let three millions of people but abandon all that they and their ancestors have been taught to believe sacred, and to forswear it publicly in terms the most degrading, scurrilous, and indecent for men of integrity and virtue, and to abuse the whole of their former lives, and to slander the education they have received, and nothing more is required of them. There is no system of folly, or impiety, or blasphemy, or atheism, into which they may not throw themselves, and which they may not profess openly, and as a system, consistently with the enjoyment of all the privileges of a free citizen in the happiest constitution in the world.

Some of the unhappy assertors of this strange scheme say they are not persecutors on account of religion. In the first place they say what is not true. For what else do they disfranchise the people? If the man gets rid of a religion through which their malice operates, he gets rid of all their prejudices and incapacities at once. They never afterwards inquire about him. I speak here of their pretexts, and not of the true spirit of the transaction, in which religious bigotry, I apprehend, has little share. Every man has his taste; but I think, if I were so miserable and undone as to be guilty of premeditated and continued violence towards any set of men, I had rather that my conduct was supposed to arise from wild conceits concerning their religious advantages than from low and ungenerous motives relative to my own selfish interest. I had rather be thought insane in my charity than rational in my malice. This much, my dear son, I have to say of this Protestant persecution; that is, a persecution of religion itself.

A very great part of the mischiefs that vex the world arises from words. People soon forget the meaning, but the impression and the passion remain. The word Protestant is the charm that locks up in the dungeon of servitude three millions of your people. It is not amiss to consider this spell of potency, this abracadabra, that is hung about the necks of the unhappy, not to heal, but to communicate disease. We sometimes hear of a Protestant *religion*, frequently of a Protestant *interest*. We hear of the latter the most frequently, because it has a positive meaning. The other has none. We hear of it the most frequently, because it has a word in the phrase, which, well or ill understood, has animated to persecution and oppression at all times infinitely more than all the dogmas in dispute between religious factions. These are indeed well formed to perplex and torment the intellect; but not half so well calculated to inflame the passions and animosities of men.

I do readily admit, that a great deal of the wars, seditions, and troubles of the world did formerly turn upon the contention between *interests* that went by the names of Protestant and Catholic. But I imagined that at this time no one was weak enough to believe, or imprudent enough to pretend, that questions of Popish and Protestant opinions, or interest, are the things by which men are at present menaced with crusades by foreign invasion, or with seditions which shake the foundations of the state at home. It is long since all this combination of things has vanished from the view of intelligent observers. The existence of quite another system of opinions and interests is now plain to the grossest sense. Are these the questions that raise a flame in the minds of men at this day? If ever the church and the constitution of England should fall in these islands, (and they will fall together,) it is not Presbyterian discipline, nor Popish hierarchy, that will rise upon their ruins. It will not be the Church of Rome nor the Church of Scotland – not the Church of Luther, nor the Church of Calvin. On the contrary, all these Churches are menaced, and menaced alike. It is the new fanatical religion, now in the heat of its first ferment, of the Rights of Man, which rejects all establishments, all discipline, all ecclesiastical, and in truth all civil, order, which will triumph, and which will lay prostrate your church; which will destroy your distinctions, and which will put all your properties to auction, and disperse you over the earth. If the present establishment should fall, it is this religion which will triumph in Ireland and in England, as it has triumphed in France. This religion, which laughs at creeds, and dogmas, and confessions of faith, may be fomented equally amongst all descriptions, and all sects; amongst nominal Catholics, and amongst nominal churchmen, and amongst those dissenters who know little, and care less, about a presbytery, or any of its discipline, or any of its doctrine.

Against this new, this growing, this exterminatory system, all these churches have a common concern to defend themselves. How the enthusiasts of this rising sect rejoice to see you of the old churches play their game, and stir and rake the cinders of animosities sunk in their ashes, in order to keep up the execution of their plan for your common ruin!

I suppress all that is in my mind about the blindness of those of our clergy, who will shut their eyes to a thing which glares in such manifest day. If some wretches amongst an indigent and disorderly part of the populace raise a riot about tithes, there are of these gentlemen ready to cry out that this is an overt act of a treasonable conspiracy. Here the bulls, and the pardons, and the crusade, and the pope, and the thunders of the Vatican, are everywhere at work. There is a plot to bring in a foreign power to destroy the church. Alas! it is not about popes, but about potatoes, that the minds of this unhappy people are agitated. It is not from the spirit of zeal, but the spirit of whiskey, that these wretches act. Is it then not conceived possible that a poor clown can be unwilling, after paying three pounds rent to a gentleman in a brown coat, to pay fourteen shillings to one in a black coat for his acre of potatoes, and tumultuously to desire some modification of the charge, without being supposed to have no other motive than a frantic zeal for being thus double-taxed to another set of landholders, and another set of priests? Have men no self-interest? no avarice? no repugnance to public imposts? Have they no sturdy and restive minds? no undisciplined habits? Is there nothing in the whole mob of irregular passions which might precipitate some of the common people, in some places, to quarrel with a legal, because they feel it to be a burdensome, imposition? According to these gentlemen, no offence can be committed by Papists but from zeal to their religion. To make room for the vices of Papists, they clear the house of all the vices of men. Some of the common people (not one however in ten thousand) commit disorders. Well! punish them as you do, and as you ought to punish them, for their violence against the just property of each individual clergyman, as each individual suffers. Support the injured rector, or the injured impropriator, in the enjoyment of the estate of which (whether on the best plan or not) the laws have put him in possession. Let the crime and the punishment stand upon their own bottom. But now we ought all of us, clergymen most particularly, to avoid assigning another cause of quarrel, in order to infuse a new source of bitterness into a dispute which personal feelings on both sides will of themselves make bitter enough, and thereby involve in it, by religious descriptions, men who have individually no share whatsoever in those irregular acts. Let us not make the malignant fictions of our own imaginations, heated with factious controversies, reasons for keeping men that are neither guilty, nor justly suspected of crime, in a servitude equally dishonourable and unsafe to religion and to the state. When men are constantly accused, but know themselves not to be guilty, they must naturally abhor their accusers. There is no character, when malignantly taken up and deliberately pursued, which more naturally excites indignation and abhorrence in mankind; especially in that part of mankind which suffers from it.

I do not pretend to take pride in an extravagant attachment to any sect. Some gentlemen in Ireland affect that sort of glory. It is to their taste. Their piety, I take it for granted, justifies the fervour of their zeal, and may palliate the excess of it. Being myself no more than a common layman, commonly informed in controversies, leading only a very common life, and having only a common citizen's interest in the church, or in the state, yet to you I will say, in justice to my own sentiments, that not one of those zealots for a Protestant interest wishes more sincerely than I do, perhaps not half so sincerely, for the support of the Established Church in both these kingdoms. It is a great link towards holding fast the connexion of religion with the state; and for keeping these two islands, in their present critical independence of constitution, in a close connexion of *opinion and affection*. I wish it well, as the religion of the greater number of the primary land-proprietors of the kingdom, with whom all establishments of church and state, for strong political reasons, ought in my opinion to be warmly connected. I wish it well, because it is more closely combined than any other of the church-systems with the *Crown*, which is the stay of the mixed constitution; because it is, as things now stand, the sole connecting *political* principle between the constitutions of the two independent kingdoms. I have another, and infinitely a stronger, reason for wishing it well; it is, that in the present time I consider it as one of the main pillars of the Christian religion itself. The body and substance of every religion I regard much more than any of the forms and dogmas of the particular sects. Its fall would leave a great void, which nothing else of which I can form any distinct idea might fill. I respect the Catholic hierarchy, and the Presbyterian republic. But I know that the hope or the fear of establishing either of them is, in these kingdoms, equally chimerical, even if I preferred one or the other of them to the Establishment, which certainly I do not.

These are some of my reasons for wishing the support of the Church of Ireland as by law established. These reasons are founded as well on the absolute as on the relative situation of that kingdom. But is it because I love the church, and the king, and the privileges of parliament, that I am to be ready for any violence, or any injustice, or any absurdity, in the means of supporting any of these powers, or all of them together? Instead of prating about Protestant ascendencies, Protestant parliaments ought, in my opinion, to think at last of becoming patriot parliaments.

The legislature of Ireland, like all legislatures, ought to frame its laws to suit the people and the circumstances of the country, and not any longer to make it their whole business to force the nature, the temper, and the inveterate habits of a nation to a conformity to speculative systems concerning any kind of laws. Ireland has an established government, and a religion legally established, which are to be preserved. It has a people who are to be preserved too, and to be led by reason, principle, sentiment, and interest to acquiesce in that government. Ireland is a country under peculiar circumstances. The people of Ireland are a very mixed people; and the quantities of the several ingredients in the mixture are very much disproportioned to each other. Are we to govern this mixed body as if it were composed of the most simple elements, comprehending the whole in one system of benevolent legislation? or are we not rather to provide for the several parts according to the various and diversified necessities of the heterogeneous nature of the mass? Would not common reason and common honesty dictate to us the policy of regulating the people in the several descriptions of which they are composed, according to the natural ranks and classes of an orderly civil society, under a common protecting sovereign, and under a form of constitution favourable at once to authority and to freedom; such as the British constitution boasts to be, and such as it is, to those who enjoy it?

You have an ecclesiastical establishment, which, though the religion of the prince, and of most of the first class of landed proprietors, is not the religion of the major part of the inhabitants, and which, consequently, does not answer to them any one purpose of a religious establishment. This is a state of things which no man in his senses can call perfectly happy. But it is the state of Ireland. Two hundred years of experiment show it to be unalterable. Many a fierce struggle has passed between the parties. The result is – you cannot make the people Protestants – and they cannot shake off a Protestant government. This is what experience teaches, and what all men of sense, of all descriptions, know. Today the question is this – are we to make the best of this situation which we cannot alter? The question is – shall the condition of the body of the people be alleviated in other things, on account of their necessary suffering from their being subject to the burdens of two religious establishments, from one of which they do not partake the least, living or dying, either of instruction or of consolation; or shall it be aggravated by stripping the people thus loaded of everything which might support and indemnify them in this state, so as to leave them naked of every sort of right, and of every name of franchise; to outlaw them from the constitution, and to cut off (perhaps) three millions of plebeian subjects, without reference to property or any other qualification, from all connexion with the popular representation of the kingdom?

As to religion, it has nothing at all to do with the proceeding. Liberty is not sacrificed to a zeal for religion; but a zeal for religion is pretended and assumed, to destroy liberty. The Catholic religion is completely free. It has no establishment; but it is recognised, permitted, and in a degree protected by the laws. If a man is satisfied to be a slave, he may be a Papist with perfect impunity. He may say mass, or hear it, as he pleases; but he must consider himself as an outlaw from the British constitution. If the constitutional liberty of the subject were not the thing aimed at, the direct reverse course would be taken. The franchise would have been permitted, and the mass exterminated. But the conscience of a man left, and a tenderness for it hypocritically pretended, is to make it a trap to catch his liberty.

So much is this the design, that the violent partisans of this scheme fairly take up all the maxims and arguments, as well as the practices, by which tyranny has fortified itself at all times. Trusting wholly in their strength and power, (and upon this they reckon, as always ready to strike wherever they wish to direct the storm,) they abandon all pretext of the general good of the community. They say that if the people, under any given modification, obtain the smallest portion or particle of constitutional freedom, it will be impossible for them to hold their property. They tell us that they act only on the defensive. They inform the public of Europe, that their estates are made up of forfeitures and confiscations from the natives: – that if the body of people obtain votes, any number of votes, however small, it will be a step to the choice of members of their own religion: – that the House of Commons, in spite of the influence of nineteen parts in twenty of the landed interest now in their hands, will be composed in the whole, or in far the major part, of Papists; that this Popish House of Commons will instantly pass a law to confiscate all their estates, which it will not be in their power to save even by entering into that Popish party themselves, because there are prior claimants to be satisfied; – that as to the House of Lords, though neither Papists nor Protestants have a share in electing them, the body of the peerage will be so obliging and disinterested as to fall in with this exterminatory scheme, which is to forfeit all their estates, the largest part of the kingdom; and, to crown all, that his Majesty will give his cheerful assent to this causeless act of attainder of his innocent and faithful Protestant subjects: – that they will be or are to be left without house or land, to the dreadful resource of living by their wits, out of which they are already frightened by the apprehension of this spoliation with which they are threatened: – that therefore they cannot so much as listen to any arguments drawn from equity or from national or constitutional policy; the sword is at their throats; beggary and famine at their door. See what it is to have a good look-out, and to see danger at the end of a sufficiently long perspective!

This is indeed to speak plain, though to speak nothing very new. The same thing has been said in all times and in all languages. The language of tyranny has been invariable; the general good is inconsistent with my personal safety. Justice and liberty seem so alarming to these gentlemen, that they are not ashamed even to slander their own titles to calumniate, and call in doubt, their right to their own estates, and to consider themselves as novel disseizors, usurpers, and intruders, rather than lose a pretext for becoming oppressors of their fellow-citizens, whom they (not I) choose to describe themselves as having robbed.

Instead of putting themselves in this odious point of light, one would think they would wish to let Time draw his oblivious veil over the unpleasant modes by which lordships and demesnes have been acquired in theirs, and almost in all other countries upon earth. It might be imagined that when the sufferer (if a sufferer exists) had forgot the wrong, they would be pleased to forget it too; that they would permit the sacred name of possession to stand in the place of the melancholy and unpleasant title of grantees of confiscation; which, though firm and valid in law, surely merits the name that a great Roman jurist gave to a title at least as valid in his nation as confiscation would be either in his or in ours, – *Tristis et luctuosa successio.*[7]

Such is the situation of every man who comes in upon the ruin of another – his succeeding, under this circumstance, is *tristis et luctuosa successio.* If it had been the fate of any gentleman to profit by the confiscation of his neighbour, one would think he would be more disposed to give him a valuable interest under him in his land; or to allow him a pension, as I understand one worthy person has done, without fear or apprehension that his benevolence to a ruined family would be construed into a recognition of the forfeited title. The public of England the other day acted in this manner towards Lord Newburgh,[8] a Catholic. Though the estate had been vested by law in the greatest of the public charities, they have given him a pension from his confiscation. They have gone further in other cases. On the last rebellion in 1745, in Scotland, several forfeitures were incurred. They had been disposed of by parliament to certain laudable uses. Parliament reversed the method, which they had adopted in Lord Newburgh's case, and, in my opinion, did better; they gave the forfeited estates to the successors of the forfeiting proprietors, chargeable in part with the uses. Is this, or anything like this, asked in favour of any human creature in Ireland? It is bounty; it is charity; wise bounty and politic charity; but no man can claim it as a right. Here no such thing is claimed as right, or begged as charity. The demand has an object as distant from all considerations of this sort as any two extremes can be. The people desire the privileges inseparably annexed, since Magna Charta, to the freehold which they have by descent, or obtain as the fruits of their industry. They call for no man's estate; they desire not to be dispossessed of their own.

But this melancholy and invidious title is a favourite (and like favourites, always of the least merit) with those who possess

every other title upon earth along with it. For this purpose they
revive the bitter memory of every dissension which has torn to
pieces their miserable country for ages. After what has passed in
1782, one would not think that decorum, to say nothing of
policy, would permit them to call up, by magic charms, the
grounds, reasons, and principles of those terrible confiscatory
and exterminatory periods. They would not set men upon calling from the quiet sleep of death any Samuel, to ask him, by what
act of arbitrary monarchs, by what inquisitions of corrupted tribunals and tortured jurors, by what fictitious tenures, invented
to dispossess whole unoffending tribes and their chieftains! They
would not conjure up the ghosts from the ruins of castles and
churches, to tell for what attempt to struggle for the independence of an Irish legislature, and to raise armies of volunteers,
without regular commissions from the Crown in support of that
independence, the estates of the old Irish nobility and gentry had
been confiscated. They would not wantonly call on those
phantoms, to tell by what English acts of parliament, forced upon
two reluctant kings, the lands of their country were put up to a
mean and scandalous auction in every goldsmith's shop in
London; or chopped to pieces, and cut into rations, to pay the
mercenary soldiery of a regicide usurper. They would not be so
fond of titles under Cromwell, who, if he avenged an Irish rebellion against the sovereign authority of the parliament of England, had himself rebelled against the very parliament whose
sovereignty he asserted full as much as the Irish nation, which he
was sent to subdue and confiscate, could rebel against that parliament, or could rebel against the king, against whom both he and
the parliament which he served, and which he betrayed, had
both of them rebelled.

The gentlemen who hold the language of the day know perfectly well that the Irish in 1641 pretended, at least, that they did
not rise against the king, nor in fact did they, whatever constructions law might put upon their act. But full surely they rebelled
against the authority of the parliament of England, and they
openly professed so to do. Admitting (I have now no time to discuss the matter) the enormous and unpardonable magnitude of
this their crime, they rued it in their persons, and in those of
their children and their grandchildren even to the fifth and sixth
generations. Admitting, then, the enormity of this unnatural
rebellion in favour of the independence of Ireland, will it follow

that it must be avenged for ever? Will it follow that it must be avenged on thousands, and perhaps hundreds of thousands, of those whom they can never trace, by the labours of the most subtle metaphysician of the traduction of crimes, or the most inquisitive genealogist of proscription, to the descendant of any one concerned in that nefarious Irish rebellion against the parliament of England?

If, however, you could find out these pedigrees of guilt, I do not think the difference would be essential. History records many things which ought to make us hate evil actions; but neither history, nor morals, nor policy can teach us to punish innocent men on that account. What lesson does the iniquity of prevalent factions read to us? It ought to lesson us into an abhorrence of the abuse of our own power in our own day; when we hate its excesses so much in other persons and in other times. To that school true statesmen ought to be satisfied to leave mankind. They ought not to call from the dead all the discussions and litigations which formerly inflamed the furious factions which had torn their country to pieces; they ought not to rake into the hideous and abominable things which were done in the turbulent fury of an injured, robbed, and persecuted people, and which were afterwards cruelly revenged in the execution, and as outrageously and shamefully exaggerated in the representation, in order, an hundred and fifty years after, to find some colour for justifying them in the eternal proscription and civil excommunication of a whole people.

Let us come to a later period of those confiscations, with the memory of which the gentlemen who triumph in the acts of 1782 are so much delighted. The Irish again rebelled against the English parliament in 1688, and the English parliament again put up to sale the greatest part of their estates. I do not presume to defend the Irish for this rebellion; nor to blame the English parliament for this confiscation. The Irish, it is true, did not revolt from King James's power. He threw himself upon their fidelity, and they supported him to the best of their feeble power. Be the crime of that obstinate adherence to an abdicated sovereign against a prince whom the parliaments of Ireland and Scotland had recognised what it may, I do not mean to justify this rebellion more than the former. It might, however, admit some palliation in them. In generous minds some small degree of compassion might be excited for an error, where they were misled, as Cicero says to a conqueror, *quâdam specie et similitudine pacis*,[9] not without a mistaken appearance of duty, and for which the guilty have suffered by exile abroad, and slavery at home, to the extent of their folly or their offence. The best calculators compute that Ireland lost 200,000 of her inhabitants in that struggle.[10] If the principle of the English and Scottish resistance at the revolution is to be justified, (as sure I am it is,) the submission of Ireland must be somewhat extenuated. For if the Irish resisted King William, they resisted him on the very same principle that the English and Scotch resisted King James. The Irish Catholics must have been the very worst and the most truly unnatural of rebels if they had not supported a prince whom they had seen attacked, not for any designs against *their* religion, or *their* liberties, but for an extreme partiality for their sect; and who, far from trespassing on *their* liberties and properties, secured both them and the independence of their country in much the same manner that we have seen the same things done at the period of 1782, – I trust the last revolution in Ireland.

That the Irish parliament of King James did in some particulars, though feebly, imitate the rigour which had been used towards the Irish, is true enough. Blameable enough they were for what they had done, though under the greatest possible provocation. I shall never praise confiscations or counter-confiscations as long as I live. When they happen by necessity I shall think the necessity lamentable and odious; I shall think that anything done under it ought not to pass into precedent, or to be adopted by choice, or to produce any of those shocking retaliations which never suffer dissensions to subside. Least of all would I fix the transitory spirit of civil fury by perpetuating and methodising it in tyrannic government. If it were permitted to argue with power, might one not ask these gentlemen whether it would not be more natural, instead of wantonly mooting these questions concerning their property, as if it were an exercise in law, to found it on the solid rock of prescription; the soundest, the most general, and the most recognised title between man and man, that is known in municipal or in public jurisprudence? a title, in which not arbitrary institutions, but the eternal order of things gives judgment; a title which is not the creature, but the master, of positive law; a title which, though not fixed in its term, is rooted in its principle, in the law of nature itself, and is, indeed, the original ground of all known property; for all property in soil will always be traced back to that source, and will rest there. The miserable natives of Ireland, who ninety-nine in a hundred are tormented with quite other cares, and are bowed down to labour for the bread of the hour, are not, as gentlemen pretend, plodding with antiquaries for titles of centuries ago to the estates of the great lords and squires for whom they labour. But if they were thinking of the titles which gentlemen labour to beat into their heads, where can they bottom their own claims but in a presumption and a proof that these lands had at some time been possessed by their ancestors? These gentlemen, for they have lawyers amongst them, know as well as I, that in England we have had always a prescription or limitation, as all nations have, against each other. The Crown was excepted; but that exception is destroyed, and we have lately established a sixty years' possession as against the Crown. All titles terminate in prescription; in which (differently from Time in the fabulous instances) the son devours the father, and the last prescription eats up all the former.

SPEECH ON THE PETITION OF
THE UNITARIAN SOCIETY[1]

11 MAY 1792

I NEVER GOVERN myself, no rational man ever did govern himself, by abstractions and universals. I do not put abstract ideas
wholly out of any question; because I well know that under that
name I should dismiss principles, and that without the guide
and light of sound, well-understood principles, all reasonings in
politics, as in everything else, would be only a confused jumble
of particular facts and details, without the means of drawing out
any sort of theoretical or practical conclusion. A statesman differs
from a professor in an university: the latter has only the general
view of society; the former, the statesman, has a number of
circumstances to combine with those general ideas, and to take
into his consideration. Circumstances are infinite, are infinitely
combined, are variable and transient: he who does not take them
into consideration is not erroneous, but stark mad; *dat operam ut
cum ratione insaniat*;[2] he is metaphysically mad. A statesman, never
losing sight of principles, is to be guided by circumstances; and
judging contrary to the exigencies of the moment, he may ruin
his country forever. I go on this ground, – that government,
representing the society, has a general superintending control
over all the actions and over all the publicly propagated doctrines
of men, without which it never could provide adequately for all
the wants of society: but then it is to use this power with an equitable discretion, the only bond of sovereign authority. For it is
not, perhaps, so much by the assumption of unlawful powers as
by the unwise or unwarrantable use of those which are most
legal, that governments oppose their true end and object: for
there is such a thing as tyranny, as well as usurpation. You can
hardly state to me a case to which legislature is the most confessedly competent, in which, if the rules of benignity and prudence
are not observed, the most mischievous and oppressive things
may not be done. So that, after all, it is a moral and virtuous
discretion, and not any abstract theory of right, which keeps
governments faithful to their ends. Crude, unconnected truths
are in the world of practice what falsehoods are in theory. A
reasonable, prudent, provident, and moderate coercion may be

a means of preventing acts of extreme ferocity and rigour: for by propagating excessive and extravagant doctrines, such extravagant disorders take place as require the most perilous and fierce corrections to oppose them.

It is not morally true that we are bound to establish in every country that form of religion which in *our* minds is most agreeable to truth, and conduces most to the eternal happiness of mankind. In the same manner, it is not true that we are, against the conviction of our own judgment, to establish a system of opinions and practices directly contrary to those ends, only because some majority of the people, told by the head, may prefer it. No conscientious man would willingly establish what he knew to be false and mischievous in religion, or in anything else. No wise man, on the contrary, would tyrannically set up his own sense so as to reprobate that of the great prevailing body of the community, and pay no regard to the established opinions and prejudices of mankind, or refuse to them the means of securing a religious instruction suitable to these prejudices. A great deal depends on the state in which you find men. . . .

An alliance between Church and State in a Christian commonwealth is, in my opinion, an idle and a fanciful speculation. An alliance is between two things that are in their nature distinct and independent, such as between two sovereign states. But in a Christian commonwealth the Church and the State are one and the same thing, being different integral parts of the same whole. For the Church has been always divided into two parts, the clergy and the laity, – of which the laity is as much an essential integral part, and has as much its duties and privileges, as the clerical member, and in the rule, order, and government of the Church has its share. Religion is so far, in my opinion, from being out of the province or the duty of a Christian magistrate, that it is, and it ought to be, not only his care, but the principal thing in his care; because it is one of the great bonds of human society, and its object the supreme good, the ultimate end and object of man himself. The magistrate, who is a man, and charged with the concerns of men, and to whom very specially nothing human is remote and indifferent, has a right and a duty to watch over it with an unceasing vigilance, to protect, to promote, to forward it by every rational, just, and prudent means. It is principally his duty to prevent the abuses which grow out of every strong and efficient principle that actuates the human mind. As religion is one of the bonds of society, he ought not to suffer it to be made the pretext of destroying its peace, order, liberty, and its security.

Above all, he ought strictly to look to it, when men begin to form new combinations, to be distinguished by new names, and especially when they mingle a political system with their religious opinions, true or false, plausible or implausible.

It is the interest, and it is the duty, and because it is the interest and the duty, it is the right of government to attend much to opinions; because, as opinions soon combine with passions, even when they do not produce them, they have much influence on actions. Factions are formed upon opinions, which factions become in effect bodies corporate in the state; nay, factions generate opinions, in order to become a centre of union, and to furnish watchwords to parties; and this may make it expedient for government to forbid things in themselves innocent and neutral. I am not fond of defining with precision what the ultimate rights of the sovereign supreme power, in providing for the safety of the commonwealth, may be, or may not extend to. It will signify very little what my notions or what their own notions on the subject may be; because, according to the exigence, they will take, in fact, the steps which seem to them necessary for the preservation of the whole: for as self-preservation in individuals is the first law of Nature, the same will prevail in societies, who will, right or wrong, make that an object paramount to all other rights whatsoever. There are ways and means by which a good man would not even save the commonwealth. ... All things founded on the idea of danger ought in a great degree to be temporary. All policy is very suspicious that sacrifices any part to the ideal good of the whole. The object of the state is (as far as may be) the happiness of the whole. Whatever makes multitudes of men utterly miserable can never answer that object; indeed, it contradicts it wholly and entirely; and the happiness or misery of mankind, estimated by their feelings and sentiments, and not by any theories of their rights, is, and ought to be, the standard for the conduct of legislators towards the people. This naturally and necessarily conducts us to the peculiar and characteristic situation of a people, and to a knowledge of their opinions, prejudices, habits, and all the circumstances that diversify and colour life. The first question a good statesman would ask himself, therefore, would be, How and in what circumstances do you find the society? and to act upon them.

To the other laws relating to other sects I have nothing to say: I only look to the petition which has given rise to this proceeding. I confine myself to that, because in my opinion its merits have little or no relation to that of the other laws which the right honourable gentleman has with so much ability blended with it. With the Catholics, with the Presbyterians, with the Anabaptists, with the Independents, with the Quakers, I have nothing at all to do. They are in *possession*, – a great title in all human affairs. The tenour and spirit of our laws, whether they were restraining or whether they were relaxing, have hitherto taken another course. The spirit of our laws has applied their penalty or their relief to the supposed abuse to be repressed or the grievance to be relieved; and the provision for a Catholic and a Quaker has been totally different, according to his exigence: you did not give a Catholic liberty to be freed from an oath, or a Quaker power of saying mass with impunity. You have done this, because you never have laid it down as an universal proposition, as a maxim, that nothing relative to religion was your concern, but the direct contrary; and therefore you have always examined whether there was a grievance. It has been so at all times: the legislature, whether right or wrong, went no other way to work but by circumstances, times, and necessities. My mind marches the same road; my school is the practice and usage of Parliament.

Old religious factions are volcanoes burnt out; on the lava and ashes and squalid scoriæ of old eruptions grow the peaceful olive, the cheering vine, and the sustaining corn. Such was the first, such the second condition of Vesuvius. But when a new fire bursts out, a face of desolations comes on, not to be rectified in ages. Therefore, when men come before us, and rise up like an exhalation from the ground, they come in a questionable shape, and we must *exorcise* them, and try whether their intents be wicked or charitable, whether they bring airs from heaven or blasts from hell. This is the first time that our records of Parliament have heard, or our experience or history given us an account of any religious congregation or association known by the name which these petitioners have assumed. We are now to see by what people, of what character, and under what temporary circumstances, this business is brought before you. We are to see whether there be any and what mixture of political dogmas and political practices with their religious tenets, of what nature they are, and how far they are at present practically separable from them. This faction (the authors of the petition) are not confined to a *theological* sect, but are also a *political* faction. 1st, As theological, we are to show that they do not aim at the quiet enjoyment of their own liberty, but are *associated* for the express purpose of proselytism. In proof of this first proposition, read their primary association. 2nd, That their purpose of proselytism is to collect a multitude sufficient by force and violence to overturn the Church. In proof of the second proposition, see the letter of Priestley to Mr. Pitt, and extracts from his works. 3rd, That the designs against the Church are concurrent with a design to subvert the State. In proof of the third proposition, read the advertisement of the Unitarian Society for celebrating the 14th of July. 4th, On what *model* they intend to build, – that it is the *French*. In proof of the fourth proposition, read the correspondence of the Revolution Society with the clubs of France, read Priestley's adherence to their opinions. 5th, What the *French* is with regard to religious toleration, and with regard to, 1. Religion, – 2. Civil happiness, – 3. Virtue, order, and real liberty, – 4. Commercial opulence, – 5. National defence. In proof of the fifth proposition, read the representation of the French minister of the Home Department, and the report of the committee upon it.

Formerly, when the superiority of two parties contending for dogmas and an establishment was the question, we knew in such a contest the whole of the evil. We knew, for instance, that Calvinism would prevail according to the Westminster Catechism with regard to *tenets*. We knew that Presbytery would prevail in *church government*. But we do not know what opinions would prevail, if the present Dissenters should become masters. They will not tell us their present opinions; and one principle of modern Dissent is, not to discover them. Next, as their religion is in a continual fluctuation, and is so by principle and in profession, it is impossible for us to know what it will be. If religion only related to the individual, and was a question between God and the conscience, it would not be wise, nor in my opinion equitable, for human authority to step in. But when religion is embodied into faction, and factions have objects to pursue, it will and must, more or less, become a question of power between them. If even, when embodied into congregations, they limited their principle to their own congregations, and were satisfied themselves to abstain from what they thought unlawful, it would be cruel, in my opinion, to molest them in that tenet, and a consequent practice. But we know that they not only entertain these opinions, but entertain them with a zeal for propagating them by force, and employing the power of law and place to destroy establishments, if ever they should come to power sufficient to effect their purpose: that is, in other words, they declare they would persecute the heads of our Church; and the question is, whether you should keep them within the bounds of toleration, or subject yourself to their persecution.

A bad and very censurable practice it is to warp doubtful and ambiguous expressions to a perverted sense, which makes the charge not the crime of others, but the construction of your own malice; nor is it allowed to draw conclusions from allowed premises, which those who lay down the premises utterly deny, and disown as their conclusions. For this, though it may possibly be good logic, cannot by any possibility whatsoever be a fair or charitable representation of any man or any set of men. It may show the erroneous nature of principles, but it argues nothing as to dispositions and intentions. Far be such a mode from me! A mean and unworthy jealousy it would be to do anything upon the mere speculative apprehension of what men will do. But let us pass by *our* opinions concerning the danger of the Church. What do the gentlemen themselves think of that danger? They from whom the danger is apprehended, what do they declare to be their own designs? What do they conceive to be their own forces? And what do they proclaim to be their means? Their designs they declare to be to destroy the Established Church; and not to set up a new one of their own. See Priestley. If they should find the State stick to the Church, the question is, whether they love the constitution in *State* so well as that they would not destroy the constitution of the State in order to destroy that of the Church. Most certainly they do not.

The foundations on which obedience to governments is founded are not to be constantly discussed. That we are here supposes the discussion already made and the dispute settled. We must assume the rights of what represents the public to control the individual, to make his will and his acts to submit to their will, until some intolerable grievance shall make us know that it does not answer its end, and will submit neither to reformation nor restraint. Otherwise we should dispute all the points of morality, before we can punish a murderer, robber, and adulterer; we should analyse all society. Dangers by being despised grow great; so they do by absurd provision against them. *Stulti est dixisse, Non putâram.*[3] Whether an early discovery of evil designs, an early declaration, and an early precaution against them be more wise than to stifle all inquiry about them, for fear they should declare themselves more early than otherwise they would, and therefore precipitate the evil, – all this depends on the reality of the danger. Is it only an unbookish jealousy, as Shakspeare calls it? It is a question of fact. Does a design against the Constitution of this country exist? If it does, and if it is carried on with increasing vigour and activity by a restless faction, and if it receives countenance by the most ardent and enthusiastic applauses of its object in the great council of this kingdom, by men of the first parts which this kingdom produces, perhaps by the first it has ever produced, can I think that there is no danger? If there be danger, must there be no precaution at all against it? If you ask whether I think the danger urgent and immediate, I answer, Thank God, I do not. The body of the people is yet sound, the Constitution is in their hearts, while wicked men are endeavouring to put another into their heads. But if I see the very same beginnings which have commonly ended in great calamities, I ought to act as if they might produce the very same effects. Early and provident fear is the mother of safety; because in that state of things the mind is firm and collected, and the judgment unembarrassed. But when the fear and the evil feared come on together, and press at once upon us, deliberation itself is ruinous, which saves upon all other occasions; because, when perils are instant, it delays decision: the man is in a flutter, and in a hurry, and his judgment is gone, – as the judgment of the deposed King of France and his ministers was gone, if the latter did not premeditately betray him. He was just come from his usual amusement of hunting, when the head of the column of treason and assassination was arrived at his house. Let not the king, let not the Prince of Wales, be surprised in this manner. Let not both Houses of Parliament be led in triumph along with him, and have law dictated to them, by the Constitutional, the Revolution, and the Unitarian Societies. These insect reptiles, whilst they go on only caballing and toasting, only fill us with disgust; if they get above their natural size, and increase the quantity whilst they keep the quality of their venom, they become objects of the greatest terror. A spider in his natural size is only a spider, ugly and loathsome; and his flimsy net is only fit for catching flies.

But, good God! suppose a spider as large as an ox, and that he spread cables about us, all the wilds of Africa would not produce anything so dreadful: –

> Quale portentum neque militaris
> Daunia in latis alit esculetis,
> Nec Jubæ tellus generat, leonum
> Arida nutrix.[4]

Think of them who dare menace in the way they do in their present state, what would they do, if they had power commensurate to their malice? God forbid I ever should have a despotic master! – but if I must, my choice is made. I will have Louis the Sixteenth rather than Monsieur Bailly, or Brissot, or Chabot, – rather George the Third, or George the Fourth, than Dr. Priestley, or Dr. Kippis,[5] – persons who would not load a tyrannous power by the poisoned taunts of a vulgar, low-bred insolence. I hope we have still spirit enough to keep us from the one or the other. The contumelies of tyranny are the worst parts of it.

But if the danger be existing in reality, and silently maturing itself to our destruction, what! is it not better to take *treason* unprepared than that *treason* should come by surprise upon us and take us unprepared? If we must have a conflict, let us have it with all our forces fresh about us, with our government in full function and full strength, our troops uncorrupted, our revenues in the legal hands, our arsenals filled and possessed by government, – and not wait till the conspirators met to commemorate the 14th of July shall seize on the Tower of London and the magazines it contains, murder the governor, and the mayor of London, seize upon the king's person, drive out the House of Lords, occupy your gallery, and thence, as from an high tribunal, dictate to you. The degree of danger is not only from the circumstances which threaten, but from the value of the objects which are threatened. A small danger menacing an inestimable object is of more importance than the greatest perils which regard one that is indifferent to us. The whole question of the danger depends upon facts. The first fact is, whether those who sway in France at present confine themselves to the regulation of their internal affairs, – or whether upon system they nourish cabals in all other countries, to extend their power by producing revolutions similar to their own. 2. The next is, whether we have any cabals formed or forming within these kingdoms, to co-operate with them for the

destruction of our Constitution. On the solution of these two
questions, joined with our opinion of the value of the object to
be affected by their machinations, the justness of our alarm and
the necessity of our vigilance must depend. Every private conspiracy, every open attack upon the laws, is dangerous. One robbery is an alarm to all property; else I am sure we exceed measure
in our punishment. As robberies increase in number and audacity, the alarm increases. These wretches are at war with us upon
principle. They hold this government to be an usurpation. See
the language of the Department.

The whole question is on the *reality* of the danger. Is it such
a danger as would justify that fear *qui cadere potest in hominem
constantem et non metuentem*?[6] This is the fear which the principles
of jurisprudence declare to be a lawful and justifiable fear. When
a man threatens my life openly and publicly, I may demand from
him securities of the peace. When every act of a man's life manifests such a design stronger than by words, even though he does
not make such a declaration, I am justified in being on my guard.
They are of opinion that they are already one fifth of the kingdom. If so, their force is naturally not contemptible. To say that in
all contests the decision will of course be in favour of the greater
number is by no means true in fact. For, first, the greater number
is generally composed of men of sluggish tempers, slow to act,
and unwilling to attempt, and, by being in possession, are so disposed to peace that they are unwilling to take early and vigorous
measures for their defence, and they are almost always caught
unprepared: –

> Nec coïere pares: alter vergentibus annis
> In senium, longoque togæ tranquillior usu.
> Dedidicit jam pace ducem; . . .
> Nec reparare novas vires, multumque priori
> Credere fortunæ: stat magni nominis umbra.[7]

A smaller number, more expedite, awakened, active, vigorous,
and courageous, who make amends for what they want in weight
by their superabundance of velocity, will create an acting power
of the greatest possible strength. When men are furiously and
fanatically fond of an object, they will prefer it, as is well known,
to their own peace, to their own property, and to their own lives:
and can there be a doubt, in such a case, that they would prefer
it to the peace of their country? Is it to be doubted, that, if they

have not strength enough at home, they will call in foreign force to aid them?

Would you deny them *what is reasonable*, for fear they should? Certainly not. It would be barbarous to pretend to look into the minds of men. I would go further: it would not be just even to trace consequences from principles which, though evident to me, were denied by them. Let them disband as a faction, and let them act as individuals, and when I see them with no other views than to enjoy their own conscience in peace, I, for one, shall most cheerfully vote for their relief.

A tender conscience, of all things, ought to be tenderly handled; for if you do not, you injure not only the conscience, but the whole moral frame and constitution is injured, recurring at times to remorse, and seeking refuge only in making the conscience callous. But the conscience of faction, – the conscience of sedition, – the conscience of conspiracy, war, and confusion. . . .

Whether anything be proper to be denied, which is right in itself, because it may lead to the demand of others which it is improper to grant? Abstractedly speaking, there can be no doubt that this question ought to be decided in the negative. But as no moral questions are ever abstract questions, this, before I judge upon any abstract proposition, must be embodied in circumstances; for, since things are right or wrong, morally speaking, only by their relation and connection with other things, this very question of what it is politically right to grant depends upon this relation to its effects. It is the direct office of wisdom to look to the consequences of the acts we do: if it be not this, it is worth nothing, it is out of place and of function, and a downright fool is as capable of government as Charles Fox. A man desires a sword: why should he be refused? A sword is a means of defence, and defence is the natural right of man, – nay, the first of all his rights, and which comprehends them all. But if I know that the sword desired is to be employed to cut my own throat, common sense, and my own self-defence, dictate to me to keep out of his hands this natural right of the sword. But whether this denial be wise or foolish, just or unjust, prudent or cowardly, depends entirely on the state of the man's means. A man may have very ill dispositions, and yet be so very weak as to make all precaution foolish. See whether this be the case of these Dissenters, as to their designs, as to their means, numbers, activity, zeal, foreign assistance.

The first question, to be decided, when we talk of the Church's being in danger from any particular measure, is, whether the danger to the Church is a public evil: for to those who think that the national Church Establishment is itself a national grievance, to desire them to forward or to resist any measure, upon account of its conducing to the safety of the Church or averting its danger, would be to the last degree absurd. If you have reason to think thus of it, take the reformation instantly into your own hands, whilst you are yet cool, and can do it in measure and proportion, and not under the influence of election tests and popular fury. But here I assume that by far the greater number of those who compose the House are of opinion that this national Church Establishment is a great national benefit, a great public blessing, and that its existence or its non-existence of course is a thing by no means indifferent to the public welfare: then to them its danger or its safety must enter deeply into every question which has a relation to it. It is not because ungrounded alarms have been given that there never can exist a real danger: perhaps the worst effect of an ungrounded alarm is to make people insensible to the approach of a real peril. Quakerism is strict, methodical, in its nature highly aristocratical, and so regular that it has brought the whole community to the condition of one family; but it does not actually interfere with the government. The principle of your petitioners is no passive conscientious dissent, on account of an overscrupulous habit of mind: the dissent on their part is fundamental, goes to the very root; and it is at issue not upon this rite or that ceremony, on this or that school opinion, but upon this one question of an Establishment, as unchristian, unlawful, contrary to the Gospel and to natural right, Popish and idolatrous. These are the principles violently and fanatically held and pursued, – taught to their children, who are sworn at the altar like Hannibal.[8] The war is with the Establishment itself, – no quarter, no compromise. As a party, they are infinitely mischievous: see the declarations of Priestley and Price, – declarations, you will say, of *hot* men. Likely enough: but who are the *cool* men who have disclaimed them? Not one, – no, not one. Which of them has ever told you that they do not mean to *destroy the Church*, if ever it should be in their power? Which of them has told you that this would not be the first and favourite use of any power they should get? Not one, – no, not one. Declarations of hot men! The danger is thence, that they are under the *conduct* of hot men: *falsos in amore odia non fingere.*[9]

They say they are well affected to the State, and mean only to destroy the Church. If this be the utmost of their meaning, you must first consider whether you wish your Church Establishment to be destroyed. If you do, you had much better do it now in temper, in a grave, moderate, and parliamentary way. But if you think otherwise, and that you think it to be an invaluable blessing, a way fully sufficient to nourish a manly, rational, solid, and at the same time humble piety, – if you find it well fitted to the frame and pattern of your civil constitution, – if you find it a barrier against fanaticism, infidelity, and atheism, – if you find that it furnishes support to the human mind in the afflictions and distresses of the world, consolation in sickness, pain, poverty, and death, – if it dignifies our nature with the hope of immortality, leaves inquiry free, whilst it preserves an authority to teach, where authority only can teach, *communia altaria, æque ac patriam, diligite, colite, fovete.*[10]

In the discussion of this subject which took place in the year 1790, Mr. Burke declared his intention, in case the motion for repealing the Test Acts[11] had been agreed to, of proposing to substitute the following test in the room of what was intended to be repealed: –

"I, *A.B.*, do, in the presence of God, sincerely profess and believe that a religious establishment in this state is not contrary to the law of God, or disagreeable to the law of Nature, or to the true principles of the Christian religion, or that it is noxious to the community; and I do sincerely promise and engage, before God, that I never will, by any conspiracy, contrivance, or political device whatever, attempt, or abet others in any attempt, to subvert the constitution of the Church of England, as the same is now by law established, and that I will not employ any power or influence which I may derive from any office corporate, or any other office which I hold or shall hold under his Majesty, his heirs and successors, to destroy and subvert the same, or to cause members to be elected into any corporation or into Parliament, give my vote in the election of any member or members of Parliament, or into any office, for or on account of their attachment to any other or different religious opinions or establishments, or with any hope that they may promote the same to the prejudice of the Established Church, but will dutifully and peaceably content myself with my private liberty of conscience, as the same is allowed by law. So help me God."

SPEECH ON WAR
WITH FRANCE[1]

12 FEBRUARY 1793

MR. BURKE BEGAN with declaring, that, in his opinion, his majesty's ministers had so clearly, so satisfactorily, and so completely justified their conduct in regard to the war, that he thought it unnecessary to add any thing in vindication of that measure. So much, however, had been thrown out, in the course of the speech of the right hon. gentleman touching the acknowledged policy and fundamental principles of that House, that, notwithstanding the lateness of the hour, and his own want of strength, he had to request the attention of the House. It must have occurred to a gentleman possessing such clear, perceptive powers, as the right hon. gentleman who moved the amendment, that an attempt to reconcile discordant parts, and connect contradictory opinions, served only to confound them. The right hon. gentleman, on a former occasion, lamented the smallness of his party,[2] and it now seemed as if that party endeavoured to make amends for the smallness of their numbers by the discordancy of their voices. He imagined some of them would find it difficult to account for their conduct in opposing the measures of ministers on the present critical occasion. In their censures on France gentlemen had shown a great deal of dexterity; but it certainly had too much the appearance of stratagem. The right hon. gentleman had complained bitterly of the misrepresentation of his expressions in that House. To him it appeared very extraordinary how a person of talents, so clear, so powerful, and so perspicuous, could possibly be misunderstood – how a person who took so much pains by repetition, and going over the same ground again and again, to bring his superior powers to the low level of the vulgar eye, could possibly be subject to misrepresentation – how a gentleman, whose friends out of doors neglected no human art to display his talents to their utmost advantage, and to detail his speeches to the public in such a manner, that he, though a close observer of the right hon. gentleman, had never been able to recollect a single idea of his that had escaped the industrious attention of his friends, while those of a right hon. friend of his (Mr. Windham[3]), whose abilities were equal to his virtues, were so mangled and so confused, in the reports that were made of them, as to be utterly unintelligible to the public. That the right hon. gentleman should be misrepresented or misunderstood, under such circumstances, was hard indeed. The right hon. gentleman had said, that he hoped he was not reputed an advocate for France. To this he would say, that, if the cause of France was an honest cause, it was justice to this country, and to mankind, to undertake her defence. The true skill of an advocate was, to put forward the strong part of his client's case, and gloss over or hide the weak; to exhibit all its right in the brightest point of view, and palliate the wrong; when he could no longer palliate, to contrive that the punishment should be as slight as possible, or to bring his writ of error, and by every quirk evade it as well as he could; and no man possessed that power in a greater degree than the right hon. gentleman. To his speeches he always attended with admiration and respect. That which he had just heard he could not help estimating less highly, seeing that he had read every part of it in Brissot's speeches in the National Convention,[4] one part only excepted, and that was the part in which the right hon. gentleman had asserted, "that France had used every means to conciliate the regards and good will of Great Britain."

The right hon. gentleman had taken great pains to acquit himself, and apologise for his vehement endeavours to exculpate France from the charge of aggression. He professed that he was almost at a loss to see what it was that made him so prompt to exculpation. If France meant nothing but what was right, and England nothing but what was wrong, he certainly owed no apology for the part he had taken in her cause. But to take the right hon. gentleman's speech in a serious view, it insinuated that the charge of the French was, that the king of Great Britain had determined on war against the sense of his ministers, against the sense of the parliament, and against the sense of the people, in order to augment his own power. If this was the case, ministers had betrayed their country by their acquiescence, and it was the duty of the house to address the king to remove them, and put into their places those whom they thought more fit for advice, more fit to do the duty of a minister, and more likely to possess the confidence of the nation, if such there were. – The right hon. gentleman had contended, that when ministers brought the nation into a war, they should declare how they intended to prosecute it, to what length they intended to carry it, and what the object of it was. For his part, he had never heard or read of any such principle, or of any such practice. The first question he conceived to be, was, whether there was just cause or foundation for the war? The second, how it should be carried on to the greatest effect? He said, that in no instance whatever had any power, at the commencement of a war, declared what period was intended to end it, what means to carry it on, or what the object of it was. It was contrary to the policy of this and every other country; it was never heard of. In this, and in every case of the kind, the common object of the alliance should be pursued to gain the grand end. War had been declared by the French; but they had not declared that they did not intend the ruin, the destruction, and total subversion of this country and every establishment in it. Was it pretended that they had done, in declaring war, that which gentlemen had prescribed as the duty of this country? No; they declared war with the professed intention to bring it, in the most formidable shape, attended with insurrection and anarchy, into the bowels of this country, to strike at the head of the stadtholder, and to put no limits to their views in the war; while gentlemen would have Britain cramped and tied by a premature declaration of her object.

As to the sentiments of the right hon. gentleman respecting the declaration of a specific object of the war, as well as the delicacy of interfering in the internal government of France, were they adopted by the House, this should be their language – "France! you have endeavoured to destroy the repose of all the countries of Europe, and particularly of England: you have reduced your own country to anarchy and ruin, and murdered your king; nevertheless, you may be assured, that, however horrible your crimes, though to the murder of your king you should add that of his infant son, his unfortunate queen and sister, and the whole remains of his family, not one hair of your heads shall be hurt. You may war against us, threaten us with destruction, and bring ruin to our very doors; yet shall you not be injured." Was ever, he exclaimed, such a declaration made in such circumstances? Much pains had been taken by the right hon. gentleman to make light of the power of France, and to persuade the House that there was nothing to be feared from it. He would answer this by showing what the right hon. gentleman had said on a former occasion. Here Mr. Burke began to read a part of a speech spoken by Mr. Fox on the commercial treaty, strongly demonstrative of the necessity of keeping down the overgrown power of France – [The Speaker called Mr. Burke to order; it being disorderly to read any debate on a former occasion. Mr. Burke said he would beg leave to read from a pamphlet in his hand. The House called Read! read! Here he read from a speech of Mr. Fox, that the effect of all our wars had been carried on with a view to repress the power of France, and to support all the other powers of Europe against her; that France only changed her means, but that her ends were ever the same. – The Speaker again interrupted Mr. Burke, and requested that he would abstain from reading, as he knew it was against the orders of the House.] Mr. Burke said, he could not but lament that the rules of the House some-times weakened the force of argument; but he considered order to be so far more necessary than argument, that he would will-ingly forego the latter to maintain the former. To return, there-fore, to his argument, without the conclusive aid he should derive from the right hon. gentleman's own language, in the book in his hand, he contended, that the whole body of policy of this country for ages was, that whatever country was the enemy of France was naturally the ally of Great Britain. If that opinion was founded in true policy before the revolution, what reason was there to alter that opinion since? If the new republic has shown no disposition to increase her dominions, if she has not annexed Savoy, Avignon, Liege, Nice, &c., to her territorial possessions, if she has not declared war against all subsisting governments, and confiscated the properties of all corporations, if she has not held out the mask of confraternity as a signal and temptation to rebellion in all countries, but particularly in Eng-land, then statesmen have a right to change their opinions and systems of policy with respect to her.

Unlimited monarchy, the right hon. gentleman had said, was the object against which France directed the shafts of her enmity. But he would be glad to know whether gentlemen would pretend to say that she was a friend to limited monarchy. No; she was an enemy to limited monarchy, as monarchy, and to the limitation, as limitation. The aristocracy of this country, all corporations, all bodies, whether civil or ecclesiastic, were the objects of her enmity. She showed the most determinate malice, in the most express terms, against all parts of the British govern-ment, equally to those that limit as those that would extend monarchy; not to this or to that, but to the whole. If conquered by Louis 16th, we might be sure of our established forms being unmolested; but if by republican France, of total extinction. Gentlemen had, with much pertinacity, asked, "Have you demanded satisfaction for this?" This, he contended, was all an error, either of misconception or of will. The acts of France were acts of hostility to this country; her whole system, every speech, every decree, every act, bespoke an intention preclusive of accommodation. No man, he would venture to say, had a more lively sense of importance of the question before the House, or of the evils of war, than himself. A war with France, under such circumstances as now governed her conduct, must be terrible, but peace much more so. A nation that had abandoned all its valuable distinctions, arts, sciences, religion, law order, every thing but the sword, was most formidable and dreadful to all nations composed of citizens who only used soldiers as a defence; as such, France should be resisted with spirit and temper, without fear or scruple. In a case of such importance to this country and to mankind, as the present was, gentlemen should examine whether they had any sinister motive, as if in the Divine presence, and act upon the pure result of such examination. He declared he had no hesitation to pronounce, as if before that presence, that ministers had not precipitated the nation into a war, but were brought into it by over-ruling necessity. I possess, said he, as deep a sense of the severe inflictions of war as any man can possibly do − "Trembling I touch it, but with honest zeal." I always held it as one of the last of evils, and wish only to adopt it now from the conviction that at no distant period we shall be obliged to encounter it at much greater disadvantage. For four years past it has grieved me to the soul, it has almost reduced me to death, when I observed how things were going on, and felt my utmost exertions unable to produce upon the government of the country, or in the public mind, a conviction of the danger that approached them. At length the infatuation was removed − ministers awoke to the peril that menaced them ere it was too late; and our enemies, finding those arts fail in which they so much confided, are reduced to attack us in open war, and have declared against us. He should therefore give ministers his clear, steady, uniform, unequivocal support; not as some gentlemen did, pretend support on one day, to lessen their authority, impair their power, and obstruct their plans on another, but in the fullest

manner he could. If any blame was to be laid to the share of ministers, it was that of too long delay; but if from that delay any
accident should arise from want of timely precaution, he would
acquit them of it; knowing, as he did, that it was not possible for
them, with prudence, to do otherwise; for had they done it at an
earlier period they would not have been supported. In his
opposition to the views and proceedings of France, for two years,
he was convinced he had not the feelings of the nation: nor was
it till full-blown mischief had alarmed the people and roused the
king, that the government could have a proper support. For his
part, he thought himself bound in honour to support ministers;
and, if bound to support them, certainly to oppose those who
acted adversely to them. From such men – men who could
neither vindicate the principles nor deny the power of France,
yet impeded the measures taken to secure us against that power
– he differed fundamentally and essentially, in every principle of
morals, in every principle of manners, in sentiment, in disposition, and in taste.

France, he said, had for some time been guilty of a continued
series of hostile acts against this country, both external and internal: first, she directed her pursuits to universal empire, under the
name of fraternity, in order to overturn the fabric of our laws and
government; next, she invented a new law of nations, subsidiary
to that intention: then she acted on that law. Next, she had directed the principal operations of that law to Great Britain; and
lastly, she had established a horrible tyranny within herself,
chased every honest person out of her territory, held out temptations the most seductive to the enlightened lower orders of all
countries, and furnished instruments for the overthrow of their
government. The putting the king of France to death was done,
not as an example to France, not to extinguish the race, not to
put an end to monarchy, but as a terror to monarchs, and particularly to the monarch of Great Britain. This newly-created empire
of theirs, Mr. Burke said, was only secondary to the accomplishment of their plans for the overthrow of all governments. This
had been professed out of the mouth of their minister Cambon.[5]
He had declared, that the limits of their empire should be those
that nature had set, not those of justice and reason; that was to
say, the sea on one side, and the Alps and the Rhine on the other,
together with a large cut of the Appenines – and all for the benefit
of mankind, of liberty and equality! Should we be deterred

by our wealth from resisting these outrages? They directed their invectives and reproaches more at England than any other country. They executed their unhappy, innocent monarch, whom they well knew to be no tyrant, principally, as they alleged, by way of warning to all other tyrants, and an example to all other nations. Even a few hours after the execution of Louis 16th, their minister of justice, Garat,[6] addressing the Convention, said, "We have now thrown down the gauntlet to all tyrants – which gauntlet is the head of a tyrant." Mr. Burke next read the declaration of the members who voted for the death of the king, some saying, "the tree of liberty could not flourish till sprinkled with the blood of tyrants;" others declaring, "that kings were no longer useful but in their deaths," &c.

Some gentlemen had asserted, that if lord Gower[7] had been left at Paris, or another ambassador had been sent in his place, the unhappy fate of the king of France might have been prevented. This, he said, was answered by the fate of the king of Spain's ambassador, who had made, at the desire of his court, a requisition, but was refused. The murder of the king was intended only as a step to the murder of the other kings of Europe; for they had declared, that no monarchical country could have alliance with them: this, too, at the very moment that they were affecting to conciliate and explain away the decree of the 19th of November.[8] War to the palace, and peace to the cottage, was the plan of their new system: wherever their power extended, they put the poor to judge upon the life and property of the rich; they formed a corps of desertion, a corps of assassination, and gave a pension to the wife and children of the assassin that was put to death for attempting to murder the king of Prussia. They declared all treaties with despots void; they were outlaws of humanity, an uncommunicable people, who acknowledged no God but the sacred right of insurrection, no law but the sovereignty of the people; nor had they any judges but *sans culottes*,[9] whom they made arbiters of the lives and properties of all. As to the rights of the poor, he hoped he understood them as well as the right hon. gentleman; the riches of the rich were held in trust for the poor; this the common people little understood, nor could they be made to understand it, if people held out false communications to corrupt them. Here he read a part of a letter from Dumourier, general of the bare-breeched corps, to Anacharsis Cloots,[10] orator of the naked posteriors. In this letter, after describing the blessings of atheism, and that which he called liberty, he says, "these are the sweets of philosophy! What pity it is that bayonets and cannon are the necessary means of propagating it!" Atheism, Mr. Burke said, was the centre from which ray emanated their mischiefs and villainies, and they proceeded to establish it with the sword.

He readily allowed that this was the most dangerous war we were ever engaged in; that we had to contend with a set of men now enured to warfare, and led on by enthusiasm and the ardour of conquest to such a degree, that they bartered the arts, commerce, industry, manufactures, and civilisation itself, for the sword. The alliances we had it in our power to form gave us, however, a good prospect of subduing them; whereas, were they allowed to proceed, we might singly and in the end become their easy prey. He then recited a variety of instances in which the French manifested the most envious and malignant disposition towards this country, and left no effort untried to do it every possible mischief. He read from the Moniteur[11] an account of the meeting of the English friends of the people in Paris; their address to the National Convention; with their fraternal reception, and their toasts after dinner. Of the latter, one was, the health of citizens Fox, Mackintosh, Sheridan, Paine, Barlow, and the other friends of liberty who have enlightened the people of England. – Should we be deterred by our wealth from resisting these outrages? What! exclaimed Mr. Burke, shall we live in a temporary, abject state of timid ease, to fatten ourselves like swine to be killed to-morrow, and to become the easier prey to our enemies? No; God forbid! If we have the spirit that has ever distinguished Britons, that very wealth will be our strength – with it we shall be more than a match for their blind fury. With regard to the means the French have of carrying on the war, the plan of supply they had proposed was worthy of attention. Their minister stated that the country had been purged of 70,000 men of property, all whose effects were to be confiscated, to the amount of 200 million sterling. Thus, like a band of robbers in a cave, they were reckoning the strength of their plunder. He said that they had two terms for raising supplies – confiscation and loan. The common people were relieved by confiscation of the property of the rich and they reckoned on the confiscation of property in every country they entered, with the brotherly intent of fraternising, as a sufficient supply for their exigencies in that

country, and their resource for making war; thus they made war
supply them with plunder, and plunder with the means of war.
– The right hon. gentleman had spoken with some asperity of
an intention in ministers to restore the ancient government. He
would not compare that government with the government of
Great Britain; but certain it was, that it would be felicity and
comfort, compared to the present state of tyranny exercised in
France; for the very same papers out of which he had read the
preceding extracts, contained the melancholy account that thirty
thousand manufacturers were perishing for want in Lyons alone.
Thus their enormities had produced misery; their misery would
drive them to despair; and out of that despair they would look
for a remedy in the destruction of all other countries, and particularly that of Great Britain.[12]

THOUGHTS AND DETAILS
ON SCARCITY[1]

NOVEMBER 1795

OF ALL THINGS, an indiscreet tampering with the trade of provisions is the most dangerous, and it is always worst in the time when men are most disposed to it; that is, in the time of scarcity. Because there is nothing on which the passions of men are so violent, and their judgment so weak, and on which there exists such a multitude of ill-founded popular prejudices.

The great use of government is as a restraint; and there is no restraint which it ought to put upon others, and upon itself too, rather than that which is imposed on the fury of speculating under circumstances of irritation. The number of idle tales, spread about by the industry of faction, and by the zeal of foolish good-intention, and greedily devoured by the malignant credulity of mankind, tends infinitely to aggravate prejudices, which, in themselves, are more than sufficiently strong. In that state of affairs, and of the public with relation to them, the first thing that government owes to us, the people, is *information*; the next is timely coercion: – the one to guide our judgment; the other to regulate our tempers.

To provide for us in our necessities is not in the power of government. It would be a vain presumption in statesmen to think they can do it. The people maintain them, and not they the people. It is in the power of government to prevent much evil; it can do very little positive good in this, or perhaps in anything else. It is not only so of the state and statesman, but of all the classes and descriptions of the rich – they are the pensioners of the poor, and are maintained by their superfluity. They are under an absolute, hereditary, and indefeasible dependence on those who labour, and are miscalled the poor.

The labouring people are only poor, because they are numerous. Numbers in their nature imply poverty. In a fair distribution among a vast multitude none can have much. That class of dependent pensioners called the rich is so extremely small, that if all their throats were cut, and a distribution made of all they consume in a year, it would not give a bit of bread and cheese for one night's supper to those who labour, and who in reality feed both the pensioners and themselves.

But the throats of the rich ought not to be cut, nor their magazines plundered; because in their persons they are trustees for those who labour, and their hoards are the banking houses of these latter. Whether they mean it or not, they do, in effect, execute their trust – some with more, some with less, fidelity and judgment. But, on the whole, the duty is performed, and everything returns, deducting some very trifling commission and discount, to the place from whence it arose. When the poor rise to destroy the rich, they act as wisely for their own purposes, as when they burn mills, and throw corn into the river, to make bread cheap.

When I say, that we of the people ought to be informed, inclusively I say, we ought not to be flattered; flattery is the reverse of instruction. The *poor* in that case would be rendered as improvident as the rich, which would not be at all good for them.

Nothing can be so base and so wicked as the political canting language, "The labouring *poor*." Let compassion be shown in action, the more the better, according to every man's ability; but let there be no lamentation of their condition. It is no relief to their miserable circumstances; it is only an insult to their miserable understandings. It arises from a total want of charity, or a total want of thought. Want of one kind was never relieved by want of any other kind. Patience, labour, sobriety, frugality, and religion, should be recommended to them; all the rest is downright *fraud*. It is horrible to call them "The *once happy* labourer."

Whether what may be called the moral or philosophical happiness of the laborious classes is increased or not, I cannot say. The seat of that species of happiness is in the mind and there are few data to ascertain the comparative state of the mind at any two periods. Philosophical happiness is, to want little. Civil or vulgar happiness is, to want much, and to enjoy much.

If the happiness of the animal man (which certainly goes somewhere towards the happiness of the rational man) be the object of our estimate, then I assert without the least hesitation, that the condition of those who labour (in all descriptions of labour, and in all gradations of labour, from the highest to the lowest inclusively) is on the whole extremely meliorated, if more and better food is any standard of melioration. They work more, it is certain; but they have the advantage of their augmented labour; yet whether that increase of labour be on the whole a *good* or an *evil*, is a consideration that would lead us a great way, and is not for my present purpose. But as to the fact of the melioration of their diet, I shall enter into the detail of proof whenever I am called upon: in the mean time, the known difficulty of contenting them with anything but bread made of the finest flour, and meat of the first quality, is proof sufficient.

I further assert, that even under all the hardships of the last year, the labouring people did, either out of their direct gains, or from charity, (which it seems is now an insult to them,) in fact, fare better than they did in seasons of common plenty, fifty or sixty years ago; or even at the period of my English observation, which is about forty-four years. I even assert, that full as many in that class as ever were known to do it before continued to save money; and this I can prove, so far as my own information and experience extend.

It is not true that the rate of wages has not increased with the nominal price of provisions. I allow it has not fluctuated with that price, nor ought it; and the squires of Norfolk had dined, when they gave it as their opinion, that it might or it ought to rise and fall with the market of provisions. The rate of wages in truth has no *direct* relation to that price. Labour is a commodity like every other, and rises or falls according to the demand. This is in the nature of things; however, the nature of things has provided for their necessities. Wages have been twice raised in my time; and they bear a full proportion, or even a greater than formerly, to the medium of provision during the last bad cycle of twenty years. They bear a full proportion to the result of their labour. If we were wildly to attempt to force them beyond it, the stone which we had forced up the hill would only fall back upon them in a diminished demand, or, what indeed is the far lesser evil, an aggravated price, of all the provisions which are the result of their manual toil.

There is an implied contract, much stronger than any instrument or article of agreement between the labourer in any occupation and his employer – that the labour, so far as that labour is concerned, shall be sufficient to pay to the employer a profit on his capital, and a compensation for his risk; in a word, that the labour shall produce an advantage equal to the payment. Whatever is above that is a direct *tax*; and if the amount of that tax be left to the will and pleasure of another, it is an *arbitrary tax*.

If I understand it rightly, the tax proposed on the farming interest[2] of this kingdom is to be levied at what is called the discretion of justices of peace.

The questions arising on this scheme of arbitrary taxation are these, – Whether it is better to leave all dealing, in which there is no force or fraud, collusion or combination, entirely to the persons mutually concerned in the matter contracted for; or to put the contract into the hands of those who can have none, or a very remote interest in it, and little or no knowledge of the subject.

It might be imagined that there would be very little difficulty in solving this question; for what man of any degree of reflection can think, that a want of interest in any subject closely connected with a want of skill in it, qualifies a person to intermeddle in any the least affair; much less in affairs that vitally concern the agriculture of the kingdom, the first of all its concerns, and the foundation of all its prosperity in every other matter by which that prosperity is produced.

The vulgar error on this subject arises from a total confusion in the very idea of things widely different in themselves; – those of convention, and those of judicature. When a contract is making, it is a matter of discretion and of interest between the parties. In that intercourse, and in what is to arise from it, the parties are the masters. If they are not completely so, they are not free, and therefore their contracts are void.

But this freedom has no further extent, when the contract is made; then their discretionary powers expire, and a new order of things takes its origin. Then, and not till then, and on a difference between the parties, the office of the judge commences. He cannot dictate the contract. It is his business to see that it be *enforced*; provided that it is not contrary to pre-existing laws, or obtained by force or fraud. If he is in any way a maker or regulator of the contract, in so much he is disqualified from being a judge. But this sort of confused distribution of administrative and judicial characters, (of which we have already as much as is sufficient, and a little more,) is not the only perplexity of notions and passions which trouble us in the present hour.

What is doing supposes, or pretends, that the farmer and the labourer have opposite interests; that the farmer oppresses the labourer; and that a gentleman, called a justice of peace, is the protector of the latter, and a control and restraint on the former; and this is a point I wish to examine in a manner a good deal different from that in which gentlemen proceed, who confide more in their abilities than is fit, and suppose them capable of more than any natural abilities, fed with no other than the provender furnished by their own private speculations, can accomplish. Legislative acts attempting to regulate this part of economy do, at least as much as any other, require the exactest detail of circumstances, guided by the surest general principles that are necessary to direct experiment and inquiry, in order again from those details to elicit principles, firm and luminous general principles, to direct a practical legislative proceeding.

First, then, I deny that it is in this case, as in any other of necessary implication, that contracting parties should originally have had different interests. By accident it may be so undoubtedly at the outset; but then the contract is of the nature of a compromise; and compromise is founded on circumstances that suppose it the interest of the parties to be reconciled in some medium. The principle of compromise adopted, of consequence the interests cease to be different.

But in the case of the farmer and the labourer, their interests are always the same, and it is absolutely impossible that their free contracts can be onerous to either party. It is the interest of the farmer, that his work should be done with effect and celerity; and that cannot be, unless the labourer is well fed, and otherwise found with such necessaries of animal life, according to his habitudes, as may keep the body in full force, and the mind gay and cheerful. For of all the instruments of his trade, the labour of man (what the ancient writers have called the *instrumentum vocale*)[3] is that on which he is most to rely for the repayment of his capital. The other two, the *semivocale* in the ancient classification, that is, the working stock of cattle, and the *instrumentum mutum*, such as carts, ploughs, spades, and so forth, though not all inconsiderable in themselves, are very much inferior in utility or in expense; and, without a given portion of the first, are nothing at all. For in all things whatever, the mind is the most valuable and the most important; and in this scale the whole of agriculture is in a natural and just order; the beast is as an informing principle to the plough and cart; the labourer is as reason to the beast; and the farmer is as a thinking and presiding principle to the labourer. An attempt to break this chain of subordination in any part is equally absurd; but the absurdity is the most mischievous in practical operation, where it is the most easy, that is, where it is the most subject to an erroneous judgment.

It is plainly more the farmer's interest that his men should thrive, than that his horses should be well fed, sleek, plump, and fit for use, or than that his waggon and ploughs should be strong, in good repair, and fit for service.

On the other hand, if the farmer cease to profit of the labourer, and that his capital is not continually manured and fructified, it is impossible that he should continue that abundant nutriment, and clothing, and lodging, proper for the protection of the instruments he employs.

It is therefore the first and fundamental interest of the labourer, that the farmer should have a full incoming profit on the product of his labour. The proposition is self-evident, and nothing but the malignity, perverseness, and ill-governed passions of mankind, and particularly the envy they bear to each other's prosperity, could prevent their seeing and acknowledging it, with thankfulness to the benign and wise Disposer of all things, who obliges men, whether they will or not, in pursuing their own selfish interests, to connect the general good with their own individual success.

But who are to judge what that profit and advantage ought to be? Certainly no authority on earth. It is a matter of convention dictated by the reciprocal conveniences of the parties, and indeed by their reciprocal necessities. – But, if the farmer is excessively avaricious? – why so much the better – the more he desires to increase his gains, the more interested is he in the good condition of those, upon whose labour his gains must principally depend.

I shall be told by the zealots of the sect of regulation, that this may be true, and may be safely committed to the convention of the farmer and the labourer, when the latter is in the prime of his youth, and at the time of his health and vigour, and in ordinary times of abundance. But in calamitous seasons, under accidental illness, in declining life, and with the pressure of a numerous off-spring, the future nourishers of the community, but the present drains and bloodsuckers of those who produce them, what is to be done? When a man cannot live and maintain his family by the natural hire of his labour, ought it not to be raised by authority?

On this head I must be allowed to submit, what my opinions have ever been; and somewhat at large.

And, first, I premise that labour is, as I have already intimated, a commodity, and, as such, an article of trade. If I am right in this notion, then labour must be subject to all the laws and principles of trade, and not to regulations foreign to them, and that may be totally inconsistent with those principles and those laws. When any commodity is carried to market, it is not the necessity of the vender, but the necessity of the purchaser, that raises the price. The extreme want of the seller has rather (by the nature of things with which we shall in vain contend) the direct contrary operation. If the goods at market are beyond the demand, they fall in their value; if below it, they rise. The impossibility of the subsistence of a man, who carries his labour to a market, is totally beside the question in this way of viewing it. The only question is, what is it worth to the buyer?

But if authority comes in and forces the buyer to a price, what is this in the case (say) of a farmer who buys the labour of ten or twelve labouring men, and three or four handy-crafts, what is it, but to make an arbitrary division of his property among them?

The whole of his gains, I say it with the most certain conviction, never do amount anything like in value to what he pays to his labourers and artificers; so that a very small advance upon what *one* man pays to *many* may absorb the whole of what he possesses, and amount to an actual partition of all his substance among them. A perfect equality will indeed be produced; – that is to say, equal want, equal wretchedness, equal beggary, and on the part of the petitioners, a woeful, helpless, and desperate disappointment. Such is the event of all compulsory equalisations. They pull down what is above. They never raise what is below: and they depress high and low together beneath the level of what was originally the lowest.

If a commodity is raised by authority above what it will yield with a profit to the buyer, that commodity will be the less dealt in. If a second blundering interposition be used to correct the blunder of the first, and an attempt is made to force the purchase of the commodity, (of labour for instance,) the one of these two things must happen, either that the forced buyer is ruined, or the price of the product of the labour, in that proportion, is raised. Then the wheel turns round, and the evil complained of falls with aggravated weight on the complainant. The price of corn, which is the result of the expense of all the operations of husbandry taken together, and for some time continued, will rise on the labourer, considered as a consumer. The very best will be, that he remains where he was. But if the price of the corn should not compensate the price of labour, what is far more to be feared, the most serious evil, the very destruction of agriculture itself, is to be apprehended.

Nothing is such an enemy to accuracy of judgment as a coarse discrimination; a want of such classification and distribution as the subject admits of. Increase the rate of wages to the labourer, say the regulators – as if labour was but one thing, and of one value. But this very broad, generic term, *labour*, admits, at least, of two or three specific descriptions: and these will suffice, at least, to let gentlemen discern a little the necessity of proceeding with caution in their coercive guidance of those, whose existence depends upon the observance of still nicer distinctions and sub-divisions, than commonly they resort to in forming their judgments on this very enlarged part of economy.

The labourers in husbandry may be divided: 1st, into those who are able to perform the full work of a man; that is, what can be done by a person from twenty-one years of age to fifty. I know no husbandry work (mowing hardly excepted) that is not equally within the power of all persons within those ages, the more advanced fully compensating by knack and habit what they lose in activity. Unquestionably, there is a good deal of difference between the value of one man's labour and that of another, from strength, dexterity, and honest application. But I am quite sure, from my best observation, that any given five men will, in their total, afford a proportion of labour equal to any other five within the periods of life I have stated; that is, that among such five men there will be one possessing all the qualifications of a good workman, one bad, and the other three middling, and approximating to the first and the last. So that in so small a platoon as that of even five, you will find the full complement of all that five men *can* earn. Taking five and five throughout the kingdom, they are equal: therefore, an error with regard to the equalisation of their wages by those who employ five, as farmers do at the very least, cannot be considerable.

2dly, Those who are able to work, but not the complete task of a day-labourer. This class is infinitely diversified, but will aptly enough fall into principal divisions. *Men*, from the decline, which after fifty becomes every year more sensible, to the period of debility and decrepitude, and the maladies that precede a final dissolution. *Women*, whose employment on husbandry is but occasional, and who differ more in effective labour one from another, than men do, on account of gestation, nursing, and domestic management, over and above the difference they have in common with men in advancing, in stationary, and in declining life. *Children*, who proceed on the reverse order, growing from less to greater utility, but with a still greater disproportion of nutriment to labour than is found in the second of these sub-divisions; as is visible to those who will give themselves the trouble of examining into the interior economy of a poor-house.

This inferior classification is introduced to show, that laws prescribing, or magistrates exercising, a very stiff and often inapplicable rule, or a blind and rash discretion, never can provide the just proportions between earning and salary on the one hand, and nutriment on the other: whereas interest, habit, and the tacit convention, that arise from a thousand nameless circumstances, produce a *tact* that regulates without difficulty, what laws and magistrates cannot regulate at all. The first class of labour wants nothing to equalise it; it equalises itself. The second and third are not capable of any equalisation.

But what if the rate of hire to the labourer comes far short of his necessary subsistence, and the calamity of the time is so great as to threaten actual famine? Is the poor labourer to be abandoned to the flinty heart and griping hand of base self-interest, supported by the sword of law, especially when there is reason to suppose that the very avarice of farmers themselves has concurred with the errors of government to bring famine on the land?

In that case, my opinion is this: Whenever it happens that a man can claim nothing according to the rules of commerce and the principles of justice, he passes out of that department, and comes within the jurisdiction of mercy. In that province the magistrate has nothing at all to do: his interference is a violation of the property which it is his office to protect. Without all doubt, charity to the poor is a direct and obligatory duty upon all Christians, next in order after the payment of debts, full as strong, and by nature made infinitely more delightful to us. Puffendorff,[4] and other casuists, do not, I think, denominate it quite properly, when they call it a duty of imperfect obligation.

But the manner, mode, time, choice of objects, and proportion, are left to private discretion; and, perhaps, for that very reason it is performed with the greater satisfaction, because the discharge of it has more the appearance of freedom; recommending us besides very specially to the Divine favour, as the exercise of a virtue most suitable to a being sensible of its own infirmity.

The cry of the people in cities and towns, though unfortunately (from a fear of their multitude and combination) the most regarded, ought, in *fact*, to be the *least* attended to upon this subject; for citizens are in a state of utter ignorance of the means by which they are to be fed, and they contribute little or nothing, except in an infinitely circuitous manner, to their own maintenance. They are truly, "*Fruges consumere nati.*"[5] They are to be heard with great respect and attention upon matters within their province, that is, on trades and manufactures; but on anything that relates to agriculture, they are to be listened to with the same *reverence* which we pay to the dogmas of other ignorant and presumptuous men.

If any one were to tell them, that they were to give in an account of all the stock in their shops; that attempts would be made to limit their profits, or raise the price of the labouring manufacturers upon them, or recommend to government, out of a capital from the public revenues, to set up a shop of the same commodities, in order to rival them, and keep them to reasonable dealing, they would very soon see the impudence, injustice, and oppression of such a course. They would not be mistaken; but they are of opinion, that agriculture is to be subject to other laws, and to be governed by other principles.

A greater and more ruinous mistake cannot be fallen into, than that the trades of agriculture and grazing can be conducted upon any other than the common principles of commerce; namely, that the producer should be permitted, and even expected, to look to all possible profit, which, without fraud or violence, he can make; to turn plenty or scarcity to the best advantage he can; to keep back or to bring forward his commodities at his pleasure; to account to no one for his stock or for his gain.[6] On any other terms he is the slave of the consumer; and that he should be so is of no benefit to the consumer. No slave was ever so beneficial to the master, as a freeman that deals with him on an equal footing by convention, formed on the rules and principles of contending interests and compromised advantages. The consumer, if he were suffered, would in the end always be the dupe of his own tyranny and injustice. The landed gentleman is never to forget, that the farmer is his representative.

It is a perilous thing to try experiments on the farmer. The farmer's capital (except in a few persons, and in a very few places) is far more feeble than commonly is imagined. The trade is a very poor trade; it is subject to great risks and losses. The capital, such as it is, is turned but once in the year; in some branches it requires three years before the money is paid. I believe never less than three in the turnip and grass land course, which is the prevalent course on the more or less fertile, sandy and gravelly loams, and these compose the soil in the south and south-east of England, the best adapted, and perhaps the only ones that are adapted, to the turnip husbandry.

It is very rare that the most prosperous farmer, counting the value of his quick and dead stock, the interest of the money he turns, together with his own wages as a bailiff or overseer, ever does make 12 or 15 *per centum* by the year on his capital. I speak of the prosperous. In most of the parts of England which have fallen within my observation, I have rarely known a farmer who to his own trade has not added some other employment or traffic, that, after a course of the most unremitting parsimony and labour, (such for the greater part is theirs,) and persevering in his business for a long course of years, died worth more than paid his debts, leaving his posterity to continue in nearly the same equal conflict between industry and want, in which the last predecessor, and a long line of predecessors before him, lived and died.

Observe that I speak of the generality of farmers, who have not more than from one hundred and fifty to three or four hundred acres. There are few in this part of the country within the former, or much beyond the latter extent. Unquestionably in other places there are much larger. But, I am convinced, whatever part of England be the theatre of his operations, a farmer, who cultivates twelve hundred acres, which I consider as a large farm, though I know there are larger, cannot proceed, with any degree of safety and effect, with a smaller capital than ten thousand pounds: and that he cannot, in the ordinary course of culture, make more upon that great capital of ten thousand pounds, than twelve hundred a year.

As to the weaker capitals, an easy judgment may be formed by what very small errors they may be further attenuated, enervated, rendered unproductive, and perhaps totally destroyed.

This constant precariousness, and ultimately moderate limits of a farmer's fortune, on the strongest capital, I press, not only on account of the hazardous speculations of the times, but because the excellent and most useful works of my friend, Mr. Arthur Young,[7] tend to propagate that error, (such I am very certain it is,) of the largeness of a farmer's profits. It is not that his account of the produce does often greatly exceed, but he by no means makes the proper allowance for accidents and losses. I might enter into a convincing detail, if other more troublesome and more necessary details were not before me.

This proposed discretionary tax on labour militates with the recommendations of the board of agriculture: they recommend a general use of the drill culture. I agree with the board, that where the soil is not excessively heavy, or encumbered with large loose stones, (which however is the case with much otherwise good land,) that course is the best, and most productive; provided that the most accurate eye, the most vigilant superintendence, the most prompt activity, which has no such day as to-morrow in its calendar, the most steady foresight and pre-disposing order to have everybody and everything ready in its place, and prepared to take advantage of the fortunate, fugitive moment, in this coquetting climate of ours – provided, I say, all these combine to speed the plough, I admit its superiority over the old and general methods. But under procrastinating, improvident, ordinary husbandmen, who may neglect or let slip the few opportunities of sweetening and purifying their ground with perpetually renovated toil, and undissipated attention, nothing, when tried to any extent, can be worse, or more dangerous: the farm may be ruined, instead of having the soil enriched and sweetened by it.

But the excellence of the method on a proper soil, and conducted by husbandmen, of whom there are few, being readily granted, how, and on what conditions, is this culture obtained? Why, by a very great increase of labour; by an augmentation of the third part, at least, of the hand-labour, to say nothing of the horses and machinery employed in ordinary tillage. Now, every man must be sensible how little becoming the gravity of legislature it is to encourage a board which recommends to us, and upon very weighty reasons unquestionably, an enlargement of the capital we employ in the operations of the hand, and then to pass an act, which taxes that manual labour, already at a very high rate; thus compelling us to diminish the quantity of labour which in the vulgar course we actually employ.

What is true of the farmer is equally true of the middle man; whether the middle man acts as factor, jobber, salesman, or speculator, in the markets of grain. These traders are to be left to their free course; and the more they make, and the richer they are, and the more largely they deal, the better both for the farmer and consumer, between whom they form a natural and most useful link of connexion; though, by the machinations of the old evil counsellor, *Envy*, they are hated and maligned by both parties.

I hear that middle men are accused of monopoly. Without question, the monopoly of authority is, in every instance and in every degree, an evil; but the monopoly of capital is the contrary. It is a great benefit, and a benefit particularly to the poor. A tradesman who has but an hundred pounds capital, which (say) he can turn but once a year, cannot live upon a *profit* of 10 *per cent* because he cannot live upon ten pounds a year; but a man of ten thousand pounds capital can live and thrive upon 5 *per cent* profit in the year, because he has five hundred pounds a year. The same proportion holds in turning it twice or thrice. These principles are plain and simple; and it is not our ignorance, so much as the levity, the envy, and the malignity of our nature, that hinders us from perceiving and yielding to them: but we are not to suffer our vices to usurp the place of our judgment.

The balance between consumption and production makes price. The market settles, and alone can settle, that price. Market is the meeting and conference of the *consumer* and *producer*, when they mutually discover each other's wants. Nobody, I believe, has observed with any reflection what market is, without being astonished at the truth, the correctness, the celerity, the general equity, with which the balance of wants is settled. They, who wish the destruction of that balance, and would fain by arbitrary regulation decree, that defective production should not be compensated by increased price, directly lay their *axe* to the root of production itself.

They may, even in one year of such false policy, do mischiefs incalculable; because the trade of a farmer is, as I have before explained, one of the most precarious in its advantages, the most liable to losses, and the least profitable of any that is carried on.

It requires ten times more labour, of vigilance, of attention, of skill, and, let me add, of good fortune also, to carry on the business of a farmer with success, than what belongs to any other trade. Seeing things in this light, I am far from presuming to censure the late circular instruction of council to lord-lieutenants – but I confess I do not clearly discern its object.[8] I am greatly afraid that the inquiry will raise some alarm as a measure, leading to the French system of putting corn into requisition. For that was preceded by an inquisition somewhat similar in its principle, though, according to their mode, their principles are full of that violence, *which here* is not much to be feared. It goes on a principle directly opposite to mine: it presumes, that the market is no fair *test* of plenty or scarcity. It raises a suspicion, which may affect the tranquillity of the public mind, "that the farmer keeps back, and takes unfair advantages by delay;" on the part of the dealer, it gives rise obviously to a thousand nefarious speculations.

In case the return should on the whole prove favourable, is it meant to ground a measure for encouraging exportation and checking the import of corn? If it is not, what end can it answer? And, I believe, it is not.

This opinion may be fortified by a report gone abroad, that intentions are entertained of erecting public granaries, and that this inquiry is to give government an advantage in its purchases.

I hear that such a measure has been proposed, and is under deliberation; that is, for government to set up a granary in every market town, at the expense of the state, in order to extinguish the dealer, and to subject the farmer to the consumer, by securing corn to the latter at a certain and steady price.[9]

If such a scheme is adopted, I should not like to answer for the safety of the granary, of the agents, or of the town itself, in which the granary was erected – the first storm of popular phrensy would fall upon that granary.

So far in a political light.

In an economical light, I must observe, that the construction of such granaries throughout the kingdom would be at an expense beyond all calculation. The keeping them up would be at a great charge. The management and attendance would require an army of agents, storekeepers, clerks, and servants. The capital to be employed in the purchase of grain would be enormous. The waste, decay, and corruption, would be a dreadful drawback on the whole dealing; and the dissatisfaction of the people, at having decayed, tainted, or corrupted corn sold to them, as must be the case, would be serious.

This climate (whatever others may be) is not favourable to granaries, where wheat is to be kept for any time. The best, and indeed the only good granary, is the rick yard of the farmer, where the corn is preserved in its own straw, sweet, clean, wholesome, free from vermin and from insects, and comparatively at a trifle of expense. This, and the barn, enjoying many of the same advantages, have been the sole granaries of England from the foundation of its agriculture to this day. All this is done at the expense of the undertaker, and at his sole risk. He contributes to government, he receives nothing from it but protection, and to this he has a *claim*.

The moment that government appears at market, all the principles of market will be subverted. I don't know whether the farmer will suffer by it as long as there is a tolerable market of competition; but I am sure that, in the first place, the trading government will speedily become a bankrupt, and the consumer in the end will suffer. If government makes all its purchases at once it will instantly raise the market upon itself. If it makes them by degrees, it must follow the course of the market. If it follows the course of the market, it will produce no effect, and the consumer may as well buy as he wants – therefore all the expense is incurred gratis.

But if the object of this scheme should be, what I suspect it is, to destroy the dealer, commonly called the middle man, and by incurring a voluntary loss to carry the baker to deal with government, I am to tell them that they must set up another trade, that of a miller or a mealman, attended with a new train of expenses and risks. If in both these trades they should succeed, so as to exclude those who trade on natural and private capitals, then they will have a monopoly in their hands, which, under the appearance of a monopoly of capital, will, in reality, be a monopoly of authority, and will ruin whatever it touches. The agriculture of the kingdom cannot stand before it.

A little place like Geneva, of not more than from twenty-five to thirty thousand inhabitants, which has no territory, or next to none; which depends for its existence on the good-will of three neighbouring powers, and is of course continually in a state of something like a *siege*, or in the speculation of it, might find some resource in state granaries, and some revenue from the monopoly of what was sold to the keepers of public-houses. This is a policy for a state too small for agriculture. It is not (for instance) fit for so great a country as the Pope possesses, where, however, it is adopted and pursued in a greater extent, and with more strictness. Certain of the Pope's territories, from whence the city of Rome is supplied, being obliged to furnish Rome and the granaries of his Holiness with corn at a certain price, that part of the papal territories is utterly ruined. That ruin may be traced with certainty to this sole cause, and it appears indubitably by a comparison of their state and condition with that of the other part of the ecclesiastical dominions not subjected to the same regulations, which are in circumstances highly flourishing.

The reformation of this evil system is in a manner impracticable; for, first, it does keep bread and all other provisions equally subject to the chamber of supply, at a pretty reasonable and regular price, in the city of Rome. This preserves quiet among the numerous poor, idle, and naturally mutinous people of a very great capital. But the quiet of the town is purchased by the ruin of the country, and the ultimate wretchedness of both. The next cause which renders this evil incurable, is, the jobs which have grown out of it, and which, in spite of all precautions, would grow out of such things, even under governments far more potent than the feeble authority of the Pope.

This example of Rome, which has been derived from the most ancient times, and the most flourishing period of the Roman empire, (but not of the Roman agriculture,) may serve as a great caution to all governments, not to attempt to feed the people out of the hands of the magistrates. If once they are habituated to it, though but for one half year, they will never be satisfied to have it otherwise. And having looked to government for bread, on the very first scarcity they will turn and bite the hand that fed them. To avoid that evil, government will redouble the causes of it; and then it will become inveterate and incurable.

I beseech the government (which I take in the largest sense of the word, comprehending the two Houses of parliament) seriously to consider that years of scarcity or plenty do not come alternately, or at short intervals, but in pretty long cycles and irregularly, and consequently that we cannot assure ourselves, if we take a wrong measure, from the temporary necessities of one season; but that the next, and probably more, will drive us to the continuance of it; so that, in my opinion, there is no way of preventing this evil, which goes to the destruction of all our agriculture, and of that part of our internal commerce which touches our agriculture the most nearly, as well as the safety and very being of government, but manfully to resist the very first idea, speculative or practical, that it is within the competence of government, taken as government, or even of the rich, as rich, to supply to the poor those necessaries which it has pleased the Divine Providence for a while to withhold from them. We, the people, ought to be made sensible, that it is not in breaking the laws of commerce, which are the laws of nature, and consequently the laws of God, that we are to place our hope of softening the Divine displeasure to remove any calamity under which we suffer, or which hangs over us.

So far as to the principles of general policy.

As to the state of things which is urged as a reason to deviate from them, these are the circumstances of the harvest of 1794 and 1795. With regard to the harvest of 1794, in relation to the noblest grain – wheat, it is allowed to have been somewhat short, but not excessively; and, in quality, for the seven-and-twenty years, during which I have been a farmer, I never remember wheat to have been so good. The world were, however, deceived in their speculations upon it – the farmer as well as the dealer. Accordingly the price fluctuated beyond anything I can remember; for, at one time of the year, I sold my wheat at £14 a load, (I sold off all I had, as I thought this was a reasonable price,) when at the end of the season, if I had then had any to sell, I might have got thirty guineas for the same sort of grain. I sold all that I had, as I said, at a comparatively low price, because I thought it a good price, compared with what I thought the general produce of the harvest; but when I came to consider what my own *total* was, I found that the quantity had not answered my expectation. It must be remembered, that this year of produce, (the year 1794,) short, but excellent, followed a year which was not extraordinary in production, nor of a superior quality, and left but little in store. At first this was not felt, because the harvest came in unusually early – earlier than common, by a full month.

The winter, at the end of 1794, and beginning of 1795, was more than usually unfavourable both to corn and grass, owing to the sudden relaxation of very rigorous frosts, followed by rains, which were again rapidly succeeded by frosts of still greater rigour than the first.

Much wheat was utterly destroyed. The clover grass suffered in many places. What I never observed before, the rye-grass, or coarse bent, suffered more than the clover. Even the meadow-grass in some places was killed to the very roots. In the spring, appearances were better than we expected. All the early sown grain recovered itself, and came up with great vigour; but that which was late sown, was feeble, and did not promise to resist any blights in the spring, which, however, with all its unpleasant vicissitudes, passed off very well; and nothing looked better than the wheat at the time of blooming: – but at the most critical time of all, a cold, dry east wind, attended with very sharp frosts, longer and stronger than I recollect at that time of year, destroyed the flowers, and withered up, in an astonishing manner, the whole side of the ear next to the wind. At that time I brought to town some of the ears, for the purpose of showing to my friends the operation of those unnatural frosts, and according to their extent I predicted a great scarcity. But such is the pleasure of agreeable prospects, that my opinion was little regarded.

On threshing, I found things as I expected – the ears not filled, some of the capsules quite empty, and several others containing only withered, hungry grain, inferior to the appearance of rye. My best ears and grains were not fine; never had I grain of so low a quality – yet I sold one load for £21. At the same time I bought my seed wheat (it was excellent) at £23. Since then the price has risen, and I have sold about two loads of the same sort at £23. Such was the state of the market when I left home last Monday. Little remains in my barn. I hope some in the rick may be better; since it was earlier sown, as well as I can recollect. Some of my neighbours have better, some quite as bad, or even worse. I suspect it will be found, that, wherever the blighting wind and those frosts at blooming time have prevailed, the produce of the wheat crop will turn out very indifferent. Those parts which have escaped will, I can hardly doubt, have a reasonable produce.

As to the other grains, it is to be observed, as the wheat ripened very late, (on account, I conceive, of the blights,) the barley got the start of it, and was ripe first. The crop was with me, and wherever my inquiry could reach, excellent; in some places far superior to mine.

The clover, which came up with the barley, was the finest I remember to have seen.

The turnips of this year are generally good.

The clover sown last year, where not totally destroyed, gave two good crops, or one crop and a plentiful feed; and bating the loss of the rye-grass, I do not remember a better produce.

The meadow-grass yielded but a middling crop, and neither of the sown or natural grass was there in any farmer's possession any remainder from the year worth taking into account. In most places, there was none at all.

Oats with me were not in a quantity more considerable than in commonly good seasons; but I have never known them heavier than they were in other places. The oat was not only a heavy but an uncommonly abundant crop. My ground under pease did not exceed an acre, or thereabouts, but the crop was great indeed. I believe it is throughout the country exuberant.

It is however to be remarked, as generally of all the grains, so particularly of the pease, that there was not the smallest quantity in reserve.

The demand of the year must depend solely on its own produce; and the price of the spring-corn is not to be expected to fall very soon, or at any time very low.

Uxbridge is a great corn market. As I came through that town, I found that, at the last market-day, barley was at forty shillings a quarter; oats there were literally none; and the innkeeper was obliged to send for them to London. I forgot to ask about pease. Potatoes were 5s. the bushel.

In the debate on this subject in the House, I am told that a leading member of great ability,[10] *little conversant in these matters*, observed, that the general uniform dearness of butcher's meat, butter, and cheese, could not be owing to a defective produce of wheat; and on this ground insinuated a suspicion of some unfair practice on the subject, that called for inquiry.

Unquestionably the mere deficiency of wheat could not cause the dearness of the other articles, which extends not only to the provisions he mentioned, but to every other without exception.

The cause is indeed so very plain and obvious, that the wonder is the other way. When a properly directed inquiry is made, the gentlemen who are amazed at the price of these commodities will find, that when hay is at six pounds a load, as they must know it is, herbage, and for more than one year, must be scanty, and

they will conclude, that if grass be scarce, beef, veal, mutton, butter, milk, and cheese, *must* be dear.

But to take up the matter somewhat more in detail – if the
wheat harvest in 1794, excellent in quality, was defective in
quantity, the barley harvest was in quality ordinary enough, and
in quantity deficient. This was soon felt in the price of malt.

Another article of produce (beans) was not at all plentiful. The
crop of pease was wholly destroyed, so that several farmers pretty
early gave up all hopes on that head, and cut the green haulm as
fodder for the cattle, then perishing for want of food in that dry
and burning summer. I myself came off better than most – I had
about the fourth of a crop of pease.

It will be recollected, that, in a manner, all the bacon and pork
consumed in this country (the far largest consumption of meat
out of towns) is, when growing, fed on grass, and on whey, or
skimmed milk; and when fatting, partly on the latter. This is the
case in the dairy countries, all of them great breeders and feeders
of swine; but for the much greater part, and in all the corn countries, they are fattened on beans, barley meal, and pease. When
the food of the animal is scarce, his flesh must be dear. This, one
would suppose, would require no great penetration to discover.

This failure of so very large a supply of flesh in one species,
naturally throws the whole demand of the consumer on the
diminished supply of all kinds of flesh, and, indeed, on all the
matters of human sustenance. Nor, in my opinion, are we to
expect a greater cheapness in that article for this year, even
though corn should grow cheaper, as it is to be hoped it will.
The store swine, from the failure of subsistence last year, are now
at an extravagant price. Pigs, at our fairs, have sold lately for fifty
shillings, which, two years ago, would not have brought more
than twenty.

As to sheep, none, I thought, were strangers to the general
failure of the article of turnips last year; the early having been
burned, as they came up, by the great drought and heat; the late,
and those of the early which had escaped, were destroyed by the
chilling frosts of the winter, and the wet and severe weather of
the spring. In many places a full fourth of the sheep or the lambs
were lost; what remained of the lambs were poor and ill-fed, the
ewes having had no milk. The calves came late, and they were
generally an article, the want of which was as much to be dreaded
as any other. So that article of food, formerly so abundant in the

early part of the summer, particularly in London, and which in a great part supplied the place of mutton for nearly two months, did little less than totally fail.

All the productions of the earth link in with each other. All the sources of plenty, in all and every article, were dried or frozen up. The scarcity was not, as gentlemen seem to suppose, in wheat only.

Another cause, and that not of inconsiderable operation, tended to produce a scarcity in flesh provision. It is one that on many accounts cannot be too much regretted, and the rather, as it was the sole *cause* of a scarcity in that article, which arose from the proceedings of men themselves. I mean the stop put to the distillery.[11]

The hogs (and that would be sufficient) which were fed with the waste wash of that produce, did not demand the fourth part of the corn used by farmers in fattening them. The spirit was nearly so much clear gain to the nation. It is an odd way of making flesh cheap, to stop or check the distillery.

The distillery in itself produces an immense article of trade almost all over the world, to Africa, to North America, and to various parts of Europe. It is of great use, next to food itself, to our fisheries and to our whole navigation. A great part of the distillery was carried on by damaged corn, unfit for bread, and by barley and malt of the lowest quality. These things could not be more unexceptionably employed. The domestic consumption of spirits produced, without complaints, a very great revenue, applicable, if we pleased, in bounties to the bringing corn from other places, far beyond the value of that consumed in making it, or to the encouragement of its increased production at home.

As to what is said, in a physical and moral view, against the home consumption of spirits, experience has long since taught me very little to respect the declamations on that subject – Whether the thunder of the laws, or the thunder of eloquence, "is hurled on *gin*," always I am thunder proof. The alembic, in my mind, has furnished to the world a far greater benefit and blessing, than if the *opus maximum*[12] had been really found by chemistry, and, like Midas, we could turn everything into gold.

Undoubtedly there may be a dangerous abuse in the excess of spirits; and at one time I am ready to believe the abuse was great. When spirits are cheap, the business of drunkenness is achieved with little time or labour; but that evil I consider to be wholly done away. Observation for the last forty years, and very particularly for the last thirty, has furnished me with ten instances of drunkenness from other causes, for one from this. Ardent spirit is a great medicine, often to remove distempers – much more frequently to prevent them, or to chase them away in their beginnings. It is not nutritive in *any great* degree. But, if not food, it greatly alleviates the want of it. It invigorates the stomach for the digestion of poor meagre diet, not easily alliable to the human constitution. Wine the poor cannot touch. Beer, as applied to many occasions, (as among seamen and fishermen for instance,) will by no means do the business. Let me add, what wits inspired with champaign and claret will turn into ridicule – it is a medicine for the mind. Under the pressure of the cares and sorrows of our mortal condition, men have at all times, and in all countries, called in some physical aid to their moral consolations, – wine, beer, opium, brandy, or tobacco.

I consider therefore the stopping of the distillery, economically, financially, commercially, medicinally, and, in some degree, morally too, as a measure rather well meant than well considered. It is too precious a sacrifice to prejudice.

Gentlemen well know whether there be a scarcity of partridges, and whether that be an effect of hoarding and combination. All the tame race of birds live and die as the wild do.

As to the lesser articles, they are like the greater. They have followed the fortune of the season. Why are fowls dear? was not this the farmer's or jobber's fault? I sold from my yard to a jobber, six young and lean fowls, for four and twenty shillings; fowls, for which, two years ago, the same man would not have given a shilling apiece. – He sold them afterwards at Uxbridge, and they were taken to London to receive the last hand.

As to the operation of the war in causing the scarcity of provisions, I understand that Mr. Pitt has given a particular answer to it – but I do not think it worth powder and shot.

I do not wonder the papers are so full of this sort of matter, but I am a little surprised it should be mentioned in parliament. Like all great state questions, peace and war may be discussed, and different opinions fairly formed, on political grounds, but on a question of the present price of provisions, when peace with the regicides is always uppermost, I can only say that great is the love of it.

After all, have we not reason to be thankful to the Giver of all good? In our history, and when the "labourer of England is said to have been once happy," we find constantly, after certain intervals, a period of real famine; by which a melancholy havoc was made among the human race. The price of provisions fluctuated dreadfully, demonstrating a deficiency very different from the worst failures of the present moment. Never, since I have known England, have I known more than a comparative scarcity. The price of wheat, taking a number of years together, has had no very considerable fluctuation, nor has it risen exceedingly until within this twelvemonth. Even now, I do not know of one man, woman, or child, that has perished from famine;[13] fewer, if any, I believe, than in years of plenty, when such a thing may happen by accident. This is owing to a care and superintendence of the poor, far greater than any I remember.

The consideration of this ought to bind us all, rich and poor together, against those wicked writers of the newspapers, who would inflame the poor against their friends, guardians, patrons, and protectors. Not only very few (I have observed that I know of none, though I live in a place as poor as most) have actually died of want, but we have seen no traces of those dreadful exterminating epidemics, which, in consequence of scanty and unwholesome food, in former times, not unfrequently wasted whole nations. Let us be saved from too much wisdom of our own, and we shall do tolerably well.

It is one of the finest problems in legislation, and what has often engaged my thoughts whilst I followed that profession, "What the state ought to take upon itself to direct by the public wisdom, and what it ought to leave, with as little interference as possible, to individual discretion." Nothing, certainly, can be laid down on the subject that will not admit of exceptions, many permanent, some occasional. But the clearest line of distinction, which I could draw, whilst I had my chalk to draw any line, was this; that the state ought to confine itself to what regards the state, or the creatures of the state, namely, the exterior establishment of its religion; its magistracy; its revenue; its military force by sea and land; the corporations that owe their existence to its fiat; in a word, to everything that is *truly and properly* public, to the public peace, to the public safety, to the public order, to the public prosperity. In its preventive police it ought to be sparing of its efforts, and to employ means, rather few, unfrequent, and strong, than

many, and frequent, and, of course, as they multiply their puny
politic race, and dwindle, small and feeble. Statesmen who know
themselves will, with the dignity which belongs to wisdom, proceed only in this the superior orb and first mover of their duty
steadily, vigilantly, severely, courageously: whatever remains
will, in a manner, provide for itself. But as they descend from the
state to a province, from a province to a parish, and from a parish
to a private house, they go on accelerated in their fall. They
cannot do the lower duty; and, in proportion as they try it, they
will certainly fail in the higher. They ought to know the different
departments of things; what belongs to laws, and what manners
alone can regulate. To these, great politicians may give a leaning,
but they cannot give a law.

Our legislature has fallen into this fault as well as other governments; all have fallen into it more or less. The once mighty state,
which was nearest to us locally,[14] nearest to us in every way, and
whose ruins threaten to fall upon our heads, is a strong instance
of this error. I can never quote France without a foreboding sigh
– ΕΣΕΤΑΙ 'ΗΜΑΡ![15] Scipio[16] said it to his recording Greek
friend amidst the flames of the great rival of his country. That
state has fallen by the hands of the parricides of their country,
called the revolutionists, and constitutionalists, of France, a
species of traitors, of whose fury and atrocious wickedness nothing in the annals of the phrensy and depravation of mankind had
before furnished an example, and of whom I can never think or
speak without a mixed sensation of disgust, of horror, and of
detestation, not easy to be expressed. These nefarious monsters
destroyed their country for what was good in it: for much good
there was in the constitution of that noble monarchy, which, in
all kinds, formed and nourished great men, and great patterns of
virtue to the world. But though its enemies were not enemies to
its faults, its faults furnished them with means for its destruction.
My dear departed friend, whose loss is even greater to the public
than to me, had often remarked, that the leading vice of the
French monarchy, (which he had well studied,) was in good
intention ill-directed, and a restless desire of governing too
much. The hand of authority was seen in everything, and in
every place. All, therefore, that happened amiss in the course
even of domestic affairs, was attributed to the government; and
as it always happens in this kind of officious universal interference, what began in odious power, ended always, I may say

without an exception, in contemptible imbecility. For this reason, as far as I can approve of any novelty, I thought well of the provincial administrations. Those, if the superior power had been severe, and vigilant, and vigorous, might have been of much use politically in removing government from many invidious details. But as everything is good or bad, as it is related or combined, government being relaxed above as it was relaxed below, and the brains of the people growing more and more addle with every sort of visionary speculation, the shiftings of the scene in the provincial theatres became only preparatives to a revolution in the kingdom, and the popular actings there only the rehearsals of the terrible drama of the republic.

Tyranny and cruelty may make men justly wish the downfall of abused powers, but I believe that no government ever yet perished from any other direct cause than its own weakness. My opinion is against an over-doing of any sort of administration, and more especially against this most momentous of all meddling on the part of authority; the meddling with the subsistence of the people.

From FIRST LETTER ON
A REGICIDE PEACE[1]

1796

MY DEAR SIR,

OUR LAST CONVERSATION, though not in the tone of absolute
despondency, was far from cheerful. We could not easily account
for some unpleasant appearances. They were represented to us as
indicating the state of the popular mind; and they were not at all
what we should have expected from our old ideas even of the
faults and vices of the English character. The disastrous events,
which have followed one upon another in a long, unbroken,
funereal train; moving in a procession that seemed to have no
end, – these were not the principal causes of our dejection. We
feared more from what threatened to fail within, than what menaced to oppress us from abroad. To a people who have once been
proud and great, and great because they were proud, a change in
the national spirit is the most terrible of all revolutions.

I shall not live to behold the unravelling of the intricate plot,
which saddens and perplexes the awful drama of Providence,
now acting on the moral theatre of the world. Whether for
thought or for action, I am at the end of my career. You are in
the middle of yours. In what part of its orbit the nation, with
which we are carried along, moves at this instant, it is not easy
to conjecture. It may, perhaps, be far advanced in its aphelion. –
But when to return.

Not to lose ourselves in the infinite void of the conjectural
world, our business is with what is likely to be affected, for the
better or the worse, by the wisdom or weakness of our plans.
In all speculations upon men and human affairs, it is of no small
moment to distinguish things of accident from permanent
causes, and from effects that cannot be altered. It is not every
irregularity in our movement that is a total deviation from our
course. I am not quite of the mind of those speculators, who seem
assured, that necessarily, and by the constitution of things, all
states have the same periods of infancy, manhood, and decrepitude, that are found in the individuals who compose them.
Parallels of this sort rather furnish similitudes to illustrate or to
adorn, than supply analogies from whence to reason. The objects

which are attempted to be forced into an analogy are not found in the same classes of existence. Individuals are physical beings subject to laws universal and invariable. The immediate cause acting in these laws may be obscure; the general results are subjects of certain calculation. But commonwealths are not physical but moral essences. They are artificial combinations, and, in their proximate efficient cause, the arbitrary productions of the human mind. We are not yet acquainted with the laws which necessarily influence the stability of that kind of work made by that kind of agent. There is not in the physical order (with which they do not appear to hold any assignable connexion) a distinct cause by which any of those fabrics must necessarily grow, flourish, or decay; nor, in my opinion, does the moral world produce anything more determinate on that subject, than what may serve as an amusement (liberal indeed, and ingenious, but still only an amusement) for speculative men. I doubt whether the history of mankind is yet complete enough, if ever it can be so, to furnish grounds for a sure theory on the internal causes which necessarily affect the fortune of a state. I am far from denying the operation of such causes: but they are infinitely uncertain, and much more obscure, and much more difficult to trace, than the foreign causes that tend to raise, to depress, and sometimes to overwhelm a community.

It is often impossible, in these political inquiries, to find any proportion between the apparent force of any moral causes we may assign and their known operation. We are therefore obliged to deliver up that operation to mere chance, or, more piously, (perhaps more rationally,) to the occasional interposition and irresistible hand of the Great Disposer. We have seen states of considerable duration, which for ages have remained nearly as they have begun, and could hardly be said to ebb or flow. Some appear to have spent their vigour at their commencement. Some have blazed out in their glory a little before their extinction. The meridian of some has been the most splendid. Others, and they the greatest number, have fluctuated, and experienced at different periods of their existence a great variety of fortune. At the very moment when some of them seemed plunged in unfathomable abysses of disgrace and disaster, they have suddenly emerged. They have begun a new course and opened a new reckoning; and, even in the depths of their calamity, and on the very ruins of their country, have laid the foundations of a towering and durable greatness. All this has happened without any apparent previous change in the general circumstances which had brought on their distress. The death of a man at a critical juncture, his disgust, his retreat, his disgrace, have brought innumerable calamities on a whole nation. A common soldier, a child, a girl at the door of an inn, have changed the face of fortune, and almost of nature.

Such, and often influenced by such causes, has commonly been the fate of monarchies of long duration. They have their ebbs and their flows. This has been eminently the fate of the monarchy of France. There have been times in which no power has ever been brought so low. Few have ever flourished in greater glory. By turns elevated and depressed, that power had been, on the whole, rather on the increase; and it continued not only powerful but formidable to the hour of total ruin of the monarchy. This fall of the monarchy was far from being preceded by any exterior symptoms of decline. The interior were not visible to every eye; and a thousand accidents might have prevented the operation of what the most clear-sighted were not able to discern, nor the most provident to divine. A very little time before its dreadful catastrophe, there was a kind of exterior splendour in the situation of the Crown, which usually adds to government strength and authority at home. The Crown seemed then to have obtained some of the most splendid objects of state ambition. None of the continental powers of Europe were the enemies of France. They were all, either tacitly disposed to her, or publicly connected with her; and in those who kept the most aloof there was little appearance of jealousy; of animosity there was no appearance at all. The British nation, her great preponderating rival, she had humbled; to all appearance she had weakened; certainly had endangered, by cutting off a very large, and by far the most growing, part of her empire.[2] In that its acmé of human prosperity and greatness, in the high and palmy state of the monarchy of France, it fell to the ground without a struggle. It fell without any of those vices in the monarch, which have sometimes been the causes of the fall of kingdoms, but which existed, without any visible effect on the state, in the highest degree in many other princes; and, far from destroying their power, had only left some slight stains on their character. The financial difficulties were only pretexts and instruments of those who accomplished the ruin of that monarchy. They were not the causes of it.

Deprived of the old government, deprived in a manner of all government, France fallen as a monarchy, to common speculators might have appeared more likely to be an object of pity or insult, according to the disposition of the circumjacent powers, than to be the scourge and terror of them all: but out of the tomb of the murdered monarchy in France has arisen a vast, tremendous, unformed spectre, in a far more terrific guise than any which ever yet have overpowered the imagination, and subdued the fortitude of man. Going straight forward to its end, unappalled by peril, unchecked by remorse, despising all common maxims and all common means, that hideous phantom overpowered those who could not believe it was possible she could at all exist, except on the principles, which habit rather than nature had persuaded them were necessary to their own particular welfare, and to their own ordinary modes of action. But the constitution of any political being, as well as that of any physical being, ought to be known, before one can venture to say what is fit for its conservation, or what is the proper means of its power. The poison of other states is the food of the new republic. The bankruptcy, the very apprehension of which is one of the causes assigned for the fall of the monarchy, was the capital on which she opened her traffic with the world.

The republic of regicide with an annihilated revenue, with defaced manufactures, with a ruined commerce, with an uncultivated and half-depopulated country, with a discontented, distressed, enslaved, and famished people, passing with a rapid, eccentric, incalculable course, from the wildest anarchy to the sternest despotism, has actually conquered the finest parts of Europe, has distressed, disunited, deranged, and broken to pieces all the rest; and so subdued the minds of the rulers in every nation, that hardly any resource presents itself to them, except that of entitling themselves to a contemptuous mercy by a display of their imbecility and meanness. Even in their greatest military efforts, and the greatest display of their fortitude, they seem not to hope, they do not even appear to wish, the extinction of what subsists to their certain ruin. Their ambition is only to be admitted to a more favoured class in the order of servitude under that domineering power.

This seems the temper of the day. At first the French force was too much despised. Now it is too much dreaded. As inconsiderate courage has given way to irrational fear, so it may be hoped, that, through the medium of deliberate sober apprehension, we may arrive at steady fortitude. Who knows whether indignation may not succeed to terror, and the revival of high sentiment, spurning away the delusion of a safety purchased at the expense of glory, may not yet drive us to that generous despair, which has often subdued distempers in the state for which no remedy could be found in the wisest councils?

Other great states, having been without any regular, certain course of elevation, or decline, we may hope that the British fortune may fluctuate also; because the public mind, which greatly influences that fortune, may have its changes. We are therefore never authorised to abandon our country to its fate, or to act or advise as if it had no resource. There is no reason to apprehend, because ordinary means threatened to fail, that no others can spring up. Whilst our heart is whole, it will find means, or make them. The heart of the citizen is a perennial spring of energy to the state. Because the pulse seems to intermit, we must not presume that it will cease instantly to beat. The public must never be regarded as incurable. I remember in the beginning of what has lately been called the seven years' war,[3] that an eloquent writer and ingenious speculator, Dr. Brown,[4] upon some reverses which happened in the beginning of that war, published an elaborate philosophical discourse, to prove that the distinguishing features of the people of England had been totally changed, and that a frivolous effeminacy was become the national character. Nothing could be more popular than that work. It was thought a great consolation to us, the light people of this country, (who were and are light, but who were not and are not effeminate,) that we had found the causes of our misfortunes in our vices. Pythagoras could not be more pleased with his leading discovery. But whilst in that splenetic mood we amused ourselves in a sour, critical speculation, of which we were ourselves the objects, and in which every man lost his particular sense of the public disgrace in the epidemic nature of the distemper; whilst, as in the Alps, *Goitre*[5] kept *Goitre* in countenance; whilst we were thus abandoning ourselves to a direct confession of our inferiority to France, and whilst many, very many, were ready to act upon a sense of that inferiority, a few months effected a total change in our variable minds. We emerged from the gulf of that speculative despondency; and were buoyed up to the highest point of practical vigour. Never did the masculine spirit of England display itself with more energy, nor ever did its genius soar with a prouder pre-eminence over France, than at the time when frivolity and effeminacy had been at least tacitly acknowledged as their national character, by the good people of this kingdom.

For one, (if they be properly treated,) I despair neither of the public fortune, nor the public mind. There is much to be done undoubtedly, and much to be retrieved. We must walk in new ways, or we can never encounter our enemy in his devious march. We are not at an end of our struggle, nor near it. Let us not deceive ourselves: we are at the beginning of great troubles. I readily acknowledge that the state of public affairs is infinitely more unpromising, than at the period I have just now alluded to, and the position of all the powers of Europe in relation to us, and in relation to each other, is more intricate and critical beyond all comparison. Difficult indeed is our situation. In all situations of difficulty men will be influenced in the part they take, not only by the reason of the case, but by the peculiar turn of their own character. The same ways to safety do not present themselves to all men, nor to the same men in different tempers. There is a courageous wisdom: there is also a false, reptile prudence, the result not of caution, but of fear. Under misfortunes it often happens that the nerves of the understanding are so relaxed, the pressing peril of the hour so completely confounds all the faculties, that no future danger can be properly provided for, can be justly estimated, can be so much as fully seen. The eye of the mind is dazzled and vanquished. An abject distrust of ourselves, an extravagant admiration of the enemy, present us with no hope but in a compromise with his pride, by a submission to his will. This short plan of policy is the only counsel which will obtain a hearing. We plunge into a dark gulf with all the rash precipitation of fear. The nature of courage is, without a question, to be conversant with danger: but in the palpable night of their terrors, men under consternation suppose, not that it is the danger, which, by a sure instinct, calls out the courage to resist it, but that it is the courage which produces the danger. They therefore seek for a refuge from their fears in the fears themselves, and consider a temporising meanness as the only source of safety.

The rules and definitions of prudence can rarely be exact; never universal. I do not deny, that, in small, truckling states, a timely compromise with power has often been the means, and the only means, of drawling out their puny existence: but a great state is

too much envied, too much dreaded, to find safety in humiliation. To be secure, it must be respected. Power, and eminence,
and consideration, are things not to be begged. They must be
commanded: and they, who supplicate for mercy from others, can
never hope for justice through themselves. What justice they are
to obtain, as the alms of an enemy, depends upon his character:
and that they ought well to know before they implicitly confide.

Much controversy there has been in parliament, and not a little
amongst us out of doors, about the instrumental means of this
nation towards the maintenance of her dignity, and the assertion
of her rights. On the most elaborate and correct detail of facts,
the result seems to be, that at no time has the wealth and power
of Great Britain been so considerable as it is at this very perilous
moment. We have a vast interest to preserve, and we possess great
means of preserving it: but it is to be remembered that the arti-
ficer may be encumbered by his tools, and that resources may be
among impediments. If wealth is the obedient and laborious slave
of virtue and of public honour, then wealth is in its place, and has
its use: but if this order is changed, and honour is to be sacrificed
to the conservation of riches, riches, which have neither eyes nor
hands, nor anything truly vital in them, cannot long survive the
being of their vivifying powers, their legitimate masters, and
their potent protectors. If we command our wealth, we shall be
rich and free: if our wealth commands us, we are poor indeed.
We are bought by the enemy with the treasure from our own
coffers. Too great a sense of the value of a subordinate interest
may be the very source of its danger, as well as the certain ruin
of interests of a superior order. Often has a man lost his all because
he would not submit to hazard all in defending it. A display of
our wealth before robbers is not the way to restrain their boldness,
or to lessen their rapacity. This display is made, I know, to persuade the people of England that thereby we shall awe the enemy,
and improve the terms of our capitulation: it is made, not that we
should fight with more animation, but that we should supplicate
with better hopes. We are mistaken. We have an enemy to
deal with who never regarded our contest as a measuring and
weighing of purses. He is the Gaul that puts his *sword* into the
scale. He is more tempted with our wealth as booty, than terrified
with it as power. But let us be rich or poor, let us be either in
what proportion we may, nature is false or this is true, that where
the essential public force (of which money is but a part) is in any

degree upon a par in a conflict between nations, that state, which is resolved to hazard its existence rather than to abandon its object, must have an infinite advantage over that which is resolved to yield rather than to carry its resistance beyond a certain point. Humanly speaking, that people which bounds its efforts only with its being, must give the law to that nation which will not push its opposition beyond its convenience.

If we look to nothing but our domestic condition, the state of the nation is full even to plethory: but if we imagine that this country can long maintain its blood and its food, as disjoined from the community of mankind, such an opinion does not deserve refutation as absurd, but pity as insane.

I do not know that such an improvident and stupid selfishness deserves the discussion, which, perhaps, I may bestow upon it hereafter. We cannot arrange with our enemy in the present conjuncture, without abandoning the interest of mankind. If we look only to our own petty peculium[6] in the war, we have had some advantages; advantages ambiguous in their nature, and dearly bought. We have not in the slightest degree impaired the strength of the common enemy in any one of those points in which his particular force consists; at the same time that new enemies to ourselves, new allies to the regicide republic, have been made out of the wrecks and fragments of the general confederacy.[7] So far as to the selfish part. As composing a part of the community of Europe, and interested in its fate, it is not easy to conceive a state of things more doubtful and perplexing. When Louis XIV had made himself master of one of the largest and most important provinces of Spain;[8] when he had in a manner overrun Lombardy, and was thundering at the gates of Turin; when he had mastered almost all Germany on this side the Rhine; when he was on the point of ruining the august fabric of the empire; when, with the elector of Bavaria[9] in his alliance, hardly anything interposed between him and Vienna; when the Turk hung with a mighty force over the empire on the other side; I do not know, that in the beginning of 1704 (that is, in the third year of the renovated war with Louis XIV) the state of Europe was so truly alarming. To England it certainly was not. Holland (and Holland is a matter to England of value inestimable) was then powerful, was then independent, and, though greatly endangered, was then full of energy and spirit. But the great resource of Europe was in England: not in a sort of England detached from the rest of the world, and amusing herself with the puppet-show of a naval power, (it can be no better, whilst all the sources of that power, and of every sort of power, are precarious,) but in that sort of England, who considered herself as embodied with Europe; but in that sort of England, who, sympathetic with the adversity or the happiness of mankind, felt that nothing in human affairs was foreign to her. We may consider it as a sure axiom, that, as on the one hand no confederacy of the least effect or duration can exist against France, of which England is not only a part, but the head, so neither can England pretend to cope with France but as connected with the body of Christendom.

Our account of the war, *as a war of communion*, to the very point in which we began to throw out lures, oglings, and glances for peace, was a war of disaster and of little else. The independent advantages obtained by us at the beginning of the war, and which were made at the expense of that common cause, if they deceive us about our largest and our surest interest, are to be reckoned amongst our heaviest losses.[10]

The allies, and Great Britain amongst the rest, (and perhaps amongst the foremost,) have been miserably deluded by this great fundamental error: That it was in our power to make peace with this monster of a state, whenever we chose to forget the crimes that made it great, and the designs that made it formidable. People imagined that their ceasing to resist was the sure way to be secure. This "pale cast of thought" sicklied over all their enterprises, and turned all their politics awry. They could not, or rather they would not, read, in the most unequivocal declarations of the enemy, and his uniform conduct, that more safety was to be found in the most arduous war, than in the friendship of that kind of being. Its hostile amity can be obtained on no terms that do not imply an inability hereafter to resist its designs. This great, prolific error (I mean that peace was always in our power) has been the cause that rendered the allies indifferent about the *direction* of the war; and persuaded them that they might always risk a choice, and even a change in its objects. They seldom improved any advantage; hoping that the enemy, affected by it, would make a proffer of peace. Hence it was, that all their early victories have been followed almost immediately with the usual effects of a defeat; whilst all the advantages obtained by the regicides have been followed by the consequences that were natural. The discomfitures, which the republic of assassins has suffered, have uniformly called forth new exertions, which not only repaired old losses, but prepared new conquests. The losses of the allies, on the contrary, (no provision having been made on the speculation of such an event,) have been followed by desertion, by dismay, by disunion, by a dereliction of their policy, by a flight from their principles, by an admiration of the enemy, by mutual accusations, by a distrust in every member of the alliance of its fellow, of its cause, its power, and its courage.

Great difficulties in consequence of our erroneous policy, as I have said, press upon every side of us. Far from desiring to conceal, or even to palliate, the evil in the representation, I wish to lay it down as my foundation, that never greater existed. In a moment when sudden panic is apprehended, it may be wise for a while to conceal some great public disaster, or to reveal it by degrees, until the minds of the people have time to be recollected, that their understanding may have leisure to rally, and that more steady councils may prevent their doing something desperate under the first impressions of rage or terror. But with regard to a *general* state of things, growing out of events and causes already known in the gross, there is no piety in the fraud that covers its true nature; because nothing but erroneous resolutions can be the result of false representations. Those measures, which, in common distress, might be available, in greater, are no better than playing with the evil. That the effort may bear a proportion to the exigence, it is fit it should be known; known in its quality, in its extent, and in all the circumstances which attend it. Great reverses of fortune there have been, and great embarrassments in council: a principled regicide enemy possessed of the most important part of Europe, and struggling for the rest: within ourselves a total relaxation of all authority, whilst a cry is raised against it, as if it were the most ferocious of all despotism. A worse phenomenon; – our government disowned by the most efficient member of its tribunals; ill supported by any of their constituent parts; and the highest tribunal of all, (from causes not for our present purpose to examine,) deprived of all that dignity and all that efficiency which might enforce, or regulate, or, if the case required it, might supply the want of every other court.[11] Public prosecutions are become little better than schools for treason;[12] of no use but to improve the dexterity of criminals in the mystery of evasion; or to show with what complete impunity men may conspire against the commonwealth; with what safety assassins may attempt its awful head. Everything is secure, except what the laws have made sacred; everything is tameness and languor that is not fury and faction. Whilst the distempers of a relaxed fibre prognosticate and prepare all the morbid force of convulsion in the body of the state, the steadiness of the physician is overpowered by the very aspect of the disease.* The doctor of the constitution, pretending to underrate what he is not able to contend with, shrinks from his own operation. He doubts and questions the salutary but critical terrors of the cautery and the knife. He takes a poor credit even from his defeat; and covers impotence under the mask of lenity. He praises the moderation of the laws, as, in his hands, he sees them baffled and despised. Is all this, because in our day the statutes of the kingdom are not engrossed in as firm a character, and imprinted in as black and legible a type, as ever? No! the law is a clear, but it is a dead letter. Dead and putrid, it is insufficient to save the state, but potent to infect and to kill. Living law, full of reason, and of equity and justice, (as it is, or it should not exist,) ought to be severe and awful too; or the words of menace, whether written on the parchment roll of England, or cut into the brazen tablet of Rome, will excite nothing but contempt. How comes it, that in all the state prosecutions of magnitude, from the Revolution to within these two or three years, the Crown has scarcely ever retired disgraced and defeated from its courts? Whence this alarming change? By a connexion easily felt, and not impossible to be traced to its cause, all the parts of the state have their correspondence and consent. They who bow to the enemy abroad will not be of power to subdue the conspirator at home. It is impossible not to observe, that, in proportion as we approximate to the poisonous jaws of anarchy, the fascination grows irresistible. In proportion as we are attracted towards the focus of illegality, irreligion, and desperate enterprise, all the venomous and blighting insects of the state are awakened into life. The promise of the year is blasted, and shrivelled, and burned up before them. Our most salutary and most beautiful institutions yield nothing but dust and smut: the harvest of our law is no more than stubble. It is in the nature of these eruptive diseases in the state to sink in by fits, and re-appear. But the fuel of the malady remains; and in my opinion is not in the smallest degree mitigated in its malignity,

---

* "Mussabat tacito medicina timore."[3]

though it waits the favourable moment of a freer communication with the source of regicide to exert and to increase its force.

Is it that the people are changed, that the commonwealth cannot be protected by its laws? I hardly think it. On the contrary, I conceive, that these things happen because men are not changed, but remain always what they always were; they remain what the bulk of us must ever be, when abandoned to our vulgar propensities, without guide, leader, or control; that is, made to be full of a blind elevation in prosperity; to despise untried dangers; to be overpowered with unexpected reverses; to find no clue in a labyrinth of difficulties, to get out of a present inconvenience with any risk of future ruin; to follow and to bow to fortune; to admire successful though wicked enterprise, and to imitate what we admire; to contemn the government which announces danger from sacrilege and regicide, whilst they are only in their infancy and their struggle, but which finds nothing that can alarm in their adult state, and in the power and triumph of those destructive principles. In a mass we cannot be left to ourselves. We must have leaders. If none will undertake to lead us right, we shall find guides who will contrive to conduct us to shame and ruin.

We are in a war of a *peculiar* nature. It is not with an ordinary community, which is hostile or friendly as passion or as interest may veer about: not with a state which makes war through wantonness, and abandons it through lassitude. We are at war with a system, which, by its essence, is inimical to all other governments, and which makes peace or war, as peace and war may best contribute to their subversion. It is with an *armed doctrine* that we are at war. It has, by its essence, a faction of opinion, and of interest, and of enthusiasm, in every country. To us it is a Colossus which bestrides our channel. It has one foot on a foreign shore, the other upon the British soil. Thus advantaged, if it can at all exist, it must finally prevail. Nothing can so completely ruin any of the old governments, ours in particular, as the acknowledgment, directly, or by implication, of any kind of superiority in this new power. This acknowledgment we make, if, in a bad or doubtful situation of our affairs, we solicit peace; or if we yield to the modes of new humiliation, in which alone she is content to give us a hearing. By that means the terms cannot be of our choosing; no, not in any part.

It is laid in the unalterable constitution of things: – None can aspire to act greatly, but those who are of force greatly to suffer. They who make their arrangements in the first run of misadventure, and in a temper of mind the common fruit of disappointment and dismay, put a seal on their calamities. To their power they take a security against any favours which they might hope from the usual inconstancy of fortune. I am therefore, my dear friend, invariably of your opinion, (though full of respect for those who think differently,) that neither the time chosen for it, nor the manner of soliciting a negotiation, were properly considered; even though I had allowed, (I hardly shall allow,) that with the horde of regicides we could by any selection of time, or use of means, obtain anything at all deserving the name of peace.

In one point we are lucky. The regicide has received our advances with scorn.[14] We have an enemy, to whose virtues we can owe nothing; but on this occasion we are infinitely obliged to one of his vices. We owe more to his insolence than to our own precaution. The haughtiness by which the proud repel us, has this of good in it; that in making us keep our distance, they must keep their distance too. In the present case, the pride of the regicide may be our safety. He has given time for our reason to operate; and for British dignity to recover from its surprise. From first to last he has rejected all our advances. Far as we have gone, he has still left a way open to our retreat.

There is always an augury to be taken of what a peace is likely to be, from the preliminary steps that are made to bring it about. We may gather something from the time in which the first overtures are made; from the quarter whence they come; from the manner in which they are received. These discover the temper of the parties. If your enemy offers peace in the moment of success, it indicates that he is satisfied with something. It shows that there are limits to his ambition or his resentment. If he offers nothing under misfortune, it is probable, that it is more painful to him to abandon the prospect of advantage than to endure calamity. If he rejects solicitation, and will not give even a nod to the suppliants for peace, until a change in the fortune of the war threatens him with ruin, then I think it evident, that he wishes nothing more than to disarm his adversary to gain time. Afterwards a question arises, which of the parties is likely to obtain the greater advantages, by continuing disarmed and by the use of time.

With these few plain indications in our minds, it will not be improper to reconsider the conduct of the enemy together with our own, from the day that a question of peace has been in agitation. In considering this part of the question, I do not proceed on my own hypothesis. I suppose, for a moment, that this body of regicide, calling itself a republic, is a politic person, with whom something deserving the name of peace may be made. On that supposition, let us examine our own proceeding. Let us compute the profit it has brought, and the advantage that it is likely to bring hereafter. A peace too eagerly sought is not always the sooner obtained. The discovery of vehement wishes generally frustrates their attainment; and your adversary has gained a great advantage over you when he finds you impatient to conclude a treaty. There is in reserve, not only something of dignity, but a great deal of prudence too. A sort of courage belongs to negotiation, as well as to operations of the field. A negotiator must often seem willing to hazard the whole issue of his treaty, if he wishes to secure any one material point.

[. . .]

If the war made to prevent the union of two crowns upon one head was a just war; this, which is made to prevent the tearing of all crowns from all heads which ought to wear them, and with the crowns to smite off the sacred heads themselves, this is a just war.

If a war to prevent Louis XIV from imposing his religion was just, a war to prevent the murderers of Lous XVI from imposing their irreligion upon us is just; a war to prevent the operation of a system, which makes life without dignity, and death without hope, is a just war.

If to preserve political independence and civil freedom to nations was a just ground of war; a war to preserve national independence, property, liberty, life, and honour, from certain, universal havoc, is a war just, necessary, manly, pious: and we are bound to persevere in it by every principle, Divine and human, as long as the system which menaces them all, and all equally, has an existence in the world.

You, who have looked at this matter with as fair and impartial an eye as can be united with a feeling heart, you will not think it a hardy assertion, when I affirm, that it were far better to be conquered by any other nation, than to have this faction for a neighbour. Before I felt myself authorised to say this, I considered the state of all the countries in Europe for these last three hundred years, which have been obliged to submit to a foreign law. In most of those I found the condition of the annexed countries even better, certainly not worse, than the lot of those which were the patrimony of the conqueror. They wanted some blessings – but they were free from many great evils. They were rich and tranquil. Such was Artois, Flanders, Lorrain, Alsatia, under the old government of France. Such was Silesia under the king of Prussia. They, who are to live in the vicinity of this new fabric, are to prepare to live in perpetual conspiracies and seditions; and to end at last, in being conquered, if not to her dominion, to her resemblance. But when we talk of conquest by other nations, it is only to put a case. This is the only power in Europe by which it is *possible* we should be conquered. To live under the continual dread of such immeasurable evils is itself a grievous calamity. To live without the dread of them is to turn the danger into the disaster. The influence of such a France is equal to a war, its example was more wasting than a hostile irruption. The hostility with any other power is separable and accidental; this power, by the very condition of its existence, by its very essential constitution, is in a state of hostility with us, and with all civilised people.*

A government of the nature of that set up at our very door has never been hitherto seen, or even imagined, in Europe. What our relation to it will be cannot be judged by other relations. It is a serious thing to have connexion with a people, who live only under positive, arbitrary, and changeable institutions; and those not perfected, nor supplied, nor explained, by any common acknowledged rule of moral science. I remember that in one of my last conversations with the late Lord Camden,[15] we were struck much in the same manner with the abolition in France of the law, as a science of methodised and artificial equity. France, since her revolution, is under the sway of a sect, whose leaders have deliberately, at one stroke, demolished the whole body of that jurisprudence which France had pretty nearly in common with other civilised countries. In that jurisprudence were contained the elements and principles of the law of nations, the great ligament of mankind. With the law they have of course destroyed all seminaries in which jurisprudence was taught, as well as all the corporations established for its conservation.[16] I have not heard of

* See Declaration, Whitehall, October 29, 1793.

any country, whether in Europe or Asia, or even in Africa on this side of Mount Atlas, which is wholly without some such colleges and such corporations, except France. No man in a public or private concern, can divine by what rule or principle her judgments are to be directed; nor is there to be found a professor in any university, or a practitioner in any court, who will hazard an opinion of what is or is not law in France, in any case whatever. They have not only annulled all their old treaties, but they have renounced the law of nations, from whence treaties have their force. With a fixed design they have outlawed themselves, and to their power outlawed all other nations.

Instead of the religion and the law by which they were in a great politic communion with the Christian world, they have constructed their republic on three bases, all fundamentally opposite to those on which the communities of Europe are built. Its foundation is laid in regicide, in Jacobinism,[17] and in atheism;[18] and it has joined to those principles a body of systematic manners, which secures their operation.

If I am asked, how I would be understood in the use of these terms, regicide, Jacobinism, atheism, and a system of corresponding manners, and their establishment? I will tell you:

I call a commonwealth *regicide*, which lays it down as a fixed law of nature, and a fundamental right of man, that all government, not being a democracy, is an usurpation.* That all kings, as such, are usurpers; and for being kings may and ought to be put to death, with their wives, families, and adherents. The commonwealth which acts uniformly upon those principles, and which, after abolishing every festival of religion, chooses the most flagrant act of a murderous regicide treason for a feast of eternal commemoration, and which forces all her people to observe it – this I call *regicide by establishment*.

Jacobinism is the revolt of the enterprising talents of a country against its property. When private men form themselves into associations for the purpose of destroying the pre-existing laws and institutions of their country; when they secure to themselves

---

* Nothing could be more solemn than their promulgation of this principle as a preamble to the destructive code of their famous articles for the decomposition of society, into whatever country they should enter. "La Convention Nationale, après avoir entendu le rapport de ses comités de finances, de la guerre et diplomatiques réunis, fidelle *au principe de souveraineté de peuples qui ne lui permet pas de reconnoître aucune institution, qui y porte atteinte*,"[19] &c. &c. Décret sur le Rapport de Cambon, Dec. 18, 1792, and see the subsequent proclamation.

an army, by dividing amongst the people of no property the estates of the ancient and lawful proprietors; when a state recognises those acts; when it does not make confiscations for crimes, but makes crimes for confiscations; when it has its principal strength, and all its resources, in such a violation of property; when it stands chiefly upon such a violation; massacring by judgments, or otherwise, those who make any struggle for their old legal government, and their legal, hereditary, or acquired possessions – I call this *Jacobinism by establishment*.

I call it *atheism by establishment*, when any state, as such, shall not acknowledge the existence of God as a moral governor of the world; when it shall offer to him no religious or moral worship; – when it shall abolish the Christian religion by a regular decree; – when it shall persecute with a cold, unrelenting, steady cruelty, by every mode of confiscation, imprisonment, exile, and death, all its ministers; – when it shall generally shut up or pull down churches; when the few buildings which remain of this kind shall be opened only for the purpose of making a profane apotheosis of monsters, whose vices and crimes have no parallel amongst men, and whom all other men consider as objects of general detestation, and the severest animadversion of law. When, in the place of that religion of social benevolence, and of individual self-denial, in mockery of all religion, they institute impious, blasphemous, indecent theatric rites, in honour of their vitiated, perverted reason, and erect altars to the personification of their own corrupted and bloody republic; – when schools and seminaries are founded at the public expense to poison mankind, from generation to generation, with the horrible maxims of this impiety; – when wearied out with incessant martyrdom, and the cries of a people hungering and thirsting for religion, they permit it, only as a tolerated evil – I call this *atheism by establishment*.

When to these establishments of regicide, of Jacobinism, and of atheism, you add the *correspondent system of manners*, no doubt can be left on the mind of a thinking man concerning their determined hostility to the human race. Manners are of more importance than laws. Upon them, in a great measure, the laws depend. The law touches us but here and there, and now and then. Manners are what vex or soothe, corrupt or purify, exalt or debase, barbarise or refine us, by a constant, steady, uniform, insensible operation, like that of the air we breathe in. They give their whole form and colour to our lives. According to their quality, they aid morals, they supply them, or they totally destroy them. Of this the new French legislators were aware; therefore, with the same method, and under the same authority, they settled a system of manners, the most licentious, prostitute, and abandoned, that ever has been known, and at the same time the most coarse, rude, savage, and ferocious. Nothing in the Revolution, no, not to a phrase or a gesture, not to the fashion of a hat or a shoe, was left to accident. All has been the result of design; all has been matter of institution. No mechanical means could be devised in favour of this incredible system of wickedness and vice, that has not been employed. The noblest passions, the love of glory, the love of country, have been debauched into means of its preservation and its propagation. All sorts of shows and exhibitions, calculated to inflame and vitiate the imagination, and pervert the moral sense, have been contrived. They have sometimes brought forth five or six hundred drunken women, calling at the bar of the Assembly for the blood of their own children, as being royalists or constitutionalists. Sometimes they have got a body of wretches, calling themselves fathers, to demand the murder of their sons, boasting that Rome had but one Brutus,[20] but that they could show five hundred. There were instances, in which they inverted, and retaliated the impiety, and produced sons, who called for the execution of their parents. The foundation of their republic is laid in moral paradoxes. Their patriotism is always prodigy. All those instances to be found in history, whether real or fabulous, of a doubtful public spirit at which morality is perplexed, reason is staggered, and from which affrighted nature recoils, are their chosen, and almost sole, examples for the instruction of their youth.

The whole drift of their institution is contrary to that of the wise legislators of all countries, who aimed at improving instincts into morals, and at grafting the virtues on the stock of the natural affections. They, on the contrary, have omitted no pains to eradicate every benevolent and noble propensity in the mind of men. In their culture it is a rule always to graft virtues on vices. They think everything unworthy of the name of public virtue, unless it indicates violence on the private. All their new institutions (and with them everything is new) strike at the root of our social nature. Other legislators, knowing that marriage is the origin of all relations, and consequently the first element of all duties, have endeavoured, by every art, to make it sacred. The

Christian religion, by confining it to the pairs, and by rendering that relation indissoluble, has by these two things done more towards the peace, happiness, settlement, and civilisation of the world, than by any other part in this whole scheme of Divine Wisdom. The direct contrary course has been taken in the syn-agogue of antichrist, I mean in that forge and manufactory of all evil, the sect which predominated in the Constituent Assembly of 1789. Those monsters employed the same, or greater industry, to desecrate and degrade that state, which other legislators have used to render it holy and honourable. By a strange, uncalled-for declaration, they pronounced, that marriage was no better than a common, civil contract.[21] It was one of their ordinary tricks, to put their sentiments into the mouths of certain personated characters, which they theatrically exhibited at the bar of what ought to be a serious assembly. One of these was brought out in the figure of a prostitute, whom they called by the affected name of "a mother without being a wife." This creature they made to call for a repeal of the incapacities, which in civilised states are put upon bastards. The prostitutes of the Assembly gave to this their puppet the sanction of their greater impudence. In con-sequence of the principles laid down, and the manners authorised, bastards were not long after put on the footing of the issue of lawful unions.[22] Proceeding in the spirit of the first authors of their constitution, succeeding assemblies went the full length of the principle, and gave a licence to divorce at the mere pleasure of either party, and at a month's notice. With them the matrimonial connexion is brought into so degraded a state of concubinage, that I believe, none of the wretches in London who keep warehouses of infamy, would give out one of their victims to private custody on so short and insolent a tenure. There was indeed a kind of profligate equity in giving to women the same licentious power. The reason they assigned was as infamous as the act; declaring that women had been too long under the tyranny of parents and of husbands. It is not necessary to observe upon the horrible consequences of taking one half of the species wholly out of the guardianship and protection of the other.

The practice of divorce, though in some countries permitted, has been discouraged in all. In the East, polygamy and divorce are in discredit; and the manners correct the laws. In Rome, whilst Rome was in its integrity, the few causes allowed for divorce amounted in effect to prohibition. They were only three. The arbitrary was totally excluded, and accordingly some hundreds of years passed, without a single example of that kind. When manners were corrupted, the laws were relaxed; as the latter always follows the former, when they are not able to regulate them, or to vanquish them. Of this circumstance the legislators of vice and crime were pleased to take notice, as an inducement to adopt their regulation; holding out a hope, that the permission would as rarely be made use of. They knew the contrary to be true; and they had taken good care, that the laws should be well seconded by the manners. Their law of divorce, like all their laws, had not for its object the relief of domestic uneasiness, but the total corruption of all morals, the total disconnexion of social life.

It is a matter of curiosity to observe the operation of this encouragement to disorder. I have before me the Paris paper, correspondent to the usual register of births, marriages, and deaths. Divorce, happily, is no regular head of registry amongst civilised nations. With the Jacobins it is remarkable, that divorce is not only a regular head, but it has the post of honour. It occupies the first place in the list. In the three first months of the year 1793, the number of divorces in that city amounted to 562. The marriages were 1785; so that the proportion of divorces to marriages was not much less than one to three; a thing unexampled, I believe, among mankind. I caused an inquiry to be made at Doctors' Commons, concerning the number of divorces; and found, that all the divorces (which, except by special act of parliament, are separations, and not proper divorces) did not amount in all those courts, and in a hundred years, to much more than one-fifth of those that passed, in the single city of Paris, in three months. I followed up the inquiry relative to that city through several of the subsequent months until I was tired, and found the proportions still the same. Since then I have heard that they have declared for a revisal of these laws; but I know of nothing done. It appears as if the contract that renovates the world was under no law at all. From this we may take our estimate of the havoc that has been made through all the relations of life. With the Jacobins of France, vague intercourse is without reproach; marriage is reduced to the vilest concubinage; children are encouraged to cut the throats of their parents; mothers are taught that tenderness is no part of their character, and, to demonstrate their attachment to their party, that they ought to make no scruple to rake with their bloody hands in the bowels of those who came from their own.

To all this let us join the practice of *cannibalism*, with which, in the proper terms, and with the greatest truth, their several factions accuse each other. By cannibalism, I mean their devouring as a nutriment of their ferocity, some part of the bodies of those they have murdered; their drinking the blood of their victims, and forcing the victims themselves to drink the blood of their kindred slaughtered before their faces. By cannibalism, I mean also to signify all their nameless, unmanly, and abominable insults on the bodies of those they slaughter.

As to those whom they suffer to die a natural death, they do not permit them to enjoy the last consolations of mankind, or those rights of sepulture, which indicate hope, and which mere nature has taught to mankind, in all countries, to soothe the afflictions, and to cover the infirmity, of mortal condition. They disgrace men in the entry into life, they vitiate and enslave them through the whole course of it, and they deprive them of all comfort at the conclusion of their dishonoured and depraved existence. Endeavouring to persuade the people that they are no better than beasts, the whole body of their institution tends to make them beasts of prey, furious and savage. For this purpose the active part of them is disciplined into a ferocity which has no parallel. To this ferocity there is joined not one of the rude, unfashioned virtues, which accompany the vices, where the whole are left to grow up together in the rankness of uncultivated nature. But nothing is left to nature in their systems.

The same discipline which hardens their hearts relaxes their morals. Whilst courts of justice were thrust out by revolutionary tribunals, and silent churches were only the funeral monuments of departed religion, there were no fewer than nineteen or twenty theatres, great and small, most of them kept open at the public expense, and all of them crowded every night. Among the gaunt, haggard forms of famine and nakedness, amidst the yells of murder, the tears of affliction, and the cries of despair, the song, the dance, the mimic scene, the buffoon laughter, went on as regularly as in the gay hour of festive peace. I have it from good authority, that under the scaffold of judicial murder, and the gaping planks that poured down blood on the spectators, the space was hired out for a show of dancing dogs. I think, without concert, we have made the very same remark on reading some of their pieces, which being written for other purposes, let us into a view of their social life. It struck us that the habits of Paris had no resemblance to the finished virtues, or to the polished vice, and elegant, though not blameless, luxury, of the capital of a great empire. Their society was more like that of a den of outlaws upon a doubtful frontier; of a lewd tavern for the revels and debauches of banditti, assassins, bravos, smugglers, and their more desperate paramours, mixed with bombastic players, the refuse and rejected offal of strolling theatres, puffing out ill-sorted verses about virtue, mixed with the licentious and blasphemous songs, proper to the brutal and hardened course of life belonging to that sort of wretches. This system of manners in itself is at war with all orderly and moral society, and is in its neighbourhood unsafe. If great bodies of that kind were anywhere established in a bordering territory, we should have a right to demand of their governments the suppression of such a nuisance. What are we to do if the government and the whole community is of the same description? Yet that government has thought proper to invite ours to lay by its unjust hatred, and to listen to the voice of humanity as taught by their example.

The operation of dangerous and delusive first principles obliges us to have recourse to the true ones. In the intercourse between nations, we are apt to rely too much on the instrumental part. We lay too much weight upon the formality of treaties and compacts. We do not act much more wisely when we trust to the interests of men as guarantees of their engagements. The interests frequently tear to pieces the engagements; and the passions trample upon both. Entirely to trust to either, is to disregard our own safety, or not to know mankind. Men are not tied to one another by papers and seals. They are led to associate by resemblances, by conformities, by sympathies. It is with nations as with individuals. Nothing is so strong a tie of amity between nation and nation as correspondence in laws, customs, manners, and habits of life. They have more than the force of treaties in themselves. They are obligations written in the heart. They approximate men to men, without their knowledge, and sometimes against their intentions. The secret, unseen, but irrefragable bond of habitual intercourse holds them together, even when their perverse and litigious nature sets them to equivocate, scuffle, and fight, about the terms of their written obligations.

As to war, if it be the means of wrong and violence, it is the sole

means of justice amongst nations. Nothing can banish it from the
world. They who say otherwise, intending to impose upon us,
do not impose upon themselves. But it is one of the greatest
objects of human wisdom to mitigate those evils which we are
unable to remove. The conformity and analogy of which I speak,
incapable, like everything else, of preserving perfect trust and
tranquillity among men, has a strong tendency to facilitate
accommodation, and to produce a generous oblivion of the
rancour of their quarrels. With this similitude, peace is more of
peace, and war is less of war. I will go further. There have been
periods of time in which communities, apparently in peace with
each other, have been more perfectly separated than, in latter
times, many nations in Europe have been in the course of long
and bloody wars. The cause must be sought in the similitude
throughout Europe of religion, laws, and manners. At bottom,
these are all the same. The writers on public law have often called
this *aggregate* of nations a commonwealth. They had reason. It is
virtually one great state having the same basis of general law, with
some diversity of provincial customs and local establishments.
The nations of Europe have had the very same Christian religion, agreeing in the fundamental parts, varying a little in the
ceremonies and in the subordinate doctrines. The whole of the
polity and economy of every country in Europe has been derived
from the same sources. It was drawn from the old Germanic or
Gothic custumary, from the feudal institutions which must be
considered as an emanation from that custumary; and the whole
has been improved and digested into system and discipline by
the Roman law. From hence arose the several orders, with or
without a monarch, (which are called states,) in every European
country; the strong traces of which, where monarchy predominated, were never wholly extinguished or merged in despotism.
In the few places where monarchy was cast off, the spirit of European monarchy was still left. Those countries still continued
countries of states; that is, of classes, orders, and distinctions
such as had before subsisted, or nearly so. Indeed the force and
form of the institution called states continued in greater perfection in those republican communities than under monarchies.
From all those sources arose a system of manners and of education which was nearly similar in all this quarter of the globe; and
which softened, blended, and harmonised the colours of the
whole. There was little difference in the form of the universities

for the education of their youth, whether with regard to faculties, to sciences, or to the more liberal and elegant kinds of erudition. From this resemblance in the modes of intercourse, and in the whole form and fashion of life, no citizen of Europe could be altogether an exile in any part of it. There was nothing more than a pleasing variety to recreate and instruct the mind, to enrich the imagination, and to meliorate the heart. When a man travelled or resided for health, pleasure, business, or necessity from his own country, he never felt himself quite abroad.

The whole body of this new scheme of manners, in support of the new scheme of politics, I consider as a strong and decisive proof of determined ambition and systematic hostility. I defy the most refining ingenuity to invent any other cause for the total departure of the Jacobin republic from every one of the ideas and usages, religious, legal, moral, or social, of this civilised world, and for her tearing herself from its communion with such studied violence, but from a formed resolution of keeping no terms with that world. It has not been, as has been falsely and insidiously represented, that these miscreants had only broke with their old government. They made a schism with the whole universe, and that schism extended to almost everything great and small. For one, I wish, since it is gone thus far, that the breach had been so complete, as to make all intercourse impracticable: but partly by accident, partly by design, partly from the resistance of the matter, enough is left to preserve intercourse, whilst amity is destroyed or corrupted in its principle.

This violent breach of the community of Europe we must conclude to have been made (even if they had not expressly declared it over and over again) either to force mankind into an adoption of their system, or to live in perpetual enmity with a community the most potent we have ever known. Can any person imagine, that, in offering to mankind this desperate alternative, there is no indication of a hostile mind, because men in possession of the ruling authority are supposed to have a right to act without coercion in their own territories? As to the right of men to act anywhere according to their pleasure, without any moral tie, no such right exists. Men are never in a state of *total* independence of each other. It is not the condition of our nature: nor is it conceivable how any man can pursue a considerable course of action without its having some effect upon others; or, of course, without producing some degree of responsibility

for his conduct. The *situations* in which men relatively stand produce the rules and principles of that responsibility, and afford directions to prudence in exacting it.

Distance of place does not extinguish the duties or the rights of
men: but it often renders their exercise impracticable. The same
circumstance of distance renders the noxious effects of an evil
system in any community less pernicious. But there are situations
where this difficulty does not occur; and in which, therefore,
these duties are obligatory, and these rights are to be asserted.
It has ever been the method of public jurists to draw a great part
of the analogies, on which they form the law of nations, from
the principles of law which prevail in civil community. Civil laws
are not all of them merely positive. Those, which are rather conclusions of legal reason than matters of statutable provision,
belong to universal equity, and are universally applicable. Almost
the whole prætorian law is such. There is a *Law of Neighbourhood*
which does not leave a man perfectly master on his own ground.
When a neighbour sees a *new erection*, in the nature of a nuisance,
set up at his door, he has a right to represent it to the judge; who,
on his part, has a right to order the work to be stayed; or, if established, to be removed. On this head the parent law is express and
clear, and has made many wise provisions, which, without
destroying, regulate and restrain the right of *ownership*, by the
right of *vicinage*. No *innovation* is permitted that may redound,
even secondarily, to the prejudice of a neighbour. The whole
doctrine of that important head of prætorian law, "*De novi operis
nunciatione*,"[23] is founded on the principle, that no *new* use should
be made of a man's private liberty of operating upon his private
property, from whence a detriment may be justly apprehended
by his neighbour. This law of denunciation is prospective. It is
to anticipate what is called *damnum infectum*,[24] or *damnum nondum
factum*,[25] that is, a damage justly apprehended, but not actually
done. Even before it is clearly known, whether the innovation
be damageable or not, the judge is competent to issue a prohibition to innovate, until the point can be determined. This prompt
interference is grounded on principles favourable to both parties.
It is preventive of mischief difficult to be repaired, and of ill blood
difficult to be softened. The rule of law, therefore, which comes
before the evil, is amongst the very best parts of equity, and justifies the promptness of the remedy; because, as it is well observed,
Res damni infecti celeritatem desiderat, et periculosa est dilatio.[26] This

right of denunciation does not hold, when things continue, however inconveniently to the neighbourhood, according to the *ancient* mode. For there is a sort of presumption against novelty, drawn out of a deep consideration of human nature and human affairs; and the maxim of jurisprudence is well laid down, *Vetustas pro lege semper habetur.*[27]

Such is the law of civil vicinity. Now, where there is no constituted judge, as between independent states there is not, the vicinage itself is the natural judge. It is, preventively, the assessor of its own rights, or remedially, their avenger. Neighbours are presumed to take cognisance of each other's acts. *"Vicini vicinorum facta presumuntur scire."*[28] This principle, which, like the rest, is as true of nations as of individual men, has bestowed on the grand vicinage of Europe a duty to know, and a right to prevent, any capital innovation which may amount to the erection of a dangerous nuisance.* Of the importance of that innovation, and the mischief of that nuisance, they are, to be sure, bound to judge, not litigiously; but it is in their competence to judge. They have uniformly acted on this right. What in civil society is a ground of action, in politic society is a ground of war. But the exercise of that competent jurisdiction is a matter of moral prudence. As suits in civil society, so war in the political, must ever be a matter of great deliberation. It is not this or that particular proceeding, picked out here and there, as a subject of quarrel, that will do. There must be an aggregate of mischief. There must be marks of deliberation, there must be traces of design, there must be indications of malice, there must be tokens of ambition. There must be force in the body where they exist, there must be energy in the mind. When all these circumstances are combined, or the important parts of them, the duty of the vicinity calls for the exercise of its competence; and the rules of prudence do not restrain, but demand it.

In describing the nuisance erected by so pestilential a manufactory, by the construction of so infamous a brothel, by digging a night-cellar for such thieves, murderers, and house-breakers, as never infested the world, I am so far from aggravating, that I have fallen infinitely short of the evil. No man who has attended to

---

* "This state of things cannot exist in France without involving all the surrounding powers in one common danger, without giving them the right, without imposing on them as a duty, to stop the progress of an evil which attacks the fundamental principles by which mankind is united in civil society." Declaration, 29th Oct. 1793.

the particulars of what has been done in France, and combined them with the principles there asserted, can possibly doubt it. When I compare with this great cause of nations, the trifling points of honour, the still more contemptible points of interest, the light ceremonies and undefinable punctilios, the disputes about precedency, the lowering or the hoisting of a sail, the dealing in a hundred or two of wild cat-skins on the other side of the globe, which have often kindled up the flames of war between nations, I stand astonished at those persons, who do not feel a resentment, not more natural than politic, at the atrocious insults that this monstrous compound offers to the dignity of every nation, and who are not alarmed with what it threatens to their safety.

I have therefore been decidedly of opinion, with our declaration at Whitehall, in the beginning of this war, that the vicinage of Europe had not only a right, but an indispensable duty, and an exigent interest, to denunciate this new work before it had produced the danger we have so sorely felt, and which we shall long feel. The example of what is done by France is too important not to have a vast and extensive influence; and that example, backed with its power, must bear with great force on those who are near it; especially on those who shall recognise the pretended republic on the principle upon which it now stands. It is not an old structure which you have found as it is, and are not to dispute of the original end and design with which it had been so fashioned. It is a recent wrong, and can plead no prescription. It violates the rights upon which not only the community of France, but those on which all communities are founded. The principles on which they proceed are *general* principles, and are as true in England as in any other country. They, who (though with the purest intentions) recognise the authority of these regicides and robbers upon principle, justify their acts and establish them as precedents. It is a question not between France and England. It is a question between property and force. The property claims; and its claim has been allowed. The property of the nation is the nation. They, who massacre, plunder, and expel the body of the proprietary, are murderers and robbers. The state, in its essence, must be moral and just: and it may be so, though a tyrant or usurper should be accidentally at the head of it. This is a thing to be lamented: but this notwithstanding, the body of the commonwealth may remain in all its integrity and be perfectly sound in its composition. The present case is different. It is not a revolution in government. It is not the victory of party over party. It is a destruction and decomposition of the whole society; which never can be made of right by any faction, however powerful, nor without terrible consequences to all about it, both in the act and in the example. This pretended republic is founded in crimes, and exists by wrong and robbery; and wrong and robbery, far from a title to anything, is war with mankind. To be at peace with robbery is to be an accomplice with it.

Mere locality does not constitute a body politic. Had Cade[29] and his gang got possession of London, they would not have been the lord mayor, aldermen, and common council. The body politic of France existed in the majesty of its throne, in the dignity of its nobility, in the honour of its gentry, in the sanctity of its clergy, in the reverence of its magistracy, in the weight and consideration due to its landed property in the several bailliages, in the respect due to its moveable substance represented by the corporations of the kingdom. All these particular *moleculæ* united form the great mass of what is truly the body politic in all countries. They are so many deposits and receptacles of justice; because they can only exist by justice. Nation is a moral essence, not a geographical arrangement, or a denomination of the nomenclator. France, though out of her territorial possession, exists; because the sole possible claimant, I mean the proprietary, and the government to which the proprietary adheres, exists, and claims. God forbid, that if you were expelled from your house by ruffians and assassins, that I should call the material walls, doors, and windows of ——, the ancient and honourable family of ——. Am I to transfer to the intruders, who, not content to turn you out naked to the world, would rob you of your very name, all the esteem and respect I owe to you? The regicides in France are not France. France is out of her bounds, but the kingdom is the same.

To illustrate my opinions on this subject, let us suppose a case, which, after what has happened, we cannot think absolutely impossible, though the augury is to be abominated, and the event deprecated with our most ardent prayers. Let us suppose then, that our gracious sovereign was sacrilegiously murdered; his exemplary queen, at the head of the matronage of this land, murdered in the same manner; that those princesses, whose beauty and modest elegance are the ornaments of the country, and who

are the leaders and patterns of the ingenuous youth of their sex,
were put to a cruel and ignominious death, with hundreds of
others, mothers and daughters, ladies of the first distinction; –
that the Prince of Wales and the Duke of York, princes the hope
and pride of the nation, with all their brethren, were forced to fly
from the knives of assassins – that the whole body of our excellent
clergy were either massacred or robbed of all, and transported
– the Christian religion in all its denominations, forbidden and
persecuted – the law totally, fundamentally, and in all its parts
destroyed – the judges put to death by revolutionary tribunals –
the peers and commons robbed to the last acre of their estates;
massacred if they stayed, or obliged to seek life in flight, in exile
and in beggary – that the whole landed property should share the
very same fate – that every military and naval officer of honour
and rank, almost to a man, should be placed in the same description of confiscation and exile – that the principal merchants and
bankers should be drawn out, as from a hen-coop, for slaughter
– that the citizens of our greatest and most flourishing cities,
when the hand and the machinery of the hangman were not
found sufficient, should have been collected in the public
squares, and massacred by thousands with cannon; – if three hundred thousand others should have been doomed to a situation
worse than death in noisome and pestilential prisons; – in such a
case, is it in the faction of robbers I am to look for my country?
Would this be the England that you and I, and even strangers,
admired, honoured, loved, and cherished? Would not the exiles
of England alone be my government and my fellow-citizens?
Would not their places of refuge be my temporary country?
Would not all my duties and all my affections be there, and there
only? Should I consider myself as a traitor to my country, and
deserving of death, if I knocked at the door and heart of every
potentate in Christendom to succour my friends, and to avenge
them on their enemies? Could I, in any way, show myself more
a patriot? What should I think of those potentates who insulted
their suffering brethren; who treated them as vagrants, or at least
as mendicants; and could find no allies, no friends, but in regicide
murderers and robbers? What ought I to think and feel, if, being
geographers instead of kings, they recognised the desolated
cities, the wasted fields, and the rivers polluted with blood, of this
geometrical measurement, as the honourable member of Europe
called England? In that condition what should we think of

Sweden, Denmark, or Holland, or whatever power afforded us a churlish and treacherous hospitality, if they should invite us to join the standard of our king, our laws, and our religion, if they should give us a direct promise of protection – if, after all this, taking advantage of our deplorable situation, which left us no choice, they were to treat us as the lowest and vilest of all mercenaries? If they were to send us far from the aid of our king, and our suffering country, to squander us away in the most pestilential climates for a venal enlargement of their own territories, for the purpose of trucking them, when obtained, with those very robbers and murderers they had called upon us to oppose with our blood? What would be our sentiments, if in that miserable service we were not to be considered either as English, or as Swedes, Dutch, Danes, but as outcasts of the human race? Whilst we were fighting those battles of their interest, and as their soldiers, how should we feel if we were to be excluded from all their cartels? How must we feel, if the pride and flower of the English nobility and gentry, who might escape the pestilential clime, and the devouring sword, should, if taken prisoners, be delivered over as rebel subjects, to be condemned as rebels, as traitors, as the vilest of all criminals, by tribunals formed of Maroon negro slaves,[30] covered over with the blood of their masters, who were made free and organised into judges, for their robberies and murders? What should we feel under this inhuman, insulting, and barbarous protection of Muscovites, Swedes, or Hollanders? Should we not obtest Heaven, and whatever justice there is yet on earth? Oppression makes wise men mad; but the distemper is still the madness of the wise, which is better than the sobriety of fools. The cry is the voice of sacred misery, exalted not into wild raving, but into the sanctified phrensy of prophecy and inspiration – in that bitterness of soul, in that indignation of suffering virtue, in that exaltation of despair, would not persecuted English loyalty cry out, with an awful warning voice, and denounce the destruction that waits on monarchs, who consider fidelity to them as the most degrading of all vices; who suffer it to be punished as the most abominable of all crimes; and who have no respect but for rebels, traitors, regicides, and furious negro slaves, whose crimes have broke their chains? Would not this warm language of high indignation have more of sound reason in it, more of real affection, more of true attachment, than all the lullabies of flatterers, who would hush monarchs to sleep in the arms of death? Let them be well convinced, that if ever this example should prevail in its whole extent, it will have its full operation. Whilst kings stand firm on their base, though under that base there is a sure-wrought mine, there will not be wanting to their levees a single person of those who are attached to their fortune, and not to their persons or cause: but hereafter none will support a tottering throne. Some will fly for fear of being crushed under the ruin, some will join in making it. They will seek in the destruction of royalty, fame, and power, and wealth, and the homage of kings, with *Reubel*, with *Carnot*, with *Revelliere*,[31] and with the *Merlins* and the *Talliens*, rather than suffer exile and beggary with the *Condés* or the *Broglios*, the *Castries*, the *D'Avrais*, the *Serrents*, the *Cazalés*, and the long line of loyal suffering, patriot nobility, or to be butchered with the oracles and the victims of the laws, the *D'Ormesons*, the *D'Espremenils*, and the *Malesherbes*. This example we shall give, if instead of adhering to our fellows in a cause which is an honour to us all, we abandon the lawful government and lawful corporate body of France, to hunt for a shameful and ruinous fraternity, with this odious usurpation that disgraces civilised society and the human race.

And is then example nothing? It is everything. Example is the school of mankind, and they will learn at no other. This war is a war against that example. It is not a war for Louis the Eighteenth, or even for the property, virtue, fidelity of France. It is a war for George the Third, for Francis the Second, and for the dignity, property, honour, virtue, and religion of England, of Germany, and of all nations.

I know that all I have said of the systematic unsociability of this new-invented species of republic, and the impossibility of preserving peace, is answered by asserting that the scheme of manners, morals, and even of maxims and principles of state, is of no weight in a question of peace or war between communities. This doctrine is supported by example. The case of Algiers[32] is cited, with a hint, as if it were the stronger case. I should take no notice of this sort of inducement, if I had found it only where first it was. I do not want respect for those from whom I first heard it – but having no controversy at present with them, I only think it not amiss to rest on it a little, as I find it adopted, with much more of the same kind, by several of those on whom such reasoning had formerly made no apparent impression. If it had no force to prevent us from submitting to this necessary war, it furnishes no better ground for our making an unnecessary and ruinous peace.

This analogical argument drawn from the case of Algiers would lead us a good way. The fact is, we ourselves with a little cover, others more directly, pay a *tribute* to the republic of Algiers. Is it meant to reconcile us to the payment of a *tribute* to the French republic? That this, with other things more ruinous, will be demanded hereafter, I little doubt; but for the present, this will not be avowed – though our minds are to be gradually prepared for it. In truth, the arguments from this case are worth little, even to those who approve the buying an Algerine forbearance of piracy.[33] There are many things which men do not approve, that they must do to avoid a greater evil. To argue from thence, that they are to act in the same manner in all cases, is turning necessity into a law. Upon what is matter of prudence, the argument concludes the contrary way. Because we have done one humiliating act, we ought with infinite caution to admit more acts of the same nature, lest humiliation should become our habitual state. Matters of prudence are under the dominion of circumstances, and not of logical analogies. It is absurd to take it otherwise.

I, for one, do more than doubt the policy of this kind of convention with Algiers. On those who think as I do, the argument *ad hominem* can make no sort of impression. I know something of the constitution and composition of this very extraordinary republic. It has a constitution, I admit, similar to the present tumultuous military tyranny of France. by which a handful of obscure ruffians domineer over a fertile country and a brave people. For the composition, too, I admit the Algerine community resembles that of France; being formed out of the very scum, scandal, disgrace, and pest of the Turkish Asia. The Grand Seignior, to disburthen the country, suffers the dey to recruit in his dominions the corps of janizaries, or asaphs, which form the directory and council of elders of the African republic one and indivisible.[34] But notwithstanding this resemblance, which I allow, I never shall so far injure the janizarian republic of Algiers as to put it in comparison for every sort of crime, turpitude, and oppression with the Jacobin republic of Paris. There is no question with me to which of the two I should choose to be a neighbour or a subject. But situated as I am, I am in no danger of becoming to Algiers either the one or the other. It is not so in my relation to the atheistical fanatics of France. I *am* their neighbour; I *may* become their subject. Have the gentlemen, who borrowed this happy parallel, no idea, of the different conduct to be held with regard to the very same evil at an immense distance, and when it is at your door? when its power is enormous, as when it is comparatively as feeble as its distance is remote? when there is a barrier of language and usages, which prevents corruption through certain old correspondences and habitudes, from the contagion of the horrible novelties that are introduced into everything else? I can contemplate, without dread, a royal or a national tiger on the borders of Pegu. I can look at him, with an easy curiosity, as prisoner within bars in the menagerie of the Tower. But if, by habeas corpus, or otherwise, he was to come into the lobby of the House of Commons whilst your door was open, any of you would be more stout than wise, who would not gladly make your escape out of the back windows. I certainly should dread more from a wild cat in my bedchamber, than from all the lions that roar in the deserts behind Algiers. But in this parallel it is the cat that is at a distance, and the lions and tigers that are in our ante-chambers and our lobbies. Algiers is not near; Algiers is not powerful; Algiers is not our neighbour; Algiers is not infectious. Algiers, whatever it may be, is an old creation and we have good data to calculate all the mischief to be apprehended from it. When I find Algiers transferred to Calais, I will tell you what I think of that point. In the mean time, the case quoted from the Algerine reports will not apply as authority. We shall put it out of court; and so far as that goes, let the counsel for the Jacobin peace take nothing by their motion.

When we voted, as you and I did, with many more whom you and I respect and love, to resist this enemy, we were providing for dangers that were direct, home, pressing, and not remote, contingent, uncertain, and formed upon loose analogies. We judged of the danger with which we were menaced by Jacobin France, from the whole tenor of her conduct; not from one or two doubtful or detached acts or expressions. I not only concurred in the idea of combining with Europe in this war, but to the best of my power even stimulated ministers to that conjunction of interests and of efforts. I joined them with all my soul, on the principles contained in that manly and masterly state-paper, which I have two or three times referred to,* and may still more frequently hereafter. The diplomatic collection never was more enriched than with this piece. The historic facts justify every stroke of the master. "Thus painters write their names at Co."[35]

Various persons may concur in the same measure on various grounds. They may be various, without being contrary to or exclusive of each other. I thought the insolent, unprovoked aggression of the regicide upon our ally of Holland, a good ground of war. I think his manifest attempt to overturn the balance of Europe, a good ground of war. As a good ground of war, I consider his declaration of war on his Majesty and his kingdom. But though I have taken all these to my aid, I consider them as nothing more than as a sort of evidence to indicate the treasonable mind within. Long before their acts of aggression, and their declaration of war, the faction in France had assumed a form, had adopted a body of principles and maxims, and had regularly and systematically acted on them, by which she virtually had put herself in a posture, which was in itself a declaration of war against mankind.

It is said by the directory in their several manifestoes, that we of the people are tumultuous for peace; and that ministers pretend negotiation to amuse us. This they have learned from the language of many amongst ourselves, whose conversations have been one main cause of whatever extent the opinion for peace with regicide may be. But I, who think the ministers unfortunately to be but too serious in their proceedings, find myself obliged to say a little more on this subject of the popular opinion.

Before our opinions are quoted against ourselves, it is proper that, from our serious deliberation, they may be worth quoting. It is without reason we praise the wisdom of our constitution, in putting under the discretion of the Crown the awful trust of war and peace, if the ministers of the Crown virtually return it again into our hands. The trust was placed there as a sacred deposit, to secure us against popular rashness in plunging into wars, and against the effects of popular dismay, disgust, or lassitude, in getting out of them as imprudently as we might first engage in them. To have no other measure in judging of those great objects than our momentary opinions and desires, is to throw us back upon

---

* Declaration, Whitehall, Oct. 29, 1793.

that very democracy which, in this part, our constitution was formed to avoid.

It is no excuse at all for a minister, who at our desire takes a measure contrary to our safety, that it is our own act. He who does not stay the hand of suicide, is guilty of murder. On our part, I say, that to be instructed, is not to be degraded or enslaved. Information is an advantage to us; and we have a right to demand it. He that is bound to act in the dark cannot be said to act freely. When it appears evident to our governors that our desires and our interests are at variance, they ought not to gratify the former at the expense of the latter. Statesmen are placed on an eminence, that they may have a larger horizon than we can possibly command. They have a whole before them, which we can contemplate only in the parts, and often without the necessary relations. Ministers are not only our natural rulers, but our natural guides. Reason clearly and manfully delivered, has in itself a mighty force; but reason in the mouth of legal authority, is, I may fairly say, irresistible.

I admit that reason of state will not, in many circumstances, permit the disclosure of the true ground of a public proceeding. In that case silence is manly, and it is wise. It is fair to call for trust when the principle of reason itself suspends its public use. I take the distinction to be this: The ground of a particular measure, making a part of a plan, it is rarely proper to divulge; all the broader grounds of policy, on which the general plan is to be adopted, ought as rarely to be concealed. They, who have not the whole cause before them, call them politicians, call them people, call them what you will, are no judges. The difficulties of the case, as well as its fair side, ought to be presented. This ought to be done; and it is all that can be done. When we have our true situation distinctly presented to us, if then we resolve, with a blind and headlong violence, to resist the admonitions of our friends, and to cast ourselves into the hands of our potent and irreconcilable foes, then, and not till then, the ministers stand acquitted before God and man, for whatever may come.

Lamenting as I do, that the matter has not had so full and free a discussion as it requires, I mean to omit none of the points which seem to me necessary for consideration, previous to an arrangement which is for ever to decide the form and the fate of Europe. In the course, therefore, of what I shall have the honour to address to you, I propose the following questions to your serious thought:

– 1. Whether the present system, which stands for a government in France, be such as in peace and war affects the neighbouring states in a manner different from the internal government that formerly prevailed in that country? – 2. Whether that system, supposing its views hostile to other nations, possesses any means of being hurtful to them peculiar to itself? – 3. Whether there has been lately such a change in France, as to alter the nature of its system, or its effect upon other powers? – 4. Whether any public declarations or engagements exist, on the part of the allied powers, which stand in the way of a treaty of peace, which supposes the right and confirms the power of the regicide faction in France? – 5. What the state of the other powers of Europe will be with respect to each other, and their colonies, on the conclusion of a regicide peace? – 6. Whether we are driven to the absolute necessity of making that kind of peace?

These heads of inquiry will enable us to make the application of the several matters of fact and topics of argument, that occur in this vast discussion, to certain fixed principles. I do not mean to confine myself to the order in which they stand. I shall discuss them in such a manner as shall appear to me the best adapted for showing their mutual bearings and relations. Here then I close the public matter of my letter; but before I have done let me say one word in apology for myself.

In wishing this nominal peace not to be precipitated, I am sure no man living is less disposed to blame the present ministry than I am. Some of my oldest friends (and I wish I could say it of more of them) make a part in that ministry. There are some indeed, "whom my dim eyes in vain explore."[36] In my mind, a greater calamity could not have fallen on the public than the exclusion of one of them.[37] But I drive away that, with other melancholy thoughts. A great deal ought to be said upon that subject, or nothing. As to the distinguished persons to whom my friends who remain are joined, if benefits, nobly and generously conferred, ought to procure good wishes, they are entitled to my best vows; and they have them all. They have administered to me the only consolation I am capable of receiving, which is to know that no individual will suffer by my thirty years service to the public. If things should give us the comparative happiness of a struggle, I shall be found, I was going to say fighting, (that would be foolish,) but dying by the side of Mr. Pitt. I must add, that if anything defensive in our domestic system can possibly save us from the disasters of a regicide peace, he is the man to save us. If the finances in such a case can be repaired, he is the man to repair them. If I should lament any of his acts, it is only when they appear to me to have no resemblance to acts of his. But let him not have a confidence in himself, which no human abilities can warrant. His abilities are fully equal (and that is to say much for any man) to those which are opposed to him. But if we look to him as our security against the consequences of a regicide peace, let us be assured, that a regicide peace and a constitutional minis-try are terms that will not agree. With a regicide peace the king cannot long have a minister to serve him, nor the minister a king to serve. If the Great Disposer, in reward of the royal and the private virtues of our sovereign, should call him from the calami-tous spectacles, which will attend a state of amity with regicide, his successor will surely see them, unless the same Providence greatly anticipates the course of nature. Thinking thus, (and not, as I conceive, on light grounds,) I dare not flatter the reigning sovereign, nor any minister he has or can have, nor his successor apparent, nor any of those who may be called to serve him, with what appears to me a false state of their situation. We cannot have them and that peace together.

I do not forget that there had been a considerable difference between several of our friends, (with my insignificant self,) and the great man at the head of ministry, in an early stage of these discussions. But I am sure there was a period in which we agreed better in the danger of a Jacobin existence in France. At one time he and all Europe seemed to feel it. But why am not I converted with so many great powers, and so many great ministers? It is because I am old and slow. – I am in this year, 1796, only where all the powers of Europe were in 1793. I cannot move with this precession of the equinoxes, which is preparing for us the return of some very old, I am afraid no golden, æra, or the commence-ment of some new æra that must be denominated from some new metal. In this crisis I must hold my tongue, or I must speak with freedom. Falsehood and delusion are allowed in no case what-ever: but, as in the exercise of all the virtues, there is an economy of truth. It is a sort of temperance, by which a man speaks truth with measure that he may speak it the longer. But as the same rules do not hold in all cases – what would be right for you, who may presume on a series of years before you, would have no sense for me, who cannot, without absurdity, calculate on six months of life. What I say, I *must* say at once. Whatever I write is in its nature testamentary. It may have the weakness, but it has the sincerity, of a dying declaration. For the few days I have to linger here, I am removed completely from the busy scene of the world; but I hold myself to be still responsible for everything that I have done whilst I continued on the place of action. If the rawest Tyro in politics has been influenced by the authority of my grey hairs, and led by anything in my speeches, or my writings, to enter into this war, he has a right to call upon me to know why I have changed my opinions, or why, when those I voted with have adopted better notions, I persevere in exploded error?

When I seem not to acquiesce in the acts of those I respect in every degree short of superstition, I am obliged to give my reasons fully. I cannot set my authority against their authority. But to exert reason is not to revolt against authority. Reason and authority do not move in the same parallel. That reason is an *amicus curiæ*[38] who speaks *de plano*, not *pro tribunali*.[39] It is a friend who makes an useful suggestion to the court, without questioning its jurisdiction. Whilst he acknowledges its competence, he promotes its efficiency. I shall pursue the plan I have chalked out in my letters that follow this.

LETTER TO A NOBLE LORD

1796

MY LORD,

I COULD HARDLY flatter myself with the hope, that so very early in the season I should have to acknowledge obligations to the Duke of BEDFORD[1], and to the Earl of LAUDERDALE.[2] These noble persons have lost no time in conferring upon me that sort of honour, which it is alone within their competence, and which it is certainly most congenial to their nature, and to their manners, to bestow.

To be ill spoken of, in whatever language they speak, by the zealots of the new sect in philosophy and politics, of which these noble persons think so charitably, and of which others think so justly, to me, is no matter of uneasiness or surprise. To have incurred the displeasure of the Duke of Orleans[3] or the Duke of Bedford, to fall under the censure of citizen Brissot[4] or of his friend the Earl of Lauderdale, I ought to consider as proofs, not the least satisfactory, that I have produced some part of the effect I proposed by my endeavours. I have laboured hard to earn, what the noble lords are generous enough to pay. Personal offence I have given them none. The part they take against me is from zeal to the cause. It is well! It is perfectly well! I have to do homage to their justice. I have to thank the Bedfords and the Lauderdales for having so faithfully and so fully acquitted towards me whatever arrear of debt was left undischarged by the Priestleys and the Paines.[5]

Some, perhaps, may think them executors in their own wrong: I at least have nothing to complain of. They have gone beyond the demands of justice. They have been (a little perhaps beyond their intention) favourable to me. They have been the means of bringing out, by their invectives, the handsome things which Lord Grenville[6] has had the goodness and condescension to say in my behalf. Retired as I am from the world, and from all its affairs and all its pleasures, I confess it does kindle, in my nearly extinguished feelings, a very vivid satisfaction to be so attacked and so commended. It is soothing to my wounded mind, to be commended by an able, vigorous, and well-informed statesman, and at the very moment when he stands forth with a manliness and resolution, worthy of himself and of his cause, for the preservation of the person and government of our sovereign, and therein for the security of the laws, the liberties, the morals, and the lives of his people. To be in any fair way connected with such things, is indeed a distinction. No philosophy can make me above it: no melancholy can depress me so low, as to make me wholly insensible to such an honour.

Why will they not let me remain in obscurity and inaction? Are they apprehensive, that if an atom of me remains, the sect has something to fear? Must I be annihilated, lest, like old *John Zisca's*,[7] my skin might be made into a drum, to animate Europe to eternal battle, against a tyranny that threatens to overwhelm all Europe, and all the human race?

My Lord, it is a subject of awful meditation. Before this of France, the annals of all time have not furnished an instance of a *complete* revolution. That Revolution seems to have extended even to the constitution of the mind of man. It has this of wonderful in it, that it resembles what Lord Verulam[8] says of the operations of nature. It was perfect, not only in its elements and principles, but in all its members and its organs from the very beginning. The moral scheme of France furnishes the only pattern ever known, which they who admire will *instantly* resemble. It is indeed an inexhaustible repertory of one kind of examples. In my wretched condition, though hardly to be classed with the living, I am not safe from them. They have tigers to fall upon animated strength. They have hyenas to prey upon carcasses. The national menagerie is collected by the first physiologists of the time; and it is defective in no description of savage nature. They pursue even such as me, into the obscurest retreats, and haul them before their revolutionary tribunals. Neither sex, nor age, nor the sanctuary of the tomb, is sacred to them. They have so determined a hatred to all privileged orders, that they deny even to the departed the sad immunities of the grave. They are not wholly without an object. Their turpitude purveys to their malice; and they unplumb the dead for bullets to assassinate the living. If all revolutionists were not proof against all caution, I should recommend it to their consideration, that no persons were ever known in history, either sacred or profane, to vex the sepulchre, and, by their sorceries, to call up the prophetic dead, with any other event, than the prediction of their own disastrous fate – "Leave me, oh leave me to repose!"

In one thing I can excuse the Duke of Bedford for his attack upon me and my mortuary pension. He cannot readily comprehend the transaction he condemns. What I have obtained was the fruit of no bargain; the production of no intrigue; the result of no compromise; the effect of no solicitation. The first suggestion of it never came from me, mediately or immediately, to his Majesty or any of his ministers. It was long known that the instant my engagements would permit it, and before the heaviest of all calamities had for ever condemned me to obscurity and sorrow, I had resolved on a total retreat. I had executed that design. I was entirely out of the way of serving or of hurting any statesman, or any party, when the ministers so generously and so nobly carried into effect the spontaneous bounty of the crown. Both descriptions have acted as became them. When I could no longer serve them, the ministers have considered my situation. When I could no longer hurt them, the revolutionists have trampled on my infirmity. My gratitude, I trust, is equal to the manner in which the benefit was conferred. It came to me indeed, at a time of life, and in a state of mind and body, in which no circumstance of fortune could afford me any real pleasure. But this was no fault in the royal donor, or in his ministers, who were pleased, in acknowledging the merits of an invalid servant of the public, to assuage the sorrows of a desolate old man.

It would ill become me to boast of anything. It would as ill become me, thus called upon, to depreciate the value of a long life, spent with unexampled toil in the service of my country. Since the total body of my services, on account of the industry which was shown in them, and the fairness of my intentions, have obtained the acceptance of my sovereign, it would be absurd in me to range myself on the side of the Duke of Bedford and the corresponding society,[9] or, as far as in me lies, to permit a dispute on the rate at which the authority appointed by *our* constitution to estimate such things has been pleased to set them.

Loose libels ought to be passed by in silence and contempt. By me they have been so always. I knew that as long as I remained in public, I should live down the calumnies of malice, and the judgments of ignorance. If I happened to be now and then in the wrong, (as who is not?) like all other men, I must bear the consequence of my faults and my mistakes. The libels of the present day are just of the same stuff as the libels of the past. But they derive an importance from the rank of the persons they come from, and the gravity of the place where they were uttered. In some way or other I ought to take some notice of them. To assert myself thus traduced is not vanity or arrogance. It is a demand of justice; it is a demonstration of gratitude. If I am unworthy, the ministers are worse than prodigal. On that hypothesis, I perfectly agree with the Duke of Bedford.

For whatever I have been (I am now no more) I put myself on my country. I ought to be allowed a reasonable freedom, because I stand upon my deliverance; and no culprit ought to plead in irons. Even in the utmost latitude of defensive liberty, I wish to preserve all possible decorum. Whatever it may be in the eyes of these noble persons themselves, to me their situation calls for the most profound respect. If I should happen to trespass a little, which I trust I shall not, let it always be supposed, that a confusion of characters may produce mistakes; that, in the masquerades of the grand carnival of our age, whimsical adventures happen; odd things are said and pass off. If I should fail a single point in the high respect I owe to those illustrious persons, I cannot be supposed to mean the Duke of Bedford and the Earl of Lauderdale of the House of Peers, but the Duke of Bedford and the Earl of Lauderdale of Palace-Yard! – The Dukes and Earls of Brentford. There they are on the pavement; there they seem to come nearer to my humble level; and, virtually at least, to have waived their high privilege.

Making this protestation, I refuse all revolutionary tribunals, where men have been put to death for no other reason, than that they had obtained favours from the Crown. I claim, not the letter, but the spirit, of the old English law, that is, to be tried by my peers. I decline his Grace's jurisdiction as a judge. I challenge the Duke of Bedford as a juror to pass upon the value of my services. Whatever his natural parts may be, I cannot recognise, in his few and idle years, the competence to judge of my long and laborious life. If I can help it, he shall not be on the inquest of my *quantum meruit*.[10] Poor rich man! He can hardly know anything of public industry in its exertions, or can estimate its compensations when its work is done. I have no doubt of his Grace's readiness in all the calculations of vulgar arithmetic; but I shrewdly suspect, that he is little studied in the theory of moral proportions; and has never learned the rule of three in the arithmetic of policy and state.

His Grace thinks I have obtained too much. I answer, that my exertions, whatever they have been, were such as no hopes of pecuniary reward could possibly excite; and no pecuniary compensation can possibly reward them. Between money and such services, if done by abler men than I am, there is no common principle of comparison; they are quantities incommensurable. Money is made for the comfort and convenience of animal life. It cannot be a reward for what mere animal life must indeed sustain, but never can inspire. With submission to his Grace, I have not had more than sufficient. As to any noble use, I trust I know how to employ, as well as he, a much greater fortune than he possesses. In a more confined application, I certainly stand in need of every kind of relief and easement much more than he does. When I say I have not received more than I deserve, is this the language I hold to Majesty? No! Far, very far, from it! Before that presence, I claim no merit at all. Everything towards me is favour, and bounty. One style to a gracious benefactor; another to a proud and insulting foe.

His Grace is pleased to aggravate my guilt, by charging my acceptance of his Majesty's grant as a departure from my ideas, and the spirit of my conduct with regard to economy. If it be, my ideas of economy were false and ill-founded. But they are the Duke of Bedford's ideas of economy I have contradicted, and not my own. If he means to allude to certain bills brought in by me on a message from the throne in 1782, I tell him that there is nothing in my conduct that can contradict either the letter or the spirit of those acts. Does he mean the pay-office act?[11] I take it for granted he does not. The act to which he alludes, is, I suppose, the establishment act.[12] I greatly doubt whether his Grace has ever read the one or the other. The first of these systems cost me, with every assistance which my then situation gave me, pains incredible. I found an opinion common through all the offices, and general in the public at large, that it would prove impossible to reform and methodise the office of paymaster-general. I undertook it, however; and I succeeded in my undertaking. Whether the military service, or whether the general economy of our finances, have profited by that act, I leave to those who are acquainted with the army, and with the treasury, to judge.

An opinion full as general prevailed also at the same time, that nothing could be done for the regulation of the civil-list establishment. The very attempt to introduce method into it, and any limitations to its services, was held absurd. I had not seen the man, who so much as suggested one economical principle, or an economical expedient, upon that subject. Nothing but coarse amputation, or coarser taxation, were then talked of, both of them without design, combination, or the least shadow of principle. Blind and headlong zeal, or factious fury, were the whole contribution brought by the most noisy on that occasion, towards the satisfaction of the public, or the relief of the Crown.

Let me tell my youthful censor, that the necessities of that time required something very different from what others then suggested, or what his Grace now conceives. Let me inform him, that it was one of the most critical periods in our annals.

Astronomers have supposed, that if a certain comet, whose path intercepted the ecliptic, had met the earth in some (I forget what) sign, it would have whirled us along with it, in its eccentric course, into God knows what regions of heat and cold. Had the portentous comet of the rights of man, (which "from its horrid hair shakes pestilence and war," and "with fear of change perplexes monarchs,") had that comet crossed upon us in that internal state of England, nothing human could have prevented our being irresistibly hurried, out of the highway of heaven, into all the vices, crimes, horrors, and miseries of the French Revolution.

Happily, France was not then Jacobinised. Her hostility was at a good distance. We had a limb cut off; but we preserved the body. We lost our colonies; but we kept our constitution. There was, indeed, much intestine heat; there was a dreadful fermentation. Wild and savage insurrection quitted the woods, and prowled about our streets in the name of reform. Such was the distemper of the public mind, that there was no madman, in his maddest ideas, and maddest projects, who might not count upon numbers to support his principles and execute his designs.

Many of the changes, by a great misnomer called parliamentary reforms, went, not in the intention of all the professors and supporters of them, undoubtedly, but went in their certain, and, in my opinion, not very remote effect, home to the utter destruction of the constitution of this kingdom. Had they taken place, not France, but England, would have had the honour of leading up the death-dance of democratic revolution. Other projects, exactly coincident in time with those, struck at the very existence of the kingdom under any constitution. There are who

remember the blind fury of some, and the lamentable help-
lessness of others; here, a torpid confusion, from a panic fear of
the danger; there, the same inaction from a stupid insensibility
to it; here, well-wishers to the mischief; there, indifferent
lookers-on. At the same time, a sort of national convention,[13]
dubious in its nature, and perilous in its example, nosed parliament in the very seat of its authority; sat with a sort of superintendence over it; and little less than dictated to it, not only laws,
but the very form and essence of legislature itself. In Ireland
things ran in a still more eccentric course. Government was un-
nerved, confounded, and in a manner suspended. Its equipoise
was totally gone. I do not mean to speak disrespectfully of Lord
North.[14] He was a man of admirable parts; of general knowledge;
of a versatile understanding fitted for every sort of business; of
infinite wit and pleasantry; of a delightful temper; and with a
mind most perfectly disinterested. But it would be only to
degrade myself by a weak adulation, and not to honour the
memory of a great man, to deny that he wanted something of the
vigilance and spirit of command, that the time required. Indeed,
a darkness, next to the fog of this awful day, loured over the
whole region. For a little time the helm appeared abandoned –

> *Ipse diem noctemque negat discernere cælo,*
> *Nec meminisse viæ mediâ Palinurus in undâ.*[15]

At that time I was connected with men of high place in the
community. They loved liberty as much as the Duke of Bedford
can do; and they understood it at least as well. Perhaps their
politics, as usual, took a tincture from their character, and they
cultivated what they loved. The liberty they pursued was a liberty
inseparable from order, from virtue, from morals, and from religion; and was neither hypocritically nor fanatically followed.
They did not wish, that liberty, in itself one of the first of blessings, should in its perversion become the greatest curse which
could fall upon mankind. To preserve the constitution entire,
and practically equal to all the great ends of its formation, not in
one single part, but in all its parts, was to them the first object.
Popularity and power they regarded alike. These were with them
only different means of obtaining that object; and had no preference over each other in their minds, but as one or the other might
afford a surer or a less certain prospect of arriving at that end. It is
some consolation to me in the cheerless gloom, which darkens

the evening of my life, that with them I commenced my political career, and never for a moment, in reality, nor in appearance, for any length of time, was separated from their good wishes and good opinion.

By what accident it matters not, nor upon what desert, but just then, and in the midst of that hunt of obloquy, which ever has pursued me with a full cry through life, I had obtained a very considerable degree of public confidence. I know well enough how equivocal a test this kind of popular opinion forms of the merit that obtained it. I am no stranger to the insecurity of its tenure. I do not boast of it. It is mentioned to show, not how highly I prize the thing, but my right to value the use I made of it. I endeavoured to turn that short-lived advantage to myself into a permanent benefit to my country. Far am I from detracting from the merit of some gentlemen, out of office or in it, on that occasion. No! – It is not my way to refuse a full and heaped measure of justice to the aids that I receive. I have, through life, been willing to give everything to others; and to reserve nothing for myself, but the inward conscience, that I had omitted no pains to discover, to animate, to discipline, to direct the abilities of the country for its service, and to place them in the best light to improve their age, or to adorn it. This conscience I have. I have never suppressed any man; never checked him for a moment in his course, by any jealousy, or by any policy. I was always ready, to the height of my means, (and they were always infinitely below my desires,) to forward those abilities which overpowered my own. He is an ill-furnished undertaker, who has no machinery but his own hands to work with. Poor in my own faculties, I ever thought myself rich in theirs. In that period of difficulty and danger, more especially, I consulted, and sincerely co-operated with, men of all parties, who seemed disposed to the same ends, or to any main part of them. Nothing to prevent disorder was omitted: when it appeared, nothing to subdue it was left uncounselled, nor unexecuted, as far as I could prevail. At the time I speak of, and having a momentary lead, so aided and so encouraged, and as a feeble instrument in a mighty hand – I do not say I saved my country; I am sure I did my country important service. There were few, indeed, that did not at that time acknowledge it, and that time was thirteen years ago. It was but one voice, that no man in the kingdom better deserved an honourable provision should be made for him.

So much for my general conduct through the whole of the portentous crisis from 1780 to 1782, and the general sense then entertained of that conduct by my country. But my character, as a reformer, in the particular instances which the Duke of Bedford refers to, is so connected in principle with my opinions on the hideous changes, which have since barbarised France, and, spreading thence, threaten the political and moral order of the whole world, that it seems to demand something of a more detailed discussion.

My economical reforms were not, as his Grace may think, the suppression of a paltry pension or employment, more or less. Economy in my plans was, as it ought to be, secondary, subordinate, instrumental. I acted on state principles. I found a great distemper in the commonwealth; and, according to the nature of the evil and of the object, I treated it. The malady was deep; it was complicated, in the causes and in the symptoms. Throughout it was full of contra-indicants. On one hand government, daily growing more invidious from an apparent increase of the means of strength, was every day growing more contemptible by real weakness. Nor was this dissolution confined to government commonly so called. It extended to parliament; which was losing not a little in its dignity and estimation, by an opinion of its not acting on worthy motives. On the other hand, the desires of the people (partly natural and partly infused into them by art) appeared in so wild and inconsiderate a manner, with regard to the economical object, (for I set aside for a moment the dreadful tampering with the body of the constitution itself,) that, if their petitions had literally been complied with, the state would have been convulsed; and a gate would have been opened, through which all property might be sacked and ravaged. Nothing could have saved the public from the mischiefs of the false reform but its absurdity; which would soon have brought itself, and with it all real reform, into discredit. This would have left a rankling wound in the hearts of the people, who would know they had failed in the accomplishment of their wishes, but who, like the rest of mankind in all ages, would impute the blame to anything rather than to their own proceedings. But there were then persons in the world, who nourished complaint; and would have been thoroughly disappointed if the people were ever satisfied. I was not of that humour. I wished that they *should* be satisfied.

It was my aim to give to the people the substance of what I knew they desired, and what I thought was right, whether they desired it or not, before it had been modified for them into senseless petitions. I knew that there is a manifest, marked distinction, which ill men with ill designs, or weak men incapable of any design, will constantly be confounding, that is, a marked distinction between change and reformation. The former alters the substance of the objects themselves; and gets rid of all their essential good, as well as of all the accidental evil, annexed to them. Change is novelty; and whether it is to operate any one of the effects of reformation at all, or whether it may not contradict the very principle upon which reformation is desired, cannot be certainly known beforehand. Reform is, not a change in the substance, or in the primary modification, of the object, but, a direct application of a remedy to the grievance complained of. So far as that is removed, all is sure. It stops there; and, if it fails, the substance which underwent the operation, at the very worst, is but where it was.

All this, in effect, I think, but am not sure, I have said elsewhere. It cannot at this time be too often repeated; line upon line; precept upon precept; until it comes into the currency of a proverb, *to innovate is not to reform*. The French revolutionists complained of everything; they refused to reform anything; and they left nothing, no, nothing at all *unchanged*. The consequences are *before* us, – not in remote history; not in future prognostication: they are about us; they are upon us. They shake the public security; they menace private enjoyment. They dwarf the growth of the young; they break the quiet of the old. If we travel, they stop our way. They infest us in town; they pursue us to the country. Our business is interrupted; our repose is troubled; our pleasures are saddened; our very studies are poisoned and perverted, and knowledge is rendered worse than ignorance, by the enormous evils of this dreadful innovation. The revolution harpies of France, sprung from night and hell, or from that chaotic anarchy, which generates equivocally "all monstrous, all prodigious things," cuckoo-like, adulterously lay their eggs, and brood over, and hatch them in the nest of every neighbouring state. These obscene harpies, who deck themselves in I know not what divine attributes, but who in reality are foul and ravenous birds of prey, (both mothers and daughters,) flutter over our heads, and souse down upon our tables, and leave nothing unrent, unrifled, unravaged, or unpolluted with the slime of their filthy offal.*

If his Grace can contemplate the result of this complete innovation, or, as some friends of his will call it, *reform*, in the whole body of its solidity and compounded mass, at which, as Hamlet says, the face of heaven glows with horror and indignation, and which, in truth, makes every reflecting mind, and every feeling heart, perfectly thought-sick, without a thorough abhorrence of everything they say, and everything they do, I am amazed at the morbid strength or the natural infirmity of his mind.

It was then not my love, but my hatred, to innovation, that produced my plan of reform. Without troubling myself with the exactness of the logical diagram, I considered them as things substantially opposite. It was to prevent that evil, that I proposed the measures, which his Grace is pleased, and I am not sorry he is pleased, to recall to my recollection. I had (what I hope that noble duke will remember in all its operations) a state to preserve, as well as a state to reform. I had a people to gratify, but not to inflame, or to mislead. I do not claim half the credit for what I did, as for what I prevented from being done. In that situation of the public mind, I did not undertake, as was then proposed, to new-model the House of Commons or the House of Lords; or to change the authority under which any officer of the Crown acted, who was suffered at all to exist. Crown, Lords, Commons, judicial system, system of administration, existed as they had existed before; and in the mode and manner in which they had always existed. My measures were, what I then truly stated them to the House to be, in their intent, healing and mediatorial. A complaint was made of too much influence in the House of Commons; I reduced it in both Houses; and I gave my reasons

---

*Tristius haud illis monstrum, nec sævior ulla
 Pestis, et ira Deûm Stygiis sese extulit undis.
 Virginei volucrum vultus; fædissima ventris
 Proluvies; uncæque manus; et pallida semper
 Ora fame —[16]

Here the poet breaks the line, because he (and that he is Virgil) had not verse or language to describe that monster even as he had conceived her. Had he lived in our time, he would have been more overpowered with the reality than he was with the imagination. Virgil only knew the horror of the times before him. Had he lived to see the revolutionists and constitutionalists of France, he would have had more horrid and disgusting features of his harpies to describe, and more frequent failures in the attempt to describe them.

article by article for every reduction, and showed why I thought it safe for the service of the state.[17] I heaved the lead every inch of way I made. A disposition to expense was complained of; to that I opposed, not mere retrenchment, but a system of economy, which would make a random expense, without plan or foresight, in future not easily practicable. I proceeded upon principles of research to put me in possession of my matter; on principles of method to regulate it; and on principles in the human mind and in civil affairs to secure and perpetuate the operation. I conceived nothing arbitrarily; nor proposed anything to be done by the will and pleasure of others, or my own; but by reason, and by reason only. I have ever abhorred, since the first dawn of my understanding to this its obscure twilight, all the operations of opinion, fancy, inclination, and will, in the affairs of government, where only a sovereign reason, paramount to all forms of legislation and administration, should dictate. Government is made for the very purpose of opposing that reason to will and caprice, in the reformers or in the reformed, in the governors or in the governed, in kings, in senates, or in people.

On a careful review, therefore, and analysis, of all the component parts of the civil list, and on weighing them against each other, in order to make, as much as possible, all of them a subject of estimate, (the foundation and cornerstone of all regular provident economy,) it appeared to me evident, that this was impracticable, whilst that part, called the pension list, was totally discretionary in its amount. For this reason, and for this only, I proposed to reduce it, both in its gross quantity, and in its larger individual proportions, to a certainty; lest, if it were left without a *general* limit, it might eat up the civil-list service; if suffered to be granted in portions too great for the fund, it might defeat its own end; and, by unlimited allowances to some, it might disable the Crown in means of providing for others. The pension list was to be kept as a sacred fund; but it could not be kept as a constant, open fund, sufficient for growing demands, if some demands would wholly devour it. The tenor of the act will show that it regarded the civil list *only*, the reduction of which to some sort of estimate was my great object.

No other of the Crown funds did I meddle with, because they had not the same relations. This of the four and a half per cents[18] does his Grace imagine had escaped me, or had escaped all the men of business, who acted with me in those regulations? I knew that such a fund existed, and that pensions had been always granted on it, before his Grace was born. This fund was full in my eye. It was full in the eyes of those who worked with me. It was left on principle. On principle I did what was then done; and on principle what was left undone was omitted. I did not dare to rob the nation of all funds to reward merit. If I pressed this point too close, I acted contrary to the avowed principles on which I went. Gentlemen are very fond of quoting me; but if any one thinks it worth his while to know the rules that guided me in my plan of reform, he will read my printed speech on that subject; at least what is contained from page 230 to page 241 in the second volume of the collection which a friend has given himself the trouble to make of my publications.[19] Be this as it may, these two bills, (though achieved with the greatest labour, and management of every sort, both within and without the House,) were only a part, and but a small part, of a very large system, comprehending all the objects I stated in opening my proposition, and, indeed, many more, which I just hinted at in my speech to the electors of Bristol, when I was put out of that representation. All these, in some state or other of forwardness, I have long had by me.

But do I justify his Majesty's grace on these grounds? I think them the least of my services! The time gave them an occasional value. What I have done in the way of political economy was far from confined to this body of measures. I did not come into parliament to con my lesson. I had earned my pension before I set my foot in St. Stephen's chapel. I was prepared and disciplined to this political warfare. The first session I sat in parliament, I found it necessary to analyse the whole commercial, financial, constitutional, and foreign interests of Great Britain and its empire. A great deal was then done; and more, far more, would have been done, if more had been permitted by events. Then, in the vigour of my manhood, my constitution sunk under my labour. Had I then died, (and I seemed to myself very near death,) I had then earned for those who belonged to me, more than the Duke of Bedford's ideas of service are of power to estimate. But, in truth, these services I am called to account for are not those on which I value myself the most. If I were to call for a reward, (which I have never done,) it should be for those in which for fourteen years, without intermission, I showed the most indus- try, and had the least success; I mean in the affairs of India. They are those on which I value myself the most; most for the importance; most for the labour; most for the judgment; most for constancy and perseverance in the pursuit. Others may value them most for the *intention*. In that, surely, they are not mistaken.

Does his Grace think, that they, who advised the Crown to make my retreat easy, considered me only as an economist? That, well understood, however, is a good deal. If I had not deemed it of some value, I should not have made political economy an object of my humble studies, from my very early youth to near the end of my service in parliament, even before (at least to any knowledge of mine) it had employed the thoughts of speculative men in other parts of Europe. At that time it was still in its infancy in England, where, in the last century, it had its origin. Great and learned men thought my studies were not wholly thrown away, and deigned to communicate with me now and then on some particulars of their immortal works. Something of these studies may appear incidentally in some of the earliest things I published. The House has been witness to their effect, and has profited of them more or less for above eight and twenty years.

To their estimate I leave the matter. I was not, like his Grace of Bedford, swaddled, and rocked, and dandled into a legislator; "*Nitor in adversum*"[20] is the motto for a man like me. I possessed not one of the qualities, nor cultivated one of the arts, that recommend men to the favour and protection of the great. I was not made for a minion or a tool. As little did I follow the trade of winning the hearts, by imposing on the understandings, of the people. At every step of my progress in life, (for in every step was I traversed and opposed,) and at every turnpike I met, I was obliged to show my passport, and again and again to prove my sole title to the honour of being useful to my country, by a proof that I was not wholly unacquainted with its laws, and the whole system of its interests both abroad and at home. Otherwise no rank, no toleration, even for me. I had no arts but manly arts. On them I have stood, and, please God, in spite of the Duke of Bedford and the Earl of Lauderdale, to the last gasp will I stand.

Had his Grace condescended to inquire concerning the person, whom he has not thought it below him to reproach, he might have found, that, in the whole course of my life, I have never, on any pretence of economy, or on any other pretence, so much as in a single instance, stood between any man and his reward of service, or his encouragement in useful talent and pursuit, from the highest of those services and pursuits to the lowest. On the contrary I have, on an hundred occasions, exerted myself with singular zeal to forward every man's even tolerable pretensions. I have more than once had good-natured reprehensions from my friends for carrying the matter to something bordering on abuse. This line of conduct, whatever its merits might be, was partly owing to natural disposition; but I think full as much to reason and principle. I looked on the consideration of public service, or public ornament, to be real and very justice: and I ever held a scanty and penurious justice to partake of the nature of a wrong. I held it to be, in its consequences, the worst economy in the world. In saving money, I soon can count up all the good I do; but when, by a cold penury, I blast the abilities of a nation, and stunt the growth of its active energies, the ill I may do is beyond all calculation. Whether it be too much or too little, whatever I have done has been general and systematic. I have never entered into those trifling vexations, and oppressive details, that have been falsely, and most ridiculously, laid to my charge.

Did I blame the pensions given to Mr. Barré and Mr. Dunning[21] between the proposition and execution of my plan? No! surely no! Those pensions were within my principles. I assert it, those gentlemen deserved their pensions, their titles – all they had; and more had they had, I should have been but pleased the more. They were men of talents; they were men of service. I put the profession of the law out of the question in one of them. It is a service that rewards itself. But their *public service*, though, from their abilities unquestionably of more value than mine, in its quantity and it duration was not to be mentioned with it. But I never could drive a hard bargain in my life, concerning any matter whatever; and least of all do I know how to haggle and huckster with merit. Pension for myself I obtained none; nor did I solicit any. Yet I was loaded with hatred for everything that was withheld, and with obloquy for everything that was given. I was thus left to support the grants of a name ever dear to me, and ever venerable to the world, in favour of those, who were no friends of mine or of his, against the rude attacks of those who were at that time friends to the grantees, and their own zealous partisans. I have never heard the Earl of Lauderdale complain of these pensions. He finds nothing wrong till he comes to me. This is impartiality, in the true, modern, revolutionary style.

Whatever I did at that time, so far as it regarded order and economy, is stable and eternal; as all principles must be. A particular order of things may be altered; order itself cannot lose its value. As to other particulars, they are variable by time and by circumstances. Laws of regulation are not fundamental laws. The public exigencies are the masters of all such laws. They rule the laws, and are not to be ruled by them. They who exercise the legislative power at the time must judge.

It may be new to his Grace, but I beg leave to tell him, that mere parsimony is not economy. It is separable in theory from it; and in fact it may, or it may not, be a *part* of economy, according to circumstances. Expense, and great expense, may be an essential part in true economy. If parsimony were to be considered as one of the kinds of that virtue, there is however another and a higher economy. Economy is a distributive virtue, and consists not in saving, but in selection. Parsimony requires no providence, no sagacity, no powers of combination, no comparison, no judgment. Mere instinct, and that not an instinct of the noblest kind, may produce this false economy in perfection. The other economy has larger views. It demands a discriminating judgment, and a firm, sagacious mind. It shuts one door to impudent importunity, only to open another, and a wider, to unpresuming merit. If none but meritorious service or real talent were to be rewarded, this nation has not wanted, and this nation will not want, the means of rewarding all the service it ever will receive, and encouraging all the merit it ever will produce. No state, since the foundation of society, has been impoverished by that species of profusion. Had the economy of selection and proportion been at all times observed, we should not now have had an overgrown Duke of Bedford, to oppress the industry of humble men, and to limit, by the standard of his own conceptions, the justice, the bounty, or, if he pleases, the charity of the Crown.

His Grace may think as meanly as he will of my deserts in the far greater part of my conduct in life. It is free for him to do so. There will always be some difference of opinion in the value of political services. But there is one merit of mine, which he, of all men living, ought to be the last to call in question. I have supported with very great zeal, and I am told with some degree of success, those opinions, or if his Grace likes another expression better, those old prejudices, which buoy up the ponderous mass of his nobility, wealth and titles. I have omitted no exertion to prevent him and them from sinking to that level, to which the meretricious French faction, his Grace at least coquets with, omit no exertion to reduce both. I have done all I could to discountenance their inquiries into the fortunes of those, who hold large portions of wealth without any apparent merit of their own. I have strained every nerve to keep the Duke of Bedford in that situation, which alone makes him my superior. Your Lordship has been a witness of the use he makes of that pre-eminence.

But be it, that this is virtue! Be it, that there is virtue in this well-selected rigour; yet all virtues are not equally becoming to all men and at all times. There are crimes, undoubtedly there are crimes, which in all seasons of our existence, ought to put a generous antipathy in action; crimes that provoke an indignant justice, and call forth a warm and animated pursuit. But all things that concern, what I may call, the preventive police of morality, all things merely rigid, harsh, and censorial, the antiquated moralists, at whose feet I was brought up, would not have thought these the fittest matter to form the favourite virtues of young men of rank. What might have been well enough, and have been received with a veneration mixed with awe and terror, from an old, severe, crabbed Cato,[22] would have wanted something of propriety in the young Scipios,[23] the ornament of the Roman nobility, in the flower of their life. But the times, the morals, the masters, the scholars, have all undergone a thorough revolution. It is a vile illiberal school, this new French academy of the *sans culottes*. There is nothing in it that is fit for a gentleman to learn.

Whatever its vogue may be, I still flatter myself, that the parents of the growing generation will be satisfied with what is to be taught to their children in Westminster, in Eton, or in Winchester: I still indulge the hope that no *grown* gentleman or nobleman of our time will think of finishing at Mr. Thelwall's[24] lecture whatever may have been left incomplete at the old universities of his country. I would give to Lord Grenville and Mr. Pitt for a motto, what was said of a Roman censor or prætor (or what was he?) who, in virtue of a Senatus consultum,[25] shut up certain academies,

"Cludere ludum impudentiæ jussit."[26]

Every honest father of a family in the kingdom will rejoice at the breaking up for the holidays, and will pray that there may be a very long vacation in all such schools.

The awful state of the time, and not myself, or my own justification, is my true object in what I now write; or in what I shall ever write or say. It little signifies to the world what becomes of such things as me, or even as the Duke of Bedford. What I say about either of us is nothing more than a vehicle, as you, my Lord, will easily perceive, to convey my sentiments on matters far more worthy of your attention. It is when I stick to my apparent first subject that I ought to apologise, not when I depart from it. I therefore must beg your Lordship's pardon for again resuming it after this very short digression; assuring you that I shall never altogether lose sight of such matter as persons abler than I am may turn to some profit.

The Duke of Bedford conceives, that he is obliged to call the attention of the House of Peers to his Majesty's grant to me, which he considers as excessive, and out of all bounds.

I know not how it has happened, but it really seems, that, whilst his Grace was meditating his well-considered censure upon me, he fell into a sort of sleep. Homer nods; and the Duke of Bedford may dream; and as dreams (even his golden dreams) are apt to be ill-pieced and incongruously put together, his Grace preserved his idea of reproach to *me*, but took the subject-matter from the Crown grants *to his own family*. This is "the stuff of which his dreams are made." In that way of putting things together his Grace is perfectly in the right. The grants to the house of Russell were so enormous, as not only to outrage economy, but even to stagger credibility. The Duke of Bedford is the leviathan among all the creatures of the Crown. He tumbles about his unwieldy bulk; he plays and frolics in the ocean of the royal bounty. Huge as he is, and whilst "he lies floating many a rood,"[27] he is still a creature. His ribs, his fins, his whalebone, his blubber, the very spiracles through which he spouts a torrent of brine against his origin, and covers me all over with the spray, – everything of him and about him is from the throne. Is it for *him* to question the dispensation of the royal favour?

I really am at a loss to draw any sort of parallel between the public merits of his Grace, by which he justifies the grants he holds, and these services of mine, on the favourable construction of which I have obtained what his Grace so much disapproves. In private life, I have not at all the honour of acquaintance with the noble Duke. But I ought to presume, and it costs me nothing to do so, that he abundantly deserves the

esteem and love of all who live with him. But as to public
service, why truly it would not be more ridiculous for me to
compare myself in rank, in fortune, in splendid descent, in
youth, strength, or figure, with the Duke of Bedford, than to
make a parallel between his services and my attempts to be useful to my country. It would not be in gross adulation, but uncivil
irony, to say, that he has any public merit of his own to keep
alive the idea of the services, by which his vast landed pensions
were obtained. My merits, whatever they are, are original and
personal; his are derivative. It is his ancestor, the original pensioner, that has laid up this inexhaustible fund of merit, which
makes his Grace so very delicate and exceptious about the merit
of all other grantees of the Crown. Had he permitted me to
remain in quiet, I should have said, 'tis his estate; that's enough.
It is his by law; what have I to do with it or its history? He
would naturally have said on his side, 'tis this man's fortune. –
He is as good now as my ancestor was two hundred and fifty
years ago. I am a young man with very old pensions; he is an
old man with very young pensions, – that's all.

Why will his Grace, by attacking me, force me reluctantly
to compare my little merit with that which obtained from the
Crown those prodigies of profuse donation, by which he
tramples on the mediocrity of humble and laborious individuals?
I would willingly leave him to the herald's college, which the
philosophy of the sans culottes (prouder by far than all the
Garters, and Norroys, and Clarencieux, and Rouge Dragons,[28]
that ever pranced in a procession of what his friends call aristocrats and despots) will abolish with contumely and scorn. These
historians, recorders, and blazoners of virtues and arms, differ
wholly from that other description of historians, who never
assign any act of politicians to a good motive. These gentle historians, on the contrary, dip their pens in nothing but the milk of
human kindness. They seek no further for merit than the preamble of a patent, or the inscription on a tomb. With them every
man created a peer is first a hero ready made. They judge of
every man's capacity for office by the offices he has filled; and the
more offices the more ability. Every general officer with them
is a Marlborough;[29] every statesman a Burleigh;[30] every judge a
Murray or a Yorke.[31] They who, alive, were laughed at or pitied
by all their acquaintance, make as good a figure as the best of
them in the pages of Guillim, Edmondson, and Collins.[32]

To these recorders, so full of good nature to the great and prosperous, I would willingly leave the first Baron Russell, and Earl of Bedford, and the merits of his grants. But the aulnager, the weigher, the meter of grants, will not suffer us to acquiesce in the judgment of the prince reigning at the time when they were made. They are never good to those who earn them. Well then; since the new grantees have war made on them by the old, and that the word of the sovereign is not to be taken, let us turn our eyes to history, in which great men have always a pleasure in contemplating the heroic origin of their house.

The first peer of the name, the first purchaser of the grants, was a Mr. Russell, a person of an ancient gentleman's family raised by being a minion of Henry the Eighth. As there generally is some resemblance of character to create these relations, the favourite was in all likelihood much such another as his master. The first of those immoderate grants was not taken from the ancient demesne of the Crown but from the recent confiscation of the ancient nobility of the land.[33] The lion having sucked the blood of his prey, threw the offal carcass to the jackal in waiting. Having tasted once the food of confiscation, the favourites became fierce and ravenous. This worthy favourite's first grant was from the lay nobility. The second, infinitely improving on the enormity of the first, was from the plunder of the church. In truth his Grace is somewhat excusable for his dislike to a grant like mine, not only in its quantity, but in its kind so different from his own.

Mine was from a mild and benevolent sovereign; his from Henry the Eighth.

Mine had not its fund in the murder of any innocent person of illustrious rank,* or in the pillage of any body of unoffending men. His grants were from the aggregate and consolidated funds of judgments iniquitously legal, and from possessions voluntarily surrendered by the lawful proprietors, with the gibbet at their door.

The merit of the grantee whom he derives from was that of being a prompt and greedy instrument of a *levelling* tyrant, who oppressed all descriptions of his people, but who fell with particular fury on everything that was *great and noble*. Mine has been, in endeavouring to screen every man, in every class, from

* See the history of the melancholy catastrophe of the Duke of Buckingham. Temp. Hen. 8.

oppression, and particularly its defending the high and eminent, who in the bad times of confiscating princes, confiscating chief governors, or confiscating demagogues, are the most exposed to jealousy, avarice, and envy.

The merit of the original grantee of his Grace's pensions was in giving his hand to the work and partaking the spoil with a prince, who plundered a part of the national church of his time and country. Mine was in defending the whole of the national church of my own time and my own country, and the whole of the national churches of all countries, from the principles and the examples which lead to ecclesiastical pillage, thence to a contempt of *all* prescriptive titles, thence to the pillage of *all* property, and thence to universal desolation.

The merit of the origin of his Grace's fortune was in being a favourite and chief adviser to a prince, who left no liberty to their native country. My endeavour was to obtain liberty for the municipal country in which I was born, and for all descriptions and denominations in it. Mine was to support with unrelaxing vigilance every right, every privilege, every franchise, in this my adopted, my dearer, and more comprehensive country; and not only to preserve those rights in this chief seat of empire, but in every nation, in every land, in every climate, language, and religion, in the vast domain that is still under the protection, and the larger that was once under the protection, of the British Crown.

His founder's merits were, by arts in which he served his master and made his fortune, to bring poverty, wretchedness, and depopulation on his country. Mine were, under a benevolent prince, in promoting the commerce, manufactures, and agriculture of his kingdom; in which his Majesty shows an eminent example, who even in his amusements is a patriot, and in hours of leisure an improver of his native soil.

His founder's merit was the merit of a gentleman raised by the arts of a court, and the protection of a Wolsey,[34] to the eminence of a great and potent lord. His merit in that eminence was, by instigating a tyrant to injustice, to provoke a people to rebellion. My merit was, to awaken the sober part of the country, that they might put themselves on their guard against any one potent lord, or any greater number of potent lords, or any combination of great leading men of any sort, if ever they should attempt to proceed in the same courses, but in the reverse order; that is, by instigating a corrupted populace to rebellion, and, through that rebellion, introducing a tyranny yet worse than the tyranny which his Grace's ancestor supported, and of which he profited in the manner we behold in the despotism of Henry the Eighth.

The political merit of the first pensioner of his Grace's house was that of being concerned as a counsellor of state in advising, and in his person executing, the conditions of a dishonourable peace with France; the surrendering the fortress of Boulogne, then our out-guard on the continent. By that surrender, Calais, the key of France, and the bridle in the mouth of that power, was, not many years afterwards, finally lost. My merit has been in resisting the power and pride of France, under any form of its rule; but in opposing it with the greatest zeal and earnestness, when that rule appeared in the worst form it could assume; the worst indeed which the prime cause and principle of all evil could possibly give it. It was my endeavour by every means to excite a spirit in the House where I had the honour of a seat, for carrying on, with early vigour and decision, the most clearly just and necessary war, that this or any nation ever carried on; in order to save my country from the iron yoke of its power, and from the more dreadful contagion of its principles; to preserve, while they can be preserved, pure and untainted, the ancient, inbred integrity, piety, good nature, and good humour of the people of England, from the dreadful pestilence, which, beginning in France, threatens to lay waste the whole moral, and in a great degree the whole physical, world, having done both in the focus of its most intense malignity.

The labours of his Grace's founder merited the curses, not loud but deep, of the Commons of England, on whom *he* and his master had effected a *complete parliamentary reform*, by making them, in their slavery and humiliation, the true and adequate representatives of a debased, degraded, and undone people. My merits were, in having had an active, though not always an ostentatious, share, in every one act, without exception, of undisputed constitutional utility in my time, and in having supported, on all occasions, the authority, the efficiency, and the privileges of the Commons of Great Britain. I ended my services by a recorded and fully reasoned assertion on their own journals of their constitutional rights, and a vindication of their constitutional conduct. I laboured in all things to merit their inward approbation, and (along with the assistance of the largest, the greatest, and best of my endeavours) I received their free, unbiassed, public, and solemn thanks.

Thus stands the account of the comparative merits of the Crown grants which compose the Duke of Bedford's fortune as balanced against mine. In the name of common sense, why should the Duke of Bedford think, that none but of the House of Russell are entitled to the favour of the Crown? Why should he imagine that no king of England has been capable of judging of merit but King Henry the Eighth? Indeed, he will pardon me; he is a little mistaken; all virtue did not end in the first Earl of Bedford. All discernment did not lose its vision when his Creator closed his eyes. Let him remit his rigour on the disproportion between merit and reward in others, and they will make no inquiry into the origin of his fortune. They will regard with much more satisfaction, as he will contemplate with infinitely more advantage, whatever in his pedigree has been dulcified by an exposure to the influence of heaven in a long flow of generations, from the hard, acidulous, metallic tincture of the spring. It is little to be doubted, that several of his forefathers in that long series have degenerated into honour and virtue. Let the Duke of Bedford (I am sure he will) reject with scorn and horror the counsels of the lecturers, those wicked panders to avarice and ambition, who would tempt him, in the troubles of his country, to seek another enormous fortune from the forfeitures of another nobility, and the plunder of another church. Let him (and I trust that yet he will) employ all the energy of his youth, and all the resources of his wealth, to crush rebellious principles which have no foundation in morals, and rebellious movements that have no provocation in tyranny.

Then will be forgot the rebellions, which, by a doubtful priority in crime, his ancestor had provoked and extinguished. On such a conduct in the noble Duke, many of his countrymen might, and with some excuse might, give way to the enthusiasm of their gratitude, and, in the dashing style of some of the old declaimers, cry out, that if the fates had found no other way in which they could give a* Duke of Bedford and his opulence as props to a tottering world, then the butchery of the Duke of Buckingham might be tolerated; it might be regarded even with complacency, whilst in the heir of confiscation they saw the

* At si non aliam venturo fata Neroni, &c.[35]

sympathising comforter of the martyrs, who suffer under the cruel confiscation of this day; whilst they behold with admiration his zealous protection of the virtuous and loyal nobility of France, and his manly support of his brethren, the yet standing nobility and gentry of his native land. Then his Grace's merit would be pure, and new, and sharp, as fresh from the mint of honour. As he pleased he might reflect honour on his predecessors, or throw it forward on those who were to succeed him. He might be the propagator of the stock of honour, or the root of it, as he thought proper.

Had it pleased God to continue to me the hopes of succession, I should have been, according to my mediocrity, and the mediocrity of the age I live in, a sort of founder of a family: I should have left a son, who, in all the points in which personal merit can be viewed, in science, in erudition, in genius, in taste, in honour, in generosity, in humanity, in every liberal sentiment, and every liberal accomplishment, would not have shown himself inferior to the Duke of Bedford, or to any of those whom he traces in his line. His Grace very soon would have wanted all plausibility in his attack upon that provision which belonged more to mine than to me. HE would soon have supplied every deficiency, and symmetrised every disproportion. It would not have been for that successor to resort to any stagnant wasting reservoir of merit in me, or in any ancestry. He had in himself a salient, living spring of generous and manly action. Every day he lived he would have re-purchased the bounty of the Crown, and ten times more, if ten times more he had received. He was made a public creature; and had no enjoyment whatever, but in the performance of some duty. At this exigent moment, the loss of a finished man is not easily supplied.

But a Disposer whose power we are little able to resist, and whose wisdom it behoves us not at all to dispute, has ordained it in another manner, and (whatever my querulous weakness might suggest) a far better. The storm has gone over me; and I lie like one of those old oaks which the late hurricane has scattered about me. I am stripped of all my honours, I am torn up by the roots, and lie prostrate on the earth! There, and prostrate there, I most unfeignedly recognise the Divine justice, and in some degree submit to it. But whilst I humble myself before God, I do not know that it is forbidden to repel the attacks of unjust and inconsiderate men. The patience of Job is proverbial. After some of the convulsive struggles of our irritable nature, he submitted himself, and repented in dust and ashes. But even so, I do not find him blamed for reprehending, and with a considerable degree of verbal asperity, those ill-natured neighbours of his, who visited his dunghill to read moral, political, and economical lectures on his misery. I am alone. I have none to meet my enemies in the gate. Indeed, my Lord, I greatly deceive myself, if in this hard season I would give a peck of refuse wheat for all that is called fame and honour in the world. This is the appetite but of a few. It is a luxury, it is a privilege, it is an indulgence for those who are at their ease. But we are all of us made to shun disgrace, as we are made to shrink from pain, and poverty, and disease. It is an instinct; and under the direction of reason, instinct is always in the right. I live in an inverted order. They who ought to have succeeded me are gone before me. They who should have been to me as posterity are in the place of ancestors. I owe to the dearest relation (which ever must subsist in memory) that act of piety, which he would have performed to me; I owe it to him to show that he was not descended, as the Duke of Bedford would have it, from an unworthy parent.

The Crown has considered me after long service: the Crown has paid the Duke of Bedford by advance. He has had a long credit for any service which he may perform hereafter. He is secure, and long may he be secure, in his advance, whether he performs any services or not. But let him take care how he endangers the safety of that constitution which secures his own utility or his own insignificance; or how he discourages those, who take up, even puny arms, to defend an order of things, which, like the sun of heaven, shines alike on the useful and the worthless. His grants are ingrafted on the public law of Europe, covered with the awful hoar of innumerable ages. They are guarded by the sacred rules of prescription, found in that full treasury of jurisprudence from which the jejuneness and penury of our municipal law has, by degrees, been enriched and strengthened. This prescription I had my share (a very full share) in bringing to its perfection.* The Duke of Bedford will stand as long as prescriptive law endures: as long as the great stable laws of property, common to us with all civilised nations, are kept in their integrity, and without the smallest intermixture of laws,

* Sir George Savile's Act called The *Nullum Tempus* Act.[36]

maxims, principles, or precedents of the grand Revolution.
They are secure against all changes but one. The whole revolutionary system, institutes, digest, code, novels, text, gloss, comment, are, not only not the same, but they are the very reverse,
and the reverse fundamentally, of all the laws, on which civil life
has hitherto been upheld in all the governments of the world.
The learned professors of the rights of man regard prescription,
not as a title to bar all claim, set up against all possession – but
they look on prescription as itself a bar against the possessor and
proprietor. They hold an immemorial possession to be no more
than a long-continued, and therefore an aggravated injustice.

Such are *their* ideas; such *their* religion, and such *their* law.
But as to *our* country and *our* race, as long as the well-compacted
structure of our church and state, the sanctuary, the holy of holies
of that ancient law, defended by reverence, defended by power,
a fortress at once and a temple,* shall stand inviolate on the brow
of the British Sion – as long as the British monarchy, not more
limited than fenced by the orders of the state, shall, like the proud
Keep of Windsor, rising in the majesty of proportion, and girt
with the double belt of its kindred and coeval towers, as long as
this awful structure shall oversee and guard the subjected land –
so long the mounds and dykes of the low, fat Bedford level will
have nothing to fear from all the pickaxes of all the levellers of
France. As long as our sovereign lord the king, and his faithful
subjects, the Lords and Commons of this realm, – the triple cord,
which no man can break; the solemn, sworn, constitutional
frank-pledge of this nation; the firm guarantees of each other's
being, and each other's rights; the joint and several securities,
each in its place and order, for every kind and every quality, of
property and of dignity; – as long as these endure, so long the
Duke of Bedford is safe: and we are all safe together – the high
from the blights of envy and the spoliations of rapacity; the low
from the iron hand of oppression and the insolent spurn of
contempt. Amen! and so be it: and so it will be,

> *Dum domus Æneæ Capitoli immobile saxum*
> *Accolet; imperiumque pater Romanus habebit.* – [37]

But if the rude inroad of Gallic tumult, with its sophistical
rights of man, to falsify the account, and its sword as a make-
weight to throw into the scale, shall be introduced into our city

---

* *Templum in modum arcis.* Tacitus, of the Temple of Jerusalem.[38]

by a misguided populace, set on by proud great men, themselves blinded and intoxicated by a frantic ambition, we shall, all of us, perish and be overwhelmed in a common ruin. If a great storm blow on our coast, it will cast the whales on the strand as well as the periwinkles. His Grace will not survive the poor grantee he despises, no, not for a twelvemonth. If the great look for safety in the services they render to this Gallic cause, it is to be foolish, even above the weight of privilege allowed to wealth. If his Grace be one of these whom they endeavour to proselytise, he ought to be aware of the character of the sect, whose doctrines he is invited to embrace. With them insurrection is the most sacred of revolutionary duties to the state. Ingratitude to bene-factors is the first of revolutionary virtues. Ingratitude is indeed their four cardinal virtues compacted and amalgamated into one; and he will find it in everything that has happened since the com-mencement of the philosophic Revolution to this hour. If he pleads the merit of having performed the duty of insurrection against the order he lives, (God forbid he ever should,) the merit of others will be to perform the duty of insurrection against him. If he pleads (again God forbid he should, and I do not suspect he will) his ingratitude to the Crown for its creation of his family, others will plead their right and duty to pay him in kind. They will laugh, indeed they will laugh, at his parchment and his wax. His deeds will be drawn out with the rest of the lumber of his evidence room, and burnt to the tune of *ça ira*[39] or in the courts of Bedford (then Equality) house.

Am I to blame, if I attempt to pay his Grace's hostile reproaches to me with a friendly admonition to himself? Can I be blamed, for pointing out to him in what manner he is likely to be affected, if the sect of the cannibal philosophers of France should proselytise any considerable part of this people, and, by their joint proselytising arms, should conquer that government, to which his Grace does not seem to me to give all the support his own security demands? Surely it is proper, that he, and that others like him, should know the true genius of this sect; what their opinions are, what they have done; and to whom; and what (if a prognostic is to be formed from the dispositions and actions of men) it is certain they will do hereafter. He ought to know, that they have sworn assistance, the only engagement they ever will keep, to all in this country, who bear a resemblance to themselves, and who think as such, that *The whole duty of man* consists in destruction.

They are a misallied and disparaged branch of the house of Nimrod.[40] They are the Duke of Bedford's natural hunters; and he is their natural game. Because he is not very profoundly reflecting, he sleeps in profound security: they, on the contrary, are always vigilant, active, enterprising, and, though far removed from any knowledge which makes men estimable or useful, in all the instruments and resources of evil, their leaders are not meanly instructed, or insufficiently furnished. In the French Revolution everything is new; and from want of preparation to meet so unlooked-for an evil, everything is dangerous. Never, before this time, was a set of literary men converted into a gang of robbers and assassins. Never before did a den of bravoes and banditti assume the garb and tone of an academy of philosophers.

Let me tell his Grace, that an union of such characters, monstrous as it seems, is not made for producing despicable enemies. But if they are formidable as foes, as friends they are dreadful indeed. The men of property in France confiding in a force, which seemed to be irresistible, because it had never been tried, neglected to prepare for a conflict with their enemies at their own weapons. They were found in such a situation as the Mexicans were, when they were attacked by the dogs, the cavalry, the iron, and the gunpowder, of a handful of bearded men, whom they did not know to exist in nature. This is a comparison that some, I think, have made; and it is just. In France they had their enemies within their houses. They were even in the bosoms of many of them. But they had not sagacity to discern their savage character. They seemed tame, and even caressing. They had nothing but *douce humanité* in their mouth. They could not bear the punishment of the mildest laws on the greatest criminals. The slightest severity of justice made their flesh creep. The very idea that war existed in the world disturbed their repose. Military glory was no more, with them, than a splendid infamy. Hardly would they hear of self-defence, which they reduced within such bounds, as to leave it no defence at all. All this while they meditated the confiscations and massacres we have seen. Had any one told these unfortunate noblemen and gentlemen, how, and by whom, the grand fabric of the French monarchy under which they flourished would be subverted, they would not have pitied him as a visionary, but would have turned from him as what they call a *mauvais plaisant*.[41] Yet we have seen what has happened. The persons who have suffered from the cannibal philosophy of

France, are so like the Duke of Bedford, that nothing but his
Grace's probably not speaking quite so good French could enable
us to find out any difference. A great many of them had as pom-
pous titles as he, and were of full as illustrious a race: some few
of them had fortunes as ample: several of them, without meaning
the least disparagement to the Duke of Bedford, were as wise,
and as virtuous, and as valiant, and as well educated, and as complete in all the lineaments of men of honour, as he is: and to all
this they had added the powerful out-guard of a military profession, which, in its nature, renders men somewhat more cautious
than those, who have nothing to attend to but the lazy enjoyment
of undisturbed possessions. But security was their ruin. They are
dashed to pieces in the storm, and our shores are covered with
the wrecks. If they had been aware that such a thing might
happen, such a thing never could have happened.

I assure his Grace, that if I state to him the designs of his
enemies, in a manner which may appear to him ludicrous and
impossible, I tell him nothing that has not exactly happened,
point by point, but twenty-four miles from our own shore.
I assure him that the Frenchified faction, more encouraged, than
others are warned, by what has happened in France, look at him
and his landed possessions as an object at once of curiosity and
rapacity. He is made for them in every part of their double character. As robbers, to them he is a noble booty; as speculatists, he
is a glorious subject for their experimental philosophy. He affords
matter for an extensive analysis, in all the branches of their
science, geometrical, physical, civil, and political. These philosophers are fanatics; independent of any interest, which if it operated alone would make them much more tractable, they are
carried with such a headlong rage towards every desperate trial,
that they would sacrifice the whole human race to the slightest
of their experiments. I am better able to enter into the character
of this description of men than the noble Duke can be. I have
lived long and variously in the world. Without any considerable
pretensions to literature in myself, I have aspired to the love of
letters. I have lived for a great many years in habitudes with those
who professed them. I can form a tolerable estimate of what is
likely to happen from a character, chiefly dependent for fame and
fortune on knowledge and talent, as well in its morbid and
perverted state, as in that which is sound and natural. Naturally
men so formed and finished are the first gifts of Providence to

the world. But when they have once thrown off the fear of God, which was in all ages too often the case, and the fear of man, which is now the case, and when in that state they come to understand one another, and to act in corps, a more dreadful calamity cannot arise out of hell to scourge mankind. Nothing can be conceived more hard than the heart of a thoroughbred metaphysician. It comes nearer to the cold malignity of a wicked spirit than to the frailty and passion of a man. It is like that of the principle of evil himself, incorporeal, pure, unmixed, dephlegmated, defecated evil. It is no easy operation to eradicate humanity from the human breast. What Shakspeare calls "the compunctious visitings of nature" will sometimes knock at their hearts, and protest against their murderous speculations. But they have a means of compounding with their nature. Their humanity is not dissolved. They only give it a long prorogation. They are ready to declare, that they do not think two thousand years too long a period for the good that they pursue. It is remarkable, that they never see any way to their projected good but by the road of some evil. Their imagination is not fatigued with the contemplaton of human suffering through the wild waste of centuries added to centuries of misery and desolation. Their humanity is at their horizon – and, like the horizon, it always flies before them. The geometricians, and the chemists, bring, the one from the dry bones of their diagrams, and the other from the soot of their furnaces, dispositions that make them worse than indifferent about those feelings and habitudes, which are the support of the moral world. Ambition is come upon them suddenly; they are intoxicated with it, and it has rendered them fearless of the danger, which may from thence arise to others or to themselves. These philosophers consider men in their experiments, no more than they do mice in an air pump, or in a recipient of mephitic gas. Whatever his Grace may think of himself, they look upon him, and everything that belongs to him, with no more regard than they do upon the whiskers of that little long-tailed animal, that has been long the game of the grave, demure, insidious, spring-nailed, velvet-pawed, green-eyed philosophers, whether going upon two legs, or upon four.

His Grace's landed possessions are irresistibly inviting to an *agrarian* experiment. They are a downright insult upon the rights of man. They are more extensive than the territory of many of the Grecian republics; and they are without comparison more fertile than most of them. There are now republics in Italy, in Germany, and in Switzerland, which do not possess anything like so fair and ample a domain. There is scope for seven philosophers to proceed in their analytical experiments, upon Harrington's seven different forms of republics,[42] in the acres of this one duke. Hitherto they have been wholly unproductive to speculation; fitted for nothing but to fatten bullocks, and to produce grain for beer, still more to stupify the dull English understanding. Abbé Sieyes[43] has whole nests of pigeon-holes full of constitutions ready made, ticketed, sorted, and numbered; suited to every person and every fancy; some with the top of the pattern at the bottom, and some with the bottom at the top; some plain, some flowered; some distinguished for their simplicity, others for their complexity; some of blood colour; some of *boue de Paris*;[44] some with directories, others without a direction; some with councils of elders, and councils of youngsters; some without any council at all. Some where the electors choose the representatives; others, where the representatives choose the electors. Some in long coats, and some in short cloaks; some with pantaloons; some without breeches. Some with five-shilling qualifications; some totally unqualified. So that no constitution-fancier may go unsuited from his shop, provided he loves a pattern of pillage, oppression, arbitrary imprisonment, confiscation, exile, revolutionary judgment, and legalised premeditated murder, in any shapes into which they can be put. What a pity it is, that the progress of experimental philosophy should be checked by his Grace's monopoly! Such are their sentiments, I assure him; such is their language, when they dare to speak; and such are their proceedings, when they have the means to act.

Their geographers and geometricians have been some time out of practice. It is some time since they have divided their own country into squares. That figure has lost the charms of its novelty. They want new lands for new trials. It is not only the geometricians of the republic that find him a good subject, the chemists have bespoken him after the geometricians have done with him. As the first set have an eye on his Grace's lands, the chemists are not less taken with his buildings. They consider mortar as a very anti-revolutionary invention in its present state; but properly employed, an admirable material for overturning all establishments. They have found that the gunpowder of *ruins* is far the fittest for making other *ruins*, and so *ad infinitum*. They have calculated what quantity of matter convertible into nitre is to be found in Bedford House, in Woburn Abbey, and in what his Grace and his trustees have still suffered to stand of that foolish royalist Inigo Jones,[45] in Covent Garden. Churches, play-houses, coffee-houses, all alike are destined to be mingled, and equalised, and blended into one common rubbish; and, well sifted and lixiviated, to crystallise into true, democratic, explosive, insurrectionary nitre. Their academy del *Cimento* (per antiphrasin)[46] with Morveau and Hassenfrats[47] at its head, have computed that the brave sans culottes may make war on all the aristocracy of Europe for a twelve-month, out of the rubbish of the Duke of Bedford's buildings.*

While the Morveaux and Priestleys are proceeding with these experiments upon the Duke of Bedford's houses, the Sieyes, and the rest of the analytical legislators, and constitution-venders, are quite as busy in their trade of decomposing organisation, in forming his Grace's vassals into primary assemblies, national guards, first, second, and third requisitioners, committees of research, conductors of the travelling guillotine, judges of revolutionary tribunals, legislative hangmen, supervisors of domiciliary visitation, exactors of forced loans, and assessors of the maximum.

The din of all this smithery may some time or other possibly wake this noble Duke, and push him to an endeavour to save some little matter from their experimental philosophy. If he pleads his grants from the Crown, he is ruined at the outset. If he pleads he has received them from the pillage of superstitious

---

* There is nothing, on which the leaders of the republic, one and indivisible, value themselves, more than on the chemical operations, by which, through science, they convert the pride of aristocracy to an instrument of its own destruction – on the operations by which they reduce the magnificent, ancient country seats of the nobility, decorated with the *feudal* titles of Duke, Marquis, or Earl, into magazines of what they call *revolutionary* gunpowder. They tell us, that hitherto things "had not yet been properly and in a *revolutionary* manner explored." – "The strong *chateaus*, those *feudal* fortresses that *were ordered to be demolished*, attracted next the attention of your committee. *Nature* there had *secretly* regained her *rights*, and had produced saltpetre for the *purpose*, as it should seem, *of facilitating the execution of your decree by preparing the means of destruction*. From these *ruins*, which *still frown* on the liberties of the republic, we have extracted the means of producing good; and those piles, which have hitherto glutted the *pride of despots*, and covered the plots of La Vendée,[48] will soon furnish wherewithal to tame the traitors, and to overwhelm the disaffected." – "The *rebellious cities*, also, have afforded a large quantity of saltpetre, *Commune Affranchie*, (that is, the noble city of Lyons reduced in many parts to a heap of ruins,) and Toulon, will pay a *second* tribute to our artillery." Report, 1st February, 1794.

corporations, this indeed will stagger them a little, because they are enemies to all corporations, and to all religion. However, they will soon recover themselves, and will tell his Grace, or his learned council, that all such property belongs to the *nation*; and that it would be more wise for him, if he wishes to live the natural term of a *citizen*, (that is, according to Condorcet's calculation,[49] six months on an average,) not to pass for an usurper upon the national property. This is what the *serjeants* at law of the rights of man will say to the puny *apprentices* of the common law of England.

Is the genius of philosophy not yet known? You may as well think the garden of the Tuilleries was well protected with the cords of ribbon insultingly stretched by the National Assembly to keep the sovereign canaille from intruding on the retirement of the poor king of the French, as that such flimsy cobwebs will stand between the savages of the Revolution and their natural prey. Deep philosophers are no triflers; brave sans-culottes are no formalists. They will no more regard a Marquis of Tavistock than an Abbot of Tavistock; the Lord of Woburn will not be more respectable in their eyes than the Prior of Woburn; they will make no difference between the superior of a Covent Garden of nuns, and of a Covent Garden of another description. They will not care a rush whether his coat is long or short; whether the colour be purple or blue and buff. They will not trouble *their* heads, with what part of *his* head his hair is cut from; and they will look with equal respect on a tonsure and a crop. Their only question will be that of their *Legendre*,[50] or some other of their legislative butchers, how he cuts up? how he tallows in the cawl, or on the kidneys?

Is it not a singular phenomenon, that whilst the sans-culotte carcass-butchers, and the philosophers of the shambles, are pricking their dotted lines upon his hide, and, like the print of the poor ox that we see in the shop-windows at Charing Cross, alive as he is, and thinking no harm in the world, he is divided into rumps, and sirloins, and briskets, and into all sorts of pieces for roasting, boiling, and stewing, that all the while they are measuring *him*, his Grace is measuring *me*; is invidiously comparing the bounty of the Crown with the deserts of the defender of his order, and in the same moment fawning on those who have the knife half out of the sheath – poor innocent!

"Pleas'd to the last, he crops the flow'ry food,
And licks the hand just raised to shed his blood"[51]

No man lives too long, who lives to do with spirit, and suffer with resignation, what Providence pleases to command, or inflict; but indeed they are sharp incommodities which beset old age. It was but the other day, that, on putting in order some things which had been brought here on my taking leave of London for ever, I looked over a number of fine portraits, most of them of persons now dead, but whose society, in my better days, made this a proud and happy place. Amongst these was the picture of Lord Keppel.[52] It was painted by an artist worthy of the subject, the excellent friend of that excellent man from their earliest youth, and a common friend of us both, with whom we lived for many years without a moment of coldness, of peevishness, of jealousy, or of jar, to the day of our final separation.

I ever looked on Lord Keppel as one of the greatest and best men of his age; and I loved and cultivated him accordingly. He was much in my heart, and I believe I was in his to the very last beat. It was after his trial at Portsmouth that he gave me this picture. With what zeal and anxious affection I attended him through that his agony of glory, what part my son took in the early flush and enthusiasm of his virtue, and the pious passion with which he attached himself to all my connexions, with what prodigality we both squandered ourselves in courting almost every sort of enmity for his sake, I believe he felt, just as I should have felt such friendship on such an occasion. I partook indeed of this honour, with several of the first, and best, and ablest in the kingdom, but I was behindhand with none of them; and I am sure, that if to the eternal disgrace of this nation, and to the total annihilation of every trace of honour and virtue in it, things had taken a different turn from what they did, I should have attended him to the quarter-deck with no less good will and more pride, though with far other feelings, than I partook of the general flow of national joy that attended the justice that was done to his virtue.

Pardon, my Lord, the feeble garrulity of age, which loves to diffuse itself in discourse of the departed great. At my years we live in retrospect alone: and, wholly unfitted for the society of vigorous life, we enjoy the best balm to all wounds, the consolation of friendship, in those only whom we have lost for ever.

Feeling the loss of Lord Keppel at all times, at no time did I feel it so much as on the first day when I was attacked in the House of Lords.

Had he lived, that reverend form would have risen in its place, and, with a mild, parental reprehension to his nephew the Duke of Bedford, he would have told him that the favour of that gracious Prince, who had honoured his virtues with the government of the navy of Great Britain, and with a seat in the hereditary great council of his kingdom, was not undeservedly shown to the friend of the best portion of his life, and his faithful companion and counsellor under his rudest trials. He would have told him, that to whomever else these reproaches might be becoming, they were not decorous in his near kindred. He would have told him, that when men in that rank lose decorum they lose everything.

On that day I had a loss in Lord Keppel; but the public loss of him in this awful crisis −! I speak from much knowledge of the person, he never would have listened to any compromise with the rabble rout of this sans-culotterie of France. His goodness of heart, his reason, his taste, his public duty, his principles, his prejudices, would have repelled him for ever from all connexion with that horrid medley of madness, vice, impiety, and crime.

Lord Keppel had two countries; one of descent, and one of birth. Their interest and their glory are the same; and his mind was capacious of both. His family was noble, and it was Dutch: that is, he was of the oldest and purest nobility that Europe can boast, among a people renowned above all others for love of their native land. Though it was never shown in insult to any human being, Lord Keppel was something high. It was a wild stock of pride, on which the tenderest of all hearts had grafted the milder virtues. He valued ancient nobility; and he was not disinclined to augment it with new honours. He valued the old nobility and the new, not as an excuse for inglorious sloth, but as an incitement to virtuous activity. He considered it as a sort of cure for selfishness and a narrow mind; conceiving that a man born in an elevated place in himself was nothing, but everything in what went before and what was to come after him. Without much speculation, but by the sure instinct of ingenuous feelings, and by the dictates of plain, unsophisticated, natural understanding, he felt, that no great commonwealth could by any possibility long subsist, without a body of some kind or other of nobility, decorated with honour, and fortified by privilege. This nobility forms the chain that connects the ages of a nation, which otherwise (with Mr. Paine) would soon be taught that no one generation can bind another. He felt that no political fabric could be well made without some such order of things as might, through a series of time, afford a rational hope of securing unity, coherence, consistency, and stability to the state. He felt that nothing else can protect it against the levity of courts, and the greater levity of the multitude. That to talk of hereditary monarchy, without anything else of hereditary reverence in the commonwealth, was a low-minded absurdity, fit only for those detestable "fools aspiring to be knaves," who began to forge in 1789 the false money of the French constitution − That it is one fatal objection to all *new* fancied and *new fabricated* republics, (among a people, who, once possessing such an advantage, have wickedly and insolently rejected it,) that the *prejudice* of an old nobility is a thing that *cannot* be made. It may be improved, it may be corrected, it may be replenished: men may be taken from it or aggregated to it, but the *thing itself* is matter of *inveterate* opinion, and therefore *cannot* be matter of mere positive institution. He felt that this nobility in fact does not exist in wrong of other orders of the state, but by them, and for them.

I knew the man I speak of: and, if we can divine the future, out of what we collect from the past, no person living would look with more scorn and horror on the impious parricide committed on all their ancestry, and on the desperate attainder passed on all their posterity, by the Orleans, and the Rochefoucaults,[53] and the Fayettes,[54] and the Viscomtes de Noailles,[55] and the false Perigords,[56] and the long *et cætera* of the perfidious sans-culottes of the court, who like demoniacs, possessed with a spirit of fallen pride, and inverted ambition, abdicated their dignities, disowned their families, betrayed the most sacred of all trusts, and, by breaking to pieces a great link of society and all the cramps and holdings of the state, brought eternal confusion and desolation on their country. For the fate of the miscreant parricides themselves he would have had no pity. Compassion for the myriads of men, of whom the world was not worthy, who by their means have perished in prisons, or on scaffolds, or are pining in beggary and exile, would leave no room in his, or in any well-formed mind, for any such sensation. We are not made at once to pity the oppressor and the oppressed.

Looking to his Batavian descent, how could he bear to behold his kindred, the descendants of the brave nobility of Holland, whose blood, prodigally poured out, had, more than all the canals, meres, and inundations of their country, protected their independence, to behold them bowed in the basest servitude to the basest and vilest of the human race; in servitude to those who in no respect were superior in dignity, or could aspire to a better place than that of hangmen to the tyrants, to whose sceptered pride they had opposed an elevation of soul, that surmounted, and overpowered, the loftiness of Castile, the haughtiness of Austria, and the overbearing arrogance of France?

Could he with patience bear, that the children of that nobility, who would have deluged their country and given it to the sea, rather than submit to Louis XIV, who was then in his meridian glory, when his arms were conducted by the Turennes, by the Luxembourgs, by the Boufflers; when his councils were directed by the Colberts, and the Louvois; when his tribunals were filled by the Lamoignons and the Daguessaus – that these should be given up to the cruel sport of the Pichegrus, the Jourdans, the Santerres, under the Rolands, the Brissots, and Gorfas, and Robespierres, the Reubels, the Carnots, and Talliens, and Dantons,[37] and the whole tribe of regicides, robbers, and revolutionary judges, that, from the rotten carcass of their own murdered country, have poured out innumerable swarms of the lowest, and at once the most destructive, of the classes of animated nature, which, like columns of locusts, have laid waste the fairest part of the world?

Would Keppel have borne to see the ruin of the virtuous patricians, that happy union of the noble and the burgher, who, with signal prudence and integrity, had long governed the cities of the confederate republic, the cherishing fathers of their country, who, denying commerce to themselves, made it flourish in a manner unexampled under their protection? Could Keppel have borne that a vile faction should totally destroy this harmonious construction, in favour of a robbing democracy, founded on the spurious rights of man?

He was no great clerk, but he was perfectly well versed in the interests of Europe, and he could not have heard with patience, that the country of Grotius,[38] the cradle of the law of nations, and one of the richest repositories of all law, should be taught a new code by the ignorant flippancy of Thomas Paine, the presumptuous foppery of La Fayette, with his stolen rights of man in his hand, the wild, profligate intrigue, and turbulency, of Marat,[59] and the impious sophistry of Condorcet, in his insolent addresses to the Batavian republic.

Could Keppel, who idolised the house of Nassau,[60] who was himself given to England along with the blessings of the British and Dutch revolutions; with revolutions of stability; with revolutions which consolidated and married the liberties and the interests of the two nations for ever, could he see the fountain of British liberty itself in servitude to France? Could he see with patience a Prince of Orange expelled as a sort of diminutive despot, with every kind of contumely, from the country, which that family of deliverers had so often rescued from slavery, and obliged to live in exile in another country, which owes its liberty to his house?

Would Keppel have heard with patience, that the conduct to be held on such occasions was to become short by the knees to the faction of the homicides, to entreat them quietly to retire? or, if the fortune of war should drive them from their first wicked and unprovoked invasion, that no security should be taken, no arrangement made, no barrier formed, no alliance entered into for the security of that, which under a foreign name is the most precious part of England? What would he have said, if it was even proposed that the Austrian Netherlands[61] (which ought to be a barrier to Holland, and the tie of an alliance, to protect her against any species of rule that might be erected, or even be restored in France) should be formed into a republic under her influence, and dependent upon her power?

But above all, what would he have said, if he had heard it made a matter of accusation against me, by his nephew the Duke of Bedford, that I was the author of the war? Had I a mind to keep that high distinction to myself, as from pride I might, but from justice I dare not, he would have snatched his share of it from my hand, and held it with the grasp of a dying convulsion to his end.

It would be a most arrogant presumption in me to assume to myself the glory of what belongs to his Majesty, and to his ministers, and to his parliament, and to the far greater majority of his faithful people: but had I stood alone to counsel, and that all were determined to be guided by my advice, and to follow it implicitly – then I should have been the sole author of a war. But it should have been a war on my ideas and my principles. However, let his

Grace think as he may of my demerits with regard to the war with regicide, he will find my guilt confined to that alone. He never shall, with the smallest colour of reason, accuse me of being the author of a peace with regicide. But that is high matter; and ought not to be mixed with anything of so little moment, as what may belong to me, or even to the Duke of Bedford.

I have the honour to be, &c.

EDMUND BURKE

PRIVATE
LETTERS

TO RICHARD SHACKLETON[1]

When he left school and returned to Dublin to study at Trinity College, Burke kept up an active correspondence with his close friend, Richard Shackleton, who remained at Ballitore.

DUBN 15 FEBRUARY 1745 [O.S.]

I received your favour which I am much concerned to find in the usual Strain – alas how are our Letters Changd of Late? Instead of jests, merriment and Congratulations now they are filled with nothing but the narration of misfortunes and Condolements for them. Not that I am a bit displeas'd at your manner of writing I only lament the Cause of it, the Stile of the heart tho ever so melancholy is more agreeable to me than a forc'd Calmness, which only serves to aggravate your own affliction and keep me ignorant of it – indulge then your Sorrows I beg you in what you write, to me, but pardon me if I am so Curious and impertinent as not to be satisfied with what you have already acquainted me, I cannot thoroughly Sympathise with you, I cannot make your Case my own 'till I am inform'd of its Cause, and tho' the whole narration may be too long for the Compass of a Letter, I beg you'l abridge it omitting no material Circumstance in your next. Conceal not the Villians[2] name who is the Cause of your afflictions that I may always hate the Idea of the wretch who dares betray the Secrets of his friend, is it Tr— is it — who is it? fear not to write the whole for no one sees your Letters but I: but Let us wave this –

I Was told t'other day by Rhames[3] that Our old friend Herbert[4] was taken by the french. I was informd Since, that he was retaken and brought into Porsmouth. – I sometimes See Sisson,[5] I told him that some misfortunes had befallen you without mentioning what they were – he seem's much concernd and allways speaks of you with the greatest affection – I beleive he's good natur'd, if So you have a friend more than you expected. There is no Evil I beleive but carries Some good along with it and if you make a proper use of the present, tho it does no more, will give you a little experience and teach you more Caution and reserve in trusting your acquaintance we live in a world where every one is on the Catch, and the only way to be Safe is to be Silent, Silent in any affair of Consequence, and I think it would not be a bad rule for every man to keep within what he thinks of others, of himself, and of his own Affairs. I wish the next account

I hear from you may be a good one, no one more sincerely wishes it than he whom you may beleive your friend.

My love to brother. I hope he's a good boy.
My Respects to your father and Mother.

TO THE DUKE OF RICHMOND[1]

Far from being the lackey of the great Whig aristocrats, as some claimed, Burke was in fact an energetic – and fearless – party manager. This incomplete draft letter shows him at his most pungent.

POST 15 NOVEMBER 1772[2]

MY DEAR LORD,

I am much obliged to your Grace for your very kind Letter of the 15th which I received by the Machine. Whatever others might have imagined I never thought your Grace too tenacious of your opinion. If you had rather leand to that extreme I should not have esteemd you the less for it. I have seen so many woful examples of the Effect of Levity, both that which arises from Temper, and that which is owing to Interest, that a small degree of obstinacy is a Quality not very odious in my Eyes, whether it be complexional or from principle. When a man makes great sacrifices to his honest opinion, it is no wonder that he should grow fond of it. I am sure that nothing can hinder the possession of publick Spirit from being very suspicious except great consistency; Those who do not much admire the security itself nor perhaps the Virtue it secures will represent it as a mark, as an obstinate and intractable disposition. Those who think in that manner of your Grace form that opinion on your steady attachment to your principles. They know nothing of your compliance and practicability in carrying on Business among your friends. I can bear witness that it has always been full as much as was necessary towards keeping a great System well compacted together in all its parts. I have known some good Effects of that practicability, I agree too, that there have been instances where we may now have reason to wish you had less facility. After all, Every political question that I have ever known, has had so much of the pro and con in it, that nothing but the success could decide which proposition ought to have been adopted. People in a constant minority can have no success; and therefore have not even that uncertain way of solving any problem of political Conduct. I believe we have had more divisions among ourselves than we ought to have had; and have made many mistakes in our Conduct, both as a body and as individuals. Comparing our proceedings with any abstract standard, we have been very faulty and imperfect; but if you try yourselves by comparison with any other existing body of men; I believe you will find a more decent regular consistent, and prudent series of proceeding among yourselves than among any of them or all of those put together. Have you in any place where you have had an Interest undone yourselves so compleatly, as a certain party[3] which was lately in possession of the Corporation of London? a Set of Gentlemen who cannot plead innocence and simplicity as an excuse for their innumerable Blunders. In the house of Lords, have the chiefs of you ever passed such injudicious motions, paid so little attention to your mutual honour, or contrived to reconcile your proceedings at one time to your declarations at another with so little finesse and dexterity as some persons of very high Name in this Country?[4] You have not, like them, while they were miserably distracted among themselves, formed a thousand childish and mischievous plots to break to pieces the only people who could possibly serve them, and in whom if they had common sense they would for their own Sakes have placed great confidence as well as have endeavourd to acquire the like from them by every method of fair and conciliatory conduct. If you look turning from them to the factions that make what is called administration, surely you are guiltless of that Tissue of absurdities by which Government that by mear abuses can hardly be more than odious, has been renderd the most contemptible thing in the world. Look at home one has much to complain of. Look abroad one has ten times more. So that on the whole I am inclined to think that the faults in your body are no more than the ordinary frailties of human Nature, some of them too inseperably attached to the Cause of all your strength and reputation. You are in general somewhat Languid, scrupulous and unsystematick. But men of high Birth and great property are rarely as enterprising as others and for reasons that are very natural; Men of integrity are curious, sometimes too curious, in the Choice of means; and great Bodies can seldom be brought to System and discipline, except by Instruments that while you are out of Government, you have not in your power. However with all these faults it is better you should be rich and honest and numerous than needy, and profligate and composed of a few desperate politicians though they have advantages in their own way which you must always want. It is with such reflexions I compose and comfort myself in the occasional dejections and vexations that I am subject to, like other men and which your Grace has seen but too much of and they will in my cool moments always put me at ease and reconcile me to everything you do, as long as I can act in publick whether I agree in opinion with the rest of you or not.

As to your Graces situation in the party and in the world, it would be the greatest injustice, for Lord Rm[5] not to say that he Sees and feels his obligations to you in their full extent; and has spoke a thousand [times] as he ought of the unparralled part you have acted. His nearest and oldest friends are, much in the same degree, your own. There can be but one opinion on your Conduct and abilities. With regard to others Your Grace is very sensible that you have not made your Court to the world by forming yourself to a flattering exterior but you put me in mind of Mr Wilkes's observation[6] when he makes love, that he will engage in such a pursuit against the handsomest fellow in England, and only desires a month start of his Rival on account of his face; your month is past; and if your Grace does not, every one else does remark, how much you grow on the publick by the exertion of real Talents and substantial Virtue. You know you have already some fruits of them, and you will gather in such fruits every day until your Barns are full as they can hold. One thing and but one I see against it which is, that your Grace dissipates your mind with too great a variety of minute pursuits, all of which from the natural Vehemence of your Temper you follow almost with equal passion. It is wise indeed considering the many many positive vexations, and the unnumerable bitter disappointments of pleasure in the world to have as many rescources of satisfaction as possible within ones power. When we concenter the mind on one sole object that object and Life itself must go together. But though it is right to have reserves of employment still some one object must be kept principal; greatly and eminently so; and the other masses and figures must preserve their due subordination to make out the grand composition of an important Life, upon those sound principles which your Grace

would require in some of those arts that you protect. Your publick business with all its discouragements and mortifications
ought to be so much principal figures with you that the rest in
comparison of it should be next to nothing; and even in that
principal figure of publick Life it will be necessary to avoid the
exquisiteness of an over attention to smaller parts and to over precision and to a spirit of detail, which acute understandings and
precise reasonings, which without great Care all are apt to get
into, and which, gives in some degree a Sort of hardness and
what you connoisseurs call the dry manner to all our Actions;
Your Grace has abundant reason not to be ⟨discouraged⟩ from
the great exhibition that I wish to see you chiefly intent. In the
Course of publick business, by degrees your Grace developes
your true Character. You would be in a bad condition, if with
the doors shut after the manner of the French, but on the principles of the English constitution, you were to be tried only by
your peers. But this is not so. Business, by degrees, brings various
kinds and descriptions of men into contact with you; and they
all go off with the best impressions and communicate them to
the world. Why have I rambled thus far – why truly, because it
became an amusement to my mind, and that I see your Grace
wants some amusement too? but is the indulgence of a Loqua-
cious vein any amusement? I will try by going on further. I agree
with your Grace, that our Condition is very bad. It is certainly
so. It can be conceald neither from friends nor Enemies. The
time for Secession[7] is past, and no other such opportunity is
in prospect. It would have done I am persuaded, but none of
our friends are to blame for the rejection of that Idea; on the
first proposal Lord Temple, Lord Lyttelton, and Lord Camden[8]
shewed such invincible repugnance to it that in your then situation, it could not be thought of; and it was impossible at that
time to take a seperate walk from them. With regard to the Transaction of 1767.[9] I do recollect, that I as well as others did in some
particulars differ from your Graces opinion. I think you will do
me the justice to believe that it was not out of any particular
regard to Bedford House. Indeed independently of my former
observations I saw clearly during the supper at Lord Rockinghams[10] not only the most unamiable dispositions, but a behaviour
in some of them that was scarcely polite, and a reserve, which
Wine circulated briskly until the sunbeams drove us from it, was

not able to dispel though these people are, not indeed candid but naturally very loose and careless talkers. But I thought I saw too, that the whole Treaty on the part of the Duke of Grafton[11] and Lord Camden and much more of another was merely an imposition both on you and on Conway,[12] principally meant to bring the Latter to act the part he did afterwards; I can scarcely forbear being still of opinion they never meant to bring you in except on Terms that when they became explicit you could neither have accepted nor rejected without great detriment and disgrace to you. I conclude this not only from the Closet disavowal in the middle of your proceedings but from a conversation with General Conway a few days after all was broke off in which he very frankly told me, that the intention never was to bring in the whole even of your body, but about half a dozen (I think) of the principal people, and to let you make way for the rest as opportunities should offer. Constituted as the remaining part of the ministry was this was no real plan of power which would enable you to serve your ⟨Cause⟩. Your Grace I dare say recollects, that we did all in effect and substance, at last accede to your Grace's opinion, when after a long consultation protracted to near two o Clock in the morning, and after frequent Messages backward and forward, your Grace at length carried the ultimatum to General Conway, and never received an answer from that day to this. On the whole I saw so little real intention towards you at that time either in the D. of G. or Lord Camden or General Conway or in the first movers that I cannot without great difficulty, attribute our present condition to our rejection of the proposals of the Court; for in Effect if they had been such as your Grace thought them the Treaty never could have broken off on account of Bedford house which had broken with you and that in a manner equally violent and scandalous before that Business concluded.

Your Grace remember well the Character of the D. of N.[13] who always treated with his Enemies in beginning by putting himself into their power and offering more than they would think of asking; and whose jealousy little short of Phrensy of Lord Rm about Objects which he neither would nor could have held, drove him headlong into any snare his adversaries laid for him. Lord Albemarle[14] too had his attentions to the D of Bedford;[15] but I must say with as great as just suspicions of him and his, as with attachment to you in the total. Yet it was very necessary to look to both these persons; and they, at least one of them and the most material, required nothing more than an empty compliment; and this the Court knew or might have known as well as we did.

But whether I am mistaken or not the thing being past, it only gives me pain [to] attribute our misfortunes to our faults, where circumstances will not suffer our repentance to amend them. Bad they are indeed; But where things are desperate with regard to power, they are not always in a Situation the most unfavourable to Character. Decorum, firmness, consistency, Courage, patient manly perseverance those are the Virtues of despair; They are worth something surely; and none has profited of that situation so much as your Grace nor could you have shewn of what materials you are made in any other. Persons in your Station of Life ought [to] have long Views. You people of great families and hereditary Trusts and fortunes are not like such as I am, who whatever we may be by the Rapidity of our growth and of the fruit we bear, flatter ourselves that while we creep on the Ground we belly into melons that are exquisite for size and flavour, yet still we are but annual plants that perish with our Season and leave no sort of Traces behind us. You if you are what you ought to be are the great Oaks that shade a Country and perpetuate your benefits from Generation to Generation. In my Eye – The immediate power of a D. of Richmond or a Marquis of Rm is not so much of moment but if their conduct and example hands down their principles to their successors; then their houses become the publick repositories and offices of Record for the constitution, Not like the Tower or Rolls Chappel[16] where it is searched for and sometimes in Vain, in rotten parchments under dripping and perishing Walls; but in full vigour and acting with vital Energy and power in the Characters of the leading men and natural interests of the Country. It has been remarked that there were two eminent families at Rome that for several Ages were distinguished uniformly, by opposite Characters and principles. The Claudian and Valerian.[17] The former were high and haughty but publick spirited, firm, and active and attached to the aristocracy. The latter were popular in their Tempers manners and principles. So far this remark; but I add that any one who looks attentively to their History will see that the ballance of that famous constitution was kept up for some ages by the personal Characters, dispositions, and traditionary politicks of certain families as by any thing in the Laws and order of the State. So that I do not look upon your time or lives lost, if in this sliding away from the genuine Spirit of the Country, certain parties if possible, if not the heads of certain families should make it their Business by the whole Course of their Lives principally by their Example to mould into their very vital Stamina of their descendants those principles which ought to be transmitted pure and *uncorrupted* to posterity. Neither Lord R. or your Grace have children; however you do not want successors of your Blood; nor I trust heirs of your Qualities, and your Virtues, and of the power which sooner or Later will be derived from them. This I say to comfort myself and possibly your Grace in the present Melancholy View of our Affairs; Although the field is lost all is not lost − to give you a Line of your Milton who has somewhat reconciled you to Poetry − and he is an able Advocate. For the rest − I can only tell your Grace, that

TO JANE BURKE

Burke had a notably loving and tender relationship with his wife Jane.

8 NOVEMBER 1774[1]

My dearest Jane, My worthy friend Mr Buller[2] has just arrived, charmed with your Ladyship; pleased with William;[3] in Raptures with Sir Joshua Reynolds. I write from Mr Nobles,[4] (of the Corporation) who is one of our very best friends, and this day gave us a very handsome dinner, to which the Committee and their Ladies were invited. Two Enemies, I think, very willing to be reconciled, were invited also. I begin to breathe, though my Visits are not half over. However I dispatch them at a great Rate. Two days more will, I think, carry me through most of them. The Visits will then be over. The dinners would never end. But we close the Poll of engagements next Saturday. That day Richard[5] gives a dinner at the Bush Tavern to our Committee; but to none else. Little Popham[6] will call on you in Town very shortly. He leaves this tomorrow. He has been friendly and serviceable here beyond expression; at much trouble and at no small expence to himself. He gave us a grand entertainment; by us, I mean, the two Committees, Crugers[7] and mine; and invited the Sheriffs and several other Gentlemen.

Now my dearest Jane I entertain some glimpse of hope that I shall see you shortly. I am sure I long for it. Sunday morning with the blessing of God We go to Bath. That day and the next, or a great part of it, we spend there. Tuesday we move to Oxford – Richard desires it much; and it is not above fifteen Miles out of the way. There you may meet us. But if that cannot be done conveniently; Why you will be for certain at Beconsfield; Where I do really long to have a quiet day or two. Adieu my ever dear Jane, my dearest William adieu. Embrace my father, Jack, and Mrs Nugent[8] – Joe Hickey[9] our Knight,[10] and every other friend that Wishes us well. God send Haslemere[11] may end as it ought. Adieu! Adieu.

TUESDAY 8 NOV.

TO PHILIP FRANCIS

Philip Francis (1740–1818) had made Burke's acquaintance in 1769 or 1770. In 1774 he was appointed to the new Council of Bengal where he very quickly clashed with Warren Hastings. They would later fight a duel. Through a common friend, the London merchant John Bourke (*c.* 1722–1806), Francis had tried to gain Burke's support against the Governor General. This letter was carried to India by William Burke.

WESTMINSTER, 9 JUNE 1777

MY DEAR SIR,

Our common friend, John Bourke, informs me that you still retain that kindness which you were so good to express towards me before you left London. This wide disconnected empire will frequently disperse those who are dear to one another; but, if this dispersion of their persons does not loosen their regards, it every now and then gives such unexpected opportunities of meeting as almost compensate the pain of separation, and furnishes means of kind offices and mutual services which make even absence and distance the causes of new endearment and continued remembrance. These thoughts occur to me too naturally, as my only comforts in parting with a friend, whom I have tenderly loved, highly valued, and continually lived with, in an union not to be expressed, quite since our boyish years. Indemnify me, my dear Sir, as well as you can, for such a loss, by contributing to the fortune of my friend. Bring him home with you an obliged person and at his ease, under the protection of your opulence. You know what his situation has been, and what things he might have surely kept, and infinitely increased, if he had not those feelings which make a man worthy of fortune, but do not put him in the way of securing it. Remember that he asks those favours which nothing but his sense of honour prevented his having it in his power to bestow. This will be a powerful recommendation to a heart like yours. Let Bengal protect a spirit and rectitude, which are no longer tolerated in England.

I do not know, indeed, that he will visit your kingdom, but if he should, I trust he will find a friend there whose manner of serving him will not be in the style of those who acquit themselves of a burthen. Mr Bourke's first views, indeed, are at Madras; but all India is now closely connected, and your influence and power are such, that you may serve him very materially even there. I will not wrong your friendship by pressing this matter[1] any farther, but it is indeed near to my heart.

I say nothing of your Eastern politics. The affairs of America, which are as important, and more distracted, have almost entirely engrossed the attention which I am able to give to any thing. I wished, and laboured to keep war at a distance; never having been able to discover any advantage which could be derived from the greatest success; I never approved of our engaging in it, and I am sure it might have been avoided. The Ministers this year hold out to us the strongest hopes of what they call a victorious campaign. I am, indeed, ready enough to believe that we shall obtain those delusive advantages, which will encourage us to proceed, but will not bring matters nearer to an happy termination. France gives all the assistance to the colonies which is consistent with the appearance of neutrality. Time is to shew whether she will proceed farther, or whether America can maintain herself in the present struggle, without a more open declaration and more decided effort from that power. At present, the Ministers seem confident that France is resolved to be quiet. If the Court of Versailles be so pacific, I assure you it is in defiance of the wishes and opinions of that whole nation.

Adieu, my dear Sir. Be assured that no person rejoices more

sincerely than I do in hearing every circumstance of fortune and honour that attends you. I am, with the most sincere esteem and affection, ever your most faithful and obedient humble servant,

EDMUND BURKE

I need not say with what affection John Bourke salutes you.

Francis received this letter – fowarded to him from Madras – on 29 September, noting in his diary: "Poor Will Burke! without an appointment at Madras, and as much to seek as if he had never had a friend: what shall I do for him? what an excellent heart breathes through Edmund's letter!" He wrote to Will on 1 October delaying his visit which never in fact took place.

TO CHARLES JAMES FOX

8 OCTOBER 1777

Fox had informed Burke in a letter sent from Chatsworth[1] on 8 September 1777 that he would shortly be leaving for Ireland to visit friends in the company of a young protégé, John Townshend.[2] The prevailing view that the Opposition "must wait for events to form a plan of operation", he wrote, had always served as a justification for indolence. He remarked: "I have been living here some time with very pleasant and very amiable people but altogether as unfit to storm a citadel as they would be proper for the defence of it."

MY DEAR CHARLES,

I am, on many accounts, exceedingly pleased with your journey to Ireland. I do not think it was possible to dispose better of the interval between this and the meeting of Parliament. I told you as much, in the same general terms, by the post. My opinion of the infidelity of that conveyance hinderd me from being particular. I now sit down with malice prepense, to kill you with a very long letter; and must take my chance for some safe method of conveying the dose. Before I say any thing to you of the place you are in, or the business of it, on which by the way a great deal may be said, I will turn myself to the concluding part of your letter from Chatsworth.

You are sensible, that I do not differ from you in many things; and most certainly I do not dissent from the main of your doctrine concerning the Heresy of depending upon contingencies. You must recollect how uniform my sentiments have been on that Subject. I have ever wishd a settled plan of our own, founded in the very essence of the American Business, wholly unconnected with the Events of the war, and framed in such a manner as to keep up our Credit and maintain our System at home, in spite of any thing which may happen abroad. I am now convinced by a long and somewhat vexatious experience that such a plan is absolutely impracticable. I think with you, that some faults in the constitution of those whom we most love and trust are among the causes of this impracticability. They are faults too, that one can hardly wish them perfectly cured of, as I am afraid they are intimately connected with honest disinterested intentions, plentiful fortunes, assured rank, and quiet homes. A great deal of activity and enterprize can scarcely ever be expected from such men, unless some horrible calamity is just over their heads; or unless they suffer some gross personal insults from power, the resentment of which may be as unquiet and stimulating a principle in their minds, as ambition is in those of a different complexion. To say the truth, I cannot greatly blame them. We live at a time, when men are not repaid in fame, for what they sacrifice in Interest or repose. On the whole, when I consider of what discordant, and particularly of what fleeting materials the opposition has been all along composed, and at the same time review what Lord Rockingham has done, with that and with his own shatterd constitution, for these last twelve years, I confess I am rather surprized that he has done so much and perseverd so long, than that he has felt now and then some cold fits, and that he grows somewhat languid and desponding at last. I know that he and those who are most prevalent with him, though they are not thought so much devoted to popularity as others, do very much look to the people; and more than I think is wise in them, who do so little to guide and direct the public opinion. Without this, they act indeed; but they act as it were from compulsion, and because it is impossible in their situation to avoid taking some part. All this it is impossible to change, and to no purpose to complain of.

As to that popular humour which is the medium we float in, if I can discern any thing at all of its present state, it is far worse than I have ever known, or could ever imagine it. The faults of the people are not *popular* vices; at least they are not such as grow out of what we used to take to be the English temper and Character. The greatest number have a sort of an heavy lumpish acquiescence in Government, without much respect or esteem for those that compose it. I really cannot avoid making some very unpleasant prognostics from this disposition of the people. I think that many of the Symptoms must have struck you. I will mention one or two that are to me very remarkable. You must know that at Bristol we grow, as an Election Interest, and even as a party Interest, rather stronger than we were when I was chosen. We have just now a Majority in the Corporation. In this state of matters what think you they have done? They have voted their freedom to Lord Sandwich and Lord Suffolk – to the first at the very moment when the American Privateers were domineering in the Irish Sea and taking the Bristol traders in the Bristol Channel – to the latter when his remonstrances on the subject of Captures were the jest of Paris and of Europe. This fine step was taken, it seems, in honour of the zeal of these two profound Statesmen in the prosecution of John the Painter – So totally negligent are they of every thing essential; and so long, and so deeply affected with Trash the most low and contemptible; Just as if they thought the merit of Sir John Fielding³ was ⟨the⟩ most shining point in the Character of great Ministers, in the most critical of all times and of all others the most deeply interesting to the commercial world! My best friends in the Corporation had no other doubts on the occasion, than whether it did not belong to me, by right of my representative capacity, to be the bearer of this auspicious Compliment. In addition to this, if it could receive any addition, they now employ me to solicit as a favour of no small magnitude, that after the example of Newcastle they may be sufferd to arm Vessels for their own defence in the Channel. Their Memorial under the Seal of Merchants-hall is now lying on the Table before me. Not a Soul has the least Sensibility on finding themselves, now for the first time, obliged to act as if the Community were dissolved, and after enormous payments towards the common protection, to defend each part as if it were a separate State.

I don't mention Bristol, as if that were the part furthest gone in this mortification. Far from it. I know that there is rather a little more life in us than in any other place. In Liverpoole they are literally almost ruined by this American War; but they love it as they suffer from it. In short from whatever I see and from whatever Quarter I hear, I am convinced that every thing that is not absolute Stagnation, is evidently a party Spirit, very adverse to our politics and to the principles from whence they arise. There are most manifest marks of the resurrection of the Tory party. They no longer criticise, as all disengaged people in the world will, on the acts of Government; but they are silent under every evil, and hide and cover up every ministerial blunder and misfortune with the officious zeal of men, who think they have a party of their own to support in power. The Tories do universally think their power and consequence involved in the Success of this American business. The Clergy are astonishingly warm in it – and what the Tories are when embodied, united with their natural head the Crown, and animated by their Clergy, no man knows better than yourself. As to the Whigs I think them far from extinct. They are what they always were (except by the able use of opportunities) by far the weakest party in this Country. They have not yet learnd the application of their principles to the present state of things; and as to the dissenters, the main effective part of the Whig strength, they are, to use a favourite expression of our American Campaign Style – not at all *in force*. They will do very little; and as far as I can discern, are rather intimidated than provoked at the denunciations of the Court in the Archbishop of Yorks Sermon.[4] I thought that Sermon rather imprudent when I first saw it – But it seems to have done its business.

In this temper of the people, I do not wholly wonder that our Northern friends[5] look a little towards Events. In war particularly I am afraid it must be so. There is something so weighty and decisive in the Events of war, something that so completely overpowers the imagination of the Vulgar, that all Counsels must in a great degree be subordinate to and attendant on them. I am sure it was so in the last war[6] very eminently. So that on the whole, what with the temper of the people, the temper of our own friends, and the domineering necessities of war, we must quietly give up all Ideas of any settled, preconcerted plan. We shall be lucky enough, if keeping ourselves attentive and alert, we can contrive to profit of the occasions as they arise; tho I am sensible, that those who are best provided with a general Scheme, are fittest to take advantage of all contingencies. However, to act with any people with the least degree of comfort, I believe we must contrive a little to assimilate to their Character. We must gravitate towards them, if we would keep in the same System, or expect that they would approach towards us. They are indeed worthy of much concession and management. I am quite convinced that they are the honestest public men that ever appeard in this Country, and I am sure that they are the wisest by far of those who appear in it at present. Not one of those who are continually complaining of them, but are themselves just as chargeable with all their faults, and have a decent stock of their own into the bargain. They are, (our friends) I admit, as you very truly represent them, but indifferently qualifyd for storming a Citadel. After all, God knows whether this Citadel is to be stormed by them or by anybody else, by the means they use or by any means. I know that as they are, abstractedly speaking, to blame, so there are those who cry out against them for it, not with a friendly complaint as we do, but with the bitterness of Enemies. But I know too that those who blame them for want of Enterprize have shewn no activity at all against the common Enemy; All their Skill and all their Spirit has been shewn only in weakning, dividing, and indeed destroying their Allies. What they are, and what we are, is now pretty evidently experienced, and it is certain, that partly by our common faults, but much more by the difficulties of our Situation, and some circumstances of unavoidable misfortune, we are in little better than a sort of Cul-de-Sac. For my part, I do all I can to give ease to my mind in this strange position. I remember some years ago, when I was pressing some points with much eagerness and anxiety, and complaining with great vexation to the Duke of Richmond of the little progress I made, he told me kindly and I believe very truly, that, tho he was far from thinking so himself, other people could not be persuaded, I had not some latent private Interest in pushing these matters, which I urged with an earnestness so extreme, and so much approaching to passion. He was certainly in the right. I am thoroughly resolved to give both to myself and my friends, less vexation on these subjects than hitherto I have done; much less indeed.

If *you* should grow too earnest, you will be still more inexcusable than I was. Your having enterd into Affairs so much younger ought to make them too familiar to you, to be a cause of much agitation, and you have much more day before you for your work. Do not be in haste. Lay your foundations deep in public opinion. Though (as you are sensible) I have never given you the least hint of advice about joining yourself[7] in a declared connexion with our party, nor do I now – yet as I love that party very well, and am clear that you are better able to serve them than any man I know, I wish that things should be so kept, as to leave you mutually very open to one another in all changes and contingencies. And I wish this the rather, because in order to be very great, as I am anxious that you should be, (always presuming that you are disposed to make a good use of power) you will certainly want some better support than merely that of the Crown. For I much doubt, whether, with all your parts, you are the man formed for acquiring real interior favour in this Court or in any. I therefore wish you a firm ground in the Country; and I do not know so firm and sound a bottom to build on as our party. Well, I have done with this matter; and you think I ought to have finished it long ago. Now I turn to Ireland.

Observe that I have not heard a word of any news relative to it from thence or from London. So that I am only going to state to you my conjectures as to facts, and to speculate again on these conjectures. I have a strong notion that the lateness of our meeting is owing to the previous managements intended in Ireland. I suspect that they mean, that Ireland should take a sort of lead and act an efficient part in this war both with men and money.[8] It will sound well when we meet to tell us of the active zeal and loyalty of the people of Ireland and contrast it with the Rebellious spirit of America. It will be a popular topic the perfect confidence of Ireland in the power of the British Parliament. From thence they will argue the little danger which any dependency of the Crown has to apprehend from the enforcement of that Authority. It will be too somewhat flattering to the Country Gentlemen who might otherwise begin to be sullen, to hold out that the Burthen is not wholly to rest upon them; and it will pique our pride to be told that Ireland has chearfully steppd forward; and when a dependent of this Kingdom has already engaged itself in another years war, merely for our dignity, how can we who are principals in the quarrell hold off. This Scheme of policy seems to me so very obvious, and is likely to be of so much service to the present System, that I cannot conceive it possible they should neglect it or something like it. They have already put the people of Ireland to the proof. Have they not borne the Earl of Buckinghamshire?[9] The person who was employed to move the fiery committee in the House of Lords in order to stimulate the Ministry to this war; who was in the chair; and who moved the Resolutions.

It is within a few days of Eleven years since I was in Ireland and then after an absence of two.[10] Those who have been absent from any Scene for even a much shorter time generally lose the true practical notion of the Country, and what may or may not be done in it. When I knew Ireland it was very different from the state of England, where Government is a vast deal, the public some thing, but individuals comparatively very little. But if Ireland bears any resemblance to what it was some years ago, neither Government nor public opinion can do a great deal; almost the whole is in the hands of a few leading people. The populace of Dublin and some parts in the North are in some sort an exception. But the Primate, Lord Hillsborough and Lord Hertford[11] have great sway in the latter, and the former may be considerable or not, pretty much as the Duke of Leinster[12] pleases. On the whole the success of Government usually depended on the bargain made with a very few men. The resident Lieutenancy[13] may have made some change, and given a strength to Government which formerly I know it had not; still however, I am of opinion, the former state, tho in other hands perhaps, and in another manner, still continues. The house you are connected with is grown into a much greater degree of power than it had, tho it was very considerable at the period I speak of. If the D. of L. takes a popular part, he is sure of the City of Dublin, and he has a young man[14] attachd to him who stands very forward in Parliament and in Profession, and by what I hear, with more good will and less envy than usually attend so rapid a progress. The movement of one or two principal men, especially if they manage the little popular strength which is to be found in Dublin and Ulster, may do a great deal, especially where money is to be saved and taxes kept off. I confess I should despair of your succeeding with any of them, if they could not be satisfyd, that every jobb which they can look for on account of carrying *this* measure, would be just as sure to them for their ordinary support of Government. They are essential to Government, which at this time must not be disturbed ⟨or their⟩ neutrality will be pu⟨rchased⟩ at as high a price as their alliance offensive and defensive. Now as by sup⟨por⟩ting they may get as much by betraying their Country, it must be a great leaning to turpitude, that could make them take a part in this war; I am satisfied, that if the Duke of Leinster and Lord Shannon[15] would act together, this business could not go on; or if either of them took part with Ponsonby,[16] it would have no better success. Hutchinsons situation is much alterd since I saw you. To please Tisdall,[17] he had been in a manner, laid aside at the Castle. It is now to be seen, whether he preferrs the gratification of his resentment, and his appetite for popularity, both of which are strong enough in him, to the advantages which his independance gives him of making a new bargain, and accumulating new Offices on his heap. For Godsake, do not be asleep in this Scene of action; at this time, if I am right, the Principal. The Protestants of Ireland will be I think in general backward. They are the landed, and the monied Interests, for the infinitely greater part; and they will not like to pay. The papists are reduced to beasts of Burthen; they will give all they have, their Shoulders, readily enough if they are flatterd. Surely the state of Ireland ought for ever to teach parties moderation in their victories. People crushd by law have no hopes but from power. If laws are their enemies, they will be enemies to laws; and those who have much to hope and nothing to lose will always be dangerous more or less. But this is not our present business. If all this should prove a dream however, let it not hinder you from writing to me and telling me so. You will easily refute in your conversations the little topics which they will set afloat; such as that Ireland is a boat and must go with the Ship; That if the Americans contended only for their liberties it would be different – but since they have declared independence and so forth. You are happy in young Townsend⟨'s comp⟩any. Remember me to him. How does he like his private situation in a Country where he was the Son of the Sovereign?[18] Mrs Burke and the two Rds salute you cordially.

EB
BEACD 8 OCTR 1777

TO JOSEPH HARFORD[1]

27 SEPTEMBER 1780

Burke had recently pulled out of the election campaign in Bristol and was temporarily without a seat. In this letter, addressed to the most radical of his Bristol friends, he explains that divisions within the Rockingham group over parliamentary reform make him reluctant to return to Parliament.

MY DEAR SIR,

The fatigues of the Election are over; and I congratulate you on your return to quiet. I congratulate you too on the order, vigour, and spirit of decision, that shortened your work, and rendered the Election itself less tedious to the City and less vexatious and expensive to the Parties than it would have been but for your exertions. Give my best compliments on this occasion to your Colleague.[2]

As to the Event of the Election, it has been just what it *ought to be*. It was the natural result of the conduct of *all* parties; and it may have a tendency to reform the conduct of *some* of them. The Tories have not acquired a great deal of Glory by the Victory they have obtained, and by the use they have made of their strength. On the other hand, I am perfectly convinced that the defeat both of Mr Cruger[3] and myself was a thing proper and necessary. If *I* had not been defeated, the Whigs never could be taught the necessity of Vigour, activity, Vigilance, and foresight. If *Mr Cruger* had not been defeated, his friends could not have had the *Chance* they now have, of being cured of presumption, and weak crooked politicks. *Both parties* could never have been taught the necessity of cordial Union, the Mischief of Gentlemens neglecting to cultivate an Interest among the common people, and the madness of the common peoples dream, that they could be any thing without the Aid of better fortunes and better heads than their own – None of us could be *practically* taught these essential Truths, but by the *Aid* of a defeat.

One great advantage towards our converting our loss into profit is, that we have lost neither temper nor Credit by it. At present all our prospects depend upon the use we make of these Circumstances. Our Numbers, though respectable, are not large. But then all the flesh we have is sound, and firm, and fit for action; and it is my earnest Wish, that no accession, however flattering, may be admitted, if it tends more to swell our Bulk than to augment our force. If it be, you will find it a weight to carry, not strength to carry away any thing else.

One thing, my dear friend, your manly sense will guard you against – the admitting any *Visionary* Politicians amongst us. We are sufficiently secured, (by our exclusion from the Court), from the *mercenary* of that Tribe. But the Bane of the Whiggs has been the admission among them of the Corps of Schemers; who in reality, and at bottom, mean little more than to indulge themselves with Speculations; but who do us infinite Mischief, by persuading many sober and well meaning people, that we have designs inconsistent with the Constitution left us by our forefathers. You know how many are startled with the Idea of innovation. Would to God it were in our power to keep things *where they are*, in point of *form*; provided we were able to improve them in point of *Substance*. The *Machine itself* is well enough to answer any good purpose, provided the *materials* were sound. But what signifies the Arrangement of rottenness?

It is our business to take care, that we who are Electors, or corporate Magistrates, or Freeholders, or Members of Parliament, or Peers, (or whatever we may be,) that we hold good principles, and that we steadily oppose all bad principles and bad men. If the Nation at large has *disposition* enough for this End, its *form* of Government is, in my opinion, fully sufficient for it. But if the *general* disposition be *against* a virtuous and manly line of publick conduct, there is no *form* into which it can be thrown that will improve its Nature or add to its Energy. I know that many Gentlemen in other parts of the Kingdom think it practicable to make the remedy of our publick disorders *attend* on an alteration in our actual constitution, and to bring about the former as a consequence of the Latter. But I believe that no people, who could think of deferring the redress of such Grievances as ours, and the Animadversion on such palpable misconduct as there has been lately in our Affairs, untill the material Alterations in the Constitution which they propose can be brought about; will ever do any mighty matter when they have carried these alterations; even if they should find themselves *able* to carry them.

As to myself, I am come to no resolution relative to my making one in the consultation of these matters. I believe, that without much intrigue, I might contrive to come into Parliament through some door or other. But when I consider on one hand, the power and prostitution of the faction which has long domineerd, and does still domineer in this Country, and on the other, the strange

distraction not only in Interests, but in views and plans of conduct, that prevails among those who oppose that faction, I do,
something more than, hesitate about the wisdom and propriety
of *my* making one in this general Scene of confusion. I will say
nothing about that Tail, which draggles in the dirt, and which
every party in every state *must* carry about it; *That* can only flirt
a little of the Mud in our faces now and then. It is no great matter.
But some of our *capital* Men entertain thoughts so very different
from mine, that if I come into Parliament, I must either fly in the
face of the clearest lights of my own understanding, and the
firmest conviction of my own conscience, or I must oppose those
for whom I have the highest value. The D. of Richmond has
voluntarily proposed to open the Election of England to all those,
without exception, who have [the] qualification of being 18 years
old; and has swept away at one stroke all the privileges of Freeholders, Cities, and Burroughs throughout the Kingdom, and
sends every Member of Parliament, every year, to the Judgment
and discretion of such Electors. Sir Geo: Saville[4] has *consented* to
adopt, the Scheme of more *frequent Elections* as a remedy for disorders, which in my opinion, have a great part of their Root in
Elections themselves; and while the Duke of Richmond proposes
to annihilate the Freeholders, Sir Geo: Saville consents to a plan
for a vast encrease of their *power* by choice of an hundred new
Knights of the Shire. Which of these am I to adhere to? or shall
I put myself into the graceful situation of opposing both? If I am
asked who the D. of Richmond and Sir G: Saville are, and what
is my own inward opinion of them, I must fairly say, that I look
upon them to be the first Men of their Age and their Country;
that I do not know Men of more parts or more honour; of the
latter you remember, what I said in the Guildhall, and I cannot
retract a word of it.

In this situation with regard to those whom I esteem the most,
how shall I act with those for whom I have no Esteem at all? Such
there are, not only in the Ministry, but in the opposition. There
is indeed the M. of Rockingham and there are some more, with
whom I do not think I differ materially; but I am quite certain,
that though they make our greatest Number, yet it is a Number
by no means sufficient with any Effect to oppose the Court, with
the little or no aid we have from the people. These are my
thoughts; or rather a very small part of the inducements, which

make me content, I had almost said desirous, of continuing where the larger part of our City was of opinion I ought to continue.

On recollection, I have perhaps gone further than I intended on the subject of my difference with my friends; and since I have troubled you with so long a letter I ought to take the Benefit of your present patience and explain myself a little.

As to the shortening the duration of Parliaments, I confess I see no cause to change or to modifye my opinion on that subject. The reason remains the same; the Desires of the people go along with the reason of the thing. I do not know any thing more *practically* unpopular. It is true, that many people are fond of *talking* on short parliaments, as a subject of ingenuity; and they will come to resolutions on the point, if any one wishes that they should; but when they come to the Touchstone, to *the Election itself* they vomit up all these Notions. You have, I dare say, remarked that, (except in one place only) not *one* Candidate has ventured, in an Advertisement, or in a declaration from the Hustings, to say one Syllable on the subject of short Parliaments, nor has any one Elector thought proper to propose a Test,[5] or to give an Instruction, or even the Slightest recommendation of such a Measure. You know how every one in Bristol feels upon that matter; and I have reason to be persuaded, that they do not at all differ from the Majority of the Kingdom.

As to *some* remedy to the present State of the representation, I do by no means object to it. But it is an Affair of great difficulty; and to be touched with great delicacy; and by an hand of great power. Power and delicacy do not often unite. But without great power, I do not hesitate to say, it *cannot* be done. By power I mean the *executive* power of the Kingdom. It is, (according to my Ideas of such a reformation) a thing in which the executive Government is more concerned (in all matters of detail it is much concerned) than it is in short Parliaments; and I know that in business of this sort, if Administration does not concurr, they are able to defeat the Scheme, even though it should be carried by a Majority in Parliament; and not only to defeat it, but to render it in a short time odious and contemptible. The people shew no disposition to exert themselves for putting power into the hands of those from whom they expect the performance of Tasks that require a great deal of strength; and that too a strength regular, systematick, and progressive. If they can find none to Trust there is an End of this and of all Questions of reformation.

Before I finished the first Sheet of this I received your Letter; and I thank you heartily for it. I am extremely pleased with the Turn that things have taken in Somersetshire; and that solely on account of Coxe; for as to Mr Trevillion[6] I am not quite certain about his disposition. I find too, with at least as much satisfaction, that you and our friends agree with me about the Constitution of our Club,[7] and the Spirit in which it ought to proceed. Hereafter, and when we have fully cut off Treachery, all our Measures ought to be healing. No revenge, and no reproach.

You see in what a way Westminster was carried. There is in that City a sort of Whiggs, perfectly resembling the corrupt part of ours, and who would have done just as much Mischief, if they had been under any head. Fortunately they were not, and therefore instead of being detrimental to the Cause, their activity rendered them very useful.

Give my most affectionate compliments to all our friends. I hope to hear that Noble[8] is quite well again. He deserves to be so on all accounts. Remember me and my Brother (whom I left in Town behind me) to Mrs Harford and the young Ladies, and to Mrs Kile.[9] When you write to Warrington[10] do not forget me there. Believe me always and with unalterable regard My dear Sir your most faithful

and Obedient humble Servant

E.B.

BEACONSFIELD 27 SEPTR 1780

Burke's presence in Parliament was, however, essential to the Rockingham party, and the Marquis turned out the newly elected Member for Malton, Yorkshire – a pocket borough in his gift – where Burke was returned in a by-election in December 1780.

TO WILLIAM BAKER

Between the last letter and this one the Rockingham party had had a taste of power, cut short after only three months by the death of Lord Rockingham in July 1782. In April 1783, their new leader Charles James Fox had botched together a pragmatic and much ridiculed alliance with Lord North, their former foe, which fell in December 1783 over its attempt to reform the organisation of the East India Company, a subject dear to Burke's heart. Now Burke was in opposition again, and Pitt the Younger, enjoying full royal support and patronage, had just won a convincing general election in April 1784.

22 JUNE 1784

MY DEAR BAKER,[1]

I am sincerely sorry for the cause of your confinement. I hope soon to hear better news; and that the Object of your family sollicitude, will leave you at leisure to think of other things, and to think of him with more Tranquillity.

As to the publick Object of your Care, it is certainly not in my power to give you any comfort about it. I consider the House of Commons as something worse than extinguishd. We have been labouring for near twenty years to make it independent; and as soon as we had accomplishd what we had in View, we found that its independence led to its destruction. The people did not like our work; and they joind the Court to pull it down. The demolition is very complete. Others may be more sanguine; but for me to look forward to the Event of another twenty years toil – it is quite ridiculous. I am sure the Task was more easy at first than it is now. The examples which have been made must operate. I can conceive that men of spirit might be persuaded to persevere in a great and worthy undertaking for many years, at the hazard, and even with the certainty of the utmost indignation of a Court; but to become Objects of that indignation only to expose themselves to popular indignation, and to be rejected by both Court and Country, is more perhaps than any one could expect; certainly a great deal more than one will meet, except perhaps in three or four men, who will be more marked for their singularity and obstinacy, than pitied for their feeble good intentions. It is rather difficult to form a judgment of an whole people. But at present the picture of the English Nation does not appear to me in a very favourable light. I do not conceive them to be under any delusion at all. If I am not mistaken, they are perfectly well aware of the Nature and Tendency of what they have done, and they by no means repent of it. To be sure they do not intend, formally to deliver over themselves and their posterity to servitude. This is not their primary intention. But they are so fond of aggrandising the Crown, and of humbling every thing which does not derive its importance directly from that Scource, that they are totally indifferent to the consequences. A More frightful Symptom, in my Mind, than this, appears in the Nation at present; to which I do not think any thing was correspondent, even in the worst times of the Roman Republick. That is that all the Tyranny, robbery, and destruction of mankind practised by the Company and their servants in the East,[2] is popular and pleasing in this Country; and that the Court and Ministry who evidently abet that iniquitous System, are somewhat the better liked on that account. The factions of the great gave countenance to the ruin of the provinces in the days of the Roman domination; But such men as Verres,[3] and such practices as his, were always odious to the people at Large.

You ask me why my Motion[4] was not supported by the party? Truly I can give no good reason for it. Such was their pleasure. If I had followed the prevailing opinion I never would have made that Motion. But I was resolved to take my own way, and to leave them to take theirs. So I made the motion; and the Event is such as you have seen. I am happy to find you think me in the Right: I am sure I should not have slept as well as I have done since that time, if I had been persuaded to omit a protest against the doctrines in the Speech from the Throne, and a defence of the worthy persons with whom I had the honour of acting in the last Parliament, and who had no longer any parliamentary means of defending themselves. A certain Routine, of Conduct, some weak hopes of the present parliament, an expectation that the popular tide would turn; that we must not too strongly oppose ourselves to the prevailing humour, and many other Topics of the same Metal, not in my opinion at all worthy of our Cause, of ourselves, or of the occasion, prevented several from coinciding with me with regard to the seasonableness of our making our defence, or of our setting our faces against the first declaration of the New Doctrines. For my own part I was thoroughly convinced, not only of the rectitude, but of the prudence and propriety of the act; and I am so little ashamed of the reception which my Motion met with (which was indeed with apparent uneasiness on our side, and with all kind of Boyish petulance and insolence on the other) that I am resolved to reprint it in a seperate Pamphlet with Notes and references; to send it to every part of the Kingdom; and to get

it translated into French, and to circulate it in every Country in
Europe. It may be perhaps the last free act we shall [be] permitted to do: and that last act ought not to be such as to disgrace all
the Rest. Adieu my dear friend and beleive me ever

> most faithfully
> and affectionately Yours &c
> EDM BURKE
> BECONSFIELD 22 JUNE 1784

TO MISS MARY PALMER

19 JANUARY 1786

Mary Palmer[1] (1751–1820), Sir Joshua Reynolds's niece, had
lived with her uncle almost continuously since 1773 and was well
acquainted with all the Burkes. Evidently she was disturbed by
the manner in which one of her correspondents in India spoke of
Edmund's activities. Edmund tried to reply to the correspondent
through her.

MY DEAR MISS PALMER,

How could you apologise, and apologise to me too, for an act of
good nature and kindness? I hear enough of my faults from my
Enemies; shall I not bear to hear them from my friends? Shall
I bear wounds in the field of Battle, and quarrel with my Surgeons, who open them only to heal them, in my Tent? Tell your
worthy correspondent,[2] who is so good as to take an Interest in
me, that I am truly thankful, to him or her (whoever it may be)
for their obliging solicitude. I am an old acquaintance of your
House; I believe of not much less than thirty years standing;
though a much later personal acquaintance of *yours*; and you,
according to your ages, are best Judges, whether I am that very
intemperate man, that I am described to be in the cool and
moderate Climate of Bengal. I am far from the least Title to
Great; perhaps I am not much nearer to that of *good*, though
I endeavour all I can at the latter – nothing at all, I assure you at
the former. However I am not, at my years, a person of a childish
credulity – nor apt to run away with every report. Having been
employd for years in the Business of arranging and stating, as well

as collecting, *Evidence*, it would not much become me, of all men, to be light and careless about matter of fact. It is indeed much the Interest of those on whom facts bear hard, so to represent me; and I do not blame them for doing the only thing which can be done in their Cause. It is not uncommon, nor blameable, to make use of a *report*, when a motion is made in the House of Commons, for papers that may, verify, contradict, or qualifye the matter of the report, according to its nature. Almost all motions for papers are made upon that Ground. However, I am, perhaps, the only active man in the House, that never did make a motion, without a very good previous knowlege of the paper I moved for. I will tell you this Business just as it is. I found, that they had received at the India House, a paper of Instructions from Mr Hastings to Mr Bristow,[3] one of which was to apprehend, and to put to Death a certain Gentleman "called" Almas Âli Khân.[4] I had a copy of that curious secret instruction in my Pocket. I moved,[5] that this Instruction should be laid before the House; stating, as my Ground, the precarious Tenure, on which people of distinction in that Country, held their honours, fortunes, and lives; – but never, either directly or indirectly, said one word of his Wife, children, parents, or relations; not having reason to know, that he had any Wife – nor having, receivd any report, made directly to me, or thro' the intervention of any other person, that should lead me to such a conclusion. If I had mentiond any such thing it must have been a mere fiction of my own brain.[6] My motion, which stands on the Journals, will verifye this; in which there is not a word of his Widow – nor of his Death – but solely of the *Order* to seize upon him, and to cause him to be put to death. The paper was given. It appeard just as I had represented. It was printed by order of the House. It excited a general indignation; and the Newspapers fell to work on that ground, to frame petitions from his Wife and Children &ca &c – The only favour I have to beg of my friends, is, that they will form their Judgments of me, by what the records of Parliament, and not the fictions of Newspapers, relate concerning me. In those records, they will find eleven pretty large Volumes; *some* of which are *entirely* mine; and the materials of *all* of which I have diligently perused, and compared – and if on collation with the authorities at home or abroad, they find, that I have abused the Trust placed in me by Parliament, by recording rumours, instead of facts, taken from official Papers, or oral Evidence judicially given at a Committee

Table, I shall be very ready to excuse them in supposing me to be, what, at my age, and with my very large experience, it is very unfit I should be, a man of a giddy credulous nature, apt to be run away with every idle rumour, and to commit myself rashly upon it. I certainly do not expect, (and I should be a fool if I did) that the reports of my conduct and Character, from the Bengal Gentlemen in London, to the Bengal Gentlemen at Calcutta, should be favourable to me. Mr Hastings has given their stations to several of them; and if they wish to imitate his Conduct – it is certain that they can never have me for their friend. I have not fallen into any Traps laid by their Patron against my reputation; He was *very* near falling into a Trap, laid, not by me, but by himself; and from which he escaped, if he has escaped, by greater Trap mechanists[7] than he has ever been, or can be. I know him very well; though never having seen him, but in the dusk of one Evening, in a walk with you and your Uncle, and in the midst of a squadron; I am sure I could not distinguish his face; but I know him in his actions and his writings. I likewise am an old acquaintance of Almas ali Khân of whom there is a great deal in the Papers before our Committee not yet reported – and on the whole, perhaps, there are not very many Gentlemen at Calcutta, so well informed of the State of the upper provinces, as I am; at least to a certain period – and that I am as little likely to fall into a gross Errour, as to persons or facts, as any of them. Your correspondent says, and does me only Justice in saying, that "I do all the good in my power to the party I represent". But I must beg leave to inform you, that in India affairs, I have not acted at all with any party from the beginning to the End. I know of no party which goes in a body upon this subject; they are all so distracted with personal considerations; and that perhaps may be among the causes of the Cry against myself in particular. I began this India Business in the administration of Lord North to which in all its periods [I was] in direct opposition, and acted in it with several of those who voted on his side of the House;[8] and against some of my own description, who have been among the Loudest against me on that account. I have no party in this Business, my dear Miss Palmer, but among a set of people, who have none of your Lilies and Roses in their faces; but who are the images of the great Pattern as well as you and I. I know what I am doing; whether the white people like it or not. They hear, it seems, at Calcutta, that "I am declined in popular favour". That cannot

be; for I never had any to lose. I never conformed myself to the
humours of the people. I cannot say that opinion is indifferent
to me: but I will take it, if I can, as my companion; never as my
Guide. I see, that the same imputation of *intemperance* has been
laid upon me by a Gentleman, at the meeting to remonstrate
against Mr Pitts Bill.[9] It is natural, from his connexions, that he
should do so; and should take an occasion (from a measure
I abhor, and certainly had no share in, except in expressing my
detestation of it, and hoping, that no man who had a regard to
his Character would suffer himself to be ballotted for the execution of it) to cast reflexions upon me, rather than upon those
whose act he opposes. I have always wished, that no man should
be prosecuted for offences, but before Tribunals known to the
Law; and that when inquisitions were made, they should be into
the actions, and not the fortunes, of persons under accusation.[10]
I never found men guilty in the Mass; nor proceeded against their
Estates, without knowing whether I had any fault to find with
their proceedings. I found the general Tenour of the Companies
internal and external System to be bad. The actors and advisers
of that Evil System; I knew; I pointed out; and would have pun-
ishd if I could. But I never wished to make a previous Enquiry
into what they were worth, in order to drive them to a composition for the delinquencies, I should presume from the degree of
their power in ransoming themselves. There are those, who like
neither the Methods of the present Ministry nor mine – but some
lately returnd, I am sure, would greatly prefer that of the persons
now in power to mine. They, therefore, support the Ministry and
they persecute me, in the only way they can, by their calumnies.
As to the Gentlemen who serve in India, as a *body*, I have nothing
to say to them; because I have nothing to say to men in *bodies*.
I attach myself to the guilty, where alone guilt can lie, *individually*; and if the Servants in general think, that my charges against
Sir Elijah Impey,[11] Mr Hastings, and Mr Benfield, are ill founded,
or frivolous, it would give me a worse opinion of them than
I have yet entertaind, who have a most sincere Esteem for several
of them. Is not this, my dear Miss Palmer, a strange ⟨account⟩
to you, who care not three Straws for such things? But it is written *thro'* you, not *to* you; and I wish you to send it (blots and all,
for I have written in a good deal of haste) to your Indian friend.
It is, as a friend to you, I write it – from my real love to all of
your Connexions; who, (if I had taken ways to power which

I never could prevail on myself to take) would have found some results from my goodwishes to some of them; as well as to other persons in India; I, whom you know, to be so *far from* a general Enemy, and persecutor of any description of men, that I would not hurt any Creature on earth, 'till I found him intollerable to every other Creature. My dearest Miss Palmer, God bless you; and send your friend home to you Rich and innocent; and may you long enjoy your own swe⟨et⟩ repose; and the love and esteem of all those who know how to value, elegance, Taste, abilities, and simplicity. I am ever

> Your affectionate friend
> EDM BURKE
> BECONSFIELD 19 JANY 1786

TO CHARLES-JEAN-FRANÇOIS DEPONT

NOVEMBER 1789

Burke gave his first important judgement on the French Revolution in this letter written in reply to the young French politician Charles Depont.[1]

DEAR SIR,

We are extremely happy in your giving us leave to promise ourselves a renewal of the pleasure we formerly had in your Company at Beconsfield and in London. It was too lively to be speedily forgotten on our part; and we are highly flatter'd to find that You keep so exactly in your Memory all the particulars of the few attentions which You were so good to accept from us during your stay in England. We indulge ourselves in the hope, that you will be able to execute what you intend in our favour; and that we shall be more fortunate in the coming Spring, than we were in the last.

You have reason to imagine that I have not been as early as I ought in acquainting you with my thankful acceptance of the Correspondence you have been pleased to Offer. Do not think me insensible to the honour you have done me. I confess I did hesitate for a time, on a doubt, whether it would be prudent to yield to my earnest desire of such a Correspondence.

Your frank and ingenuous manner of writing, would be ill

answer'd by a cold, dry, and guarded reserve on my part.
It would indeed be adverse to my habits and my Nature to make
use of that sort of Caution in my intercourse with any friend.
Besides as you are pleased to think that your splendid flame of
Liberty was first lighted up at My faint and glimmering taper,
I thought you had a right to call upon me for my undisguised
sentiments on whatever related to that Subject. On the other
hand, I was not without apprehension, that in this free mode of
intercourse, I might say something not only disagreeable to Your
formed opinions, upon points, on which of all others we are
most impatient of Contradiction, but not pleasing to the Power
which should happen to be prevalent at the time of your receiving my letter. I was well aware, that, in Seasons of Jealousy, suspicion is vigilant and active; that it is not extremely scrupulous
in its means of Enquiry; not perfectly equitable in its Judgments;
and not altogether deliberate in its Resolutions. In the ill connected and inconclusive logick of the Passions, whatever may
appear blameable, is easily transferr'd from the guilty Writer to
the innocent Receiver. It is an aukward, as well as unpleasant
Accident; but it is one that has sometimes happen'd. A Man may
be made a Martyr to tenets the most opposite to his own. At
length a friend of mine, lately come from Paris, informed me
that heats are beginning to abate, and that intercourse is thought
to be more safe. This has given me some Courage; and the
Reflexion, that the sentiments of a Person of no more consideration than I am either Abroad or at home, could be of little
consequence to the success of any Cause or any Party, has at
length decided me to accept of the honour you are willing to
confer upon me.

You may easily believe, that I have had my Eyes turned with
great Curiosity to the astonishing scene now displayed in France.
It has certainly given rise in my Mind to many Reflexions, and
to some Emotions. These are natural and unavoidable; but it
would ill become Me to be too ready in forming a positive opinion upon matters transacted in a Country, with the correct, political Map of which I must be very imperfectly acquainted.
Things indeed have already happen'd so much beyond the scope
of all speculation, that persons of infinitely more sagacity than
I am ought to be ashamed of any thing like confidence in their
reasoning upon the operation of any principle or the effect of
any measure. It would become me least of all to be so confident,

who ought at my time of life, to have well learn'd the important lesson of self distrust; A lesson of no small Value in company with the best information; but which alone can make any sort of amends for our not having learn'd other lessons so well as it was our business to learn them. I beg you, once for all, to apply this corrective of the diffidence I have on my own Judgment to whatever I may happen to say with more positiveness than suits my knowledge and situation. If I should seem any where to express myself in the language of disapprobation, be so good to consider it as no more than the expression of doubt.

You hope, Sir, that I think the French deserving of Liberty? I certainly do. I certainly think that all Men who desire it, deserve it. It is not the Reward of our Merit or the acquisition of our Industry. It is our Inheritance. It is the birthright of our Species. We cannot forfeit our right to it, but by what forfeits our title to the privileges of our kind; I mean the abuse or oblivion of our rational faculties, and a ferocious indocility, which makes us prompt to wrong and Violence, destroys our social Nature, and transforms us into something little better than the description of Wild beasts. To Men so degraded, a state of strong constraint is a sort of necessary substitute for freedom; since, bad as it is, it may deliver them in some Measure from the worst of all Slavery, that is the despotism of their own blind and brutal passions.

You have kindly said, that You began to love freedom from Your intercourse with Me. This is the more necessary because of all the loose Terms in the world Liberty is the most indefinite. Permit me then to continue our conversation, and to tell You what the freedom is that I love and that to which I think all men intitled. It is not solitary, unconnected, individual, selfish Liberty. As if every Man was to regulate the whole of his Conduct by his own will. The Liberty I mean is *social* freedom. It is that state of things in which Liberty is secured by the equality of Restraint; A Constitution of things in which the liberty of no one Man, and no body of Men and no Number of men can find Means to trespass on the liberty of any Person or any description of Persons in the Society. This kind of liberty is indeed but another name for Justice, ascertained by wise Laws, and secured by well constructed institutions. I am sure, that Liberty, so incorporated, and in a manner, identified, with justice, must be infinitely dear to every one, who is capable of conceiving what it is. But whenever a separation is made between Liberty and

Justice, neither is, in my opinion, safe. I do not believe that Men ever did submit, certain I am that they never ought to have submitted, to the arbitrary pleasure of one Man, but under circumstances in which the arbitrary pleasure of many Persons in the Community, pressed with an intolerable hardship upon the just and equal Rights of their fellows. Such a choice might be made as among Evils. The moment *Will* is set above Reason and Justice in any Community, a great Question may arise in sober Minds, in what part or portion of the Community that dangerous dominion of *Will* may be the least Mischievously placed.

If I think all men who cultivate Justice entitled to Liberty, and when joined in States, entitled to a Constitution framed to perpetuate and secure it; You may be assured, Sir, that I think Your Countrymen eminently worthy of a blessing, which is peculiarly adapted to noble, generous and humane Natures. Such I found the French, when more than fifteen Years ago, I had the happiness, tho' but for too short a time, of visiting your Country; and I trust their Character is not alter'd since that period.

I have nothing to check my wishes towards the establishment of a solid and rational scheme of Liberty in France. On the subject of the Relative power of Nations I may have my prejudices; but I envy internal freedom, security, and good order to none. When therefore I shall learn, that in France, the Citizen, by whatever description he is qualified, is in a perfect state of legal security, with regard to his life, to his property, to the uncontrolled disposal of his Person, to the free use of his Industry and his faculties; – When I hear that he is protected in the beneficial Enjoyment of the Estates, to which, by the course of settled Law, he was born, or is provided with a fair compensation for them; – that he is maintain'd in the full fruition of the advantages belonging to the state and condition of life, in which he had lawfully engaged himself, or is supplied with a substantial, equitable Equivalent; – When I am assured, that a simple Citizen may decently express his sentiments upon Publick Affairs, without hazard to his life or safety, even tho' against a predominant and fashionable opinion; When I know all this of France, I shall be as well pleased as every one must be, who has not forgot the general communion of Mankind, nor lost his natural sympathy in local and accidental connexions.

If a Constitution is settled in France upon those principles and calculated for those ends, I believe there is no Man in this

Country whose heart and Voice would not go along with You. I am sure it will give me, for one, an heartfelt pleasure when I hear, that, in France, the great publick Assemblies, the natural securities for individual freedom, are perfectly free themselves; when there can be no suspicion, that they are under the coercion of a Military Power[2] of any description; When it may be truly said, that no armed force can be seen which is not called into existence by their creative Voice, and which must not instantly disappear at their dissolving word, – When such Assemblies after being freely chosen shall proceed with the weight of Magistracy and not with the arts of Candidates; – When they do not find themselves under the necessity of feeding one part of the Community at the grievous Charge[3] of other parts as necessitous as those who are so fed; – When they are not obliged, (in order to flatter those who have their lives in their disposal) to tolerate acts of doubtful influence on Commerce and on Agriculture, and for the sake of a precarious Relief under temporary scarcity, to sow (if I may be allowed the expression) the seeds of lasting want; – When they are not compell'd daily to stimulate an irregular and juvenile imagination for supplies, which they are not in a condition, firmly to demand; – When they are not obliged to diet the State from hand to Mouth, upon the casual alms of Choice, fancy, Vanity, or Caprice,[4] on which plan the value of the object to the Publick which Receives, often bears no sort of proportion to the loss of the Individual who gives; – When they are not necessitated to call for contributions to be estimated on the conscience of the Contributor,[5] by which the most pernicious sorts of exemptions and immunities may be establish'd; by which Virtue is taxed, and Vice privileged; and honour and Publick spirit are obliged to bear the burthens of Craft, selfishness and avarice; When they shall not be driven to be the instruments of the Violence of others, from a sense of their own weakness; and from a want of Authority to Assess equal and proportion'd Charges upon all, they are not compelled to lay a strong hand upon the entire possessions of a part; – When under the exigencies of the State (aggravated if not caused by the imbecillity of their own Government, and of all Government) they are not obliged to Resort to *confiscation* to supply the defect of *taxation*, and thereby to hold out a pernicious example to teach the different descriptions of the Community, to prey upon one another; – When they abstain religiously from all general and extrajudicial declarations concerning the property of the Subject;[6] – When they look with horrour upon all Arbitrary decisions in their Legislative Capacity, striking at prescriptive Right, long undisturbed Possession, opposing an uninterrupted stream of Regular judicial determinations, by which sort of decisions they are conscious no Man's possession could be safe, and Individual Property, to the very idea would be extinguish'd; – When I see your great Sovereign Bodies, Your now Supreme Power; in this condition of deliberative freedom, and guided by these or similar principles in acting and forbearing, I shall be happy to behold in Assemblies, whose name is venerable to my understanding, and dear to My heart, an Authority, a dignity, and a Moderation, which in all Countries, and Governments ought ever to accompany the collected Reason and Representative Majesty of the Commonwealth.

I shall rejoice no less in seeing a judicial Power establish'd in France, correspondent to such a Legislature as I have presumed to hint at, and worthy to second it in its endeavours to secure the freedom and property of the Subject. When your Courts of Justice[7] shall obtain an ascertain'd Condition before they are made to decide on the condition of other Men; – When they shall not be called upon to take cognisance of publick Offences, whilst they themselves are consider'd only to exist as a tolerated abuse; – When under doubts on the legality of their Rules of decision, their forms and modes of proceeding, and even of the validity of that system of Authority to which they owe their existence; When amidst circumstances of Suspense, fear, and humiliation, they shall not be put to judge on the Lives, Liberties, Properties or estimation of their fellow Citizens; – When they are not called upon to put any Man to his trial upon undefined Crimes of State, not ascertain'd by any previous Rule, Statute or course of precedent; – When Victims shall not be snatched from the fury of the People, to be brought before a Tribunal itself subject to the effects of the same fury, and where the acquittal of the Parties accused might only place the Judge in the situation of the Criminal; – When I see Tribunals placed in this state of Independence of every thing but Law, and with a clear Law for their direction, – as a true lover of equal Justice, (under the Shadow of which alone, true liberty can live) I shall Rejoice in seeing such a happy order establish'd in France as much as I do in my consciousness, that an order of the same kind, or one not very

Remote from it, has been long settled, and I hope on a firm foundation in England. I am not so narrow minded as to be unable to conceive, that the same Object may be attain'd in many ways, and perhaps in ways very different from those which we have follow'd in this Country. If this real *practical* Liberty, with a Government powerful to Protect, impotent to invade it, be establish'd, or is in a fair train of being establish'd in the Democracy, or rather collection of Democracies, which seem to be chosen for the future frame of Society in France, it is not my having long enjoyed a sober share of freedom under a qualified Monarchy that shall render Me incapable of admiring and praising your System of Republicks. I shall rejoice, even tho' England should hereafter be reckon'd only as one among the happy Nations; and should no longer retain her proud distinction, her Monopoly of fame for a practical Constitution, in which the grand secret had been found of reconciling a Government of real energy for all foreign and all domestick Purposes, with the most perfect security to the liberty and safety of Individuals. The Government whatever its name or form may be, that shall be found, substantially and practically, to unite these advantages, will most Merit the applause of all discerning Men.

But if (for in my present want of information I must only speak hypothetically) neither your great Assemblies, nor your Judicatures nor your Municipalities Act and forbear to Act in the particulars, upon the principles, and in the spirit that I have stated, I must delay my congratulations on your acquisition of Liberty. You may have made a Revolution, but not a Reformation. You may have subverted Monarchy, but not recover'd freedom.

You see, Sir, that I have nearly confined myself in my few observations, on what has been done, and is doing in France, to the topics of the liberty, property, and safety of the Subject. I have not said much on the influence of the present measures upon your Country as a State. It is not my business, as a Citizen of the World; and it is unnecessary to take up much time about it, as it is sufficiently visible.

You are now to live in a new order of things; under a plan of Government of which no Man can speak from experience. Your talents, Your publick spirit, and your fortune give you fair pretensions to a considerable share in it. Your settlement may be at hand; But that it is still at some distance is more likely. The French may be yet to go through more transmigrations. They may pass, as one of our Poets says, "thro' many varieties of untried being"[8] before their State obtains its final form. In that progress thro' Chaos and darkness, you will find it necessary (at all times it is more or less so) to fix Rules to keep your life and Conduct in some steady course. You have theories enough concerning the Rights of Men. It may not be amiss to add a small degree of attention to their Nature and disposition. It is with Man in the concrete, it is with common human life and human Actions you are to be concerned. I have taken so many liberties with You, that I am almost got the length of venturing to suggest something which may appear in the assuming tone of advice. You will however be so good as to receive my very few hints with your usual indulgence, tho' some of them I confess are not in the taste of this enlighten'd age, and indeed are no better than the late ripe fruit of mere experience. – Never wholly seperate in your Mind the merits of any Political Question from the Men who are concerned in it. You will be told, that if a measure is good, what have you [to] do with the Character and views of those who bring it forward. But designing Men never seperate their Plans from their Interests; and if You assist them in their Schemes, You will find the pretended good in the end thrown aside or perverted, and the interested object alone compassed, and that perhaps thro' Your means. The power of bad Men is no indifferent thing.

At this Moment, you may not perceive the full sense of this Rule, but you will recollect it, when the Cases are before you; You will then see and find its use. It will often keep your Virtue from becoming a tool of the Ambition and ill designs of others. Let me add, what, I think has some connexion with the Rule I mention: That you ought not to be so fond of any Political Object, as not to think the means of compassing it a serious consideration. No Man is less disposed than I am to put You under the Tuition of a petty Pedantick scruple in the management of arduous affairs: All I recommend is, that whenever the sacrifice of any subordinate point of Morality, or of honour, or even of common liberal sentiment and feeling is called for, one ought to be tolerably sure, that the object is worth it. Nothing is good, but in proportion, and with Reference. There are several who give an air of consequence to very petty designs and Actions, by the Crimes thro' which they make their way to their objects. Whatever is obtain'd smoothly and by easy means appears of no value

in their Eyes. But when violent Methods are in agitation, one
ought to be pretty clear, that there are no others to which we can
Resort, and that a predilection from Character to such Methods
is not the true cause of their being proposed. The State was
Reformed by Sylla and by Caesar;[9] But the Cornelian Law and
the Julian Law were not worth the proscription. The Pride of the
Roman Nobility deserved a check; But I cannot, for that Reason
admire the Conduct of Cinna, and Marius, and Saturninus.[10]

I admit that Evils may be so very great and urgent that other
Evils are to be submitted to for the mere hope of their Removal.
A War, for instance, may be necessary, and we know what are the
Rights of War, But before we use those Rights, We ought to be
clearly in the state which alone can justify them; and not, in the
very fold of Peace and security, by a bloody sophistry, to act
towards any persons, at once as Citizens and as Enemies; and
without the necessary formalities and evident distinctive lines of
War, to exercise upon our Countrymen the most dreadful of all
hostilities. Strong Party contentions, and a very violent opposition to our desires and opinions, are not War, nor can justify any
one of its operations.

One form of Government may be better than another; and
this difference may be worth a struggle. I think so. I do not mean
to treat any of those forms, which are often the contrivances of
deep human Wisdom (not the Rights of Men, as some people,
in my opinion, not very wisely, talk of them) with slight or disrespect; Nor do I mean to level them.

A positively Vicious and abusive Government ought to be
chang'd, and if necessary, by Violence, if it cannot be, (as sometimes it is the case) Reformed: But when the Question is concerning the more or the less *perfection* in the organisation of a
Government, the allowance to *means* is not of so much latitude.
There is, by the essential fundamental Constitution of things a
radical infirmity in all human contrivances, and the weakness is
often so attached to the very perfection of our political Mechanism, that some defect in it, something that stops short of its
principle, something that controls, that mitigates, that moderates
it, becomes a necessary corrective to the Evils that the Theoretick Perfection would produce. I am pretty sure it often is so, and
this truth may be exemplified abundantly.

It is true, that every defect is not of course, such a corrective
as I state; but supposing it is not, an imperfect good is still a good;

The defect may be tolerable, and may be Removed at some future time. In that Case, Prudence (in all things a Virtue, in Politicks the first of Virtues) will lead us rather to acquiesce in some qualified plan that does not come up to the full perfection of the abstract Idea, than to push for the more perfect, which cannot be attain'd without tearing to pieces the whole contexture of the Commonwealth, and creating an heart-ache in a thousand worthy bosoms. In that case combining the means and end, the less perfect is the more desirable. The *means* to any end, being first in order, are *immediate* in their good or their Evil, they are always, in a manner, *certainties*; The *End* is doubly problematical; first whether it is to be attain'd; then, whether supposing it obtaind, we obtain the true object we sought for.

But allow it in any degree probable, that theoretick and practical Perfection may differ, that an object pure and absolute may not be so good as one lower'd, mixed, and qualified, then, what we abate in our demand in favour of moderation and Justice and tenderness to Individuals, would be neither more nor less than a real improvement which a wise Legislator would make if he had no collateral Motive whatsoever, and only look'd in the formation of his Scheme, to its own independent Ends and purposes. Would it then be right to make way, thro' Temerity and Crime, to a form of things, which when obtained, evident Reason, perhaps imperious Necessity would compel us to alter, with the disgrace of inconsistency in our Conduct, and of want of foresight in our designs.

Believe me, Sir, in all changes in the State, Moderation is a Virtue not only amiable but powerful. It is a disposing, arranging, conciliating, cementing Virtue. In the formation of New Constitutions it is in its Province: Great Powers reside in those who can make great Changes. Their own Moderation is their only check; and if this Virtue is not paramount in their minds, their Acts will taste more of their Power than of their Wisdom or their benevolence. Whatever they do will be in extremes; it will be crude, harsh, precipitate. It will be submitted to with grudging and Reluctance; Revenge will be smother'd and hoarded; and the duration of schemes made in that temper will be as precarious as their Establishment was odious. This Virtue of Moderation (which times and Situations will clearly distinguish from the counterfeits of pusillanimity and indecision) is the Virtue only of superior Minds. It requires a deep Courage,

and full of ⟨Ref⟩lexion, to be temperate, when the voice of
Multitudes (the speci⟨ous⟩⟨m⟩imick of fame and Reputation)
passes Judgment against you; ⟨the⟩ impetuous desires of an
unthinking Publick will endure no course but what conducts to
splendid and perilous extremes. Then to dare to be fearful, when
all about you are full of presumption and confidence, and
when those who are bold at the hazard of others, would punish
your caution as disaffection, is to shew a Mind prepared for its
trial; it discovers in the midst of general levity, a self possessing
and collected Character which sooner or later bids fair to attract
every thing to it, as to a Center. If however the Tempest should
prove to be so very violent that it would make Publick Prudence
itself unseasonable, and therefore little less than madness for the
Individual and the Publick too, perhaps a Young Man could not
do better than to retreat for a while into Study – to leave the
field to those whose duty or inclination, or the Necessities of
their Condition, have put them in possession of it; – and wait
for the settlement of such a Commonwealth as an honest Man
may act in with satisfaction and Credit. This he can never do
when those who counsel the Publick or the Prince are under
terror, let the authority under which they are made to speak
other than the dictates of their conscience, be never so imposing
in its name and attributes.

This Moderation is no Enemy to Zeal and Enthusiasm. There
is room enough for them; for the restraint is no more than the
restraint of principle, and the restraint of Reason.

I have been led further than I intended. But every days account
shews more and more, in my opinion, the ill consequence of
keeping good principles and good general views within no
bounds. Pardon the liberty I have taken; though it seems somewhat singular, that I, whose opinions have so little weight in my
own Country, where I have some share in a Publick Trust, should
write as if it were possible they should affect one Man, with
regard to Affairs in which I have no concern. But for the present,
my time is my own, and to tire your patience is the only injury
I can do You.

TO CAPTAIN THOMAS MERCER[1]

26 FEBRUARY 1790

During a debate on the Army Estimates on 9 February 1790, before his *Reflections* had been published, Burke had for the first time publicly condemned both the French Revolution and its English admirers. Fox had refused to be drawn, but Sheridan had not, and the two men never made it up. The debate was reported in the newspapers, causing some surprise to a public who regarded Burke as a liberal and a reformer. Captain Thomas Mercer, a recent acquaintance of Burke, shared the general wonder and in his letter of 19 February defended the revolution and praised the new French government as the only kind "fit for rational beings to live under and submit to".

DEAR SIR,

The speedy answer I return to your letter, I hope, will convince you of the high value I set upon the regard you are so good to express for me, and the obliging trouble which you take to inform my judgment upon matters in which we are all very deeply concerned. I think perfectly well of your heart and your principles, and of the strength of your natural understanding, which, according to your opportunities, you have not been wanting in pains to improve. If you are mistaken, it is perhaps owing to the impression almost inevitably made by the various careless conversations which we are engaged in through life; conversations in which those who propagate their doctrines have not been called upon for much reflection concerning their end and tendency; and in which those, who imperceptibly imbibe the doctrines taught, are not required, by a particular duty, very closely to examine them, or to act from the impressions they receive. I am obliged to *act*, and am therefore bound to call my principles and sentiments to a strict account. As far as my share of a public trust goes, I am in *trust* religiously to maintain the rights and properties of all descriptions of people in the *possession* which legally they hold; and in the *rule* by which alone they can be secure in any possession. I do not find myself at liberty, either as a man, or as a trustee for men, to take a *vested* property from one man, and to give it to another, because *I* think that the portion of one is too great, and that of another too small. From my first juvenile rudiments of speculative study to the grey hairs of my present experience, I have never learned any thing else. I can never be taught any thing else by *reason*; and when *force* comes, I shall consider whether I am to submit to it, or how I am to resist it. This I am very sure of, that an early guard against the manifest tendency of a contrary doctrine is the only way by which those who love order can be prepared to resist such force.

The calling men by the names of "pampered and luxurious prelates",[2] &c. is in you no more than a mark of your dislike to intemperance and idle expence; but in others it is used for other purposes. It is often used to extinguish the sense of justice in our minds, and the natural feelings of humanity in our bosoms. Such language does not mitigate the cruel effects of reducing men of opulent condition, and their innumerable dependents, to the last distress. If I were to adopt the plan of a spoliatory reformation, I should probably employ such language; but it would aggravate instead of extenuating my guilt in overturning the sacred principles of property.

Sir, I say that church and state, and human society too, for which church and state are made, are subverted by such doctrines, joined to such practices, as leave no foundation for property in *long possessions*. My dear Captain Mercer, it is not my calling the use you make of your plate in your house, either of dwelling or of prayer, "pageantry and hypocrisy", that can justify me in taking from you your own property, and your own liberty to use your own property according to your own ideas of ornament. When you find me attempting to break into your house to take your plate, under any pretence whatsoever, but most of all under pretence of purity of religion and Christian charity, shoot me for a robber and an hypocrite, as in that case I shall certainly be. The "true Christian Religion" never taught me any such practices, nor did the religion of my nature, nor any religion, nor any law.

Let those who never abstained from a full meal, and as much wine as they could swallow, for a single day of their whole lives, satirise "luxurious and pampered prelates", if they will. Let them abuse such prelates, and such lords, and such squires, provided it be only to correct their vices. I care not much about the language of this moral satire, if they go no further than satire. But there are occasions when the language of Falstaff, reproaching the Londoners, whom he robbed in their way to Canterbury, with their gorbellies and their city luxury, is not so becoming.

It is not calling the landed estates, possessed by old *prescriptive rights*, the "accumulations of ignorance and superstition", that can support me in shaking that grand title, which supersedes all other title, and which all my studies of general jurisprudence have taught me to consider as one principal cause of the formation of states; I mean the ascertaining and securing *prescription*. But these are donations made in "ages of ignorance and superstition". Be it so. It proves that these donations were made long ago; and this is *prescription*; and this gives right and title. It is possible that many estates about you were originally obtained by arms, that is, by violence,[3] a thing almost as bad as superstition, and not much short of ignorance: but it is *old violence*; and that which might be wrong in the beginning, is consecrated by time, and becomes lawful. This may be superstition in me, and ignorance; but I had rather remain in ignorance and superstition than be enlightened and purified out of the first principles of law and natural justice. I never will suffer you, if I can help it, to be deprived of the well-earned fruits of your industry, because others may want your fortune more than you do, and may have laboured, and do now labour, in vain, to acquire even a subsistence. Nor on the contrary, if success had less smiled on your endeavours, and you had come home insolvent, would I take from any "pampered and luxurious lord" in your neighbourhood one acre of his land, or one spoon from his sideboard, to compensate your losses, though incurred (as they would have been incurred) in the course of a well-spent, virtuous, and industrious life. God is the distributor of his own blessings. I will not impiously attempt to usurp his throne, but will keep according to the subordinate place and trust in which he has stationed me, to secure the order of property which I find established in my country. No guiltless man has ever been, nor ever will, I trust, be able to say with truth, that he has been obliged to retrench a dish at his table for any reformations of mine.

You pay me the compliment to suppose me a foe to tyranny and oppression, and you are therefore surprised at the sentiments I have lately delivered in Parliament. I am that determined foe to tyranny, or I greatly deceive myself in my character: and I am sure I am an ideot in my conduct. It is because I am, and mean to continue so, that I abominate the example of France for this country. I know that tyranny seldom attacks the poor, never in the first instance. They are not its proper prey. It falls on the wealthy and the great, whom by rendering objects of envy, and otherwise obnoxious to the multitude, they may more easily destroy; and, when they are destroyed, that multitude which was led to that ill work by the arts of bad men, is itself undone for ever.

I hate tyranny, at least I think so; but I hate it most of all where most are concerned in it. The tyranny of a multitude is a multiplied tyranny. If, as society is constituted in these large countries of France and England, full of unequal property, I must make my choice (which God avert!) between the despotism of a single person, or of the many, my election is made. As much injustice and tyranny has been practised in a few months by a French democracy, as in all the arbitrary monarchies in Europe in the forty years of my observation. I speak of publick glaring acts of tyranny; I say nothing of the common effects of old abusive governments, because I do not know that as bad may not be found in the new. This democracy begins very ill; and I feel no security, that what has been rapacious and bloody in its commencement, will be mild and protecting in its final settlement. They cannot, indeed, in future, rob so much, because they have left little that can be taken. I go to the full length of my principle. I should think the government of the deposed King of France, or of the late King of Prussia, or the present Emperor, or the present Czarina,[4] none of them, perhaps, perfectly good people, to be far better than the government of twenty-four millions of men, *all as good as you*; and I do not know any body better; supposing that those twenty-four millions would be subject, as infallibly they would, to the same unrestrained, though virtuous, impulses; because it is plain, that their majority would think every thing justified by their warm good intentions – they would heat one another by their common zeal – counsel and advice would be lost on them – they would not listen to temperate individuals, and they would be less capable, infinitely, of moderation, than the most heady of those princes.

What have I to do with France, but as the common interest of humanity, and its example to this country, engages me? I know France, by observation and enquiry, pretty tolerably for a stranger: and I am not a man to fall in love with the faults or follies of the old or new government. You reason as if I were running a parallel between its former abusive government and the present tyranny. What had all this to do with the opinions I delivered in

Parliament, which ran a parallel between the liberty they might have had, and this frantic delusion. This is the way by which you blind and deceive yourself, and beat the air in your argument with me. Why do you instruct me on a state of the case which has no existence? You know how to reason very well. What most of the newspapers make me say, I know not, nor do I much care. I don't think, however, they have thus stated me. There is a very fair *abstract* of my speech printed in a little pamphlet,[5] which I would send you if it were worth putting you to the expence.

To discuss the affairs of France and its Revolution would require a volume, perhaps many volumes. Your general reflections[6] about revolutions may be right or wrong: they conclude nothing. I don't find myself disposed to controvert them, for I do not think they apply to the present affairs, nay, I am sure they do not. I conceive you have got very imperfect accounts of these transactions. I believe I am much more exactly informed of them.

I am sorry, indeed, to find that our opinions do differ essentially, fundamentally, and are at the utmost possible distance from each other, if I understand you or myself clearly on this subject. Your freedom is far from displeasing to me; I love it; for I always wish to know the full of what is in the mind of the friend I converse with. I give you mine as freely; and I hope I shall offend you as little as you do me. I shall have no objection to your shewing my letter to as many as you please. I have no secrets with regard to the public. I have never shrunk from obloquy; and I have never courted popular applause. If I have met with any share of it, "*non recepi sed rapui*".[7] No difference of opinion, however, shall hinder me from cultivating your friendship, while you permit me to do so. I have not written this to discuss these matters in a prolonged controversy (I wish we may never say more about them), but to comply with your commands, which ever shall have due weight with me. I am most respectfully, and

> most affectionately your's,
> EDMD BURKE
> LONDON, 26 FEBRUARY 1790

Mercer was neither crushed nor converted by Burke's letter. He composed a ten-page answer to it in August 1790, but did not forward it to Burke until 8 November, after seeing advertisements for the publication of the *Reflections*. Burke does not seem to have replied to it.

TO ARTHUR MURPHY[1]

8 DECEMBER 1793

Burke appears to be writing a second letter, after an interval of nearly six months, to thank Arthur Murphy for a present of his translation in four volumes of the *Works of Cornelius Tacitus*[2] which he had dedicated to Burke.

MY DEAR SIR,

I have not been as early as, to all appearance, I ought to have been, in my acknowledgments for your present. I received it in due time, but my delay was not from the want of a due sense of the value of what you have sent, or of the honour you have done me in sending it. But I have had some visitors to whom I was obliged to attend; and I have had some business to do, which, though it is not worth your while to be troubled with it, occupied almost every hour of the time I could spare from my guests: until yesterday, it was not in my power so much as to open your Tacitus.

I have read the first book through; besides dipping here and there into other parts. I am extremely delighted with it. You have done what hitherto, I think, has not been done in England: you have given us a translation of a Latin prose-writer which may be read with pleasure. It would be no compliment at all to prefer your translation to the last, which appeared with such a pomp of patronage. Gordon[3] was an author fashionable in his time; but he never wrote any thing worthy of much notice but that work, by which he has obtained a kind of eminence in bad writing: so that one cannot pass it by with mere neglect. It is clear to me that he did not understand the language from which he ventured to translate; and that he had formed a very whimsical idea of excellence with regard to ours. His work is wholly remote from the genius of the tongue, in its purity, or in any of its jargons. It is not English, nor Irish, nor even his native Scotch. It is not fish, nor flesh, nor good red herring. Yours is written with facility and spirit, and you do not often depart from the genuine native idiom of the language. Without attempting, therefore, to modernise terms of art, or to disguise ancient customs under new habits, you have contrived things in such a manner that your readers will find themselves at home. The other translators do not familiarise

you with ancient Rome: they carry you into a new world. By
their uncouth modes of expression, they prevent you from taking
an interest in any of its concerns. In spite of you, they turn your
mind from the subject, to attend with disgust to their unskilful
manner of treating it: from such authors we can learn nothing.
I have always thought the world much obliged to good translators, like you. Such are some of the French. They who understand the original are not those who are under the smallest
obligations to you; it is a great satisfaction to see the sense of one
good author in the language of another. He is thus *alias et idem*.[4]
Seeing your author in a new point of view, you become better
acquainted with him: his thoughts make a new and deeper
impression on the mind. I have always recommended it to young
men in their studies, when they had made themselves thorough
masters of a work in the original, then (but not till then) to read
it in a translation, if in any modern language a readable translation was to be found. What I say of your translation is really no
more than very cold justice to my sentiments of your great
undertaking. I never expected to see so good a translation. I do
not pretend that it is wholly free from faults; but at the same time
I think it more easy to discover them than to correct them. There
is a style, which daily gains ground amongst us, which I should
be sorry to see farther advanced by the authority of a writer of
your just reputation. The tendency of the mode to which I allude
is, to establish two very different idioms amongst us, and to introduce a marked distinction between the English that is written
and the English that is spoken. This practice, if grown a little
more general, would confirm this distemper (such I must think
it) in our language, and perhaps render it incurable.

From this feigned manner of *falsetto*, as I think the musicians
call something of the same sort in singing, no one modern historian, Robertson[5] only excepted, is perfectly free. It is assumed,
I know, to give dignity and variety to the style; but, whatever
success the attempt may sometimes have, it is always obtained at
the expence of purity, and of the graces that are natural and
appropriate to our language. It is true, that when the exigence
calls for auxiliaries of all sorts, and common language becomes
unequal to the demands of extraordinary thoughts, something
ought to be conceded to the necessities which make "Ambition
Virtue:"[6] but the allowances to necessities ought not to grow into
a practice. Those portents and prodigies ought not to grow too

common. If you have here and there (much more rarely, however, than others of great and not unmerited fame) fallen into an
error, which is not that of the dull or careless, you have an author
who is himself guilty, in his own tongue, of the same fault in a
very high degree. No author thinks more deeply or paints more
strongly, but he seldom or ever expresses himself naturally. It is
plain, that comparing him with Plautus and Terence, or the beautiful fragments of Publilius Syrus,[7] he did not write the language
of good conversation. Cicero[8] is much nearer to it. Tacitus and
the writers of his time have fallen into that vice, by aiming at a
poetical style. It is true, that eloquence in both modes of rhet-
orick is fundamentally the same; but the manner of handling is
totally different, even where words and phrases may be transferred from the one of these departments of writing to the other.

I have accepted the licence you have allowed me, and blotted
your book in such a manner that I must call for another for my
shelves. I wish you would come hither for a day or two. Twenty
coaches come almost to our very door. In an hour's conversation,
we can do more than in twenty sheets of writing. Do come, and
make us all happy. My affectionate compliments to our worthy
Doctor.[9] Pray believe me, with most sincere respect and regard,
my dear Sir,

Your most faithful
and obedient humble servant,
EDMUND BURKE
BEACONSFIELD, 8 DEC. 1793

TO FRENCH LAURENCE

BATH 28 JULY 1796

French Laurence (1757–1809) was one of Burke's most devoted
disciples. They had met during the Hastings impeachment trial
when Laurence, a civil lawyer, was appointed Chamber Counsel
to the Managers in the prosecution, earning the nickname of
Burke's 'Drum Major'. Burke, who had left Parliament after the
prosecution of Hastings was completed in June 1794, had asked
Laurence to help him prepare and publish a history of the
Impeachment.[1]

MY DEAR LAURENCE,

I thank you for employing the short moment you were able to snatch from being useful, in being kind and compassionate. Here I am in the last retreat of hunted infirmity. I am indeed aux abois:[2] But, as thro the whole of a various and long Life I have been more indebted than thankful to Providence, so I am now. Singularly so, in being dismissed, as hitherto I appear to be so gently from Life and sent to follow, those who in Course ought to have followd me, whom, I trust, I shall yet, in some inconceivable manner, see and know; and by whom I shall be seen and known. But enough of this. However as it is possible that my stay on this side of the Grave, may be yet shorter, than I compute it, let me now beg to call to your Recollection, the solemn charge and trust I gave you on my Departure from the publick Stage. I fancy I must make you the sole operator, in a work, in which, even if I were enabled to undertake it you must have been ever the assistance on which alone I could rely. Let not this cruel, daring, unexampled act of publick corruption, guilt, and meanness go down – to a posterity, perhaps as careless as the present race, without its due animadversion, which will be best found in its own acts and monuments. Let my endeavours to save the Nation from that Shame and guilt, be my monument; The only one I ever will have. Let every thing I have done, said, or written be forgotten but this. I have struggled with the great and the little on this point during the greater part of my active Life; and I wish after death, to have my Defiance of the Judgments of those, who consider the dominion of the glorious Empire given by an incomprehensible dispensation of the Divine providence into our hands as nothing more than an opportunity of gratifying for the lowest of their purposes, the lowest of their passions – and that for such poor rewards, and for the most part, indirect and silly Bribes, as indicate even more the folly than the corruption of these infamous and contemptible wretches. I blame myself exceedingly for not having employd the last year in this work and beg forgiveness of God for such a Neglect. I had strength enough for it, if I had not wasted some of it in compromising Grief with drowsiness and forgetfulness; and employing some of the moments in which *I* have been rouzed to mental exertion, in feeble endeavours to rescue this dull and thoughtless people from the punishments which their neglect and stupidity will bring upon them for their Systematick iniquity and oppression: But you are made to continue all that is good of me; and to augment it with the various rescources of a mind fertile in Virtues, and cultivated with every sort of Talent, and of knowlege. Above all make out the cruelty of this pretended acquittal, but in reality this barbarous and inhuman condemnation of whole Tribes and nations, and of all the abuses they contain. If ever Europe recovers its civilisation that work will be useful. Remember! Remember! Remember!

It is not that I want you to sacrifice yourself blindly and unfruitfully, at this Instant. But there will be a Season for the appearance of such a Record; and it ought to be in Store for that Season. Get every thing that Troward[3] has.

Your kindness will make you wish to hear more particulars of me. To compare my State with that of the three first days after my arrival, I feel on the whole less uneasiness – But my flesh is wasted in a manner which in so short a time no one could imagine. My limbs look about to find the Rags that cover them. My strength is declined in the full proportion; and at my time of life new flesh is never supplied; and lost strength is never recoverd. If God has any thing to do for me here – here he will keep me. If not, I am tolerably resigned to his Divine pleasure. I have not been yet more than a day in condition to drink the Waters – but they seem rather to compose than to disorder my Stomach. My illness has not sufferd Mrs Burke to profit as she ought of this situation. But she will bathe to Night. Give Woodford[4] a thousand kind remembrances. Please God, I shall write to him tomorrow. Adieu.

Your ever true friend
EDM BURKE

Mrs Burke never forgets you nor what remains of poor William.

TO UNKNOWN

FEBRUARY 1797

This letter was dictated, and extensively corrected, by an ailing Burke from his couch in Bath, where he had gone to take the waters a few months before his death. It sets out his views on the situation in Ireland and was probably intended for publication.

In the reduced state of body, and in the dejected state of mind in which I find myself at this very advanced period of my Life, it is a great consolation to me to know, that a cause, I ever have had so very near my heart, is taken up by a man of your activity and Talents.

It is very true that your late friend, my ever dear and honored Son,[1] was in the highest degree solicitous about the final event of a business which he also had pursued for a long time with infinite Zeal, and no small degree of success. It was not above half an hour before he left me for ever, that He spoke with considerable earnestness on this very subject. If I had needed any incentives to do my best for freeing the body of my Country from the grievances under which they labour, this alone would certainly call forth ⟨all⟩ my endeavours.

The Person[2] who succeeded to the Government ⟨of⟩ Ireland about the time of that afflicting event had been all along of my Sentiments and yours, upon this Subject; and far from needing to be stimulated by me, that incomparable person and those in whom he strictly confided, even went before me in their resolution to pursue the great end of Government, the satisfaction and concord of the people with whose welfare they were charged. I cannot bear to think on the causes by which this great plan of policy so manifestly beneficial to both kingdoms has been defeated.

Your mistake with regard to me lies in supposing that I did not, when his removal was in agitation, strongly and personally represent to several of his Majesty's Ministers, to whom I could have the most ready access, the true state of Ireland and the mischiefs which sooner or later must arise from subjecting the Mass of the people to the capricious and interested domination of an exceeding small faction and its dependencies.

That representation was made the last time, or very nearly the last time, that I have ever had the honour of seeing these ministers. I am so far from having any credit with them on this, or any other public matter, that I have reason to be certain if it were known, that any person in office in Ireland from the highest to the lowest, were influenced by my Opinions and disposed to act upon them, such a one would be instantly turned out of his employment. You have formed, to my person a flattering, yet

in truth a very erroneous Opinion of my power with those
who direct the public measures. I never have been directly or
indirectly consulted about any thing that is done. The Judgment
of the eminent and able persons who conduct public Affairs is
undoubtedly superior to mine; but self partiality induces almost
every man to defer something to his own. Nothing is more
notorious than that I have the misfortune of thinking, that no
one capital measure relative to political arrangements, and that
no one military plan for the defence of either Kingdom in this
arduous War has been taken upon any other principle, than such
as must conduct us to inevitable ruin.

In the state of my mind, so discordant with the tone of
ministers, and still more discordant with the tone of Opposition,
you may judge what degree of weight I am likely to have with
either of the parties who divide this Kingdom; even tho' I were
endowed with strength of body, or were possessed of any active
situation in the Government which might give success to my
endeavours. But the fact is, since the day of my unspeakable
calamity, except in the attentions of a very few old and compassionate friends, I am totally out of all social intercourse. My
health has gone down very rapidly; and I have been brought
hither with very faint hopes of Life, and enfeebled to such a
degree, as those, who had known me some time ago, could
scarcely think credible. Since I came hither my Sufferings have
been greatly aggravated, and my little strength still further
reduced; so, that though I am told the Symptoms of my disorder
begin to carry a more favourable aspect, I pass the far larger part
of the twenty four hours, indeed almost the whole, either in my
Bed, or lying upon the Couch, from which I dictate this. Had
you been apprised of this circumstance you could not have
expected any thing, as you seem to do, from my active exertions.
I could do nothing if I was still stronger, not even "Si 〈. . .〉 meus
adforet Hector".[3]

There is no hope for the body of the people of Ireland, as long
as those who are in power with you shall make it the great Object
of their policy to propagate an Opinion on this side of the Water,
that the mass of their Countrymen are not to be trusted by their
Government; and that the only hold which England has upon
Ireland, consists in preserving a certain very small Number of
Gentlemen in full possession of a monopoly of that Kingdom.

This System has disgusted many others besides Catholicks and dissenters.

As to those, who, on your side of the Channel are in the Opposition to *oppose* Government, they are composed of Persons several of whom I love and revere. They have been irritated by a treatment too much for the ordinary patience of mankind to bear, into the adoption of Schemes which, however *argumentatively* specious, would go *practically* to the inevitable ruin of the Kingdom. The Opposition always connects the emancipation of the Catholics with these Schemes of reformation: Indeed it makes the former only a member of the latter project. The Gentlemen who compose that opposition are in my opinion playing the game of their adversaries with all their might; and there is no third party in Ireland, (nor in England neither) to seperate things that are in themselves so distinct, I mean the admitting people to the benefits of the constitution, and a change in the form of the Constitution itself.

As every one knows, that a great part of the Constitution of the Irish House of Commons was founded about the year 1614, expressly for bringing that House into a state of dependance; and that the new Representative was at that time seated and installed by force and violence, nothing can be more impolitic than for those who wish the House to stand on its present basis, (as for one I most sincerely do) to make it appear to have kept too much the principle of its first institution, and to continue to be as little a virtual, as it is an actual representative of the Commons. It is the *degeneracy* of such an institution *so vicious in its principle*, that is to be wished for. If Men have the real Benefit of a *Sympathetic* Representation, none but those who are heated and intoxicated with Theory will look for any other. This sort of Representation, my dear Sir, must wholly depend not on the force with which it is upheld, but upon the *prudence* of those who have influence upon it. Indeed without some such prudence in the use of Authority, I do not know, at least in the present time, how any power can long continue.

If it be true that both parties are carrying things to extremities in different ways, the object which you and I have in common, that is to say the Union and concord of our Country *on the basis of the actual representative* without risquing those evils which any change in the form of our Legislature must inevitably bring on can never be obtaind. On the part of the Catholics (that is to say, of the body of the people of the Kingdom) it is a terrible alternative, either to submit to the Yoke of declared and insulting Enemies, or to seek a remedy in plunging themselves into the horrours and Crimes of that Jacobinism, which unfortunately is not disagreeable to the principles and inclinations of, I am afraid, the Majority of what we call the Protestants of Ireland. The protestant part of that Kingdom is represented by the Government itself to be, by whole Counties, in nothing less than open Rebellion. I am sure that it is everywhere teeming with dangerous conspiracy.

I beleive it will be found, that tho' the principles of the Catholics and the incessant endeavours of their Clergy have kept them from being generally infected with the Systems of this time, yet wherever their situation brings them nearer into contact with the Jacobin Protestants, they are more or less infected with their doctrines.

It is a matter for mellancholly reflexion; but I am fully convinced, that many persons in Ireland would be glad, that the Catholics should become more and more infected with the Jacobin madness in order to furnish new arguments for fortifying them in their monopoly. On any other ground, it is impossible to account for the late language of your Men in power. If Statesmen (let me suppose for Argument) upon the most solid political principles conceive themselves obliged to resist the wishes of the far more numerous, and as things stand, not the worse part of the Community, one would think, they would naturally put their refusal as much as possible upon temporary grounds, and that they would act towards them in the most conciliatory manner, and would talk to them in the most gentle and soothing language. For refusal, in itself, is not a very gracious thing; and, unfortunately, men are very quickly irritated out of their principles. Nothing is more discouraging to the loyalty of any description of men than to represent to them, that their humiliation and subjection make a principal part in the fundamental and invariable policy which regards the conjunction of these two Kingdoms. This is not the way to give them a warm interest in that conjunction.

My poor opinion is, that the closest connexion between Great Britain and Ireland, is essential to the well being, I had almost said, to the very being, of the two Kingdoms. For that purpose

I humbly conceive that the whole of the Superiour, and, what I should call, *Imperial* politics, ought to have its residence here; and that Ireland, locally, civilly, and commercially independent, ought politically to look up to Great Britain in all matters of peace and of War, in all those points to be guided by her, and, in a word with her to live and to die. At Bottom Ireland has no other choice, I mean no other rational choice.

I think indeed that Great Britain would be ruined by the seperation of Ireland; but, as there are degrees even in ruin, it would fall the most heavily on Ireland. By such a seperation Ireland would be the most compleatly undone Country in the world; the most wretched, the most distracted and, in the end, the most desolate part of the habitable Globe. Little do many people in Ireland consider, how much of its prosperity has been owing to, and still depends upon, its intimate connexion with this Kingdom but more sensible of this great Truth than perhaps any other man, I have never conceivd, or can conceive, that the connexion is strengthened by making the major part of the Inhabitants of your Country beleive, that their ease, and their satisfaction, and their equalisation with the rest of their fellow subjects of Ireland, are things adverse to the principles of that connexion, or that their Subjection to a small monopolising Junto, composed of one of the smallest of their own internal factions, is the very condition upon which the harmony of the two Kingdoms essentially depends. I was sorry to hear that this principle or something not unlike it was publickly and fully avowed by persons of great rank and authority in the House of Lords in Ireland.

As to a participation on the part of the Catholics in the privileges and capacities which are with-held without meaning wholly to depreciate their importance, if I had the honour of being an Irish Catholic, I should be content to expect satisfaction upon that Subject with patience until the minds of my adversaries, (few but powerful,) were come to a proper temper: because, if, the Catholics, did enjoy without fraud, chicane, or partiality, some fair portion of those advantages which the Law, even as now the Law is, leaves open to them, and if the Rod were not shaken over them at every turn, their present condition would be tolerable as compared with their former condition, it would be happy, but the most favourable Laws can do very little towards the happiness of a people, when the disposition of the ruling power is adverse to them. Men do not live upon blotted paper. The favourable or the hostile mind of the ruling power is of far more importance to mankind; for Good or evil, than the black Letter of any Statute. Late acts of Parliament,[4] whilst they fixed at least a temporary bar to the hopes and progress of the larger description of the Nation, opened to them certain subordinate objects of equality, but it is impossible that the people should imagine, that any fair measure of advantage is intended to them, when they hear the Laws, by which they were admitted to this limited qualification, publickly reprobated, as excessive and inconsiderate. They must think that there is a hankering after the old penal and persecuting code – Their alarm must be great, when that declaration is made by a person in very high and important Office,[5] in the House of Commons, and as the very first specimen and auspice of a new Government.

All this is very unfortunate. I have the honour of an old acquaintance, and entertain, in common with you, a very high esteem for the few English persons who are concerned in the Government of Ireland; but I am not ignorant of the relation, these transitory ministers bear to the more settled Irish part of your Administration. It is a delicate topic, upon which I wish to say but little; tho' my reflexions upon it, are many, and serious. There is a great cry against English influence. I am quite sure that [it] is Irish influence that dreads the English Cabinet.

I cannot, however, avoid adverting to the course which justice has taken of late Years in cases of tumult, and disorder, where the body of the people are of the Catholic persuasion, or where the same or greater disorders have broken out in other descriptions. You must readily recollect many things in the nature of the prosecution, the character of evidence, the temper of the tryal; the mode and circumstance of the Executions; and many other points more capable of giving alarm than any thing of privileges and immunities with-held. Partiality, tho' not very laudable is tolerated in the grant of favours; but where it extends to the Courts of Justice no man can think himself safe.

Great disorders have long prevailed in Ireland. It is not long since, that the Catholics were the suffering party from those disorders. I am sure they were not protected as the Case required. Not one person has been punished on that account; or, that I can find, so much as questioned. Their sufferings became a matter of discussion in Parliament. It produced the most infuriated declaration against them that I have ever read. An enquiry was moved into the facts. The declamation was at least tolerated, if not approved. The enquiry was absolutely rejected.[6] Very soon after we find, that many if not most of that description so covered were represented by the Government which had covered those excesses as in Open rebellion, or conspirant against the State. In that case, what is left for those who are abandoned by Government, but to join with the persons who are capable of injuring them or protecting them, as they oppose or concur in their designs. This will produce a very fatal kind of union amongst the people; but it is an union which an unequal administration of justice tends necessarily to produce.

If any thing could astonish one at this time, it is the War that the rulers in Ireland think it proper to carry on against the person, whom they call the Pope, and against all his adherents, whenever they think they have the power of manifesting their hostility. Without in the least derrogating from the talents of your Theological politicians, or from the military abilities of your Commanders, (who act on the same principles,) in Ireland, and without derogating from the Zeal of either, it appears to me that the Protestant Directory of Paris, as Statesmen, and the Protestant Hero Buonaparté, as a General, have done more to destroy the said Pope, and all his adherents in all their capacities, than the Junto in Ireland have been ever able to effect. You must submit your fasces to theirs; and at best be contented to follow, with Songs of gratulation, or invectives, according to your humour, the triumphal Car of those great Conquerors. Had that true Protestant *Hoche*,[7] with an Army not infected with the slightest tincture of Popery, made good his landing in Ireland, he would have saved you from a great deal of the trouble which is taken to keep under a description of your fellow Citizens obnoxious to you from their religion. It would not have a months existence supposing his Success. This is the Alliance, which, under the appearance of hostility, we act as if we wished to promote. All is well, provided we are safe from Popery.

It was not necessary for you, My dear Sir, to explain yourself to *me*, (in justification of your good wishes to your fellow Citizens) concerning your total alienation from the principles of the Catholics. I am more concerned in what we agree, than in what we differ. You know the impossibility of our forming any judgment upon the Opinions, religious, moral, or political, of those who

in the largest sense are called Protestants; at least as these Opinions and tenets form a qualification for holding any civil, Judicial,
Military, or even ecclesiastical situation. I have no doubt of the
Orthodox Opinion of many both of the Clergy, and Laity,
professing the established religion in Ireland, and of many even
amongst the Dissenters, relative to the great points of the Christian faith: But that Orthodoxy concerns them only as *individuals*.
As a Qualification for employment, we all know that in Ireland,
it is not necessary that they should profess any religion at all. So
that the War that we make is upon certain Theological tenets,
about which, scholastic disputes are carried *aequó Marte*[8] by con-
trovertists on their side as able and as learned and, perhaps, as well
intentioned as those are who fight the Battle on the other part.
To them I would leave those controversies – I would turn my
mind to what is more within its competence and has been more
my study, (tho' for a man of the world I have thought of those
things) I mean the moral, civil, and political good of the Countries we belong to, and in which God has appointed your station
and mine. Let every man be as pious as he pleases; and in the way
that He pleases; but it is agreeable neither to piety nor to policy
to give exclusively all manner of civil privileges and advantages
to a *negative* Religion; – (such is the Protestant without a certain
Creed) that is to say, to no religion at all; and at the same time,
to deny those priveleges to men whom we who beleive according to the Establishment here, know to agree to an Iota in every
one *positive* doctrine, which all of those who profess the religion
authoritatively taught in England, hold ourselves according to
our faculties bound to beleive. The Catholics of Ireland (as I have
said) have the whole of our *positive* religion; our difference is only
a Negation of certain Tenets of theirs. If we strip ourselves of *that*
part of Catholicity we injure Christianity. If we drive them from
that holding without engaging them in some other positive religion, (which you know by our qualifying Laws we do not) what
do we better than to hold out to them terrours on the one side
and bounties on the other, in favour of that which, for any thing
we know to the contrary, may be pure Atheism.

You are well aware that when a Man renounces the Roman
Religion, there is no civil inconvenience or incapacity whatsoever which shall hinder him from joining any new or old sect of
Dissenters, or of forming a sect of his own invention upon the
most Antichristian principles. Let Mr Thomas Paine[9] obtain a

pardon (as on change of Ministry not improbable he may), there is nothing to hinder him from starting up a church of his own in the very midst of you; He is a natural born British Subject. His French Citizenship does not disqualify him, at least upon a peace. This protestant Apostle is as much above all suspicion of Popery as the greatest and most Zealous of your Sanhedrim[10] in Ireland can possibly be. On purchasing a qualification (which his friends of the Directory are not so poor as to be unable to effect) he may sit in Parliament, and there is no doubt that there is not one of your tests against Popery, that He will not take as fairly, and as much *ex animo* as the best of your zealot Statesmen. I push this point no further, and only adduce this example (a pretty strong one, and fully in point) to shew what I take to be the madness and folly, of driving men under the existing circumstances from any *positive* religion whatever into the irreligion of the times, and its sure concomitant principles of Anarchy.

When Religion is brought into a question of civil and political arrangement, it must be considered more politically than Theologically; at least by us who are nothing more than meer Laymen. In that light the case of the Catholics of Ireland is peculiarly hard whether they be layity or Clergy. If any of them take part, like the Gentleman you mention, with some of the most accredited Protestants of the Country and with the far the most suspicious body of the Protestants in projects (which cannot be more abhorrent to your nature and disposition than they are to mine) in that Case, however few these Catholic factions who are united with factious Protestants may be, (and very few they are now whatever shortly they may become) on their account the whole Body is considered as of suspected fidelity to the Crown; and as wholly undeserving of its favour. But if on the contrary in those districts of the Kingdom where their numbers are the greatest, where they make in a manner the whole body of the people (as out of Cities in 3/4ths of the Kingdom they do) these Catholicks shew every mark of loyalty and zeal in support of the Government which at best looks on them with an evil eye, then their very loyalty is turned against their claims. They [are] represented as a contented and happy people, and that it is unnecessary to do any thing more in their favour. Thus the factious disposition of a few among the Catholicks and the loyalty of the whole mass are equally assigned as reasons for not putting them on a par with those Protestants, who are asserted by the Government itself which frowns upon Papists, to be in a state of nothing short of actual rebellion, and in a strong disposition to make common cause with the worst foreign Enemy that these Countries have ever had to deal with. What in the End can come of all this?

As to the Irish Catholic Clergy, their condition is likewise most critical, if they endeavour by their influence to keep a dissatisfied layity in quiet, They are in danger of losing the little credit they possess, by being considered as the instruments of a Government adverse to the civil interest of their flock. If they Let things take their course, they will be represented as colluding with sedition or at least tacitly encouraging it. – If they remonstrate against persecution they propagate rebellion. Whilst Government publickly avows hostility to that people as a part of a regular System – there is no road they can take which does not lead to their ruin.

If nothing can be done on your side of the Water, I promise you that nothing will be done here. Whether in reality or only on appearances I cannot positively determine, but you will be left to yourselves by the ruling power here. It is thus ostensibly and above Board; and in part I believe the disposition is real. As to the people at large in this Country, I am sure they have no disposition to intermeddle in your affairs. They mean you no ill whatever; and they are too ignorant of the state of your affairs to be able to do you any good. Whatever Opinion they have on your Subject is very faint and indistinct; and if there is any thing like a formed Notion even that amounts to no more than a sort of humming, that remains on their ears of the burthen of the old Song about Popery. Poor souls they are to be pitied; who think of nothing but dangers long past by; and but little of the perils that actually surround them.

I have been long, but it is almost a necessary consequence of dictating and that by snatches as a relief from pain gives me the means of expressing my sentiments. They can have little weight as coming from me and I have not power enough of mind or body to bring them out with their natural force, but I do not wish to have it concealed, that I am of the same opinion to my last breath, which I entertained when my faculties were at the best; and I have not held back from men in power in this Kingdom, to whom I have very good wishes any part of my sentiments on this melancholy subject, so long as I had means of access to persons of their consideration. I have the honor to be &c.

NOTES

A VINDICATION OF NATURAL SOCIETY (1)

[Full title: *A Vindication of Natural Society: or, A View of the Miseries and Evils arising to Mankind from every Species of Artificial Society. In a Letter to Lord ★★★★ By a late Noble Writer*]

1 The First Edition: published anonymously by Robert Dodsley on 18 May 1756.

2 Lord Bolingbroke (Henry St John, 1st Viscount Bolingbroke, 1678–1751): Tory politician and political philosopher. As Secretary of State under Queen Anne he had negotiated the terms of the Treaty of Utrecht at the end of the War of Spanish Succession in 1713. After the Hanoverian succession in 1714, Bolingbroke fled to Paris where he supported the rival claim to the throne of James Edward Stuart, 'the Old Pretender'. He was convicted of high treason, but received a royal pardon in 1723 when he returned to England and took up the cudgels against the Walpole administration for its excessive use of patronage in the pages of his influential political journal, *The Craftsman*. His friends and admirers included Swift, Pope and Voltaire. Bolingbroke's collected philosophical works had been published in 1754, gaining him posthumous notoriety as a deist, sceptical of scriptural revelation and opposed to organized religion. Burke disagreed strongly with his views, as did Samuel Johnson and William Warburton, among others. Burke's parody of Bolingbroke's philosophy and writing style in *A Vindication of Natural Society* was perhaps a little too perfect, as many critics believed its arguments were sincere – or even mistook it for a lost work by Bolingbroke. He wrote the preface to the second edition (1757) to explain his intentions.

3 Isocrates (436–338 BC): Athenian orator.

4 Lord Coke's Reports: 'In many cases an embroidered falsehood appears more likely, and often defeats the plain truth by reasoning.' Sir Edward Coke (1552–1634), English jurist. As Attorney General he had represented the Crown at the trials of the Earls of Essex and Southampton (1601), Sir Walter Raleigh (1603) and the Gunpowder Plot conspirators (1605). In 1606 he was made Chief Justice of the Common Pleas but quarrelled with James I on questions of royal prerogative, and was removed to the less lucrative though more senior office of Chief Justice of the King's Bench in 1613, and from the bench altogether in 1616, by which time he had become a celebrated champion of the Common Law. In 1621 he returned to the House of Commons where his constitutional expertise enabled him to take a lead in defending and upholding its authority against the Crown. He was instrumental in drawing up the Petition of Right in 1628. His *Reports* (1600–15) consisted principally of summaries and comments on cases he had attended or presided over. They became the first textbook of early modern law, with which Burke would have been familiar from his own studies at the Middle Temple. Coke's other major work, the *Institutes of the Laws of England*, was published between 1628 and 1644.

5 Lord ★★★★: the lord to whom the work is addressed remains anonymous.

6 Guicciardini (Francesco Guicciardini, 1483–1540): Florentine statesman, diplomat, lawyer and historian, a close friend of Machiavelli (*see* n.7, below). He was the author of the classic *Storia d'Italia*, an important contemporary history of Italy, and is regarded as the pioneer of modern historical method.

7 Machiavel (Niccolò Machiavelli, 1469–1527): Florentine statesman, diplomat, political philosopher and historian. His notorious treatise on statecraft, *Il principe* (*The Prince*) was written in 1513 and published in 1532.

8 old Hobbes (Thomas Hobbes, 1588–1679): English philosopher. The work referred to is his *Leviathan* (1651).

9 the distressed Portuguese: at the behest of George II, Parliament voted a sum of £100,000 to assist the Portuguese following a major earthquake in Lisbon in November 1755.

10 Sesostris: a composite heroic Middle Kingdom ruler described by Greek and Roman historians, to whom the foreign exploits of the Twelfth-Dynasty Egyptian pharaohs Senusret I (*c.* 1956–1911 BC) and Senusret III (*c.* 1870–1831 BC) substantially contributed.

11 Justin (Marcus Julianus Justinus): Roman historian of the second or third century AD. His *History* is an abridgement of a universal history by Pompeius Trogus, now lost.

12 Semiramis: according to the legend related by Justin and the ancient Greek historian Diodorus Siculus (*fl. c.* 60–30 BC) – one of Burke's sources – Semiramis was an Assyrian queen, who, after the death of her husband King Ninus, founded Babylon and conquered much of western Asia. Her prototype may have been the historical queen Shammu-ramat, wife of the Assyrian ruler Shamshi-Adad V, who ruled the Assyrian Empire as sole regent for their son in the early ninth century BC.

13 Xerxes (*c.* 519–465 BC): King of Persia from 486 BC. He launched the second Persian war against Greece in 480 BC, for which his elaborate military and naval preparations took three years. His first attempt to lead his army across the Hellespont on two bridges of boats was thwarted by a storm (he was reputed to have had the sea whipped as a punishment); the bridges were rebuilt and his army – having been held back for two days by the Spartan army of King Leonidas at Thermopylae – reached and sacked Athens. However, the Persian navy was shortly afterwards crushed at the battle of Salamis and Xerxes returned to Persia. The numbers given by Herodotus and other ancient Greek historians for the size of the Persian force are fantastic; modern estimates are in the region of 200,000 men for the army and a navy of some 600 ships. Xerxes was the son and successor of Darius, who invaded Greece in 490 BC, launching the first Persian war.

14 Agesilaus … Alexander: Agesilaus (*c.* 444–361 BC) was a Spartan king who invaded Persia in 396 BC. Alexander the Great of Macedon (356–323 BC) invaded Persia in 334 BC and by 325 BC had conquered most of western Asia and India. His death precipitated a series of wars and power struggles which continued until Rome came to dominate the region in the second century BC.

15 Athenians and Lacedæmonians: the Peloponnesian war between Athens and the Lacedæmonians (or Spartans) took place between 431 and 404 BC.

16 Aceldama (Aramaic 'Field of Blood'): the name of a field near Jerusalem purchased by Judas with the money he had received for betraying Jesus, and where he met a violent death (Acts 1:19). (The account in Matthew 27:7 varies slightly: the guilty Judas hangs himself, having returned the money to the Temple; regarded as blood money which could serve no sacred purpose, it was used to purchase the field as a cemetery for foreigners.)

17 Sicily: the Greeks colonized Sicily during the eighth century BC. From the sixth century BC they were involved in a lengthy and bloody series of wars with the Carthaginians who sought to add the island to their own empire. It was eventually annexed by Rome during the first Punic war (264–241 BC).

18 Grecia-Magna (Greater Greece): the collective name for the Greek cities of southern Italy colonized during the eighth and seventh centuries BC.

19 Punic wars: three wars (264–261 BC, 218–201 BC, 149–146 BC) in which Rome successfully contended with Carthage for dominance of the western Mediterranean. They culminated in the sacking of Carthage itself in 146 BC.

20 Mithridates (reigned 120–63 BC): King of Pontus on the Black Sea, who fought three wars against the Roman Republic. During the first of these he overran the Roman province of Asia (eastern Anatolia), and on a particular day in 88 BC he ordered every Roman and Italian living there to be put to death. In 86 BC he captured Athens but the city was retaken by Sulla after a five-month siege, and sacked. In the same year his army was twice defeated by the Romans under Sulla, at Chaeronia and at Orchomenus. After holding his own in the second war he suffered defeat at the beginning of the third by Lucullus at Cyzicum in 73 BC. He sought shelter with his son-in-law, Tigranes, King of Armenia, whose forces were routed by Lucullus at Tigranocerta and the city destroyed in 69 BC. Tigranes finally made peace with the Romans under Pompey in 66 BC. Mithridates was driven back to his own territory, where he was unable to raise another army and faced a revolt led by his son Pharnaces. Choosing death over captivity, he found himself immune to poison as a result of taking so many antidotes, so ordered a slave to stab him.

21 Sylla (Lucius Cornelius Sulla, c. 138–78 BC): Roman consul and general, leader of the aristocratic party (the *optimates*) against the *popularis* party of Marius in two civil wars. Denied the promised command of the army against Mithridates, he had already marched against Rome once in 88 BC – an unprecedented event – and taken it by force. After defeating Mithridates he once again seized control of Rome in 82 BC, with the assistance of Pompey and Crassus. He was elected dictator, whereupon he set about exterminating his enemies. Infamously he adopted the system of proscription, publishing the names of victims who could be killed without trial and their property confiscated, and rewarding those who carried out such murders. Having reformed the Roman constitution to his satisfaction he retired to private life.

22 Julius Caesar (100–44 BC): as governor of Gaul, he waged war on the Gallic tribes (58–51 BC), resulting in the subjugation of the province. Pliny the Elder (*Natural History*) gives 1,192,000 as the figure of those killed in Caesar's Gallic wars; Plutarch (*Life of Julius Caesar*) around one million, with a further million taken prisoner.

23 no more a nation: a Jewish revolt in AD 66–73 was crushed by the Romans.
The temple in Jerusalem was destroyed, and many of the people were scattered or sold into slavery. This was the first of three Jewish–Roman wars.
After the third, a revolt led by Simon Bar Kokhba in AD 132–136 which
temporarily set up an independent Jewish state, the Emperor Hadrian set
about the systematic destruction of Judaism, even renaming Judaea Syria
Palaestina.

24 *Vastum ubique ... obvius*: ' ... a vast silence all around, desolate hills, the distant smoke of burning houses, and not a living soul descried by the scouts,
displayed more amply the face of victory' (Tacitus, *Agricola*).

25 poured out of the south: the Muslim invasions from Africa in the eighth
century.

26 ye Orpheuses ... Numas!: Orpheus was a legendary musician and poet,
regarded as the founder of Orphism, a mystic religion of ancient Greece;
Moses (*fl.* 14th–13th centuries BC), law-giver and leader of the Hebrews;
Minos, legendary King of Crete; Solon (*fl. c.* 600 BC), poet and statesman
who reformed the Athenian constitution; Theseus, legendary Greek hero
who unified the state of Attica; Lycurgus, legendary founder of Sparta;
Numa Pompilius (*c.* 715–673 BC), Roman king who introduced religious
and cultural reforms.

A PHILOSOPHICAL INQUIRY INTO THE ORIGIN OF OUR IDEAS OF THE SUBLIME AND BEAUTIFUL (2)

1 *Circa vilem ... lex*: ' ... we will waste our time on a common and obvious
ground ... from which either shame or the laws which govern the work
will prevent us from putting a foot forward' (Horace, *Ars Poetica*, slightly
misquoted).

2 bolus of squills: diuretic pills made from extract of sea onion.

3 Locke (John Locke, 1632–1704): English philosopher; Burke refers here
to Locke's *Essay on Human Understanding*.

4 a Turkish emperor: Mehmed II, conqueror of Constantinople. In 1479 at
the conclusion of a long war with Venice, he requested that a 'good painter'
might be sent to the Ottoman court. The Venetians sent their best: Gentile
Bellini. In order to illustrate his point about the defect mentioned by
Burke, Mehmed ordered a slave to be beheaded on the spot.

5 Don Bellianis: hero of a sixteenth-century Spanish romance by Geronimo
Fernandez, *Historia del valeroso é invincible Principe don Belianis de Grecia*.
Translated by 'L. A.', it was collected by Francis Kirkman in 1673 as *The
Famous and Delectable History of Don Bellienis of Greece*.

6 a shipwreck on the coast of Bohemia: in Shakespeare, *The Winter's
Tale*.

7 Horace: Roman poet (65–8 BC). Burke refers here to *Ars Poetica*.

8 *Molle meum ... semper amem*: 'My heart is tender and easily pierced by the
light shaft, and there is always a reason why I should always be in love'
(Ovid, *Heroides*, slightly misquoted).

9 *elegans formarum spectator*: 'a fastidious observer of beauty' (Terence, *Eunachus*).

10 & 11 As when a wretch ... ; Still in short intervals ... : translations from Homer by Alexander Pope (1688–1774), the former slightly misquoted.

12 regicide in France: Robert Francis Damiens (1714–57) tried to assassinate Louis XV on 5 January 1757. He was subjected to barbaric torture before being executed on 28 March.

13 its unhappy prince: Alexander the Great of Macedon died of fever at Babylon in 323 BC at the age of thirty-two; his empire was immediately plunged into civil war.

14 Scipio and Cato: Publius Cornelius Scipio Africanus (236–183 BC) was a brilliant and successful general in the second Punic war who drove the Carthaginians out of Spain and crossed over to Africa to defeat Hannibal at Zama in 202 BC. Marcus Porcius Cato (or Cato the Younger, 95–46 BC), statesman and Stoic, was known for his uncompromising integrity. He was a champion of republicanism and an outspoken critic of Julius Caesar. During the civil war he took up arms against him, and learning of the defeat of his allies at the battle of Thapsus, committed suicide.

15 *Quod latet ... fibrâ*: 'How the secret entrails lie unfathomable' (Persius, *Satires*).

16 Milton (John Milton, 1608–74): English poet and man of letters, a civil servant for the Commonwealth under Oliver Cromwell. He is best known for his epic poem *Paradise Lost* (1667), from which the following eight lines are taken (ii, 666–73).

17 *Segnius irritant ... fidelibus*: 'Impressions of what is heard affect the mind less vividly than those seen by the eyes, which do not lie' (Horace, *Ars Poetica*).

18 Abbé du Bos (Jean-Baptiste Dubos, 1670–1742): French author and political agent also known as l'Abbé Du Bos.

19 Chevy-chace or the Children in the Wood: referred to by Joseph Addison (1672–1719), essayist and politician, in the magazine he founded with Richard Steele, the *Spectator*.

20 He above the rest ... monarchs: *Paradise Lost* (*see* n.16, above), i, 589–99.

21 passage in the book of Job: 4:13–17.

22 temptations of St. Anthony ... serious passion: many sixteenth- and seventeenth-century European painters, Dutch, Flemish and Spanish, painted the temptations of St Anthony, often in grotesque detail.

23 Virgil's Fame: *Aeneid*, 4.

24 Homer's Discord: *Iliad*, 4.

25 Mr. Blacklock (Thomas Blacklock, 1721–91): Scottish poet left blind by smallpox at the age of six months. He attended Edinburgh University and published his *Poems* in 1746. David Hume introduced his work to Joseph Spence, a former Oxford Professor of Poetry, whose subsequent essay, *An Account of the Life, Character and Poems of Mr Blacklock*, was reprinted as a preface to the second edition of the *Poems* in 1756.

26 Mr. Saunderson (Dr Nicholas Saunderson, 1682–1739): also blinded by smallpox at an early age, he was a talented mathematician who rose to become Lucasian Professor of Mathematics at Cambridge in 1711.

27 Belphebe: a character in Edmund Spenser's poem *The Faerie Queene* (1590), who was intended to represent Elizabeth I.

28 Lucretius (*c.* 99–*c.* 55 BC): Roman poet. The following lines translate as 'When the life of man lay foul to see and grovelling upon the earth, crushed by the weight of religion, which showed her face from the realms of heaven, lowering upon mortals with a dreadful mien, 'twas a man of Greece who dared first to raise his mortal eyes to meet her ...' (*De rerum natura*, English translation by Cyril Bailey, 1910).

29 *animi motus effert interprete lingua*: 'the tongue, its interpreter, expresses the emotions of the soul' (Horace, *Ars Poetica*).

30 Sanguine ... ignes: 'Staining with his blood the fires which he himself had sanctified' (Virgil, *Aeneid*).

31 O'er many ... death: Milton (*see* n.16, above), *Paradise Lost*, 2.

AN ESSAY TOWARDS AN ABRIDGMENT OF THE ENGLISH HISTORY (3)

1 Reign of John: born in 1166, John was King of England between 1199 and 1216. Burke's principal source for the events of his reign is the *Chronica Majora* of Matthew of Paris (*c.* 1200–1250).

2 all of them uncertain: the Angevin 'empire' (the area ruled over by the House of Plantagenet) had been established by John's father King Henry II (r. 1154–89), Count of Anjou and Duke of Normandy, arguably the most powerful ruler in Europe. Broadly, it comprised the western half of France, all of England and the eastern half of Ireland.

3 Arthur (1187–1203): three-year-old Arthur, posthumous son of Geoffrey Plantagenet, had been named as his successor by Richard I before he set off on crusade in 1190. However, on his deathbed in 1199 Richard had named John his heir.

4 Hubert ... and Glanville: Hubert Walter (d. 1205), Archbishop of Canterbury from 1193, had also been Chief Justiciar (the King's principal minister) from 1193 to 1198. He became John's Lord Chancellor. 'Glanville' may refer to Ranulf de Glanville, uncle of Hubert Walter and Justiciar from 1180 to 1189. However, he had died in 1190. Justiciar in 1199 was Geoffrey FitzPeter, who also supported John's succession and was made 1st Earl of Essex as a result. The support of the powerful royal marshal, William Marshal (1146/7–1219), created Earl of Pembroke on John's accession, was also critical.

5 his new subjects: Henry II decided in 1177 to give the lordship of Ireland to the youngest of his four surviving sons (previously nicknamed 'John Lackland'). John was sent to govern Ireland in 1185, at the age of eighteen.

6 Avisa: also known as Isabella (*c.* 1173–1217) was a rich heiress, Countess of Gloucester in her own right. She had married John in 1189 but the couple were second cousins and the marriage was immediately challenged by the

Archbishop of Canterbury as contrary to canon law. A formal papal dispensation had never been sought – perhaps because John wished to keep his options open. In the early 1190s he was considering marrying Alice, sister of Philip Augustus of France. Isabella did not contest the annulment. Henry II had made her a royal ward, so both she and her lands were in the keeping of the Crown. She was not allowed to remarry until 1214 when John forced the 2nd Earl of Essex, Geoffrey FitzGeoffrey de Mandeville, to pay 20,000 marks for her hand. Unsurprisingly the Earl was among the barons who rebelled against John the following year.

7 Hugh, Count of Marche (Hugh IX de Lusignan, Count of La Marche, d. 1219): John's marriage to Isabella of Angoulême took place on 24 August 1200. To add insult to injury John also confiscated La Marche and gave it to Hugh's greatest rival, his new father-in-law, Aymer, Count of Angoulême. Isabella was just twelve years old at the time; after John's death she married her former fiancé's son, Hugh X.

8 the emperor and the Earl of Flanders: Emperor Otto IV (1175–1218), John's nephew, was one of two rival German emperors (the other being Philip, Duke of Swabia). He had been crowned King of the Romans in 1198 but did not become sole Holy Roman Emperor until 1208, after Philip's death. He was forced to abdicate in 1215. Baldwin IX (1172–1205), Count of Flanders, shortly afterwards led the Fourth Crusade and was elected as Latin Emperor of Constantinople. He was captured at the battle of Adrianople and died a prisoner of the Emperor of Bulgaria.

9 he renounced his alliance: the Treaty was made at Le Goulet, on the Seine, on 22 May 1200. The English barons nicknamed him 'John Softsword' as a result.

10 He found that his enemies ... was besieged: John's mother was Eleanor (c. 1122–1204), Duchess of Aquitaine and Gascony (territories also known as Guyenne) and Countess of Poitou in her own right. She had been the wife of Louis VII of France before marrying Henry II of England, bringing her large French possessions into the Angevin empire. At the age of eighty she was none the less determined to protect her lands from the French and was on her way to rally Poitiers when besieged at Mirebeau (Mirabel) castle by her grandson Arthur of Brittany and three of the Lusignan family, who were seemingly obsessed with the idea of kidnapping her (this was their third attempt).

11 the castle of Bristol: Arthur's sister Eleanor (c. 1184–1241), 'the Fair Maid of Brittany', spent the rest of her life as a prisoner in England, regarded as a potential threat by John and by his successor Henry III, because of her claim to the English throne.

12 Rollo (c. 846–c. 932): Viking warrior who was granted lands around Rouen by Charles III of France in 911. He and his successors came to control the whole of Normandy (from 'Northmen') and to style themselves as dukes. William the Conqueror was descended from him.

13 part of Guienne: Gascony (Guyenne) held out under the Archbishop of Bordeaux. It would remain in English hands until the end of the Hundred Years' War in 1453.

14 his subsequent conduct: as Lord Chancellor Hubert had done much to improve the administrative and legal system and to increase the efficiency

of tax collection. However, he was suspected of being on too friendly terms with Philip Augustus and John no doubt resented the part he played in frustrating his plan to attack France in 1205.

15 a person recommended by the king: John de Grey (d. 1214), Bishop of Norwich.

16 the pope: Innocent III, Pope between 1198 and 1216. He reasserted papal authority within the Church and over secular affairs throughout Europe.

17 Stephen Langton (*c.* 1150–1228): educated in Paris, he later lectured there at the University, gaining a wide reputation for his learning. Lotario di Segni, the future Pope Innocent III, had been one of his students. Innocent called him to Rome in 1206 and made him cardinal-priest of San Crisogono.

18 The Earl of Flanders: Portuguese Prince Ferdinand (1188–1233), who had married Countess Joan of Flanders, who had succeeded her father Baldwin (*see* n.8 above) in 1205. Like his father, he allied against France because of French aggression towards Flanders.

19 a battle which entirely broke his strength: fought near Lille on 27 July 1214. Otto's defeat led to his deposition the following year by Frederick II (son of Otto's predecessor Emperor Henry VI), whose claim was supported by the Pope.

20 He took the cross ... sacred: a promise to go on a crusade to free Jerusalem from Muslim rule. The Fifth Crusade, preached by Innocent III, was under way at this time.

21 as our historians ... assert: e.g. David Hume's *History of England* (1754–61).

22 fines and amercements: fine – a sum of money paid to an individual (in this case the king) in return for the grant of some right or benefit. Amercement – a financial penalty.

23 disseized: to have property appropriated (often wrongfully).

24 the censures of the holy see: Innocent III issued a Bull annulling the Magna Carta on 24 August 1215. He would particularly have objected to the clause stating that 'the English Church shall be free'. He ordered Stephen Langton to excommunicate the barons who had signed the document and did so himself when Langton refused. Langton was soon afterwards suspended by the papal legate Pandulph.

25 He retired to the Isle of Wight ... popular: this story (from the *Chronica Majora*) is now thought to be apocryphal.

26 perished at sea: according to Matthew Paris, Hugh de Boves, a knight from Picardy who had been a commander in the Anglo-Imperial army at Bouvines, was bringing an army of French mercenaries to join King John which was shipwrecked off the Suffolk coast in September 1215.

27 Stephen's wars: the civil war which followed the death of Henry I in 1135 between his daughter and named successor Matilda and his nephew Stephen who seized the throne. It continued until Stephen's death in 1154 when, by his prior agreement, Matilda's son Henry Plantagenet took the throne as Henry II.

28 Lewis: Louis (1187–1226) was proclaimed King in London in 1216. He

had a very slender claim to the throne through his wife Blanche, a grand-daughter of Henry II. In 1223 he succeeded his father as King of France.

ON PARTIES (4)
[Manuscript essay]

1 Whig & Tory: the division of English politicians into two opposing parties, the Whigs and the Tories, took place during the Exclusion Crisis of 1679–81. Charles II's heir was his Catholic brother James, Duke of York, and popular fear of Catholicism with its traditional links to arbitrary power had reached a climax of paranoia during the recent 'Popish Plot', a wholly fictitious conspiracy to kill the King and put James on the throne in his place. The party names were originally terms of abuse: the 'Whigs' (or Whiggamores – an old Scottish name for Presbyterian rebels), led by a group of Protestant aristocrats, demanded that James be excluded from the throne by Act of Parliament; the 'Tories' (an old Irish name for Catholic rebels) believed in the Divine Right of Kings and opposed exclusion on principle. Tories were firm supporters of the Anglican Church and tended to oppose toleration of religious dissenters; Whigs included both Anglicans and dissenters and generally favoured toleration. Burke notes that the division had its roots in the Civil War. The Tories were heirs to the Cavaliers, the Whigs, to a lesser extent, to the Parliamentarians. Charles II dissolved three parliaments and ruled for the last four years of his life without one in order to prevent an Exclusion Act from being passed.

2 the Jacobite: Tory beliefs were challenged during the reign of James II (1685–88), whom both parties suspected of trying to introduce a Catholic absolutist monarchy on the French model. Many Tories joined the Whigs in support of the Revolution in 1688 or were at any rate willing to acquiesce. Those whose belief in Divine Right overrode all other considerations opposed it and became known as Jacobites ('Jacobus' being the Latin for James). There were a number of Jacobite plots to reverse the Revolution during the 1690s.

3 the abdicated family: James II never abdicated, but finding he could not trust the loyalty of his own army, fled the country after William of Orange landed. The Convention Parliament shortly afterwards declared that he had abdicated and offered the crown to William (his nephew) and his wife Mary, James's eldest daughter, who were both Protestants. The 'abdicated family' refers to the deposed James II and his son by his second wife Mary of Modena. The birth of James Edward, in 1688, acted as a catalyst for revolution since it looked like the start of a Catholic dynasty: no one could now view a Catholic monarch as a merely temporary aberration. The Prince was brought up in France, declared himself King James III of England and Ireland (James VIII of Scotland) on his father's death in 1701, and was recognized as such by France, Spain, Modena and the Pope. For measures taken to exclude this family, *see* Thoughts on the Present Discontents (6), nn.8, 11.

4 But a long exclusion ... that Party: party politics remained vigorous during the reigns of William and Mary and Anne, with monarchs often favouring mixed ministries of Whigs and Tories. However, George I distrusted the Tories and his first ministry was almost entirely Whig even though Tories

had a majority in both houses. A general election speedily returned a huge Whig majority and reasons were found to impeach Tory ministers of the previous administration. The Jacobite rebellion of 1715 and subsequent plots in 1719 and 1722 made Whig ministers nervous and their leader Robert Walpole played upon popular fears to associate all Tories with the taint of Jacobitism. The second 'unsuccessful war' of 1745 entrenched the Whigs still further and there were no Tory ministers until the reign of George III (1760–1820). The tradition was kept alive in the country among the staunchly Anglican landowning gentry class.

5 Green & Blue ... Caesar & Pompey ... Anthony & Octavian ... York & Lancaster: the Greens and the Blues were circus factions who supported rival teams in the Byzantine Empire's favourite sport of chariot racing. Their fanaticism not infrequently turned into appalling violence and became a factor in the politics of the period. (Both fell foul of the Emperor Justinian and were trapped in the Hippodrome and massacred together after the Nika riots of 532.) In the last days of the Roman Republic former allies Caesar and Pompey fought each other in 49–48 BC; Antony and Octavian did the same in 32 BC, the victory of the latter ushering in the Roman Empire with Octavian as the first Emperor (Augustus). The houses of York and Lancaster were branches of the royal House of Plantagenet, who fought the Wars of the Roses (1455–87) over their rival claims to the English throne.

6 Prince of Orange: the house of Orange-Nassau had owned vast swathes of land across a number of European countries; its close association with the Netherlands (also known as the United Provinces) had begun when William the Silent, Prince of Orange, led a rebellion against Spanish rule in the sixteenth century. The seven provinces (of which Holland was one) formed a federal republic (the United Provinces), each with its own States; a prince of Orange was generally nominated as 'stadtholder' (steward or chief executive) and Captain General of the army in the majority of the provinces, with powers as limited or as absolute as he could manage to secure. For two centuries the stadtholders were engaged in a tug of war for power with the republican oligarchy. After the death of William III (also William III of England) the Netherlands had lost its status as a Great Power. The dynasty had also lost Orange itself, a small principality near Avignon which was annexed by Louis XIV and incorporated into France in 1713. In 1747 a popular revolution had enabled William IV to become Stadtholder of all seven provinces, and to create a hereditary post of Stadtholder General. He was succeeded in 1751 by his son William V, a minor, whose government was weak and corrupt. However, his regime tottered on until he was overthrown in the Batavian Revolution of 1795.

7 Marius & Sylla (Sulla): see A Vindication of Natural Society (1), n.21.

CONSIDERATIONS ON A MILITIA (5)
[Manuscript essay]

1 a standing Army: in spite of the long-standing English fear and suspicion of standing armies (armies which were not disbanded in peacetime) as a menace to civil liberties, there had been a standing army in England since the Restoration. When Parliament's New Model Army was disbanded,

Charles II was allowed to keep a small army for his protection. Although James II's augmentation of this army had provoked enormous hostility, William's wars had necessitated the maintenance of an even larger force, and defence of the new dynasty combined with Britain's growing imperial expansion to ensure that the army became a permanent feature of Hanoverian rule. However, since 1689 such an army could only be maintained with the consent of Parliament. Numbers fluctuated depending on whether the country was at war. In 1757 Britain was involved in the Seven Years' War, during which the army rose to nearly 65,000 men. Before the war it had dropped to 19,000. Compared to the army of France, these numbers were tiny.

2 militia: ancient territorial force with its origins in Saxon England which assumed greater importance after the decline of the feudal system. The militia was the responsibility of Lord Lieutenants, royal officials (generally peers) in the counties. Its purpose was to preserve local order or to defend the locality against an invader. Trained bands (the more active section of the militia) played a significant role in the Civil War. The force had become moribund during the eighteenth century. Pitt the Elder was keen to revive it during the Seven Years' War. His first Militia Bill failed to pass in 1756, and Newcastle had been obliged to call in soldiers from Hesse and Hanover. These were sent back to Germany when the second Militia Bill passed in 1757. Militia regiments remained active through the remainder of the eighteenth and throughout the nineteenth century, particularly during the Napoleonic Wars. They were converted to 'Special Reserve' in 1906, and they became effectively training units during World War I. Redesignated militia following the war, they were no longer active and were formally disbanded in 1953.

THOUGHTS ON THE CAUSE OF THE PRESENT DISCONTENTS (6)

1 *Hoc vero … potueris*: 'But this hidden evil in the heart of a man's own household not only remains invisible but also surprises him before he can watch and reconnoitre' (Cicero, *Verrine Orations*, slightly misquoted). This refers to the treachery of Verres, who in 83 BC during the Roman civil wars deserted his commander Carbo and joined Sulla, his adversary, taking with him the money entrusted to him for payment of Carbo's army. The suggestion is of similar treachery in the Court and House of Commons towards the English nation.

2 the great parties: *see* On Parties (4), n.1.

3 Mem. de Sully: 'The revolutions which take place in great states are not the result of chance or the whim of the people. Nothing provokes the nobility of a kingdom like a weak and disorderly government. As for the populace, it is never from a desire to attack that it rebels, but from impatience with suffering.' Quotation from the memoirs of the Duc de Sully (1560–1641), the chief minister of Henri IV of France between 1598 and 1610. He was a good administrator and a highly successful superintendent of finance.

4 King John … King James … Henry the Eighth … Richard the Second: four monarchs popularly supposed to be tyrants. John's misgovernment was

seen as the prime cause of the Magna Carta (1215). Catholic James II was accused of arbitrary rule and lost his throne in the Glorious Revolution of 1688. Henry VIII (r. 1509–47) was considered the architect of a Tudor despotism. Richard II's alleged misrule was used as a justification for his deposition by Henry IV in 1399.

5 *Ship-money ... Forest laws*: during his 'personal rule' without Parliament in the 1630s Charles I needed to find a means of raising money. He reasserted the Crown's rights over large areas of forests which had fallen into desuetude since the fourteenth century. Ship Money, levied on coastal towns in time of war, was still a current tax, but his attempt to extend it to inland counties aroused considerable opposition, aggravated by the suspicion that the King would treat this as a permanent source of revenue. In 1638 the MP John Hampden was famously put on trial for making a principled stand against this form of unparliamentary taxation.

6 *usufruct ... fee and inheritance*: usufruct is the right to enjoy the use and advantage of a property; fee and inheritance refers to outright ownership with the right to pass on a property to one's heirs. Individual MPs might be susceptible to bribery by ministers but would never surrender the rights of Parliament itself.

7 Uxor Hugonis ... Hugone de Nevill: 'The wife of Hugh de Nevill fined two hundred hens, that she might lie with her husband at night.'

8 the Revolution: the 'Glorious Revolution' of 1688, when the reigning monarch, James II (r. 1685–88), deeply unpopular and a Catholic (with all the connotations of arbitrary government which accrued to it at the time), was replaced by invitation of Parliament with the joint monarchs William III (James's nephew), Prince of Orange, and his wife Mary (James's eldest daughter), both of whom were Protestants. For the first time constitutional legislation was introduced – notably the Bill of Rights (1689) and the Act of Settlement (1701), which placed restrictions on the power of the Crown. Both monarch and consort had to be Protestant, and the King was forbidden to raise a standing army, levy taxes, make or suspend laws without the consent of Parliament. In fact many powers remained: to call and dismiss Parliament, to appoint ministers (provided they were Anglican and British) and to reject legislation. The Crown had considerable financial resources and Hanoverian kings could and did exercise influence in areas of interest such as foreign policy.

9 so new and unsettled a government: Burke hereafter refers approvingly to the Whig oligarchy under prime ministers Robert Walpole (1721–42), Henry Pelham (1743–54) and his brother the Duke of Newcastle (1754–56; 1757–62) which came to an end soon after the accession of George III.

10 mortmain: perpetual ownership of land by ecclesiastical or other corporation.

11 House of Brunswick: the House of Hanover. The Kings of Hanover were also the Dukes of Brunswick-Lüneburg. Protestant cousins of the Stuarts, they acceded to the British throne in 1714 as provided for in the Act of Settlement (1701) on the death without heirs of the last Stuart monarch, Queen Anne. George I had ruled until 1727, George II from 1727 to 1760. Britain and Hanover were ruled by the same monarch until 1837.

12 Frederic Prince of Wales: George III had succeeded his grandfather,

George II, in 1760. His father, Frederick, Prince of Wales, had died in 1751. Notoriously, the Hanoverian monarchs did not get on with their eldest sons, and the household of the Princes of Wales acted as a focus for opposition ministers with a view to their future careers. Frederick had been a particularly active politician, his 'Leicester House Set' harrying the government during the 1730s, finally bringing down prime minister Robert Walpole in 1742.

13 a person ... little known or considered in the kingdom: John Stuart, 3rd Earl Bute (1713–92) had been George III's tutor and was a close friend. His introduction to the Cabinet in 1760 and even his swift elevation to First Lord of the Treasury in 1762 was widely considered quite natural, though his opponents chose to regard it as a plot to introduce personal government by the King. He proved very unpopular and, finding political life not to his taste, resigned in 1763.

14 *A party ... against the ministry*: the King's Friends, followers of George III and Lord Bute during the 1760s. Never a formal grouping, they were seen by Burke and the Rockingham Whigs as an inner 'Cabal' of court placemen and careerists. They liked to see themselves as a group of patriots who put country before party.

15 His Majesty: George III (r. 1760–1820).

16 the Pretender: Charles Edward Stuart (1720–88), known as 'The Young Pretender', grandson of the deposed James II. He led the ultimately unsuccessful Jacobite rebellion of 1745–46, the last attempt of the Stuarts to regain the throne. In later years his drunken, debauched life on the continent brought discredit to his cause.

17 a mighty war: the Seven Years' War (1756–63). It involved all the European Great Powers, pitting France, Austria, Saxony, Sweden and Russia against Prussia, Hanover and Britain. Britain's principal interest was to increase its trade and colonial possessions at the expense of France.

18 a monarch ... reversionary hope: George III (*see* n.12, above) came to the throne at the age of twenty-two. There was no mature heir to the throne around whom opposition could concentrate until the 1780s.

19 the Duke of Newcastle and Mr. Pitt: George III inherited a successful war administration run in uneasy alliance by William Pitt the Elder (1708–78), Secretary of State for the Southern Department, and Thomas Pelham-Holles, Duke of Newcastle (1683–1768), First Lord of the Treasury. Pitt had proved an inspired war leader; Newcastle, one of the richest Whig landowners in England and a strong supporter of the Hanoverian succession in 1714, had been Secretary of State for the Southern Department for thirty years before landing the top job in 1754, and was a tireless and indispensable manager of patronage – the system of distributing posts, sinecures and pensions that kept an administration together before the advent of parties. Pitt, known as 'The Great Commoner', resigned in 1761 and sacrificed some popularity by his ready acceptance of a pension for himself and a peerage for his wife. Newcastle's resignation in 1762 was followed by a purge of his placemen – though it was not systematic, and those who were happy to change allegiance kept their positions.

20 Sentiments of an Honest Man: actually *Seasonable Hints of an Honest Man* by John Douglas (1761).

21 *Atè*: in Greek mythology Ate personified blind folly.

22 *Mettre le Roy hors de page*: making the King his own master.

23 a triennial parliament, or a place-bill: a Triennial Act in 1694 had re-estab-
    lished the tradition of more frequent parliaments. It was replaced by the
    Septennial Act in 1716.

24 The Earl of Bute: (*see* n.13, above) he continued to advise the King on
    major issues after he left office in 1763, though probably not as often as his
    enemies claimed. He spoke out against the Rockingham ministry in the
    House of Lords as the embodiment of 'faction and party' on 17 March
    1766. George's last letters to him are from the same year; they had no fur-
    ther contact.

25 *Idem sentire de republicâ*: to think alike on political matters (an allusion to
    Cicero's *De Amicitia*).

26 *necessitudo sortis*: the loyalty that was imposed on men whom chance had
    thrown together as colleagues in office (e.g. in the relationship of the quaes-
    tor Verres and his praetor Cecilius, *see* n.1, above).

27 *plus sages que les sages*: Molière in *La critique de l'école des femmes*.

28 Queen Anne (r. 1701–14): younger sister of Queen Mary. Her reign was
    dominated by the War of Spanish Succession, which Britain joined in 1702.

29 Addison (Joseph Addison, 1672–1719): a Whig politician as well as a man
    of letters. The quotation is from 'The Campaign', written to commemor-
    ate the Duke of Marlborough's victory at Blenheim (1704).

30 Lord Sunderland, Lord Godolphin, Lord Somers, and Lord Marlborough:
    Charles Spencer, 3rd Earl of Sunderland (1675–1722) and John Somers,
    Baron Somers (1651–1716) were members of a so-called Whig junto which
    collectively led the Whig party after 1696 during the reigns of William III
    and Queen Anne. Sidney Godolphin, 1st Earl of Godolphin (1645–1712),
    and John Churchill, 1st Duke of Marlborough (1650–1722) were moderate
    Tories who co-operated with the junto in a joint ministry between 1702
    and 1710.

31 *Not men but measures*: a catchphrase which became Pitt's political maxim.
    It appealed to George III and brought about a *rapprochement* between them.
    From 1766 to 1768 Pitt led a less successful second administration, though
    often incapacitated by ill health, from the House of Lords as Earl of
    Chatham.

SPEECH ON THE MIDDLESEX ELECTION (7)

[Full title: *Speech on the Motion made in the House of Commons, February 7,
1771, Relative to the Middlesex Election*]

1   Mr. Wilkes (John Wilkes, 1725–97): English politician, journalist, radical.
    Elected to Parliament in 1757, he came to prominence when he attacked
    the new prime minister Lord Bute – *see* Thoughts on the Present Discon-
    tents (6), n.13 – in his political periodical *The North Briton*. In 1763 his
    arrest for seditious libel under a general warrant launched him on his career
    as a champion of Liberty against the tyranny of the Administration.

Pleading parliamentary privilege he was released from the Tower but shortly afterwards his obscene satire *Essay on Woman* fell into government hands, creating a furore in both Houses which eventually drove him abroad. In 1764 he was tried and convicted of sedition and blasphemy *in absentia*, and outlawed by the House of Lords; the House of Commons expelled him. Mob hysteria accompanied his return and election as MP for Middlesex in the general election of 1768. When he surrendered himself to imprisonment his supporters rioted, leading to the so-called St George's Fields Massacre and adding the bonus of martyrdom to his cause. Expelled from the Commons in February 1769 he was enthusiastically re-elected, unopposed, in by-elections three times, to the great embarrassment of Lord Grafton's government, who secured his expulsion on each occasion. Opponents were found to stand against him at a fourth by-election in April 1769; this time the House of Commons declared the runner-up, Henry Luttrell, the victor. On release from prison in 1770, Wilkes cultivated the radicals in the City of London, founding the Society for the Supporters of the Bill of Rights, and successfully campaigning for the right of printers to publish accurate reports of parliamentary debates. He became Lord Mayor in 1774 and finally re-entered the House of Commons the same year. He introduced the first reform bill (1776), and supported the rebels during the American War of Independence. His motion that the House should expunge from the record his expulsion of February 1769 finally passed in 1782. In later life, however, he had become more conservative, and he helped suppress the Gordon Riots in 1780. His popularity on the wane, he withdrew early from the Middlesex election in 1790.

2   subverts the constitution: the constitutional implications of Wilkes's expulsion and replacement were much discussed in the Commons. The first attempts to clarify and confirm the rights of electors were made by Rockinghamite leader William Dowdeswell in January 1770; independent Sir George Savile followed up with no fewer than four motions of which that of 7 February 1771 was the first. The fourth was in 1774, after which Wilkes was able to take up the issue for himself.

3   the usurping House of Commons ... constituents: Cromwell's 'Rump' Parliament (1648–53) abolished the House of Lords and the monarchy following Charles I's execution in 1649. Both were restored in 1660 with the return of Charles II.

4   *ex vi termini*: by force of the term, i.e. by definition.

5   Lord Coke: *see* A Vindication of Natural Society (1), n.4.

6   golden metwand of the law: metwand, measuring rod used by Lord Coke as a symbol of how issues should be defined according to a fixed rule (the Golden Metwand) rather than 'the crooked cord of discretion'.

SPEECH AT THE CONCLUSION OF THE POLL AT BRISTOL (8)

[Full title: *Mr Edmund Burke's Speech to the Electors of Bristol, On his being declared by the Sheriffs, duly elected one of the Representatives in Parliament for that City, on Thursday the 3d of November, 1774*]

1   the same honour ... conferred on me: Bristol returned two MPs; Henry

Cruger (1739–1827), who finished ahead of Burke in the poll, was the other. Originally from New York, he was a merchant and radical, already active in local politics. No love was lost between the fellow members, who became rivals rather than colleagues.

2 the Candidate: Matthew Brickdale (1735–1831), who had just lost his seat to Burke. In 1768 he had been returned unopposed for Bristol as candidate for the Tory Steadfast Society (*see* To Joseph Harford, n.7) though once in Parliament he had pursued a relatively independent line. He petitioned unsuccessfully against the return of Burke and Cruger. He was re-elected, again as Steadfast Society candidate, in 1780, but did not stand in 1790 and ended his life in reduced circumstances.

SPEECH ON CONCILIATION WITH AMERICA (9)

[Full title: *The Speech of Edmund Burke, Esq. on moving his Resolutions for Conciliation with the Colonies, March 22, 1775*]

1 Mr. Rose Fuller (?1708–77): Sussex landowner, iron-master and planter in Jamaica, in Parliament 1756–77. He was a supporter of the Administration, but opposed coercion in America.

2 Lord North (Frederick North, 2nd Earl of Guilford, 1732–92): prime minister for twelve years from 1770, putting an end to the ministerial instability of the 1760s. He had entered Parliament in 1756 and proved a useful servant of several administrations, becoming Chancellor of the Exchequer in 1767. Although his connections were Whig he led no faction but attracted the support of a large portion of the country gentry, having the advantage of sitting in the Commons (his father was in the Lords). His premiership was fully endorsed by George III. He proved a competent financial manager, was a persuasive speaker and a man known for his wit and good humour. North's policy towards the American colonies was vigorously opposed by the Rockingam group. His popularity melted away when the American War began to go badly for Britain and the King finally permitted him to resign in 1782.

3 Mr. Glover (Richard Glover, 1712–85): merchant and poet, author of epic poem *Leonidas*, member for Weymouth and Melcombe Regis 1761–68.

4 my lord Bathurst (Allen Bathurst, 1st Earl Bathurst, 1684–1775): prominent Tory, member for Cirencester 1705–11 until raised to peerage. Privy Councillor (1742), made Earl Bathurst 1772.

5 *acta ... virtus*: 'he could review his ancestors' behaviour and thus know what virtue is' (Virgil, *Eclogues*).

6 Blackstone's Commentaries: treatise on England's common law by Sir William Blackstone (1723–80), first published 1765–69. A readable, accessible, four-volume work (on rights of persons, rights of things, private wrongs and public wrongs), it became the standard source on the development (relying on precedent rather than statute) of English law.

7 General Gage (Thomas Gage, 1719/20–87): British general, military commander during the American Revolution, military governor of Massachusetts (1774). His attempts to inflict punishment for the Boston Tea Party resulted in the battles of Lexington and Concord, and sparked the American War of Independence. He was replaced by General William Howe in 1775.

8 *Abeunt studia in mores*: 'Customary behaviour becomes character' (Ovid, *Herodias*).

9 Lord Dunmore (John Murray, 4th Earl of Dunmore, 1732–1809): Governor of Virginia from 1771, until his loyalist troops were defeated at Great Bridge (1775). He returned to England and to Parliament, and served as Governor of the Bahamas (1787–96).

10 *Spoliatis arma supersunt*: 'Those who are robbed take up arms' (Juvenal, *Satires*).

11 Sir Edward Coke ... Sir Walter Raleigh: *see* A Vindication of Natural Society (1), n.4. Coke put the government's case (that Walter Raleigh in 1603 had supported Lady Arabella Stuart's claim to the throne and accepted a bribe from the Spanish goverment) in Raleigh's subsequent trial for treason, calling him a 'notorious traitor', a 'vile viper' and a 'damnable atheist', and succeeded in having him found guilty, imprisoned in the Tower of London and eventually executed. Coke was widely criticized for ignoring the weakness and bias of the case against Raleigh.

12 *ex vi termini*: by force of the term, i.e. by definition.

13 *great Serbonian bog ...* : John Milton, *Paradise Lost*.

14 Mr. Rice (George Rice, *c.* 1724–79): Welsh politician and courtier, Member of Parliament 1754–79.

15 Sir John Davis (1569–1626): English lawyer, politician and poet. As Attorney General for Ireland, he formulated a number of legal principles underpinning the British Empire.

16 glorious Revolution (1688): revolution resulting in the deposition of (the Catholic) James II and his replacement with his daughter Mary II and her husband, William III, Prince of Orange and Stadtholder of the Dutch Republic.

17 *Simul alba nautis ... Unda recumbit*: ' ... soon as gleam / Their stars at sea, / The lash'd spray trickles from the steep, / The wind sinks down, the storm-cloud flies, / The threatening billow on the deep / Obedient lies' (Horace, *Odes*).

18 Judge Barrington (Daines Barrington, 1727–1800): English lawyer, naturalist and antiquary. His 1767 estimate of the population of Merioneth, Carnavon and Anglesey (50,000), in *Archaeologia* (1770), is thought to be an underestimate (it was probably almost twice that size).

19 Republic of Plato ... Utopia of More ... Oceana of Harrington: imaginary commonwealths/utopias proposed by Plato (*The Republic*, 380 BC), Sir Thomas More (*Utopia*, 1516) and James Harrington (*The Commonwealth of Oceana*, 1656).

20 *Non meus ... sapiens*: 'Not my writing, but the wisdom of Ofellus, a rustic' (Horace, *Satires*).

21 stamp act: passed by Parliament in 1765, requiring American colonists to pay a tax on printed paper (ships' papers, licences, legal documents etc.) to defray the costs of defending the American frontier.

22 Lord Hillsborough (Wills Hill, 1st Earl of Hillsborough, 1718–93): as Secretary of State for the Colonies (1768–72), he told the colonial governors

of America that no further taxes would be levied there, and that the existing duties on glass, paper and colours would be removed.

23 Mr. Grenville (George Grenville, 1712–70): as prime minister (1763–65), he tried to curb public spending, bringing in the Stamp Act (*see* n.21, above), only to see it subsequently repealed. Grenville was dismissed in 1765 and replaced by Lord Rockingham.

24 Lord Chatham (William Pitt, 1st Earl of Chatham, 1708–78): British Whig statesman, 'Pitt the Elder' (*see* Thoughts on the Present Discontents (6), nn.19, 31). In 1766, he and Grenville (*see* n.23, above) argued about the meanings of the preambles of two Acts concerned with revenue-raising.

25 *Experimentum in corpore vili*: Let the experiment be carried out using a worthless body.

26 *Posita luditur arca*: 'Treasure is the stake in the game' (Juvenal, *Satires*).

27 "*Ease would retract vows made in pain, as violent and void*": John Milton, *Paradise Lost*.

28 revenue from Bengal: in 1767, Chatham (*see* n.24, above) attempted to extract revenue from the East India Company, rendering it impecunious enough to need a loan from Parliament in 1773.

29 *Sursum corda*: lift up your hearts.

30 *quod felix faustumque sit*: let it be happy and prosperous.

LETTER TO THE SHERIFFS OF BRISTOL (10)

[Full title: *A Letter from Edmund Burke, Esq; One of the Representatives in Parliament for the City of Bristol, to John Farr and John Harris, Esqrs, Sheriffs of that City, on the Affairs of America*. Burke had been criticized in Bristol for his party's boycott of Parliament in the early months of 1777. This letter was written to explain their conduct.]

1 'the two last acts': both passed in February 1777. The Letters of Marque Act enabled the Admiralty to grant commissions to commanders of private ships to capture American ships and seize their cargoes. The American Treason Act suspended *Habeas Corpus* (*see* n.2 below) for anyone accused or suspected of high treason out of the realm or of piracy against British subjects at sea.

2 *Habeas Corpus* (Latin – you have the body): writ commanding an official to produce a prisoner on request in order that a court might determine the legality of the imprisonment.

3 Lord Coke: *see* A Vindication of Natural Society (1), n.4.

4 Lord Balmerino (1688–1746): Arthur Elphinstone, 6th Lord Balmerino, Scottish nobleman, was an officer in the Jacobite army during the 1715 uprising, then served with the French army until 1733 when he received a pardon and returned to Scotland. He was involved in the 1745 Jacobite rebellion, captured at Culloden, tried before Parliament and beheaded.

5 Tyburn: gallows, main execution site for London and Middlesex until 1783. Soldiers were also shot there for military offences.

6 commission of Oyer and Terminer: authorizes English judges (as High Court judges on circuit) to hear, at the assizes, treason, felony or misdemeanour cases.

7 breathed the same air with them: a reference to the landmark case of James Somerset (1772), a slave who was released by Chief Justice Lord Mansfield on a writ of *Habeas Corpus*.

8 I have not debated ... correct it: Burke's absence from the debates in February 1777 when these two Acts were debated and passed had caused particular concern in Bristol, especially amongst the radicals who expected to see any suppression of individual rights strongly opposed. The practice of secession, as it was known, in principle distanced the opposition from government policies of which it disapproved but could not defeat, but in practice made such policies easier to implement. The Rockingham boycott was not a success. It attracted little public attention and was only partial since Charles James Fox and Sir George Savile had decided to break it very early on in order to speak against these very Acts. The party as a whole returned to Parliament on 16 April.

9 Mr. *Hume* (David Hume, 1711–76): the greatest philosopher to write in the English language. In his 'Of Civil Liberty' he wrote: 'Private property seems to me almost as secure in a civilized European monarchy, as in a republic; nor is danger much apprehended in such a government, from the violence of the sovereign; more than we commonly dread harm from thunder, or earthquakes, or any accident the most unusual and extraordinary.' Hume was an acquaintance of Burke. His other works include *A Treatise of Human Nature* (1739–40), the *Political Discourses* (1752) and a bestselling History of England (1754–62).

10 Colonel Raille ... Fort Kniphausen: Johann Rall/Rahl (1726–76) and Lieutenant General Wilhelm von Knyphausen (1716–1800) were commanders of Hessian mercenaries supporting Britain during the American War of Independence. Rall distinguished himself by scattering American militia at the battle of White Plains (28 October 1776); Fort Washington, captured by British troops under General William Howe on 16 November 1776, was renamed Fort Knyphausen.

11 court gazette ... attempted in vain: the royal proclamation of 23 August 1775 in support of suppressing rebellion in the colonies was printed in newspapers throughout the country and elicited a flood of loyal addresses. From 12 September to 12 December 1775 the *London Gazette*, the official instrument of the government, had printed all of the addresses, together with all the signatures, in specially enlarged editions.

12 the author of the celebrated pamphlet ... irresistible: Thomas Paine (1737–1809) had written, 'The last cord is now broken, the people of England are presenting addresses against us' in his pamphlet *Common Sense* (January 1776) which sold widely throughout the American colonies. Paine was an Englishman, an excise officer dismissed from employment in Lewes, Sussex, for leading a movement for an increase in pay. He emigrated to America in 1774 and became editor of the *Pennsylvania Gazette*. From 1776 to 1783 he published the *American Crisis* pamphlets, encouraging resistance to England. In 1777 he became secretary to the Congressional committee

on foreign affairs. He accompanied Colonel John Laurens on a successful mission to France to obtain financial aid for the Americans, and later served with the American army. (For Paine's subsequent career, *see* Letter to Unknown, n.9.)

13 Lord Howe ... General Howe: the British naval and army commanders-in-chief in North America in 1777 were two brothers, Richard Howe, 1st Earl Howe (1726–99) and Sir William Howe (1729–1814). At their own request, they were also appointed peace commissioners, but their discretionary powers were strictly limited. Having taken New York, the brothers issued a proclamation of conciliation on 30 November 1776.

14 Mr. Tryon (William Tryon, 1729–88): British soldier, colonial administrator. Governor of Province of North Carolina (1765–71) and New York (1771–80).

15 massacre at Amboyna (1623): ten English, ten Japanese and one Portuguese were executed by the Dutch authorities, who believed them guilty of plotting to kill the local Dutch Governor in the power struggle between the British and Dutch East India Companies over the Spice Islands (Amboyna is now Ambon, Indonesia).

16 high-commission court and the star-chamber: prerogative courts, source of considerable tension between Parliament, Church and Crown during Charles I's personal rule. The latter, the temporal counterpart to the High Commission Court (which practised a union of Church and civil law), was a conciliar court presided over by members of the King's council, judges and lords spiritual, and (unlike the procedure of Common Law) operated on the principle that the accused was guilty until innocence was proven.

17 convocation of the clergy: thought to originate in the seventh century this body later became in effect a parliament in which ecclesiastical matters were deliberated and the clergy settled their own taxation for the royal exchequer. There were in fact two convocations, one at Canterbury and one at York, but the former had become more important. After the fourteenth century both assemblies were divided into an upper and lower house. Their powers had been restricted by Henry VIII but they had exercised considerable influence on the Reformation settlement. The convocations lost their right to determine clerical taxation shortly after the Restoration. Tensions had run high between the upper and lower houses during Queen Anne's reign, the latter being generally Tory and high church, the former predominantly Whig with some sympathy for the views of Protestant dissenters. These tensions came to a head in the Bangorian theological controversy of 1716–17 which resulted in George I proroguing the convocations. Until the mid-nineteenth century they met to conduct formal business only at the beginning of each Parliament.

18 Cutchery court (India): public administrative or judicial office.

19 that man and his excellent associates ... 1766: the Marquis of Rockingham (*see* Inscription on the Tomb of Lord Rockingham (16)) and the Rockingham party who secured the repeal of the Stamp Act in March 1766.

20 I was one of those ... respected its honour: Burke refers to his support of the Declaratory Act which accompanied the repeal of the Stamp Act, and asserted Britain's right in principle to tax the colonies.

21 the Saviles ... the Saunderses: all associated with the Rockingham group. Sir George Savile (1726–84), MP for Yorkshire, was a friend of Rockingham though had declined to join his administration, preferring to maintain his independence; William Dowdeswell (1721–75), the group's leader in the Commons and Chancellor of the Exchequer 1765–66; Charles Watson Wentworth, 2nd Marquis of Rockingham (1730–82), party leader (*see* Inscription on the Tomb of Lord Rockingham (16)); William Henry Cavendish Bentinck, 3rd Duke of Portland (1738–1809); Charles Lennox, 3rd Duke of Richmond (*see* Letter to the Duke of Richmond, n.1); George Montagu, 4th Duke of Manchester (1737–88) – more closely associated with Chatham than Rockingham but none the less on good terms with the latter; George Keppel, 3rd Earl Albemarle (*see* Letter to the Duke of Richmond, n.14) and his brother, Augustus Keppel, 1st Viscount Keppel (*see* Letter to a Noble Lord (29), n.52); Sir Charles Saunders (*c.* 1713–75).

22 House of Cavendish: Lord John Cavendish (1732–96) who led the Rockingham group in the Commons after the death of Dowdeswell; his two older brothers Lord Frederick (1729–1803) and Lord George Augustus (1727–94); their cousins Lord George Augustus Henry (1754–1834) and Lord Richard (1752–81) – all of whom sat in the House of Commons – and their nephew William, 5th Duke of Devonshire (1748–1811).

23 *Titius and Mœvius*: i.e. John Doe and Richard Roe, *see* Reflections on the Revolution in France (20), n.184.

SPEECH ON ECONOMICAL REFORM (11)

[*Full title*: *Speech of Edmund Burke Esq., Member of Parliament for the City of Bristol, on Presenting to the House of Commons (on the 11th of February, 1780,) a Plan for the better Security of the Independence of Parliament and the Oeconomical Reformation of the Civil and Other Establishments*]

1 Pyrrhus (319–272 BC): King of Hellenistic Epirus. His successful (but costly) military campaigns against the Romans and Macedonians gave the world the phrase 'Pyrrhic victory'.

2 The noble lord in the blue riband: Lord North. *See* On Conciliation with America (9), n.2.

3 Neckar (Jacques Necker, 1732–1804): *see* Reflections on the Revolution in France (20), n.110.

4 "*before any new burthens ... public money*": from the petition drawn up by the Yorkshire Association, presented to the House of Commons in February 1780. The Association or petitioning movement had begun in late 1779 when a Yorkshire clergyman, Christopher Wyvill, rallied the county gentry to call for reform. It had quickly spread across the country, and a central committee was established in London. Initially the demands were for 'economical reform' – reductions in government spending, and limitations on Crown patronage – which the Rockingham group were happy to support – and increased representation for the counties in the House of Commons. However, the movement was soon to take on a more radical agenda which they viewed with some alarm.

5 Thomas Gilbert (*c.* 1719–98): English land agent, early advocate of poor relief, Member of Parliament for Newcastle-under-Lyme (1763–68) and for Lichfield (1768–95).

6 John Probert: appointed by the Treasury in 1778 to improve Wales's revenue, he was asked to desist following protests.

7 King Edward, and the massacre of the bards: Edward I of England executed a number of bards following their failure to sing his praises during a banquet at Montgomery Castle in 1277. The incident is the subject of a poem by Thomas Gray.

8 Hanse towns: confederation of merchant guilds and their respective market towns formed for commercial and defensive purposes. Stretching from the North Sea to the Baltic, the Hanseatic League dominated trade in that area from the thirteenth to the seventeenth century.

9 Edward the Black Prince (1330–76): son of Edward III of England and Philippa of Hainault, father of Richard II, famous for his victories against the French in the Hundred Years' War. He became Prince of Wales in 1343, but died (probably of amoebic dysentery contracted on one of his many military campaigns) before inheriting the throne.

10 *sibi et heredibus suis regibus Angliæ*: to himself and his heirs from the Kings of England.

11 *Duke Humphrey*: Duke Humphrey's Walk, in Old St Paul's, was a gathering place for the indigent gentry, giving rise to the phrase 'to dine with Duke Humphrey' (to go without dinner).

12 *par multis regnis*: equal to many kingdoms.

13 Cromwell: Thomas Cromwell (?1485–1540), chief minister to Henry VIII from 1533, was closely involved in the dissolution of the monasteries and was also responsible for large-scale reform and centralization of government administration. Henry created him 1st Earl of Essex just three months before ordering his execution.

14 *two chief justices in Eyre*: wardens of the forest, the highest magistrates in medieval forest law (*eyre* [circuit] points to the practice of moving the relevant court between various royal forests). There were two justices, *citra* (on the same side of) and *ultra* (across) the Trent, referring to the location of the royal court.

15 "Boreas, and Eurus, and Canrus, and Argestes loud": John Milton, *Paradise Lost*.

16 *Old Sarum*: on the site of the original settlement of Salisbury, Old Sarum was an archetypal 'rotten borough', though more rotten than most, later described by *The Times* as a 'large circular mound of earth, surmounted by a smaller mound'. It had an electorate of one (its proprietor) and returned two members to Parliament. Old Sarum was abolished in the Reform Act (1832).

17 Lord Talbot (William Talbot, 1st Earl Talbot, 1710–82): Member of Parliament for Glamorganshire (1734–37), Privy Councillor from 1761.

18 "entire affection scorneth nicer hands": Spenser, *Faerie Queene*.

19 board of Green Cloth: named after the green baize tablecloth that covered

the table at which it sat, a board of officials that audited the Royal House-hold's accounts, oversaw royal travel and made judgments upon offences committed in palace grounds.

20 Summum jus summa injuria: the highest law is the highest wrong, quoted by Cicero (*De Officiis*).

21 *Expedit reipublicæ ut sit finis litium*: the state's interests demand an end to litigation.

22 Lord Holland (Henry Fox, 1st Baron Holland, 1705–74): Member of Parliament from 1735 who amassed a huge fortune as Paymaster General, created Baron Holland in 1763. He was the father of Whig leader Charles James Fox.

23 Lord Somers (John Somers, 1st Baron Somers, 1651–1716): English Whig statesman and jurist, Lord Chancellor under William III. He delivered his most famous judgment in the bankers' case, in which bankers who had lost money in the Great Stop of the Exchequer (1672) sued for its return. The Court of Exchequer Chamber initially found for the bankers, but Somers reversed the judgment on a technicality, a decision itself overturned by the House of Lords in 1700.

24 Townshends (Charles Townshend, 2nd Viscount Townshend, 1674–1738): Whig statesman, Secretary of State for the Northern Department 1714–16, 1721–30.

25 Duke of Newcastle (Henry Pelham Clinton, 2nd Duke of Newcastle, 1720–94): second son of the 7th Earl of Lincoln, he was also nephew of the 1st Duke of Newcastle (*see* Thoughts on the Present Discontents (6), n.19), who became his guardian, made him his heir and bestowed upon him lucrative sinecures including Controller of Customs for the port of London and Auditor of the Exchequer, which he held for the rest of his life.

26 *Atlas*: Greek mythological figure, a Titan holding up the celestial spheres.

27 manufacturer of administrations: Lord Bute, *see* Thoughts on the Present Discontents (6), nn.13, 24.

28 Earl of Suffolk (Henry Howard, 12th Earl of Suffolk, 1739–79): Secretary of State for the Northern Department, 1771–79.

29 Lord Weymouth (Thomas Thynne, Viscount Weymouth, 1734–96): Secretary of State for the Southern Department, 1768–70, 1775–79 and of the Northern Department briefly in 1768 and 1779.

30 *Nil horum*: none of these.

31 new-year's ode: honours (such as the 'Georges, and Thistles, and medals' Burke mentions above) were bestowed on their recipients on New Year's Eve.

32 Bacon (Francis Bacon, 1st Viscount St Alban, 1561–1626): English philosopher, statesman, author and scientist (regarded as the father of empiricism), created Baron of Verulam in 1618.

33 W. Dowdeswell: *see* Letter to the Sheriffs of Bristol (10), n.21. He was a close friend of Burke, who composed his epitaph on his death in 1775.

34 Lord Shelburne's motion: on 15 December 1779, Lord Shelburne moved two resolutions, each advocating governmental economy. See *Parliamentary History*, xx, pp. 1285–93.

SPEECH ON A BILL FOR SHORTENING THE DURATION OF PARLIAMENTS (12)

[Speech delivered in opposition to a motion made on 8 May 1780 by John Sawbridge (*see also* Letter to the Duke of Richmond, nn.3, 4) for leave to introduce a bill. The motion was, as usual, defeated, but the debate was unusually animated and the final result was 90 votes in favour and 182 against.]

1 on which there are three opinions: favouring septennial (as established by the Septennial Act of 1716), triennial, or annual parliaments. Burke's opposition to this motion underlined the split in the Rockingham group at the time of the Association movement: Lord John Cavendish and Charles James Fox were amongst those who supported it. Rockingham himself had indicated that he would be prepared to support triennial though opposing annual parliaments. Burke's position on this subject did not endear him to the radical electorate in Bristol.

2 *Multum in Fabiâ ... curule*: 'This rules the Fabian, that the Veline clan; / Just as he likes, he seats or ousts his man' (Horace, *Epistles*, trans. John Conington).

3 the peace of Utrecht (April 1713–September 1714): the treaties between European powers concluding the War of Spanish Succession (1701–14). France recognized Queen Anne and undertook to stop supporting the claims of James Edward, the deposed James II's son. Newfoundland, Nova Scotia, the Hudson Bay Territory and St Kitts were ceded to Britain. Spain ceded Gibraltar and Minorca to Britain, having also (courtesy of the *assiento* agreement) granted her the right to supply Spanish colonies with slaves for the next thirty years. The peace was masterminded by Bolingbroke (*see* A Vindication of Natural Society (1), n.2) and condemned by Whigs as being far too favourable to France.

4 The Protestant succession (to the throne): secured by the Act of Settlement (1701), which strengthened both parliamentary government, and the Bill of Rights (1689), which had already guaranteed the succession rights of Mary's heirs. The majority of Tories supported the Hanoverian succession in 1714 but rumours of Bolingbroke's involvement in a Jacobite plot were happily spread by Whigs.

5 Sir W. Musgrave: error of initial in MS – Burke is referring to Sir Christopher Musgrave (*c.* 1632–1704), an MP from 1661 to his death (*see also* n.6 below).

6 Bishop Burnet (Gilbert Burnet, 1643–1715): Scottish theologian, historian and Bishop of Salisbury, associated with the Whig party. In his *History of His Own Times*, Burnet claims that Sir Christopher Musgrave (*see* n.5 above) accepted bribes totalling £12,000 in return for parliamentary influence.

7 the great plague at Athens: epidemic that devastated the city-state (and much of the eastern Mediterranean) during the Peloponnesian War (430 BC), returning the following year and during the winter of 427/426 BC.

8 the plague of London (1665): so-called 'Great Plague' caused by insanitary conditions in the Stuart capital, which enabled rats (and their disease-carrying fleas) to prosper. The Great Fire of London (1666) stopped the disease in its tracks by destroying the city slums that had hosted it.

9 Acheron: 'river of woe', one of the five rivers of the Greek underworld, across which Charon would ferry the recently dead. A son of Helios and Gaia (or Demeter), Acheron was transformed into the river as a punishment for giving the Titans revitalizing refreshment during their dispute with Zeus.

10 Ixion: pardoned for kin-slaying (he killed his father-in-law) and brought to Olympus by Zeus, Ixion abused this leniency by lusting after Zeus's wife, Hera, coupling with a cloud in her shape and producing the Centaurs. As punishment, he was blasted with a thunderbolt and bound to a spinning solar wheel for all eternity.

SKETCH OF THE NEGRO CODE (13)

[Full title: *A Letter to the Right Honourable Henry Dundas, one of his Majesty's principal Secretaries of State. With the Sketch of a Negro Code*]

1 NEGRO CODE: Burke sent his 'Negro Code' on request to Henry Dundas (1742–1811), Home Secretary and close political confidant of Pitt the Younger, on 9 April 1792. Just one week before this, on 2 April, William Wilberforce (*see* Speech on the Slave Trade (19), nn.1, 2) had introduced his second motion to abolish the slave trade. A heated debate ensued (in which both Pitt and Fox argued for abolition) and Dundas had proposed adding the word 'gradual' to the motion, 'as a moderate and middle way of proceeding'. This was adopted and the amended motion then passed by 230 votes to 85. A date of 1 January 1796 was settled upon for achieving complete abolition. However, on 5 June the Lords, who had begun the process of examining the subject in committee, voted for postponement, and a year later declined to fix a date for 'gradual abolition'.

2 near twelve years ago: Burke's 'code' had not seen the light of day since he drew it up in 1780 – either while, or just after, he was MP for Bristol, an important slave-trading port. He was the first statesman to elaborate a plan for the ending of the slave trade, and it was before its time: the popular movement against the slave trade did not begin until after the formation of the Society for Effecting the Abolition of the Slave Trade in 1787 (*see* n.4 below). However, Burke was not entirely alone. The Quakers had been quietly condemning slavery for some decades; civil servant Granville Sharp had begun his challenge to the legality of slavery in England, and had won a qualified but significant victory in the James Somerset case (1772) – approved in the pages of Burke's *Annual Register*. Sharp, who was the first chairman of the Abolition Society, published the first British tract against slavery in 1769; in 1774 John Wesley added his voice to the protest. However, the abolitionist literature of this period received little publicity.

3 marginal heads: these are omitted, as Burke's original headings have been lost.

4 carried it through: between 1787 and 1794 Thomas Clarkson of the Abolition Society travelled about the country in an ambitious project to gather

detailed evidence against the slave trade, particularly from the major slave-trading ports of Liverpool and Bristol. This was fed to Wilberforce for his parliamentary campaign, laid before a committee of the Privy Council established in 1788 to investigate 'the present state of the African trade', and later published. The Abolition Society also publicized their campaign throughout the British Isles via a network of local committees. Lectures were held, pamphlets circulated, fliers and merchandise produced carrying the symbol (designed at Josiah Wedgwood's pottery) of a kneeling slave in chains and the words 'Am I not a man and a brother'. They also initiated a popular petitioning movement in 1788 and again in 1792 when the 519 petitions received by the House of Commons was the largest number ever presented on a single subject in one session.

5 *Hic labor, hoc opus*: 'This is the labour, this is the work' (Virgil, *Aeneid*).

6 *Horatian* keeping: in his *Ars Poetica* Horace recommends a nine-year gap between composition and publication to give a writer ample time to reflect and revise.

7 the African Company: after 1750 the slave trade was mainly handled by the 'Company of Merchants Trading to Africa', successors to Charles II's Royal Africa Company. The latter had been confined to London merchants, but the new company was opened up to merchants from Liverpool and Bristol. It continued to receive a grant from the government for maintaining forts on the Gold Coast to protect its interests against French and Dutch competitors.

FIRST SPEECH ON THE SEIZURE AND CONFISCATION OF PRIVATE PROPERTY IN THE ISLAND OF ST. EUSTATIUS (14)

1 ST. EUSTATIUS: The West Indian island of St Eustatius had been colonized by the Dutch in 1636. During the seventeenth century it changed hands several times but by the 1680s the Dutch West India Company had secured control. Its geographical position amongst a multinational cluster of islands – English, French, Spanish and Danish – and a harbour which could accommodate 200 ships, had made St Eustatius, nicknamed 'the golden rock', a perfect hub for commerce; its status as a free port (it had abolished customs duties in 1756) coupled with Dutch neutrality during the Seven Years' War had vastly increased its prosperity. In defiance of the British Navigation Acts, it had become the principal depot for the transshipment of goods to and from America, and although the Dutch government had placed an embargo on contraband in 1775, the merchants of St Eustatius were at this time engaged in the lucrative if dangerous business of shipping military supplies to the American colonists. British merchants also used the island for the same purpose.

2 the Manifesto: on 20 December 1780 the prime minister Lord North had sent Sir Joseph Yorke (1724–92), former general and British Ambassador in The Hague since 1751, a Manifesto severing diplomatic relations with the United Provinces. It listed five reasons for the ensuing war (the fourth Anglo-Dutch War, 1780–84), one of which was the discovery that the authorities in Amsterdam had made a secret treaty with the Americans (currently fighting for their independence against Britain), another that Dutch traders were providing the rebels with war supplies. (Equally important, if

not mentioned, was the fact that the United Provinces had just joined the League of Armed Neutrality, sponsored by Catherine the Great of Russia, which Britain regarded as tantamount to a declaration of war.)

3   a hurricane: the Great Hurricane of 9–20 October 1780 remains the deadliest Atlantic hurricane of all time, killing an estimated 23,000 people in the West Indies. British and French ships contesting for control of the region during the American War of Independence suffered heavy losses.

4   Dr Franklin: writing from Paris, where he successfully represented American interests between 1776 and 1785, Benjamin Franklin (1706–90, printer, author, inventor, scientist and philanthropist, and one of the founding fathers of the United States) responded in February 1781 to a request for assistance from the citizens of Dublin, by ordering American armed ships to allow vessels carrying relief supplies to the West Indies to pass unmolested, 'as the principles of common humanity require'.

5   *lusus naturæ*: a freak of nature.

6   Tyre: Phoenician city which became centre of the commerce of the ancient world. Tyre is today a major port in Lebanon.

7   United States: that is, the United Provinces (Dutch Republic).

8   the Jews: the first Sephardic Jews had settled on St Eustatius in 1660, in flight from the Spanish invasion of Brazil. The community had grown, and was joined by Ashkenazic Jews. In 1730 they had gained equal rights with gentiles, to vote, hold office and engage in commerce. They were free to practise their religion, and dispensation to build a synagogue was granted in 1737. In the years 1760–80 they had grown in prosperity. The mercantile community was divided between those who engaged in trade with the American colonists and those who refused. Although the Jews slowly re-established themselves after the war, most of them left when the island was under French control (1795–1816) when taxes on merchants were punitively high, and of those remaining the last died in 1846.

9   sir William Howe (1729–1814): British Commander-in-Chief in North America, 1775–78.

10 St. Christopher's Gazette: newspaper published on the island of St Kitts (St Christopher's), five miles south-east of St Eustatius and the closest island in British hands, between 1747 and 1908.

11 sir George Rodney (1718–92): admiral who had made a name for himself in the Seven Years' War, notably commanding naval operations at the capture of Martinique in 1762. During the American War of Independence he had successfully relieved Gibraltar (under siege by the French and Spanish 1779–83) after defeating the Spanish fleet at the battle of Cape St Vincent. On the outbreak of war with the Dutch Republic (but before news of the war had reached St Eustatius) he was ordered to seize the island, which had been acting as a base for supplying the American revolutionaries. This he achieved, in conjunction with General Vaughan, with minimal bloodshed, in February 1781. The diversion in St Eustatius, with all its opportunities for plunder, delayed their providing support to beleaguered British forces in North America. Rodney's morale-boosting victory against the French at the battle of the Saintes in 1782, however, made him a national hero. He was rewarded with a peerage and a pension, and spent his last ten years in retirement.

12 the Grenada Act, the Tobacco Act, and the Cotton Act: three Acts passed in 1780. Grenada was taken by British troops in 1762 during the Seven Years' War and ceded to Britain at the Treaty of Paris the following year. It was in French hands from 1779 and was returned to Britain by the Treaty of Paris in 1783. The Grenada Act was passed to protect Grenadian exports carried in neutral vessels to neutral ports. The Tobacco Act gave permission for tobacco to be imported into Britain (with duties attached) from places other than its country of origin (this sort of trade flourished in St Eustatius), for the duration of the war; the Cotton Act permitted the import of cotton from places other than the Levant and India (cotton was just beginning to take off in the West Indies).

13 lord Beauchamp: Francis Ingram-Seymour-Conway, Viscount Beauchamp, was the eldest son of the 1st Earl of Hertford (*see* Letter to Charles James Fox, n.11) and nephew of General Conway (*see* Letter to the Duke of Richmond, n.12). He was Secretary to Ireland when his father was Lord Lieutenant (1765–66) during the Rockingham administration. He was a Lord of the Treasury under Lord North from 1774 and Cofferer of the Household 1780–82.

14 sir Grey Cooper (*c.* 1726–1801): a successful lawyer, he had been appointed Secretary to the Treasury by Rockingham in 1765 and found a seat in Parliament. He remained at the Treasury under successive premierships until the fall of Lord North in 1782.

15 Vattel (Emer de Vattel, 1714–67): Swiss legal expert and political philosopher, author of the influential *The Law of Nations* (1758). His theories laid some of the foundations of modern international law.

16 count D'Estaing (Charles Hector, comte d'Estaing, 1729–94): French general and admiral. He captured Grenada from the British in July 1779.

17 her cause in the Baltic: the League of Armed Neutrality (1780) had been initiated by the Baltic states – Russia, Sweden and Denmark – and effectively excluded the Royal Navy from the Baltic. After some diplomatic manoeuvring to ensure the safety of British merchant shipping (essential naval stores were obtained from the Baltic) Britain had no problem in accepting this. However, outside the Baltic British ships continued to search and arrest the convoys of neutral states for 'contraband', ignoring their armed escorts, though possibly a little more circumspectly than before.

18 sir Samuel Hood (later 1st Viscount Hood, 1724–1816): British admiral acting as second-in-command to Rodney in the West Indies. The two did not always see eye to eye. He was Commander-in-Chief of the Mediterranean Fleet 1793–94.

19 the Caribbees: British military and naval forces had been mobilized against the Black Caribs on St Vincent's in 1772. Orders to pursue this policy of coercion had come via Lord Hillsborough (1718–93), Secretary of State for the Colonies at the time (later Secretary of State for the Southern Department 1779–82). The Caribs feared deportation or even extirpation, and sent to the French islands for help. The subsequent war ended in stalemate in 1773.

20 he therefore moved ... West Indies: Burke's motion calling for an enquiry was defeated by 160 votes to 86. Rodney returned briefly to England and

when on 4 December 1781 Burke renewed his call for an enquiry, personally replied to his accusations. Again the motion was defeated and the Admiral returned to the West Indies. By this time St Eustatius had already been retaken by the French. Burke made a final impassioned appeal against Rodney in February 1782, but the government remained unmoved. The new Rockingham administration recalled Rodney in March, but, before receiving this instruction, the admiral had won his decisive victory at the battle of the Saintes (9–12 April). In the circumstances Burke announced (30 May) that he would not be pursuing the matter of an enquiry unless requested by the House. When the French retook St Eustatius in November 1781 they restored property in so far as they were able. The British government was obliged to compensate French merchants operating there. The island was returned to the Dutch in 1784 and had regained its former prosperity by 1790. Rodney faced lawsuits from British merchants for the rest of his life, some of them hugely successful. Much of his loot had never reached England; of the 34 merchant ships carrying it home, 22 were seized by a French squadron in June 1781.

SPEECH ON FOX'S EAST-INDIA BILL (15)

[Full title: *Mr. Burke's Speech, On the 1st December 1783, upon the Question for the Speaker's leaving the Chair, in order for the House to resolve itself into a committee on Mr. Fox's East-India Bill*]

1 FOX'S EAST-INDIA BILL: Charles James Fox (1749–1806) had entered Parliament in 1768 at the age of just nineteen. Rich and well-connected, he was known for his dissolute lifestyle, but he had considerable personal charisma and was a formidable debater in the House; in spite of differences of age and character, he and Burke became close friends. Fox was Britain's first Foreign Secretary during Rockingham's second administration (March–July 1782), and took over the leadership of the party after Rockingham's death, refusing, like Burke, to serve under Shelburne. He returned as Foreign Secretary in a much criticized and short-lived coalition with his former opponent Lord North (April–December 1783). He was heartily disliked by George III, not least because he was a favourite drinking companion of the Prince of Wales. (For Fox's later career, *see* Speech on War with France (26), n.2.)

2 *quo warranto* (Latin: by what warrant?): prerogative writ to ensure that warrant-holders are acting with due authority. The City of London had lost its charter by a writ of *Quo Warranto* in 1683.

3 *mandamus* (Latin: we command): writ from superior jurisdiction to inferior tribunal or corporation or individual governing the performance (or non-performance) of an act the performance (or non-performance) of which is legally obligatory.

4 *certiorari* (Latin: to be informed of/made certain in regard to): original writ (from Chancery or King's Bench) obliging officers of inferior courts to submit a pending case's records in order to ensure speedy and certain justice.

5 secretary of state for the home department: Lord North. The Fox-North coalition was formed in April 1783, with the Duke of Portland as First Lord of the Treasury. Burke was Paymaster General.

6 Mr. Powis: Thomas Powys (1748–1800), an independent MP who had

been the first to attack the bill. It was, he said, founded upon the 'old system of prerogative' which had characterized the previous government of Lord North, that 'champion of influence', notwithstanding that it had been introduced by Fox, 'the man of the people'. 'Its voice was indeed the voice of Jacob, but its hands were those of Esau.' (*Parliamentary History*, xxiii, p. 1309.) (In the Book of Genesis Jacob deceived his blind father Isaac into giving him the birthright of his brother Esau by smothering his smooth hands with goat's hair so they would feel like his brother's.)

7 Mr. Pitt: William Pitt led the attack on the East-India Bill in particular and the coalition in general. When the bill – which passed in the Commons – was sent up to the Lords and defeated (the King's wishes being more decisive there), the coalition was dismissed and Pitt was asked to form a government, becoming Britain's youngest prime minister at the age of twenty-four. The younger Pitt (1759–1806), son of William Pitt the Elder, had begun his political career as a Foxite in 1781, but Fox never forgave him for accepting office as Chancellor of the Exchequer under Shelburne (1782–83). Pitt remained prime minister from December 1783 until 1801 and returned again from 1804 to 1806. Fox remained his greatest critic and rival.

8 charters of ... Henry the Third: 'Forest' Charter, limiting size of royal forests, issued in 1217 alongside a new version of Magna Carta (now, for the first time, called this to distinguish between the charters).

9 treaty of Westphalia (1648): endpoint of Thirty Years' War, involving 176 representatives of 196 European rulers. It brought an end to the age of religious wars in Germany, recognizing and enshrining both full territorial sovereignty and mutual religious toleration in the Holy Roman Empire. The 'three religions' referred to are Catholicism, Lutheranism and Calvinism.

10 statute of tallege (1297): granting of certain liberties to his Commons by Edward I. The Petition of Right (1628) prohibited the King (then Charles I) from infringing specific liberties of the subject; the Declaration of Rights (1689), after the Glorious Revolution, was an Act declaring the rights and liberties of the subject and settling the succession of the Crown.

11 Mr. Hastings (Warren Hastings): *See* Speech in Opening the Impeachment of Warren Hastings (18), n.1.

12 Mr. Hornby (William Hornby, 1723–1803): Governor of Bombay, 1771–84.

13 Maratta (Maratha) peace: Treaty of Salbai (1782), bringing first of three Anglo-Maratha wars (between the British East India Company and the Maratha Empire) to a close.

14 Henry the Fourth of France: Fox was descended from Charles II through his mother, Georgiana Lennox; Charles II's mother, Henrietta Maria, was the daughter of Henri IV of France.

15 *Indole proh quanta juvenis ... linguæ*: 'How noble was his youthful promise! and how great the immortal descendant he was to give to Italy! That voice shall fill the earth and be heard beyond the Ganges and the peoples of India; with the thunders of his tongue shall he quell the frenzy of war' (Silius Italicus, *Punica*).

INSCRIPTION ON THE TOMB OF LORD ROCKINGHAM (16)

1 Charles Watson-Wentworth, 2nd Marquis of Rockingham, was an exact contemporary of Burke, born in 1730 at the family seat of Wentworth Woodhouse in Yorkshire. He was educated at Westminster School. His father, a court Whig, was elevated to the peerage in 1746, and his son inherited the title in 1750, together with extensive lands in Yorkshire, Nottinghamshire and Ireland which brought him considerable electoral influence. Already rich, he married the heiress Mary Bright in 1752, and became one of the wealthiest men in the country. He was an exemplary landowner and employer. In the House of Lords he was first associated with the Duke of Newcastle and lost his post as Lord of the Bedchamber and his Lord Lieutenancies in the 'purge' of the Duke's supporters in 1762. After opposing first Bute and then Grenville he was asked to form a ministry in 1765 which notably repealed Grenville's hated Stamp Act. When it fell in 1766 he led his group of around fifty into opposition, and, though plagued by ill-health and distracted by a fondness for racing and gambling, continued to inspire their loyalty. A retiring man and no great debater he none the less spoke out often against Lord North's colonial policy, supported the removal of civil disabilities on both dissenters and Catholics, and was a strong advocate of economic reform. Returning briefly to the premiership in 1782 he was able to secure an element of the latter as well as legislative independence for Ireland. He had employed Burke as his private secretary in 1765 and was a generous patron, making him loans, offering pocket boroughs when required, and annulling his debts shortly before his untimely death in July 1782. Rockingham had no children. The monument at Wentworth Woodhouse—both a cenotaph and a Temple of Friendship—was commissioned by his nephew and heir, Earl Fitzwilliam, and built by John Carr of York.

SPEECH ON THE REFORM OF THE REPRESENTATION OF THE COMMONS IN PARLIAMENT (17)

[Full title: *Speech on a Motion in the House of Commons for a Committee to Inquire into the State of the Representation of the Commons in Parliament*. The speech has been dated to 16 June 1784.]

1 in *forma pauperis*: in the character of a pauper, a legal phrase referring to the court's permission to a pauper to enter into a legal action without incurring court fees or costs.

2 one *third* only of the legislature: the Crown, the House of Lords and the House of Commons together made up the tripartite legislature.

3 Prescription ... Government: entitlement to own property based on a long and uncontested possession of it.

4 *Neque decipitur ratio, neque decipit unquam*: as none deceiving, so of none deceived (Walter Harte, *An Essay on Reason*).

5 ★★★: (and elsewhere) indicates blank space in first published version (the 10-vol. edition of Burke's *Works* published by his literary executors).

6 receipt tax ... Mr Fox's ambition: a tax on receipts for payments had been introduced in the May 1783 budget by Lord John Cavendish, Chancellor

of the Exchequer in the Fox-North coalition of that year. Stamps to the value of 2d were required for payments between £2.00 and £20.00; 4d for higher amounts. The tax had met with vigorous opposition from the commercial and manufacturing interests throughout the country, notably in Yorkshire, centre of the Rockingham interest, for which Cavendish was one of the two county MPs. Fox's East-India Bill had likewise proved deeply unpopular. A county meeting was called at which Wyvill's reformers (*see* Speech on Economical Reform (11) n.4) combined with Pittites and Tories to approve an Address to the Throne in March 1784 denouncing Fox's 'late attempt to seize the property and violate the chartered rights of the East India Company' as an act of unconstitutional ambition (*see also* Speech on Fox's East-India Bill (15)). Unsurprisingly not just Cavendish but all four candidates put forward by Fitzwilliam (Rockingham's nephew and heir) in both York and Yorkshire lost their seats in the general election of April 1784 which gave popular endorsement to Pitt the Younger's premiership.

7 statical chair: a machine to measure perspiration designed by the Italian physician Sanctorius (1561–1636).

8 associations: these had been set up during the petitioning movement (*see* Speech on Economical Reform (11) n.4).

SPEECH IN OPENING THE IMPEACHMENT OF WARREN HASTINGS (18)

1 Mr. Hastings (Warren Hastings, 1732–1818): first Governor-General of Bengal. Warren Hastings had made his career in the East India Company, first arriving in Bengal in 1750 as a teenager and rising through the ranks over thirty-five years. He was appointed Governor-General in 1773. Hastings had received a classical education and was a cultured man with a genuine interest in Indian civilization. He initiated successful reforms but wielded an enormous amount of personal power which he used to manipulate Indian rulers to the Company's advantage, making more money than his official allowances in the process. He had proved particularly successful in a series of wars and the India he left in 1785 was peaceful with British dominions intact. Accused of corruption he was impeached in 1787, with Burke playing a leading role. The trial dragged on for seven years and ended in his acquittal. Hastings received financial compensation from the East India Company and lived the rest of his life in retirement.

2 Lord Macclesfield (Thomas Parker, 1st Earl of Macclesfield, 1666–1732): Whig politician, Lord Chief Justice (1710–18), Lord Chancellor (1718–25). Disgraced in 1725, impeached, tried in the House of Lords and convicted of corruption (he received more than £100,000 – over £11 million in today's money – in bribes), he saw his wealth confiscated and died at Shirburn Castle, Oxfordshire.

3 Dey of Algiers: title applied to the governor of Algiers prior to the French conquest (1830). The (French) word is derived from the Turkish for maternal uncle, or protector.

4 Dr. Shawe (Thomas Shaw, 1694–1751): English cleric, traveller. This quotation is from his 1757 work *Travels or Observations relating to several parts of Barbary and the Levant*.

5 19 FEBRUARY 1788: Burke's speech at Westminster Hall was delivered over four days (the court did not meet on the 17th, which was a Sunday).

6 Gunga Govin Sing (Ganga Govind Singh [Ganga Gobinda Sinha], *fl.* 1750–95): Warren Hastings's revenue administrator in Bengal. Founded influential family in nineteenth-century Bengal courtesy of the huge fortune he amassed in the process.

7 Rajahs Kelleram and Cullian Sing: tax farmers in the province of Bahar, Sing the Dewan to the Patna Council, Kelleram his Naib (deputy).

8 a minor Rajah ... Debi Sing: the Rajah of Dinajpur, a minor, had his large agricultural estate (Zemindary) granted to Debi Sing, who managed Dinajpur, Rangpur and Idrakpur (the 'three great provinces' Burke mentions below).

SPEECH ON THE SLAVE TRADE (19)

1 committee: on 12 May 1789 the report of the Privy Council committee set up the previous year to examine the slave trade was presented to the House of Commons. The papers were referred to a Committee of the Whole House, before which Wilberforce (*see* n.2 below) made a powerful speech calling for abolition and moved twelve resolutions condemning the trade. Resistance from the planters' lobby was strong. It was agreed that evidence should be heard both for and against the slave trade, and when Wilberforce's motion to ban it was finally put to the vote in April 1791 it was defeated by 163 votes to 88.

2 the hon. gentleman: William Wilberforce (1759–1833), English politician and philanthropist. He was a friend of Pitt the Younger whom he met at Cambridge. Both men entered the House of Commons in the same year, Wilberforce representing Hull (1780–84) and then Yorkshire (1784–1812). After becoming an evangelical Christian in 1785, he was persuaded to carry into Parliament the campaign for the abolition of the slave trade – a campaign that would not succeed until 1807. He was an early member of the Society for Effecting the Abolition of the Slave Trade (*see* Sketch of the Negro Code (13), n.4) and later became a prominent figure in the Clapham sect, an influential group of well-to-do Anglicans who in addition to supporting the abolition movement promoted missionary work at home and abroad and espoused such causes as prison and factory reform. He died just three days after being assured of the passage through Parliament of the Slavery Abolition Act 1833, which prohibited slavery in most of the British Empire.

3 Demosthenes (384–322 BC): statesman and celebrated orator in ancient Athens.

4 admiral Barrington (Admiral Samuel Barrington, 1729–1800): British admiral who served in the West Indies in 1778, taking Saint Lucia from the French. Son of the 1st Viscount Barrington and brother of Daines Barrington (*see* Speech on Economical Reform (11), n.18).

5 Mr. Glover: *see* Speech on Conciliation with America (9), n.3.

REFLECTIONS ON THE REVOLUTION IN FRANCE (20)

[Full title: *Reflections on the Revolution in France, and on the Proceedings in Certain Societies in London Relative to that Event. In a Letter Intended to have been sent to a Gentleman in Paris. By the Right Honourable Edmund Burke*]

1 a very young gentleman at Paris (Charles-Jean-François Depont, 1767–96): Depont had been a guest at Gregories in September 1785, accompanying his father Jean, a magistrate from Metz, who had been recommended to Burke by the writer and educational theorist Madame de Genlis. The young man wrote to Burke enthusiastically on 4 November about the Revolution, soliciting his views. It was to Charles that his *Reflections on the Revolution in France* was later addressed.

2 the Constitutional Society, and the Revolution Society: the Constitutional Society, founded by John Horne (Tooke) in 1771, reconstituted as the Society for Constitutional Information (1780) and newly active from 1791. Many Whig noblemen were members. The Revolution Society was founded in 1788 on the centenary of the 1688 Revolution. Its chairman at this time was Charles Stanhope (*see* n.5, below). Both organizations promoted parliamentary reform.

3 the National Assembly of France: later the Constituent Assembly, the first of the revolutionary parliaments in France. Having framed a new Constitution it dissolved itself on 30 September 1791 and was superseded by the Legislative Assembly.

4 Dr. Price ... Duke de Rochefaucault ... Archbishop of Aix: Richard Price (1723–91) was a radical and dissenting minister who wrote largely on ethical and economical questions. He vigorously opposed the war with America and was a close friend of Benjamin Franklin. Price had moved a congratulatory Address to the National Assembly at the Revolution Society on 4 November 1789. This was presented to the National Assembly by Louis-Alexandre, duc de La Rochefoucauld-d'Anville (1743–92), a leading French liberal, who would later be killed during the September Massacres in Gisors. Jean de Dieu-Raymond de Boisgelin de Cucé (1732–1804), Archbishop of Aix, replied to the Address on behalf of the National Assembly.

5 Earl Stanhope (Charles, 3rd Earl Stanhope, 1753–1816): brother-in-law of Pitt the Younger, who first entered Parliament in the interest of Lord Shelburne and whose radical politics later earned him the nickname of 'Citizen Stanhope'. In 1790 he wrote a reply to Burke's *Reflections*. He was also a scientist of some note.

6 *philippises*: to 'philippize' is to speak in support of a cause as the result of corrupt influence. Demosthenes (384–322 BC) claimed that the Delphic Oracle gave prophecies biased in favour of Philip of Macedon.

7 Rev. Hugh Peters (1598–1660): independent minister and republican who returned from America to join the English Civil War. He preached regularly at Whitehall during the Protectorate. He was executed as a regicide after the Restoration in 1660.

8 your league: the Catholic League (1576), an aristocratic alliance formed by the duc de Guise in the French Wars of Religion for the suppression of Protestantism. The Solemn League and Covenant (1643) between the

English Parliament and the Scots Presbyterians guaranteed Presbyterianism in Scotland (in return for assistance against Charles I).

9 reverend lay-divine: the Duke of Grafton (*see* Letter to the Duke of Richmond, n.11), former prime minister, was Chancellor of Cambridge University from 1768, which he managed to combine with being a Unitarian and a member of the Revolution Society. He had written a pamphlet in favour of church reform. Among the other lay-divines of rank was Lord Shelburne, Burke's bugbear, who also favoured Unitarianism.

10 *Seekers*: an informal religious society which developed in the early seventeenth century. Seekers regarded any organized church as corrupt. They had no clergy and held meetings in silence, awaiting divine inspiration. They respected all religions. The movement continued into the eighteenth century, though many of its members joined the Quakers.

11 *hortus siccus*: a dry garden.

12 *Mess-Johns*: an old Scottish term for a priest.

13 "*utinam nugis ... sævitiæ*": 'would that he had spent all that time of violence on trifles' (Juvenal on the Emperor Domitian in his *Satires*).

14 *Condo ... possim*: 'I amass and arrange my stores, so that afterwards I may be able to bring them forth' (Horace, *Epistles*).

15 the Brunswick line: descendants of Sophia, Duchess of Brunswick-Lüneburg (and Electress of Hanover), James I's granddaughter. The line of succession was established by the Act of Settlement (1701).

16 *Declaration of Right*: or Bill of Rights, March 1689.

17 *Privilegium non transit in exemplum*: a maxim of civil law – a special case must not be made a general rule.

18 undoubtedly his: the birth in 1688 of Prince James Edward, James II's son by his second wife, Mary of Modena, displaced the Protestant Princess Mary as heir presumptive; convenient and groundless rumours soon arose that he had been smuggled into the Queen's bedchamber in a warming pan.

19 Lord Somers (John, 1st Baron Somers, 1651–1716): *see* Speech on Economical Reform (11), n.23.

20 *communi sponsione reipublicæ*: the consent of the entire commonwealth.

21 heir *per capita* ... heir *per stirpes*: *per capita* and *per stirpes* (terms borrowed from Roman law), two different schemes for the distribution of an estate among heirs, which Burke indirectly applies to the respective claims to the throne of James II and William of Orange. By the *per capita* ('by head') rule of inheritance James II had the greater claim, being the senior male in the family and closest in relationship to Charles I (second son and only surviving child); indeed, his claim would even have prevailed over that of a legitimate son of Charles II, had there been one. By the rule of *per stirpes* ('by root'), each branch of the family – in this case, all the children of Charles I – possessed an equal claim which passed down through the generations. According to this rule, William, who had no siblings, was the sole representative of his deceased mother, Princess Mary, eldest daughter of Charles I, and inherited in full her right of inheritance, which was equal to her brother James's, in Roman law no distinction being made between males

and females. However, in England since the Norman conquest the rule of male primogeniture had entered into the equation; the Crown had sometimes passed to the male heir *per capita* (King John was the last, *see* p.74) but the male heir *per stirpes* had been declared the indisputable successor of landed estates during the reign of Henry III and the monarchy thereafter descended similarly (though there were notable exceptions – both Henry IV and Henry VII had a more distant claim to the throne than the incumbent they displaced). William's claim *per stirpes* was therefore not as strong as James's as he was descended through the female line. This was recognized by the Revolution settlement, which, though it made them joint monarchs, confirmed that the succession would pass specifically to the heirs of Queen Mary, as James II's oldest daughter, and in the event of there being none, to Mary's sister Anne. However, Burke's point is that while the principle of inheritance can be defined in various ways, it is the principle itself that is important.

22 *multosque ... avorum*: on bees: 'for many a year the fortune of the house stands firm, and grandsires' grandsires swell the pedigree' (Virgil, *Georgics*).

23 statute *de tallagio ... habeas corpus*: these were regarded as important advances in guaranteeing individual liberties. *Tallagio non concedendo* (1297) was a tax on the towns and demesne lands of the Crown which was not to be taken without all consenting to it. Charles I assented to the Petition of Right in 1628; the Habeas Corpus Act of 1679 gave protection from illegal imprisonment.

24 Princess Sophia: Electress of Hanover (1630–1714). She was actually fifty-sixth in line to the throne but the first fifty-five were disqualified as Roman Catholics.

25 "no pardon ... in parliament": this resolved a constitutional problem raised by the impeachment of the Earl of Danby for high treason in 1678. Danby had pleaded the King's pardon (but was committed to the Tower anyway). The Act of Settlement allowed the King to issue a pardon only after conviction, thus upholding the constitutional principle of ministerial responsibility.

26 "*Haec memoratio est quasi exprobatio*": 'This reminder smacks of a reproach.' A steward in Terence's *Andria* resents being reminded of his former slavery.

27 the signet of "the Fisherman": the Pope commonly used the title 'Servus servorum Dei'. As Bishop of Rome he was the successor to St Peter, hence 'The Fisherman'.

28 *Justicia* of Aragon: the Justiciar of the medieval kingdom of Aragon was endowed by the Cortes (a parliament lively in its defence of popular rights) with considerable authority to guard against oppressive rule.

29 "*Justa bella quibus necessaria*": 'Wars are righteous in so far as they are inevitable' (Livy).

30 Magna Charta: the Magna Carta/Charta or 'Great Charter' was a political charter King John was forced to sign by his barons at Runnymede (*see* An Abridgment of the English History (3)) which placed certain limitations on royal power. Although it was often flouted it came to be regarded as a seminal document of English constitutional practice. One of its provisions was that no one should be imprisoned or exiled except by the law of the land.

31 Sir Edward Coke: *see* A Vindication of Natural Society (1), n.4.

32 Blackstone (Sir William Blackstone, 1723–80): legal authority whose *Commentaries on the Laws of England* (1765–69) became a standard text in the eighteenth century. *See* Speech on Conciliation with America (9), n.6.

33 Henry I: his Coronation Charter in 1100 bound him to certain laws in his treatment of nobles and clergy, who had suffered under the oppressive rule of his brother William Rufus. The Magna Carta (*see* n.30, above) is largely based upon it.

34 *Petition of Right*: in 1628 Parliament forced Charles I to agree to a Petition of Right in return for granting him supply (revenue). Their grievances included non-parliamentary taxation, imprisonment without trial, the introduction of martial law in peacetime, and the quartering of soldiers on subjects. Charles prevaricated, only granting the petition by his grace and not 'of right'.

35 Selden (John Selden, 1584–1654): famous jurist and orientalist, legal historian and theologian. He took a leading part in the parliamentary opposition to James I and Charles I and was twice imprisoned.

36 Abbé Sieyes (Emmanuel-Joseph Sieyès, 1748–1836): priest and writer, major contributor to the Constitution of 1791.

37 mortmain: *see* Thoughts on the Present Discontents (6), n.10.

38 your old states: the Estates (or States) General, which had not met between 1614 and 1789 ('suspended before it was perfected'). This national assembly had first met in 1302 and represented the three 'estates' of the realm: clergy, nobility and commoners. It had never been summoned frequently, especially since the French kings levied a permanent tax (the *taille*) which did not require its involvement. From the mid-sixteenth century it had been convoked only in times of crisis. (Provincial estates had been suppressed in the heartlands of France but existed in a number of peripheral provinces, known as the *pays d'états*, where they retained at least the theoretical right to negotiate taxation. The *pays d'états* were more recent additions to the kingdom. Among them were Brittany, Burgundy and Provence, incorporated into France in the fifteenth century, and others such as Artois and Flanders added by Louis XIV's wars.)

39 Maroon slaves: fugitive slaves in the Americas who formed their own colonies (from French, *marron*; Spanish, *cimarron*, 'wild').

40 your parliament of Paris: there were thirteen *parlements* in France in 1789, of which the oldest, the *parlement* of Paris – which evolved during the thirteenth century – was the most important, its jurisdiction covering one-third of the country. Their functions were initially judicial and they came to be run by a hereditary caste of magistrates. Purchase of a seat guaranteed entry into the *noblesse de la robe*, the 'administrative' nobility (*see* n.112, below). One of their functions was to register royal edicts, and by the mid-eighteenth century they were arguing that their consent was required before any edict became law. They began to conceive of themselves as intermediaries between the people and the King and freely exercised their 'right of remonstrance'. By 1771 they had irritated the government so much that they were abolished, but they were restored by Louis XVI on his accession in 1774. Though their systematic opposition to the Crown

was generally self-interested, the *parlements* did act as a focus for discontent. By 1787 they enjoyed enormous popular support and continually resisted all government proposals for taxation. Their suspension in 1788 provoked nationwide riots. The King capitulated to their demands and summoned the Estates General. The privileged position of the *parlements* did not long survive the Revolution. They were abolished in September 1790.

41 their shoe-buckles: a reference to the *dons patriotiques*. Free gifts of money, jewellery or other articles of value to the state, had been encouraged by the National Assembly.

42 *Tiers Etat*: the Third Estate, or commoners. It comprised the educated middle classes, among them professional civil servants, lawyers, clerks, merchants, bankers, engineers, doctors and chemists, artists and writers – all of whom felt keenly their social and political exclusion. As a class it had grown in numbers and wealth since the Estates General had last been convened in 1614, and it immediately began to demand greater representation.

43 states-general: the Estates General was summoned in August 1788 to meet in May 1789. The doubling of the Third Estate was conceded by Louis XVI in December 1788, in order to outweigh the privileged orders, who were resisting necessary taxation. The nobles and clergy had 300 members apiece.

44 that body: the Estates met at Versailles on 4 May and on 17 June the radical Third Estate broke away, forming the National Assembly, and granting itself control of taxation. On 22 June the Archbishops of Vienne and Bordeaux led 250 members of the First Estate to join them and three days later the duc d'Orléans brought over nearly fifty members of the Second Estate. Louis XVI had little choice but to command the three Orders to sit together as a single body.

45 practitioners in the law: lawyers were numerous in France (Montaigne had described them as a Fourth Estate) owing to the varied systems of common law that prevailed in different districts. But they were not in a majority in the States: out of 652 members the lawyers numbered 272.

46 country clowns: there were some seventy or eighty farmers and perhaps the same number of merchants. There were just sixteen physicians.

47 breakers of law in India … England: the impeachment of Warren Hastings for misconduct in India was in progress, but Burke may have had in mind the financier Paul Benfield, whose shady dealings in India had led to his recall in 1779. However, Benfield had successfully defended himself and in the meantime got himself elected to Parliament as MP for Cricklade (1780–84). His conduct had occasioned one of Burke's more celebrated speeches, on the debts of the Nawab of the Carnatic. He became an MP again between 1790 and 1792, lost his fortune in speculations and died in needy circumstances in Paris in 1810.

48 mere country curates: in the clergy there were forty-eight bishops, thirty-five abbots and canons and 208 parish priests.

49 none but traitors: first among these would be Louis Philippe Joseph, duc d'Orléans (1747–93), a relation of the King. He was well known in England and the friend of Fox, Richard Sheridan, Lord Lansdowne (the former Earl

of Shelburne) and the Prince of Wales. An active supporter of the Revolution, he adopted the name Philippe Egalité and opened up the Palais Royal to the Jacobins; rumour reported that he had been behind the riots of 14 July and 5–6 October. He was guillotined during the Reign of Terror.

50 Earl of Holland (Henry Rich, 1st Earl of Holland, 1590–1649): a favourite of Charles I and Henrietta Maria, he had joined the Parliamentary forces in 1642, vacillating between the two sides throughout the Civil War until Cromwell put an end to his indecision by beheading him.

51 "Still as *you* rise ... destroys": Edmund Waller (1606–87), 'A Panegyric to My Lord Protector'.

52 Guises, Condés, and Colignis: three important families of the French nobility, all of whom had played a prominent role in the Wars of Religion (1562–98). François de Guise, the second duke (1519–63) was the virtual ruler of France in the reign of François II, setting himself to crush Protestantism with the able assistance of his brother Charles (1527–74), Cardinal of Lorraine. The third duke, Henri de Guise (1550–88) was responsible for the formation of the Catholic League and helped plan the St Bartholomew's Day Massacre. In 1588 he led a revolt against Henri III and became de facto ruler of France; the King feigned a reconciliation and had him murdered, along with his brother Louis, Cardinal of Lorraine (1555–88), during a meeting at Blois. The Condés were a collateral branch of the House of Bourbon. Louis, Prince of Condé (1530–69), a spirited soldier, became a Protestant and opposed the Guises. The second Louis (1621–86), 'the great Condé', was equally distinguished in arms and in letters. The Coligny family originated in Burgundy and served the French kings for many centuries. The three sons of Gaspard I de Coligny, Marshal of France (d. 1522), were active in the Protestant cause. Gaspard II (1519–72), a distinguished admiral, was the first victim of the St Bartholomew's Day Massacre. Odet (1517–71) was already a cardinal when he decided to embrace Calvinism – and marry his mistress. He was promptly excommunicated as a heretic and died in suspicious circumstances while fundraising in England. Their brother François (1521–69) was a colonel.

53 the Richelieus: Armand-Jean du Plessis, Cardinal de Richelieu (1585–1642) was chief minister of Louis XIII from 1624 to 1642 and strove to subdue the French Protestants as a military and political force; to curtail the power of the nobles; and to humiliate the Habsburgs, who ruled in Spain and Austria. He had a genius for detailed administration and effected many reforms in finance, legislation and the army. He also founded the Académie Française.

54 your Henry the Fourth and your Sully: Henri IV (1553–1611), King of France 1589, and his principal minister Maximilien de Béthune, duc de Sully (1560–1641), soldier and statesman, tried to follow a policy of religious reconciliation in the aftermath of the civil war – hence the Edict of Nantes (1598) allowing limited toleration for Huguenots. Henri, himself Protestant, had reconverted to Catholicism in order to be anointed King, famously remarking that 'Paris is worth a Mass'.

55 Jews: unlike Protestants, they were not covered by the Declaration of Human and Civil Rights on 26 August 1789 but full emancipation for Jews was granted in September 1791.

56 the lamp-post for its second: referring to the street lynchings in Paris in the summer of 1789, when the mob hanged its victims from lamp-posts. Two of these were Joseph-François Foullon, the very unpopular Comptroller General of Finances, and Berthier de Sauvigny, the *Intendant* of Paris.

57 A man: Dr Joseph Priestley (1733–1804), dissenting minister and theologian. He had long been associated with the radical politics of Lord Shelburne's Bowood Circle, and, like his patron, became a Unitarian. Priestley was also a noted scientist, whose chief work was on the chemistry of gases, and he discovered 'dephlogisticated air' (oxygen) in 1774. His house and laboratory in Birmingham were destroyed during 'Church and King' riots in 1791. The following year he was awarded French citizenship for his support of the French Revolution – much to Burke's disgust. He emigrated to Pennsylvania in 1794. The quotation here is from his *History of the Corruptions of Christianity* (1782).

58 "Illa *se jactat … regnet*": 'In that hall let Aeolus bluster, there let him reign when he has closed the dungeon of the winds' (Virgil, *Aeneid*).

59 *Liceat perire poetis … Ardentem frigidus Ætnam insiluit*: 'Let poets have the right to die if they please' … 'He leapt in cold blood into burning Etna' (Horace, *Ars Poetica*). The reference is to Empedocles, the Greek philosopher, born in Sicily, who according to legend leapt into the crater of Mount Etna in order that he should be thought a god.

60 franchises of Parnassus: liberties or privileges accorded to poets, Parnassus being a mountain in Greece sacred to Apollo and the muses.

61 mercury sublimate … cantharides: two highly toxic stimulants. Mercury sublimate was used in the treatment of syphilis. Cantharides was made from dried green beetles, and among other things was used as a diuretic and an aphrodisiac.

62 *cum perimit … tyrannos*: 'when many a class annihilates the cruel despots' (Juvenal, *Satires*).

63 Pisgah: the hill from which Moses looked across Jordan to the land of Canaan (Deuteronomy 34).

64 *nunc dimittis*: the Song of Simeon from Luke 2, beginning 'Nunc dimittis servum tuum, Domine, secundum verbum tuum in pace', translated in the Book of Common Prayer as 'Lord, now lettest thou thy servant depart in peace: according to thy word'. Simeon had been promised by God that he should not die until he had seen the Messiah.

65 Onondaga: refers to the march which triumphantly escorted the royal family from Versailles to the Tuileries Palace in Paris on 6 October 1789. The majority of marchers were women; poor harvests had led to bread shortages, and as 'father of the people' they applied to the King to see that markets were provisioned; but there was also another agenda – in Paris the King would be in a weaker position to resist the revolutionaries' demands. Onondaga was an Indian settlement in New York State near the site of the present town of Syracuse. It was the site of a French Jesuit mission, whose records Burke had researched for a book on the early European settlers in America.

66 an army: the National Guard, a voluntary citizens' militia, generally drawn from the middle class, hastily formed in mid-July 1789 in view of the

deteriorating situation in the capital. The new municipal authorities appointed the marquis de La Fayette (*see* n.175, below) as its commander. The Guard was augmented by a core of professional soldiers from a former royal household regiment, the Gardes Françaises, who had mutinied and joined the attack on the Bastille. Similar bodies were formed in provincial towns. Later, under the constitution of 1791, all adult 'active citizens' were obliged to join as reservists and officers were elected to serve for terms of one year. Many of the National Guard sympathized with the marchers who left Paris on 5 October. Unable to restrain them, La Fayette escorted them in the hope of maintaining public order and protecting the King.

67 a gang of assassins: on arrival at Versailles on 5 October the marchers had poured into the National Assembly, shouting down the speakers. The Assembly, too, was obliged to remove to Paris. Some fifty-six monarchist deputies, fearing mob violence in the capital, declined to go. By 19 October 1789 nearly 300 members of the National Assembly had either resigned, abandoned their seats or emigrated.

68 Catiline ... Cethegus: Catiline was an able but ambitious Roman, who formed an unscrupulous conspiracy against the state, the discovery of which by Cicero forced him to leave the city and attempt a rebellion. This was put down, and Catiline died in the engagement (62 BC). Gaius Cornelius Cethegus was one of Catiline's fellow conspirators, whose strangling in the Capitol dungeons (63 BC), urged by Cato and Cicero, was opposed as illegal by Julius Caesar.

69 *nec color ... senatûs*: the quotation, paraphrased in the preceding phrase, is from Lucan, *Pharsalia*.

70 "that the vessel ... more speed than ever": the words are Mirabeau's. Honoré Gabriel Riqueti, comte de Mirabeau was well known for his scandalous private life but also for his indictment of *lettres de cachet*, the system by which under the *ancien régime* a subject might be imprisoned without trial. Visiting London in 1784 he had been welcomed into Whig literary and political society, and his English friends included Lord Shelburne and Sir Samuel Romilly. He was introduced to Richard Price at this time. He also met Burke. In 1789 he had become a deputy of the Third Estate for Aix-en-Provence at the Estates General, and as a moderate favouring a constitutional monarchy he played a leading role in the National Assembly, becoming its President in 1791, the year of his death (from natural causes).

71 "the blood ... pure!": Barnave's remark on hearing of the hanging of Foullon and Berthier (*see* n.56, above). (Antoine Barnave, another moderate constitutionalist, was one of the best orators in the National Assembly. He was guillotined in 1793.)

72 *leze nation*: offence against the nation. This had replaced the old concept of *lèse-majesté*, an offence against the sovereign.

73 the sentinel: M. de Miomandre, who in fact recovered from his wounds, as Burke's critics were quick to inform him.

74 A band of cruel ruffians ... for a moment: the accuracy of this account of the events of 5–6 October was often called into question by eye-witnesses and by Burke's political opponents. Thomas Paine, in *Rights of Man*, his reply to Burke's *Reflections* published in 1791, dismissed it as no more than 'a dramatic performance'.

75 Theban and Thracian orgies: driven mad by the god Bacchus/Dionysus, the women of Thebes tear King Pentheus apart (Euripides, *Bacchae*); Orpheus suffers the same fate at the hands of the women of Thrace.

76 Io Pæan: hymn of praise to Apollo.

77 the projected fifth monarchy: millenarian beliefs had become particularly prevalent during the turmoil of the Civil War in England, and various dissenting sects including the Fifth Monarchists looked for the imminent Second Coming of Christ on earth which – according to the Books of Daniel and of Revelations – would follow four kingdoms or eras of history, which they reckoned to be the Babylonian, Persian, Greek and Roman Empires. The anticipated Millennium – the thousand years in which Christ would rule as king – was to be hastened by His saints endeavouring to throw over the old order, if necessary by violence. They therefore supported the execution of Charles I in 1649. They were put down by Cromwell, and again soon after the Restoration.

78 *M. de Lally Tollendal*: Trophime Gérard, comte de Lally-Tollendal (1751–1830). A member of the Estates General for the nobility of Paris, he opposed Mirabeau in the National Assembly, where he gained little support for his conservative monarchist views. He fled to England after the October Days in 1789. There had evidently been some personal contact in the past between him and Burke, for Lally-Tollendal had met Burke's son Richard in Paris at the end of 1785. Although their views on constitutional monarchy were not dissimilar, they argued over Burke's interpretation of the events of 1789, and his disapproval of the *monarchiens* expressed later in his Letter to a Member of the National Assembly (21) (1791).

79 *Non satis ... sunto*: 'For poems to have beauty of style is not enough, they must have feeling too' (Horace, *Ars Poetica*).

80 Bailly and Condorcet: two revolutionaries who would fall victim to the Reign of Terror. Sylvain Bailly (1736–93), philosopher and astronomer, Mayor of Paris 1789–91, was guillotined. Marie-Jean-Antoine-Nicolas de Caritat, marquis de Condorcet (1743–94), was a leading philosopher of the Enlightenment, mathematician, educational theorist, and, according to Burke, 'a fanatic atheist and a furious democratic Republican'. He had not sat in the National Assembly but became President of the Legislative Assembly in 1792. He either took poison or was murdered after his arrest in 1794.

81 *gentis incunabula nostræ*: 'the cradle of our race' (Virgil, *Aeneid*).

82 Garrick ... Siddons: David Garrick (1717–79) was the most celebrated actor of his day. He had been a friend of Burke. Sarah Siddons, *née* Kemble (1755–1831), was a well-known tragedienne.

83 Nero ... Monaldeschi: a blacklist of the most abhorred despots of the Whigs. Among his other crimes, the Roman emperor Nero (r. 54–68) infamously raised money by 'inviting' rich noblemen to commit suicide, leaving their estates to him. His mother Agrippina, as Empress of Rome, had proved adept at eliminating potential rivals and finally eliminated the Emperor Claudius himself with a plate of deadly mushrooms – though not before she had got him to name Nero, his stepson, as his successor. Nero had her murdered. Louis XI (r. 1461–83) broke the resistance of feudal

princes, extended the bounds of the state and was considered to have inaugurated an absolute tyranny which culminated only with the Revolution; Charles IX (r. 1560–74) ordered the Massacre of St Bartholomew and the persecution of the Huguenots. John Patkul was a nobleman from Livonia (present-day Latvia/Estonia, then ruled by Sweden), whom Charles XII (r. 1697–1718) had broken on the wheel for treason in 1707; Monaldeschi was the Master of Horse and possibly the lover of Queen Christina of Sweden (r. 1633–54) who had settled in Rome after her abdication. Accused of betraying to the Pope her plans to seize Naples with military backing from France, he was horribly murdered in her presence by members of her entourage at the palace of Fontainebleau near Paris.

84 flower-de-luce: for certain offences criminals in the *ancien régime* could be branded with a *fleur de luce/lys* on the shoulder.

85 Lord George Gordon (1751–93): he had been convicted of libelling the French Queen in 1787, and spent the rest of his life in Newgate prison. He had been President of the Protestant Association and the mob that he raised was in connection with the very violent 'No Popery' or 'Gordon' riots of 1780. He converted to Judaism in 1787 and while in prison lived the life of an Orthodox Jew (hence the reference to 'our Protestant Rabbin', below).

86 the Gallican church: the French Roman Catholic Church. Although it recognized the Pope as its head it had negotiated considerable autonomy under the King.

87 the victor in the field: Jean II of France (r. 1350–64) had been taken by the Black Prince at Poitiers in 1356. Brought to England, he was regally lodged in the Savoy Palace, and granted full royal privileges.

88 Rousseau ... Voltaire ... Helvetius: François-Marie Arouet, known as Voltaire (1694–1778), Claude-Adrien Helvétius (1715–71) and Jean-Jacques Rousseau (1712–78), three prominent thinkers associated with the Enlightenment.

89 Collins ... and Morgan ... Bolingbroke: prominent deists who advocated a rationalist approach to Christianity. Much of their work was based on the spirit and teaching of John Locke. For Bolingbroke, *see* A Vindication of Natural Society (1), n.2. Burke regarded deism, widely adopted during the French Enlightenment, as little better than atheism.

90 Sit igitur hoc ... sententia: 'Let this, therefore, be a fundamental principle in all societies, that the gods are the supreme lords and governors of all things, that all events are directed by their influence and wisdom, and that they are loving and benevolent to mankind. They likewise know what every person really is; they observe his actions, whether good or bad; they discern whether our religious professions are sincere and heart-felt, and are sure to make a difference between good men and the wicked. When once our minds are confirmed in these views, it will not be difficult to inspire them with true and useful sentiments' (Cicero, *De Legibus*, tr. Francis Barham, 1842).

91 janissaries: Christian-born infantry troops of the Ottoman Empire who formed the Sultan's bodyguard. In the seventeenth and eighteenth centuries they frequently engineered palace coups.

92 Quicquid multis peccatur inultem: 'Whatever wrong is wrought by the many, goes unpunished' (Lucan, *Pharsalia*).

93 "Quod illi principi ... appellantur": 'For nothing on earth is more agree-
    able to God, the Supreme Governor of the Universe, than the assemblies
    and societies of men united together by laws, which are called States'
    (Cicero, *De Republica*, tr. Francis Barham, 1842).

94 Euripus: the strait between the island of Euboea and mainland Greece
    where, contrary to most of the Mediterranean Sea, there is a considerable
    rise and fall of tides.

95 the *Palais Royal*, and the *Jacobins*: the Palais Royal was the home of the duc
    d'Orléans (*see* n.49, above). The courtyard was a favourite spot for political
    discussions. The Jacobin Club, or the Société des Amis de la Constitution,
    was formed after the October Days when the National Assembly moved
    from Versailles to Paris. It was open to non-deputies and by July 1790 its
    membership – mainly professional men, or bourgeoisie – was around 1,200
    in Paris, and there were 152 affiliated clubs throughout France. ('Jacobins'
    was the Parisian term for the Dominicans, whose earliest houses had been
    dedicated to St James; the revolutionary group took the name as they met
    in the hall of an old Dominican convent.) The Jacobin Club remained rela-
    tively moderate until its more conservative members left to form the Feuill-
    lants Club in July 1791. A Jacobin coup in 1793 brought the republican
    extremists under Robespierre to power in France, ushering in the Reign
    of Terror.

96 *jus retractus*: the right of recovery, by which, for example, a lord could com-
    pulsorily repurchase alienated lands which had at any previous time formed
    part of his fief.

97 the regent: Philippe II d'Orléans, Regent of France 1715–22 during the
    minority of Louis XV.

98 the two academies of France: the most famous was the Académie Française,
    founded by Richelieu in 1635, which jealously guarded the purity of the
    French language. But there were other academies founded under Louis
    XIV – of Science, Inscriptions and *Belles-Lettres*, Painting and Sculpture,
    Music, and Architecture.

99 the Encyclopædia: the *Encyclopédie* was begun by Denis Diderot (1713–84)
    and Jean le Rond d'Alembert (1717–83) in 1751 as a dictionary of universal
    knowledge, with articles by leading intellectuals of the age. It became a
    vehicle of the Enlightenment, propagating rationalist and sceptical views
    of philosophy and religion, and as such attracted the hostility of both
    Church and State. This was a sure recipe for popular success. By 1772 when
    the project was complete, seventeen volumes of text and eleven of plates
    had been published; five additional volumes appeared in 1776–77.

100 the late king of Prussia: Frederick the Great (r. 1740–86) had corresponded
    with a number of the *philosophes*, but particularly Voltaire, who spent three
    years at the Prussian court, 1750–53.

101 Turgot (Anne-Robert-Jacques Turgot, 1727–81): Comptroller General of
    Finances 1774–76, was a scientific economist associated with the Physio-
    crats. Resistance from the privileged classes dealt the death-blow to his
    reform programme.

102 comptrollers-general: the *Controlleur-général des finances* was the most
    important ministerial post under the *ancien régime* but also the most insec-
    ure. In the thirty-five years preceding the Revolution turnover was high

– nineteen ministers came and went, and it was hardly surprising that the official residence was dubbed the *hotel des déménagements* (the house of removals). In addition to finances the *Controlleur-général* was responsible for agriculture, industry and commerce, bridges and roads.

103 M. Laborde (Jean Joseph de Laborde, 1724–94): a Spaniard by birth, he was a prosperous Bayonne merchant, who became a financial contractor for the government of Louis XV, and received a marquisate. Under the Reign of Terror in 1794 he was condemned for exporting bullion and guillotined.

104 Duke de Choiseul (Etienne-François, duc de Choiseul, 1719–85): Foreign Minister under Louis XV (twice). He presided over France's defeat in the Seven Years' War (1756–63) and afterwards worked to rebuild French military and global prestige. In 1770 he pressed ruthlessly for war with Britain in support of Spanish claims to the Falkland Islands. The King would not accept a further drain on the treasury, and Choiseul's enemies at court – notably the King's new mistress, Mme du Barry – were able to secure his dismissal.

105 Duke d'Aiguillon (1720–88): as military Governor of Brittany from 1753, he became involved in an interminable dispute with the Breton *parlement* over taxation in the province. He was brought to trial for abuse of power in 1770 but Louis XV ordered the case to be quashed. The Duke succeeded Choiseul as Foreign Minister and is remembered for his supineness in the partition of Poland. After the death of Louis XV he quickly fell foul of the young queen Marie Antoinette and was dismissed in 1774.

106 The noble family of Noailles: two former ducs de Noailles had served with distinction as Marshals of France; Louis de Noailles, the fourth duke, bore the title though his military record was indifferent. He died in 1793 and many of his family were guillotined the following year. Louis-Marie, vicomte de Noailles (1756–1804), a member of a cadet branch of the Noailles family, fought brilliantly against the British in the War of American Independence, and took the surrender of Yorktown. He was well-known in England as a liberal, sat in the National Assembly and was one of the original members of the Jacobin Club (*see* n.95, above). On 4 August 1789 he put forward a motion for the abolition of feudal dues – supported by the duc d'Aiguillon (1761–1800), son of the former Foreign Minister (*see* n.105, above). He later emigrated to Pennsylvania and became a banker. His wife, a granddaughter of the fourth duke, remained in France and was executed in 1794.

107 Duke de Rochefoucauld ... Cardinal de Rochefoucauld: the former is either the duc de La Rochefoucauld in n.4 above, or his cousin, François-Alexandre-Frédéric, duc de La Rochefoucauld-Liancourt (1747–1827), who had held a lucrative court appointment as Master of the King's Wardrobe. He too was a reformer who had spent some time in England studying agriculture, and was a founder of schools, hospitals and prisons. He had become President of the National Assembly in July 1789. He was given command of a military division in Normandy and offered Louis XVI a safe haven there. He fled France after the King's capture in August 1792 and spent seven years in exile before returning in 1799. Dominique de La Rochefoucauld (1713–1800), the elderly Cardinal Archbishop of Rouen, came from an impoverished branch of the same family. He was President

of the Estate of the Clergy in the Estates General, where he had resisted
the merging of the three estates. In the Assembly he resolutely opposed the
new laws regarding the clergy and the Church. He was given to charitable
works and much loved in his diocese. He emigrated to Germany in 1792.

108 *crudelem illam hastam*: that cruel spear – refers to the Roman custom of
sticking a spear in the ground at public auctions, originally the sign of booty
gained in battle.

109 Mariuses and Syllas: *see* A Vindication of Natural Society (1), n.21.

110 M. Necker (Jacques Necker, 1732–1804): a banker from Geneva, who
served as Director General of Finance in France 1771–81 (he could not be
Comptroller General as he was a Protestant). His *Compte Rendu au roi*
(1781), effectively the first public lecture on finance, had been a bestseller
in France. He had remained powerful and popular, even after his dismissal,
and was reinstated in 1788 as financial director and de facto prime minister
to cope with the political crisis. His account of the state of French finances
was given to the Estates General on 5 May 1789.

111 Tahmas Kouli Khân: Nadir Shah, who ruled Persia 1736–47.

112 Intendants of the generalities of France: under the *ancien régime* the country
was divided into administrative units known as *généralités*. In 1789 there
were thirty-three of these, each meticou0lsy overseen by a royal *intendant*.
Under Louis XIV the feudal aristocracy or *noblesse d'épée* had been eliminated from administrative office; *intendants* were drawn from the ranks of
the *noblesse de la robe* or administrative nobility but held a royal commission
direct from the King (many other posts were hereditary) to ensure their
loyalty and efficiency.

113 M. de Calonne (Charles-Alexandre de Calonne, 1734–1802): Comptroller
General of Finance 1783–87, he had inherited a debt augmented by
France's participation in the American War of Independence (1775–83).
His failure to persuade the nobles and clergy to accept his suggested reform
of the land tax would lead two years later to the summoning of the Estates
General. It led immediately to his dismissal. He settled in England, where
he became well known in Whig society, and wrote many books and
pamphlets about the situation in France.

114 Hanse-towns ... *Orsini* and *Vitelli* ... *Mamelukes* ... *Nayres*: for the Hanseatic
League, *see* Speech on Economical Reform (11), n.8. The Orsini were a
powerful princely family whose endless feuds with the Colonna had dominated the history of early Renaissance Rome. The Vitelli were fifteenth-
century *condottieri* (Italian mercenaries). The Mamelukes or Mamluks were
a Turkoman warrior people originally brought to Egypt as slaves, who
became sultans of Egypt and Syria from the mid-thirteenth century until
defeated by the Ottoman Turks in 1517. The Mamluks were well known
for political violence. The 'Nayrs' who gained such a reputation for piracy
were in fact a dynasty of Muslim traders, the Kunjali Marakkars, who carried out successful naval warfare against the incursions of the Portuguese
throughout the sixteenth century, with the support of the local Hindu
('Nayr') kings of Calicut.

115 voluntarily surrendered: the National Assembly abolished hereditary
nobility and the use of all aristocratic titles in June 1790. But their loss of

tax privileges had already been approved in August 1789, when two aristo-crats – the vicomte de Noailles and the duc d'Aiguillon (*see* nn. 105 and 106, above) – put forward a motion for the abolition of feudalism.

116 Henry the Fourth: Henri IV of France (r. 1572–1610), formerly Henri III of Navarre (*see* n.54, above).

117 *Omnes boni nobilitati semper favemus*: 'True nobility is esteemed by every one of us' (Cicero, *Pro Sestio*).

118 The Massacre of St. Bartholomew: on 24 August 1572, thousands of French Protestants (Huguenots) were butchered in Paris. Plotted by the regent Catherine de Medici and masterminded by the Guise faction, the killing quickly gained a momentum of its own, spreading to the provinces and continuing until the beginning of October. The Pope celebrated a *Te Deum* when told of it.

119 Cardinal of Lorraine ... Guises: for the Guise family and the Cardinal of Lorraine, *see* n.52, above.

120 a *Fenelon*: François Fénelon (1651–1715), Archbishop of Cambrai, famous French theologian and man of letters, best known for his *Télémaque*, written for Louis XIV's grandson the duc de Bourgogne (1682–1712), to whom he was tutor.

121 an hundred and twenty bishops: there were in fact 130 bishops, reduced to eighty-three, one for each department of the country (the old provinces had been broken up into equal units based on area).

122 Burnet (Gilbert Burnet, 1643–1715): *see* On the Duration of Parliaments (12), n.6.

123 long parliament: following the execution of Charles I in 1649, the Long Parliament (so called because it was summoned in 1640 and not officially dissolved until 1660), had passed a series of measures confiscating Church, Crown and Royalist lands, which were then sold to pay off wage arrears to the army and to retire some of the national debt. These lands were largely restored at the Restoration, with compensation paid to the buyers.

124 Domat (Jean Domat, 1625–96): French jurist and scholar of Roman law, author of the influential *Les lois civiles dans leur ordre naturel*.

125 Anabaptists of Munster: name given to radical Protestant reformers who believed in adult baptism. During the 1520s the movement was spreading across Germany, the Low Countries, Switzerland, Austria and Moravia. In 1534–35 a group of Anabaptists had tried to set up a popular sectarian government in Munster.

126 Mr. Camus: Armand-Gaston Camus (1740–1804), advocate and expert in canon law, who played a large part in the drafting of the Civil Constitution of the Clergy (July 1790).

127 "Si plures sunt ... latius" ... "Sic par est agere ... continere": 'Thus even though they to whom property has been wrongfully awarded be more in number than they from whom it has been unjustly taken, they do not for that reason have more influence; for in such matters influence is measured not by numbers but by weight. And how is it fair that a man who never had any property should take possession of lands that had been occupied for many years or even generations, and that he who had them before

should lose possession of them? Now, it was on account of just this sort of wrong-doing that the Spartans banished their ephor Lysander, and put their king Agis to death – an act without precedent in the history of Sparta. From that time on – and for the same reason – dissensions so serious ensued that tyrants arose, the nobles were sent into exile, and the state, though most admirably constituted, crumbled to pieces. Nor did it fall alone, but by the contagion of the ills that, starting in Lacedaemon, spread widely and more widely, it dragged the rest of Greece down to ruin.' ... 'That is the right way to deal with one's fellow-citizens, and not, as we have already witnessed on two occasions to plant the spear in the forum and knock down the property of the citizens under the auctioneer's hammer. But yon Greek, like a wise and excellent man, thought that he must look out for the welfare of all. And this is the highest statesmanship and the soundest wisdom on the part of a good citizen, not to divide the interests of the citizens but to unite all on the basis of impartial justice' (Cicero, *De Officiis*, translation by Walter Miller, 1913).

128 See two books ... 1787: these books refer to the secret society of the Illuminati, the discovery of which produced a panic out of all proportion to its importance. The society arose at Ingolstadt in Bavaria in 1776 as a kind of political variety of freemasonry that aimed at combating the obscurantism of the Jesuits.

129 *Spartam nactus es; hanc exorna*: 'Your lot is cast in Sparta, be a credit to it'; 'having made your bed, now lie on it as comfortably as you can'. The proverb is frequent in Latin literature, being adapted from the *Telephus* of Euripides, where it is addressed by Agamemnon to Menelaus.

130 monks into pensioners: monastic orders were dissolved in France by decree on 13 February 1790.

131 *Munera Terræ*: 'The gifts of the earth' (Horace, *Odes*) – the things that pass away as opposed to things eternal.

132 *Pater ... voluit*: 'The great Father himself would not have the path of tillage an easy one' (Virgil, *Georgics*).

133 M. Rabaud de St. Etienne ... the *Quinze-vingt* or the *Petits Maisons*: Jean-Paul Rabat de St Etienne (1743–93), a Protestant minister, was active on the Constitutional Committee and made many policy speeches in the National Assembly. Les Quinze-Vingts was a hospital in Paris for 300 blind men; *Petites Maisons* were lunatic asylums.

134 Cicero ... Cato: Marcus Tullius Cicero (106–43 BC), statesman and orator, widely considered Rome's greatest prose stylist. His surviving works include speeches, letters, treatises on rhetoric, and philosophical essays. He was particularly revered by Enlightenment thinkers; Burke himself was a great admirer. Cicero supported the return to republican government after the death of Julius Caesar, and made an implacable enemy of Mark Antony, who had him murdered. Cato the Younger: *see* An Inquiry into the Sublime and Beautiful (2), n.14.

135 Stoic philosophy: Stoicism was an ancient Greek philosophy which became popular among the Roman upper classes. Stoics argued that virtue was the highest good and that only the wise could attain it. The wise live in harmony with divine reason and are indifferent to pleasure, pain and the fickleness of fortune.

136 *pede nudo Catonem*: Burke quotes from Horace (*Epistles*). 'Suppose a man with rough and stern countenance, barefoot and with the texture of a scanty toga, were to ape Cato, would he, therefore, reproduce the virtues and morals of Cato?' It takes something more than the philosopher's garb to make a philosopher.

137 Mr. Hume ... Rousseau: for David Hume *see* Letter to the Sheriffs of Bristol (10), n.9. From 1763−65 Hume was secretary to the embassy in Paris, and mixed in French literary society, there meeting Rousseau, whom he brought to England where they had a much publicized falling-out.

138 *Cantons*: Jacques Guillaume Thouret (1746−94) a lawyer from Normandy, and member of the Constitution Committee, was responsible for the administrative reorganization of France into eighty-three departments, each named for an element of nature or geographical feature. The old provinces and the *généralités* (which seldom corresponded to them − *see* n.112, above) were alike abolished.

139 Empedocles and Buffon: Empedocles (*see* n.59, above) of Sicily (*c.* 490−430 BC) conceived the story of the universe as an everlasting evolution, a series of endless cycles in which the two motive principles, love and hate, alternately prevail over the four elements fire, air, earth and water. Georges-Louis Leclerc, comte de Buffon (1707−80) was a naturalist, anthropologist and palaeontologist, author of a monumental thirty-six-volume *Natural History* (1749−1804) which systematically sought to present everything then known about these subjects.

140 "But soft − by regular degrees, not yet": Alexander Pope, 'Epistle to Richard Boyle, Earl of Burlington'.

141 Servius Tullius (578−534 BC): the sixth king of Rome.

142 *Hominem non sapiunt*: 'They do not take cognizance of man'.

143 Tacitus (AD 56/57 − d. after 117): Roman historian (*see* Letter to Sir Arthur Murphy).

144 *facies Hippocratica*: The Hippocratic face − physical changes in the face prior to death described by Hippocrates, 'the father of medicine', in the fifth century BC.

145 Non, ut olim ... quam colonia: 'For whole legions were no longer transplanted, as in former days, with tribunes and centurions and soldiers of every grade, so as to form a state by their unity and mutual attachment, but strangers to one another from different companies, without a head or any community of sentiment, were suddenly gathered together, as it might be out of any other class of human beings, and became a mere crowd rather than a colony' (Tacitus, *Annals*, tr. Church and Brodribb, 1869).

146 Montesquieu (Charles-Louis de Secondat, baron de Montesquieu, 1689−1755): political philosopher, whose chief work was *The Spirit of the Laws* (1748). The work here referred to is his *Considerations on the Causes of the Grandeur and Decadence of the Romans* (1734). His theories were highly influential in Europe and also in the drafting of the American constitution.

147 Qualitas ... Habitus: Quality, relation, action, passion, place, time, situation, condition − together with substance and quantity, these are the ten categories in the philosophy of Aristotle.

148 *Limbus Patrum*: in medieval Catholic theology, limbo was a temporary place on the edge of hell for the souls of righteous people who had died before the time of Christ. It was divided between the limbo of the Fathers (*Limbus Patrum*) where the great patriarchs of the Old Testament awaited Christ's coming, and the limbo of unbaptized infants.

149 Latonian kindness ... Delos ... *oras et littora circum*: Latona (or Leto) was a Greek goddess, mother of the twins Artemis and Apollo, whose father was Zeus. Shunned by all for fear of the anger of Hera – wife of Zeus – she could find nowhere to give birth but the floating island of Ortygia (later identified with Delos), which she sensibly anchored to the ocean bed. *Ora et littora circum* – 'Around the shores and coasts' (Virgil, *Aeneid*).

150 a holy bishop: Charles Maurice de Talleyrand-Périgord (1754–1838), created Bishop of Autun in 1789, had first proposed the Civil Constitution of the Clergy and consecrated the first bishops established under its provisions. The eldest son of an aristocratic family, he was (on account of a childhood injury) earmarked early for an ecclesiastical career. In 1780 he became Agent-General of the Clergy, and was involved in the drafting of an inventory of Church properties in France, experience that no doubt proved useful later when he presided over their dismantling. He resigned as bishop after being excommunicated by Pope Pius VI in 1791. His report on public education, clearly influenced by the theories of the Enlightenment, was widely praised but never adopted. He emigrated in 1792, first to England where he was welcomed in advanced circles, then to America. On his return he became Napoleon's Foreign Minister, represented France at the Congress of Vienna and was a key supporter of the Bourbon restoration. Under Louis-Philippe he was the French Ambassador in London. A gifted statesman, wily diplomat and pragmatic survivor of regime change, Talleyrand was not above intriguing with France's enemies, and was a notorious taker of bribes. Unsurprisingly, he became very rich. He was created a duke in 1817, but with the title of prince.

151 "Diis immortalibus sero": 'I sow for the immortal gods'. Paraphrase of Cicero, *De Senectute*. The farmer explains that it is the will of the gods that just as he inherited the land from his forebears, so he should prepare it for his successors.

152 *Caisse d'Escompte* (discount house): a bank in all but name (the failure of John Law's Banque royale – *see* n.195, below – had given the term a negative connotation in France). It was founded in 1769, failed, and was refounded in 1776 by Turgot (*see* n.101, above), with its activities carefully prescribed. It was closely linked to the government to which it advanced money and, like Law's bank, it was over-generous in its issue of bank notes during the financial crisis of the 1780s, leading to hyperinflation and public panic. The revolutionary government took over its assets in 1793.

153 "*Beatus ille*": 'Happy is the man ... ', the opening words of Horace's second Epode, in which Alphius the moneylender reviews the idyllic prospect of life in the country. However, the epode ends, 'Having said this, the moneylender Alphius, on the point of becoming a farmer, called in all his money on the Ides [mid-month] and is seeking to invest it again on the Kalends [month-end].'

154 *Caisse d'Eglise*: The 'Church Bank' – a mocking allusion to the fact that the new currency is based on confiscated Church lands.

155 the Mississippi and South Sea: two joint stock companies which had ridden high on a fever of speculation and taken over much of the national debt. In Britain the failure of the South Sea Company in 1720 – the notorious 'South Sea Bubble' – had ruined many individual investors and compromised a number of government ministers. At the same time the Mississippi Company in France also failed, ending the spectacular career of its founder, Scottish banker and adventurer John Law (see n.195, below).

156 assignats: paper currency issued by the National Assembly, backed by the proceeds of the first sale of Church lands at the end of 1789. The idea was to release the lands gradually, and use the proceeds to amortize the national debt. The assignats were to be bought in and destroyed as money returned to the Treasury from the sales, thus dissipating the fear of inflation. However, there was no control over the amount printed. A shortage of currency in France before the Revolution allowed the new government two years' grace before castastrophic hyperinflation set in.

157 "the Serbonian bog": Milton, *Paradise Lost*. ('A gulf profound as that Serbonian bog / Betwixt Damatia and Mount Casius old / Where Armies whole have sunk.')

158 Solons and Numas: see A Vindication of Natural Society (1), n.26.

159 Louis the Thirteenth ... Richelieu: Louis XIII (r. 1610–43); Richelieu, see n.53, above.

160 Louis the Fourteenth ... Mazarin ... Louvois: Louis XIV (r. 1643–1715), son of Louis XIII. Jules Mazarin (1602–61), an Italian papal diplomat and protégé of Richelieu (see n.53, above), who became a naturalized Frenchman, gained a Cardinal's hat in 1641 and succeeded his mentor as Louis XIII's chief minister in 1642. During the minority of Louis XIV, he was effectively co-ruler with the young King's mother, Anne of Austria. He took up Richelieu's policies, continuing the war against the Habsburgs and increasing royal power at the expense of the nobility and the *parlements*. His unpopularity provoked the disturbances known as the Frondes (1648–53), but he was able to defeat his enemies and to restore royal absolutism intact. After Mazarin's death in 1661 Louis XIV resolved to rule without a chief minister, but as Secretary of State for War during a reign in which war was an almost permanent state of affairs, François-Michel Le Tellier, marquis de Louvois (1639–91) had by the mid-1680s made himself both powerful and indispensable. He had been carefully groomed for the position by its previous incumbent, his father Michel Le Tellier. The father devised and the son effected reforms which made the French army one of the most formidable in Europe.

161 George the Second took Mr Pitt: Pitt the Elder had made himself particularly disagreeable to George II during the early 1740s, criticizing the conduct of the War of Austrian Succession and waxing eloquent on the subject of the 'despicable electorate' (Hanover). He was made Paymaster General in 1746 when the ministry dominated by the Pelham brothers forced the King's hand by the unprecedented method of resigning en bloc. When in 1757 Pitt became Secretary of State, a monarch for the first time bowed to popular pressure in his choice of war leader.

162 M. de Montmorin (Armand-Marc, comte de Montmorin de Saint-Hérem, 1745–92): Louis XVI's Foreign Minister from 1787. He trod a

difficult path in the Nootka Sound diplomatic crisis between Spain and Britain in 1790, the National Assembly being more kindly disposed towards Britain than France's traditional ally, Spain. On 22 May the Assembly put itself in charge of foreign policy, though the King's consent was still required for a declaration of war. Montmorin died in the September Massacres of 1792.

163 M. Necker ... *sed multæ* ... *vicerunt*: 'but the public prayers of all those cities gained the day' (Juvenal, *Satires*). For Necker, *see* n.110, above. He and Burke had had some correspondence.

164 Areopagus: rocky hill in Athens where in classical times the highest governmental council sat, and later a judicial court.

165 *psephismata*: decrees passed by a vote of the Athenian Assembly.

166 *Chatelet*: in October 1789 the National Assembly had decreed that those accused of the new crime of *lèse-nation* (*see* n.72, above) should be tried before the Chatelet, one of the principal courts of Paris. Like other courts of the *ancien régime*, it was suppressed in August 1790.

167 *committee of research*: the Comité des Recherches, an agency with powers to investigate and to prosecute, established by the Paris municipal council during the early days of the Revolution in the summer of 1789. It functioned as the capital's political police.

168 M. de la Tour du Pin (Jean-Frédéric, comte de la Tour du Pin, 1727–94): the speech referred to was made in June 1790, when there were many disturbances in the army which lasted into the autumn. He was replaced by Duportail in November 1790, and guillotined during the Reign of Terror.

169 *risum teneatis?*: could you keep from laughing?

170 *prêtés ... solemnité*: sworn with the most impressive solemnity.

171 "comitia, comices": group of comrades, often soldiers.

172 Comme sa majesté ... confederacies: *Discours de M. de la Tour du Pin*, June 1790.

173 *Si isti ... recusem!*: 'If that lot gave me leave to return to childhood again from my present time of life, to bawl once more in their cradle, I should vigorously refuse!' (paraphrase of Cicero, *De Senectute*).

174 Armies ... your whole republic: events were to prove Burke perfectly correct in this prediction. The Jacobins soon began to fear their revolution being hijacked by a military dictator, and began to look out for any potential French 'Cromwell' figure, both Lafayette (*see* n.175, below) and Dumouriez early coming under suspicion. Napoleon's coup of 18 Brumaire (9 November) 1799 realized Burke's worst fears.

175 Marquis de la Fayette (Marie-Joseph Paul Yves Roch Gilbert du Motier, marquis de La Fayette, 1757–1834): he came from a military family and was famed for his youthful exploits during the American War of Independence, in which he espoused the colonists' cause. On return to France he had abandoned his long name and title in favour of the simple Lafayette (hence Burke's taunt). He was a member of the Second (noble) estate in the Estates General, joined the National Assembly and was made commander of the National Guard in July 1789. Lafayette favoured a new

constitution on American lines and was well known in Whig circles in England. He was appointed to army command in 1791 but, alarmed by the radicalism of the Legislative Assembly, he turned royalist and was obliged to flee France in 1792. He returned in 1799, living in retirement during the First Empire but playing an active part in public affairs as a constitutionalist in the post-Napoleonic era.

176 As the colonists rise ... : this is what happened in the French West Indian colony of Saint Domingue where colonists and slaves alike were inspired by the revolutionary 'Declaration of the Rights of Man'. A major slave rebellion against the white planters in 1791 was led by former slave Toussaint l'Ouverture, whose armies went on to defeat both French and (during the Revolutionary Wars) British forces. Napoleon also attempted unsuccessfully to restore French rule and slavery on the island. In 1804 it declared its independence and was renamed Haiti.

177 In consequence ... troops against them: though the decree of 4 August 1789 had abolished feudal dues, the National Assembly (which contained many landowners) had had second thoughts and in March 1790 decreed that certain specified feudal rights required reimbursement.

178 rochet: a vestment resembling a surplice, used by bishops and abbots.

179 gabelles: a notoriously unpopular tax levied on salt in the *ancien régime*.

180 systasis of Crete ... confederation of Poland: Hellenistic Cretan cities, generally engaged in fighting each other, agreed to unite for defence if attacked by a common enemy. This seldom worked in practice and the Romans annexed the island in 69 BC. The Polish confederations from the thirteenth century to the eighteenth were ad hoc groups of nobles, clergy, cities or military forces which were by law entitled to combine to seek redress of specific grievances. Their activities led to a weakening of royal authority and ultimately to Russian intervention and the second partition of Poland in 1793.

181 M. Vernier (Théodore Vernier, comte de Mont-Orient, 1731–1818): financial expert in the National Assembly.

182 *Cedò ... tam cito*: 'Say, how lost you so great a state so soon?' (Cicero, *De Senectute*) – to which the reply is given: 'A brood came of new leaders, foolish striplings' (Andrew P. Peabody, 1887).

183 The National Assembly ... were to pay: a *contribution patriotique* of a quarter of incomes above 400 livres p.a. had been decreed in October 1789.

184 John Doe ... Richard Roe: in the old common law action of ejectment (to recover the possession of or title to land) instead of the real parties being named, the fictitious John Doe, plaintiff, would sue the fictitious Richard Roe, defendant. The practice was not abolished until 1852.

185 Memoirs of the Duke de St. Simon: Louis de Rouvroy, duc de Saint-Simon (1673–1755), soldier and diplomat, was well known for his *Mémoires*, a detailed record of court life between 1694 and 1723, spanning the reigns of Louis XIV and XV.

186 'Change: the London money market, or Exchange.

187 church mummy: gum used in medicine.

188 *Mais si ... assignare*: But if the disease in opinion does not wish to cure itself, what is to be done? Issue assignats – then more assignats, followed by more assignats (dog Latin).

189 a pious and venerable prelate: Talleyrand, Bishop of Autun (*see* n.150, above).

190 *Fisc*: the public exchequer.

191 La Bruyère of Bossuet: the essayist Jean de la Bruyère (1645–96) had thus described Jacques-Bénigne Bossuet (1627–1704), Bishop of Meaux, celebrated preacher and royal tutor.

192 bishop of Nancy: Anne-Louis-Henri de La Fare (1752–1829), Bishop of Nancy, left France in 1791, returning after the Restoration when he was made Archbishop of Sens, and later a Cardinal.

193 the club at Dundee: the Dundee Friends of Liberty, founded in early 1791 by Unitarian minister Thomas Fyshe Palmer, one of many similar organizations springing up throughout the country in the early years of the French Revolution. Initially inspired by the Friends of the People, a society formed by Whig politicians in favour of parliamentary reform, their agenda became increasingly radical, especially in Scotland where the subscription rate was lower and many working men joined. Such societies became subject to severe government repression in 1793–94.

194 *Judæus Apella*: 'Let the Jew Apella, believe it, not me' (Horace, *Satires*). 'Apella' came to be a by-word for a credulous man.

195 Mr. Law: John Law (1671–1729), son of a Scots goldsmith, had in 1694 escaped from Newgate prison (where he was under sentence of death for killing an opponent in a duel), and reappeared on the continent, gambling for high stakes, mixing with high society and charming his way into the confidence of the duc d'Orléans, future regent of France. He was convinced of the importance of paper money as credit and promoted the establishment of a national bank in France in 1716. When Orléans made him Comptroller General of Finances, he used the bank money to finance monopoly companies, stimulating massive speculation and subsequent panic. Forced to flee the country, Law died in poverty in Venice.

196 "smitten with the cold, dry, petrific mace": Milton, *Paradise Lost*.

197 tontines: loan from which subscribers receive an annuity which increases as each person dies, until the last of the subscribers receives all the income. Called after its originator, Neapolitan banker Lorenzo Tonti, who introduced them in France in the mid-seventeenth century.

198 Lucan and Corneille: the former was Roman poet Marcus Annaeus Lucanus (AD 39–65); Pierre Corneille (1606–84), French dramatist, was regarded as the founder of French classical tragedy.

199 "through great varieties of untried being": Joseph Addison, *Cato*.

LETTER TO A MEMBER OF THE NATIONAL ASSEMBLY (21)

[Full title: *A letter from Mr. Burke, to a Member of the National Assembly: in Answer to Some Objections to his Book on French Affairs*]

1 A MEMBER OF THE NATIONAL ASSEMBLY: the letter is addressed to François-Louis-Thibault de Menonville, deputy for Mirecourt in Lorraine. He had

written to Burke in November 1790 from Paris, praising his *Reflections* but also pointing out factual mistakes and defending some of the moderate members of the Assembly whom Burke had criticized. It was published first in Paris in April 1791 and in London in May.

2 *Nulla nova mihi res inopinave surgit*: 'I have no new or unexpected things' (Virgil, *Aeneid*).

3 *deductio ad absurdum*: process of reasoning relying on the recognition either that an absurd result follows from a statement's denial, or that a statement is false because its acceptance would result in a undeniable absurdity.

4 *Nihil non arrogant armis*: 'they claim everything by force of arms' (Horace, *Ars Poetica*).

5 *ardentis massæ fuligine lippos*: 'bleary-eyed with the reek of a burning mass' (Juvenal, *Satires*).

6 lanterne: symbol of street justice in revolutionary France, a *lanterne* (lamp-post) serving as a means enabling mobs to perform improvised lynchings by hanging enemies of the Revolution from them.

7 Cromwell ... Hale (Oliver Cromwell, 1599–1658; Sir Matthew Hale, 1609–76): Cromwell, MP and military commander for Parliament during the English Civil War, later Lord Protector of the Commonwealth (1653–58). He appointed Hale, a widely respected barrister (who had defended a number of royalists) Justice of the Common Pleas in 1654. Hale's successful judicial career continued after the Restoration and he became Chief Justice of the King's Bench in 1671. He gained a posthumous reputation as a jurist and scholar of English common law.

8 Burnet (Gilbert Burnet, 1643–1715): *see* On the Duration of Parliaments (12), n.6. Burnet wrote a life of Sir Matthew Hale (*see* n.7, above).

9 M. Mirabeau (Honoré Gabriel Riqueti, comte de Mirabeau, 1749–91): *see* Reflections on the Revolution in France (20), n.70.

10 the holy prelate of Autun: Talleyrand. *See* Reflections on the Revolution in France (20), n.150.

11 Gamaliel: first-century master of Jewish law, referred to here ironically by Burke.

12 *terra australis*: term used to designate any mythical, faraway (barren) land.

13 *Mahomet*, hid: refers either to Muhammad's desert sojourn with the Bedouin, or to his taking refuge in the oasis of Taif during his Hegira.

14 in *luce Asiae*: in plain sight, visible to everyone.

15 The king of Prussia ... confusion: in 1786 the Dutch Stadtholder William V was engaged in fighting the 'Patriots', a band of young revolutionaries. His brother-in-law, Frederick William II of Prussia, sent an army to restore him in 1787, with Britain's encouragement. (In 1795 the Patriots in conjunction with the French revolutionary army, would succeed in deposing him for good.) In July 1790 Prussia and Austria concluded the Treaty of Reisenbach, after which Prussia ceased frustrating Emperor Leopold II's attempts to regain control of the Austrian Netherlands following a rebellion (supported by Dutch Patriots) in 1789, which had resulted in a declaration of independence and the establishment of the United States of Belgium. Full imperial control was established by the end of the year.

16 the Grand Seignior: Austria had been at war with the Ottoman Empire since 1787 but on Prussia's threatened intervention returned to the Sultan (the 'Grand Seignior') by the same Treaty of Reisenbach (*see* n.15 above) all the territory gained from him during that period.

17 the bishop of Liege: a revolution in August 1789 had removed the Prince-Bishop of Liège, and its instigators had expected support from both France and Prussia; when Austrian troops retook the city in December 1790, however, they did so unopposed by Prussia.

18 Provident patriots ... Lacedæmonian enemy: elements in the Roman Senate advised against the destruction of Carthage in 146 BC; King Pausanias of Sparta, in a similar manner, was unwilling to exploit the divisions in Athens to destroy that city's power in 403 BC.

19 Bajazet: immortalized by Racine, the younger brother of Sultan Murad IV of Turkey, put to death by him in 1639.

20 *Polycletus* (Polyclitus/Polyklitos/Polycleitus – 'much-renowned'): 5th-century BC Greek (bronze) sculptor, seen as one of the most important and influential artistic figures of classical antiquity.

21 *preceptorum sancti voluere parentis esse loco*: 'who consider that a teacher stood in for a parent' (Juvenal, *Satires*).

22 *Nouvelle Eloise* (*Julie, ou la nouvelle Héloïse*): novel in letters by Jean-Jacques Rousseau, published in Amsterdam in 1761.

23 *Cum ventum ... æqui*: 'One's character is repulsed when the truth is at issue, and justice and equity are born from expediency' (Horace, *Satires*).

24 *Debet ... tutissimum*: paraphrase from Cicero, regretting the lack of protection from persecution provided either by home or senate.

25 Helvetius (Claude Adrien Helvétius, 1715–71): French philosopher, author of *De l'esprit* (On Mind).

26 Virgil ... Pollios: Gaius Asinius Pollio, a Roman soldier and politician, was the addressee of Virgil's fourth and eighth Eclogues. Mirabeau warned the Assembly in summer 1790 not to expect peace either 'from the smallest of our hamlets [or] from the entire world'.

27 General Monk (George Monck, 1st Duke of Albemarle, 1608–70): English soldier who rose to prominence during the Thirty Years' War, fought for Charles I during the English Civil War, but was pardoned by Parliament, later becoming a vital figure in the Restoration of Charles II.

28 *ubi miseriarum ... aspici*: 'to see and be seen was a significant part of one's misery' (Tacitus, *Agricola*).

29 Abbé Maury (Jean-Siffrein Maury, 1746–1817): French cardinal, defender of the *ancien régime* until he emigrated in 1792. He was made Archbishop of Paris in 1810 after coming to an accommodation with Napoleon.

30 M. Cazales (Jacques-Antoine-Marie Cazalès, 1758–1805): French orator, politician. He emigrated in 1792, fighting in the émigrés' army against revolutionary France, lived in both Switzerland and England (where he met Burke), but returned to France in 1803.

31 M. Mounier and M. Lally: Assembly members who, being leaders of the Right, left Paris in 1789, Mounier travelling to Switzerland, Lally-Tollendal (*see* Reflections on the Revolution in France (20), n.78) to England.

32 *tiers état* (Third Estate): *see* Reflections on the Revolution in France (20), n.42.

33 *ea visa salus morientibus una*: 'this seemed the only hope to preserve them from death' (Virgil, *Georgics*).

34 *Mox erat ... dentibus artus*: 'afterwards, even this was their destruction, and they burned with fury; in the pangs of death, they lacerated their limbs with their bare teeth' (Virgil, *Georgics*).

35 first I would say: Greek means 'give me a place to stand [and I will move the world]', Archimedes' famous boast, explaining the principles of leverage.

36 "a work of labour long, and endless praise": a quotation from Spenser's *Faerie Queene*.

37 Fairfaxes (Thomas Fairfax, 3rd Baron Fairfax, 1612–71): General, commander of Parliamentary forces during the English Civil War, but resigned, unwilling to countenance the execution of Charles I. He was later active in the Restoration of Charles II (1660).

38 committee of research: the French National Assembly set up the *comité de recherches* to root out conspiracies and subversion.

AN APPEAL FROM THE NEW TO THE OLD WHIGS (22)

[Full title: *An Appeal from the New to the Old Whigs, in consequence of some late discussions in Parliament, relative to the* Reflections on the French Revolution]

1 *petere honestam dimissionem*: to ask for an honourable discharge.

2 Diogenes the Cynic (412/404–323 BC): Greek thinker. He reportedly saw contemporary Athenian society as corrupt and espoused a simple lifestyle.

3 authentic organ: reference to Charles James Fox and Burke's confrontation with him during the debates on 6 and 11 May 1791 on the Quebec Bill (*see* below, n.5). Both men used the bill to expound upon their very different views of the new French constitution, in the course of which they publicly ended their friendship of twenty-two years.

4 Avignon ... Carpentras: papal enclaves shortly afterwards annexed by France.

5 the Quebec bill: when passed, the Constitutional Act of 1791 superseded the Quebec Act (1774), with the intention of accommodating the large numbers of English-speaking loyalists who had fled to Quebec after the American Revolution. The province was divided into two, Upper Canada being governed by English law and institutions and Lower Canada by French. Representative legislative assemblies were established in both. The Roman Catholic Church was confirmed in its privileges in Lower Canada while it was hoped that grants of land to Protestant clergy in Upper Canada would encourage the creation of an established church there.

6 Marcus Aurelius (AD 121–180): Roman Emperor (161–180) and Stoic philosopher.

7 Trajan (AD 53–117): Roman Emperor (98–117). He presided over the Empire's greatest era of military expansion, but also (as one of the Five Good Emperors – one of whom was Marcus Aurelius, *see* n.6 above) oversaw ambitious building projects and implemented social welfare policies resulting in an era of peace and prosperity for the Mediterranean world.

8 Nero (AD 37–68): Roman Emperor (54–68), described as a tyrant by Suetonius and Tacitus but portrayed more favourably by other contemporary sources.

9 *more majorum*: after the custom of our ancestors.

10 Galba (3 BC–AD 69): Roman Emperor (68–69), Governor of Hispania Tarreconensis, assassinated after disputing the right of the Praetorians to hail Otho (Governor of Lusitania) as their emperor.

11 *dura mater*: (literally: tough mother), membrane, outermost of three layers surrounding the brain and spinal cord, used here to refer to the birth of Athena, who sprang fully formed from the head of Jupiter (Zeus).

12 *Si genus ... nefandi*: 'Even if you have no respect for the human race and mortal arms, you should beware the gods, who remember right and wrong' (Virgil, *Aeneid*).

13 *artifices officiorum*: manufacturers of official duties.

14 *Quid summus? ... et humana qua parte locatus es in re?*: 'learn what we are, and for what sort of lives we were born; what place was assigned to us at the start; how to round the turning-post gently, and from what point to begin the turn; what limit should be placed on wealth; what prayers may rightfully be offered; what good there is in fresh-minted coin; how much should be spent on country and on kin; what part God has ordered you to play, and at what point of the human commonwealth you have been stationed' (Persius, *Satires*, English translation by G. C. Ramsay, 1918).

15 *numero plures ... virtute et honore majores*: more in number ... greater in honour and virtue.

16 *satis est equitem mihi plaudere*: 'it is enough if the knights applaud me' (Horace, *Satires*).

17 *Jacquerie*: uprising of the French peasantry against the nobility in 1358, later applied to any popular revolt.

18 *Captal de Buche* (Sir Jean III de Grailly, d. 1376): French military leader in the Hundred Years' War, praised for his chivalry by chronicler Jean Froissart, but severe in his treatment of the Jacquerie (*see* n.17 above).

19 Cade, Ket, and Straw: leaders of revolts – Jack Cade led a popular uprising against Henry VI (1450); Robert 'Ben' Kett led a 1549 revolt against the enclosure of land in Norfolk; Jack Straw was one of three leaders of the Peasants' Revolt in 1381.

20 Abbé John Ball ... Abbé Gregoire: John Ball was a fourteenth-century cleric who was removed from his post as a priest for preaching sermons criticizing the feudal system; Abbé Grégoire (1750–1831) was a French Catholic priest, revolutionary leader and proponent of universal suffrage.

21 When Adam delved ... gentleman?: quotation from speech made by John
    Ball to Kentish rebels gathered on Blackheath in the Peasants' Revolt
    which continues, 'From the beginning all men were created alike, and our
    bondage or servitude came in by the unjust oppression of naughty men.'
    Burke's lengthy footnote, in which he elaborates on the theme that the
    peasants' uprisings of old 'contain more good morality and less bad politics'
    than to be found amongst the radicals of the 1790s, and quotes at length in
    Latin from Thomas Walsingham's *Historia Anglicana*, is here omitted.

22 bailliages: areas of interest or authority.

23 A name ... joy to hear: from Abraham Cowley, *Davideis*.

24 *Ferrum est quod amant*: The sword is what they love.

25 Proteus: legendary oracular Old Man of the Sea based on the island of
    Pharos, off the coast of the Nile Delta.

26 *Finita* potestas ... haerens: 'What law limits the scope of each thing, and
    where is its boundary stone?' (Lucretius, *De Rerum Natura*).

27 "*Octingentorum annorum fortuna ... non potest*": 'Eight hundred years of pros-
    perity and order have consolidated this fabric of empire; it cannot be over-
    thrown without destroying those who overthrow it' (Tacitus, *Historiae*).

28 'Tis not the hasty ... delay: from John Dryden's *Astraea Redux*.

29 *Knaves Acre*: eighteenth-century name for Little Pulteney Street, Soho,
    London, mentioned in John Strype's 1720 survey, an updated edition of
    A Survey of London by John Stow (1598).

30 *Eadem semper causa ... vocabulara usurparet*: 'It is always the same reason: lust,
    avarice and a desire to change their situation. The pretext is provided by
    liberty and specious words; the same cant is always used by those who desire
    slavery for others and dominion for themselves' (Tacitus, *Historiae*).

31 Montesquieu: *see* Reflections on the Revolution in France (20), n.146.

32 Milton (John Milton, 1608–74): *see* Inquiry into the Sublime and Beautiful
    (2), n.16.

33 Sir Joshua Reynolds (1723–92): English painter, specializing in portraits,
    founder and first president of the Royal Academy. A close friend of Burke.

LETTER TO SIR HERCULES LANGRISHE (23)

[Full title: *A Letter from the Right Hon. Edmund Burke, M.P. in the Kingdom
of Great Britain, to Sir Hercules Langrishe, Bart. M.P. on the Subject of Roman
Catholics of Ireland and the Propriety of Admitting them to the Elective Franchise,
Consistently with the Principles of the Constitution as Established at the
Revolution*]

1 SIR HERCULES LANGRISHE: the Irish politician Sir Hercules Langrishe (1731–
   1811), was a friend and contemporary of Burke with known Catholic sympathies. Like Burke, he was a graduate of Trinity College, Dublin. He
   owned his own borough and sat in the Irish House of Commons as an
   independent from 1761 until the Union with Great Britain in 1800 when
   he retired from active politics.

2 I really think ... commencement: Catholics driven to throw in their lot
with those Protestants and dissenters who have been inspired by the ideas
of the French Revolution. The Society of United Irishmen, just such an
organization, had been established in 1791. This would cause considerable
alarm to the British government and helped persuade them that further
Catholic relief was necessary.

3 Popery laws: otherwise known as the Penal Laws and used to describe anti-
Catholic Acts and proclamations in Ireland since the Reformation, penalizing the practice of the Roman Catholic religion and imposing civil disabilities on Catholics. Some of these had lapsed since the Restoration; the
term is sometimes used more specifically for the code of anti-Catholic laws
passed by the Protestant Parliament of Ireland between 1691 and 1759, after
the defeat of the Catholics by William III.

4 senseless projects: schemes to solicit French military intervention in favour
of a similar revolution in Ireland. (These later bore fruit in a sizeable but
abortive naval invasion in 1796, and a small, unsuccessful French landing
during the Irish Rebellion of 1798.)

5 absurd persons: possibly Theobald Wolfe Tone (1763–98) and James Napper Tandy (1740–1803), two of the founders of the United Irishmen. Their
original object of parliamentary reform would soon give way to a more
radical agenda of independence and republicanism.

6 *Servorum non est respublica*: This is not a republic of slaves.

7 test acts: in England (1661 and 1673) and Ireland (1704) these required civil
and military office holders under the Crown to take Holy Communion
according to Anglican rites, to subscribe to a declaration against transub-
stantiation and to swear oaths of supremacy and allegiance. They were directed against both Catholics and Protestant nonconformists. The latter,
however, were readmitted to public life by a series of Indemnity Acts. In
Ireland the first of these was passed as early as 1719. In England annual acts
were passed after 1728.

8 Popery laws since repealed: the process of slowly dismantling the Penal Acts
had already begun, with Catholic relief acts passed in 1771, 1774, 1778 and
1782.

9 octennial act (1768): provided for general elections every eight years and
was passed after a radical campaign for shorter parliaments during the
1760s. Before that the Irish Parliament had existed for the lifetime of the
King.

10 inclined to favour: Protestant landlords might be inclined to dispossess
Catholic tenants in favour of Protestant freeholders who had the right to
vote, and who would vote in the Protestant interest.

11 Thirty-nine Articles (of Religion, 1563–71): part of the Elizabethan religious settlement, the result of three decades of attempting to define the
doctrinal position of the Church of England vis à vis the Roman Catholic
Church. Largely the work of Matthew Parker, Archbishop of Canterbury
1559–75, they were confirmed and ratified by Crown, Convocation and
Parliament, and printed in the Book of Common Prayer. Anglican clergy
were obliged to subscribe to them. (They were adopted by the Church of
Ireland, which had previously used its own articles, in 1634.)

12 Protestant toleration itself: the Toleration Act of 1689 had granted freedom
    of religious worship to Protestant dissenters in England who swore the oath
    of allegiance and supremacy. Their ministers were expected to subscribe
    to those of the Thirty-Nine Articles not directly concerned with Anglican
    Church government. A Dissenters' Relief Act in 1779 released them from
    this obligation.

13 *adulta et prævalida*: 'strong and matured vices' (Tacitus, *Annals*).

14 *the Confession of Faith*: largely written by John Knox in 1560, the Confession
    of Faith defined the reformed religion in Scotland; the presbyterian struc-
    ture of the Kirk was set out in his *First Book of Discipline* the same year.
    During the Commonwealth, both were superseded by the Westminster
    Confession of Faith (1646–48) which established a Presbyterian Church in
    England and Scotland alike. This in turn was nullified at the Restoration,
    but ratified for Scotland alone by the Scottish Parliament in 1690 and con-
    firmed again in the Act of Union (1707) between England and Scotland.

15 the *Directory*: the Westminster Assembly (1643–48) of Puritan divines pro-
    duced a Directory of Public Worship designed to replace the Anglican
    Book of Common Prayer, and a shorter and longer catechism for religious
    instruction.

16 the king ... *church of England*: as stipulated in the Act of Settlement (1701).

17 it is so in Ireland: in 1782 the efforts of the Irish Patriot leader Henry Grat-
    tan – a friend of Burke – were crowned with success when the Rock-
    ingham administration repealed the Declaratory Act of 1719 and amended
    Poynings' Law (*see* n.31 below), thereby conceding the Irish Parliament
    legislative independence under the Crown. The Act of Renunciation
    (1783) confirmed this as a right 'established for ever, and shall at no time
    hereafter be questioned or questionable'.

18 the test as to Protestant dissenters: in 1780 the Irish Test Act of 1704 was
    repealed to allow dissenters to hold public office.

19 acts of the 2nd and 8th of Anne: laws were introduced in Ireland during
    Queen Anne's reign preventing Catholics from voting in parliamentary or
    local elections unless they had taken the oaths of allegiance and abjuration.
    It was under George II in 1728 that all Catholics were completely
    disenfranchised.

20 edict of Nantz [Nantes] (1598): issued by Henri IV, himself a former
    Huguenot. Richelieu destroyed the Huguenots as a political and military
    threat to the French state, but allowed them freedom of worship and equal-
    ity before the law (Peace of Alès, 1629). When Louis XIV revoked the edict
    and issued the repressive Edict of Fontainebleau in 1685 around 200,000
    Huguenots immediately fled the country, a quarter of them settling in Eng-
    land and Ireland. By 1760, some 300,000 had left France.

21 Guelph or Ghibelline: two competing factions in medieval Italy, the
    Guelphs supporting the Pope, the Ghibellines the Holy Roman Emperor.

22 Cerealis (Ceralis Petilius, b. *c.* AD 30–d. after 83): Roman general.

23 "*Nos quamvis ... colite*": 'We, though so often provoked, have used the
    right of conquest to burden you only with the cost of maintaining peace;
    for the tranquillity of nations cannot be preserved without armies; armies

cannot exist without pay; pay cannot be furnished without tribute; all else is common between us. You often command our legions. You rule these and other provinces. There is no privilege, no exclusion ... Give, therefore, your love and respect to the cause of peace, and to that capital in which we, conquerors and conquered, claim an equal right' (Tacitus, *Histories*, tr. Church and Brodribb, 1869).

24 statutes of Kilkenny (1366): by these, Edward III sought to secure his weakening hold over the eastern counties which still remained loyal to him, and to keep them English. His English subjects were enjoined to have nothing to do with 'Irish enemies' – no intermarriage, no hurling, no Irish minstrels, no horse-trading, etc. – while Irishmen living in the colony could not own land, hold ecclesiastical office or bring a court case, and were obliged to have English surnames, speak English and follow English customs.

25 Baron Finglass, Spenser, and Sir John Davis: Patrick Finglas (d. 1537) was an Irish judge during the reign of Henry VIII, regarded as one of the chief supporters of English rule in Ireland; the poet Edmund Spenser (1552–99) served as secretary to Lord Grey of Wilton, Lord Deputy of Ireland, and received land following the plantation of Munster in 1580; John Davis (1569–1626), lawyer, poet and politician, was Attorney General in Ireland during the reign of James I and was involved in a government project to establish a plantation in Ulster. All three men wrote about the condition of Ireland under English rule.

26 Chichester's time: Sir Arthur Chichester (1563–1625) was Lord Deputy of Ireland from 1604 to 1616 in the years following the Tyrone rebellion, which he had helped to subdue ruthlessly. A persecutor of Catholics, whom he saw as a threat to the English Crown, he was also heavily involved in the plantation of Ulster.

27 Lord Strafford (Thomas Wentworth, 1st Earl of Strafford, 1593–1641): English statesman, Lord Deputy of Ireland 1632–39, made government more efficient, improved the economy and raised a great deal of revenue for the English exchequer. He received his earldom in 1640 and was appointed Lord Lieutenant of Ireland, charged by Charles I with the raising of an army to fight against Scotland in the Bishops' War. Fear that this would be used in England was one reason for his impeachment and subsequent execution in May 1641.

28 Earl of Clarendon (Edward Hyde, 1st Earl of Clarendon, 1609–74): Charles II's chief minister at the Restoration. A staunch Anglican who nonetheless favoured the King's more tolerant attitude to religious nonconformity, he was not in fact the author of the so-called Clarendon Code, a series of laws penalizing dissenters introduced by the Cavalier Parliament in the 1660s.

29 Irish Revolution of 1782: *see* n.17 above.

30 burned all the journals: James II had fled to Ireland and called a Parliament in 1689, the majority of whose members were Anglo-Catholics. After the defeat of James II the Parliament called in 1695 was wholly Protestant, subordinate to England and intent upon subduing the Irish Catholics. It cancelled all the legislation passed under James II and burnt the parliamentary records for that period.

31 Poyning's law: Sir Edward Poynings (1459–1521), Lord Deputy of Ireland,

placed the Parliament of Ireland under the authority of the English Parliament in 1494. (It had not in fact been repealed under James nor mentioned in the address to William and Mary in 1692.)

32 the Cardinal of York: Henry Benedict Stuart (1725–1807), Cardinal Duke of York, was the younger son of the 'Old Pretender', and the last Stuart heir to the throne. Styled Henry IX by Jacobites, he never laid claim to it.

33 a man of some property: Edward Byrne (d. 1804), who became Chairman of the Catholic Committee in December 1791, a merchant who was said to have an annual tax bill of £100,000. The Catholic Committee was a political organization founded in 1757 to campaign for relief from the Penal Acts. The old aristocratic leaders had been conservative in their aims and methods; Byrne represented the rising Catholic commercial interest, men of substance whose methods were more aggressive but whose prime aim was to participate in public life. Their coming to power provoked a secession of sixty-eight prominent Catholics led by Lords Fingal and Kenmare.

34 Polybius ... Cato: the ancient Greek historian Polybius (c. 204–122 BC); Marcus Porcius Cato ('the Elder') (234–149 BC), Roman statesman, great-grandfather of the younger Cato.

35 draft you have sent me: probably a reference to a Declaration issued by the Catholic Committee of Dublin at the end of 1791, asserting its right to form an association in order to achieve the repeal of Catholic disabilities by constitutional means.

36 Mr. Butler and Mr. Tandy: Simon Butler (1757–97) and James Napper Tandy (1740–1803), prominent members of the Dublin Society of United Irishmen.

37 "artful folds of sacred lawn": Matthew Prior, from *Alma: or, The Progress of the Mind* (1718).

38 *væ victis*: 'woe to the conquered!' (Livy).

39 Mr. Flood (Henry Flood, 1732–91): orator and statesman, founder of the Irish opposition party in the 1760s and from 1782 an MP at Westminster, where he introduced a bill for parliamentary reform on 4 March 1790. Both Pitt and Burke spoke against it, and it was withdrawn.

40 a person of the very highest rank: Charles Lennox, 3rd Duke of Richmond (*see also* Letter to the Duke of Richmond, n.1), one of the more radical of the Rockingham group, tried to push the Whigs into action on parliamentary reform by introducing his own bill in the House of Lords in June 1780. His proposals for manhood suffrage, equal electoral districts and annual parliaments went far beyond what even reforming peers would entertain, and the bill was rejected without a vote.

41 Lord Coke (Sir Edward Coke): *see* A Vindication of Natural Society (1), n.4.

42 an union with Great Britain: as would happen in 1800 after the failed Irish rebellion of 1798.

43 Lord Kenmare (Thomas Browne, 4th Viscount Kenmare, 1726–95): Catholic landowner and politician. In the 1770s and 1780s he was the leader of the conservative wing of the Catholic Committee along with Lord Fingal and Sir Patrick Bellew.

44 another distressed people ... : the people of India under British rule.

45 French conquered country of Canada: for the Quebec Act and the Constitutional Act *see* An Appeal from the New to the Old Whigs (22) n.5.

46 take what part you please at this hour: in the event, the concessions won
   by Catholics in 1792 were very moderate indeed. The British Cabinet had
   required some token of reform, but the Irish government contented itself
   with asking Sir Hercules to introduce a modest measure as a private member's bill which passed almost without opposition. The resulting Act
   opened the legal profession to Catholics, legalized marriages between
   Catholics and Protestants and removed restrictions on Catholic schools and
   apprenticeships. It roused the Catholic Committee to further efforts and
   in 1793, with Britain on the brink of war with France, Pitt and Dundas
   brought greater pressure to bear on the Irish junta, resulting in more substantial concessions (*see* Letter to Unknown, n. 4).

LETTER TO RICHARD BURKE (24)

[Full title: *A Letter to Richard Burke, Esq., on the Protestant Ascendancy in Ireland*, first published in *Works* (1793). On 19 February 1792 Burke informed
Richard, then in Dublin, that he was writing him a long letter. It was never
finished.]

1 similar in principal to mine: Burke compares his involvement in the
  impeachment of Warren Hastings to his son's mission in Ireland. Richard,
  a practising barrister, was employed as an agent by the Catholic Committee
  between 1790 and 1792. He had held hopeful talks with Pitt and Dundas
  in London during 1791 and in Dublin lobbied the Irish government on
  the Committee's behalf for a Relief Act which included voting rights for
  Catholics. He regarded Langrishe's bill as a betrayal and on 25 January 1792
  while trying to conduct a protest in the Irish House of Commons narrowly
  avoided arrest. But he was as assiduous as his father could have desired,
  and his chief adversary, Major Hobart, Chief Secretary of Ireland, admitted
  when Richard returned to Dublin later in the year that 'the Catholics seem
  to have acquired fresh vigour since the arrival of Mr Richard Burke'. By
  this time Richard had already lost his job as Secretary to the Committee
  to Wolfe Tone.

2 *honestum nomen imponitur vitio*: an honest name is placed over vice.

3 Castle of Dublin: Dublin Castle was the seat of government.

4 a touch of the corporation: the Corporation of Dublin had on 20 January
  1792 approved an address to the King pleading that the Protestant Ascendancy in Ireland be preserved.

5 Horace ... *parcè detortum* (*parce detorsum*): 'sparingly altered' (Horace, *Ars
  Poetica*).

6 Cowley (Abraham Cowley, 1618–67): son of London stationer, poet,
  scholar and one of the founders of the Royal Society. Burke is here referring to Cowley's 'Of Wit': 'What is it then, which like the *Power Divine* /
  We only can by *Negatives* define?'

7 *Tristis et luctuosa successio*: sad and doleful inheritance.

8 Lord Newburgh (Anthony James Radclyffe, 5th Earl of Newburgh, 1757–1814): born in Slindon, Sussex, son of James Bartholomew Radclyffe, 4th Earl of Newburgh.

9 *quâdam specie et similitudine pacis*: under false cover and likeness of peace.

10 Ireland lost 200,000 of her inhabitants: future Whig historians chose to overlook that the 'Bloodless Revolution' had been far from bloodless in Ireland and Scotland.

SPEECH ON THE PETITION OF THE UNITARIAN SOCIETY (25)

1 UNITARIAN SOCIETY: Unitarian beliefs were gaining ground in England during the eighteenth century, drawing adherents from within the Anglican Church as well as amongst dissenters. Theophilus Lindsey, a former Anglican clergyman, founded the first Unitarian church in London in 1774; Joseph Priestley (*see* Reflections on the French Revolution (20), n.57) helped to establish Unitarian patterns of worship and institutional structure in his *Forms of Prayer; and other Offices for the Use of Unitarian Societies* (1783). A number of prominent politicians had Unitarian sympathies (*see also* Reflections on the French Revolution (20), n.9), and the movement was increasingly associated with radicalism. Unitarians were not covered by the 1779 Act giving relief to dissenters, because of their non-trinitarian theology. They organized a petition to Parliament for the repeal of the Blasphemy Act of 1697, which was presented by Fox on 8 March 1792. On 11 May his bill for the relief of Unitarians was rejected by a majority of 142 to 63. A Relief Act eventually passed in 1813.

2 *dat operam ut cum ratione insaniat*: he strives to make his mind unsound by means of his reason.

3 *Stulti est dixisse, Non putâram*: Self-evident nonsense, I would have thought.

4 Quale portentum neque militaris ... Arida nutrix: 'Ebullient Apulia does not support an omen like this in the wide oak forests, and Juba, dry nurse of lions, does not produce such either' (Horace, *Odes*).

5 Monsieur Bailly, or Brissot, or Chabot [...] Dr. Kippis: all men, in Burke's opinion, who would 'load a tyrannous power by the poisonous taunts of the vulgar'. Jean-Sylvain Bailly (1736–93), French astronomer, mathematician, mayor of Paris (1789–91); Jacques Pierre Brissot (1754–93), leading Girondist (*see* Speech on War with France (26), n.4); François Chabot (1756–94), radical French politician; Andrew Kippis (1725–95), English nonconformist clergyman, biographer.

6 *qui cadere potest in hominem constantem et non metuentem*: which is able to seize any constant, fearless man.

7 Nec coïere pares ... nominis umbra: 'the two contenders were not well matched: one was weakened by ageing, having worn the toga for a long time and, trusting his former greatness, had forgotten, in peacetime, how to lead ... he did nothing to gain fresh power, standing as a mere shadow of a mighty name' (Lucan, *Pharsalia*).

8 Hannibal (Hannibal Barca, 247–183?BC): Carthaginian military commander.

9 *falsos in amore odia non fingere*: men do not necessarily feign hatred because they are false in friendship.

10 *communia altaria, æque ac patriam, diligite, colite, fovete*: love, embrace and esteem high altars as well as their native country.

11 Test Acts: English penal laws ensuring that Roman Catholics and nonconformists were excluded from public office. *See also* Letter to Sir Hercules Langrishe (23), n.7.

SPEECH ON WAR WITH FRANCE (26)

[From *Debate in the Commons on the King's Message respecting the Declaration of War with France*, Cobbett's Parliamentary History of England, 1793]

1 WAR WITH FRANCE: on 21 January 1793, Louis XVI was guillotined, and on 1 February the Convention unanimously voted for war with Great Britain. On 11 February Secretary Dundas presented George III's Message calling for 'the firm and effectual support of the House of Commons, and of the jealous exertions of a brave and loyal people, in prosecuting a just and necessary war and endeavouring, under the blessing of Providence, to oppose an effectual barrier to the farther progress of a system which strikes at the security and peace of all independent nations, and is pursued in open defiance of every principle of moderation, good faith, humanity, and justice.' The debate took place the following day. Pitt the Younger proposed an address promising the expected support; Fox, while accepting war as a *fait accompli*, nevertheless accused ministers of misrepresenting the causes of the war and called for an amendment to the address.

2 the right hon. gentleman ... the smallness of his party: Fox's enthusiasm for the French Revolution was causing increasing discomfort to moderate Whigs. He could no longer rely on the support of moderates like Fitzwilliam and Portland who had been outraged when in December 1792 he accused George III and Pitt of playing upon popular fear of Jacobinism to curtail civil liberties and increase executive power – an amendment which he lost by 290 votes to 50. The break finally came in 1794 when Portland and others joined Pitt's ministry. Fox and his diminished group of friends continued to call for parliamentary reform and to champion civil liberties against repressive legislation introduced by Pitt during the war with France (Fox's notable victory had already come in securing the passage of the Libel Act in 1792). He was briefly Foreign Secretary again in Lord Grenville's government (1806) and proposed the bill which would finally abolish the slave trade the following year. Already in poor health, he died before it had passed. (For Fox's earlier career, *see* Speech on Mr Fox's East-India Bill (15), n.1.)

3 Mr. Windham (William Windham, 1750–1810): Whig statesman, noted orator in the House of Commons from his election (1784) onwards. Although originally supporting the French Revolution, he was a leading anti-Jacobin by 1792 and in the process of breaking with Fox to form a 'third party'.

4 Brissot's speeches in the National Convention: Brissot (Jacques Pierre Brissot, 1754–93) was a leading member of the more moderate 'Girondin'

grouping during the Revolution. He was celebrated for his oratory, especially in favour of keeping Louis XVI alive both for the King's value as a bargaining chip and as a means of preventing a royalist rebellion. He was guillotined during the Reign of Terror.

5 their minister Cambon (Pierre-Joseph Cambon, 1756–1820): served the French Revolutionary government (1791–95) by stabilizing its finances.

6 Garat (Dominique Joseph Garat, 1749–1833): French politician and writer. As a deputy to the Estates General (elected 1789), he recorded the Assembly's proceedings in the *Journal de Paris*, and as Minister of Justice (appointed 1792) he was entrusted by Georges Danton with the task of informing Louis XVI of his death sentence.

7 lord Gower (George Granville Leveson-Gower, 1st Duke of Sutherland, 1758–1833): ambassador to Paris (1790–92), withdrawn on the imprisonment of the French royal family.

8 decree of the 19th of November: 1792 decree promising French support ('fraternity and assistance to all people') for any rebellion against a king. Chauvelin, the French ambassador in London, whose mission was to secure British neutrality, had attempted and failed to interpret this declaration as unthreatening to Foreign Secretary William Grenville.

9 *sans culottes*: lower classes, who did not wear the silk knee-breeches, or *culottes*, of the nobility. They became the grassroots radicals of the French Revolution, protesting against the excesses of the *ancien régime*.

10 Dumourier ... to Anacharsis Cloots: Charles-François du Périer Dumouriez (1739–1823) was a general in the French Revolutionary Wars who deserted the revolutionary cause during Napoleon's reign; Jean-Baptiste du Val-de-Grâce, baron de Cloots/z (1755–94), known as 'Anarchasis', was a Prussian nobleman who hastened joyfully to Paris on the outbreak of revolution. After congratulating the National Assembly on behalf of the human race, he joined the Jacobin Club, became a naturalized French citizen and was elected to the National Convention, where he called for a revolutionary crusade to spread democracy throughout Europe. He voted in favour of Louis XVI's execution but was accused by Robespierre of being a foreign agent and guillotined the following year.

11 the Moniteur (*Le Moniteur Universel*): French newspaper (founded 1789), official journal of the French government, of considerable value as a purveyor of propaganda during the Napoleonic regime. It ceased publication in 1901.

12 Great Britain: when Burke had finished, Sheridan rose to defend Fox, and after several more speeches Fox's amendment was negatived and the address agreed to without a division. On 18 February Fox put twelve resolutions against the war which Burke again opposed; they were rejected by a majority of 270 to 44.

THOUGHTS AND DETAILS ON SCARCITY (27)

[Full title: *Thoughts and Details on Scarcity, originally presented to the Right Hon. William Pitt, in the month of November, 1795.* Burke described this as 'a paper' which he had 'hurriedly scribbled'; it was edited and printed from a transcription found amongst Burke's papers by his executors in 1800.]

1 THOUGHTS ON SCARCITY: after two years of war and poor harvests in both 1794 and 1795, the House of Commons at Pitt's behest had on 3 November set up a select committee 'to enquire into the circumstance of the present scarcity and the best means of remedying it'. Burke, by now in retirement, was concerned by a project to fix agricultural wages in times of shortage. Ill-health prevented him from expanding it into the economic treatise he had planned.

2 tax proposed on the farming interest: the 'Speenhamland system', as it came to be known. In view of the distress caused by the high price of corn in 1795, the magistrates of Berkshire met on 6 May at the Pelican Inn in Speenhamland and devised a scheme to guarantee agricultural labourers a living wage by fixing a minimum wage on a sliding scale according to the price of corn and adjusted according to size of family. If the wages paid to them by their employers fell below that, they would be supplemented from the poor rates. The idea was adopted in other counties, particularly in the south of England, but was never passed into legislation. When Samuel Whitbread in December 1795 put forward a miminum wage bill it was opposed by Pitt who argued that it represented 'legislative interference into that which ought to be allowed to take its natural course'.

3 *instrumentum vocale*: talking (agricultural) implements (i.e. slaves), referred to by Marcus Terentius Varro in his *Rerum Rusticarum Libri Tres* (Three Books on Agriculture).

4 Puffendorff (Baron Samuel von Pufendorf, 1632–94): German political philosopher, legal theorist and historian. Burke here refers to Pufendorf's *De jure natura et gentium* (1672).

5 "*Fruges consumere nati*": 'born to consume natural resources' (Horace, *Epistles*).

6 to account to no one ... for his gain: Burke had served on a committee in 1772 to draw up a bill for the repeal of the common law offences of engrossing, forestalling and regrating – all of which involved influencing the market in some way – and the law providing for the licensing of 'badgers', traders who bought corn from a market in order to sell it on. In 1787 he spoke strongly against their revival.

7 Arthur Young (1741–1820): famous agricultural theorist, farmer, writer and political economist. During the 1760s he had undertaken a series of journeys through England and Wales, conducting detailed research into agriculture and publishing the results in three popular books. His *Tour of Ireland* was published in 1780; his *Travels in France* in 1782. In 1793 he helped to establish the Board of Agriculture. His friendship with Burke began in the 1770s when Burke was making improvements to his farm at Gregories.

8 I confess ... discern its object: in October 1795 the Home Secretary, the Duke of Portland, had sent a letter to all Lords Lieutenant (England and

Wales) and Sheriff Deputies (Scotland) requesting them to oblige magistrates to provide details of the harvest in their areas. (The information gathered was insufficient to be of use and the enquiry was dropped.)

9 certain and steady price: during 1795 the government had been importing corn on a large scale and dispatching it to wherever the supply was particularly short. The scheme to introduce public granaries was not pursued. There was a significant decrease in regular grain imports; purchase prices were high and private merchants probably felt they could only lose out by competing with the government. This contributed to a significant shortfall, much hardship, and food riots throughout 1795–6 (John Bohstedt, *The Politics of Provisions*, 2010).

10 a leading member of great ability: Fox had wondered whether an increase in consumption might be a possible explanation (2 November 1795).

11 stop put to the distillery: the use of wheat, barley or malt for the distillation of spirits was prohibited from June 1795 to February 1797 when a Select Committee of the House of Commons was able to dissuade the government from intervening.

12 *opus maximum*: the heart of the matter.

13 perished from famine: records reveal that in the years 1794–1801 mortality rates did not reach crisis levels – being defined as a 10 per cent uptrend in one year, or a 25 per cent uptrend in any one month – though 1795 was close. In October 1795 the government stopped its grain import programme and offered import bounties instead. Private merchants began to trade again. Many were ruined when in March 1796 the government released stockpiles of grain on to the market (John Bohstedt, *The Politics of Provisions*, 2010).

14 nearest to us locally: during 1793 the Convention had brought in a policy of fixing the price for foodstuffs (the Law of the Maximum), with penalties for forestalling, which was followed until the end of 1794.

15 'ΕΣΤΑΙ 'ΗΜΑΡ!: 'The day will come' (Homer, *Iliad*).

16 Scipio (Publius Cornelius Scipio Africanus, 236–183 BC): Scipio the African, Roman statesman and general in the second Punic war.

FIRST LETTER ON A REGICIDE PEACE (28)

[Full title: *Two Letters Addressed to A Member of the Present Parliament, on the Proposals for Peace with the Regicide Directory of France By the Right Hon. Edmund Burke*. Burke had finished writing the work by March 1796 but publication was delayed until October.]

1 A REGICIDE PEACE: by the end of 1795 the coalition against France was collapsing; Prussia and Spain, defeated, had made peace; the French had overrun the Austrian Netherlands and a client state had been established in the United Provinces. Duing 1796 Sardinia and other Italian allies also capitulated. Austria was Britain's only ally left in the field. The possibility of making peace overtures had first been raised in Parliament early in 1795. The war had become unpopular, and was damaging British commercial interests. When in the autumn a new French constitution was promulgated, Pitt was encouraged that the new Directory would prove more

moderate than the Convention and attempted to open negotiations. Burke regarded the Directory as no less 'regicide' than its predecessor.

2   cutting off ... part of her empire: the French had assisted the American colonists in the War of Independence. The British conceded independence to the colonists at the Treaty of Paris in 1783.

3   seven years' war (1756–63): *see* Thoughts on the Present Discontents (6), n.17.

4   Dr. Brown (John Brown, 1715–66): minister from Carlisle, writer on diverse topics ranging from satire and drama to philosophy, also a nature poet. Burke here refers to Brown's *An Estimate of the manners and principles of the time* (1757–58), which castigated the decadence and ignorance of the upper classes.

5   *Goitre* kept *Goitre* in countenance: this is thought to be a reference to Juvenal (*Satires*, xiii), who asks: 'Who will marvel at a goitre in the Alps?'

6   peculium: property a father or master allowed a child or slave to hold as his own.

7   new allies ... general confederacy: the Batavian (formerly Dutch) Republic and Britain had been in a state of undeclared war since the French invasion of 1795; in 1797 the British navy won a major victory against the Dutch at the battle of Camperdown. Spain had allied with France and declared war on Britain in October 1796 and a naval blockade of Spain began the next year.

8   one of the largest and most important provinces of Spain: refers to the occupation, in 1701, of the Spanish Netherlands by France.

9   elector of Bavaria (Maximilian II Emanuel, 1679–1726): fought against the Ottoman Empire and was an ally of France in the War of the Spanish Succession (1701–14).

10   independent advantages ... heaviest losses: there were early successes for the British in the West Indies, including the recapture of Tobago which was rapidly turned into a slave and sugar colony.

11   the highest tribunal of all ... every other court: reference to the acquittal of Warren Hastings by the House of Lords in April 1795.

12   schools for treason: at the end of 1794 three leading radical reformers, John Horne Tooke, Thomas Hardy and John Thelwall, were tried for treason at the Old Bailey and found not guilty.

13   "Mussabat tacito medicina timore": 'Medicine muttered underneath her breath' (Lucretius, *De Rerum Natura*).

14   The regicide ... scorn: peace overtures made to the French in March 1796 at Basle (where the marquis de Barthélemy was acting, in Burke's words 'as a sort of factor to deal in the degradation of the crowned heads of Europe') were repulsed. Diplomatic efforts to get the King of Prussia to act as a mediator (August) ended in failure. In October the Earl of Malmesbury was permitted by the Directory to travel to Paris where his negotiations with foreign minister Charles Delacroix broke down over the restoration of the Austrian Netherlands (Belgium) to Austria as a *sine qua non*. He was ordered to leave on 19 December.

15 Lord Camden (Charles Pratt, 1st Earl and 1st Baron Camden, 1714–94): English judge and Whig politician, prominent proponent of civil liberties. He was Chief Justice of the Common Pleas, Attorney General and Lord Chancellor.

16 With the law ... conservation: major changes to French civil law were made in 1789; in 1791 a new Penal Code was introduced. The courts of the *ancien régime* were abolished and a new system of courts with elected judges gradually introduced; from 1793 judges were not obliged to have degrees in law and amongst those elected were a gardener, a painter, a gem-cutter and a rent collector. In 1790 the *parlements* (*see* Reflections on the Revolution in France (20), n.40) were swept away and in 1793 the schools of law were closed down.

17 Jacobinism: radical republicanism in the French Revolution (*see* Reflections on the Revolution in France (20), n.95).

18 aetheism: the Cult of Reason was established by Jacques Hébert and Pierre Gaspard Chaumette during the early days of the Republic with the intention of replacing Christianity. A number of church buildings in Paris were converted into temples of reason and a Festival of Reason was held at the cathedral of Notre Dame on 10 November 1793. Robespierre replaced the Cult of Reason with his own brand of deism – the Cult of the Supreme Being – and an even bigger festival took place on 8 June in the Champ de mars. He was guillotined the following month and this new state religion did not survive him.

19 "La Convention ... ": 'The National Convention, having heard the report of its finance, war and diplomatic committees, in accordance with the principle of the people's sovereignty, which does not allow the recognition of any institution that undermines ... '.

20 Brutus (Marcus Junius Brutus, 85–42 BC): politician of the late Roman Republic, one of the assassins of Julius Caesar (44 BC).

21 civil contract: the National Assembly had sanctioned divorce in August 1789 and in September 1792 had laid down the grounds for a quick divorce by mutual consent.

22 lawful unions: Madame Gravel's petition had been presented in March 1792. A committee had been set up to consider the matter and in June 1793 it was decreed that illegitimate children could inherit through both parents; in November 1793 those born after 14 July 1789 were declared to have the same inheritance rights as legitimate children.

23 "*De novi operis nunciatione*": term in civil law dealing with aggrieved party's right to institute an interdict or injunction to hinder any action intended to injure.

24 *damnum infectum*: a threatened injury, not carried out.

25 *damnum nondum factum*: an injury yet to be carried out.

26 *Res damni infecti celeritatem desiderat, et periculosa est dilatio*: a matter involving a threatened injury should be speedily and safely dealt with.

27 *Vetustas pro lege semper habetur*: established custom is always regarded as law.

28 "*Vicini vicinorum facta presumuntur scire*": neighbours can be assumed to know the neighbourhood.

29 Cade (John/Jack Cade, d. 1450): leader of the Kentish rising that attempted to take London.

30 Maroon negro slaves: *see* Reflections on the Revolution in France (20), n.39.

31 *Reubel*, with *Carnot*, with *Revelliere*: three of the five Directors of France. To qualify for the position it was necessary to have served in the Convention and to have voted for the King's execution.

32 The case of Algiers: Fox (1792) denied that having a consul in Algiers implied approval of the administration there.

33 forbearance of piracy: piracy flourished in Algiers. A number of European countries, Britain excluded, paid the Dey for (relative) immunity.

34 The Grand Seignior. ... one and indivisible: Algiers was nominally a Turkish province but from the seventeenth century the Sultan (Grand Seignior) allowed the governor (Dey) to be elected by the soldiery (Janissaries), who were dominant in the country. The Janissaries were recruited in Constantinople, Smyrna and Anatolia.

35 Thus painters write their names at Co: from Matthew Prior's 'Protogenes and Appelles': 'On the plain ground Appelles drew / A circle regularly true. / And will you please, Sweet-heart, said he, / To show your master this from me? / By it he presently will know / How painters write their names at Co.'

36 "whom my dim eyes in vain explore": Homer, *Iliad* (Pope's translation).

37 Some of my oldest friends ... exclusion of one of them: the Duke of Portland (Home Secretary), William Windham (Secretary at War) and other moderate Whigs who had formed a coalition with Pitt in July 1794. Lord Fitzwilliam had left the government in March 1795, having resigned as Lord Lieutenant of Ireland (*see* Letter to Unknown, n.2).

38 *amicus curiae*: literally, a friend of the court, who offers information or argument relevant to a case, but is not actually a party to it.

39 *de plano*, not *pro tribunali*: not on or from the Bench (literally on level ground), not in front of the tribunal.

LETTER TO A NOBLE LORD (29)

[Full title: *A Letter from the Right Honourable Edmund Burke to a Noble Lord, on the Attacks made upon him and his Pension in The House of Lords, by the Duke of Bedford and the Earl of Lauderdale.* Burke's letter was published in February 1796. The addressee is Lord Grenville (*see* n.6 below).]

1 Duke of Bedford (Francis Russell, 5th Duke of Bedford, 1765–1802): one of the younger generation of Whig politicians, a devoted friend of Fox – to whom he would leave a considerable legacy – and a prominent member of the Prince of Wales's circle. Earlier in 1795 he had led a revolt against a new tax on hair powder (a luxury item targeted by Pitt to raise revenue for

the war against France) by sporting what became known as the 'Bedford crop', a fashion followed by many opponents of the war. He was also a pioneer of scientific farming, and an original member of the Board of Agriculture (1793). He and Lauderdale managed to introduce the subject of Burke's pension during a debate on Pitt's Treasonable Practices Act on 13 November 1795. (Burke had retired from the House of Commons in 1794, in straitened financial circumstances. Pitt organized a pension for him, which was finalized during the summer of 1795.)

2 Earl of Lauderdale (James Maitland, 8th Earl of Lauderdale, 1759–1839): Scottish peer, Keeper of the Great Seal of Scotland; leading Foxite and radical. Entered the House of Commons in 1780, made his maiden speech in support of Burke's Civil List bill (1781) and was one of the managers in the impeachment of Warren Hastings. Sat in the House of Lords after 1789 where he was consistently hostile to Pitt's policies. In 1792 he co-founded the Society of the Friends of the People to campaign for parliamentary reform. An impassioned supporter of the French Revolution, he visited Paris the same year, meeting Brissot (*see* Speech on War with France (26), n.4); on return he opposed war with France. Later in life 'Citizen Maitland' became a Tory.

3 Duke of Orleans (Louis Philippe Joseph d'Orléans, 1747–93): member of House of Bourbon (cadet branch), France's ruling dynasty. Although supporting the French Revolution, he was guillotined during the Terror. After the July Revolution (1830), his son Louis-Philippe became King of the French. Gave his name to the Orléanists, proponents of constitutional monarchy.

4 citizen Brissot: *see* Speech on War with France (26), n.4.

5 The Priestleys and the Paines: Joseph Priestley, *see* Reflections on the French Revolution (20), n.57. Thomas Paine, *see* Letter to the Sheriffs of Bristol (10), n.12. and Letter to Unknown, n.9.

6 Lord Grenville (William Wyndham Grenville, 1st Baron Grenville, 1759–1834): Whig statesman, Foreign Secretary from 1791. Later prime minister (1806–07) in the so-called Ministry of All the Talents. He defended Burke's pension as 'the well-earned reward of merit' for a lifetime's public service in the debate in the House of Lords on 13 November 1795.

7 John Zisca (John Zizka, *c.* 1376–1424): Hussite general who requested that his body should be flayed on his death and his skin be used to make a drum, to be played to terrify his enemies.

8 Lord Verulam: *see* Speech on Economical Reform (11), n.32.

9 corresponding society: founded in 1792 by shoemaker Thomas Hardy in London with branches in Sheffield, Manchester, Stockport and Norwich, the Corresponding Society supported radical reform including annual parliaments, manhood suffrage, cheaper government, an end to unfair enclosures and a simpler legal system. The subscription of 1d a week was considerably lower than that of the Constitutional Society (*see* Reflections on the Revolution in France (20), n.2) and it drew much of its membership from the artisan class. Like other radical societies, it maintained links with the French Convention. It was suppressed in 1799.

10 *quantum meruit*: as much as he deserves.

11 pay-office act: Act for the Better Regulation of the Office of Paymaster General of His Majesty's Forces (1783).

12 establishment act: Act for enabling His Majesty to discharge the Debt contracted upon his Civil List Revenues (1782).

13 a sort of national convention: when the petitioning movement (*see* Speech on Economical Reform (11), n.4) was at its height in April 1780, representatives from thirteen counties, three cities and two towns met at the St Albans tavern in Pall Mall, with Christopher Wyvill in the chair, to draw up their reform programme.

14 Lord North: *see* Speech on Conciliation with America (9), n.2.

15 *Ipse diem … in undâ*: 'Even Palinurus cannot distinguish between day and night in the sky; nor does he remember the way through the waters' (Virgil, *Aeneid*).

16 Tristius haud … Ora fame: 'no more baneful monster, no plague or wrath of the gods more fierce, ever emerged from the Stygian waves. These birds have maidens' faces, they drop disgusting filth, have clawed hands and faces ravaged by hunger' (Virgil, *Aeneid*).

17 service of the state: *See* Speech on Economical Reform (11).

18 This of the four and a half per cents: the financial package arranged for Burke included two annuities on the West Indian $4\frac{1}{2}$ per cent fund (raised from customs duties granted to the Crown in the reign of Charles II and classed as hereditary revenue). These did not have to be approved by Parliament.

19 What is contained from page 230 … my publications: see *Works* (1792–1827), ii, pp. 230–41, edited by French Laurence (*see* Letter to French Laurence) and Rev. Walker King.

20 "*Nitor in adversum*": 'I have to contend against this' (Ovid, *Metamorphoses*).

21 Mr. Barré and Mr. Dunning: Isaac Barré (1726–1802), Treasurer of the Navy, was promised a pension of £3,200 on leaving office; John Dunning, 1st Baron Ashburton (1731–83), Chancellor of the Duchy of Lancaster, was granted a pension of £4,000 a year on the formation of the Rockingham administration.

22 Cato (Marcus Porcius Cato, 234–149 BC), Roman statesman known as Cato the Elder (his great-grandson is known as Cato the Younger).

23 the young Scipios: could be either Publius Cornelius Scipio Africanus (237–183 BC) or Publius Cornelius Scipio Aemilianus Africanus (*c.* 187–129 BC). Both were young when in high office.

24 Mr. Thelwall's lecture: John Thelwall (1764–1834) was a prominent radical orator, writer and elecutionist. Tried for high treason (and acquitted) in 1794, he gave many public lectures on parliamentary reform and universal suffrage.

25 Senatus consultum: text from the Senate, ancient Rome.

26 "*Cludere ludum impudentiæ jussit*": refers to the shutting down of the 'school of shamelessness' (Cicero's term) of the Greek rhetoricians and their expulsion from Rome by the censors L. Crassus and Ch. Domitius Ahenobardus (Tacitus, *Dialogus de Oratoribus*).

27 "he lies floating many a rood": Milton, *Paradise Lost*.

28 Garters ... Dragons: officers of the College of Arms.

29 Marlborough (John Churchill, 1st Duke of Marlborough, 1650–1722): English soldier and statesman who made his reputation as one of Europe's greatest generals at the battles of Blenheim (1704), Ramillies (1706) and Oudenarde (1708).

30 Burleigh (William Cecil, 1st Baron Burghley, 1520–98): English statesman, adviser to Elizabeth I.

31 Murray or a Yorke: William Murray (1705–93), MP, 1st Earl of Mansfield, Lord Chief Justice of the King's Bench 1756–88; Philip Yorke (1690–1764), MP, 1st Earl of Hardwicke, Lord Chancellor 1737–56.

32 Guillim, Edmondson, and Collins: writers on heraldry and genealogy.

33 ancient nobility of the land: Henry VIII granted John Russell (*c.*1485–1555) lands which had belonged to Edward Stafford, 3rd Duke of Buckingham (1478–1521), who was convicted of treason and executed. Russell received his earldom from Edward VI in 1550.

34 Wolsey (Thomas Wolsey, 1473–1530): English politician and Cardinal, Lord Chancellor and chief adviser to Henry VIII.

35 At si non aliam venturo fata Neroni: 'if this was the only way for Fate to bring about the advent of Nero' (Lucan, *Pharsalia*, reflecting on the dreadful carnage of the battle of Pharsalia and its consequences).

36 Sir George Savile's ... *Nullum Tempus* Act: legislation drawn up in 1768 by George Savile (1726–84) securing subjects' land (after sixty years' possession) from recovery by the Crown.

37 *Dum domus ... Romanus habebit*: 'While Aeneas's house remains on the Capitol's unmoveable rock, and the father of Rome rules' (Virgil, *Aeneid*).

38 *Templum in modem arcis*: 'a temple constructed like a citadel' (Tacitus, *Histories*).

39 *ça ira*: it will survive (French Revolutionary song).

40 Nimrod: King of Shinar, great-grandson of Noah, celebrated as a mighty hunter (Genesis, Books of Chronicles).

41 *mauvais plaisant*: hoaxer.

42 Harrington's seven different forms of republics: James Harrington (1611–77), English political theorist, posited a utopian republic in his *The Commonwealth of Oceana* (1656).

43 Abbé Sieyes (comte Emmanuel-Joseph Sieyès, 1748–1836): *see* Reflections on the Revolution in France (20), n.36.

44 *boue de Paris*: mud of Paris.

45 Inigo Jones (1573–1652): British painter, designer, architect, often considered the founder of the English classical tradition of architecture, most celebrated for the Banqueting House (1619–22) in Whitehall.

46 academy del *Cimento* (per antiphrasin): L'Accademia del Cimento, founded

in Florence in 1657 by students of Galileo – Giovanni Alfonso Borelli (physiologist, physicist, mathematician) and mathematician Vincenzo Viviani – existed to champion objective, experimental science (hence Burke's comment on the inapplicability of its name in this context).

47 Morveau and Hassenfrats: Louis-Bernard Guyton de Morveau (1737–1816) was a chemist and balloon-warfare pioneer; Jean-Henri Hassenfratz (1755–1827) was a meteorologist and prominent Jacobin.

48 La Vendée: a peasant revolt against the Revolutionary government, sparked by the imposition of military conscription; nearly a quarter of a million lives were lost before it ended in 1796.

49 Condorcet's calculation: for Condorcet see Reflections on the Revolution in France (20), n.80. His predictions on the outcome of votes, given changes in the make-up of electorates, are used here to make a satirical point about the durability of the Revolution.

50 Legendre: Louis Legendre (1756–97) extreme Jacobin, supporter of Danton, member of the Convention. He was actually a butcher, owning a shop in Paris.

51 "Pleas'd to the last ... his blood": from Pope's Essay on Man, Epistle 1.

52 Lord Keppel (Admiral Augustus Keppel, 1st Viscount Keppel, 1725–86): Royal Navy officer during the Seven Years' War and the War of American Independence. He was an opposition Whig, and his court martial (in 1779, for supposed fecklessness in the battle of Ushant the previous year) was seen by many as politically motivated. He was acquitted (Burke helped him with his defence). Lord Keppel was the grandson of Arnold Joost van Keppel, favourite of William III, who had accompanied him to England in 1688 and was created 1st Earl of Albemarle. Lord Keppel's sister Elizabeth was the Duke of Bedford's mother.

53 Rochefoucault (Louis Alexandre, duc de La Rochefoucault D'Anville, 1743–92): see Reflections on the Revolution in France (20), n.4.

54 Fayette (Marie-Joseph Paul Yves Gilbert du Motier, marquis de La Fayette, 1757–1834): see Reflections on the Revolution in France (20), n.175.

55 Viscomte de Noailles (Louis-Marie Noailles, 1756–1804): son of Philippe, duc de Mouchy, played a prominent part in the American Revolutionary War under La Fayette, then in the National Assembly at the beginning of the French Revolution, where he proposed methods for abolishing feudalism. He emigrated to America in 1793.

56 Périgord (Charles Maurice de Talleyrand-Périgord, 1754–1838): see Reflections on the Revolution in France (20), n.150.

57 the Turennes ... the Daguessaus ... and Dantons: prominent Marshals of France (Henri de La Tour d'Auvergne, vicomte de Turenne, 1611–75; François Henri de Montmorency-Bouteville, duc de Luxembourg, 1628–95; Louis François, duc de Boufflers, 1644–1711). Jean-Baptiste Colbert (1619–83) was Finance Minister under Louis XIV, and François-Michel Le Tellier, marquis de Louvois (1639–91) War Minister. The de Lamoignon and d'Aguesseau families were represented by several generations of public servants, in the seventeenth and eighteenth centuries. Jean-Charles Pichegru (1761–1804) was a successful general, but was relieved of his

command in 1795, suspected of royalist intrigue; Burke then lists the 'Regicides, robbers and revolutionary judges ... [who] have laid waste the fairest part of the world'.

58 Grotius (Hugo Grotius, 1583–1645): Dutch jurist, philosopher, playwright, statesman and diplomat.

59 Marat (Jean-Paul Marat, 1743–93): physician, revolutionary political theorist and scientist, famously murdered in his bath by Charlotte Corday.

60 the house of Nassau: *see* On Parties (4), n.6.

61 Austrian Netherlands: overrun and annexed by the French Revolutionary army in 1794.

PRIVATE LETTERS (30)

TO RICHARD SHACKLETON

1 Richard Shackleton (1726–92): the son of Abraham Shackleton, a Quaker, who ran the non-denominational boarding school at Ballitore, some thirty miles from Dublin, which Burke attended between the ages of eleven and fourteen. Shackleton, who attended Trinity College after Burke had finished there – the first Quaker to do so (though he was not permitted to receive a degree) – became headmaster of his father's school in 1756. He and Burke remained friends for life.

2 Villians name: perhaps James Trimble, engaged as an usher at Ballitore School the previous year.

3 Rhames: probably Joseph Rhames, Dublin printer and bookseller.

4 Our old friend Herbert: Newcomen Herbert had left Ballitore School before Burke arrived there, but through Shackleton the two had become friends in Dublin, where Herbert was living with an uncle, preparing himself for a career with the East India Company. He sailed for India in October 1745, a hazardous undertaking in time of war (Britain was engaged in the War of Austrian Succession). He evidently made another attempt, and either died on the voyage or after his arrival.

5 Sisson (Richard Sisson, d. 1767): he had left Ballitore School and was apprenticed to the portrait painter Francis Bindon in Dublin. Burke took great interest in his later career, and commissioned him to paint Richard Shackleton in the 1760s. After Sisson's death he may have provided for his son.

TO THE DUKE OF RICHMOND

1 the Duke of Richmond: Charles Lennox, 3rd Duke of Richmond (1735–1806), a keen and impetuous supporter of the Rockingham group, and an admirer of Burke, with whom he kept in close touch. He had seen distinguished service in the army before entering the House of Commons, was briefly a Secretary of State in Rockingham's first administration (1766) and temporarily took over the leadership of the opposition in 1771 when Rockingham was kept from Parliament by his wife's health. He was a

strenuous opponent of Lord North, particularly outspoken on his American policy. His extreme views on parliamentary reform would later alienate him from Burke. Rockingham made him Master General of the Ordnance in his second administration (1782), with a seat in the Cabinet, and Pitt the Younger later persuaded him to serve in the same capacity. Though his views became increasingly Tory his past became an embarrassment to a government trying to stifle political radicalism, and he was removed from office in 1795.

2 Post 15 November 1772: Richmond had written to Burke on 15 November, discouraged, like many of the Rockinghamites, by the group's lack of effectiveness in opposition. He continued to dally on his Goodwood estate, hunting and entertaining, in spite of Burke's exhortations to return to London. He had observed: 'You say the Party is an object of too much importance to be let go to pieces. Indeed Burke you have more merit than any man in keeping us together, but I believe our greatest Bond is the Pride of the individuals, which Unfortunately tho' it keeps us from breaking, hinders us from acting like men of Sense.' (Though Richmond was late for the parliamentary session when he did arrive he threw himself with his customary energy into opposing Lord North's East India Company legislation in the House of Lords, just as Burke was doing in the Commons.)

3 a certain party: the Chatham-Shelburne group and their supporters in the City. The two principal opposition groups in 1772, early in Lord North's ministry, were the Rockingham Whigs and the supporters of the Earls of Chatham and Shelburne. Both were competing to gain support in the City but the Rockinghamites were less keen to be involved with the activities of radicals like John Wilkes. Shelburne had the better contacts, including several aldermen who were also radical MPs, such as John Sawbridge and James Townsend. They had joined John Wilkes in establishing the Society of the Supporters of the Bill of Rights in 1769. Two years later the society split acrimoniously, resulting in the ministerial candidate being elected mayor instead of Sawbridge.

4 some persons of very high Name in this Country: Shelburne and Chatham had to lead their opposition from the House of Lords. In 1771 they backed a bill to shorten the duration of parliaments introduced by Sawbridge in the House of Commons (he did this every year for the next ten years) as well as other radical motions on economical reform including a place and pensions bill – all with little chance of success. It did much for their standing in the City (which Shelburne now wished to wean away from the influence of Wilkes) but created tension with the Rockingham Whigs, most of whom preferred a more cautious approach.

5 Lord Rm: the Marquis of Rockingham (1730–82), party leader, prime minister 1765–66 and again from March 1782 until his unexpected death just over three months later. *See* Inscription on the Tomb of Lord Rockingham (16).

6 Mr Wilkes's observation: John Wilkes – *see* Speech on the Middlesex Election (7), n.1 – champion of civil liberties, had a parallel career as a philanderer, in spite of the squint and prognathous jaw which rendered him exceptionally ugly. He often made this boast, though one month seems to be his most cautious estimate; sometimes he reduced the time to ten minutes.

7 Secession: refusal to attend Parliament. Richmond had expressed the opinion that the Rockinghamites should have seceded after Wilkes's election
as MP for Middlesex, so provocatively mishandled by Grafton's administration during 1768–69. The party would later secede, though rather half-
heartedly, in 1777 over Lord North's colonial policy (*see* Letter to the Sheriffs of Bristol (10), n.8).

8 Lord Temple, Lord Lyttelton, and Lord Camden: friends and political allies
of Chatham in the House of Lords. Along with Richmond himself, all had
spoken in support of Chatham's motion in May 1770 to reverse the adjudication of the House of Commons that Wilkes's election had been illegal. It
was defeated by 89 votes to 43. Richard Grenville-Temple, 2nd Earl Temple
(1711–79), was a patron and close friend of Wilkes. He was Pitt the Elder's
brother-in-law, often described as his evil genius, and a great political
intriguer. He served as Lord Privy Seal in Pitt's wartime ministry and
encouraged Wilkes (they were neighbours in Buckinghamshire) to enter
Parliament as MP for Aylesbury in 1757. Temple subsidized Wilkes's controversial periodical *The North Briton*, and later paid the litigation costs he
incurred in challenging the legality of general warrants. George Lyttelton,
1st Baron Lyttelton (1709–73), was a cousin of the Grenvilles, had been at
Oxford University with Pitt and entered Parliament the same year (1735).
He had seen office as Chancellor of the Exchequer under Newcastle in
1755–56. He was also a man of letters and a friend of Burke who was much
saddened by his death the following year. Charles Pratt, Baron Camden
(1714–94), had known Pitt since their schooldays at Eton. A practising lawyer, he was Attorney General, then Chief Justice of the Common Pleas during the Pitt–Newcastle administration, and became a popular hero for his
numerous rulings against the use of general warrants. He was made Lord
Chancellor when Chatham returned to power in 1766. The two men shared
the same views on Wilkes and America and Camden continued to support
Chatham's policies when the latter was in opposition. This eventually
proved too much for the King, who dismissed him in January 1770.

9 the Transaction of 1767: negotiations which took place in July 1767 with
a view to bringing the Rockingham and Bedford groups into the administration which was struggling in the absence of Chatham (suffering from
illness and depression). Rockingham had declined to accept office merely
to alter the balance of the ministry and demanded an entirely new administration with whose views (particularly on America) he was in sympathy.
Richmond had criticized Rockingham's handling of the negotiations.

10 the supper at Lord Rockinghams: at this supper, held on 3 July 1767, Rockingham made it known to members of the Bedford group (Lords Weymouth and Gower are known to have attended) that Grafton had invited
him to join the government. The Bedfords were an archetypal faction, and
John Russell, 4th Duke of Bedford (1710–71), had served under several
different administrations, variously supporting and opposing the Pelhams,
Pitt, Bute and Grenville. They had been in opposition during Rockingham's first ministry and were divided about whether they wanted to work
with Chatham. Rockingham at this point did not put forward any plan
to work with them because he objected to their current association with
Grenville (they in turn objected to his friendship with Conway). The King
disliked them for the same reason, but they were eventually brought into
the ministry – having severed connections with Grenville – in 1768.

11 the Duke of Grafton: the young Augustus Henry Fitzroy, 3rd Duke of Grafton (1735–1811), was a staunch supporter of Pitt. With Pitt's agreement he had served as Secretary of State in Rockingham's government (1765–66) and afterwards became First Lord of the Treasury in Chatham's own administration, though doubtful of being up to the job (Chatham himself held the post of Lord Privy Seal). When Pitt became incapacitated through illness, Grafton was naturally involved in attempting to boost the ministry with some heavyweight replacements. After failing with Rockingham he finally succeeded with Bedford, and the ministry continued, beset by problems, until Grafton had enough and resigned in 1770.

12 Conway (Henry Seymour Conway, 1719–95): brother of the Earl of Hertford, who had served in the army and risen to the rank of lieutenant general. He had served as a Secretary of State for the Northern Department in Rockingham's first ministry, and upset some of his colleagues by staying on under Chatham in 1766. He was replaced by Lord Weymouth, a Bedfordite, in 1768, and resumed his military career.

13 D. of N: elderly but still active in the House of Lords, Newcastle tried to promote the accession of both Rockingham (his one-time protégé) and Bedford to the Cabinet. Newcastle also disapproved of Rockingham's handling of this episode.

14 Lord Albemarle (George Keppel, 3rd Earl Albemarle, 1724–72): he entered Parliament in 1746 but during George II's reign he was more interested in his military career, where rapid advancement was ensured by his friendship with the Duke of Cumberland, the King's favourite son. In 1762 during the Seven Years' War he commanded a successful expedition to seize Cuba from the Spanish, for which George II awarded him the Garter. Returning home, he followed Cumberland in supporting Rockingham's first ministry in 1765, and went into opposition with him in 1766. His sister had married the Duke of Bedford's eldest son, and it was he who had handled negotiations with the Bedford group for the Rockinghamites.

15 D of Bedford: the Duke of Bedford's declining health led him to retire from political affairs after the successful conclusion of his negotiations with Grafton. He did not accept office for himself and died three years later in January 1771.

16 Rolls Chappel: the records (Rolls) of the Court of Chancery had been stored since 1377 in a building formerly used as a residence and chapel for Jews who had converted to Christianity. It was rebuilt in 1617, possibly by Inigo Jones, and demolished in 1895.

17 The Claudian and Valerian: the Valeria were an ancient and celebrated patrician family who traced their origins back to the early days of Rome in the eighth century BC. From the time of Publius Valerius, who helped found the Roman Republic and was elected consul in 509 BC, members of the *gens* featured in public life for a thousand years. During the Republic they often pressed for the rights of the plebeians. They later furnished a number of emperors, among them Diocletian and Constantine the Great. The Claudia arrived in Rome at the beginning of the Republic, gaining their first consulship in 495 BC. Rome's first five emperors – Augustus, Tiberius, Caligula, Claudius and Nero – were members of the Julio-Claudian dynasty.

1 8 November 1774: Burke wrote to Jane from Bristol a few days after he had won the election there. His son Richard had been assisting in the campaign.

2 Mr Buller (William Buller): Richard Burke described him as 'one of our most active as well as able and ingenious friends'.

3 William (or Will Burke, 1729–98): a friend of Edmund Burke from his early days in London. They called each other cousin but were probably not related. He lived with Edmund and Jane at Gregories, their estate in Buckinghamshire.

4 Mr Nobles: John Noble (1743–1828) was a prominent Bristol merchant who had supported Burke's election.

5 Richard: Burke's son (1758–94).

6 Little Popham: Stephen Popham (1745–95), another supporter.

7 Crugers: *see* Speech at the Conclusion of the Poll at Bristol (8), n.1.

8 my father, Jack, and Mrs Nugent: his father-in-law Christopher Nugent (1698–1775), his brother-in-law John Nugent (1737–1813) and John's wife Elizabeth (d. 1779).

9 Joe (Joseph) Hickey (*c.* 1714–94): Burke's solicitor and friend.

10 our Knight: Sir Joshua Reynolds. *See* An Appeal from the New Whigs to the Old (22), n.33.

11 Haslemere: Will Burke was standing for election at Haslemere, evidently put forward by the Duke of Portland, but lost.

1 this matter: William Burke had been MP for Great Bedwyn from 1766 to 1774. His patron, the Buckinghamshire landowner Lord Verney, had several parliamentary seats at his disposal and had generously supported both Burkes. He could no longer afford to do so after disastrous speculations in East India Company stock in which all three men had been involved (Edmund probably only indirectly). Rockingham provided for Edmund, but Will, having failed in another attempt to gain a seat (Haslemere in Surrey) was no longer immune from prosecution for debt. Hence the project to seek his fortune in India. He did indeed find employment, though not through Francis, becoming the Agent of the Rajah of Tanjore. He returned to England in 1778 but was back in India in 1780, remaining there for seven years. He came home for good in 1793, in broken health, and still financially ruined.

1 Chatsworth: seat of the dukes of Devonshire. William Cavendish, the 5th Duke, was an enormously wealthy Whig politician with a strong interest group in Parliament which had allied with the Rockinghamites. Fox's particular champion was the Duchess, the former Lady Georgiana Spencer, to whom he was distantly related.

2 John Townshend (Lord John Townshend, 1757–1833): though only twenty years old he was already a member of the Devonshire House circle and remained intimate with Fox throughout the latter's life, though this largely condemned him to the political wilderness. He entered the House of Commons in 1780 and in 1782 was appointed a Lord of the Admiralty in Rockingham's short-lived administration. After some years without a seat he served as MP for Knaresborough from 1793 to 1818, holding office briefly alongside Fox in the Ministry of All the Talents (1806).

3 They have voted their freedom ... John the Painter ... Sir John Fielding: in August 1777 Bristol voted the freedom of the city to John Montagu, 4th Earl of Sandwich (1718–92), First Lord of the Admiralty, and Henry Howard, 12th Earl of Suffolk (1739–79), Secretary of State, for their part in the prosecution of James Aitken (1752–77), nicknamed 'John the Painter', a young Scot who had taken early to a life of crime, fled to the colonies and returned to England in 1775 where he hoped for sponsorship from the American revolutionaries for his new career as a political arsonist. He proved largely incompetent but while his attacks on shipyards in royal dockyards in Portsmouth and Bristol did little damage the impression that a large band of terrorists was at large caused panic in the government and throughout the country. An irresistibly large reward being offered for his capture, he was eventually apprehended and brought to trial by Sir John Fielding (1721–80), the celebrated blind magistrate and social reformer. (The younger half-brother of the novelist and magistrate Henry Fielding, he had taken over with great success his brother's work in establishing the Bow Street Runners as London's first effective police force, and was knighted for his services in 1761.) Aitken was hanged in March 1777; the mizzenmast of HMS *Arethusa* was re-erected in the Portsmouth dockyard for the purpose, guaranteeing a good view for all.

4 the Archbishop of Yorks sermon: the Archbishop was William Markham, an old friend of Burke's. On 21 February 1777 he had preached a contro-versial sermon before the Society for the Propagation of the Gospel, attacking the Whigs in general for their support of the American cause and in particular the dissenters whose prominence in politics and ideas on civil liberties greatly alarmed him. He proposed that dissenters should be put under the same legal restraints as Roman Catholics.

5 our Northern friends: particularly Rockingham and the Cavendishes, who had family seats in Yorkshire and Derbyshire respectively. It was Lord John Cavendish (1732–96) rather than Burke who led the Rockingham group in the House of Commons, since he represented the family interest of the Duke of Devonshire. (He was not himself a peer, being the youngest son of the 3rd Duke.) However, he was more interested in fox hunting than politics.

6 the last war: the Seven Years' War (1756–63).

7 joining yourself: Burke had been working on Fox (who had twice joined Lord North's government) since 1774 to join the Rockingham group. Around this time, possibly while he was at Chatsworth, he decided to do so.

8 men and money: Lord Harcourt, Lord Lieutenant of Ireland 1772–77, had already succeeded in getting the Irish Parliament to agree to send 4,000 troops to America in 1775 in spite of the British parliamentary opposition's

attempt to persuade them to stand aloof from the conflict and refuse. The Dublin government had also proposed and carried two resolutions pledging loyalty to the Crown and abhorrence of revolution.

9 the Earl of Buckinghamshire (John Hobart, 2nd Earl of Buckinghamshire, 1723–93): succeeded Lord Harcourt as Lord Lieutenant of Ireland in 1777. Burke's reference here is probably to a motion of 1 February 1774 for papers concerning the 'Boston Tea Party' to be laid before the House of Lords, which Burke regarded as provocative and counter-productive. The motion was later withdrawn.

10 an absence of two: Burke had gone to Ireland in August 1766 after the fall of the Rockingham ministry, staying there two months.

11 the Primate, Lord Hillsborough and Lord Hertford: the Primate was Dr Richard Robinson, Archbishop of Armagh and Primate of all Ireland since 1765. He was created Baron Rokeby in 1777. Wills Hill, Earl of Hillsborough (1718–93), was one of the largest Irish landowners, controlling a number of seats in the Irish House of Commons. His own political career was spent in England. He had been Secretary of State for the Colonies 1768–72 and would return to office again as Secretary of State for the Southern Department in 1779. Francis Seymour Conway, 1st Earl of Hertford (1718–94), had been Lord Lieutenant of Ireland, 1765–66, and was Lord Chamberlain, 1766–82. He held extensive lands in County Antrim.

12 Duke of Leinster (William Robert Fitzgerald, 2nd Duke of Leinster, 1749–1804): a large landowner who controlled a number of boroughs in County Kildare. Fox was his cousin.

13 resident Lieutenancy: the Chatham ministry had made residence in Ireland compulsory for the Lord Lieutenant in 1767.

14 a young man: thought to be Walter Hussey Burgh (1742–83), MP for Athy and later for Dublin University.

15 Lord Shannon (Richard Boyle, 2nd Earl of Shannon, 1727–1807): a strong supporter of the Dublin government and member of the Privy Council of Ireland.

16 Ponsonby (John Ponsonby, 1713–87): the Ponsonbys were related to the Cavendishes – the Dukes of Devonshire had large estates in Ireland and exercised political influence there.

17 Hutchinsons ... Tisdall: John Hely Hutchinson (1724–94), controversially appointed Provost of Trinity College, Dublin in 1774 (he was not in holy orders), was an unashamed place hunter but also an active MP in the Dublin House of Commons who supported both Catholic relief and parliamentary reform. He succeeded his bitter rival Philip Tisdal (1703–77) as Secretary of State in 1777.

18 Son of the Sovereign: John Townshend's father, George, 4th Viscount Townshend, had been Lord Lieutenant of Ireland, 1768–72.

1 Joseph Harford (1741–1802): one of a group of Quaker merchants who were partners in Harfords' & Bristol Brass Company.

2 your Colleague: Edward Brice (c. 1737–1809), a fellow Sheriff.

3 Mr Cruger: Henry Cruger (*see* Speech at the Conclusion of the Poll at Bristol (8), n.1) had been badly defeated at the polls, not helped by the abstention of Burke's supporters, and failed again at a by-election the following year. However, he was returned in 1784 as a follower of the younger Pitt. He went back to America in 1790.

4 Sir Geo: Saville (George Savile, 8th Baronet, 1726–84): *see* Letter to the Sheriffs of Bristol (10), n.21 and Speech on the Middlesex Election (7), n.2. The views Burke cites were put forward in his election address in September 1780.

5 propose a Test: require candidates standing for election to Parliament to sign a pledge to support a particular measure or measures stipulated by their constituents (as Wilkes did in Middlesex in 1774).

6 Coxe ... Mr Trevillion: Richard Hippisley Coxe (1742–86), MP for Somerset since 1768 and Sir John Trevelyan, 4th Baronet (1735–1828), were returned unopposed for Somerset when the other sitting member, Edward Phelps (1725–97), withdrew from the contest. Trevelyan was a consistent opponent of the North administration from 1779.

7 our Club: political clubs flourished in Bristol. The Union Club had been organized by the Whigs in the 1730s, with dissenting and low church backing. The Tories, around the same time, established the Steadfast Society, with support from the Anglican clergy. The clubs sponsored parliamentary candidates and gave them instructions and financial assistance; occasionally they tried to influence national legislation. For some years before Burke's arrival in Bristol, the rival clubs had begun to co-operate in order to curb election expenditure, and their activities had lapsed somewhat. The Steadfast Society, renamed the Loyal and Constitutional Club, however, was in full swing in 1780, which partly accounted for the victory of the two government candidates in the election. Before his departure Burke took measures to revive the Union Club. According to Richard Champion, his campaign manager, it was 'to be extended to all the honest part of the Whigs' – those who would consider 'the ruin of Mr Cruger and his friends, as the Basis, upon which their building must be constructed'. However, they decided to support him in 1784 and the Whig party in Bristol was reunited.

8 Noble: *see* Letter to Jane Burke, n.4.

9 Mrs Kile: Harford had married Hannah Kill (1741–1811). The 'young ladies' were Mrs Harford's three sisters, Martha, Elizabeth and Mary. Mrs Kill was Harford's mother-in-law.

10 Warrington: Harford's only son, Charles Joseph Harford (1764–1830), had entered Warrington Academy in 1779.

1 William Baker (1743–1824): MP for Aldborough, a close personal and political friend of Burke. On 14 June Burke had given a lengthy defence of the coalition in Parliament, for which Baker sent his congratulations.

2 the Company and their servants in the East: George III had been active in encouraging opposition to the East-India Bill in the House of Lords. Lord Temple and John Moore, Archbishop of Canterbury, had acted as his agents.

3 Verres: Gaius Verres was a Roman governor of Sicily (73–71 BC) who ruthlessly exploited the province for his own enrichment – much as Burke considered Warren Hastings had done in India. With powerful allies and ample funds to bribe the authorities, Verres expected to survive prosecution in the extortion courts, but had not counted on the legal skills and oratorical prowess of Cicero. Cicero's *Verrine Orations*, recounting his crimes, ensured his lasting notoriety.

4 my Motion: in defence of the Fox-North coalition, which even his own party had found embarrassing. It was rejected without division.

1 Mary Palmer: Reynolds never married and Mary Palmer inherited most of her uncle's property and income on his death in 1792. She thereupon married an Irish peer, the Earl of Inchiquin, and eventually became Marchioness of Thomond.

2 your worthy correspondent: Miss Palmer's most frequent Indian correspondent was her cousin William Johnson (1756–99), who had gone to India in 1774 and was Clerk of the Peace to the Supreme Court. But William's younger brother Richard (b. *c.* 1760) was also in India at the time, as was his brother-in-law Philip Yonge (1755–88), who had written to Burke in 1785.

3 Mr Bristow (John Bristow, 1750–1802): Resident at Lucknow.

4 Almas Âli Khân: the most influential revenue farmer in Oudh. Hastings admitted the 'secret instruction' (dated 23 October 1782) during his impeachment in 1787, but drew attention to the conditional clauses stipulating that Bristow should act only if Almas had been guilty of a criminal offence.

5 I moved: in his motion of 30 July 1784 Burke denounced Hastings as 'the scourge of India' who had 'reduced the whole to a waste, howling desert, where no creature could exist'. His remarks caused some amusement and much indignation, and when he rose again to defend them the order of the day was called, putting a stop to the debate (*Parliamentary History*, vol. xxiv).

6 a mere fiction of my own brain: Burke had been infuriated by the sensational reporting of the episode in the opposition press. During the following week, the *English Chronicle*, for example, had printed a letter purporting to be from Almas's wife, begging for the life of 'the father of my children' and describing how her husband had been 'immediately strangled'. Those

au fait with Indian affairs would have known that Almas was still alive; he was also known to be a eunuch.

7 Trap mechanists: Burke was convinced that Pitt's administration was an ally of the East India Company, with some justification. In March 1786 both Pitt and Henry Dundas – his future Home Secretary – would defend Hastings's conduct in the Mahratta war, declaring that it had saved the British Empire in Asia.

8 on his side of the House: notably Charles Jenkinson, Secretary at War 1778–82 and Lord Loughborough (Alexander Wedderburn, one-time supporter of John Wilkes, who owed his peerage and rapid rise through the legal hierarchy to Chief Justice of the Common Pleas to his former political enemy, Lord North). There is no evidence that his own party disagreed with Burke's stand on Indian affairs during the North administration (1770–82), but Burke took much of the blame for the failure of Fox's East-India Bill in 1783.

9 Mr Pitts Bill: Pitt's government passed their own India Act in August 1784, introducing dual control of India by the Company and the Crown. It would remain effective until 1857. While it did much to rectify past abuses and to improve adminstrative efficiency, Burke interpreted it as an attempt to increase government patronage and opposed it vigorously. The meeting referred to here took place in Calcutta on 25 July 1785. George Dallas (1758–1833), a protégé of Warren Hastings, opposed the new legislation and also complained of the 'intemperate public debate' in England which was giving the servants of the East India Company an undeservedly bad name.

10 persons under accusation: Burke had opposed the so-called 'inquisitional clause' of Pitt's Act, which set up a special tribunal for Indian offences. He also objected to the requirement that company officials should deliver an inventory of their property on returning home, though this clause was never enforced and was repealed in 1786.

11 Sir Elijah Impey ... Mr Benfield: Impey (1732–1809) was Chief Justice of the Supreme Court at Calcutta. Burke would be the prime mover in an attempt to impeach him on a charge of judicial murder in 1788 but government backing and a convincing defence, which Impey delivered himself, ensured that the matter was not taken beyond committee stage. Paul Benfield (1741–1810) was a particular *bête noire* of Burke's, an East India Company financier who had made a huge personal fortune in Madras, largely through personal loans (most infamously, to the Nawab of Arcot, a British client ruler) repayable by the Exchequer.

TO CHARLES-JEAN-FRANÇOIS DEPONT

1 Depont (Charles Depont, 1767–96): *see* Reflections on the Revolution in France (20), n.1. Since his visit to England in 1785, Depont had become involved in French politics, first as a member of the Paris *parlement*, and in 1789 as the representative for Metz in the National Assembly.

2 Military Power: Burke presumably alludes to the National Guard, but this was in fact the Assembly's chief means of defence against mob violence.

3   the grievous Charge: fear of social disorder made it a government priority
    that grain should be supplied to Paris, regardless of the need in the country-
    side. In this respect it followed the example of the *ancien régime* which after
    a bad harvest would requisition food stocks and fix the price of grain.

4   alms of Choice ... Caprice: *dons patriotiques*. *See* Reflections on the Revolu-
    tion in France (20), n.41.

5   conscience of the Contributor: a *contribution patriotique*. *See* Reflections on
    the Revolution in France (20), n.183.

6   the property of the Subject: presumably refers to the August Decrees of
    1789, abolishing feudalism.

7   your Courts of Justice: this and the following passage refer to the *parlements*
    which had been temporarily suspended in November. Their judicial func-
    tions were being exercised by the *chambres de vacation* until a new system of
    courts could be established. *See also* Reflections on the Revolution in
    France (20), n.40.

8   "thro' many varieties of untried being": Joseph Addison, from *Cato* (1713).

9   Sylla ... Caesar: Lucius Cornelius Sulla: *see* A Vindication of Natural Soci-
    ety (1), n.21. Julius Caesar's reform of the constitution between 49 and 44
    BC was designed to restore strong centralized government after an era of
    civil war and political chaos.

10 Cinna, and Marius, and Saturninus: Cornelius Cinna, Caius Marius
    and Lucius Appuleius Saturninus were all leaders of the *popularis* party in
    Rome who introduced punitive legislation against the senatorial class
    (*c.* 120–84 BC).

TO CAPTAIN THOMAS MERCER

1   Mercer: Thomas Mercer (*c.* 1733–1801) had been a ship's captain and gen-
    eral merchant in the East India Company for twenty years and had managed
    to make an honest fortune. He had appeared as a witness before the House
    of Commons in 1787 in the run-up to the impeachment of Warren Has-
    tings and had then retired to his native Ulster.

2   "pampered and luxurious prelates": Mercer had written: 'For the rest – if
    to take from pampered and luxurious prelates a part of those sumptuous
    livings which were accumulated in the times of ignorance and superstition,
    and to provide for the more comfortable subsistence of parish priests, be
    the subversion of a church, millions of good men and good Christians will
    heartily wish (for the honour of true religion, distinct from pageantry and
    hypocrisy) that all such may in this manner be speedily subverted.' The
    confiscation of Church property had been accompanied by proposals that
    a stipend of 2,000 *livres* be paid by the State to all parish priests – a consider-
    able increase for most of them.

3   by violence: many of the estates in Ulster had passed into Protestant and
    English hands after the defeat of the Irish revolt of 1598 and the 'plantation'
    of the province under James I; others had changed hands by force as a result
    of the reconquests of the province under Cromwell (1649–52) and William
    III (1688–91).

4 the deposed King of France ... present Czarina: Burke lists four contemporary monarchs. Louis XVI, King of France since 1774 was effectively a prisoner in the Tuileries but was not formally deposed until August 1792 when a Republic was declared; Frederick II ('the Great') of Prussia (r. 1740–86); the Habsburg Emperor Joseph II of Austria, news of whose death a week previously had not yet reached England; Catherine II ('the Great') of Russia (1762–96).

5 a little pamphlet: Burke had arranged publication of the *Substance of the Speech of the Right Honourable Edmund Burke, in the Debate on the Army Estimates* on 20 February.

6 your general reflections: Mercer had written that a revolution 'cannot be effected without some convulsion; nor is it possible so to order the matter, but in some cases many individuals may suffer injury and outrage; and this, as far as it goes, is to be lamented. But, if it ends in freedom, in the deliverance of a nation from the despotism of one man, no price can be thought too dear to pay for it.'

7 "*non recepi sed rapui*": 'Non rapui sed recepi' ('I did not steal it, but I received it') was the motto inserted under the arms of William, Prince of Orange, on his accession to the English Crown.

TO ARTHUR MURPHY

1 Arthur Murphy (1727–1805): actor, playwright and classical scholar. He was an old friend of Burke who had probably first met him in 1752. His translation of Tacitus was still being reprinted in the twentieth century.

2 Tacitus (Gaius Cornelius Tacitus, b. AD 56/57–d. after 117): Roman historian. His principal works were the *Annals*, covering the history of the Roman Empire during the years 14–68, and the *Histories*, covering the years 69–96. His monographs included the *Germania*, an ethnographic work about the German tribes, and a life of his father in law *Agricola*, general and one-time governor of Britain.

3 Gordon (Thomas Gordon, d. *c.* 1750): published his *Works of Tacitus* in two volumes, the first in 1728, the second in 1731. He was also the writer of political and religious tracts.

4 *alias et idem*: different and the same.

5 Robertson (William Robertson, 1721–93): Burke was well acquainted with his *History of Scotland* (1759) and *History of Charles V* (1769) and described his *History of America* (1777) as 'your incomparable Work'.

6 which make "Ambition Virtue": from Shakespeare's *Othello*.

7 Plautus ... Terence ... Publius Syrus: Plautus (*c.* 250–184 BC) and Terence (d. *c.* 159 BC) were writers of comedies; Publilius Syrus (1st century BC) was a writer of mimes and *sententiæ*.

8 Cicero: *see* Reflections on the Revolution in France (20), n.134.

9 our worthy Doctor: probably Ralph Griffiths, LL.D. (1720–1803), editor and proprietor of the *Monthly Review*, and a neighbour and close friend of Murphy in his later years.

1 French Laurence ... Impeachment: Laurence was active politically and probably first came to Burke's attention in the early 1780s when he wrote pamphlets in support of Charles James Fox and the Whig party. He resigned with Burke from the Whig Club in 1793. Burke persuaded Fitzwilliam (*see* To Unknown, n.2) to provide his friend with a parliamentary seat at Peterborough in October 1796. In the same year Laurence became Regius Professor of Civil Law in the University of Oxford. He was a writer of poetry, pamphlets and biblical commentary; after 1792 he took over the editorship of the *Annual Register*. He was with Burke at Beaconsfield when he died and was one of his literary executors. Together he and Walker King brought out the first eight of a sixteen-volume collected *Works* before Laurence's death in 1809. Laurence had continued to sit in Parliament but his attempts to gain office were thwarted. The history of the Impeachment was never written.

2 aux abois: at bay – waiting for the inevitable end. Burke had generally enjoyed robust health but now he had succumbed to the gastric ailment which would kill him the following year. He was at Bath with Jane, taking the waters.

3 Troward (Richard Troward, d. 1815): one of the prosecution solicitors at the Hastings trial.

4 Woodford (Captain Emperor John Alexander Woodford): an army officer brought into increasingly close contact with the Burkes since 1791 by his knowledge of France and his royalist sympathies.

1 my ever dear and honored Son: refers to Richard Burke's work on behalf of the Catholic Committee (*see* Letter to Richard Burke (24), n.1). His sudden death in 1794 is the 'unspeakable calamity' Burke speaks of later in the letter.

2 The Person who succeeded to the Government of Ireland: William Wentworth-Fitzwilliam, 4th Earl Fitzwilliam (1748–1833). He was the nephew of the Marquis of Rockingham and had inherited his estates in 1782. Alienated by Fox's support of the French Revolution he had joined the government in 1794 as Lord President of the Council during the coalition of the Portland Whigs with Pitt. Burke had worked to secure his appointment as Lord Lieutenant of Ireland the same year. Asssured of the coalition's commitment to the defeat of Jacobinism, Fitzwilliam had expected Pitt to back him up in his attempt to break the Protestant Ascendancy, since Irish Catholics with a stake in the constitution would be less likely to stage an insurrection with the aid of Revolutionary France. Pitt, however, was more interested in keeping Ireland quiet, and George III was opposed to his programme of reform. He was recalled after only three months in Dublin.

3 "Si [...] meus adforet Hector": 'Non si ipse meus nunc adforet Hector'; 'no, not though my own [son] Hector were here himself' (Virgil, *Aeneid*).

4 Late acts of Parliament: the Catholic Relief Act (1793) offered substantial concessions, extending the right to vote to Irish Catholics on the same

terms as Protestants. They were also allowed to attend university, sit on juries, become magistrates and hold commissions, but were excluded from Parliament and higher office.

5 a person ... Office: the Whig politician Thomas Pelham (1756–1826), who became Chief Secretary for Ireland when Lord Camden (the 2nd Earl, 1759–1840) succeeded Fitzwilliam as Lord Lieutenant, a position which necessitated sitting in the Irish Parliament as an MP. During a debate on 4 May 1795 on Grattan's Catholic Relief Bill, Pelham stated that the government was opposed to the admission of Catholics to Parliament.

6 The enquiry was absolutely rejected: in early 1796 the Indemnity and Insurrection Bills were introduced in response to sectarian violence in the north of the country and fear of open rebellion. On 22 February Henry Grattan (1746–1820, champion of Catholic emancipation in the Irish House of Commons) made a powerful speech on the sufferings of the Catholics in the north of Ireland at the hands of the Orange militias, against which they had no legal redress. Before each bill was passed he moved unsuccessfully that the House should hear further evidence in Committee about the disturbances.

7 that true Protestant *Hoche*: Lazare Hoche (1768–97), a general in the French Revolutionary Army who led a naval invasion of Ireland in December 1796. It was foiled by bad weather, England's 'luckiest escape since the Armada', according to Wolfe Tone, leader of the United Irishmen, at whose request the French – at war, of course, with England – had intervened.

8 *aequó Mane*: even in battle.

9 Thomas Paine (1737–1809): writer and political activist who had taken part in both the American and French revolutions. For his career in America, *see* Letter to the Sheriffs of Bristol (10), n.12. He returned to London in 1787 and in 1791 published the first part of his celebrated *Rights of Man* in reply to Burke's *Reflections on the Revolution in France*. The second part appeared the following year. Warned of impending arrest for seditious libel he fled to France where he accepted honorary French citizenship and was elected to the National Convention. However, he opposed the execution of Louis XVI and spent a year in prison, narrowly escaping the guillotine. During this time (1793–94) he wrote and published *The Age of Reason*, an attack on Christianity and the Bible. He returned to the Convention and after its dissolution in October 1795 remained in France. In 1796 he published a letter denouncing George Washington, whom he believed had conspired with Robespierre to have him imprisoned. In late 1797 he was consorting with Napoleon about his projected invasion of Britain. But he condemned Napoleon's progress towards dictatorship and at President Jefferson's invitation, returned to America in 1802.

10 Sanhedrim: the highest Jewish council in ancient Israel.

INDEX

ABOUT THE EDITOR

JESSE NORMAN is the Member of Parliament for Hereford and South Herefordshire. His books include *Edmund Burke: Philosopher, Politician, Prophet*; *Compassionate Conservatism* and *The Big Society*.

CHINUA ACHEBE
The African Trilogy
Things Fall Apart

AESCHYLUS
The Oresteia

ISABEL ALLENDE
The House of the Spirits

MARTIN AMIS
London Fields

THE ARABIAN NIGHTS

ISAAC ASIMOV
Foundation
Foundation and Empire
Second Foundation
(in 1 vol.)

MARGARET ATWOOD
The Handmaid's Tale

JOHN JAMES AUDUBON
The Audubon Reader

AUGUSTINE
The Confessions

JANE AUSTEN
Emma
Mansfield Park
Northanger Abbey
Persuasion
Pride and Prejudice
Sanditon and Other Stories
Sense and Sensibility

HONORÉ DE BALZAC
Cousin Bette
Eugénie Grandet
Old Goriot

MIKLOS BANFFY
The Transylvanian Trilogy
(in 2 vols)

JOHN BANVILLE
The Book of Evidence
The Sea (in 1 vol.)

JULIAN BARNES
Flaubert's Parrot
A History of the World in
10½ Chapters (in 1 vol.)

GIORGIO BASSANI
The Garden of the Finzi-Continis

SIMONE DE BEAUVOIR
The Second Sex

SAMUEL BECKETT
Molloy, Malone Dies,
The Unnamable

SAUL BELLOW
The Adventures of Augie March

HECTOR BERLIOZ
The Memoirs of Hector Berlioz

THE BIBLE
(King James Version)
The Old Testament
The New Testament

WILLIAM BLAKE
Poems and Prophecies

GIOVANNI BOCCACCIO
Decameron

JORGE LUIS BORGES
Ficciones

JAMES BOSWELL
The Life of Samuel Johnson
The Journal of a Tour to
the Hebrides

RAY BRADBURY
The Stories of Ray Bradbury

JEAN ANTHELME
BRILLAT-SAVARIN
The Physiology of Taste

ANNE BRONTË
Agnes Grey and The Tenant of
Wildfell Hall

CHARLOTTE BRONTË
Jane Eyre
Villette
Shirley and The Professor

EMILY BRONTË
Wuthering Heights

MIKHAIL BULGAKOV
The Master and Margarita

EDMUND BURKE
Reflections on the Revolution in
France and Other Writings

SAMUEL BUTLER
The Way of all Flesh

This book is set in BEMBO which was cut
by the punch-cutter Francesco Griffo
for the Venetian printer-publisher
Aldus Manutius in early 1495
and first used in a pamphlet
by a young scholar
named Pietro
Bembo.